'. . . when it comes to helping wine drinkers make sense of the
now thousands of wines being produced in this country,
(Halliday) is in a class of his own.'
— *Sunday Herald Sun*

'An annual "must have" for those racing to keep up with the hurly-
burly of the Australian wine industry, and it's easy to see why.'
— *The Age*

'Halliday has refined the art of tucking diverse information . . . into a
readable and compact package.'
— *Melbourne Times*

'Halliday brings a vast knowledge to the subject, so even a few words
carry a weight unmatched by lesser mortals.'
— *Gold Coast Bulletin*

'(Wine) buyers will find his assessments expert and informative,
and those with cellars, however modest, will be helped by his assessment
of past vintages.'
— *Herald Sun*

james halliday

australia

wine

companion

2003 EDITION

HarperCollins*Publishers*

HarperCollins*Publishers*

First published as *Australia and New Zealand Wine Companion* in Australia in 1997
Subsequent editions published annually, in 1998, 1999, 2000, 2001
This edition published in 2002
Reprinted in 2002 (twice)
by HarperCollins*Publishers* Pty Limited
ABN 36 009 913 517
A member of HarperCollins*Publishers* (Australia) Pty Limited Group
www.harpercollins.com.au

Copyright © James Halliday 1997, 2002

The right of James Halliday to be identified as the moral rights
author of this work has been asserted by him in accordance with
the *Copyright Amendment (Moral Rights) Act 2000 (Cth).*

HarperCollins*Publishers*
25 Ryde Road, Pymble, Sydney, NSW 2073, Australia
31 View Road, Glenfield, Auckland 10, New Zealand
77–85 Fulham Palace Road, London W6 8JB, United Kingdom
Hazelton Lanes, 55 Avenue Road, Suite 2900, Toronto, Ontario M5R 3L2
and 1995 Markham Road, Scarborough, Ontario M1B 5M8, Canada
10 East 53rd Street, New York NY 10022, USA

ISBN 0 7322 7534 2
ISSN 1445-5447

Cover inset photograph by Kevin Judd
Typeset in Bembo 8/9.5 by HarperCollins Design Studio
Printed and bound in Australia by Griffin Press on 60gsm Bulky Paperback White

8 7 6 5 4 3   02 03 04 05

about the author

James Halliday is Australia's most respected wine writer. Over the past thirty-odd years he has worn many hats: lawyer, winemaker and grape grower, wine judge, wine consultant, journalist and author. He has discarded his legal hat, but actively continues in his other roles, incessantly travelling, researching and tasting wines in all the major wine-producing countries. He judges regularly at wine shows in Australia, the UK, the US, South Africa and New Zealand.

James Halliday has written or contributed to over 40 books on wine since he began writing in 1979 (notable contributions include the *Oxford Companion* and *Larousse Encylopedia of Wine*). His books have been translated into Japanese, French and German, and have been published in the UK and the US as well as Australia.

His most recent works include *Classic Wines of Australia and New Zealand, An Introduction to Australian Wine, Wine Atlas of Australia and New Zealand* and *Collecting Wine:You and Your Cellar.*

Co-founder of the wine website, www.winepros.com.au, Halliday is proving to be as popular on the World Wide Web as he is in other mediums.

contents

how to use this book

for the first time the 2003 *Wine Companion* provides a guide to Australian wineries only, rather than Australia and New Zealand. This change has been necessary due to the huge growth in the number of Australian wineries to describe and for which to provide tasting notes. Sadly consraints of space has meant New Zealand simply could not be included.

The *Wine Companion* is arranged with wineries in alphabetical order. The entries should be self-explanatory, but here I will briefly take you through the information for each entry.

winery entries

cape mentelle ★★★★☆
Off Wallcliffe Road, Margaret River, WA 6285 **region** Margaret River
phone (08) 9757 3266 **fax** (08) 9757 3233 **open** 7 days 10–4.30
winemaker John Durham **production** 55 000 **est.** 1970
product range ($15.50–55 R) Semillon Sauvignon Blanc, Sauvignon Blanc Semillon Wallcliffe Reserve, Georgiana, Marmaduke, Chardonnay, Shiraz, Zinfandel, Trinders Vineyard Cabernet Merlot, Cabernet Sauvignon.
summary Notwithstanding ownership by Veuve Clicquot, David Hohnen remains in command of one of Australia's foremost medium-sized wineries. Exceptional marketing skills and wine of the highest quality, with the backup of New Zealand's Cloudy Bay, are a potent combination. The Chardonnay and Semillon Sauvignon Blanc are among Australia's best, the potent Shiraz usually superb, and the berry/spicy Zinfandel makes one wonder why this grape is not as widespread in Australia as it is in California. Enlarged its business by the slightly quixotic acquisition of Mountadam in September 2000. Exports to Asia and the US.

winery name	Cape Mentelle

Although it might seem that stating the winery name is straightforward, this is not necessarily so. To avoid confusion, wherever possible I use the name that appears most prominently on the wine label and do not refer to any associated trading name.

ratings ★★★★☆

The winery star system may be interpreted as follows:

★★★★★ Outstanding winery regularly producing exemplary wines.
★★★★☆ Extremely good; virtually on a par with a five-star winery.
★★★★ Consistently produces high-quality wines.
★★★☆ A solid, reliable producer of good wine.
★★★ Typically good, but may have a few lesser wines.
★★☆ Adequate.
★★ Hard to recommend.

If the ratings seem generous, so be it. The fact is that Australia is blessed with a marvellous climate for growing grapes, a high degree of technological skill, and a remarkable degree of enthusiasm and dedication on the part of its winemakers. Across the price spectrum, Australian wines stand tall in the markets of the world. I see no reason, therefore, to shrink from recognising excellence. NR = not rated, either because the winery is new or because I have not tasted enough of its wines.

address Off Wallcliffe Road, Margaret River, WA 6285
phone (08) 9757 3266 **fax** (08) 9757 3233

The details are usually those of the winery and cellar door but in a few instances may simply be of the winery; this occurs when the wine is made at another winery under contract and is sold only through retail.

region Margaret River

The mapping of Australia into Zones and Regions with legally defined boundaries is now well underway. This edition sees radical changes (and additions) to the regional names and boundaries. Wherever possible the official 'Geographic Indication' name has been adopted, and where the registration process is incomplete, I have used the most likely name.

cellar door sales hours **open** 7 days 10–4.30

Although a winery might be listed as not open or only open on weekends, some may in fact be prepared to open by appointment. Many will, some won't; a telephone call will establish whether it is possible or not. Also, virtually every winery that is shown as being open only for weekends is in fact open for public holidays as well. Once again, a telephone call will confirm this.

winemaker John Durham

In the large companies the winemaker is simply the head of a team; there may be many executive winemakers actually responsible for specific wines.

production 55 000

This figure (representing the number of cases produced each year) is merely an indication of the size of the operation. Some wineries (principally but not exclusively the large companies) regard this information as confidential; in that event, NFP (not for publication) will appear. NA = information was not available.

year of establishment **est.** 1970

A more or less self-explanatory item, but keep in mind that some makers consider the year in which they purchased the land to be the year of establishment, others the year in which they first planted grapes, others the year they first made wine, others the year they first offered wine for sale, and so on. There may also be minor complications where there has been a change of ownership or a break in production.

price range and prod. range ($15.50–55 R) Semillon Sauvignon Blanc, Sauvignon Blanc Semillon Wallcliffe Reserve, Georgiana, Marmaduke, Chardonnay, Shiraz, Zinfandel, Trinders Vineyard Cabernet Merlot, Cabernet Sauvignon.

The **price range** covers the least expensive through to the most expensive wines usually made by the winery in question (where the information was available). Hence there may be a significant spread. That spread, however, may not fully cover fluctuations that occur in retail pricing, particularly with the larger companies. Erratic and often savage discounting remains a feature of the wine industry, and prices must therefore be seen as approximate.

For Australia, this spread has been compounded by the introduction on July 1 2000 of the Goods and Services Tax (GST) of 10 per cent and the special and uniquely discriminatory Wine Equalisation Tax (WET) of 29 per cent imposed on top of one another in a tax-on-tax pyramid.

I have indicated whether the price is cellar door (CD), mailing list (ML) or retail (R). By and large, the choice has been determined by which of the three methods of sale is most important to the winery. The price of Australian wines in other countries is affected by a number of factors, including excise and customs duty, distribution mark-up and currency fluctuations. Contact the winery for details.

product range

Particularly with the larger companies, it is not possible to give a complete list of the wines. The saving grace is that these days most of the wines are simply identified on their label by their varietal composition.

> **summary** Notwithstanding ownership by Veuve Clicquot, David Hohnen remains in command of one of Australia's foremost medium-sized wineries. Exceptional marketing skills and wine of the highest quality, with the backup of New Zealand's Cloudy Bay, are a potent combination. The Chardonnay and Semillon Sauvignon Blanc are among Australia's best, the potent Shiraz usually superb, and the berry/spicy Zinfandel makes one wonder why this grape is not as widespread in Australia as it is in California. Enlarged its business by the slightly quixotic acquisition of Mountadam in September 2000. Exports to Asia and the US.

My summary of the winery. Little needs to be said, except that I have tried to vary the subjects I discuss in this part of the winery entry.

🍂 The vine leaf symbol indicates wineries that are new entries in this year's listing.

tasting notes

Cape Mentelle Cabernet Sauvignon

ΥΥΥΥ 1998 Medium red-purple; the moderately intense bouquet has a mix of savoury, earthy, cedary aromas, those cedary oak characters coming through quite clearly on the palate. There is a typical core of red berry fruit on the mid-palate, then lingering, fine tannins on the finish. Overall, an austere style, but none the worse for that. **rating:** 88

best drinking 2003–2008 **best vintages** '76, '78, '82, '83, '86, '90, '91, '93, '94, '95 **drink with** Loin of lamb • $55

wine name Cape Mentelle Cabernet Sauvignon

In most instances, the wine's name will be prefaced by the name of the winery.

ratings ΥΥΥΥΥ

Two ratings are given for each wine; the ratings apply to the vintage reviewed, and may vary from one year to the next.

Points scale	Glass symbol	
98–100	–	Perfection which exists only as an idea.
94–97	ΥΥΥΥΥ	As close to perfection as the real world will allow.
90–93	ΥΥΥΥΥ	Excellent wine full of character; of gold medal standard.
85–89	ΥΥΥΥ	Very good wine; clear varietal definition/style; silver verging on gold medal standard.
80–84	ΥΥΥΥ	Good fault-free, flavoursome; high bronze to silver medal standard.

You will see that most of the wines reviewed in this book rate 80–84 points (3½ glasses) or better. This is not wanton generosity on my part. It simply reflects the fact that the 2000 or so wines selected for specific review are the tip of more than 5000 tasting notes accumulated over the past year. In other words, the wines described are among Australia's top 20 per cent.

▼▼▼▼ **1998** Medium red-purple; the moderately intense bouquet has a mix of savoury, earthy, cedary aromas, those cedary oak characters coming through quite clearly on the palate. There is a typical core of red berry fruit on the mid-palate, then lingering, fine tannins on the finish. Overall, an austere style, but none the worse for that.   **rating: 88**

The tasting note opens with the vintage of the wine tasted. With the exception of a very occasional classic wine, this tasting note will have been made within the 12 months prior to publication. Even that is a long time, and during the life of this book the wine will almost certainly change. More than this, remember that tasting is a highly subjective and imperfect art. NV = non-vintage.

best drinking   2003–2008

I will usually give a range of years or a more specific comment (such as 'quick-developing style'), but whatever my best drinking recommendation, always consider it with extreme caution and as an approximate guide at best. When to drink a given wine is an intensely personal decision, which only you can make.

best vintages   '76, '78, '82, '83, '86, '90, '91, '93, '94, '95

Self-explanatory information, but a note of caution: wines do change in the bottle, and it may be that were I to taste all of the best vintages listed, I would demote some and elevate some not mentioned.

drink with   Loin of lamb

Again, merely a suggestion – a subliminal guide to the style of wine.

price   • $55

This is a guide only.

$NA = information not available.

Abbreviation: mlf = malolactic fermentation.

key to regions

1 Lower Hunter Valley
2 Upper Hunter Valley
3 Hastings River
4 Mudgee
5 Orange
6 Cowra
7 Swan Hill
8 Murray Darling
9 Riverina
10 Perricoota
11 Hilltops
12 Canberra District
13 Tumbarumba
14 Shoalhaven
15 Henty
16 Grampians
17 Pyrenees
18 Ballarat
19 Bendigo
20 Goulburn Valley
21 Central Victorian High Country
22 Rutherglen and Glenrowan
23 King Valley
24 Alpine Valleys and Beechworth
25 Gippsland
26 Mornington Peninsula
27 Yarra Valley
28 Geelong
29 Sunbury
30 Macedon Ranges
31 Northern Tasmania
32 Southern Tasmania
33 Mount Gambier
34 Coonawarra
35 Wrattonbully
36 Mount Benson
37 Padthaway
38 Langhorne Creek
39 McLaren Vale
40 Adelaide Hills
41 Eden Valley
42 Adelaide Plains
43 Barossa Valley
44 Riverland
45 Clare Valley
46 Southern Eyre Peninsula
47 Great Southern
48 Pemberton and Manjimup
49 Blackwood Valley
50 Margaret River
51 Geographe
52 Peel
53 Perth Hills
54 Swan District
55 South Burnett
56 Granite Belt

wine regions of australia

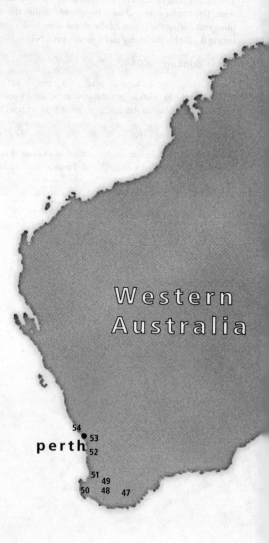

Western Australia

perth

54
53
52
51
49
50 48 47

Northern Territory

Queensland

South Australia

55
brisbane
56

New South Wales

2
3
4
1
5
6
11
sydney
12

8
9
45
43
46
42 41
40
44
adelaide
39 38
1
10
ACT
37
20
22
13
35
17 19
21 23
14
36 34
16
18 30 29
24
33 15
28 27
Victoria
melbourne
26
25

launceston
31

Tasmania 32 hobart

australia's geographical indications

the process of formally mapping Australia's wine regions continues to ever-so-slowly inch forward. The division into States, Zones, Regions and Sub Regions follows; those Regions or Sub Regions marked with an asterisk are variously in an early or late stage of determination. In two instances I have gone beyond the likely finalisation: it makes no sense to me that the Hunter Valley should be a Zone, the Region Hunter, and then Sub Regions which are all in the Lower Hunter Valley. I have elected to stick with the traditional division between the Upper Hunter Valley on the one hand, and the Lower on the other.

I am also ahead of the game with Tasmania, dividing it into Northern and Southern, and, to a lesser degree, have anticipated that the Coastal Hinterland Region of Queensland will seek recognition under this or some similar name.

state/zone	region	sub region
New South Wales		
Big Rivers	Lachlan Valley*	
	Murray Darling	
	Perricoota	
	Riverina	
	Swan Hill	
Central Ranges	Cowra	
	Mudgee	
	Orange	
Hunter Valley	Hunter	Allandale*
		Belford*
		Broke Fordwich*
		Dalwood*
		Pokolbin*
		Rothbury*
Northern Rivers	Hastings River	
Northern Slopes		
South Coast	Shoalhaven Coast*	
	Southern Highlands	
Southern New South Wales	Canberra District	
	Gundagai	
	Hilltops	
	Tumbarumba	
Western Plains		

state/zone	region	sub region
South Australia		
Adelaide (Super Zone, above Mount Lofty Ranges, Fleurieu and Barossa)		
Mount Lofty Ranges	Adelaide Hills	Gumeracha*
		Lenswood
		Piccadilly Valley
	Adelaide Plains	
	Clare Valley	Auburn*
		Clare*
		Hill River*
		Polish Hill River*
		Sevenhill*
		Watervale*
Fleurieu	Currency Creek	
	Kangaroo Island	
	Langhorne Creek	
	McLaren Vale	Clarendon*
	Southern Fleurieu	
Limestone Coast	Coonawarra	
	Mount Benson	
	Penola*	
	Padthaway	
	Wrattonbully*	
The Peninsulas	Southern Eyre Peninsula	
Lower Murray	Riverland	
Far North		
Barossa	Barossa Valley	
	Eden Valley	High Eden
		Springton*
Victoria		
Central Victoria	Bendigo	
	Central Victoria High Country*	
	Goulburn Valley	Nagambie Lakes
	Heathcote*	
	Strathbogie Ranges	
Gippsland		

state/zone	region	sub region
North East Victoria	Alpine Valleys	Kiewa Valley*
		Ovens Valley*
	Beechworth	
	Glenrowan*	
	King Valley*	Myrrhee*
		Whitlands*
	Rutherglen	Wahgunyah*
North West Victoria	Murray Darling	
	Swan Hill	
Port Phillip	Geelong	
	Macedon Ranges*	
	Mornington Peninsula	
	Sunbury	
	Yarra Valley	
Western Victoria	Grampians	
	Henty	
	Pyrenees	

Western Australia

state/zone	region	sub region
Eastern Plains, Inland and North of Western Australia		
West Australian		
South East Coastal	Esperance*	
South West Australia	Blackwood Valley	
	Geographe	
	Great Southern	Albany
		Frankland River
		Mount Barker
		Porongurup
	Manjimup*	
	Margaret River	
	Pemberton*	
Central Western Australia		
Greater Perth	Peel	
	Perth Hills	
	Swan District	Swan Valley*

Queensland

state/zone	region	sub region
Queensland	Granite Belt	
	Coastal Hinterland*	
	South Burnett	

Tasmania

Tasmania

Australian Capital Territory

Northern Territory

The best of the best of Australian wine

this year follows in the tradition of last year by listing the top wines from well over 5000 tasting notes made between April 2001 and March 2002. As I have said before, the lists brutally expose the imperfections of assigning numbers (or points) to wines and giving those points the appearance of immutable validity. The reality is they are part of a series of snapshots, as accurate as I could make them at the time and in the varying circumstances of the particular tasting.

There are some notable omissions, most frequently because the wine in question did not cross my tasting table this year. There are also some surprising inclusions: I have resisted the temptation to edit the lists in any way.

This year I have also included some new categories for the first time: Special Value Wines, Ten of the Best New Wineries and Ten Dark Horse Wineries – wineries that deserve to be far better known and appreciated.

best of the best 2003 by variety

riesling

The shortage in premium riesling grapes became evident in the 2002 vintage and pushed grape prices for this variety skywards. This, and the positive publicity generated by the Stelvin closure debate, suggests we can expect to pay more for quality Rieslings in the years ahead. Nonetheless, it will be a long time before these wines command the price they really deserve.

2001 Ashton Hills Riesling	95
2001 Brindabella Hills Riesling	95
2001 Crawford River Reserve Riesling	95
2001 Petaluma Riesling	95
2001 Sevenhill Cellars Riesling	95
2001 Tamar Ridge Riesling	95
1996 Taylors St Andrews Riesling	95
2001 Alkoomi Frankland River Riesling	94
2001 Crabtree of Watervale Riesling	94
2001 Craigow Riesling	94
2001 Crawford River Riesling	94
2000 Geoff Weaver Lenswood Riesling	94
2001 Gilberts Riesling	94
2001 Grosset Watervale Riesling	94
2001 Houghton Frankland River Riesling	94
2001 Lark Hill Riesling	94
1998 Leo Buring Leonay Riesling	94
2001 Mitchell Watervale Riesling	94
2001 Morningside Wines Riesling	94
2001 Nepenthe Vineyards Adelaide Hills Riesling	94
2001 O'Leary Walker Watervale Riesling	94
1997 Pewsey Vale The Contours Riesling	94
1999 Seppelt Drumborg Riesling	94
2001 Stringy Brae Riesling	94
2001 Taylors Clare Riesling	94
2001 Wolf Blass Gold Label Riesling	94
2001 Wynns Coonawarra Estate Riesling	94

semillon

There are far more Semillons rating 94 or more this year than last year simply because of the exceptional quality of the 2000 and 2001 vintages for this variety in the Hunter Valley. Only three wines came from outside the Hunter Valley, and, if this indicates bias, so be it.

1996 Brokenwood ILR Reserve Semillon	96
1996 McWilliam's Mount Pleasant Lovedale Semillon	96
1996 Tyrrell's Vat 1 Semillon	96
2001 Briar Ridge Early Harvest Semillon	95
2000 Farmer's Daughter Semillon	95
2001 McLeish Estate Semillon	95
1997 McWilliam's Mount Pleasant Lovedale Semillon	95
2000 Rothbury Estate Brokenback Semillon	95
2001 Angus Sturt Ridge Semillon	94
2001 Briar Ridge Karl Stockhausen Signature Release Semillon	94
2001 Brokenwood Semillon	94
2001 Chalkers Crossing Hilltops Semillon	94
2001 McWilliam's Hunter Semillon	94
1998 McWilliam's Mount Pleasant Elizabeth	94
2001 Pothana Belford Semillon	94
2000 Pothana Belford Semillon	94
2001 Rothbury Estate Hunter Valley Semillon	94
2001 Tower Estate Hunter Valley Semillon	94
2001 Tyrrell's Lost Block Semillon	94
1997 Tyrrell's Vat 1 Semillon	94

sauvignon blanc and blends – and a few others

If 2000 wasn't kind to sauvignon blanc, 2001 was even less so – or at least, outside of the Margaret River where it has a natural affinity with semillon. These constitute the first 14 wines; there is then a small group of Rhône white varietals bringing up the rear.

2001 Grosset Semillon Sauvignon Blanc	95
2001 Pierro Semillon Sauvignon Blanc LTC	94
2001 Shaw & Smith Sauvignon Blanc	94
2001 Cape Jaffa Semillon Sauvignon Blanc	93
2001 Cape Mentelle Semillon Sauvignon Blanc	93
2001 Cullen Semillon Sauvignon Blanc	93
2000 Cullen Semillon Sauvignon Blanc	93
2001 Eldredge Semillon Sauvignon Blanc	93
2001 Starvedog Lane Sauvignon Blanc	93
1999 Voyager Estate Tom Price Semillon Sauvignon Blanc	93
2001 Willow Bridge Estate Winemaker's Reserve Semillon Sauvignon Blanc	93
2001 Forest Hill Vineyard Sauvignon Blanc Semillon	92
2001 Gapsted Ballerina Canopy Sauvignon Blanc	92
1999 Yarra Yarra Semillon Sauvignon Blanc	92
2000 Yalumba The Virgilius	94

chardonnay

My personal predilections may suggest otherwise, but you cannot argue with the proposition that high quality chardonnay grapes, coupled with appropriate winemaking techniques, produce the most complex and complete white wines.

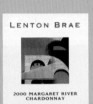

sparkling, sweet and rosé

Sparkling, rosé, and sweet white wines. An odd trio, of course, but they all deserve recognition notwithstanding special constraints.

1995 Domaine Chandon Cuvée Prestige	95
1997 Hardys Arras	95
1997 Jansz	95
1998 Bianchet Cuvée	94
1997 Hardys Sir James Vintage	94
1998 Moorilla Estate Brut	94
1992 Petaluma Croser LD	94
1997 Pipers Brook Pirie Cuvée	94
NV Rockford Black Shiraz	94
2000 Pipers Brook Vineyard Cuvée Clarke	95
2000 De Bortoli Noble One	93
2000 Margan Family Botrytis Semillon	93
2001 Mount Horrocks Cordon Cut Riesling	93
1998 Brown Brothers Noble Riesling	92
2001 Crawford River Nektar	92
2000 Ninth Island Botrytis Riesling	92
2001 Wellington Iced Riesling 375 ml	92
2001 Charles Melton Rosé of Virginia	94
2001 De Bortoli Cabernet Rosé	91
2001 Turkey Flat Rosé	90

pinot noir

I can but hope that some day soon we will have another vintage like 2000 for Pinot Noir. In last year's *Companion* nine Pinot Noirs scored 94 points or more; this year the number is 44. The brightest star is Tasmania, but all the acknowledged Pinot Noir regions performed brilliantly. Necessity being the mother of invention, those on 94 points are listed in abbreviated, running text form.

1999 Providence Miguet Reserve Pinot Noir	97
1999 Candlebark Hill Reserve Pinot Noir	96
2000 Diamond Valley Close Planted Pinot Noir	96
2000 No Regrets Pinot Noir	96
1999 Pipers Brook Vineyard The Lyre Pinot Noir	96
2000 2 Bud Spur Pinot Noir	95
2000 Apsley Gorge Pinot Noir	95
1999 Diamond Valley Close Planted Pinot Noir	95
2000 Pinot Noir by Farr	95
2000 Freycinet Pinot Noir	95
2000 Kings Creek Reserve Pinot Noir	95
2000 Knappstein Lenswood Vineyards Pinot Noir	95

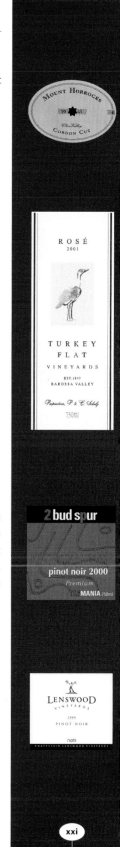

2000 Montalto Pinot Noir	95
2000 Moorooduc Estate Wild Yeast Pinot Noir	95
2000 Paringa Estate Pinot Noir	95
2000 Providence Miguet Reserve Pinot Noir	95
2000 Wedgetail Estate Reserve Pinot Noir	95

2000 Bannockburn, 2000 Bindi Original Vineyard, 1999 Bindi Original Vineyard, 2000 Brinalon, 1998 Cleveland, 2000 De Bortoli Yarra Valley, 2000 Elsewhere Vineyard Bay of Eight, 2000 Golders, 2000 Grosset, 2000 Kraanwood, 1999 Metier Wines, 2000 Montalto Pennon, 1999 Mount Mary, 2000 Nepenthe Vineyards, 2000 Panorama, 1999 Pipers Brook Vineyard The Blackwood, 2000 Port Phillip Estate Reserve, 2000 Rochford, 2000 Seville Estate, 2000 Shadowfax Geelong, 2000 Tamar Ridge, 2000 Tarrington Vineyards, 2000 Ten Minutes by Tractor, 2000 Ten Minutes by Tractor Judd Vineyard, 2000 Wedgetail Estate, 2000 Winstead, 2000 Yering Station Reserve.

shiraz

The unprecedented number of Shiraz wines scoring 94 points or more is remarkable in itself. Even more surprising, however, is the number of wines from the 1999 and 2000 vintages – years less favorable than 1998. The 52 wines on 94 points are listed in the same fashion as the Pinot Noirs.

1999 Alkoomi Jarrah Shiraz	96
2000 Bannockburn Shiraz	96
1999 Brokenwood Graveyard Shiraz	96
2000 Dalwhinnie Moonambel Shiraz	96
2000 Howard Park Scotsdale Shiraz	96
1998 McWilliam's Mount Pleasant Maurice O'Shea Shiraz	96
1997 Seppelt Great Western Shiraz	96
1998 Taylors St Andrews Shiraz	96
1999 Farmer's Daughter Shiraz	95
1999 Jim Barry The Armagh	95
2000 Petersons Back Block Shiraz	95
1997 Montrose Black Shiraz	95
2000 Punters Corner Spartacus Reserve Shiraz	95
1999 Punters Corner Spartacus Reserve Shiraz	95
1998 Saltram No. 1 Reserve Shiraz	95
1998 St Hallett Old Block Shiraz	95
1999 Torbreck The Factor	95
1998 Wirra Wirra Chook Block Shiraz	95
1998 Wolf Blass Platinum Label Shiraz	95

1999 Burra Burra Lone Star, 1999 Barossa Valley Estate E & E Black Pepper, 1998 Barossa Valley Estate Ebenezer, 2000 Berrys Bridge, 2000 Brokenwood Graveyard, 2000 Chateau Leamon Reserve, 1998

Coriole Lloyd Reserve, 1999 Coriole, 1999 Crabtree of Watervale, 1998 Craiglee, 1997 De Bortoli GS Reserve Yarra Valley, 2000 Dowie Doole, 1998 Elderton Command, 2000 Fonty's Pool, 2000 Galli Estate, 1998 Grant Burge Meshach, 2000 Hanging Rock Winery Heathcote, 2000 Henry's Drive, 1999 Heritage Wines Barossa, 1999 Hillstowe Mary's Hundred, 1999 Houghton Frankland, 2000 Huntington Estate Special Reserve, 1999 Huntington Estate Special Reserve, 1999 Huntington Estate Special Reserve, 2000 Jasper Hill Georgia's Paddock, 1999 Jasper Hill Georgia's Paddock, 1998 Jasper Hill Georgia's Paddock, 2000 Jinks Creek Yarra Valley, 1999 Kaesler Old Vine, 1998 Knight Granite Hills, 2000 McGuigan Genus 4 Old Vine, 1998 McWilliam's Mount Pleasant OP & OH, 2000 Mount Beckworth, 1999 Petaluma, 2000 Picardy, 1999 Plantagenet Mount Barker, 1999 Montrose Black, 2000 Port Phillip Estate Reserve, 2000 Red Edge, 1999 Rosemount Estate Show Reserve, 1998 Rosemount Estate Show Reserve, 2000 Seville Estate, 2000 Summerfield Reserve, 1996 Tahbilk 1933 Vines Reserve, 1999 Torbreck The RunRig, 2000 Tower Estate Hunter Valley, 2000 Turkey Flat, 1999 Turkey Flat, 1998 Warraroong Estate, 1999 Willespie, 2000 Willow Bridge Estate Winemaker's Reserve, 1999 Wirra Wirra RSW.

shiraz blends

A short list, but of high quality, emphasising the flexibility of Shiraz as a blend-mate with both Bordeaux and Rhône varietals.

1999 Annie's Lane Old Vine Grenache Shiraz Mourvèdre	94
1999 Charles Melton Nine Popes	94
1999 Jasper Hill Emily's Paddock Shiraz Cabernet Franc	94
1998 Jasper Hill Emily's Paddock Shiraz Cabernet Franc	94
2000 Torbreck The Descendant	94
1998 Yalumba Barossa Valley Shiraz + Viognier	94
2000 Cobaw Ridge Shiraz Viognier	93
2000 Gralyn Estate Shiraz Cabernet	93
1998 Tyrrell's Vat 8 Shiraz Cabernet	93

cabernet sauvignon

There are precisely the same number (23) of Cabernet Sauvignons at 94 points or above as in last year's list, but this is by no means a list I could have predicted then. There are four wines from new wineries (Epis & Williams, Gartner and Murdock), and every manner of climate, from cool to very warm.

1998 Wirra Wirra Vineyard Series Penley Cabernet Sauvignon	97
2000 Dalwhinnie Moonambel Cabernet Sauvignon	96
1996 Hardys Thomas Hardy Cabernet Sauvignon	96
1999 Houghton Margaret River Cabernet Sauvignon	95

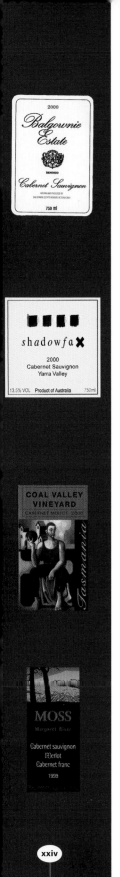

1998 Jim Barry McCrae Wood Cabernet Sauvignon 95
2000 Balgownie Estate Cabernet Sauvignon 94
2000 Balnaves Cabernet Sauvignon 94
2000 Balnaves The Tally Reserve Cabernet Sauvignon 94
1998 Balnaves The Tally Reserve Cabernet Sauvignon 94
1998 Elderton Ashmead Single Vineyard
      Cabernet Sauvignon 94
2000 Epis & Williams Cabernet Sauvignon 94
1999 Gartner Coonawarra Cabernet Sauvignon 94
2000 Gralyn Estate Cabernet Sauvignon 94
1997 Katnook Estate Odyssey Cabernet Sauvignon 94
1999 Moorilla Estate Cabernet Sauvignon 94
1999 Murdock Cabernet Sauvignon 94
1998 Murdock Cabernet Sauvignon 94
1999 Parker Coonawarra Estate Terra Rossa
      Cabernet Sauvignon 94
1999 Penfolds Bin 707 Cabernet Sauvignon 94
2000 Shadowfax Yarra Valley Cabernet Sauvignon 94
1998 Tempus Two Reserve Hollydene Cabernet Sauvignon 94
1998 Wolf Blass Platinum Label Cabernet Sauvignon 94
1996 Wyndham Estate Show Reserve Mudgee
      Cabernet Sauvignon 94

cabernet blends, and other bordeaux varieties

The Cabernet/Bordeaux blends couple Cabernet with one or more of Merlot, Cabernet Franc, Malbec and Petit Verdot. Nine of these come from the Margaret River or Great Southern regions of Western Australia. Then come the single varietal wines in this overall category.

1999 Cullen Cabernet Sauvignon Merlot 96
1999 Alkoomi Blackbutt 95
2000 Coal Valley Vineyard Cabernet Merlot 95
1998 Houghton Jack Mann 95
1999 Moss Brothers Cabernet Sauvignon Merlot 95
1999 Vasse Felix Heytesbury 95
1999 Andrew Harris Cabernet Merlot 94
1998 Bleasdale Frank Potts 94
2000 Cullen Cabernet Sauvignon Merlot 94
1997 De Bortoli Melba Barrel Select 94
1999 Devil's Lair Margaret River 94
1999 Howard Park Cabernet Sauvignon Merlot 94
2000 Keith Tulloch Forres Blend 94
1999 Voyager Estate Cabernet Sauvignon Merlot 94
1999 Pirramimma Reserve Petit Verdot 94
2000 Shaw & Smith Merlot 94
1999 Tatachilla Adelaide Hills Merlot 94

fortified wines

Against the grain, I have omitted the list of the best fortified wines because they are essentially the same, year-in, year-out. Simply use last year's list, and you won't go wrong.

special value wines

I have selected ten of the best value wines in various self-explanatory groups. Correllating price and points is never easy at the best of times, and in some instances there were 30 or 40 wines with near-equal credentials. For any number of reasons, including all of them was out of the question, and so I was compelled to make some fairly arbitrary choices. So it is that the title is 'Ten of the Best', not 'The Best Ten' for each group.

ten of the best value whites $10 and under

2001 De Bortoli Sacred Hill Semillon Chardonnay	86	$5.50
2001 De Bortoli Sacred Hill Rhine Riesling	84	$5.50
2001 Yalumba Oxford Landing Chardonnay	87	$7.95
2000 McPherson Wines Murray Darling Chardonnay	84	$7.99
2001 Orlando Jacob's Creek Chardonnay	87	$8.00
2001 Orlando Jacob's Creek Riesling	86	$8.00
2001 Jindalee Estate Chardonnay	89	$9.50
2000 Morgan Simpson Chardonnay	85	$9.50
2001 Eaglehawk Riesling	92	$9.95
NV Hardys Omni	87	$10.00

ten of the best value reds $10 and under

2001 Angove's Butterfly Ridge Shiraz Cabernet	82	$6.00
2001 Queen Adelaide Pinot Noir	82	$7.00
2001 Lindemans Bin 50 Shiraz	82	$8.50
2001 Salisbury Estate Merlot	82	$9.00
2001 Miranda Mirool Creek Reserve Durif	85	$9.95
2000 Deakin Estate Shiraz	87	$9.99
2001 Wolf Blass Eaglehawk Cabernet Sauvignon	83	$9.99
2001 Pepperjack Grenache Rosé	86	$10.00
2001 Zilzie Buloke Reserve Petit Verdot	85	$10.00
2001 De Bortoli Montage Cabernet Merlot	83	$10.00

2001 McWilliam's Hanwood Chardonnay	88	$11.50
2001 Tahbilk Semillon	90	$11.95
2001 Kingsley Riesling	91	$12.00
2001 Wolf Blass South Australia Riesling	91	$12.00
2001 Angus Sturt Ridge Semillon	94	$13.00
2000 The Willows Vineyard Semillon	92	$13.00
2001 Annie's Lane Riesling	93	$13.50
1999 McGuigan Bin 9000 Semillon	92	$13.50
2001 Macaw Creek Riesling	92	$14.00
2001 Primo Estate la biondina Colombard	92	$14.50

ten of the best value reds $10-$15

2001 De Bortoli Cabernet Rosé	91	$12.00
2001 Faber Vineyard Shiraz	91	$12.00
2001 Turkey Flat Rosé	90	$14.00
1999 Moondah Brook Shiraz	90	$14.95
2000 Cape Jaffa Brocks Reef Cabernet Merlot	90	$14.95
1999 Farmer's Daughter Shiraz	95	$15.00
2000 De Bortoli Gulf Station Shiraz	90	$15.00
1998 Lindemans Padthaway Shiraz	90	$15.00
2001 Taylors Shiraz	90	$15.00
2001 Judds Warby Range Estate Durif	90	$15.00

2001 Stringy Brae Riesling	94	$16.00
2001 Taylors Clare Riesling	94	$16.00
2001 Wolf Blass Gold Label Riesling	94	$16.00
2001 Chalkers Crossing Hilltops Semillon	94	$16.50
2001 Morningside Wines Riesling	94	$17.00
2001 Brokenwood Semillon	94	$17.00
2000 Clearview Estate Mudgee Church Creek Chardonnay	94	$17.00
1998 McWilliam's Mount Pleasant Elizabeth	94	$17.50
2001 Brindabella Hills Riesling	95	$18.00
2001 Briar Ridge Early Harvest Semillon	95	$18.50

ten of the best value reds $15-$20

1999 Steins Cabernet Sauvignon	93	$16.00
2000 Mount View Estate Reserve Shiraz	92	$16.00
2001 Faber Vineyard Riche Shiraz	92	$16.50

2001 Charles Melton Rosé Of Virginia	94	$16.90
1999 Crabtree of Watervale Shiraz	94	$18.00
2000 Mount Beckworth Shiraz	94	$18.00
2000 Montalto Pennon Pinot Noir	94	$18.50
1999 Heritage Wines Barossa Shiraz	94	$19.00
1999 Montrose Black Shiraz	94	$19.00
2000 Fettler's Rest Pinot Noir	93	$19.50

ten of the best new wineries

My heading for this piece has been chosen with particular care. This is not the ten best new wineries, simply because I do not have the wisdom of Solomon, and in a field of 183 new wineries I doubt that even Solomon could come up with a fail-safe list. I have tried to provide a spread of regions, but, beyond that, it all becomes very difficult.

Angus Wines [page 14] Adelaide Zone
Hindmarsh Island is a symbol of many things, but Susan and Alistair Angus have added another dimension with their utterly delicious Semillon and sturdy Shiraz. Clean graphic design adds to the appeal; mailing list the best purchase option.

Chalkers Crossing [page 83] Hilltops
One of the most exciting debuts, with a range of immaculately crafted wines predominantly from Hilltops and Tumbarumba via the hand of French-trained Celine Rousseau. Available through Vintage Cellars.

Epis/Epis & Williams [page 143] Macedon Ranges
Brings together three legends: Alec Epis (of Essendon fame) as owner and viticulturist; Stuart Anderson as consulting winemaker; and the late Laurie Williams, pioneer viticulturist of the Macedon region.

Hackersley [page 183] Geographe
Founded by the Ovens, Stacey and Hewitt families under the mistaken belief that growing and making their own wine would be cheaper than buying it. Houghton buys the grapes and makes a small percentage of the take into three beautifully sculpted and immaculately presented wines which do indeed represent great value.

Faber Vineyard [page 148] Swan Valley

Former Houghton winemaker John Griffiths is leading a busy life as a consultant, but has also developed his own label in the Swan Valley, deliberately opting for an unfashionably warm climate, and producing richly robed Shiraz.

Heritage Wines at Mt Tamborine [page 200] Queensland Coastal

Far from the largest of the new Queensland wineries, but at least in 1999 and 2000, making the best wines. Its viticultural foot rests in the Granite Belt, which helps.

House of Certain Views [page 211] Hunter Valley

A brilliant concept by the Margan family, utilising grapes from high altitude vineyards on the western side of the Great Dividing Range, in some instances pioneering areas hitherto unplanted. Meticulously made wines.

Murdock [page 322] Coonawarra

The Murdock family has various connections with Coonawarra, the most relevant being ten hectares of cabernet sauvignon, principally sold but with a small proportion contract-made by Pete Bissell. The two first vintages are, quite simply, great.

O'Leary Walker Wines [page 333] Clare Valley

Some might say notwithstanding 30 years combined experience in the industry, David O'Leary and Nick Walker have set out on their own, with vineyards in the Clare Valley and Adelaide Hills providing a perfect spectrum of varietal fruit for their undoubted talents.

Ten Minutes by Tractor Wine Co [page 446] Mornington Peninsula

The seemingly impossible name is wrapped around a highly sophisticated and brilliantly presented joint venture between three Mornington Peninsula grape grower families, co-operating to provide thoroughly impressive wines led by Chardonnay and Pinot Noir.

ten dark horses

As with the ten best new wineries, this is a highly subjective list of wineries which have either shown recent but impressive improvement in their wines, or which simply deserve greater recognition. With one exception (Stanton & Killeen) they are all rated at 4.5 stars, rather than five. Without wishing to appear presumptuous, a five-star rating is recognition in itself.

Bremerton Wines [page 53] Langhorne Creek

From the slightly unfashionable Langhorne Creek region this winery regularly produces attractively priced red wines with silky, soft mouthfeel and stacks of flavour.

Crabtree of Watervale [page 107] Clare Valley

Quiet and self-effacing Robert Crabtree has made a stellar 2001 Riesling and 1999 Shiraz, both at mouthwatering prices.

Jindalee Estate [page 226] Geelong

A business with two distinct parts: the elegant, high quality Fettler's Rest wines from the former Idyll Estate at Geelong, and one of the best value Chardonnays on the market from the Riverland.

Jinks Creek Winery [page 227] Gippsland

Andrew Clarke hit the jackpot in 2000, but the sold-out sign will have doubtless gone up. Well worth watching in 2002, in particular.

Poet's Corner Wines [page 365] Mudgee

The Poet's Corner and Montrose wines have gone from strength to strength in recent years, notwithstanding challenging Mudgee vintages. Bargain basement prices for terrific wines.

Pothana [page 368] Lower Hunter Valley

Those on the mailing list will know just how good these wines are, but I had lost track of them, partly due to my lack of understanding of the labelling structure. Highly skilled winemaking shines through.

Shantell [page 415] Yarra Valley

Without question, the most under-rated producer in the Yarra Valley. An excellent, fully mature vineyard is complemented by largely non-interventionist winemaking which highlights the quality of the grapes. Watch for the 2000 vintage reds

Stanton & Killeen [page 423] Rutherglen

Like Shantell, deserves more recognition, although I have done my bit with the five-star rating. Chris Killeen's skills are as evident in the rich red wines as they are in one of Australia's greatest Vintage Ports.

Tahbilk [page 436] Goulburn Valley

Has gone from strength to strength in recent years; the current range of releases is utterly exemplary.

Taylors [page 443] Clare Valley

The darkest of dark horses, simply because it is so large and has been around for so long. Yet, stand back and look objectively at the quality of its wines since 1997 and you will see why it is challenging for a fifth star. If that is not enough, the prices are the clincher.

australian vintage charts

Each number represents a mark out of ten for the quality of vintages in each region. NR denotes no rating.

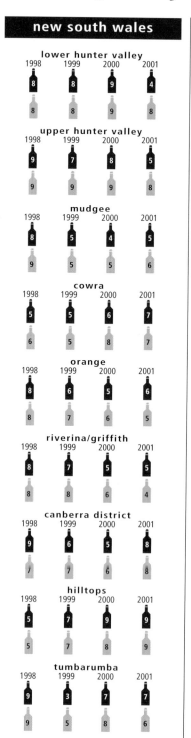

new south wales

lower hunter valley
1998	1999	2000	2001
8	8	9	4
8	8	9	8

upper hunter valley
1998	1999	2000	2001
9	7	8	5
9	9	9	8

mudgee
1998	1999	2000	2001
8	5	4	5
9	5	5	6

cowra
1998	1999	2000	2001
5	5	6	7
6	5	8	7

orange
1998	1999	2000	2001
8	6	5	6
8	7	6	5

riverina/griffith
1998	1999	2000	2001
8	7	5	5
8	8	6	4

canberra district
1998	1999	2000	2001
9	6	5	8
7	7	6	8

hilltops
1998	1999	2000	2001
5	7	9	9
5	7	8	9

tumbarumba
1998	1999	2000	2001
9	3	7	7
9	5	8	6

hastings river
1998	1999	2000	2001
7	6	8	5
9	6	9	7

shoalhaven
1998	1999	2000	2001
9	5	NR	4
9	6	NR	5

victoria

yarra valley
1998	1999	2000	2001
9	6	9	7
8	6	9	6

mornington peninsula
1998	1999	2000	2001
9	7	9	8
9	7	8	8

geelong
1998	1999	2000	2001
NR	8	9	6
NR	6	8	6

macedon
1998	1999	2000	2001
9	9	8	7
8	8	8	7

sunbury
1998	1999	2000	2001
9	9	8	8
9	8	8	9

grampians
1998	1999	2000	2001
9	10	8	8
7	8	9	7

pyrenees
1998	1999	2000	2001
8	8	8	9
8	9	8	7

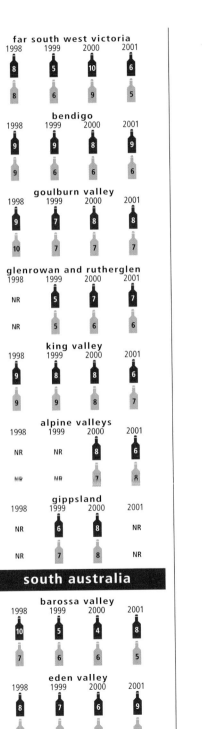

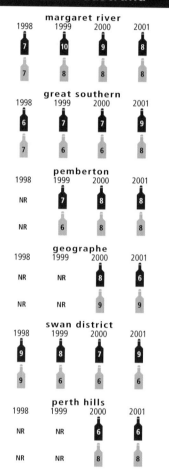

western australia

margaret river
1998	1999	2000	2001
7	10	9	8
7	8	8	8

great southern
1998	1999	2000	2001
6	7	7	9
7	6	6	8

pemberton
1998	1999	2000	2001
NR	7	8	8
NR	6	8	8

geographe
1998	1999	2000	2001
NR	NR	8	6
NR	NR	9	9

swan district
1998	1999	2000	2001
9	8	7	9
9	6	6	6

perth hills
1998	1999	2000	2001
NR	NR	6	6
NR	NR	8	8

queensland

granite belt
1998	1999	2000	2001
9	8	10	8
5	6	9	7

tasmania

northern tasmania
1998	1999	2000	2001
10	9	9	8
9	9	9	8

southern tasmania
1998	1999	2000	2001
9	8	10	8
8	7	9	8

australian vintage 2002:
a snapshot

t he star performer for the 2002 vintage was an unlikely one: the Riverland. It had its best and its largest vintage ever, which might seem like the hackneyed 'vintage of the century' call, except it happens to be true. Tonnage was up because of new plantings coming on stream, rather than a large yield per hectare, and the quality has come from the absence of any really hot days. One Barossa winemaker, with absolutely no axe to grind, commented the red wines had more Barossa Valley feel about them than Riverland.

The Hunter Valley had a typical vintage: an absolute deluge of rain shortly after picking commenced. Until the rain, everything was looking superb, and — characteristically — the semillon emerged unscathed. Chardonnay falls somewhere in the middle, while the shiraz will be an unpredictable mixed bag: the best vineyards with the best soil and management dried out without the onset of rot, and produced very good shiraz. This, however, was far from universal, and extreme care will be needed when the time comes for buying the red wines of 2002.

Clare Valley Riesling, Western Australia (both Margaret River and Great Southern, and with the white wines particularly brilliant), the Yarra Valley (outstanding) and Mornington Peninsula fared particularly well. The berry size, bunch weight and overall yield in the Yarra Valley and Mornington Peninsula (and likewise Geelong, Gippsland and Macedon) were all microscopic: bunches weighing one-fifth of the normal amount (20 grammes instead of 100 grammes) and yields down to half a ton to the acre or even less were commonplace.

Northern Tasmania shared with the rest of the cooler parts of south eastern Australia a wet and cool spring, then a very cool summer. Just when things looked decidedly dodgy, the weather turned fine around February 23, and between then and the first week of April was more or less continuously fine and warm. While the yield was down between 30 per cent and 50 per cent (far better than southern Victoria) expectations were high for quality; the sparkling bases were good, and the table wine grapes were finished at what would be classed as a normal time. The low yields clearly helped the ripening process. Southern Tasmania did not have the same good fortune: there the weather continued cold and wet for a further 14 days, and did not turn until the end of the first week of March.

Indeed, the whole of the bottom half of south eastern Australia suffered from depressed yields, including the key areas of Coonawarra, Padthaway and elsewhere on the Limestone Coast. This was due to the coldest summer on record following on the heels of the hottest summer on record in 2001. The cold and often wet conditions during flowering resulted in these depressed yields, and in a late to very late vintage.

Elsewhere in South Australia yields were down between 20 and 50 per cent. There is colour in abundance, and in many cases tannins likewise, but the concern is there may be an absence of vinosity, of mid-palate fruit. Relatively speaking,

Coonawarra Cabernet Sauvignon fared better than Shiraz, and this may be part of a wider-spread pattern. Overall, and notwithstanding the colour, the red wines from across South Australia will most likely be lighter in body, not unlike the '97 vintage.

The one common feature right across Australia was the high natural acidity. One major company calculated that halfway through vintage it had already saved one million dollars in tartaric acid additions (or rather lack thereof) while in the Yarra Valley the cost was zero.

The 2001 vintage produced 1.39 million tonnes; the 2002 crush will increase somewhat to around 1.52 million tonnes.

abbey vale ★★★★

Wildwood Road, Yallingup, WA 6282 **region** Margaret River
phone (08) 9755 2121 **fax** (08) 9755 2286 **open** 7 days 10–5
winemaker Dorham Mann, Kevin McKay **production** 42 000 **est.** 1986
product range ($14.50–49 CD) Semillon, Semillon Sauvignon Blanc, Verdelho, Sauvignon Blanc, Sunburst Verdelho, Contessa, Chardonnay, Monseigneur, Shiraz, Merlot, Merlot Shiraz, Monseigneur (Cabernet blend), Cabernet Merlot, Reserve Cabernet Sauvignon, Port.
summary Abbey Vale has gone from strength to strength, vinifying an ever-increasing proportion of the production from its 30-hectare vineyard (plus another 60 under contract), and winning a significant number of show awards. It was no doubt this success which led to its acquisition by Swiss interests in 2000. The wines are exported to the US, the UK, France, Switzerland and Italy.

Abbey Vale Sauvignon Blanc

▼▼▼▽ **2001** Light green-yellow; the aromas of the bouquet are in the ripe spectrum, with sweet gooseberry and just a touch of herb. The palate doesn't deliver the promise of the bouquet; it lacks persistence, but nonetheless a pleasant flavour. **rating:** 84

best drinking 2001–2003 **best vintages** NA **drink with** Calamari • $19.50

Abbey Vale Dry Verdelho

▼▼▼▽ **2001** Light green-yellow; the bouquet is clean, with touches of apple, fruit salad and spice. The palate is crisp, again with some apple flavours, and adequate length and balance. Could mature with age into a generous wine. **rating:** 83

best drinking 2002–2005 **best vintages** '92, '94, '95, '96 **drink with** Honey-baked ham • $19.50

Abbey Vale Chardonnay

▼▼▼▼ **2000** Light green-yellow; a clean, fruit-driven bouquet with melon and citrus fruit is logically followed by an elegant, still quite tight palate showing citrus and stone fruit in the foreground, and oak in the background. Good development potential. **rating:** 87

best drinking 2001–2004 **best vintages** NA **drink with** Deep-fried calamari • $22.50

Abbey Vale Shiraz

▼▼▼▼ **2000** Medium to full red-purple; the bouquet is clean, with raspberry/cherry/spice aromas and subtle oak. The palate is very youthful and unformed, but has plenty of fruit, and will improve with cellaring. **rating:** 85

best drinking 2003–2007 **best vintages** '99 **drink with** Diced lamb • $22

Abbey Vale Merlot

▼▼▼▽ **1999** Medium red, with some purple hues; the light, savoury/spicy/cedary bouquet has positive varietal character, as do the savoury and olive flavours of the palate. The tannins are silky, but the core of sweet fruit is hard to find. **rating:** 84

best drinking 2002–2006 **best vintages** NA **drink with** Roast veal • $21

Abbey Vale Monseigneur

▼▼▼▼▽ **1998** Medium to full red-purple; the bouquet opens with quite sweet blackcurrant fruit, then has a slightly earthy/savoury twist which adds to the appeal. The medium-bodied palate offers blackberry, blackcurrant and chocolate flavours supported by attractive cedary oak and fine tannins. **rating:** 90

best drinking 2003–2008 **best vintages** '98 **drink with** Beef in black bean sauce • $49

abercorn ★★★★

Cassilis Road, Mudgee, NSW 2850 **region** Mudgee
phone 1800 000 959 **fax** (02) 6373 3108 **open** Thurs–Mon 10.30–4.30
winemaker Tim Stevens **production** 7000 **est.** 1996
product range ($14.95–34.95 R) Chardonnay, Unwooded Chardonnay, Reserve Chardonnay, Shiraz, A Reserve Shiraz, Shiraz Cabernet; Barons Court is second label, comprising Chardonnay and Shiraz.
summary Tim and Connie Stevens acquired the 25-year-old Abercorn Vineyard in 1996; while admirably located, next door to Huntington Estate, it had become somewhat run down. Rejuvenation of the vineyard is largely complete, and the tasting room, opened in January 2001, has proved a major success. The wine is starting to find retail distribution throughout Sydney in addition to its cellar-door and mail-order business. National distribution through National Wine & Beer Distributors; exports to the UK.

Abercorn Unwooded Chardonnay

ŦŦŦŸ 2001 Light straw-green; clean, light melon fruit aromas lead into a fresh, unfussed palate with melon fruit and a clean, balanced finish. **rating: 84**

best drinking 2002–2003 **best vintages** NA **drink with** Seafood • $14.95

Abercorn Shiraz

ŦŦŦŦ 2000 Bright purple-red; the bouquet offers a regional/varietal mix with earthy overtones to sweet, red berry fruit; a powerful, sturdy palate with black cherry fruit and pervasive tannins needing at least five years to resolve. Well-handled oak. **rating: 88**

best drinking 2006–2011 **best vintages** '98, '99 **drink with** Rare roast beef • $19.95

Abercorn A Reserve Shiraz

ŦŦŦŦŸ 1999 Medium purple-red; a fragrant bouquet with distinctly ripe plum and berry fruit is followed by a complex palate powered by red fruit, chocolate, vanilla oak and relatively powerful tannins. Demands and deserves time. **rating: 91**

best drinking 2006–2016 **best vintages** NA **drink with** Leave it in the cellar • $35.95

ada river ★★★☆

2330 Main Road, Neerim South, Vic 3831 **region** Gippsland
phone (03) 5628 1661 **fax** (03) 5628 1661 **open** 10–6 weekends and public holidays
winemaker Peter Kelliher, Chris Kelliher **production** 1500 **est.** 1983
product range ($12-26 CD) From Gippsland-grown grapes Chardonnay, Pinot Noir, Cabernet Sauvignon, Cabernets; from Yarra Valley grapes Traminer, Chardonnay, Pinot Noir; Heathcote Shiraz, Gewürztraminer Baw Baw Port.
summary The Kelliher family first planted vines on their dairy farm at Neerim South in 1983, extending the original Millstream Vineyard in 1989 and increasing plantings yet further by establishing the nearby Manilla Vineyard in 1994. Until 2000, Ada River leased a Yarra Valley vineyard; it has since relinquished that lease and in its place established a vineyard at Heathcote, in conjunction with a local grower.

Ada River Yarra Valley Gewürztraminer

ŦŦŦŸ 2001 Very pale straw-green; a clean but delicate and light bouquet has a faint tickle of spice, the palate flavour likewise light to the point of attenuation, yet with quite good mouthfeel. The varietal character should build, although this wine seems to go through extreme style gyrations from one vintage to the next. **rating: 83**

best drinking 2002–2003 **best vintages** NA **drink with** Asian prawns • $14

Ada River Gippsland Chardonnay

ŦŦŦŸ 1999 Medium to full yellow-green; a toasty and complex bouquet, with faint medicinal overtones, possibly a yeast fermentation residue. A similar toasty palate dips slightly in the middle, but has good acidity to close. **rating: 84**

best drinking 2002–2003 **best vintages** NA **drink with** Salmon pizza • $16

Ada River Special Release Gippsland Chardonnay

ŦŦŦŦ 1992 Glowing yellow-green; complex toasty oak and attractive melon/citrus fruit on the bouquet lead into a palate which is primarily held together by pronounced acidity, which may or may not please. Plenty of flavour and length. **rating: 87**

best drinking 2002–2003 **best vintages** NA **drink with** Crumbed brains • $12

Ada River Special Release Yarra Valley Chardonnay

ŦŦŦŦ 1991 Glowing yellow-green, a quite fragrant melon/citrus bouquet with gentle oak, then a palate which is hanging in well, particularly for a hot Yarra vintage; has good structure and balance, sustained by acidity. **rating: 89**

best drinking 2002–2003 **best vintages** '91 **drink with** Grilled spatchcock • $12

Ada River Gippsland Pinot Noir

ŦŦŦŦ 2000 Light to medium red-purple; light cherry, mint and leaf aromas suggest less than total ripening; the palate is indubitably light, but has more complexity and better style than the bouquet suggests. **rating: 86**

best drinking 2002–2003 **best vintages** NA **drink with** Smoked quail • $18

Ada River Yarra Valley Pinot Noir

▼▼▼▼ **2000** Light to medium red-purple, a fraction brighter than the Gippsland version; clean, gentle plum and cherry fruit on the bouquet leads into a tighter palate, better focused and structured, with direct cherry/plum fruit and a touch of sappiness on the finish.   **rating: 88**

best drinking 2002–2004 **best vintages** NA **drink with** Breast of duck • $17

Ada River Heathcote Shiraz

▼▼▼▼♡ **2000** Medium to full red-purple; the bouquet has classic regional/varietal fruit in the plum and licorice spectrum, supported by subtle oak. Powerful but not extractive plum/blackberry/prune flavours on the palate are supported by nice tannins and neatly judged oak. A top wine, well made.   **rating: 93**

best drinking 2005–2015 **best vintages** '00 **drink with** Beef casserole • $26

Ada River Cabernet Sauvignon

▼▼▼▼ **2000** Medium purple-red; the moderately intense bouquet has firm red and blackcurrant fruit allied with a touch of oak. The similarly firm palate offers a mix of blackcurrant, olive and herb flavours, and fine tannins.   **rating: 85**

best drinking 2004–2008 **best vintages** NA **drink with** Lamb shashlik • $16

affleck   NR

154 Millynn Road off Bungendore Road, Bungendore, NSW 2621 **region** Canberra District
phone (02) 6236 9276 **fax** (02) 6236 9090 **open** 7 days 9–5
winemaker Ian Hendry **production** 300 **est.** 1976
product range ($14–24 CD) Chardonnay, Semillon, Late Picked Sauvignon Blanc, Sweet White, Pinot Noir, Cabernet Shiraz, Muscat, Ruby Port.
summary The cellar-door and mail-order price list says that the wines are 'grown, produced and bottled on the estate by Ian and Susie Hendry with much dedicated help from family and friends'. The original 2.5-hectare vineyard has been expanded to 7 hectares, and a new tasting room (offering light lunches) opened in 1999.

ainsworth estate   NR

110 Ducks Lane, Seville, Vic 3139 **region** Yarra Valley
phone (03) 5964 4711 **fax** (03) 5964 4311 **open** 7 days 10.30–5
winemaker Denis Craig **production** 2500 **est.** 1994
product range ($17.95–25.65 CD) Unoaked Chardonnay, Chardonnay, Shiraz, Cabernet Sauvignon.
summary Denis Craig and wife Kerri planted their first two hectares of chardonnay and shiraz near Healesville in 1994. The grapes from this vineyard were sold until the 2000 vintage, when the first wines were made under the Ainsworth Estate label. In the intervening period they established a second vineyard at Ducks Lane, Seville, with another two hectares of vines, here planted to shiraz and pinot noir. They have also turned from selling to purchasing grapes with a total of just under 3 hectares of chardonnay, shiraz and cabernet sauvignon grown for them under contract. Their cellar-door and barbecue area at Ducks Lane opened in March 2001; for the time being, at least, Denis Craig and Al Fencaros make the wines at Fencaros' Allinda Winery in Dixons Creek.

🐢 albert river wines   ★★★

1-117 Mundoolun Connection Road, Tamborine, Qld 4270 **region** Queensland Coastal
phone (07) 5543 6622 **fax** (07) 5543 6627 **open** 7 days 10–4
winemaker Peter Scudamore-Smith **production** 5000 **est.** 1998
product range ($15–32 ML) Jacaranda Semillon, Unwooded Chardonnay, Chardonnay, Sparkling White, Sparkling Red, Roundelay (Shiraz Merlot Cabernet blend), Grand Masters Shiraz, Merlot, Shiraz Cabernet Merlot, Red Belly Black Port.
summary Albert River is yet another high-profile winery to open on the Gold Coast hinterland, with all its distribution through cellar door, mail order and local restaurants. The proprietors are David and Janette Bladin, with a combined 30 years' experience in tourism and hospitality, who have acquired and relocated two of Queensland's most historic buildings: Tamborine House and Auchenflower House. The winery itself is housed in a newly constructed annex to Auchenflower House, and the Bladins have established 10 hectares of vineyards on the property, and have another 50 hectares under contract. The first releases were acquired for Albert River Wines by its consultant winemaker, Peter Scudamore-Smith, from various sources, but from 2000 all the wines have been made from Queensland-grown grapes.

Albert River Unwooded Chardonnay

♥♥♥♡ **2000** Light green-yellow; the bouquet is clean, with light melon varietal character, the palate similarly lacking fruit intensity, but well enough made, and fairly priced. **rating: 82**

best drinking 2001–2002 **best vintages** NA **drink with** Vegetable terrine • $15

Albert River Chardonnay

♥♥♥♡ **2000** Medium yellow-green; the bouquet shows powerful and slightly raw oak, oak which also dominates the palate. Either less oak or better quality would have been a better option. **rating: 83**

best drinking 2001–2003 **best vintages** NA **drink with** Pasta marinara • $19

Albert River Grand Masters Shiraz

♥♥♥♡ **2000** Medium red-purple; light cherry fruit with subtle oak on the bouquet is repeated on the palate, but sharp, corrected acidity unbalances the wine. It has spent 15 months in French and American oak, and comes from the Inglewood Vineyard, which is situated west of Stanthorpe. **rating: 83**

best drinking 2002–2003 **best vintages** NA **drink with** Pizza • $32

Albert River Roundelay

♥♥♥♡ **2001** Light red-purple; clean, fresh apple and cherry aromas are followed by a well-balanced and made palate, with a nice dry finish after sweet fruit on the mid palate. A blend of Shiraz, Merlot and Cabernet Sauvignon purpose-built for early drinking. **rating: 85**

best drinking 2002–2003 **best vintages** NA **drink with** Cold meat salad • $17

Albert River Merlot

♥♥♥♡ **2000** Light to medium red-purple; the bouquet shows some spicy oak over light fruit; nice juicy/berry fruit on the mid palate has been legitimately protected by early bottling, although there is a shadow suggestive of low SO$_2$ on the aftertaste. **rating: 83**

best drinking 2001–2004 **best vintages** NA **drink with** Lamb cutlets • $22

🐗 aldgate ridge ★★★★

23 Nation Ridge Road, Aldgate, SA 5154 **region** Adelaide Hills
phone (08) 8388 5225 **fax** (08) 8388 5856 **open** By appointment
winemaker David Powell (Contract) **production** 350 **est.** 1992
product range ($27.50–29 ML) Pinot Noir.
summary Jill and Chris Whisson acquired their vineyard property in 1988, when the land was still being used as a market garden. The 2.5 hectares of pinot noir now established were planted in two stages, in 1992 and 1997, the first block with some of the first of the new Burgundian clones to be propagated in Australia. One and a half hectares of sauvignon blanc were added in 2000. The vineyard is typical of the Adelaide Hills region, on a rolling to steep southeast-facing hillside at the 440-metre altitude line. The wine is contract-made by the celebrated David Powell of Torbreck Wines in the Barossa Valley, and apart from mail order, has limited fine wine retail distribution.

Aldgate Ridge Pinot Noir

♥♥♥♥♡ **1999** Strong colour, deep red with the last vestiges of purple; a rich, ripe, complex and quite concentrated bouquet with obvious oak, then a palate with lots of texture to the rich, dark plum fruit. Verges on dry red, but will undoubtedly please those who like Pinot with punch. **rating: 90**

best drinking 2003–2009 **best vintages** NA **drink with** Rich game • $27.50

aldinga bay winery ★★★

Main South Road, Aldinga, SA 5173 **region** McLaren Vale
phone (08) 8556 3179 **fax** (08) 8556 3350 **open** 7 days 10–5
winemaker Nick Girolamo **production** 8000 **est.** 1979
product range ($13–21 CD) Verdelho, Chardonnay, Shiraz, Sangiovese, Petit Verdot, Reserve Tawny Port.
summary The former Donolga Winery has had a name and image change since Nick Girolamo, the son of founders Don and Olga Girolamo, returned from Roseworthy College with a degree in oenology. Nick Girolamo has taken over both the winemaking and marketing; prices remain modest, though not as low as they once were, reflecting an increase in the quality and an upgrade in packaging. Aldinga Bay also has some very interesting varietal plantings, 16 varieties in all, including petit verdot, nebbiolo, barbera and sangiovese.

alexandra bridge estate   NR

Brockman Highway, Karridale, WA 6288 **region** Margaret River
phone (08) 9758 5000 **fax** (08) 9384 4811 **open** 7 days 10–4.30
winemaker Philip Tubb **production** 20 000 **est.** 1994
product range ($15–30 R) Semillon, Sauvignon Blanc, Chardonnay, Margaret River Classic, Shiraz, Cabernet Sauvignon.
summary The dynamic Mike Calneggia has taken effective control of the former Hotham Wine Group, which announced a loss of over $8 million for the six months ending 30 December 2001, and has restructured the entire operation, amongst other things changing the name of Hotham to Australian Wine Holdings, and phasing out the Hotham brand. The 30-hectare Alexandra Bridge Estate vineyard and the 97-hectare Bridgeland Vineyard (on a 207-hectare property) are the principal vineyard assets; they may be sold and leased back as a means of reducing debt. The marketing plan is to have vineyard-specific wines at a premium price point, with a second tier of cheaper wines.

alkoomi   ★★★★★

Wingebellup Road, Frankland, WA 6396 **region** Great Southern
phone (08) 9855 2229 **fax** (08) 9855 2284 **open** 7 days 10.30–5
winemaker Michael Staniford, Merv Lange **production** 80 000 **est.** 1971
product range ($11.50–59 CD) Frankland River Riesling, Wandoo (Semillon), Sauvignon Blanc, Southlands White, Southlands Unwooded Chardonnay, Chardonnay, Sparkling Shiraz, Late Harvest, Southlands Red, Shiraz, Jarrah Shiraz, Cabernet Sauvignon, Blackbutt, Shiraz Cabernet Merlot, Pedro Ximinez Liqueur.
summary For those who see the wineries of Western Australia as suffering from the tyranny of distance, this most remote of all wineries shows there is no tyranny after all. It is a story of unqualified success due to sheer hard work, and, no doubt, to Merv and Judy Lange's aversion to borrowing a single dollar from the bank. The substantial production is entirely drawn from the ever-expanding estate vineyards, which by 2001 amounted to over 70 hectares. Wine quality across the range is impeccable, always with precisely defined varietal character. National retail distribution; exports to Hong Kong, Singapore, Japan, Malaysia, the UK, the US, Denmark and Germany.

Alkoomi Frankland River Riesling
▼▼▼▼▼ 2001 Elegant, fine, clean and flowery lime aromas show no signs of slow ferment (sometimes a problem), the palate equally fine and having the intensity and length to underwrite a long future. **rating:** 94
best drinking 2002–2012 **best vintages** '94, '95, '96, '98, '99, '01 **drink with** Salad Nicoise • $19

Alkoomi Sauvignon Blanc
▼▼▼▼▽ 2001 Light straw-green; a crisp, light minerally bouquet is followed by a lively, fresh, clean, zippy seafood style, with no flavour forcing. **rating:** 90
best drinking 2001–2003 **best vintages** '95, '96, '97, '98, '00, '01 **drink with** Ginger prawns • $20

Alkoomi Jarrah Shiraz
▼▼▼▼▼ 1999 Bright purple-red; abundant dark cherry and licorice aromas are followed by a classy palate with a savoury cool-climate twist of spice, fine tannins and restrained oak. Finesse and subtlety, not raw power. Gold medal Great Australian Shiraz Challenge 2001. **rating:** 96
best drinking 2004–2009 **best vintages** '99 **drink with** Roast venison • $39

Alkoomi Southlands Shiraz Cabernet Merlot
▼▼▼▽ 2001 Vivid purple-red; fresh, juicy, berry fruit with little or no oak on the bouquet is followed by a quite substantial palate, with dark berry fruit and some tannins. Has the awkwardness of a wine rushed to bottle, and doesn't appeal overmuch on price. **rating:** 83
best drinking 2001–2003 **best vintages** NA **drink with** Takeaway • $14

Alkoomi Blackbutt
▼▼▼▼▼ 1999 Medium to full red-purple; pristine blackcurrant and blackberry fruit on the bouquet is followed by a powerful, concentrated palate, densely packed with flavour, the tannins fine, the oak subservient to the fruit; long-lived but elegant. The best Blackbutt for years. **rating:** 95
best drinking 2003–2018 **best vintages** '94, '95, '96, '97, '98, '99 **drink with** Rare beef • $59

Alkoomi Frankland River Cabernet Sauvignon

ŶŶŶŶ 1999 Bright purple-red; blackberry and confit/jam aromas together with subtle oak on the bouquet settle down somewhat on the soft, sweet berry fruit and fine tannins of the palate; just a little loose overall.

rating: 89

best drinking 2003–2008 **best vintages** '83, '84, '86, '90, '93, '94, '95 **drink with** Rare rump steak • $27

allandale ★★★★

Lovedale Road, Lovedale, NSW 2320 **region** Lower Hunter Valley
phone (02) 4990 4526 **fax** (02) 4990 1714 **open** Mon-Sat 9–5, Sun 10–5
winemaker Bill Sneddon, Steve Langham **production** 18 000 **est.** 1978
product range ($17–26 CD) Semillon, Verdelho, Chardonnay, Matthew Shiraz, McLaren Vale Shiraz, Hilltops Cabernet Sauvignon.
summary Without ostentation, this medium-sized winery has been under the control of winemaker Bill Sneddon for well over a decade. Allandale has developed something of a reputation as a Chardonnay specialist, but does offer a broad range of wines of consistently good quality, with several red wines sourced from outside the Hunter Valley. The wines are exported to the UK, Switzerland, Singapore, Malyasia and Fiji.

Allandale Hunter Valley Semillon

ŶŶŶŶŶ 2000 Light to medium yellow-green; a clean, fresh bouquet with gentle lemon citrus aromas opens with similarly fresh fruit, the palate then lengthens and tightens, lingering, with minerally acidity. Trophy Boutique Winemakers Show 2001.

rating: 90

best drinking 2004–2010 **best vintages** '86, '91, '94, '96, '97, '00 **drink with** Summer salads • $17

Allandale Verdelho

ŶŶŶŶ 2001 Light yellow-green; the moderately intense bouquet has typical fruit salad aromas, characters which flow into the well-balanced palate, which is in turn enlivened by some lemon/citrus notes; good flavour, and not phenolic. Gold medal Royal Perth Wine Show 2001. Perth loves Verdelho. **rating: 87**

best drinking 2002–2003 **best vintages** NA **drink with** Smoked salmon pasta • $18

Allandale Matthew Shiraz

ŶŶŶŶŶ 2000 Medium red-purple; a regional mix of berry, earth and spice on the bouquet is complexed by partial barrel fermentation in French and American oak. A powerful, complex but well-balanced wine on the palate which cries out for five years or more in the cellar, as all the makings are there (including 14° alcohol).

rating: 91

best drinking 2005–2015 **best vintages** '86, '87, '91, '00 **drink with** Smoked beef • $23

Allandale Hilltops Cabernet Sauvignon

ŶŶŶŶ 2000 Medium to full purple-red; a bouquet of toasty/charry oak and blackberry fruit is faithfully reflected on the palate, where those two components are in balance; distinctly firm finish, and will reward patience.

rating: 89

best drinking 2005–2010 **best vintages** NA **drink with** Rack of lamb • $26

allanmere NR

Allandale Road, Allandale via Pokolbin, NSW 2321 **region** Lower Hunter Valley
phone (02) 4930 7387 **fax** (02) 4930 7900 **open** 7 days 9.30–5
winemaker Greg Silkman **production** 7000 **est.** 1984
product range ($15–20 CD) Gold Label Chardonnay, Semillon, Trinity White (Chardonnay, Semillon, Sauvignon Blanc), Cabernet Sauvignon, Trinity Red (Cabernet blend), Cabernet Shiraz. Durham Chardonnay is top-of-the-range Chardonnay.
summary Now owned by Monarch Winemaking Services. While it has a relatively low profile in conventional retail markets, cellar-door sales are flourishing in response to the ever-increasing tourist traffic in the Hunter Valley. No recent tastings. Exports to Japan, Switzerland, the US, Taiwan and the UK.

allinda NR

119 Lorimers Lane, Dixons Creek, Vic 3775 **region** Yarra Valley
phone (03) 5965 2450 **fax** (03) 5965 2467 **open** Weekends and public holidays 11–5
winemaker Al Fencaros **production** 2500 **est.** 1991

product range ($16.50–24.50 CD) Riesling, Sauvignon Blanc, Chardonnay, Late Harvest Riesling, Shiraz, Cabernets.

summary Winemaker Al Fencaros has a Bachelor of Wine Science (Charles Sturt University) and was formerly employed by De Bortoli in the Yarra Valley. All of the Allinda wines are produced on site; all except the Shiraz (from Heathcote) are estate-grown from a little over 3 hectares of vineyards. Limited retail distribution in Melbourne and Sydney.

all saints estate   ★★★★

All Saints Road, Wahgunyah, Vic 3687 **region** Rutherglen
phone (02) 6033 1922 **fax** (02) 6033 3515 **open** Mon–Sat 9–5.30, Sun 10–5.30
winemaker Peter Brown **production** 35 000 **est.** 1864
product range ($9.80–395 CD) At the top of the table wines come Carlyle Chardonnay, Sparkling Red, Shiraz, Ruby Cabernet, Durif; then come All Saints Riesling, Marsanne, Images White, Méthode Traditionelle, Late Harvest Semillon, Images Rosé, Images Shiraz, Shiraz, Merlot, Cabernet Sauvignon; Heritage Tawny Port and Tokays and Muscats are headed by Museum Release, then Rare, then Grand, and finally Classic Rutherglen.

summary The winery rating principally reflects the Show Reserve fortified wines, but the table wines are more than adequate. An excellent winery restaurant makes this a compulsory and most enjoyable stop for any visitor to the northeast. All Saints and St Leonards are now wholly owned by Peter Brown; the vast majority of the wines are sold through the cellar door and by mailing list.

All Saints Riesling

▼▼▼▽ **2001** Light to medium yellow-green; the bouquet is quite floral and aromatic, with soft tropical fruit; the flavoursome palate has distinctly tropical characters, making it an ideal candidate for the cellar door.   **rating:** 83

best drinking 2001–2002 **best vintages** NA **drink with** Sashimi • $13.90

All Saints Shiraz

▼▼▼▼ **1999** Youthful red-purple; a fresh, clean and direct bouquet of cherry and touches of plum is repeated on the medium-bodied palate, with touches of vanilla oak. It looks as if it spent time in tank.   **rating:** 85

best drinking 2003–2007 **best vintages** '92, '96, '98 **drink with** Venison • $18.60

All Saints Carlyle Shiraz

▼▼▼▼▽ **1998** Medium to full red-purple; a rich, concentrated bouquet with sweet black fruit and well-balanced and integrated vanilla oak is followed by an equally concentrated palate with cigar-box overtones to the blackberry and cherry fruit, moving through to appropriately structured tannins on the finish.   **rating:** 92

best drinking 2005–2015 **best vintages** NA **drink with** Chargrilled rump • $37.30

All Saints Carlyle Durif

▼▼▼▼▽ **1999** Inky red-purple; a powerful, dense and ripe bouquet with warm earthy/spicy aromas foreshadows a massive palate with huge fruit, oak (French) and tannins, demanding a minimum of ten years' cellaring.   **rating:** 90

best drinking 2009–2019 **best vintages** '99 **drink with** Ox • $32

All Saints Carlyle Ruby Cabernet

▼▼▼▼ **1999** Deep red-purple; clean, slightly lifted fruit on the bouquet is followed by a palate with totally unexpected concentration and extract, especially for Ruby Cabernet; the tannins are slightly dry/bitter, underlining the work done in the winery.   **rating:** 85

best drinking 2004–2009 **best vintages** NA **drink with** Aussie barbecue • $24.80

All Saints Classic Rutherglen Tokay (500 ml)

▼▼▼▼▽ **NV** Amber-brown; a clean bouquet with a mix of tea leaf, toffee and butterscotch leads into a sweet, quite raisiny palate with very good balancing acidity on the finish.   **rating:** 91

best drinking 2002–2003 **best vintages** NA **drink with** Espresso coffee and dark chocolate • $24

All Saints Grand Rutherglen Tokay (375 ml)

TTTTT NV Deep olive-amber brown; the bouquet is spicy and rich with some plum pudding aromas, the palate powerful and concentrated, less overtly sweet/raisiny than the Classic, but more complex and spicy; has excellent length, and good acidity. **rating: 94**

best drinking 2001–2002 **best vintages** NA **drink with** Espresso coffee and dark chocolate • $32

All Saints Rare Rutherglen Tokay (375 ml)

TTTTT NV Deep olive; a rich, intense, complex and deep bouquet flows onto a palate with exceptional length and balance, having significantly more finesse than the Grand Tokay. The flavours are of tea leaf and brown toffee, but no fish oil (a quite common varietal character for tokay). Fantastic length. **rating: 97**

best drinking 2001–2002 **best vintages** NA **drink with** Espresso coffee and dark chocolate • $65

All Saints Classic Rutherglen Muscat

TTTTY NV Some reddish tints to the medium tawny-brown colour are evidence of (relative) youth. A perfumed, grapey, raisiny bouquet leads into a lively, highly flavoured, grapey/raisiny palate. A very pure varietal expression of young Muscat. **rating: 90**

best drinking 2002–2003 **best vintages** NA **drink with** Espresso coffee and walnuts • $24

All Saints Grand Rutherglen Muscat

TTTTY NV Deeper brown than the Classic, and quite viscous when swirled in the glass. A rich and compelling bouquet is loaded with raisin and plum pudding aromas; the palate is intensely grapey and spicy, with fruit, not spirit, dominant. **rating: 93**

best drinking 2001–2002 **best vintages** NA **drink with** Espresso coffee and walnuts • $32

All Saints Rare Rutherglen Muscat

TTTTT NV Deep, dark brown with an olive rim; both the bouquet and palate are as complex and concentrated as one might expect, but, like the Rare Tokay, with remarkable finesse: this is not a raw expression of power or age. Once again, finishes with great acidity. **rating: 97**

best drinking 2001–2002 **best vintages** NA **drink with** Espresso coffee and walnuts • $65

🐦 allusion wines   NR

Smith Hill Road, Yankalilla, SA 5203 **region** Southern Fleurieu
phone (08) 8558 3333 **fax** (08) 8558 3333 **open** Thu–Sun 11–5
winemaker Contract (previously Normans) **production** 750 **est.** 1996
product range ($17–35 CD) Semillon Sauvignon Blanc, Viognier, Shiraz Viognier, Cabernet Sauvignon.
summary Steve and Wendy Taylor purchased the property on which Allusion Wines is established in 1980, and have since planted 4 hectares of vines and 35 000 trees. Steve Taylor's 20 years as a chef have strongly influenced both the varietal plantings and the wine styles made; not altogether surprisingly, they are designed to be consumed with good food. The wine is fermented off-site, then matured on-site before being contract-bottled.

🐦 allyn river wines   NR

Torryburn Road, East Gresford, NSW 2311 **region** Upper Hunter Valley
phone (02) 4938 9279 **fax** (02) 4938 9279 **open** Fri–Mon and public holidays 9–5 or by appointment
winemaker David Hook (Contract) **production** 650 **est.** 1996
product range ($14.50–16.50 CD) Semillon, Chardonnay Semillon, Chambourcin.
summary Allyn River is situated on the alluvial soils on the banks of the stream which has given the vineyard its name. The plantings of 1.5 hectares each of semillon and chambourcin were in part inspired by the knowledge that Dr Henry Lindeman had established his famous Cawarra Vineyard in the locality, and since Allyn River's foundation in 1996, others have moved to the area to establish vineyards totalling more than 20 hectares within a 10-kilometre radius of Allyn River. As well as a wine-tasting room and picnic facilities, self-contained cottage accommodation is available on the property, known as the Maples Cottage.

amberley estate   ★★★★

Thornton Road, Yallingup, WA 6282 **region** Margaret River
phone (08) 9755 2288 **fax** (08) 9755 2171 **open** 7 days 10–4.30
winemaker Eddie Price, David Watson **production** 90 000 **est.** 1986

product range ($16–63 R) Semillon, Sauvignon Blanc, Semillon Sauvignon Blanc, Chenin Blanc, Chardonnay, Charlotte Street Chardonnay Semillon, Shiraz, First Selection Shiraz, Charlotte Street Shiraz Chardonnay Cabernet, Cabernet Merlot, Cabernet Sauvignon, Cabernet Reserve.

summary Based its initial growth on the basis of its ultra-commercial, fairly sweet Chenin Blanc, which continues to provide the volume for the brand, selling out well prior to the following release. However, the quality of all the other wines has risen markedly over recent years as the 31 hectares of estate plantings have become fully mature. Exports to the UK, France, Germany, Singapore, Japan, Hong Kong and the US.

Amberley Estate First Selection Shiraz

▼▼▼▼ 2000 Light to medium purple-red; the bouquet has earthy notes accompanied by spice, the palate with direct, red berry fruit and restrained oak. Not especially complex, but will develop.   **rating: 88**

best drinking 2004–2009 **best vintages** NA **drink with** Grilled T-bone • NA

amietta vineyard and winery   NR

30 Steddy Road, Lethbridge, Vic 3332 **region** Geelong
phone (03) 5281 7427 **fax** (03) 5281 7427 **open** By appointment
winemaker Nicholas Clark, Janet Cockbill **production** NA **est.** 1995
product range Riesling, Cabernet.

summary Janet Cockbill and Nicholas Clark are multi-talented. Both are archaeologists, but Janet manages to combine part-time archaeology, part-time radiography at Geelong Hospital and part-time organic viticulture. Nicholas Clark is in his final (part-time) year of a viticulture degree at Charles Sturt University. When they purchased the property (which had half a hectare each of cabernet sauvignon and riesling already established), they decided to convert to a full-on organic vineyard regime. Engagingly, Nicholas goes on to say 'We are garagistes – literally. One day, when we grow up, we might even be wine producers.' They planted an additional 0.9 hectares of shiraz and 0.5 hectares of chardonnay in 2000, and their first Cabernet and Riesling became available in September 2001.

🐌 amulet vineyard   NR

Wangaratta Road, Beechworth, Vic 3747 **region** Beechworth
phone (03) 5727 0420 **fax** (03) 5727 0421 **open** Fri–Mon, public and school holidays 10–6 or by appointment
winemaker Sue Thornton, Eric Thornton, Contract **production** 1600 **est.** 1998
product range ($15–30 ML) Pinot Gris, Chardonnay, Rosato, Sangiovese Shiraz, Barbera, Orange Muscat.

summary Sue and Eric Thornton have planted a patchwork quilt four-hectare vineyard, with sangiovese taking one hectare, the other varieties half a hectare or less. In descending order of magnitude they are barbera, shiraz, cabernet sauvignon, merlot, nebbiolo, orange muscat, pinot gris and pinot blanc. The vineyard (and cellar door) is 11 kilometres west of Beechworth on the road to Wangaratta, the vines planted on gentle slopes at an elevation of 300 metres. The cellar door enjoys panoramic views, and wine sales are both by the glass and by the bottle. The quixotic label, featuring a scarecrow riding an airborne bicycle, bears testament to the vines' co-habitation with birds.

anderson   NR

Lot 12 Chiltern Road, Rutherglen, Vic 3685 **region** Rutherglen
phone (02) 6032 8111 **fax** (02) 6032 9028 **open** 7 days 10–5
winemaker Howard Anderson **production** 1500 **est.** 1992
product range ($13–25 CD) Chenin Blanc, Doux Blanc, Unoaked Chardonnay, Chardonnay, Shiraz, Merlot, Cabernet Merlot, Cabernet Sauvignon, Late Harvest Tokay, Méthode Champenoise range of Pinot Noir Chardonnay, Chenin Blanc, Doux Blanc, Shiraz.

summary Having notched up a winemaking career spanning over 30 years, including a stint at Seppelt Great Western, Howard Anderson and family have started their own winery, with a particular focus on sparkling wine made entirely on-site.

andraos bros   ★★★★

Winilba Vineyard, 150 Vineyard Road, Sunbury, Vic 3429 **region** Sunbury
phone (03) 9740 9703 **fax** (03) 9740 9795 **open** Fri–Sun and public holidays 11–5 or by appointment
winemaker Fred Andraos, Mario Marson (Consultant) **production** 2500 **est.** 1989

product range ($18–70 CD) Released under the Olde Winilba label are Riesling, Semillon, Semillon Sauvignon Blanc, Chardonnay, Pinot Shiraz, Pinot Noir, Shiraz, Cabernet Shiraz, Cabernet Sauvignon.

summary The original Winilba Vineyard was first planted in 1863, and remained in production until 1889. Exactly 100 years later the Andraos brothers commenced replanting the vineyard on the property they had purchased five years earlier. Over the following years they built a winery from the ruins of the original bluestone cellar, making the inaugural vintage in 1996. They have also established Estelle's Cellar Restaurant on the second floor of the building, which is open for dinner from Tuesday to Sunday and for lunch on Friday, Saturday, Sunday and public holidays.

andrew garrett vineyard estates ★★★☆

134a The Parade, Norwood, SA 5067 (postal) **region** Yarra Valley
phone (08) 8364 0555 **fax** (08) 8364 5799 **open** at The Grand Hotel, Yarra Glen
winemaker Andrew Garrett **production** 100 000 **est.** 1986
product range ($10–52 R) There are two premium wine ranges: from the Yarra Valley in Victoria comes the Yarra Glen label, from the Adelaide Hills in South Australia the Springwood Park label. In the lower price category come the Kelly's Promise (previously McLarens on the Lake) wines of Chardonnay, Shiraz, Cabernet Merlot and Brut Cuvée and the Ironwood range of Chardonnay, Shiraz, Merlot and Cabernet Sauvignon.

summary The irrepressible Andrew Garrett has risen once again after 20 years in the wine industry as 'winemaker, innovator, entrepreneur, marketer and personality' (to use his own words). Andrew Garrett Vineyard Estates is now the umbrella for the Yarra Valley-based Yarra Glen label, the Adelaide Hills-based Springwood Park label, and the Kelly's Promise range (previously known as McLarens on the Lake). The 117-hectare Yarra Valley vineyards are the fruit source for all the Yarra Glen wines. Martindale Hall (Clare Valley) and Macedon Range are the most recent additions. The wines are exported to the UK, Europe, Asia and the US.

Springwood Park Sauvignon Blanc

▼▼▼▼ **2001** Light to medium yellow-green; a clean mix of herb, grass and asparagus on the bouquet is followed by a palate with good mouthfeel, rather softer and riper than the bouquet suggests, providing a pleasant counterplay. **rating:** 87

best drinking 2002–2003 **best vintages** NA **drink with** Grilled scallops • $16.60

Yarra Glen Sauvignon Blanc

▼▼▼▼ **2000** Light to medium yellow-green; the bouquet is complex, with a hint of reduction to the tropical/gooseberry fruit. The palate thickens up somewhat, raising the question whether skin contact was used. **rating:** 85

best drinking 2002–2003 **best vintages** NA **drink with** Smoked salmon • $14.50

Yarra Glen Marsanne

▼▼▼▽ **2001** Medium yellow-straw; the bouquet is neutral, pretty much in line with what one expects from young Marsanne. The palate moves up a gear, with some honeysuckle characters, good mouthfeel, and nice lemony acidity. Could develop into something special with bottle age. **rating:** 83

best drinking 2002–2006 **best vintages** NA **drink with** Light seafood • $14.95

Yarra Glen Unoaked Chardonnay

▼▼▼▼ **2000** Medium yellow-green; strong, sweet melon and stone fruit aromas are distinctively regional and appealing. The palate is less powerful than the bouquet suggests it will be, but has pleasant fruit and pleasingly crisp acidity to close. **rating:** 85

best drinking 2001–2003 **best vintages** NA **drink with** Poached chicken breast • $17.95

Springwood Park Chardonnay

▼▼▼▼▽ **1998** Glowing yellow-green; some buttery/honey overtones to the melon fruit have developed with bottle age; there are similar dynamics at work on the palate, with peachy melon fruit offset by nicely balanced acidity, and a touch of toasty, spicy oak. **rating:** 90

best drinking 2001–2004 **best vintages** '98 **drink with** Pan-fried veal • $29.95

Yarra Glen Pinot Noir

▼▼▼▽ **2000** Medium red-purple; the wine is quite aromatic, with a core of cherry/strawberry fruit, but both the bouquet and the palate have some leafy/minty overtones. On the other side of the coin, the mouthfeel and structure are good. **rating:** 84

ȲȲȲ 1999 Medium red-purple; an earthy/foresty/stemmy bouquet leads into a light-bodied palate with some strawberry fruit joining the more foresty characters of the bouquet. However, it lacks structure, which is not surprising given the vintage. **rating: 82**

best drinking 2001–2003 **best vintages** NA **drink with** Coq au vin • $19.95

Ironwood Shiraz
ȲȲȲȲ 2000 Light to medium red-purple; a light, savoury, almost lemony bouquet is followed by a palate with surprising spicy plum and cherry fruit, finishing with soft tannins. **rating: 84**

best drinking 2002–2004 **best vintages** NA **drink with** Takeaway • $12.50

Nicholas Shiraz
ȲȲȲȲ 1998 Medium red-purple; the bouquet is flooded with American vanilla oak, but with fruit poking through the thickets; the palate is a replica of the bouquet. Far too much oak for my liking, but others, I know, will love the wine. Thus it was given five stars by *Winestate Magazine* on two occasions. **rating: 85**

best drinking 2002–2007 **best vintages** NA **drink with** Smoked beef • $53

Yarra Glen Shiraz
ȲȲȲȲ 2000 Medium red-purple; clean, fresh red fruit aromas and minimal oak lead into a palate with more intensity and depth, albeit still fruit-driven, with berry, mint and cherry supported by fine tannins. **rating: 87**

best drinking 2004–2008 **best vintages** NA **drink with** Osso buco • $16.60

King Valley Tom Merlot
ȲȲȲȲ 1998 Medium red-purple; the ripe bouquet has abundant fruit with mercifully subtle French oak, followed by a palate with substantial structure and extract; olive, earth and plum flavours are supported by controlled oak. 14.5° is a rare achievement for the King Valley, but the wine carries the alcohol. **rating: 87**

best drinking 2003–2008 **best vintages** NA **drink with** Venison • $53

Kelly's Promise Cabernet Sauvignon
ȲȲȲȲ 1998 Medium red-purple; the light and clean bouquet has a mix of berry fruit, some earthy overtones and a dusting of oak; the palate has a mix of cedar, earth, chocolate and light berry fruit, but lacks concentration. **rating: 84**

best drinking 2002–2005 **best vintages** NA **drink with** Pizza • $15.80

Yarra Glen Cabernet Sauvignon
ȲȲȲ 2000 Medium red-purple; the bouquet is very youthful, with somewhat callow juicy berry fruit, the palate entirely fruit-driven, with gentle berry fruit, soft tannins and the faintest touch of French oak on the finish. **rating: 84**

best drinking 2002–2006 **best vintages** NA **drink with** Fillet steak • $19.95

andrew garrett/ingoldby   ★★★★
Ingoldby Road, McLaren Flat, SA 5171 **region** McLaren Vale
phone (08) 8383 0005 **fax** (08) 8383 0790 **open** 7 days 10–4
winemaker Charles Hargrave **production** NFP **est.** 1983
product range ($9–27 R) Andrew Garrett range of Sauvignon Blanc Semillon, Marsanne, Chardonnay, Cabernet Merlot, Bold Shiraz, Vintage Chardonnay Pinot Noir, Vintage Sparkling Shiraz, Pinot Noir Chardonnay, Sparkling Burgundy; and Garrett range of Sauvignon Blanc, Chardonnay Semillon, Sparkling Chardonnay, Shiraz Cabernet. Under the Ingoldby label are Sauvignon Blanc, Chardonnay, Shiraz, Reserve Shiraz, Roadblock Grenache Shiraz, Tawny Port.
summary Andrew Garrett and Ingoldby are brands within the Beringer Blass wine group, with many of the wines now not having a sole McLaren Vale source but instead being drawn from regions across southeastern Australia. Over the past few years, winemaker Charles Hargrave has produced some excellent wines which provide great value for money.

Andrew Garrett Chardonnay
ȲȲȲȲ 2001 Light green-yellow; the bouquet is quite complex, with obvious but not excessive nutty/smoky/cashew oak aromas. The palate has length and balance, with gentle fruit and oak flavours tied off with good acidity on the finish. Particularly good value. **rating: 88**

best drinking 2001–2002 **best vintages** '95, '97 **drink with** Loin of pork • $13.50

Andrew Garrett Shiraz

ŦŦŦŸ **2000** Medium red-purple; the bouquet is fresh and firm, with touches of mint and leaf to red fruits. The medium-bodied palate has a similar mix of red berry and mint fruit, not complex, but honest; prior vintages have impressed more.   **rating: 84**

best drinking 2002–2005 **best vintages** '96, '98 **drink with** Wood-fired pizza • $14.50

Ingoldby Shiraz

ŦŦŦŦ **2000** Excellent purple-red colour; fresh under fragrant red berry/cherry aromas, with an appealing hint of underlying game; there is fresh, yet quite soft mid palate fruit flowing into slightly savoury, soft tannins on the finish. Particularly good value.   **rating: 87**

best drinking 2002–2006 **best vintages** '99 **drink with** Shepherd's pie • $15

Ingoldby Reserve Shiraz

ŦŦŦŦŸ **1999** Dense red-purple; an archetypal, regional bouquet loaded with rich berry and dark chocolate aromas. The powerful, dense palate follows precisely down the same track, with dark berry and chocolate flavours supported by well-handled oak and tannins. 900 made.   **rating: 93**

best drinking 2004–2014 **best vintages** '98, '99 **drink with** Marinated venison • $29

Ingoldby Roadblock Grenache Shiraz

ŦŦŦŸ **2000** Medium red-purple; the clean bouquet has moderately intense, slightly minty fruit, the light to medium-bodied palate with similarly fresh, juicy/minty/berry flavours. The d'Arenberg penchant for quirky names is there, but not the d'Arenberg flavour.   **rating: 83**

ŦŦŦŦ **1998** Light to medium red-purple; juicy berry fruit on the bouquet is followed by a palate with much more structure and texture than that bouquet suggests, ripe and luscious, carrying (just) its 14.5° alcohol; minimal oak.   **rating: 88**

best drinking 2002–2003 **best vintages** NA **drink with** Ravioli • $19.95

andrew harris vineyards   ★★★★

Sydney Road, Mudgee, NSW 2850 **region** Mudgee
phone (02) 6373 1213 **fax** (02) 6373 1296 **open** Not
winemaker Frank Nepean **production** 40 000 **est.** 1991
product range ($16–45 ML) Semillon, Verdelho, Chardonnay, Shiraz, Merlot, Cabernet Sauvignon; Reserve Range of Chardonnay, Shiraz, Merlot, Cabernet Merlot, Cabernet Sauvignon; limited range of Double Vision (sparkling Shiraz) and The Vision (Shiraz Cabernet Sauvignon).
summary Andrew and Debbie Harris lost no time after purchasing a 300-hectare sheep station southeast of Mudgee in 1991. The first six hectares of vineyard were planted in that year and have since been expanded   to
101 hectares. A substantial portion of the production is sold to others, but production under the Andrew Harris label has risen significantly in recent years. There is now a spread of price and quality, with the difficult vintages of 1999, 2000 and 2001 also impacting, so care is needed in choosing the wines. Exports to the US, New Zealand, Malaysia and Japan.

Andrew Harris Semillon

ŦŦŦŦ **2001** Light green-yellow; quite intense spicy oak comes through on the bouquet, reflecting the six months the wine spent in new French oak; the palate is tangy, lively and crisp; the use of oak gives a legitimate alternative style, and does not obscure the varietal character.   **rating: 89**

best drinking 2002–2004 **best vintages** '01 **drink with** Asian fish • $15.95

Andrew Harris Reserve Chardonnay

ŦŦŦŸ **2000** Medium to full yellow-green, relatively advanced. The solid bouquet with some yellow peach and oak influence is a fair but not exciting start, although the palate is picked up to a degree by the acidity on the finish.   **rating: 84**

best drinking 2002–2003 **best vintages** '95 **drink with** Roast pork • $25.95

Andrew Harris Shiraz

ŦŦŦŸ **2001** Medium to full red; spicy dark plum, with hints of spice, earth and prune on both bouquet and palate are the strength of the wine, the texture of the palate doesn't quite live up to the flavour.   **rating: 88**

best drinking 2004–2010 **best vintages** '97 **drink with** Butterfly leg of lamb • $15.95

Andrew Harris Reserve Shiraz

ŸŸŸŸ **1999** Light to medium red-purple; the bouquet is fragrant, but light, with slightly minty/leafy aromas; vanillin oak makes some positive contribution to the palate in balancing the aromas, but the wine lacks concentration, which is not surprising given the vintage. **rating: 84**

best drinking 2002–2006 **best vintages** '97 **drink with** Braised oxtail • $25.95

Andrew Harris The Vision

ŸŸŸŸŸ **1998** Medium red-purple; a moderately complex blend of cedar, earth, berry, chocolate and vanilla on the bouquet leads into an attractive palate, with plum, black cherry and currant fruit, rounded off by soft tannins and subtle oak. **rating: 90**

best drinking 2003–2008 **best vintages** '96, '97, '98 **drink with** Steak and kidney pie • $44.95

Andrew Harris Cabernet Merlot

ŸŸŸŸŸ **1999** Medium purple-red; the bouquet has appealing red berry fruit with a hint of sweet earth, the palate has nicely balanced berry fruit and oak in a distinctly elegant, fruit-driven style. Gold medal Mudgee Wine Show 2001. **rating: 94**

best drinking 2004–2009 **best vintages** '99 **drink with** Rack of lamb • $25.95

Andrew Harris Reserve Cabernet Merlot

ŸŸŸŸ **1999** Light to medium red-purple; the bouquet is quite fresh, with light red berry fruit, but is not especially complex. The palate has distinctly savoury, almost lemony, spicy characters, no doubt deriving from the 50 per cent Merlot component. Intriguingly, shows little impact of the 18 months the wine spent in new French oak. **rating: 85**

best drinking 2003–2007 **best vintages** NA **drink with** Fillet of lamb • $25.95

Andrew Harris Reserve Cabernet Sauvignon

ŸŸŸŸ **1999** Medium red-purple; attractive red berry fruit on both the bouquet and palate is subverted by too much sweet oak, which does not sit happily with the varietal character of cabernet sauvignon. A pity, because there is some good wine hiding under that oak. **rating: 86**

best drinking 2003–2008 **best vintages** '94 **drink with** Sitr-fried beef • $25.95

andrew peace wines ★★★☆

PO Box 92, Piangil, Vic 3597 **region** Swan Hill
phone (03) 5030 5291 **fax** (03) 5030 5605 **open** By appointment
winemaker Andrew Peace **production** 50 000 **est.** 1995
product range ($9.95–15.95 R) Sauvignon Blanc, Chardonnay, Colombard Chardonnay, Mourvedre Shiraz, Grenache Shiraz, Shiraz, Cabernet, Merlot.
summary The Peace family has been a major Swan Hill grape grower since 1980, and moved into winemaking with the opening of a $3 million winery in 1997. The modestly priced wines are aimed at supermarket-type outlets in Australia and, in particular, at the export market in the major destinations for Australian wine. The quality of the wines is consistently good.

angove's ★★★

Bookmark Avenue, Renmark, SA 5341 **region** Riverland
phone (08) 8580 3100 **fax** (08) 8580 3155 **open** Mon–Fri 9–5
winemaker Jane Gilham **production** 1 million **est.** 1886
product range ($4.50–14 CD) A range of new label designs and packaging for the six ranges. At the top comes Sarnia Farm, with Chardonnay and Cabernet Sauvignon; Classic Reserve, covering virtually all varieties; Bear Crossing Chardonnay and Cabernet Merlot; Stonegate Semillon Chardonnay, Verdelho, Chardonnay and Cabernet Shiraz; Butterfly Ridge Riesling, Colombard Chardonnay, Spatlese Lexia and Shiraz Cabernet; and bringing up the rear, Misty Vineyards with Dry White, Fruity White, Late Harvest Sweet White and Traditional Dry Red.
summary Exemplifies the economies of scale achievable in the Australian Riverland without compromising potential quality. Very good technology provides wines which are never poor and which can sometimes exceed their theoretical station in life; the white varietals are best. Angove's expansion into Padthaway has resulted in estate-grown premium wines at the top of the range. As well as national distribution, Angove's is exported to virtually all the major markets in Europe, North America and Asia. For good measure, it also acts as a distributor of Perrier Jouet Champagne and several small Australian wineries.

Angove's Classic Reserve Chardonnay

TTTY 2001 Medium yellow-green; the bouquet has peachy fruit and some slightly nutty characters in the background; there is plenty of soft peachy fruit on the palate, with well-balanced acidity. Good value.

rating: 84

best drinking 2002–2003 **best vintages** NA **drink with** Pork fillet • $10

Angove's Butterfly Ridge Shiraz Cabernet

TTTY 2001 Light to medium red-purple; the bouquet has somewhat plain red berry fruit and a touch of spice, the palate has more weight, the flavours a mix of berry, plum and a flick of vanilla. Very cleverly made, and exceptional value at the price.

rating: 82

best drinking 2002–2003 **best vintages** NA **drink with** Pizza, pasta • $6

angus wines ★★★★

Captain Sturt Road, Hindmarsh Island, SA 5214 **region** Southern Fleurieu
phone (08) 8555 2320 **fax** (08) 8555 2323 **open** By appointment
winemaker Mike Farmilo (Contract) **production** 1000 **est.** 1995
product range ($13-21.50 ML) Semillon, Shiraz.
summary Susan and Alistair Angus are the pioneer viticulturists on Hindmarsh Island, an island which has never been far from the headlines, but for reasons entirely divorced from viticulture. If the Bridge has had problems to contend with, so have the Anguses as they have progressed from a test plot of vines planted in 1992 through to the first tiny commercial crop in 1998 and a far larger crop in 1999. They have established 4.5 hectares of shiraz, and 1.5 hectares of semillon, the wine being contract-made for them by Mike Farmilo at The Fleurieu Winery in McLaren Vale. Part is bottled under the Angus Wines label, but a larger amount is sold in bulk to other wineries. Every aspect of packaging and marketing has a sophisticated touch.

Angus Sturt Ridge Semillon

TTTTT 2001 Light straw-green; an aromatic and stylish bouquet, with intense grassy fruit and a subliminal hint of French oak; the palate is vibrantly lively and fresh, with a long, lingering finish, the oak once again imperceptible (30 per cent of the wine spent six weeks in new French oak). Truly outstanding. **rating: 94**
TTTT 2000 Very pale straw-green; a crisp, light, minerally bouquet, happily unforced by excessive oak or skin contact. A crisp, light and clean bouquet, for all the world like a young Hunter Semillon; could develop equally well. Terrific value.

rating: 86

best drinking 2002–2006 **best vintages** '01 **drink with** Light shellfish • $13

Angus Sturt Ridge Shiraz

TTTT 2000 Medium purple-red; the bouquet is clean and fresh, with red berry fruit accompanied by hints of spice and vanilla; the palate has attractive red berry fruit with heaps of smooth vanilla oak, well integrated, but slightly over the top. The oak is an equal mix of French and American, but, as ever, it is the American which dominates. **rating: 87**
TTTT 1999 Medium red-purple; scented, lively, savoury, almost lemony fruit combines with soft vanillin oak on the bouquet; the medium-bodied palate once again shows savoury, slightly earthy fruit with well-integrated American oak.

rating: 86

best drinking 2002–2007 **best vintages** NA **drink with** Designer sausages • $21.50

annie's lane ★★★★☆

Quelltaler Road, Watervale, SA 5452 **region** Clare Valley
phone (00) 0010 0000 **fax** (00) 0010 0090 **open** Mon Fri 0.00 5, weekends 11 1
winemaker Wendy Stuckey, Nigel Dolan **production** NFP **est.** 1856
product range ($12–34 CD) Riesling, Semillon, Reserve Semillon, Shiraz, Copper Trail Shiraz, Old Vine Shiraz, Grenache Mourvedre, Clare/Barossa Cabernet Merlot, Chardonnay.
summary The Clare Valley portfolio of Beringer Blass formerly made at Quelltaler is sold under the Annie's Lane label, the name coming from Annie Weyman, a turn-of-the-century local identity. Since 1996, a series of outstanding wines have appeared under the Annie's Lane label. The Quelltaler winery has been leased to some Clare Valley vignerons determined to keep it in going-concern condition, but that lease is due to expire soon.

Annie's Lane Riesling

ŢŢŢŢŸ **2001** Light but brilliant green-yellow, with fragrant aromas of lime, passionfruit and apple blossom, the excellent palate is tightened up by precisely judged acidity on the finish. **rating: 93**

best drinking 2001–2002 **best vintages** '96, '97, '98, '01 **drink with** Summer salad • $13.50

Annie's Lane Semillon

ŢŢŢŢ **2001** Glowing, medium to full yellow-green; rich, ripe fruit on the bouquet is followed by a palate with abundant fruit weight and complexity, round, full and rich. A rare beast – a drink-now Semillon. **rating: 87**

best drinking 2001–2002 **best vintages** '94, '96, '00 **drink with** Rich seafood • $15

Annie's Lane Chardonnay

ŢŢŢŢ **2001** Light to medium green-yellow; the bouquet is clean, with neither fruit nor oak especially expressive. However, the fruit-driven palate has some length, with nice citrus and melon flavours and, once again, subliminal oak. **rating: 85**

best drinking 2001–2002 **best vintages** '94, '96 **drink with** Grilled chicken • $13.50

Annie's Lane Shiraz

ŢŢŢŢŸ **2000** Medium to full red-purple; deep, dark berry/black cherry fruit aromas are followed by a typically voluminous palate, with masses of blackberry and dark cherry fruit; well-balanced oak and tannins; the same great value as ever. **rating: 90**

best drinking 2004–2014 **best vintages** '94, '96, '98, '99, '00 **drink with** Grilled porterhouse • $17

Annie's Lane Old Vine Grenache Shiraz Mourvèdre

ŢŢŢŢŢ **1999** Medium red-purple; the aroma is strongly reminiscent of good quality Rhône Valley red, with a mix of licorice and game aromas, then an attractive medium-bodied and particularly well-balanced palate. Gold and trophy winner Clare Valley Regional Wine Show 2001. **rating: 94**

best drinking 2003–2009 **best vintages** '98, '99 **drink with** Beef in red wine • $21

Annie's Lane Cabernet Merlot

ŢŢŢŢŸ **2000** Bright red-purple; aromatic red berry fruit and a hint of slightly dusty oak on the bouquet; picks up the pace dramatically on the palate, featuring abundant sweet, red and blackcurrant fruit, a touch of mint, the tannins, extract and oak all perfectly balanced and integrated. Excellent value. **rating: 90**

best drinking 2003–2009 **best vintages** '94, '95, '97, '99, '00 **drink with** Devilled kidneys • $17

annvers wines ★★★☆

Lot 10, Razorback Road, Kangarilla, SA 5157 **region** Adelaide Hills
phone (08) 8374 1787 **fax** (08) 8374 2102 **open** Not
winemaker Contract **production** 3500 **est.** 1998
product range ($28 R) Shiraz, Cabernet Sauvignon.
summary Myriam and Wayne Keoghan established Annvers Wines with the emphasis on quality rather than quantity. The first Cabernet Sauvignon was made in 1998, and volume has increased to the point where 3500 cases of Cabernet Sauvignon and Shiraz will be released in 2002. The grapes come from vineyards in Langhorne Creek, McLaren Vale and the Annvers Estate Vineyard in the Adelaide Hills. The quality of the 2000 Shiraz and 2000 Cabernet Sauvignon show that the Keoghans have indeed succeeded in their aim: the wines border on a four-star rating. Since the wine was first released, it has been sold in the United States and Singapore; it has limited retail distribution in SA, NSW and Qld.

Annvers Shiraz

ŢŢŢŢ **2000** Strong, youthful purple-red; the bouquet opens up with quality dark plum and licorice fruit, before American oak proceeds to flex its muscles. The palate is rich and full flavoured, with masses of plum and vanilla; a little more polishing might have produced an even better result, but this is a more than useful wine. **rating: 87**

best drinking 2004–2009 **best vintages** NA **drink with** Braised oxtail • $28

Annvers Cabernet Sauvignon

ŢŢŢŢ **2000** Deep red-purple; clean, ripe, smooth dark berry fruit and subtle oak aromas are repeated on the impressive palate, which has lots of character and stuffing, particularly for the vintage; equally obvious development potential. **rating: 88**

best drinking 2005–2011 **best vintages** NA **drink with** Roast saltbush lamb • $28

antcliff's chase ★★★☆

RMB 4510, Caveat via Seymour, Vic 3660 **region** Central Victorian High Country
phone (03) 5790 4333 **fax** (03) 5790 4333 **open** Weekends 10–5
winemaker Chris Bennett, Ian Leamon **production** 800 **est.** 1982
product range ($14–30 CD) Riesling, Chardonnay, Pinot Noir, Ultra Pinot Noir, Cabernet Merlot.
summary A small family enterprise which commenced planting the vineyards at an elevation of 600 metres in the Strathbogie Ranges in 1982; wine production from the four-hectare vineyard began in the early 1990s. After an uncertain start, wine quality has picked up considerably.

🐂 anthony dale ★★★☆

Lot 202 Robe Road, Bray, SA 5276 **region** Mount Benson
phone (08) 8735 7255 **fax** (08) 8735 7255 **open** Not
winemaker John Bird (Contract) **production** 1700 **est.** 1994
product range Shiraz Cabernet Sauvignon.
summary Anthony Dale has meticulously planned every aspect and detail of the vineyard and winery which bears his name. The vineyard was planted between 1995 and 1998 inclusive; situated on the leeward side of the Woakwine Range, the light sandy soil is heavily impregnated with limestone. The decision has been taken to limit the crop to 1 tonne per acre (2.5 tonnes per hectare). Only one wine has been and will be made: a blend of shiraz and cabernet sauvignon; the winemaker is John Bird, a former senior Penfolds red winemaker with experience in helping make all of the Penfolds top red wines (including Grange). As well as limited local distribution, the wines are exported to the United States.

Anthony Dale Limited Release Shiraz Cabernet

ɥɥɥ 2000 Medium red-purple; a solid bouquet with expansive use of French and American oak. The palate precisely follows down the track of the bouquet; structurally smooth, but the fruit struggles to keep up with the impact of the oak. Greater maturity of the vines may help redress the balance in the years ahead. **rating: 83**

best drinking 2003–2007 **best vintages** NA **drink with** Smoked beef • $49

apsley gorge vineyard ★★★★☆

The Gulch, Bicheno, Tas 7215 **region** Southern Tasmania
phone (03) 6375 1221 **fax** (03) 6375 1589 **open** 7 days in summer 11–6 or by appointment
winemaker Brian Franklin **production** 2000 **est.** 1988
product range ($21–36 CD) Chardonnay, Pinot Noir.
summary While nominally situated at Bicheno on the east coast, Apsley Gorge is in fact some distance inland, taking its name from a mountain pass. Clearly, it shares with the other east coast wineries the capacity to produce Chardonnay and Pinot Noir of excellent quality.

Apsley Gorge Pinot Noir

ɥɥɥɥɥ 2000 Good depth to the deep red colour, still with a touch of purple; obvious charry oak adds to the complexity of the damson plum fruit of the bouquet, but the wine changes up a gear with the classy, layered and rich palate, with its mix of plum and spice powering the wine through to a long finish. Multiple trophy winner. **rating: 95**

best drinking 2002–2007 **best vintages** '94, '95, '00 **drink with** Breast of squab • $21

aquila estate ★★★★

85 Carabooda Road, Carabooda, WA 6033 **region** Swan District
phone (08) 9561 8166 **fax** (08) 9561 8177 **open** Mon–Fri 11–3, weekends and public holidays 11–5
winemaker Andrew Spencer-Wright **production** 25 000 **est.** 1993
product range ($12–40 CD) Riesling, Chenin Blanc, Sauvignon Blanc Semillon, Reflections (white blend), Chardonnay Semillon, Chardonnay, Shiraz, Merlot, Flame (red blend), Cabernet Sauvignon.
summary As Aquila Estate has matured, so have its grape sources centred on the Margaret River (principally) and Blackwood Valley. The wines on release in 2002 are of high quality. Exports to the UK, Singapore, Mauritius and Japan.

Aquila Estate Blackwood Valley Riesling

ɥɥɥɥ 2001 Light green-yellow; the fragrant bouquet has a mix of delicate passionfruit and apple aromas, the palate a more minerally accent, but nonetheless continuing the pleasing delicacy of the bouquet. **rating: 90**

best drinking 2002–2005 **best vintages** '01 **drink with** Shellfish • $19

Aquila Estate Margaret River Blackwood Valley Cabernet Sauvignon
▼▼▼▼▽ **2000** Excellent, bright red-purple; clean, sweet blackberry and blackcurrant fruit aromas flow through into the opening stanza of the palate, which has lots of substance and built-in tannins on the finish. Good oak handling throughout.   **rating: 91**
best drinking 2005–2010 **best vintages** NA **drink with** Lamb shanks • $19

arakoon   ★★★☆

229 Main Road, McLaren Vale, SA 5171 **region** McLaren Vale
phone (08) 8323 7339 **fax** (02) 6566 6288 **open** Not
winemaker Patrik Jones, Raymond Jones **production** 1000 **est.** 1999
product range ($15–44 CD) Chardonnay, Pinot Black (Pinot Noir), Doyen Shiraz, Reserve Shiraz, Sellick Beach Shiraz Grenache, Big, Fat and Gutsy (Shiraz Grenache), Dingabledinga Blend (Cabernet Shiraz), The Lighthouse Cabernet Sauvignon Shiraz.
summary Ray and Patrik (sic correct spelling) Jones' first venture into wine came to nothing: a 1990 proposal for a film about the Australian wine industry with myself as anchorman. Five years too early, say the Jones'. In 1991 they opened an agency for Australian wine in Stockholm, and they started exporting wine to that country, the UK, Germany and Switzerland in 1994. In 1999 they took the plunge into making their own wine, and exporting it as well as the wines of others. Patrik is the winemaker, having completed a degree at the Waite Campus of the University of Adelaide. The graphic design of the labels, incidentally, is as outrageous as the names of the wines.

Arakoon Doyen Shiraz
▼▼▼▼ **2000** Incredibly deep and dense colour; prune, jam and licorice aromas lead into the thickly textured palate, featuring very ripe (read overripe) fruit, though the tannins are soft. Robert Parker might well be disposed to give it 100 points.   **rating: 86**
best drinking 2005–2015 **best vintages** NA **drink with** Game • $44

Arakoon Reserve Shiraz
▼▼▼▼ **2000** Full red-purple; ripe, dark berry fruit and lots of oak, said to be French, is followed by a rich, ripe and luscious palate, better balanced, and less a caricature than Doyen.   **rating: 88**
best drinking 2005–2010 **best vintages** NA **drink with** Braised ox cheek • $32

Arakoon Sellicks Beach Shiraz Grenache
▼▼▼▼ **2000** Medium red-purple; a complex spicy/leathery/licorice bouquet is followed by a palate with stacks of flavour and character, replaying the bouquet.   **rating: 87**
best drinking 2002–2006 **best vintages** NA **drink with** Ragout of lamb • $22

arlewood estate   ★★★☆

Harmans Road South, Wilyabrup, WA 6284 **region** Margaret River
phone (08) 9755 6267 **fax** (08) 9755 6267 **open** Weekends 11–5
winemaker Voyager Estate (Contract) **production** 4000 **est.** 1988
product range ($19–35 CD) Semillon, Sauvignon Blanc, Reserve Chardonnay, Shiraz, Cabernet Merlot, Cabernet Reserve (Cabernet Sauvignon Merlot Cabernet Franc).
summary The Heydon and Gosatti families acquired Arlewood Estate in October 1999, having previously established a small vineyard in Cowaramup in 1995. George Heydon is a Perth dentist whose passion for wine has led him to study viticulture at the University of Western Australia, while Garry Gosatti has been involved in the boutique brewing and hospitality industries for many years. The area under vine has now been expanded to 15 hectares, and Arlewood has entered into a long-term winemaking contract with Voyager Estate, with consultancy advice from Janice McDonald. The partners have significantly lifted the standard of the wines, and continuing improvements seem highly likely. Retail distribution in most states and exports to Switzerland.

Arlewood Estate Cabernet Reserve
▼▼▼▼ **1998** Medium red-purple; the bouquet is complex and fragrant, with a strong French oak input; the palate has good structure, with a cedary/berry/chocolatey mid-palate, and fine, silky tannins running through to the finish.   **rating: 89**
best drinking 2003–2008 **best vintages** NA **drink with** Osso buco • $29

armstrong vineyards ★★★★☆

Lot 1 Military Road, Armstrong, Vic 3381 **region** Grampians
phone (08) 8277 6073 **fax** (08) 8277 6035 **open** Not
winemaker Tony Royal **production** 800 **est.** 1989
product range ($48 R) Shiraz.
summary Armstrong Vineyards is the brain- or love-child of Tony Royal, former Seppelt Great Western winemaker who now runs the Australian business of Seguin Moreau, the largest of the French coopers. Armstrong Vineyards has 5 hectares of shiraz, the first 2 hectares planted in 1989, the remainder in 1995–96. Low yields (4.5 to 5.5 tonnes per hectare) mean the wine will always be produced in limited quantities.

Armstrong Vineyards Shiraz

♟♟♟♟♟ **2000** Medium to full purple-red; clean, ripe black cherry fruit with hints of spice and subtle French (Seguin Moreau, of course) oak is followed by a powerful palate with black cherry fruit, pervasive lingering tannins and quality oak. Demands and deserves patience. **rating:** 93
♟♟♟♟ **1999** Medium red-purple; the moderately intense bouquet is clean, with a cedary/savoury/spicy spectrum of aromas. The palate, likewise, shows cedary French oak and attractive, fine tannins. One wonders whether the 22 months it spent in oak may be around four months too long. **rating:** 88
best drinking 2006–2016 **best vintages** '96, '98, '00 **drink with** Yearling steak • $48

arranmore vineyard NR

Rangeview Road, Carey Gully, SA 5144 **region** Adelaide Hills
phone (08) 8390 3034 **fax** (08) 8390 0005 **open** By appointment
winemaker John Venus **production** 400 **est.** 1998
product range ($25–26.50 CD) Chardonnay, Black Pinot Noir.
summary One of the tiny operations which are appearing all over the beautiful Adelaide Hills. The two-hectare vineyard is planted to pinot noir, chardonnay and sauvignon blanc, and the wines are distributed by Australian Premium Boutique Wines, and are sold by mail order.

arrowfield ★★★☆

Denman Road, Jerrys Plains, NSW 2330 **region** Upper Hunter Valley
phone (02) 6576 4041 **fax** (02) 6576 4144 **open** 7 days 10–5
winemaker Blair Duncan **production** 70 000 **est.** 1968
product range ($12–21 R) Top-of-the-range Show Reserve range of Chardonnay, Semillon, Shiraz, Merlot, Cabernet Sauvignon, Late Harvest Botrytis Semillon; Hunter Valley Chardonnay, Semillon, Shiraz; Cowra Chardonnay, Merlot; Arrowfield varietals Chardonnay, Semillon Chardonnay, Sauvignon Blanc, Verdelho, Sauvignon Blanc, Shiraz, Cabernet Merlot.
summary After largely dropping the Arrowfield name in favour of Mountarrow and a plethora of other brands, this Japanese-owned company has come full circle, once again marketing the wines solely under the Arrowfield label. Its principal grape sources are Cowra and the Upper Hunter, but it does venture further afield from time to time. Exports to the US, the UK, New Zealand, Germany, Malaysia and Hong Kong.

Arrowfield Semillon Chardonnay

♟♟♟♟ **2001** Light to medium yellow-green; the bouquet is quite crisp and lemony, with the semillon component dominant. Much the same occurs on the palate, with early-picked semillon fruit sweetened by later-picked chardonnay; sounds simple, but it rarely works as well as it does with this wine. **rating:** 89
best drinking 2002–2004 **best vintages** NA **drink with** Grilled fish • $12

Arrowfield Hunter Valley Shiraz

♟♟♟♟ **2000** Medium red-purple; ripe black cherry and plum fruit on the bouquet flows into a rich and ripe opening to the cherry-flavoured palate, although corrected acidity pokes through on the finish. **rating:** 86
best drinking 2003–2007 **best vintages** NA **drink with** Red meats • $15

artamus ★★★★

PO Box 489, Margaret River, WA 6285 **region** Margaret River
phone (08) 9757 8131 **fax** (08) 9757 8131 **open** Not
winemaker Michael Gadd **production** 250 **est.** 1994
product range ($15 R) Chardonnay.

summary Ann Dewar and Ian Parmenter (the celebrated television food presenter) planted a hectare of chardonnay cuttings (from Cape Mentelle) at their property on the north bank of the Margaret River. Their first wine was produced in 1998, made for them by Michael Gadd, and the style of each succeeding vintage has been remarkably consistent.

Artamus Margaret River Chardonnay

▼▼▼▼ 2000 Light to medium yellow-green; has the typically clean and subtle integration and balance of fruit and oak; the light to medium-bodied palate flows along the same track, with hints of cashew and melon; its main strength is the length of its finish, auguring well for short-term cellaring.　　**rating: 87**

best drinking 2002–2005 best vintages '99 drink with Margaret River marron • $16.25

arthurs creek estate　　★★★★☆

Strathewen Road, Arthurs Creek, Vic 3099 **region** Yarra Valley
phone (03) 9714 8202 **fax** (03) 9824 0252 **open** Not
winemaker Tom Carson (Contract), Gary Baldwin (Consultant) **production** 1500 **est.** 1975
product range ($28–46 R) Chardonnay, Cabernet Sauvignon.
summary A latter-day folly of leading Melbourne QC S E K Hulme, who began the planting of 3 hectares of chardonnay, 4.3 hectares of cabernet sauvignon and 0.7 hectares of merlot at Arthurs Creek in the mid-1970s, and commenced to have wine made by various people for 15 years before deciding to sell any of it. A ruthless weeding-out process followed, with only the best of the older vintages offered. The Cabernets from the 1990s are absolutely outstanding: deeply fruited and marvellously structured. Exports to the UK, the US, Denmark and Japan.

Arthurs Creek Chardonnay

▼▼▼▼▼ 2000 Medium yellow-green; melon, fig and cashew aromas mark a bouquet with excellent fruit and oak balance and integration; the palate has that hard-to-describe squeaky feel of high-quality Chardonnay, with nectarine and melon at the core of a long, graceful wine.　　**rating: 94**

best drinking 2002–2007 best vintages '90, '92, '93, '94, '95, '97, '99, '00 drink with Veal fricassee • $26

Arthurs Creek Cabernet Sauvignon

▼▼▼▼ 1998 Medium red-purple; the bouquet is clean, with fresh red berry fruit, but not particularly complex; the same characters come through on the palate, which is not as concentrated as expected.　　**rating: 85**

▼▼▼▼ 1997 Medium red-purple; the moderately intense bouquet offers a range of cedar, spice, berry and leaf aromas, all reminiscent of Bordeaux. The palate has good texture, tannins and oak balance, but there is a distinctly savoury/earthy edge to the fruit which is just a little too pronounced. Near, but not quite.　　**rating: 88**

best drinking 2002–2006 best vintages '82, '87, '89, '91, '92, '93, '94, '95, '96 drink with Lamb fillets • $43

🐘 arundel farm estate　　NR

Arundel Road, Keilor, Vic 3036 **region** Sunbury
phone (03) 9335 3422 **fax** (03) 9335 4912 **open** Not
winemaker Bianca Conwell **production** 150 **est.** 1995
product range ($25 R) Shiraz.
summary Arundel Farm Estate has been built around a single acre of cabernet and shiraz planted by a previous owner in the 1970s, but abandoned for many years. When the Conwell family purchased the property in the early 1990s, the vineyard was resurrected, the first vintage being made by Rick Kinzbrunner in 1995. Thereafter the cabernet was grafted over to shiraz, the block being slowly increased to 1.6 hectares. After the 1999 vintage, Bianca Conwell took over the responsibility for winemaking on-site, with consultancy advice from Kinzbrunner. Over the past two years an additional four hectares of shiraz and 1.6 hectares of viognier and marsanne have been planted, which will lead to significantly increased production in the future.

ashbrook estate　　★★★★☆

Harmans Road South, Wilyabrup, WA 6284 **region** Margaret River
phone (08) 9755 6262 **fax** (08) 9755 6290 **open** 7 days 11–5
winemaker Tony Devitt, Brian Devitt **production** 8000 **est.** 1975
product range ($15–25 CD) Gold Label Riesling, Black Label Riesling, Semillon, Sauvignon Blanc, Chardonnay, Verdelho, Cabernet Merlot.

summary A fastidious maker of consistently outstanding estate-grown table wines but which shuns publicity and the wine show system alike and is less well known than it deserves to be, selling much of its wine through the cellar door and by an understandably very loyal mailing list clientele. All of the white wines are of the highest quality, year in, year out. Small quantities of the wines now find their way to Japan, Singapore, Hong Kong, Indonesia and Holland.

Ashbrook Estate Semillon

TTTTT 2001 Glowing green-yellow; the complex and rich bouquet is suggestive of lees contact or a small percentage of barrel ferment, but in fact simply comes from the richness of the fruit. The palate is similarly rich and soft, with supple mouthfeel, having the weight of Chardonnay, and the taste of (Margaret River) Semillon. **rating:** 92

best drinking 2002–2005 **best vintages** '93, '94, '95, '97, '99, '01 **drink with** Blanquette of veal • $16

Ashbrook Estate Sauvignon Blanc

TTTTT 2001 Light to medium green-yellow; a mix of gooseberry, tropical and grass aromas, then a palate with abundant flavour and more weight than many, counterbalanced by fine acidity on the finish. Silver medal Sheraton Wine Awards 2001 (remembering there is only one gold, one silver and one bronze awarded in each wine group). **rating:** 90

best drinking 2002–2003 **best vintages** '01 **drink with** Marron • $18

Ashbrook Estate Chardonnay

TTTTT 2000 Medium yellow-green; an intense, aromatic and complex bouquet with smoky barrel ferment and tangy fruit aromas; the palate is high powered, long and intense, more fruit than oak driven. **rating:** 94

best drinking 2002–2005 **best vintages** '92, '93, '94, '95, '98, '99, '00 **drink with** Grilled spatchcock • $23

Ashbrook Estate Cabernet Merlot

TTTTT 1998 Medium red, with the purple starting to diminish; the bouquet offers sweetly savoury/spicy aromas over a core of blackberry fruit; the palate has good texture and structure with fine, bottle-developed flavours, and savoury tannins to close. As always, has overtones of Bordeaux (in a good year). **rating:** 90

best drinking 2003–2008 **best vintages** '98 **drink with** Braised beef • $27

ashton hills ★★★★★

Tregarthen Road, Ashton, SA 5137 **region** Adelaide Hills
phone (08) 8390 1243 **fax** (08) 8390 1243 **open** Weekends 11–5.30
winemaker Stephen George **production** 1500 **est.** 1982
product range ($25–42 CD) Chardonnay, Riesling, Salmon Brut, Blanc de Blanc, Pinot Noir, Piccadilly Valley Pinot Noir, Burra Burra Lone Star Shiraz, Obliqua (Cabernet Merlot).
summary Stephen George wears three winemaker hats: one for Ashton Hills, drawing upon a 3.5-hectare estate vineyard high in the Adelaide Hills; one for Galah Wines; and one for Wendouree. It would be hard to imagine three wineries producing more diverse styles, with the elegance and finesse of Ashton Hills at one end of the spectrum, the awesome power of Wendouree at the other. The Riesling and Pinot Noir have moved into the highest echelon. 2001 saw the release of the single-vineyard Burra Burra Lone Star Shiraz, the first vintage being 1998, but with some earlier experimental vintages also available. The grapes for this wine come from a vineyard established and owned by Stephen George's father. Export markets have been developed in the UK, the US and Japan.

Ashton Hills Riesling

TTTTT 2001 Pale straw-green; a highly aromatic, floral bouquet with lemon blossom and a touch of passionfruit flows into a crisp, intense and long palate, offering a mix of mineral flavours and the fruit flavours promised by the bouquet. Trophy for Best Wine of Show at the 2001 Adelaide Hills Wine Show. Stelvin cap. **rating:** 95

best drinking 2003–2013 **best vintages** '89, '90, '91, '93, '94, '96, '97, '98, '01 **drink with** Fresh asparagus • $20

Ashton Hills Chardonnay

TTTTT 2000 Glowing yellow-green; complex barrel-ferment aromas surround the nectarine, fig, melon and citrus fruit of the bouquet; the powerful fruit of the palate has some additional cashew, with oak underneath, and a long, clean finish. **rating:** 94

ΥΥΥΥΥ **1999** Glowing yellow-green, identical to that of the 2000; the bouquet is complex yet subtle, with excellent fruit and oak balance and integration, in consistent Ashton Hills style. The palate is particularly appealing, with fine, elegant, melon, fig and cashew woven through with subtle oak. **rating: 95**

best drinking 2003–2008 **best vintages** '95, '97, '98, '99, '00 **drink with** Bouillabaisse • $25

Ashton Hills Pinot Noir

ΥΥΥΥΫ **2000** Medium red, with some purple; fragrant, sweet plum and spice aromas then a very ripe, juicy/plummy, fruit-driven palate, finishing with soft, fine tannins; despite the ripeness of the fruit, a lighter style than immediately prior vintages. **rating: 92**

best drinking 2001–2005 **best vintages** '88, '91, '92, '93, '94, '97, '98, '99, '00 **drink with** Smoked duck • $42

Ashton Hills Piccadilly Valley Pinot Noir

ΥΥΥΥ **2000** Medium red, showing a distinct colour shift away from purple; the moderately intense bouquet has savoury/spicy/foresty aromas, characters which drive the palate, which seems to have already lost some of its primary fruit. Either the wine or the taster is at fault. **rating: 85**

best drinking 2003–2006 **best vintages** NA **drink with** Braised duck • $25

Burra Burra Lone Star Shiraz

ΥΥΥΥΥ **1999** Medium purple-red; a solid and ripe bouquet with a mix of plum, blackberry and cherry is followed by an opulent, ripe and rich palate with a core of black plum fruit, attractive oak and soft tannins; truly excellent for the vintage. Spent 18 months in new French oak. **rating: 94**

ΥΥΥΥΫ **1998** Medium purple-red; the moderately intense bouquet is clean, with fresh cherry/red berry fruit, the palate supple, showing ripe plum, black cherry, soft, fine tannins and excellent oak. The first commercial release from the vineyard established by Stephen George's father near Burra (experimental vintages from '95 onwards). **rating: 93**

best drinking 2004–2009 **best vintages** '96, '98, '99 **drink with** Venison • $30

ashworths hill   NR

Ashworths Road, Lancefield, Vic 3435 **region** Macedon Ranges
phone (03) 5429 1689 **fax** (03) 5429 1689 **open** 7 days 10–6
winemaker Anne Manning, John Ellis **production** 100 **est.** 1982
product range ($12–20 CD) Macedon Ranges Cabernet Sauvignon is the flagship; Victorian Riesling and Chardonnay are also available.
summary Peg and Ken Reaburn offer light refreshments throughout the day, and the property has scenic views of the Macedon Ranges.

audrey wilkinson   ★ ★ ★ ☆

Oakdale, De Beyers Road, Pokolbin, NSW 2320 **region** Lower Hunter Valley
phone (02) 4998 7411 **fax** (02) 4998 7303 **open** Mon–Fri 9–5, weekends 9.30–5
winemaker Chris Cameron **production** 2755 **est.** 1999
product range ($16–30 CD) Traminer, Semillon, Unwooded Chardonnay, Chardonnay, Shiraz, Reserve Shiraz, Reserve Coonawarra Cabernet Sauvignon, Pepper Tree Reserve Malbec.
summary One of the most historic properties in the Hunter Valley, with a particularly beautiful location. The four wines come from the old plantings on the property, which has a very attractive cellar door. It is part of the James Fairfax wine group (headed by Pepper Tree).

Audrey Wilkinson Traminer

ΥΥΥΫ **2002** Light yellow-green; the youthful bouquet is light, with faint rose petal aromas and a whiff of SO_2; the clean, pleasant palate, fractionally off-dry, has light citrus and a touch of spice. From a 1.4-hectare plot at Oakdale, hand-picked late January and released 15 March 2002. **rating: 82**

best drinking 2002–2003 **best vintages** NA **drink with** Light Asian dishes • $19

Audrey Wilkinson Semillon

ΥΥΥΥ **2001** Medium yellow-green; a solid bouquet, predominantly minerally, but with a touch of herb, leads into a palate with plenty of weight and solidity, arguably a trifle leaden-footed, but with plenty of presence. **rating: 85**

best drinking 2003–2007 **best vintages** NA **drink with** Leave it in the cellar • $19

Audrey Wilkinson Chardonnay

ŦŦŦŦ 2000 Medium yellow-green; the moderately aromatic bouquet with good fruit and oak balance and integration leads into a lively, fresh citrus and melon-flavoured palate, with good length. **rating: 87**

best drinking 2001–2003 **best vintages** NA **drink with** Veal • $20

Audrey Wilkinson Pepper Tree Reserve Malbec

ŦŦŦŦ 1991 Medium red; the bouquet is redolent with jammy varietal character in a striking and totally unexpected mode. The palate, likewise, is rich and powerful, still with a slightly tannic finish. A rarity. **rating: 88**

best drinking 2001–2006 **best vintages** NA **drink with** Braised ox cheek • NA

august hill estate   NR

763 Woodbridge Hill Road, Gardners Bay, Tas 7112 **region** Southern Tasmania
phone (03) 6229 2316 **fax** (03) 6229 2326 **open** Not
winemaker David Masterton **production** 600 **est.** 1996
product range ($14–45 ML) Pinot Noir, Directors Reserve Pinot Noir, Fruit Liqueur.
summary A relatively new and equally small venture in the Huon Valley which has elected to make its own wines rather than use the contract winemaking services of Andrew Hood or others in the field. It is a pinot noir specialist, with 3 hectares planted. The early results have been somewhat erratic, but there are better things on the way.

auldstone   ★★★

Booths Road, Taminick via Glenrowan, Vic 3675 **region** Glenrowan
phone (03) 5766 2237 **fax** (03) 5766 2131 **open** Thur–Sat and school holidays 9–5, Sun 10–5
winemaker Michael Reid **production** 2000 **est.** 1987
product range ($12–26 CD) Riesling, Traminer Riesling, Chardonnay, Late Picked Riesling, Sparkling Shiraz, Shiraz, Cabernet Merlot, Cabernet Sauvignon, Herceynia Tawny Port, Liqueur Muscat.
summary Michael and Nancy Reid have restored a century-old stone winery and have replanted the largely abandoned 26-hectare vineyard around it. Gourmet lunches are available on weekends.

Auldstone Chardonnay

ŦŦŦŦ♈ 1999 Medium yellow-green; a solid, full bouquet with tangy fruit and well-integrated French and American oak. A big, generous palate in traditional Australian White Burgundy style. **rating: 84**

best drinking 2002–2003 **best vintages** NA **drink with** KFC • $15

Auldstone Late Picked Riesling

ŦŦŦŦ♈ 2000 Light to medium yellow-green; some tropical lime aromas come through on the palate, with no botrytis but spatlese-level residual sugar. Might surprise with bottle age. **rating: 84**

best drinking 2003–2008 **best vintages** NA **drink with** Soft cheese, dried fruit • $16

austin's barrabool   ★★★

50 Lemins Road, Waurn Ponds, Vic 3221 **region** Geelong
phone (03) 5241 8114 **fax** (03) 5241 8122 **open** By appointment
winemaker John Ellis (Contract), Pamela Austin **production** 3000 **est.** 1982
product range ($18–40 CD) Riesling, Sauvignon Blanc, Chardonnay, Pinot Noir, Shiraz, Cabernet Sauvignon.
summary Pamela and Richard Austin have quietly built their business from a tiny base, but one which is now poised for much bigger things. The vineyard has been progressively extended to 55 hectares, and production has risen from 700 cases in 1998 to 3000 cases in 2001. Strangely, no recent tastings.

avalon vineyard   ★★★

RMB 9556 Whitfield Road, Wangaratta, Vic 3678 **region** King Valley
phone (03) 5729 3629 **fax** (03) 5729 3635 **open** 7 days 10–5
winemaker Doug Groom **production** 1000 **est.** 1981
product range ($12–20 CD) Riesling, Semillon, Sauvignon Blanc, Chardonnay, Late Harvest Semillon, Pinot Noir, Shiraz, Cabernet Sauvignon, Pinot Noir Méthode Champenoise.

summary Avalon Vineyard is in the King Valley, four kilometres north of Whitfield. Much of the production from the ten-hectare vineyard is sold to other makers, with limited quantities made by Doug Groom, a graduate of Roseworthy, and one of the owners of the property. Exports to the US.

avalon wines   NR

1605 Bailey Road, Glen Forrest, WA 6071 **region** Perth Hills
phone (08) 9298 8049 **fax** (08) 9298 8049 **open** By appointment
winemaker Rob Marshall **production** 700 **est.** 1986
product range ($13–17 CD) Semillon, Chardonnay, Cane-Cut Semillon, Cabernet Merlot.
summary One of the smaller wineries in the Perth Hills, drawing upon three-quarters of a hectare each of chardonnay, semillon and cabernet sauvignon.

avenel park   NR

24/25 Ewings Road, Avenel, Vic 3664 **region** Goulburn Valley
phone (03) 9347 5444 **fax** (03) 9349 3278 **open** By appointment
winemaker David Traeger (Contract) **production** 500 **est.** 1994
product range ($24 CD) Shiraz, Shiraz Cabernet Sauvignon, Cabernet Sauvignon.
summary Jed and Sue Hart have, in their words, 'turned the rocky, ironstone soils of Lovers Hill into a 22-acre vineyard over back-breaking years'. Seven of the 10 hectares are planted to shiraz and cabernet sauvignon, with a small amount each of merlot, semillon and chardonnay. Most of the grapes have been and will continue to be sold to Southcorp, but since 2000 the equivalent of 500 cases of wine have been retained and contract-made by David Traeger. Over the next 3–5 years this may increase to 1000 cases, but the Harts' main viticultural business (Jed Hart is in aviation) will be grape growing.

Avenel Park Shiraz Cabernet Sauvignon
TTTTT 2000 Medium to full red-purple; attractive dark berry fruit with touches of spice and vanilla on the bouquet is followed by a medium-bodied palate, with a core of dark berry fruits surrounded by well-judged extract of tannins and oak. An impressive debut.   **rating:** 90

best drinking 2004–2009 **best vintages** NA **drink with** Braised beef • $24

avonmore estate   NR

Mayreef–Avonmore Road, Avonmore, Vic 3558 **region** Bendigo
phone (03) 5432 6291 **fax** (03) 5432 6291 **open** Not
winemaker Don Buchanan (Contract), Shaun Bryans **production** 1500 **est.** 1996
product range Viognier, Shiraz, Sangiovese, Cabernet Sauvignon.
summary Rob and Pauline Bryans own and operate a certified Grade A Bio-Dynamic farm, producing and selling beef, lamb and cereals as well as establishing nine hectares of viognier, sangiovese, cabernet sauvignon, cabernet franc and shiraz, which produced its first crop in 2000. Most of the wine is contract-made by Don Buchanan at the Tisdall Winery at Echuca, but a small amount is made on the property. The wine will be marketed under the Avonmore Estate label, but with the worldwide Demeter logo. Several of the unbottled wines have been awarded medals at Victorian wine shows, and the Bryans plan to have a cellar door and small winery up and running within two years.

bacchanalia estate   NR

Taverner Street, Bacchus Marsh, Vic 3340 **region** Sunbury
phone (03) 5367 6416 **fax** (03) 5367 6416 **open** Sundays by appointment
winemaker Pat Carmody (Contract), John Reid **production** 500 **est.** 1994
product range ($15–25 R) Semillon, Shiraz.
summary Noted ABC broadcaster and journalist John Reid and wife Val established Bacchanalia Estate in 1994 on the fertile black soils of Bacchus Marsh, adjacent to the Werribee River. Consultancy viticultural advice from Dr Richard Smart pointed to the inevitably vigorous growth to be expected from the rich, black soil, and so a Geneva Double Curtain (GDC) trellis and canopy was utilised from the outset. Two hectares of shiraz, 0.6 ha semillon, 0.4 ha cabernet sauvignon and 0.2 ha viognier have been established. For several years now Pat Carmody (of Craiglee) has been making the wine, the only wine he makes other than for his own label. Apart from local distribution through Geelong and Ballarat, the wine is available at Nick's Wine Merchants throughout Melbourne.

badger's brook ★★★

874 Maroondah Highway, Coldstream, Vic 3770 **region** Yarra Valley
phone (03) 5962 4130 **fax** (03) 5962 4238 **open** Thurs–Mon 11–5
winemaker Contract **production** 5000 **est.** 1993
product range ($16–25 CD) The Badger's Brook range, all of which are from the Yarra Valley, mostly said to be estate-grown, and the Storm Ridge range, coming from various regions including the Mornington Peninsula and as far away as Margaret River, but also with some Yarra component.
summary Situated prominently on the Maroondah Highway next door to the well-known Eyton-on-Yarra. Location is all, although not for all the wines. As is proper, the Badger's Brook-branded wines are significantly better than the Storm Ridge range. Domestic distribution on the east coast by The Wine Company. Exports to Europe and Asia.

Badger's Brook Sauvignon Blanc
▼▼▼▼ 2001 Light green-yellow; a light, fresh and crisp bouquet with some gooseberry fruit aromas is followed by a cleverly made wine, the finish pushed out by just a touch of sweetness. One hundred per cent hand-picked, estate-grown grapes.   **rating:** 86
best drinking 2002–2003 **best vintages** NA **drink with** Light seafood • $18

Badger's Brook Pinot Noir
▼▼▼▼ 2000 Full red; the moderately fragrant bouquet has a mix of foresty/savoury and plum fruit aromas; on the palate, ripe, plummy fruit shows clear varietal character, the palate shortening off slightly on the finish.   **rating:** 87
best drinking 2002–2005 **best vintages** NA **drink with** Quail • $25

Badger's Brook Shiraz
▼▼▼▼ 2000 Medium purple-red; clean, smooth cherry and raspberry aromas flow into a palate with ripe, black cherry fruit and a hint of oak; not particularly complex, but certainly has flavour. Like the Pinot Noir, estate-grown.   **rating:** 86
best drinking 2003–2007 **best vintages** NA **drink with** Smoked lamb • $22

bago vineyards ★★★

Milligans Road, off Bago Road, Wauchope, NSW 2446 **region** Hastings River
phone (02) 6585 7099 **fax** (02) 6585 7099 **open** 7 days 11–5
winemaker John Steel, John Cassegrain (Contract) **production** 5000 **est.** 1985
product range ($10–21.50 CD) Chardonnay, Jazz White Classic, Verdelho, Chambourcin, Merlot Chambourcin, Jazz Red Classic, Sparkling Pinot Noir Chardonnay, Sparkling Chambourcin, Tawny Port.
summary Jim and Kay Mobs commenced planting the Broken Bago Vineyards in 1985 with one hectare of chardonnay, and have now increased the total plantings to 12.5 hectares. Regional specialist John Cassegrain is contract winemaker.

Bago Vineyards Chambourcin
▼▼▼▼ 2000 Bright purple-red; the spotlessly clean bouquet has gentle red berry fruit; the palate has similar earthy/red berry fruit flavours, but by far its most impressive feature is its structure: it does not tail off or dip like the vast majority of wines made from this variety. Into the bargain, it is also holding well.   **rating:** 86
best drinking 2002–2003 **best vintages** NA **drink with** Lamb kidneys • $14.50

baileys of glenrowan ★★★★★

Cnr Taminick Gap and Upper Taminick Roads, Glenrowan, Vic 3675 **region** Glenrowan
phone (03) 5766 2392 **fax** (03) 5766 2596 **open** Mon–Fri 9–5, weekends 10–5
winemaker Matt Steel **production** 30 0000 **est.** 1870
product range ($16–40 R) Shiraz, 1904 Block Shiraz, 1920s Block Shiraz and Cabernet Sauvignon are the principal wines; also Founder Tokay, Muscat and Port.
summary Now part of the sprawling Beringer Blass empire, inherited via the Rothbury takeover. Has made some excellent Shiraz in recent years, but its greatest strength lies in its fortified wines. It is for these wines that the winery rating is given.

Baileys of Glenrowan 1904 Block Shiraz

❚❚❚❚❚ 1999 Bright red-purple; the bouquet offers good fruit and oak balance and integration, the sweet, ripe cherry/berry fruit both there and on the palate. A wine which verges on elegance, with fine tannins and subtle oak. **rating:** 92

best drinking 2003–2009 **best vintages** '98, '99 **drink with** Leave it in the cellar • $37

Baileys 1920s Block Shiraz

❚❚❚❚❚ 1999 Medium red-purple; savoury berry and chocolate aromas are followed by an intense and long palate, with a similar, quite elegant, range of flavours to those of the bouquet; not what one might expect, but pretty impressive. **rating:** 90

best drinking 2004–2009 **best vintages** '91, '92, '93, '96, '97, '99 **drink with** Rare rump steak, venison • $23

Baileys Founder Liqueur Tokay

❚❚❚❚ NV Medium golden brown; full, complex sweeter style of Tokay, with clean spirit. The palate is rich, full and textured, with flavours of butterscotch and sweet biscuit and a chewy texture, but finishing long and clean. **rating:** 89

best drinking 2002–2003 **best vintages** NA **drink with** Winter aperitif; summer after dinner • $17.95

Baileys Founder Liqueur Muscat

❚❚❚❚ NV Medium red-brown; an arresting bouquet with hints of spice to the sweet, ripe, complex fruit. The same unusual spicy/cinnamon aspects are apparent on the rich and complex palate. **rating:** 88

best drinking 2002–2003 **best vintages** NA **drink with** After coffee; alternative to Cognac • $17.95

bainton family wines   NR

390 Milbrodale Road, Fordwich, NSW 2330 **region** Lower Hunter Valley
phone (02) 9968 1764 **fax** (02) 9960 3454 **open** Not
winemaker Tony Bainton **production** 10 000 **est.** 1998
product range ($11–30 ML) Wollemi Semillon, Unwooded Chardonnay, Shiraz; Q Shiraz Chambourcin; Wollemi GOLD Botrytis Semillon, Wollemi GOLD Shiraz.
summary The Bainton family, headed by eminent Sydney QC Russell Bainton, has 48 hectares of vineyard, currently selling most of the grapes but intending to steadily increase production in-house.

bald mountain   ★★★☆

Hickling Lane, Wallangarra, Qld 4383 **region** Granite Belt
phone (07) 4684 3186 **fax** (07) 4684 3433 **open** 7 days 10–5
winemaker Simon Gilbert (Contract) **production** 5000 **est.** 1985
product range ($11–19 CD) Classic Queenslander (in fact 100 per cent Sauvignon Blanc), Chardonnay, Reserve Chardonnay, Dancing Brolga (Sauvignon Blanc Verdelho), Late Harvest Sauvignon Blanc, Shiraz, Shiraz Cabernet, Reserve Shiraz Cabernet.
summary Denis Parsons is a self-taught but exceptionally competent vigneron who has turned Bald Mountain into the viticultural showpiece of the Granite Belt. In various regional and national shows since 1988, Bald Mountain has won almost 70 show awards, placing it at the forefront of the Granite Belt wineries. The two Sauvignon Blanc-based wines, Classic Queenslander and the occasional non-vintage Late Harvest Sauvignon Blanc, are interesting alternatives to mainstream wines. Future production will also see grapes coming from new vineyards near Tenterfield just across the border in NSW. No recent tastings. Significant exports to the Netherlands.

balgownie estate   ★★★★☆

Hermitage Road, Maiden Gully, Vic 3551 **region** Bendigo
phone (03) 5449 6222 **fax** (03) 5449 6506 **open** 7 days 11–5
winemaker Tobias Ansted **production** 7000 **est.** 1969
product range ($14–30 CD) Chardonnay, Pinot Noir, Shiraz, Cabernet Sauvignon; Maiden Gully Chardonnay, Cabernet Shiraz.
summary The sale of Balgownie foreshadowed in the previous edition of the *Wine Companion* has now eventuated, and major changes have followed. Vineyard plantings have been doubled to 36 hectares; Tobias Ansted has replaced Lindsay Ross as winemaker in the wake of a $3 million upgrade to the winery; and the Maiden Gully range has been introduced. Making a concerted move back to top form. Exports to the UK, the US, Switzerland, New Zealand, Hong Kong, Indonesia, Singapore and Malaysia.

Balgownie Estate Chardonnay

♥♥♥♡ 2001 Light to medium yellow-green; smoky/charry barrel-ferment oak dominates the bouquet and the palate. The fruit is there somewhere, but is suppressed. **rating: 84**

best drinking 2002–2005 **best vintages** NA **drink with** Smoked chicken • $26

Balgownie Estate Pinot Noir

♥♥♥♥ 2001 Medium red-purple; surprisingly positive varietal aromas involving a mix of plum (chiefly) and sappy (less), plus oak. The palate has strong flavour and good length, but is slightly hard in the mouth, needing time to soften. A surprise packet, although the Pinot Noir has always been there in the vineyard. **rating: 87**

best drinking 2003–2008 **best vintages** NA **drink with** Braised duck • $30

Balgownie Estate Shiraz

♥♥♥♥♡ 1999 Medium to full red-purple; the bouquet is quite complex, with lifted dark cherry fruit supported by cedar and spice. The powerful palate exudes dark cherry and plum fruit, with lingering, but ripe, tannins, and the oak well controlled. Shows the concentration of a low-yield vintage due to spring frost. **rating: 91**

best drinking 2004–2014 **best vintages** '91, '93, '96, '97, '98, '99, '00 **drink with** Beef in red wine • $30

Balgownie Estate Cabernet Sauvignon

♥♥♥♥♥ 2000 Medium to full red-purple; the bouquet has blackberry and blackcurrant fruit with well-integrated oak, and the palate is marvellously sweet and rich, without being heavy, over-extracted or tannic; here blackberry, blackcurrant and a touch of chocolate all come together in an excellent wine. **rating: 94**

♥♥♥♥ 1999 Medium red, with some purple; the fragrant and strongly varietal bouquet has a mix of cedar, earth, leaf and olive aromatics; concentrated, powerful red and blackcurrant fruit comes through on the palate with slightly chewy tannins and a nice touch of oak. Will quite likely develop into a seriously good wine, but was a little tough on the gums early in its life. **rating: 88**

best drinking 2005–2015 **best vintages** '75, '76, '80, '94, '96, '97, '98, '00 **drink with** Beef casserole • $30

ballabourneen vineyard   NR

Talga Road, Rothbury, NSW 2330 **region** Lower Hunter Valley
phone (02) 9420 9992 **fax** (02) 9420 9993 **open** Weekends 10–5 or by appointment
winemaker Alasdair Sutherland, Greg Silkman **production** 1500 **est.** 1994
product range ($12.50–15 R) Verdelho, Chardonnay Verdelho.
summary Alex and Di Stuart planted their first vines, 1.6 hectares of chardonnay and 1.2 hectares of verdelho, in 1994. They followed up these plantings in 1998 with 1.6 hectares of shiraz; the viticulture is gently organic, with the use of natural sprays, fertilisers, mulches and compost, and with a permanent sward maintained between the rows. Competent contract winemaking by Alasdair Sutherland has brought show success for every vintage of the Verdelho, the high point being a trophy at the 1999 Hunter Valley Wine Show; the Chardonnay Verdelho, made by Greg Silkman, has also won several medals.

ballandean estate   ★★★

Sundown Road, Ballandean, Qld 4382 **region** Granite Belt
phone (07) 4684 1226 **fax** (07) 4684 1288 **open** 7 days 9–5
winemaker Dylan Rhymer, Angelo Puglisi **production** 12 000 **est.** 1970
product range ($10–40 CD) Semillon, Semillon Sauvignon Blanc, Black Label Sauvignon Blanc, Black Label Viognier, Black Label Chardonnay, Classic White, Sylvaner Late Harvest, White Pearl (semi-sweet white), Lambrusco, Classic Red (Shiraz Cabernet), Estate Shiraz, Black Label Shiraz, Black Label Cabernet Merlot, Cabernet Sauvignon, Fortifieds.
summary The senior winery of the Granite Belt and by far the largest. The white wines are of diverse but interesting styles, the red wines smooth and usually well made. The estate specialty, Sylvaner Late Harvest, is a particularly interesting wine of good flavour. Exports to the UK.

ballast stone estate wines   NR

Myrtle Grove Road, Currency Creek, SA 5214 **region** Currency Creek
phone (08) 8555 4215 **fax** (08) 8555 4216 **open** Mon–Fri 10–4.30, weekends and public holidays 12–5
winemaker F John Loxton **production** 5000 **est.** 2001
product range ($12–20 CD) Riesling, Sauvignon Blanc, Chardonnay, Sparkling Chardonnay, Sparkling Shiraz, Grenache, Cabernet Sauvignon.

summary The Shaw family had been grape growers in McLaren Vale for 25 years before deciding to establish a large vineyard in Currency Creek in 1994. Two hundred and fifty hectares have been planted, mainly with cabernet sauvignon and shiraz, with much smaller quantities of eight other trendy varieties. A large on-site winery has been built, managed by Philip Shaw (no relation to Rosemount's Philip Shaw) and John Loxton (formerly senior winemaker at Maglieri); it handled the 1500 tonnes of grapes crushed in 2001, a crush expected to rise to 5000 tonnes by 2003. Only a small part of the production will be sold under the Ballast Stone Estate label; most will be sold in bulk. A cellar door is to be established on the main Strathalbyn to Victor Harbor road, tapping into the tourism trade of the Southern Fleurieu Peninsula.

balnaves of coonawarra ★★★★★

Main Road, Coonawarra, SA 5263 **region** Coonawarra
phone (08) 8737 2946 **fax** (08) 8737 2945 **open** Mon–Fri 9–5, weekends 10–5
winemaker Peter Bissell **production** 10 000 **est.** 1975
product range ($16–80 R) Chardonnay, Cheeky Red, The Blend (Merlot Cabernet Franc), Shiraz, Cabernet Merlot, The Tally Reserve Cabernet Sauvignon.
summary Former Hungerford Hill vineyard manager and now viticultural consultant-cum-grape grower Doug Balnaves established his vineyard in 1975 but did not launch into winemaking until 1990, with colleague Ralph Fowler as contract winemaker in the early years. A striking new 300-tonne winery was built and in operation for the 1996 vintage, with former Wynns Coonawarra Estate assistant winemaker Peter Bissell in charge. The expected leap in quality has indeed materialised and been maintained. The wines are exported to the UK, the US, Switzerland, the Netherlands and Japan. Note – all the 200 reds were tasted as tank samples immediately prior to bottling late in February 2002.

Balnaves Chardonnay

♥♥♥♥♥ 2000 Medium yellow-green; a clean, fruit-forward bouquet with nectarine and subtle oak moves into top gear on the palate, with excellent, lively and fresh nectarine and melon fruit, and exemplary oak handling sustaining both the balance and length. **rating:** 94

best drinking 2002–2006 **best vintages** '92, '93, '94, '96, '98, '99, '00 **drink with** Robe crayfish • $28

Balnaves The Blend

♥♥♥♥♡ 2000 Medium red-purple; the bouquet has red and blackcurrant fruit, together with touches of spice and mint; the palate has plenty of depth and substance, driven by layers of black fruit and finishing with soft tannins. **rating:** 91

best drinking 2005–2011 **best vintages** '00 **drink with** Lamb loin • $24

Balnaves Cabernet Merlot

♥♥♥♥♡ 2000 Medium to full red-purple; the bouquet offers dark berry, blackcurrant and a hint of mulberry; on the palate, ripe, dark berry fruits and a faint touch of chocolate, plus well-handled oak, provide more depth even than The Blend. **rating:** 92

best drinking 2005–2012 **best vintages** '90, '91, '92, '96, '99, '00 **drink with** Calf's liver Italian style • $24

Balnaves Cabernet Sauvignon

♥♥♥♥♥ 2000 Dense red-purple; rich blackberry/blackcurrant fruit and sweet oak on the bouquet are followed by a similarly dense, rich and powerful palate, flooded with cassis and blackberry fruit, and soft but persistent tannins on the finish. **rating:** 94

best drinking 2005–2015 **best vintages** '90, '91, '96, '98, '99 **drink with** Veal chops • $31

Balnaves The Tally Reserve Cabernet Sauvignon

♥♥♥♥♥ 2000 Dense red-purple; the complex bouquet has obvious charry oak, doubtless deriving from the 100 per cent new wood in which the wine has been matured. A massively concentrated palate, made in the John Riddoch fashion; a huge wine demanding time. **rating:** 94

♥♥♥♥♥ 1998 Medium red-purple; the bouquet offers a restrained mix of cedar/blackcurrant/mulberry/spice aromas; the palate is intense and focussed, opening with cedar, vanilla and black fruits, finishing with balanced but firm tannins. **rating:** 94

best drinking 2007–2020 **best vintages** '98 **drink with** Braised beef • $80

bannockburn vineyards ★★★★★

Midland Highway, Bannockburn, Vic 3331 **region** Geelong
phone (03) 5281 1363 **fax** (03) 5281 1349 **open** Not
winemaker Gary Farr **production** 8000 **est.** 1974

product range ($20–120 R) Riesling, Sauvignon Blanc, Chardonnay, SRH Chardonnay (named in honour of the late Stuart Reginald Hooper, founder of Bannockburn), Pinot Noir, Saignee (Rosé), Serre, Shiraz, Cabernet Merlot.

summary With the qualified exception of the Cabernet Merlot, which can be a little leafy and gamey, produces outstanding wines across the range, all with individuality, style, great complexity and depth of flavour. The low-yielding estate vineyards play their role, but so does the French-influenced winemaking of Gary Farr. Export markets have been established in the UK, Brussels, the US, Hong Kong, New Zealand and Indonesia.

Bannockburn Chardonnay

TTTT 2000 Medium yellow-green; a fairly massive bouquet, with ripe melon and fig fruit framed by positive but not aggressive oak, then a fruit-driven, rich palate ranging through yellow peach/nectarine/melon fruit. The alcohol does show, reflecting the very hot vintage. **rating:** 89

best drinking 2002–2005 **best vintages** '88, '90, '91, '92, '94, '96, '98 **drink with** Rich white meat dishes • $45

Bannockburn Pinot Noir

TTTTT 2000 Outstanding purple-red; rich, deep plum fruit with underlying spice and forest aromas sets the tone for the very powerful, pure palate which, while complex, shows relatively little sign of whole-bunch maceration. Will be very long-lived. **rating:** 94

TTTTY 1999 Appealing and healthy red, with none of the grey/blue tinges which sometimes bedevil Pinot. A clean, complex bouquet has plum, cherry, strawberry and spice fruit with some savoury undertones. The palate has very good balance, structure and length; the amalgam of fruit and more savoury characters is bonded by good oak handling and fine tannins. On the very brink of five stars. **rating:** 93

best drinking 2004–2010 **best vintages** '84, '86, '88, '89, '90, '91, '92, '94, '97, '99, '00 **drink with** Rare roast squab • $45

Bannockburn Shiraz

TTTTT 2000 Deep purple-red; a spotlessly clean bouquet with rich, complex black cherry, licorice and spice is followed by a palate with great depth of flavour, a silky, velvety richness, and fine, ripe tannins.

rating: 96

best drinking 2005–2015 **best vintages** '88, '91, '92, '94, '95, '98, '00 **drink with** Roast marinated venison • $45

banrock station ★★★☆

Holmes Road, off Sturt Highway, Kingston-on-Murray, SA 5331 **region** Riverland
phone (08) 8583 0299 **fax** (08) 8583 0288 **open** 7 days 10–4, except public holidays
winemaker Glenn James **production** NFP **est.** 1994
product range ($6.30–14.95 R) Semillon Chardonnay, Chardonnay, Shiraz Cabernet, Cabernet Merlot; Premium Range includes Wigley Reach Unwooded Chardonnay, Napper's Verdelho, Ball Island Shiraz, Cave Cliff Merlot and Sparkling Chardonnay and Shiraz.

summary The $1 million visitors centre at Banrock Station was opened in February 1999. Owned by BRL Hardy, the Banrock Station property covers over 1700 hectares, with 230 hectares of vineyard and the remainder being a major wildlife and wetland preservation area. The wines have consistently offered excellent value for money.

Banrock Station Cave Cliff Merlot

TTTY 2000 Medium red-purple; the moderately intense bouquet is clean, with spice and dark fruit aromas, moving through to a strong, dry red palate with little or no varietal character evident. **rating:** 82

best drinking 2001–2004 **best vintages** '98 **drink with** Kransky sausages • $12.50

barak estate NR

Barak Road, Moorooduc, Vic 3933 **region** Mornington Peninsula
phone (03) 5978 8439 **fax** (03) 5978 8439 **open** Weekends and public holidays 11–5
winemaker James Williamson **production** 500 **est.** 1996
product range ($17–20 CD) Chardonnay, Shiraz, Cabernet Sauvignon.

summary When James Williamson decided to plant vines on his 4-hectare Moorooduc property and establish a micro-winery, he already knew it was far cheaper to buy wine by the bottle than to make it. Undeterred, he ventured into grape growing and winemaking, picking the first grapes in 1993 and opening Barak Estate in 1996. Old telegraph poles, railway sleepers, old palings and timber shingles have all been used in the construction of the picturesque winery.

barambah ridge   NR

79 Goschnicks Road, Redgate via Murgon, Qld 4605 **region** South Burnett
phone (07) 4168 4766 **fax** (07) 4168 4770 **open** 7 days 10–5
winemaker Stuart Pierce **production** 12 000 **est.** 1997
product range ($10–19.50 CD) Semillon, Chardonnay Semillon, Ridge White, Unwooded Chardonnay, Oaked Chardonnay, Ridge Red, Reserve Claret, Reserve Shiraz, Merlot, Cabernet Sauvignon, Old Feedlot Port, Mayoral Muscat, Cafe Liqueur.
summary Barambah Ridge is owned by Tambarambah Limited, an unlisted public company, and is a major new entrant on the Queensland wine scene. Tambarambah also owns Mount Tamborine Winery, and Barambah Ridge has four outlets: 79 Goschnicks Road, Redgate; 313 Flaxton Drive, Flaxton; On the Boardwalk, Noosa Harbour Marine Village, Tewantin; and South Maryborough Travel Stop, Bruce Highway, Maryborough.

baratto's   NR

Farm 678, Hanwood, NSW 2680 **region** Riverina
phone (02) 6963 0171 **fax** (02) 6963 0171 **open** 7 days 10–5
winemaker Peter Baratto **production** 6250 **est.** 1975
product range ($6–18 CD) Chardonnay, Trebbiano Semillon (Late Harvest), Botrytis Semillon, Shiraz Cabernet Sauvignon, Cabernet Sauvignon; also a variety of casks and cleanskins.
summary Baratto's is in many ways a throwback to the old days. Peter Baratto has 15 hectares of vineyards and sells the wine in bulk or in 10- and 20-litre casks from the cellar door at old-time prices, from as little as $2 per litre.

barletta bros   NR

95a Walkerville Terrace, Walkerville, SA 5081 **region** Clare Valley
phone (08) 8342 3395 **fax** (08) 8269 4008 **open** By appointment
winemaker Neil Pike (Polish Hill River Winery) **production** 3000 **est.** 1993
product range ($9–11 CD) Shiraz, Dry Grown Grenache Shiraz.
summary There have been many twists since 1993 when Mario, Ben and Julio Barletta started an 'own brand' for their then-retail business, Walkerville Cellars. They no longer own Walkerville Cellars, and the winemaking business is now the sole business of Mario, who has an active involvement with contract winemaker Neil Pike. The Barletta tanks and barrels reside at Pikes, but Mario Barletta intends to ultimately establish his own independent vineyard and winery and operation. Retail distribution in South Australia and Melbourne; exports to the US, Canada, Singapore, the UK and Germany.

barnadown run   ★★★★

390 Cornella Road, Toolleen, Vic 3551 **region** Heathcote
phone (03) 5433 6376 **fax** (03) 5433 6386 **open** 7 days 10–5
winemaker Andrew Millis **production** 1500 **est.** 1995
product range ($17–30 CD) Chardonnay, Reserve Chardonnay, Shiraz, Cabernet Sauvignon.
summary Named after the original pastoral lease of which the vineyard forms part, and established on rich terra rossa soil for which the best Heathcote vineyards are famous. Owner Andrew Millis carries out both the viticulture and winemaking at the 5-hectare vineyard. After a slightly uncertain start, he is producing wines worthy of the best of Heathcote. Exports to the US.

Barnadown Run Shiraz
▼▼▼▼ 2000 Deep, bright red-purple; a powerful bouquet with a somewhat unusual set of shoe leather, prune and plum aromas; the palate provides dense, ripe, plummy fruit, with some of the prune of the bouquet, but the leather disappears; brisk acidity on the finish despite the 13.9° alcohol; obviously enough, needs time.   **rating:** 89

best drinking 2005–2015 **best vintages** NA **drink with** Leave it in the cellar • $25

Barnadown Run Cabernet Sauvignon
▼▼▼▼▽ 2000 Medium red-purple; a lifted, aromatic bouquet with mint/peppermint and berry fruit, which comes through in an abundant display of red and dark berry fruit on the palate, finishing with supple tannins.   **rating:** 92

best drinking 2005–2015 **best vintages** '00 **drink with** Rare beef • $25

barossa ridge wine estate ★★★★

Light Pass Road, Tanunda, SA 5352 **region** Barossa Valley
phone (08) 8563 2811 **fax** (08) 8563 2811 **open** By appointment
winemaker Marco Litterini **production** 2000 **est.** 1987
product range ($24–26 CD) Valley of Vines Merlot Cabernet Sauvignon Petit Verdot Cabernet Franc, Old Creek Shiraz, Mardia's Vineyard Cabernet Franc, Bamboo Creek Merlot, Rocky Valley Cabernet Sauvignon.
summary A grape grower turned winemaker with a small list of interesting red varietals, including the Valley of Vines blend of Merlot, Cabernet Franc, Cabernet Sauvignon and Petit Verdot, the only such wine produced in the Barossa Valley. Production has doubled, and the wines have retail distribution in New South Wales. All of its wines are built in an impressively heroic style. Exports to Switzerland, Germany, Malaysia and Thailand.

barossa settlers ★★★

Trial Hill Road, Lyndoch, SA 5351 **region** Barossa Valley
phone (08) 8524 4017 **fax** (08) 8524 4519 **open** Mon–Sat 10–4, Sun 11–4
winemaker Howard Haese **production** 800 **est.** 1983
product range ($12.50–35 CD) Gully Winds Riesling, Megan's Woolshed Flat Chardonnay, Joachim's Festive, Millowstowe Royale (Sparkling Red), Late Harvest Riesling, Joan's Block Grenache, Hoffnungsthal Settlement Shiraz, Howard's Bin 1927 Shiraz, Tom's Rostock Red (Cabernet Sauvignon), James Cabernet Sauvignon, Port, Sherry.
summary A superbly located cellar door is the only outlet (other than mail order) for the wines from this excellent vineyard owned by the Haese family. Production has slowed in recent years, with the grapes from the 31-hectare vineyard being sold to others.

barossa valley estate ★★★★

Seppeltsfield Road, Marananga, SA 5355 **region** Barossa Valley
phone (08) 8562 3599 **fax** (08) 8562 4255 **open** 7 days 10–4.30
winemaker Stuart Bourne **production** 150 000 **est.** 1984
product range ($9–65 R) Spires Chardonnay Semillon, Shiraz Cabernet Sauvignon; Moculta Chardonnay, Shiraz, Grenache, Cabernet Merlot; Ebenezer Chardonnay, Shiraz, Cabernet Sauvignon Merlot; and the premium E & E Sparkling Shiraz and Black Pepper Shiraz.
summary Barossa Valley Estate is now part-owned by BRL Hardy, marking the end of a period during which it was one of the last significant co-operative-owned wineries in Australia. Across the board, the wines are full flavoured and honest. E & E Black Pepper Shiraz is an upmarket label with a strong reputation and following, the Ebenezer range likewise. Overenthusiastic use of American oak (particularly with the red wines) has been the Achilles heel in the past. The wines are distributed in Australia and the UK by BRL Hardy, and by independent distributors in North America.

Barossa Valley Estate E & E Black Pepper Shiraz
▼▼▼▼▼ 1999 Full red-purple; the bouquet has abundant sweet chocolate, prune and plum aromas flowing through into an excellently constructed palate, with fruit, oak and tannin all showing excellent balance.

rating: 94

best drinking 2003–2013 **best vintages** '90, '91, '94, '96, '99 **drink with** Rich red meat dishes • $45

Barossa Valley Estate Ebenezer Shiraz
▼▼▼▼▼ 1998 Medium red-purple; a firm and complex bouquet with savoury/spicy overtones to the black berry fruit. The palate has good structure, depth and length, featuring black fruits, chocolate and some vanilla from the oak.

rating: 94

best drinking 2003–2013 **best vintages** '90, '91, '94, '96, '98 **drink with** Lamb, rabbit or hare • $27.50

barratt ★★★★★

PO Box 204, Summertown, SA 5141 **region** Adelaide Hills
phone (08) 8390 1788 **fax** (08) 8390 1788 **open** By appointment
winemaker Lindsay Barrat, Jeffrey Grosset (Contract) **production** 1000 **est.** 1993
product range ($26.50–39.50 ML) Chardonnay, Pinot Noir.

summary Former medical practitioner Lindsay and his wife Carolyn Barratt own two vineyards at Summertown: the Uley Vineyard, purchased from the late Ian Wilson in August 1990, and the Bonython Vineyard. They have 8.4 hectares of vines, some coming into production, and they will be adding sauvignon blanc and merlot to the wine range from 2002. Part of the production from the vineyards is sold to other makers, with Jeffrey Grosset the maker of the Chardonnay and Pinot Noir. Both wines are complex and of high quality. Limited quantities are sold in the UK, the US, Germany, Belgium and Japan.

Barratt Chardonnay

▼▼▼▼ **2000** Yellow-straw, a little developed. The bouquet has a complex array of toasty cashew and melon aromas; the big, mouthfilling, rich and soft palate looks as if it will develop quickly, and is close to its peak now. **rating:** 89

best drinking 2001–2003 **best vintages** '97, '99 **drink with** Trout mousse • $26.50

Barratt Piccadilly Valley Pinot Noir

▼▼▼▼ **2000** Medium red, not bright, and indicating that the wine was not filtered; this is hardly surprising given that only 100 cases were made. There is a complex array of cinnamon and nutmeg spice aromas alongside the more traditional foresty/savoury fruit on the bouquet. The palate has ultra-ripe, almost stewed, dark plum fruit which seems to have been picked too late, an impression underlined by the 14.5° alcohol. **rating:** 88

best drinking 2001–2003 **best vintages** '96, '97, '99 **drink with** Jugged hare • $39.50

barretts wines NR

Portland–Nelson Highway, Portland, Vic 3305 **region** Henty
phone (03) 5526 5251 **open** 7 days 11–5
winemaker Rod Barrett **production** 1000 **est.** 1983
product range ($14–18 CD) Riesling, Traminer, Late Harvest Riesling, Pinot Noir, Cabernet Sauvignon, Port.
summary Has a low profile, selling its wines locally. The initial releases were made at Best's, but since 1992 all wines have been made on the property by Rod Barrett.

barrymore estate NR

76 Tuerong Road, Tuerong, Vic 3933 **region** Mornington Peninsula
phone (03) 5974 8999 **fax** (03) 9789 0821 **open** Most days 11–5
winemaker Peter Cotter, Brian Wilson **production** 2500 **est.** 1998
product range ($26–30 CD) Sauvignon Blanc, Pinot Gris, Chardonnay, Pinot Noir; associated brands are Tuerong Station, Peninsula Pinot Noir and Tuerong Valley.
summary Barrymore Estate is part of a much larger property first settled in the 1840s; the abundance of water and wetlands, with the confluence of the Devil Bend and Balcombe Creeks nearby, has sustained grazing and farming since the first settlement. Peter Cotter has planted 8 hectares of pinot noir, 1.5 hectares of chardonnay and 1.5 hectares of sauvignon blanc, selling part of the grapes and making part under the Barrymore label.

Barrymore Estate Pinot Gris

▼▼▼▼ **2001** Medium yellow-green, with no bronze evident; the bouquet is quite aromatic, with ripe apple/pear/dried flowers/hay aromas; the palate has abundant flavour, with the sweetness apparent deriving largely from the 14.5° alcohol; an impressive example of the variety, sourced from a Tuerong vineyard. **rating:** 88

best drinking 2002–2004 **best vintages** NA **drink with** Antipasto • $26

Barrymore Estate Pinot Noir

▼▼▼▼ **2001** Bright red-purple; the clean bouquet has light plum aromas interspersed with hints of spice and oak; the palate builds on the theme, with abundant plummy fruit, good intensity and length; will develop yet more complexity as it ages. Sophisticated winemaking. **rating:** 89

best drinking 2002–2004 **best vintages** NA **drink with** Braised quail • $30

barwang vineyard ★★★★☆

Barwang Road, Young, NSW 2594 **region** Hilltops
phone (02) 6382 3594 **fax** (02) 6382 2594 **open** Not
winemaker Jim Brayne, Russell Cody, Scott Zrna **production** NA **est.** 1969

product range ($15.95–30 R) Chardonnay, Semillon, Shiraz, Merlot, Cabernet Sauvignon.

summary Peter Robertson pioneered viticulture in the Young region when he planted his first vines in 1969 as part of a diversification programme for his 400-hectare grazing property. When McWilliam's acquired Barwang in 1989, the vineyard amounted to 13 hectares; today the plantings exceed 100 hectares. Wine quality has been exemplary from the word go: always elegant, restrained and deliberately understated, repaying extended cellaring.

Barwang Vineyard Shiraz

TTTTY 2000 Medium red-purple; the bouquet offers dark cherry/plum fruit with hints of spice and earth; the palate is round and soft, with supple fruit a feature of the mid-palate in particular. Oak handling is restrained throughout. **rating:** 91

best drinking 2005–2010 **best vintages** '90, '91, '92, '93, '94, '97, '98, '00 **drink with** Parmesan cheese • $24

Barwang Vineyard Merlot

TTTTY 2000 Medium red-purple; a mix of spice, leaf and olive aromas precede a palate with very good structure, and fine, savoury tannins running through the sweet raspberry fruit; finishes with nicely balanced acidity. **rating:** 92

best drinking 2004–2009 **best vintages** '00 **drink with** Braised veal • $30

Barwang Vineyard Cabernet Sauvignon

TTTTY 2000 Medium red-purple; gentle blackberry and blackcurrant fruit on the bouquet lead into a palate with similar blackcurrant fruit, and surprisingly soft tannins, the oak in restraint. All of these wines from Barwang share the same sweet fruit. **rating:** 91

best drinking 2005–2010 **best vintages** '89, '91, '92, '93, '96, '97, '98, '00 **drink with** Beef Wellington • $24

basedow ★★★☆

161–165 Murray Street, Tanunda, SA 5352 **region** Barossa Valley
phone (08) 8563 3666 **fax** (08) 8563 3597 **open** Mon–Fri 10–5, weekends and public holidays 11–5
winemaker Craig Stansborough **production** 100 000 **est.** 1896
product range ($6.95–65 CD) Sauvignon Blanc Semillon, Bush Vine Grenache, Shiraz, Pinot Noir Chardonnay, Late Harvest, Mistella, Old Tawny Port; Barossa Valley Riesling, Semillon, Chardonnay; Johannes Barossa Shiraz is the flagship wine.
summary An old and proud label, particularly well known for its oak-matured Semillon (once called White Burgundy on the Australian market); it underwent a number of changes of ownership during the 1990s. Overall, a reliable producer of solidly flavoured wines, although the appointment of a receiver to owner Hill International in February 2002 threw a shadow over the business. Exports to the US, Canada, Brazil, the UK, Denmark, Germany, Holland, Switzerland, Fiji, Singapore, Thailand and New Zealand.

Basedow Johannes Shiraz

TTTTY 1998 Medium red-purple; the wine has good fruit aroma, flavour, structure and length; it is not over-extracted nor forced by oak, and has a harmonious finish. **rating:** 91

best drinking 2003–2008 **best vintages** '89 **drink with** Braised veal • $65

basket range wines NR

c/o PO, Basket Range, SA 5138 **region** Adelaide Hills
phone (08) 8390 1515 **fax** (08) 8390 0499 **open** Not
winemaker Phillip Broderick **production** 500 **est.** 1980
product range ($18 ML) A single Bordeaux blend of Cabernet Sauvignon, Cabernet Franc, Merlot and Malbec drawn from 3 hectares of estate plantings.
summary A tiny operation known to very few, run by civil and Aboriginal rights lawyer Phillip Broderick, a most engaging man with a disarmingly laid-back manner.

bass fine wines ★★★☆

Deviot Road, Gravelly Beach, Tas 7276 **region** Northern Tasmania
phone (03) 6231 6222 **fax** (03) 6231 6222 **open** Not
winemaker Guy Wagner **production** 1000 **est.** 1999
product range ($19–28 R) Strait Chardonnay, Block 1 Pinot Noir, Strait Pinot Noir.

summary Bass Fine Wines runs entirely counter to the usual Tasmanian pattern of tiny, estate-based businesses. Guy Wagner has set up Bass as a classic negociant operation, working backwards from the marketplace. He is currently completing a wine marketing degree at the University of Adelaide, and intends to continue studies in oenology. The wines have been purchased from various vineyards in bottle and in barrel, but from the 2000 vintage he has also purchased grapes. The winery has been set up to focus on Pinot Noir, with three levels of Pinot in the business plan: Strait Pinot in the fighting sector of the market, then Bass as a premium brand, and ultimately a super-premium Pinot, possibly to come from 30-year-old plantings which have been contracted.

Bass Fine Wines Block 1 Pinot Noir

TTTT 2000 Strong purple-red, bright but deep, notwithstanding the fact that the wine is unfiltered. A clean, smooth bouquet with plum and dark cherry fruit with a dash of oak leads into a powerful palate with fairly high acidity, needing time to resolve. If it all comes together, it will be an outstanding wine.   **rating:** 89

best drinking 2003–2007 **best vintages** NA **drink with** Venison • $28

Bass Fine Wines Strait Pinot Noir

TTTT 2001 Youthful red-purple; a clean, moderately intense bouquet with cherry fruit and subtle oak is followed by a clean, no-frills palate, making one wonder whether the wine has seen much oak. Tailored to a price.   **rating:** 85

best drinking 2003–2006 **best vintages** NA **drink with** Quail • $18.95

bass phillip   ★★★★★

Tosch's Road, Leongatha South, Vic 3953 **region** Gippsland
phone (03) 5664 3341 **fax** (03) 5664 3209 **open** By appointment
winemaker Phillip Jones **production** 1500 **est.** 1979
product range ($27–145) Tiny quantities of Pinot Noir in three categories: standard, Premium and an occasional barrel of Reserve. A hatful of Chardonnay also made, plus Pinot Rosé and Gamay.
summary Phillip Jones has retired from the Melbourne rat-race to handcraft tiny quantities of superlative Pinot Noir which, at its best, has no equal in Australia. Painstaking site selection, ultra-close vine spacing and the very, very cool climate of South Gippsland are the keys to the magic of Bass Phillip and its eerily Burgundian Pinots.

batista   NR

Franklin Road, Middlesex, WA 6258 **region** Manjimup
phone (08) 9772 3530 **fax** (08) 9772 3530 **open** By appointment
winemaker Bob Peruch **production** 1200 **est.** 1993
product range ($19–28 CD) Pinot Noir, Shiraz, Shiraz Cabernet, Pinot Chardonnay Reserve Brut.
summary Batista is in fact the baptismal name of owner Bob Peruch, a Pinot Noir devotee whose father planted 1 hectare of vines back in the 1950s (these have since gone). Between 1993 and 1996 Bob Peruch planted 1.5 hectares of pinot noir, 1.85 hectares of shiraz and the cabernet family, and half a hectare of chardonnay destined for sparkling wine. The estate has two vineyards, one selected for pinot noir and chardonnay, and the other, 2 kilometres away, for shiraz, cabernet sauvignon, cabernet franc and merlot. The well-drained soils are of quartz and ironstone gravel; yields are restricted to around seven tonnes per hectare.

baxter stokes wines   NR

65 Memorial Avenue, Baskerville, WA 6065 **region** Swan District
phone (08) 9296 4831 **fax** (08) 9296 4831 **open** 9.30–5 weekends and public holidays
winemaker Greg Stokes **production** 750 **est.** 1988
product range ($10–14 CD) Chardonnay, Verdelho, Shiraz Pinot Noir, Shiraz Cabernet Sauvignon.
summary A weekend and holiday operation for Greg and Lucy Stokes, with the production sold by mail order and through the cellar door.

🐌 bayview estate   NR

365 Purves Road, Main Ridge, Vic 3928 **region** Mornington Peninsula
phone (03) 5989 6130 **fax** (03) 5989 6373 **open** 7 days 12–5
winemaker Dean Burford **production** 1500 **est.** 1984
product range ($20–29 CD) Pinot Gris, The Big Pig Red Cabernet Merlot, Cabernet Sauvignon Reserve.

summary Few enterprises have cast such a broad net over the tourist traffic in the Mornington Peninsula. It has a hotel with 45 beers from around the world, a 120-seat restaurant, an 80-seat beer garden, offers fly fishing on the vineyard dam, and rosé and lavender gardens. Almost incidental are the ten hectares of pinot gris, pinot noir and pinot grigio which produce 6000 cases of wine a year sold through the cellar door, the Hilton Hotel, and Mornington Peninsula restaurants.

🐦 beaumont estate ★★★☆

Lot 20, 155 Milbrodale Road, Broke, NSW 2330 **region** Lower Hunter Valley
phone (02) 5449 8906 **fax** (02) 5474 3722 **open** Not
winemaker Adrian Lockhart (Contract) **production** 860 **est.** 1998
product range ($21 ML) Hand Picked Semillon, Merlot.
summary The estate vineyards were planted in September 1999 on the river flats of Parson Creek, nestled between the Yengo and Wollemi National Parks. The soils were enhanced with organic preparations; after 17 months the 2.2 hectares of semillon and 1.3 hectares of merlot produced a substantial crop, the vine growth, so it is said, equivalent to three years under normal conditions. The intention is to continue the organic farming approach, and to eventually become certified Biodynamic. Currently the wines are sold by phone, mail order and email; future plans include a cellar door.

Beaumont Estate Hand Picked Semillon

▼▼▼▼ 2001 Light, bright green-yellow; a crisp, clean and correct bouquet with a mix of mineral and lemongrass leads into a powerful, rich palate, with ripe fruit; avoids phenolics, but will develop quickly.
rating: 88

best drinking 2002–2005 **best vintages** NA **drink with** Balmain bugs • $21

beckett's flat ★★★☆

Beckett Road, Metricup, WA 6280 **region** Margaret River
phone (08) 9755 7402 **fax** (08) 9755 7344 **open** 7 days 10–6
winemaker Belizar Ilic **production** 5000 **est.** 1992
product range ($14–27 CD) Sauvignon Blanc Semillon, Chardonnay, Autumn Harvest, Liqueur Chardonnay, Sparkling Shiraz, Reserve Shiraz, Merlot, Cabernet Sauvignon.
summary Bill and Noni Ilic opened Beckett's Flat in September 1997. Situated just off the Bussell Highway, at Metricup, midway between Busselton and the Margaret River, it draws upon 14 hectares of estate vineyards, first planted in 1992. As from 1998 the wines have been made at the on-site winery. Accommodation is available.

Beckett's Flat Sauvignon Blanc Semillon

▼▼▼▼ 2000 Pale straw; the relatively light bouquet has a mix of mineral, spice and citrus/grapefruit, the palate crisp, and with a degree of textural complexity deriving from the portion of the Semillon that is barrel-fermented. **rating: 85**

best drinking 2001–2003 **best vintages** NA **drink with** Delicate white-fleshed fish • $18

Beckett's Flat Chardonnay

▼▼▼▼ 2000 Medium yellow-green; the bouquet is light, fresh and clean, with less intense fruit than one might expect from the Mendoza clone. There is more fruit on the palate, with sweet melon and citrus on the mid-palate before moving through to a dry finish. **rating: 86**

best drinking 2001–2004 **best vintages** NA **drink with** Roast turkey • $24.80

Beckett's Flat Cabernet Sauvignon

▼▼▼▼ 2000 Medium red-purple; a clean, moderately intense bouquet with clear-cut varietal blackcurrant and earth fruit flows into a palate with sweet cassis/blackcurrant fruit, good depth and subtle oak. **rating: 89**

best drinking 2004–2009 **best vintages** '97, '00 **drink with** Ox kidney • $21

🐦 beckingham wines NR

7/477 Warrigal Road, Moorabbin, Vic 3189 **region** Warehouse
phone (03) 9258 7352 **fax** (03) 9360 0713 **open** Weekends 10–5
winemaker Peter Beckingham **production** 2500 **est.** 1998
product range ($9–20 CD) Burnt Creek Riesling, Zibibbo, Edgehill Unwooded Chardonnay, Edgehill Chardonnay, Pas de Deux Sparkling, Botrytis Riesling, Chardonnay Liqueur, Cabernet Pink, Strathbogie Shiraz, Strathbogie Merlot, Strathbogie Cabernet, Cornelia Creek Cabernet, Pinot Noir Liqueur.

summary Peter Beckingham is a chemical engineer who has turned a hobby into a part-time business, moving operations from the driveway of his house to a warehouse in Moorabbin. The situation of the winery may not be romantic, but it is eminently practical, and more than a few winemakers have adopted the same solution in California. His friends grow the grapes, and he makes the wine; the Mornington Peninsula, Echuca and the Strathbogie Ranges are the prime source of grapes, but other regions (such as the Yarra Valley) contribute from time to time. Peter Beckingham professes to be passionate about his wines, and is doubtless learning more as each vintage goes by.

belbourie   NR

Branxton Road, Rothbury, NSW 2330 **region** Lower Hunter Valley
phone (02) 4938 1556 **open** Weekends, holidays 10–sunset
winemaker Bob Davies **production** 2000 **est.** 1963
product range ($15–16 CD) Barramundi Chardonnay, Belah Semillon Chardonnay, Hermitage.
summary A winery with a rich, and at times highly controversial history of wine and winemaking, but these days tending more to the conventional. It has always sought to encourage cellar door and mailing list sales, focusing on monthly wine and food events, and has a loyal clientele.

belgenny vineyard   ★★★☆

92 De Beyers Road, Pokolbin, NSW 2320 **region** Lower Hunter Valley
phone (02) 9634 4439 **fax** (02) 9634 4439 **open** Not
winemaker Monarch Winemaking Services (Contract) **production** 7000 **est.** 1990
product range ($12–30 R) Semillon, Unwooded Chardonnay, Partner's Reserve Chardonnay, Chardonnay, Proprietor's Reserve Chardonnay, Petit Rosé, Merlot, Shiraz, Cabernet Sauvignon.
summary In 1999 partners Norman Seckold and Dudley Leitch realised a long-held ambition to establish a vineyard in the Hunter Valley with the acquisition of their 17-hectare site. Plantings have steadily increased, and are presently chardonnay (5.7 hectares), shiraz (4.9 ha), merlot (2 ha), semillon (1.2), and a carefully thought out marketing strategy has been put in place. A cellar door and restaurant were scheduled for completion mid-2002. Exports to Hong Kong and Singapore.

bellarine estate   NR

2270 Portarlington Road, Bellarine, Vic 3222 **region** Geelong
phone (03) 5259 3310 **fax** (03) 5259 3393 **open** Weekends 10–5
winemaker Robin Brockett **production** 7000 **est.** 1995
product range ($16.50–25 ML) Sauvignon Blanc, Unwooded Chardonnay, James' Paddock Chardonnay, Portarlington Ridge Pinot Noir, Shiraz, Portarlington Ridge Shiraz, Portarlington Ridge Merlot.
summary A new arrival on the Bellarine Peninsula, but a substantial one, with 4 hectares each of chardonnay and pinot noir, 3 hectares of shiraz, 1 hectare of merlot and half a hectare each of pinot gris and viognier. The wines are made by Robin Brockett at Scotchman's Hill. Bella's offers a seafood/Tuscan menu Friday–Sunday from 11 am for lunch and Fri and Sat from 6 pm for dinner.

belubula valley vineyards   NR

Golden Gully, Mandurama, NSW 2798 **region** Orange
phone (02) 6367 5236 **fax** (02) 6362 4726 **open** Not
winemaker David Somervaille **production** 1000 **est.** 1986
product range Cabernet Sauvignon.
summary Belubula Valley is a foundation member of the Central Highlands Grapegrowers Association (now ORVA), centred on Orange; the vineyard is located on the Belubula River, near Carcoar, and the small amounts of wine made to date have not yet been commercially released. David Somervaille, incidentally, was the chairman of partners of the national law firm Blake Dawson Waldron.

🍷 benarra vineyards   NR

PO Box 1081, Mt Gambier, SA 5290 **region** Mount Gambier
phone (08) 8738 9355 **fax** (08) 8738 9355 **open** Not
winemaker Martin Slocombe **production** 150 **est.** 1998
product range Flint Bed Pinot Noir.

summary Lisle Pudney has planted a substantial vineyard with the help of investors. In all there are over 26 hectares of pinot noir and 4 hectares each of sauvignon blanc and chardonnay, with another 40 hectares to be planted over the next three years. The vineyard is situated 20 kilometres from the Southern Ocean on ancient flint beds; a million-year-old mollusc found on the property by Lisle Pudney is depicted on the label of the Pinot Noir. Most of the grapes are sold; a small portion is contract-made for the Benarra label.

Benarra Vineyards Flint Bed Pinot Noir

YYYY 2001 Light to medium purple-red; a light but fragrant and spotlessly clean bouquet offers a mix of plum, spice and forest, with the barest touch of oak. The light-bodied palate is strongly varietal, in a spicy plum spectrum; while light, the wine shows more pinot varietal character than most others from the Limestone Coast Zone. **rating: 89**

best drinking 2002–2004 **best vintages** NA **drink with** Squab • NA

☙ ben's run ★★★☆

71 Adams Peak Road, Broke, NSW 2330 **region** Lower Hunter Valley
phone (02) 6579 1310 **fax** (02) 6579 1370 **open** Not
winemaker Andrew Margan (Contract) **production** 520 **est.** 1997
product range ($30 R) Shiraz.
summary Ben's Run has an interesting, almost schizophrenic, background. On the one hand, say the owners, 'it is named for our kelpie dog for graciously allowing part of his retirement run to be converted into a showpiece shiraz-only vineyard.' On the other hand, patriarch Norman Marran was one of the pioneers of the Australian cotton industry, has had a long and distinguished career as a director of both the Australian Wheat Board and Grains Research Corporation, and is currently chairman of a leading food research company. The decision has been taken to produce only 500 cases of wine a year from the 3-hectare, low-yielding shiraz-only vineyard; the remainder is sold to Andrew Margan.

Ben's Run Shiraz

YYYY 2000 Youthful purple-red; slightly dusty/pencilly/smoky American oak is still to integrate on the bouquet, but on the palate luscious, rich and ripe fruit reflecting a dry Hunter vintage takes over, with plum running into prune and licorice flavours. **rating: 87**

best drinking 2003–2010 **best vintages** NA **drink with** Rump steak • $30

beresford wines ★★★

49 Fraser Avenue, Happy Valley, SA 5159 **region** McLaren Vale
phone (08) 8322 3611 **fax** (08) 8322 3610 **open** Mon–Fri 9–5, weekends 11–5
winemaker Scott McIntosh **production** 250 000 **est.** 1985
product range ($8.50–21 CD) At the bottom of the three-tier structure comes Beacon Hill Semillon Chardonnay and Shiraz; the second level is the Highwood range of Sauvignon Blanc, Chardonnay and Shiraz; then under the premier Beresford label are Clare Valley Riesling, Adelaide Hills Chardonnay, Clare Valley Shiraz, McLaren Vale Shiraz and McLaren Vale Cabernet Sauvignon.
summary The Beresford brand sits at the top of a range of labels primarily and successfully aimed at export markets in the UK, the US, Hong Kong and China. The intention is that ultimately most, if not all, of the wines will be sourced from grapes grown in McLaren Vale, with a new cellar door and boutique winery planned for the second half of 2002. Incidentally, it is run as an entirely separate operation from its sister winery, Step Road in Langhorne Creek.

Beresford Crooked Road Clare Valley Riesling

YYYY 2000 Medium yellow-green; a powerful and complex mix of keroséne and herbs on the bouquet, then a similarly powerful and intense palate, finishing with firm acid. Unconventional but interesting. **rating: 87**

best drinking 2002–2005 **best vintages** NA **drink with** Strongly flavoured fish • $16.50

Beresford Highwood Sauvignon Blanc

YYYY 2001 Light straw-green; the light bouquet has aromatic gooseberry, herb and a hint of tropical fruit; there is authentic flavour to the palate, with good length, mouthfeel and balance. **rating: 88**

best drinking 2002–2003 **best vintages** NA **drink with** Blue swimmer crab • $12.50

Beresford Wines Adelaide Hills Chardonnay

♥♥♥♥ **2001** Medium yellow-green; the bouquet is quite complex, with well-integrated barrel ferment, malolactic ferment, and oak inputs to fig, cashew and melon. The light to medium-bodied palate is stylish and well made, with pleasing citrus and melon fruit.   **rating:** 89

best drinking 2002–2004 **best vintages** NA **drink with** Creamy pasta • $11.00

St Yvette Chardonnay

♥♥♥♡ **2000** Light to medium green-yellow; the bouquet is not intense, but does have a touch of complexity, suggesting that the wine may have been given some lees contact. A clean, simple palate, but well made and balanced, with gentle acidity on the finish.   **rating:** 84

best drinking 2002–2003 **best vintages** NA **drink with** Calamari • $10.50

Belleville Estate Shiraz

♥♥♥♡ **1999** Medium red-purple; aromas of spice, leaf, earth and red berry lead into a fresh, light to medium-bodied palate with juicy berry flavours; oak is barely perceptible throughout, and the wine does not aspire to complexity.   **rating:** 83

best drinking 2002–2004 **best vintages** NA **drink with** Pizza • $21

Beresford Clare Valley Shiraz

♥♥♥♥♡ **2000** Bright red-purple; solid, ripe dark plum and black cherry fruit on the bouquet flows into a palate with good weight and structure; hints of cedar accompany the fruit; soft tannins to close. **rating:** 90

best drinking 2004–2009 **best vintages** NA **drink with** Saddle of kangaroo • NA

Highwood McLaren Vale Shiraz

♥♥♥♥ **2000** Medium purple-red; the firm, clean and fresh bouquet offers cherry fruit and a splash of oak; the palate has plenty of juicy berry fruit in a no-frills, easily enjoyed style.   **rating:** 85

best drinking 2001–2003 **best vintages** NA **drink with** Takeaway • $12

Beresford McLaren Vale Shiraz

♥♥♥♥ **2000** Medium red-purple; the moderately complex bouquet offers a pleasing blend of ripe, red and black fruits and a hint of vanilla oak. The medium-bodied palate provides a replay, with well-balanced red and black fruit flavours, soft tannins and evident but not excessive American oak.   **rating:** 87

best drinking 2003–2008 **best vintages** NA **drink with** Lamb cutlets • NA

Belleville Estate Cabernet Merlot

♥♥♥♡ **1999** Light to medium red-purple; a fresh, light mix of red berry fruit, mint and leaf, together with a whisker of oak on the bouquet, then a pleasant palate with red berry fruit to the fore, but a touch of oak phenolics on the finish.   **rating:** 84

best drinking 2002–2005 **best vintages** NA **drink with** Braised lamb • $19

Beresford McLaren Vale Cabernet Sauvignon

♥♥♥♥ **2000** Medium to full red-purple; clean, full blackberry fruit is joined on the palate by some typically regional chocolate and earth characters, providing a savoury finish to a wine which has the grip of cabernet throughout.   **rating:** 87

best drinking 2004–2009 **best vintages** NA **drink with** Braised lamb shanks • NA

berlingieri wines   NR

218 Glen Osmond Road, Fullarton, SA 5063 **region** McLaren Vale
phone (08) 8338 4111 **fax** (08) 8338 4122 **open** Not
winemaker Vincenzo Berlingieri **production** 18 000 **est.** 1992
product range ($10–24 R) Chardonnay, Sparkling Shiraz, Pinot Noir Shiraz Cabernet, Cabernet Franc; under the Charleston label Semillon Riesling Chardonnay, Sparkling Chenin Blanc, Sparkling Shiraz, Shiraz Cabernet Merlot, Cabernet Shiraz, Liqueur Muscat, Tawny Liqueur Port.
summary Vincenzo Berlingieri, one of the great characters of the wine industry, arrived in Sydney with beard flowing and arms waving in the 1970s and gained considerable publicity for his then McLaren Vale winery. Fortune did not follow marketing success for this research scientist who had arrived to work in plant genetics at Melbourne University's Botany Department in 1964, armed with a doctorate in agricultural science from Perugia University, Italy. However, after various moves he is in business again with his children, Jason, John and Annika, sourcing most of the grapes from Langhorne Creek and McLaren Vale. Most of the business is in unlabelled cleanskin form at yesterday's prices, sold only through a mailing list/direct order system.

berri estates ★★☆

Sturt Highway, Glossop, SA 5344 **region** Riverland
phone (08) 8582 0300 **fax** (08) 8583 2224 **open** Mon–Sat 9–5, Sundays on long weekends 10–4
winemaker Paul Kasselbaum, Peter Hensel, Graham Buller **production** NFP **est.** 1916
product range Light Fruity Lexia, Fruity Gordo Moselle, Chablis, Claret, Rosé, White Lambrusco, all in cask form.
summary Part of the BRL Hardy Group, with no pretensions to grandeur, its visible business is almost entirely restricted to 5-litre casks, many with generic names to be phased out under Australia's wine agreement with the EU.

berrys bridge ★★★★☆

Forsters Road, Carapooee, St Arnaud, Vic 3478 **region** Pyrenees
phone (03) 5496 3220 **fax** (03) 5496 3322 **open** By appointment
winemaker Jane Holt **production** 1300 **est.** 1990
product range ($32 CD) Shiraz, Merlot, Cabernet Sauvignon.
summary While the date of establishment is 1990, Roger Milner purchased the property in 1975, intending to plant a vineyard, having worked for three years at Reynell winery in South Australia. In the mid-1980s he returned with Jane Holt, and together they began the construction of the stone house-cum-winery. Planting of existing seven hectares of vineyard commenced in 1990, around the time that Jane commenced her viticultural studies at Charles Sturt University (completed in 1993, and a subsequent wine science degree course in 2000). Until 1997 the grapes were sold to others, the first vintage (from 1997) being released in November 1998 when Ian McDonald joined the business and became responsible for marketing and export. The wines are distributed in Victoria through Winestock to a number of well-known retailers. Not surprisingly, the limited quantity sells out with great speed. Exports to the US, Germany and Switzerland.

Berrys Bridge Shiraz

♥♥♥♥♥ 2000 Full purple-red; as concentrated and complex as ever, with strong plum and dark berry fruit on the bouquet, the oak in restraint. The palate follows on logically, very concentrated, with this depth doubtless coming from the vineyard. **rating:** 94

best drinking 2005–2015 **best vintages** '98, '00 **drink with** Flame-grilled rump steak • $30

Berrys Bridge Merlot

♥♥♥♥ 2000 Medium to full red-purple; there is a complex blend of fruit and oak on the bouquet, with some slightly savoury varietal aspects despite the fruit ripeness; the palate has very ripe juicy berry flavours, and at this stage the wine is somewhat disjunctive. Time needed. **rating:** 87

best drinking 2005–2010 **best vintages** NA **drink with** Marinated beef • $30

Berrys Bridge Cabernet Sauvignon

♥♥♥♥ 2000 Medium red-purple, with a fair bit of gas showing in the glass. The clean, moderately intense bouquet is not as concentrated as the Shiraz, and the palate has a mix of red berry, cassis and blackberry, but is well adrift of the prior releases. I don't know what is going on here. **rating:** 86

best drinking 2005–2009 **best vintages** '98 **drink with** Garlic and herb-studded leg of lamb • $28

best's wines ★★★★★

1 kilometre off Western Highway, Great Western, Vic 3377 **region** Grampians
phone (03) 5356 2250 **fax** (03) 5356 2430 **open** 7 days 10–5
winemaker Viv Thomson, Hamish Seabrook **production** 30 000 **est.** 1866
product range ($17–29 R) Great Western Riesling, Great Western Chardonnay, Concongella Chardonnay, Great Western Pinot Noir, Bin O Shiraz, Thomson Family Shiraz, Great Western Cabernet Sauvignon, Great Western Merlot together with a large range of fortified wines sourced from St Andrews at Lake Boga. Some of these wines are available only at the cellar door.
summary A historic winery, owning some priceless vineyards planted as long ago as 1867 (other plantings are, of course, much more recent), which has consistently produced elegant, supple wines which deserve far greater recognition than they in fact receive. The Shiraz is a classic; the Thomson Family Shiraz magnificent. Exports to the UK, Canada, Holland, Belgium and Switzerland.

Best's Wines Great Western Riesling

♥♥♥♥♡ **2001** Light green-yellow; a clean, fresh aromatic lime blossom bouquet leads into a delicate, lively, lime-accented fore- to mid-palate, with a faintly dusty/minerally aftertaste. Very good, though, and the best Riesling for some time. **rating: 90**

best drinking 2002–2005 **best vintages** '01 **drink with** Grilled fish • $17

Best's Wines Great Western Chardonnay

♥♥♥♥♡ **2000** Very good green-yellow; fine, elegant melon and stone fruit aromas with subtle spicy oak, then a long, smooth palate with melon and grapefruit supported by an echo of oak. Understated and elegant in true Best's style. **rating: 93**

best drinking 2002–2004 **best vintages** '00 **drink with** Slow-cooked ocean trout • $28

Best's Great Western Pinot Noir

♥♥♥♥ **2000** Bright, deep red-purple; the bouquet is clean and ranges through strawberry, mint and ripe cherry. Very clearly presented cherry and strawberry flavours, with touches of spice and mint in the background provide another surprising wine for the region. The only drawback at this stage is the slightly hard profile; this will soften with age. **rating: 89**

best drinking 2005–2009 **best vintages** '00 **drink with** Game • $28

Best's Great Western Merlot

♥♥♥♥♡ **2000** Light to medium red-purple; the bouquet has juicy redcurrant fruit aromas supported by subtle oak, characters which come through on the palate with its attractive flow and balance, sustained by subtle oak and fine tannins. **rating: 90**

best drinking 2003–2008 **best vintages** NA **drink with** Grilled spatchcock • $28

Best's Great Western Cabernet Sauvignon

♥♥♥♥♡ **1999** Medium red-purple; clean cassis berry fruit on the bouquet is followed by that hallmark, elegant palate bringing together cassis, red berry fruit, sweet, fine tannins and neatly judged oak. **rating: 91**

best drinking 2004–2009 **best vintages** '88, '91, '92, '93, '96, '99 **drink with** Sirloin of beef • $29

bethany wines ★★★☆

Bethany Road, Bethany via Tanunda, SA 5352 **region** Barossa Valley
phone (08) 8563 2086 **fax** (08) 8563 0046 **open** Mon–Sat 10–5, Sun 1–5
winemaker Geoff Schrapel, Robert Schrapel **production** 30 000 **est.** 1977
product range ($14–70 CD) Riesling, Chardonnay, Wood Aged Semillon, Steinbruch, Select Late Harvest Riesling, Shiraz, GR4 Shiraz, Shiraz Cabernet, Grenache, Cabernet Merlot, GR5 Reserve Cabernet Sauvignon, Old Quarry Barossa Tawny Port, Old Quarry Barossa Fronti (White Port), Cuvée Chardonnay Pinot, Sparkling Black Pinot.
summary The Schrapel family has been growing grapes in the Barossa Valley for over 140 years, but the winery has only been in operation since 1977. Nestling high on a hillside on the site of an old quarry, it is run by Geoff and Rob Schrapel, who produce a range of consistently well made and attractively packaged wines. They have 36 hectares of vineyards in the Barossa Valley, eight in the Eden Valley and (recently and interestingly) 2 hectares each of chardonnay and cabernet sauvignon on Kangaroo Island. The wines enjoy national distribution in Australia, and are exported to the UK, New Zealand, Europe, Japan and the US.

Bethany Riesling

♥♥♥♥ **2001** Light green-yellow; a clean but firm bouquet with herb, lemon and mineral notes, not particularly aromatic, flowing on logically into the full-favoured, moderately long palate. Well made, but not helped by the hot vintage. **rating: 85**

best drinking 2002–2004 **best vintages** NA **drink with** Seafood risotto • $13.90

Bethany Barrel Fermented Semillon

♥♥♥♥ **2001** Medium to full yellow-green; a solid, traditional bouquet with some tangy fruit is followed by a palate in similar mould; not over-oaked, but tending short. **rating: 83**

best drinking 2002–2003 **best vintages** NA **drink with** Salmon pizza • $13.90

Bethany Select Late Harvest Riesling

♥♥♥♥ **1999** Golden yellow; the bouquet has the honey, mead and peach aromas which often come from cordon-cut wines, and the flavours of the palate continue the thread, with the addition of some cumquat. Of Auslese sweetness, but not particularly complex. **rating: 84**

best drinking 2002–2004 **best vintages** '89, '90, '92, '93 **drink with** Fresh fruit • $16

Bethany Shiraz

▼▼▼▽ 1999 Medium red; a cedary, spicy, slightly jammy bouquet leads into a palate with a similar range of flavours, appealing in their own way, but lacking density.　　　　　　　　　**rating: 84**

best drinking 2003–2007 **best vintages** '88, '90, '91, '92, '94, '96 **drink with** Mild curry • $25

Bethany Shiraz Cabernet

▼▼▼▼ 2001 Youthful purple-red; a fresh, juicy berry, fruit-driven bouquet is followed by a flavoursome, softly sweet, berry fruit-driven palate in easy drinking style.　　　　　　　　　**rating: 87**

best drinking 2002–2005 **best vintages** NA **drink with** Spaghetti Milanese • $19

Bethany GR5 Reserve Cabernet Sauvignon

▼▼▼▼ 1997 Medium red-purple; a fresh, light juicy red berry bouquet, amazingly youthful for its age. The palate does nothing to disturb the impression of the bouquet, and is in a style all of its own. Very difficult to rate precisely.　　　　　　　　　**rating: 86**

best drinking 2002–2007 **best vintages** NA **drink with** Spiced lamb • $70

beyond broke vineyard　　　NR

Cobcroft Road, Broke, NSW 2330 **region** Lower Hunter Valley
phone (02) 6026 2043 **fax** (02) 6026 2043 **open** Tastings available at Broke Village Store 10–4
winemaker Pete Howland (Contract) **production** 4000 **est.** 1996
product range ($14–22 R) Semillon, Verdelho, Chardonnay, Unwooded Chardonnay, Sparkling Semillon, Shiraz.
summary Beyond Broke Vineyard is the reincarnation of a former Lindemans vineyard purchased by Bob and Terry Kennedy in 1996. In a more than slightly ironic twist, the 1997 Beyond Broke Semillon won two trophies at the Hunter Valley Wine Show of that year, the first for the Best Current Vintage Semillon and the second, the Henry John Lindeman Memorial Trophy for the Best Current Vintage Dry White Wine. Subsequent shows have been less spectacularly kind, but there is nothing surprising in that, and its turn will come again when vintage conditions permit.

bianchet　　★★★☆

Lot 3 Victoria Road, Lilydale, Vic 3140 **region** Yarra Valley
phone (03) 9739 1779 **fax** (03) 9739 1277 **open** Thurs–Mon 11–5
winemaker Keith Salter **production** 2500 **est.** 1976
product range ($16–25 CD) Traminer, Semillon, Copestone Semillon Sauvignon Blanc, Marsanne, Chardonnay Cuvée, Duet (Gewürztraminer Semillon), Verduzzo, Pinot Noir, Copestone Shiraz, Cabernets.
summary Now owned by a small Melbourne-based syndicate, with Keith Salter taking on winemaking responsibilities. One of the most unusual wines from the winery is Verduzzo Gold, a late-harvest sweet white wine made from the Italian grape variety. The wines are still basically sold through the cellar door.

Bianchet Copestone Semillon Sauvignon Blanc

▼▼▼▽ 1999 Medium to full yellow-green; the bottle-developed aromas have a slightly vegetal cast, but are quite complex. The palate is firm, with mineral, grass and herb flavours preceding a slightly stalky finish. A dual medal winner in 2000, and was quite possibly better when younger. A blend of Yarra Valley Semillon and Mornington Peninsula Sauvignon Blanc.　　　　　　　　　**rating: 84**

best drinking 2002–2003 **best vintages** NA **drink with** Mixed seafood • $16

Bianchet Verduzzo

▼▼▼▽ 1999 Glowing yellow green; the quite complex bouquet has a mix of tangy, dried fruit and honey aromas; the palate is big, broad and rich, with a slightly soapy, short finish. A rare example of yet another Italian grape variety.　　　　　　　　　**rating: 84**

best drinking 2002–2003 **best vintages** NA **drink with** Veal scallopine • $25

Bianchet Marsanne

▼▼▼▽ 1999 Bright yellow-green; the bouquet is solid, and as ever with the variety, not aromatic. Having spent 20 months in old French oak, the palate is likewise chunky and solid, with disparate touches of talc and dried fruits, then a dry finish.　　　　　　　　　**rating: 84**

best drinking 2002–2005 **best vintages** NA **drink with** Smoked turkey • $23

Bianchet Cuvée

TTTTT 1998 Medium but brilliant green-yellow; a clean, seamless marriage of nectarine/melon fruit and subtle oak on the bouquet, with a similarly seamless range of melon, cashew and oak flavours; won two trophies, including Best White Wine of Show, at the Victorian Wines Show 2001. However, very much a drink-now rather than a cellaring proposition. **rating:** 94

best drinking 2002–2003 **best vintages** '98 **drink with** Chicken fricassee • $23

Bianchet Duet (375 ml)

TTTTY NV Light green-yellow; highly fragrant, spicy gewürztraminer totally dominates the bouquet; the richly flavoured palate is of spatlese sweetness, the semillon doubtless cutting back on any propensity to show excess phenolics. Excellent aperitif/terrace wine. **rating:** 90

best drinking 2002–2003 **best vintages** NA **drink with** Aperitif • $15

Bianchet Pinot Noir

TTTTY 2000 Medium to full red-purple; a ripe, rich and quite concentrated bouquet has plum and spice in abundance; the palate delivers much the same in a slightly rustic but flavourful style. **rating:** 90

best drinking 2002–2004 **best vintages** '00 **drink with** Wild mushroom risotto • $22

Bianchet Cabernet

TTTT 1999 Medium red-purple; the bouquet has ripe, almost jammy, redcurrant fruit and evident oak, the palate following down the same track, with the vanilla oak, if anything, even more evident, finishing with soft tannins. **rating:** 85

best drinking 2002–2006 **best vintages** NA **drink with** Osso buco • $23

🐾 bidgeebong wine   NR

352 Byrnes Road, Bomen, Wagga Wagga, NSW 2650 **region** Southern New South Wales Zone
phone (02) 6931 9955 **fax** (02) 6931 9966 **open** Not
winemaker Andrew Birks **production** NA **est.** 2000
product range ($16 R) Tumbarumba Chardonnay.
summary Bidgeebong is a made-up name using a combination of Murrumbidgee and Billabong. It encompasses what the founders refer to as the Bidgeebong triangle, lying between Young, Wagga Wagga, Tumbarumba and Gundagai, these being the four regions which will provide grapes for the Bidgeebong brand. Two of the partners in the venture are Andrew Birks, with a 30-year career as a lecturer and educator at Charles Sturt University, and Simon Robertson, who studied viticulture and wine science at Charles Sturt University, and after working in Europe and the Barwang Vineyard established by his father Peter in 1969, built a substantial viticultural management business in the area. A winery was completed for the 2002 vintage; it will eventually be capable of handling 2000 tonnes of grapes. As well as meeting Bidgeebong's own needs, it will process grapes for other local growers and larger producers who purchase grapes from the region.

Bidgeebong Tumbarumba Chardonnay

TTTY 2000 Light green-yellow; the clean bouquet has a range of citrussy, minerally and grassy aromas, with the barest whiff of oak lurking in the background. The citrussy/minerally palate is definitively cool-grown, and should handsomely repay cellaring, but needs a little more generosity. **rating:** 84

best drinking 2003–2007 **best vintages** NA **drink with** Shellfish • $16

big hill vineyard   NR

Cnr Calder Highway and Belvoir Park Road, Big Hill, Bendigo, Vic 3550 **region** Bendigo
phone (03) 5435 3366 **fax** (03) 5435 3311 **open** 7 days 10–5
winemaker John Ellis, Robert Fiumara (Contract) **production** 1000 **est.** 1998
product range ($11.60–25 CD) Granite White, Sauvignon Blanc, Chardonnay, Granite Botrytis, Granite Red, Shiraz, Big Hill Shiraz, Cabernet Sauvignon, Granite Port, Curly Port, Curly Muscat.
summary A partnership headed by Nick Cugura began the re-establishment of what is now called Big Hill Vineyard on a site which was first planted to grapes almost 150 years ago. That was in the height of the gold rush, and there was even a long-disappeared pub, the Granite Rock Hotel. The wheel has come full circle, for Big Hill Vineyard now has a cafe-restaurant overlooking the vineyard, with plans for bed and breakfast cottages. The restaurant specialises in wedding receptions, and provides limited conference facilities. The modern-day plantings began with two hectares of shiraz in 1998 (which provided the first wine in May 2000), followed by one hectare each of merlot and cabernet sauvignon.

bimbadgen estate ★★★☆

Lot 21 McDonalds Road, Pokolbin, NSW 2320 **region** Lower Hunter Valley
phone (02) 4998 7585 **fax** (02) 4998 7732 **open** 7 days 9.30–5
winemaker Kees Van De Scheur, Simon Thistlewood **production** 50 000 **est.** 1968
product range ($12.50–28 R) Semillon, Limited Edition Art Series Semillon Verdelho, Verdelho, Chardonnay, Botrytis Semillon, Pinot Noir, Shiraz, Limited Edition Art Series Cabernet Franc Merlot, Port; Signature range is the super-premium range of Semillon, Chardonnay, Shiraz; Grand Ridge Estate is the lower-priced label, with Semillon Chardonnay, Verdelho, Chardonnay, Sparkling Semillon, Shiraz Cabernet, Cabernet Merlot.
summary Established as McPherson Wines, then successively Tamalee, then Sobels, then Parker Wines and now Bimbadgen, this substantial winery has had what might politely be termed a turbulent history. It has the great advantage of having 88.5 hectares of estate plantings, mostly with now relatively old vines, supplemented by a separate estate vineyard at Yenda for the lower-priced Grand Ridge series. The restaurant is open seven days for lunch and from Wednesday to Saturday inclusive for dinner. Exports to Hong Kong, Japan, the UK and the US.

Bimbadgen Estate Semillon

▼▼▼▼ **2001** Medium straw-green; the bouquet is quite ripe and aromatic, showing lemon and citrus fruit; the palate has good weight, length and balance. **rating:** 87

best drinking 2002–2007 **best vintages** '00 **drink with** Pasta • $17.50

Bimbadgen Estate Signature Semillon

▼▼▼▼ **2000** Light to medium green-yellow; a solid and quite complex bouquet, the palate, like the bouquet, having depth. However, the wine is starting to go through a closed period, making it very difficult to judge. Will almost certainly emerge in three or four years' time with a great deal of character. **rating:** 86

best drinking 2003–2008 **best vintages** NA **drink with** Trout mousse • $22.50

Bimbadgen Estate Hunter Valley Verdelho

▼▼▼▼ **2001** Light green-yellow; a clean and fresh bouquet with light fruit salad and citrus aromas leads into a lively, crisp and tangy palate with some length; very well made, almost turning a sow's ear into a silk purse. **rating:** 86

best drinking 2002–2003 **best vintages** NA **drink with** Chicken salad • $17.50

Bimbadgen Estate Grand Ridge Chardonnay

▼▼▼▽ **2000** Light to medium green-yellow; the bouquet is clean and fresh, with a mix of melon and faint vanilla oak, presumably from chips or innerstaves. A no-frills wine on the palate but has good length and balanced oak infusion. Well worth a look at the price. **rating:** 83

best drinking 2002–2003 **best vintages** NA **drink with** Takeaway • $12.50

Bimbadgen Estate Hunter Valley Chardonnay

▼▼▼▼ **2001** Light to medium yellow-green; a clean and fresh bouquet with melon and peach fruit and a touch of smoky oak. The palate has nice mouthfeel, but there is not overmuch concentration, and the wine is likely best drunk young. **rating:** 85

best drinking 2002–2003 **best vintages** NA **drink with** Roast chicken • $17.50

Bimbadgen Estate Myall Road Botrytis Semillon (375 ml)

▼▼▼▼ **1999** Deep golden-yellow; an array of rich cumquat, pineapple and peach aromas flow through directly into the palate, which has good balancing acidity, and little or no oak evident. From the Yenda vineyard. **rating:** 88

best drinking 2002–2004 **best vintages** NA **drink with** Rich desserts • $18.50

bindi wine growers ★★★★★

343 Melton Road, Gisborne, Vic 3437 **region** Macedon Ranges
phone (03) 5428 2564 **fax** (03) 5428 2564 **open** Not
winemaker Michael Dhillon, Stuart Anderson (Consultant) **production** 1000 **est.** 1988
product range ($32.50–65 ML) Chardonnay, Quartz Chardonnay, Macedon Méthode Champenoise Cuvée II, Original Vineyard Pinot Noir, Block 5 Pinot Noir.

summary One of the icons of Macedon, indeed Victoria. The Chardonnay is top-shelf, the Pinot Noir as remarkable (albeit in a very different idiom) as Bass Phillip, Giaconda or any of the other tiny-production icon wines. Notwithstanding the tiny production, the wines are exported (in small quantities, of course) to the UK, Italy, Singapore and the US.

Bindi Quartz Chardonnay

ϒϒϒϒϒ 2000 Medium yellow-green; the bouquet offers a subtle yet complex interplay between ripe nectarine fruit and oak; the palate is typically concentrated and powerful, yet held in a tightly contained mould. **rating:** 94

best drinking 2002–2006 **best vintages** '00 **drink with** Salmon risotto • $45

Bindi Wine Growers Cuvée II Chardonnay Pinot

ϒϒϒϒϒ NV Medium to full yellow-green; notwithstanding that the base wines were held in oak for several years, and came from blocks yielding below two tonnes to the acre, the bouquet is rich and complex, but neither oaky nor aldehydic, while the palate is surprisingly elegant and fresh. The wine spent over three and a half years on lees, and the acidity at harvest must have been daunting. A blend of Chardonnay and Pinot Noir from the 1993–1996 vintages. **rating:** 90

best drinking 2002–2003 **best vintages** NA **drink with** Antipasto • $40

Bindi Block 5 Pinot Noir

ϒϒϒϒϒ 2000 Medium red-purple; a lively, aromatic, tangy/spicy bouquet, then an elegant yet intense and long palate, the fruit flavours in the strawberry/cherry/plum spectrum. **rating:** 93

best drinking 2002–2006 **best vintages** '97, '00 **drink with** Rich game • $65

Bindi Original Vineyard Pinot Noir

ϒϒϒϒϒ 2000 The colour is fractionally deeper than that of the Block 5; a clean and fragrant bouquet of dark plum is followed by a palate with significantly greater grip, intensity and length than Block 5 and, like the bouquet, oriented towards plum. **rating:** 94

ϒϒϒϒϒ 1999 Medium red-purple; a typical exotic array of savoury, spicy plum fruit aromas, the palate with near-identical grip and length to that of the 2000, with tangy, lingering plum fruit. In all of these wines quality French oak is a contributor, but it is the fruit which does the talking. **rating:** 94

best drinking 2002–2008 **best vintages** '93, '94, '96, '97, '98, '99, '00 **drink with** Squab • $50

birdwood estate   NR

Mannum Road, Birdwood, SA 5234 **region** Adelaide Hills
phone (08) 8263 0986 **fax** (08) 8263 0986 **open** Not
winemaker Oli Cucchiarelli **production** 600 **est.** 1990
product range ($14–23 ML) Chardonnay, Riesling, Merlot, Cabernet Sauvignon.
summary Birdwood Estate draws upon 7 hectares of estate vineyards progressively established since 1990. The quality of the white wines, and in particular the Chardonnay, has generally been good. The tiny production is principally sold through retail in Adelaide, with limited distribution in Sydney and Melbourne. No recent tastings.

birnam wood wines   ★★★

Turanville Road, Scone, NSW 2337 **region** Upper Hunter Valley
phone (02) 6545 3286 **fax** (02) 6545 3431 **open** Weekends and public holidays 11–4
winemaker Monarch Wines (Contract) **production** 8000 **est.** 1994
product range ($7–20 R) Shakespeare Range: The Bards Tipple Hunter Valley Fruity, The Bards Tipple Hunter Valley Semillon, The Witches Brew Chardonnay, The Kings Cup Shiraz. Family Range: Semillon, Sauvignon Blanc, Semillon Sauvignon Blanc, Verdelho, Unwooded Chardonnay, Premium Reserve Chardonnay, Premium Reserve Shiraz.
summary Former Sydney car dealer Mike Eagan and wife Min moved to Scone to establish a horse stud; the vineyard came later (in 1994) but is now a major part of the business, with 32 hectares of vines. Most of the grapes are sold; part only is vinified for Birnam Wood. Exports to Switzerland, Canada and China. Son Matthew has now joined the business after working for five years for Tyrrell's in its export department.

Birnam Wood Semillon

♥♥♥♡ **2001** Light to medium yellow-green; the relatively solid bouquet has citrus and herb aromas, the palate following suit with weight and complexity, but early in its life the wine needed to settle down and smooth out. **rating:** 83

best drinking 2003–2008 **best vintages** NA **drink with** Fresh asparagus • $10

black george ★★★★

Black Georges Road, Manjimup, WA 6258 **region** Manjimup
phone (08) 9772 3569 **fax** (08) 9317 2084 **open** 7 days 10.30–4.45
winemaker Dr Shelley E Wilson, Gregory Chinery **production** 9000 **est.** 1991
product range ($17.50–28.50 CD) Sauvignon Blanc, Sauvignon Blanc Chardonnay, Classic White, Captain's Reserve Chardonnay, Late Picked Verdelho, Pinot Noir, Merlot Cabernet Franc, Cabernet Merlot, White Port.
summary Black George arrived with particular aspirations to make high-quality Pinot Noir. As with so much of the Manjimup region, it remains to be seen whether the combination of soil and climate will permit this; the quality of the Black George Merlot Cabernet Franc once again points in a different direction. Retail distribution in NSW, Vic, WA and Qld; exports to the UK and the Netherlands.

ℬ blackgum estate NR

166 Malmsbury Road, Metcalfe, Vic 3448 **region** Macedon Ranges
phone (03) 5423 2933 **fax** (03) 5423 2944 **open** Not
winemaker Simonette Sherman **production** 400 **est.** 1990
product range ($15–25 CD) Riesling, Chardonnay, Cabernet Sauvignon.
summary Simonette Sherman is the sole proprietor, executive winemaker and marketing manager of Blackgum Estate. It is situated 9 kilometres north-east of the historic village of Malmsbury, and 1.6 kilometres from the town of Metcalfe. The 4.5-hectare ten-year-old vineyard is planted to riesling, chardonnay, shiraz and cabernet sauvignon, with a planting of sagrantino (which sent me scuttling to Jancis Robinson's *Oxford Companion to Wine*) planned for the near future. Sagrantino is a red variety grown strictly around the Italian university town of Perugia, and is said to produce wines of great concentration and, usually, liveliness, with deep ruby colour and some bitterness. So there; the varietal atlas of Australia continues to expand. Ms Sherman has retained Llew Knight of Granite Hills to make the 2001 Riesling, while the Cabernet Sauvignon and Chardonnay will be made on-site in consultation with Tom Gyorffy.

blackjack vineyards ★★★☆

Cnr Blackjack Road and Calder Highway, Harcourt, Vic 3453 **region** Bendigo
phone (03) 5474 2355 **fax** (03) 5474 2355 **open** Weekends and public holidays 11–5, when stock available
winemaker Ian McKenzie, Ken Pollock **production** 2500 **est.** 1987
product range ($22 CD) Shiraz, Cabernet Merlot.
summary Established by the McKenzie and Pollock families on the site of an old apple and pear orchard in the Harcourt Valley. Best known for some very good Shirazs. Ian McKenzie, incidentally, is not to be confused with Ian McKenzie of Seppelt Great Western. Exports to New Zealand.

blackwood crest wines ★★★☆

RMB 404A, Boyup Brook, WA 6244 **region** Blackwood Valley
phone (08) 9767 3029 **fax** (08) 9767 3029 **open** 7 days 10–6
winemaker Max Fairbrass **production** 2000 **est.** 1976
product range ($13–21 CD) Riesling, Sauvignon Blanc, Semillon Sauvignon Blanc, Chardonnay, Shiraz, Cabernet Sauvignon, Ruby Port, Liqueur Muscat.
summary A remote and small winery which has produced one or two notable red wines full of flavour and character; worth watching, particularly now that it has added the striking Riesling to the mix.

blackwood wines NR

Kearney Street, Nannup, WA 6275 **region** Blackwood Valley
phone (08) 9756 0088 **fax** (08) 9756 0089 **open** Thurs–Tues 10–4
winemaker Andrew Mountford (Contract) **production** 2500 **est.** 1998

product range ($15–20 CD) Blackwood White, Chenin Blanc, Unwooded Chardonnay, Late Harvest Verdelho, Clay Pit Pinot Noir, Merlot Cabernet Sauvignon Shiraz, Merlot Cabernet Franc Malbec.
summary Blackwood Wines draws upon 1 hectare each of chardonnay, merlot and chenin blanc and half a hectare of pinot noir, supplemented by contract-grown fruit, which significantly broadens the product range. It also operates a Cellar Club with discounted prices for members, and a restaurant is open each day except Wednesday.

blanche barkly wines ★★★

Rheola Road, Kingower, Vic 3517 **region** Bendigo
phone (03) 5438 8223 **open** Weekends and public holidays 10–5, or by appointment
winemaker David Reimers, Arleen Reimers **production** 1000 **est.** 1972
product range ($25 CD) Mary Eileen Kingower Shiraz, Johann Kingower Cabernet Sauvignon.
summary After a long hiatus, the tasting of the 2000 vintage wines happily renewed my acquaintance with the winery. The tasting notes should speak for themselves.

Blanche Barkly Mary Eileen Shiraz

▼▼▼▼ **2000** Medium purple-red; the bouquet has a quite fragrant mix of red cherry and earth aromas, and the medium-bodied palate is fruit-driven, with soft, fine tannins. Perhaps not quite as concentrated as might have been expected, but well made.   **rating:** 85

best drinking 2002–2006 **best vintages** NA **drink with** Lasagne • $25

Blanche Barkly Johann Cabernet Sauvignon

▼▼▼▼ **2000** Medium red-purple; like the Mary Eileen Shiraz, the mix of berry, leaf, mint and earth on the bouquet is quite fragrant; sweet blackberry/cassis fruit comes through on the soft palate, finishing with fine tannins. Once again, well made.   **rating:** 86

best drinking 2002–2006 **best vintages** NA **drink with** Rack of lamb • $25

blaxlands wines NR

Broke Road, Pokolbin, NSW 2320 **region** Lower Hunter Valley
phone (02) 4998 7550 **fax** (02) 4998 7802 **open** 7 days 10.30–4.30
winemaker Contract **production** 1000 **est.** 1976
product range ($17–18 CD) Chardonnay, Chardonnay Semillon, Shiraz.
summary Chris Barnes was an industry veteran who ran Blaxlands Restaurant and Wine Centre in Pokolbin for almost 20 years before selling it to Len Evans in 1999. One and a half hectares each of chardonnay and semillon provide wines which are included in the comprehensive range of Hunter Valley wines available from the Wine Centre (and the restaurant).

bleasdale vineyards ★★★★

Wellington Road, Langhorne Creek, SA 5255 **region** Langhorne Creek
phone (08) 8537 3001 **fax** (08) 8537 3224 **open** Mon–Sat 9–5, Sun 11–5
winemaker Michael Potts **production** 150 000 **est.** 1850
product range ($9–38 CD) Langhorne Crossing White and Dry Red; Verdelho, Chardonnay, Malbec, Generations Shiraz, Cabernet Shiraz, Mulberry Tree Cabernet Sauvignon, Bremerview Shiraz, Frank Potts Cabernet Malbec Merlot Petit Verdot, Sparkling, Fortified.
summary One of the most historic wineries in Australia, drawing upon vineyards that are flooded every winter by diversion of the Bremer River, which provides moisture throughout the dry, cool, growing season. The wines offer excellent value for money, all showing that particular softness which is the hallmark of the Langhorne Creek region. Production has soared; export markets established in the UK, the US, Canada, New Zealand, Germany and Switzerland.

Bleasdale Generations Shiraz

▼▼▼▼▽ **1997** Medium red-purple; a solid, traditional style with plenty of vanilla oak on savoury fruit aromatics; the medium to full-bodied palate ranges through chocolate, dark berry and a touch of licorice; has the supple concentration one expects from premium Shiraz.   **rating:** 90

best drinking 2002–2010 **best vintages** NA **drink with** Porterhouse steak • $38

Bleasdale Frank Potts

ŢŢŢŢ **1998** Dense red-purple; the sweet, ripe and concentrated cassis/berry fruit of the bouquet avoids porty or jammy characters; the palate offers seductively supple ripe fruit with equally supple tannins and a dusting of vanilla ex the American oak. Fully deserves its medals and represents very good value. **rating:** 94

best drinking 2002–2010 **best vintages** '92, '94, '97, '98 **drink with** Rich casserole dishes • $28

bloodwood ★★★★☆

4 Griffin Road, Orange, NSW 2800 **region** Orange
phone (02) 6362 5631 **fax** (02) 6361 1173 **open** By appointment
winemaker Stephen Doyle **production** 4000 **est.** 1983
product range ($13–28 ML) Riesling, Chardonnay, Schubert Chardonnay, Chirac (Pinot Chardonnay), Noble Riesling, Big Men in Tights (Rosé), Rosé of Malbec, Maurice (Bordeaux blend), Cabernet Sauvignon, Shiraz.
summary Rhonda and Stephen Doyle are two of the pioneers of the burgeoning Orange district. The wines are sold mainly through the cellar door and an energetically and informatively run mailing list; the principal retail outlet is Ian Cook's Fiveways Cellar, Paddington, Sydney. Bloodwood has done best with elegant but intense Chardonnay and the intermittent releases of super-late-harvest Ice Riesling.

Bloodwood Riesling

ŢŢŢŢŢ **2001** Bright, light green-yellow; the bouquet offers abundant lime together with some more tropical aromas; the palate is full of rich, gently sweet lime, citrus and pineapple fruit flavours, generous but not phenolic. **rating:** 91

best drinking 2002–2006 **best vintages** '88, '90, '92, '94, '95, '98, '01 **drink with** Grilled scallops • $18

Bloodwood Chardonnay

ŢŢŢŢ **2000** Medium to full yellow-green, somewhat advanced; a concentrated bouquet with toasty/nutty/figgy/melon aromas, and a commensurately rich palate with good texture and layered flavours of fig, melon, nectarine and nuts with a creamy feel. Shows the concentration of a tiny vintage: only five barrels were made. **rating:** 90

best drinking 2002–2004 **best vintages** NA **drink with** White-fleshed fish • $21

Bloodwood Chirac

ŢŢŢŢ **1999** Light green-yellow; some obvious lees autolysis provides complexity for the bouquet, the tangy/herby/lemony/citrussy palate speaking more of the Chardonnay component than the Pinot; a slightly short finish. **rating:** 84

best drinking 2002–2003 **best vintages** NA **drink with** Aperitif • $30

Bloodwood Shiraz

ŢŢŢŢ **2000** Medium red-purple; some gamey varietal aromas, supported by hints of spice and earth, then a lively palate led by black cherry fruit plus spice, earth and licorice, finishing with savoury tannins. Superior outcome for a very difficult vintage. **rating:** 88

best drinking 2003–2008 **best vintages** NA **drink with** Lamb casserole • $21

Bloodwood Cabernet Sauvignon

ŢŢŢŢ **1999** Medium red-purple; a very high-toned and aromatic mix of spice, leaf and berry with slightly porty undertones is followed by a palate with similarly intense, slightly edgy, fruit characters, showing some sweet and sour characteristics, but with lots of character. **rating:** 86

best drinking 2002–2006 **best vintages** NA **drink with** Rib of veal • $21

bluebush estate NR

Wilderness Road, Cessnock, NSW 2325 **region** Lower Hunter Valley
phone (02) 4930 7177 **fax** (02) 4930 7666 **open** Not
winemaker Contract **production** 200 **est.** 1991
product range ($15 R) Chardonnay.
summary Two hectares of vineyards (half chardonnay, half shiraz) have been established by David McGain; the Chardonnay is contract-made and sold by mail order.

blue pyrenees estate ★★★☆

Vinoca Road, Avoca, Vic 3467 **region** Pyrenees
phone (03) 5465 3202 **fax** (03) 5465 3529 **open** Mon–Fri 10–4.30, weekends and public holidays 10–5
winemaker Greg Dedman **production** 100 000 **est.** 1963
product range ($10–60 CD) A four-tiered structure for the table wines sees Ghost Gum (sourced from south-east Australia) at the bottom; next Fiddlers Creek, sourced from Victoria but including estate-grown grapes; then Blue Pyrenees, varietal range of Sauvignon Blanc, Chardonnay, Shiraz, Merlot and Cabernet Sauvignon sourced exclusively from the Pyrenees' region; and at the top the two Estate Reserve wines of Chardonnay and Red (a Bordeaux blend). Alongside are the two sparkling wines, Vintage Brut and Midnight Cuvée.
summary Perseverance has finally started to pay dividends, with a decided lift in quality of the table wines in particular, which also offer good value for money. Not surprisingly, the wines are exported throughout Asia (frequently through Remy subsidiaries), and to the UK, Belgium, Switzerland, the US and Canada.

Blue Pyrenees Estate Reserve Chardonnay
ɪɪɪɪ **2000** Light to medium yellow-green; the clean bouquet has light melon fruit and a gentle touch of oak, the palate flowing logically on, with moderately sweet melon fruit and an overall soft structure. **rating:** 85

best drinking 2001–2003 **best vintages** NA **drink with** Veal fricassee • $23.95

Blue Pyrenees Fiddlers Creek Chardonnay
ɪɪɪɣ **1999** Light to medium yellow-green; there is not much happening on the bouquet, but it is quite a different story with the palate, which is pleasant and well balanced, with quite a deal of peachy fruit. A straightforward profile. Good value. **rating:** 84

best drinking 2001–2002 **best vintages** NA **drink with** Takeaway • $12

Blue Pyrenees Victoria Chardonnay
ɪɪɪɣ **2001** Light to medium green-yellow; a clean, smooth bouquet, then a melon and citrus-flavoured palate, with the barest touch of oak; a simple wine, but no fault. **rating:** 83

best drinking 2002–2003 **best vintages** NA **drink with** KFC • $16.50

Blue Pyrenees Victoria Shiraz
ɪɪɪɪ **2000** Medium red-purple; the moderately intense bouquet offers dark berry fruit and a light lick of vanilla oak; pleasantly ripe and quite sweet, plum, mulberry and dark cherry fruit melds with soft tannins on the finish; good value. **rating:** 85

best drinking 2002–2005 **best vintages** NA **drink with** Red-sauced pasta • $16.50

Blue Pyrenees Victoria Merlot
ɪɪɪɪ **2000** Medium red-purple; fresh, slightly spicy, sweet red berry/raspberry fruit aromas are a promising start, and the palate delivers good flavour and structure, with savoury edges to the core of sweet fruit. Good tannins and oak. Great value. **rating:** 89

best drinking 2003–2008 **best vintages** NA **drink with** Game • $16.50

Blue Pyrenees Estate Reserve Red
ɪɪɪɪ **1999** Medium red-purple; the moderately intense bouquet has savoury/spicy/cedary overtones to the berry fruit; soft, smooth, ripe dark berry flavours are supported by soft tannins and subtle oak. **rating:** 89

best drinking 2003–2008 **best vintages** '86, '89, '91, '94, '98 **drink with** Beef Bordelaise • $27.95

Blue Pyrenees Fiddlers Creek Victoria Cabernet Merlot
ɪɪɪɪ **1999** Medium red, with a touch of purple; clean, spicy/savoury aromas are followed by a palate with chocolate and red berry fruit added to the mix; lots of character and flavour for this price. **rating:** 85

best drinking 2001–2003 **best vintages** NA **drink with** Lamb shashlick • $12

Blue Pyrenees Estate Cabernet Sauvignon
ɪɪɪɪ **2000** Medium red-purple; the fresh bouquet has pleasantly ripe cassis berry fruit and well-integrated oak; the attractive palate has mouthfilling dark berry flavours, then savoury tannins to finish. Excellent value. **rating:** 88

best drinking 2003–2008 **best vintages** NA **drink with** Hard cheese • $16.95

Blue Pyrenees Estate Victoria Cabernet Sauvignon
ɪɪɪɣ **2000** Medium red-purple; moderately ripe blackberry fruit and subtle oak heralds a neatly assembled wine, with a light berry/savoury mix; neither rich nor complex, but honest. **rating:** 84

best drinking 2003–2007 **best vintages** NA **drink with** Beef spare ribs • $15

blue wren ★★★★

1 Cassilis Road, Mudgee, NSW 2850 **region** Mudgee
phone (02) 6372 6205 **fax** (02) 6372 6206 **open** Wed–Sun 10.30–4.30
winemaker Various contract **production** 3000 **est.** 1985
product range ($15–26 CD) Semillon, Chardonnay, Cabernet Sauvignon.
summary James and Diana Anderson have two vineyards. The first is called Stoney Creek, planted in 1985 and acquired from the Britten family in early 1999. It has 2 hectares each of chardonnay and semillon, 1.5 hectares of cabernet and 0.5 hectares of merlot, and is 20 kilometres north of Mudgee; the vines are dry-grown. The second vineyard has been planted to 2.4 hectares of shiraz and 1.4 hectares of verdelho, leaving more than 20 hectares as yet unplanted. The Bombira Vineyard, as it is known, is adjacent to the old Augustine vineyards owned by Beringer Blass. The capacious on-site restaurant is recommended – as are the wines.

Blue Wren Semillon

▼▼▼▼ **2001** Pale straw-green; an excellent aromatic bouquet with ripe lemon, even into tropical, is followed by a similarly accented palate with lots of flavour, but no phenolics. Tasted very early in its life with the CO_2 evident, in turn lifting the apparent acidity. Will settle down with age. **rating: 88**

best drinking 2003–2008 **best vintages** '00 **drink with** Calamari • $15

Blue Wren Cabernet Sauvignon

▼▼▼▼▼ **1999** Full red-purple; complex, spicy edges to the blackberry fruit of the bouquet are a promising opening, the powerful palate living up to expectations, with ripe, concentrated blackberry/blackcurrant fruit, and precisely judged extract and tannins. **rating: 93**

best drinking 2005–2015 **best vintages** '99 **drink with** Lamb shanks • $26

☙ boatshed vineyard ★★★

703 Milbrodale Road, Broke, NSW 2330 **region** Lower Hunter Valley
phone (02) 9876 5761 **fax** (02) 9876 5761 **open** Not
winemaker Mark Davidson (Contract) **production** 3500 **est.** 1989
product range ($14–18 ML) Verdelho, Estate Chardonnay, Hunter Range Chardonnay, Botrytis Chardonnay.
summary Mark Hill and wife Helen acquired the property in June 1998. At that time it had 5 hectares of chardonnay, and in the spring of 1999 the plantings were extended with 2 hectares each of verdelho, merlot, chambourcin and cabernet sauvignon. Mark Hill says the new name of the vineyard has to do with his lifetime involvement with rowing, first as a schoolboy competitor and thereafter as a coach of his school's senior IVs. Sustainable viticultural practices are used, and no insecticides have been applied for the past ten years. The wines are made under contract by Mark Davidson at Tamburlaine, with approximately 25 per cent of the wine made and bottled for Boatshed, the remainder being taken by Tamburlaine. There is no cellar door, and all sales are mail order or ex the vineyard on a wholesale basis to Sydney restaurants.

Boatshed Vineyard Wooded Chardonnay

▼▼▼▼ **1999** Light to medium yellow-green; the tangy, melon fruit of the bouquet is accompanied by pronounced spicy oak; the palate is developing relatively slowly (always a good thing with a Hunter Chardonnay) and, while oaky, is not oppressively so. **rating: 84**

best drinking 2001–2003 **best vintages** NA **drink with** Gnocchi • $18

boireann NR

Donnellys Castle Road, The Summit, Qld 4377 **region** Granite Belt
phone (07) 4683 2194 **open** 7 days 10–4.30
winemaker Peter Stark **production** 350 **est.** 1998
product range ($14–22 CD) Shiraz Grenache Mourvedre, Merlot, Cabernet Merlot, Granite Belt Cabernet Sauvignon.
summary Peter and Therese Stark have a ten-hectare property set amongst the great granite boulders and trees which are so much part of the Granite Belt. Luxury accommodation is provided and supplements the winemaking activities. They have established a little over 1 hectare of vines planted to no less than seven varieties, including the four Bordeaux varieties which go to make a Bordeaux blend; grenache and mourvedre provide a Rhône blend, and there will also be a straight Merlot.

boneo plains   NR

RMB 1400, Browns Road, South Rosébud, Vic 3939 **region** Mornington Peninsula
phone (03) 5988 6208 **fax** (03) 5988 6208 **open** By appointment
winemaker R D Tallarida **production** 2500 **est.** 1988
product range ($10–22 CD) Chardonnay, Cabernet Sauvignon; Roch Unwooded Chardonnay, Roch Rosé.
summary A 9-hectare vineyard and winery established by the Tallarida family, well known as manufacturers and suppliers of winemaking equipment to the industry. The Chardonnay is the best of the wines so far released.

bonneyview   NR

Sturt Highway, Barmera, SA 5345 **region** Riverland
phone (08) 8588 2279 **open** 7 days 9–5.30
winemaker Robert Minns **production** 5000 **est.** 1975
product range ($6–25 CD) Riesling, Chardonnay, Frontignan Blanc, Shiraz Petit Verdot, Cabernet Petit Verdot, Cabernet Blend, Fortifieds.
summary The smallest Riverland winery selling exclusively cellar door, with an ex-Kent cricketer and Oxford University graduate as its owner/winemaker. The Shiraz Petit Verdot (unique to Bonneyview) and Cabernet Petit Verdot add a particular dimension of interest to the wine portfolio.

booth's taminick cellars   NR

Taminick via Glenrowan, Vic 3675 **region** Glenrowan
phone (03) 5766 2282 **fax** (03) 5766 2151 **open** Mon–Sat 9–5, Sun 10–5
winemaker Peter Booth **production** 4000 **est.** 1904
product range ($6.50–12 CD) Trebbiano, Chardonnay, Late Harvest Trebbiano, Shiraz, Cabernet Merlot, Cabernet Sauvignon, Ports, Muscat.
summary Ultra-conservative producer of massively flavoured and concentrated red wines, usually with more than a few rough edges, which time may or may not smooth over.

boston bay wines   ★★★

Lincoln Highway, Port Lincoln, SA 5606 **region** Southern Eyre Peninsula
phone (08) 8684 3600 **fax** (08) 8684 3637 **open** Weekends, school/public holidays 11.30–4.30
winemaker David O'Leary, Nick Walker **production** 3500 **est.** 1984
product range ($11–21 CD) Riesling, Spätlese Riesling, Chardonnay, Riesling Mistelle, Shiraz, Merlot, Cabernet Sauvignon.
summary A strongly tourist-oriented operation which has extended the viticultural map in South Australia. It is situated at the same latitude as Adelaide, overlooking the Spencer Gulf at the southern tip of the Eyre Peninsula. Say proprietors Graham and Mary Ford, 'It is the only vineyard in the world to offer frequent sightings of whales at play in the waters at its foot.' No recent tastings.

botobolar   ★★★☆

89 Botobolar Road, Mudgee, NSW 2850 **region** Mudgee
phone (02) 6373 3840 **fax** (02) 6373 3789 **open** Mon–Sat 10–5, Sun 10–3
winemaker Kevin Karstrom **production** 5000 **est.** 1971
product range ($8–22.50 CD) Sauvignon Blanc, Rain Goddess Dry White, Rain Goddess Sweet White, Marsanne, Chardonnay, Rain Goddess Red, Pinot Noir, Shiraz, R&B Shiraz, Cabernet Sauvignon; The King, The Saviour (both Cabernet Shiraz blends); Low Preservative Chardonnay and Preservative Free Shiraz.
summary One of the first organic vineyards in Australia, with present owner Kevin Karstrom continuing the practices established by founder Gil Wahlquist. Preservative Free Dry White and Dry Red extend the organic practice of the vineyard to the winery. Shiraz is consistently the best wine to appear under the Botobolar label. Exports to the UK, Denmark and Germany.

Botobolar Marsanne

TTTT 2001 Medium yellow-green; the bouquet is very typical of the variety, initially neutral, but then faint flower and apple blossom aromas can be teased out. The crisp, medium-bodied palate is similarly reticent, seemingly neutral, but with crisp apple there in the background. All in all, an impressive result for a finicky variety. **rating:** 87

best drinking 2002–2006 **best vintages** NA **drink with** Antipasto • $15

Botobolar Shiraz

ŢŢŢŢ 2000 Medium red-purple; the aromas run through the full array of earth, chocolate, berry, sweet leather and spice, but the palate doesn't quite deliver; it is primarily earthy/leathery, with a slightly green finish. Given the ordinary vintage, a good outcome. **rating:** 85

best drinking 2003–2007 **best vintages** NA **drink with** Rich beef stew • $14

bowen estate ★★★★☆

Riddoch Highway, Coonawarra, SA 5263 **region** Coonawarra
phone (08) 8737 2229 **fax** (08) 8737 2173 **open** 7 days 10–5
winemaker Doug Bowen, Emma Bowen **production** 12 000 **est.** 1972
product range ($26.50–55 R) Chardonnay, Shiraz, Ampelon (Shiraz), The Blend, Cabernet Sauvignon.
summary One of the best-known names among the smaller Coonawarra wineries, with a great track record of red winemaking; Chardonnay and Sanderson Sparkling have joined the band, but the Riesling ended with the '93 vintage. Full-bodied reds at the top end of the ripeness spectrum are the winery trademarks; they have a chewy richness uncommon in Coonawarra. Exports to the UK, Germany, Switzerland, Japan, Singapore, Indonesia, Vietnam, Hong Kong and New Zealand.

Bowen Estate Shiraz

ŢŢŢŢ 1999 Medium red-purple; the bouquet is quite fragrant, with a mix of black cherry, mulberry, vanilla and spice; the rich and powerful palate has voluminous dark fruit flavours and the usual hefty boost from 14.5° alcohol. **rating:** 89

best drinking 2004–2014 **best vintages** '86, '90, '91, '92, '94, '95, '97 **drink with** Kangaroo fillet • $26.50

Bowen Estate Ampelon

ŢŢŢŢŢ 1998 Medium to full red-purple; ultra-ripe, rich black cherry, plum and prune aromas flow into voluptuous, mouth-coating fruit on the palate, which is not overly extractive or tannic; fine oak sits in the background. Made in the take it or leave it hallmark style of Doug Bowen. A single vineyard wine from hand-pruned, 28-year-old vines. **rating:** 92

best drinking 2005–2015 **best vintages** '98 **drink with** Venison and wild mushroom ragout • $55

Bowen Estate Cabernet Sauvignon

ŢŢŢŢŢ 1999 Medium red-purple; the bouquet has an elegant mix of cedary and blackberry aromas, the medium-bodied palate following down the same path, replete with ripe tannins and a long finish. **rating:** 90

best drinking 2004–2014 **best vintages** '86, '90, '91, '93, '94 **drink with** Richly sauced beef casserole • $27.30

boynton's ★★★☆

Great Alpine Road, Porepunkah, Vic 3741 **region** Alpine Valleys
phone (03) 5756 2356 **fax** (03) 5756 2610 **open** 7 days 10–5
winemaker Kel Boynton, Eleana Anderson **production** 11 000 **est.** 1987
product range ($14–60 CD) Riesling, Sauvignon Blanc, Chardonnay, Boynton's Gold (Noble Riesling Chardonnay blend), Pinots (Pinot Meunier Pinot Noir), Shiraz, Merlot, Cabernet Sauvignon, Alluvium (Cabernet Sauvignon Merlot Petit Verdot), Vintage Brut.
summary The original 12.5-hectare vineyard, expanded to almost 16 hectares by 1996 plantings of pinot gris, durif and sauvignon blanc, is situated in the Ovens Valley, north of the township of Bright, under the lee of Mount Buffalo. In the early years a substantial part of the crop was sold, but virtually all is now vinified at the winery. Overall, the red wines have always outshone the whites, initially with very strong American oak input, but in more recent years with better fruit/oak balance. Striking, indeed strident, new labelling has led to a minor name change – with the dropping of the words 'of Bright'. The wines have distribution through the east coast of Australia; exports to Germany, Austria and the US.

braewattie ★★★★

Woodend Road, Rochford, Vic 3442 **region** Macedon Ranges
phone (03) 9818 5742 **fax** (03) 9818 8361 **open** By appointment
winemaker John Flynn, John Ellis **production** 250 **est.** 1993

product range ($18–25 R) Chardonnay, Pinot Noir, Pinot Noir Chardonnay.
summary A tiny operation with the wines sold by mail order to friends and acquaintances.

Braewattie Pinot Noir Chardonnay
▼▼▼▼▽ NV Medium to full straw-yellow; the complex bouquet offers a subtle mix of aldehyde and autolysis characters, and a hint of underlying oak. The palate is no less complex, with some true Méthode Champenoise style, and showing exemplary balance and length. **rating:** 93
best drinking 2001–2003 **best vintages** NA **drink with** Aperitif • $29

Braewattie Pinot Noir
▼▼▼▽ 2000 Light red; a relatively simple, clean and light bouquet is followed by a palate with delicate strawberry fruit, providing an attractive early-drinking, summer lunch style. **rating:** 83
best drinking 2001–2002 **best vintages** NA **drink with** Cold meat salad • $26

brahams creek winery   NR
Woods Point Road, East Warburton, Vic 3799 **region** Yarra Valley
phone (03) 9566 2802 **fax** (03) 9566 2802 **open** Weekends and public holidays 11–5
winemaker Geoff Richardson, Chris Young **production** 1200 **est.** 1990
product range ($11–13.50 CD) Chardonnay, Pinot Noir, Merlot, Cabernet Sauvignon, Tawny Port.
summary Owner Geoffrey Richardson did not start marketing his wines until 1994, and a string of older vintages are available for sale at cellar door at an enticing price. Part of the grape production is sold to other Yarra Valley winemakers.

bramley wood   NR
RMB 205, Rosa Brook Road, Margaret River, WA 6285 **region** Margaret River
phone (08) 9757 9291 **fax** (08) 9757 9291 **open** Not
winemaker Cliff Royle, Mike Edwards (Voyager Estate) **production** 200 **est.** 1994
product range ($25 ML) Cabernet Sauvignon.
summary David and Rebecca McInerney planted 2 hectares of cabernet sauvignon in 1994, with an inaugural vintage in 1998, released in December 2000. Encouraged by the quality of that wine and, in particular, the 1999 which followed it, the McInerneys are extending the plantings with 14 hectares of cabernet sauvignon, merlot and chardonnay in the spring of 2002. For the time being, the tiny production is sold by mail order and through the two self-contained chalets on the property, each capable of hosting 4–6 adults.

brand's of coonawarra   ★★★★☆
Riddoch Highway, Coonawarra, SA 5263 **region** Coonawarra
phone (08) 8736 3260 **fax** (08) 8736 3208 **open** Mon–Fri 8–5, weekends 10–4
winemaker Jim Brand, Jim Brayne **production** NFP **est.** 1966
product range ($10.95–27.95 R) Riesling, Chardonnay, Sparkling Cabernet Sauvignon, Cabernet Merlot, Shiraz, Stentiford's Reserve Shiraz, Merlot, Cabernet Sauvignon, Patron's Reserve.
summary Part of a very substantial investment in Coonawarra by McWilliam's, which first acquired a 50 per cent interest from the founding Brand family then moved to 100 per cent, and followed this with the purchase of 100 hectares of additional vineyard land. Significantly increased production of the smooth wines for which Brand's is known will follow past the end of the decade.

Brand's of Coonawarra Riesling
▼▼▼▼▽ 2001 Light yellow-green; a clean and crisp bouquet brings lime, lemon and mineral, the firm, minerally palate having good length and tightness; guaranteed to develop marvellously over the next five years or more. **rating:** 90
best drinking 2004–2009 **best vintages** '98, '01 **drink with** Caesar salad • $18

Brand's of Coonawarra Shiraz
▼▼▼▼▽ 1999 Medium to full red-purple; the bouquet has good intensity, with smooth, dark berry, a hint of briar and nicely integrated oak. The palate opens with sweet plummy fruit, moving through to an appealing mix of savoury tannins and gentle oak on the finish. **rating:** 90
best drinking 2004–2010 **best vintages** '90, '91, '96, '98, '99 **drink with** Braised lamb shanks • $23

Brand's of Coonawarra Cabernet Sauvignon

TTTT 1999 Medium red-purple; varietal cabernet aromas of red and blackcurrant, together with more savoury/earthy undertones, lead into a palate with quite spicy, tangy berry fruit. It is less conventionally varietal than the bouquet, but has garnered three gold medals. **rating: 88**

best drinking 2004–2011 **best vintages** '86, '90, '91, '93, '94, '95, '98 **drink with** Lamb Provençale • $23

brangayne of orange ★★★★

49 Pinnacle Road, Orange, NSW 2880 **region** Orange
phone (02) 6365 3229 **fax** (02) 6365 3170 **open** By appointment
winemaker Simon Gilbert (Contract) **production** 5000 **est.** 1994
product range ($18–26 CD) Sauvignon Blanc, Premium Chardonnay, Isolde Reserve Chardonnay, Pinot Noir, The Tristan (Cabernet blend).
summary Orchardists Don and Pamela Hoskins decided to diversify into grape growing in 1994, and have progressively established 25 hectares of high-quality vineyards. With viticultural consultancy advice from Dr Richard Smart and skilled contract winemaking by Simon Gilbert, Brangayne made an extraordinarily auspicious debut, underlining the potential of the Orange region. Exports to the UK, Hong Kong and Singapore.

Brangayne of Orange Sauvignon Blanc

TTTT 2001 Light green-yellow; the clean, delicate bouquet has grass and faint citrus aromatics; the palate is bright, fresh and brisk, well-balanced and well made, with a pleasant aftertaste. Simply needs more varietal definition for top points. **rating: 87**

best drinking 2002–2003 **best vintages** NA **drink with** Caesar salad • $20

Brangayne of Orange Premium Chardonnay

TTTT 2001 Light straw-green; the light, almost grassy, bouquet has a wisp of reduction, but the palate more or less rights the ship, with crisp citrus, a touch of melon and an airbrush of oak. Despite its 13° alcohol, the wine lacks ripeness; this is perhaps not surprising given the vintage. **rating: 87**

best drinking 2002–2005 **best vintages** '97 **drink with** Calamari • $18

Brangayne Orange Pinot Noir

TTTT 2000 Excellent, bright red-purple; the aromatic bouquet has light cherry stone, wild strawberry and plum aromas, all in the fruit spectrum. The palate has honest varietal plum and strawberry fruit; neither the winemaking nor the oak choice is particularly inspired, but the fruit base is at once interesting and impressive. **rating: 88**

best drinking 2002–2006 **best vintages** '98 **drink with** Jugged hare • $22

bream creek ★★★☆

Marion Bay Road, Bream Creek, Tas 7175 **region** Southern Tasmania
phone (03) 6231 4646 **fax** (03) 6231 4646 **open** At Potters Croft, Dunally, phone (03) 6253 5469
winemaker Steve Lubiana (Contract) **production** 3000 **est.** 1975
product range ($17–22 CD) Riesling, Traminer, Sauvignon Blanc, Schönburger, Chardonnay, Pinot Noir, Cabernet Sauvignon.
summary Until 1990 the Bream Creek fruit was sold to Moorilla Estate, but since that time the winery has been independently owned, and managed by Fred Peacock; the care he bestows on the vines under his direction is legendary. Peacock's skills have seen both an increase in production and also a vast lift in wine quality across the range, headed by the Pinot Noir. The 1996 acquisition of a second vineyard in the Tamar Valley has significantly strengthened the business base of the venture.

Bream Creek Riesling

TTTT 2001 Light green-yellow; crisp, dry and minerally aromas have a faint tinge of lime blossom in the background, and those delicate blossom and passionfruit characters come through on the attractive, albeit light, palate. **rating: 88**

best drinking 2002–2006 **best vintages** NA **drink with** Spring rolls • $17

Bream Creek Chardonnay

TTTT 2000 Light to medium yellow-green; a mix of melon and citrus/grapefruit is backed by a touch of oak on the bouquet, that oak coming through with a slight vanilla overtone on the clean and smooth palate. Perhaps the choice of oak is not entirely convincing. **rating: 85**

best drinking 2002–2005 **best vintages** NA **drink with** Crumbed brains • $18

Bream Creek Pinot Noir

▼▼▼▼ 2000 Purple-red, with good hue and depth; a strongly herbal/vegetal edge to the bouquet is followed by a powerful palate showing a mix of sweeter plum and sour cherry fruit; an up-and-down wine with curate's egg qualities. **rating: 87**

best drinking 2002–2005 best vintages '97 drink with Braised duck • $22

bremerton wines ★★★★☆

Strathalbyn Road, Langhorne Creek, SA 5255 **region** Langhorne Creek
phone (08) 8537 3093 **fax** (08) 8537 3109 **open** 7 days 10–5
winemaker Rebecca Willson **production** 22 500 **est.** 1988
product range ($15–35 R) Sauvignon Blanc, Verdelho, Old Adam Shiraz, Selkirk Shiraz, Bremerton Blend (red), Walter's Cabernet Sauvignon, Tamblyn (Cabernet Shiraz Merlot).
summary The Willsons have been grape growers in the Langhorne Creek region for some considerable time, but their dual business as grape growers and winemakers has expanded significantly over the past few years. Their vineyards have more than doubled to over 100 hectares (predominantly cabernet sauvignon, shiraz and merlot), as has their production of wine under the Bremerton label, no doubt in recognition of the quality of the wines. Wholesale distribution in all states of Australia; exports to the UK, the US, Canada, Singapore, Holland, Germany, New Zealand and Switzerland.

Bremerton Old Adam Shiraz

▼▼▼▼▽ 1999 Medium to full red-purple; rich, savoury blackberry and plum fruit on the bouquet leads into a powerful palate with flavours in the same spectrum as the bouquet, supplemented by positive tannins on the finish. **rating: 91**

best drinking 2004–2009 best vintages '97, '98, '99 drink with Parmesan cheese • $30

Bremerton Selkirk Shiraz

▼▼▼▼ 2000 Medium red-purple; the moderately intense bouquet ranges through dark cherry, plum and spice; sweet berry fruit and controlled oak and tannins provide good balance and mouthfeel. Good value. **rating: 89**

best drinking 2003–2007 best vintages NA drink with Beef shashlik • $17

Bremerton Tamblyn

▼▼▼▼ 2000 Medium purple-red; quite complex fruit, augmented by oak, gives a spicy overtone to the bouquet. The palate is similarly flavoursome, tangy and lively; fine tannins and good length from the blend of Cabernet Sauvignon, Shiraz, Malbec and Merlot. **rating: 88**

best drinking 2003–2007 best vintages NA drink with Osso buco • $17

Bremerton Walter's Cabernet Sauvignon

▼▼▼▼▽ 1999 Medium to full red, with a touch of purple; savoury, earthy, blackberry fruit on the bouquet is followed by a palate with abundant blackberry, blackcurrant and chocolate fruit, riper and denser than the bouquet suggests. **rating: 92**

best drinking 2004–2009 best vintages '91, '96, '97, '99 drink with Braised beef in red wine • $30

brewery hill winery NR

Olivers Road, McLaren Vale, SA 5171 **region** McLaren Vale
phone (08) 8323 7344 **fax** (08) 8323 7355 **open** Mon–Fri 9–5, weekends 10–5
winemaker Contract **production** 12 000 **est.** 1869
product range ($10–22.50 CD) Riesling, Classic Spätlese, Chardonnay, Classic Dry Red, Shiraz, Cabernet Sauvignon, Sparkling and Fortifieds.
summary A change of name and of address for the former St Francis Winery, which has moved into the former Manning Park Winery and is now known as Brewery Hill Winery. Exports to Japan.

briagolong estate NR

Valencia–Briagolong Road, Briagolong, Vic 3860 **region** Gippsland
phone (03) 5147 2322 **fax** (03) 5147 2400 **open** By appointment
winemaker Gordon McIntosh **production** 300 **est.** 1979
product range ($31–35 ML) Chardonnay, Pinot Noir.

summary This is very much a weekend hobby for medical practitioner Gordon McIntosh, who tries hard to invest his wines with Burgundian complexity, although with mixed success. Dr McIntosh must have established an all-time record with the 15.4° alcohol in the '92 Pinot Noir. No recent tastings.

brian barry wines ★★★☆

PO Box 128, Stepney, SA 5069 **region** Clare Valley
phone (08) 8363 6211 **fax** (08) 8362 0498 **open** Not
winemaker Brian Barry, Judson Barry **production** 8000 **est.** 1977
product range ($18–35 R) Jud's Hill Handpicked Riesling, Handpicked Merlot, Handpicked Cabernet Sauvignon; McLaren Vale Shiraz.
summary Brian Barry is an industry veteran with a wealth of winemaking and show-judging experience. His is nonetheless in reality a vineyard-only operation, with a substantial part of the output sold as grapes to other wineries and the wines made under contract at various wineries, albeit under Brian Barry's supervision. As one would expect, the quality is reliably good. Retail distribution through all states, and exports to the UK.

Brian Barry Jud's Hill Handpicked Riesling

TTTTY **2001** Light green-yellow; highly fragrant lime aromas, with a sprinkling of mineral, lead into an attractive, moderately intense palate with similar fruit registers, though in a slightly softer mould, making the wine an each-way, drink now or later, proposition. **rating:** 90

best drinking 2002–2006 **best vintages** '91, '92, '94, '95, '00, '01 **drink with** Caesar salad • $18

Brian Barry Special Release Shiraz

TTTT **2000** Medium red-purple; the moderately intense, clean bouquet is driven by appealing red berry/plum/cherry fruit, the light to medium-bodied palate with cherry and plum flavours, finishing with soft tannins. **rating:** 85

best drinking 2004–2008 **best vintages** NA **drink with** Rare rump steak • $28

Brian Barry Jud's Hill Handpicked Cabernet Sauvignon

TTTT **1999** Medium purple-red; clean, fresh and bright berry fruit on the bouquet is followed by a palate which is rather more savoury, with cedar, earth and chocolate flavours. **rating:** 85

best drinking 2003–2007 **best vintages** '90, '92 **drink with** Rack of lamb • $25

briar ridge ★★★★☆

Mount View Road, Mount View, NSW 2325 **region** Lower Hunter Valley
phone (02) 4990 3670 **fax** (02) 4990 7802 **open** 7 days 10–5
winemaker Neil McGuigan, Karl Stockhausen, Adrian Lockhart **production** 27 000 **est.** 1972
product range ($17.50–50 CD) Premium range of Early Harvest Semillon, Verdelho, Hand Picked Chardonnay, Mèthode Champenoise, Late Harvest Gewürztraminer, Botrytis Semillon, Old Vines Shiraz, Cabernet Sauvignon, Liqueur Muscat; Signature Release range of Stockhausen Semillon, McGuigan Chardonnay, Stockhausen Shiraz, McGuigan Cabernet Merlot, The Reserve Red.
summary Semillon and Hermitage, each in various guises, have been the most consistent performers, underlying the suitability of these varieties to the Hunter Valley. The Semillon, in particular, invariably shows intense fruit and cellars well. Briar Ridge has been a model of stability with the winemaking duo of Neil McGuigan and Karl Stockhausen, and also has the comfort of over 48 hectares of estate vineyards, from which it is able to select the best grapes. Exports to the US and Canada.

Briar Ridge Early Harvest Semillon

TTTTT **2001** Light to medium green-yellow; a complex and deep bouquet which derives its intensity from very pure semillon fruit. The palate is similarly intense, very fine and long, with delicious lemony flavour and acidity. Two trophies at the 2001 Hunter Valley Wine Show for Best Current Vintage Semillon and Best Current Vintage Dry White Wine, All Varieties. **rating:** 95

best drinking 2002–2012 **best vintages** '00, '01 **drink with** Crab or shellfish • $18.50

Briar Ridge Karl Stockhausen Signature Release Semillon

TTTTT **2001** Light green-yellow; a fresh, crisp and spotlessly clean bouquet has appealing lemony fruit aromas; the palate is particularly well-balanced, with excellent mouthfeel and length; clean, dry finish. **rating:** 94

best drinking 2005–2015 **best vintages** '01 **drink with** Flathead fillets • $23

Briar Ridge Verdelho

TTTT 2001 Medium green-yellow; the bouquet seems to show some complexity over and above the varietal character of the wine. The same impression comes on the palate, with ripe fruit salad flavours expected of the variety, but neither that flavour nor the alcohol of 12.5° explained why the wine has better than average character, given no-frills winemaking. Don't look a gift horse...   **rating: 85**

best drinking 2002–2003 **best vintages** NA **drink with** Anything other than rump • $18.50

Briar Ridge Cellar Reserve Chardonnay

TTTTT 2000 Medium green-yellow; complex, classy barrel ferment characters are the cornerstone of a stylish wine with good balance, length and flavour, driven by its nectarine/melon fruit. Gold medal 2001 Hunter Valley Wine Show.   **rating: 94**

best drinking 2002–2005 **best vintages** '00 **drink with** Balmain bugs • $20

Briar Ridge Hand Picked Chardonnay

TTTTT 2001 Light to medium green-yellow; the moderately intense bouquet has obvious smoky/spicy barrel-ferment characters which do not, however, overwhelm the fruit, which comes through nicely on the palate with nectarine and a touch of cashew. In stark contrast to the Adrian Lockhart Chardonnay of the same year, which is literally swamped with smoky bacon oak.   **rating: 90**

best drinking 2002–2004 **best vintages** '87, '89, '91, '92, '97, '01 **drink with** Breast of chicken • $18.50

Briar Ridge Signature McGuigan Chardonnay

TTTT 2000 Light to medium yellow-green; both the bouquet and palate are driven by charry and aggressive oak. The fruit is there, but the oak does the talking. Split the judges at the 2001 Hunter Valley Wine Show right down the middle, three giving the wine gold medal points, and three giving it no medal at all, the ultimate outcome a compromise between the two views.   **rating: 86**

best drinking 2002–2005 **best vintages** NA **drink with** Smoked trout • $23

Briar Ridge Karl Stockhausen Shiraz

TTTT 2000 Medium red-purple; the complex bouquet has dark berry and licorice fruit with a nice hint of bacony oak; that oak comes through more strongly on the palate, but should settle down with time, as there is ample fruit there and appropriate soft tannins.   **rating: 89**

best drinking 2004–2009 **best vintages** '86, '87, '89, '91, '93, '94, '96 **drink with** Braised lamb shanks • $25.50

Briar Ridge Old Vines Shiraz

TTTT 2000 Medium purple-red; clean, fresh earth and cherry varietal fruit aromas are supported by subtle oak; the well-balanced, light to medium-bodied palate likewise offers ripe cherry fruit and controlled oak. Does not show its alcohol of 14°, which is a good thing; the wine could develop very well over the long term.   **rating: 88**

best drinking 2004–2010 **best vintages** NA **drink with** Beef casserole • $19.50

bridgeman downs   NR

Barambah Road, Moffatdale via Murgon, Qld 4605 **region** South Burnett
phone (07) 4168 4784 **fax** (07) 4168 4767 **open** 10–4
winemaker Bruce Humphery-Smith **production** NA **est.** NA
product range ($12–18.50 CD) Cellar White and Red; Chardonnay, Verdelho, Shiraz, Merlot Cabernet.
summary A substantial, albeit new, vineyard with 4 hectares of vines, the major plantings being of verdelho, chardonnay and shiraz, with lesser amounts of merlot and cabernet sauvignon. The perpetual-motion Bruce Humphery-Smith has been retained as consultant winemaker, which should ensure wine quality. However, no tastings.

bridgewater mill   ★★★★

Mount Barker Road, Bridgewater, SA 5155 **region** Adelaide Hills
phone (08) 8339 3422 **fax** (08) 8339 5311 **open** Mon–Fri 9.30–5, weekends 10–5
winemaker Brian Croser **production** 50 000 **est.** 1986
product range ($10–19 CD) 3 Districts Sauvignon Blanc, Chardonnay, Sparkling Riesling Brut, Sharefarmers Botrytis Semillon, Millstone Shiraz, Sharefarmers Red Blend (Malbec, Cabernet Sauvignon, Merlot, Cabernet Franc).
summary The second label of Petaluma, which consistently provides wines most makers would love to have as their top label. The fruit sources are diverse, with the majority of the sauvignon blanc and chardonnay coming from Petaluma-owned or managed vineyards; the Shiraz is made from purchased grapes.

Bridgewater Mill Sauvignon Blanc

YYYY 2001 Light green-yellow; a soft, ripe bouquet with the fruit aromas ranging from gooseberry to tropical is followed by a palate which is rather less exotic than the bouquet, but with plenty of flavour in an early-drinking style. **rating: 88**

best drinking 2001–2002 **best vintages** '92, '94, '95, '00, '01 **drink with** Mousseline of scallops • $19

brinalon ★★★★

18 Paringa Road, Red Hill South, Vic 3937 **region** Mornington Peninsula
phone (03) 5989 2105 **fax** (03) 5989 3159 **open** Weekends and public holidays 11–5, or by appointment
winemaker David Coy **production** 1400 **est.** 1995
product range ($17–24 CD) Sauvignon Blanc, Chardonnay, Pinot Noir, Shiraz.
summary In 1992 Jeff and Robin Seager selected a property at Red Hill South with the specific intention of establishing a vineyard. It nestles on the side of a valley, with the vines planted on a north-facing slope running down to a small creek, which provides a natural dam site. A little under 4 hectares of vines were planted in 1995 (pinot noir 1.7 hectares, chardonnay one hectare, shiraz 0.7 hectares and sauvignon blanc 0.4 hectares); the Brinalon wines are made entirely from estate-grown grapes. Currently all wines are sold by mail order and through the cellar door; there is the possibility of limited retail distribution down the track. At the time of going to print, Brinalon was being offered for sale.

Brinalon Chardonnay

YYYY 2000 Light to medium yellow-green; a clean, quite aromatic bouquet with a mix of citrus and citrus blossom is logically reflected in the grapefruit and citrus flavours of the palate; the wine has gobbled up the French oak in which it spent 12 months, and also belies its 13.8° alcohol. **rating: 88**

best drinking 2002–2005 **best vintages** NA **drink with** Cold smoked salmon • $20

Brinalon Pinot Noir

YYYYY 2000 Deep red-purple; the bouquet has a complex array of dark plum fruit plus hints of forest and spice; the palate is very attractive and focussed, with masses of depth and power to the plummy fruit. Yet another tribute to the great pinot vintage of 2000. **rating: 94**

best drinking 2002–2006 **best vintages** '00 **drink with** Squab • $24

brindabella hills ★★★★☆

Woodgrove Close via Hall, ACT 2618 **region** Canberra District
phone (02) 6230 2583 **fax** (02) 6230 2023 **open** Weekends, public holidays 10–5
winemaker Dr Roger Harris **production** 2500 **est.** 1989
product range ($18–20 CD) Riesling, Sauvignon Blanc Semillon, Chardonnay, Reserve Chardonnay, Shiraz, Tumbarumba Merlot, Cabernets, Cabernet, Reserve Cabernet.
summary Distinguished research scientist Dr Roger Harris presides over Brindabella Hills, which increasingly relies on estate-produced grapes, with small plantings of cabernet sauvignon, cabernet franc, merlot, shiraz, chardonnay, sauvignon blanc, semillon and riesling. Wine quality has been consistently impressive. Limited retail distribution in NSW and the ACT.

Brindabella Hills Riesling

YYYYY 2001 Light green-yellow; a fresh, clean, lively and fragrant bouquet has tropical/lime fruit, the promise being fully realised on the delicious palate, at once delicate yet intense, with lingering lime juice flavours. **rating: 95**

best drinking 2002–2008 **best vintages** '90, '92, '93, '95, '01 **drink with** Grilled fish • $18

Brindabella Hills Sauvignon Blanc Semillon

YYYYY 2001 Light to medium yellow-green; quite complex, with a typical Brindabella interplay between herb and riper fruit aromas; the light but intense palate shows Semillon to the fore, underwriting the development potential of the wine. **rating: 90**

best drinking 2002–2005 **best vintages** '01 **drink with** Gravlax • $18

Brindabella Hills Chardonnay

YYYY 2001 Glowing yellow-green; the complex and quite rich bouquet offers tangy fruit and nicely judged oak, the palate opening in similar fashion, but the fruit sweetness seems to diminish the total impact.**rating: 86**

best drinking 2002–2004 **best vintages** NA **drink with** Pan-fried veal • $20

Brindabella Hills Shiraz Cabernet

YYYY 2000 Medium red-purple; a mix of spicy, cherry, earthy, savoury aromas flow into a quite smooth, medium-bodied palate with a mix of cherry, red berry and plum fruit. A blend of Canberra and Hilltops material, with Shiraz dominant. **rating: 87**

best drinking 2004–2010 **best vintages** NA **drink with** Beef stroganoff • $8

britannia creek wines NR

75 Britannia Creek Road, Wesburn, Vic 3799 **region** Yarra Valley
phone (03) 5780 1426 **fax** (03) 5780 1426 **open** Weekends 10–6
winemaker Charlie Brydon **production** 1200 **est.** 1982
product range ($12–18 CD) Sauvignon Blanc, Semillon, Cabernets.
summary The wines (from Britannia Creek Wines) are made under the Britannia Falls label from 4 hectares of estate-grown grapes. A range of vintages are available from the cellar door, with some interesting, full-flavoured Semillon.

broadview estate NR

Rowbottoms Road, Granton, Tas 7030 **region** Southern Tasmania
phone (03) 6263 6882 **fax** (03) 6263 6840 **open** Tues–Sun 10–5
winemaker Andrew Hood (Contract) **production** 250 **est.** 1996
product range ($16–18 CD) Stoney Ridge Riesling, Erin Vale Chardonnay.
summary David and Kaye O'Neil planted half a hectare of chardonnay and a quarter of a hectare each of riesling and pinot noir in the spring of 1996, producing limited quantities of Riesling and Chardonnay.

broke estate/ryan family wines ★★★★

Wollombi Road, Broke, NSW 2330 **region** Lower Hunter Valley
phone (02) 9664 3000 **fax** (02) 9665 3303 **open** Weekends and public holidays 10–5 or by appointment
winemaker Matthew Ryan **production** 18 000 **est.** 1988
product range ($13–38 ML) Broke Estate is the premium label, with Semillon, Chardonnay, Sparkling Cabernets, Lacrima Angelorum (sweet white), Cabernet Sauvignon; the second label is Ryan Free Run Chardonnay and Single Vineyard Cabernets.
summary With a high-profile consultant viticulturist (Dr Richard Smart) achieving some spectacular early results, Broke Estate has seldom been far from the headlines. It has taken full advantage of the 2000 and 2001 vintages.

Broke Estate Semillon

YYYY 2001 Pale straw-green; a delicate bouquet with flint, mineral and lime is mirrored in the delicate, clean, fresh and well-balanced palate. **rating: 88**

best drinking 2003–2008 **best vintages** NA **drink with** Caesar salad • $22

Broke Estate Chardonnay

YYYY 2000 Light green-yellow; the bouquet has some errant, plastic-like aromas, notwithstanding the natural cork; after this thoroughly unpropitious start, the palate is fine, harmonious and well balanced, with melon and cashew fruit neatly balanced against quality French oak. Were it not for the uncertainty of the bouquet, would have rated even higher points. **rating: 89**

best drinking 2002–2006 **best vintages** '91, '93, '94 **drink with** Creamy pasta • $25

Broke Estate Lacrima Angelorum

YYYY 2000 Full golden-yellow; mead and honey aromas and flavours come through on a quite intense late-harvest wine, with a long palate and good acidity. **rating: 88**

best drinking 2001–2003 **best vintages** NA **drink with** Pistachio icecream • $38

brokenwood ★★★★★

McDonalds Road, Pokolbin, NSW 2320 **region** Lower Hunter Valley
phone (02) 4998 7559 **fax** (02) 4998 7893 **open** 7 days 10–5
winemaker Iain Riggs **production** 70 000 **est.** 1970
product range ($10–90 CD) Semillon, Cricket Pitch Sauvignon Blanc Semillon, ILR Reserve Semillon, Verdelho, Chardonnay, Graveyard Chardonnay, Harlequin White, Jelka Riesling (dessert), Cricket Pitch

Red, Harlequin Red, Pinot Noir, Shiraz (regional blend and Hunter Dry Red), Rayner Vineyard Shiraz, Mistress Block Shiraz, Graveyard Shiraz, Cabernet Sauvignon Merlot.

summary Deservedly fashionable winery producing consistently excellent wines. Cricket Pitch Sauvignon Blanc Semillon has an especially strong following, as has Cabernet Sauvignon; the Graveyard Shiraz is one of the best Hunter reds available today, the unwooded Semillon a modern classic. In 1997 the winery acquired a controlling interest in Seville Estate (Yarra Valley); it has also been involved in the establishment of substantial vineyards in Cowra. National distribution in Australia; exports to the US, the UK, Canada and Sweden.

Brokenwood Semillon

▼▼▼▼▼ 2001 Bright mineral, grass and herb aromas expand in the mouth, with gently sweet fruit on the mid-palate providing exemplary balance right through to the lingering finish. **rating:** 94

best drinking 2001–2006 **best vintages** '85, '86, '89, '92, '94, '95, '96, '97, '98, '99, '00, '01 **drink with** Balmain bugs • $17

Brokenwood ILR Reserve Semillon

▼▼▼▼▼ 1996 Complex, rich toasty overtones to lemony fruit on the bouquet, then a palate with lovely sweet lemony fruit allied with toast, the freshness sustained by the last vestiges of CO_2. **rating:** 96

best drinking 2001–2006 **best vintages** '94, '96 **drink with** Veal saltimbocca • $35

Brokenwood Cricket Pitch Sauvignon Blanc Semillon

▼▼▼▼ 2001 Light to medium green-yellow; a clean, fresh bouquet with gentle grass and lemon aromas is followed by a clean, firm and crisp palate with grassy flavours and fair length, the oak contributing more to texture than to flavour. **rating:** 87

best drinking 2001–2002 **best vintages** NA **drink with** All seafood and white meat dishes • $14.50

Brokenwood Graveyard Shiraz

▼▼▼▼▼ 2000 Full red-purple; a complex array of dark fruits, prune and charry oak on the bouquet lead into a powerful wine, flooded with dark berry fruit, and lots of extract and depth. Built for the long haul. **rating:** 94

▼▼▼▼▼ 1999 Medium to full red-purple; oak is quite assertive on the complex bouquet, but the wine comes together on the palate which, while trenchantly demanding patience, has masses of earthy black fruit supported by excellent tannin management. **rating:** 96

best drinking 2007–2027 **best vintages** '85, '86, '87, '88, '89, '91, '93, '94, '95, '98, '99, '00 **drink with** Chargrilled rump • $90

broke's promise wines ★★★☆

725 Milbrodale Road, Broke, NSW 2330 **region** Lower Hunter Valley
phone (02) 6579 1165 **fax** (02) 9438 4985 **open** By appointment
winemaker Andrew Margan (Contract) **production** 2500 **est.** 1996
product range ($16–19 R) Hunter Valley Semillon, Jesse's Eclipse Chardonnay, Hunter Valley Shiraz, Hunter Valley Reserve Shiraz.
summary Jane Marquard and Dennis Karp (and their young children) have established Broke's Promise on the banks of the Wollombi Brook, adjacent to the Yengo National Park. They have followed tradition in planting shiraz, chardonnay and semillon, and broken with it by planting barbera and olive trees – the latter two inspired by a long stay in Italy.

Broke's Promise Semillon

▼▼▼▽ 2001 Medium yellow-green, quite developed; the bouquet is soft and broad, with some ripe herb aromas, the palate with full flavour, already developed. **rating:** 84

best drinking 2002–2003 **best vintages** NA **drink with** Stuffed crab claw • $16

brook eden vineyard NR

Adams Road, Lebrina, Tas 7254 **region** Northern Tasmania
phone (03) 6395 6244 **fax** (03) 6395 6211 **open** 7 days 10–5
winemaker Mike Fogarty (Contract) **production** 600 **est.** 1988
product range ($17–28 CD) Riesling, Unwooded Chardonnay, Tribute Chardonnay, Pinot Noir Reserve, Cabernet Sauvignon.

summary Sheila and the late Jan Bezemer established a 2.2-hectare vineyard on the 60-hectare Angus beef property which they purchased in 1987. The vineyard site is beautiful, with viticultural advice from the noted Fred Peacock.

Brook Eden Vineyard Riesling

▼▼▼▼ **2001** Light straw-yellow, very pale; as with many of the 2001 Rieslings from Tasmania, the aromatics are subdued, and while the structure of the palate is good, the wine needs more fruit intensity to score gold medal points. Good acidity is a distinct plus. **rating:** 88

best drinking 2002–2005 **best vintages** NA **drink with** Asparagus • $18

Brook Eden Vineyard Pinot Noir

▼▼▼▼ **2000** Medium to full red-purple; the bouquet is not particularly fragrant, and there is the subliminal suggestion of some aldehydes; the palate, in contrast, is mouthfilling and very persistent, with flavours verging on chocolate. A thoroughly controversial wine which split opinions at the Tasmanian Wines Show 2002. **rating:** 87

best drinking 2002–2006 **best vintages** NA **drink with** Saddle of hare • $28

🐌 brookhampton estate NR

South West Highway, Donnybrook, WA 6239 **region** Geographe
phone (08) 9226 4100 **fax** (08) 9226 4110 **open** Not
winemaker Contract **production** 1200 **est.** 1998
product range ($18–22 ML) Semillon Sauvignon Blanc, Chardonnay, Shiraz, Cabernet Merlot.
summary Brookhampton Estate, situated 3 kilometres south of Donnybrook, has wasted no time since its establishment in 1998. One hundred and twelve hectares of vines have been established, with three fashionable red varietals to the fore: cabernet sauvignon (34 hectares), shiraz (25 hectares) and merlot (17 hectares). One hectare of tempranillo and 3 hectares of grenache can safely be classed as experimental. The three white varieties planted are chardonnay, sauvignon blanc and semillon. The first contract-made vintage was in 2001, understandably in small quantities given the youth of the vineyard.

brookland valley ★★★★☆

Caves Road, Wilyabrup, WA 6284 **region** Margaret River
phone (08) 9755 6250 **fax** (08) 9755 6214 **open** 7 days 10–5
winemaker Larry Cherubino, Malcolm Jones **production** 60 000 **est.** 1984
product range ($15.99–36 R) Sauvignon Blanc, Chardonnay, Merlot, Cabernet Merlot; Verse 1 Semillon Sauvignon Blanc, Chardonnay, Shiraz and Cabernet Sauvignon Merlot.
summary Brookland Valley has an idyllic setting, with its much enlarged Flutes Cafe one of the best winery restaurants in the Margaret River region, and its Gallery of Wine Arts, which houses an eclectic collection of wine and food-related art and wine accessories. In 1997 BRL Hardy acquired a 50 per cent interest in the venture and took responsibility for viticulture and winemaking. The move towards richer and more complex red wines evident before the takeover has continued; the white wines now also have an extra degree of finesse and elegance. Exports to the UK, Germany, Switzerland, Japan and Hong Kong.

Brookland Valley Chardonnay

▼▼▼▼ **2000** Light green-yellow; the bouquet is light, fresh and crisp, with a mix of nectarine and citrus fruit, the palate following on in a similarly light vein – perhaps a little too much so. **rating:** 85

best drinking 2001–2002 **best vintages** NA **drink with** Seafood salad • $24.15

Brookland Valley Verse 1 Chardonnay

▼▼▼▼ **2001** Light straw-green; a clean, fresh, fruit-driven bouquet with grapefruit and melon aromas, then a long, firm, citrus, melon and grapefruit-flavoured palate; the oak is largely invisible, but there is a slight grip to the finish. **rating:** 86

best drinking 2002–2004 **best vintages** '99 **drink with** Lemon chicken • $19.99

Brookland Valley Verse 1 Shiraz

▼▼▼▼ **2000** Very bright purple-red; the youthful, fresh fruit and charry oak of the bouquet are yet to integrate; the palate is firm and youthful, once again with the parts still coming together. Should settle down with more time. **rating:** 86

best drinking 2003–2008 **best vintages** NA **drink with** Beef shashlik • $20.95

Brookland Valley Merlot

▼▼▼▼▽ **1999** Medium to full red-purple; the bouquet has a complex mix of red berry and more savoury fruit, the oak is balanced. The palate is very powerful, with strong and insistent varietal fruit providing savoury/gamey characters throughout. Overall, somewhat aggressive, but with time could be a particularly interesting wine. **rating:** 92

best drinking 2005–2011 **best vintages** '99 **drink with** Devilled steak • $29.50

Brookland Valley Cabernet Sauvignon Merlot

▼▼▼▼▽ **1999** Medium to full red-purple; a quite complex bouquet of blackberry and faintly gamey fruit is followed by a very concentrated, dense and rich palate, fruit-driven, perhaps concentrated through juice run-off. **rating:** 93

best drinking 2004–2009 **best vintages** '90, '91, '92, '93, '95, '97, '99 **drink with** Chargrilled steak • $28

Brookland Valley Verse 1 Cabernet Sauvignon Merlot

▼▼▼▼▽ **2000** Medium purple-red; a clean, quite fragrant bouquet, with spicy/leafy/juicy berry fruit and just a twist of oak, is followed by an attractive palate with sweet, lively berry fruit, ripe tannins and controlled oak adding to the length. **rating:** 92

best drinking 2004–2009 **best vintages** '98, '00 **drink with** Pasta • $20.95

brookside vineyard   NR

5 Loaring Road, Bickley Valley, WA 6076 **region** Perth Hills
phone (08) 9291 8705 **fax** (08) 9291 5316 **open** Weekends and public holidays 11–5
winemaker Darlington Estate (Contract) **production** 450 **est.** 1984
product range ($17–20 CD) Chardonnay, Cabernet Sauvignon, Mèthode Champenoise.
summary Brookside is one of the many doll's house-scale vineyard operations which dot the Perth Hills. It has a quarter of a hectare each of chardonnay and cabernet sauvignon, and basically sells the wine through a mailing list. It does, however, offer bed and breakfast accommodation at the house, which has attractive views of the Bickley Valley.

brookwood estate   ★★★☆

Treeton Road, Cowaramup, WA 6284 **region** Margaret River
phone (08) 9755 5604 **open** 7 days 10–6
winemaker Trevor Mann, Lyn Mann **production** 2500 **est.** 1999
product range ($13–24 R) Sauvignon Blanc, Semillon Sauvignon Blanc, Chenin Blanc, Shiraz, Cabernet Sauvignon.
summary Trevor and Lyn Mann began the development of their 50-hectare property in 1996, and now have 1.3 hectares each of shiraz, cabernet sauvignon, semillon, sauvignon blanc and chenin blanc planted. An on-site winery was constructed in 1999 to accommodate the first vintage. Viticultural consultants provide advice on management in the vineyard, and the Manns are in the course of establishing export markets.

Brookwood Estate Shiraz

▼▼▼▼ **2000** Dense red-purple; a rich, concentrated bouquet with black plum and dark berry fruit aromas is followed by a very concentrated and youthful palate; however, the wine is not callow or undermade, and should handsomely repay patience. **rating:** 89

best drinking 2005–2012 **best vintages** NA **drink with** Leave it in the cellar • $24

broussard's chum creek winery   NR

52 Cunninghams Road, Healesville, Vic 3777 **region** Yarra Valley
phone (03) 5962 5551 **fax** (03) 5962 5551 **open** Weekends and public holidays 10–6 or by appointment
winemaker Contract **production** 250 **est.** 1977
product range ($17 CD) Chardonnay, Pinot Noir, Cabernet Sauvignon.
summary As at February 2002, 75-year-old owner/winemaker James Broussard was seeking to lease the vineyard and winery. If he is unsuccessful, he will close the winery, and seek a buyer for the grapes. If that, too, fails, he will take out the vines, which, as he says, would be 'a bit sad after 20 years'.

brown brothers ★★★★

Snow Road, Milawa, Vic 3678 **region** King Valley
phone (03) 5720 5500 **fax** (03) 5720 5511 **open** 7 days 9–5
winemaker Terry Barnett, Wendy Cameron **production** 770 000 **est.** 1885
product range ($10–44 R) A kaleidoscopic array of varietal wines, with a cross-hatch of appellations, the broadest being Victorian (e.g. Victorian Shiraz), more specific being King Valley (e.g. NV Brut and Pinot Chardonnay) and Milawa (e.g. Noble Riesling), then the Limited Release, Family Selection (e.g. Very Old Tokay and King Valley Chardonnay) and the Family Reserve ranges. Dinning's Shiraz is a cellar door special; other wines also exclusive to the cellar door include Viognier, Tempranillo, Graciano and a range of Limited Release mainstream varietals.
summary Brown Brothers draws upon a considerable number of vineyards spread throughout a range of site climates, ranging from very warm to very cool, with the climate varying according to altitude. It is also known for the diversity of varieties with which it works; the wines always represent excellent value for money. Deservedly one of the most successful family wineries in Australia. The wines are exported to over 20 countries spread throughout Europe, the UK, Asia and the Far East. Conspicuously, Brown Brothers still remains out of the US market.

Brown Brothers Limited Release King Valley Riesling

ΨΨΨΨ 1999 Bright light to medium yellow-green, excellent for the age of the wine. Clean, ripe fruit with tropical nuances on the bouquet, then a palate with good length and weight, braced by firm, minerally acidity on the finish. The slightly disparate characters of the bouquet and palate in fact work quite well. **rating:** 88

best drinking 2002–2005 **best vintages** NA **drink with** Avocado salad • $26.50

Brown Brothers Gewürztraminer

ΨΨΨΨ 2000 Light to medium green-yellow; the bouquet offers light but clear spice and lychee varietal fruit, the palate backing off the pace a bit, but still with spicy characters, and, mercifully not loaded with residual sugar on the finish. **rating:** 86

best drinking 2001–2002 **best vintages** '98 **drink with** Asian food • $17

Brown Brothers Victorian Semillon

ΨΨΨΫ 1998 Medium to full yellow-green; as expected, there is some bottle development in the lightly browned toast, but the varietal fruit is still quite herbal. The palate has a mix of gentle citrus and herb flavours, with a touch of slightly fuzzy vanilla oak. At the price there is no cause for complaint. **rating:** 84

best drinking 2002–2004 **best vintages** NA **drink with** KFC • $15

Brown Brothers Victorian Chardonnay

ΨΨΨΨ 2000 Light green-yellow; the bouquet is quite fragrant and floral, with peach blossom aromas and minimal oak. A light, well-balanced palate with stone fruit flavours offers modest cellaring potential.**rating:** 85

best drinking 2001–2003 **best vintages** NA **drink with** Poached chicken • $18.60

Brown Brothers NV Pinot Chardonnay Brut

ΨΨΨΨ NV Light to medium yellow-green; a spotlessly clean, fresh and flowery bouquet has a palate to match; ultra-user-friendly, not complex, but with delicious flavours. **rating:** 87

best drinking 2001–2002 **best vintages** NA **drink with** Aperitif • $17.80

Brown Brothers Limited Release King Valley Sparkling Shiraz

ΨΨΨΨ 1998 Deep red-purple; strong blackberry/spice/anise fruit aromas and flavours lead into a well-balanced palate, with a pleasingly dry finish. **rating:** 87

best drinking 2002–2010 **best vintages** NA **drink with** Meat-based antipasto • $24.30

Brown Brothers Noble Riesling

ΨΨΨΨΫ 1998 Golden bronze; spicy, brulee overtones to peach/tropical fruit mark the bouquet, and similar biscuity/brulée characters appear on the complex palate; altogether in its own idiom, but showing good length and acidity. **rating:** 92

best drinking 2002–2005 **best vintages** '92, '94, '96, '98 **drink with** Sticky date pudding • $26

Brown Brothers Victorian Shiraz

▼▼▼▼ **1999** Medium to full red-purple; the bouquet offers some savoury complexity, with a suspicion of green/canopy characters lurking in the background. The palate is a replay of the bouquet, opening with gently sweet fruit, then moving to a savoury/foresty finish. **rating: 85**

best drinking 2003–2007 **best vintages** '91, '92, '93, '94, '98 **drink with** Braised beef Chinese-style • $19

Brown Brothers Milawa Shiraz Mondeuse Cabernet

▼▼▼▼▽ **1996** Medium red-purple; a clean and smooth bouquet with gentle fruit and oak provides a complex and savoury whole; the palate is nicely tempered and balanced, with dark fruits supported by persistent but fine tannins. **rating: 91**

best drinking 2001–2006 **best vintages** '96 **drink with** Shepherd's pie • $29.10

Brown Brothers Nebbiolo

▼▼▼▼ **1999** Light to medium red, showing a marked colour shift towards brick; a strongly savoury/woodsy bouquet with spice and bracken, then a palate which opens with soft, spicy, cedary flavours, finishing with dusty, slightly furry tannins; quite varietal overall. **rating: 85**

best drinking 2002–2005 **best vintages** NA **drink with** Veal saltimbocca • $15.60

Brown Brothers Cellar Door Release Tempranillo

▼▼▼▽ **2000** Medium to full red-purple; the sweet berry fruit of the bouquet is unfortunately smothered by American oak, as is the lush, dark berry fruit of the palate. I simply do not understand why the wine should have been matured for 16 months in a mix of new American and older French oak. It would have been much more interesting to see the varietal fruit express itself. **rating: 84**

best drinking 2003–2005 **best vintages** NA **drink with** Air-dried Spanish ham • $18.80

Brown Brothers Milawa Graciano

▼▼▼▼ **1999** Medium red-purple; aromas of blackcurrant, spice and earth are followed by a palate with most appealing texture and mouthfeel, with lingering berry flavours and an intriguing hint of lemon zest. Contrasts with the Tempranillo, matured in old oak, which does not interfere with the fruit. **rating: 87**

best drinking 2003–2006 **best vintages** NA **drink with** Roast kid • $18.80

Brown Brothers Victorian Merlot

▼▼▼▼ **1999** Medium red-purple; some savoury complexity adds interest to the bouquet; the palate has good texture and weight. A mix of red berry fruit and savoury overtones, supported by fine tannins, is convincing; better than the majority of Merlots at this price. **rating: 87**

best drinking 2002–2007 **best vintages** NA **drink with** Veal casserole • $18

Brown Brothers Classic Release Cabernet Sauvignon Malbec Shiraz Merlot

▼▼▼▼ **1994** Medium to full red-purple; quite complex fruit does battle with heaps of American oak on the bouquet; the oak attack diminishes on the palate, where solid, ripe mulberry and plum fruit flavours and well-balanced tannins come together with the oak. A traditional style. **rating: 88**

best drinking 2000–2009 **best vintages** NA **drink with** Beef ragout with olives • NA

Brown Brothers Family Reserve Cabernet Shiraz

▼▼▼▼ **1997** Medium red-purple; dusty/cinnamon spice oak and gentle fruit aromas are followed by a palate with redcurrant/berry fruit, soft tannins and less obvious oak. **rating: 87**

best drinking 2002–2007 **best vintages** NA **drink with** Yearling steak • $43.60

Brown Brothers Victorian Cabernet Sauvignon

▼▼▼▼ 2000 Medium red-purple, balanced blackberry, earth and small red berry aromas precede a pleasant palate with light berry fruit, light oak and gently savoury tannins. **rating: 86**

best drinking 2002–2005 **best vintages** NA **drink with** Roast beef • $18.60

Brown Brothers Very Old Tokay

▼▼▼▼ **NV** Good olive-brown colour; the varietal character is clear but not intense, in a sweet tea-leaf spectrum. That same flavour comes through on the medium-bodied palate, with gentle spirit helping to provide a cleansing finish. **rating: 88**

best drinking 2002–2003 **best vintages** NA **drink with** After coffee • $27.90

Brown Brothers Liqueur Muscat

TTTT NV Deep olive-brown; the wine shows obvious age, with luscious raisiny liqueur aromas; the palate has abundant raisin/plum pudding flavours, again showing mature characters. **rating: 88**

best drinking 2002–2003 **best vintages** NA **drink with** Nuts, dried fruits • $29.80

brown hill estate ★★★

Cnr Rosa Brook and Barrett Roads, Rosa Brook, WA 6285 **region** Margaret River
phone (08) 9757 4003 **fax** (08) 9757 4004 **open** 7 days 10–5
winemaker Nathan Bailey **production** 2000 **est.** 1995
product range ($14–16 CD) Sauvignon Blanc, Semillon Sauvignon Blanc, Desert Rosé, Shiraz, Cabernet Sauvignon.
summary The Bailey family's stated aim is to produce top-quality wines at affordable prices. This is to be achieved by uncompromising viticultural practices emphasising low yields per hectare, in conjunction with the family being involved in all stages of production, with minimum outside help. They have established 7 hectares each of shiraz and cabernet sauvignon, 4 hectares of semillon, and 2 hectares each of sauvignon blanc and merlot, and by the standards of the Margaret River, the prices are indeed affordable.

Brown Hill Estate Sauvignon Blanc

TTTY 2001 Very pale colour, with a faintly grey cast; the clean but light bouquet has flecks of mineral, the light to medium-bodied palate is clean, well enough balanced, but there is not much fruit or varietal impact. **rating: 84**

best drinking 2002–2003 **best vintages** NA **drink with** Shellfish • NA

Brown Hill Estate Semillon Sauvignon Blanc

TTTY 2001 Very pale; a crisp, minerally/grassy bouquet, then a palate with similar characters to the Sauvignon Blanc; nice mouthfeel and length, subtle oak. **rating: 84**

best drinking 2002–2004 **best vintages** NA **drink with** Summer salads • NA

browns of padthaway ★★★★

Keith Road, Padthaway, SA 5271 **region** Padthaway
phone (08) 8765 6063 **fax** (08) 8765 6083 **open** At Padthaway Estate
winemaker Contract **production** 35 000 **est.** 1993
product range ($10–24 R) Classic Diamond, Riesling, Sauvignon Blanc, Non Wooded Chardonnay, Verdelho, T-Trellis Shiraz, Ernest Shiraz, Redwood Cabernet Malbec, Myra Family Reserve Cabernet Sauvignon, Sparkling Shiraz.
summary The Brown family has for many years been the largest independent grape grower in Padthaway, a district in which most of the vineyards were established and owned by Wynns, Seppelt, Lindemans and Hardys, respectively. After a slow start, has produced some excellent wines since 1998.

Browns of Padthaway Melba Family Reserve Chardonnay

TTTT 1999 Light to medium yellow-green; lots of barrel ferment oak drives the bouquet, the palate delivering ripe melon and nectarine fruit, warming up on the finish with its alcohol of 14°. Plenty of overall presence; some might regard my points as niggardly. **rating: 89**

best drinking 2001–2002 **best vintages** NA **drink with** Roast chicken • $24

Browns of Padthaway Ernest Family Reserve Shiraz

TTTTY 1998 Deep red-purple; a complex, dark cherry and licorice bouquet is followed by a very rich, full and ripe, almost viscous, palate with spicy berry fruit and oak. While definitely at the big end of the spectrum, the wine hangs together impressively. The best under $25 wine at the 2001 Great Australian Shiraz Challenge. **rating: 93**

best drinking 2005–2015 **best vintages** '98 **drink with** Irish stew • $24.60

brush box vineyard NR

c/o 6 Grandview Parade, Mona Vale, NSW 2103 **region** Lower Hunter Valley
phone (02) 9979 4468 **fax** (02) 9999 5303 **open** Not
winemaker Contract **production** 1000 **est.** 1997
product range ($13–17 CD) Verdelho, Chardonnay, Cabernet Merlot.

summary Paul and Suzanne Mackay have established their 6.5-hectare Brush Box Vineyard at Broke. It is situated in a secluded part of the Fordwich Hills, with views across the Wollombi Valley to the northern perimeter of Yengo National Park. It is planted to chardonnay, verdelho, cabernet sauvignon and merlot, and so far the wine is sold by mail order only.

bullers beverford ★★★

Murray Valley Highway, Beverford, Vic 3590 **region** Swan Hill
phone (03) 5037 6305 **fax** (03) 5037 6803 **open** Mon–Sat 9–5
winemaker Richard Buller (Jnr) **production** 50 000 **est.** 1952
product range ($5.50–60 CD) Victoria Riesling, Victoria Spatlese Lexia, Semillon, Magee Semillon Chardonnay, Chenin Blanc, Sails Unwooded Chardonnay, Chardonnay, Victoria Chardonnay, Sparkling Spumante, Victoria Rosé, Shiraz, White Label Shiraz, Victoria Shiraz Grenache Mourvedre, Sails Shiraz Merlot Cabernet, Merlot, Magee Cabernet Sauvignon Shiraz, Cabernet Sauvignon; Fortifieds with Port, Tokay and Muscat.
summary Traditional wines which in the final analysis reflect both their Riverland origin and a fairly low-key approach to style in the winery. It is, however, one of the few remaining sources of reasonable quality bulk fortified wine available to the public, provided in 22-litre Valorex barrels at $6.50 per litre.

Bullers Beverford White Label Shiraz

▼▼▼▽ 1999 Medium red-purple; the bouquet has a range of predominantly earthy/spicy aromas, with notes of chocolate and hay in the background. The medium-bodied palate is clean and well-balanced, with pleasant earthy/chocolatey varietal character but not a lot of structure. **rating:** 84

best drinking 2002–2005 **best vintages** NA **drink with** Steak and kidney pie • $15

Bullers Sails Shiraz Merlot Cabernet

▼▼▼▽ 2000 Medium red-purple; soft, sweet red berry fruit on the bouquet is followed by pleasant redcurrant/raspberry fruit on the palate. If oak has been used, it is not obvious. **rating:** 83

best drinking 2002–2003 **best vintages** NA **drink with** Takeaway • $14

bullers calliope ★★★★☆

Three Chain Road, Rutherglen, Vic 3685 **region** Rutherglen
phone (02) 6032 9660 **fax** (02) 6032 8005 **open** Mon–Sat 9–5, Sun 10–5
winemaker Andrew Buller **production** 4000 **est.** 1921
product range ($14–55 CD) Limited Release Rutherglen Shiraz, Mondeuse Shiraz, Grenache Cinsaut Shiraz, Merlot Cabernet Sauvignon Cabernet Franc; Premium Black Label range and Museum Release range of old and rare material.
summary The winery rating is very much influenced by the superb releases of Museum fortified wines. Limited releases of Calliope Shiraz and Shiraz Mondeuse can also be very good. The rating is primarily for the fortified wines.

Bullers Calliope Shiraz

▼▼▼▽ 1997 Bright red-purple, very youthful. Ripe prune and milk chocolate aromas on the bouquet are the precursors of an unusual combination of ripe fruit and high acidity on the palate. Both the colour and the flavour of the wine suggest that there may have been an over-correction of acidity. Further time in bottle could be rewarded. **rating:** 83

best drinking 2004–2007 **best vintages** NA **drink with** Marinated beef • $35

Bullers Calliope Rare Liqueur Tokay

▼▼▼▼▼ NV Deep golden brown; a classic mix of sweet tea-leaf and crème brûlée aromas is followed by an outstanding palate showing the complexity which only age (and first-class base material) can bring; some nutty characters join the tea-leaf and crème brûlée of the bouquet. **rating:** 95

best drinking 2002–2003 **best vintages** NA **drink with** Strictly unnecessary, a meal in itself • NA

Bullers Calliope Rare Liqueur Muscat

▼▼▼▼▼ NV Deep brown with a touch of olive on the rim; full and deep, almost into chocolate, with intense raisined fruit; richly textured, with great structure to the raisined/plum pudding fruit flavours, and obvious rancio age. **rating:** 94

best drinking 2002–2003 **best vintages** NA **drink with** Strictly unnecessary, a meal in itself • $60

🐃 bulong estate ★★★☆

70 Summerhill Road, Yarra Junction, Vic 3797 **region** Yarra Valley
phone (03) 5967 2487 **fax** (03) 5967 2487 **open** Not
winemaker Contract **production** 500 **est.** 1994
product range ($14–24 ML) Sauvignon Blanc, Pinot Gris, Chardonnay, Pinot Noir, Merlot, Cabernets, Cabernet Franc.
summary Judy and Howard Carter purchased their 45-hectare property in 1994. They are beautifully situated, looking down into the valley below and across to the nearby ranges with Mount Donna Buang at their peak. Most of the grapes from the immaculately tended vineyard are sold, with limited quantities made for the Bulong Estate label – made, as the tasting notes indicate, with considerable skill.

Bulong Estate Sauvignon Blanc

▼▼▼▽ **2001** Light green-yellow; a clean, fresh, crisp but light bouquet – what is there is correct. Similarly, light grassy fruit on the palate does not have much weight, but has been immaculately handled in the winery. **rating:** 84

best drinking 2002–2003 **best vintages** NA **drink with** Fresh seafood • $14

Bulong Estate Cabernet Franc

▼▼▼▼ **2000** Medium purple-red; the bouquet is clean and fresh, with light raspberry fruit and just a hint of oak. The smooth palate has a mix of currant, raspberry and mint fruit, with minimal tannins. A polished wine, as well made as the Sauvignon Blanc. **rating:** 86

best drinking 2002–2004 **best vintages** NA **drink with** Roast veal • $24

bungawarra NR

Bents Road, Ballandean, Qld 4382 **region** Granite Belt
phone (07) 4684 1128 **fax** (07) 4684 1128 **open** 7 days 10.30–4.30
winemaker Bruce Humphery-Smith, Jeff Harden **production** 1000 **est.** 1975
product range ($10–17 CD) Traminer, Thomas Semillon, Foundation Chardonnay, Reserve Chardonnay, Bliss, Festival Red, Shiraz, Cabernet Sauvignon, Liquid Amber, Paragon Liqueur, Liqueur Muscat.
summary Now owned by Jeff Harden. It draws upon 5 hectares of mature vineyards which over the years have shown themselves capable of producing red wines of considerable character.

🐃 bunnamagoo estate ★★★☆

Bunnamagoo, Rockley, NSW 2795 **region** Southern New South Wales Zone
phone (02) 6377 5216 **fax** (02) 6377 5231 **open** Not
winemaker Jon Reynolds (Contract) **production** 2500 **est.** 1995
product range ($19–30 ML) Chardonnay, Cabernet Sauvignon.
summary Bunnamagoo Estate (on one of the first land grants in the region) is situated near the historic town of Rockley, itself equidistant from Bathurst and Oberon. Here a 7-hectare vineyard planted to chardonnay, merlot and cabernet sauvignon has been established by Paspaley Pearls, a famous name in the pearl industry. The wines are contract-made under the direction of Jon Reynolds at the Cabonne Winery in Orange, and are sold by mail order and email. As at April 2002, three vintages of Chardonnay and two vintages of Cabernet Sauvignon were on sale. Interestingly, these seemed to be priced according to the quality of the vintage (and hence the quality of the wine).

Bunnamagoo Estate Chardonnay

▼▼▼▼ **2000** Light to medium yellow-green; the clean, fresh bouquet has a mix of citrus, subtle oak, oak spice and smoky malolactic fermentation influences. The palate has excellent mouthfeel, supple and smooth, with lively citrus fruit running through to the finish. **rating:** 88
▼▼▼▼▽ **1999** Medium yellow-green; quite pronounced creamy malolactic fermentation and toasty barrel ferment characters accompany ripe fig and melon fruit on the bouquet. The palate has good length and intensity, with subtle oak and strong malolactic influences. Like the 2000 vintage, 13.4° alcohol. **rating:** 90

best drinking 2002–2005 **best vintages** '99 **drink with** Steamed abalone • $24.10

Bunnamagoo Estate Cabernet Sauvignon

▼▼▼▼ **2000** Light to medium red-purple; the wine spent 18 months in a mix of new and older French oak barriques, and the spicy oak influence is very evident on the bouquet. The palate shows the cool climate (and of course oak), with a range of savoury/spicy/leathery/foresty characters. For the record, 12.5° alcohol. **rating:** 86

▼▼▼▼ **1999** Medium red-purple; the rich and complex bouquet has dark berry fruit and well-integrated but powerful oak; despite the lower alcohol (12.2°), it has more dark berry fruit to the palate than the 2000; persistent but quite ripe tannins to close. 1999 was obviously a good vintage. **rating: 89**

best drinking 2003–2008 **best vintages** NA **drink with** Herbed rack of lamb • $27.50

burge family winemakers ★★★★

Barossa Way, Lyndoch, SA 5351 **region** Barossa Valley
phone (08) 8524 4644 **fax** (08) 8524 4444 **open** 7 days 10–5
winemaker Rick Burge **production** 2500 **est.** 1928
product range ($16–34 CD) Olive Hill Semillon, Olive Hill Shiraz Mourvedre Grenache, Clochmerle (Grenache Cabernet), Garnacha Old Vine Grenache, A Nice Red, Draycott Shiraz.
summary Rick Burge came back to the family winery after a number of years successfully running St Leonards; there was much work to be done, but he has achieved much, using the base of very good fortified wines and markedly improving table wine quality, with Draycott Shiraz (both standard and the brilliant Reserve) leading the way. The wines are exported to the US, Canada, the UK, Germany, New Zealand, Hong Kong, Singapore and Japan.

Burge Family Draycott Shiraz

▼▼▼▼▽ **2000** Medium to full red-purple; typical, super-ripe cherry, plum and prune fruit, then a palate flooded with sweet, ripe fruit; despite its 14.5°, not obviously alcoholic, nor hot or extractive. **rating: 90**

best drinking 2004–2008 **best vintages** '88, '91, '94, '95, '98, '99, '00 **drink with** Wild duck, or failing that, domestic duck • $35

Burge Family Olive Hill Shiraz Mourvedre Grenache

▼▼▼▼ **2000** Medium red-purple; a hyper-fragrant bouquet with slightly jammy fruit which seems to flow from the Grenache, even though this comprises only 21 per cent of the blend. The palate has a complex web of ripe fruit flavours, licorice and spice, all in slightly jammy, idiosyncratic style. **rating: 86**

best drinking 2003–2008 **best vintages** NA **drink with** Game • $35

Burge Family A Nice Red

▼▼▼▼ **2000** Medium purple-red; ripe, redcurrant and raspberry fruit aromas, then a sweet, ripe, supple palate with soft fruit. The front label shows the wine being from Lane Block Ridge Creek Station Run Classic Reserve and the Hill of Goannas; the back label (printed partially upside down) suggests that the wine comes from Australia's premier regions. Rick Burge is having not only a friendly riposte at those who come to the cellar door asking for 'a nice red' but also a not-so-gentle jab at the nonsense labels fabricated for export wines. **rating: 86**

best drinking 2002–2007 **best vintages** NA **drink with** A nice hamburger • $19.80

Burge Family Garnacha Old Vine Grenache

▼▼▼▼▽ **2000** Medium red-purple; the bouquet has attractive ripe, spicy but not jammy varietal aromas, marking a wine of some distinction. The palate is riper and more luscious than the bouquet, veering towards the jammy end of the spectrum; for lovers of big-framed Grenache from the Barossa. **rating: 90**

best drinking 2003–2008 **best vintages** '00 **drink with** Game pie • $35

Burge Family Clochemerle (Grenache Cabernet)

▼▼▼▼ **2000** Medium red-purple; the bouquet has a mix of savoury/spicy and ripe berry aromas; the palate has ripples of spice, ripe fruit and savoury characters through the middle, moving back to particularly sweet fruit on the finish. **rating: 87**

best drinking 2003–2008 **best vintages** NA **drink with** Irish stew • $15.80

burnbrae ★★★★

Hill End Road, Erudgere via Mudgee, NSW 2850 **region** Mudgee
phone (02) 6373 3504 **fax** (02) 6373 3601 **open** Wed–Mon 9–5
winemaker Alan Cox **production** NFP **est.** 1976
product range ($10–18 CD) Sauvignon Blanc, Chardonnay, Pinot Noir, Shiraz, Malbec, Cabernet Shiraz, Cabernet Sauvignon, Vintage Port, Liqueur Muscat.
summary The founding Mace family sold Burnbrae to Alan Cox in 1996. It continues as an estate-based operation with 23 hectares of vineyards. Since that time the Burnbrae wines have gone from strength to

strength, improving beyond all recognition between 1996 and 2001, attesting to the value of the old, dry-grown vines and the accumulation of winemaking experience by Alan Cox. Given the difficult vintages, the quality of the red wines from 1999 and 2000 is quite remarkable.

Burnbrae Shiraz

YYYY 2000 Medium red-purple; nicely balanced fresh cherry fruit and oak on the bouquet flow into a well-made wine, which is well-balanced, and not over-extracted, paying substantial dividends in a difficult vintage. **rating: 89**

YYYY 1999 Medium to full red-purple; rich, dark plum aromas on the bouquet flow into a rich and ripe palate with dark berry and plum flavours, soft tannins and subtle oak. **rating: 89**

best drinking 2003–2008 **best vintages** NA **drink with** Rare roast beef • NA

Burnbrae Cabernet Shiraz

YYYY 1999 Medium to full red-purple; lifted, spicy, savoury berry aromas are repeated on the palate, with slightly dusty tannins to close. **rating: 89**

best drinking 2003–2007 **best vintages** NA **drink with** Lamb shanks • NA

Burnbrae Cabernet Sauvignon

YYYY 2000 Medium red-purple; the bouquet is clean and firm, with oak evident but not oppressive. The light to medium-bodied palate has nicely balanced red berry and savoury characters, with the same positive oak contribution as is evident on the bouquet. **rating: 88**

YYYYY 1999 Dense red-purple; clean berry and chocolate fruit is still slightly locked up on the bouquet, with corresponding dynamics on the palate, which has masses of fruit but dips towards the finish before the tannins take over. All of this will undoubtedly resolve with time. Gold medal Mudgee Wine Show 2001. **rating: 93**

YYYY 1997 Medium to full red-purple; the sweet, ripe, cassis bouquet has a touch of confection about it; the palate is similarly ripe and sweet, with chewy/toffee characters, which are not the least bit unpleasant. Simply less classical and conventional than the '99 vintage. **rating: 86**

best drinking 2004–2010 **best vintages** '99 **drink with** Braised leg of lamb • NA

burramurra ★★★☆

Barwood Park, Nagambie, Vic 3608 **region** Goulburn Valley
phone (03) 5794 2181 **fax** (03) 5794 2755 **open** Most weekends by appointment
winemaker Mitchelton (Contract) **production** 1000 **est.** 1988
product range ($18 R) Cabernet Merlot.
summary Burramurra is the relatively low-profile vineyard operation of the Honourable Pat McNamara. Most of the grapes are sold to Mitchelton; a small amount is contract-made for the Burramurra label. Glowing reviews in the US have led to a brisk export business with that country and to the selection of Burramurra by various international airlines.

burrundulla NR

Sydney Road, Mudgee, NSW 2850 **region** Mudgee
phone (02) 6372 1620 **fax** (02) 6372 4058 **open** Not
winemaker Contract **production** NA **est.** 1996
product range NA
summary A very substantial venture but one which is still in its infancy; the Cox family (Chris, Michael and Ted) are in the course of establishing 54 hectares of vineyards planted to chardonnay, shiraz and cabernet sauvignon.

calais estate ★★★

Palmers Lane, Pokolbin, NSW 2320 **region** Lower Hunter Valley
phone (02) 4998 7654 **fax** (02) 4998 7813 **open** 7 days 9–5
winemaker Adrian Sheridan **production** 11 000 **est.** 1987
product range ($14.50–40 CD) Semillon, Viognier, Shiraz, Chambourcin.
summary Richard and Susan Bradley purchased the substantial Calais Estate winery in April 2000. Long-serving winemaker Adrian Sheridan continues his role, and the estate offers a wide range of facilities for visitors, ranging from private function rooms to picnic spots to an undercover outdoor entertaining area.

cambewarra estate ★★★☆

520 Illaroo Road, Cambewarra, NSW 2540 **region** Shoalhaven
phone (02) 4446 0170 **fax** (02) 4446 0170 **open** Thurs–Sun 10–5 and public holidays falling on a Monday
winemaker Tamburlaine (Contract) **production** 3500 **est.** 1991
product range ($15.50–36 CD) Verdelho, Unwooded Chardonnay, Wooded Chardonnay, Louise Botrytis Chardonnay, Sparkling Reserve Chambourcin, Reserve Pettillance Noir (sparkling Chambourcin), Petit Rouge, Chambourcin, Cabernet Sauvignon, Vintage Port.
summary Geoffrey and Louise Cole founded Cambewarra Estate near the Shoalhaven River on the central southern coast of NSW, with contract winemaking competently carried out (a considerable distance away) at Tamburlaine Winery in the Hunter Valley. Cambewarra continues to produce attractive wines which have had significant success in wine shows.

Cambewarra Estate Reserve Pettillance Noir

▼▼▼▼ **1998** Medium to full red-purple; a complex bouquet with a mix of biscuit, marmite, chocolate and vanilla, then a palate which is mercifully quite dry and balanced, with chocolate and dried plum fruit to the fore, and vanilla American oak present but not too aggressive. The strange name in fact means sparkling Chambourcin. **rating: 85**

best drinking 2002–2005 **best vintages** NA **drink with** Pâté, terrine, rillette • NA

Cambewarra Estate Louise Botrytis Chardonnay

▼▼▼▼ **NV** Medium to full yellow-green; the soft bouquet has gentle peach and apricot aromas, the palate similarly showing gently sweet peachy fruit; unoaked, and a little simple. One is left to wonder about the non vintage status; perhaps botrytis is a frequent visitor in the vineyards. **rating: 84**

best drinking 2002–2003 **best vintages** NA **drink with** Fruit tart • $22

campbells ★★★★

Murray Valley Highway, Rutherglen, Vic 3685 **region** Rutherglen
phone (02) 6032 9458 **fax** (02) 6032 9870 **open** Mon–Sat 9–5, Sun 10–5
winemaker Colin Campbell **production** 60 000 **est.** 1870
product range ($9–89 CD) Riesling, Gewürztraminer, Semillon, Chardonnay Semillon, Cellar White, Pedro Ximinez, Trebbiano, Limited Release Chardonnay, Chardonnay, Autumn Harvest, Bobbie Burns Shiraz, Cellar Red, The Barkly Durif, Shiraz Durif Cabernet, Ruby Cabernet, Cabernets, Cabernet Sauvignon, Rutherglen Tokay, Liquid Gold Tokay, Isabella Tokay, Rutherglen Muscat, Merchant Prince Muscat, Classic Muscat, Ports.
summary A wide range of table and fortified wines of ascending quality and price, which are always honest; as so often happens in this part of the world, the fortified wines are the best, with the extremely elegant Isabella Tokay and Merchant Prince Muscat at the top of the tree. For all that, the table wines are impressive in a full-bodied style; the winery rating is something of a compromise between that for the fortified wines and for the table wines. A feature of the cellar door is an extensive range of back vintage releases of small parcels of wine not available through any other outlet. National distribution through Red + White; exports to the UK, the US and Canada.

Campbells Semillon

▼▼▼▼ **2000** Light to medium green-yellow; the clean bouquet offers a mix of herb, spice, lemon and citrus, the palate with good early to middle flavour, but shortening on the finish. **rating: 84**

best drinking 2002–2005 **best vintages** NA **drink with** Yabbies • $15.80

Campbells Trebbiano

▼▼▼▼ **2001** Light straw-green; dry, faintly herbal/spicy aromas are followed by a palate with the particular acidity of trebbiano, almost making a silk purse from a sow's ear. Used to be sold under the Chablis label, and, if nothing else, is long-lived. **rating: 84**

best drinking 2002–2007 **best vintages** NA **drink with** Antipasto • $15.95

Campbells Bobbie Burns Shiraz

▼▼▼▼ **1999** Medium to full red-purple; the bouquet is solid, with savoury/earthy overtones to the plum and berry fruit, the oak subservient to the fruit. The mouthfilling palate with savoury/chocolatey/plummy/berry fruit is relatively soft despite its size, the alcohol (14.5°) creeping through on the finish. **rating: 87**

best drinking 2004–2009 **best vintages** '86, '88, '90, '91, '92, '94, '96, '98 **drink with** Rich game dishes • $21

Campbells The Barkly Durif

TTTT 1998 Medium to full red, with tinges of purple remaining; ripe blackberry, prune and plum aromas lead into a luscious and rich palate, with prune, chocolate and plum flavours supported by soft tannins. A wine in its own inimitable style, driven by fruit, not oak. **rating:** 89

TTTT 1996 Medium red; the moderately intense bouquet has a complex mix of chocolate, spice, earth and savoury berry aromatics. Strong chocolate, spice and savoury dark berry fruit flavours finish with lingering tannins. Powered along with 14.9° alcohol. **rating:** 85

best drinking 2003–2008 **best vintages** '98 **drink with** Jugged hare • $38.20

Campbells Limited Release Malbec

TTTT 1998 Medium to full red-purple; very strong juicy berry malbec varietal aromas are joined by an intriguing twist of 'lemon fab' spice. An interesting wine with lots of flavour and intensity in the mouth; all in all, somewhat confrontational. **rating:** 86

best drinking 2003–2008 **best vintages** NA **drink with** Lamb casserole • $19

Campbells Limited Release Cabernets

TTTY 1998 Medium red-purple; a clean, moderately intense bouquet with earth and savoury chocolate aromas swirls out into a palate which is sweeter than the bouquet, offering blackberry and chocolate flavours, finishing with appropriate tannins. **rating:** 84

best drinking 2002–2007 **best vintages** NA **drink with** Braised beef • $20.80

Campbells Cabernet Sauvignon

TTTY 1999 Medium red-purple; a savoury, slightly earthy bouquet is followed by a light to medium-bodied palate, with austere cabernet fruit and a touch of oak to provide balancing sweetness; fine tannins. **rating:** 83

best drinking 2003–2007 **best vintages** NA **drink with** Grilled meat • $17.25

Campbells Isabella Tokay

TTTTY NV Light tawny-gold; fragrant grapey, sweet tea-leaf aromas with clean spirit; the palate is luscious with sweet juicy berry and tea-leaf flavours, finishing with good acidity and a very clean aftertaste. **rating:** 93

best drinking 2002–2003 **best vintages** NA **drink with** As fine an aperitif as it is a digestif • $89

Campbells Liquid Gold Tokay

TTTTY NV Glowing golden brown; totally delicious, sweet tea-leaf and caramel varietal aromas leap from the glass, with the flavour precisely tracking the bouquet. Clean spirit; sweet but not the least bit cloying. **rating:** 91

best drinking 2002–2003 **best vintages** NA **drink with** Cake and coffee • $34.60

Campbells Rutherglen Tokay (375 ml)

TTTTT NV Bright golden brown; lovely young cold tea, tea-leaf varietal aromas flowing without a break into the palate, where the spirit is harmonious and does not threaten the wonderful tokay flavour. **rating:** 94

best drinking 2002–2003 **best vintages** NA **drink with** As fine an aperitif as it is a digestif • $16.60

Campbells Merchant Prince Muscat

TTTTT NV Light to medium brown; intense but fragrant spice and raisin aromas with clean spirit. The palate is remarkably fresh and light given the age of the wine, with raisin, spice, malt and toffee flavours all intermingling, followed by cleansing acidity. **rating:** 94

best drinking 2002–2003 **best vintages** NA **drink with** Coffee, high-quality biscuits • $89

Campbells Rutherglen Muscat (375 ml)

TTTTY NV Light tawny red; very youthful raisiny fruit aromas, with the spirit fractionally jumpy – quite why, I am not sure. High-toned fruit on the palate adds a haunting edge to the flavour, almost floral. Intriguing and delicious. **rating:** 90

best drinking 2002–2003 **best vintages** NA **drink with** Fruit cake • $16.60

candlebark hill ★★★★

Fordes Lane, Kyneton, Vic 3444 **region** Macedon Ranges
phone (03) 9836 2712 **fax** (03) 9836 2712 **open** By appointment
winemaker David Forster, Vincent Lakey, Llew Knight (Consultant) **production** 600 **est.** 1987
product range ($25–49 CD) Chardonnay, Pinot Noir, Cabernet Merlot, Cabernet Shiraz; Reserve Pinot Noir, Cabernet Merlot.

summary Candlebark Hill has been established by David Forster on the northern end of the Macedon Ranges. It enjoys magnificent views over the central Victorian countryside north of the Great Dividing Range. The 3.5-hectare vineyard is planted to pinot noir (1.5 hectares) together with one hectare each of chardonnay and the three main Bordeaux varieties, complete with half a hectare of shiraz and malbec.

Candlebark Hill Pinot Noir

♥♥♥♥♡ 1999 Bright red-purple, holding its hue well; a clean, cherry-accented bouquet with subtle oak swirls markedly on the attractive palate, where positive varietal character comes through in the slightly sappy but deep flavours and a finish which is still slightly firm. **rating: 90**

best drinking 2003–2008 **best vintages** '97, '99 **drink with** Roast duck • $25

Candlebark Hill Reserve Pinot Noir

♥♥♥♥♥ 1999 Has more depth to the colour than the varietal; the bouquet is distinctly more complex, with an array of tangy, savoury plum and cherry aromas. The powerful palate is even more complex, with layer upon layer of sweet plummy fruit providing excellent texture; has soaked up the new French oak in which it spent 20 months. Outstanding wine. **rating: 96**

best drinking 2002–2009 **best vintages** '99 **drink with** Rich game • $49

Candlebark Hill Shiraz

♥♥♥♥ 1999 Medium red-purple; a clean, bright and fresh bouquet with spicy, small berry fruit aromas leads into a light to medium-bodied palate, which is fractionally simple, and has emphatically gobbled up the new French and American oak in which it spent 20 months. **rating: 86**

best drinking 2004–2009 **best vintages** NA **drink with** Ravioli • $25

Candlebark Hill Cabernet Merlot

♥♥♥♥ 1999 Medium red-purple; the clean and fresh bouquet has an array of leafy, minty, berry aromas; the pleasant light to medium-bodied palate has fresh berry fruit followed by soft tannins. Here, too, the oak treatment has had relatively little obvious effect; I marginally prefer this wine to the Reserve Cabernet Merlot. **rating: 85**

best drinking 2002–2007 **best vintages** NA **drink with** Veal chop • $25

🐾 cannibal creek vineyard ★★★☆

260 Tynong North Road, Tynong North, Vic 3813 **region** Gippsland
phone (03) 5942 8380 **fax** (03) 5942 8202 **open** Weekends and public holidays 10–5
winemaker Patrick Hardiker **production** 1800 **est.** 1997
product range ($20–22 ML) Sauvignon Blanc, Gilgai Chardonnay, Chardonnay, Pinot Noir, Merlot.
summary The Hardiker family moved to Tynong North in 1988, initially only grazing beef cattle, but aware of the viticultural potential of the sandy clay loam and bleached sub-surface soils weathered from the granite foothills of Tynong North. Plantings began in 1997, using organically based cultivation methods, and by 1999 the vines were already producing grapes. The family decided to make their own wine, and a heritage shed built from locally milled timber has been converted into a winery and small cellar door facility.

Cannibal Creek Vineyard Sauvignon Blanc

♥♥♥♥ 2001 Light green-yellow; a clean, crisp, minerally/grassy bouquet is followed by a well-balanced and focussed palate; a well-made wine in every way, the downside being the low varietal fruit profile. **rating: 85**

best drinking 2001–2002 **best vintages** NA **drink with** Shellfish • $19.80

Cannibal Creek Pinot Noir

♥♥♥♥♡ 2000 Positive red-purple colour; a clean, firm bouquet with cherryish fruit and subtle oak, and a most attractive palate, with primary cherry, strawberry and plum fruit flavours, nigh on certain to develop complexity with bottle age. **rating: 90**

best drinking 2002–2006 **best vintages** '00 **drink with** Coq au vin • $22

canobolas-smith ★★★☆

Boree Lane, off Cargo Road, Lidster via Orange, NSW 2800 **region** Orange
phone (02) 6365 6113 **fax** (02) 6365 6113 **open** Weekends, public holidays 11–5
winemaker Murray Smith **production** 2000 **est.** 1986
product range ($24–30 CD) Chardonnay, Merlot, Alchemy (Cabernet blend).

summary Canobolas-Smith has established itself as one of the leading Orange district wineries with its distinctive blue wraparound labels. Much of the wine is sold from the cellar door, which is well worth a visit. Exports to the US.

canonbah bridge NR

Merryanbone Station, Warren, NSW 2824 **region** Central Western New South Wales
phone (02) 6833 9966 **fax** (02) 6833 9980 **open** Not
winemaker Simon Gilbert (Contract) **production** 3600 **est.** 1999
product range ($13–30 ML) Semillon, Semillon Sauvignon Blanc, Ram's Leap Semillon Sauvignon Blanc, Reserve Sparkling, Ram's Leap Shiraz, Reserve Shiraz, Shiraz Grenache Mourvedre.
summary If you ever wondered why the Western Plains Zone was the largest in NSW, Canonbah Bridge provides an answer. The 29-hectare vineyard has been established by Shane McLaughlin on the very large Merryanbone Station, a grazing property. If you head out of Dubbo towards Bourke, you will pass Warren, which is north-west of Dubbo. The wine is made by Simon Gilbert in his new, large winery at Mudgee, and is sold by mail order, with exports to the US.

canungra valley vineyards NR

Lamington National Park Road, Canungra Valley, Qld 4275 **region** Queensland Coastal
phone (07) 5543 4011 **fax** (07) 5543 4162 **open** 7 days 9–5
winemaker Andrew Hickinbotham, Mark Davidson (Contract) **production** NFP **est.** 1997
product range ($13.50–37.50 CD) Picnic range of White, Red, Semillon Chardonnay and Bubbles; Platypus range of Semillon Sauvignon Blanc, Chardonnay, Shiraz, Cabernet Merlot, Cabernet and Platypus Play Port; Preston Peak Cabernet Merlot; Molly's Reserve Chardonnay, Golden Gleam, Vince Peter's Muscat, Argyle Blanc de Noirs, Bernard O'Reilly Chambourcin.
summary Canungra Valley Vineyards has been established in the hinterland of the Gold Coast with a clear focus on broad-based tourism. Two hectares of vines have been established around the 19th-century homestead (relocated to the site from its original location in Warwick) but these provide only a small part of the wine offered for sale. In deference to the climate, 70 per cent of the estate planting is chambourcin, the rain and mildew-resistent hybrid, the remainder being semillon. As the product range makes perfectly obvious, all the wine being offered at this early stage has been purchased from other winemakers. On the other hand, Canungra Valley offers a great deal of natural beauty for the general tourist.

Canungra Valley Vineyards Molly's Reserve Chardonnay

▼▼▼▽ **2001** Light to medium yellow-green; the bouquet is clean, light and tending neutral, as is the palate. No regional claim or inference is made on either the front or back label. The wine is competently made, but the price seems out of all proportion. **rating: 82**

best drinking 2002–2003 **best vintages** NA **drink with** Grilled fish • $28.50

Canungra Valley Vineyards Bernard O'Reilly Chambourcin

▼▼▼▽ **2000** Medium red-purple, with the typically bright hue of the variety; the bouquet is clean, with pleasant French oak inputs along with red berry fruit; the palate is fresh and clean, the high acidity on the finish injecting a degree of pungency. The first vintage of Chambourcin from Cangungra Valley Vineyards' own plantings. Once again, a hefty price tag. **rating: 84**

best drinking 2002–2003 **best vintages** NA **drink with** Braised duck • $37.50

cape bouvard NR

Mount John Road, Mandurah, WA 6210 **region** Peel
phone (08) 9739 1360 **fax** (08) 9739 1360 **open** 7 days 10–5
winemaker Gary Grierson **production** 2000 **est.** 1990
product range ($13–20 CD) Chenin Blanc, Dry White, Tuart Shiraz, Cabernet Sauvignon, Port.
summary Doggerel poet-cum-winemaker Gary Grierson draws upon 1 hectare of estate plantings but also purchases grapes from other growers for the new Cape Bouvard label. The few wines tasted have been light but inoffensive.

cape horn vineyard NR

Echuca-Picola Road, Kanyapella, Vic 3564 **region** Goulburn Valley
phone (03) 5480 6013 **fax** (03) 5480 6013 **open** 7 days 10.30–5
winemaker John Ellis (Contract) **production** 1000 **est.** 1993

product range ($17–21 CD) Chardonnay, Sparkling Shiraz Durif, Shiraz, Durif, Cabernet Durif, Cabernet Sauvignon.

summary The unusual name comes from a bend in the Murray River which was considered by the riverboat owners of the 19th century to resemble Cape Horn, a resemblance now depicted on the wine label. The property was acquired by Echuca GP Dr Sue Harrison and her schoolteacher husband Ian in 1993. Ian Harrison set about planting 3 hectares each of chardonnay, shiraz and cabernet sauvignon, together with 1 hectare of durif: 2 hectares of marsanne followed in 1999, and 2 hectares of zinfandel in 2000. A new tasting room facility and residence on the property are under construction, and accommodation units in the vineyard are planned.

cape jaffa wines ★★★★☆

Limestone Coast Road, Cape Jaffa, SA 5276 **region** Mount Benson
phone (08) 8768 5053 **fax** (08) 8768 5040 **open** 7 days 10–5
winemaker Derek Hooper **production** 10 000 **est.** 1993
product range ($15–35 CD) Unwooded Chardonnay (McLaren Vale), Semillon Sauvignon Blanc, Sauvignon Blanc, Barrel Fermented Chardonnay (Mount Benson and Padthaway), Shiraz (McLaren Vale), Siberia Shiraz, Cabernet Sauvignon (Mount Benson), Brocks Reef Cabernet Merlot.
summary Cape Jaffa is the first of the Mount Benson wineries to come into production, albeit with most of the initial releases coming from other regions. Ultimately all of the wines will come from the substantial estate plantings of 25 hectares, which include the four major Bordeaux red varieties, shiraz, plus chardonnay, sauvignon blanc and semillon. It is a joint venture between the Hooper and Fowler families, and the winery (built of local paddock rock) has been designed to allow eventual expansion to 1000 tonnes, or 70 000 cases. Exports to the UK, the US, China and New Zealand.

Cape Jaffa Sauvignon Blanc

▼▼▼▼ **2001** Light to medium yellow-green; a moderately rich bouquet with gooseberry and touches of tropical fruit; the palate has good texture, the making techniques having successfully added to the complexity of the wine without making it ponderous. **rating:** 88

best drinking 2001–2003 **best vintages** NA **drink with** Steamed mussels • $18.95

Cape Jaffa Semillon Sauvignon Blanc

▼▼▼▼▽ **2001** Light to medium yellow-green; the bouquet is complex, successfully merging clean, new world style with echoes of White Bordeaux; the clever winemaking comes through strongly on the palate, which has good depth, concentration and style in a pleasing citrus framework. **rating:** 93

best drinking 2001–2004 **best vintages** '01 **drink with** Robe crayfish • $18.95

Cape Jaffa Brocks Reef Cabernet Merlot

▼▼▼▼▽ **2000** Medium red-purple; youthful, sweet, redcurrant/red berry aromas with a well-balanced touch of oak lead into a palate with good flavour, length and balance, the fruit ripe, but not jammy, and once again, the gentle touch of oak. **rating:** 90

best drinking 2003–2008 **best vintages** '00 **drink with** Lamb casserole • $14.95

cape mentelle ★★★★☆

Off Wallcliffe Road, Margaret River, WA 6285 **region** Margaret River
phone (08) 9757 3266 **fax** (08) 9757 3233 **open** 7 days 10–4.30
winemaker John Durham **production** 55 000 **est.** 1970
product range ($15.50–55 R) Semillon Sauvignon Blanc, Sauvignon Blanc Semillon Wallcliffe Reserve, Georgiana, Marmaduke, Chardonnay, Shiraz, Zinfandel, Trinders Vineyard Cabernet Merlot, Cabernet Sauvignon.
summary Notwithstanding ownership by Veuve Clicquot, David Hohnen remains in command of one of Australia's foremost medium-sized wineries. Exceptional marketing skills and wine of the highest quality, with the backup of New Zealand's Cloudy Bay, are a potent combination. The Chardonnay and Semillon Sauvignon Blanc are among Australia's best, the potent Shiraz usually superb, and the berry/spicy Zinfandel makes one wonder why this grape is not as widespread in Australia as it is in California. Enlarged its business by the slightly quixotic acquisition of Mountadam in September 2000. Exports to Asia and the US.

Cape Mentelle Wallcliffe Reserve Sauvignon Blanc Semillon

ŢŢŢŸ **2000** Light to medium yellow-green; the rich and complex bouquet has strong barrel-ferment oak characters which wind up for a toast and vanilla knockout punch on the palate, leaving the fruit unconscious. **rating:** 84

best drinking 2002–2003 **best vintages** NA **drink with** Sweetbreads • $20.80

Cape Mentelle Semillon Sauvignon Blanc

ŢŢŢŢŸ **2001** Light green-yellow; a vibrantly crisp and clean bouquet with lemony/grassy fruit is followed by a fresh, crisp and clean palate with well above average intensity and length. **rating:** 93

best drinking 2001–2004 **best vintages** '85, '88, '91, '93, '95, '96, '97, '98, '99, '00, '01 **drink with** Fish, Asian cuisine • $22.30

Cape Mentelle Georgiana

ŢŢŢŢ **2001** Light green-yellow; the bouquet is of light to medium intensity, offering a mix of herb, grass and gooseberry, the palate follows down the same track, with a faint whiff of reduction which will likely dissipate with age. **rating:** 86

best drinking 2001–2003 **best vintages** NA **drink with** Carpaccio of Tasmanian salmon • $15.30

Cape Mentelle Chardonnay

ŢŢŢŢŢ **2000** Charges out of the blocks, instantly proclaiming another great Margaret River Chardonnay. It has a typically ultra-complex yet elegant bouquet, showing barrel-ferment and malolactic fermentation characters with a mix of fig, melon and creamy cashew. The palate is an instant replay, intense, complex and long. **rating:** 96

best drinking 2001–2010 **best vintages** '90, '91, '92, '93, '94, '95, '96, '97, '98, '99, '00 **drink with** Veal sweetbreads • $32.20

Cape Mentelle Shiraz

ŢŢŢŢŸ **2000** Medium to full red-purple; the complex bouquet has a range of savoury, sweet leather, spice and plum aromas; the palate is very much headed towards secondary characters, supported by fine tannins. **rating:** 90

best drinking 2005–2010 **best vintages** '90, '91, '93, '94, '96, '97, '98, '99, '00 **drink with** Stir-fried Asian beef • $30.60

Cape Mentelle Zinfandel

ŢŢŢŢŸ **2000** Medium to full red-purple; the bouquet has ripe prune, licorice and chocolate aromas; the palate offers lusciously ripe and dense black fruits dipped in chocolate, with fine tannins to balance. **rating:** 92

best drinking 2004–2009 **best vintages** '91, '92, '93, '94, '95, '97, '98, '99, '00 **drink with** Rare chargrilled rump steak • $33.20

Cape Mentelle Trinders Vineyard Cabernet Merlot

ŢŢŢŢ **2000** Medium red-purple; the moderately intense bouquet has a mix of savoury/spicy/cedary aromas which yield to a quite luscious mix of dark berry and bitter chocolate flavours on the palate, with notes of cedar returning on the finish. Comprehensively the best Trinders to date. **rating:** 89

best drinking 2003–2008 **best vintages** '00 **drink with** Butterfly leg of lamb • $28.25

Cape Mentelle Cabernet Sauvignon

ŢŢŢŢ **1998** Medium red-purple; the moderately intense bouquet has a mix of savoury, earthy, cedary aromas, those cedary oak characters coming through quite clearly on the palate. There is a typical core of red berry fruit on the mid-palate, then lingering, fine tannins on the finish. Overall, an austere style, but none the worse for that. **rating:** 88

best drinking 2003–2008 **best vintages** '76, '78, '82, '83, '86, '90, '91, '93, '94, '95 **drink with** Loin of lamb • $55

capel vale ★★★★

Lot 5 Stirling Estate, Mallokup Road, Capel, WA 6271 **region** Geographe
phone (08) 9727 1986 **fax** (08) 9727 1904 **open** Cellar door 7 days 10–4, Cafe Thu–Mon 10–4
winemaker Nicole Esdaile **production** 150 000 **est.** 1979
product range ($12.50–48 ML) CV Bistro range of Sauvignon Blanc, Chenin, Unwooded Chardonnay, Pinot Noir, Shiraz, Cabernet Merlot; Capel Vale Fine Dining range of Riesling, Semillon, Sauvignon Blanc, Sauvignon Blanc Semillon, Verdelho, Chardonnay, Late Harvest, Shiraz, Merlot, Cabernet

Sauvignon; Connoisseur range of Whispering Hill Riesling, Seven Day Road Sauvignon Blanc, Frederick Chardonnay, Kinnaird Shiraz, Howecroft Merlot, Howecroft Cabernet Sauvignon Merlot; Sassy Sparkling Chardonnay, Botrytis Riesling, Tawny Port.

summary Capel Vale continues to expand its viticultural empire, its contract-grape sources and its marketing, the last through the introduction of a series of vineyard or similarly named super-premium wines. Against the run of play, as it were, the most successful of these super-premiums are the red wines, for it was the Riesling which first captured attention. The strong marketing focus the company has always had is driven by its indefatigable owner, Dr Peter Pratten, who has developed export markets throughout Europe, Asia and the US.

Capel Vale WA Riesling

▼▼▼▼ 2001 Medium yellow-green; the bouquet is quite full, with soft lime/tropical fruit, the palate similarly full-flavoured, a fraction broad, although CO_2 and acidity brace and tighten up the finish.   **rating:** 88

best drinking 2001–2006 **best vintages** '86, '87, '91, '92, '93, '95, '96, '99 **drink with** Caesar salad • $16

Capel Vale Semillon Sauvignon Blanc

▼▼▼▼ 2001 Light yellow-green; a delicate mix of citrus, herb and grass aromas foreshadow a light palate, with some tropical fruit coming into play, and of moderate length.   **rating:** 85

best drinking 2002–2003 **best vintages** NA **drink with** Shellfish • $16

Capel Vale Chardonnay

▼▼▼▼▽ 1999 Light to medium yellow-green; the bouquet is still fresh and youthful, the oak subtle. The fruit-driven palate, with a flavoursome mix of melon, stone fruit and a touch of grapefruit/citrus, has particularly good length and persistence.   **rating:** 93

best drinking 2001–2006 **best vintages** '86, '87, '91, '92, '95, '99 **drink with** Marron • $22

Capel Vale Kinnaird Shiraz

▼▼▼▼ 2000 Medium red, the purples starting to diminish. The moderately intense bouquet has gentle spice and soft red berry fruit; the medium-bodied palate is in a more distinctly savoury spectrum, finishing with fine tannins.   **rating:** 86

best drinking 2003–2008 **best vintages** NA **drink with** Game pie • $48

Capel Vale Howecroft Merlot

▼▼▼▼ 1999 Medium to full red-purple; a complex bouquet with fine cedary/savoury overtones, then a palate with dark berry fruit, cedary oak and fine tannins, the varietal character of merlot coming through more in terms of structure than flavour, but a good wine nonetheless.   **rating:** 89

best drinking 2004–2009 **best vintages** '95, '97, '98 **drink with** Rare eye fillet • $48

capercaillie   ★★★★

Londons Road, Lovedale, NSW 2325 **region** Lower Hunter Valley
phone (02) 4990 2904 **fax** (02) 4991 1886 **open** Mon–Sat 9–5, Sun 10–5
winemaker Alasdair Sutherland **production** 6000 **est.** 1995
product range ($17–40 CD) Watervale Riesling, Hunter Valley Gewürztraminer, Hunter Valley Semillon, Hunter Valley Chardonnay, Dessert Gewürztraminer, C Sparkling Red, Hunter Valley Rosé, Hunter Valley Chambourcin, The Ghillie Shiraz, Ceilidh Shiraz, Orange Highlands Merlot, The Clan (Cabernet Sauvignon Merlot Cabernet Franc).

summary The former Dawson Estate, now run by Hunter Valley veteran Alasdair Sutherland (no relation to Neil Sutherland of Sutherland Estate). The Capercaillie wines are very well made, with generous flavour. Following the example of Brokenwood, its fruit sources are spread across southeast Australia. The wines are exported to the UK and Singapore.

Capercaillie Hunter Valley Semillon

▼▼▼▼ 2001 Light green-yellow; the bouquet is light, fresh, crisp and minerally, the palate providing more of the same. As with so many of the 2001 Semillons, quite classic in character.   **rating:** 89

▼▼▼▼▽ 2000 Very light straw-green; a clean, crisp bouquet with delicate lemon, mineral and grass aromas, then a long, intense and crisp lemony palate with tingling acidity; a classic style for a long life.   **rating:** 93

best drinking 2002–2007 **best vintages** '98, '00, '01 **drink with** Lemon chicken • $17

Capercaillie Hunter Valley Chardonnay

▼▼▼▼▽ **2001** Light to medium green-yellow; fragrant melon and nectarine fruit is supported by a light touch of French oak on the bouquet; the palate is well-balanced, with a subtle oak infusion to the smoky melon fruit; smooth, fine finish. **rating:** 90

best drinking 2002–2005 **best vintages** '01 **drink with** Rich fish dishes • $19

Capercaillie Ceilidh Shiraz

▼▼▼▼ **2000** Medium red-purple; clean, sweet, dark plum and subtle oak on the bouquet is followed by a sweet, soft palate with supple fruit and minimal tannins. Nicely put together, but lacks depth. A blend of Hunter Valley, Langhorne Creek and McLaren Vale grapes. **rating:** 85

best drinking 2003–2007 **best vintages** NA **drink with** Rack of veal • $23

Capercaillie The Ghillie Shiraz

▼▼▼▼▽ **2000** Bright purple-red; clean, fresh black cherry/blackberry fruit and nicely controlled oak on the bouquet leads into a medium-bodied palate, with excellent fruit focus. Very well made and balanced, combining elegance and flavour, finishing with fine tannins. A much gentler touch than the '99 vintage. **rating:** 92

best drinking 2005–2015 **best vintages** '00 **drink with** Marinated beef • $40

Capercaillie The Clan

▼▼▼▼ **2000** Medium purple-red; quite fragrant, sweet red berry and spice aromas, then a light to medium-bodied palate with sweet, small red berry fruit flavours and gentle oak. A touch of confection, perhaps, but this in no way spoils the palate. A blend of Langhorne Creek and Barossa Valley (90 per cent) and Orange (ten per cent) Cabernet Sauvignon, Merlot and Petit Verdot. **rating:** 86

best drinking 2003–2007 **best vintages** NA **drink with** Lasagne • $22

capogreco estate NR

Riverside Avenue, Mildura, Vic 3500 **region** Murray Darling
phone (03) 5023 3060 **open** Mon–Sat 10–6
winemaker Bruno Capogreco **production** NFP **est.** 1976
product range ($8–12 CD) Riesling, Moselle, Shiraz Mataro, Cabernet Sauvignon, Claret, Rosé, Fortifieds.
summary Italian-owned and run, the wines are a blend of Italian and Australian Riverland influences.

captain's paddock NR

Booie–Crawford Road, Kingaroy, Qld 4610 **region** South Burnett
phone (07) 4162 4534 **fax** (07) 4162 4502 **open** Weekends 9–4
winemaker Charles Williams **production** 660 **est.** 1995
product range ($10–17 CD) Chardonnay, Captain's White, Shiraz, Captain's Red (semi-sweet).
summary Don and Judy McCallum planted the first hectare of vineyard in 1995, followed by a further 3 hectares in 1996, focusing on shiraz and chardonnay. It is a family affair; the mudbrick cellar door building was made with bricks crafted by Don McCallum, and Judy's screenprinting adorns the tables and chairs and printed linen for sale to the public. Their two children are both sculptors, with works on display at the winery. Captain's Paddock is fully licensed, offering either light platters or full dishes incorporating local produce. Meals are served either inside or alfresco in the courtyard, which has views over the Booie Ranges.

carabooda estate NR

297 Carabooda Road, Carabooda, WA 6033 **region** Swan District
phone (08) 9407 5283 **fax** (08) 9407 5283 **open** 7 days 10–6
winemaker Terry Ord **production** 2000 **est.** 1989
product range ($12.50–18 CD) Sauvignon Blanc, Chenin Blanc, Shiraz, Cabernet Shiraz, Cabernet Sauvignon.
summary 1989 is the year of establishment given by Terry Ord, but it might as well have been 1979 (when he made his first wine) or 1981 (when he and wife Simonne planted their first vines). It has been a slowly, slowly exercise, with production from the 3 hectares of estate plantings now supplemented by purchased grapes, the first public release not being made until mid-1994. Since that time production has risen significantly.

carbunup estate NR

Bussel Highway, Carbunup, WA 6280 **region** Margaret River
phone (08) 9755 1111 **open** 7 days 10–5
winemaker Robert Credaro **production** NFP **est.** 1988
product range ($12–16 CD) Under the premium Vasse River Wines label: Chardonnay, Semillon, Sauvignon Blanc; under Carbunup Estate label: Verdelho, Shiraz.
summary The estate sells part of the grapes produced from the 18 hectares of vineyards but keeps part for release under the Carbunup Estate and Vasse River labels – strikingly different in design, and giving no clue that they emanate from the same winery. It had early success with its white wines, in particular its Chardonnay and Semillon. No recent tastings.

🐌 cardinham estate ★★★☆

Main North Road, Stanley Flat, SA 5453 **region** Clare Valley
phone (08) 8842 3802 **fax** (08) 8842 3802 **open** Fri–Mon 10–5
winemaker Smith John Wine Co. **production** 500 **est.** 1980
product range ($13–25 CD) Clare Valley Riesling, Clare Valley Semillon, Sangiovese Merlot, Stradbroke Shiraz, Cabernet Merlot, Cabernet.
summary The Smith family began the development of Cardinham Estate in 1980, over the years building the vineyard size up to its present level of 60 hectares, the largest plantings being of cabernet sauvignon (23 hectares), shiraz (15 hectares) and riesling (10.5 hectares). It entered into a grape supply contract with Wolf Blass, which led to an association with then Quelltaler winemaker Stephen John. After 15 years supplying Wolf Blass and others, Stephen John and the Smiths formed the Smith John Wine Company in 1999. Its purpose is to provide contract winemaking services to small producers in the valley, and to supply bulk wine to others. The development of the Cardinham brand is a small but important part of the business. This will see production rise to 1000 cases, with the three staples of Riesling, Cabernet Merlot and Stradbroke Shiraz available from the winery and through retail distribution, and additional wines made in small volume available only at the cellar door and by mail order.

Cardinham Estate Riesling

▼▼▼▼ 2001 Light straw-green; a restrained, clean, minerally bouquet is followed by a moderately long, lemony/minerally palate which may simply be biding its time before fully expressing itself.   **rating:** 86
best drinking 2003–2007 **best vintages** NA **drink with** Summer salad • $13

Cardinham Estate Stradbroke Shiraz

▼▼▼▼ 2000 Medium red-purple; the moderately intense bouquet has plum, spice, prune and earth aromas which continue through to the mid-palate for a fractionally tart finish.   **rating:** 86
best drinking 2004–2009 **best vintages** NA **drink with** Braised rabbit • $18

Cardinham Estate Cabernet Merlot

▼▼▼▼ 2000 Medium red-purple; the clean, dark berry fruit of the bouquet is made complex by touches of chocolate and earth; there is a similar mix of chocolate and blackcurrant fruit on the palate, supported by fine tannins and subtle, cedary oak.   **rating:** 87
best drinking 2005–2010 **best vintages** NA **drink with** Braised rabbit • $18

cargo road wines NR

Cargo Road, Orange, NSW 2800 **region** Orange
phone (02) 6365 6100 **open** Weekends 11–5
winemaker James Sweetapple **production** 1800 **est.** 1983
product range ($14–22.50 CD) Riesling, Gewürztraminer, Sauvignon Blanc, Merlot, Zinfandel, Cabernet Merlot.
summary Originally called The Midas Tree, the vineyard was planted in 1984 by Roseworthy graduate John Swanson. He established a 2.5-hectare vineyard that included zinfandel 15 years ahead of its time. The property was acquired in 1997 by a syndicate, which is expanding the vineyard, particularly zinfandel.

carilley estate NR

Lot 2 Hyem Road, Herne Hill, WA 6056 **region** Swan District
phone (08) 9296 1116 **fax** (08) 9296 1735 **open** By appointment
winemaker Rod Marshall **production** 1000 **est.** 1985

product range ($10–17 R) Chenin Blanc, Chardonnay, Shiraz.
summary Doctors Laura and Isavel Carija have 2 hectares each of chenin blanc, shiraz and chardonnay, and 1 hectare of merlot. Most of the grapes are sold, with only a small proportion made under the Carilley Estate label, with very limited retail mail order or distribution. Carilley Estate is in the process of acquiring acres of adjoining land and plans to build cellars.

carindale wines   NR

Palmers Lane, Pokolbin, NSW 2320 **region** Lower Hunter Valley
phone (02) 4998 7665 **fax** (02) 4998 7065 **open** Fri–Mon 10–4.30
winemaker Brian Walsh (Contract) **production** 1000 **est.** 1996
product range ($21–26.50 CD) Chardonnay, Blackthorn (Cabernet blend).
summary Carindale draws upon 2 hectares of chardonnay, 1.2 hectares of cabernet franc and 0.2 hectares of merlot (together with few muscat vines). Exports to the US and Canada.

carosa   ★★★

310 Houston Street, Mount Helena, WA 6082 **region** Perth Hills
phone (08) 9572 1603 **fax** (08) 9572 1604 **open** Weekends, holidays 11–5 or by appointment
winemaker James Elson **production** 450 **est.** 1984
product range ($14–19 CD) Chardonnay, Summer White, Classic Dry White, Pinot Noir, Cabernet Merlot, Cabernet Sauvignon, Sparkling Pinot Noir, Pinot Noir, Old Tawny Port, White Port.
summary Very limited production and small-scale winemaking result in wines which can only be described as rustic, but which sell readily enough into the local market. Winemaker Jim Elson has extensive eastern Australia winemaking experience (with Seppelt), which is reflected in the steady quality of the 1999 vintage reds. The wines are sold through the cellar door and by mailing list.

casa fontana   NR

4 Cook Street, Lutana, Tas 7009 **region** Southern Tasmania
phone (03) 6272 3180 **open** Not
winemaker Mark Fontana, Steve Lubiana (Contract) **production** 250 **est.** 1994
product range ($22 ML) Chardonnay, Pinot Noir.
summary Mark Fontana and his Japanese wife Shige planted their first pinot noir in 1994, and over the following two years expanded the vineyard to its present level of 2.6 hectares, 1 hectare each of pinot noir and chardonnay, and 0.6 hectares of riesling. Mark Fontana is a metallurgist with Pasminco and came into grape growing through his love of fine wine. The 1999 Chardonnay was a lovely wine.

casa freschi   ★★★☆

30 Jackson Avenue, Strathalbyn, SA 5255 **region** Langhorne Creek
phone (08) 8536 4569 **fax** (08) 8536 4569 **open** Not
winemaker David Freschi **production** 800 **est.** 1998
product range ($34–54 R) Profondo, La Signora.
summary David Freschi graduated with a degree in Oenology from Roséworthy in 1991, and spent most of the decade working in California, Italy and New Zealand, culminating in a senior winemaking position with Corbans in New Zealand in 1997. In 1998 he and his wife decided to trade in the corporate world for a small family-owned winemaking business, with a core of 2.5 hectares of vines established by David Freschi's parents in 1972, and an additional 2 hectares of nebbiolo planted adjacent to the original vineyard. Says David Freschi 'the names of the wines were chosen to best express the personality of the wines grown in our vineyard, as well as to express our heritage'. I suspect some outstanding wines will come from Casa Freschi in good vintages; it is a pity they missed out on 1998. Exports to the US, Germany, Switzerland, Singapore and New Zealand.

Casa Freschi Profundo

TTTT **2000** Medium purple-red; the clean bouquet has well-balanced fruit and oak; the medium-bodied palate is elegant, with a nice conjunction of plum, spice and oak, but not particularly complex or deep – as the price would suggest it should be. **rating:** 88
TTTT **1999** Medium red-purple; a clean, well-balanced, moderately ripe bouquet with dark berry fruit and nicely handled oak leads into a palate with good concentration and balance, with blackberry and mulberry fruit supported by positive oak. Eight hundred and forty bottles made. **rating:** 89

best drinking 2004–2008 **best vintages** NA **drink with** Fillet of beef • $54

Casa Freschi La Signora

▼▼▼▼ **2000** Medium red-purple; the moderately intense bouquet has fresh red and black berry fruit together with touches of licorice and spice; the pleasant, albeit fairly light-bodied, palate has sweet fruit and a dusting of vanilla oak, but not a great deal of structure. **rating: 86**

▼▼▼▽ **1999** Light to medium red-purple; the relatively light bouquet is clean, but with slightly squashy fruit aromatics. The palate has a mix of sweet berry, mint, vanilla and leaf flavours in a light to medium-bodied mode. Four thousand five hundred bottles made. **rating: 84**

best drinking 2003–2007 **best vintages** NA **drink with** Ragout of veal • $34

cascabel ★★★★

Rogers Road, Willunga, SA 5172 **region** McLaren Vale
phone (08) 8557 4434 **fax** (08) 8557 4435 **open** By appointment
winemaker Susana Fernandez, Duncan Ferguson **production** 2000 **est.** 1997
product range ($18–30 R) Eden Valley Riesling, Fleurieu Shiraz, McLaren Vale Grenache et al.
summary Cascabel's proprietors, Duncan Ferguson and Susana Fernandez, established Cascabel when they purchased a property at Willunga on the Fleurieu Peninsula and planted it to roussanne, tempranillo, graciano, monastrel, grenache, shiraz and viognier. The choice of grapes reflects the winemaking experience of the proprietors in Australia, the Rhône Valley, Bordeaux, Italy, Germany and New Zealand – and also Susana Fernandez's birthplace, Spain. Both are fully qualified and intend to move the production base steadily towards the style of the Rhône Valley, Rioja and other parts of Spain. In the meantime, the 4000-case capacity winery which they erected on site prior to the 1998 vintage is being kept busy with grapes sourced from areas throughout SA. The initial releases left no doubt that the proprietors know what they are doing, and it will be interesting to watch the development of the wines from the estate plantings. Exports to the US, the UK, Switzerland, New Zealand, Hong Kong, Singapore and Japan.

Cascabel Eden Valley Riesling

▼▼▼▼ **2001** Light to medium yellow-green; the bouquet is solid, not particularly aromatic, but with some varietal lime; the palate follows down a similarly solid, rich track, showing the warm vintage. **rating: 87**

best drinking 2001–2005 **best vintages** '99 **drink with** Stir-fried prawns • $16

Cascabel Fleurieu Peninsula Shiraz

▼▼▼▼▽ **2000** Medium red, the purple starting to fade a little, suggesting that the wine may develop reasonably quickly. The bouquet is quite complex, with savoury/briary overtones to the fruit, and nicely controlled oak. The palate is similarly powerful, with pleasingly savoury tannins giving the wine a European touch; carries its 14° alcohol well. **rating: 93**

best drinking 2003–2008 **best vintages** '98, '99, '00 **drink with** Ox cheek • $27

Cascabel Grenache et al

▼▼▼▼ **2000** Light to medium red-purple; a clean, light, fresh fruity/jammy varietal bouquet, which does not aspire to complexity, leads into a palate with more weight and fruit sweetness than the bouquet suggests; it is soft and ripe, with soft tannins bracing the finish. **rating: 86**

best drinking 2002–2004 **best vintages** NA **drink with** Beef stew • $23

casella ★★★

Wakely Road, Yenda, NSW 2681 **region** Riverina
phone (02) 6968 1346 **fax** (02) 6968 1196 **open** Not
winemaker Alan Kennett **production** 1.65 million **est.** 1969
product range ($4.95–19.50 R) Chardonnay, Shiraz, Cabernet Sauvignon; under the Carramar Estate label Semillon Sauvignon Blanc, Chardonnay, Unwooded Chardonnay, Botrytis Semillon, Merlot, Shiraz, Shiraz Cabernet, Cabernet Sauvignon; Yenda Vale Durif, Tempranillo, Cabernet Sauvignon Petit Verdot; also Cottlers Bridge at significantly lower prices. The Yellow Tail range of wines (Chardonnay, Shiraz, Merlot) is for the export market.
summary Casella is typical of the new wave sweeping through the Riverina. It draws upon 100 hectares of estate vineyards, selling much of its wine in bulk or as cleanskin bottled wine to other producers, but also marketing a range of varietals under the Carramar Estate label. Casella is part of the Semillon of the Riverina group (promoting dry Semillon), and overall its wines offer good value for money. Predictably, the Botrytis Semillon is the outstanding release. Retail distribution through the eastern states and SA; exports to the US, the UK, Japan and New Zealand.

Casella Yellow Tail Chardonnay

♈♈♈♀ **2001** Glowing yellow-green; rich, ripe yellow peach and vanilla fruit on the bouquet and palate provides a full-bodied, fast maturing style; good value. **rating: 83**

best drinking 2002–2003 **best vintages** NA **drink with** KFC • $12.99

Casella Carramar Estate Botrytis Semillon

♈♈♈♀ **2000** Golden bronze, very advanced; the bouquet shows the complexity and impact of a high degree of botrytis, although the palate is slightly less rich and dense than expected, perhaps a function of its rapid development. **rating: 84**

best drinking 2002–2003 **best vintages** '97 **drink with** Any rich dessert • $19.99

Casella Yenda Vale Durif

♈♈♈♈ **2000** Medium red-purple; clean blackcurrant fruit and subtle oak on the bouquet lead into a quite rich and concentrated palate with some savoury/dark chocolate flavours; the tannins dry up the fruit somewhat on the finish. **rating: 85**

best drinking 2002–2004 **best vintages** NA **drink with** Barbecued rump steak • $16.99

Casella Yenda Vale Tempranillo

♈♈♈♈ **2000** Medium red-purple; a clean, moderately intense bouquet with spicy, Christmas cake aromas; an interesting palate, probably best when very young, but the tannin structure and length are impressive, silky and long. Gold and trophy Perth 2000; top gold Class 9, Canberra 2000. **rating: 89**

best drinking 2002–2003 **best vintages** NA **drink with** Moussaka • $16.99

Casella Yellow Tail Merlot

♈♈♈♀ **2001** Light to medium purple-red; the light bouquet has an almost lemony fragrance, together with savoury spices; sweet, dark berry fruit comes through on the palate with above average substance. Excellent value. **rating: 84**

best drinking 2002–2003 **best vintages** NA **drink with** Pizza • $12.99

cassegrain ★★★★

Hastings River Winery, Fernbank Creek Road, Port Macquarie, NSW 2444 **region** Hastings River
phone (02) 6583 7777 **fax** (02) 6584 0354 **open** 7 days 9–5
winemaker John Cassegrain **production** 45 000 **est.** 1980
product range ($12–25 CD) Semillon, Verdelho, Pinot Gris, Unwooded Chardonnay, Chardonnay, White Pinot, Brut, Rosé, Chambourcin, Pinot Noir, Shiraz, Cabernet Franc Cabernet Sauvignon; Five Mile Hollow Chardonnay Semillon, White, Red, Sparkling Cuvée; Discovery Semillon, Chambourcin; The Premiere Collection series of Reserve Semillon, Fromenteau Reserve Chardonnay, Reserve Chambourcin; Fortifieds.
summary A very substantial operation based in the Hastings Valley on the north coast of NSW. In earlier years it drew fruit from many parts of Australia but it is now entirely supplied by the 154 hectares of estate plantings which offer 14 varieties, including the rare chambourcin, a French-bred cross. In February 2002 Cassegrain purchased Hungerford Hill from Southcorp, and secured the services of Phillip John as senior Hungerford Hill winemaker. The identity of Hungerford Hill as a separate venture will be preserved, and it is thus separately listed in this book. Exports to the UK, Netherlands, Malaysia, Thailand, Philippines, Singapore and Japan.

Cassegrain Discovery Semillon

♈♈♈♈♀ **2000** Light but bright straw-green; a clean, lemon/citrus bouquet, soft but not flabby; the palate has excellent length and intensity, the citrus-tinged fruit providing prolonged carry through the length of the palate and finish. **rating: 92**

best drinking 2003–2008 **best vintages** '00 **drink with** Tempura oysters • $17.95

Cassegrain Hastings River Semillon

♈♈♈♈ **2001** Light straw-green; a firm, grassy and powerful bouquet is followed by an equally powerful and firm palate with grassy/herbaceous flavours and lingering acidity. **rating: 89**

best drinking 2004–2010 **best vintages** '97, '98, '00, '01 **drink with** Oysters • $17.50

Cassegrain Unwooded Chardonnay

♈♈♈♈ **2001** Light to medium yellow-green; the bouquet is clean, with a light citrus edge to the fruit; there is pleasant mouthfeel and texture; not bad at the price. **rating: 83**

best drinking 2002–2003 **best vintages** NA **drink with** Fish and chips • $14.50

Cassegrain Hastings River Chardonnay

♥♥♥♥ 2000 Light to medium green-yellow; the bouquet offers some complexity, with ripe apple and melon fruit, and a hint of oak. The unusual apple character comes through again on the palate, allied with melon; finishes with crunchy acidity. **rating: 85**

best drinking 2002–2004 best vintages '96 drink with Fish terrine • $16.95

Cassegrain Shiraz

♥♥♥♥ 2000 Medium red-purple; interesting high-toned spice, prune, licorice and cherry aromatics are followed by a similar range of flavours on the palate; fruit-dominant, with a touch of clove of uncertain origin. **rating: 89**

best drinking 2003–2007 best vintages NA drink with Italian • $18.50

Cassegrain Chambourcin

♥♥♥♡ 2001 Light to medium red-purple; a light, fresh, juicy bouquet with hints of fresh-mown hay, then a similarly fresh, juicy, early-drinking palate with zero tannins. **rating: 84**

best drinking 2002–2003 best vintages '89, '90, '92, '95, '96 drink with Italian cuisine • $17.95

Cassegrain Discovery Chambourcin

♥♥♥♥ 2000 Medium to full red-purple, much deeper than the varietal version. The bouquet, likewise, has more depth, with plum and spice aromas, while on the palate the difference is massive: very concentrated, and with some of those 'wild' characters typical of the variety. This is love it or leave it stuff. **rating: 86**

best drinking 2002–2003 best vintages NA drink with Game pie • $17.95

Cassegrain Cabernet Franc Cabernet Sauvignon

♥♥♥♥ 2000 Light to medium red-purple; a lively, fresh, minty juicy berry bouquet is effectively repeated on the palate; another fresh, friendly, early-drinking style requiring no great thought or contemplation. **rating: 85**

best drinking 2002–2003 best vintages NA drink with Pizza • $18.50

castagna vineyard   NR

Ressom Lane, Beechworth, Vic 3747 **region** Beechworth
phone (03) 5728 2888 **fax** (03) 5728 2898 **open** By appointment
winemaker Julian Castagna **production** 2000 **est.** 1997
product range ($25–45 ML) Allegro, Genesis Syrah, La Chiave, Sauvage.
summary The elegantly labelled wines of Castagna will ultimately come from 4 hectares of estate shiraz and viognier in the course of establishment (the latter making up 15 per cent of the total). Winemaker Julian Castagna is intent on making wines which reflect the terroir as closely as possible, declining to use cultured yeast or filtration. The initial release of 1998 Genesis Syrah was in fact made from grapes purchased from a next-door neighbour, but all susbequent wines have been estate-grown.

castle rock estate

Porongurup Road, Porongurup, WA 6324 **region** Great Southern
phone (08) 9853 1035 **fax** (08) 9853 1010 **open** Mon–Fri 10–4, weekends and public holidays 10–5
winemaker Robert Diletti **production** 5000 **est.** 1983
product range ($12–27 CD) Riesling, Robert Reserve White, Chardonnay, Late Harvest Riesling, Della (sparkling), Pinot Noir, Cabernet Franc Merlot, Cabernet Sauvignon Merlot, Liqueur Muscat.
summary An exceptionally beautifully sited vineyard and cellar-door sales area with sweeping vistas from the Porongurups, operated by the Diletti family. The standard of viticulture is very high, and the site itself ideally situated (quite apart from its beauty). The Rieslings have always been elegant and handsomely repaid time in bottle.

Castle Rock Estate Riesling

♥♥♥♥ 2001 Light green-yellow; a chalky, dusty bouquet with some dried apple aromas is followed by a palate with gently sweet fruit, pleasant but with a curious lack of definition/focus. Makes you wonder whether the cork is to blame; the first wine made on the on-site winery by son Robert Diletti after returning from winemaking in Alsace. **rating: 86**

best drinking 2003–2008 best vintages '86, '89, '90, '91, '93, '94, '96, '97, '98, '00 drink with Seafood salad • $18

cathcart ridge estate   NR

Moyston Road, Cathcart via Ararat, Vic 3377 **region** Grampians
phone (03) 5352 1997 **fax** (03) 5352 1558 **open** 7 days 10–5
winemaker David Farnhill, Michael Unwin (Consultant) **production** 10 000 **est.** 1977
product range ($11–28 CD) Estate range of Chardonnay, Shiraz, Cabernet; Rhymney Reef Chardonnay,
Shiraz, Merlot, Cabernet Merlot, Old Tawny Port; and, at the bottom of the price range, Mount Ararat
Colombard, Shiraz.
summary In recent years has raised capital to fund a significant expansion programme of both vineyards
and the winery, but is still little known in the wider retail trade. Exports to Ireland and the US.

cathedral lane wines   ★★★☆

228 Cathedral Lane, Taggerty, Vic 3714 **region** Central Victorian High Country
phone (03) 5774 7305 **fax** (03) 5774 7305 **open** By appointment
winemaker Martin Williams MW **production** 400 **est.** 1997
product range ($25 ML) Pinot Noir.
summary Rod Needham and Heather Campbell formed the Acheron Valley Wine Company, which
makes the Cathedral Lane wines, in 1997. The 3.2-hectare vineyard is situated on the lower slopes of
Mount Cathedral at a height of 280 metres. A variant of the Scott Henry trellis system, with high-density
1-metre spacing between the vines, alternately trained up or down, has been employed. The vineyard
planning was supervised by former Coldstream Hills viticulturist Bill Christophersen.

Cathedral Lane Pinot Noir

▼▼▼▼ 2000 Medium red, with some purple tinges remaining; the bouquet is complex, with soft, dark
plum and black cherry fruit supported by gentle oak; the palate moves more towards a secondary mode,
with attractive, slightly briary, foresty flavours before a fractionally hard finish.   **rating:** 87

best drinking 2002–2006 **best vintages** NA **drink with** Tea-smoked duck • $25

catherine vale vineyard   ★★★☆

656 Milbrodale Road, Bulga, NSW 2330 **region** Lower Hunter Valley
phone (02) 6579 1334 **fax** (02) 6579 1334 **open** Weekends and public holidays 10–5 or by appointment
winemaker John Hordern (Contract) **production** 1125 **est.** 1994
product range ($12–16 CD) Semillon, Chardonnay, Semillon Chardonnay, Gabrielle Dolcetto.
summary Former schoolteachers Bill and Wendy Lawson have established Catherine Vale as a not-so-idle
retirement venture. Both were involved in school athletics and sports programmes, handy training for do-it-
yourself viticulturists. Most of the grapes from the 5.8-hectare vineyard are sold to contract winemaker John
Hordern; a small proportion is vinified for the Catherine Vale label.

Catherine Vale Semillon

▼▼▼▼ 2000 Light green-yellow; citrus, grass and lemon aromas precede a finely structured palate with
lemony acidity lengthening the finish. Very good value.   **rating:** 88

best drinking 2005–2010 **best vintages** '98, '00 **drink with** Shellfish • $14

Catherine Vale Chardonnay

▼▼▼▼ 2000 Light to medium green-yellow; the light bouquet is clean, the partial barrel ferment working
well with the basically light fruit. The light to medium-bodied palate tracks the bouquet with pleasant
nectarine flavour and subtle oak.   **rating:** 87

best drinking 2002–2004 **best vintages** '98 **drink with** Poached scallops • $16

Catherine Vale Vineyard Gabrielle Dolcetto

▼▼▼▽ 2001 Light to medium red-purple; light spice, berry and chocolate aromas, then a palate which,
while clean, is lighter and somewhat less interesting than the bouquet. There may well have been no oak
used; certainly none is evident. Of interest as the first example of this variety from the Hunter Valley.
rating: 83

best drinking 2002–2003 **best vintages** NA **drink with** Veal scallopine • $15

catspaw farm   NR

Texas Road, Stanthorpe, Qld 4380 **region** Granite Belt
phone (07) 4683 6229 **fax** (07) 4683 6386 **open** Thurs–Sun 10–5
winemaker Christopher Whitfort **production** 1000 **est.** 1989

product range ($12–21 CD) Sauvignon Blanc Semillon, Chardonnay, Sweet White, Golden Queen, Cabernet Shiraz, Liqueur Muscat, Liqueur Muscat Gold Label.

summary The foundations for Catspaw Farm were laid back in 1989 when planting of the vineyard began with chardonnay, riesling, cabernet franc, cabernet sauvignon, merlot, chambourcin and shiraz, totalling 4.6 hectares. More recently, Catspaw has moved with the times in planting rousanne, semillon, barbera and sangiovese, lifting total plantings to just under 8 hectares. The newer plantings are yet to come into bearing and the wines are some time away from release. In the meantime a mixed bag of wines is available, some dating back to 1996. Catspaw, incidentally, also offers on-farm accommodation in a self-contained farmhouse (with disabled access) and picnic facilities.

cedar creek estate NR

104 Hartley Road, Mount Tamborine, Qld 4272 **region** Queensland Coastal
phone (07) 5545 1666 **fax** (07) 5545 4762 **open** 7 days 10–5
winemaker Contact **production** NA **est.** 2000
product range ($17.50 CD) Genesis Chardonnay Semillon.

summary Opened in November 2000, Cedar Creek Estate takes its name from the creek which flows through the property at an altitude of 550 metres on Tamborine Mountain. A small vineyard has been planted, but has yet to come into bearing, and the focus will always be on general tourism, with a host of facilities for visitors. It also offers Granite Belt wines made by Ballandean, Hidden Creek and Robinson Family. The single wine offered under the Cedar Creek Estate label at the present time is unambiguously directed to the cellar door trade, being equally unambiguously sweet.

celtic farm ★★★☆

39 Sweyn Street, North Balwyn, Vic 3104 **region** Warehouse
phone (03) 9857 3600 **fax** (03) 9857 3601 **open** Not
winemaker Gerry Taggert **production** 3800 **est.** 1997
product range ($18.50–20 R) South Block Riesling (Clare Valley), The Gridge Pinot Grigio (King Valley), Far Canal Shiraz (Coonawarra), Merlot (Alpine and King Valleys), Raisin Hell Rutherglen Muscat.

summary Yet another Warehouse winery, the brainchild of a marketing and sales team of Mark McKenzie and Gerry Taggert. The proprietors say, 'Celtic Farm is produced from classic varieties selected from Australia's premium wine regions and made with a total commitment to quality. While we have a desire to pay homage to our Celtic (drinking) heritage we are also acutely aware that wine should be about enjoyment, fun and not taking yourself too seriously.'

Celtic Farm South Block Riesling

▼▼▼▼ 2001 Light green-yellow; the bouquet is firm, with distinctly herbaceous aromas, the palate similarly firm and herbaceous; an unusual style, but has abundant flavour. From the Clare Valley. **rating:** 87

best drinking 2002–2005 **best vintages** '98 **drink with** Vegetable terrine • $18.50

Celtic Farm The Gridge Pinot Gris

▼▼▼▼ 2001 Light straw-green; a clean, fresh and lively bouquet with apple/apple blossom aromas is followed by an apple and citrus-flavoured palate; good length, and no alcohol heat. An altogether superior example; from the King and Alpine Valleys. **rating:** 88

best drinking 2002–2003 **best vintages** NA **drink with** Antipasto • $20

chain of ponds ★★★★

Adelaide Road, Gumeracha, SA 5233 **region** Adelaide Hills
phone (08) 8389 1415 **fax** (08) 8389 1877 **open** 7 days 10.30–4.30
winemaker Neville Falkenberg **production** 8000 **est.** 1993
product range ($10–35 CD) Purple Patch Riesling, Square Cut Semillon, Black Thursday Sauvignon Blanc Semillon, Special Release Sauvignon Blanc, Nether Hill Unwooded Chardonnay, The Morning Star Chardonnay, Corkscrew Road Chardonnay, Novello Rosso, Pinot Noir, Salem Pinot Noir, Ledge Shiraz, Grave's Gate Shiraz, Sangiovese, Amadeus Cabernet Sauvignon, Diva Pinot Chardonnay.

summary Caj and Genny Amadio are the largest growers in the Adelaide Hills, with 100 hectares of vineyards established on a Scott Henry trellis producing 1000 tonnes of grapes a year, almost all sold to Penfolds, but with a small amount made into wine for sale under the Chain of Ponds label. The full-flavoured wines have enjoyed consistent show success, and the arrival of energetic Adelaide man-about-town Zar Brooks as general manager has enlivened the marketing of the brand and led to the birth of a rash of new wine names and prolix back labels. The Vineyard Balcony restaurant provides lunches on weekends and public holidays.

Chain Of Ponds Purple Patch Riesling

ŢŢŢŢ 2001 Light green-yellow; a firm, clean, mineral/herb bouquet with slightly suppressed fruit is followed by a relatively austere palate, with distinct slate/talc/mineral characters. Deserves time in bottle. **rating: 86**

best drinking 2004–2009 **best vintages** '98 **drink with** Globe artichoke • $17.50

Chain of Ponds Black Thursday Sauvignon Blanc

ŢŢŢŢ 2001 Light green-straw; the bouquet is delicate, with some light passionfruit aromas, the palate similarly light and crisp, getting there as a shellfish style. **rating: 85**

best drinking 2001–2002 **best vintages** NA **drink with** Shellfish • $20

Chain of Ponds Nether Hill Unwooded Chardonnay

ŢŢŢŢ 2001 Light green-yellow; light melon fruit on the bouquet leads into a light to medium-bodied palate with a varietally precise array of melon/nectarine/citrus fruit. **rating: 85**

best drinking 2001–2002 **best vintages** NA **drink with** Prawn salad • $20

Chain of Ponds Corkscrew Road Chardonnay

ŢŢŢŢ 2000 Light to medium green-yellow; quite refined, citrussy overtones to the varietal fruit of the bouquet move into lemony/herbal characters on the palate, well away from classical chardonnay varietal character, but certainly making a statement. **rating: 86**

best drinking 2001–2005 **best vintages** NA **drink with** Grilled whiting • $35

Chain Of Ponds The Morning Star Chardonnay

ŢŢŢŢ 1999 Light to medium yellow-green; a stylish and subtle mix of fruit, oak and malolactic influences. On the palate nectarine fruit comes more to the fore, together with touches of cashew and nicely controlled oak. Has barely changed over the last 12 months, developing remarkably slowly. **rating: 89**

best drinking 2002–2006 **best vintages** '94, '97, '98 **drink with** Veal saltimbocca • $25

Chain of Ponds Jerusalem Section Pinot Noir

ŢŢŢŢŢ 2000 Medium red, with some purple remaining; complex dark plum and spice fruit aromas show excellent (and unexpected) varietal character. The palate is rich, powerful and complex, richly robed and plush; at the baroque end of the spectrum, but without losing varietal integrity. **rating: 93**

ŢŢŢŢ 1999 Medium red-purple; the bouquet is fresh for its age, with quite savoury, tangy complexity; there is more of the same on the palate, albeit with slightly drying stem tannins; good attempt at style. **rating: 88**

best drinking 2002–2005 **best vintages** NA **drink with** Game pie • $35

Chain of Ponds Grave's Gate Shiraz

ŢŢŢŢŢ 1999 Deep, bright red-purple; clean, fresh juicy/berry fruit on the bouquet is followed by luscious and sweet berry fruit on the palate. Neither the oak, nor the extract, nor the alcohol (13.5°) has been overdone. **rating: 90**

best drinking 2003–2008 **best vintages** NA **drink with** Spaghetti bolognese • $35

🐞 chalkers crossing ★★★★☆

387 Grenfell Road, Young, NSW 2594 **region** Hilltops
phone (02) 6382 6900 **fax** (02) 6382 5068 **open** Mon–Fri 9–5, weekends 10–4
winemaker Celine Rousseau **production** 10 000 **est.** 2000
product range ($14.50–18 CD) Hilltops range of Riesling, Semillon, Shiraz, Cabernet Sauvignon; Tumbarumba range of Sauvignon Blanc, Chardonnay, Rosé, Pinot Noir.
summary Owned and operated by Ted and Wendy Ambler, Chalkers Crossing is based near Young, where the first vines were planted at the Rockleigh vineyard in late 1997, with follow-up plantings in 1998 lifting the total to 10 hectares. It also purchases grapes from Tumbarumba and Gundagai to supplement the intake. A winery was opened for the 2000 vintage, with Celine Rousseau as winemaker. Born in France's Loire Valley and trained in Bordeaux, Celine has worked in Bordeaux, Champagne, Languedoc, Margaret River and in the Perth Hills, an eclectic mix of climates if ever there was one. This French Flying Winemaker (and now Australian citizen) has exceptional skills and dedication.

Chalkers Crossing Hilltops Riesling

▼▼▼▼ 2001 Light green-yellow; a clean, correct, herb, mineral and lime-accented bouquet, then a crisp, minerally palate which is well made but lacks fruit intensity; not quite what one would expect from a very good vintage. May well surprise with bottle development. **rating: 86**

▼▼▼▼ 2000 Light to medium green-yellow; quite powerful Germanic lime juice aromas lead into a palate with corresponding power on entry and through to the middle, before shortening slightly on the finish. **rating: 87**

best drinking 2003–2007 **best vintages** NA **drink with** Asparagus and salmon terrine • $16.50

Chalkers Crossing Hilltops Semillon

▼▼▼▼▼ 2001 Light green-yellow; a clean, crisp, ultra-correct bouquet with a range of grass, lemon and herb aromas, followed by an intense palate with excellent structure and length, combining complexity and finesse; 50 per cent was barrel-fermented in used oak, adding to texture rather than flavour. **rating: 94**

▼▼▼▼▽ 2000 Light green-yellow; the bouquet is still youthful and minerally, the palate similarly lively, crisp and minerally, with good length and style. **rating: 92**

best drinking 2004–2010 **best vintages** '00, '01 **drink with** Caesar salad • $16.50

Chalkers Crossing Tumbarumba Sauvignon Blanc

▼▼▼▼ 2001 Light green-yellow; quite fragrant gooseberry, asparagus and lemon aromas show no sweaty or extended ferment characters. The palate stays in the asparagus/herbal spectrum, with good length and balance; as with all these wines, well made. **rating: 88**

best drinking 2002–2003 **best vintages** NA **drink with** Marinated octopus • $16.50

Chalkers Crossing Tumbarumba Chardonnay

▼▼▼▼ 2000 Very pale green-yellow; the clean, light citrussy bouquet is fruit-driven, barely showing the effect of barrel fermentation, lees contact and 9 months' maturation in French oak. The fine, elegant palate proclaims its cool climate, but the varietal character is not lost. **rating: 89**

best drinking 2002–2005 **best vintages** NA **drink with** Gravlax • $17.50

Chalkers Crossing Tumbarumba Rosé

▼▼▼▼ 2000 Light salmon-pink; the highly fragrant, tangy, spicy bouquet is followed by a fresh, crisp and lively palate with spicy/leafy flavours and subliminal oak. A very interesting wine which was barrel-fermented and spent 9 months on lees. **rating: 86**

best drinking 2002–2003 **best vintages** NA **drink with** Consommé • $17.50

Chalkers Crossing Tumbarumba Pinot Noir

▼▼▼▼▽ 2000 Medium purple-red; perfumed bouquet with ripe plum, five spice and scented powder aromas, then a palate with impressive depth and complexity, ranging through dark plum and forest. Truly excellent value. **rating: 90**

best drinking 2002–2005 **best vintages** NA **drink with** Squab • $18

Chalkers Crossing Hilltops Shiraz

▼▼▼▼ 2000 Bright red-purple; the moderately intense bouquet has clean cherry and spice aromas, but are not particularly concentrated. The palate is firm and savoury, with cherry coming through on the mid-palate, then slightly edgy tannins on the finish. **rating: 85**

best drinking 2003–2007 **best vintages** NA **drink with** Lasagne • $18

Chalkers Crossing Hilltops Cabernet Sauvignon

▼▼▼▼▽ 2000 Vivid purple-red; fresh and vibrantly juicy blackberry and blackcurrant fruit on the bouquet are followed by a clean and lively palate with berry fruit, and fine, gently savoury tannins. Another very well made wine. **rating: 90**

best drinking 2005–2010 **best vintages** NA **drink with** Braised ox cheek • $18

chalk hill ★★★★

Field Street, McLaren Vale, SA 5171 **region** McLaren Vale
phone (08) 8556 2121 **fax** (08) 8556 2221 **open** Not
winemaker Contract **production** 2000 **est.** 1973
product range ($15–25 CD) Chardonnay, Shiraz, Cabernet Sauvignon.
summary Chalk Hill is in full flight again, drawing upon the 12.5 hectares of vineyards of grape-growing owners John and Di Harvey, who acquired Chalk Hill in 1996. Domestic distribution is solely through the cellar door and by mail order; a small portion is exported to Holland, Germany and the US (under Wits End label).

chambers rosewood ★★★★☆

Barkly Street, Rutherglen, Vic 3685 **region** Rutherglen
phone (02) 6032 8641 **fax** (02) 6032 8101 **open** Mon–Sat 9–5, Sun 11–5
winemaker Bill Chambers, Stephen Chambers **production** 10 000 **est.** 1858
product range ($6–35 CD) A wide range of table wines, including such rarities as a Riesling and Gouias blend, Blue Imperial (which is in fact Cinsaut) and a wide range of fortified wines. The supremely great wines are the Rare Tokay and Rare Muscat, and the very good Special Muscat and Special Tokay. These are now offered in 375 ml bottles at prices which are starting to reflect their intrinsic value, and are rather higher than the prices for the same wines when last offered in 750 ml bottles.
summary The winery rating is given for the Muscats and Tokays and is in fact a compromise between the Special Muscat and Tokay (rated 'grand' under the Rutherglen Classification system) and the Rare wines, which are on a level all of their own, somewhere higher than five stars. The chief virtue of the table wines is that they are cheap. Exports to the US, the UK and Belgium.

Chambers Rosewood Rutherglen Tokay

▼▼▼♀ **NV** Golden brown. The bouquet is fresh, but there is a slight cosmetic edge, verging on dishwashing soap. The palate is better, with tea leaf/fish oil varietal character. **rating:** 83

best drinking 2002–2003 **best vintages** NA **drink with** After dinner biscuits • $12.50

🐂 chanters ridge NR

440 Chanters Lane, Tylden, Vic 3444 **region** Macedon Ranges
phone (03) 9509 7233 **fax** (03) 9509 8046 **open** Not
winemaker John Ellis **production** 300 **est.** 1995
product range ($25 R) Pinot Noir.
summary Orthopedic surgeon Barry Elliott, as well as running the surgery unit at Melbourne's Alfred Hospital, became involved with the Kyneton Hospital five years ago. Through a convoluted series of events, he and his wife acquired the 24-hectare property without any clear idea of what they might do with it; later his lifelong interest in wine steered him towards the idea of establishing a vineyard. He retained local overlord John Ellis as his consultant, and this led to the planting of 2 hectares of pinot noir, and the first tiny make in 2000. Barry Elliott intends to retire from surgery and devote himself full-time to the challenge of making Pinot Noir in one of the more difficult parts of Australia, but one which will richly reward success.

Chanters Ridge Pinot Noir

▼▼▼▼ **2000** Light to medium purple-red; fresh cherry and plum fruit and subtle oak define a clean but not complex bouquet. The palate moves along with nice plummy fruit, but both the texture and the 12° alcohol raise the question whether the grapes might have been picked a little too early. **rating:** 87

best drinking 2001–2004 **best vintages** NA **drink with** Pot-roasted quail • $25

chapel hill ★★★★

Chapel Hill Road, McLaren Vale, SA 5171 **region** McLaren Vale
phone (08) 8323 8429 **fax** (08) 8323 9245 **open** 7 days 12–5
winemaker Pam Dunsford (Consultant), Angela Meaney **production** 60 000 **est.** 1979
product range ($14–40 CD) Verdelho, Unwooded Chardonnay, Reserve Chardonnay, McLaren Vale Shiraz, The Vicar (Cabernet Shiraz), McLaren Vale/Coonawarra Cabernet Sauvignon, The Devil Tawny Port.
summary A leading medium-sized winery in the region; in the second half of 2000 Chapel Hill was sold to the diversified Swiss Thomas Schmidheiny group, which owns the respected Cuvaison winery in California, as well as vineyards in Switzerland and Argentina. From my knowledge of Cuvaison, which stretches back 16 years or so, I am confident Chapel Hill is in safe hands. Exports to the UK, the US, Switzerland, Germany and Hong Kong.

Chapel Hill Unwooded Chardonnay

▼▼▼♀ **2001** Light to medium yellow-green; pleasant melon/nectarine varietal fruit is evident both on the bouquet and on the light to medium-bodied palate. Nicely balanced, but constrained by its birth. **rating:** 84

best drinking 2001–2002 **best vintages** NA **drink with** Pasta, salads • $14.50

Chapel Hill Shiraz

▼▼▼♀ **1999** Light to medium red-purple; the bouquet is light, seemingly lacking concentration, although there is a little more red cherry fruit on the palate; overall, lacks focus. **rating:** 84

best drinking 2002–2005 **best vintages** '91, '94, '95, '96 **drink with** Grilled calf's liver • $28

Chapel Hill McLaren Vale/Coonawarra Cabernet Sauvignon
ŸŸŸŸŸ 1999 Medium red-purple, showing some colour shift; a solid bouquet with a mix of earthy/briary/blackberry/chocolate aromas, the palate with plenty of depth, well weighted and structured; ripe tannins round off a good outcome for the vintage. The oak is not overplayed. **rating:** 90

best drinking 2004–2009 **best vintages** '88, '90, '91, '92, '95, '98, '99 **drink with** Marinated beef • $28

chapman's creek vineyard   NR

RMS 447, Yelverton Road, Wilyabrup, WA 6280 **region** Margaret River
phone (08) 9755 7545 **fax** (08) 9755 7571 **open** 7 days 10.30–4.30
winemaker Various Contract **production** 5000 **est.** 1989
product range ($15–26 R) Chenin Blanc, Unoaked Chardonnay, Chardonnay, Merlot, Cabernet Merlot, Tawny Port.
summary Chapman's Creek was founded by Tony Lord, an extremely experienced wine journalist who for many years was editor and part-owner of *Decanter* magazine of the United Kingdom, one of the leaders in the field. Notwithstanding this, he was always reticent about seeking any publicity for Chapman's Creek; why, I do not know. Regrettably, it is now too late to find out, as he died in February 2002. Chapman's Creek will continue to be managed by his long-term pal Chris Leach, who was one of those who kept an eye on him throughout his prolonged illness.

charles cimicky   ★★★☆

Gomersal Road, Lyndoch, SA 5351 **region** Barossa Valley
phone (08) 8524 4025 **fax** (08) 8524 4772 **open** Tues–Sat 10.30–4.30
winemaker Charles Cimicky **production** 15 000 **est.** 1972
product range ($15–25 CD) Sauvignon Blanc, Chardonnay, Cabernet Franc, Classic Merlot, Cabernet Sauvignon, Signature Shiraz, Old Fireside Tawny Port.
summary These wines are of very good quality, thanks to the lavish (but sophisticated) use of new French oak in tandem with high-quality grapes. The intense, long-flavoured Sauvignon Blanc has been a particularly consistent performer, as has the rich, voluptuous American-oaked Signature Shiraz. Limited retail distribution in SA, Victoria, NSW and WA, with exports to the UK, the US, Switzerland, Canada, Malaysia and Hong Kong.

charles melton   ★★★★★

Krondorf Road, Tanunda, SA 5352 **region** Barossa Valley
phone (08) 8563 3606 **fax** (08) 8563 3422 **open** 7 days 11–5
winemaker Charlie Melton **production** 15 000 **est.** 1984
product range ($15.90–36.90 CD) Rosé of Virginia, Pinot Hermitage, Shiraz, Laura Shiraz, Nine Popes (Shiraz Grenache Mourvedre), Grenache, Cabernet Sauvignon, Sotto di Ferro (sweet white).
summary Charlie Melton, one of the Barossa Valley's great characters, with wife Virginia by his side, makes some of the most eagerly sought à la mode wines in Australia. Inevitably, the Melton empire grew in response to the insatiable demand, with a doubling of estate vineyards to 13 hectares (and the exclusive management and offtake of a further 10 hectares) and the erection of a new barrel store in 1996. The expanded volume has had no adverse effect on the wonderfully rich, sweet and well-made wines. Exports to the UK, Ireland, Switzerland, France, the US and Southeast Asia.

Charles Melton Rosé Of Virginia
ŸŸŸŸŸ 2001 Vivid colour, vivid aroma and vivid flavour all achieved without sugary sweetness, just cherry/cherry blossom fruit. **rating:** 94

best drinking 2001–2002 **best vintages** '97, '98, '00, '01 **drink with** Anything • $16.80

Charles Melton Shiraz
ŸŸŸŸŸ 1999 Medium red-purple; complex, ripe, scented spicy/cherry fruit aromas provide a most attractive start; the medium-bodied palate flows logically on, with soft, ripe, spicy/cherry fruit, and subtle but complementary oak. Vaguely reminiscent of some of the best wines from the 1989 vintage. **rating:** 93

best drinking 2001–2008 **best vintages** '95, '96, '98, '99 **drink with** Spiced lamb • $38.80

Charles Melton Laura Shiraz

❚❚❚❚ **1999** Medium red, with the purple starting to fade; there is a whiff of hay and straw behind red berry fruit on the bouquet, then a smooth entry through to the mid-palate before a twist on the finish with faintly citrussy acidity. Very interesting. **rating:** 87

best drinking 2002–2006 **best vintages** NA **drink with** Lebanese • $31.80

Charles Melton Nine Popes

❚❚❚❚❚ **1999** The bouquet is spicy and lively, with excellent fruit and oak balance and integration; the juicy/spicy palate is likewise complex but elegant and long, a true reflection of southern Rhône style.

rating: 94

best drinking 2002–2009 **best vintages** '90, '91, '92, '93, '94, '95, '96, '98, '99 **drink with** Roasted veal kidney • $38.80

Charles Melton Cabernet Sauvignon

❚❚❚❚ **1999** Medium red-purple; the smooth bouquet is at the spicy/savoury end of the spectrum, rather than the opulent one. The elegance promised by the bouquet manifests itself on the palate with savoury/earthy cabernet varietal fruit, fine tannins and controlled oak. **rating:** 88

best drinking 2004–2009 **best vintages** '96 **drink with** Braised ox cheek with demi glaze • $36.80

charles reuben estate   NR

777 Middle Tea Tree Road, Tea Tree, Tas 7017 **region** Southern Tasmania
phone (03) 6268 1702 **fax** (03) 6231 3571 **open** Wed–Sun 10–5
winemaker Tim Krushka **production** 350 **est.** 1990
product range ($15–22 CD) Riesling, Chardonnay, Unwooded Chardonnay, Pinot Noir.
summary Charles Reuben Estate has 1.5 hectares of pinot noir, 0.5 hectare of chardonnay and a few rows of riesling in production. It has also planted 1.2 hectares of the four Bordeaux varieties, headed by cabernet sauvignon with a little cabernet franc, merlot and petit verdot, and 0.6 hectare of sauvignon blanc accompanied by a few rows of semillon. The principal wines will be Pinot Noir, Chardonnay, a Bordeaux-blend red and a Sauvignon Blanc Semillon, although there is an element of trial in the plantings to establish which varieties succeed best on the estate.

charles sturt university winery   ★★★☆

Boorooma Street, North Wagga Wagga, NSW 2650 **region** Southern New South Wales Zone
phone (02) 6933 2435 **fax** (02) 6933 4072 **open** Mon–Fri 11–5, weekends 11–4
winemaker Greg Gallagher **production** 20 000 cases **est.** 1977
product range ($10–22 R) The precise composition varies from one release to the next, but is divided into two sections: the top-of-the-range Limited Release Series (e.g. Cabernet Sauvignon Shiraz, Cowra Chardonnay, Méthode Champenoise, Cabernet Sauvignon, Botrytis Semillon, Liqueur Port and Liqueur Muscat) and a basic range of lower-priced varietals, including Chardonnay, Traminer Riesling, Sauvignon Blanc Semillon and Cabernet Sauvignon Shiraz.
summary A totally new $2.5 million commercial winery (replacing the 1977 winery) was opened on 9 April 2002, complementing the $1 million experimental winery opened in June 2001. The commercial winery has been funded through the sale of wines produced under the Charles Sturt University brand, wines which always offer the consumer good value. It seems reasonable to expect that the quality will rise in the wake of the opening of the two new facilities.

Charles Sturt Cellar Reserve Pinot Gris

❚❚❚❙ **2000** Light straw-green; a flowery bouquet with some herbal/grassy aromas is followed by a palate which has some presence on entry, with more of those lemony/grassy notes of the bouquet, but then tails off rather abruptly on the finish. **rating:** 83

best drinking 2001–2002 **best vintages** NA **drink with** Light seafood • $16.50

Charles Sturt Chardonnay

❚❚❚❙ **2000** Light to medium green-yellow; a fresh, light and clean bouquet with gentle citrus aromas flows into a pleasant melon and citrus-flavoured palate in easy-drinking style. **rating:** 84

best drinking 2001–2003 **best vintages** '98 **drink with** Grilled chicken • $12

charley brothers ★★☆

The Ruins Way, Inneslake, Port Macquarie, NSW 2444 **region** Hastings River
phone (02) 6581 1332 **fax** (02) 6581 0391 **open** Mon–Fri 11–5, weekends 10–5
winemaker John Cassegrain (Contract), Nick Charley **production** 1000 **est.** 1988
product range ($11–16 CD) Semillon, Chardonnay, Summer White, Pinot Noir, Shiraz, Cabernet
Merlot, Cabernet Sauvignon, Inneslake Mist, Tawny Port.
summary The property upon which the Charley Brothers vineyard is established has been in the family's
ownership since the turn of the century, but in fact had been planted to vines by a Major Innes in the
1840s. After carrying on logging and fruit growing at various times, the Charley family planted vines in
1988 with the encouragement of John Cassegrain. Around 7.5 hectares of vines have been established.

Charley Brothers Cabernet Merlot

TTTT **1998** Light red, very advanced; the earthy/spicy bouquet is almost lemony; the light-bodied palate
has mature cedary/earthy/berry flavours and soft tannins; a pleasant, drink-now style.   **rating:** 84
best drinking 2002–2003 **best vintages** '91, '93 **drink with** Lamb shanks • NA

charlotte plains   NR

RMB 3180, Dooleys Road, Maryborough, Vic 3465 **region** Bendigo
phone (03) 5361 3137 **open** By appointment
winemaker Roland Kaval **production** 80 **est.** 1990
product range ($16 ML) Shiraz.
summary Charlotte Plains is a classic example of miniaturism. Production comes from a close-planted
vineyard which is only 0.3 hectare, a quarter being shiraz, the remainder sauvignon blanc. The minuscule
production is sold solely through the mailing list and by phone.

🐢 chateau champsaur   NR

Wandang Lane, Forbes, NSW 2871 **region** Central Ranges Zone
phone (02) 6852 3908 **fax** (02) 6852 3902 **open** Sat 10–5, or by appointment
winemaker Pierre Dalle, Andrew McEwin **production** 200 **est.** 1866
product range ($10–13 CD) Colombard Semillon, Chateau Dry White, Shiraz, Shiraz Cabernet,
Fortified and Peach Wine.
summary No, the establishment date of 1866 is correct. In that year Frenchmen Joseph Bernard Raymond
and Auguste Nicolas took up a 130-hectare selection and erected a large wooden winery and cellar, with
production ranging up to 360 000 litres in a year in its heyday. They named it Champsaur after Raymond's
native valley in France, and it is said to be the oldest French winery in the southern hemisphere. In recent
years it traded as Lachlan Valley Wines, but under the ownership of Pierre Dalle it has reverted to its
traditional name and French ownership. Its business is in transition; most of the wines on offer at the
moment are derived from the Lachlan Valley days of the Chislett family, but with the new plantings and
consultancy winemaking by Andrew McEwin, changes are almost certain.

chateau dore   NR

303 Mandurang Road, Mandurang near Bendigo, Vic 3551 **region** Bendigo
phone (03) 5439 5278 **open** 7 days 10–5
winemaker Ivan Grose **production** 1000 **est.** 1860
product range ($9–14 CD) Riesling, Shiraz, Cabernet Sauvignon, Tawny Port.
summary Has been in the ownership of the Grose family since 1860, with the winery buildings dating
back respectively to 1860 and 1893. All wine is sold through the cellar door.

chateau dorrien   NR

Cnr Seppeltsfield Road and Barossa Valley Way, Dorrien, SA 5352 **region** Barossa Valley
phone (08) 8562 2850 **fax** (08) 8562 1416 **open** 7 days 10–5
winemaker Fernando Martin **production** 2000 **est.** 1983
product range ($10–18 CD) Riesling, Semillon Chardonnay, Traminer, Frontignac Traminer, Frontignac
Spätlese, Late Harvest Frontignac, Semillon Chardonnay Sparkling Brut, Prima Vera (light red), Limited
Release Grenache, Shiraz, Cabernet Sauvignon, Tawny Port.
summary Unashamedly and successfully directed at the tourist trade.

chateau francois ★★★

Broke Road, Pokolbin, NSW 2320 **region** Lower Hunter Valley
phone (02) 4998 7548 **fax** (02) 4998 7805 **open** Weekends 9–5 or by appointment
winemaker Don Francois **production** 700 **est.** 1969
product range ($11 ML) Pokolbin Mallee Semillon, Chardonnay, Shiraz Pinot Noir.
summary The retirement hobby of former NSW Director of Fisheries, Don Francois. Soft-flavoured and structured wines which frequently show regional characters but which are modestly priced and are all sold through the cellar door and by mailing list to a loyal following. The tasting room is available for private dinners for 12–16 people. Don Francois sailed through a quadruple-bypass followed by a mild stroke with his sense of humour intact, if not enhanced. A subsequent newsletter said (inter alia) '... my brush with destiny has changed my grizzly personality and I am now sweetness and light ... Can you believe? Well, almost!' He even promises comfortable tasting facilities.

chateau hornsby NR

Petrick Road, Alice Springs, NT 0870 **region** Alice Springs
phone (08) 8955 5133 **fax** (08) 8955 5133 **open** 7 days 11–4
winemaker Gordon Cook **production** 1000 **est.** 1976
product range ($12–17 CD) Riesling, Semillon, Chardonnay, Shiraz, Cabernet Sauvignon.
summary Draws in part upon 3 hectares of estate plantings, and in part from grapes and wines purchased from other regions. Very much a tourist-oriented operation, with numerous allied entertainments on offer.

chateau leamon ★★★★

5528 Calder Highway, Bendigo, Vic 3550 **region** Bendigo
phone (03) 5447 7995 **fax** (03) 5447 0855 **open** Wed–Mon 10–5
winemaker Ian Leamon **production** 2000 **est.** 1973
product range ($17–38 CD) Riesling, Semillon, Chardonnay, Shiraz, Reserve Shiraz, Cabernet Sauvignon Cabernet Franc Merlot, Reserve Cabernet Sauvignon.
summary After a period of uncertainty, Chateau Leamon is returning to some of its former glory. Ian Leamon is using locally grown grapes but is also looking to the Strathbogie Ranges for grapes for other wines, including Pinot Noir. Limited retail distribution in Vic, NSW and Qld; exports to Asia, the US, Canada, the UK and Germany.

Chateau Leamon Riesling

▼▼▼▽ 2001 Light green-yellow; early in its life, mineral and slate aromas are evident, but not much of the fruit escapes; similarly, the palate is vibrantly crisp but relatively austere early in its life. Paradoxically, this all adds up to the near certainty of significant fruit development over the years ahead. **rating:** 84

best drinking 2003–2008 **best vintages** NA **drink with** Shellfish • $17

Chateau Leamon Semillon

▼▼▼▼ 2001 Light to medium green-yellow; the bouquet is clean, fresh and tight, showing clear lemony/grassy varietal character, the oak barely evident. The palate has good flavour, the oak making its presence felt in terms of texture and structure (along with the malolactic ferment component) rather than flavour. Sophisticated winemaking. **rating:** 88

best drinking 2003–2007 **best vintages** NA **drink with** Richer fish dishes • $17

Chateau Leamon Shiraz

▼▼▼▼ 2000 Medium red-purple; the fresh, moderately intense bouquet has cherry, a touch of mint and a light dressing of vanilla. All of these characters contribute to the palate, with its mix of cherry, mint and sweet vanilla oak, finishing with soft tannins. A thoroughly easy-drinking style. **rating:** 88

best drinking 2001–2004 **best vintages** NA **drink with** Spaghetti bolognaise • $22

Chateau Leamon Reserve Shiraz

▼▼▼▼▼ 2000 Medium to full red-purple; the bouquet offers rich, dark plum and blackberry fruit married with attractive oak, the palate fulfilling the promise of the bouquet, with smooth, sweet dark plum fruit, hints of spice and soft tannins. The best for some time from a distinguished producer. **rating:** 94

best drinking 2002–2015 **best vintages** '97, '00 **drink with** Rich game • $38

chateau pato   ★★★★☆

Thompson's Road, Pokolbin, NSW 2320 **region** Lower Hunter Valley
phone (02) 4998 7634 **fax** (02) 4998 7860 **open** By appointment
winemaker Nicholas Paterson **production** 300 **est.** 1980
product range ($35 CD) Shiraz.
summary Nicholas and Roger Paterson took over responsibility for this tiny winery following the death
of their father David Paterson during the 1993 vintage. Two and a half hectares of shiraz, 1 hectare of
chardonnay and 0.5 hectare of pinot noir are grown; most of the grapes are sold, with a tiny quantity of
shiraz being made into a marvellous wine. David Paterson's inheritance is being handsomely guarded.

Chateau Pato Shiraz

▼▼▼▼▽ 2000 Medium to full red-purple; solid, savoury, slightly earthy/regional dark berry fruit and a
whisk of oak on the bouquet are followed by a rich, ripe and concentrated palate with dark
cherry/berry/plum, a hint of chocolate; finishes with fine, ripe tannins.   **rating:** 93

best drinking 2005–2015 **best vintages** '86, '87, '90, '91, '94, '98, '99, '00 **drink with** Barbecued beef • $35

chateau tanunda   NR

9 Basedow Road, Tanunda, SA 5352 **region** Barossa Valley
phone (08) 8563 3888 **fax** (08) 8563 1422 **open** 7 days 10–5
winemaker Simon Gilbert, Ralph Fowler (Contract) **production** 8000 **est.** 1890
product range ($14–36 CD) The Chateau Riesling, Chardonnay, Shiraz and Cabernet Sauvignon;
Chateau Cadet Frontignac, Chardonnay, Cabernet Rosé, Shiraz, Merlot, Cabernet Sauvignon Shiraz,
Shiraz, Cabernet Sauvignon.
summary This is one of the most imposing winery buildings in the Barossa Valley, built from stone
quarried at nearby Bethany in the late 1880s. It started life as a winery, then became a specialist brandy
distillery until the death of the Australian brandy industry, whereafter it was simply used as storage cellars. It
has now been completely restored, and converted to a major convention facility catering for groups up to
400. The large complex also houses a cellar door where the Chateau Tanunda wines are sold; Chateau
Bistro, gardens and a croquet lawn; the Barossa Small Winemakers Centre, offering wines made by small
independent winemakers in the region; and, finally, specialist support services for tour operators.

chatsfield   ★★★★

O'Neil Road, Mount Barker, WA 6324 **region** Great Southern
phone (08) 9851 1704 **fax** (08) 9851 1704 **open** Tues-Sun, public holidays 10.30–4.30
winemaker Rob Lee, John Wade (Consultant) **production** 4500 **est.** 1976
product range ($14–20 CD) Mount Barker Riesling, Gewürztraminer, Chardonnay, Cabernet Franc, Shiraz.
summary Irish-born medical practitioner Ken Lynch can be proud of his achievements at Chatsfield, as
can most of the various contract winemakers who have taken the high-quality estate-grown material and
made some impressive wines, notably the Riesling, the vibrant Cabernet Franc (as an unwooded nouveau
style) and the spicy licorice Shiraz. Exports to Ireland, the UK, Ireland, Japan, Hong Kong and Singapore.

Chatsfield Mount Barker Riesling

▼▼▼▼ 2001 Light green-yellow; the aromatic bouquet has light apple blossom and lime aromas; the palate
is quite delicate, with crisp apple and a touch of mineral flavour; will undoubtedly develop with time in
bottle.   **rating:** 89

best drinking 2003–2008 **best vintages** '85, '87, '89, '90, '93, '94, '96, '01 **drink with** Spring salads • $16

chepstowe vineyard   ★★★☆

Fitzpatricks Lane, Carngham, Vic 3351 **region** Ballarat
phone (03) 5344 9412 **fax** (03) 5344 9403 **open** 7 days 10–5
winemaker John Ellis (Contract) **production** 700 **est.** 1994
product range ($25–30 CD) Chardonnay, Pinot Noir.
summary Way back in 1983 Bill Wallace asked the then Yellowglen winemaker Dominique Landragin
what he thought about the suitability of a block of steeply sloping grazing land on the side of the
Chepstowe Hill, looking north-east across to the Grampians and its various mountains, including Mount
Misery. Landragin replied, 'it might be possible to grow grapes there', and Wallace subsequently acquired
the property. It was not until November 1994 that 1 hectare each of pinot noir and chardonnay was

planted, followed by an additional hectare of pinot noir in 1996. In the warmest of vintages it is possible to obtain full ripeness for table wines, but in normal years I suspect sparkling wine (of potentially high quality) might be the best option.

chestnut grove ★★★★

Chestnut Grove Road, Manjimup, WA 6258 **region** Manjimup
phone (08) 9772 4345 **fax** (08) 9772 4543 **open** 7 days 10–4
winemaker Kim Horton **production** 12 000 **est.** 1988
product range ($14–38 R) Sauvignon Blanc, Verdelho, Chardonnay, Pinot Noir, Cabernet Merlot, Merlot, Vermilion, Platinum.
summary A substantial vineyard which is now reaching maturity and the erection of an on-site winery are the most obvious signs of change, but ownership, too, has been passed on by the late founder Vic Kordic to his sons Paul (a Perth lawyer) and Mark (the general manager of the wine business). Exports to Canada, Denmark, Germany, Hong Kong, Singapore and the UK.

Chestnut Grove Sauvignon Blanc

▼▼▼▼ **2001** Exceptionally pale, almost water white; varietal character comes through the light bouquet with hints of passionfruit and an odd touch of overripe kiwi fruit. The wine is quite well structured until its finish, when the 13.5° alcohol heats up the mouthfeel. **rating:** 85

best drinking 2002–2003 **best vintages** '98 **drink with** Chinese prawns • $18

Chestnut Grove Pinot Noir

▼▼▼▼ **2001** Strong colour; the complex bouquet has savoury aspects to the dark plum skin aromas, characters which come through on the rich, dark plum-flavoured palate, which has plenty of weight and depth, but, like the Sauvignon Blanc, is slightly let down by the hot finish from the 14.5° alcohol. **rating:** 89

best drinking 2004–2009 **best vintages** '01 **drink with** Pot-roasted quail • $37

Chestnut Grove Merlot

▼▼▼▼ **2000** Medium to full red-purple; the bouquet has positive fruit with faintly earthy/olivaceous aromas which are distinctly varietal. The palate has good texture and structure, with nice berryish fruit, but is dominated (at the moment) by cedar and vanilla oak. Needs time to come together. **rating:** 89

best drinking 2004–2009 **best vintages** '99 **drink with** Milk-fed veal • $37

chestnut hill vineyard NR

1280 Pakenham Road, Mount Burnett, Vic 3781 **region** Gippsland
phone (03) 5942 7314 **fax** (03) 5942 7314 **open** Weekends and public holidays 10.30–5.30, or by appointment
winemaker Charlie Javor **production** 1100 **est.** 1995
product range ($15–18 CD) Chardonnay, Sauvignon Blanc, Shiraz.
summary Charlie and Ivka Javor started Chestnut Hill with small plantings of chardonnay and shiraz in 1985 and have slowly increased the vineyards to their present total of a little over 3 hectares. The first wines were made in 1995, and all distribution is through the cellar door and direct to a few restaurants. Situated less than 1 hour's drive from Melbourne, the picturesque vineyard lies among the rolling hills in the southeast of the Dandenongs near Mount Burnett. The wines reflect the cool climate.

🐂 cheviot bridge ★★★★

10/499 St Kilda Road, Melbourne, Vic 3004 **region** Central Victorian High Country
phone (03) 9820 9080 **fax** (03) 9820 9070 **open** Not
winemaker Hugh Cuthbertson **production** 50 000 **est.** 1998
product range ($14–25 R) CB range from southeast Australia of Chardonnay, Shiraz and Cabernet Merlot, primarily desined for export; top drawer Yea Valley range of Chardonnay, Pinot Noir, Shiraz, Merlot, Cabernet Merlot.
summary After 15 years at Mildara Blass, Hugh Cuthbertson heads up a highly experienced group of wine professionals who own Cheviot Bridge, armed with a lifetime experience in sales and marketing. Murrindindi Vineyards, his parents' venture, continues as a totally separate entity; the top echelon Cheviot Bridge Yea Valley range comes from four large vineyards in the Yea Valley. The wines are made under the direction of Hugh Cuthbertson at Yering Station, and are distributed by T3 Fine Wines. The CB range is made under the direction of O'Leary Walker. Exports to the US, which will be the major market.

Cheviot Bridge CB Chardonnay

TTTY 2001 Light green-yellow; a clean, quite fresh bouquet with light melon and nectarine fruit supported by subtle oak. The light to medium-bodied palate has gentle fruit; pleasantly unforced. **rating:** 84

best drinking 2002–2003 **best vintages** NA **drink with** Fried chicken • $14

Cheviot Bridge Yea Valley Chardonnay

TTTY 2000 Light to medium yellow-green; strong oak dominates the bouquet and the palate at this stage (12 months after vintage), and it is hard to imagine that the wine will come back into balance, but you never know. **rating:** 84

best drinking 2002–2005 **best vintages** NA **drink with** Brains in black butter • $25

Cheviot Bridge CB Shiraz

TTTT 2000 Medium purple-red; the clean bouquet offers cherry, a touch of plum and a hint of oak; an attractive fruit-forward style on the palate, with clean fruit and fine tannins. **rating:** 85

best drinking 2002–2004 **best vintages** NA **drink with** Hamburger • $14

Cheviot Bridge Yea Valley Shiraz

TTTT 2000 Deep purple-red; a complex barrel-ferment and oak characters surround the dark cherry fruit of the bouquet, and strongly toasty/charry oak comes rocketing through on the palate, which does, however, seem to have the density to soak up the oak given time. **rating:** 89

best drinking 2004–2009 **best vintages** NA **drink with** Leave it in the cellar • $25

Cheviot Bridge CB Cabernet Merlot

TTTY 2000 Medium red-purple; the clean, lively bouquet has small, red berry fruit aromas; no oak evident. The commensurately fresh, juicy berry palate is in uncompromising early-drinking style. **rating:** 84

best drinking 2004–2004 **best vintages** NA **drink with** Pizza • $14

Cheviot Bridge Yea Valley Cabernet Merlot

TTTTY 1999 Medium red-purple; sweet blackberry and blackcurrant fruit marries with well-balanced and integrated oak on the bouquet, showing a similar match of dark berry fruit, a hint of bitter chocolate, oak and tannins on the palate. **rating:** 90

best drinking 2004–2010 **best vintages** '99 **drink with** Lamb shanks • $25

ciavarella ★★★

Evans Lane, Oxley, Vic 3678 **region** King Valley
phone (03) 5727 3384 **fax** (03) 5727 3384 **open** Mon–Sat 9–6, Sun 10–6
winemaker Cyril Ciavarella **production** 3000 **est.** 1978
product range ($13–18 CD) Semillon, Verdelho, Chardonnay, Sweet White, Rosé, Durif, Dolcino (medium-bodied sweet red), Shiraz, Cabernet Sauvignon.
summary Cyril and Jan Ciavarella both entered the wine industry from other professions and have been producing wine since 1992. The vineyard was planted in 1978, with plantings and varieties being extended over the years. One variety, aucerot (first released in 375 ml bottles late 2001) was produced by Maurice O'Shea of McWilliam's Mount Pleasant in the Hunter Valley 50 or more years ago; the Ciavarella vines have been grown from cuttings collected from an old Glenrowan vineyard before the parent plants were removed in the mid-1980s.

clairault ★★★★

Henry Road (off Puzey Road), Wilyabrup, WA 6280 **region** Margaret River
phone (08) 9755 6225 **fax** (08) 9755 6229 **open** 7 days 10–5
winemaker Peter Stark **production** 49 000 **est.** 1976
product range ($17–50 CD) Riesling, Sauvignon Blanc, Semillon Sauvignon Blanc, Claireau (sweet white), Cabernet Merlot, Cabernet Sauvignon, Reserve (Cabernet blend, replacing The Clairault); also Swagman's Kiss Premium White, Chardonnay, Premium Red, Shiraz.
summary Bill and Ena Martin, with sons Conor, Brian and Shane, have purchased Clairault from the founders, Ian and Ani Lewis. The acquisition has led to a major expansion of the vineyards on the 120-hectare property. The 12 hectares of vines established by the Lewises, and up to 25-years-old, are being supplemented by the development of another 70 hectares of vines on the property, with an end-point ratio of 70 per cent red varieties to 30 per cent white varieties. This will see continuing steep increases in production. A restaurant has been opened for lunch seven days. Domestic distribution throughout all states; exports to the US and Ireland.

Clairault Riesling

▼▼▼▼▽ **2001** Light green-yellow; a crisp, clean and lively bouquet with minerally notes to the fore leads into an elegant wine with very good structure; quite outstanding in the context of Margaret River.   **rating:** 91

best drinking 2004–2010 **best vintages** '85, '88, '91, '92, '93, '01 **drink with** Shellfish • $19

Clairault Sauvignon Blanc

▼▼▼▼ **2001** Light straw-green; the bouquet is without fault, but does not exhibit a lot of character; however, the flavours build on the palate around a core of grass, herb and mineral.   **rating:** 86

best drinking 2002–2003 **best vintages** '93, '95, '97 **drink with** Shellfish • $20

Clairault Semillon Sauvignon Blanc

▼▼▼▼▽ **2001** Light to medium yellow-green; the bouquet has attractive fruit with a mix of lemon, lanolin and just a hint of gooseberry, followed by a palate with abundant, ripe citrus flavour; good length and balance. A blend of 90 per cent Semillon and 10 per cent Sauvignon Blanc.   **rating:** 90

best drinking 2002–2004 **best vintages** '88, '91, '92, '93, '95, '97, '01 **drink with** Seafood salad • $20

Clairault Swagman's Kiss Chardonnay

▼▼▼▼ **2001** Light green-yellow; a solid nectarine and peach bouquet in an apparently unoaked style, then a palate showing lively fruit with particularly good acidity and structure in full-on nectarine mould. **rating:** 86

best drinking 2002–2004 **best vintages** NA **drink with** Barbecued chicken • $17

Clairault Reserve

▼▼▼▼ **1998** Medium red-purple; both the bouquet and palate seem to have entered the secondary phase of development, accentuating the savoury/earthy characters, and diminishing the primary fruit flavours. The palate is long, cedary and savoury in an underplayed style. A blend of 85 per cent Cabernet Sauvignon, 12 per cent Cabernet Franc and 3 per cent Merlot.   **rating:** 88

best drinking 2002–2007 **best vintages** '82, '85, '86, '90, '91, '95 **drink with** Margaret River Chevre • $50

Clairault Cabernet Merlot

▼▼▼▼ **2000** Medium purple-red; clean, fresh, sweet berry aromas are followed by a palate offering a mix of light but sweet berry fruit, then a more savoury finish around fine tannins.   **rating:** 85

best drinking 2004–2009 **best vintages** NA **drink with** Braised lamb • $28

Clairault Cabernet Sauvignon

▼▼▼▼▽ **2000** Medium red-purple; the bouquet has cedary, savoury, spicy overtones to fractionally subdued blackberry fruit, but the wine leaps into top gear with the powerful and penetrating palate, driven by a mix of intense blackberry and savoury dark chocolate flavours.   **rating:** 91

best drinking 2007–2012 **best vintages** '00 **drink with** Boned leg of lamb • $32

🐌 clarence hill   NR

PO Box 530, McLaren Vale, SA 5171 **region** McLaren Vale
phone (08) 8323 8946 **fax** (08) 8323 9644 **open** Not
winemaker Claudio Curtis, Brian Light (Contract) **production** NA **est.** 1990
product range ($11–20 R) Clarence Hill range of Semillon, Chardonnay, Shiraz, Cabernet Sauvignon Merlot.
summary This is indeed a complicated story, with the Curtis family as its core, encompassing a wine history dating back to the 15th century in Italy. In 1956 the family emigrated to Australia, purchased its first vineyard land from one Clarence William Torrens Rivers, and renamed it Clarence Hill. Further land was acquired in the 1980s and 1990s, establishing the Landcross Farm and California Rise vineyards, which, together with Clarence Hill, now have over 100 hectares in production. In 1990 Claudio Curtis, having previously acquired a science degree from the University of Adelaide, formed the Tiers Wine Co. (Australia) Pty Ltd to undertake wine production and sales. That company, obviously enough, has nothing to do with Petaluma (who produce Tiers Chardonnay), and just to complicate matters yet further, a new winery adjacent to the company's vineyards, operational for the 2002 vintage, is called Landcross Estate Winery.

Clarence Hill

▼▼▼▼▽ **1998** Dark red-purple; a powerful, indeed massive, wine with super-charged fruit and oak, and what would appear to be commensurately high alcohol.   **rating:** 92

best drinking 2004–2014 **best vintages** '98 **drink with** Chargrilled rump steak • $19.50

clarendon hills ★★★★☆

Brookmans Road, Blewitt Springs, SA 5171 **region** McLaren Vale
phone (08) 8364 1484 **fax** (08) 8364 1484 **open** By appointment
winemaker Roman Bratasiuk **production** 15 000 **est.** 1989
product range ($45—120 R) Hickinbotham Chardonnay, Hickinbotham Pinot Noir, Liandra Shiraz, Moritz Vineyard Shiraz, Piggott Range Shiraz, Romas Grenache, Hickinbotham Merlot, Hickinbotham Cabernet Sauvignon.
summary Clarendon Hills produces some of the most startlingly concentrated, rich and full-bodied red wines to be found in Australia, rivalled in this respect only by Wendouree. Roman Bratasiuk is a larger-than-life figure who makes larger-than-life wines. Technocrats may quibble about this or that aspect, but influential judges such as Robert Parker have neither reservations about nor problems with the immense, brooding red wines which Bratasiuk regularly produces from small patches of old, low-yielding vines which he ferrets out. Moreover, even the technocrats were silenced by the technical excellence of the 1998 and 1999 vintage wines. Exports to New Zealand, the US, Canada, Germany, Switzerland, Belgium, the Netherlands, Sweden, the UK and Japan.

Clarendon Hills Hickinbotham Vineyard Chardonnay
TTTT 1999 Medium yellow-green; the bouquet charges with full-on complexity from charry barrel ferment over melon fruit; the palate is a replay, full-bodied and oak-dominated; the bouquet is a bit more convincing than the palate. **rating:** 87
best drinking 2002–2006 **best vintages** NA **drink with** Crumbed brains • $45

Clarendon Hills Hickinbotham Vineyard Pinot Noir
TTTT 1999 Medium red, not 100 per cent bright, and, like all of the reds, presumably not filtered. The bouquet is complex and savoury, with the varietal fruit suppressed. The palate is complex and savoury, likely to dry out with further age. As with the Chardonnay, will doubtless have its fierce supporters. **rating:** 85
best drinking 2002–2004 **best vintages** NA **drink with** Chinese deep-fried quail • $65

Clarendon Hills Liandra Shiraz
TTTT 1999 Slightly hazy red-purple; the clean, moderately intense bouquet offers complex dark plum fruit, with hints of earth and spice, the palate adding some vanilla to those earthy, spicy characters. Notwithstanding that all three 1999 Clarendon Hills Shiraz wines have 14.5° alcohol, this is the lightest of the three. **rating:** 87
best drinking 2004–2009 **best vintages** '98 **drink with** Oxtail • $80

Clarendon Hills Moritz Vineyard Shiraz
TTTT 1999 Medium red-purple, slightly brighter than the Liandra. Firm, clean dark cherry and plum fruit on the bouquet leads the palate down the same path, finishing with dusty tannins. **rating:** 88
best drinking 2004–2011 **best vintages** NA **drink with** Osso buco • $80

Clarendon Hills Piggott Range Vineyard Shiraz
TTTTY 1999 Slightly more accent on the purple components than the other two 1999 Clarendon Hills wines. A firm bouquet, with savoury, dark berry fruit and a touch of mint, then the most concentrated and firmly fruited palate, with dusty tannins running through its length. All three of the Shiraz wines are 14.5°; happily, none seems to show any heat or heaviness from the alcohol. **rating:** 90
best drinking 2004–2014 **best vintages** '98 **drink with** Seared beef • $120

Clarendon Hills Romas Vineyard Old Vine Grenache
TTTTY 1999 Medium red-purple; clean, firm, juicy berry fruit, which is not jammy, and has well-balanced and integrated oak joining it on the bouquet. The palate is very well-balanced and structured, with dark, slightly spicy/savoury berry fruit, and smooth, ripe tannins. **rating:** 93
best drinking 2002–2009 **best vintages** '99 **drink with** Beef in red wine sauce • $80

Clarendon Hills Hickinbotham Vineyard Cabernet Sauvignon
TTTT 1999 Medium to full red-purple; the bouquet has hints of hay and straw over ripe blackberry fruit; powerful black fruits are at the centre of a fairly austere palate, finishing with lingering tannins. **rating:** 89
best drinking 2004–2014 **best vintages** '98 **drink with** Kangaroo fillet • $65

classic mclaren wines ★★★★

Lot B Coppermine Road, McLaren Vale, SA 5171 **region** McLaren Vale
phone (08) 8323 9551 **fax** (08) 8323 9551 **open** By appointment
winemaker Tony De Lisio **production** 4500 **est.** 1996
product range ($20–110 R) CMC Shiraz and Grenache; and La Testa range of Chardonnay, Shiraz, Blend (Shiraz Grenache Cabernet Sauvignon), Merlot, Grenache and Cabernet Sauvignon.
summary Tony and Krystina De Lisio have established a substantial business in a relatively short period of time. They have established vineyard plantings of shiraz (20.47 hectares), merlot (11.34 hectares), cabernet sauvignon (9.29 hectares), semillon (3.9 hectares) and chardonnay (0.41 hectare), and are currently building a new winery and underground cellar storage for wine in barrel and packaged wine. When the new buildings are completed, there will be facilities for tastings, promotions and the possibility of limited cellar door sales. The wines are distributed in Sydney and Melbourne by Ultimo Wine Centre, Adelaide being serviced direct from the winery. Exports to the US, Thailand, Germany, Belgium, Switzerland and New Zealand have been established at impressively high prices.

Classic McLaren Wines La Testa Shiraz

TTTT **1999** Medium to full red-purple; a powerful, concentrated oak-driven bouquet is followed by a palate with rich dark fruits, chocolate, soft tannins and massive American oak. Both the style and the price will doubtless appeal to some more than others. **rating:** 88

best drinking 2004–2009 **best vintages** NA **drink with** Rump steak • $120

Classic McLaren Wines La Testa Blend

TTTTY **2000** Youthful red-purple; a direct, fresh, clean, sweet berry bouquet with controlled oak leads into a palate with good concentration and length; sweet juicy varietal character is complexed by subtle oak and soft, fine tannins. **rating:** 90

best drinking 2003–2010 **best vintages** NA **drink with** Bistecca Fiorentina • $54.95

Classic McLaren Wines La Testa Grenache

TTTT **1999** Medium to full red-purple; the ripe and rich bouquet is primarily driven by spicy berry fruit, with a touch of oak in the background. The palate shows plenty of grenache fruit in full varietal mode, but is not too jammy or confection-like. Not surprisingly, the first release from the great 1998 vintage was an even better wine. **rating:** 87

best drinking 2002–2006 **best vintages** NA **drink with** Game pie • $44.95

Classic McLaren Wines La Testa Cabernet Sauvignon

TTTTY **1999** Medium red-purple; the moderately intense bouquet is spotlessly clean, with gently savoury cabernet varietal fruit and sweetly spicy oak. The palate has good structure and texture, with savoury berryflavours, fine tannins and good length; the oak is far from overwhelming. Once again, the '98 was the outstanding wine. **rating:** 90

best drinking 2004–2010 **best vintages** '98, '99 **drink with** Fillet of beef • $54.95

claymore wines NR

Leasingham Road, Leasingham, SA 5452 **region** Clare Valley
phone 0412 822 250 **fax** (08) 8284 2899 **open** Weekends and public holidays 10–5
winemaker Justin Ardill, Hugh Mathews **production** 2000 **est.** 1998
product range ($14–30 CD) Riesling, Joshua Tree Riesling, Semillon Chardonnay, Duet Red, Nocturne Shiraz, Nocturne Cabernet.
summary Claymore Wines draws on various vineyards, some situated in the Clare Valley, others in McLaren Vale. The Kupu-Kupu vineyard at Penwortham has 9 hectares of shiraz and 2 hectares of merlot, all planted in 1997; the Nocturne series of wines come from the Wilpena and Moray Park vineyards, owned by the Trott family; the Joshua Tree Watervale Riesling comes from old vines on the Leasingham to Mintaro road which are not estate-owned (although the story is, I must admit, somewhat complex). It is the Joshua Tree Riesling which has attracted high ratings from magazines and at the Clare Valley Wine Show.

Claymore Joshua Tree Riesling

TTTTY **2001** Light to medium yellow-green; herb, apple and lime aromas on the bouquet are followed by abundant fruit flavour, body and length on the palate; big, yet not heavy. Gold medal winner at the 2001 Clare Valley Regional Wine Show. **rating:** 92

best drinking 2001–2007 **best vintages** '01 **drink with** Salmon and asparagus terrine • $18

clearview estate mudgee ★★★★

Cnr Sydney and Rocky Water Hole Roads, Mudgee, NSW 2850 **region** Mudgee
phone (02) 6372 4546 **fax** (02) 6372 7577 **open** Fri–Mon 10–4 or by appointment
winemaker Letitia (Tish) Cecchini **production** 2200 **est.** 1995
product range ($14–19 CD) Church Creek Chardonnay (oaked and unoaked); Rocky Waterhole Red Shiraz and Cabernet Sauvignon.
summary No relationship with the famous Hawke's Bay winery, but doubtless John E Hickey would be delighted to achieve the same quality. They have progressively planted 4.16 hectares of shiraz, 2.16 hectares each of chardonnay and cabernet sauvignon, 1.5 hectare of merlot, and small amounts of cabernet franc, semillon, pinot grigio, barbera and sangiovese (yet to come into bearing) since 1995, and send the grapes to the Hunter Valley for contract making. An 'Aussie Farm' style cellar door, with a timber deck looking out over the vineyard and surrounding vista, was opened in September 2000. Exports to the US.

Clearview Estate Mudgee Church Creek Chardonnay

▼▼▼▼▼ **2000** Light to medium green-yellow; the bouquet is complex, with a mix of cashew and oak, the fruit still to fully express itself. However, the palate provides a very different picture: it is well-balanced and constructed, with melon/nectarine fruit to the fore providing excellent mouthfeel. **rating:** 94

best drinking 2002–2005 **best vintages** '00 **drink with** Pan-fried veal • $17

Clearview Estate Mudgee Rocky Waterhole Red Shiraz

▼▼▼▼ **1999** Bright purple-red; the bouquet is ripe and full, with slightly gamey overtones which some will regard as simply varietal, others as suggestive of brettanomyces. The palate is full-bodied, with ripe black cherry and plum fruit, finishing with soft tannins. **rating:** 85

best drinking 2003–2007 **best vintages** NA **drink with** Steak and kidney pie • $17

clemens hill ★★★

686 Richmond Road, Cambridge, Tas 7170 **region** Southern Tasmania
phone (03) 6248 5985 **fax** (03) 6248 5985 **open** By appointment
winemaker Julian Alcorso (Contract) **production** 650 **est.** 1994
product range ($16.50–19.50 CD) Sauvignon Blanc, Chardonnay, Pinot Noir.
summary The Shepherd family acquired Clemens Hill in June 2001 after selling their Rosabrook winery in the Margaret River to Palandri Wines. They also have a shareholding in Winemaking Tasmania, the newly established contract winemaking facility run by Julian Alcorso, who will henceforth make the Clemens Hill wines. A trebling of the estate vineyards from 1 hectare to over 3 hectares is also planned.

Clemens Hill Chardonnay

▼▼▼▼ **2001** Light to medium yellow-green; clean, fresh, citrus-toned aromas lead into a palate which has good length, in austere, cool-climate style. No oak evident. **rating:** 86

best drinking 2002–2006 **best vintages** NA **drink with** Delicate seafood • $18

Clemens Hill Pinot Noir

▼▼▼▽ **2000** Light to medium red-purple; a clean bouquet with some strawberry fruit is followed by a pleasant palate, again with strawberry accents, but lacking the firepower of the better wines of the vintage. **rating:** 81

best drinking 2002–2003 **best vintages** NA **drink with** Fresh grilled salmon • $16.50

cleveland ★★★★

Shannons Road, Lancefield, Vic 3435 **region** Macedon Ranges
phone (03) 5429 1449 **fax** (03) 5429 2017 **open** 7 days 9–5
winemaker Keith Brien **production** 2500 **est.** 1985
product range ($10–45 CD) Chardonnay, Pinot Gris, Macedon Brut, Brut Rosé, Pinot Noir, Heathcote Shiraz, Minus Five Cabernet Merlot; Brien Family Chardonnay Gordo, Muscat Gordo Blanco, Shiraz.
summary The Cleveland homestead was built in 1889 in the style of a Gothic Revival manor house, but had been abandoned for 40 years when purchased by the Briens in 1983. It has since been painstakingly restored, and 3.8 hectares of surrounding vineyard established. In January 2002 a partnership was formed between Keith Brien and the Grange Group of Conference Centres, which initiated fast-track development of The Grange at Cleveland Winery, with 22 suites, plus a large conference room and facilities alongside a new winery and warehouse. Exports to the UK.

Cleveland Macedon Brut

▼▼▼▼ **1997** Medium to full yellow-green; a complex but fruit-driven bouquet is followed by a palate with equally plentiful fruit, quite rich but well balanced. Strongly supported at the 2001 Macedon Ranges Wine Exhibition. **rating:** 89

best drinking 2001–2005 **best vintages** NA **drink with** Oysters • $30

Cleveland Pinot Noir

▼▼▼▼▼ **1998** Strong red-purple; the bouquet is quite powerful, with rich plummy and black cherry fruit. The palate, likewise, has masses of fruit flavour in a dark plum spectrum, with considerable extract and complexity. Will go on from here. **rating:** 94

best drinking 2001–2006 **best vintages** '91, '92, '94, '98 **drink with** Coq au vin • $26

Cleveland Minus Five Cabernet Merlot

▼▼▼▼ **1998** Medium red-purple; there are two distinct strands to the bouquet, with jammy berry on the one hand and more minty notes (and light oak) on the other. The palate has good depth and structure, with quite surprising tannins. **rating:** 85

best drinking 2003–2008 **best vintages** NA **drink with** Braised lamb • $30

cliff house NR

57 Camms Road, Kayena, Tas 7270 **region** Northern Tasmania
phone (03) 6394 7454 **fax** (03) 6394 7454 **open** By appointment
winemaker Julian Alcorso (Contract) **production** 2500 **est.** 1983
product range ($18–20 R) Riesling, Chardonnay, Pinot Noir, Devil's Elbow (Pinot Cabernet blend), Cabernet Sauvignon.
summary Cliff House has undergone a metamorphosis. In 1999 Geoff and Cheryl Hewitt sold the 4-hectare vineyard they established in the Tamar Valley area in 1983. They have now turned a two-hole golf course around their house into a second, new vineyard, planted to riesling and pinot noir. No recent tastings.

clonakilla ★★★★☆

Crisps Lane, Murrumbateman, NSW 2582 **region** Canberra District
phone (02) 6227 5877 **fax** (02) 6227 5871 **open** 7 days 11–5
winemaker Tim Kirk **production** 3500 **est.** 1971
product range ($16–42 CD) Riesling, Semillon Sauvignon Blanc, Viognier, Chardonnay, Shiraz Viognier, Hilltops Shiraz, Cabernet Merlot.
summary The indefatigable Tim Kirk, who has many of the same personality characteristics as Frank Tate (of Evans & Tate), has taken over the management of Clonakilla from father and scientist Dr John Kirk. The quality of the wines is excellent, none more so than the highly regarded Shiraz Viognier, which sells out quickly every year. Exports to the UK, the US, Canada, Singapore and Hong Kong.

Clonakilla Riesling

▼▼▼▼▼ **2001** Light green-yellow; fine lemon and apple, with hints of herb and spice, drive an attractive bouquet. The palate offers well-balanced, sweet citrus fruit flavours which run evenly through the long palate. **rating:** 92

best drinking 2002–2007 **best vintages** '91, '93, '94, '95, '97, '00, '01 **drink with** Spiced Asian dishes • $19

Clonakilla Viognier

▼▼▼▼▼ **2001** Medium green-yellow; the bouquet has a mix of aromas, running through blossom to dried fruits and a hint of lychee; the palate has mouth-coating flavour and rich texture, seemingly even higher than the 13.5°. All in all, strongly varietal. **rating:** 91

best drinking 2002–2004 **best vintages** '00, '01 **drink with** Carpaccio of salmon • $30

Clonakilla Chardonnay

▼▼▼▼ **2000** Medium yellow-green; a moderately intense bouquet with smooth nectarine/peach fruit and subtle oak, then a generous palate with a mix of yellow peach and fig fruit in a soft, mouthfilling style. A very good outcome for the vintage, but to be drunk sooner rather than later. **rating:** 89

best drinking 2002–2003 **best vintages** NA **drink with** Creamy pasta • $24

Clonakilla Hilltops Shiraz

♥♥♥♡ 2000 Youthful red-purple; a complex bouquet, with spice, licorice and a distinct overlay of gaminess; a big, powerful, chunky/gamey style in the mouth, with no shortage of flavour, but a question mark on the origins of that game. **rating:** 84

best drinking 2002–2005 **best vintages** NA **drink with** Game pie • $19

Clonakilla Shiraz Viognier

♥♥♥♥♡ 2000 Medium red-purple; a complex and aromatic bouquet with a mix of spice, licorice, berry and game; a high-toned and accented palate, extremely complex, and again raising the question where those gamey characters come from. **rating:** 90

best drinking 2002–2006 **best vintages** '90, '92, '93, '94, '95, '97, '98, '99 **drink with** Jugged hare • $42

clos clare ★★★★

Old Road, Watervale, SA 5452 **region** Clare Valley
phone (08) 8843 0161 **fax** (08) 8843 0161 **open** Weekends and public holidays 10–5
winemaker Various Contract **production** 1000 **est.** 1993
product range ($17–22 CD) Riesling, Shiraz.
summary Clos Clare is based on a small (2 hectares), unirrigated section of the original Florita Vineyard once owned by Leo Buring and which produces Riesling of extraordinary concentration and power. Exports to the US and Ireland.

Clos Clare Riesling

♥♥♥♥ 2001 Light to medium green-yellow; a crisp, light, minerally bouquet has a substrate of floral passionfruit which comes through quite strongly on the very lively palate. A very pretty, slightly sweet, wine. **rating:** 88

best drinking 2002–2006 **best vintages** NA **drink with** Thai cuisine • $16.50

Clos Clare Shiraz

♥♥♥♥ 2000 Medium purple-red; savoury/spicy fruit aromas are accompanied by pronounced oak on the bouquet; there is a similar array of spicy/savoury/oaky flavours on the palate, supported by fair tannins. **rating:** 88

best drinking 2004–2009 **best vintages** '99 **drink with** Venison ragout • $23.50

clovely estate NR

Steinhardts Road, Moffatdale via Murgon, Qld 4605 **region** South Burnett
phone (07) 3876 5200 **fax** (07) 3876 5200 **open** 7 days 10–5
winemaker David Lowe, Adam Chapman (Contract) **production** 15 000 **est.** 1998
product range ($12.95–14.95 CD) Left Field Semillon Chardonnay, Chardonnay, Shiraz; Fifth Row Chardonnay, Shiraz Cabernet.
summary Although new-born, Clovely Estate has the largest vineyards in Queensland, having established 174 hectares of vines at two locations just to the east of Murgon in the Burnett Valley. There are 127 hectares of red grapes (including 74 hectares of shiraz) and 47 hectares of white grapes. The attractively packaged wines are sold in four tiers: Clovely Estate at the top end (this will not be produced every year); Left Field, strongly fruity and designed to age; Fifth Row, for early drinking; and Outback, primarily designed for the export market.

clover hill ★★★★☆

Clover Hill Road, Lebrina, Tas 7254 **region** Northern Tasmania
phone (03) 6395 6114 **fax** (03) 6395 6257 **open** 7 days 10–5, by appointment in winter
winemaker Shane Clohesy, Peter Steer, Loic Le Calvez **production** 4000 **est.** 1986
product range ($33 R) Clover Hill (Sparkling).
summary Clover Hill was established by Taltarni in 1986 with the sole purpose of making a premium sparkling wine. Its 20 hectares of vineyards, comprising 12 hectares of chardonnay, 6.5 of pinot noir and 1.5 of pinot meunier, are still coming into bearing, and production is steadily increasing. Wine quality is excellent, combining finesse with power and length.

Clover Hill
▼▼▼▼ **1998** Light straw-green; a very closed bouquet, which may or may not have been due to subliminal cork taint, then a very fine, crisp, taut citrussy palate of well above average length. A strange series of circumstances prevented the tasting of the second bottle. Rated as tasted. **rating:** 88

best drinking 2002–2005 **best vintages** '90, '91, '92, '95, '96 **drink with** Caviar, shellfish • $33

coal valley vineyard ★★★★
257 Richmond Road, Cambridge, Tas 7170 **region** Southern Tasmania
phone (03) 6248 5367 **fax** (03) 6248 4175 **open** Fri–Sun 12–5 or by appointment
winemaker Andrew Hood (Contract) **production** 500 **est.** 1991
product range ($19–35 CD) Riesling, Chardonnay, Pinot Noir, Cabernet Merlot.
summary Coal Valley Vineyard is the new name for Treehouse Vineyard and Wine Centre, the change brought about by the fact that Treehouse had been trademarked by the Pemberton winery, Salitage. The vineyard was purchased by Todd Goebel and wife Gillian Christian in 1999. They have set about doubling the size of the existing riesling vineyard, and establishing 1.5 hectares of another vineyard planted to pinot noir, with a few vines of cabernet. Their plans also include the renovation of the Wine Centre to incorporate a full commercial kitchen and windows overlooking the existing vineyard and the Coal River Valley; this renovation was completed in 2002.

Coal Valley Vineyard Riesling
▼▼▼▼ **2001** Pale yellow-green; the bouquet is light, fresh and clean, but not particularly aromatic; the palate likewise is fractionally spongy; strangely, the wine creeps up on you when retasted. **rating:** 86

best drinking 2002–2005 **best vintages** '99 **drink with** Caesar salad • $19

Coal Valley Vineyard Chardonnay
▼▼▼▼ **2000** Light green-yellow; fragrant, citrus blossom and peach aromas are followed by a fresh and lively palate, with white peach/stone fruit flavours, and crisp acidity to close. **rating:** 86

best drinking 2001–2004 **best vintages** '98, '99 **drink with** Grilled white-fleshed fish • $15

Coal Valley Vineyard Pinot Noir
▼▼▼▽ **2000** The moderately intense colour has good hue; the bouquet is clean, but neither expressive nor complex, and the palate has a linear, low pH style, with relatively high acidity. Needs time to soften. **rating:** 83

best drinking 2003–2007 **best vintages** NA **drink with** Grilled chicken livers • $22

Coal Valley Vineyard Cabernet Merlot
▼▼▼▼▼ **2000** Medium to full red-purple; a luscious, sweet and concentrated bouquet, then a similarly ripe and luscious palate, swollen with sweet cassis fruit, and tempered by very good oak and appropriate tannins. Trophy winner 2002 Tasmanian Wines Show. **rating:** 95

best drinking 2005–2010 **best vintages** '00 **drink with** Venison • $35

coalville vineyard NR
RMB 4750, Moe South Road, Moe South, Vic 3825 **region** Gippsland
phone (03) 5127 4229 **fax** (03) 5127 2148 **open** 7 days 10–5
winemaker Peter Beasley **production** 3000 **est.** 1985
product range ($15–18 CD) Chardonnay, Malbec, Merlot, Cabernet Merlot, Cabernet Sauvignon.
summary This is the new name for Mair's Coalville, following the sale of the property by Dr Stewart Mair to Peter Beasley, who had significantly increased not only the volume but the range of wines available.

cobanov NR
Stock Road, Herne Hill, WA 6056 **region** Swan District
phone (08) 9296 4210 **open** Wed–Sun 9–5.30
winemaker Steve Cobanov **production** 10 000 **est.** 1960
product range ($6–10 CD) Chenin Blanc, Chardonnay, Sauvignon Blanc, Verdelho, Shiraz, Grenache, Cabernet Sauvignon.
summary A substantial family-owned operation producing a mix of bulk and bottled wine from 21 hectares of estate grapes. Part of the annual production is sold as grapes to other producers, including Houghton, part is sold in bulk, part is sold in two-litre flagons, and the remainder is sold in modestly priced bottles.

cobaw ridge ★★★★☆

31 Perc Boyer's Lane, East Pastoria via Kyneton, Vic 3444 **region** Macedon Ranges
phone (03) 5423 5227 **fax** (03) 5423 5227 **open** 7 days 10–5
winemaker Alan Cooper **production** 1500 **est.** 1985
product range ($28–45 CD) Chardonnay, Lagrein, Shiraz, Shiraz Viognier.
summary Nelly and Alan Cooper established Cobaw Ridge's 6-hectare vineyard at an altitude of 610 metres in the hills above Kyneton, complete with self-constructed pole-framed mudbrick house and winery. The plantings of cabernet sauvignon have been removed and partially replaced by lagrein, a variety which sent me scuttling to Jancis Robinson's seminal book on grape varieties, from which I learned that it is a northeast Italian variety typically used to make delicate Rosé, but at Cobaw Ridge it is made into an impressive full-bodied dry red. The Coopers sold the winery in 2002, but Alan will remain as consultant winemaker, and says the wine styles won't change.

Cobaw Ridge Chardonnay

▼▼▼▼ 2000 Light to medium green-yellow; the moderately intense bouquet is developing very slowly, with melon fruit and gentle oak, well-balanced and integrated; the fine, elegant and long palate comes in an understated style which is still developing. **rating:** 88

best drinking 2002–2007 **best vintages** '99 **drink with** Honey chicken • $30

Cobaw Ridge Shiraz Viognier

▼▼▼▼▽ 2000 Medium red-purple; a fragrant, aromatic and exotic mix of spicy/earthy aromas on the bouquet are followed by an elegant, light to medium-bodied palate, the feel, structure and flavours strongly reminiscent of the wines of the northern Rhône Valley. **rating:** 93

best drinking 2004–2010 **best vintages** '00 **drink with** Salmon • $35

Cobaw Ridge Lagrein

▼▼▼▼ 2000 Full red-purple; the sweet, faintly jammy bouquet has aromas of raspberry, cigar and spice, characters which carry the palate, which then finishes with terse acidity, and needing time. **rating:** 86

best drinking 2005–2010 **best vintages** '99 **drink with** Braised ox cheek • $45

cobbitty wines NR

Cobbitty Road, Cobbitty, NSW 2570 **region** South Coast Zone
phone (02) 4651 2281 **fax** (02) 4651 2671 **open** Mon–Sat 10–5, Sun 12–6
winemaker Giovanni Cogno **production** 5000 **est.** 1964
product range ($5–14 CD) A full range of generic table, fortified and sparkling wines under the Cobbitty Wines label; also cocktail wines.
summary Draws upon 10 hectares of estate plantings of muscat, barbera, grenache and trebbiano, relying very much on local and ethnic custom.

🐌 cobb's hill NR

Oakwood Road, Oakbank, SA 5243 **region** Adelaide Hills
phone (08) 8388 4054 **fax** (08) 8388 4820 **open** Not
winemaker Martin Shaw, Willie Lunn **production** 700 **est.** 1997
product range ($15 ML) Riesling, Sauvignon Blanc, Chardonnay, Merlot.
summary Sally and Roger Cook have a 140-hectare property in the Adelaide Hills that takes its name from Cobb and Co., which used it as a staging post and resting place for 1000 horses. The Cooks now use the property to raise Angus cattle, grow cherries and, more recently, grow grapes. Three different sites on the property, amounting to just over 10 hectares, were planted to selected clones of sauvignon blanc, chardonnay, semillon and merlot, with riesling in the pipeline. Part of the production is sold to Shaw and Smith, who vinify the remainder for Cobb's Hill.

cockfighter's ghost vineyard ★★★★

Lot 251 Milbrodale Road, Broke, NSW 2330 **region** Lower Hunter Valley
phone (02) 9667 1622 **fax** (02) 9667 1442 **open** By appointment
winemaker Patrick Auld **production** 7500 **est.** 1994
product range ($16.50–28.50 R) Semillon, Verdelho, Unwooded Chardonnay, Chardonnay, Pinot Noir, Shiraz, Coonawarra Premium Reserve Cabernet Sauvignon.

summary Like Poole's Rock Vineyard, this vineyard is part of a rapidly expanding wine empire owned by eminent Sydney merchant banker David Clarke. It will be housed at the former Tulloch winery as from 2003. Accommodation is, however, available at the Milbrodale property. The wine has retail distribution throughout Australia and is exported to the UK, the US, Canada, New Zealand and Asia.

Cockfighter's Ghost Semillon

▼▼▼▼ **2001** Bright, light green-yellow; a crisp, flinty, minerally bouquet is followed by a lively palate with lemon and citrus on top of the mineral structure. CO_2 is evident, but the wine has good balance and potential. **rating:** 89

▼▼▼▼▽ **2000** Bright, light green-yellow; attractive lemon/herb/grass aromas on the bouquet lead into a palate with excellent focus and balance, and which belies its 12.5° alcohol. **rating:** 90

best drinking 2003–2010 **best vintages** '96, '98, '00, '01 **drink with** Fresh asparagus • $16.95

Cockfighter's Ghost Verdelho

▼▼▼▼ **2001** Light green-yellow; the bouquet is clean, with fruit salad aromas; the lemony palate has attractive mouthfeel, well above average for the standard fare which verdelho usually delivers. A major but pleasant surprise. **rating:** 86

▼▼▼▽ **2000** Light green-yellow; some citrus/lemon notes on the bouquet add interest, and the palate has above average flavour and length; good balance. **rating:** 84

best drinking 2001–2003 **best vintages** NA **drink with** Seafood pasta • $16.95

Cockfighter's Ghost Unwooded Chardonnay

▼▼▼▼ **2000** Bright, light green-yellow; the bouquet is quite fragrant, with gently ripe melon fruit, the palate likewise content to let the melon and nectarine fruit express itself; well-balanced and not forced. A good example, if such there be, of unwooded Chardonnay. **rating:** 86

best drinking 2002–2003 **best vintages** NA **drink with** Light Asian cuisine • $16.95

Cockfighter's Ghost Chardonnay

▼▼▼▼ **1999** Medium to full yellow-green; the bouquet is quite rich and ripe, with nice peachy fruit and a slightly tangy cross-cut. The palate opens with peach and a touch of citrus, but high levels of CO_2 then interfere and need time to dissipate. **rating:** 86

best drinking 2002–2005 **best vintages** NA **drink with** Pasta • $18.95

Cockfighter's Ghost Shiraz

▼▼▼▼ **1999** Light to medium red-purple; clean, gentle cherry fruit and subtle oak on the bouquet are followed by a medium-bodied palate, with a similar gentle mix of cherry, spice and a hint of vanilla. **rating:** 85

best drinking 2003–2007 **best vintages** NA **drink with** Ravioli • $21.95

Cockfighter's Ghost Vineyard Coonawarra Premium Reserve Cabernet Sauvignon

▼▼▼▼▽ **1999** Medium red-purple; the bouquet is fresh and clean, with pure, direct cassis/berry fruit, characters joined on the palate by a touch of mint. Fruit-driven and youthful, and will certainly flower with some years in bottle. **rating:** 90

best drinking 2004–2009 **best vintages** '99 **drink with** Braised lamb • $28.95

cofield wines ★★★★

Distillery Road, Wahgunyah, Vic 3687 **region** Rutherglen
phone (02) 6033 3798 **fax** (02) 6033 0798 **open** Mon–Sat 9–5, Sun 10–5
winemaker Max Cofield, Damien Cofield **production** 11 000 **est.** 1990
product range ($12–28 CD) Semillon, Semillon Chardonnay, Chenin Blanc, Max's Blend White, Chardonnay, Late Harvest Muscadelle, Shiraz, Gamay, Merlot, Max's Blend Red, Cabernet Franc, Cabernet Sauvignon, Sparkling, Fortified.
summary District veteran Max Cofield, together with wife Karen and sons Damien, Ben and Andrew, is developing a strong cellar-door sales base by staging in-winery functions with guest chefs, and also providing a large barbecue and picnic area. (The Pickled Sisters Cafe is open for lunch Wed–Mon; telephone (02) 6033 2377.) The quality of the red wines, in particular, is most impressive; it is for these wines that the rating is given. Limited retail distribution through Prime Wines in Melbourne, exports to the US.

Cofield Shiraz

▼▼▼▼ **2000** Bright medium red-purple; clean, sweet damson plum and black cherry aromas introduce a palate with good weight and flavour, with ample tannins running throughout its length; will richly repay cellaring. **rating: 89**

best drinking 2004–2009 **best vintages** '00 **drink with** Marinated beef • $18

Cofield Cabernet Franc

▼▼▼▼ **2000** Light to medium red-purple; the moderately intense bouquet has spicy, leafy berry aromas, not particularly complex, but varietal; the same characters appear on the palate, but there is a nice skein of red berry fruit running through its core. **rating: 85**

best drinking 2003–2007 **best vintages** NA **drink with** Veal goulash • $18

Cofield Rutherglen Merlot

▼▼▼▼▽ **2000** Medium red-purple; surprisingly rich, ripe, deep, dark berry aromas, with abundant early to mid-palate fruit, tightening up somewhat on the finish; not much varietal character, but a very good wine. **rating: 90**

best drinking 2004–2014 **best vintages** '00 **drink with** Veal piccata • $18

coldstream hills NR

31 Maddens Lane, Coldstream, Vic 3770 **region** Yarra Valley
phone (03) 5964 9410 **fax** (03) 5964 9389 **open** 7 days 10–5
winemaker Andrew Fleming, James Halliday (Consultant) **production** 50 000 **est.** 1985
product range ($20–54 CD) Pinot Gris, Sauvignon Blanc, Chardonnay, Reserve Chardonnay, Pinot Noir, Reserve Pinot Noir, Merlot, Reserve Merlot, Briarston (Cabernet Merlot), Reserve Cabernet Sauvignon, Pinot Noir Chardonnay Brut; occasional limited release wines sold chiefly through the cellar door.
summary Founded by the author, who continues to be involved with the winemaking, but acquired by Southcorp in mid-1996. Expansion plans already then underway have been maintained, with well in excess of 100 hectares of owned or managed estate vineyards as the base. Chardonnay and Pinot Noir continue to be the principal focus; Merlot came on-stream from the 1997 vintage. Vintage conditions permitting, these three wines are made in both varietal and Reserve form, the latter in restricted quantities.

Coldstream Hills Sauvignon Blanc

1997 was the first varietal Sauvignon Blanc produced by Coldstream Hills. In prior years the Sauvignon Blanc was blended with a greater volume of Semillon to produce a wine labelled Fumé Blanc. It is a blend of 90 per cent Sauvignon Blanc cold-fermented in stainless steel, principally sourced from Upper Yarra Valley vineyards, and ten per cent barrel-fermented Semillon.

2001 Light yellow-green; the bouquet is fragrant, with tropical fruits, lantana and gooseberry; a lively wine with sweet fruit flavours and soft acidity. **rating: 0**

best drinking 2002–2003 **best vintages** '97, '98 **drink with** Salad • $27.50

Coldstream Hills Pinot Gris

2000 Light straw; the bouquet offers delicate aromas of apple and pear. While relatively light-bodied, there is arresting fruit sweetness on the mid-palate, perhaps partly from the alcohol which is part and parcel of properly ripened pinot gris, but the finish is fresh and crisp, showing no alcohol heat. **rating: 0**

best drinking 2002–2004 **best vintages** NA **drink with** Seafood, chicken or pasta dishes. • $27.50

Coldstream Hills Chardonnay

2001 Light green-yellow; the bouquet has fragrant citrus blossom, melon and nectarine fruit aromas, which are supported by typically subtle French oak; excellent texture, balance and weight, with fruit in a riper melon spectrum, complexed by a gentle touch of spicy oak. There is no alcohol heat or burn on the long finish. No Reserve Chardonnay made in 2001.
rating: 0
2000 Light to medium yellow-green; aromas of sweet fig and white peach are interwoven with spicy barrel ferment character on the bouquet; similar flavours of peach, nectarine and fig which are no doubt drawing from the warm vintage come through on the palate, with hallmark length of flavour, rich middle palate and fine acidity. **rating: 0**

best drinking 2002–2006 **best vintages** '86, '88, '91, '92, '93, '94, '96, '97 **drink with** Oven-roasted blue-eye cod • $22

Coldstream Hills Reserve Chardonnay

2000 Light to medium yellow-green; much tighter than the '99 Reserve in style, quite apart from being one year younger. The fruit flavours of the palate range through nectarine, melon and some citrus; the oak is in restraint, and the wine carries its alcohol well. **rating:** 0

best drinking 2002–2008 **best vintages** '88, '91, '92, '93, '94, '96, '97, '00 **drink with** Veal, chicken • $41.50

Coldstream Hills Pinot Noir

2001 Strong red-purple; a deep and powerful bouquet, with a base of dark plum, spice and briar, yet to develop the aromatics which will progressively appear over 2002/2003; the palate shows plum, with underlying touches of cherry and raspberry in a cradle of evenly distributed tannins, which start to make their presence felt on the mid-palate, and run through to the hallmark long finish. Will richly repay cellaring; no Reserve Pinot Noir this year. **rating:** 0

2000 Medium red, dense hues; the bouquet has a classic mix of plum, cherry and ripe aromas supported by very fine spicy oak. A complex and mouthfilling palate, lovely sweet plum fruit on the mid-palate, then a long, soft finish. **rating:** 0

best drinking 2002–2007 **best vintages** '87, '88, '91, '92, '94, '96, '97 **drink with** Seared or slow-cooked salmon, Asian cuisine • $26.50

Coldstream Hills Reserve Pinot Noir

2000 Vibrant full purple-red; there is an excellent balance and integration of the fruit and oak; dark cherry plum and ripe fruit aromas are abundant in the bouquet. A very tightly structured palate, requiring many years in bottle, during which time it will emerge as one of the best Reserve Pinot Noirs to date. **rating:** 0

best drinking 2003–2006 **best vintages** '87, '88, '91, '92, '94, '96, '97, '00 **drink with** Quail, Asian cuisine • NA

Coldstream Hills Merlot

2000 Medium to full red purple; the bouquet has an array of blackberry, mocha, chocalate, spice and earth aromas, the fruit having all but swallowed the oak. The palate is rich and ripe, with pronounced mid-palate fruit sweetness, then fine-grained tannins and neatly balanced oak on the finish. **rating:** 0

best drinking 2003–2010 **best vintages** '90, '97, '98, '00 **drink with** All red meats, cheeses and game • $27.50

Coldstream Hills Reserve Merlot

2000 Deep red-purple; an array of various red berry fruits, hints of chocolate, spice and vanilla mark the bouquet; the palate is soft, rich and textured throughout its entire length, with soft, fluffy tannins and supple mouthfeel. Particular mid-palate richness is a feature of the best Reserve Merlot made to date by Coldstream Hills. Winner of two trophies at the 2002 Royal Sydney Wine Show, for Best Merlot and Best 2000 Vintage Wine. **rating:** 0

best drinking 2005–2012 **best vintages** '00 **drink with** All red meats, cheeses and game • $55

Coldstream Hills Reserve Cabernet Sauvignon

2000 Full purple-red; a very fragrant and pure bouquet of cassis and earth varietal fruit, allied with cedary oak aromas, then a perfectly balanced palate with long, persistent flavours tracking those of the bouquet, finishing with fine, ripe tannins. By far the best Reserve Cabernet since 1992. Winner of six trophies at the end of 2002, including Best Red Wine at the 2001 Liquorland National Wine Show, Canberra. **rating:** 0

best drinking 2005–2020 **best vintages** '92, '93, '94, '97, '00 **drink with** Rump steak • $57.50

collina wines   NR

Princes Highway, Mogo, NSW 2536 **region** South Coast Zone
phone (02) 4474 0005 **open** 7 days 10–5
winemaker Nicola Collins **production** NA **est.** 1999
product range ($15–22 CD) Chardonnay, Classic White, Gewürztraminer, Late Harvest Riesling Traminer, South Coast Cabernets, Rougon (semi-sweet red).
summary In the spring of 1980, Jim Collins planted the first vines on the south coast at Bega's Grevillea Estate. His daughter Nicola was winemaker from the outset and, having completed 16 vintages, encouraged her father to build a second winery, at Mogo, in the Eurobodalla region. The winery does not have vineyards of its own, sourcing grapes in part from Grevillea Estate and from the growing number of South Coast vineyards. As with Grevillea Estate, the operation is aimed at the general tourist rather than the wine connoisseur.

colmaur ★★★★

447 Native Corners Road, Campania, Tas 7026 **region** Southern Tasmania
phone (03) 6260 4312 **fax** (03) 6260 4580 **open** By appointment
winemaker Michael Vishacki (Contract) **production** 120 **est.** 1994
product range ($20 R) Chardonnay, Pinot Noir.
summary Colmaur is sufficiently small for the vines to be counted: presently 1100 chardonnay and 1700 pinot noir are in production. In 2000/2001 a further 600 chardonnay, 1350 pinot noir and 250 cabernet sauvignon were planted, and that will be the total extent of the vineyard. Likewise, production will be limited to the five new French oak barrels purchased in 2000, producing 100 to 120 cases of wine per year; any surplus grapes will be sold. Likewise, there are 700 olive trees in production, and Colmaur has its own oil press.

Colmaur Chardonnay

▼▼▼▼♀ **2001** Medium yellow-green; citrus and melon fruit aromas are woven through subtle oak, the same balance neatly achieved on the palate, with obvious malolactic and barrel-ferment influences. **rating:** 90
▼▼▼▼ **2000** Light green-yellow; a light, clean, fresh and crisp bouquet leaves no doubt about the cool climate from where the wine comes. The palate, likewise, is fresh and crisp, with tangy, lemony, juicy fruit flavours on the edge of ripeness, notwithstanding the 13.4° alcohol. **rating:** 85
best drinking 2002–2004 **best vintages** NA **drink with** Shellfish • $20

Colmaur Pinot Noir

▼▼▼▼ **2000** Medium red; the bouquet is moderately intense, with plummy fruit in the background; that fruit comes through on the forepalate, but grippy tannins and acid need to soften on the finish. **rating:** 87
best drinking 2003–2008 **best vintages** NA **drink with** Osso buco • $20

connor park winery NR

59 Connors Road, Leichardt, Vic 3516 **region** Bendigo
phone (03) 5437 5234 **fax** (03) 5437 5204 **open** 7 days 10–6
winemaker Ross Lougoon **production** 2000 **est.** 1994
product range ($12–28 CD) Riesling, Semillon, Sparkling Shiraz, Merlot, Shiraz, Cabernet, Port, Muscat.
summary The original planting of 2 hectares of vineyard dates back to the mid-1960s and to the uncle of the present owners, who had plans for designing an automatic grape harvester. The plans came to nothing, and when the present owners purchased the property in 1985 the vineyard had run wild. They resuscitated it (it formed part of a much larger mixed farming operation), and until 1994 were content to sell the grapes to other winemakers. Since then the vineyard has been expanded to 10 hectares, and while some of the grapes are sold to others, significant quantities are made into wine under the Connor Park label and sold through the cellar door and by mail order.

constable & hershon ★★★☆

1 Gillards Road, Pokolbin, NSW 2320 **region** Lower Hunter Valley
phone (02) 4998 7887 **fax** (02) 4998 7887 **open** 7 days 10–5
winemaker Neil McGuigan (Contract) **production** 5000 **est.** 1981
product range ($20–24 CD) Semillon, Chardonnay, Unwooded Chardonnay, Vintage Collection Chardonnay, Shiraz, Merlot.
summary Features four spectacular formal gardens, the Rosé, Knot and Herb, Secret and Sculpture; a free garden tour is conducted every Monday to Friday at 10.30 am (the tour lasts 30 minutes). The 9.75-hectare vineyard is itself spectacularly situated, with a backdrop of the Brokenback Range. Typically offers a range of several vintages of each variety ex cellar door or by mailing list. The quality is good, sometimes very good.

coolangatta estate ★★★☆

1335 Bolong Road, Shoalhaven Heads, NSW 2535 **region** Shoalhaven
phone (02) 4448 7131 **fax** (02) 4448 7997 **open** 7 days 10–5
winemaker Tyrrell's (Contract) **production** 5000 **est.** 1988
product range ($15–25 CD) Semillon, Sauvignon Blanc Chardonnay, Chardonnay, Alexander Berry Chardonnay, Verdelho, Chardonnay Brut, Chambourcin, Shiraz Cabernet, Merlot, Vintage Port.
summary Coolangatta Estate is part of a 150-hectare resort with accommodation, restaurants, golf course, etc, with some of the oldest buildings convict-built in 1822. It might be thought that the wines are tailored purely for the tourist market, but in fact the standard of viticulture is exceptionally high (immaculate Scott-Henry trellising), and the winemaking is wholly professional (contract by Tyrrell's).

Coolangatta Estate Semillon

▼▼▼▼ 2001 Pale straw-green; the bouquet is very taut, with a mix of herb, spice and mineral aromas carrying through to a lemon-tingle palate, finishing with lively acidity. A striking wine which will likely develop very well, and a gold medal winner at the Australian Boutique Winemakers Show.　**rating:** 87

best drinking 2002–2008 **best vintages** '98 **drink with** Grilled fish • $17

Coolangatta Estate Sauvignon Blanc Chardonnay

▼▼▼▽ 2001 Very pale; light herbal fruit with some spicy notes is followed by a palate which is stuffed full of CO₂, it will need time to absorb this and settle down.　**rating:** 83

best drinking 2002–2003 **best vintages** '91, '94, '98 **drink with** Whitebait • $15

Coolangatta Estate Verdelho

▼▼▼▽ 2001 Very pale colour; a clean, neutral bouquet with some varietal fruit salad is followed by a palate with fruit appeal, but showing a lot of CO₂. The judges at the Australian Boutique Wine Awards were not fussed by this, giving the wine a top gold medal.　**rating:** 84

best drinking 2002–2003 **best vintages** NA **drink with** Pasta • $18

Coolangatta Estate Alexander Berry Chardonnay

▼▼▼▼ 2001 Light to medium green-yellow; the light bouquet has a mix of grassy/herbal/citrus fruit and a gentle flick of oak. The light to medium-bodied palate is clean, fresh and gentle, with pleasant mouthfeel.　**rating:** 85

best drinking 2002–2004 **best vintages** '91, '94, '96, '97, '00 **drink with** Avocado and seafood • $22

Coolangatta Estate Merlot

▼▼▼▽ 2001 Light to medium purple-red; fresh, bright, juicy raspberry aromas and flavours, with a touch of mint coming through on the palate, are in harmony with the virtual absence of tannins and discernible oak. For summer gulping.　**rating:** 83

best drinking 2002–2003 **best vintages** NA **drink with** Cold meats • $20

coombend estate　★★★★

Coombend via Swansea, Tas 7190 **region** Southern Tasmania
phone (03) 6257 8881 **fax** (03) 6257 8484 **open** 7 days 9–6
winemaker Andrew Hood (Contract) **production** 2000 **est.** 1985
product range ($19–26 CD) Riesling, Sauvignon Blanc, Cabernet Sauvignon.
summary John Fenn Smith originally established 1.75 hectares of cabernet sauvignon, 2.25 hectares of sauvignon blanc and 0.3 hectare of riesling (together with a little cabernet franc) on his 2600-hectare sheep station, choosing that part of his property which is immediately adjacent to Freycinet. This slightly quixotic choice of variety has been justified by the success of the wine in limited show entries. In December 1998 Coombend opened a brand new, purpose-built cellar-door sales area; it has also significantly expanded its plantings to include riesling and sauvignon blanc.

Coombend Estate Riesling

▼▼▼▼ 2000 Medium yellow-green; a big and rich bouquet, with ripe lime and tropical fruit, is followed by a similarly big and slightly broad palate; whatever the wine might lack, it is not flavour.　**rating:** 86

best drinking 2002–2004 **best vintages** '99 **drink with** Avocado salad • $19

Coombend Estate Sauvignon Blanc Late Harvest

▼▼▼▼▽ 2001 Medium yellow-green; the bouquet initially shows a touch of reduction, which dissipates with aeration to reveal intense tropical/guava fruit; the palate is very rich, the syrupy sweetness cut by good acidity on the finish. One of the most striking examples of late harvest Sauvignon Blanc made in Australia thus far.　**rating:** 90

best drinking 2002–2005 **best vintages** '01 **drink with** Honey ice cream • $22

cooperage estate　NR

15 Markovitch Lane, Junortoun, Vic 3551 **region** Bendigo
phone 0418 544 743 **open** Not
winemaker Graham Gregurek **production** NA **est.** 1995
product range NA

summary The Gregurek family has established 2.2. hectares of shiraz and cabernet sauvignon at their vineyard on the southern outskirts of the town of Bendigo. As the name suggests, there is also a cooperage on-site.

coorinja ★★☆

Toodyay Road, Toodyay, WA 6566 **region** Greater Perth Zone
phone (08) 9574 2280 **open** Mon–Sat 10–5
winemaker Michael Wood **production** 3200 **est.** 1870
product range ($8–10.50 CD) Dry White, Claret, Hermitage, Burgundy, Fortifieds; the latter account for 50 per cent of Coorinja's production.
summary An evocative and historic winery nestling in a small gully which seems to be in a time-warp, begging to be used as a set for a film. A recent revamp of the packaging accompanied a more than respectable Hermitage, with lots of dark chocolate and sweet berry flavour, finishing with soft tannins.

cope-williams ★★★☆

Glenfern Road, Romsey, Vic 3434 **region** Macedon Ranges
phone (03) 5429 5428 **fax** (03) 5429 5655 **open** 7 days 11–5
winemaker David Cowburn **production** 7000 **est.** 1977
product range ($14–25 R) Chardonnay, Cabernet Merlot; d'Vine is second label, with Riesling, Chardonnay and Cabernet Sauvignon; winery specialty is sparkling wine Macedon R.O.M.S.E.Y.
summary One of the high country Macedon pioneers, specialising in sparkling wines which are full flavoured, but also producing excellent Chardonnay and Pinot Noir table wines in the warmer vintages. A traditional 'English Green'-type cricket ground is available for hire and booked out most days of the week from spring through till autumn.

coriole ★★★★☆

Chaffeys Road, McLaren Vale, SA 5171 **region** McLaren Vale
phone (08) 8323 8305 **fax** (08) 8323 9136 **open** Mon–Fri 10–5, weekends and public holidays 11–5
winemaker Grant Harrison **production** 52 000 **est.** 1967
product range ($16–70 R) Lalla Rookh Semillon, Semillon Sauvignon Blanc, Chenin Blanc, Shiraz, Lloyd Reserve Shiraz, Redstone Shiraz Cabernet, Sangiovese Shiraz, Lloyd Sangiovese Cabernet, Mary Kathleen Reserve Cabernet Merlot.
summary Justifiably best known for its Shiraz, which – both in the rare Lloyd Reserve and standard forms – is extremely impressive. It has spread its wings in recent years, being one of the first wineries to catch onto the Italian fashion with its Sangiovese, but its white varietal wines lose nothing by comparison. It is also a producer of high-quality olive oil, which is distributed commercially through all Australian states. The wines are exported to the UK, the US, Canada, Switzerland, Germany, the Netherlands, Sweden, Taiwan, Malaysia, Japan, Singapore and New Zealand.

Coriole Lalla Rookh Semillon

 2000 Light green-yellow; typically full and quite ripe citrus, a hint of tropical fruit, and equally subtle oak on the bouquet are followed by a complex palate with lots of flavour and structure. **rating:** 91
best drinking 2001–2004 **best vintages** '93, '94 '95, '97, '98 **drink with** Salad, seafood • NA

Coriole Semillon Sauvignon Blanc

ꭡꭡꭡꭡ 2001 Medium yellow-green; the bouquet is quite complex and ripe, suggestive of some oak influence, although there is in fact none; the same characters come through on the palate in excellent lunch-style. **rating:** 84

best drinking 2001–2001 best vintages NA drink with Deep fried calamari • NA

Coriole Shiraz

ꭡꭡꭡꭡ 2000 Medium red-purple; ripe, sweet red and black cherry fruit and an appropriate flick of oak on the bouquet is followed by a palate with lots of sweet fruit and dark chocolate in classic regional style; the tannins and oak have been well managed in an exceptionally good outcome for the vintage. **rating:** 93
ꭡꭡꭡꭡꭡ 1999 Vivid purple-red, the bouquet emanates black cherry fruit with oak in the background. The palate is a replay, with an exceptional concentration of black cherry fruit, particularly given the somewhat indifferent vintage, and avoids the high alcohol trap. **rating:** 94

best drinking 2004–2010 **best vintages** '90, '91, '96, '98, '99, '00 **drink with** Daube of lamb • $27.95

Coriole Lloyd Reserve Shiraz

♥♥♥♥♀ 1999 Deep red-purple; the bouquet has abundant rich dark cherry fruit framed with powerful oak still to fully integrate; mouthfilling fruit, oak and tannins all guarantee a long life, but need patience.   **rating:** 93

♥♥♥♥♥ 1998 Excellent purple-red; powerful, concentrated, lush, black cherry fruit offset by fine oak on the bouquet, then an archetypal McLaren Vale palate with concentrated fruit, tannins, oak and alcohol; will age.   **rating:** 94

best drinking 2004–2014 **best vintages** '70, '74, '84, '88, '89, '90, '91, '92, '94, '95, '96, '97, '98 **drink with** Ragout of lamb • $70

Coriole Redstone

♥♥♥♥ 2000 Strong red-purple; the bouquet offers ripe, sweet dark berry/cassis fruit and a waft of oak; the palate has good fruit flavour, although the structure is less convincing, fractionally hollow and short.   **rating:** 85

♥♥♥♥♀ 1999 Bright red-purple; sweet, rich and appealing red berry fruit with a twitch of oak on the bouquet, then abundant black cherry, plum and chocolate flavours, with a savoury tweak on the finish; very good wine at the price.   **rating:** 91

best drinking 2003–2007 **best vintages** '99 **drink with** Lamb's fry • $19

Coriole Mary Kathleen Cabernet Merlot

♥♥♥♥ 1998 Medium to full red-purple; a dense, ripe juicy/jammy/berry/minty bouquet, followed by a massively constructed palate, as only McLaren Vale can provide. The big surprise is that the alcohol is only 13.5°.   **rating:** 88

best drinking 2003–2013 **best vintages** '90, '91, '92, '94, '95, '96, '97 **drink with** Mature cheddar • $38

cosham   NR

101 Union Road, Carmel via Kalamunda, WA 6076 **region** Perth Hills
phone (08) 9293 5424 **fax** (08) 9293 5062 **open** Weekends and public holidays 10–5
winemaker Julie White **production** 1000 **est.** 1989
product range ($12–22 CD) Chardonnay, Pinot Noir, Cabernet Merlot, Mèthode Champenoise Brut.
summary Has grown significantly over recent years, though admittedly from a small base. A complex Mèthode Champenoise and savoury/earthy Cabernet Merlot are both creditable wines.

cowra estate   ★★★

Boorowa Road, Cowra, NSW 2794 **region** Cowra
phone (02) 6342 1136 **fax** (02) 6342 4286 **open** 7 days 9–6
winemaker Simon Gilbert (Contract) **production** 15 000 **est.** 1973
product range ($6–15 CD) Chardonnay, Cool Classic Chardonnay, Cabernet Rosé, Cabernets. The Classic Bat series of Chardonnay and Cabernet Merlot is now at the head of the range.
summary Cowra Estate was purchased from the family of founder Tony Gray by South African-born food and beverage entrepreneur John Geber in 1995. A vigorous promotional campaign has gained a higher domestic profile for the once export-oriented brand. John Geber is actively involved in the promotional effort and rightly proud of the excellent value for money which the wines represent. The Quarry Wine Cellars and Restaurant offer visitors a full range of all of the Cowra Estate's wines and wines from the other producers in the region, including Richmond Grove, Hungerford Hill, Arrowfield, Mulyan and Chiverton.

crabtree of watervale   ★★★★☆

North Terrace, Watervale, SA 5452 **region** Clare Valley
phone (08) 8843 0069 **fax** (08) 8843 0144 **open** 7 days 11–5
winemaker Robert Crabtree **production** 5000 **est.** 1979
product range ($16–20 CD) Riesling, Semillon, Grenache, Bay of Biscay Grenache Rosé, Shiraz, Cabernet Sauvignon, Muscat, Windmill Tawny.
summary The gently mannered Robert Crabtree and his wife Elizabeth are once again very much part of the business, making full-flavoured, classic Clare Valley styles with outstanding success in 1999 and 2001. Exports to the UK and Kuala Lumpur.

Crabtree of Watervale Riesling

▼▼▼▼▼ **2001** Light green-yellow; a firm but highly aromatic bouquet of lime, apple and slate is followed by a palate with exceptional intensity, length and depth to the flavours, which replicate those of the bouquet. Multiple trophies at the 2001 Clare Valley Regional Wine Show, including Best Wine of Show. However, some variation has been noticed; the wine is finished with a cork, not Stelvin. **rating:** 94

best drinking 2001–2010 **best vintages** '99, '00, '01 **drink with** Ginger prawns • $18

Crabtree of Watervale Shiraz

▼▼▼▼▼ **1999** Medium purple-red; a clean, smooth and elegant bouquet with neatly counterpoised black cherry and oak is faithfully mirrored on the harmonious and elegant palate. **rating:** 94

best drinking 2004–2009 **best vintages** '99 **drink with** Rack of lamb • $18

Crabtree of Watervale Bay of Biscay Grenache

▼▼▼▼ **2001** Light red-purple; the bouquet is bright, clean and fresh, the palate not too sweet; a touch more fruit would have made an outstanding Rosé. **rating:** 87

best drinking 2001–2002 **best vintages** NA **drink with** An ice block • $16

craig avon vineyard ★★★

Craig Avon Lane, Merricks North, Vic 3926 **region** Mornington Peninsula
phone (03) 5989 7465 **fax** (03) 5989 7615 **open** Weekends and public holidays 12–5
winemaker Ken Lang **production** 1000 **est.** 1986
product range ($29–33 CD) Chardonnay, Pinot Noir, Cabernet.
summary All of the wines are sold through the cellar door and by mailing list. The wines are competently made, clean, and with pleasant fruit flavour.

craigie knowe ★★★

Glen Gala Road, Cranbrook, Tas 7190 **region** Southern Tasmania
phone (03) 6223 5620 **fax** (03) 6223 5009 **open** Weekends or by appointment
winemaker Dr John Austwick **production** 500 **est.** 1979
product range ($20–23 ML) Cabernet Sauvignon, Pinot Noir.
summary John Austwick makes a small quantity of full-flavoured, robust Cabernet Sauvignon in a tiny winery as a weekend relief from a busy metropolitan dental practice. The Pinot Noir is made in a style which will appeal to confirmed Cabernet Sauvignon drinkers, and John Austwick had a couple of barrels of 1998 Cabernet Sauvignon which, if bottled separately, would have appealed to everyone who has ever lifted a wine glass.

craiglee ★★★★★

Sunbury Road, Sunbury, Vic 3429 **region** Sunbury
phone (03) 9744 4489 **fax** (03) 9744 4489 **open** Sun, public holidays 10–5 or by appointment
winemaker Patrick Carmody **production** 3000 **est.** 1976
product range ($16–34 CD) Sauvignon Blanc, Chardonnay, Pinot Noir, Shiraz, Cabernet Sauvignon.
summary A historic winery with a proud 19th-century record, which recommenced winemaking in 1976 after a prolonged hiatus. Produces one of the finest cool-climate Shirazs in Australia, redolent of cherry, liquorice and spice in the better (i.e. warmer) vintages, lighter-bodied in the cooler ones. Maturing vines and improved viticulture have made the wines more consistent (and even better) over the past ten years or so. Exports to the UK, the US and New Zealand.

Craiglee Shiraz

▼▼▼▼▼ **1998** Medium to full red-purple; the bouquet is redolent of dark plums, spice being little more than a background whisper. Luscious, round palate offering a mix of ripe plum and sweet cherry moves through to a soft tannin finish. The oak handling cannot be faulted. It's not often that Craiglee Shiraz reaches 14° alcohol, but it did in this great vintage. **rating:** 94

best drinking 2003–2008 **best vintages** '84, '86, '88, '91, '92, '93, '94, '96, '97, '98 **drink with** Italian cuisine • $34

craigow ★★★★☆

528 Richmond Road, Cambridge, Tas 7170 **region** Southern Tasmania
phone (03) 6248 4210 **fax** (03) 6248 5482 **open** Fri–Sun 10–5 or by appointment
winemaker Julian Alcorso (Contract) **production** 500 **est.** 1989

product range ($18.50–25 CD) Riesling, Gewürztraminer, Chardonnay, Pinot Noir.

summary Craigow has substantial vineyards, with 5 hectares of pinot noir and another 5 hectares divided between riesling, chardonnay and gewürztraminer. Barry and Cathy Edwards have moved from being grape growers with only one wine made for sale to having a portfolio of four wines, while continuing to sell most of their grapes. Their cellar door opened early in December 1999.

Craigow Riesling

▼▼▼▼▼ 2001 Light to medium green-yellow; an intense bouquet with lime juice and a touch of tropical fruit follows through on the intensely flavoured palate with substantial weight and length. Top gold medal 2002 Tasmanian Wines Show. **rating:** 94

best drinking 2002–2006 **best vintages** '00, '01 **drink with** Fish terrine • $18.50

Craigow Pinot Noir

▼▼▼▼ 2000 Medium to full red-purple; a dense, powerful bouquet has ripe plum and a touch of prune, leaving little doubt about the powerful, dense and very ripe palate to follow. Will evoke varying responses, but will certainly improve with time in bottle. **rating:** 89

best drinking 2004–2008 **best vintages** NA **drink with** Leave it in the cellar • $25

craneford ★★★★

Moorundie Street, Truro, SA 5356 **region** Barossa Valley
phone (08) 8564 0003 **fax** (08) 8564 0008 **open** 7 days 10–5
winemaker John Zilm, Colin Forbes (Consultant) **production** 25 000 **est.** 1978
product range ($14–33 CD) Eden Valley Riesling, Barossa Semillon, Barossa Valley Chardonnay, Barossa Valley Unwooded Chardonnay, Shiraz, Quartet (Petit Verdot Cabernet Sauvignon Cabernet Franc Shiraz), Grenache, Coonawarra Cabernet Sauvignon, Mistelle (fortified), Sparkling Shiraz Petit Verdot.

summary The purchase of Craneford by owner/winemaker John Zilm has wrought many changes. It has moved to a new winery (and cafcre) and is supported by contract-grown grapes, with the purchase price paid per hectare, not per tonne, giving Craneford total control over yield and (hopefully) quality. Colin Forbes continues to provide consultancy advice. Retail distribution in Sydney and Melbourne, and exports to Japan through Australian Prestige Wines.

Craneford Eden Valley Riesling

▼▼▼▼ 2001 Light green-yellow; a crisp bouquet with a mix of lemon, apple and mineral aromas, moving more to sweet citrus on the palate, although some CO_2 spritz is still settling down on the finish. Stelvin sealed, and should age impeccably. **rating:** 88

best drinking 2004–2010 **best vintages** NA **drink with** Caesar salad • $18

Craneford Chardonnay

▼▼▼▼ 2001 Light to medium yellow-green; the moderately intense bouquet has well-balanced and integrated stone fruit and oak aromas, with a replay on the smooth, quick developing palate. **rating:** 85

best drinking 2002–2003 **best vintages** NA **drink with** Creamy pasta • $15

Craneford Coonawarra Cabernet Sauvignon

▼▼▼▼▽ 2000 Medium to full red-purple; blackberry, mulberry, cedar and earth aromas flow into a rich, ripe and powerful palate; abundant blackberry and blackcurrant provide an intensely fruit-driven finish. **rating:** 92

best drinking 2005–2010 **best vintages** '00 **drink with** Marinated beef • $30

crane winery NR

Haydens Road, Kingaroy, Qld 4610 **region** South Burnett
phone (07) 4162 7647 **fax** (07) 4162 8381 **open** 7 days 10–4
winemaker John Crane **production** 4000 **est.** 1996
product range ($10–25 ML) Semillon, Semillon Chardonnay, Moscato, Verdelho, Marsanne, Hillside White, Chardonnay, Late Harvest Frontignac, Sparkling Burgundy, Pinot Semillon Chardonnay Sparkling, Estate Sparkling Cuvée, Pinot Noir, Shiraz, Shiraz Cabernet Sauvignon, Ruby Cabernet, Merlot, Cabernet Sauvignon, Liqueur Shiraz, Cream Sherry.

summary Established by John and Sue Crane, Crane Winery is one of several in the burgeoning Kingaroy (or South Burnett) region in Queensland, drawing upon 4 hectares of estate plantings but also purchasing grapes from 20 other growers in the region. Interestingly, Sue Crane's great-grandfather established a vineyard planted to shiraz 100 years ago (in 1898) and which remained in production until 1970.

cranswick estate ★★★

Walla Avenue, Griffith, NSW 2680 **region** Riverina
phone (02) 6962 4133 **fax** (02) 6962 2888 **open** 7 days 10–4
winemaker Andrew Schulz, Tim Pearce, Eddie Bonato, Sam Mittiga **production** 1.3 million **est.** 1976
product range ($6–25 ML) There are several ranges; at the top comes the Pioneer Old Vine Series comprising Semillon, Chardonnay, Shiraz and Cabernet Sauvignon; Autumn Gold Botrytis Semillon; then the Cocoparra range of Marsanne, Shiraz, Merlot and Cabernet Sauvignon; next is the Image range of Verdelho, Chardonnay and Cabernet Merlot; then there is the volume-selling Vignette Range of Semillon, Verdelho, Chardonnay, Pinot Chardonnay, Unoaked Botrytis Semillon, Shiraz, Cabernet Merlot and Estate Selection Cabernet Sauvignon (export only); Aldridge Sparkling Brut; also lower-priced ranges of The Masters, Kidman Way, Cedar Creek and Barramundi Varietal.
summary Taking full advantage of the buoyant share market and the continuing export success of Australian wines, Cranswick Estate made a successful entry to the lists of the Australian Associated Stock Exchanges in 1997. The substantial capital raised has seen the further expansion of the business, firmly aimed at the export market in the UK and Europe, the US, Japan and Iceland, and Southeast Asia. It did, however, make the headlines in 2002 when it offered some of its growers $100 per tonne to leave their grapes on the vine. Merged with Evans and Tate in June 2002

Cedar Creek Chardonnay

♥♥♥♡ 2000 Medium to full yellow-green; charry oak on the bouquet outweighs the rather lean fruit, but there is more weight and sweetness to the fruit on the palate. At least the wine has some character. **rating:** 84
best drinking 2001–2003 **best vintages** NA **drink with** Light pasta • $8

crawford river wines ★★★★★

Hotspur Upper Road, Condah, Vic 3303 **region** Henty
phone (03) 5578 2267 **fax** (03) 5578 2240 **open** 7 days 10–4 by appointment
winemaker John Thomson **production** 4000 **est.** 1975
product range ($20–33 CD) Riesling, Reserve Riesling, Semillon Sauvignon Blanc, Cabernet Merlot, Cabernet Sauvignon, Nektar.
summary Exemplary wines right across the range are made by part-time winemaker John Thomson, who clearly has the winemaker's equivalent of the gardener's green thumb. The Riesling is consistently outstanding, the Cabernet-based wines excellent in warmer vintages. Exports to the UK, Germany, Denmark, Singapore, the US and Canada.

Crawford River Riesling

♥♥♥♥♥ 2001 Pristine, fragrant aromas of passionfruit, lime and fresh-cut apple are repeated on the fresh, lively palate with an additional hint of spice, and a tingle to the crisp finish. Guaranteed to age superbly. **rating:** 94
best drinking 2002–2012 **best vintages** '86, '88, '89, '91, '94, '96, '97, '98, '99, '00, '01 **drink with** Antipasto • $27

Crawford River Reserve Riesling

♥♥♥♥♥ 2001 Light green-yellow; crisp, mineral herb and lime blossom aromas are followed by an exceptionally intense and powerful palate, with green lime flavours; long and balanced. However, needs time. **rating:** 95
best drinking 2005–2015 **best vintages** '99, '00, '01 **drink with** Richer fish dishes • $33

Crawford River Semillon Sauvignon Blanc

♥♥♥♥♡ 2001 Light green-yellow; a clean, light, fresh and crisp grassy bouquet together with mineral characters is faithfully repeated on the crystal clear, clean and crisp palate. **rating:** 91
best drinking 2001–2003 **best vintages** '96, '97, '01 **drink with** Crab or shellfish • $21

Crawford River Nektar

♥♥♥♥♡ 2001 Light green-yellow; intense lime juice aromas on both the bouquet and palate show the clearest possible varietal character notwithstanding the botrytis; the palate is of auslese sweetness, long and pure. **rating:** 92
best drinking 2002–2007 **best vintages** '99, '01 **drink with** Any rich dessert • $25

Crawford River Cabernet Merlot
▼▼▼▼ 2000 Light to medium purple-red; light cedary/savoury/spicy/earthy aromas are not as rich or ripe as expected on the bouquet; however, the wine comes together on the palate, all the components marrying seamlessly, and further bolstered by quite sweet, ripe tannins. **rating:** 88

best drinking 2004–2009 best vintages NA drink with Rib of veal • $25

Crawford River Cabernet Sauvignon
▼▼▼▼ 1999 Medium red-purple; distinctly savoury/spicy/fragrant aromas attesting to the cool climate. There are similar spicy/savoury flavours on the palate, yet not nearly as green as expected, if at all. On the other hand, the tannins are almost transparent. **rating:** 88

best drinking 2003–2008 best vintages '86, '88, '90, '91, '93, '97 drink with Roast veal • $35

crisford winery   NR
556 Hermitage Road, Pokolbin, NSW 2320 **region** Lower Hunter Valley
phone (02) 9387 1100 **fax** (02) 9387 6688 **open** Not
winemaker Steve Dodd **production** 340 **est.** 1990
product range A single wine – Synergy (Merlot Cabernet Franc blend).
summary Carol and Neal Crisford have established 2.6 hectares of merlot and cabernet franc which go to produce Synergy (a name which I fancy has been trademarked by Hamilton). Neal Crisford produces educational videos on wine used in TAFE colleges and by the Australian Society of Wine Education. The wine is sold through the Hunter Valley Wine Society.

crooked river wines   NR
11 Willow Vale Road, Gerringong, NSW 2534 **region** South Coast Zone
phone (02) 4234 0975 **fax** (02) 4234 4477 **open** Not
winemaker Bevan Wilson **production** NA **est.** 1998
product range Verdelho, Chardonnay, Illawarra Flame, Shiraz, Chambourcin, Cabernet Merlot, Cabernet Sauvignon.
summary With 14 hectares of vineyard planted to chardonnay, verdelho, arneis, shiraz, cabernet sauvignon, merlot, ruby cabernet, sangiovese and chambourcin, Crooked River Wines has the largest vineyard on the South Coast. Production is expected to increase to 10 000 cases by 2003 through a winery being constructed on-site. Cellar door sales, plus a craft shop and cafe, opened in December 2001.

crosswinds vineyard   ★★★★
10 Vineyard Drive, Tea Tree, Tas 7017 **region** Southern Tasmania
phone (03) 6268 1091 **fax** (03) 6268 1091 **open** Mon–Fri 10–5, weekends by appointment
winemaker Andrew Vasiljuk **production** 1500 **est.** 1990
product range ($16–20 ML) Riesling, Unwooded Chardonnay, Chardonnay, Pinot Noir, Cabernet Sauvignon.
summary Crosswinds has two vineyards, with the 1-hectare Tea Tree Vineyard and the 2-hectare Margate Vineyard. As well as cellar-door sales, there is retail distribution in Melbourne and small exports to the UK and Southeast Asia. Both Chardonnay and Pinot Noir have excelled in recent years.

Crosswinds Chardonnay
▼▼▼▼ 1998 Glowing yellow-green; the bouquet is clean, with a mix of citrus, melon and stone fruit supported by a touch of oak; the wine comes into its own with intense citrus and stone fruit flavours, and above-average length. Driven by fruit and not oak, but quite developed for its age. **rating:** 89

best drinking 2001–2003 best vintages NA drink with Full-flavoured fish • $20

Crosswinds Pinot Noir
▼▼▼▼▽ 1998 Medium red, with just a touch of purple remaining; a stylish and aromatic bouquet with a mix of tangy and more savoury fruit characters is followed by a palate which likewise shows considerable intensity and length, the potent varietal character expressing itself in a savoury/tangy mix. **rating:** 90

best drinking 2001–2004 best vintages '98 drink with Braised duck • $20

cruickshank callatoota estate   ★★☆
2656 Wybong Road, Wybong, NSW 2333 **region** Upper Hunter Valley
phone (02) 6547 8149 **fax** (02) 6547 8144 **open** 7 days 9–5
winemaker John Cruickshank, Andrew Thomas (Consultant) **production** 7000 **est.** 1973

product range ($10–16 CD) Cabernet Rosé, Shiraz, Two Cabernets, Cabernet Franc, Cabernet Sauvignon, Cabernet Sauvignon Carbonic Maceration, Cabernet Sauvignon Pressings, Old Tawny Port.

summary Owned by Sydney management consultant John Cruickshank and family. Wine quality definitely improved in the 1990s, although the wines still show strong regional, rather earthy, characters; the label itself likewise doggedly remains old-fashioned. The Cabernet Rosé is typically delicate, clean and crisp and the most appealing of the range. Other wines tend to have rather harsh, earthy tannins, but clearly have their supporters.

cubbaroo cellars   NR

Cubbaroo Station, Wee Waa, NSW 2388 **region** Western Plains Zone
phone (02) 6796 1741 **fax** (02) 6796 1751 **open** Thurs–Sun 12–10
winemaker Simon Gilbert (Contract) **production** NA **est.** 1972
product range ($10–15 CD) Shiraz, Port.

summary Cubbaroo Cellars has led a shadowy existence since the early 1970s, in the heart of the Namoi Valley cotton country. For a while it seemed that it had ceased production under the Cubbaroo Cellars label, selling its grapes to wineries in the Hunter Valley. However, the 10.8 hectares of shiraz planted long ago has now been supplemented by 4 hectares of cabernet sauvignon, so its fortunes may be on the rise. The two wines presently available are sold only through the cellar door.

cullen wines   ★★★★★

Caves Road, Cowaramup, WA 6284 **region** Margaret River
phone (08) 9755 5277 **fax** (08) 9755 5550 **open** 7 days 10–4
winemaker Vanya Cullen, Trevor Kent **production** 18 000 **est.** 1971
product range ($16.50–75 CD) Flagship wines: Chardonnay, Sauvignon Blanc, Pinot Noir, Semillon Sauvignon Blanc, Mangan Malbec Petit Verdot Merlot, Reserve Cabernet Sauvignon Merlot; premium wines: Classic Dry White, Blanc de Noir, Velvet Red, Autumn Harvest.

summary One of the pioneers of Margaret River which has always produced long-lived wines of highly individual style from the substantial and mature estate vineyards. Winemaking is now in the hands of Vanya Cullen, daughter of the founders; she is possessed of an extraordinarily good palate. The Chardonnay is superb, while the Cabernet Merlot goes from strength to strength; indeed, I would rate it Australia's best. The wines are distributed throughout Australia and also make their way to significant export markets in the UK, the US, Europe and Asia.

Cullen Semillon Sauvignon Blanc

TTTTY **2001** Light straw-green; the bouquet offers a typically complex and subtle interplay between the two varietal components (in a 65/35 ratio) and between the fruit and the oak. The palate is spotlessly clean, in texture headed directly to white Bordeaux, and has swallowed up the 100 per cent new French oak in which it was fermented (with a mix of cultured and wild yeasts) and matured.   **rating:** 93

TTTTY **2000** Light to medium yellow-green; a complex and ripe bouquet with passionfruit, gooseberry and dried apple fruit aromas is followed by a rich, very complex and ripe mouthfilling, fleshy palate which carries its 14° alcohol with ease. Unusually, the 2000 vintage is 60 per cent Semillon and 40 per cent Sauvignon Blanc.   **rating:** 93

best drinking 2002–2007 **best vintages** '97, '98, '99, '00, '01 **drink with** Margaret River marron • $26

Cullen Chardonnay

TTTTT **2000** Medium yellow-green; the complex bouquet offers a subtle interweaving of fruit, oak and malolactic influences; the long and elegant palate carries on in the same fashion with cashew, melon and stone fruit supported by beautifully integrated French oak.   **rating:** 95

best drinking 2002–2010 best vintages '93, '94, '96, '98, '99, '00 drink with Marron • $48

Cullen Mangan Malbec Petit Verdot Merlot

TTTT **2001** Inky, youthful purple; the bouquet has clean, intense, juicy blackberry fruit, and the palate is similarly powerful and concentrated, the tannins there as expected with any Cullen red, but not over the top. From brother Rick Cullen and wife Bettina Mangan's vineyard planted in 1995. Seems to have been bottled prematurely, but patience is sure to be rewarded.   **rating:** 89

best drinking 2006–2011 **best vintages** NA **drink with** Leave it in the cellar • $45

Cullen Cabernet Sauvignon Merlot

▼▼▼▼▼ **2000** Medium to full red-purple; the bouquet is clean and fresh, with small red berry fruit aromas and subtle oak, half suggesting the palate may be down in power. Nothing could be further from the truth, for there are lush red and black berry fruits in abundance, followed by the pillars of tannin which are so much part of the structure of this distinguished wine. A blend of 65 per cent Cabernet Sauvignon, 21 per cent Merlot, 5 per cent each Petit Verdot and Malbec, and 4 per cent Cabernet Franc. **rating:** 94

▼▼▼▼▼ **1999** Strong purple-red; the powerful but pristine bouquet proclaims the blackberry/blackcurrant/cassis fruit of the palate framed by the inimitable Cullen tannins which run through from the mid-palate to the finish. **rating:** 96

best drinking 2008 - 2018 **best vintages** '77, '84, '86, '90, '91, '92, '93, '95, '96, '97, '98, '99, '00 **drink with** Braised ox tail • $75

curlewis winery ★★★★☆

55 Navarre Road, Curlewis, Vic 3222 **region** Geelong
phone (03) 5250 4567 **fax** (03) 5250 4567 **open** By appointment
winemaker Rainer Breit **production** 1000 **est.** 1998
product range ($28–32 R) Chardonnay, Pinot Noir, Reserve Pinot Noir, Shiraz.
summary Rainer Breit and partner Wendy Oliver have achieved a great deal in a remarkably short period of time. In 1996 they purchased their property at Curlewis with 1.6 hectares of what were then 11-year-old pinot noir vines; previously (and until 1998) the grapes had been sold to Scotchman's Hill. They set to and established an on-site winery, making 800 cases of very good Pinot Noir in their first vintage, 1998. Rainer Breit is a self-taught winemaker, but the full bag of pinot noir winemaking tricks was used in 1998. While Breit and Oliver are self-confessed 'pinotphiles', they have planted a little chardonnay and buy a little locally grown shiraz and chardonnay.

Curlewis Pinot Noir

▼▼▼▼♈ **2000** Light to medium red-purple; a fragrant, spicy, savoury, tangy bouquet is followed by a similarly intense tangy, sappy, savoury palate with fine tannins and very good length. In consistent style for the winery, with strongly Burgundian overtones. **rating:** 92

best drinking 2002–2006 **best vintages** '98, '00 **drink with** Tea-smoked duck • $32

Curlewis Shiraz

▼▼▼▼♈ **2000** Medium red-purple; a woodsy, savoury, spicy bouquet with the emphasis away from primary fruit, but the palate powers forward with abundant black plum and spicy fruit. Fine tannins and a long finish. Grown on three nearby vineyards, all low-yielding. **rating:** 93

best drinking 2004–2010 **best vintages** NA **drink with** Game • $28

🐌 curly flat ★★★★

Collivers Road, Lancefield, Vic 3435 **region** Macedon Ranges
phone (03) 5429 1956 **fax** (03) 5429 2256 **open** Not
winemaker Phillip Moraghan, Llew Knight (Consultant) **production** 1000 **est.** 1991
product range ($35–44 ML) Chardonnay, Lacuna Chardonnay (unwooded), Pinot Noir.
summary Phillip and Jeni Moraghan began the development of Curly Flat in 1992, drawing in part upon the inspiration Phillip Moraghan experienced when working in Switzerland in the late 1980s, and with a passing nod to Michael Leunig. With ceaseless help and guidance from the late Laurie Williams (who died unexpectedly in mid-2001) the Moraghans have painstakingly established 14 hectares of vineyard, principally pinot noir, with lesser amounts of chardonnay and pinot gris. Half of the targeted 10 000-case production will be exported, half sold in Australia, none passing through the retail trade. Plans have already been drawn up for the erection of an on-site winery, due for completion by the end of 2002, with 2003 the first on-site vintage.

currency creek wines ★★★☆

Winery Road, Currency Creek, SA 5214 **region** Currency Creek
phone (08) 8555 4069 **fax** (08) 8555 4100 **open** 7 days 10–5
winemaker John Loxton (Consultant) **production** 8000 **est.** 1969
product range ($9.95–25.95 CD) Sauvignon Blanc, The Creek Station Sweet White, Princess Alexandrina Noble Riesling and Semillon, The Creek Station Grenache Shiraz, Ostrich Hill Shiraz, Cabernet Sauvignon, Fortifieds.

summary Constant name changes early in the piece (Santa Rosa, Tonkins have also been tried) did not help the quest for identity or recognition in the marketplace, but the winery has nonetheless produced some outstanding wood-matured whites and pleasant, soft reds selling at attractive prices.

dalfarras ★★★☆

PO Box 123, Nagambie, Vic 3608 **region** Goulburn Valley
phone (03) 5794 2637 **fax** (03) 5794 2360 **open** Not
winemaker Alister Purbrick, Alan George **production** 20 000 **est.** 1991
product range ($12.95-49.95 R) Sauvignon Blanc, Marsanne, Verdelho Chardonnay, Shiraz, Merlot Cabernet Sauvignon.
summary The personal project of Alister Purbrick and artist-wife Rosa (née) Dalfarra, whose paintings adorn the labels of the wines. Alister, of course, is best known as winemaker at Tahbilk, the family winery and home, but this range of wines is intended to (in Alister's words) 'allow me to expand my winemaking horizons and mould wines in styles different to Tahbilk'. It now draws upon 23 hectares of its own plantings in the Goulburn Valley, and the business continues to grow.

Dalfarras Sauvignon Blanc

▼▼▼▼ **2001** Light to medium green-yellow; the clean and smooth bouquet has soft gooseberry fruit, the palate with quite good depth, the varietal character picking up intensity; well-balanced. **rating:** 85

best drinking 2001–2002 **best vintages** '96 **drink with** Smoked eel • $13.95

Dalfarras Shiraz

▼▼▼▽ **1998** Medium red-purple; the moderately intense, clean and smooth bouquet leads into a palate with gentle red berry fruit, but not overmuch structure. **rating:** 84

best drinking 2001–2004 **best vintages** NA **drink with** Steak and kidney pie • $19.95

dalrymple ★★★★

1337 Pipers Brook Road, Pipers Brook, Tas 7254 **region** Northern Tasmania
phone (03) 6382 7222 **fax** (03) 6382 7222 **open** 7 days 10–5
winemaker Bertel Sundstrup **production** 4500 **est.** 1987
product range ($15–35 CD) Chardonnay, Unwooded Chardonnay, Sauvignon Blanc, Blanc de Blanc, Pinot Noir, Special Bin Pinot Noir.
summary A partnership between Jill Mitchell and her sister and brother-in-law, Anne and Bertel Sundstrup, inspired by father Bill Mitchell's establishment of the Tamarway Vineyard in the late 1960s. In 1991 Tamarway reverted to the Sundstrup and Mitchell families, and it, too, will be producing wine in the future, probably under its own label but sold ex the Dalrymple cellar door. As production has grown (significantly), so has wine quality, across the board, often led by its Sauvignon Blanc.

Dalrymple Blanc de Blanc

▼▼▼▼▽ **1998** Pale green-gold; a clean, fresh and citrussy bouquet is followed by a palate which, while not especially complex, echoes the clean and fresh aromas of the bouquet with ripe citrus flavours and substantial length. A strong silver medal at the 2002 Tasmanian Wines Show. **rating:** 90

best drinking 2002–2004 **best vintages** '98 **drink with** Aperitif • $25

Dalrymple Pinot Noir

▼▼▼▽ **2000** Light to medium red-purple; lifted sappy/leafy/spicy/cherry aromas are precursors to a palate which is slightly betrayed on the aftertaste, where the green leaf edges leave a touch of bitterness. **rating:** 84

best drinking 2002–2004 **best vintages** '98 **drink with** Roast rabbit • $25

Dalrymple Special Bin Pinot Noir

▼▼▼▼▽ **2000** Medium red-purple; a fragrant and stylish bouquet with touches of savoury herb is mirrored on the complex and similarly stylish palate; the only criticism might be a lack of fruit density. **rating:** 90

best drinking 2002–2005 **best vintages** '99 **drink with** Wild mushroom risotto • $35

dalwhinnie ★★★★★

RMB 4378 Taltarni Road, Moonambel, Vic 3478 **region** Pyrenees
phone (03) 5467 2388 **fax** (03) 5467 2237 **open** 7 days 10–5
winemaker David Jones, Gary Baldwin (Consultant) **production** 5500 **est.** 1976

product range ($27–120 CD) Dalwhinnie Pinot Noir; Moonambel Chardonnay, Shiraz and Cabernet; Eagle Series Shiraz.

summary David and Jenny Jones have acquired full ownership of Dalwhinnie from Ewan Jones. Dalwhinnie goes from strength to strength, making outstanding wines right across the board. The wines all show tremendous depth of fruit flavour, reflecting the relatively low-yielding but very well-maintained vineyards. It is hard to say whether the Chardonnay, the Cabernet Sauvignon or the Shiraz is the more distinguished, and the Pinot Noir is a startling arrival from out of nowhere. A further 8 hectares of shiraz (with a little viognier) were planted in the spring of 1999 on a newly acquired block on Taltarni Road, permitting the further development of exports to the UK, the US, Canada, Switzerland, New Zealand and Hong Kong. A 50-tonne contemporary high-tech winery was built prior to the 2002 vintage, allowing the Eagle Series and Pinot Noir to be made on-site.

Dalwhinnie Chardonnay

▼▼▼▼▽ **2000** Light to medium yellow-green; the bouquet shows obvious toasty barrel-ferment characters interwoven with fig, stone fruit and cashew, the palate with a typically complex web of fruit, barrel-ferment and cashew sweeping through to an ultra-smooth finish.   **rating:** 92

best drinking 2003–2008 **best vintages** '87, '88, '90, '92, '93, '94, '96, '98, '99, '00 **drink with** Turkey • $27

Dalwhinnie Pinot Noir

▼▼▼▼▽ **2000** Light to medium red-purple; the bouquet ranges through sappy/foresty/cedary/cigar box aromas, the palate producing surprising plum-oriented varietal fruit and all of the complexity of the bouquet in a fine, elegant and moderately intense mode. Theoretically, it shouldn't be possible, but there it is.   **rating:** 90

best drinking 2002–2005 **best vintages** '00 **drink with** Game • $35

Dalwhinnie Moonambel Shiraz

▼▼▼▼▼ **2000** Deep but bright full purple-red; a smooth, classy bouquet with sweet damson plum fruit, followed by the usual immaculately sculpted palate offering sumptuous plum and dark cherry, positive but not overly assertive oak, and lingering, ripe tannins.   **rating:** 96

best drinking 2005–2015 **best vintages** '86, '88, '90, '91, '92, '94, '95, '97, '98, '99, '00 **drink with** Potent cheeses, strong red meats • $45

Dalwhinnie Moonambel Cabernet Sauvignon

▼▼▼▼▼ **2000** Medium to full red-purple, typically bright; a smooth, seductive, fruit-driven blackcurrant bouquet flows into a palate with great mouthfeel and structure; red and blackcurrant, cassis, soft fine tannins and quality oak all merge seamlessly.   **rating:** 96

best drinking 2005–2015 **best vintages** '92, '93, '00 **drink with** Rare chargrilled rump steak • $40

dalyup river estate   NR

Murrays Road, Esperance, WA 6450 **region** South West Australia Zone
phone (08) 9076 5027 **fax** (08) 9076 5027 **open** Weekends 10–4
winemaker Tom Murray **production** 700 **est.** 1987
product range ($12–15 CD) Hellfire White, Esperance Sauvignon Blanc, Esperance Shiraz, Esperance Cabernet Sauvignon, Port.
summary Arguably the most remote winery in Australia other than Chateau Hornsby in Alice Springs. The quantities are as small as the cellar-door prices are modest; this apart, the light but fragrant wines show the cool climate of this ocean-side vineyard. Came from out of the clouds to win the trophy for Best Wine of Show at the West Australian Show in 1999 with its Shiraz.

dal zotto wines   ★★★☆

Edi Road, Cheshunt, Vic 3678 **region** King Valley
phone (03) 5729 8321 **fax** (03) 5729 8490 **open** 7 days 11–5
winemaker Otto Dal Zotto, Warren Proft **production** 6000 **est.** 1987
product range ($15–24 CD) Riesling, Chardonnay, Shiraz, Merlot, Cabernet Merlot, Cabernet Sauvignon.
summary Dal Zotto Wines remains primarily a contract grape grower, with almost 26 hectares of vineyards (predominantly chardonnay, cabernet sauvignon and merlot, but with trial plantings of sangiovese, barbera and marzemino), but does make a small amount of wine for local sale (and sale by mail order).

Dal Zotto Shiraz

ŶŶŶŶ 2000 Youthful red-purple; the clean, moderately intense bouquet has small berry fruit aromas and a touch of spice; pleasing cherry/plum fruit teams with soft but persistent tannins and subtle oak on the palate. **rating:** 87

ŶŶŶŶ 1999 Medium red-purple; the bouquet has some complexity, with plum, spice and vanilla oak intermingling; the palate has surprising concentration, with persistent tannins and plenty of all-over flavour. **rating:** 88

best drinking 2003–2007 **best vintages** NA **drink with** Beef shishkebabs • $24

Dal Zotto Cabernet Merlot

ŶŶŶŶ 2000 Medium red-purple; the bouquet is driven by sweet berry fruit, with little or no oak impact; the palate is similarly driven by nicely ripened fruit and tannins. **rating:** 85

best drinking 2002–2005 **best vintages** NA **drink with** Veal kidneys • $19

Dal Zotto Cabernet Sauvignon

ŶŶŶŶ 1999 Medium red-purple; earthy/savoury cabernet varietal fruit comes through on both the bouquet and palate, with minimal oak influence, in typical Dal Zotto style. **rating:** 85

best drinking 2003–2007 **best vintages** NA **drink with** Wood-fired pizza • $19

danbury estate   NR

Billimari, NSW 2794 (PO Box 605, Cowra, NSW 2794) **region** Cowra
phone (02) 6341 2204 **fax** (02) 6341 4690 **open** Tues–Sun 10–4 at Chill Restaurant, Japanese Garden, Cowra
winemaker Hope Estate (Contract) **production** 6000 **est.** 1996
product range ($12.95–15.30 CD) Middleton Chardonnay, Middleton Sparkling, Reserve.
summary A specialist Chardonnay producer established by Jonathon Middleton, with 22 hectares in production and the wines made under contract. The Quarry Restaurant at the winery is open Tuesday to Sunday 10–4.

d'arenberg   ★★★★☆

Osborn Road, McLaren Vale, SA 5171 **region** McLaren Vale
phone (08) 8323 8206 **fax** (08) 8323 8423 **open** 7 days 10–5
winemaker Chester Osborn, Phillip Dean **production** 150 000 **est.** 1912
product range ($11–90 R) Dry Dam Riesling, Broken Fishplate Sauvignon Blanc, Last Ditch Viognier, Money Spider Roussanne, Stump Jump Riesling Marsanne Sauvignon Blanc, The Hermit Crab Marsanne Viognier, Olive Grove Chardonnay, Other Side Chardonnay, Noble Riesling, Noble Semillon, Peppermint Paddock Sparkling Chambourcin, Dead Arm Shiraz, Footbolt Old Vine Shiraz, Laughing Magpie Shiraz Viognier, Twenty Eight Road Mourvedre, d'Arry's Original Shiraz Grenache, Stump Jump Grenache Shiraz, Ironstone Pressings Grenache Shiraz Mourvedre, Custodian Grenache, Peppermint Paddock Chambourcin, High Trellis Cabernet Sauvignon, Coppermine Road Cabernet Sauvignon; Vintage Fortified Shiraz, Nostalgia Rare Tawny.
summary Originally a conservative, traditional business (albeit successful), d'Arenberg adopted a much higher profile in the second half of the 1990s, with a cascade of volubly worded labels and the opening of a spectacularly situated and high-quality restaurant, d'Arry's Verandah. Happily, wine quality has more than kept pace with the label uplifts. An incredible number of export markets spread across Europe, North America and Asia, with all of the major countries represented.

d'Arenberg The Last Ditch Viognier

ŶŶŶŶ 2001 Medium yellow-green; complex inputs from barrel fermentation, but the oak pit is is not too assertive; a big, rich, mouthfilling wine in which oak plays an important role, but does not entirely obscure pear and peach flavours. Full barrel fermentation and French oak maturation, wild yeast, hand-picked, etc. **rating:** 89

best drinking 2002–2004 **best vintages** NA **drink with** Cassoulet • $20

d'Arenberg The Money Spider Roussanne

ŶŶŶŶ 2001 Medium to full yellow-green; a moderately rich, faintly honeyed bouquet is followed by a quite generous palate, again with a whisper of honey, not unlike ripe pinot gris. A varietal curiosity for McLaren Vale. **rating:** 85

best drinking 2001–2003 **best vintages** NA **drink with** Crumbed brains • $19.95

d'Arenberg Dead Arm Shiraz

▼▼▼▼▽ **1999** Dense red-purple; powerful, concentrated, deep black cherry and plum fruit on the bouquet is replicated on the rich and concentrated palate; fruit-driven plus a boost from 14.5° alcohol; the tannins and oak present no problem. **rating:** 93

best drinking 2004–2014 best vintages '94, '95, '96, '97, '98, '99 drink with Marinated beef • $65

d'Arenberg d'Arry's Original Shiraz Grenache

▼▼▼▼ **2000** Medium red-purple; a distinctly fragrant bouquet with the sweet, bright cherry jam of grenache coming through strongly, then a similarly sweetly complex berry, jam and mint palate. **rating:** 87

best drinking 2002–2007 best vintages '63, '76, '86, '87, '88, '91, '95, '96, '97 drink with Jugged hare • $19.50

d'Arenberg The Laughing Magpie

▼▼▼▼ **2000** Medium red-purple; the aromas are complex and quite scented, with licorice and a range of small, dark berry fruits; the palate is ripe and savoury, slightly thick and chewy thanks to the abundant tannins. Should settle down well with a few more years in bottle. **rating:** 88

best drinking 2004–2010 best vintages NA drink with Marinated venison • $30

d'Arenberg Ironstone Pressings

▼▼▼▼▽ **1999** Medium red-purple; the bouquet has spotlessly clean and fresh red berry fruit, the expected tannins not making their appearance on the palate until the finish. Does need time to knit and soften, but is sufficiently balanced for that process to yield a fine wine. **rating:** 90

best drinking 2004–2009 best vintages '91, '94, '95, '97, '98, '99 drink with Leave it in the cellar • $90

d'Arenberg The Coppermine Road Cabernet Sauvignon

▼▼▼▼▽ **1999** Medium red-purple; clean, ripe fruit with a mix of mint and berry on the bouquet flows into a solid, rich and ripe palate with blackberry and mint on the middle moving through to firm tannins on the finish. **rating:** 90

best drinking 2004–2014 best vintages '97, '99 drink with Leave it in the cellar • $35

d'Arenberg The High Trellis Cabernet Sauvignon

▼▼▼▼ **2000** Bright purple-red; aromatic red berry/blackcurrant/cassis fruit on the bouquet leads into a palate with plenty of red berry fruit, but a slightly smudgy finish. **rating:** 85

best drinking 2004–2008 best vintages '98 drink with Rack of lamb • $20.50

d'Arenberg Nostalgia Rare Tawny

▼▼▼▼ **NV** Golden tawny; honey, Christmas cake, nutty, rancio aromas lead into a quite fine Christmas cake palate, followed by a distinctly biscuity aftertaste. **rating:** 89

best drinking 2002–2003 best vintages NA drink with Coffee • $30

dargo valley winery   NR

Lower Dargo Road, Dargo, Vic 3682 **region** Gippsland
phone (03) 5140 1228 **fax** (03) 5140 1388 **open** Mon–Thurs 12–8, weekends, holidays 10–8
winemaker Hermann Bila **production** 500 **est.** 1985
product range ($12–14 CD) Traminer, Rhine Riesling, Sauvignon Blanc, Chardonnay, Cabernet Sauvignon, Port, Muscat.
summary Two and a half hectares are situated in mountain country north of Maffra and looking towards the Bogong National Park. Hermann Bila comes from a family of European winemakers; there is an on-site restaurant, and Devonshire teas and ploughman's lunches are provided – very useful given the remote locality. The white wines tend to be rustic, the sappy/earthy/cherry Pinot Noir the pick of the red wines. Bed and breakfast accommodation is available.

darling estate   ★★★

Whitfield Road, Cheshunt, Vic 3678 **region** King Valley
phone (03) 5729 8396 **fax** (03) 5729 8396 **open** By appointment
winemaker Guy Darling, Rick Kinzbrunner (Consultant) **production** 200 **est.** 1990
product range ($6.25–18.75 ML) Koombahla Riesling, Nambucca Chenin Blanc, Koombahla Chardonnay, Koombahla Pinot Noir, Nambucca Gamay, Koombahla Shiraz, Koombahla Cabernet Franc, Koombahla Cabernet Sauvignon.

summary Guy Darling was one of the pioneers of the King Valley when he planted his first vines in 1970. For many years the entire production was purchased by Brown Brothers, providing their well-known Koombahla Estate label. Much of the production from the 23 hectares is still sold to Brown Brothers (and others), but since 1991 Guy Darling has had a fully functional winery established on the vineyard, making a small portion of the production into wine; this was, in fact, his motivation for planting the original vines. All the wines on sale have considerable bottle age.

darling park ★★★★

232 Red Hill Road, Red Hill, Vic 3937 **region** Mornington Peninsula
phone (03) 5989 2324 **fax** (03) 5989 2324 **open** Weekends and public holidays 11–5 and any time the vineyard gates are open
winemaker Various **production** 1200 **est.** 1986
product range ($17–25 CD) Chardonnay, Pinot Gris, Querida (Rosé), Te Quiero, Decadence, Pinot Noir, Pinot Noir Reserve, Merlot, Cabernet Sauvignon.
summary John Liberman (and wife Karen) and David Coe purchased Darling Park prior to the 2002 vintage. The Winenet consultancy group is providing advice on both the viticultural and winemaking side, and the product range has been revamped.

darlington estate ★★★☆

Lot 39 Nelson Road, Darlington, WA 6070 **region** Perth Hills
phone (08) 9299 6268 **fax** (08) 9299 7107 **open** Thurs–Sun and holidays 12–5
winemaker John Griffiths (Consultant) **production** 2000 **est.** 1983
product range ($13–30 CD) Sonata (Sauvignon Blanc), Semillon, Chardonnay, Symphony (Verdelho), Serenade (Chardonnay), Shiraz, Cabernet Sauvignon, Brut, Ruby Port; Darling Red (Grenache), Darling White (Unwooded Chardonnay), Darling Rosé (Grenache).
summary By far the largest producer in the Perth Hills region, and the best. Winemaking responsibilities passed to Caspar van der Meer, Balt's son, who graduated from Roseworthy in 1995 and, after a vintage at Chateau de Landiras in Bordeaux, joined the family business in 1996, returning to Languedoc in 1997 to make a large quantity of wine for the American market. He has now left to pursue further overseas winemaking opportunities, with winemaking passing to John Griffiths, who is possessed of an excellent palate.

david traeger ★★★☆

139 High Street, Nagambie, Vic 3608 **region** Goulburn Valley
phone (03) 5794 2514 **fax** (03) 5794 1776 **open** 7 days 10–5
winemaker David Traeger **production** 10 000 **est.** 1986
product range ($11–29.50 R) Verdelho, Shiraz, Cabernet; Helvetia (available from the cellar door only), Classic Dry (Riesling Semillon), Late Harvest (Riesling Verdelho), Cabernet Dolce, Cabernet Shiraz Merlot, Tawny Port.
summary David Traeger learned much during his years as assistant winemaker at Mitchelton, and knows central Victoria well. The red wines are solidly crafted, the Verdelho interesting but more variable in quality. Reasonably active retail distribution through Victoria, NSW and Queensland, with exports to the UK, the US, Japan and Singapore.

deakin estate ★★★

Kulkyne Way via Red Cliffs, Vic 3496 **region** Murray Darling
phone (03) 5029 1666 **fax** (03) 5024 3316 **open** Not
winemaker Linda Jukubans **production** 200 000 **est.** 1980
product range ($10 R) Sauvignon Blanc, Chardonnay, Brut, Shiraz, Merlot, Cabernet Sauvignon; Select range of Chardonnay, Shiraz, Merlot.
summary Effectively replaces the Sunnycliff label in the Katnook Estate, Riddoch and (now) Deakin Estate triumvirate, which constitutes the Wingara Wine Group, now 60 per cent owned by Freixenet of Spain. Sunnycliff is still used for export purposes but does not appear on the domestic market any more. Deakin Estate draws on over 300 hectares of its own vineyards, making it largely self-sufficient, and produces competitively priced wines of consistent quality and impressive value, getting better year by year. Exports to the UK, the US, Canada, New Zealand and Asia.

Deakin Estate Select Chardonnay

ŸŸŸŸ **2000** Medium yellow-green; the bouquet is complex, though smoky/charry oak is a little assertive, but on the palate some nectarine and melon come through before the slightly grippy finish which is (almost always) a sure sign of oak chips and/or oak inner staves. **rating:** 84

best drinking 2002–2003 **best vintages** NA **drink with** Takeaway • $9.99

Deakin Estate Shiraz

ŸŸŸŸ **2000** Clean, direct red fruit and restrained oak on the bouquet are followed by an attractive fruit-driven palate which has fleshed out very well since being bottled. Very good value. **rating:** 87

best drinking 2001–2003 **best vintages** '00 **drink with** One size fits all • $9.99

Deakin Estate Merlot

ŸŸŸŸ **2001** Medium red-purple; a light, leafy/earthy bouquet with savoury varietal character; the fractionally lean and simple palate provides more of the same, but what can one expect at the price? **rating:** 82

best drinking 2002–2003 **best vintages** NA **drink with** Pizza • $10

Deakin Estate Cabernet Sauvignon

ŸŸŸŸ **2001** Medium red-purple; light blackberry/earth with minimal oak on the bouquet is followed by a light to medium-bodied palate with savoury, blackberry fruit and not much length or depth. However, fair value. **rating:** 82

best drinking 2002–2003 **best vintages** NA **drink with** Steak and kidney pie • $10

de bortoli ★★★★

De Bortoli Road, Bilbul, NSW 2680 **region** Riverina
phone (02) 6964 9444 **fax** (02) 6964 9400 **open** Mon–Sat 9–5, Sun 9–4
winemaker Nick Guy, Ralph Graham, Julie Mortlock, Helen Foggo-Paschkow **production** 3 million
est. 1928
product range ($4.90–42.50 CD) Noble One Botrytis Semillon is the flagship wine; Premium varietals under Deen De Bortoli label; mid-priced range of varietal and blended wines under the Montage and Wild Vine labels; low-priced range of varietal and generic wines under the Sacred Hill label; Sparkling, Fortified. Substantial exports in bulk.
summary Famous among the cognoscenti for its superb Botrytis Semillon, which in fact accounts for only a minute part of its total production, this winery turns around low-priced varietal and generic wines which are invariably competently made and equally invariably provide value for money. Exports include Canada, Singapore, Japan, Hong Kong, Sweden and Thailand.

De Bortoli Sacred Hill Rhine Riesling

ŸŸŸŸ **2001** Light to medium yellow-green; the moderately intense bouquet is clean, with some citrus fruit, the palate soft, a little broad, but full in flavour. **rating:** 84

best drinking 2001–2002 **best vintages** NA **drink with** Fish, white meats, salad • $5.50

De Bortoli Sacred Hill Traminer Riesling

ŸŸŸŸ **2001** Light yellow-green; light spice and lime aromas are followed by a palate with flavoursome fruit in much the same spectrum, and distinct residual sweetness. Precisely styled and targeted, and excellent value. **rating:** 82

ŸŸŸŸ **2000** Pale yellow-green; the bouquet has distinct varietal spice, and, as expected, the palate has obvious residual sugar which pumps up the flavour. If you are looking for the style, irresistible at the price. **rating:** 81

best drinking 2002–2003 **best vintages** NA **drink with** Thai green chicken curry • $6

De Bortoli Montage Semillon Sauvignon Blanc

ŸŸŸŸ **2001** Light green-yellow; the bouquet is light, fresh and crisp, the fruit in neutral mode, the minerally and fresh palate with no obvious sweetness on the finish, which is highly commendable. **rating:** 83

best drinking 2002–2003 **best vintages** NA **drink with** Seafood • $10

De Bortoli Sacred Hill Semillon Chardonnay

ŸŸŸŸ **2001** Light to medium yellow-green; surprisingly fragrant tangy/lemony aromas which reappear in abundance in the tangy/tropical fruit of the palate, which also has good acidity and length. Outstanding value. **rating:** 86

best drinking 2001–2002 **best vintages** '01 **drink with** Any seafood • $5.50

De Bortoli Montage Chardonnay Semillon

♥♥♥♡ 2000 Light to medium yellow-green; the bouquet is not particularly intense, but is complex, and the oak, while evident, is not over the top. The palate is quite rich and soft, even if a fraction broad; good value at the price.   rating: 81

best drinking 2001–2002 best vintages NA drink with Caesar salad • $9

De Bortoli Deen De Bortoli Vat 7 Chardonnay

♥♥♥♥ 2000 Light to medium yellow-green; there is some complexity and style to the bouquet, triggered by the first stages of bottle development; flows easily across the tongue, with a fruit-driven range of ripe melon, nectarine and peach. Excellent value.   rating: 85

best drinking 2001–2002 best vintages '90, '92, '93, '99 drink with Pasta marinara • $10

De Bortoli Deen De Bortoli Vat 5 Botrytis Semillon(375 ml)

♥♥♥♥ 1997 Golden orange-bronze; rich cumquat, toffee and mandarin aromas are reflected in the flavours of the palate; as with prior vintages, the wine does not have the same intense sweetness as Noble One, but for some will be all the better, and the price is emphatically right.   rating: 88

best drinking 2002–2003 best vintages NA drink with Light cakes • $10

De Bortoli Noble One

♥♥♥♥♡ 2000 Glowing yellow-green; the spotlessly clean bouquet has neatly balanced citrus fruit and oak, the palate still tight, long and lingering. The best makers of this style of wine are working hard to build in longevity; this is a case in point, because the corollary is that such wines are less flashy at the very start of their life.   rating: 93

best drinking 2003–2009 best vintages '82, '84, '87, '90, '91, '94, '95, '96, '97, '98, '99, '00 drink with Crème brûlée • $22

De Bortoli Montage Cabernet Merlot

♥♥♥♡ 2001 Medium purple-red; light, clean, simple berry fruit aromas are reflected in the soft, red berry fruit flavours of the palate; balanced acidity and no oak chips to be seen.   rating: 83

best drinking 2002–2003 best vintages NA drink with Pizza • $10

de bortoli (victoria)   ★★★★★

Pinnacle Lane, Dixons Creek, Vic 3775 region Yarra Valley
phone (03) 5965 2271 fax (03) 5965 2442 open 7 days 10–5
winemaker Stephen Webber, David Slingsby-Smith, David Bicknell production 170 000 est. 1987
product range ($12–55 R) At the top comes the premium Melba (Cabernet blend), followed by Yarra Valley Gewürztraminer, Chardonnay, Pinot Noir, Shiraz, Cabernet Sauvignon; then comes the intermediate Gulf Station range of Riesling, Semillon Sauvignon Blanc, Unwooded Chardonnay, Chardonnay, Pinot Noir, Shiraz, Merlot and Cabernet Sauvignon; the Windy Peak range of Riesling, Chardonnay, Cabernet Rosé, Pinot Noir, Cabernet Shiraz Merlot.
summary The quality arm of the bustling De Bortoli group, run by Leanne De Bortoli and husband Stephen Webber, ex-Lindeman winemaker. The top label (De Bortoli), the second (Gulf Station) and the third (Windy Peak) all offer wines of consistently good quality and excellent value – the complex Chardonnay is of outstanding quality. Exports to the UK, Europe, Asia and the US.

De Bortoli Gulf Station Riesling

♥♥♥♥ 2001 Medium to full yellow-green, quite developed; the bouquet is similarly ripe and developed, with some secondary characters, possibly due to botrytis; the palate is soft and forward, with spice and old fashioned kerosene flavours. Very much the product of a schizophrenic vintage.   rating: 86

best drinking 2002–2003 best vintages NA drink with Artichoke with hollandaise sauce • $15

De Bortoli Windy Peak Riesling

♥♥♥♥♡ 2001 Light green-yellow; the tight bouquet ranges through mineral, herb, apple and a touch of spice; the palate is as attractive as ever; flows well; sweet lime fruit is followed by good acidity on the finish.   rating: 90

best drinking 2001–2004 best vintages '90, '92, '94, '95, '96, '97, '99, '01 drink with Fresh asparagus • $12

De Bortoli Gulf Station Semillon Sauvignon Blanc

TTTT 2001 Light green-yellow; attractive, light, gooseberry aromas mingle with some grass and herb; the palate has fruit sweetness on entry rather than on the finish, with good length and extract, and nicely balanced acidity to close. In this vintage, Sauvignon Blanc was the major component. **rating: 88**

best drinking 2001–2002 **best vintages** NA **drink with** Summer seafood • $15

De Bortoli Gulf Station Chardonnay

TTTT 2001 Light to medium yellow-green; gentle grapefruit and melon fruit on the bouquet are mirrored in the well-balanced and structured palate with its gentle citrus fruit. Good value. **rating: 88**

TTTT 2000 Medium straw-yellow; an unmistakable Yarra style, with nutty melon fruit on the bouquet and soft, rounded and quite sweet melon fruit on the palate. Minimal oak, and good acidity to close; held in check by the unusually warm vintage. **rating: 86**

best drinking 2002–2004 **best vintages** '95, '96, '97, '98 **drink with** Yabbies • $15

De Bortoli Windy Peak Chardonnay

TTTT 2001 Light to medium yellow-green; clean, fresh, light nectarine and subtle oak aromas lead into a lively, fresh, citrussy palate with lingering acidity and light oak nuances. **rating: 87**

best drinking 2001–2003 **best vintages** '90, '92, '93, '94, '97, '00 **drink with** Sashimi • $12

De Bortoli Yarra Valley Chardonnay

TTTTY 2001 Light green-straw; a clean, fresh, crisp bouquet is very understated, with the oak held in tight restraint. The fruit-driven, delicate palate has melon and nectarine flowing evenly to the finish. There is no alcohol burn, and the oak, while there, is subtle. **rating: 93**

TTTTY 2000 Light green-yellow; the complex, distinctly nutty bouquet shows barrel ferment and malolactic ferment influences on the melon fruit. The palate has well above average length and intensity, with lively stone fruit flavours, sophisticated oak and good acidity. **rating: 93**

best drinking 2003–2006 **best vintages** '90, '92, '93, '94, '96, '97, '98, '99, '00, '01 **drink with** Braised pork neck • $23

De Bortoli Cabernet Rosé

TTTTY 2001 Vivid red-purple; cherry, rose petal and lemon blossom aromas lead into a palate with good length and minimal sweetness. Immaculate winemaking. **rating: 91**

best drinking 2001–2002 **best vintages** '00 **drink with** Antipasto, aperitif • $12

De Bortoli Gulf Station Pinot Noir

TTTT 2001 Light to medium purple-red; strawberry, strawberry jam and plum fruit on the bouquet move emphatically into the plum spectrum on the palate, supported by fine tannins and neatly judged acidity. As ever, one of the best value Pinot Noirs in Australia. **rating: 88**

best drinking 2002–2005 **best vintages** '00 **drink with** Roast pigeon • $15

De Bortoli Windy Peak Pinot Noir

TTTT 2001 Bright red-purple; fresh plum and cherry fruit aromas lead into a light to medium-bodied palate, again showing plum and cherry fruit, still slightly firm and needing another 12 months. A whole bag of winemaking tricks in a wine costing only $12. It's absurd. **rating: 87**

TTTT 2000 Medium red-purple; some gamey notes (not brettanomyces) add complexity to the bouquet. Gamey/cherry fruit to the palate has good length; very good value. **rating: 87**

best drinking 2003–2004 **best vintages** '00, '01 **drink with** Chinese dry-fried shredded beef • $12

De Bortoli Yarra Valley Pinot Noir

TTTTT 2000 Bright purple-red; a clean, firmish, dark plum bouquet is repeated on the palate, which has good depth to the fruit, balanced acidity, and good length. Will develop well. **rating: 94**

best drinking 2002–2007 **best vintages** '95, '96, '97, '00 **drink with** Duck casserole • $29

De Bortoli GS Reserve Yarra Valley Shiraz

TTTTT 1997 Medium red-purple; the mature, complex bouquet has an array of sweet leather, spice, cedar and plum, the palate tightening up considerably, especially via its tannins. Overall, very complex. Spent 18 months in French oak; 3000 bottles made. **rating: 94**

best drinking 2002–2007 **best vintages** NA **drink with** Smoked quail • NA

De Bortoli Gulf Station Shiraz

▼▼▼▼▽ **2000** Rich, complex dark berry and earthy fruit aromas are followed by a concentrated and weighty palate of ripe blood plums, finishing with fine tannins. Subtle oak throughout. **rating:** 90

best drinking 2002–2008 **best vintages** '99, '00 **drink with** Osso buco • $15

De Bortoli Melba Barrel Select

▼▼▼▼▼ **1997** Medium red, with a touch of purple; a complex array of spicy/earthy/cedary/blackberry fruit aromas, then a mix of blackberry and blackcurrant, before surprising tannins which still bolster the long finish. Two years in French oak; 7500 bottles made; 95 per cent Cabernet Sauvignon, 5 per cent Merlot and Shiraz. **rating:** 94

best drinking 2002–2010 **best vintages** '93, '94, '95, '97 **drink with** Yarra Valley venison • $55

De Bortoli Windy Peak Cabernet Shiraz Merlot

▼▼▼▼ **2000** Medium red-purple; the bouquet has quite rich fruit with nicely balanced berry, spice and oak aromas. The palate has substantial structure, weight and flavour, with good tannin and extract management. Excellent value. **rating:** 87

best drinking 2002–2006 **best vintages** NA **drink with** Braised lamb • $12

De Bortoli Gulf Station Cabernet Sauvignon

▼▼▼▼ **2000** Medium purple-red; pristine redcurrant fruit aromas with touches of cedar and earth lead into a luscious palate with red and blackcurrant fruit, ripe tannins and minimal oak influence. Excellent value. **rating:** 89

best drinking 2004–2009 **best vintages** '00 **drink with** Parmesan or aged cheddar • $16

deep dene vineyard   NR

36 Glenisla Road, Bickley, WA 6076 **region** Perth Hills
phone (08) 9293 0077 **fax** (08) 9293 0077 **open** By appointment
winemaker Contract **production** 4000 **est.** 1994
product range ($25–28 R) Pinot Noir, Shiraz.
summary Deep Dene is the largest of the Perth Hills vineyards, drawing upon 4 hectares of pinot noir and 0.5 hectare of shiraz, continuing the near obsession of the Perth Hills vignerons with pinot noir in a climate which, to put it mildly, is difficult for the variety.

deep woods estate   ★★★★

Lot 10 Commonage Road, Yallingup, WA 6282 **region** Margaret River
phone (08) 9756 6066 **fax** (08) 9756 6066 **open** Tues–Sun 11–5, 7 days during holidays
winemaker Bruce Dukes, Ben Gould **production** 16 000 **est.** 1987
product range ($14–30 CD) Semillon, Semillon Sauvignon Blanc, Ivory (Semillon Sauvignon Blanc), Verdelho, Eden (Botrytis Semillon), Shiraz, Ebony (Cabernet Sauvignon Shiraz), Cabernet Sauvignon, Cabernet Reserve.
summary The Gould family acquired Deep Woods Estate in 1991, 4 years after the commencement of the estate plantings. There are 15 hectares of estate vines planted to nine varieties, with the intake supplemented by contract-grown grapes for the Ebony and Ivory wines. At the top of the tree are the occasional and tiny releases under the Boneyard label: the first such release was of 600 bottles of 2001 Cabernet Franc. These wines are only available to mailing list customers, and are likely to be pre-sold to those on a waiting list.

Deep Woods Estate Margaret River Semillon

▼▼▼▼ 2000 Light straw green; hints of lemon blossom, apple and whispers of spicy French oak on the bouquet flow through into a slow-developing palate which has gobbled up the French oak in which the wine was fermented, and which carries its 13+° with impressive ease. **rating:** 88

best drinking 2002–2006 **best vintages** NA **drink with** Calamari • $18

Deep Woods Estate Semillon Sauvignon Blanc

▼▼▼▼▽ **2001** Light green-yellow; a light, crisp, gently herbaceous bouquet leads into a light to medium-bodied palate which has good focus and length; a touch of spritz on the finish does not intrude on the harmonious palate feel. **rating:** 90

best drinking 2001–2003 **best vintages** '00, '01 **drink with** Margaret River abalone • $16

Deep Woods Estate Eden

♥♥♥♥ **2000** Light to medium yellow-green; the clean, gently aromatic bouquet only hints at the palate, with its mix of citrus, lemon and pineapple, providing both balance and focus. **rating:** 86

best drinking 2002–2003 **best vintages** NA **drink with** Fruit tart • $19.50

Deep Woods Estate Shiraz

♥♥♥♥ **2000** Medium red-purple; the fresh, moderately intense bouquet has some spicy/savoury undertones to the fruit, then a palate with good length and structure, showing cherry and small berries building progressively on the mid-palate to the finish. **rating:** 89

best drinking 2004–2010 **best vintages** NA **drink with** Lamb casserole • $17

de iuliis ★★★☆

12 Broke Road, Pokolbin, NSW 2320 **region** Lower Hunter Valley
phone (02) 4993 8000 **fax** (02) 4998 7168 **open** 7 days 10–5
winemaker Michael De Iuliis **production** 8500 **est.** 1990
product range ($14–38 CD) Semillon, Show Reserve Verdelho, Chardonnay, Show Reserve Chardonnay, Pinot Chardonnay, Botrytis Semillon Shiraz, McLaren Vale Shiraz, Cabernet Merlot.
summary Three generations of the De Iuliis family have been involved in the establishment of their 19.5-hectare vineyard at Keinbah in the Lower Hunter Valley. The family acquired the property in 1986 and planted the first vines in 1990, selling the grapes from the first few vintages to Tyrrell's but retaining small amounts of grapes for release under the De Iuliis label. Winemaker Michael De Iuliis, the third-generation family member, has completed postgraduate studies in oenology at the Roseworthy Campus of Adelaide University. The overall quality of the wines is good; at this juncture, they are only available by mail order or at the cellar door.

delacolline estate NR

Whillas Road, Port Lincoln, SA 5606 **region** Southern Eyre Peninsula
phone (08) 8682 5277 **fax** (08) 8682 4455 **open** Weekends 9–5
winemaker Andrew Mitchell (Contract) **production** 650 **est.** 1984
product range ($10–15 R) Riesling, Fumé Blanc, Cabernet Sauvignon.
summary Joins Boston Bay as the second Port Lincoln producer; the white wines are made under contract in the Clare Valley. The 3-hectare vineyard, run under the direction of Tony Bassett, reflects the cool maritime influence, with ocean currents that sweep up from the Antarctic. No recent tastings.

delamere ★★★

Bridport Road, Pipers Brook, Tas 7254 **region** Northern Tasmania
phone (03) 6382 7190 **fax** (03) 6382 7250 **open** 7 days 10–5
winemaker Richard Richardson **production** 2500 **est.** 1983
product range ($16–28.50 CD) Chardonnay, Chardonnay Reserve, Pinot Noir, Pinot Noir Reserve), Sparkling Rosé, Sparkling Cuvée.
summary Richie Richardson produces elegant, rather light-bodied wines that have a strong following. The Chardonnay has been most successful, with a textured, complex, malolactic-influenced wine with great, creamy feel in the mouth. The Pinots typically show pleasant varietal fruit, but seem to suffer from handling problems with oak and a touch of oxidation. Retail distribution through Prime Wines.

delaney's creek winery NR

70 Hennessey Road, Delaneys Creek, Qld 4514 **region** Queensland Coastal
phone (07) 5496 4925 **fax** (07) 5496 4926 **open** Mon–Fri 10–4, weekends and public holidays 10–5
winemaker Brian Wilson **production** 3000 **est.** 1997
product range ($9.50–14.50 CD) Verdelho, Marsanne Blanc, Muscat Rosé, Cabernet Franc, Shiraz Cabernet Franc, Fortifieds.
summary Tom Weidmann established Delaney's Creek Winery in 1997 and by doing so has expanded the vineyard map of Queensland yet further. Delaney's Creek is situated near the town of Woodford, itself not far northwest of Caboolture. In 1998 Weidmann planted an exotic mix of 1 hectare each of shiraz, chardonnay, sangiovese, touriga nacional and verdelho. In the meantime he is obtaining his grapes from 4 hectares of contract-grown fruit, including cabernet sauvignon, cabernet franc, merlot, shiraz, chardonnay, marsanne and verdelho.

delatite ★★★★

Stoneys Road, Mansfield, Vic 3722 **region** Central Victorian High Country
phone (03) 5775 2922 **fax** (03) 5775 2911 **open** 7 days 10–4
winemaker Rosalind Ritchie **production** 12 000 **est.** 1982
product range ($15–35 CD) Riesling, Dead Man's Hill Gewürztraminer, Sauvignon Blanc, Pinot Gris, Unoaked Chardonnay, Chardonnay, Delmelza Pinot Chardonnay, Late Picked Riesling, Rosé, Pinot Noir, Shiraz, Merlot, Malbec, Dungeon Gully, Devil's River (Cabernet Sauvignon Malbec Shiraz), Cabernet Sauvignon, Fortifieds; V.S. Limited Edition Riesling, R.J. Limited Edition (Cabernet blend).
summary With its sweeping views across to the snow-clad alps, this is uncompromising cool-climate viticulture, and the wines naturally reflect the climate. Light but intense Riesling and spicy Traminer flower with a year or two in bottle, and in the warmer vintages the red wines achieve flavour and mouthfeel, albeit with a distinctive mintiness. Exports to the UK, Switzerland, Malaysia and Singapore.

Delatite Riesling

▼▼▼▼ 2001 Typical ultra-pale colour; light, floral, apple cake spice and mineral aromas, the crisp palate with firm, minerally mouthfeel, but still to flower and open the fruit locked up inside; as ever, needs time.

rating: 88

best drinking 2004–2010 **best vintages** '82, '86, '87, '93, '97, '99 **drink with** Grilled fish • $18

Delatite Chardonnay

▼▼▼▼ 2001 Medium yellow-green; the moderately intense bouquet ranges through toasty/nutty/cashew characters to fig and melon; the light to medium-bodied palate is smooth, but derives complexity from the assemblage of flavours which parallel the characters of the bouquet.

rating: 86

best drinking 2002–2004 **best vintages** '88, '91, '92, '98 **drink with** Crab • $23

Delatite Delmelza Pinot Chardonnay

▼▼▼▼ 1996 Light straw-green; a clean, bright and fresh bouquet with a hint of bready/biscuity autolysis and perhaps the 100 per cent Pinot Noir base wine; the tangy, flavoursome palate has length and grip, still fresh, and with brisk acidity.

rating: 87

best drinking 2002–2003 **best vintages** NA **drink with** Aperitif • $27.50

Delatite Dungeon Gully

▼▼▼▽ 2001 Medium purple-red; raspberry and cherry fruit aromas lead into a light but pleasant palate with sweet, juicy berry (not minty) flavours in unabashed, early-drinking style.

rating: 84

best drinking 2002–2003 **best vintages** NA **drink with** Italian • $18

Delatite Cabernet Sauvignon

▼▼▼▽ 1999 Light to medium red-purple; a tangy leafy bouquet is followed by a palate which opens up with sweet red berry fruit, followed by rather green tannins on the finish. Delatite is confident it will cellar well and soften and open up over the next 8 years. I hope it does.

rating: 82

best drinking 2002–2007 **best vintages** NA **drink with** Roast veal • $25

del rios vineyard ★★★☆

2320 Ballan Road, Anakie, Vic 3221 **region** Geelong
phone (03) 9497 4644 **fax** (03) 9497 4644 **open** Weekends 10–4, bus tours by appointment
winemaker Scott Ireland, Peter Flewellyn (Contract) **production** 6500 **est.** 1996
product range ($18–23 ML) Sauvignon Blanc, Sauvignon Blanc Crisp, Chardonnay, Marsanne, Pinot Noir, Shiraz, Cabernet Sauvignon.
summary German del Rio was born in northern Spain (in 1920) where his family owned vineyards. After three generations in Australia, his family has established 16 hectares of vines on their 104-hectare property on the slopes of Mount Anakie, the principal focus being chardonnay, pinot noir and cabernet sauvignon (4 hectares each) then marsanne, sauvignon blanc, merlot and shiraz (1 hectare each). Planting commenced in 1996, and vintage 2000 was the first commercial release.

del Rios Sauvignon Blanc

▼▼▼▼ 2001 Light straw-green; the relatively light bouquet has a mix of grassy/herbal/gooseberry/asparagus aromas, the herb and asparagus driving the fairly austere palate. An interesting wine with plenty of character.

rating: 87

best drinking 2002–2003 **best vintages** NA **drink with** Delicate seafood • $24.50

del Rios Chardonnay

▼▼▼▽ **2000** Medium yellow-green; the bouquet is complex, but there is slightly raw/bitter oak; the softer palate has some tropical edges, and the oak is not overly intrusive; slight lack of overall focus.   **rating:** 84

best drinking 2001–2002 **best vintages** NA **drink with** Salmon pizza • $19

del Rios Pinot Noir

▼▼▼▼ **2000** Medium red, with a touch of purple; not 100 per cent bright; unfiltered? The bouquet is predominantly in the gamey/foresty spectrum, with some plum; the medium-bodied palate goes down much the same track, with soft plummy fruit and those foresty/gamey characters. Some would doubtless suggest the presence of brettanomyces; I am not so sure.   **rating:** 86

best drinking 2001–2004 **best vintages** NA **drink with** Smoked quail • $23

del Rios Shiraz

▼▼▼▼▽ **2000** Medium to full red; complex, ripe spice and cinnamon on dark plum and prune aromas move into a palate with masses of flavour, character and style; ripe but distinctly Rhône-ish; soft tannins.   **rating:** 92

best drinking 2003–2010 **best vintages** '00 **drink with** Braised duck • $23

del Rios Cabernet Sauvignon

▼▼▼▽ **2000** Medium red-purple; a spicy/savoury/leafy bouquet leads into a light to medium-bodied palate, with all the fruit in a spicy/savoury/leafy track, and really needing a touch more ripeness/sweetness.   **rating:** 84

best drinking 2003–2007 **best vintages** NA **drink with** Lamb shanks • $21

demondrille vineyards ★★★☆

RMB 97, Prunevale Road, Kingsvale, NSW 2587 **region** Hilltops
phone (02) 6384 4272 **fax** (02) 6384 4292 **open** Weekends 10.30–5 or by appointment
winemaker Contract **production** 1000 **est.** 1979
product range ($8–22 CD) Riesling, The Dove (Sauvignon Blanc Semillon), Stan (Dessert style), Precious (Botrytis Riesling), Purgatory (Rosé style), Bloodline (Pinot Noir), The Raven (Shiraz) and Black Rosé (Cabernet Sauvignon), together with lesser quantities of cellar-door-only wines (from the Tin Shed range).
summary Pamela Gillespie and Robert Provan purchased the former Hercynia Vineyard and winery in 1995. Pam Gillespie has an Associate Diploma in Winemaking and Marketing from Adelaide University, Roseworthy, and has been in the hospitality industry since 1989. Her partner had a remarkable career and is part way through a Bachelor of Science degree at Sydney University (as a mature-age student) majoring in agriculture. Most of the wines from Demondrille are made at Charles Sturt University, with smaller quantities made on site. Specially created food platters featuring local produce are available at the winery each weekend.

Demondrille Precious Botrytis Riesling

▼▼▼▼ **1999** Bright yellow-gold; a complex, rich bouquet, with a mix of peach, lime and apricot is followed by a moderately sweet palate with cleansing and balancing acidity. 10.2° alcohol.   **rating:** 85

best drinking 2002–2003 **best vintages** NA **drink with** Fruit tart • $12

Demondrille Bloodline Pinot Noir

▼▼▼▼ **1999** Dark red-purple; a foresty/savoury/spicy bouquet is followed by a palate with pleasing spice and dark plum fruit, held in check by the inappropriate choice of vanilla oak.   **rating:** 85

best drinking 2002–2004 **best vintages** NA **drink with** Braised hare • $22

Demondrille The Raven Shiraz

▼▼▼▽ **1999** Medium to full red-purple; a clean bouquet with an array of briary, savoury, spicy fruit aromas, moving more to plum and cherry on the palate, then a slightly sharp, acid finish.   **rating:** 84

best drinking 2002–2006 **best vintages** NA **drink with** Wild duck • $22

Demondrille Black Rosé

▼▼▼▼ **1999** Medium red-purple; clean, red berry fruit with a touch of mint on the bouquet follows through into a light to medium-bodied palate with sweet, red berry fruit, soft tannins and gently sweet oak. Nice wine.   **rating:** 87

best drinking 2003–2008 **best vintages** NA **drink with** Lamb casserole • $22

dennis ★★★

Kangarilla Road, McLaren Vale, SA 5171 **region** McLaren Vale
phone (08) 8323 8665 **fax** (08) 8323 9121 **open** Mon–Fri 10–5, weekends, holidays 11–5
winemaker Peter Dennis **production** 10 000 **est.** 1970
product range ($14–40 CD) Sauvignon Blanc, Chardonnay, Shiraz, Cabernet Sauvignon, Grenache, Merlot, Egerton Vintage Port, Old Tawny Port.
summary A low-profile winery which has, from time to time, made some excellent wines, most notably typically full-blown, buttery/peachy Chardonnay. However, in 1998 the pendulum swung towards the Shiraz and Cabernet Sauvignon.

d'entrecasteaux NR

Boorara Road, Northcliffe, WA 6262 **region** Pemberton
phone (08) 9776 7232 **open** By appointment
winemaker Alkoomi (Contract) **production** 600 **est.** 1988
product range Chardonnay, Sauvignon Blanc, Pinot Noir, Cabernet Sauvignon.
summary Not to be confused with the now moribund Tasmanian winery of the same name but likewise taking its name from the French explorer Admiral Bruni D'Entrecasteaux, who visited both Tasmania and the southwest coast of Western Australia. Four hectares of estate vineyards, planted on rich Karri loam, produce grapes for the wines which are contract-made at Alkoomi.

derwent estate ★★★★☆

329 Lyell Highway, Granton, Tas 7070 **region** Southern Tasmania
phone (03) 6248 5073 **fax** (03) 6248 5073 **open** Not
winemaker Stefano Lubiana (Contract) **production** 300 **est.** 1993
product range ($17.50 ML) Riesling, Chardonnay, Pinot Noir.
summary The Hanigan family has established Derwent Estate as part of a diversification programme for their 400-hectare mixed farming property. Five hectares of vineyard have been progressively planted since 1993, initially to riesling, followed by chardonnay and pinot noir.

devil's lair ★★★★☆

Rocky Road, Forest Grove via Margaret River, WA 6286 **region** Margaret River
phone (08) 9757 7573 **fax** (08) 9757 7533 **open** By appointment
winemaker Stuart Pym **production** 40 000 **est.** 1985
product range ($20–54 R) Chardonnay, Margaret River (Cabernet blend); Fifth Leg Dry White and Dry Red.
summary Having rapidly carved out a high reputation for itself through a combination of clever packaging and marketing allied with impressive wine quality, Devil's Lair was acquired by Southcorp Wine Group (Penfolds, etc) in December 1996, and production is projected to increase to over 50 000 cases.

Devil's Lair Margaret River Cabernet Blend

▼▼▼▼▼ 1999 Medium to full red-purple; the rich yet restrained savoury, dark berry complexity of the bouquet is the opening stanza for a palate crammed with dark berry, cassis and blackberry fruit, with exemplary oak and tannin management. There can be no doubt this is the best Devil's Lair to date. **rating:** 94
best drinking 2004–2014 **best vintages** '97, '98, '99 **drink with** Chargrilled rump • $55

diamond valley vineyards ▲▲▲▲▲

2130 Kinglake Road, St Andrews, Vic 3761 **region** Yarra Valley
phone (03) 9710 1484 **fax** (03) 9710 1369 **open** Not
winemaker David Lance, James Lance **production** 7000 **est.** 1976
product range ($20.50–65 R) Chardonnay, Pinot Noir, Cabernet; Yarra Valley (formerly Blue Label) Sauvignon Blanc, Chardonnay, Pinot Noir, Cabernet Merlot; Close Planted Pinot Noir, Cabernet Sauvignon.
summary One of the Yarra Valley's finest producers of Pinot Noir and an early pacesetter for the variety, making wines of tremendous style and crystal-clear varietal character. They are not Cabernet Sauvignon lookalikes but true Pinot Noir, fragrant and intense. Much of the wine is sold through an informative and well-presented mailing list, supplemented by national distribution through Red + White. Exports to the UK, Holland, Indonesia, Singapore and Malaysia.

Diamond Valley Yarra Valley Sauvignon Blanc

▼▼▼▼ 2001 Light green-yellow; a clean, crisp and fresh bouquet has no sweaty characters whatsoever, instead having appealing apple and passionfruit aromas. The palate is minerally and tight, with some grassy fruit in proper varietal mode, finishing with firm acidity.   **rating: 89**

best drinking 2001–2003 **best vintages** '00 **drink with** Mussels • $17.50

Diamond Valley Estate Chardonnay

▼▼▼▼▽ 2000 Medium yellow-green; ripe nectarine, peach and fig are accompanied by slightly more obvious barrel-ferment oak than one often encounters with this wine; the palate is similarly rich, ripe and powerful, very much the product of an unusually warm vintage, yet still retaining finesse.   **rating: 92**

best drinking 2002–2005 **best vintages** '90, '92, '94, '96, '00 **drink with** Cold smoked trout • $31.50

Diamond Valley Yarra Valley Chardonnay

▼▼▼▼▽ 2000 Glowing yellow-green; complex, toasty barrel-ferment oak with rich, ripe fruit on the bouquet is followed by a palate with sweet, peachy/nectarine fruit in a round and soft mode.   **rating: 90**

▼▼▼▼▽ 1999 Glowing yellow-green; the ripe stone fruit and subtle, well-integrated oak of the bouquet are followed by a palate with more of the ripe stone fruit flavours in a structure which is still quite tight, and seems to shorten fractionally on the finish. Time should see it swell out and, very likely, lengthen. **rating: 90**

best drinking 2002–2004 **best vintages** '99, '00 **drink with** Coquilles St Jacques • NA

Diamond Valley Close Planted Pinot Noir

▼▼▼▼▼ 2000 Deep red-purple; powerful dark plum, spice and subtle oak on the bouquet foreshadow an ultra-powerful, concentrated and complex palate with plum and forest flavours, and extreme length. 140 dozen made.   **rating: 96**

▼▼▼▼▼ 1999 Quite strong red-purple; intense dark plum fruit is offset by attractive savoury/spice notes on the bouquet; intense plummy fruit on the long, well-structured palate has all the hallmarks of a serious wine.   **rating: 95**

best drinking 2003–2010 **best vintages** '97, '99, '00 **drink with** Braised duck • $65

Diamond Valley Yarra Valley Pinot Noir

▼▼▼▼ 2001 Medium to full red-purple; an aromatic bouquet with spicy, foresty, berry aromas which flow through into the mid-palate, but then the wine seems to tighten up on the finish.   **rating: 89**

▼▼▼▼▽ 2000 The bouquet has intriguing savoury bacony oak aromas alongside plummy fruit. The palate follows suit with complex flavour and texture, providing a mix of savoury/foresty/dark plum flavours and silky tannins.   **rating: 93**

best drinking 2003–2007 **best vintages** '91, '92, '94, '96, '97, '99, '00 **drink with** Game pie • $25.50

Diamond Valley Yarra Valley Cabernet Merlot

▼▼▼▼ 2000 Medium to full red-purple; ripe blackcurrant/blackberry/cassis fruit on the bouquet moves more towards mint and leaf on the palate, braced by crisp acidity. A difficult wine to point.   **rating: 87**

best drinking 2003–2008 **best vintages** NA **drink with** Yearling steak • $21.50

Diamond Valley Estate Cabernet Sauvignon

▼▼▼▼▽ 1999 Medium red-purple; a clean, fresh and soft bouquet with gently ripe red and blackcurrant fruit together with some cedary notes, then a palate with quite firm backbone provided by acidity and (less so) tannins; attractive berry fruit, and subtle oak.   **rating: 90**

best drinking 2003–2008 **best vintages** NA **drink with** Marinated beef • $31.50

diggers rest   NR

205 Old Vineyard Road, Sunbury, Vic 3429 **region** Sunbury
phone (03) 9740 1660 **fax** (03) 9740 1660 **open** By appointment
winemaker Peter Dredge **production** 1000 **est.** 1987
product range ($16.50–22 CD) Chardonnay, Pinot Noir, Shiraz, Cabernet Sauvignon.
summary Diggers Rest was purchased from the founders, Frank and Judith Hogan, in July 1998; the new owners, Elias and Joseph Obeid, intend to expand the vineyard resources and, by that means, significantly increase production.

djinta djinta winery   NR

10 Stevens Road, Kardella South, Vic 3950 **region** Gippsland
phone (03) 5658 1163 **fax** (03) 5658 1863 **open** Weekends and public holidays 10–5 or by appointment

winemaker Peter Harley **production** 170 **est.** 1991
product range ($15–21 CD) Semillon, Sauvignon Blanc, Marsanne, Cabernet Merlot, Cabernet Sauvignon.
summary One of a group of wineries situated between Leongatha and Korumburra, the most famous being Bass Phillip. Vines were first planted in 1986 but were largely neglected until Peter and Helen Harley acquired the property in 1991, set about reviving the 2 hectares of sauvignon blanc and a little cabernet sauvignon, planting an additional 3 hectares (in total) of merlot, cabernet franc, cabernet sauvignon, semillon, marsanne, roussanne and viognier. The first vintage was 1995, during the time when Peter Harley was completing a Bachelor of Applied Science (Wine Science) at Charles Sturt University. They are deliberately adopting a low-technology approach to both vineyard and winery practices, using organic methods wherever possible.

domaine a   NR

Campania, Tas 7026 **region** Southern Tasmania
phone (03) 6260 4174 **fax** (03) 6260 4390 **open** Mon–Fri 9–4, weekends by appointment
winemaker Peter Althaus **production** 5000 **est.** 1973
product range ($20–60 CD) Domaine A is the top label, with Lady A Fumé Blanc, Pinot Noir and Cabernet Sauvignon; second label is Stoney Vineyard, with Aurora (wood-matured Sylvaner), Sauvignon Blanc and Cabernet Sauvignon.
summary The striking black label of the premium Stoney Vineyard wine, dominated by the single, multicoloured 'A', signified the change of ownership from George Park to Swiss businessman Peter Althaus. The NR rating for the winery is given in deference to Peter Althaus, who has no faith whatsoever in Australian wine judges or critics, and profoundly disagrees with their ratings. Exports to the US, Singapore, Hong Kong and Switzerland.

domaine chandon   ★★★★★

Green Point, Maroondah Highway, Coldstream, Vic 3770 **region** Yarra Valley
phone (03) 9739 1110 **fax** (03) 9739 1095 **open** 7 days 10.30–4.30
winemaker Dr Tony Jordan, Neville Rowe, James Gosper, John Harris **production** 135 000 **est.** 1986
product range ($22–45 CD) The most important sparkling wine is the Vintage Brut; then there is a range of special vintage cuvées, including Blanc de Noir, Blanc de Blanc and Brut Rosé, together with a vintage Prestige Cuvée (the most expensive in the range) which is given up to 6 years on lees prior to disgorgement. The non vintage Cuvée Riche is line-priced with the vintage cuvées, and its sales are surprisingly large. The sparkling range is rounded off with non vintage Brut and a Sparkling Pinot Shiraz. The table wines are released under the Green Point label, the Chardonnay and Pinot Noir appearing in both varietal and reserve mode.
summary Wholly owned by Moët et Chandon, and one of the two most important wine facilities in the Yarra Valley, the Green Point tasting room having a national and international reputation and winning a number of major tourism awards in recent years. Not only has the sparkling wine product range evolved, but there has been increasing emphasis placed on the table wines. The return of Dr Tony Jordan, the first CEO of Domaine Chandon, should further strengthen both the focus and quality of the brand. Exports to the UK, Asia and Japan.

Domaine Chandon Green Point Chardonnay

♟♟♟♟♟ **2000** Medium yellow-green; a smooth but stylish bouquet with ripe melon fruit and restrained oak flows through into a palate with excellent mouthfeel and an array of ripe, yellow peach and rounded melon flavours.   **rating:** 93

best drinking 2003–2004 **best vintages** '92, '93, '96, '00 **drink with** Veal in white sauce • $21.95

Domaine Chandon Green Point Reserve Chardonnay

♟♟♟♟♟ **2000** Medium yellow-green; a finer and tighter bouquet and palate than that of the varietal release, and not necessarily richer. Fig and melon fruit is neatly supported by high-quality French oak as a background prop.   **rating:** 94

best drinking 2003–2007 **best vintages** '98, '00 **drink with** Grilled spatchcock • $35

Domaine Chandon NV

♟♟♟♟ **NV** Medium to full straw-bronze; the broad bouquet has full fruit, and the palate is soft and moderately flavoursome.   **rating:** 86

best drinking 2001–2002 **best vintages** NA **drink with** Prawn salad • $22.95

Cuvée Prestige

YYYYY 1995 Excellent mousse; both the bouquet and palate attest to a complete wine, with biscuit and brioche aromas and flavours running through a seamless palate, with a hint of pinot noir on the finish. Six years on yeast lees has given the wine that extra degree of complexity, without sacrificing finesse. **rating:** 95

best drinking 2002–2006 **best vintages** '95 **drink with** Light seafood • $45

Domaine Chandon Sparkling Pinot Shiraz

YYYYY NV Medium red-purple; an extremely complex and interesting fruit base (Yarra Valley pinot noir and McLaren Vale shiraz), with some spicy aspects; the palate works equally well, with the sweetness coming from the fruit as much as dosage; should have very broad appeal, and will improve with time in bottle. **rating:** 92

best drinking 2002–2012 **best vintages** NA **drink with** Chicken liver pate • $24.95

Domaine Chandon Green Point Pinot Noir

YYYY 2000 Medium to full red-purple; solid, dark plummy fruit is followed by a palate which basically offers identical ripe, plummy fruit, bordering on heavy. Will improve with cellaring, however. **rating:** 88

best drinking 2003–2008 **best vintages** '96, '97 **drink with** Smoked quail • $24.95

Domaine Chandon Green Point Reserve Pinot Noir

YYYYY 2000 Medium to full red-purple; a bigger and more concentrated version of the varietal, with the degree of power and depth one associates with Tarrawarra. With a yield of 1.8 tonnes to the acre providing the fruit base, will be very long-lived for a Pinot Noir. **rating:** 93

best drinking 2003–2009 **best vintages** NA **drink with** Jugged hare • $35

Domaine Chandon Green Point McLaren Vale Shiraz

YYYY 1999 Medium to full red-purple; most unusual aromatics of gum leaf and spice along with some regional chocolate; a big, powerful wine on the palate, with dark berry, black chocolate and tannins; fractionally brutish. **rating:** 88

best drinking 2004–2009 **best vintages** '98 **drink with** Kangaroo fillet • $26.95

dominion wines ★★★

Upton Road, Strathbogie Ranges via Avenel, Vic 3664 **region** Central Victorian High Country
phone (03) 5796 2718 **fax** (03) 5796 2719 **open** 7 days 10–5
winemaker Travis Bush **production** 32 000 **est.** 1999
product range ($10–34.95 CD) Wines released in three tiers: the cheaper Vinus range of Muscat Gordo, Riesling, Chardonnay, Shiraz Cabernet, Sparkling Shiraz; followed by the Alexander Park label offering Riesling, Sauvignon Blanc, Unwooded Chardonnay, Chardonnay, Pinot Noir, Shiraz, Cabernet Sauvignon; then the Alexander Park Reserve Chardonnay and Shiraz.
summary Dominion is a major newcomer in the wine industry. Between December 1996 and September 1999, 91 hectares of vines were planted at Alexander Park, with sauvignon blanc, chardonnay, pinot noir, shiraz and cabernet sauvignon the principal varieties, and smaller amounts of riesling, verdelho and merlot. Prior to the 2000 vintage a winery designed by award-winning architect Scott Shelton was erected at Alexander Park; at full capacity it will be able to process up to 7500 tonnes of fruit. It will have two functions: firstly, the production of the company's own brands of Dominion Estate, Alexander Park, Vinus and Saddle Mountain; secondly, contract winemaking services for other major Australian wine companies.

Dominion Alexander Park Reserve Chardonnay

YYYY 2000 Medium to full yellow-green, very advanced for a 12-month-old wine. The bouquet is complex but very oaky, and the same strong, clove/spice oak obliterates the fruit on the palate. **rating:** 83

best drinking 2001–2003 **best vintages** NA **drink with** Spicy Asian • $28.95

Dominion Alexander Park Shiraz

YYYY 2000 Medium red-purple; clean, fresh red cherry/berry fruit on the bouquet is replicated with the sweet cherry fruit of the palate, which has good depth and length. A direct, straightforward style, but with pleasing fruit. **rating:** 86

best drinking 2002–2006 **best vintages** NA **drink with** Steak and kidney pie • $18

Dominion Alexander Park Reserve Shiraz

YYYY 1999 Medium red-purple; strong, charry/spicy American oak is very evident on the bouquet and palate, but in the mouth some black cherry and plum flavour comes through, and the tannins are good. **rating:** 85

best drinking 2003–2008 **best vintages** NA **drink with** Spiced beef • $34.95

dominique portet ★★★★

870–872 Maroondah Highway, Coldstream, Vic 3770 **region** Yarra Valley
phone (03) 5962 5760 **fax** (03) 5962 4938 **open** 7 days 10–5
winemaker Dominique Portet, Marcus Satchell **production** 8000 **est.** 2000
product range ($16–35 ML) Sauvignon Blanc, Rosé Fontaine, Fontaine (Cabernet Merlot Shiraz), Heathcote Shiraz, Yarra Valley Cabernet Sauvignon.
summary Dominique Portet was bred in the purple. He spent his early years at Chateau Lafite (where his father was regisseur) and was one of the very first flying winemakers, commuting to Clos du Val in the Napa Valley where his brother is winemaker and helping with the initial vintages. Since 1976 he has lived in Australia, spending more than 20 years as managing director of Taltarni, and also developed the Clover Hill Vineyard in Tasmania. After retiring from Taltarni, he spent six months in Provence, with his family, making wine and setting up an international distribution network, but always intended to return to Australia and to set himself up in the Yarra Valley, a region he has been closely observing since the mid-1980s. In 2001 he found the perfect site, and in a twinkling of an eye, built his winery and cellar door, and planted a quixotic mix of viognier (0.9 hectare) and merlot (0.7 hectare) net to the winery (which, incidentally, can also be accessed from Maddens Lane). Exports to New Zealand, Malaysia and Hong Kong.

Dominique Portet Fontaine Rosé

▼▼▼▼ **2001** Salmon pink; a fragrant bouquet has a touch of spice alongside the light red berry fruit, the clean palate showing a similar mix of light berry fruit and spice, then a dry finish. **rating:** 86

best drinking 2001–2002 **best vintages** NA **drink with** Yabbie risotto • $17.50

Dominique Portet Heathcote Shiraz

▼▼▼▼▽ **2000** Medium red-purple; the moderately intense bouquet offers fresh red cherry fruit, some spice and subtle oak; very attractive cherry fruit and fine tannins on the fresh palate mark a wine utterly different from the Taltarni style of old. **rating:** 90

best drinking 2003–2008 **best vintages** NA **drink with** Milk-fed veal • $35

Dominique Portet Fontaine

▼▼▼▼ **2000** Light to medium red-purple; there is a nice savoury edge to the dark berry fruit and balanced oak on the moderately intense palate. The palate has appealing juicy berry fruit and fine tannins; the oak has most assuredly not been overplayed. **rating:** 85

best drinking 2001–2004 **best vintages** NA **drink with** Braised oxtail • $17.50

Dominique Portet Yarra Valley Cabernet Sauvignon

▼▼▼▼ **2000** Medium red-purple; an aromatic mix of berry, cedar and earth leads into a light to medium-bodied palate with cedary/spicy overtones; surprisingly developed, and will come along quickly. **rating:** 85

best drinking 2002–2004 **best vintages** NA **drink with** Lamb shanks • $35

donnelly river wines ★★★

Lot 159 Vasse Highway, Pemberton, WA 6260 **region** Pemberton
phone (08) 9776 2052 **fax** (08) 9776 2053 **open** 7 days 9.30–4.30
winemaker Blair Meiklejohn **production** 15 000 **est.** 1986
product range ($13–26 CD) Sauvignon Blanc, Chardonnay, Mist (white blend), Pinot Noir, Shiraz, Karri, Cabernet Sauvignon, Cascade, Mistella, Port, Liqueur Muscat.
summary Donnelly River Wines draws upon 16 hectares of estate vineyards. They were planted in 1986 and produced their first wines in 1990. The Chardonnay has performed consistently well. Exports to the UK, Denmark, Germany, Singapore, Malaysia and Japan.

donovan wines ★★★

RMB 2017 Pomonal Road, Stawell, Vic 3380 **region** Grampians
phone (03) 5358 2727 **fax** (03) 5358 2727 **open** By appointment
winemaker Chris Peters **production** 2000 **est.** 1977
product range ($14–27 ML) Chardonnay, Shiraz, Cabernet Sauvignon, Sparkling.

summary Donovan quietly makes some concentrated, powerful Shiraz, with several vintages of the latter typically on offer. Limited wholesale distribution in Melbourne through Dilettare; otherwise most of the wine is sold via mail order with some bottle age.

doonkuna estate ★★★☆

Barton Highway, Murrumbateman, NSW 2582 **region** Canberra District
phone (02) 6227 5811 **fax** (02) 6227 5085 **open** 7 days 11–4
winemaker Malcolm Burdett **production** 3000 **est.** 1973
product range ($14–24 CD) Riesling, Sauvignon Blanc Semillon, Sauvignon Blanc, Clan (Pinot Noir Chardonnay), Chardonnay, Rosé, Pinot Noir, Shiraz; Rising Ground Chardonnay, Shiraz, Cabernet Sauvignon.
summary Following the acquisition of Doonokuna by Barry and Maureen Moran in late 1996, the plantings have been increased from a little under 4 hectares to 20 hectares. The cellar door prices remain modest, and increased production will follow in the wake of the new plantings. Exports to the UK and US.

Doonkuna Estate Riesling

▼▼▼▼ 2001 Light green-yellow; a clean, crisp, dry mineral and apple bouquet foretells the palate, which does, however, have elevated CO_2 and needs time for this to settle down. Has all the basics and deserves the chance. **rating:** 87

best drinking 2004–2010 **best vintages** '88, '90, '91, '92, '95, '97, '01 **drink with** Antipasto • $14

Doonkuna Estate Sauvignon Blanc Semillon

▼▼▼▼▽ 2001 Light straw-green; in consistent style with prior releases, the bouquet is in the grassy/herbal/mineral spectrum, the clean, crisp, minerally palate with balanced, lingering acidity providing a fresh aftertaste. **rating:** 90

best drinking 2002–2003 **best vintages** '01 **drink with** Thai • $16

Doonkuna Estate Chardonnay

▼▼▼▼ 2000 Light green-yellow; a clean, fruit-driven bouquet with melon and citrus aromas is repeated on the palate, which, while not complex, is neatly composed and balanced. **rating:** 86

best drinking 2002–2004 **best vintages** '88, '90, '91, '92, '95, '97, '98 **drink with** Snowy Mountains trout • $18

dorrien estate NR

Cnr Barossa Valley Way and Siegersdorf Road, Tanunda, SA 5352 **region** Barossa Valley
phone (08) 8561 2200 **fax** (08) 8561 2299 **open** Not
winemaker Simon Adams, Steve Chapman, Nick Badrice, John Schwartzkopff, Sally Blackwell, Mark Starick **production** NFP **est.** 1982
product range ($10.50–21 CD) Produces a substantial number of wines under proprietary labels (Dorrien Estate, Rare Print, New Eden, Avon Brae) for the Cellarmaster Group; notable are Storton Hill, Di Fabio, Black Wattle Mount Benson, Wright's Bay, Addison Selection 49, Bosworth Edge, Vasarelli and numerous others.
summary The Cellarmaster Group was acquired by Beringer Blass in 1997. Dorrien Estate is the physical base of the vast Cellarmaster network; wearing its retailer's hat, this is by far the largest direct-sale outlet in Australia. It buys substantial quantities of wine from other makers, both in bulk and as cleanskin (ie unlabelled bottles), and with recognisable but subtly different labels of the producers concerned. It is also making increasing quantities of wine on its own account at Dorrien Estate, many of which are quite excellent, and of trophy quality. The labelling of these wines is becoming increasingly sophisticated, giving little or no clue to the Cellarmaster link.

dowie doole ★★★★

182 Main Road, McLaren Vale, SA 5171 **region** McLaren Vale
phone (08) 8323 7535 **fax** (08) 8323 7536 **open** At Ingleburne, Willunga Road: Mon–Fri 10–5, weekends and public holidays 11–5
winemaker Brian Light (Contract) **production** 7000 **est.** 1996
product range ($12.50–22 CD) Semillon, Chenin Blanc, Semillon Sauvignon Blanc, Chardonnay, Shiraz, Cabernet Sauvignon.
summary The imaginatively packaged and interestingly named Dowie Doole was a joint venture between two McLaren Vale grape growers: architect Drew Dowie and one-time international banker Norm Doole.

Between them they have over 40 hectares of vineyards, and only a small proportion of their grapes are used to produce the Dowie Doole wines. In 1999 the partnership was expanded to include industry marketing veteran Leigh Gilligan, who returned to his native McLaren Vale after five years in Coonawarra (Gilligan is also involved with Boar's Rock). The wines have retail distribution in South Australia and the eastern states, and are exported to the US, Canada and Germany.

Dowie Doole Semillon

♥♥♥♥ 2001 Light green-yellow; the moderately intense bouquet shows positive grassy/lemony varietal character, as does the medium-bodied palate, which already has sufficient weight and character for early rather than later consumption.   **rating:** 87

best drinking 2002–2005 **best vintages** NA **drink with** Seafood salad • $16.50

Dowie Doole Shiraz

♥♥♥♥♥ 2000 Medium to full red-purple; ripe plum, prune and spice aromas drive the bouquet, rather than oak; the palate has a similar abundance of plum, prune and chocolate flavours, carrying its 14° alcohol with ease; by far the best wine so far under the Dowie Doole label.   **rating:** 94

best drinking 2004–2010 **best vintages** '00 **drink with** Beef in black bean sauce • $22

Dowie Doole Cabernet Sauvignon

♥♥♥♥ 2000 Light to medium red-purple; the relatively light bouquet has leafy berry aromas plus a touch of mint; the palate has more blackberry and chocolate fruit than the bouquet suggests, finishing with soft tannins and minimal oak.   **rating:** 86

best drinking 2003–2008 **best vintages** NA **drink with** Kangaroo fillet • $21

drayton's family wines   ★★★☆

Oakey Creek Road, Cessnock, NSW 2321 **region** Lower Hunter Valley
phone (02) 4998 7513 **fax** (02) 4998 7743 **open** Mon–Fri 8–5, weekends and public holidays 10–5
winemaker Trevor Drayton **production** 90 000 **est.** 1853
product range ($7–70 CD) Several label ranges, including budget-priced Oakey Creek, New Generation and Hunter Valley; Vineyard Reserve Chardonnay, Semillon, Cabernet Sauvignon, Pinot Noir, Shiraz, Merlot; Sparkling and Fortifieds; top-of-the-range Limited Release Chardonnay, Shiraz, Susanne Semillon, William Shiraz, Joseph Shiraz, Bin 5555 Shiraz, Botrytis Semillon, Old Vineyard Sherry and Liqueur Muscat.
summary A family-owned and run stalwart of the Valley, producing honest, full-flavoured wines which sometimes excel themselves and are invariably modestly priced. The size of the production will come as a surprise to many but it is a clear indication of the good standing of the brand, notwithstanding the low profile of recent years. It is not to be confused with Reg Drayton Wines; national retail distribution with exports to New Zealand, the US, Japan, Singapore, Taiwan, Samoa and Switzerland.

Drayton's Semillon

♥♥♥♡ 2001 Pale straw; both the bouquet and palate have quite intense and relatively ripe citrus/lemon fruit. While the CO_2 is a little bit evident, the wine has good potential.   **rating:** 84

best drinking 2003–2008 **best vintages** '84, '85, '86, '88, '94, '95 **drink with** Sushi • $14.50

Drayton's Vineyard Reserve Pokolbin Merlot

♥♥♥♡ 1999 Medium red-purple; earthy/savoury overtones to the bouquet are followed by a pleasant palate, with a mix of savoury/chocolatey/berry flavours and soft tannins.   **rating:** 83

best drinking 2002–2005 **best vintages** NA **drink with** Beef stroganoff • $22

Drayton's Cabernet Sauvignon

♥♥♥♥ 1999 Medium red-purple; an intriguing bouquet with overtones of pine needles and fir cones gives way to a more conventional mint and berry-flavoured palate. The tannins, oak and extract are all well handled.   **rating:** 85

best drinking 2003–2007 **best vintages** '81, '83, '85, '88, '91 **drink with** Soft ripened cheese • $16.50

drews creek wines   NR

558 Wollombi Road, Broke, NSW 2330 **region** Lower Hunter Valley
phone (02) 6579 1062 **fax** (02) 6579 1062 **open** By appointment
winemaker David Lowe (Contract) **production** 300 **est.** 1993
product range ($10–16 R) Chardonnay, Unoaked Chardonnay, Merlot.

summary Graeme Gibson and his partners are developing Drews Creek step by step. The initial planting of 2 hectares of chardonnay and 3 hectares of merlot was made in 1991, and the first grapes were produced in 1993. A further 2.5 hectares of sangiovese were planted in September 1999. Most of the grapes have been sold to contract winemaker David Lowe, but a small quantity of wine has been made for sale to friends and through the mailing list. A cellar door has opened, and ultimately several holiday cabins overlooking the vineyard and Wollombi Brook will be opened.

driftwood estate ★★★★

Lot 13 Caves Road, Yallingup, WA 6282 **region** Margaret River
phone (08) 9755 6323 **fax** (08) 9755 6343 **open** 7 days 11–4.30
winemaker Barney Mitchell, Severine Madoux **production** 15 000 **est.** 1989
product range ($13.50–29 CD) Classic White, Meadow Wood Dry White, Semillon, Sauvignon Blanc Semillon, Chardonnay, Cane Cut Semillon (dessert style), Shiraz, Merlot, Cabernet Sauvignon, Sparkling, Tawny Port.
summary Driftwood Estate is yet another remarkable new entrant on the vibrant Margaret River scene. Quite apart from offering a brasserie restaurant capable of seating 200 people (open seven days for lunch and dinner) and a mock Greek open-air theatre, its wines feature striking and stylish packaging (even if strongly reminiscent of that of Devil's Lair) and opulently flavoured wines. The winery architecture is, it must be said, opulent but not stylish. The wines are exported to Japan, the UK and Malaysia.

dromana estate ★★★★

Cnr Harrison's and Bittern–Dromana Roads, Dromana, Vic 3936 **region** Mornington Peninsula
phone (03) 5987 3800 **fax** (03) 5981 0714 **open** 7 days 11–4
winemaker Garry Crittenden, Judy Gifford Watson **production** 20 000 **est.** 1982
product range ($15–49 CD) Dromana Estate Sauvignon Blanc, Blanc Semillon, Chardonnay, Reserve Chardonnay, Pinot Noir, Reserve Pinot Noir, Shiraz, Reserve Merlot, Cabernet Merlot; second label Schinus range of Riesling, Chenin Blanc, Sauvignon Blanc, Chardonnay, Melia, Merlot, Longest Lunch Brut, Rosé, Pinot Noir; and a newly packaged range of Italian varietals – Arneis, Barbera, Dolcetto, Sangiovese, Granaccia, Riserva, Nebbiolo and Rosato – under the Garry Crittenden i label.
summary Since it was first established, Dromana Estate has never been far from the headlines. The energetic marketing genius of Garry Crittenden has driven it hither and thither, launching a brief but highly successful foray into the UK market, and since then concentrating much of its efforts on a no less successful restaurant and cellar door with a kaleidoscopic array of wines – first under the Dromana Estate label, then under the Schinus label – and in late 1995, a strikingly revamped range of Italian-accented wines, the i wines. In late 2000 became the head of an expanded empire, yet another winery to raise significant working capital from outside investors. Exports to the UK, the US and Asia.

Schinus Sauvignon Blanc

▼▼▼▼ 2001 Light green-yellow; the bouquet is clean, quite fresh, with some gooseberry; the palate is moderately intense, aided by good acidity and a relatively long finish **rating:** 86

best drinking 2001–2002 **best vintages** NA **drink with** Seafood • $14.90

Dromana Estate Sauvignon Blanc Semillon

▼▼▼▼ 2001 Light straw-green; a light and crisp bouquet is followed by a fresh, clean and delicate palate; very appealing within its term of reference, and well-balanced. **rating:** 87

best drinking 2001–2002 **best vintages** NA **drink with** Seafood • $19.50

Garry Crittenden Schinus Chardonnay

▼▼▼▼ 2001 Light to medium yellow-green; the bouquet is quite complex, with nectarine, citrus and melon tweaked by the barest touch of oak. The palate has well above average intensity and length, with melon and citrus fruit driving the flavour. **rating:** 87

▼▼▼▽ 2000 Medium yellow-green; a clean, light melon and stone fruit bouquet is followed by a palate with pleasing balance and flavour in a no-frills style. **rating:** 84

best drinking 2001–2003 **best vintages** '01 **drink with** Any and all cold dishes • $15

Dromana Estate Reserve Chardonnay

▼▼▼▼▼ 2000 Light to medium yellow-green; a typically subtle and elegant bouquet with creamy cashew, fig and melon aromas followed by very fine and elegant, light to medium-bodied palate, developing slowly; has some Chablis affinities. **rating:** 94

best drinking 2001–2005 **best vintages** '91, '94, '96, '97, '99, '00 **drink with** Kassler • $49

Garry Crittenden i rosato

▼▼▼ 2001 Salmon-pink; a spicy, lemony, zippy bouquet and palate provide a made to measure brasserie/summer style for the aficionados of the i range. **rating:** 84

best drinking 2001–2002 **best vintages** NA **drink with** Brasserie food • $16

Dromana Estate Pinot Noir

▼▼▼▼ 2000 Medium red, with some tinges of purple remaining; the bouquet is a little closed at this juncture, with some cherry fruit, but little else. The palate, however, is in stark contrast, with very good structure and length; plum and cherry fruit run through a gently spicy, long finish, supported by fine tannins. Reflects the superior vintage. **rating:** 92

best drinking 2002–2005 **best vintages** '97, '00 **drink with** Grilled quail • $29

Dromana Estate Reserve Pinot Noir

▼▼▼▼ 2000 Light to medium purple-red; a quite fragrant bouquet with cherry and mint aromas is followed by a long and intense palate featuring cherry, plum and mint; the oak influence throughout is restrained. **rating:** 93

best drinking 2002–2006 **best vintages** '00 **drink with** Braised duck • $49

Garry Crittenden i Barbera

▼▼▼ 2000 Light to medium purple-red; fresh crushed berry, leaf and mint aromas are followed by a palate with lots of sweet, juicy berry flavours and soft tannins, very similar to the impact of grenache. If oak has been used, it is not obvious. **rating:** 85

best drinking 2001–2004 **best vintages** '99 **drink with** Anything Italian • $22

Garry Crittenden i Dolcetto

▼▼▼▼ 2001 Vivid red-purple; a clean, fresh, lively cherry stone bouquet comes through on the palate, which finishes with lively acidity. Good varietal character; all about fresh, early drinking. **rating:** 90

best drinking 2002–2003 **best vintages** NA **drink with** Pizza • $20

Garry Crittenden i Sangiovese

▼▼▼ 2000 Light to medium red-purple; light but lively savoury/spicy edges to the red fruit of the bouquet is replicated on the cherry/cherry pip flavours of the light to medium-bodied palate. **rating:** 85

best drinking 2001–2004 **best vintages** '99 **drink with** Osso buco • $22

Schinus Merlot

▼▼▼ 2000 Light to medium red-purple; a lively, scented bouquet with fresh berry fruit is followed by an uncomplicated, light-bodied, fruity palate in an emphatic drink-now style. **rating:** 83

best drinking 2001–2002 **best vintages** NA **drink with** Tapas • $15

dulcinea ★★★☆

Jubilee Road, Sulky, Ballarat, Vic 3352 **region** Ballarat
phone (03) 5334 6440 **fax** (03) 5334 6828 **open** 7 days 9–5
winemaker Rod Stott **production** 2000 **est.** 1983
product range ($15–16 CD) Sauvignon Blanc, Chardonnay, Pinot Noir, Shiraz, Merlot, Cabernet Sauvignon.
summary Rod Stott is passionate grape grower and winemaker who chose the name Dulcinea from 'The Man of La Mancha', where only a fool fights windmills. With winemaking help from various sources, he has produced a series of very interesting and often complex wines. Exports to Japan.

Dulcinea Sauvignon Blanc

▼▼▼ 2000 Light straw-green; a light, crisp, clean and minerally bouquet is a conventional opening, the mineral/grass palate and its potent, lemony acidity reflecting the ultra-cool climate. **rating:** 85

best drinking 2002–2004 **best vintages** NA **drink with** Shellfish • $15

Dulcinea Pinot Noir

▼▼▼ 1999 Medium red, faintly hazy; very ripe plum aromas almost verge into prune, leading into a palate flooded with ripe plum and sweet forest characters. **rating:** 87

best drinking 2002–2005 **best vintages** '96, '97, '98 **drink with** Roast duck • $16

Dulcinea Merlot

▼▼▼▽ **2000** Medium red-purple; light, savoury, leafy, earthy aromas reflect the relatively austere palate, which has a varietal mix of olive, earth and leaf, and needs more ripe fruit.   **rating:** 83

best drinking 2003–2006 **best vintages** NA **drink with** Veal pizzicata • $16

Dulcinea Cabernet Sauvignon

▼▼▼▽ **1999** Light to medium red-purple; the bouquet shows light, leafy blackcurrant fruit, but the palate is riper than the bouquet suggests, with a mix of blackberry and blackcurrant, and just a touch of that leafy character.   **rating:** 84

best drinking 2003–2007 **best vintages** '96 **drink with** Lasagne • $16

dusty hill vineyard   NR

Barambah Road, Moffatdale via Murgon, Qld 4605 **region** South Burnett
phone (07) 4168 4700 **fax** (07) 4168 4888 **open** 7 days 10–5
winemaker Contract **production** 2000 **est.** 1996
product range ($15–20 R) Semillon Chardonnay, Rosé, Dusty Rosé, Shiraz, Shiraz Cabernet Sauvignon, Joe's Muscat.
summary Joe Prendergast and family have established 2 hectares each of shiraz and cabernet sauvignon, 1 hectare each of merlot and verdelho, 0.75 hectare of semillon and 0.5 hectare of black muscat. The vines are crop-thinned to obtain maximum ripeness in the fruit and to maximise tannin extract, although the winery's specialty is the Dusty Rosé, continuing a long tradition of rosé/Beaujolais style wines from Queensland. The 2000 vintage of this wine won a bronze medal at the 2000 Melbourne Royal Wine Show.

dutschke wines   NR

Lyndoch Valley Road, Lyndoch, SA 5351 **region** Barossa Valley
phone (08) 8265 6567 **fax** (08) 8265 2635 **open** Not
winemaker Wayne Dutschke **production** 2500 **est.** 1990
product range ($25–45 R) Oscar Semmler Shiraz, St Jakobi Shiraz, Willowbend Merlot Shiraz Cabernet.
summary Wayne Dutschke has had 10 years of winemaking experience with major wine companies in SA, Victoria and NSW, but has returned to SA to join his uncle, Ken Semmler, a leading grape grower in the Barossa Valley and now in the Adelaide Hills. No recent tastings, simply because Dutschke sells out of wine in less than six months each year. Exports to the US, the UK, Germany and Singapore.

Dutschke St Jakobi Shiraz

▼▼▼▽ **1999** Medium red-purple; sweet plum and cherry fruit leads the bouquet, but more oak, indeed much more, comes through on the palate, largely overwhelming the fruit. A lighter hand would have been so much better.   **rating:** 83

best drinking 2004–2009 **best vintages** NA **drink with** Smoked beef • $35

dyson wines   NR

Sherriff Road, Maslin Beach, SA 5170 **region** McLaren Vale
phone (08) 8386 1092 **fax** (08) 8327 0066 **open** 7 days 10–5
winemaker Allan Dyson **production** 2000 **est.** 1976
product range ($16–20 CD) Chardonnay, Viognier, Cabernet Sauvignon.
summary Allan Dyson, who describes himself as 'a young man of 50 years' has recently established 1.5 hectares of viognier and has absolutely no thoughts of slowing down or retiring.

east arm vineyard   ★★★★

111 Archers Road, Hillwood, Tas 7250 **region** Northern Tasmania
phone (03) 6334 0266 **fax** (03) 6334 1405 **open** Weekends and public holidays or by appointment
winemaker Andrew Hood, Bert Sundstrup, Nicholas Butler (Contract) **production** 1200 **est.** 1993
product range ($14–21 ML) Riesling, Chardonnay, Pinot Noir.
summary East Arm Vineyard was established by Launceston gastroenterologist Dr John Wettenhall and partner Anita James, who happens to have completed the Charles Sturt University Diploma in Applied Science (wine growing). The 2 hectares of vineyard which came into full production in 1998 are more or less equally divided between riesling, chardonnay and pinot noir. It is established on a historic block, part of a grant made to retired British soldiers of the Georgetown garrison in 1821, and slopes down to the Tamar

River. The property is 25 hectares, and there are plans for further planting and, somewhere down the track, a winery. The Riesling is always excellent. Exports to Hong Kong.

East Arm Riesling

▼▼▼▼▽ **2001** Light to medium yellow-green; a mix of lime and mineral aromas are followed by a well-balanced, moderately light palate, which has more persistence of flavour than many others, and even a touch of kerosene-like development. Looks as if it will develop rapidly.   **rating:** 90

best drinking 2002–2003 **best vintages** '98, '99, '00 **drink with** Scallops • $18.50

East Arm Chardonnay

▼▼▼▼ **1998** Exceptionally youthful green-yellow; a tight, citrussy and lively bouquet is followed by a similarly fresh and tangy palate with pronounced citrussy fruit. An excellent unoaked style, with a long cellaring future. Top value.   **rating:** 87

best drinking 2002–2008 **best vintages** NA **drink with** Seafood • $14

East Arm Pinot Noir

▼▼▼▽ **2000** Strong and deep red-purple; a powerful bouquet with plum and beetroot aromas, coupled with the colour, suggest a degree of over-extraction, a suggestion confirmed by the powerful and tannic palate. Some will thoroughly enjoy the power, and the wine will undoubtedly soften and improve with time in bottle.   **rating:** 83

best drinking 2003–2008 **best vintages** NA **drink with** Roast baby kid • $21

eastern peake   NR

Clunes Road, Coghills Creek, Vic 3364 **region** Ballarat
phone (03) 5343 4245 **fax** (03) 5343 4365 **open** 7 days 10–5
winemaker Norman Latta **production** 3000 **est.** 1983
product range ($17–30 CD) Reserve Chardonnay, Persuasion (Pinot Rosé), Pinot Noir, Morillon Pinot Noir, Reserve Pinot Noir.
summary Norm Latta and Di Pym commenced the establishment of Eastern Peake, situated 25 kilometres northeast of Ballarat on a high plateau overlooking the Creswick Valley, almost 15 years ago. In the early years the grapes were sold to Trevor Mast of Mount Chalambar and Mount Langi Ghiran, but the 5 hectares of vines are now dedicated to the production of Eastern Peake wines. The Pinot Noir is on the minerally/stemmy side; earlier bottling might preserve more of the sweet fruit. Exports to the UK and Northern Ireland.

🐌 eden springs   NR

Boehm Springs Road, Springton, SA 5235 **region** Eden Valley
phone (08) 8564 1166 **fax** (08) 8564 1265 **open** Not
winemaker Andrew Ewart (Contract) **production** 1000 **est.** 2000
product range ($15.50–24.50 ML) High Eden range of Riesling, Shiraz, Cabernet Sauvignon.
summary Richard Wiencke and Meredith Hodgson opened the Eden Springs wine doors on 1 July 2000, offering the first wines from the 17 hectares of vines made in 1999 (Shiraz and Cabernet Sauvignon) and the inaugural release of Riesling from 2000, contract-made by Andrew Ewart. It is a remote vineyard (6 kilometres by dirt road from Springton) and sells its wine through a high-quality newsletter to mailing list customers, and a website, which has brought export orders from the US, Denmark and Malaysia.

eden valley wines   NR

Main Street, Eden Valley, SA 5235 **region** Eden Valley
phone (08) 8564 1111 **fax** (08) 8564 1110 **open** 7 days 10–5
winemaker Peter Thompson **production** 1500 **est.** 1994
product range ($9–15 CD) Riesling, Spätlese Frontignac, Shiraz, Mourvedre, Golden Port.
summary Eden Valley Wines has waxed and waned over the years, but seems now in the ascendant. The venture now has 30 hectares each of recently planted riesling, cabernet sauvignon and shiraz, with 5 hectares of much older mourvedre. A major part of the production is sold as grapes to others; the wines currently on sale have varied backgrounds, now moving to an estate-grown base. Exports to Malaysia.

edwards & chaffey   ★★★★

Chaffey's Road, McLaren Vale, SA 5171 **region** McLaren Vale
phone (08) 8323 8250 **fax** (08) 8323 9308 **open** Mon–Sat 10–5, Sun 11–4

winemaker Fiona Donald **production** NFP **est.** 1850
product range ($15–32 R) The table wines are no more, but the Seaview and Edwards & Chaffey (E&C) sparkling range of Brut, Brut de Brut, Chardonnay, Pinot Chardonnay, Blanc de Blancs, Grand Cuvée, Gull Rock, Pinot Noir Chardonnay Brut continues, although it is not produced from McLaren Vale grapes.
summary The former Seaview, now limited to sparkling wine production under the Seaview and Edwards & Chaffey labels, and with an uncertain future.

Seaview Blanc de Blancs

▼▼▼▼ **1999** Medium to full straw-yellow; a powerful, complex bouquet with some aldehydes, then a rich, full-flavoured palate with some bite from the aldehydic characters (which are quite deliberately part of the style). **rating:** 87

best drinking 2001–2002 **best vintages** NA **drink with** Antipasto • $18

Seaview Pinot Noir Chardonnay Brut

▼▼▼▼▽ **1998** Good mousse, and both elegance and complexity, with touches of biscuit and citrus to the bouquet; the palate has good balance and length, the citrus and bready/biscuity characters intermingling. **rating:** 90

best drinking 2001–2002 **best vintages** NA **drink with** Seafood • $18

Edwards & Chaffey Section 353 Pinot Chardonnay

▼▼▼▼▽ **1994** RD. Medium to full straw-yellow; an unusually rich bready/toasty/biscuity bouquet attests to the long period on yeast lees; the palate is similarly rich and mouthfilling, with overtones of honey and toast. Particularly good value. **rating:** 90

best drinking 2002–2003 **best vintages** NA **drink with** Full-flavoured canapés • $25

edwards vineyard ★★★★

Cnr Caves and Ellensbrook Roads, Cowaramup, WA 6284 **region** Margaret River
phone (08) 9755 5999 **fax** (08) 9755 5988 **open** Thurs–Sun and public holidays 10.30–5.30 or by appointment
winemaker Michael Edwards, Stuart Pym (Contract) **production** 1200 **est.** 1994
product range ($19–25 CD) Semillon, Semillon Sauvignon Blanc, Chardonnay, Shiraz, Cabernet Sauvignon.
summary This is very much a family affair, headed by parents Brian and Jenny Edwards. Michael Edwards is the assistant winemaker at Voyager Estate, while overseeing the winemaking of the Edwards Vineyard wines; Chris Edwards is vineyard manager, while Fiona and Bianca Edwards are involved in sales and marketing. They have a substantial vineyard, planted to chardonnay (3 hectares), semillon (2.5 hectares), sauvignon blanc (2.1 hectares), shiraz (4.8 hectares) and cabernet sauvignon (7.6 hectares), and have plans to build a winery in time for the 2004 vintage. One of the local attractions is the Tiger Moth 'Matilda', flown from England to Australia in 1990 as a fundraiser – it is now kept at the Edwards Vineyard and can be seen flying locally. Exports to Holland.

Edwards Vineyard Sauvignon Blanc

▼▼▼▼ **2001** Light green-yellow; the bouquet is clean, with gooseberry fruit, a dash of mineral and a whisper of oak; the subtle oak use adds to the texture of the palate without unduly distracting from the gentle gooseberry/tropical fruit. **rating:** 86

best drinking 2002–2003 **best vintages** NA **drink with** Scallop terrine • $19

Edwards Vineyard Semillon Sauvignon Blanc

▼▼▼▼▽ **2001** Light to medium green-yellow; a quite intense bouquet with lemon and herb allied with faintly spicy oak, then a palate with sweet lemon/citrus fruit, a touch of gooseberry, and again high-quality oak used with ultimate discretion. Trophy Best Wooded White - 2001 Wine Show of Western Australia. **rating:** 91

best drinking 2002–2004 **best vintages** '01 **drink with** Abalone • $19

Edwards Vineyard Shiraz

▼▼▼▼ **2000** Medium red-purple; the bouquet has an attractive, savoury mix of fruit and cedary oak, a combination which continues on the elegant, medium-bodied palate, with spicy/cedary notes; all in all, very much less aggressive than the '99 vintage, and all the better for that. **rating:** 88

best drinking 2004–2009 **best vintages** NA **drink with** Smoked lamb • $23

Edwards Vineyard Cabernet Sauvignon

▼▼▼▼ **2000** Full red-purple; a mix of cedary/earthy/spicy/blackberry aromas come through on the medium-bodied palate, which dries fractionally on the finish, but has stacks of character and flavour.   **rating: 87**

best drinking 2004–2009 **best vintages** NA **drink with** Moroccan lamb • $25

elan vineyard   NR

17 Turners Road, Bittern, Vic 3918 **region** Mornington Peninsula
phone (03) 5983 1858 **fax** (03) 5983 2821 **open** First weekend of month, public holidays 11–5 or by appointment
winemaker Selma Lowther **production** 600 **est.** 1980
product range ($13–16 CD) Olive's Paddock Riesling, Chardonnay, Shiraz, Gamay, Cabernet Merlot.
summary Selma Lowther, fresh from Charles Sturt University (as a mature-age student) made an impressive debut with her spicy, fresh, crisp Chardonnay. Most of the grapes from the 2.5 hectares of estate vineyards are sold; production remains minuscule.

elderton   ★★★★☆

3 Tanunda Road, Nuriootpa, SA 5355 **region** Barossa Valley
phone (08) 8562 1058 **fax** (08) 8562 2844 **open** Mon–Fri 8.30–5, weekends, holidays 11–4
winemaker James Irvine (Consultant) **production** 32 000 **est.** 1984
product range ($13.95–85 CD) Riesling, Sauvignon Blanc Verdelho, Chardonnay, Botrytis Semillon, Pinot Chardonnay, Cabernet Rosé, Merlot, Shiraz, CSM, Tantalus Shiraz Cabernet, Cabernet Sauvignon; Command Shiraz and Ashmead Single Vineyard Cabernet Sauvignon are flagbearers.
summary The wines are based on some old, high-quality Barossa floor estate vineyards, and all are driven to a lesser or greater degree by lashings of American oak; the Command Shiraz is at the baroque end of the spectrum and has to be given considerable respect within the parameters of its style. The range of wines on offer in 2002 is particularly impressive. National retail distribution, with exports to the UK, the US, Europe and Asia.

Elderton Riesling

▼▼▼▽ **2001** Light to medium yellow-green; a quite rich and ripe bouquet with lime-accented fruit, the palate flavoursome but slightly short; a quick-developing style.   **rating: 84**

best drinking 2002–2003 **best vintages** NA **drink with** Pasta marinara • $14.95

Elderton Chardonnay

▼▼▼▼ **2001** Medium yellow-green; quite complex, with an obvious oak infusion on the bouquet; on the palate, elegant nectarine, cashew and citrus pushes the oak further back.   **rating: 85**

best drinking 2002–2005 **best vintages** NA **drink with** KFC • $16.95

Elderton Riverina Botrytis Semillon (375 ml)

▼▼▼▼ **2001** Deep gold, very advanced for its age; complex toffee and cumquat aromas and flavours provide a rich, unctuous liquid feast, but the wine has developed very quickly and should be drunk immediately.   **rating: 89**

best drinking 2002–2003 **best vintages** NA **drink with** Pecan pie • $17.95

Elderton Shiraz

▼▼▼▼ **2000** Medium to full red-purple; a quite fragrant bouquet with plum and vanilla, then a palate which is not particularly lush, but does have firm, plummy fruit, the oak held in some restraint. **rating: 86**

best drinking 2002–2007 best vintages '86 '88 '90 '91 '92 '94 drink with Steak and kidney pie • $26.95

Elderton Command Shiraz

▼▼▼▼▼ **1998** Medium to full red-purple; the deep and complex bouquet has an array of rich, dark berry, plum, chocolate and vanilla aromas; the rich palate has an unctuously sweet fruit, chocolate and vanilla mix; the overall extract is well handled – this is a very good example of the full-on American-oaked Shiraz style.   **rating: 94**

best drinking 2002–2013 **best vintages** '98 **drink with** Kangaroo • $85

Elderton Merlot

▼▼▼▼ **1998** Medium red-purple; ripe and sweet dark berry fruit on the bouquet is followed by a very luscious palate, with sweet berry and plum fruit, all in all seeming to have nothing much to do with merlot; a nice wine nonetheless. **rating: 88**

best drinking 2003–2008 **best vintages** NA **drink with** Rib of veal • $28.95

Elderton CSM

▼▼▼▼♀ **1998** Medium to full red-purple; dark berry/blackberry fruit with positive French and American oak is followed by a commensurately ripe and sweet palate with blackberry, prune and a touch of chocolate. A blend of Cabernet Sauvignon, Shiraz and Merlot, hence the name. **rating: 90**

best drinking 2003–2010 **best vintages** '95, '98 **drink with** Wild duck • $40

Elderton Ashmead Single Vineyard Cabernet Sauvignon

▼▼▼▼▼ **1998** Medium to full red-purple; sweet blackberry and blackcurrant fruit is matched by subtle French oak on the bouquet; similarly, the attractive blackcurrant fruit of the palate is complemented by the positive use and integration of French oak; a long and polished finish. **rating: 94**

best drinking 2005–2015 **best vintages** '98 **drink with** Baby leg of lamb • $85

eldredge ★★★★

Spring Gully Road, Clare, SA 5453 **region** Clare Valley
phone (08) 8842 3086 **fax** (08) 8842 3086 **open** 7 days 11–5
winemaker Leigh Eldredge **production** 6000 **est.** 1993
product range ($13–40 CD) Watervale Riesling, Semillon Sauvignon Blanc, C.V. Gold (Late Picked Riesling), Blue Chip Shiraz, Gilt Edge Shiraz, M.S.G., Boundary Sangiovese, Cabernet Sauvignon, Tawny Port.
summary Leigh and Karen Eldredge have established their winery and cellar-door sales area in the Sevenhill Ranges at an altitude of 500 metres, above the town of Watervale. Hit a purple patch with its 2001 white wines, complementing the very good Cabernet Sauvignon. The wines are distributed in Victoria and Queensland and exported to Ireland and Canada.

Eldredge Watervale Riesling

▼▼▼▼♀ **2001** Light green-yellow; the firm bouquet has a mix of spice, mineral and herb; the palate has excellent length and balance, with the focus moving more to lemony fruit, a hint of passionfruit, and neatly balanced acidity. **rating: 92**

best drinking 2002–2010 **best vintages** '98, '01 **drink with** Bruschetta • $16

Eldredge Semillon Sauvignon Blanc

▼▼▼▼♀ **2001** Light straw-green; a clean, fresh, firm bouquet with the Semillon dominant leads into a tangy, strongly lemony, lively palate with masses of character and flavour, yet not at all heavy. Good length and a real surprise packet. Great value. **rating: 93**

best drinking 2002–2005 **best vintages** '01 **drink with** Fish cakes • $16

Eldredge Blue Chip Shiraz

▼▼▼▼ **2000** Medium purple-red; clean, dark berry fruit with a gentle waft of vanilla oak on the bouquet, then a palate with fully ripe, sweet berry and plum fruit making all the statements; a user-friendly style, finishing with soft tannins. **rating: 88**

best drinking 2002–2006 **best vintages** NA **drink with** Braised beef • $21

Eldredge Cabernet Sauvignon

▼▼▼▼ **1999** Medium red-purple; the fresh and clean bouquet exudes fully ripe cassis and blackberry aromas, the same spectrum coming on the fruit-driven palate, adding a touch of mint to the mix, and concluding with ripe tannins. **rating: 87**

best drinking 2002–2009 **best vintages** '95, '98 **drink with** Barbecued lamb • $21

eldridge estate ★★★★

Red Hill Road, Red Hill, Vic 3937 **region** Mornington Peninsula
phone (03) 5989 2644 **fax** (03) 5989 2644 **open** Weekends, public holidays and January 1–26 11–5
winemaker David Lloyd **production** 800 **est.** 1985
product range ($18–34 CD) Semillon Sauvignon Blanc, Chardonnay, Gamay, Pinot Noir, Cabernet Merlot, Sparkling.

summary The Eldridge Estate vineyard, with seven varieties included in its 3.5 hectares, was purchased by Wendy and David Lloyd in 1995. Major retrellising work has been undertaken, changing to Scott-Henry, and all of the wines will now be estate-grown and made. The wines are available at the Victorian Wine Centre and Tastings, Armadale, in Melbourne, and at a few leading restaurants in Melbourne and Sydney.

Eldridge Estate Semillon Sauvignon Blanc

▼▼▼▼ **2001** Light straw-green; the bouquet is crisp and minerally, but with very little fruit aromatics; the palate follows logically on – clean, firm and minerally in unabashed seafood style. **rating: 86**

best drinking 2002–2003 **best vintages** NA **drink with** Shellfish • $18

Eldridge Estate Chardonnay

▼▼▼▼▼ **2000** Light to medium yellow-green; the clean but complex bouquet offers a subtle interplay between fruit, oak and malolactic influences; the palate has excellent feel, featuring nectarine, melon, white peach and a touch of cashew; fine, subtle oak. Winner of three trophies, including Best White of Show, at the 2001 Southern Victorian Wines Show. **rating: 94**

best drinking 2002–2006 **best vintages** '99, '00 **drink with** Poached fish • $34

Eldridge Estate Gamay Nouveau

▼▼▼▼ **2001** Bright, light purple-red; a clean, fresh, light bouquet with a mix of cherry, mint and spice is followed by a clean and fresh palate, bordering on Rosé in style. A lovely springtime drink. **rating: 85**

best drinking 2002–2003 **best vintages** NA **drink with** Alfresco • $16

Eldridge Estate Pinot Noir

▼▼▼▼ **2000** Light to medium red-purple; an extremely foresty/gamey bouquet will have some noses quivering, but the palate should reassure, with foresty/sappy/stemmy overtones to cherry and plum fruit. A Pinot with attitude. **rating: 87**

best drinking 2002–2006 **best vintages** NA **drink with** Braised duck • $34

elgee park ★★★★

Wallaces Road, Merricks North, Vic 3926 **region** Mornington Peninsula
phone (03) 5989 7338 **fax** (03) 5989 7338 **open** Sunday of Queen's Birthday weekend
winemaker Stonier, T'Gallant (Contract) **production** 1500 **est.** 1972
product range ($14–30 R) Excellence (Riesling), Chardonnay, Pinot Gris, Pinot Noir, Cabernet, Cuvée Brut; Baillieu Myer Family Reserve Riesling, Viognier, Chardonnay, Pinot Noir and Cabernet Merlot.
summary The pioneer of the Mornington Peninsula in its 20th century rebirth, owned by Baillieu Myer and family. The wines are now made at Stonier and T'Gallant, Elgee Park's own winery having been closed, and the overall level of activity decreased. Melbourne retail distribution through Flinders Wholesale.

Elgee Park Family Reserve Chardonnay

▼▼▼▼▽ **2000** Medium yellow-straw; the smooth and clean bouquet offers nectarine with a subtle web of oak and malolactic fermentation influences; nectarine with hints of fig and cashew run through the ultra-smooth palate; good length. **rating: 91**

best drinking 2002–2005 **best vintages** '00 **drink with** Seafood risotto • $30

eling forest winery ★★★

Hume Highway, Sutton Forest, NSW 2577 **region** Southern New South Wales Zone
phone (02) 4878 9499 **fax** (02) 4878 9499 **open** 7 days 10–5
winemaker Leslie Fritz, Michelle Crockett **production** 3500 **est.** 1987
product range ($8–45 CD) Riesling, Traminal (Traminer), Furmint, Linden Leaf Harselvelu, Chardonnay, Lunel, Catherine Hill, Botrytis Riesling, Rosé, Carla (Red), Cabernet Sauvignon, Peach Brandy, Peach Ambrosia, Cherry Port.
summary Eling Forest's mentally agile and innovative founder Leslie Fritz celebrated his 80th birthday not long after he planted the first vines at his Sutton Forest vineyard in 1987. He proceeded to celebrate his 88th birthday by expanding the vineyards from 3 hectares to 4, primarily with additional plantings of the Hungarian varieties. He has also developed a Cherry Port and is using the spinning cone technology to produce various peach-based liqueurs, utilising second-class peach waste. Right across the extensive range, the wines are increasingly technically well made, even if far more European than Australian in terms of fruit weight.

elliot rocke estate   ★★★☆

Craigmoor Road, Mudgee, NSW 2850 **region** Mudgee
phone (02) 6372 7722 **fax** (02) 6372 0680 **open** Wed–Sun and public holidays 9–4
winemaker Simon Gilbert (Contract) **production** 6100 **est.** 1999
product range ($13–33 ML) Traminer, Semillon, Unwooded Chardonnay, Premium Chardonnay, Late Harvest, McLaren Vale Shiraz, Cabernet Sauvignon Merlot.
summary Elliot Rocke Estate is a new label for Mudgee, but planting of its 34 hectares of vineyards dates back to 1987, when the property was known as Seldom Seen. Twelve hectares of shiraz, 9 hectares of semillon, and 5 hectares each of chardonnay and cabernet sauvignon and 1 hectare of traminer are the main plantings, and contract winemaking by Simon Gilbert has resulted in an impressive range of wines which already have a strong show record. The wines are available through the cellar door, by mailing list, and from a number of Sydney retailers.

Elliot Rocke Estate Semillon

▼▼▼▼ **2001** Light yellow-green; both the bouquet and palate are in the style established by Elliot Rocke over the past few years. The bouquet is light and crisp, with clear varietal definition in a herby mode, the palate very pure, with lemon and grass flavours, backed by good acidity. Another classic.   **rating:** 89
▼▼▼▼ **2000** Very light straw-green; the bouquet is crisp and correct, with herb and lemon aromas, the palate still tight and youthful, with minerally grip and some varietal herbaceousness. Certain to develop slowly, and quite classic.   **rating:** 89
▼▼▼▼ **1999** Light to medium yellow-straw; a delicate and fragrant bouquet with flowery lemon blossom overtones. Grass, herb, lemon and spice are all to be found on the delicate, slow-maturing palate. **rating:** 88
best drinking 2003–2010 **best vintages** NA **drink with** Light seafood • $14.95

Elliot Rocke Estate Premium Chardonnay

▼▼▼▼ **1999** Very light green-yellow, particularly given its age. A delicate citrus and melon bouquet with integrated oak is followed by a very light and youthful palate. One wonders how long the wine spent in tank and just when it was bottled.   **rating:** 85
best drinking 2001–2005 **best vintages** NA **drink with** Deep-fried calamari • $20

Elliot Rocke Estate Late Harvest

▼▼▼▼ **1999** Glowing green-gold; the bouquet has a mix of spicy notes from the traminer together with citrus and pineapple. A surprising wine, with good length and impact.   **rating:** 87
best drinking 2001–2003 **best vintages** NA **drink with** Ice-cream • $14

Elliot Rocke Estate McLaren Vale Shiraz

▼▼▼▼ **1998** Medium to full red with some purples remaining; the moderately intense bouquet is clean, with good fruit and oak balance and integration. Black cherry, chocolate and vanilla (the last ex-oak) mark a palate with plenty of substance, and neatly balanced acidity and tannins.   **rating:** 86
best drinking 2003–2008 **best vintages** NA **drink with** Roast beef • $33

elmslie   ★★☆

Upper McEwans Road, Legana, Tas 7277 **region** Northern Tasmania
phone (03) 6330 1225 **fax** (03) 6330 2161 **open** By appointment
winemaker Ralph Power **production** 600 **est.** 1972
product range ($18 ML) Pinot Noir, Cabernet Sauvignon.
summary A small, specialist red winemaker, from time to time blending Pinot Noir with Cabernet. The fruit from the now fully mature vineyard (0.5 hectare of pinot noir and 1.5 hectares of cabernet sauvignon) has depth and character, but operational constraints mean that the style of the wine is often somewhat rustic.

elmswood estate   ★★★☆

75 Monbulk–Seville Road, Wandin East, Vic 3139 **region** Yarra Valley
phone (03) 5964 3015 **fax** (03) 5964 3405 **open** Weekends 10–5 and by appointment
winemaker Contract **production** 2000 **est.** 1981
product range ($18–26 ML) Unoaked Chardonnay, Chardonnay, Cabernet Merlot, Cabernet Sauvignon, Barrel Select Cabernet.
summary Rod and Dianne Keller purchased their 9.5-hectare vineyard in June 1999; it had been planted in 1981 on the red volcanic soils of the far-southern side of the valley which stretches from Wandin to Warburton. Prior to their acquisition of the vineyard, the grapes had been sold to other Yarra Valley

winemakers, but the Kellers immediately set about having their own wine made from the estate. The cellar door offers spectacular views across the Upper Yarra Valley to Mount Donna Buang and Warburton. The wines are sold chiefly through the cellar door and a mailing list, with limited restaurant listings.

Elmswood Estate Cabernet Merlot

♥♥♥♥ 2000 Medium red-purple; the moderately intense bouquet is clean, with a mix of red berry and blackberry fruit supported by appropriate oak. Nicely ripened, juicy red berry fruits and fine tannins reflect the near-perfect vintage conditions for these varieties; rounded off with gentle oak. **rating: 86**

best drinking 2003–2007 best vintages NA drink with Braised veal • $23

Elmswood Estate Barrel Select Cabernet

♥♥♥♥ 2000 Medium red-purple; fragrant, ripe cassis/blackcurrant fruit on the bouquet is followed by an attractively framed and sculpted palate, with ripe cassis cabernet flavours, soft oak and fine tannins. **rating: 88**

best drinking 2003–2008 best vintages NA drink with Baby rack of lamb • $26

elsewhere vineyard ★★★★☆

42 Dillons Hill Road, Glaziers Bay, Tas 7109 **region** Southern Tasmania
phone (03) 6295 1228 **fax** (03) 6295 1591 **open** Not
winemaker Andrew Hood (Contract), Steve Lubiana (Contract) **production** 4000 **est.** 1984
product range ($20–30 ML) Riesling, Chardonnay, Pinot Noir, Mèthode Champenoise.
summary Kylie and Andrew Cameron's evocatively named Elsewhere Vineyard used to jostle for space with a commercial flower farm. It is a mark of the success of the wines that in 1993 some of the long-established flowers made way for additional chardonnay and riesling, although it is Elsewhere's long-lived Pinot Noirs that are so stunning. The estate-produced range comes from the 6 hectares of pinot noir, 3 hectares of chardonnay and 1 hectare of riesling which constitute the immaculately tended vineyard.

Elsewhere Vineyard Riesling

♥♥♥♥ 2001 Light green-yellow; a light, crisp mineral lime and blossom bouquet is slightly hindered by high SO_2. The palate is elegant, with lime/lemon flavours, crisp acidity and good length. Will undoubtedly benefit from time in bottle, which will see the SO_2 diminish. **rating: 89**

best drinking 2004–2010 best vintages '99 drink with Seafood bisque • $22

Elsewhere Vineyard Gewürztraminer

♥♥♥♥ 2001 Medium yellow-green; tropical spice aromas on the bouquet provide complexity. There is abundant flavour and weight on the mid-palate, which is quite Alsace-like, but the wine has a distinctly short finish. **rating: 86**

best drinking 2001–2004 best vintages NA drink with Chinese • $18

Elsewhere Vineyard Bay of Eight Pinot Noir

♥♥♥♥♥ 2000 Medium to full red-purple; strongly lifted aromas with a mix of leaf, spice and strawberry, moving through to a palate with plum, spice, strawberry, leaf and mint. From a similar base wine to that of the No Regrets, but shows distinct differences. Gold medal 2002 Tasmanian Wines Show. **rating: 94**

best drinking 2002–2006 best vintages '00 drink with Braised duck • $30

elsmore's caprera grove NR

657 Milbrodale Road, Broke, NSW 2330 **region** Lower Hunter Valley
phone (02) 6579 1344 **fax** (02) 6579 1355 **open** By appointment
winemaker Jim Chatto, Gary Reid (Contract) **production** 500 **est.** 1995
product range ($15–20 CD) Chardonnay, Peregrinus Methode Champenoise, Bartolomeo Botrytis Chardonnay.
summary Bindy and Chris Elsmore purchased their 16-hectare property at Broke in 1995, subsequently establishing a little over 4 hectares of chardonnay, verdelho and shiraz, with chardonnay taking the lion's share of the plantings. Their interest in wine came not from their professional lives – Chris is a retired commodore of the Royal Australian Navy and Bindy had a career in advertising, marketing and personnel – but from numerous trips to the wine regions of France, Italy and Spain.

Elsmore's Caprera Grove Chardonnay

♥♥♥♥ 2000 Medium yellow-green; gentle nectarine and peach aromas and flavours are supported by appropriately subtle oak on both bouquet and palate; fresh and with a pleasing finish. **rating: 87**

♥♥♥♥♥ **1999** Excellent medium green-yellow; the bouquet is quite tight and tangy, with the oak well-balanced and integrated both on the bouquet and on the stylish, nectarine palate. Top gold medal in its class at the 2001 Hunter Valley Wine Show. **rating: 94**

best drinking 2001–2003 **best vintages** '99 **drink with** Avocado and prawns • $15

eltham vineyards ★★★

225 Shaws Road, Arthurs Creek, Vic 3099 **region** Yarra Valley
phone (03) 9439 4688 **fax** (03) 9439 5121 **open** By appointment
winemaker George Apted, John Graves **production** 850 **est.** 1990
product range ($14.95–18.95 ML) Chardonnay, Pinot Noir, Cabernet Sauvignon.
summary Drawing upon vineyards at Arthurs Creek and Eltham, John Graves (brother of David Graves, of the illustrious Californian Pinot producer Saintsbury) produces tiny quantities of quite stylish Chardonnay and Pinot Noir, the former showing nice barrel-ferment characters.

elysium vineyard NR

393 Milbrodale Road, Broke, NSW 2330 **region** Lower Hunter Valley
phone (02) 9664 2368 **fax** (02) 9664 2368 **open** By appointment
winemaker Tyrrell's (Contract) **production** 350 **est.** 1990
product range ($20 R) Verdelho.
summary Elysium was once part of a much larger vineyard established by John Tulloch. John Tulloch (not part of the Tulloch operation previously owned by Southcorp) continues to look after the viticulture, with the 1 hectare of verdelho being vinified at Tyrrell's. The Elysium Cottage, large enough to accommodate six people, has won a number of tourism awards, and proprietor Victoria Foster conducts wine education weekends on request, with meals prepared by a chef brought in for the occasion. The cost per person for a gourmet weekend is $300–400, depending on numbers.

england's creek NR

Butt's Road, Murrumbateman, NSW 2582 (PO Box 6, Murrumbateman, NSW 2582) **region** Canberra District
phone (02) 6227 5550 **fax** (02) 6227 5550 **open** Not
winemaker Ken Helm (Contract) **production** 250 **est.** 1995
product range ($17–20 ML) Riesling, Hand Picked Riesling, Shiraz, Hand Picked Shiraz.
summary The diminutive England's Creek was established in 1995 by Stephen Carney and Virginia Rawling, with the planting of 1 hectare each of riesling and shiraz. The wines are available at selected Canberra restaurants and Vintage Cellars, Manuka or by contacting the winery.

ensay winery NR

Great Alpine Road, Ensay, Vic 3895 **region** Gippsland
phone (03) 5157 3203 **fax** (03) 5157 3372 **open** Weekends, public and school holidays 11–5 or by appointment
winemaker David Coy **production** 1500 **est.** 1992
product range ($17–20 R) Chardonnay, Pinot Noir, Shiraz, Cabernet Sauvignon.
summary A weekend and holiday business for the Coy family, headed by David Coy, with 2.5 hectares of chardonnay, pinot noir, merlot, shiraz and cabernet sauvignon.

epis/epis & williams ★★★★☆

Lot 16 Calder Highway, Woodend, Vic 3442 **region** Macedon Ranges
phone (03) 5427 1204 **fax** (03) 5427 1204 **open** By appointment
winemaker Stuart Anderson **production** 800 **est.** 1990
product range ($30–40 R) Epis Chardonnay, Pinot Noir, Cabernet Sauvignon; Epis & Williams Cabernet Sauvignon.
summary Three legends are involved in the Epis and Epis & Williams wines, two of them in their own lifetime. They are long-term Essendon guru and former player Alec Epis, who owns the two quite separate vineyards and brands; Stuart Anderson, who makes the wines, with Alec Epis doing all the hard work; and the late Laurie Williams, the father of viticulture in the Macedon region and the man who established the Flynn & Williams vineyard in 1976. Alec Epis purchased that vineyard from Laurie Williams in 1999, and as

a mark of respect (and with Laurie Williams' approval) continued to use Williams' name in conjunction with his own. The cabernet sauvignon comes from this vineyard, the chardonnay and pinot noir from the vineyard at Woodend, where a small winery will have been completed prior to the 2002 vintage.

Epis Macedon Ranges Chardonnay

▼▼▼▼▽ 2000 Medium to full yellow-green; a very complex bouquet full of nutty/figgy character, and an equally distinctive palate with strong barrel ferment characters, not just deriving from oak but also from the apparent fermentation at ambient temperatures, investing the wine with structure and nutty flavours. Definitely slanted to white burgundy in style. **rating:** 90

best drinking 2002–2005 best vintages '00 drink with Pan-fried veal • $30

Epis Macedon Ranges Pinot Noir

▼▼▼▼▽ 2000 Medium red-purple; a fine and elegant bouquet ranging through spice, plum and black cherry, with gently sappy/foresty overtones. The palate is similarly elegant, with fine, savoury tannins; the finesse and subtlety of the wines shows the cool climate without being green. **rating:** 93

best drinking 2002–2006 best vintages NA drink with Smoked breast of duck • $40

Epis & Williams Cabernet Sauvignon

▼▼▼▼▼ 2000 Medium to full red-purple; there is a range of blackberry, blackcurrant, cedar and earth on the bouquet; the palate has a core of olive, herb and bramble intermingling with blackberry fruit, a hint of cedar, and fine but ripe tannins. Well away from the mainstream of warmer-climate Cabernet, but I like it. **rating:** 94

best drinking 2004–2010 best vintages '00 drink with Leg of lamb • $35

eppalock ridge   NR

633 North Redesdale Road, Redesdale, Vic 3444 **region** Heathcote
phone (03) 5425 3135 **fax** (03) 5425 3135 **open** 7 days 10–6 by appointment
winemaker Rod Hourigan **production** 1500 **est.** 1979
product range ($25 CD) Shiraz, Cabernet Merlot.
summary A low-key operation now focusing mainly on Shiraz produced from the 4 hectares of this variety; the other wine in the portfolio comes from the 2.7 hectares of cabernet sauvignon, merlot and cabernet franc.

ermes estate   NR

2 Godings Road, Moorooduc, Vic 3933 **region** Mornington Peninsula
phone (03) 5978 8376 **fax** (03) 5978 8396 **open** Weekends and public holidays 11–5
winemaker Ermes Zucchet, Denise Succhet **production** 1000 **est.** 1989
product range ($10–20 CD) Riesling, Chardonnay, Pinot Grigio, Merlot, Cabernet Sauvignon.
summary Ermes and Denise Zucchet began planting the 2.5-hectare estate in 1989, with chardonnay, riesling, cabernet sauvignon and merlot, adding pinot gris in 1991. In 1994 an existing piggery on the property was converted to a winery and cellar-door area (in the Zucchets' words, the pigs having been evicted); the modestly priced wines are now on sale at weekends. No recent tastings.

ese vineyards   ★★★★

1013 Tea Tree Road, Tea Tree, Tas 7017 **region** Southern Tasmania
phone 0417 319 875 **fax** (03) 6272 5398 **open** 7 days 10–5
winemaker Michael Vishacki (Contract) **production** 2500 **est.** 1994
product range ($20 CD) Chardonnay, Pinot Noir.
summary Elvio and Natalie Brianese are an architect and graphic designer couple whose extended family have centuries-old viticultural roots in the Veneto region of northern Italy. ese has 2.5 hectares of vineyard and got off to a flying start with a gold and silver medal for its 1997 Pinot Noir. Subsequent vintages have been less exhilarating, but there is no question the potential is there.

ese Vineyards Chardonnay

▼▼▼▼▼ 2001 Glowing yellow-green; has an ultra-complex bouquet with intense, tangy/citrus fruit and barrel ferment characters interwoven. The rich, intense and powerful palate has strong overtones of Burgundy in an individualistic but stylish mode. **rating:** 94

best drinking 2002–2007 best vintages '01 drink with Washed-rind cheese • NA

ese Vineyards Pinot Noir

ŢŢŢŢ **2000** Light to medium red-purple; a light, clean, slightly minty bouquet opens with similar characters on the palate, then a slightly scrappy finish. Another wine to polarise the judges; the points are very much a compromise between high a low. **rating: 83**

best drinking 2002–2003 **best vintages** '97 **drink with** Rabbit casserole • NA

🐎 etain   NR

Boodjidup Road, Margaret River, WA 6285 **region** Margaret River
phone 0407 445 570 **open** Not
winemaker Conor Lagan, Jurg Muggli **production** 5000 **est.** 2001
product range ($16–25 R) Riesling, Semillon Sauvignon Blanc, Cabernet Merlot.
summary Etain is a private label of Conor Lagan, available only to trade through distributor Prime Wines. In Gaelic mythology Etain is the horse goddess, representing birth and rebirth. It is in turn linked to the fascinating story of Conor Lagan's life, which can be found on www.etainwines.com. The wines are sourced from vineyards in the Margaret and Frankland River regions.

eumundi winery   NR

2 Bruce Highway, Eumundi, Qld 4562 **region** Queensland Coastal
phone (07) 5442 7444 **fax** (07) 5442 7455 **open** 7 days 10–6
winemaker Andrew Hickinbotham (Contract) **production** 2500 **est.** 1996
product range ($12–15 R) Semillon Chardonnay, Taminga, Shiraz, Shiraz Cabernet, Shiraz Durif, Merlot, Chambourcin, Cabernet Sauvignon.
summary Eumundi Vineyard is set on 21 hectares of riverfront land in the beautiful Eumundi Valley, 12 kilometres inland from Noosa Heads. The climate is hot, wet, humid and maritime, the only saving grace being the regular afternoon northeast sea breeze. It is a challenging environment in which to grow grapes, and over 5 years the owners, Robyn and Gerry Humphrey, have trialled 14 different grape varieties and three different trellis systems. Currently they have tempranillo, shiraz, chambourcin, petit verdot, durif and mourvedre, and verdelho. Plantings in 2001 included tannat and others, which gives some idea of their eclectic approach. The establishment of the vineyard was financed by the sale of a 19-metre charter yacht which used to sail the oceans around northern Australia. Quite a change in lifestyle for the Humphreys.

Eumundi Chambourcin

ŢŢŢŢ **2000** Bright red-purple, typical of the variety; the bouquet is clean, with soft, dark berry fruit, the palate with some richness and depth to the blackberry and spice fruit. **rating: 84**

best drinking 2002–2004 **best vintages** NA **drink with** Beef ragout • $14

evans & tate   ★★★★

Metricup Road, Wilyabrup, WA 6280 **region** Margaret River
phone (08) 9755 6244 **fax** (08) 9755 6346 **open** 7 days 10.30–4.30
winemaker Steve Warne **production** 270 000 **est.** 1970
product range ($11–50 CD) Gnangara range of Chenin Blanc, Chardonnay, Shiraz; the Margaret River range of Margaret River Classic, Semillon, Shiraz, Sauvignon Blanc Semillon, Verdelho, Chardonnay, Cane Cut Semillon, Classic Shiraz Cabernet Merlot, Merlot, Barrique 61 Cabernet Merlot; Redbrook Chardonnay and Cabernet Sauvignon.
summary Single-handedly changed perceptions of the Swan Valley red wines in the 1970s before opening its highly successful Margaret River operation, which goes from strength to strength. The most recent expansion has been the establishment of a large vineyard in the new Jindong subregion of the Margaret River, precipitating a flood of other arrivals in that area. The continuing rapid growth of the business has taken the edge off the white wines which, while immaculately crafted and ever reliable, lack the concentration and complexity of the very best wines of the region. National distribution; exports to Canada, the UK, France, Switzerland and Hong Kong.

Evans & Tate Margaret River Chardonnay

ŢŢŢŢ **2001** Medium yellow-green; well-balanced and integrated fruit and oak open proceedings on the bouquet; the light to medium-bodied palate is similarly very well crafted, with light nectarine, melon and soft oak flavours. At the end of the day, however, there is not a great deal of fruit intensity by the standards of Margaret River. **rating: 87**

best drinking 2002–2004 **best vintages** NA **drink with** Sugar-cured tuna • $20

Evans & Tate Gnangara Shiraz

▼▼▼▽ **2000** Medium red-purple; the moderately intense bouquet has quite good varietal character, with some slightly gamey aromas; the moderately intense palate has cherry and plum fruit, tailing off on the finish. Well priced. **rating: 83**

best drinking 2001–2002 **best vintages** NA **drink with** Takeaway • $10

Evans & Tate Margaret River Shiraz

▼▼▼▼ **2000** Medium purple-red; the moderately intense bouquet has some dusty oak which suppresses the fruit; the medium-bodied palate, however, allows that red and black cherry fruit to come through; pleasant and straightforward. **rating: 85**

best drinking 2003–2007 **best vintages** '86, '88, '90, '91, '92, '93, '95, '96 **drink with** Strong red meat dishes • $25

Evans & Tate Margaret River Classic Red

▼▼▼▼ **2000** Youthful red-purple; the moderately intense bouquet is clean and entirely driven by its fresh berry fruit; the palate is similarly fruity but with good texture, suggesting the use of micro-oxygenation. **rating: 86**

best drinking 2001–2004 **best vintages** NA **drink with** Roast veal • $19.60

Evans & Tate Margaret River Merlot

▼▼▼▼▽ **1998** Medium red-purple; a clean, elegant and quite complex bouquet with small, red berry fruit leads into a well-balanced and modulated palate with red fruit at the centre, then a gently savoury finish. A high-quality wine with excellent varietal character. **rating: 92**

best drinking 2003–2008 **best vintages** '98 **drink with** Osso buco • $40

Evans & Tate Barrique 61 Cabernet Merlot

▼▼▼▼ **2000** Medium red-purple; the bouquet has good fruit weight, with small, dark berry aromas which carry through to the palate, with a hint of chocolate also coming through. Excellent flavour; slightly simple structure. For all that, good value. **rating: 89**

best drinking 2003–2008 **best vintages** '99 **drink with** Gourmet sausages • $19

Evans & Tate Redbrook Cabernet Sauvignon

▼▼▼▼▽ **1999** Strong red-purple; clean, sweet cassis/berry/mulberry fruit aromas lead into a stylish, elegant, medium-bodied palate with slightly firm acidity on the finish (presenting no long-term problems); judicious use of oak throughout. **rating: 91**

best drinking 2004–2009 **best vintages** '86, '88, '90, '91, '92, '95, '96, '99 **drink with** Braised ox cheek in red wine sauce • $50

evans family ★★★★☆

Palmers Lane, Pokolbin, NSW 2320 **region** Lower Hunter Valley
phone (02) 4998 7333 **fax** (02) 4998 7798 **open** By appointment
winemaker Sarah-Kate Wilson (Contract) **production** 3000 **est.** 1979
product range ($16–29 ML) Semillon, Chardonnay, Gamay, Pinot Noir, Shiraz.
summary In the wake of the acquisition of Rothbury by Mildara Blass, Len Evans' wine interests now focus on Evans Family (estate-grown and produced from vineyards around the family home), the Evans Wine Company (a quite different, part-maker, part-negociant business) and, most recently, Tower Estate. Len Evans continues to persist with the notion that the Hunter Valley can produce Gamay and Pinot Noir of quality and, irritatingly, occasionally produces evidence to suggest he may be half right. There is, of course, no such reservation with the Semillon, the Chardonnay or the Shiraz.

Evans Family Howard Vineyard Semillon

▼▼▼▼▽ **1999** Medium yellow-green; the bouquet is complex, but in the mid-point of development, and slightly closed in consequence. The palate, however, is in full flight, with intense herb and citrus flavours; good length and persistence. **rating: 92**

best drinking 2003–2009 **best vintages** '97, '99 **drink with** Richer fish dishes • $16.50

Evans Family Chardonnay

▼▼▼▼ **1999** Glowing yellow-green; a complex buttery, peachy, toasty bouquet leads into a slightly old-fashioned but generously proportioned palate with masses of buttery, peachy fruit. **rating: 88**

best drinking 2002–2004 **best vintages** NA **drink with** Ballottine of chicken • $22.50

Evans Family Howard Shiraz

▼▼▼▼ **1999** Medium red-purple; the fresh, moderately intense bouquet opens with red cherry, then picks up touches of regional earth and chocolate; the elegant, medium-bodied palate has fine, savoury red cherry fruit and fine tannins; one of those deceptive wines which don't look as if they will age, but are in fact long-lived. **rating: 88**

best drinking 2004–2014 **best vintages** NA **drink with** Irish stew • $28.50

evelyn county estate ★★★★☆

55 Eltham–Yarra Glen Road, Kangaroo Ground, Vic 3097 **region** Yarra Valley
phone (03) 9437 2155 **fax** (03) 9437 2188 **open** Mon–Fri 9–5, weekends 8–6
winemaker James Lance, David Lance (Contract) **production** 2300 **est.** 1994
product range ($19–30 CD) Black Paddock range of Sauvignon Blanc, Chardonnay, Pinot Noir, Merlot, Cabernet Sauvignon.
summary The 10.3-hectare Evelyn County Estate has been established by former Coopers & Lybrand managing partner Roger Male and his wife Robyn, who is currently completing a degree in Applied Science (Wine Science) at Charles Sturt University. David Lance (of Diamond Valley) is currently making the wines, and an architect-designed cellar door sales, gallery and restaurant opened in April 2001. As one would expect, the quality of the wines is very good.

Evelyn County Estate Black Paddock Sauvignon Blanc

▼▼▼▼▽ **2001** Light green-yellow; the moderately intense bouquet offers ripe citrus and gooseberry aromas, the wine flowing evenly across the palate with plenty of weight and flavour; as one would expect, very well made. **rating: 91**

best drinking 2002–2003 **best vintages** '01 **drink with** White-fleshed fish • $21

Evelyn County Estate Black Paddock Chardonnay

▼▼▼▼▽ **2000** Excellent green-yellow; delicate, crisp melon fruit, with a hint of citrus, is married with subtle oak on the bouquet. The elegant palate offers citrus, nectarine and melon, made complex by a hint of oak spice. Lovely wine. **rating: 93**

best drinking 2002–2005 **best vintages** '00 **drink with** Yarra Valley trout • $23

excelsior peak NR

1927 Jingallic Road, Tumbarumba, NSW 2653 (postal) **region** Tumbarumba
phone (02) 6948 5102 **fax** (02) 6948 5102 **open** Not
winemaker Contract **production** 1150 **est.** 1980
product range ($18–22 ML) Chardonnay, Pinot Noir, Méthode Champenoise.
summary Excelsior Peak proprietor Juliet Cullen established the first vineyard in Tumbarumba in 1980. That vineyard was thereafter sold to Southcorp, and Juliet Cullen subsequently established another vineyard, now releasing wines under the Excelsior Peak label. Plantings total over 10 hectares.

eyton-on-yarra ★★★★

Cnr Maroondah Highway and Hill Road, Coldstream, Vic 3370 **region** Yarra Valley
phone (03) 5962 2119 **fax** (03) 5962 5319 **open** 7 days 10–5
winemaker David Creed **production** 13 000 **est.** 1993
product range ($22–40 R) There were three labels in the range: at the top is NDC Reserve, a tribute to the late Newell Cowan, who effectively founded Eyton-on-Yarra; the main varietal range, under the Eyton label; and the third label range of Dalry Road, the name of the second vineyard owned by Deirdre Cowan. This range will change significantly once existing stocks are depleted.
summary Late in 2001 acquired from Deirdre Cowan by Helmut and Yvonne Konecsny, who have moved the winemaking operations of Rochford to this winery, with major expansion already underway.

Eyton-on-Yarra Chardonnay

▼▼▼▼ **2000** Medium to full yellow-green; a very strong nutmeg/spice oak overlay hides the fruit on the bouquet; the palate has nice mouthfeel and texture, but the oak tends to dominate the fruit. May come back into better balance with more time in bottle, and others will be far more tolerant of the oak in any event. **rating: 87**

best drinking 2003–2007 **best vintages** '95, '99 **drink with** Veal cutlet on white truffle pasta • $24.50

faber vineyard ★★★★

233 Hadrill Road, Baskerville, WA 6056 **region** Swan District
phone (08) 9296 0619 **fax** (08) 9296 0681 **open** Not
winemaker John Griffiths **production** 1000 **est.** 1997
product range ($12–16.50 ML) Chardonnay, Riche Shiraz, Shiraz.

summary Former Houghton winemaker and now university lecturer and consultant John Griffiths has teamed with his wife Jane Micallef to found Faber Vineyard. Since 1997 they have established 1 hectare of shiraz, and 0.5 hectare each of chardonnay, verdelho, cabernet sauvignon, petit verdot and brown muscat. Says John Griffiths, 'It may be somewhat quixotic, but I'm a great fan of traditional warm area Australia wine styles – those found in areas such as Rutherglen and the Barossa. Wines made in a relatively simple manner that reflect the concentrated ripe flavours one expects in these regions. And when one searches, some of these gems can be found from the Swan Valley.' Possessed of an excellent palate, and with an impeccable winemaking background, the quality of John Griffiths' wines is guaranteed.

Faber Vineyard Chardonnay

TTTT **2001** Light to medium green-yellow; a clean, fresh bouquet with a mix of citrus and nectarine is followed by a palate in near identical style, lifted by a touch of mineral. The oak influence on both bouquet and palate is minimal. **rating:** 85

best drinking 2001–2003 **best vintages** NA **drink with** Grilled white-fleshed fish • $12

Faber Vineyard Shiraz

TTTTY **2001** Deep, dark purple-red; the intense bouquet has an array of savoury, earthy, spicy and licorice aromas; the palate has abundant fruit and good structure, the tannin management positive but not harsh. Has all the requisites for a long life. **rating:** 91

best drinking 2006–2016 **best vintages** '01 **drink with** Ox tail • $12

Faber Vineyard Riche Shiraz

TTTTY **2001** Dense, almost opaque, colour; a complex bouquet, with an obvious contribution of vanilla from the American oak interwoven with ripe, plum and prune fruit. A massive wine, like a bigger version of Houghton's Jack Mann; needs a minimum of 10 years. It is said to have been made using techniques that concentrate colour, whatever they may be. **rating:** 92

best drinking 2010 - 2020 **best vintages** '01 **drink with** Leave it in the cellar • $16.50

fairfield vineyard NR

Murray Valley Highway, Browns Plains via Rutherglen, Vic 3685 **region** Rutherglen
phone (02) 6032 9381 **open** Mon–Sat 10–5, some Sun 12–5
winemaker Andrew Sutherland-Smith **production** 4200 **est.** 1959
product range ($8.50–15 CD) White Hermitage, Riesling, Moselle, Rosé, Light Red, Shiraz, Durif, Cabernet Sauvignon, Fortified.
summary Specialist in red and fortified wines made with 19th-century wine equipment housed in the grounds of the historic Fairfield Mansion built by G F Morris. A tourist must. Offers a wide range of back vintages.

fairview wines NR

422 Elderslie Road, Branxton, NSW 2335 **region** Lower Hunter Valley
phone (02) 4938 1116 **fax** (02) 4938 1116 **open** Weekends 10–5 or by appointment
winemaker Rhys Eather (Contract) **production** 1000 **est.** 1997
product range ($16–20 CD) Semillon, Quignoc, Shiraz.
summary Greg and Elaine Searles purchased the property on which they have established Fairview Wines in 1997. For the previous 90 years it had sustained an orchard, but since that time 2 hectares of shiraz, 1 hectare each of barbera, semillon and verdelho and 0.5 hectare of chambourcin have been established, using organic procedures wherever possible. The Searles operate the cellar door in person; retail distribution in Sydney and exports to the United Kingdom have also been established.

faisan estate ★★★

Amaroo Road, Borenore, NSW 2800 **region** Orange
phone (02) 6365 2380 **open** Not
winemaker Col Walker **production** 500 **est.** 1992

product range ($8–13 ML) Semillon, Chardonnay, Canobolas Classic White, Pinot Noir, Britton's Block Cabernet Sauvignon, Cabernet Sauvignon.

summary Faisan Estate, within sight of Mount Canobolas and 20 kilometres west of the city of Orange, has been established by Trish and Col Walker. They now have almost 7 hectares of vineyards coming into bearing and have purchased grapes from other growers in the region in the interim.

Faisan Estate Semillon

♥♥♥♡ **2001** Glowing but developed yellow-green; a complex, rich bouquet is presumably the consequence of skin contact, which has played up the colour, but which also comes to haunt the back palate and finish, where phenolics catch up.   **rating: 83**

best drinking 2002–2003 **best vintages** NA **drink with** Roast chicken •$12

Faisan Estate Pinot Noir

♥♥♥♥ **1999** Medium red, with a slightly dull purple edge suggesting elevated pH. The bouquet offers secondary, spicy/foresty aromas; the palate provides more of the same, with some weight in a savoury, foresty style. Certainly no lollipop/candy fruit to be seen here.   **rating: 85**

best drinking 2002–2003 **best vintages** NA **drink with** Wild mushroom risotto • $13

Faisan Estate Cabernet Sauvignon

♥♥♥♥ **2000** Medium to full red-purple; the bouquet is distinctly varietal, with earthy, faintly cedary, blackberry aromas; a big, powerful, rough-hewn but flavoursome palate with blackberry fruit, then grippy tannins on the finish.   **rating: 85**

best drinking 2007–2012 **best vintages** NA **drink with** Leave it in the cellar • $14

🍇 farmer's daughter wines   ★★★★

791 Cassilis Road, Mudgee, NSW 2850 **region** Mudgee
phone (02) 6373 3177 **fax** (02) 6373 3759 **open** 7 days 9–5
winemaker Joe Lesnik (Contract) **production** 16 000 **est.** 1995
product range ($15–19 CD) Reserve Semillon, Chardonnay, Shiraz, Merlot, Cabernet Sauvignon.
summary The intriguingly named Farmer's Daughter Wines is a family-owned vineyard, run by daughters of a feed-lot farmer, with contract winemaking by Joe Lesnik. Seven hectares of shiraz, 6 hectares of merlot, 3 hectares each of chardonnay and cabernet sauvignon and 1 hectare of semillon provide the base for a substantial business. As well as local retail distribution (and seven-day cellar door sales) the wines are available through Porters liquor outlets in Sydney. The first two vintages have had outstanding (though somewhat controversial) show success.

Farmer's Daughter Semillon

♥♥♥♥♥ **2000** Pale straw-green; a fine, delicate and crisp bouquet flows through to an intense and exceptionally long and fine palate, with a lingering finish. Top gold and trophy winner Mudgee Wine Show 2001.   **rating: 95**

best drinking 2003–2013 **best vintages** '00 **drink with** Cold seafood • $18

Farmer's Daughter Chardonnay

♥♥♥♥♡ **2000** Light to medium green-yellow; there is a subtle interplay between fruit and oak on the bouquet, the palate unfolding with fresh, lively and crisp stone fruit and citrus flavours.   **rating: 90**

best drinking 2002–2004 **best vintages** NA **drink with** Mussels in creamy sauce • $15

Farmer's Daughter Shiraz

♥♥♥♥♥ **1999** Medium to full purple-red; clean, fresh, bright dark cherry fruit on the bouquet introduces a beautifully balanced and proportioned wine, with a rare combination of elegance and flavour. Multiple trophy winner 2001 Mudgee Wine Show.   **rating: 95**

best drinking 2003–2013 **best vintages** '99 **drink with** Shoulder of lamb • $15

Farmer's Daughter Merlot

♥♥♥♥ **1999** Bright, medium purple-red. Light, fresh berry merlot fruit on the bouquet is followed by a lively, fresh palate with just a flick of green stemmy character on the finish, a character which I am happy to attribute to the variety.   **rating: 88**

best drinking 2002–2007 **best vintages** NA **drink with** Osso buco • $19

Farmer's Daughter Cabernet Sauvignon
YYYY 1999 Medium red-purple; the bouquet and the palate are both compromised by overenthusiastic use of oak, but there is plenty of sweet fruit to be found once you peel back the oak.　　**rating:** 86

best drinking 2004–2009 **best vintages** NA **drink with** Chargrilled rump steak • $15

by farr　　★★★★★

c/o Bannockburn, Midlands Highway, Bannockburn, Vic 3331 **region** Geelong
phone (03) 5281 1979 **fax** (03) 5281 1979 **open** Not
winemaker Gary Farr **production** 2000 **est.** 1999
product range ($45 R) Viognier, Chardonnay, Pinot Noir, Shiraz.
summary In 1994 Gary Farr and family planted just under 5 hectares of clonally selected viognier, chardonnay, pinot noir and shiraz on a north-facing hill which is directly opposite the Bannockburn Winery, having acquired the land from the late Stuart Hooper (Bannockburn's then owner). For a multiplicity of reasons, in 1999 Farr decided to establish his own label for part of the grapes coming from the vineyard; the remainder go to Bannockburn. The quality of the wines is exemplary, their character subtly different from those of Bannockburn itself; this is due, in Farr's view, to the interaction of the terroir of the hill and the clonal selection. As from 2000, the reference to Bannockburn was removed from the front label.

Chardonnay by Farr
YYYYY 2000 Light to medium yellow-green; the bouquet spins a complex but subtle web of sweet stone fruit, oak and cashew; the palate is similarly complex and rich, yet in a way it is also restrained, because no one character dominates.　　**rating:** 93

best drinking 2002–2006 **best vintages** '99, '00 **drink with** Pan-fried veal • $45

Pinot Noir by Farr
YYYYY 2000 Bright red-purple; a high-toned, estery, almost citrussy bouquet, showing some (but not too much) new oak is followed by a palate with a similarly spicy/tangy undercurrent to the quite beautiful red and black cherry fruit. The wine has all the length one could wish for, and is at once similar to yet quite radically different from the 2000 Bannockburn.　　**rating:** 95

best drinking 2002–2006 **best vintages** '99, '00 **drink with** Barbecued quail • $45

farrell's limestone creek　　★★★

Mount View Road, Mount View, NSW 2325 **region** Lower Hunter Valley
phone (02) 4991 2808 **fax** (02) 4991 3414 **open** 7 days 10–5
winemaker Adrian Lockhart (Contract) **production** 3500 **est.** 1980
product range ($17–20 CD) Semillon, Chardonnay, Shiraz, Merlot, Cabernet Sauvignon Merlot.
summary The Farrell family purchased 20 hectares on Mount View in 1980 and gradually established 7.3 hectares of vineyards planted to semillon, verdelho, chardonnay, shiraz, cabernet sauvignon and merlot. Most of the grapes are sold to McWilliam's, a lesser amount is made for cellar door and mailing list orders.

Farrell's Limestone Creek Semillon
YYYY 2001 Very light straw-green; a youthful and aromatic bouquet with flint and lime is followed by a crisp, clean and fresh palate, with good length and potential.　　**rating:** 85

best drinking 2003–2008 **best vintages** NA **drink with** Balmain bugs • $17

Farrell's Limestone Creek Chardonnay
YYYY 2000 Light to medium yellow-green; a light, tangy bouquet with minimal oak is repeated on the palate, where the fresh fruit has much of the feel and structure of Semillon; should age well.　　**rating:** 84

best drinking 2001–2004 **best vintages** NA **drink with** Chinese steamed fish • $17

felsberg winery　　★★★

Townsends Road, Glen Aplin, Qld 4381 **region** Granite Belt
phone (07) 4683 4332 **fax** (07) 4683 4377 **open** 7 days 9–5
winemaker Otto Haag **production** 2000 **est.** 1983
product range ($12–20 CD) Rhine Riesling, Traminer, White Classic, Chardonnay, Shiraz, Merlot, Cabernet Shiraz, Mead, Ruby Mead.
summary Felsberg has a spectacular site, high on a rocky slope, the winery itself built on a single huge boulder. It has been offering wine for sale via the cellar door (and the mailing list) made by former master brewer Otto Haag for many years; as the 2000 Cabernet Sauvignon shows, the quality can be good.

🐦 fenton views vineyard   NR

182 Fenton Hill Road, Clarkefield, Vic 3430 **region** Sunbury
phone (03) 5428 5429 **fax** (03) 5428 5304 **open** First and last Sunday of the month or by appointment
winemaker David Spiteri **production** 500 **est.** 1994
product range ($16–22 R) Chardonnay, Pinot Noir, Shiraz.
summary Situated on the north-facing slopes of Fenton Hill at Clarkefield, just northeast of Sunbury, the Hume and Macedon Ranges providing a spectacular and tranquil setting. It is a small family operation with plantings of shiraz and chardonnay followed by pinot noir, and cabernet sauvignon. Co-owner David Spiteri studied winemaking at Charles Sturt University, and has had vintage experience both in Australia and California.

Fenton Views Chardonnay

▼▼▼▽ **2000** Light green-yellow; a clean, light bouquet with a mix of mineral and toast aromas, the fruit somewhere underneath. The palate is fresh and crisp, showing very competent winemaking, but, equally, needing more substance to carry the winemaking inputs, particularly the malolactic fermentation.

rating: 84

best drinking 2002–2006 **best vintages** NA **drink with** Fish terrine • $16

Fenton Views Shiraz

▼▼▼▽ **2000** Light to medium red-purple; a light spicy/leafy bouquet leaves little doubt about the cool climate; nor does the palate, with its supple mix of cherry, spice and leaf; the oak is sensibly held in restraint.   **rating:** 84

best drinking 2003–2007 **best vintages** NA **drink with** Roast duck Chinese-style • $18

ferguson falls estate   ★★★

Pile Road, Dardanup, WA 6236 **region** Geographe
phone (08) 9728 1083 **fax** (08) 9728 1616 **open** By appointment
winemaker James Pennington (Contract) **production** 1000 **est.** 1983
product range ($15–17 CD) Chardonnay, Cabernet Sauvignon.
summary Peter Giumelli and family are dairy farmers in the lush Ferguson Valley, 180 kilometres south of Perth. In 1983 they planted 3 hectares of cabernet sauvignon, chardonnay and merlot, making their first wines for commercial release from the 1995 and 1996 vintages, which confirmed the suitability of the region for the production of premium wine.

fergusson   ★★★☆

Wills Road, Yarra Glen, Vic 3775 **region** Yarra Valley
phone (03) 5965 2237 **fax** (03) 5965 2405 **open** 7 days 11–5
winemaker Christopher Keyes, Peter Fergusson **production** 10 000 **est.** 1968
product range ($16–50 CD) There are two basic ranges: the lower-priced Tartan Range sourced from grapes grown outside the Yarra Valley, with Chardonnay, Pinot Noir, Shiraz, Cabernet Sauvignon, Fine Old Tawny Port; and the Estate Range with Victoria Chardonnay, Victoria Reserve Chardonnay, Sparkling Pinot Noir Chardonnay, LJK Pinot Noir, Jeremy Shiraz and Benjamyn Cabernet Sauvignon.
summary Best known as a favoured tourist destination, particularly for tourist coaches, and offering hearty fare in comfortable surroundings accompanied by wines of non-Yarra Valley origin. For this reason the limited quantities of its estate wines are often ignored, but they should not be. Exports to the UK and New Zealand.

fermoy estate   ★★★★

Metricup Road, Wilyabrup, WA 6280 **region** Margaret River
phone (08) 9755 6285 **fax** (08) 9755 6251 **open** 7 days 11–4.30
winemaker Michael Kelly **production** 15 000 **est.** 1985
product range ($12–30 CD) Sauvignon Blanc, Sentinel (Sauvignon Blanc Semillon), Semillon, Reserve Semillon, Chenin Blanc, Sentinel Verdelho, Chardonnay, Reserve Chardonnay, Sentinel Rosé, Sentinel Shiraz, Merlot, Sentinel Navigator (Cabernet blend), Cabernet Sauvignon, Reserve Cabernet.
summary A change of ownership several years ago seemed to coincide with a distinct shift in style – and improvement in – the wines, notwithstanding the continuation of Michael Kelly as winemaker.

Fermoy Estate Reserve Semillon

▼▼▼ **2000** Light green-yellow; a soft, faintly funky bouquet with some tropical edges, then a rich and full palate with slightly smoky characters adding further interest to a wine with considerable character (and alcohol at 14°). **rating:** 87

best drinking 2002–2004 **best vintages** NA **drink with** Sautéed scallops • $30

Fermoy Estate Merlot

▼▼▼▽ **2000** Medium to full red-purple; rich, ripe, small red berry fruit is matched by sympathetic oak on the bouquet; there is similarly plenty of fruit concentration to the palate, ranging through sweet blueberry and raspberry flavours; gentle oak and tannins provide the appropriate texture and structure. **rating:** 90

best drinking 2003–2008 **best vintages** '00 **drink with** Ragout of veal • $30

🍷 ferngrove vineyards estate ★★★☆

Ferngrove Road, Frankland, WA 6396 **region** Great Southern
phone (08) 9855 2378 **fax** (08) 9855 2368 **open** 7 days 10–5
winemaker John Griffiths (Contract) **production** 20 000 **est.** 1997
product range ($16–22 R) Cossack Riesling, Cossack Sauvignon Blanc, Semillon Sauvignon Blanc, Chardonnay, Shiraz, Cabernet Merlot.
summary After 90 years of family beef and dairy farming heritage, Murray Burton decided to venture into premium grape growing and winemaking in 1997. Since that time he has moved with exceptional speed, establishing 414 hectares of grapes on three vineyards in the Frankland River subregion, and a 4th at Mount Barker. The operation centres around the Ferngrove Vineyard, where a large, tourist-oriented, rammed-earth winery and tourist complex was built in time for the 2000 vintage. The highly experienced John Griffiths acts as contract winemaker; as well as Australia-wide distribution through Hill International, exports to the UK through Vinus Vita.

Ferngrove Vineyards Cossack Riesling

▼▼▼▼ **2001** Pale straw-green; the crisp, minerally bouquet has faint aromas of herb, lime and apple, the light-bodied palate following down the same track, with mineral and a touch of ripe apple; needs time, but is well-balanced. **rating:** 87

best drinking 2003–2008 **best vintages** NA **drink with** Steamed crab • $22

Ferngrove Vineyards Semillon Sauvignon Blanc

▼▼▼▼ **2001** Light to medium yellow-green; focussed citrus and herbaceous fruit on the bouquet leads into a generously flavoured palate, sweetening slightly towards the finish, perhaps due to the 13.5 per cent alcohol. However, it is not hot. **rating:** 85

best drinking 2002–2004 **best vintages** NA **drink with** Asparagus with hollandaise sauce • $15.99

Ferngrove Vineyards Chardonnay

▼▼▼▽ **2001** Light straw-green; light melon fruit with a hint of citrus skin and subliminal oak lead into a palate with soft fruit, once again seeming to derive some sweetness from alcohol, closing with subtle oak (30 per cent barrel-fermented). **rating:** 84

best drinking 2002–2004 **best vintages** NA **drink with** Trout mousse • $18.99

🍷 fern gully winery NR

63 Princes Highway, Termeil, NSW 2539 **region** South Coast Zone
phone (02) 4457 1124 **open** Weekends and holidays 11–5.30 (except winter)
winemaker Max Staniford **production** 350 **est.** 1996
product range ($16–19 CD) Chardonnay, Shiraz, Chambourcin, Cabernet Sauvignon.
summary Glenda and Max Staniford planted 0.25 hectare each of chardonnay, shiraz, cabernet sauvignon and chambourcin in the 1996 and 1997 planting seasons, producing the first grapes in 1998. The wines are all estate-grown (hence the limited production) and all of the winemaking takes place on-site. The vineyard is enclosed in permanent netting, and hand picking ensures the exclusion of diseased fruit. The wines have won a number of silver and bronze medals at (unspecified) shows.

Fern Gully Cabernet Sauvignon

▼▼▼▽ **2000** Medium red-purple; the clean bouquet is moderately intense, with some varietal berry fruit and a touch of oak. The light to medium-bodied palate is clean, with touches of mint and leaf alongside the berry fruit; subtle oak. **rating:** 83

best drinking 2002–2004 **best vintages** NA **drink with** Fillet of lamb • $19

fern hill estate ★★☆

Ingoldby Road, McLaren Flat, SA 5171 **region** McLaren Vale
phone (08) 8383 0167 **fax** (08) 8383 0107 **open** 7 days 10–5
winemaker Grant Burge (Contract) **production** 7000 **est.** 1975
product range ($15.95–19.95 CD) Semillon, Chardonnay, Brut, Shiraz, Cabernet Sauvignon.
summary One suspects there have been significant changes since Wayne Thomas sold Fern Hill to the Hill International Group, and not all for the better. Further changes will flow in the wake of Hill International's major financial troubles. Exports to the US, Brazil, the UK, Switzerland, Hong Kong, Japan, Fiji, Singapore and New Zealand.

🐌 fire gully ★★★★

Metricup Road, Wilyabrup, WA 6280 **region** Margaret River
phone (08) 9755 6220 **fax** (08) 9755 6308 **open** By appointment
winemaker Dr Michael Peterkin **production** 5000 **est.** 1988
product range ($22–39 R) Semillon, Sauvignon Blanc Semillon, Merlot, Cabernet Sauvignon Merlot, Cabernet Sauvignon.
summary The Fire Gully vineyard has been established on what was first a dairy and then a beef farm. A 15-acre lake was created in the gully ravaged by bushfires and that gave the property its name. The vineyard was planted in 1998. In 1998 Mike Peterkin of Pierro purchased the property; he now manages the vineyard in conjunction with former owners Ellis and Margaret Butcher. He regards the Fire Gully wines as entirely separate from those of Pierro, being estate-grown, with just under 9 hectares planted to cabernet sauvignon, merlot, shiraz, semillon, sauvignon blanc, chardonnay and viognier. Exports to the US, Europe and Asia.

Fire Gully Semillon

▼▼▼▼▽ **2001** Light green-yellow; a light, crisp and fine bouquet with a mix of spice and herbs is followed by a palate with good life, freshness and length, finishing with excellent acidity. **rating:** 93

best drinking 2003–2008 **best vintages** '00, '01 **drink with** Marinated baby octopus • $24

Fire Gully Sauvignon Blanc Semillon

▼▼▼▼ **2001** Light to medium yellow-green; a light mix of gooseberry and mineral on the bouquet leads into a wine that is well-weighted on the mid-palate, but which softens markedly on the finish. **rating:** 85

best drinking 2001–2002 **best vintages** '00 **drink with** Grilled scampi • $21

five oaks vineyard ★★★☆

60 Aitken Road, Seville, Vic 3139 **region** Yarra Valley
phone (03) 5964 3704 **fax** (03) 5964 3064 **open** Weekends and public holidays 10–5 and by appointment
winemaker Wally Zuk **production** 2000 **est.** 1997
product range ($15–35 CD) Riesling, Chardonnay, Merlot, Cabernet Sauvignon Merlot, SGS Cabernet Sauvignon.
summary Wally and Judy Zuk purchased the Five Oaks Vineyard from Oakridge Estate, which has moved to its new premises on the other side of the Yarra Valley. Wally Zuk, with a background in nuclear physics, has completed his Wine Science degree at Charles Sturt University. He has now retired from the nuclear science world and is devoting himself (with help from his wife Judy) to running Five Oaks.

Five Oaks Merlot

▼▼▼▽ **2000** Light to medium red-purple; the bouquet is slanted towards the minty/leafy end of the spectrum, but some savoury/spicy red berry fruit comes through on the palate; fine tannins help create the correct structure. **rating:** 84

best drinking 2004–2008 **best vintages** NA **drink with** Braised veal • $25

Five Oaks Vineyard Cabernet Sauvignon

▼▼▼▼ **2000** Medium red-purple; aromatic blackcurrant and spice on the bouquet lead into a palate with gentle, redcurrant/cassis fruit, a touch of chocolate, fine tannins and nicely judged oak. **rating:** 88

best drinking 2004–2010 **best vintages** '00 **drink with** Roast beef • $23

572 richmond road ★★★☆

572 Richmond Road, Cambridge, Tas 7170 (postal 44 Lambert Street, Kangaroo Point, Qld 4169) **region** Southern Tasmania
phone 0419 878 023 **fax** (07) 3391 4565 **open** At Craigow Fri–Sun 10–5

winemaker Andrew Hood, Julian Alcorso (Contract) **production** 200 **est.** 1994
product range ($20.50–23.50 ML) Riesling, Gewürztraminer, Chardonnay.
summary It hardly needs to be said that 572 Richmond Road is both the address and the name of the vineyard. It is owned by John and Sue Carney, medical professionals, and is adjacent to Andrew Hood's winery; it is part of a spectacular vineyard development that is made up of various ownerships, all situated close to the winery.

572 Richmond Road Riesling

▼▼▼▽ **2001** Medium yellow-green; the bouquet is quite rich and full, with tropical fruit characters which come through on the surprisingly soft and broad palate; paradoxically, notwithstanding all the exotic fruit, the wine has a somewhat weak structure.   **rating:** 84

best drinking 2002–2003 **best vintages** NA **drink with** Mussels • $20.50

572 Richmond Road Pinot Noir

▼▼▼▼ **2000** Medium purple-red; a clean bouquet with pleasant plum fruit and hints of spice, the palate with plummy fruit at its core, but a higher than desirable level of acidity; this may well sort itself out with further time in bottle.   **rating:** 87

best drinking 2003–2008 **best vintages** NA **drink with** Veal kidneys • NA

flinders bay ★★★☆

Davis Road, Witchcliffe, WA 6286 **region** Margaret River
phone (08) 9757 6281 **fax** (08) 9757 6353 **open** Not
winemaker Contract **production** 15 000 **est.** 1995
product range ($15–22 R) Pericles Sauvignon Blanc Semillon, Verdelho, Chardonnay, Shiraz, Merlot, Agincourt Cabernet Malbec Merlot.
summary Flinders Bay is a joint venture between the Gillespie and Ireland families. The Gillespies have been grape growers and viticultural contractors in the Margaret River region for over 20 years, while Bill and Noel Ireland were very prominent retailers in Sydney from 1979 to 1996. All in all, a potent and synergistic combination. Fifty hectares of vines were planted between 1995 and 1998 at Karridale, an extremely cool subregion (possibly the coolest in WA), with the climate influenced by both the Indian and Southern Oceans. The wines presently being produced are blends of grapes from the northern and central parts of the Margaret River and estate-grown grapes. Ultimately, all of the wines will be estate-produced. They are contract-made at Vasse Felix, which also provides the cellar door facility for Flinders Bay. Exports to the UK and the US.

Flinders Bay Pericles Sauvignon Blanc Semillon

▼▼▼▼ **2001** Light green-yellow; the clean, moderately intense bouquet offers a mix of grass and passionfruit, the fresh palate moving more to lemon and passionfruit, with good length, balance and mouthfeel.   **rating:** 89

best drinking 2001–2003 **best vintages** NA **drink with** Margaret River marron • $16

Flinders Bay Chardonnay

▼▼▼▽ **2000** Light to medium yellow-green; the clean, relatively subdued bouquet with a gentle interplay of fruit and oak is followed by a light nectarine and peach palate; needs greater intensity for higher points.   **rating:** 84

best drinking 2001–2004 **best vintages** NA **drink with** Margaret River marron • $19

Flinders Bay Shiraz

▼▼▼▼ 2000 Youthful, deep purple red; the bouquet is clean, but not complex; on the other hand it has plenty of dark cherry fruit, leading into a smooth, quite supple palate with soft cherry fruit and gentle tannins.   **rating:** 87

best drinking 2002–2006 **best vintages** '99 **drink with** Baby lamb • $22

🍷 fluted cape vineyard ★★★★

28 Groombridge Road, Kettering, Tas 7155 **region** Southern Tasmania
phone (03) 6267 4262 **open** 7 days 10–5
winemaker Andrew Hood **production** 170 **est.** 1993
product range ($12–25 CD) Unwooded Chardonnay, Chardonnay, Pinot Noir.

summary For many years Val Dell was the senior wildlife ranger on the central plateau of Tasmania, his wife Jan running the information centre at Liawenee. I met them there on trout fishing expeditions, staying in one of the park huts. They have now retired to the Huon Valley region, having established 0.25 hectare each of pinot noir and chardonnay overlooking Kettering and Bruny Island, said to be a spectacularly beautiful site, which I wouldn't doubt. The high-quality wines are made for them by Andrew Hood, and are sold from the cellar door, and through Hartzview Cellars in Gardners Bay.

Fluted Cape Vineyard Chardonnay

TTTT **2000** Light to medium yellow-green; fragrant grapefruit and stone fruit aromas lead into a crisp, relatively light but lively palate with good length and which clearly reflects the cool growing conditions.
rating: 87

best drinking 2001–2004 **best vintages** NA **drink with** Cold seafood • $18

Fluted Cape Vineyard Pinot Noir

TTTT **2000** Medium purple-red; the clean bouquet is not particularly expressive at first blush, but some juicy, plummy fruit aromas can be teased out; the palate offers similar plummy fruit, then a tweak of acidity on the finish.
rating: 85

TTTT **1999** Medium red-purple; the moderately intense, clean bouquet has a mix of plum and more savoury notes, with just a whisper of oak. Sweet, plummy/spicy fruit is supported by fine tannins on the palate to produce a totally enjoyable wine from a particularly good vintage.
rating: 88

best drinking 2002–2005 **best vintages** '99 **drink with** Veal kidneys • $23

fonty's pool vineyards ★★★★

c/o Cape Mentelle Vineyards, PO Box 11, Margaret River, WA 6285 **region** Manjimup
phone (08) 9757 3266 **fax** (08) 9757 3233 **open** Not
winemaker Eloise Jarvis (Cape Mentelle) **production** 5000 **est.** 1998
product range ($21–25 R) Chardonnay, Pinot Noir, Shiraz.
summary The Fonty's Pool vineyards are part of the original farm owned by pioneer settler Archie Fontanini, who was granted land by the government in 1907. In the early 1920s a large dam was created to provide water for the intensive vegetable farming which was part of the farming activities. The dam became known as Fonty's Pool and to this day remains a famous local landmark and recreational facility. The first grapes were planted in 1989, and the vineyard is now one of the region's largest, supplying grapes to a number of leading WA wineries. Only a small part of the production is used for Fonty's Pool; the wines are made at Cape Mentelle by Eloise Jarvis, who is part of the Cape Mentelle winemaking team.

Fonty's Pool Chardonnay

TTTT **2000** Light to medium yellow-green; a complex bouquet with smoky/toasty barrel-ferment dominant, but not totally obscuring the melon/grapefruit notes. The palate has crisp, citrussy fruit and lively acidity on the finish, helping subdue the oak. Seems to be in a different style from the '99.
rating: 88

best drinking 2003–2007 **best vintages** NA **drink with** Oyster soup • $20.75

Fonty's Pool Pinot Noir

TTTT **2000** Medium red-purple; the bouquet has a slightly savoury bacon edge, likely contributed (at least in part) by the oak. The medium-bodied palate has pleasant plum and black cherry fruit, but lacks intensity and convincing structure.
rating: 85

best drinking 2002–2005 **best vintages** NA **drink with** Coq au vin • $24.80

Fonty's Pool Shiraz

TTTTT **2000** Bright but deep red-purple; complex spice, leather, licorice and plum fruit on the bouquet, then a finely structured and distinguished palate, with dark plum fruit, spice, and fine, ripe tannins. A particularly elegant cool-climate style, with complexity to burn.
rating: 94

best drinking 2004–2009 **best vintages** '00 **drink with** Cassoulet • $20.75

forest hill vineyard ★★★★

Muirs Highway, Mount Barker, WA 6324 **region** Great Southern
phone (08) 9284 2825 **fax** (08) 9284 2835 **open** Not
winemaker Gordon Parker **production** 15 000 **est.** 1966
product range ($15–20 CD) Riesling, Sauvignon Blanc Semillon, Chardonnay, Shiraz, Cabernet Sauvignon.

summary This is one of the oldest 'new' winemaking operations in WA, and was the site of the first grape plantings for the Great Southern region in 1966, on a farming property owned by the Pearce family. The Forest Hill brand became well known, aided by the fact that a 1975 Riesling made by Sandalford from Forest Hill grapes won nine trophies in national wine shows. In 1989 the property was acquired by Heytesbury Holdings (Janet Holmes à Court) as part of the Vasse Felix operation, and most of the grapes were used in the Vasse Felix wines. The only Forest Hill wines were a Riesling and a Cabernet Sauvignon, produced in small quantities and largely sold locally. In 1997 the property was acquired by interests associated with Perth stockbroker Tim Lyons, and a programme of renovation and expansion of the vineyards commenced. A winery is under construction near the town of Denmark and will be completed in time for the 2003 vintage.

Forest Hill Vineyard Riesling

▼▼▼▼▽ **2001** Light to medium yellow-green; intense herb, mineral and slate aromas foretell a powerful, intense, mouthfilling wine which, despite all the power, avoids phenolic toughness. **rating:** 90

best drinking 2003–2008 **best vintages** '01 **drink with** Summer salad • $15

Forest Hill Vineyard Sauvignon Blanc Semillon

▼▼▼▼▽ **2001** Light green-yellow; a clean, fragrant bouquet with herb and lemon blossom aromatics leads into a long, clean palate with good mouthfeel and balance. Outstanding value. **rating:** 92

best drinking 2002–2004 **best vintages** NA **drink with** Delicate seafood • $15

Forest Hill Vineyard Chardonnay

▼▼▼▼ **2000** Medium yellow-green; an extremely complex bouquet with cool-grown, citrussy, almost vegetal, fruit is followed by a similarly complex, cool-grown mouthfeel and flavour. **rating:** 88

best drinking 2002–2006 **best vintages** '99 **drink with** Grilled marron • $15

Forest Hill Vineyard Cabernet Sauvignon

▼▼▼▼ **1999** Medium to full red-purple; the blackberry, earth and cassis fruit of the bouquet has some leafy lift, the same assemblage coming through on the mid-palate, but then a particularly pleasing finish with slippery tannins. **rating:** 88

best drinking 2003–2009 **best vintages** NA **drink with** Rack of lamb • $20

fox creek wines ★★★★

Malpas Road, Willunga, SA 5172 **region** McLaren Vale
phone (08) 8556 2403 **fax** (08) 8556 2104 **open** 7 days 11–5
winemaker Daniel Hills, Tony Walker **production** 35 000 **est.** 1995
product range ($15.50–36 CD) Verdelho, Semillon Sauvignon Blanc, Sauvignon Blanc, Chardonnay, Vixen Sparkling Shiraz Cabernet Franc, Grenache Shiraz, Short Row Shiraz, Reserve Shiraz, Merlot, JSM Shiraz Cabernets, Duet Cabernet Merlot, Reserve Cabernet Sauvignon.
summary Fox Creek has made a major impact since coming on-stream late in 1995. It is the venture of a group of distinguished Adelaide doctors (three of them professors), with particular input from the Watts family, which established the vineyard back in 1985. The Reserve red wines, and especially the Reserve Shiraz, are outstanding, and have enjoyed considerable show success. As well as comprehensive distribution throughout Australia, the wines are exported to the UK, the US, Canada, Germany, Switzerland, Italy, France, New Zealand, Thailand and Hong Kong.

Fox Creek Verdelho

▼▼▼▼ **2001** Light green-yellow; a quite intense and flowery, blossom-like bouquet is followed by a palate with plenty of flavour, helped by a touch of sweetness. A Verdelho with this much character is a rare beast. **rating:** 86

best drinking 2001–2003 **best vintages** NA **drink with** Pasta • $17

Fox Creek Reserve Shiraz

▼▼▼▼ **2000** Medium to full red-purple; quite powerful savoury, dark berry fruit on the bouquet is followed by a palate with abundant dark berry, chocolate and blackberry flavours, restrained oak and good tannins. **rating:** 88

▼▼▼▼▽ **1999** Strong red-purple; the bouquet offers an abundance of sweet, ripe berry fruit, the palate ultra-typical of McLaren Vale: rich, with lots of chunky dark chocolate fruit in a big, thick frame. **rating:** 92

best drinking 2004–2010 **best vintages** '96, '98, '99 **drink with** Grilled beef • $36

Fox Creek Short Row Shiraz

▼▼▼▼ 2000 Medium to full red-purple; ripe, blackcurrant/cherry fruit aromas are followed by a solid, black cherry palate with moderate length and restrained oak. **rating:** 86

best drinking 2003–2008 **best vintages** NA **drink with** Beef spare ribs • $26

Fox Creek JSM Shiraz Cabernet

▼▼▼▼ 2000 Medium to full red-purple; the first waft of the bouquet is laden with chippy/stavey oak, but the palate is quite luscious, offering much more sweet, chocolatey fruit, which pushes the oak off centre stage. **rating:** 87

best drinking 2003–2008 **best vintages** '99 **drink with** Rib of beef • $23

Fox Creek Reserve Merlot

▼▼▼▼ 2000 Medium red-purple; a solid, savoury bouquet with some earth and chocolate, then a palate with ripe, dark fruits, chocolate and vanilla; a nice dry red, but not a distinctive Merlot. **rating:** 87

best drinking 2004–2009 **best vintages** NA **drink with** White Rocks veal • $36

Fox Creek Duet Cabernet Merlot

▼▼▼▼ 2000 Medium to full red-purple; dusty vanillin oak and ripe berry fruit do indeed sing a duet on the bouquet; on the palate, the fruit sings the melody, with luscious, dark berry flavours, the overall tannin and extract kept under control. **rating:** 88

best drinking 2004–2009 **best vintages** NA **drink with** Venison • $19

Fox Creek Reserve Cabernet Sauvignon

▼▼▼▼ 2000 Medium to full red-purple; rich, ripe blackberry and cassis aromas are mirrored in the palate, which does, however, dip slightly in the middle, rising again with lingering tannins and subtle oak on the finish. **rating:** 87

best drinking 2005–2010 **best vintages** '96, '97 **drink with** Game pie • $36

françois jacquard ★★★☆

14 Neil Street, Osborne Park, WA 6017 **region** Perth Hills
phone (08) 9380 9199 **fax** (08) 9380 9199 **open** Not
winemaker François Jacquard **production** 2000 **est.** 1997
product range ($17–42 R) Long Jetty Seafood Reserve Semillon Sauvignon Blanc; Terra Dura Millennium Collection Viognier, Reserve Collection Chardonnay, Millennium Collection Shiraz, De Beaux Vineyards Shiraz Viognier; Duyfken 1606 Replica Cabernet Sauvignon.
summary François (Franky) Jacquard graduated from Dijon University in 1983. He worked that vintage as a cellar hand at Domaine Dujac, then came to Australia for Bannockburn in 1985. Between then and 1992 he worked in both the northern and southern hemispheres, before moving back to become chief winemaker at Chittering Estate in the Perth Hills in 1992, a position he held until 1997 when he established his own brand. He does not have vineyards of his own, leasing one in the Chittering Valley, and having a long-term purchase arrangement with another. He now makes the wines at the new Sitella Winery in the Swan Valley. As Franky Jacquard himself recognises, the style of his wines is most definitely not mainstream Australian. He is much more interested in texture and longevity than primary fruit flavour, and is quite relaxed about a degree of controlled oxidation in his white winemaking.

François Jacquard Terra Dura Viognier

▼▼▼▽ 1999 Medium yellow-green; a solid bouquet, with some hints of dried fruits, but not particularly aromatic, is followed by a full-bodied dry white wine which is not noticeably varietal, but certainly has impact. Only 5000 bottles made. **rating:** 84

best drinking 2001–2003 **best vintages** NA **drink with** Marron • $25

François Jacquard Terra Dura Reserve Chardonnay

▼▼▼▼ 1994 Glowing yellow-gold; a honeyed, buttery bouquet with fully browned toast aromas leads into a big, slightly old-fashioned, White Burgundy style, powered by flavour more than finesse. **rating:** 85

best drinking 2001–2004 **best vintages** NA **drink with** Deep sea shrimp • $32

François Jacquard Terra Dura Shiraz

▼▼▼▽ 1999 Medium to full red-purple; solid, dark berry/blackberry fruit with some slightly aldehydic/savoury edges to the bouquet are followed by a big, chunky, chocolatey palate, with a slightly grippy finish. **rating:** 84

best drinking 2003–2008 **best vintages** NA **drink with** Venison • $22

frankland estate ★★★★

Frankland Road, Frankland, WA 6396 **region** Great Southern
phone (08) 9855 1544 **fax** (08) 9855 1549 **open** By appointment
winemaker Barrie Smith, Judi Cullam **production** 15 000 **est.** 1988
product range ($21.50–33.50 R) Under the Isolation Ridge label are Riesling, Chardonnay, Shiraz, Cabernet Sauvignon; Olmo's Reward (Bordeaux-blend) is the flagbearer; also Rivermist Riesling.
summary A significant Frankland River operation, situated on a large sheep property owned by Barrie Smith and Judi Cullam. The 29-hectare vineyard has been established progressively since 1988, and a winery was built on the site for the 1993 vintage. The Riesling, Isolation Ridge and Olmo's Reward are consistent in style, and all the wines are energetically promoted and marketed by Judi Cullam, especially the Riesling. Frankland Estate has held several important International Riesling tastings and seminars over recent years. Exports to the US, Canada, the UK, Belgium, Switzerland, Denmark, Singapore and Japan.

Frankland Estate Isolation Ridge Riesling

TTTTT 2001 Light straw-green; a solid mix of lime and lemon on the one hand, and mineral talc on the other, drives the bouquet; the powerful palate is firm and rich, with a tight, lingering finish. Very much a return to previous form. **rating:** 91

best drinking 2003–2008 **best vintages** '92, '93, '94, '96, '98, '01 **drink with** Antipasto • $21.50

Frankland Estate Rivermist Riesling

TTTT 2001 Light green-yellow; a distinctly minerally bouquet with underlying hints of lime, the palate with lighter fruit, some mineral/talc, but doesn't power through to the finish. **rating:** 87

best drinking 2002–2005 **best vintages** NA **drink with** Trout mousse • $15

Frankland Estate Isolation Ridge Shiraz

TTTT 1999 Medium red-purple; the aromas of the bouquet range through savoury, earthy and olive, not at all typical of Shiraz. The palate offers the same spectrum of flavours in a rather austere, food style frame. How much of these characters come from the vineyard, and how much from the winery is not easy to determine, but the net result is far from unpleasant. **rating:** 85

best drinking 2003–2008 **best vintages** '92, '93, '97 **drink with** Braised lamb shanks • $27

Frankland Estate Isolation Ridge Cabernet Sauvignon

TTTT 1999 Medium red-purple; the bouquet offers a mix of blackcurrant and blackberry, with oak very much in the background; the palate opens with powerful, deep blackberry fruit then moves through to moderately pervasive, lingering tannins on the finish. Once again, the best for some years. **rating:** 88

best drinking 2004–2009 **best vintages** NA **drink with** Rich lamb casserole • $23.50

🍷 freshwater point NR

Freshwater Point, Legana, Tas 7277 **region** Northern Tasmania
phone (03) 6327 4170 **open** Not
winemaker Julian Alcorso **production** 100 **est.** 1997
product range ($11 ML) Chardonnay, Pinot Noir, Cabernet Sauvignon.
summary Freshwater Point is a parallel operation to Waterton Estate, in this instance with 900 vines of pinot noir, cabernet sauvignon and chardonnay. A syndicate of 4 operates the vineyard, but there is a bed and breakfast on-site which sells whatever wine is left over.

freycinet ★★★★★

15919 Tasman Highway via Bicheno, Tas 7215 **region** Southern Tasmania
phone (03) 6257 8574 **fax** (03) 6257 8454 **open** Mon–Fri 9–5, weekends 10–5
winemaker Claudio Radenti, Lindy Bull **production** 7000 **est.** 1980
product range ($20–50 CD) Riesling, Chardonnay, Radenti (Mèthode Champenoise), Pinot Noir, Cabernet Merlot.
summary The original 9-hectare Freycinet vineyards are beautifully situated on the sloping hillsides of a small valley. The soils are podsol and decaying granite with a friable clay subsoil, and the combination of aspect, slope, soil and heat summation produces red grapes of unusual depth of colour and ripe flavours. One of Australia's foremost producers of Pinot Noir, with a wholly enviable track record of consistency – rare with such a temperamental variety.

Freycinet Riesling

TTTTY 2001 Light straw-yellow; a clean, crisp, minerally bouquet, then a well-balanced, apple, lime and mineral-flavoured palate, which is still in its infancy, and will be sustained for many years by its acidity.

rating: 92

best drinking 2004–2011 **best vintages** '00, '01 **drink with** Seared scallops • $21

Freycinet Chardonnay

TTTTY 2000 Light to medium yellow-green; a complex mix of melon and cashew on the bouquet reflects skilled oak handling; the palate equally so, with an appealing array of flavours and good texture. **rating:** 90

best drinking 2002–2006 **best vintages** '93, '94, '95, '96, '98, '99, '00 **drink with** Abalone • $32

Freycinet Pinot Noir

TTTTT 2000 Fragrant plum spice and herb aromas, then a vibrant palate, intense, complex and driven by sappy, plum and cherry pip fruit, carrying through powerfully to a long and lingering finish. Oak a sideline player. This note was not made from the 2002 Tasmanian Wines Show, where the wine was strangely off-song. **rating:** 95

best drinking 2002–2007 **best vintages** '91, '92, '94, '95, '96, '97, '98, '99, '00 **drink with** Jugged hare • $50

frog rock ★★★☆

Cassilis Road, Mudgee, NSW 2850 **region** Mudgee
phone (02) 6372 2408 **fax** (02) 6372 6924 **open** 7 days 11–4
winemaker Simon Gilbert, David Lowe (Contract) **production** 8000 **est.** 1973
product range ($15–40 ML) Chardonnay, Premium Chardonnay, Rosé, Old Vine Shiraz, Premium Shiraz Cabernet, Chambourcin, Merlot, Old Vine Cabernet Sauvignon.
summary Frog Rock is the former Tallara Vineyard, established almost 30 years ago by leading Sydney chartered accountant Rick Turner. There are now 60 hectares of vineyard, with 22 hectares each of shiraz and cabernet sauvignon, and much smaller plantings of chardonnay, semillon, merlot, petit verdot and chambourcin. The wines are exported to the UK, the US and Hong Kong.

fyffe field ★★★☆

RMB 4243, Murray Valley Highway, Yarrawonga, Vic 3730 **region** Goulburn Valley
phone (03) 5748 4282 **fax** (03) 5748 4284 **open** 7 days 10–5
winemaker Contract **production** 1300 **est.** 1993
product range ($10–16 CD) Diamond White, Byramine White, Verdelho, Byramine Red, Byramine Classic Red, Merlot, Shiraz, Tokay, Muscat, Tawny Snort.
summary Fyffe Field has been established by Graeme and Liz Diamond near the Murray River, between Cobram and Yarrawonga, in a mudbrick and leadlight tasting room opposite a historic homestead. A highlight is the ornamental pig collection, a display set up long before Babe was born.

Fyffe Field Shiraz

TTTT 2000 Medium to full red-purple; there are slightly spicy, savoury edges to the dark plum and berry fruit of the bouquet, and also good flavour on entry into the mouth. The wine doesn't quite carry through on the finish, but is an impressive wine for the region. **rating:** 87

best drinking 2003–2008 **best vintages** NA **drink with** Braised ox tail • $14

Fyffe Field Byramine Classic Red

TTTT 2000 Medium red-purple; the blend of Merlot, Cabernet Sauvignon and Petit Verdot (50/25/25) is immediately obvious in the mix of berry and earth on the clean bouquet; there is surprising character and sweetness to the fruit on the palate. Another quite good result. **rating:** 86

best drinking 2003–2007 **best vintages** NA **drink with** Moroccan lamb • $15.50

gabriel's paddocks vineyard NR

Deasys Road, Pokolbin, NSW 2320 **region** Lower Hunter Valley
phone (02) 4998 7650 **fax** (02) 4998 7603 **open** Thurs–Mon 9–5
winemaker Contract **production** NA **est.** 1979
product range ($14–20 ML) Chenin Blanc, Chardonnay, Pinot Noir, Shiraz, Cabernet Merlot.
summary Formerly Sutherlands Wines, Gabriel's Paddocks is as much about general tourism and small conference accommodation as it is about wine production, with two separate buildings able to accommodate more than 20 people. The vineyards are planted to chardonnay, chenin blanc, pinot noir, merlot, shiraz and cabernet sauvignon; the wines from these varieties are all contract-made.

galafrey ★★★☆

Quangellup Road, Mount Barker, WA 6324 **region** Great Southern
phone (08) 9851 2022 **fax** (08) 9851 2324 **open** 7 days 10–5
winemaker Ian Tyrer **production** 12 000 **est.** 1977
product range ($12–50 CD) Riesling, Muller, Art Label Semillon Sauvignon Blanc, Chardonnay, Unoaked Chardonnay, Art Label Premium Dry White, Late Harvest, Reserve Botrytis Riesling, Pinot Noir, Shiraz, Art Label Shiraz, Art Label Premium Dry Red, Cabernet Sauvignon, Reserve Cabernet Sauvignon, Tawny Port.
summary Relocated to a new purpose-built but utilitarian winery after previously inhabiting the exotic surrounds of the old Albany wool store, Galafrey makes wines with plenty of robust, if not rustic, character, drawing grapes in the main from nearly 13 hectares of estate plantings at Mount Barker. Exports to the Netherlands, Switzerland, Canada and Japan. Quality is on the rise again after a period of uncertainty.

Galafrey Art Label Semillon Sauvignon Blanc

TTTY 2000 Medium yellow-green; the wine is showing solid, secondary aromas and perhaps a hint of botrytis; the powerful palate cloys slightly, making it feel fractionally heavy in the mouth. The painting on the label is by Ian Tyrer's daughter, Kim, and works well. **rating:** 83

best drinking 2002–2003 **best vintages** NA **drink with** Sweet and sour pork • $14

Galafrey Shiraz

TTTT 1999 Medium red-purple; the moderately intense, clean and quite fragrant bouquet has berry/cherry fruit, the light to medium-bodied palate corresponding precisely with its fresh berry fruit and subtle oak. **rating:** 86
TTTT 1998 Medium red-purple; intense cherry/cherry essence and plum aromas on the bouquet are followed by a smooth, clean palate with cherry and mint-flavoured fruit, and nice mouthfeel. **rating:** 89

best drinking 2004–2008 **best vintages** '85, '90, '91, '93, '96, '98 **drink with** Washed rind cheese • $22

Galafrey Art Label Shiraz

TTTT 2000 Medium red-purple; the moderately intense bouquet has a mix of spicy/savoury/berry aromas; the light to medium-bodied palate has fresh red berry fruit, fine tannins and minimal oak, all adding up to easy drinking. Well priced. **rating:** 85

best drinking 2002–2003 **best vintages** NA **drink with** Pizza • $15

galah wine ★★★☆

Tregarthen Road, Ashton, SA 5137 **region** Adelaide Hills
phone (08) 8390 1243 **fax** (08) 8390 1243 **open** Available at Ashton Hills
winemaker Stephen George **production** 1000 **est.** 1986
product range ($25–42 ML) SE Aust Semillon Chardonnay, Brut, Sparkling Red, McLaren Vale Cabernet Shiraz, Clare Valley Cabernet Malbec Shiraz, Clare Valley Shiraz, Cabernet Sauvignon.
summary Over the years, Stephen George has built up a network of contacts across South Australia, from which he gains some very high-quality small parcels of grapes or wine for the Galah label. These are all sold direct at extremely low prices for the quality. Exports to the UK and the US.

Galah Wine Sparkling Red

TTTT 1996 Medium red, with just a touch of purple remaining; good mousse. The complex, spicy bouquet leads into a multi-flavoured palate ranging through earth, spice and berry; the dosage is a little high for my taste, but will appeal to others. **rating:** 87

best drinking 2002–2003 **best vintages** NA **drink with** Borscht • $42

Galah Cabernet Sauvignon

TTTT 1999 Medium red-purple; a powerful bouquet with some slightly jammy fruit and a whiff of hay. The palate is massively structured and tannic; truly formidable, and requiring greater longevity than I can look forward to. **rating:** 87

best drinking 2009–2019 **best vintages** NA **drink with** Leave it in the cellar • $25

gallagher estate ★★★☆

Dog Trap Road, Murrumbateman, NSW 2582 **region** Canberra District
phone (02) 6254 9957 **fax** (02) 6254 9957 **open** Not
winemaker Greg Gallagher **production** 2500 **est.** 1995
product range ($14–20 R) Chardonnay, Shiraz.

summary Greg Gallagher was senior winemaker at Taltarni for 20 years, where he worked with Dominique Portet. He began planning a change of career at much the same time as did Dominique, and began the establishment of a small vineyard at Murrumbateman in 1995, planting a little over 1 hectare each of chardonnay and shiraz. He has now moved to the region with his family, his major job at the present being winemaker at the Charles Sturt University Winery, playing a central role in training the winemakers of tomorrow. Retail distribution through Yarra Valley Wine Consultants in Vic and NSW, and Oak Barrel Wines in Canberra.

Gallagher Estate Chardonnay

TTTT 2001 Very pale colour; a light, crisp and fresh citrus-toned bouquet is followed by a light-bodied, fresh and citrussy palate, somewhat akin to a Chardonnay Sauvignon Blanc cross. Style is consistent with prior vintages. **rating: 84**

best drinking 2002–2004 best vintages NA drink with Light seafood • $18

Gallagher Estate Bin 16 Shiraz

TTTT 2000 Medium red, with diminished purple hues and already distinctly advanced; the bouquet has ripe, sweet, prune and chocolate fruit aromatics, augmented by a touch of vanilla, characters which flow through on the palate, closing with moderate tannins. **rating: 85**

best drinking 2002–2005 best vintages NA drink with Shoulder of lamb • $17.50

galli estate ★★★★☆

316 Tarletons Road, Rockbank, Vic 3335 **region** Sunbury
phone (03) 9747 1817 **fax** (03) 9747 1630 **open** 7 days 11–5
winemaker Stephen Phillips **production** 10 000 **est.** 1997
product range ($9–24 R) Sauvignon Blanc Semillon, Semillon Sauvignon Blanc, Pinot Grigio, Chardonnay, Pinot Noir, Shiraz, Cabernet Sauvignon Franc Merlot, Sangiovese, Cabernet Sauvignon.
summary Galli Estate may be a newcomer to the scene, but it is a substantial one. Lorenzo and Pam Galli have planted 32 hectares of vineyard, the lion's share to cabernet sauvignon and shiraz, but with 1–2 hectares each of semillon, sauvignon blanc, merlot, pinot noir, cabernet franc, chardonnay and pinot grigio. A large underground cellar has been constructed; already 50 metres long, it is to be extended in the future. A cellar door sales, bistro and administration centre was completed in March 2002; former Coldstream Hills winemaker Stephen Phillips is now in charge.

Galli Estate Shiraz

TTTTT 2000 Dense red-purple; an exceptionally powerful and complex bouquet of black fruits, game, spice, leather and licorice is followed by a richly succulent and layered palate, with a similar suite of complex flavours, finishing with soft tannins. **rating: 94**

best drinking 2004–2014 best vintages '00 drink with Rich casserole • $24

Galli Estate Cabernet Sauvignon

TTTT 2000 Full red-purple; the dense blackberry/blackcurrant bouquet shows fully ripe fruit, as does the palate, slightly unbalanced as yet by the persistent, savoury tannins. The wine has good length and good oak handling, and simply needs time for those tannins to soften. **rating: 90**

best drinking 2005–2012 best vintages NA drink with Leave it in the cellar • $24

gapsted wines ★★★★

Great Alpine Road, Gapsted, Vic 3737 **region** King Valley
phone (03) 5751 1383 **fax** (03) 5751 1368 **open** 7 days 10–5
winemaker Michael Cope-Williams, Shayne Cunningham **production** 14 000 **est.** 1997
product range ($17–30 ML) Ballerina Canopy range of Sauvignon Blanc, Chardonnay, Shiraz, Durif, Merlot, Cabernet Franc, Cabernet Sauvignon; Limited Release Pinot Grigio, Late Harvest Riesling, Malbec, Petit Manseng and Saperavi; Tutu Chardonnay Verdelho, Cabernet Merlot.
summary Gapsted is the premier brand of the Victorian Alps Wine Co., the latter primarily a contract-crush facility which processes grapes for 48 growers in the Alpine Valleys. The estate plantings total 10 hectares of shiraz, cabernet sauvignon, petit verdot and merlot, but the Gapsted wines come both from these estate plantings and from contract-grown fruit. All incorporate the 'ballerina canopy' tag, a reference to the open nature of this particular training method, which is ideally suited to these regions.

Gapsted Ballerina Canopy Sauvignon Blanc

▼▼▼▼▽ 2001 Light to medium green-yellow; the moderately intense and clean bouquet has attractive gooseberry fruit, the palate not only living up to but exceeding the expectations created by the bouquet, with good varietal character and length; a particularly impressive finish. Wow. Where did this come from?

rating: 92

best drinking 2002–2003 **best vintages** '01 **drink with** Salmon and asparagus terrine • $18

Gapsted Ballerina Canopy Durif

▼▼▼▼ 1999 Medium red-purple; moderately intense, fresh dark berry and spice aromas lead into a palate with lots of varietal grip and power, featuring dark fruit and bitter chocolate; wholly appropriate tannins to close.

rating: 87

best drinking 2005–2012 **best vintages** '98 **drink with** Braised ox cheek • $30

Gapsted Limited Release Saperavi

▼▼▼▼ NV Medium purple-red; a complex mix of red berry fruit, spice, mint and oak leads into a powerful, intense and concentrated palate with dark berry and spice fruit in a tangy mould, offset by some vanilla oak. The acidity leaves the wine with a slightly angular/sharp profile, but it is nonetheless full of interest.

rating: 86

best drinking 2001–2006 **best vintages** NA **drink with** Game • $25

Gapsted Ballerina Canopy Cabernet Franc

▼▼▼▼ 1999 Light to medium red-purple, holding its hue well; the fragrant bouquet has an array of savoury/cedary/leafy/spicy aromas, then a palate with dark fruit flavours, a touch of chocolate and unexpected tannins fortifying the finish. Plenty going on here with a relatively unfashionable variety.

rating: 88

best drinking 2003–2007 **best vintages** NA **drink with** Roast veal • $20

Gapsted Ballerina Canopy Merlot

▼▼▼▼ 1999 Medium red-purple; the moderately intense bouquet has a range of leafy/savoury/spice/tobacco aromas, all of which are (to me at least) varietal. The palate has similar pleasantly savoury fruit flavours, finishing with soft, fine tannins.

rating: 85

best drinking 2002–2005 **best vintages** '98 **drink with** Grilled marinated lamb fillets • $20

Gapsted Limited Release Malbec

▼▼▼▼ 1999 Medium red-purple; attractive cedary/plummy/spicy/jammy varietal aromas flow into the light to medium-bodied palate, all adding up to a drink-now style.

rating: 85

best drinking 2001–2002 **best vintages** NA **drink with** Ravioli • $20

Gapsted Tutu Cabernet Merlot

▼▼▼▼ 1999 Medium red-purple; the bouquet ranges through some leafy/gamey canopy characters, but also offers dark fruit aromas; the palate throws off the uncertainty of the bouquet, with red and blackcurrant fruit, and quite ripe tannins.

rating: 85

best drinking 2002–2005 **best vintages** NA **drink with** Pizza • $14

garbin estate ★★★

209 Toodyay Road, Middle Swan, WA 6056 **region** Swan District
phone (08) 9274 1747 **fax** (08) 9274 1747 **open** 7 days 10.30–5.30
winemaker Peter Garbin **production** 3000 **est.** 1956
product range ($14–19 CD) Chenin Blanc, Chardonnay, Unwooded Chardonnay, Shiraz, Merlot, Cabernet Merlot, Dessert Wine, Ruby Port.
summary Peter Garbin, winemaker by weekend and design draftsman by week, decided in 1990 that he would significantly upgrade the bulk fortified winemaking business commenced by his father in 1956. The vineyards have been replanted, the winery re-equipped, and the first of the new generation wines was produced in 1994. The wines have since received significant critical acclaim, both locally and nationally.

Garbin Estate Chenin Blanc

▼▼▼▽ 2001 Light green-yellow; touches of mineral and lemon are evident on an aromatic bouquet; the palate balancing is elevated by residual sugar and crisp acidity, producing a dead-set cellar-door style.

rating: 83

best drinking 2001–2003 **best vintages** NA **drink with** Summer salad • $14

Garbin Estate Chardonnay

ŸŸŸŸ 2001 Light green-yellow; a youthful, citrussy bouquet with just the faintest touch of oak is followed by a fresh, crisp, slightly lemony palate, with some CO_2 showing (and likely to help the wine age).**rating: 84**

best drinking 2001–2003 **best vintages** NA **drink with** Tiger prawns • $17

garden gully vineyards ★★★★

Western Highway, Great Western, Vic 3377 **region** Grampians
phone (03) 5356 2400 **fax** (03) 5356 2400 **open** Mon–Fri 10.30–5.30, weekends 10–5.30
winemaker Brian Fletcher, Warren Randall **production** 2000 **est.** 1987
product range ($13–28 CD) Riesling, Shiraz, Sparkling Shiraz, Tokay.
summary Given the skills and local knowledge of the syndicate which owns Garden Gully, it is not surprising that the wines are typically good: an attractive stone cellar-door sales area is an additional reason to stop and pay a visit. Shiraz produced from the 100-year-old vines adjoining the cellar door is especially good. The 4 hectares of shiraz is complemented by 3 hectares of riesling, providing another good wine.

Garden Gully Riesling

ŸŸŸŸ 2001 Light green-yellow; a delicate, floral bouquet with apple blossom and hints of lime is followed by a similarly delicate palate, with fresh, ripe apple surrounded by a minerally structure. As ever, terrific value. **rating: 88**

best drinking 2003–2009 **best vintages** '98, '00, '01 **drink with** Light seafood • $14

Garden Gully Sparkling Shiraz

ŸŸŸŸ 1999 Medium red, with strong mousse; red berries, cherry and strawberry come through on the bouquet, joined by hints of vanilla and licorice on the palate, then a pleasingly dry finish. Produced from 50-year-old shiraz vines. **rating: 89**

best drinking 2002–2020 **best vintages** '98 **drink with** Game soup • $28

garlands ★★★☆

Marmion Street, off Mount Barker Hill Road, Mount Barker, WA 6324 **region** Great Southern
phone (08) 9851 2737 **fax** (08) 9851 2686 **open** Thurs–Sun and public holidays 10–4 or by appointment
winemaker Michael Garland **production** 4000 **est.** 1996
product range ($12–22 CD) Riesling, Sauvignon Blanc Semillon, Chardonnay, Reserve Chardonnay, Shiraz, Merlot, Cabernet Franc; Barker Hill White and Red.
summary Garlands is a partnership between Michael and Julie Garland and their vigneron neighbours, Craig and Caroline Drummond. Michael Garland has come to grape growing and winemaking from a varied background in biological research, computer sales and retail clothing; he is now enrolled at Charles Sturt University for his degree in oenology, but already has significant practical experience behind him. A tiny but highly functional winery was erected prior to the 2000 vintage, the earlier wines being made elsewhere. The winery has a capacity of 150 tonnes, and will continue contract-making for other small producers in the region as well as making the wine from the 6 hectares of estate vineyards planted to cabernet franc, sauvignon blanc, chardonnay, riesling, shiraz and cabernet sauvignon. The Cabernet Franc is the winery specialty.

Garlands Riesling

ŸŸŸŸ 2001 Light to medium yellow-green; subdued mineral and herb aromas are followed by a medium-bodied but sturdy palate; the fruit is still to fully express itself. **rating: 85**

best drinking 2003–2007 **best vintages** NA **drink with** Fish terrine • $15

Garlands Reserve Chardonnay

ŸŸŸŸ 2000 Medium to full yellow-green; the bouquet has a curious nutty/biscuity edge, probably from the oak; nectarine and melon fruit come through strongly on the medium-bodied palate, which has nice balance and mouthfeel. **rating: 86**

best drinking 2002–2004 **best vintages** NA **drink with** Wiener schnitzel • $17

Garlands Shiraz

ŸŸŸŸ 2000 Medium red-purple; the moderately intense bouquet has clean, fresh, but noticeably ripe berry fruit, that ripeness manifesting itself on the powerful, slightly jammy palate, which nonetheless scores well for its abundant flavour. **rating: 86**

best drinking 2004–2009 **best vintages** NA **drink with** Game pie • $20

Garlands Cabernet Franc

YYYY 2000 Medium red-purple; a clean, fragrant and lively bouquet has fresh redcurrant fruit, the lively and tangy palate having red and blackcurrant flavours, fine tannins and subtle oak.   **rating: 88**

best drinking 2003–2008 **best vintages** '96, '98 **drink with** Venison pie • $22

gartelmann hunter estate   ★★★★

Lovedale Road, Lovedale, NSW 2321 **region** Lower Hunter Valley
phone (02) 4930 7113 **fax** (02) 4930 7114 **open** 7 days 10–5
winemaker Monarch Winemaking Services (Contract) **production** 8000 **est.** 1970
product range ($13–26 ML) Semillon, Reserve Semillon, Chenin Blanc, Chardonnay, Semillon Chenin Blanc, Méthode Champenoise, Botrytis Chenin Blanc, Rosé, Shiraz, Diedrich Shiraz, Wilhelm Shiraz, Merlot.
summary In 1996 Jan and Jorg Gartelmann purchased what was previously the George Hunter Estate, established by Sydney restaurateur Oliver Shaul in 1970. They acquired 16 hectares of mature vineyards, producing a limited amount of wine under the Gartelmann label in 1997 and moving to full production in 1998. Diedrich Shiraz is the flagship, and is consistently good. Exports to the UK, Germany and Canada.

Gartelmann Hunter Estate Semillon

YYYY 2001 Light to medium green-yellow; a crisp bouquet with flint, lemon and citrus is followed by a crisp, clean palate showing length rather than depth. Will develop.   **rating: 86**

best drinking 2002–2006 **best vintages** '99 **drink with** Shellfish • $17

Gartelmann Hunter Estate Reserve Semillon

YYYY 2001 Light straw-green; a clean, firm, minerally bouquet is matched by a crisp, flinty palate; very youthful, but well-balanced; simply needs lots of time.   **rating: 88**

best drinking 2004–2009 **best vintages** NA **drink with** Poached mussels • $22

Gartelmann Hunter Estate Chardonnay

YYYY 2000 Light green-yellow; clean melon, nectarine and citrus fruit aromas on the bouquet are barely disturbed by oak; fresh, lively citrussy/nectarine fruit is responsible for the good length of the palate, oak once again playing only a minor role. One of five Chardonnays in the Top 40 of the 2001 New South Wales Wine Awards.   **rating: 89**

best drinking 2001–2003 **best vintages** NA **drink with** Stir-fried abalone • $19

Gartelmann Hunter Estate Diedrich Shiraz

YYYYY 2000 Bright red-purple; a nice balance of dark berry fruit and oak on the bouquet flows into a palate with smooth, deep fruit, featuring excellent tannin and oak management. A very good wine from a very good vintage.   **rating: 93**

best drinking 2005–2015 **best vintages** '99, '00 **drink with** Smoked lamb • $22

Gartelmann Hunter Estate Wilhelm Shiraz

YYYY 2000 Medium red-purple; the bouquet is less intense than the Diedrich, with a mix of red and dark berry fruit; the light to medium-bodied palate has fresh red fruits and subtle oak.   **rating: 86**

best drinking 2003–2008 **best vintages** NA **drink with** Braised beef • $18

gartner family vineyards   ★★★★☆

Sydney Road, Coonawarra, SA 5263 **region** Coonawarra
phone (08) 8736 5011 **fax** (08) 8736 5006 **open** 7 days 10–4
winemaker Peter Douglas **production** 15 000 **est.** 1997
product range ($14–30 CD) Limestone Coast Semillon Chardonnay, Padthaway Chardonnay, Padthaway Shiraz, Limestone Coast Shiraz Merlot, Coonawarra Cabernet Sauvignon.
summary Gartner Family Vineyards is a major entrant on the Australian winemaking scene. The family has been farming in Coonawarra since the 1930s, planting its first vineyard in 1988, and now have more than 400 hectares of vines, including just under 330 hectares of cabernet sauvignon. In addition they are partners in 40 hectares of vineyard in Padthaway, 65 hectares in the Barossa Valley and 80 hectares in Central Victoria. The winery is being established in a disused quarry which forms part of the property, and is a spectacular sight, even when half built. Peter Douglas has returned to the region he knows so well, and has produced some outstanding first-up wines from good, but not great, vintages. Exports to the UK.

Gartner Padthaway Chardonnay

▼▼▼▼▽ 2000 Medium yellow-green; a complex bouquet with both barrel-ferment and malolactic ferment influences evident in the mix of nutty/figgy/melon aromas. The palate has good length and excellent mouthfeel, the mix of nectarine, citrus and melon fruit the dominant influence notwithstanding barrel fermentation in new French oak. **rating:** 91

best drinking 2002–2006 **best vintages** '00 **drink with** Pan-fried scallops • $20

Gartner Padthaway Shiraz

▼▼▼▼▽ 2000 Medium red-purple; a fragrant bouquet with spice, licorice and mulberry fruit aromas married with well-balanced and integrated oak, then a palate where barrel fermentation (at the end of fermentation) has put its stamp on an elegant wine, persistent, fine-grained tannins helping to lengthen the flavour and structure profile. **rating:** 92

best drinking 2004–2010 **best vintages** '00 **drink with** Veal goulash • $25

Gartner Coonawarra Cabernet Sauvignon

▼▼▼▼▼ 1999 Medium red-purple; an archetypal bouquet for Coonawarra Cabernet Sauvignon, offering a mix of cedar, earth and blackberry; a similarly classic, fine, light to medium-bodied palate with a mix of cedar and blackberry once again, supported by super-fine savoury tannins and perfectly integrated oak. **rating:** 94

best drinking 2004–2014 **best vintages** '99 **drink with** Roast lamb • $30

gecko valley   NR

Bailiff Road, via 700 Glenlyon Road, Gladstone, Qld 4680 **region** Queensland Coastal
phone (07) 4979 0400 **fax** (07) 4979 0500 **open** 7 days 10–5
winemaker Bruce Humphery-Smith (Contract) **production** 1500 **est.** 1997
product range ($12.50–18.50 CD) Lightly Oaked Chardonnay, Special Reserve Chardonnay, Special Reserve Verdelho, Lazy Lizard White, Lazy Lizard Red, Special Reserve Shiraz, Liqueur Shiraz, Liqueur Mead.
summary Gecko Valley extends the viticultural map of Queensland yet further. It is situated little more than 50 kilometres off the tropic of Capricorn, in an area better known for sugar cane farming and mineral activities. The 3-hectare vineyard (1 hectare each of chardonnay, verdelho and shiraz) provides the base for the table wines made by the omnipresent Bruce Humphery-Smith, supplemented by a range of liqueurs, ports and muscats made several thousand kilometres further south. As one would expect, the facility caters for the general tourist, with a cafe and a gift shop with a wide range of merchandise.

geebin wines   NR

3729 Channel Highway, Birchs Bay, Tas 7162 **region** Southern Tasmania
phone (03) 6267 4750 **fax** (03) 6267 5090 **open** 7 days 10–5
winemaker Andrew Hood (Contract) **production** 50 **est.** 1983
product range ($17 CD) Riesling, Cabernet Sauvignon.
summary Although production is minuscule, quality has been consistently high. The Riesling is well made, but the interesting wine from this far southern vineyard is Cabernet Sauvignon – clearly, the vineyard enjoys favourable ripening conditions. With 0.7 hectare of vineyards (including 0.3 hectare of chardonnay yet to come into bearing), Geebin claims to be the smallest commercial producer in Australia, but isn't: Scarp Valley and (temporarily) Jollymont are smaller.

gehrig estate   ★★★

Cnr Murray Valley Highway and Howlong Road, Barnawartha, Vic 3688 **region** Rutherglen
phone (02) 6026 7296 **fax** (02) 6026 7424 **open** Mon–Sat 9–5, Sun 10–5
winemaker Brian Gehrig **production** 5000 **est.** 1858
product range ($10–32 CD) Chenin Blanc, Chardonnay, Autumn Riesling, Late Harvest Muscadelle, Fine Dry Rosé, Shiraz, Shiraz Cabernet, Durif Shiraz Cabernet, Alfresco Cabernet, Fortifieds.
summary A historic winery and adjacent house are superb legacies of the 19th century. Progressive modernisation of the winemaking facilities and operations has seen the quality of the white wines improve significantly, while the red wines now receive a percentage of new oak. Another recent innovation has been the introduction of the Gourmet Courtyard, serving lunch on weekends, public holidays and Victorian school holidays.

Gehrig Estate Shiraz

???? 1999 Medium to full red; the solid bouquet offers blackberry, together with hints of chocolate and earth; the full-bodied palate has a rich, fleshy middle, moving through to firm tannins on the finish, and needing to soften. Made in classic northeast Victorian style. **rating: 86**

best drinking 2004–2009 **best vintages** NA **drink with** Rump steak • $18.50

Gehrig Estate Old Tawny Port

???? NV The colour is dark, with a few red hues still there indicating intermediate age. The bouquet is solid, with sweet fruit and some rancio; a big, rich Rutherglen style on the palate, which, like the bouquet, does not show any signs of staleness. **rating: 86**

best drinking 2001–2002 **best vintages** NA **drink with** Coffee • $25

gembrook hill ★★★☆

Launching Place Road, Gembrook, Vic 3783 **region** Yarra Valley
phone (03) 5968 1622 **fax** (03) 5968 1699 **open** By appointment
winemaker Timo Mayer **production** 2000 **est.** 1983
product range ($16.50–33 R) Sauvignon Blanc, Young Vines Sauvignon Blanc, Chardonnay, Pinot Noir.
summary The 6-hectare Gembrook Hill Vineyard is situated on rich, red volcanic soils 2 kilometres north of Gembrook in the coolest part of the Yarra Valley. The vines are not irrigated, with consequent natural vigour control.

Gembrook Hill Young Vines Sauvignon Blanc

???? 2001 Bright, light green-yellow; the clean, fresh and light to moderately intense bouquet does not have much varietal definition, but rather more comes through on the palate with a mix of grassy/citrussy/gooseberry flavours in a neatly constructed frame. **rating: 86**

best drinking 2002–2003 **best vintages** NA **drink with** Chilled seafood • $16.50

Gembrook Hill Chardonnay

???? 2000 Light to medium yellow-green; the attractive bouquet has an appealing mix of stone fruit and citrus; the palate, while light, has good mouthfeel, length and persistence. A classic cool-climate style. **rating: 89**

best drinking 2001–2004 **best vintages** '90, '91, '93, '94, '97 **drink with** Crab, prawns • $30

Gembrook Hill Pinot Noir

???? 2000 Very light red; the bouquet has a light mix of cherry, strawberry and leaf, the palate delivering rather more, with sweet fruit in a cherry, plum and strawberry spectrum, and rather more mouthfeel than the bouquet would suggest. Nonetheless, an early maturing style. **rating: 86**

best drinking 2001–2003 **best vintages** '97, '98 **drink with** Asian seafood dishes • $33

gemtree vineyards ★★★☆

Kangarilla Road, McLaren Flat, SA 5171 **region** McLaren Vale
phone (08) 8323 8199 **fax** (08) 8323 7889 **open** Not
winemaker Mike Brown **production** 3000 **est.** 1992
product range ($15–25 R) Chardonnay, Shiraz, Tatty Road (Cabernet blend).
summary The Buttery family, headed by Paul and Jill and with the active involvement of Melissa as viticulturist for Gemtree Vineyards, has been actively involved as grape growers in McLaren Vale since 1980, when they purchased their first vineyard. Today the family owns a little over 130 hectares of vines, the oldest block being of 25 hectares on Tatachilla Road, planted in 1970. Exports to the US and Switzerland.

Gemtree Vineyards Tatty Road Cabernet Blend

???? 2000 Light to medium red-purple; the moderately intense bouquet ranges through red berry, leaf and mint, redcurrant/cassis fruit coming through quite strongly on the palate, then a fractionally sharp finish. A blend of Cabernet Sauvignon, Merlot, Petit Verdot and Shiraz. **rating: 85**

best drinking 2004–2009 **best vintages** NA **drink with** Braised lamb • $18

geoff hardy wines ★★★★

c/o Pertaringa Wines, cnr Hunt and Rifle Range Roads, McLaren Vale, SA 5171 **region** Adelaide Hills
phone (08) 8323 8125 **fax** (08) 8323 7766 **open** At Pertaringa, Mon–Fri 10–5, weekends and public holidays 11–5

winemaker Geoff Hardy, Ben Riggs **production** 2000 **est.** 1993
product range ($15–32 CD) Kuitpo Sauvignon Blanc, Shiraz, Cabernet; Wirrega Vineyard Petit Verdot.
summary Geoff Hardy wines come from 20 hectares of vines, with a large percentage of the grape production being sold to other makers. Retail distribution through SA, NSW, Vic and Qld; exports to the UK, Denmark, Germany, Japan, Hong Kong, Canada and the US.

Geoff Hardy Kuitpo Shiraz
▼▼▼▼ **1999** Medium red-purple; as ever, the wine expresses the cool climate in which it is grown, with red berry, leaf and earth aromas all intermingling, joined by spice and hints of bitter chocolate on the palate. A savoury, austere style demonstrates, if nothing else, the folly of regarding all SA Shiraz as much the same.   **rating:** 87

best drinking 2004–2009 **best vintages** '93, '98 **drink with** Rich red meat dishes • $32

Geoff Hardy Kuitpo Cabernet
▼▼▼▼ **1999** Light to medium red-purple; the clean, fresh bouquet opens with light, red berry fruit, then moves to touches of cedar and earth; the light to medium-bodied palate has minty berry flavours, once again putting the wine in a category which will greatly appeal to some, and not others.   **rating:** 86

best drinking 2003–2008 **best vintages** NA **drink with** Lamb fillets • $32

geoff merrill wines   ★★★★
291 Pimpala Road, Woodcroft, SA 5162 **region** McLaren Vale
phone (08) 8381 6877 **fax** (08) 8322 2244 **open** Mon–Fri 10–5, weekends 12–5
winemaker Geoff Merrill, Scott Heidrich **production** 80 000 **est.** 1980
product range ($17–155 R) A change in brand structure has resulted in the Geoff Merrill Wines having Henley Shiraz at the top; the Reserve range representing the ultra-premium wines, the Regional range and the Varietal range; Who Cares The Whites and Who Cares The Reds; Mount Hurtle wines are sold exclusively through Vintage Cellars/Liquorland.
summary If Geoff Merrill ever loses his impish sense of humour or his zest for life, high and not-so-high, we shall all be the poorer. He is seeking to lift the profile of his wines on the domestic market; in 1998 the product range was rearranged into three tiers: premium (in fact simply varietal); reserve, the latter being the older (and best) wines, reflecting the desire for elegance and subtlety of this otherwise exuberant winemaker; and at the top, Henley Shiraz. As well as national retail distribution, significant exports to the UK, Switzerland, Austria, the US, Hong Kong, Malaysia and Singapore.

Geoff Merrill Chardonnay
▼▼▼▼ **1999** Medium green-yellow; attractive, fresh melon fruit and the barest hint of oak on the bouquet flows into a pleasant, unpretentious palate with a mix of melon and cashew flavours in an easily accessible mode.   **rating:** 89

best drinking 2001–2003 **best vintages** '84, '85, '86, '89, '91 **drink with** Poultry, rabbit • $16.50

Geoff Merrill Grenache Rosé
▼▼▼▼ **2001** Light red-purple; clean, soft cherry/berry aromas lead into a soft, easy palate, lacking a little focus, but not too sweet.   **rating:** 88

best drinking 2001–2002 **best vintages** NA **drink with** Antipasto • $16.50

Geoff Merrill Shiraz
▼▼▼▼ **1999** Youthful red-purple; there are distinctly spicy/leafy overtones to the red fruit and gentle oak of the bouquet; the medium-bodied palate likewise provides a mix of savoury and red cherry fruit; the 12 months the wine spent in French and American oak is not obvious.   **rating:** 86

best drinking 2003–2008 **best vintages** '97 **drink with** Ragout of veal • $22

Geoff Merrill Henley Shiraz
▼▼▼▼▽ **1996** Excellent colour for a 5-year-old wine. There is no shortage of dark cherry fruit on either the bouquet or palate; French oak makes its presence felt on the bouquet, but the tannins and extract have been well handled to produce a typically elegant Geoff Merrill style.   **rating:** 93

best drinking 2001–2006 **best vintages** NA **drink with** Rare roast beef • $148

Geoff Merrill Reserve Shiraz

ŦŦŦŦ 1997 Light to medium red-purple; a light, savoury, leafy/woody bouquet is largely repeated on the palate; only Geoff Merrill could make a savoury, Hunter-like wine such as this from McLaren Vale, and it constitutes a refuge for those who do not enjoy high-alcohol styles. **rating:** 87

best drinking 2002–2007 **best vintages** NA **drink with** Kangaroo fillet • $46

Geoff Merrill Merlot

ŦŦŦŦ 2000 Medium red-purple; a clean, smooth, fruit-driven bouquet with moderately ripe fruit showing some spicy varietal character. The same flavours come together well on the palate, the slightly dusty/woodsy characters towards the finish falling within varietal expectation. **rating:** 85

best drinking 2002–2005 **best vintages** NA **drink with** Ragout of veal • $22

Geoff Merrill Cabernet Shiraz

ŦŦŦŦ 2000 Light to medium red-purple; light, fresh berry fruit aromas repeat on the palate, where fruit is foremost, the tannins soft. A simple, accessible lunch style needing no patience. **rating:** 85

best drinking 2001–2002 **best vintages** NA **drink with** Beef salad • $16.50

Geoff Merrill Reserve Cabernet Sauvignon

ŦŦŦŦ 1997 Light to medium red, starting to move to brick red on the rim; the savoury/leafy bouquet is quite elegant in a Merrill way; the palate is very savoury, long and intense, but I cannot work out why it was considered necessary to leave the wine for 29 months in a mix of French and American oak. **rating:** 87

best drinking 2001–2006 **best vintages** '96 **drink with** Rack of lamb • $46

geoff weaver   ★★★★★

2 Gilpin Lane, Mitcham, SA 5062 **region** Adelaide Hills
phone (08) 8272 2105 **fax** (08) 8271 0177 **open** Not
winemaker Geoff Weaver **production** 4500 **est.** 1982
product range ($21–35 ML) Riesling, Sauvignon Blanc, Chardonnay, Pinot Noir, Cabernet Merlot.
summary This is now the full-time business of former Hardy Group chief winemaker Geoff Weaver. He draws upon a little over 11 hectares of vineyard established between 1982 and 1988; for the time being, at least, the physical winemaking is carried out by Geoff Weaver at Petaluma. He produces invariably immaculate Riesling and Sauvignon Blanc, and one of the longest-lived Chardonnays to be found in Australia, which has intense grapefruit and melon flavour. The beauty of the labels ranks with that of Pipers Brook. The wines are exported to the US and the UK.

Geoff Weaver Lenswood Riesling

ŦŦŦŦŸ 2001 Light to medium green-yellow; a spotlessly clean, fine and delicate bouquet has a mix of florals, spice and lime; the palate has excellent structure and balance, simply needing time for the fruit to fully express itself, which it will do. Stelvin closure. **rating:** 92

ŦŦŦŦŦ 2000 Light to medium green-yellow; a clean, crisp and fresh bouquet with a mix of mineral, toast, apple and lime leads into a palate with excellent intensity and balance to the gentle mix of lime, citrus and apple fruit. Stelvin-capped. **rating:** 94

best drinking 2004–2010 **best vintages** '90, '93, '94, '96, '98, '00, '01 **drink with** Fresh asparagus • $21

Geoff Weaver Sauvignon Blanc

ŦŦŦŦŸ 2001 Light straw-green; the fragrant but light bouquet has touches of passionfruit and strawberry which flow through into the fresh palate, which is not particularly intense, but is clean and lively. **rating:** 90

best drinking 2001–2003 **best vintages** '00 **drink with** Blue swimmer crab • $21

Geoff Weaver Lenswood Chardonnay

ŦŦŦŦŸ 2000 Glowing yellow-green; the bouquet has a mix of cashew, fig, melon and citrus; the palate has a similar range of flavours, lively, fresh and long, and delicate oak. Will develop slowly. **rating:** 90

ŦŦŦŦ 1999 The colour shows more development than one might expect; the bouquet is likewise a fraction errant, suggesting some botrytis. The palate does nothing to change the message, with tropical fruit flavours; the wine finishes with the typical bright acidity of the Geoff Weaver style, but is diffuse. **rating:** 87

best drinking 2004–2010 **best vintages** '95, '97, '98, '00 **drink with** Fresh prawns • $35

Geoff Weaver Cabernet Merlot

▼▼▼▼ **1999** Medium red-purple; a light but high-toned bouquet with a mix of earthy, savoury and sappy aromas is followed by a powerful, austere palate with a mix of olive, leaf, earth and berry; all in all, a wine with distinct Bordeaux affinities. **rating:** 89

▼▼▼▼▽ **1998** Medium purple-red; a bouquet of fresh, clean, berry fruit, plus a touch of mint and subtle oak, leads into a palate with good structure, balance and length, driven by red berry fruit, and supported by silky, fine tannins. **rating:** 93

best drinking 2004–2009 **best vintages** '98 **drink with** Seared rib-eye of beef • $35

giaconda ★★★★★

McClay Road, Beechworth, Vic 3747 **region** Beechworth
phone (03) 5727 0246 **fax** (03) 5727 0246 **open** By appointment
winemaker Rick Kinzbrunner **production** 2000 **est.** 1985
product range ($50–100 R) Aeolia, Nantua Les Deux, Chardonnay, Pinot Noir, Warner Vineyard Shiraz, Cabernet Sauvignon.
summary Wines which have a super-cult status and which, given the tiny production, are extremely difficult to find; they are sold chiefly through restaurants and by mail order. All have a cosmopolitan edge befitting Rick Kinzbrunner's international winemaking experience. The Chardonnay and Pinot Noir are made in contrasting styles: the Chardonnay tight and reserved, the Pinot Noir more variable, but usually opulent and ripe. Exports to the UK and the US.

Giaconda Chardonnay

▼▼▼▼▽ **2000** Medium to full yellow-green; has the expected ultra-complex bouquet with strong Burgundian overtones, the palate providing more of the same. You can see all the elements in the wine: great fruit, then barrel fermentation of partially clear juice at ambient temperatures. Way out of the mainstream for the normal more clinical Australian Chardonnay style. **rating:** 90

best drinking 2002–2007 **best vintages** '86, '88, '90, '92, '93, '94, '95, '96, '97, '98 **drink with** Slow-roasted Tasmanian salmon • $100

gidgee estate wines NR

441 Weeroona Drive, Wamboin, NSW 2621 **region** Canberra District
phone (02) 6236 9506 **fax** (02) 6236 9070 **open** Weekends 12–4
winemaker David Madew, Andrew McEwin (Contract) **production** 500 **est.** 1996
product range ($15–16 CD) Janette Murray Riesling, Chardonnay, Ensemble (Cabernet blend).
summary Brett and Cheryl Lane purchased the 1-hectare vineyard in 1996; it had been planted to riesling, chardonnay, cabernet sauvignon, cabernet franc and merlot over a ten-year period prior to its acquisition, but had been allowed to run down and needed to be rehabilitated. The Lanes intend to double the vineyard size over the next two years and have retained David Madew and Andrew McEwen as contract winemakers.

gilberts ★★★★★

RMB 438 Albany Highway, Kendenup via Mount Barker, WA 6323 **region** Great Southern
phone (08) 9851 4028 **fax** (08) 9851 4021 **open** 7 days 10–5
winemaker Plantagenet (Contract) **production** 3000 **est.** 1980
product range ($14–25 CD) Riesling, Alira (medium sweet), Chardonnay, Shiraz, Cabernet Shiraz, Old Tawny.
summary A part-time occupation for sheep and beef farmers Jim and Beverly Gilbert but a very successful one. The now mature vineyard, coupled with contract-winemaking at Plantagenet, has produced small quantities of high-quality Riesling and Chardonnay. The five-star rating is for the Riesling, which won the trophy for Best Wine of Show at the Qantas West Australian Wines Show in both 2000 and 2001. The small production sells out quickly each year, with retail distribution through NSW, Vic, the ACT and WA, and exports to the US, the UK and the Netherlands.

Gilberts Riesling

▼▼▼▼▼ **2001** Light straw-green; a spotlessly clean and crisp bouquet with a classic mix of herb, mineral and citrus followed by a palate with great intensity and length, tightly focussed, with perfect acidity on a bone-dry finish. Trophy for Best West Australian Riesling 2001 Qantas Wine Show of Western Australia, repeating the performance of the 2000 vintage at the 2000 show. **rating:** 94

best drinking 2003–2010 **best vintages** '91, '92, '94, '95, '96, '97, '00, '01 **drink with** Asparagus with prosciutto • $18

gilgai winery NR

Tingha Road, Gilgai, NSW 2360 **region** Northern Slopes Zone
phone (02) 6723 1204 **open** 7 days 10–6
winemaker Keith Whish **production** 100 **est.** 1968
product range Pinot Noir, Malbec.
summary Inverell medical practitioner Dr Keith Whish has been quietly producing wines from his 6-hectare vineyard for almost 30 years. All of the production is sold through the cellar door.

glaetzer wines ★★★☆

34 Barossa Valley Way, Tanunda, SA 5352 **region** Barossa Valley
phone (08) 8563 0288 **fax** (08) 8563 0218 **open** Mon–Sat 10.30–4.30, Sun and public holidays 1–4.30
winemaker Colin Glaetzer, Ben Glaetzer **production** NA **est.** 1996
product range ($16–45 CD) Bush Vine Semillon, Semillon Ratafia, Grenache Mourvedre; Sparkling Pinot Noir, The Bishop Shiraz, Malbec Cabernet Sauvignon, Shiraz, Sparkling Shiraz.
summary Colin and Ben Glaetzer are almost as well known in SA wine circles as Wolf Blass winemaker John Glaetzer, and, needless to say, they are all related. Glaetzer Wines purchases its grapes from third and 4th-generation Barossa Valley growers and makes an array of traditional Barossa styles. The Shiraz comes predominantly from vines 80 years or more old. National retail distribution; exports to the US, Germany, the UK, Belgium, Italy, the Netherlands and Canada.

Glaetzer Shiraz

▼▼▼▼ **1998** Bright purple-red; a clean and smooth bouquet leads into a solid, rich, dark cherry-flavoured palate, finishing with gentle oak and tannins. **rating:** 85

best drinking 2003–2008 **best vintages** NA **drink with** Braised beef • NA

glenalbyn ★★★

84 Halls Road, Kingower, Vic 3517 **region** Bendigo
phone (03) 5438 8255 **fax** (03) 5438 8255 **open** 10.30–4.30 most days
winemaker Lee (Leila) Gillespie **production** 500 **est.** 1997
product range ($16–25 CD) Sauvignon Blanc, Pinot Noir, American Oak Cabernet Sauvignon, French Oak Cabernet Sauvignon.
summary When Leila Gillespie's great-grandfather applied for his land title in 1856, he had already established a vineyard on the property. A survey plan of 1857 shows the cultivation paddocks, one marked the Grape Paddock, and a few of the original grape vines have survived in the garden which abuts the National Trust and Heritage homestead. In 1986 Leila and John Gillespie decided on a modest diversification of their sheep, wool and cereal crop farm, and began the establishment of 4 hectares of vineyards. Since 1997 Leila Gillespie has made the wine on a self-taught basis, with Cabernet Sauvignon, and more recently Pinot Noir and Sauvgnon Blanc.

Glenalbyn Sauvignon Blanc Gold

▼▼▼▼ **2001** Light green-yellow; the light, fresh bouquet has some flowery aspects; the palate has apple and gooseberry fruit followed by a crisp, clean finish. **rating:** 87

best drinking 2002–2003 **best vintages** NA **drink with** Antipasto • $16

Glenalbyn Cabernet Sauvignon

▼▼▼▼ **1999** Medium red-purple; blackberry fruit is joined by chocolate and vanilla on the bouquet; the palate has dark berry flavours, a touch of chocolate, and persistent (but ripe) tannins. **rating:** 85

best drinking 2005–2011 **best vintages** NA **drink with** Marinated beef • $25

glenara wines ★★★☆

126 Range Road North, Upper Hermitage, SA 5131 **region** Adelaide Hills
phone (08) 8380 5277 **fax** (08) 8380 5056 **open** Mon–Fri 11–5 (closed public holidays)
winemaker Trevor Jones **production** 5000 **est.** 1971
product range ($15–25 CD) Riesling, Sauvignon Blanc, Unwooded Chardonnay, White Quartz (Sparkling), Cabernet Rosé, Pinot Noir, Shiraz, Shiraz Cabernet, Cabernet Merlot, Cabernet Sauvignon, Old Tawny Port.

summary Glenara has been owned by the Verrall family since 1924; the first vines were planted in 1971, the first wine was made in 1975, and the winery was built in 1988. Has proceeded to produce many good wines, particularly the full-flavoured Rieslings, but also creditable full-bodied reds.

glenayr ★★★★

Back Tea Tree Road, Richmond, Tas 7025 region Southern Tasmania
phone (03) 6260 2388 fax (03) 6260 2691 open Mon–Fri 8–5
winemaker Andrew Hood production 500 est. 1975
product range ($18–20 CD) Riesling, Chardonnay, Pinot Noir, Cabernet Shiraz Merlot; Tolpuddle Vineyards Chardonnay and Pinot Noir.
summary The principal occupation of Chris Harrington is as viticultural manager of the substantial Tolpuddle Vineyard, the grapes of which are sold to Domaine Chandon and BRL Hardy. Tiny quantities of wine are made from an adjacent 1-hectare vineyard for mailing list sales under the GlenAyr label; chardonnay and pinot noir grapes are also purchased from Tolpuddle Vineyards.

glen erin vineyard retreat ★★★☆

Rochford Road, Lancefield, Vic 3435 region Macedon Ranges
phone (03) 5429 1041 fax (03) 5429 2053 open Weekends, public holidays 10–6
winemaker Brian Scales, John Ellis production 400 est. 1993
product range ($17–38 CD) Gewürztraminer, Chardonnay, Pinot Noir, Mystic Park Sparkling Macedon.
summary Brian Scales acquired the former Lancefield Winery and renamed it Glen Erin. Wines are contract-made from Macedon grapes and elsewhere and sold only through the cellar door and the restaurant; the conference and function facilities are supported by 24 accommodation rooms.

Glen Erin Vineyard Chardonnay

▼▼▼▼ 2000 Light straw-green; a fresh, citrussy/minerally bouquet leads into a lively and fresh citrus, passionfruit and melon-flavoured palate. Some really nice fruit flavours here.   rating: 87

best drinking 2001–2006 best vintages NA drink with Sautéed scallops • $22.50

glenfinlass NR

Elysian Farm, Parkes Road, Wellington, NSW 2820 region Central Ranges Zone
phone (02) 6845 2011 fax (02) 6845 3329 open Sat 9–5 or by appointment
winemaker Brian G Holmes production 500 est. 1971
product range ($15–25 CD) Sauvignon Blanc, Drought Drop (Shiraz, Cabernet Sauvignon, Sauvignon Blanc).
summary The weekend and holiday hobby of Wellington solicitor Brian Holmes, who has wisely decided to leave it at that. I have not tasted the wines for many years, but the last wines I did taste were competently made. Wines are in short supply owing to drought (1998), frost (1999) and flooding (2000). It is a sign of his resilience (and sense of humour) that the 1998 Drought Drop is currently on sale; it is a blend of 50 per cent Shiraz, 25 per cent Cabernet Sauvignon and 25 per cent Sauvignon Blanc.

glenguin ★★★★

River Oaks Vineyard, Lot 8 Milbrodale Road, Broke, NSW 2330 region Lower Hunter Valley
phone (02) 6579 1009 fax (02) 6579 1009 open 7 days at Boutique Wine Centre, Broke Road, Pokolbin
winemaker Robin Tedder MW production 15 000 est. 1993
product range ($16–29 R) Individual Vineyard series of The Old Broke Block Semillon, Unwooded Chardonnay, River Terrace Vineyard Chardonnay, Griffith Vineyard Botrytised Semillon, Shiraz, Schoolhouse Block Shiraz, Orange Vineyard Cabernet Sauvignon.
summary Glenguin's vineyard has been established along the banks of the Wollombi Brook by Robin, Rita and Andrew Tedder, Robin and Andrew being the grandsons of Air Chief Marshal Tedder, made Baron of Glenguin by King George VI in recognition of his wartime deeds. (Glenguin is also the name of a Scottish distillery which continues to produce a single malt but which is otherwise unconnected.) Glenguin has 15 hectares of vineyard at Broke and another 4 hectares at Orange (cabernet and merlot). Exports to the US, Canada, the UK, and Germany.

Glenguin The Old Broke Block Semillon

▼▼▼▼ 2000 Very pale; a crisp bouquet ranges through mineral, herb and grass; the palate has some sweetness at the core, and the required length and persistence. Simply needs time to start to develop real character. **rating:** 86

best drinking 2004–2009 **best vintages** '99 **drink with** Leave it in the cellar • $18

Glenguin River Terrace Vineyard Chardonnay

▼▼▼▼ 1999 Medium to full yellow-green; the solid bouquet is carried primarily by ripe peachy fruit, although the oak is undoubtedly present. The rich palate has a mix of yellow peach and fig fruit; nutty/cashew overtones come through on the back palate prior to the soft but balanced finish. **rating:** 88

best drinking 2001–2002 **best vintages** NA **drink with** Pan-fried chicken breast • $16

Glenguin Griffith Vineyard Botrytised Semillon

▼▼▼▼ 2000 Deep gold and distinctly advanced colour; the bouquet has a mix of cumquat, mandarin and toffee fruit; the palate has precisely the same flavours, is not overly sweet, and is balanced by appropriate acidity. **rating:** 88

best drinking 2002–2003 **best vintages** NA **drink with** Hazlenut tart • $23

Glenguin Shiraz

▼▼▼▼ 1999 Medium red, starting to shed its purple hues. The bouquet is savoury, with some cigar box aromatics; the palate has a range of cherry, mulberry, cedar and cigar flavours. Looks as if it will develop quickly. **rating:** 85

best drinking 2002–2005 **best vintages** NA **drink with** Smoked lamb • NA

Glenguin Schoolhouse Block Shiraz

▼▼▼▼ 2000 Medium to full red-purple; sweet plum and prune aromas and positive oak lead into a palate which opens with luscious fruit; slightly hard tannins emphasise the acidity on the finish. All arms and legs now, but virtually guaranteed to sort itself out with time in bottle. **rating:** 89

▼▼▼▼▽ 1999 Bright purple red of medium depth; the clean and fresh bouquet has black cherry/berry fruit to the fore, with a touch of spice coming through, partly oak-derived. The palate has excellent texture and feel, tighter and finer than the other Glenguin Shiraz; silky tannins run through a long finish. **rating:** 90

best drinking 2005–2010 **best vintages** '99 **drink with** Wild mushroom risotto • $29

glenhurst wines　　　NR

Jones Road, Hahndorf, SA 5245 **region** Adelaide Hills
phone (08) 8388 4439 **fax** (08) 8388 4439 **open** Wed–Sun 11–4
winemaker Bruce Crowhurst **production** 3000 **est.** 1992
product range ($20–25 CD) The Eleanor Sauvignon Blanc, The Doretta Chardonnay, The Dark Lady Pinot Noir, The Zealia Shiraz, The Nobleman Cabernet Sauvignon.
summary The Crowhurst family began the establishment of Glenhurst Wines in 1992 with the purchase of an 80-hectare property in Wrattonbully. The plantings comprise a tiny patch of dolcetto alongside the 21 hectares of cabernet sauvignon and 19 hectares of shiraz. This was followed by the 1997 purchase of a property near Hahndorf, where 21 hectares of chardonnay, pinot noir and sauvignon blanc (in more or less equal quantities) have now been planted. The wines are made at Shaw and Smith, but for the time being only part of the production is vinified for Glenhurst, the remainder being sold to others. On 28 February 2002 the business was sold as a going concern to Drumcalpin Wines, but the brand will continue to be sold under the Glenhurst label.

gloucester ridge vineyard　　　★★★★

Lot 7489 Burma Road, Pemberton, WA 6260 **region** Pemberton
phone (08) 9776 1035 **fax** (08) 9776 1390 **open** 7 days 10–5 (until late Saturday)
winemaker Brenden Smith **production** 15 000 **est.** 1985
product range ($12.50–40 CD) Semillon, Sauvignon Blanc, Pemberton Classic, Back Block White, Unwooded Chardonnay, Chardonnay, Chimère (Sparkling), Late Harvest Riesling, Pinot Noir, Reserve Pinot Noir, Shiraz, Cabernet Merlot, Cabernets, Cabernet Sauvignon, Pemberton Red, Back Block Red, Seduction, Port.
summary Gloucester Ridge is the only vineyard located within the Pemberton town boundary, within easy walking distance. It is owned and operated by Don and Sue Hancock; some of the recent releases have been most impressive. Retail distribution in Queensland, NSW, Victoria and WA.

Gloucester Ridge Vineyard Premium Reserve Shiraz

TTTT 2000 Medium red-purple; berry, leaf, mint and earth aromas lead into a light to medium-bodied palate with cherry/berry fruit and soft tannins making the impact; oak is somewhere in the background. **rating:** 85

best drinking 2003–2007 **best vintages** NA **drink with** Designer sausages • $20

Gloucester Ridge Cabernet Sauvignon

TTTTY 1999 Medium to full red-purple; clean blackberry/cassis fruit with a touch of lift and a dash of oak on the bouquet, then a medium-bodied palate with a most attractive savoury/chocolatey cast to the blackberry fruit. A well-deserved gold medal at 2001 Perth Wine Show. **rating:** 91

best drinking 2004–2009 **best vintages** '99 **drink with** Barbecued lamb chops • $40

gnadenfrei estate   NR

Seppeltsfield Road, Marananga via Nuriootpa, SA 5355 **region** Barossa Valley
phone (08) 8562 2522 **fax** (08) 8562 3470 **open** Tues–Sun 10–5.30
winemaker Malcolm Seppelt **production** 1500 **est.** 1979
product range ($12–20 CD) Riesling, Semillon, Traminer Riesling, Shiraz Grenache, Tawny Port, Sparkling.
summary A strictly cellar-door operation, which relies on a variety of sources for its wines but has a core of 2 hectares of estate shiraz and 1 hectare of grenache. A restaurant presided over by Joylene Seppelt is open for morning teas, lunches and afternoon teas. Small quantities of the wines make their way to Pennsylvania, US.

gold dust wines   NR

Southpark, Tallwood Road, Millthorpe, NSW 2798 **region** Orange
phone (02) 6366 5168 **fax** 902) 6361 9165 **open** By appointment
winemaker Jon Reynolds (Contract) **production** 1000 **est.** 1993
product range ($12.50–15 ML) Riesling, Chardonnay Riesling, Chardonnay, Late Harvest.
summary John and Jacqui Corrie have established 4 hectares each of riesling and chardonnay, electing to sell two-thirds of the production, and have the remainder contract-made, since 2001 by Jon Reynolds. Most of the wine is sold by mail order.

golden grape estate   NR

Oakey Creek Road, Pokolbin, NSW 2320 **region** Lower Hunter Valley
phone (02) 4998 7588 **fax** (02) 4998 7730 **open** 7 days 10–5
winemaker Neil McGuigan (Consultant) **production** NFP **est.** 1985
product range ($14.95–29.90 CD) Premier Semillon, Gewürztraminer, Sauvignon Blanc, Semillon Verdelho, Happy Valley Chardonnay, Five Star (light fruity), Frizzante Rosé, Mount Leonard (Cabernet Sauvignon), Domaine Springton (Shiraz), Classic Red, Fortifieds.
summary German-owned and unashamedly directed at the tourist, with a restaurant, barbecue and picnic areas, wine museum and separate tasting room for bus tours. The substantial range of wines are of diverse origins and style. The operation now has over 42 hectares of Hunter Valley plantings.

golden grove estate   ★★★☆

Sundown Road, Ballandean, Qld 4382 **region** Granite Belt
phone (07) 4684 1291 **fax** (07) 4684 1247 **open** 7 days 9–5
winemaker Sam Costanzo **production** 10 000 **est.** 1993
product range ($10–15 CD) Accommodation Creek Classic White and Classic Dry Red, Muscadean, Rosé, Shiraz, Cabernet Merlot, Liqueur Muscat.
summary Golden Grove Estate was established by Mario and Sebastiana Costanzo in 1946, producing stone fruits and table grapes for the fresh fruit market. The first wine grapes (shiraz) were planted in 1972, but it was not until 1985, when ownership passed to son Sam Costanzo and wife Grace, that the use of the property started to change. In 1993 chardonnay and merlot joined the shiraz, followed by cabernet sauvignon, sauvignon blanc and semillon. Wine quality has steadily improved, with many medals in regional shows awarded up to 2002, leading to national (though limited) retail distribution.

golden gully wines   NR

5900 Midwestern Highway, Mandurama, NSW 2792 **region** Orange
phone (02) 6367 5148 **fax** (02) 6367 4148 **open** Weekends 10–4 or by appointment
winemaker Jon Reynolds (Contract) **production** 1300 **est.** 1994
product range ($18–19 CD) Shiraz, Cabernet Merlot, Cabernet Sauvignon.
summary Kevin and Julie Bate have progressively established over 5 hectares of vineyard (2 hectares cabernet sauvignon, 1.6 shiraz, 0.5 merlot and 0.5 each of semillon and sauvignon blanc). The first commercial crop came in 2001, but tiny makes in 1999 (Cabernet Shiraz) and 2000 Cabernet Sauvignon) have both won bronze medals at the Bathurst Cool Climate Wine Show.

golders vineyard   ★★★★☆

Bridport Road, Pipers Brook, Tas 7254 **region** Northern Tasmania
phone (03) 6395 4142 **fax** (03) 6395 4142 **open** By appointment
winemaker Richard Crabtree **production** 400 **est.** 1991
product range ($18–24 R) Chardonnay, Pinot Noir.
summary The initial plantings of 1.5 hectares of pinot noir have been supplemented by 1 hectare of chardonnay. The quality of the Pinot Noir has been good from the initial vintage in 1995, hitting a high spot in 2000.

Golders Pinot Noir

▼▼▼▼▼ 2000 Medium red-purple; an intensely perfumed, sappy bouquet with a mix of tomato vine, spice and chocolate, then a palate with a combination of tingling, sappy nervosity and sweeter fruit. Far from conventional, but first-up gold medals from two of the judges ensured its ultimate award of a gold medal at the 2002 Tasmanian Wines Show.   **rating: 94**

best drinking 2002–2005 **best vintages** '95, '96, '97, '00 **drink with** Duck risotto • $24

goona warra vineyard   ★★★☆

Sunbury Road, Sunbury, Vic 3429 **region** Sunbury
phone (03) 9740 7766 **fax** (03) 9744 7648 **open** 7 days 10–5
winemaker John Barnier, Nick Bickford **production** 2500 **est.** 1863
product range ($14–28 CD) Semillon Sauvignon Blanc, Chardonnay, Black Cygnet Chardonnay, Roussanne, Pinot Noir, Cabernets, Black Cygnet Cabernet Shiraz, Black Widow Brut, Black Cygnet Tawny Port.
summary A historic stone winery, established under this name by a 19th-century Victorian premier. A capital infusion by a Melbourne-based venture capital group in early 2001 will result in a doubling of production. Excellent tasting facilities; an outstanding venue for weddings and receptions; Sunday lunch also served. Situated 30 minutes' drive from Melbourne (10 minutes north of Tullamarine Airport). Berry Bros & Rudd import the wines into the UK.

goundrey   ★★★☆

Muir Highway, Mount Barker, WA 6324 **region** Great Southern
phone (08) 9851 1777 **fax** (08) 9851 1997 **open** 7 days 10–4.30
winemaker David Martin, Michael Perkins **production** 240 000 **est.** 1976
product range ($14.50–34 R) Windy Hill range of Riesling, Chardonnay, Pinot Noir, Classic Red, Goundrey range of Chenin Blanc, Classic White, Unwooded Chardonnay, Brut, Late Picked Riesling, Shiraz Grenache, Shiraz Cabernet, Cabernet Merlot; Reserve range of Riesling, Chardonnay, Botrytis Riesling, Pinot Noir, Shiraz, Cabernet Sauvignon; second label is Fox River with Classic White, Chardonnay, Pinot Noir, Shiraz, Shiraz Cabernet.
summary Under the ownership of Perth businessman Jack Bendat, not to mention the injection of many millions of dollars into vineyard and winery expansion, Goundrey has grown significantly. There seems to be a widening gap between the quality of the Reserve wines (usually, but not invariably, good) and the varietal range (workmanlike). This may be no bad thing from a commercial viewpoint, particularly if the differential is reflected in the price, but it does make an overall rating difficult. National distribution; exports to the US, Asia, the UK and Europe.

Goundrey Classic White
ᵀᵀᵀᵀ **2001** Light to medium green-yellow; a clean, moderately intense bouquet offers grassy/lemony fruit; the light to medium-bodied palate is conventional, no frills, dry and minerally. A silver medal at the Griffith Wine Show displayed on the label says much. **rating:** 84

best drinking 2002–2003 **best vintages** '00 **drink with** Steamed Chinese fish • $15.50

Goundrey Reserve Shiraz
ᵀᵀᵀᵀ **1999** Medium red-purple; savoury, earthy aromas with the fruit in the background on the bouquet, although more black cherry/berry fruit comes through on the palate, supported by fine tannins and controlled oak. **rating:** 87

best drinking 2003–2008 **best vintages** '81, '85, '87, '91, '92, '95, '97, '99 **drink with** Osso buco • $34

Fox River Cabernet Shiraz
ᵀᵀᵀᵀ **2000** Medium red-purple; a clean, moderately intense bouquet with uncomplicated red fruit aromas is followed by a palate which has some substance and fruit ripeness, offering fair value at the price. **rating:** 84

best drinking 2002–2005 **best vintages** NA **drink with** Takeaway • $14

governor robe selection NR
Waterhouse Range Vineyards, Lot 11 Old Naracoorte Road, Robe, SA 576 **region** Limestone Coast Zone
phone (08) 8768 2083 **fax** (08) 8768 2190 **open** By appointment
winemaker Cape Jaffa Wines (Contract) **production** 500 **est.** 1998
product range ($15–25 CD) Shiraz.
summary Brothers Bill and Mick Quinlan-Watson, supported by a group of investors, began the development of Waterhouse Range Vineyards Pty Ltd in 1995, planting 15 hectares of vines that year, with further plantings over the following few years lifting the total area under vine to just over 40 hectares. The majority of the grapes are sold, with a lesser amount retained and contract-made at Cape Jaffa winery. The unusual name comes from the third Governor of South Australia, who in 1845 selected the site for a port and personally put in the first survey peg at Robe. Next door is the Customs House, which is a National Trust building, and which is depicted on the label.

governor's choice winery NR
Berghofer Road, Westbrook via Toowoomba, Qld 4350 **region** Queensland Zone
phone (07) 4630 6101 **fax** (07) 4630 6701 **open** 7 days 9–5
winemaker James Yates **production** 2500 **est.** 1999
product range ($15–30 CD) Semillon, Verdelho, Chardonnay, Shiraz, Cabernet Shiraz, Cabernet Sauvignon.
summary This is a part winery, part premium guest house accommodation venture situated 18 kilometres from the town of Toowoomba. Three hectares of estate plantings produce chardonnay, shiraz, verdelho, cabernet sauvignon and malbec, made on-site and sold through the cellar door on weekends or to guests.

gowrie mountain estate NR
2 Warrego Highway, Kingsthorpe, Qld 4400 **region** Granite Belt
phone (07) 4630 0566 **fax** (07) 4630 0366 **open** Not
winemaker Peter Howland (Contract) **production** 4000 **est.** 1998
product range ($14–22 R) Semillon, Verdelho, Chardonnay, Shiraz, Gamay, Tempranillo, Chambourcin, Cabernet Sauvignon.
summary Situated northeast of Toowoomba, in the heart of the Darling Downs, this is a substantial new entrant, having already established 32 hectares to mainstream varieties, and to new breeds: tempranillo (4 hectares) and gamay (2 hectares). Part of the production goes to Hope Estate in the Hunter Valley, which makes the red wines, and part to Preston Peak, where the white wines and Tempranillo are made. An underground barrel and bottled wine storage area has been completed with a sales, restaurant and general tourist facility expected to be open by August–September 2002. All of the Newberry family members, headed by father Ron, are involved in the venture.

gralyn estate ★★★★☆

Caves Road, Wilyabrup, WA 6280 **region** Margaret River
phone (08) 9755 6245 **fax** (08) 9755 6245 **open** 7 days 10.30–4.30
winemaker Graham Hutton, Merilyn Hutton **production** 2500 **est.** 1975
product range ($16–90 CD) Premium Dry White, Late Harvest Riesling, Old Vine Shiraz, Late Harvest
Cabernet, Shiraz Cabernet, Unoaked Cabernet, Cabernet Sauvignon, and an extensive range of fortifieds
including White Port, Vintage Port and Tawny Port.
summary The move from primarily fortified wine to table wine production has been completed, and has
brought considerable success. The red wines are made in a distinctively different style from most of those
from the Margaret River region, with an opulence (in part from American oak) which is reminiscent of
some of the bigger wines from McLaren Vale. The age of the vines (25 years plus) and the site are also
significant factors. Exports to Denmark.

Gralyn Estate Old Vine Shiraz

▼▼▼▼▽ 2000 Medium to full red-purple; solid, deep, dark savoury/earthy fruit aromas, and oak also
present; the rich and supple palate has dark fruit, good tannin management, the oak (not for the first time)
a fraction assertive. **rating:** 91

best drinking 2005–2015 **best vintages** '94, '95, '96, '00 **drink with** Strong red meat dishes • $60

Gralyn Estate Shiraz Cabernet

▼▼▼▼▽ 2000 Full red-purple; rich, dense plum, blackberry and chocolate fruit on the bouquet, then an
exceptionally powerful palate with concentrated ripe fruit and persistent tannins. A 20-year proposition.
rating: 93

best drinking 2008 – 2020 **best vintages** '95, '99, '00 **drink with** Smoked lamb • $90

Gralyn Estate Cabernet Sauvignon

▼▼▼▼▼ 2000 Full red-purple; dense, sweet blackcurrant fruit almost, but not quite, absorbs the oak on
the bouquet; a densely packed, immense palate with chewy, ripe fruit oak and tannin all intermingling in
full-blooded show style. Whatever else this wine aspires to, it is not elegance, which is exactly why it will
appeal to many. **rating:** 94

best drinking 2008 – 2015 **best vintages** '99, '00 **drink with** Marinated beef • $90

grampians estate NR

Mafeking Road, Willaura, Vic 3379 **region** Grampians
phone (03) 5354 6245 **fax** (03) 5354 6257 **open** By appointment
winemaker Simon Clayfield **production** 1300 **est.** 1989
product range ($16–20 R) Mafeking Unwooded Chardonnay, Mafeking Gold Chardonnay, Mafeking
Shiraz.
summary Ten years ago local farmers and graziers Sarah and Tom Guthrie decided to diversify their
activities, while continuing to run their fat lamb and wool production. So they planted a little over
1.5 hectares each of shiraz and chardonnay, and opened the Thermopylae Host Farm business. This offers
two farm-stay buildings, a five-bedroom shearer's cottage which sleeps 12, and a five-room miner's cottage
which sleeps 10. They also secured the services of immensely experienced local winemaker Simon Clayfield
to produce the Grampians Estate wines. These are sold to those who stay on the farm, which is able to offer
an unusually wide range of activities; the wines are also available by direct mail order and at one or two
local hotels, including the Kookaburra Rest at Halls Gap.

granite ridge wines NR

Sundown Road, Ballandean, Qld 4382 **region** Granite Belt
phone (07) 4684 1263 **fax** (07) 4684 1250 **open** 7 days 9–5
winemaker Dennis Ferguson, Juliane Ferguson **production** 1200 **est.** 1995
product range ($12–28 CD) Goldies Unwooded Chardonnay, Bilby White (Semillon), First Oak
Chardonnay, Elles Quartz (sweet Semillon), The Ridge (Shiraz Ruby Cabernet), Granite Garnet, Granite
Rock Shiraz, Fergies Hill Merlot, Millenium Cabernet Merlot, Bilby Red (Cabernet Sauvignon), Granite
Grange Cabernet Sauvignon, Granite Amber (Liqueur Muscat).
summary Formerly known as Denlana Ferguson Estate Wines, Granite Ridge had considerable success in
the mid-1990s, with both the 1995 and 1996 Cabernet Sauvignon being judged Queensland's Best
Cabernet (though quite by whom I am not sure); continues to be run by Dennis Ferguson.

grant burge ★★★★

Barossa Vines, Krondorf Road, Tanunda, SA 5352 **region** Barossa Valley
phone (08) 8563 3700 **fax** (08) 8563 2807 **open** 7 days 10–5
winemaker Grant Burge **production** 108 000 **est.** 1988
product range ($10.50–100 R) Has moved to a series of vineyard-designated varietal wines, including Thorn Vineyard Riesling, Zerk Vineyard Semillon, Kraft Vineyard Sauvignon Blanc, Barossa Ranges Chardonnay, Summers Chardonnay, Lily Farm Frontignac, Filsell Shiraz, Hillcott Merlot, and Cameron Vale Cabernet Sauvignon. Top-of-the-range reds are Meshach Shiraz, The Holy Trinity (Grenache Shiraz Mourvedre), Reserve The Holy Trinity and Shadrach Cabernet Sauvignon; also Rubycind and Virtuoso; RBG Gewürztraminer, RBS1 Semillon, RBS2 Semillon, RSHZ Eden Valley Shiraz, MSJ1 Shiraz Cabernet, RBM1 Merlot; Sparklings, Fortifieds. The budget-priced Barossa Vines range joined the band in late 1999, Miamba Shiraz in 2001.

summary As one might expect, this very experienced industry veteran makes consistently good, full-flavoured and smooth wines chosen from the pick of the crop of his extensive vineyard holdings, which total an impressive 200 hectares; the immaculately restored/rebuilt stone cellar-door sales buildings are another attraction. The provocatively named The Holy Trinity (a Grenache Shiraz Mourvedre blend) joins Shadrach and Meshach at the top of the range. In late 1999 Grant Burge repurchased the farm from Mildara Blass by acquiring the Krondorf winery (not the brand) in which he made his first fortune. He has renamed it Barossa Vines and, taking advantage of the great views it offers, has opened a cellar door offering casual food, and featuring local produce wherever possible. Exports to the UK, Europe, the US, Canada and Asia.

Grant Burge Thorn Vineyard Riesling

TTTTY 2001 Medium yellow-green; a soft, ripe lime/citrus/tropical bouquet is followed by a palate which is much tighter, crisper and more minerally than the bouquet suggests, finishing with good acidity. **rating:** 90

best drinking 2003–2008 **best vintages** '88, '90, '92, '93, '94, '96, '98, '00 **drink with** Smoked trout mousse • $16.50

Grant Burge Eden Valley Gewürztraminer

TTTT 2001 Light straw-green; the moderately intense bouquet has positive lychee and spice varietal aromas, the palate good weight, length and acidity. One of a handful of serious examples of Gewürztraminer in Australia, with promising short-term development. **rating:** 89

best drinking 2002–2005 **best vintages** NA **drink with** Asian • $25

Grant Burge Barossa Vines Semillon

TTTY 2000 Light to medium yellow-green; a solid, clean bouquet with some citrus is followed by a palate with plenty of flavour in a ripe citrus mould. There is no question that withholding oak is the right way to go. **rating:** 83

best drinking 2001–2002 **best vintages** NA **drink with** All white meat dishes • $12

Grant Burge Zerk Semillon

TTTT 2001 Glowing yellow-green; the rich and complex bouquet shows obvious oak, the solid, full-bodied wine showing the impact of skin contact, barrel fermentation, 4 months' oak maturation and 70-year-old vines, all adding up to an emphatic drink-now style before the inevitable phenolics take over. **rating:** 85

best drinking 2002–2003 **best vintages** NA **drink with** Grilled chicken • $16.55

Grant Burge Kraft Vineyard Sauvignon Blanc

TTTT 2001 Light to medium green-yellow; a clean and aromatic bouquet with a ripe mix of gooseberry and passionfruit leads into a solid, honest palate with plenty of flavour in a slightly 4-square mode. **rating:** 85

best drinking 2001–2002 **best vintages** '94, '98, '99 **drink with** Rich seafood • $13.45

Grant Burge Virtuoso

TTTT 2001 Light to medium yellow-green; a powerful bouquet, with the gooseberry and faintly herbaceous Sauvignon Blanc dominant, a dominance which continues into the quite long and intense palate, the finish pleasantly tightened up by the Semillon. Not for the first time, preferred over the Kraft Sauvignon Blanc. **rating:** 88

best drinking 2001–2003 **best vintages** '98 **drink with** Brasserie food • $13.95

Grant Burge Lily Farm Frontignac

♥♥♥♥ 2001 Light green-yellow; the flowery bouquet is strongly and appropriately grapey, the palate crisp and lively, with a mix of lemony/grapey fruit flavours in the clearest imaginable manifestation of varietal character; has good length, and the aftertaste does not cloy as the sweetness might suggest. **rating:** 86

best drinking 2001–2002 **best vintages** NA **drink with** A summer's morning • $11

Grant Burge Summers Eden Valley and Adelaide Hills Chardonnay

♥♥♥♥ 2001 Light to medium green-yellow; citrus and melon fruit intermingle with strong barrel-ferment characters on the bouquet, but on the palate it is the fruit rather than the oak which comes through, in a wine which has surprising delicacy. **rating:** 87

best drinking 2002–2004 **best vintages** NA **drink with** Calamari • $18.10

Grant Burge Barossa Vines Shiraz

♥♥♥♥ 2000 Medium red-purple; scented American oak leads the charge on the bouquet, with fruit trailing along behind. On the palate, however, there is considerable all-up flavour, with dark cherry fruit, vanilla oak and soft tannins. **rating:** 86

best drinking 2002–2006 **best vintages** NA **drink with** Cold rare roast beef • $14.95

Grant Burge Filsell Shiraz

♥♥♥♥ 1999 Medium to full red-purple; the bouquet and palate are in the mainstream of the traditional style which Grant Burge favours, featuring dark cherry fruit and ladles of vanilla oak. **rating:** 86

best drinking 2003–2008 **best vintages** '97 **drink with** Pizza • $27.30

Grant Burge Meshach Shiraz

♥♥♥♥♥ 1998 Medium red-purple; clean berry fruit and particularly well-integrated and balanced oak on the bouquet lead into a medium-bodied palate, with a near-perfect balance between fruit, oak and tannins. Manages to combine elegance and flavour. **rating:** 94

best drinking 2003–2013 **best vintages** '88, '90, '91, '92, '95, '96, '98 **drink with** Braised beef • $90

Grant Burge Miamba Shiraz

♥♥♥♥ 1999 Medium red-purple; the moderately intense and traditional bouquet offers a mix of cherry and vanilla; the palate has plenty of weight to the dark cherry fruit; the tannins and oak are both neatly balanced with the fruit. **rating:** 87

best drinking 2002–2006 **best vintages** NA **drink with** Steak and kidney pie • $20

Grant Burge The Holy Trinity Grenache Shiraz Mourvedre

♥♥♥♥♀ 1998 Medium red-purple; the bouquet is clean, with light juicy fruit, tending a little simple, but the palate is well-balanced and constituted, with fresh fruit, fine tannins and restrained oak. **rating:** 90

best drinking 2002–2007 **best vintages** '98 **drink with** Jugged hare • $33

Grant Burge Hillcott Merlot

♥♥♥♥ 2000 Medium red-purple; sweet red berry and raspberry fruit with subtle oak on the bouquet are followed by a substantial palate, with ripe, soft, full fruit, again showing good oak handling. By far the best under this label thus far. **rating:** 89

best drinking 2003–2008 **best vintages** '00 **drink with** Veal saltimbocca • $18.10

Grant Burge RBM1 Merlot

♥♥♥♥ 1998 Medium red-purple; there are quite complex cedar, cigar box, spice/anise and berry varietal aromas leading into a palate with sweet raspberry fruit plus a touch of chocolate; the feel, structure and acidity are all appropriate for Merlot, the flavour less convincingly so. **rating:** 87

best drinking 2002–2008 **best vintages** '98 **drink with** Beef stroganoff • $33.10

Grant Burge Cameron Vale Cabernet Sauvignon

♥♥♥♥ 2000 Medium red-purple; earthy cabernet varietal fruit aromas are balanced by moderate oak on the bouquet; the palate has pleasant earthy/berry fruit, with good balance and mouthfeel; controlled oak. **rating:** 87

best drinking 2004–2009 **best vintages** '92, '93, '96, '98 **drink with** Roast beef • $24

Grant Burge Shadrach Cabernet Sauvignon

▼▼▼▼ 1998 Medium red-purple; the bouquet is of light to moderate intensity, lacking the concentration expected of 1998, though with some sweet berry fruit; the palate follows down the same track, but has the considerable advantage of not being swamped by oak; structure and tannins are good. **rating:** 87

best drinking 2003–2008 **best vintages** '93, '96 **drink with** Beef Bordelaise • $44.70

great lakes wines NR

Herivals Road, Wootton, NSW 2423 **region** Hastings River
phone (02) 4997 7255 **fax** (02) 4997 7450 **open** 7 days 11–4
winemaker David Hooke, Steve Atkins **production** 3000 **est.** 1990
product range ($9–16 CD) Semillon Chardonnay, Chardonnay, Shiraz, Chambourcin, Mellow Red.
summary John Webber and family began planting their vineyard on the mid-north coast of NSW in 1990. There is a 4-hectare vineyard planted to chambourcin, shiraz, cabernet sauvignon, chardonnay, semillon and verdelho, and the Webbers are proud of the fact that (to use their words) 'we are a fair dinkum winery where we grow the grapes and we make the wine'. Given the identity of the winemakers, I'm not sure how that works, but no matter.

greenock creek wines NR

Radford Road, Seppeltsfield, SA 5360 **region** Barossa Valley
phone (08) 8562 8103 **fax** (08) 8562 8259 **open** Wed–Mon 11–5 when wine available
winemaker Michael Waugh **production** 2500 **est.** 1978
product range ($27–145 CD) Apricot Block Shiraz, Seven Acre Shiraz, Creek Block Shiraz, Roennfeldt Road Shiraz, Cornerstone Grenache, Cabernet Sauvignon, Roennfeldt Road Cabernet Sauvignon.
summary Michael and Annabelle Waugh are disciples of Rocky O'Callaghan of Rockford Wines, and have deliberately accumulated a series of old dryland, low-yielding Barossa vineyards, aiming to produce wines of unusual depth of flavour and character. They have handsomely succeeded in this aim, achieving icon status and stratospheric prices in the US, making the opinions of Australian scribes irrelevant. They also offer superior accommodation in the ancient but beautifully restored two-bedroom cottage 'Miriam's'; Michael Waugh is a skilled stonemason.

green valley vineyard ★★★★

3137 Sebbes Road, Forest Grove, WA 6286 **region** Margaret River
phone (08) 9384 3131 **open** 7 days 10–6
winemaker Keith Mugford, Clive Otto (Contract) **production** 3500 **est.** 1980
product range ($17.50–29.50 CD) Riesling, Chardonnay, Gelignite Block White, Gelignite Block Shiraz, Cabernet Sauvignon.
summary Owners Ed and Eleanore Green commenced the development of Green Valley Vineyard in 1980. It is still a part-time operation, with the wines made by contract, but production has grown steadily from the 7.7 hectares of vines, and the Cabernet Sauvignon has been a consistent medal winner. Exports to Singapore and the US.

Green Valley Vineyard Riesling

▼▼▼▼ 2001 Light green-yellow; the bouquet has aromatic citrus blossom and apple, with a faint touch of reduction in the background; the firm and crisp palate moves positively into a mineral spectrum. **rating:** 86

best drinking 2003–2008 **best vintages** NA **drink with** Asparagus with hollandaise sauce • $17.50

Green Valley Vineyard Chardonnay

▼▼▼▽ 2000 Light to medium green-yellow; a light mix of fig and citrus, plus cashew and spicy oak on the bouquet, all of which come through on the light to medium-bodied, relatively understated, palate. Should build with time. **rating:** 84

▼▼▼▼ 1999 Medium yellow-green; a clean and smooth bouquet with well-balanced and integrated fruit and oak ranging through citrus and cashew; the palate has fine melon and citrus fruit offset by neatly judged and integrated oak. **rating:** 87

best drinking 2002–2005 **best vintages** NA **drink with** Steamed mussels • $23.50

Green Valley Vineyard Gelignite Block Shiraz

▼▼▼▼ 2000 Full purple-red; an ultra-complex bouquet, with opulent berry, spice and pronounced game. The palate is rich and full, with dark berry fruit and again that gamey character of the bouquet. I suspect that various tasters will have various interpretations of the origin of that character. The points are a cowardly compromise. **rating:** 88

best drinking 2004–2009 **best vintages** NA **drink with** Venison • $23.50

Green Valley Vineyard Cabernet Sauvignon

▼▼▼▼♡ 1999 Medium red-purple; a clean bouquet with an array of gravelly/blackberry/earthy cabernet varietal aromas of clarion clarity; the palate sweetens up with both cassis, blackcurrant and oak coming through, finishing with fine tannins. **rating:** 90

best drinking 2004–2009 **best vintages** NA **drink with** Saddle of lamb • $29.50

grevillea estate ★★★

Buckajo Road, Bega, NSW 2550 **region** South Coast Zone
phone (02) 6492 3006 **fax** (02) 6492 5330 **open** 7 days 9–5
winemaker Nicola Collins **production** 3000 **est.** 1980
product range ($12–25 CD) Daisy Hill Riesling, Lunatic Hill Sauvignon Blanc, Unoaked Chardonnay, Peak Hill Chardonnay, Rosé Hill Gewürztraminer, Traminer Riesling, Rougon, Grosse's Creek Merlot, Edmund Kirby Cabernet Sauvignon, Family Reserve Cabernet Sauvignon, Old Tawny Port.
summary A tourist-oriented winery which successfully sells all of its surprisingly large production through the cellar door and to local restaurants. All of the wines have very attractive labels, and the quality has increased significantly in recent years.

Grevillea Estate Lunatic Hill Sauvignon Blanc

▼▼▼♡ 2001 Light green-yellow; the firm and fresh bouquet has some herbal notes; the crisp, clean and firm palate is sustained by brisk acidity. There is not a great deal of varietal fruit character (not surprising), but the wine is well made. **rating:** 83

best drinking 2002–2003 **best vintages** NA **drink with** Seafood • $17

Grevillea Estate Family Reserve Cabernet Sauvignon

▼▼▼▼ 1999 Medium red-purple; the clean bouquet has good dark berry fruit aromatics; the palate has sweet blackberry and blackcurrant flavours; does tail off slightly on the finish, but nonetheless an impressive wine. **rating:** 86

best drinking 2003–2007 **best vintages** NA **drink with** Lamb backstrap • $25

grey sands ★★★★

Frankford Highway, Glengarry, Tas 7275 **region** Northern Tasmania
phone (03) 6396 1167 **fax** (03) 6396 1153 **open** By appointment
winemaker Bob Richter **production** 400 **est.** 1989
product range ($19–35 CD) Pinot Gris, Merlot, Shiraz.
summary Bob and Rita Richter began the slow establishment of Grey Sands in 1988, slowly increasing the plantings over the ensuing ten years to the present total of 2.5 hectares. The ultra-high density of 8900 vines per hectare partially reflects the experience gained by the Richters during a three-year stay in England, during which time they visited many vineyards across Europe, and Bob Richter's graduate diploma in wine from Roseworthy Agricultural College (1985/86).

Grey Sands Pinot Gris

▼▼▼▼♡ 2000 Light green-yellow; a clean bouquet with floral apple/apple blossom/pear aromas, then a palate with excellent mouthfeel and weight to the rich quince and apple fruit. Top-class Pinot Gris. **rating:** 91

best drinking 2002–2004 **best vintages** '00 **drink with** Bocconcini • $22

Grey Sands Shiraz

▼▼▼♡ 2000 Light to medium red-purple; the bouquet is clean, with some spicy notes, the light to medium-bodied palate offering a mix of spice, leaf and mint. Somewhat like the dog preaching, the wonder is not that it does it well, but that it does it at all. **rating:** 84

best drinking 2002–2005 **best vintages** NA **drink with** Lamb with mint sauce • $35

Grey Sands Merlot

▼▼▼▼ 2000 Light to medium red-purple; a fragrant mix of spicy/leafy/minty aromas, then a lively, fresh and flavoursome palate, those leafy/minty characters reappearing, suggesting less than complete ripening. **rating:** 85

best drinking 2002–2005 **best vintages** '99 **drink with** Braised lamb • $30

� grimm's domain ★★★☆

Broke Road, Pokolbin, NSW 2320 **region** Lower Hunter Valley
phone (02) 4998 7025 **fax** (02) 4998 7026 **open** Not
winemaker David Lowe, Jane Wilson **production** 500 **est.** 1996
product range Sunrise Ridge Semillon, Moon River Shiraz.
summary Wolfgang Grimm arrived as general manager of Sydney's Hotel Inter-Continental in 1989, and almost immediately made his impact on the wine and hospitality industries. He encouraged the holding of wine events of all types and sizes at the Inter-Continental, and worked tirelessly for the broader tourism industry; his work was recognised with the award of an AM in 1998. In the meantime, encouraged by Len Evans, he had purchased a 30-hectare property on the northern slopes of Broke Road, Pokolbin, and in 1996 he planted 1 hectare of semillon, following with a further hectare of shiraz in 2000. Reflecting his 35 years of experience as a hotelier, he also erected a six-suite lodge development, recently given a five-star rating by the AAA. The estate-grown Sunrise Ridge Semillon and contract-grown Moon River Shiraz are more than creditable; other than through the lodge, the wines are only sold overseas.

Grimm's Domain Sunrise Ridge Semillon

▼▼▼▼ 2000 Light to medium yellow-green; the moderately intense bouquet is clean, with a mix of herb, grass, citrus and mineral aromas. Has a generous mid-palate, reflecting the warm and dry 2000 vintage, which may be why the wine seems to shorten fractionally on the finish. **rating:** 87

best drinking 2002–2007 **best vintages** '00 **drink with** Grilled fish • $20

Grimm's Domain Moon River Shiraz

▼▼▼▼ 2000 Deep red-purple; the bouquet shows some lift to the regional, savoury fruit, doubtless coming from the oak. A big, rich, concentrated palate follows, with dark berry and chocolate flavours. A little jumpy at the moment, but will smooth out and reflect the excellent vintage as it matures. **rating:** 85

best drinking 2004–2010 **best vintages** NA **drink with** Seared kangaroo fillet • $25

grosset ★★★★★

King Street, Auburn, SA 5451 **region** Clare Valley
phone (08) 8849 2175 **fax** (08) 8849 2292 **open** Wed–Sun 10–5 from 1st week of September for approx 6 weeks
winemaker Jeffrey Grosset **production** 8500 **est.** 1981
product range ($29–58 R) Watervale Riesling, Polish Hill Riesling, Semillon Sauvignon Blanc, Piccadilly Chardonnay, Gaia (a Cabernet blend), Reserve Pinot Noir.
summary Jeffrey Grosset served part of his apprenticeship at the vast Lindeman Karadoc winery, moving from the largest to one of the smallest when he established Grosset Wines in its old stone winery. He now crafts the wines with the utmost care from grapes grown to the most exacting standards; all need a certain amount of time in bottle to achieve their ultimate potential, not the least the Rieslings and Gaia, among Australia's best examples of their kind. At a Riesling Summit held in Hamburg in the latter part of 1998, Grosset was voted Riesling Winemaker of the Year. Exports to the US, Europe and Asia mean a continuous shortage of the wines in all markets.

Grosset Polish Hill Riesling

▼▼▼▼▽ 2001 Light green-yellow; a very restrained, dry, minerally bouquet with touches of herb is followed by a fresh, still neutral palate, like a young Semillon, austere and delicate, finishing with crisp acidity. The track record of these wines leaves no doubt that they will blossom with time in bottle, but, in the interim, the Watervale, at a lower price, has the greater appeal. **rating:** 91

best drinking 2004–2014 **best vintages** '87, '90, '93, '94, '96, '97, '98, '99, '00 **drink with** Grilled SA whiting • $36.50

Grosset Watervale Riesling

▼▼▼▼▼ 2001 Fresh cut apple/apple blossom aromas with hints of spice and lime meld into a lime-accented palate with great mouthfeel, its impact building progressively through to the finish. **rating:** 94

best drinking 2002–2012 **best vintages** '81, '86, '90, '93, '94, '95, '96, '97, '98, '99, '00, '01 **drink with** Grilled King George whiting • $31

Grosset Semillon Sauvignon Blanc

ŸŸŸŸŸ **2001** Light green-yellow; the fragrant bouquet has a mix of blossom, gooseberry and citrus aromas; the palate is intense and long, with impeccable balance in terms of both fruit flavours and acidity; neither has nor needs oak. **rating:** 95

best drinking 2001–2003 **best vintages** '93, '94, '95, '96, '97, '99, '00, '01 **drink with** Antipasto • $29

Grosset Piccadilly Chardonnay

ŸŸŸŸŸ **2000** Medium yellow-green; in mainstream Grosset style, the bouquet offers a subtle mix of cashew, fig, melon and stone fruit, characters which are faithfully reproduced on the very long and immaculately balanced palate. **rating:** 94

best drinking 2002–2007 **best vintages** '96, '97, '99, '00 **drink with** Milk-fed veal • $45

Grosset Pinot Noir

ŸŸŸŸŸ **2000** Medium red-purple; slightly dusty oak over glossy plum and mint fruit on the bouquet is followed by a full, ripe and lush palate with masses of plummy fruit and a velvety soft texture. **rating:** 94

best drinking 2002–2006 **best vintages** '00 **drink with** Braised duck • $58

Grosset Gaia

ŸŸŸŸŸ **1999** Medium to full red-purple; sweet, luscious, dark berry fruit aromas, with a hint of oak spice, lead into a rich and textured palate with savoury tannins surrounding the dark berry fruit at its core. **rating:** 92

best drinking 2004–2014 **best vintages** '90, '91, '92, '94, '95, '96, '98, '99 **drink with** Clare hare pie • $56

grove estate ★★★

Murringo Road, Young, NSW 2594 **region** Hilltops
phone (02) 6382 6999 **fax** (02) 6382 4527 **open** Weekends 10–5 or by appointment
winemaker Jenny Bright, Monarch Winemaking Services (Contract) **production** 2000 **est.** 1989
product range ($14–21 CD) Hilltops Semillon, Murringo Way Chardonnay, The Cellar Block Shiraz, Hilltops Zinfandel, The Partners Cabernet Sauvignon.
summary A partnership headed by Brian Mullany has established a 30-hectare vineyard planted to semillon, chardonnay, merlot, shiraz, cabernet sauvignon and zinfandel. Most of the grapes are sold (principally to Southcorp), but a limited amount of wine is contract-made by Monarch Winemaking Services for the Grove Estate label.

grove hill ★★★★

120 Old Norton Summit Road, Norton Summit, SA 5136 **region** Adelaide Hills
phone (08) 8390 1437 **fax** (08) 8390 1437 **open** Sunday 11–5
winemaker (Contract) **production** 500 **est.** 1978
product range ($22–40 ML) Riesling, Chardonnay, Reserve Chardonnay, Marguerite Pinot Chardonnay, Pinot Noir.
summary Grove Hill is a heritage property established in 1846 with the original homestead and outbuildings and held by the same family since that time. Winemaking by David Powell (of Torbreck) adds an extra degree of interest.

Grove Hill Chardonnay

ŸŸŸŸ **1998** Light to medium green-yellow; a clean but complex bouquet, then a tangy/lemony/citrussy palate, long, with high acidity and radically different to the much more advanced, ripe and quite sweet '99. A blend of the two vintages gives the perfect result. **rating:** 88

best drinking 2002–2005 best vintages NA drink with Grilled prawns • $10

🐌 growlers gully ★★★☆

21a Shaws Road, Merton, Vic 3715 **region** Central Victorian High Country
phone (03) 5778 9615 **fax** (03) 5778 9615 **open** Fri 5–7, weekends and public holidays 12–6 or by appointment
winemaker Martin Williams MW, Daniel Crane MW (Contract) **production** 380 **est.** 1997
product range ($22 CD) Shiraz.
summary Les and Wendy Oates began the establishment of the Growlers Gully vineyard in 1997, extending it in 1998 to a total of 4 hectares of shiraz and 1 hectare of cabernet sauvignon. It sits at an elevation of 375 metres with fertile brown clay loam soil. Very competent contract winemaking by Martin

Williams MW has led to richly flavoured and coloured wine. A rammed earth cellar-door sales outlet opened in early 2002, with the ambition of ultimately offering light meals and the option to visitors of using the barbecue facilities on-site.

Growlers Gully Shiraz

▼▼▼▼ 2000 Medium red-purple; clean, dark berry fruit with gentle oak leads into a palate with abundant, sweet dark berry/cherry fruit, a touch of bitter chocolate, and fine-grained, savoury tannins; not over-extracted. **rating:** 87

best drinking 2004–2009 **best vintages** NA **drink with** Braised ox cheek • $22

haan wines ★★★★☆

Siegersdorf Road, Tanunda, SA 5352 **region** Barossa Valley
phone (08) 8562 4590 **fax** (08) 8562 4590 **open** Not
winemaker James Irvine (Contract) **production** 4000 **est.** 1993
product range ($18–38 ML) Semillon, Viognier, Chanticleer Sparkling Rosé, Wilhelmus (red blend), Shiraz Prestige, Merlot Prestige.
summary Hans and Fransien Haan established their business in 1993 when they acquired a 16-hectare vineyard near Tanunda (since extended to 36.7 hectares). The primary focus is on Merlot, and in particular on the luxury Merlot Prestige, and they understandably chose James Irvine as their contract-winemaker. There are no cellar-door sales; the wines are distributed in eastern Australia through Australian Prestige Wines and exported to the UK, the US, Switzerland, Germany, Malaysia, Singapore, Hong Kong and Japan.

Haan Semillon

▼▼▼▼ 2001 Medium to full yellow-green; a massively rich and ripe bouquet is followed by a rich and striking palate; an altogether alternative face of Semillon, tipping the scales at 13.5° alcohol, and in an uncompromising drink-now style. **rating:** 89

best drinking 2001–2002 **best vintages** NA **drink with** Rich seafood • $18.50

Haan Viognier

▼▼▼▼▽ 2001 Medium to full yellow-green; rich, complex dried fruit/pastille varietal character on the bouquet smooths through to a palate with considerable viscosity and richness at the centre, tinged with apricot; a big, bold style with sweetness (probably simply varietal fruit and alcohol) quite evident. **rating:** 92

best drinking 2001–2004 **best vintages** '99, '00, '01 **drink with** Rich fish dishes • $26.50

☙ hackersley ★★★★☆

Ferguson Road, Dardanup, WA 6236 **region** Geographe
phone (08) 9384 6247 **fax** (08) 9728 3133 **open** Weekends 10–4
winemaker Jeff Ovens **production** 450 **est.** 1997
product range ($18–22 CD) Sauvignon Blanc Semillon, Shiraz, Cabernet Sauvignon.
summary Hackersley is a partnership between the Ovens, Stacey and Hewitt families, friends since their university days, and with (so they say) the misguided belief that growing and making their own wine would be cheaper than buying it. They found what they describe as a 'little piece of paradise in the Ferguson Valley just south of Dardanup', and in September 1998 they planted a little under 8 hectares, extended in August 2000 to 9.5 hectares of the mainstream varieties, interestingly, turning their back on chardonnay. The first harvest in 2000 produced 42 tonnes of fruit, most going to Houghton, as will be the pattern for the foreseeable future. However, a small quantity of immaculately packaged Semillon Sauvignon Blanc, Shiraz and Cabernet has been made for release under the Hackersley label, and is of exceptional quality for a first vintage.

Hackersley Sauvignon Blanc Semillon

▼▼▼▼ 2001 Pale straw; while not especially intense, the bouquet is complex, with a range of fruit blossom aromatics and a touch of spice, probably from the small portion barrel-fermented in French oak. The palate has good flavour and structure, with positive citrussy fruit reflecting the blend of 60 per cent Sauvignon Blanc and 40 per cent Semillon; once again, there is a whisper of oak. **rating:** 89

best drinking 2002–2003 **best vintages** NA **drink with** Any seafood • $18

Hackersley Shiraz

▼▼▼▼▽ 2000 Medium to full red-purple; solid, ripe, black fruits and chocolate aromas are folded through well-handled oak; on the palate there is abundant but not over-extracted black cherry, chocolate and spice fruit, allied with excellent tannins and oak. **rating:** 92

best drinking 2003–2010 **best vintages** '00 **drink with** Slow-braised beef • $22

Hackersley Cabernet Sauvignon

▼▼▼▼▽ 2000 Excellent red-purple, deep but clear; a smoothly complex mix of cassis, mulberry, cedar and spice on the bouquet, then an elegant but flavoursome palate with ripe cassis and impeccable oak handling. Lovely wine, outstanding value. **rating:** 93

best drinking 2003–2010 **best vintages** '00 **drink with** Milk-fed lamb • $20

haig   NR

Square Mile Road, Mount Gambier, SA 5290 **region** Mount Gambier
phone (08) 8725 5414 **fax** (08) 8725 5414 **open** 7 days 11–5
winemaker Martin Slocombe (Contract) **production** 1000 **est.** 1982
product range ($16–19 CD) Chardonnay, Late Harvest Chardonnay, Pinot Noir, Cabernet Sauvignon.
summary The 4 hectares of estate vineyards are planted on the rich volcanic soils near the slopes of the famous Blue Lake of Mount Gambier. I have neither seen nor tasted the wines.

hainault   ★★★

255 Walnut Road, Bickley, WA 6076 **region** Perth Hills
phone (08) 9226 4704 **fax** (08) 9226 4755 **open** Weekends 10–5
winemaker Contract **production** 2300 **est.** 1980
product range ($14–21 CD) The Terroir Range of Gewürztraminer, Pinot Noir, Merlot, Shiraz; Talus Sparkling.
summary Under the energetic ownership of public affairs consultant and businessman Bill Mackey and wife Vicki, the changes have come thick and fast at Hainault, with plantings increasing to 11 hectares.

halcyon daze   ★★★

19 Uplands Road, Lilydale, Vic 3140 **region** Yarra Valley
phone (03) 9726 7111 **fax** (03) 9726 7111 **open** By appointment
winemaker Richard Rackley **production** 500 **est.** 1982
product range ($28–30 ML) Merlot, Cabernet Franc Merlot.
summary One of the lower-profile wineries, with a small, estate-grown production. The winery in fact sells the major part of the grapes from its 6.5 hectares of vines to others. Immaculate viticulture ensures that the grapes have a strong market.

hamelin bay   ★★★★

Brockman Highway, Karridale, WA 6288 **region** Margaret River
phone (08) 9758 5555 **fax** (08) 9389 6020 **open** Mon–Fri 10–5 (by appointment)
winemaker Philip Tubb **production** 15 000 **est.** 1992
product range ($16–30 R) Sauvignon Blanc, Semillon Sauvignon Blanc, Chardonnay, Rampant White, Rampant Red, Shiraz, Cabernet Merlot, Cabernet Sauvignon.
summary The 25-hectare Hamelin Bay vineyard was established by the Drake-Brockman family. The initial releases were contract-made, but a winery with a cellar-door sales facility was opened in 2000. In the meantime, production has increased from 5000 to 15 000 cases. Exports to the UK, the US, Germany and Singapore.

Hamelin Bay Chardonnay

▼▼▼▼▽ 2000 Light to medium yellow-green; the clean, fresh bouquet has melon and honeydew fruit interwoven with subtle oak and malolactic influences; there is good depth, length and mouthfeel to the palate, with citrus and melon fruit followed by a crisp, bright finish. **rating:** 90

best drinking 2002–2015 **best vintages** '00 **drink with** Lemon chicken • $22.99

Hamelin Bay Rampant Red

▼▼▼▼ 2000 Medium to full red-purple; ultra-ripe black fruit, plum, prune and licorice flood both the bouquet and palate, the palate finishing with ripe tannins; 14.5° alcohol, and in very similar style to the preceding vintage. Double gold at the 2002 Sydney International Wine Competition. **rating:** 89

best drinking 2005–2015 **best vintages** NA **drink with** Barbecued bangers • $17.99

Hamelin Bay Cabernet Merlot

ŢŢŢŢŶ **2000** Medium to full red-purple; ripe blackcurrant and blackberry fruit is supported by soft oak on the bouquet; the palate is in similar soft, ripe but not jammy mould, the tannins and oak sweet, making for a very accessible style. **rating:** 90

best drinking 2002–2007 **best vintages** '00 **drink with** Spaghetti bolognese • $24.99

Hamelin Bay Cabernet Sauvignon

ŢŢŢŢ **2000** Deep red-purple; potent, brooding blackberry, spice and cedar aromas flow into a palate as powerful as the bouquet suggests, playing black fruit flavours against a savoury, slightly grippy finish. 15° alcohol; the kind of wine one expects from McLaren Vale, not Margaret River. **rating:** 89

best drinking 2005–2015 **best vintages** NA **drink with** Butterfly leg of lamb • $24.99

hamilton ★★★★

Main Road, Willunga, SA 5172 **region** McLaren Vale
phone (08) 8556 2288 **fax** (08) 8556 2868 **open** Mon–Fri 10–5, weekends 11–5
winemaker Paul Gordon **production** 25 000 **est.** 1837
product range ($13–50 R) Slate Quarry Riesling, Noble Sauvignon Blanc Semillon, Lot 148 Merlot, Gumprs' Block Shiraz, Hut Block Cabernet Sauvignon; Hamilton Reserve wines are Richard Hamilton Signature Chardonnay, Marion Vineyard Grenache Shiraz, Burton's Vineyard Grenache Shiraz, Centurion 100 Year Old Vines Shiraz, Egremont Reserve Merlot.
summary Hamilton has outstanding estate vineyards, some of great age, all fully mature, but I have often felt the end products did not seem to do full justice to those vineyards. The arrival (in 2002) of former Rouge Homme winemaker Paul Gordon should answer once and for all whether that feeling is (or was) justified. Exports to Europe, the US, Canada, and Asia.

Hamilton Slate Quarry Riesling

ŢŢŢŢ **2001** Light green-yellow; light tropical blossom aromas, almost into peach, are reflected in the flavour of the palate, but it simply doesn't have the length of top Rieslings. However, the Stelvin closure will protect the wine as it ages in bottle. **rating:** 85

best drinking 2002–2006 **best vintages** NA **drink with** Summer salads • $12.95

Richard Hamilton Synergy Semillon Sauvignon Blanc

ŢŢŢŢ **2001** Medium yellow-green; the solid bouquet has quite pronounced herbaceous fruit untrammelled by oak; the palate, likewise, has plenty of varietal inputs from both fruit components, providing a positively flavoured and structured wine. Excellent value. **rating:** 88

best drinking 2002–2004 **best vintages** NA **drink with** King George whiting • $12

Richard Hamilton Signature Chardonnay

ŢŢŢŢ **2001** Medium yellow-green; melon fruit on the bouquet is offset by a touch of citrus and lemony oak, the palate moving up a gear, with attractive, squeaky mouthfeel, and the barrel-ferment oak inputs more positive, but without threatening. Pleasing melon and nectarine fruit occupy the mid-palate **rating:** 89
ŢŢŢŶ **1999** Medium yellow-green; the bouquet has moderately ripe peach supported by solid oak inputs; overall, plenty of aroma and flavour, but slightly hard acid on the finish disrupts the palate. Disappointing after the '98. **rating:** 83

best drinking 2002–2004 **best vintages** NA **drink with** Abalone • $17.99

Hamilton Centurion 100 Year Old Shiraz

ŢŢŢŢ **1999** Medium red-purple; a very typical, lifted, scented minty edge to the aromas, followed by red berry fruit then a sharp minty edge on the finish; extraordinary that these flavours should come from a 15° alcohol wine. **rating:** 88

best drinking 2003–2008 **best vintages** '98 **drink with** Braised ox cheek • $49.95

Hamilton Gumprs' Block Shiraz

ŢŢŢŢŶ **2000** Deep red-purple; clean, rich, savoury, chocolate, plum and berry fruit on the bouquet leads into a medium-bodied palate which flows well across the tongue, the flavours tracking the bouquet. Excellent for the vintage. **rating:** 90

best drinking 2005–2010 **best vintages** '00 **drink with** Kebabs • $19.95

Richard Hamilton Burton's Vineyard Old Bush Vine Grenache Shiraz

ŢŢŢŢŢ 1998 Medium to full red-purple, still bright; sweet, smooth, ripe and supple fruit aromas on the bouquet have some gamey undertones; a powerful wine in the mouth, in uncompromising gamey Rhône-ish style; strong tannins need patience. **rating:** 90

best drinking 2004–2009 **best vintages** '91, '92, '94, '95, '98 **drink with** Cassoulet • $29.95

Hamilton Marion Vineyard Grenache Shiraz

ŢŢŢŢŢ 1998 Medium red-purple; fresh, bright aromas have a varietal gamey edge; the palate has flavoursome berryish fruit and attractive fine, ripe tannins. **rating:** 90

best drinking 2002–2007 **best vintages** '98 **drink with** Spiced beef • $29.95

Hamilton Egremont Reserve Merlot

ŢŢŢŢ 2000 Medium red-purple; has slightly curious oriental spice aromas and a touch of tobacco on the bouquet, the palate moving more to typical red berry fruit, the remnants of spice of the bouquet, a touch of chocolate, and fine, savoury tannins. **rating:** 86

best drinking 2005–2010 **best vintages** '97 **drink with** Stuffed shoulder of lamb • $44.95

Hamilton Lot 148 Merlot

ŢŢŢŢ 2000 Medium purple-red; firm, leafy/berry fruit and subtle oak open proceedings, some regional chocolate coming through on the palate to accompany dark berry flavours and moderate tannins. **rating:** 85

best drinking 2003–2007 **best vintages** NA **drink with** Grilled beef • $19.95

Hamilton Hut Block Cabernet Sauvignon

ŢŢŢŢ 2000 Medium red-purple; a clean, fresh bouquet with a mix of black and redcurrant; the palate runs with those blackcurrant flavours, adding a dash of chocolate, finishing with fine tannins. There is the faintest question as to whether the SO_2 level may be low. **rating:** 88

best drinking 2004–2010 **best vintages** '86, '90, '91, '93, '00 **drink with** Beef Provençale • $19.95

hamiltons bluff NR

Longs Corner Road, Canowindra, NSW 2804 **region** Cowra
phone (02) 6344 2079 **fax** (02) 6344 2165 **open** Weekends and holidays 10–4, Mon–Fri by appointment
winemaker Andrew Margan **production** 5000 **est.** 1995
product range ($14.50–22 CD) Canowindra Grossi range of Unwooded Chardonnay, Cabernet Sauvignon; Cowra Chardonnay, Chairman's Reserve Chardonnay, Sangiovese, Méthode Champenoise, Devonian Red NV,
summary Hamiltons Bluff is owned and operated by the Andrews family, which planted 45 hectares of vines in 1995. 1998 produced the first crop, and three different Chardonnays were contract-made by Andrew Margan. The Cowra Chardonnay and Canowindra Grossi Chardonnay received medals at the 1998 Cowra Wine Show. Cellar-door sales opened in early 1999, heralding a new stage of development for the Cowra region.

hamilton's ewell vineyards ★★★★

Siegersdorf Vineyard, Barossa Valley Way, Tanunda, SA 5352 **region** Barossa Valley
phone (08) 8231 0088 **fax** (08) 8231 0355 **open** Mon–Fri 10–5, weekends 11–5
winemaker Robert Hamilton, John Davey **production** 13 000 **est.** 1837
product range ($16–25 R) Limestone Quarry Chardonnay, Railway Chardonnay, Railway Shiraz, Fuller's Barn Shiraz, Stonegarden Grenache Shiraz, Cabernet Sauvignon
summary Mark Hamilton, an Adelaide lawyer by profession, is a sixth generation direct descendent of Richard Hamilton, who arrived in South Australia in 1838 (a year after the state was proclaimed) and made his first wine in 1841. Hamilton's Ewell Vineyards remained in the family until 1979, when it was acquired by Mildara Blass, much to Mark Hamilton's dismay. Since 1991 he has set about building yet another Hamilton wine business by a series of astute vineyard acquisitions, and buying back the name Hamilton's Ewell from Mildara. Most of the grapes are sold, but there is scope to very significantly increase production in the years ahead. Exports to the US, Canada, Hong Kong and the UK.

Hamilton's Ewell Vineyards Limestone Quarry Wrattonbully Chardonnay

TTTT 2001 Light green-yellow; a clean, direct fresh lemon and grapefruit bouquet and palate makes for a zesty unoaked style. **rating: 85**

best drinking 2002–2003 **best vintages** NA **drink with** Fish and chips • $16

Hamilton's Ewell Vineyards Railway Chardonnay

TTTT 2000 Light to medium yellow-green; the bouquet is solid, not particularly aromatic, but with some yellow peach and residual oak. The solid, no-frills palate has flavour, controlled oak, but not much zip. **rating: 85**

best drinking 2002–2003 **best vintages** NA **drink with** Roast chicken • $16

Hamilton's Ewell Vineyards Railway Shiraz

TTTT 2000 Medium to full red-purple; clean, sweet cherry/raspberry fruit and subtle oak on the bouquet, then a palate with abundant cherry, raspberry and blackberry fruit; good flow and feel. **rating: 89**

TTTTY 1999 Medium to full red-purple; a rich and complex bouquet with dark berry, dark chocolate and positive oak contributions is followed by a similarly rich and complex palate with sweet, juicy berry fruit, neither jammy nor heavy. Fine tannins and appropriate oak complete the picture. **rating: 92**

best drinking 2005–2010 **best vintages** '99 **drink with** Braised game • $25

Hamilton's Ewell Vineyards Stonegarden Grenache Shiraz

TTTT 1999 Bright, deep red-purple; the bouquet is complex and firm, not at all jammy, but sweetly expressive of grenache. The solid, powerful palate has dark chocolate, dark berry fruit, and quite powerful tannins. **rating: 88**

best drinking 2004–2009 **best vintages** NA **drink with** Game pie • $19

Hamilton's Ewell Vineyards Cabernet Sauvignon

TTTT 2000 Medium red-purple; a challenging, fragrant bouquet with distinctly earthy/spicy overtones, even cachou/licorice, all unexpected with cabernet sauvignon, is followed by a palate which veers back to familiar territory. Here red and blackcurrant fruit marry with some vanilla oak and soft tannins, suggesting a relatively early-maturing wine. **rating: 88**

best drinking 2004–2009 **best vintages** NA **drink with** Lamb shanks • $25

hanging rock winery ★★★★

88 Jim Road, Newham, Vic 3442 **region** Macedon Ranges
phone (03) 5427 0542 **fax** (03) 5427 0310 **open** 7 days 10–5
winemaker John Ellis **production** 30 000 **est.** 1982
product range ($12–55 CD) The wines are offered in 4 tiers: at the bottom the Rock range of Riesling, Chardonnay, Red and Merlot; next up the scale Victoria Chardonnay, Verdelho, S (sweet white) and Late Harvest Gewürztraminer and Riesling; then the trio of Central Highlands Pinot Noir, Victoria Shiraz and Victoria Cabernet Merlot; at the top are Jim Jim Sauvignon Blanc, Heathcote Shiraz, Macedon Cuvée and Gralaine Merlot.
summary The Macedon area has proved very marginal in spots, and the Hanging Rock vineyards, with their lovely vista towards the Rock, are no exception. John Ellis has thus elected to source additional grapes from various parts of Victoria to produce an interesting and diverse style of wines. The low-priced Rock series, with its bold packaging, has replaced the Picnic wines. Exports to the UK, Denmark, the US, Canada, New Zealand, Hong Kong, Malaysia, Taiwan and Japan.

Rock Riesling

TTTY 2001 Light straw-green; a clean, light and fresh bouquet with hints of blossom goes through into the fore and mid-palate; does fumble the finish slightly and shorten, but good value. Part of the new, strikingly packaged economy-priced range, and good value. **rating: 83**

best drinking 2002–2003 **best vintages** NA **drink with** Fish, vegetarian • $12

Hanging Rock The Jim Jim Sauvignon Blanc

TTTT 2001 Very pale straw-green; a light, crisp bouquet with touches of gooseberry, asparagus and grass peeping through; the delicate and crisp palate has a nice tight finish, giving it both length and, despite the delicacy, character. Made in a very consistent style from year to year. **rating: 89**

best drinking 2002–2004 **best vintages** '93, '95, '96, '99, '00, '01 **drink with** Oysters • $22

Hanging Rock Central Highlands Pinot Noir

▼▼▼▽ 2000 Medium red-purple; clean, red cherry/berry fruit has some fragrance on the bouquet; the palate provides similar direct red berry fruits, and a faint green tinge which does not add to the complexity of a fresh, no-frills wine. A blend of Macedon, Ballarat and Central Highlands material.   **rating:** 84

best drinking 2002–2004 **best vintages** '98 **drink with** Braised rabbit • $20

Hanging Rock Winery Heathcote Shiraz

▼▼▼▼▽ 2000 Medium to full red-purple; obvious high-toast barrel-ferment oak is the first impression on the bouquet, with strong fruit following; the palate provides a similar play, although the powerful berry fruit is there in abundance; still in its infancy, needing much time; I suspect will always show the pronounced oak influence.   **rating:** 92

best drinking 2005–2012 **best vintages** '97, '98, '99, '00 **drink with** Roast venison • $55

Hanging Rock Victoria Shiraz

▼▼▼▼▽ 2000 Good medium red-purple; the bouquet shows exemplary varietal character with damson plum, a whisker of spice, and integrated oak; the palate has luscious, sweet plum and blackberry fruit supported by fine tannins. A blend of Swan Hill and Heathcote wine. The best for years under this label and very good value.   **rating:** 90

best drinking 2003–2008 **best vintages** '90, '91, '92, '94, '00 **drink with** Marinated beef • $20

hankin estate   NR

2 Johnsons Lane, Northwood via Seymour, Vic 3660 **region** Goulburn Valley
phone (03) 5792 2396 **fax** (03) 9353 2927 **open** Weekends and public holidays 10–5
winemaker Dr Max Hankin **production** 2400 **est.** 1975
product range ($8–28 CD) Semillon, Verdelho, Rosé, Shiraz, Merlot, Merlot Cabernet Franc Malbec, Cabernet Malbec, Cabernet Sauvignon Merlot.
summary Hankin Estate is now the principal occupation of Dr Max Hankin, who has retired from full-time medical practice. He has to contend with phylloxera, which decimated the original plantings; the replanting process is still underway.

hanns creek estate   NR

Kentucky Road, Merricks North, Vic 3926 **region** Mornington Peninsula
phone (03) 5989 7266 **fax** (03) 5989 7500 **open** 7 days 11–5
winemaker Tony Aubrey-Slocock **production** 1500 **est.** 1987
product range ($18–25 CD) Chardonnay, Rosé, Pinot Noir, Cabernet Shiraz, Cabernet Sauvignon.
summary Denise and Tony Aubrey-Slocock established a 3-hectare vineyard on the slopes of Merricks North. After an uncertain start, with contract-winemaking moving around, Kevin McCarthy took control and wine style steadied. However, the vineyard was sold in April 2002; no further details available at the time of going to print.

hansen hilltops   ★★★★

Barwang Ridge, 1 Barwang Road via Young, NSW 2594 **region** Hilltops
phone (02) 6382 6363 **fax** (02) 6382 6363 **open** 7 days 11–6
winemaker Charles Sturt University (Contract) **production** 2000 **est.** 1979
product range ($15.50–18 CD) Riesling, Chardonnay Semillon, Cabernet Sauvignon.
summary The vineyard has 5 hectares of vines, 1 hectare each of riesling, chardonnay, shiraz, cabernet sauvignon, and a further hectare roughly split between semillon, merlot and malbec. The plantings date back to 1970, but the first wines were not made until the late 1990s. Peter Hansen points out that there are only two vineyards at Barwang, both part of the original Barwang sheep station: McWilliam's and his. Perhaps a little cheekily, he goes on to point out that the difference is that his wines are produced solely from non-irrigated vines which are hand-picked and hand-pruned, and, into the bargain, are 10 years older than McWilliam's.

hanson-tarrahill vineyard   ★★★

49 Cleveland Avenue, Lower Plenty, Vic 3093 (postal) **region** Yarra Valley
phone (03) 9439 7425 **fax** (03) 9439 4217 **open** Not
winemaker Dr Ian Hanson **production** 1000 **est.** 1983
product range ($21–30 R) Pinot Noir, Arundel (Cabernet blend), Tarra's Block Cabernets, Cabernet Sauvignon.

summary Dental surgeon Ian Hanson planted his first vines in the late 1960s, close to the junction of the Yarra and Plenty Rivers; in 1983 those plantings were extended (with 3000 vines), and in 1988 the Tarrahill property at Yarra Glen was established with a further 4 hectares. Hanson is the name which appears most prominently on the newly designed labels; Tarrahill Vineyard is in much smaller type.

happs ★★★★

571 Commonage Road, Dunsborough, WA 6281 **region** Margaret River
phone (08) 9755 3300 **fax** (08) 9755 3846 **open** 7 days 10–5
winemaker Erl Happ, Mark Aitken **production** 18 000 **est.** 1978
product range ($13–45 CD) Dry table wines are Anne Coralie Semillon, Semillon Verdelho, Semillon Sauvignon Blanc, Marrimée (Semillon Chenin Blanc), Viognier, Marsanne, PF White (Preservative Free), Chardonnay, PF Red (Preservative Free), Shiraz, Merlot and Cabernet Merlot; sweet table wines are Fuschia, Topaz and Late Picked Verdelho; fortifieds are Fortis (Vintage Port), 10 Year Fortis (Tawny), Fortissimo, Garnet (from Muscat à Petit Grains) and Pale Gold (White Port); Karridale Three Hills super premium range of Shiraz, Charles Andreas (Cabernet blend), Merlot, Nebbiolo and Cabernet Franc.
summary Former schoolteacher turned potter and winemaker Erl Happ is an iconoclast and compulsive experimenter. Many of the styles he makes are very unconventional, the future likely to be even more so: the Karridale vineyard planted in 1994 has no less than 28 different varieties established. Merlot has been a winery specialty for a decade. Limited retail distributed through NSW, Victoria and Queensland and, more recently, exports to Europe.

Happs Semillon Sauvignon Blanc

ΨΨΨΨ **2001** Very pale straw-green; a mainstream bouquet of crisp herb, grass and mineral plays through into the moderately long palate, with the addition of some lemony notes. A blend of 70 per cent Semillon and 30 per cent Sauvignon Blanc. **rating:** 85

best drinking 2002–2003 **best vintages** NA **drink with** Asparagus terrine • $16

Happs Marrimee Margaret River White

ΨΨΨΨ **1999** Very light straw-green, amazingly youthful for its age; the bouquet offers a mix of mineral, spice and talc, the multi-flavoured palate adding some canned peach. A blend of Semillon, Chardonnay, Chenin Blanc and Marsanne. **rating:** 83

best drinking 2002–2003 **best vintages** NA **drink with** Strongly sauced pasta • $14

Happs PF White

ΨΨΨΨ **2000** Bright green-yellow, showing no sign of browning; the bouquet is quite rich and solid, with yellow peach, and the palate, likewise, has stood the test of time remarkably well, showing no oxidation or mousiness. A 50/50 blend of Chardonnay and Semillon which one would normally seek to drink in the year of vintage. **rating:** 84

best drinking 2002–2003 **best vintages** NA **drink with** Whatever • $17

Happs Verdelho

ΨΨΨΨ **2001** Light green-yellow; a curious mix of lemon butter and more floral characters, then a quite lively/lemony palate with some grassy fruit components. **rating:** 84

best drinking 2002–2003 **best vintages** NA **drink with** Gazpacho • $16

Happs Chardonnay

ΨΨΨΨ **2000** Medium yellow-green; the bouquet is moderately intense but not without complexity, light melon fruit interwoven with subtle oak. The palate is pleasant and harmonious, but not as complex as the bouquet; elegance is the key word. **rating:** 86

best drinking 2002–2004 **best vintages** '91, '94 **drink with** Quiche • $18

Happs Three Hills Shiraz

ΨΨΨΨ **1999** Dense, deep colour; the powerful bouquet has abundant blackberry, plum and prune fruit; the palate is massive and concentrated, fully reflecting its 15.3° alcohol; an exercise in gigantism. **rating:** 89

best drinking 2004–2014 **best vintages** NA **drink with** Ox • $45

Happs Three Hills Nebbiolo

ΨΨΨΨ **1999** Typical light to medium purple-red; a gently savoury/leathery/spicy bouquet flows into a distinctly savoury palate, with a fractionally bitter finish. **rating:** 83

best drinking 2002–2006 **best vintages** NA **drink with** Pastrami • $28

Happs Three Hills Cabernet Franc

▼▼▼▼▽ **1999** Medium red-purple; the moderately intense bouquet blends spicy blackberry fruit with well-handled oak; an interesting wine on the palate, with a mix of cedary and blackberry flavours supported by good structure and length.　　　　**rating:** 90

best drinking 2003–2009　**best vintages** '99　**drink with** Ox tail • $28

Happs Three Hills Merlot

▼▼▼▼ **1999** Medium to full red-purple; the very ripe bouquet has slightly gamey overtones with some spice; there is a distinct change of direction on the palate, which is powerful and savoury rather than fruity; has depth and length, but is on the austere side, reflecting its varietal base.　　　　**rating:** 89

best drinking 2004–2009　**best vintages** NA　**drink with** White Rocks veal • $36

Happs Three Hill Charles Andreas Cabernet Blend

▼▼▼▼▽ **1999** Dense purple-red; a rich, dense bouquet with sweet berry, blackcurrant and cassis, the palate adding chocolate to the mix, offset by quite long, savoury tannins. A blend of Cabernet Sauvignon (50 per cent), Merlot and Cabernet Franc (in equal proportions).　　　　**rating:** 92

best drinking 2004–2011　**best vintages** '99　**drink with** Marinated lamb • $36

harcourt valley vineyards　　NR

Calder Highway, Harcourt, Vic 3453　**region** Bendigo
phone (03) 5474 2223　**fax** (03) 5474 2293　**open** 7 days 11–6
winemaker John Livingstone　**production** 1200　**est.** 1976
product range ($14–28 CD) Riesling, Unwooded Chardonnay, Chardonnay, Barbara's Shiraz, Cabernet Sauvignon.
summary Traditional producer of rich, full-bodied red wines typical of the district, but sporadic and largely outdated tastings since ownership changed preclude evaluation.

hardys reynella　　★★★★★

Reynell Road, Reynella, SA 5161　**region** McLaren Vale
phone (08) 8392 2294　**fax** (08) 8392 2301　**open** Mon–Fri 10–4, Sat 10–3.30, Sun 11–3.30, closed public holidays
winemaker Peter Dawson, Stephen Pannell, Glenn James, Ed Carr　**production** NFP　**est.** 1853
product range ($8–79 R) At the bottom comes the R&R range of Riesling Traminer, Colombard Chardonnay, Chardonnay, Shiraz, Merlot, Cabernet Sauvignon, Omni, Classic Cuvée; then Nottage Hill Riesling, Chardonnay, Shiraz, Cabernet Sauvignon Shiraz; Siegersdorf Riesling and Chardonnay; No Preservative Added range of Chardonnay, Shiraz and Cabernet Sauvignon; Eileen Hardy Chardonnay, Shiraz and Thomas Hardy Cabernet Sauvignon; Sir James, Arras; also superior-quality Brandies and Ports including Australia's finest Vintage Port.
summary Since the 1992 merger of Thomas Hardy and the Berri Renmano group, the business has flourished, and the shareholders have profited greatly. The merged group has confounded expectations by aggressively, and very successfully, pushing the premium end of the business, making a number of acquisitions and investments across the length and breadth of Australia, all aimed at the upper end of the market. A high level of winemaking expertise and commitment has been an essential part of this success. It is basically for these wines that the winery rating is given.

Hardys Siegersdorf Riesling

▼▼▼▼ **2001** Excellent light yellow-green; the bouquet is clean, with light citrus fruit tinged with tropical aromas; a pretty wine, fresh and delicate in the mouth, with a gently slatey/minerally finish.　　**rating:** 86

best drinking 2001–2003 best vintages '00, '90, '92, '93, '94, '90, '93 drink with Seafood • $11

Hardys Arras

▼▼▼▼▼ **1997** Chardonnay Pinot. Light straw-green; a fine, intense, elegant bouquet, lean, but showing bready autolysis from prolonged lees contact. The palate is intense, fine and lingering, the aftertaste even better. 4 trophies and 13 gold medals says it all.　　　　**rating:** 95

best drinking 2002–2003　**best vintages** '95, '97　**drink with** Aperitif • $54.99

Hardys Omni

▼▼▼▼ **NV** Medium straw, with a glint of bronze; hints of sweet, strawberryish fruit come through on the bouquet; the smooth, well-balanced palate offers particularly attractive fruit for its price range.　　**rating:** 87

best drinking 2001–2002　**best vintages** NA　**drink with** Aperitif • $10

Hardys Sir James Vintage

ŶŶŶŶŶ **1997** Light straw-green; a complex, toasty bouquet, reflecting four years on yeast lees, then a fresh, very lively citrussy palate, hints of strawberry and a very long, intense yet delicate finish. 4 trophies and 12 gold medals including at least one gold medal at every capital city wine show. **rating:** 94

best drinking 2002–2003 **best vintages** '94, '97 **drink with** Chinese dumplings • $24.99

Hardys No Preservative–Added Shiraz

ŶŶŶŶ **2001** Vivid purple-red; an essency berry/plum bouquet is followed by a palate with undeniable flavour, but little or no structure. **rating:** 83

best drinking 2001–2002 **best vintages** NA **drink with** No limits • $13.99

Hardys Padthaway Cabernet Sauvignon

ŶŶŶŶ **1999** Medium to full red-purple; a powerful, extractive, dense bouquet is followed by a massive palate with drying tannins on the aftertaste, rather than the finish. Made in a style consistent with all of the wines made at Stonehaven these days. **rating:** 87

best drinking 2005–2010 **best vintages** NA **drink with** Leave it in the cellar • $20.99

Hardys Thomas Hardy Cabernet Sauvignon

ŶŶŶŶŶ **1996** Still dense and strong in colour, the bouquet is primarily powered by sweet blackcurrant fruit; the palate is packed with dense blackcurrant/blackberry fruit, the tannins still to fully soften but in balance. **rating:** 96

best drinking 2002–2026 **best vintages** '89, '90, '91, '92, '93, '94, '95, '96 **drink with** Leave it in the cellar • $79

Hardys Vintage Port

ŶŶŶŶŶ **1996** Dense, deep red, showing the first signs of losing its purple rim. The potent blackberry and spice bouquet has that typical tangy/brandy spirit which is the hallmark of the style. The palate is rich, verging on thick, and mouth-coating, an outstanding example of old-fashioned Vintage Port, Australian style. Simply needs 20 years, give or take a decade. **rating:** 92

best drinking 2016 – 2026 **best vintages** '45, '51, '54, '56, '71, '73, '75, '81, '82, '84 **drink with** Coffee • $26.99

✿ hardys tintara ★★★★

202 Main Road, McLaren Vale, SA 5171 **region** McLaren Vale
phone (08) 8392 4124 **fax** (08) 8392 4155 **open** 7 days 10–4.30
winemaker Simon White **production** 110 000 **est.** 1876
product range ($15–35 R) Limited Release Shiraz, Grenache; Tintara Cellars Chardonnay, Shiraz and Cabernet Sauvignon.
summary Hardys Tintara is run as a separate winemaking entity, although all the Hardys wines are offered at the cellar door. The Limited Release wines are first class; the Tintara Cellars appeal on the grounds of price. The rating is a compromise between the two ranges.

Tintara Cellars Shiraz

ŶŶŶŶ **1999** Medium red-purple; slightly callow, red berry fruit and charry/chippy oak aromas are followed by a palate with an aggressive profile, needing time to settle down. **rating:** 84

best drinking 2004–2008 **best vintages** NA **drink with** Grilled chops • $16

Tintara Cellars Cabernet Sauvignon

Open-fermented and basket-pressed wines are rare beasts indeed at this price point.
ŶŶŶŶŶ **1999** Solid, dark berry fruit drives the bouquet with minimal interference from oak; the palate is equally full-flavoured; here blackberry, plum and dark chocolate fruit flavours are supported by positive but soft tannins. Impressive value. **rating:** 90

best drinking 2003–2008 **best vintages** '99 **drink with** Beef Bordelaise • $16

harewood estate ★★★☆

Scotsdale Road, Denmark, WA 6333 **region** Great Southern
phone (08) 9840 9078 **fax** (08) 9840 9053 **open** By appointment
winemaker Michael Kerrigan **production** 700 **est.** 1988
product range ($29–30 R) Chardonnay, Pinot Noir.

summary Keith and Margie Graham have established a showpiece vineyard at Binalong. The majority of the grapes are sold to Howard Park and Domaine Chandon, but gradually increasing amounts of wine are being made under the Harewood Estate label. The wines have retail distribution in Perth and are exported to the UK, but are otherwise only available by mail order.

hartz barn wines   NR

1 Truro Road, Moculta, Barossa Valley, SA 5353 **region** Eden Valley
phone (08) 8563 9002 **fax** (08) 8563 9002 **open** By appointment
winemaker David Barnett **production** 1300 **est.** 1997
product range ($36.95 CD) Shiraz, Merlot, Cabernet Sauvignon.
summary Hartz Barn Wines was formed in 1997 by Penny Hart (operations director), David Barnett (winemaker/director), Katrina Barnett (marketing director) and Matthew Barnett (viticulture/cellar director), which may suggest that the operation is rather larger than it in fact is. The business name and label have an unexpectedly complex background, too. The 'z' was added to Hart to reflect early German settler heritage in the Barossa Valley; Barn is a shortened version of Barnett; the house depicted on the label is the north-facing wall of the family's home in Moculta, built in 1866; the heart logo comes from Penny's school days, when she used the heart symbol on her school books instead of writing Hart; the HBW symbol within the heart has dual heritage, including the sheep branding iron that David Barnett's father, Henry William Barnett, used in New Zealand. The grapes come from the estate vineyards, planted to riesling, lagrein, merlot, shiraz and cabernet sauvignon.

Hartz Barn General Store Barossa Valley Shiraz
TTTT 2000 When tasted in September 2001, very, very, youthful, but with attractive fruit on both bouquet and palate, showing obvious development potential. The extract and oak handling are good.
rating: 86

best drinking 2004–2009 **best vintages** NA **drink with** Spaghetti bolognese • $36.95

hartzview wine centre   ★★★★

RSD 1034, off Cross Road, Gardners Bay, Tas 7112 **region** Southern Tasmania
phone (03) 6295 1623 **open** 7 days 9–5
winemaker Andrew Hood (Contract), Robert Patterson **production** NFP **est.** 1988
product range ($18–35 CD) Chardonnay, Pinot Noir; also a range of Pig and Whistle Hill fruit wines.
summary A combined wine centre, offering wines from a number of local Huon Valley wineries, and newly erected and very comfortable accommodation for six people in a separate, self-contained house. Hartzview table wines (produced from 3 hectares of estate plantings) are much to be preferred to the self-produced Pig and Whistle Hill fruit wines.

Hartzview Pinot Noir
TTTT 2001 Very deep red-purple; powerful black cherry fruit and charry oak ripple through the bouquet; the equally powerful palate has lots of oak, and is slightly rough around the edges. Obvious development potential for a wine which in many respects falls outside the square.   **rating: 88**

best drinking 2003–2007 **best vintages** NA **drink with** Roast kid • $35

haselgrove   ★★★★

Foggo Road, McLaren Vale, SA 5171 **region** McLaren Vale
phone (08) 8323 8706 **fax** (08) 8323 8049 **open** Mon–Fri 9–5, weekends 10–5
winemaker Nick Haselgrove **production** 216 000 **est.** 1981
product range ($10–67 R) Lost Sheep range of Chardonnay, Shiraz and Cabernet Sauvignon, McLaren Vale Pictures Series Sauvignon Blanc, Chardonnay, Grenache, Shiraz, Cabernet Sauvignon; Futures Shiraz; Bentwing Chardonnay, Shiraz, Cabernet Sauvignon; premium releases under 'H' Reserve label and Limelight McLaren Vale Syrah; Sparkling, Port; lesser priced varietals under Sovereign Series.
summary Haselgrove Wines was purchased in early 2002 by Barrington Estates. Under Nick Haselgrove's direction, the premium red wines, and in particular the 'H' Reserve range, have gone from strength to strength. Exports to the UK, New Zealand and the US.

Haselgrove 'H' Shiraz
TTTTY 1999 Deep red-purple; a big, chunky, ripe style with a voluptuous mix of chocolate and dark berry/cherry fruit, continuing the style established by earlier vintages.   **rating: 92**

best drinking 2007–2012 **best vintages** '91, '94, '96, '97, '99 **drink with** Eye fillet • $67

hastwell & lightfoot ★★★☆

Foggos Road, McLaren Vale, SA 5171 **region** McLaren Vale
phone (08) 8323 8692 **fax** (08) 8323 8098 **open** Not
winemaker Joe DiFabio (Contract) **production** 1300 **est.** 1990
product range ($16.50 ML) Shiraz, Cabernet.
summary Hastwell & Lightfoot is an offshoot of a rather larger grape-growing business, with the majority of the grapes from the 15 hectares of vineyard being sold to others; the vineyard was planted in 1988 and the first grapes produced in 1990. Until the advent of GST, the wines were under the small business sales tax exemption, hence the mouthwateringly low prices. Incidentally, the labels are once seen, never forgotten. Exports to Germany, Singapore and New Zealand.

hawley vineyard ★★★★

Hawley Beach, Hawley, Tas 7307 **region** Northern Tasmania
phone (03) 6428 6221 **fax** (03) 6428 6844 **open** 7 days
winemaker Andrew Pirie (Contract) **production** 1000 **est.** 1988
product range ($18–25 R) Rubicon Chardonnay, Unwooded Chardonnay, Rubicon Pinot Noir.
summary Hawley Vineyard overlooks Hawley Beach, and thence northeast to Bass Strait. It is established on a historic 200-hectare farming property, with Hawley House offering dining and accommodation in a grand style. There are no other vineyards in what is a unique winegrowing region, and few hoteliers-cum-viticulturists as flamboyant as owner Simon Houghton. Limited distribution in Sydney.

Hawley Vineyard Pinot Noir

▼▼▼▼▽ **2000** Medium purple-red; an exceptionally intense, high-toned and assertive bouquet heralds a very complex, very powerful and very long palate. High-octane stuff, yet does not imperil its pinot noir pedigree. **rating:** 93

best drinking 2003–2008 **best vintages** '97, '00 **drink with** Peking duck • NA

hay shed hill estate ★★★★

RMB 398, Harman's Mill Road, Wilyabrup, WA 6280 **region** Margaret River
phone (08) 9755 6234 **fax** (08) 9755 6305 **open** 7 days 10.30–5
winemaker Peter Stanlake **production** 45 000 **est.** 1987
product range ($15–55 CD) Semillon, Sauvignon Blanc, Sauvignon Blanc Semillon, Verdelho, Chardonnay, Cane Cut, Pinot Noir, Shiraz, Cabernet Franc, Cabernet Sauvignon; Pitchfork White, Pitchfork Pink (Rosé), Pitchfork Red.
summary A landmark on the Margaret River scene, with a striking 200-tonne winery, acquired in 2000 by Barrington Estate. Wine quality has been a touch inconsistent, but the 'sold-out' sign so often displayed speaks for itself. At their best, tangy and incisive. The wines are distributed through retail outlets in Perth, Melbourne and Sydney, and are exported to the UK.

Hay Shed Hill Semillon

▼▼▼▼ **2000** Light straw-green; the light bouquet offers herb and asparagus aromas, with distinct similarities to Sauvignon Blanc; the palate tightens up with mineral, lemon and asparagus flavours, with a kick (not unpleasant) on the finish. Certainly a Semillon with attitude. **rating:** 88

best drinking 2002–2004 **best vintages** '95, '96 **drink with** Lobster • $22

Hay Shed Hill Estate Sauvignon Blanc Semillon

▼▼▼▼ **2001** Light green-yellow; quite complex, with some smoky nuances from the French oak; the wine has good mouthfeel and flavour, mixing lemon with a touch of tropical fruit, then a faintly sweet finish. **rating:** 87

best drinking 2002–2004 **best vintages** NA **drink with** Carpaccio of salmon • $20

Hay Shed Hill Pinot Noir

▼▼▼▼ **2000** Medium red-purple; the bouquet is quite fragrant, with distinct savoury aspects; the palate has unexpected structure and length sustained by savoury tannins which complement the foresty/earthy overtones to the fruit. All in all, an impressive achievement utilising indigenous yeast and barrel fermentation. **rating:** 87

best drinking 2002–2004 **best vintages** NA **drink with** Smoked quail • $35

Hay Shed Hill Cabernet Franc

▼▼▼▼ **2000** Medium red-purple, very slightly cloudy; a perfumed bouquet with some slightly cedary varietal characters leads into a light-bodied but elegant palate, where fine-grained, savoury tannins provide the framework. **rating:** 86

best drinking 2002–2005 **best vintages** NA **drink with** Veal chops • $55

Hay Shed Hill Cabernet Sauvignon

▼▼▼▼▽ **1999** Medium red-purple; attractive cedary/spicy edges to the blackberry fruit of the bouquet lead into a well-balanced and structured palate in an elegant, medium-bodied frame. Blackcurrant fruit combines with super-fine tannins on the finish. **rating:** 92

best drinking 2003–2009 **best vintages** '92, '94, '96, '99 **drink with** Beef casserole • $37

hayward's whitehead creek ★★★

Lot 18A Hall Lane, Seymour, Vic 3660 **region** Goulburn Valley
phone (03) 5792 3050 **open** Mon–Sat 9–6, Sun 10–6
winemaker Sid Hayward, David Hayward **production** 1000 **est.** 1975
product range ($9.50–14.50 CD) Riesling, Shiraz, Cabernet Sauvignon.
summary The 4.5 hectares of low-yielding 25-year-old vines make powerful wines in a somewhat rustic mode, perhaps, but at low prices by the standards of today.

heathcote winery ★★★★

183–185 High Street, Heathcote, Vic 3523 **region** Heathcote
phone (03) 5433 2595 **fax** (03) 5433 3081 **open** 7 days 11–5
winemaker Jonathan Mepham **production** 10 000 **est.** 1978
product range ($12.50–40.50 CD) Cellar Door Thomas Craven range of MCV (Marsanne Chardonnay Viognier), Viognier, Chardonnay and Shiraz; Premium range of Chardonnay, Cane Cut (Chenin Blanc), Violet (Rosé style) and Mail Coach Shiraz; Super Premium Curagee range of Viognier and Shiraz.
summary The Heathcote Winery is back in business with a vengeance. The wines are being produced predominantly from the 26 hectares of estate vineyard, and some from local and other growers under long-term contracts, and the tasting room facilities have been restored and upgraded. Exports to the UK.

Heathcote Thomas Craven MCV

▼▼▼▽ **2001** Light to medium yellow-green; the 45 per cent Marsanne, rather than the 40 per cent Chardonnay or 15 per cent Viognier, seems to drive the bouquet in the fruit-neutral mode so typical of young Marsanne. The wine may well develop character in bottle given a few years, and certainly has varietal character. **rating:** 84

best drinking 2003–2006 **best vintages** NA **drink with** Antipasto • $13.50

Heathcote Curagee Viognier

▼▼▼▼ **2001** Light straw-green; the bouquet offers a light mix of mineral and blossom/flower aromas, the palate following down the same track, with more excitement from the label than the wine in the glass, perhaps. However, it does have the impact on the palate typical of Viognier. **rating:** 86

best drinking 2002–2005 **best vintages** '00 **drink with** Leave it in the cellar • $35

Heathcote Chardonnay

▼▼▼▼▽ **2000** Light to medium green-yellow; a clean, moderately intense bouquet has subtle fig and cashew aromas; the palate is well balanced and composed, again showing melon and cashew fruit; all in all, a sophisticated and elegant style. **rating:** 90

best drinking 2001–2004 **best vintages** 00 **drink with** Grilled spatchcock • $22

Heathcote Violet

▼▼▼▼ **2001** Light red-purple; fragrant aromas of strawberry, raspberry jam and tea leaf are followed by a palate which is more Rosé in style than anything else, needing to be chilled in summer and served in much the same context as Rosé. For the record, a blend of Shiraz and Viognier. **rating:** 86

best drinking 2002–2003 **best vintages** NA **drink with** Summer salads • $24

Heathcote Curagee Shiraz

TTTTY 1999 Medium to full red-purple; smooth, ripe, concentrated black cherry/blackberry fruit and evident but balanced oak on the bouquet; a monster wine in Leviathan style on the palate, with massive extract and tannins along with ripe fruit. Approach with extreme caution. **rating:** 90

best drinking 2009–2019 **best vintages** '98, '99 **drink with** Venison • $40.50

Heathcote Mail Coach Shiraz

TTTTY 2000 Excellent red-purple colour; a clean and smooth bouquet with black cherry/berry/plum plus well-integrated oak, then a palate which is powerful, having a good depth of similar fruit to that of the bouquet, rounded up by assertive tannins which need time to resolve, but which seem likely to do so. **rating:** 90

TTTTY 1999 Medium to full red-purple; ripe black cherry, blackberry and mint fruit aromas on the bouquet come cascading through the palate, balanced by some savoury tannins on the finish, and well-controlled oak. **rating:** 91

best drinking 2005–2010 **best vintages** '98, '99, '00 **drink with** Barbecued meat • $24

Heathcote Thomas Craven Shiraz

TTTT 2000 Medium red-purple; clean, smooth, sweet berry and plum fruit on the bouquet runs through into a palate flooded with berry and plum fruit, finishing with soft tannins. Good value. **rating:** 87

best drinking 2004–2009 **best vintages** NA **drink with** Rare beef • $16

heathvale ★★★☆

Saw Pit Gully Road via Keyneton, SA 5353 **region** Eden Valley
phone (08) 8564 8248 **fax** (08) 8564 8248 **open** By appointment
winemaker Paul Bailey (Contract) **production** 500 **est.** 1987
product range ($20–22 ML) Chardonnay, Shiraz.
summary The origins of Heathvale go back to 1865, when William Heath purchased a 60-hectare property, establishing a fruit orchard and 8 hectares of vineyard. The wine was made in the cellar of the house which stands on the property today, and is occupied by current owners Trevor and Faye March. Heath's vines disappeared in the early 1900s, but the Marchs now have 3 hectares each of shiraz and cabernet sauvignon, and 2 hectares each of chardonnay and riesling in production. Trevor March is a trained viticulturist and is completing his studies for a Master of Viticulture degree at the Waite Campus of the University of Adelaide.

Heathvale Chardonnay

TTTT 2001 Medium yellow-green; the bouquet has some complexity, in part deriving from slightly tangy barrel-ferment inputs to light melon fruit. The palate ranges through similar flavours, with grip and length, in an overall somewhat austere mould, particularly compared to the 2000 wine. **rating:** 85

best drinking 2002–2005 **best vintages** NA **drink with** Light risotto • $20

Heathvale Shiraz

TTTY 2000 Medium red, showing some development; the cherry fruit of the bouquet has savoury, earth and vanilla overtones; the medium-bodied palate is pleasant in a no-frills fashion. **rating:** 84

best drinking 2002–2006 **best vintages** NA **drink with** Chinese pork • $22

heggies vineyard ★★★★☆

Heggies Range Road, Eden Valley, SA 5235 **region** Eden Valley
phone (08) 8565 3203 **fax** (08) 8565 3380 **open** At Yalumba
winemaker Hugh Reimers **production** 12 000 **est.** 1971
product range ($17–25 R) Riesling, Viognier, Chardonnay, Botrytis Riesling, Merlot.
summary Heggies was the second of the high-altitude (570 metres) vineyards established by S Smith & Sons (Yalumba), with plantings on the 120-hectare former grazing property commencing in 1973. The once simple view of Heggies as a better white than red wine producer has become more complicated, with the pendulum swinging backwards and forwards according to vintage. Exports to all major markets.

Heggies Riesling

TTTTY 2001 Light to medium yellow-green; the clean bouquet has quite sweet lime and citrus aromatics; a delicate and fine wine which flows across the tongue, with excellent feel and structure; needs time. Surprisingly, finished with a cork, not a Stelvin. **rating:** 91

best drinking 2002–2011 **best vintages** '95, '96, '98, '99, '01 **drink with** Seafood salad • $16.95

Heggies Viognier

♥♥♥♥ 2000 Medium yellow-green; the soft, moderately intense bouquet has some fruit pastille aromas; the palate has good mouthfeel, with some authentic pastille/spice fruit. **rating: 87**

best drinking 2001–2003 best vintages '93, '95, '97, '99 drink with Pork fillet • $24.95

Heggies Chardonnay

♥♥♥♥ 2000 Medium yellow-green; the bouquet opens with smooth, ripe, stone fruit, then picking up touches of nutty/cashew aromas; there is similar flavour to the palate, which has plenty of depth and richness; flavour rather than finesse, although the oak is restrained. **rating: 88**

best drinking 2001–2003 best vintages '86, '91, '93, '97 drink with Veal, turkey • $24.95

Heggies Merlot

♥♥♥♥♥ 1998 Medium red-purple; the bouquet is complex, with distinctly savoury/earthy/olivaceous varietal fruit aromas. The powerful palate continues a long line of quality Merlots from Heggies, even if it is just a little short on finesse. **rating: 90**

best drinking 2003–2008 best vintages '93, '95, '96, '98 drink with Rack of veal • $24.95

helm ★★★☆

Butt's Road, Murrumbateman, NSW 2582 **region** Canberra District
phone (02) 6227 5953 **fax** (02) 6227 0207 **open** Thurs–Mon 10–5
winemaker Ken Helm **production** 4000 **est.** 1973
product range ($14–25 CD) Riesling Classic Dry, Cowra Riesling Classic Dry, Gewürztraminer, Traminer Riesling, Unwooded Chardonnay, Chardonnay, Reserve Merlot, Cabernet Merlot, Cabernet Shiraz, Helm Reserve Blend.
summary Ken Helm is well known as one of the more stormy petrels of the wine industry, and is an energetic promoter of his wines and of the Canberra district generally. His wines have been consistent bronze medal winners, with silvers and the occasional gold dotted here and there, such as the gold medal to the 1997 Cabernet Merlot at the 1999 Sydney Royal Wine Show. The wines have limited retail distribution in NSW, the ACT and Victoria.

Helm Reserve Merlot

♥♥♥♥ 2000 Medium red-purple; savoury/earthy aromas on the bouquet are varietally correct, the palate likewise, following down a no-compromise savoury/olive/earthy pathway. Ken Helm has resisted the temptation to sweeten the wine up with vanilla oak. **rating: 85**

best drinking 2002–2006 best vintages NA drink with Spiced quail • $20

Helm Reserve Blend

♥♥♥♥ 2000 Medium red, with the purple starting to loose vibrancy. The bouquet offers a mix of spicy/earthy/savoury notes allied with some red berry fruit; the same play is evident on the palate, except that firm red berry fruit comes first, then light savoury/spicy notes on the finish. **rating: 86**

best drinking 2002–2007 best vintages '83, '86, '88, '90, '92, '94, '96 drink with Rack of lamb • $25

Helm Cabernet Merlot

♥♥♥♥ 2000 Medium red, the purple fading; a savoury, slightly leafy bouquet is followed by a most interesting palate, almost European in character, with red berry fruits supported by lingering, persistent and fine tannins. **rating: 87**

best drinking 2002–2007 best vintages NA drink with Roast veal • $18

henke ★★☆

175 Henke Lane, Yarck, Vic 3719 **region** Central Victorian High Country
phone (03) 5797 6277 **fax** (03) 5797 6277 **open** By appointment
winemaker Tim Miller, Caroline Miller **production** 250 **est.** 1974
product range ($20–23 CD) Shiraz, Shiraz Cabernet.
summary Produces tiny quantities of deep-coloured, full-flavoured, minty red wines known only to a chosen few. Typically, a range of back vintages up to 5 years of age are available at the cellar door.

henkell wines NR

Melba Highway, Dixons Creek, Vic 3775 **region** Yarra Valley
phone (03) 9417 4144 **open** Weekends 11–5

winemaker Contract **production** 500 **est.** 1988
product range ($13–29.50 CD) Under the Henkell label are Trocken, Trocken Piccolo, Rosé, Rosé Piccolo, Brut, Adam Henkell; under Henkell Southeastern Australia are Riverland Riesling Spätlese, Riverland Chablis, Riverland Cabernet Grenache, Port; under Henkell Yarra Valley are Sauvignon Blanc, Chardonnay, Pinot Noir and Cabernet Sauvignon.
summary Hans Henkell started with a 57-variety Heinz mix in the vineyard, but has now rationalised it to a total of 17.7 hectares of sauvignon blanc, chardonnay, pinot noir and cabernet sauvignon. Most of the grapes are sold, with small amounts contract made each year. And yes, Hans Henkell is part of the family.

henley park wines   NR

6 Swan Street, Henley Brook, WA 6055 **region** Swan District
phone (08) 9296 4328 **fax** (08) 9296 1313 **open** Tues–Sun 10–5
winemaker Claus Petersen, Lisbet Petersen **production** 5000 **est.** 1935
product range ($9.95–15.95 CD) Semillon, Chenin Blanc, Classic White, Chardonnay, Muscat Gordo Blanco (late picked), Mousse Rosé Brut (Méthode Champenoise), Pinot Noir, Merlot, Shiraz, Cabernet Sauvignon, Shiraz Cabernet Merlot, Vintage Port, Old Tawny.
summary Henley Park, like so many Swan Valley wineries, was founded by a Yugoslav family, but it is now jointly owned by Danish and Malaysian interests, a multicultural mix if ever there was one. Majority owner and winemaker Claus Petersen arrived in 1986 and had his moment of glory in 1990, when Henley Park was the Most Successful Exhibitor at the Mount Barker Wine Show. Much of the production is sold through the cellar door (and exported to Denmark and Japan).

henry's drive   ★★★★☆

Riddoch Highway, Padthaway, SA 5271 **region** Padthaway
phone (08) 8765 5251 **fax** (08) 8765 5180 **open** 7 days 10–4
winemaker Sparky Marquis, Sarah Marquis **production** 8000 **est.** 1998
product range ($25–40 ML) Sparkling Shiraz, Shiraz, Reserve Shiraz, Cabernet.
summary This substantial vineyard has 53 hectares each of cabernet sauvignon and shiraz, 16 hectares of chardonnay and 8 hectares of merlot. The wines are made by Sparky and Sarah Marquis, for many years the winemaking duo at Fox Creek Wines in McLaren Vale. In no time at all, exports to the United States (through the Grateful Palate), Japan, Canada, New Zealand, South East Asia and Germany have been established, no doubt due to the reputation gained at Fox Creek.

Henry's Drive Shiraz

TTTTT 2000 Deep red-purple; complex, ripe, black cherry/blackberry fruit and high toast oak marry on the bouquet; the palate is commensurately rich, ripe, powerful and concentrated, more akin to what might be expected from a great vintage such as 1998. **rating:** 94

best drinking 2005–2015 **best vintages** '00 **drink with** Chargrilled rump steak • $30

Henry's Drive Reserve Shiraz

TTTTT 2000 Medium to full red-purple; a massively powerful and concentrated bouquet with earthy/dark berry fruit and lots of oak; the fruit on the palate appears even riper than that in the standard varietal, with flavours of plum, prune and chocolate. Was a silver medal winner at the 2001 Limestone Coast Wine Show, the gold medal going to the varietal version. **rating:** 91

best drinking 2005–2015 **best vintages** '00 **drink with** Leave it in the cellar • $40

henschke   ★★★★☆

Henschke Road, Keyneton, SA 5353 **region** Eden Valley
phone (08) 8564 8223 **fax** (08) 8564 8294 **open** Mon–Fri 9–4.30, Sat 9–12, public holidays 10–3
winemaker Stephen Henschke **production** 40 000 **est.** 1868
product range ($14–243 CD) From the Henschke Eden Valley sources, Julius Riesling, Joseph Hill Gewürztraminer, Louis Semillon, Sauvignon Blanc Semillon, Little Hampton Pinot Gris, Tilly's Vineyard, Cranes Chardonnay, Noble Rot Semillon Chardonnay, Johann's Garden Grenache Shiraz Mourvedre, Keyneton Estate, Mount Edelstone, Cyril Henschke Cabernet Sauvignon, Hill of Grace. From the Lenswood Vineyard in the Adelaide Hills, Green's Hill Riesling, Croft Chardonnay, Abbott's Prayer Cabernet Merlot.
summary Regarded as the best medium-sized red wine producer in Australia, and has gone from strength to strength over the past two decades under the guidance of Stephen and Prue Henschke. The red wines

fully capitalise on the very old, low-yielding, high-quality vines, and are superbly made with sensitive but positive use of new small oak: Hill of Grace is second only to Penfolds Grange as Australia's red wine icon. Exports to the UK, Europe, Asia and the US.

Henschke Green's Hill Riesling

▼▼▼▼ **2001** Light green-yellow; a fresh, lively green apple and herb bouquet is followed by a discrete, elegant wine in its infancy; it will flourish with time in bottle. Stelvin-capped.   **rating:** 87

best drinking 2004–2010 **best vintages** '94, '95 **drink with** Smoked trout pâté • $24.80

Henschke Julius Eden Valley Riesling

▼▼▼▼ **2001** Medium yellow-green; quite ripe fruit, with touches of spice and lime, moves through from the bouquet to the palate, which has minerally acidity to brace the finish.   **rating:** 88

best drinking 2003–2008 **best vintages** NA **drink with** Barramundi • $23.50

Henschke Joseph Hill Gewürztraminer

▼▼▼▼ **2001** Light green-yellow; light but distinctive varietal aromas offering a mix of lychee, rosé petal and spice merge into a light, crisp and dry palate, with the barest touch of phenolics on the finish – almost impossible to avoid with this variety.   **rating:** 87

best drinking 2002–2005 **best vintages** NA **drink with** Delicate Asian • $27.80

Henschke Tilly's Vineyard

▼▼▼▼ **2001** Strong green-yellow; the complex blend of tangy fruit and light oak works well; the ample palate has soft, mouthfilling flavour in an unambiguously drink-now style.   **rating:** 85

best drinking 2002–2003 **best vintages** NA **drink with** Takeaway • $14

Henschke Crane's Eden Valley Chardonnay

▼▼▼▼▼ **2001** Light green-yellow; a delicate but complex bouquet with good fruit and oak balance and integration; the elegant palate flows seamlessly on from the bouquet, with barrel-ferment and malolactic-ferment cashew characters intermingling with the fig and melon fruit; good mouthfeel.   **rating:** 90

best drinking 2002–2005 **best vintages** '01 **drink with** Tempura • $29.30

Henschke Lenswood Croft Chardonnay

▼▼▼▼▼ **2000** Medium to full yellow-green; the bouquet is nutty, and rather oaky, but on the palate, ripe fig and melon fruit asserts itself; good length and balance.   **rating:** 90

best drinking 2001–2004 **best vintages** '00 **drink with** Gravlax • $37.60

Henschke Mount Edelstone

▼▼▼▼ **1999** Medium red-purple; the potent bouquet offers ripe fruit, smoky oak and leather overtones; the palate is full of character and flavour, but falling away somewhat on the finish, perhaps reflecting a less than perfect vintage.   **rating:** 87

best drinking 2002–2007 **best vintages** '52, '56, '61, '66, '67, '78, '82, '86, '88, '90, '92, '93, '94, '95, '96, '98 **drink with** Beef bourguignon • $67

Henschke Keyneton Estate Shiraz Cabernet Malbec

▼▼▼▼▼ **1999** Bright red-purple, holding its hue well; excellent colour seems to be a continuing feature of this wine, year in, year out. The nicely balanced bouquet brings together black cherry, plum, spice and subtle oak, the palate flowing effortlessly through to the finish, with good weight, texture and mouthfeel. Arguably the best value of all of the Henschke range.   **rating:** 92

best drinking 2004–2011 **best vintages** '82, '84, '86, '88, '90, '92, '93, '94, '96, '97, '98, '99 **drink with** Veal chops • $33.70

Henschke Abbott's Prayer Cabernet Merlot

▼▼▼▼▼ **1999** Medium purple-red; a fragrant bouquet, ripe, but neither jammy nor soupy, leads into a medium-bodied palate with structure and elegance, offering raspberry and blackberry fruit, and ever-so-slightly dusty oak.   **rating:** 90

best drinking 2003–2008 **best vintages** '89, '90, '91, '92, '93, '94, '96, '97, '99 **drink with** Guinea fowl in red wine sauce • $64

Henschke Cyril Henschke Cabernet Sauvignon

▼▼▼▼▼ **1999** Medium to full red-purple; the bouquet is flooded with clean, fragrant blackcurrant and cassis fruit; quite lush fruit marks the entry through to the mid-palate, which then becomes much finer and more elegant towards the finish. A significant success for the vintage.   **rating:** 92

🍷🍷🍷🍷🍷 **1998** Medium red-purple; fresh, juicy, red berry fruit and relatively subtle oak on the bouquet flow into a well-composed and balanced palate; here there is an interplay of soft, sweet, cedary/spicy oak, redcurrant/cassis fruit, and gentle tannins. **rating:** 93

best drinking 2004–2014 **best vintages** '78, '80, '85, '86, '88, '90, '91, '92, '93, '94, '96, '98, '99 **drink with** Roast lamb • $97.40

henty brook estate NR

Box 49, Dardanup, WA 6236 **region** Geographe
phone (08) 9728 1459 **fax** (08) 9728 1459 **open** By appointment
winemaker James Pennington (Contract) **production** 350 **est.** 1994
product range ($12–16 CD) Sauvignon Blanc Semillon, Shiraz.
summary One hectare each of shiraz and sauvignon blanc and 0.5 hectare of semillon were planted in the spring of 1994. James Pennington is the contract-winemaker; the first releases are now on the market.

heritage estate ★★★

Granite Belt Drive, Cottonvale, Qld 4375 **region** Granite Belt
phone (07) 4685 2197 **fax** (07) 4685 2112 **open** 7 days 9–5
winemaker Jim Barnes **production** 5000 **est.** 1992
product range ($9.50–35 CD) Semillon, Dry White, Semillon Chardonnay, Harvest Blend, Chardonnay, Club Red, Shiraz, Roswal Shiraz, Merlot, Cabernet Merlot, Fortified and flavoured wines.
summary A very successful winery, with many awards in recent years, which showcases its wines through its cellar door at Mount Tamborine (corner Bartle Road and The Shelf Road), an old church converted into a tasting and sales area, with views over the Gold Coast hinterland; it also incorporates a restaurant, barbecue area and art gallery. The estate plantings comprise chardonnay (2 hectares), merlot (2 hectares), shiraz (1 hectare) and cabernet sauvignon (1 hectare).

heritage farm wines NR

RMB 1005, Murray Valley Highway, Cobram, Vic 3655 **region** Goulburn Valley
phone (03) 5872 2376 **fax** (03) 5872 2376 **open** 7 days 9–5
winemaker Roy Armfield **production** 2000 **est.** 1987
product range ($5–12 CD) Riesling, Traminer Riesling, Moselle, Chardonnay are varietal releases; there are a considerable number of generic releases and fortified wines on sale at the cellar door.
summary Heritage Farm claims to be the only vineyard and orchard in Australia still using horsepower, with Clydesdales used for most of the general farm work. The winery and cellar-door area also boasts a large range of restored horse-drawn farm machinery and a bottle collection. All of the wines are sold by mailing list and at the cellar door.

heritage wines ★★★★

106a Seppeltsfield Road, Marananga, SA 5355 **region** Barossa Valley
phone (08) 8562 2880 **fax** (08) 8562 2692 **open** 7 days 11–5
winemaker Stephen Hoff **production** 6000 **est.** 1984
product range ($11.50–30 CD) Riesling, Semillon, Barossa Shiraz, Rossco's Shiraz, Cabernet Malbec, Cabernet Sauvignon, Tokay, Tawny Port.
summary A little-known winery which deserves a far wider audience, for Stephen Hoff is apt to produce some startlingly good wines. At various times the Chardonnay, Riesling (from old Clare Valley vines) and Rossco's Shiraz (now the flag-bearer) have all excelled; at other times not. Exports to the UK and US.

Heritage Wines Barossa Semillon

🍷🍷🍷🍷 **2001** Exemplary green-yellow colour; both the bouquet and palate offer juicy/lemony fruit in an appealing, early drinking style. **rating:** 83

best drinking 2001–2003 **best vintages** NA **drink with** Fish and chips • $13

Heritage Wines Barossa Shiraz

🍷🍷🍷🍷🍷 **1999** Medium to full red-purple; clean, dark berry, plum and prune fruit bouquet is followed by a very attractive palate with dark berry, plum and chocolate flavours, supported by soft, ripe tannins and subtle oak. Has improved enormously since previously tasted. **rating:** 94

best drinking 2004–2009 **best vintages** '98, '99 **drink with** Steak and kidney pie • $19

🐦 heritage wines at mt tamborine ★★★★

Corner Shelf and Bartle Road, Mount Tamborine, Qld 4272 **region** Queensland Coastal
phone (07) 5545 3144 **fax** (07) 5545 3144 **open** 7 days 10–5
winemaker Contract **production** NA **est.** 2000
product range ($22.50–25 CD) Private Reserve Chardonnay, Merlot, Shiraz; Roswal Shiraz.
summary Bryce and Paddy Kassulke operate yet another Queensland winery with a thoroughly odd history. The building was originally the Infant Saviour Catholic Church at Burleigh Heads, which the Kassulkes saved from destruction by buying it just when it was to be demolished and sold as second-hand wood. The vineyard is in the Granite Belt, and was established in 1993 with plantings of chardonnay, merlot, shiraz and cabernet sauvignon. The quality of the wines is excellent; the labels, too, have a touch of class not always obvious in this part of the world. The winery is open for lunch every day and groups are welcome.

Heritage Wines at Mt Tamborine Private Reserve Chardonnay

▼▼▼▼ **2000** Light to medium yellow-green; the moderately intense bouquet is clean, with fresh nectarine fruit, and the oak is particularly well-integrated and subtle, given that the wine spent 8 months in new French barriques. The tightly knit palate is particularly well made in a restrained style, and will develop relatively slowly. **rating:** 87

best drinking 2002–2004 **best vintages** NA **drink with** Moreton Bay bugs • $22.50

Heritage Wines at Mt Tamborine Private Reserve Shiraz

▼▼▼▼▽ **1999** Medium to full red-purple; another spotlessly clean and well-made wine, with dark berry/cherry fruit intermingling with American oak on the bouquet; the palate has stacks of flavour, featuring good oak and tannin management. Thoroughly impressive. **rating:** 90

best drinking 2003–2008 **best vintages** '99 **drink with** Kangaroo fillet • $22.50

Heritage Wines at Mt Tamborine Private Reserve Merlot

▼▼▼▽ **1999** Light to medium red-purple; a light spicy/savoury/earthy/berry bouquet is followed by a palate which is very much on the light side, but has distinct varietal character, falling away slightly on the back palate. **rating:** 84

best drinking 2002–2006 **best vintages** NA **drink with** Rack of veal • $25

hermes morrison wines NR

253 Swan Ponds Road, Woodstock, NSW 2793 **region** Central Ranges Zone
phone (02) 6345 0153 **fax** (02) 6345 0153 **open** 7 days 10–5 summer, winter weekends and public holidays
winemaker Jill Lindsay (Contract) **production** 600 **est.** 1990
product range ($12–15 CD) Riesling, Semillon, Sauvignon Blanc, Chardonnay, Pinot Noir, Shiraz Cabernet.
summary The Morrison family established their Hermes Poll Dorset Stud in 1972, which continues but has now been joined by Hermes Morrison wines. The cellar door has been established by the side of a large lake fed by cold, clear water welling up from subterranean caves, and a 10-minute walk takes you to the summit of Mount Palatine, one of the highest peaks in the shire and with a spectacular view of the Canobolas Mountains 80 kilometres away.

herons rise vineyard ★★★★

Saddle Road, Kettering, Tas 7155 **region** Southern Tasmania
phone (03) 6267 4339 **fax** (03) 6267 4245 **open** By appointment
winemaker Andrew Hood **production** 500 **est.** 1984
product range ($15–25 CD) Müller Thurgau Riesling, Pinot Noir, Premium Pinot Noir.
summary Sue and Gerry White run a small stone country guesthouse in the D'Entrecasteaux Channel area and basically sell the wines produced from the surrounding 1 hectare of vineyard to those staying at the two self-contained cottages. The Pinot Noir is strongly recommended. The postal address for bookings is PO Box 271, Kettering, Tas 7155.

Herons Rise Pinot Noir

▼▼▼▼▽ **2001** Medium red-purple; the bouquet offers a nice mix of cherry and plum fruit, characters which come through the fresh, smooth and light to medium-bodied palate. Just a little more weight and intensity would lift the wine into the highest class, and there can be no question about the making of the wine. **rating:** 90

🍷🍷🍷🍷🍷 **2000** Medium red-purple; the moderately intense bouquet is clean, with pleasant plum and cherry fruit, characters which are also to be found on the palate, with good flavour and length. Lacks the complexity and depth of the very top wines of the vintage, but nonetheless is a quality wine. **rating:** 90

best drinking 2002–2005 **best vintages** '00, '01 **drink with** Breast of squab • $20

hesperos wines NR

36 Elva Street, Margaret River, WA 6285 **region** Margaret River
phone (08) 9757 3302 **fax** (08) 9757 3302 **open** By appointment
winemaker Jürg Muggli **production** 1250 **est.** 1993
product range ($18.50–30 CD) Sauvignon Blanc, Shiraz.
summary Hesperos is the venture of Jürg Muggli and Sandra Hancock. It supplies Jürg Muggli's winemaking skills to Xanadu, where Muggli has been resident winemaker for many years. It also has a 30-hectare property near Witchcliffe, between Cape Mentelle and Devil's Lair, with the potential of 15 hectares of vineyard. Planting commenced in the winter of 1999. In the meantime, the Hesperos wines are made from purchased grapes; Shiraz and Sauvignon Blanc have been produced in each vintage. Exports to Japan, Switzerland and Germany.

hewitson ★★★★☆

16 McGowan Avenue, Unley, SA 5061 **region** Warehouse
phone (08) 8271 5755 **fax** (08) 8271 5570 **open** Not
winemaker Dean Hewitson **production** 4500 **est.** 1996
product range ($18–37 R) La Source Eden Valley Riesling, L'Oizeau Shiraz, Old Garden Mourvedre, Barossa Shiraz, Barossa Valley Grenache, Miss Harry, Dry Grown and Ancient.
summary Dean Hewitson was a Petaluma winemaker for ten years, and during that time managed to do three vintages in France and one in Oregon as well as undertaking his Masters at UC Davis, California. It is hardly surprising that the Hewitson wines are immaculately made from a technical viewpoint. However, he has also managed to source 30-year-old riesling from the Eden Valley and 70-year-old shiraz from McLaren Vale, following on with a Barossa Valley Mourvedre produced from 145-year-old vines at Rowland Flat, and a Barossa Valley Shiraz and Grenache, coming from 60-year-old vines at Tanunda. The vineyards are now under long-term contracts to Ian Hewitson. Exports to New Zealand, China, Japan, Malaysia, Singapore, the US, Canada, Finland, the Netherlands, Norway, Germany and the UK.

Hewitson La Source Eden Valley Riesling

🍷🍷🍷🍷🍷 **2001** Light straw-green; the bouquet has some fragrance, with an apple blossom and mineral mix, then a clean, crisp and very delicate, finely balanced, palate. Stelvin-capped. **rating:** 90

🍷🍷🍷🍷🍷 **2000** Light to medium yellow-green; the bouquet opens with fragrant lime and passionfruit before moving through to some more minerally characters. The palate is cast in much the same mould in terms of flavour, having good mouthfeel and weight. A generous wine, but not heavy. **rating:** 91

best drinking 2004–2009 **best vintages** '98, '99, '00 **drink with** Summer salads • $19

Hewitson L'Oizeau Shiraz

🍷🍷🍷🍷 **1999** Medium red, with a slightly dull purple hue; the bouquet is clean, but somewhat muted, with chocolate, cedar and earth peeping through. The palate has a slightly curious mix of ripe plummy fruit, a hint of cedar, and brisk acidity. Less convincing than some of the earlier releases, notwithstanding the old vine source. Presumably just the less than perfect vintage. **rating:** 87

best drinking 2003–2008 **best vintages** '97, '98 **drink with** Hearty red meat dishes • $37

Hewitson Miss Harry, Dry Grown and Ancient

🍷🍷🍷🍷 **2000** Light red-purple; the bouquet is fresh, lively and fruity, with minimal oak influence evident. The palate bridges the gap between conventional dry red and rosé, with an aromatic mix of berry, mint and leaf, and a brisk finish. **rating:** 86

best drinking 2001–2004 **best vintages** NA **drink with** Pasta • $24

hickinbotham NR

Nepean Highway (near Wallaces Road), Dromana, Vic 3936 **region** Mornington Peninsula
phone (03) 5981 0355 **fax** (03) 5981 0355 **open** 7 days
winemaker Andrew Hickinbotham **production** 3000 **est.** 1981

product range ($15–30 R) Chardonnay with Aligote, Taminga, Strawberry Kiss (sparkling), Pinot Noir, Luxuriance Shiraz, Merlot, Cabernet Merlot; Strawberry Elixir.

summary After a peripatetic period and a hiatus in winemaking, Hickinbotham established a permanent vineyard and winery base at Dromana. It now makes only Mornington Peninsula wines, drawing in part on 5 hectares of estate vineyards, and in part on contract-grown fruit. The wines are principally sold through the cellar door and by mail order.

Hickinbotham Chardonnay with Aligote

▼▼▼▽ **2000** Light straw-green; a light, crisp, melon and citrus bouquet with no oak evident is followed by a pleasant melon and peach/stone fruit palate, with a slightly furry finish. So far as I can recollect, Hickinbotham remains in sole possession of aligote, the high-yielding workhorse of southern Burgundy. **rating: 84**

best drinking 2002–2003 **best vintages** NA **drink with** Thick fish soup • $28

hidden creek ★★☆

Eukey Road, Ballandean, Qld 4382 **region** Granite Belt
phone (07) 4684 1383 **fax** (07) 4684 1355 **open** Mon–Fri 12–3, weekends 10–4
winemaker Adrien Kuffer **production** 1400 **est.** 1998
product range ($13.50–18 CD) Semillon, Chardonnay, Mountain Muscat, Shiraz, First Block Shiraz, Merlot.
summary A beautifully located vineyard and winery on a ridge overlooking the Ballandean township and the Severn River valley, separated from Girraween National Park by Doctors Creek. The granite boulder-strewn hills mean that the 70-hectare property will only provide a little over 6 hectares of vineyard, in turn divided into six different blocks. The two wines tasted to date were of modest but acceptable quality.

hidden river estate NR

Mullineaux Road, Pemberton, WA 6260 **region** Pemberton
phone (08) 9776 1437 **fax** (08) 9776 0189 **open** 7 days 9–4
winemaker Brenden Smith, Phil Goldring **production** 2400 **est.** 1994
product range ($14.50–30 ML) Three Feathers Blend Semillon Sauvignon Blanc Chardonnay, Unwooded Chardonnay, Wooded Chardonnay, Sparkle Arse (Méthode Champenoise), Late Picked Riesling, Authentic Basket Press Shiraz, Cabernet Sauvignon, Aged Cell Door Tawny Port, The Muskateer.
summary Phil and Sandy Goldring spent ten years operating farm chalets in the Pemberton area before selling the business and retiring to become grape growers, with the intention of selling the grapes to others. However, they found old habits hard to kick, so opened a cellar door sales and cafe/restaurant, and plan to establish a boutique brewery on site in 2001. It is a business with a very strong marketing push, a 1901 Kalgoorlie tram having been purchased, renovated and installed on-site to provide more seating for the restaurant. I hope the Goldrings did not pay much for the tram.

highbank NR

Riddoch Highway, Coonawarra, SA 5263 **region** Coonawarra
phone (08) 8736 3311 **fax** (08) 8736 3122 **open** By appointment
winemaker Dennis Vice, Trevor Mast **production** 1000 **est.** 1986
product range ($40 CD) Chardonnay, Basket Pressed Cabernet Blend, Basket Pressed Cabernet Sauvignon.
summary Mount Gambier lecturer in viticulture Dennis Vice makes a tiny quantity of smooth, melon-accented Chardonnay and stylish Coonawarra Cabernet Blend of good quality which are sold through local restaurants and the cellar door, with limited Melbourne distribution. Intermittent exports to various countries.

highland heritage estate ★★★☆

Mitchell Highway, Orange, NSW 2800 **region** Orange
phone (02) 6361 3612 **fax** (02) 6361 3613 **open** Mon–Fri 9–3, weekends 9–5
winemaker John Hordern, Rex D'Aquino **production** 3500 **est.** 1984
product range ($10–30 CD) Under the Mount Canobolas label: Chardonnay, Sauvignon Blanc, Pinot Noir; Gosling Creek Chardonnay; and the newly released Wellwood Estate label.
summary The estate plantings have increased from 4 hectares to over 15 hectares, with plantings in 1995 and 1997 now in full production. The tasting facility is unusual: a converted railway carriage overlooking the vineyard.

🐦 high valley wines   ★★★☆

Berowra Road, Dunedoo, NSW 2844 **region** Mudgee
phone (02) 6375 0292 **fax** (02) 6375 0228 **open** By appointment
winemaker Simon Gilbert, Ian McRae (Contract) **production** 2300 **est.** 1995
product range ($13–18.50 CD) Chardonnay, Chardonnay Simon Gilbert, Premium Chardonnay, Shiraz, Reserve Shiraz.
summary The Francis family, headed by Ro and Grosvenor Francis, have operated a sheep, wheat and cattle property at Dunedoo for several generations. Concurrently with handing over the property to their sons in 1995, Ro and Grosvenor subdivided and retained a 40-hectare block on which they have since established 11 hectares of shiraz, 6 hectares of cabernet sauvignon and 5 hectares of chardonnay. A grape supply agreement was entered into with Rothbury Estate, but a decision was taken in 1998 to retain a portion of the grapes and develop the High Valley Wines label. While the property is only open by appointment, it does feature a gas and wood-fired working pottery, vineyard tours and farm tours.

High Valley Chardonnay

▼▼▼▼ 2000 Medium yellow-green; both the bouquet and palate offer a subtle interplay of melon fruit, cashew and oak in a light to medium-bodied style which should develop well over the short term. **rating:** 86
▼▼▼▼ 1999 Light green-yellow; a clean, light, fresh and crisp bouquet then a similarly very youthful, slow-developing palate with some melon fruit; the wine was barrel-fermented and oak-matured, but that oak has disappeared into the fruit. An interesting cool-grown style, and good value. **rating:** 85
best drinking 2002–2005 **best vintages** NA **drink with** Light seafood • $12.95

High Valley Reserve Shiraz

▼▼▼▼ 1999 Medium red-purple; a good marriage of red berry fruit and oak, both balanced and integrated; the palate has plenty of fruit weight and structure, offering chocolate, red berry, a touch of spice and some oak. **rating:** 88
best drinking 2004–2009 **best vintages** NA **drink with** Rump steak • $18.50

highway wines   NR

612 Great Northern Highway, Herne Hill, WA 6056 **region** Swan District
phone (08) 9296 4354 **open** Mon–Sat 8.30–6
winemaker Tony Bakranich **production** 4000 **est.** 1954
product range ($5–14.50 CD) Exclusively Fortified wines, of which 20 are available, including six different styles of Sherry, six Muscats, three Ports, and so forth.
summary A survivor of another era, when literally dozens of such wineries plied their business in the Swan Valley. It still enjoys a strong local trade, selling much of its wine in fill-your-own-containers and 2-litre flagons, with lesser quantities sold by the bottle.

🐦 hillbrook   NR

639 Doust Road, Geary's Gap via Bungendore, NSW 2621 **region** Canberra District
phone (02) 6236 9455 **fax** (02) 6236 9455 **open** Weekends and public holidays 10–5
winemaker Contract **production** 2000 **est.** 1994
product range ($19–25 CD) Riesling, Chardonnay, Pinot Noir, Merlot, Tawny Port.
summary Adolf and Levina Zanzert began the establishment of 8.5 hctares of vines at Geary's Gap in 1994. The wines have good retail distribution in the ACT, Bungendore and Cooma, and are also available through the cellar door and by mailing list.

hill-smith estate   ★★★★

PO Box 10, Angaston, SA 5353 **region** Eden Valley
phone (08) 8561 3200 **fax** (08) 8561 3393 **open** At Yalumba
winemaker Robert Hill-Smith, Hugh Reimers **production** 3500 **est.** 1973
product range ($18 R) Sauvignon Blanc, Chardonnay.
summary Part of the Yalumba stable, drawing upon its own estate plantings, comprising 23 hectares of chardonnay and sauvignon blanc. Over the years has produced some excellent wines, but quality does seem to vary significantly with vintage, and the winery rating is a compromise between the best and the least. Exports to all major markets.

Hill-Smith Estate Sauvignon Blanc

▼▼▼▼ 2001 Light to medium yellow-green; the bouquet has some complexity, notwithstanding the stainless steel fermentation and early bottling. The palate has pleasant lemon/herb/grass flavours, finishing with crisp acidity. **rating:** 87

best drinking 2001–2002 **best vintages** '86, '92, '93, '94, '95, '96, '99 **drink with** Fresh mussels • $17.95

hills of plenty NR

370 Yan Yean Road, Yarrambat, Vic 3091 **region** Yarra Valley
phone (03) 9436 2264 **fax** (03) 9436 2264 **open** Last Sun of each month 12–5 or by appointment
winemaker Karen Coulston **production** 400 **est.** 1998
product range ($15–20 ML) Riesling, Sauvignon Blanc, Chardonnay, Pinot Noir, Shiraz, Cabernet Sauvignon.
summary Hills of Plenty has been established just outside the Melbourne metropolitan area, a few minutes' drive north of Greensborough. There is a tiny 0.2-hectare vineyard of riesling, chardonnay and cabernet sauvignon around the winery, but most of the fruit is purchased from other regions, notably Geelong, Gippsland and Swan Hill. The tiny production means that the cellar door only opens once a month, but it is turned into a festive occasion, with live music, and picnics or barbecues welcome.

hillstowe ★★★★☆

104 Main Road, Hahndorf, SA 5245 **region** Adelaide Hills
phone (08) 8388 1400 **fax** (08) 8388 1411 **open** 7 days 10–5
winemaker NA **production** 14 000 **est.** 1980
product range ($15.95–48 R) A range of vineyard and varietal-designated wines of ascending price and quality: Buxton Sauvignon Blanc, Chardonnay, Buxton Shiraz, Pinto Gris, Buxton Cabernet Merlot, and at the top end, Adelaide Hills Udy's Mill Chardonnay, Udy's Mill Pinot Noir, Mary's Hundred Shiraz and The Pinch Row Lenswood Merlot.
summary Rapid-fire changes of ownership from founder Chris Lawrie to Banksia Wines then to Lion Nathan should (theoretically) not impact on the quality and style of the high-quality Hillstowe wines. Its principal vineyard, Udy's Mill at Lenswood, has 17 hectares planted, supplementing McLaren Vale grapes coming from the Buxton Vineyard. The wines are exported to the UK, Canada, the US, Europe and Asia.

Hillstowe Sauvignon Blanc

▼▼▼▼ 2001 Very light straw-green; a light, crisp bouquet opens with mineral characters, then showing gooseberry and asparagus; the light to medium-bodied palate is pleasant, but doesn't follow on with the varietal definition promised by the bouquet. **rating:** 85

best drinking 2002–2003 **best vintages** '90, '93, '94, '96 **drink with** King George whiting • $17

Hillstowe The Scrub Block Lenswood Pinot Gris

▼▼▼▼ 2001 Light straw, faintly pink, the colour deriving from the grape, rather than the absence of SO_2. The bouquet is clean, crisp and distinctly herbal, the palate with relatively tight structure and length; the texture is the strong part of the wine, which inclines more to the style of Pinot Grigio of Italy than the Pinot Gris of Alsace. **rating:** 85

best drinking 2001–2003 **best vintages** NA **drink with** Blue swimmer crab • $22

Hillstowe Buxton Lightly Oaked Chardonnay

▼▼▼▼ 2001 Medium green-yellow; a complex and stylish bouquet with excellent balance between the touch of barrel-ferment and fruit components flows through to the nicely flavoured and textured palate, where cashew, fig and melon interplay. Particularly well priced. **rating:** 89

best drinking 2002–2004 **best vintages** NA **drink with** Trout risotto • $14.95

Hillstowe Udy's Mill Chardonnay

▼▼▼▼▽ 1999 Light to medium yellow-green; the tangy bouquet has a nice mix of grapefruit, stone fruit and subtle oak; the palate is similarly fruit driven, with a mix of citrus and stone fruit running through a long and stylish finish, the oak sotto voce. **rating:** 91

best drinking 2002–2006 **best vintages** '90, '92, '93, '95, '96, '99 **drink with** Trout or salmon mousse • $19.80

Hillstowe Udy's Mill Pinot Noir

❦❦❦❦ **1999** Light to medium red-purple; while the bouquet is complex, the oak is fairly obvious and slightly dusty; the palate has moderately clear plummy/savoury varietal character, but lacks the drive of the '98, a shortcoming compounded by the indifferent choice of oak. **rating:** 86

best drinking 2001–2004 **best vintages** '98 **drink with** Rich game • $29.80

Hillstowe Mary's Hundred Shiraz

❦❦❦❦❦ **1999** Medium to full red-purple; solid, ripe, dark plum with hints of chocolate and licorice run through the bouquet; rich, luscious, mouthfilling dark fruits drive the palate, with excellent tannin and oak management. **rating:** 94

best drinking 2004–2014 **best vintages** '96, '97, '98, '99 **drink with** Rack of lamb • $45

Hillstowe The Pinch Row Lenswood Merlot

❦❦❦❦❦ **1999** Youthful red-purple; a complex bouquet with a sweet blackberry and raspberry mix, then a palate with good weight and structure, juicy berry fruit, fine tannins and nicely judged oak. **rating:** 91

best drinking 2004–2009 **best vintages** '98, '99 **drink with** Osso buco • $48

hills view vineyards ★★★☆

11 Main Avenue, Frewville, SA 5063 **region** McLaren Vale
phone (08) 8338 0666 **fax** (08) 8338 0666 **open** Not
winemaker Brett Howard **production** 12 000 **est.** 1998
product range ($10–30 R) Three ranges of wines produced: Blewitt Springs Semillon, Chardonnay, Shiraz and Cabernet Sauvignon; Howard Fleurieu Semillon and Coonawarra Shiraz; Hills View Chardonnay Verdelho, Shiraz Cabernet and Cabernet Merlot.
summary District veteran Brett Howard, with 20 years' winemaking experience, is now the winemaker for Hills View Vineyards, producing the Hills View Vineyards range of wines, the Blewitt Springs range and Howard label. A Fleurieu Semillon and a Coonawarra Shiraz released only in the best vintages.

hjt vineyards NR

Keenan Road, Glenrowan, Vic 3675 **region** Glenrowan
phone (03) 5766 2252 **fax** (03) 5765 3260 **open** Fri, Sat, 10–5 and Sun during school holidays
winemaker Wendy Tinson **production** 1200 **est.** 1979
product range ($11.50–17.50 CD) A varietal range, with occasional use of bin numbers denoting winemaking approaches, Bin 4 being more delicate, Bin 19 fuller-bodied. Wines include Riesling Bins 4 and 19, Chardonnay, Chenin Blanc Bin 19, Late Picked Riesling, Pinot Noir, Cabernet Pinot, Shiraz, Cabernet Sauvignon, Merlot, Tawny Port.
summary Founded by the late Harry Tinson after he left Baileys following a long and illustrious stewardship, and now run by his daughter Wendy Tinson, with tiny production all sold from the cellar door. No recent tastings, alas.

hochkirch wines NR

Hamilton Highway, Tarrington, Vic 3301 **region** Henty
phone (03) 5573 5200 **fax** (03) 5573 5200 **open** 11–5 by appointment
winemaker John Nagorcka **production** 1500 **est.** 1997
product range ($11–24 ML) Riesling, Semillon, Pinot Noir, Shiraz, Cabernet Sauvignon.
summary Jennifer and John Nagorcka have developed Hochkirk in response to the very cool climate, which has growing season temperatures similar to those in Burgundy. A high-density planting pattern was implemented, with a low fruiting wire to take advantage of soil warmth in the growing season, and the focus was placed on pinot noir (4.5 hectares), with lesser quantities of riesling, cabernet sauvignon, semillon and shiraz. The vines are not irrigated, and no synthetic fungicides, pesticides or fertilisers are used; currently the Nagorckas are trialling bio-dynamic practice. Wines with considerable complexity and interest are the result, the Pinot Noir having received critical acclaim in a number of quarters.

hoffmann's ★★★☆

Ingoldby Road, McLaren Flat, SA 5171 **region** McLaren Vale
phone (08) 8383 0232 **fax** (08) 8383 0232 **open** 7 days 11–5
winemaker Nick Holmes (Consultant) **production** 2000 **est.** 1996
product range ($16–22 CD) Chardonnay, Shiraz, Cabernet Sauvignon.

summary Peter and Anthea Hoffmann have been growing grapes at their property in Ingoldby Road since 1978, and Peter Hoffmann has worked at various wineries in McLaren Vale since 1979. Both he and Anthea have undertaken courses at the Regency TAFE Institute in Adelaide, and (in Peter Hoffmann's words) 'in 1996 we decided that we knew a little about winemaking and opened a small cellar door'. Exports to Germany and Malaysia.

Hoffmann's Chardonnay

ΥΥΥΫ **1999** Medium yellow-green; some bottle-developed complexity is building on the bouquet, and the palate has some intensity and weight to the tangy, citrus and melon fruit. Well priced.   **rating: 83**

best drinking 2001–2003 **best vintages** NA **drink with** Veal fricassee • $15

Hoffmann's Shiraz

ΥΥΥΫ **2000** Medium red-purple; the moderately intense bouquet offers red berry/cherry fruit, and oak in the background; that oak is more evident on the palate, with slightly dusty/chewy aspects to the texture, which will likely settle down given time.   **rating: 84**

best drinking 2003–2007 **best vintages** NA **drink with** Spaghetti bolognese • $21

Hoffmann's Cabernet Sauvignon

ΥΥΥΥ **2000** Light to medium red-purple; there are light, savoury edges to the red and blackcurrant fruit of the bouquet, the palate picking up weight with rich, dark berry and dark chocolate fruit in regional style. Subtle oak.   **rating: 87**

ΥΥΥΫ **1999** Light to medium red, the purple starting to fade; the bouquet is light and earthy, with some spicy notes, but there is rather more on the palate, with blackberry and a touch of regional chocolate.   **rating: 82**

best drinking 2004–2009 **best vintages** NA **drink with** Boned leg of lamb • $22

hollick ★★★★

Riddoch Highway, Coonawarra, SA 5263 **region** Coonawarra
phone (08) 8737 2318 **fax** (08) 8737 2952 **open** 7 days 9–5
winemaker Ian Hollick, David Norman **production** 40 000 **est.** 1983
product range ($15–60 R) A very disciplined array of products with Riesling, Sauvignon Blanc Semillon, Wilgha Vineyard Unoaked Chardonnay, Pinot Noir and Shiraz Cabernet Sauvignon at the lower end of the price range; Reserve Chardonnay, Cabernet Sauvignon Merlot, Sparkling Merlot are in the middle; Wilgha Shiraz, Neilson's Block Merlot and Ravenswood, the deluxe Cabernet Sauvignon, are at the top. Also Pinot Noir Chardonnay, as a cellar-door release only.
summary Winner of many trophies (including the most famous of all, the Jimmy Watson), its wines are well crafted and competitively priced, although sometimes a little on the light side. A $1 million cellar door and restaurant complex opened in June 2002. National distribution in all states; exports to the UK, the US, Hong Kong, Singapore, Malaysia, Denmark, Belgium, Holland, Sweden and Switzerland.

Hollick Riesling

ΥΥΥΥ **2001** Light straw-green; clean, crisp, mineral, slate and herb aromas, with some blossom in the background, lead into a palate with crisp, bracing acidity, needing another year or so to fully come together; will undoubtedly do so.   **rating: 87**

best drinking 2003–2007 **best vintages** '99 **drink with** Light seafood • $17.50

Hollick Sauvignon Blanc Semillon

ΥΥΥΫ **2001** Light green-yellow; a fresh mix of mineral and lemon aromatics lead into a crisp, delicate minerally palate which, while not overburdened with fruit, is clean and refreshing.   **rating: 84**

best drinking 2002–2003 best vintages NA drink with Grilled seafood • $17

Hollick Wilgha Unoaked Chardonnay

ΥΥΥΫ **2001** Light to medium yellow-green; citrus and nectarine aromas leads into a palate which has some length and grip, helped by zingy acidity.   **rating: 84**

best drinking 2001–2003 **best vintages** NA **drink with** Light fish or pasta • $14.95

Hollick Reserve Chardonnay

ΥΥΥΥ **2000** Light to medium yellow-green; a refreshing bouquet is light but clean, with nicely balanced stone fruit and subtle oak; the vibrant palate picks up pace and intensity with stone fruit and melon running through to a long finish.   **rating: 90**

best drinking 2001–2005 **best vintages** NA **drink with** Steamed mud crab • $20

Hollick Shiraz Cabernet

ΨΨΨΨ 2000 Medium to full red-purple; some faintly dusty/chippy oak is evident on the bouquet, but without disguising the fruit depth. That fruit comes through even more strongly on the big, juicy, strongly flavoured palate. Good value at the price, and with obvious development potential. **rating: 85**

best drinking 2003–2008 **best vintages** '98 **drink with** Porthouse • $18.95

Hollick Coonawarra Cabernet Sauvignon Merlot

ΨΨΨΨΥ 2000 Bright red-purple of good depth; the bouquet has nicely ripened cassis/berry fruit and a deft touch of oak; there is abundant ripe, rich fruit on the palate, with more concentration than some previous vintages, finishing with soft tannins. A particularly good outcome for the vintage. **rating: 90**

best drinking 2004–2009 **best vintages** '84, '88, '90, '91, '94, '98, '00 **drink with** Gently spiced Asian meat dishes • $24

Hollick Ravenswood Cabernet Sauvignon

ΨΨΨΨ 1999 Medium red-purple, not 100 per cent bright; soft blackberry/cassis fruit and subtle oak on the bouquet are followed by a typically reserved, savoury palate with fine tannins; as much European as Australian in style. **rating: 87**

best drinking 2004–2011 **best vintages** '88, '90, '91, '93, '94 **drink with** Scotch fillet • $60

hollyclare   NR

940 Milbrodale Road, Broke, NSW 2330 **region** Lower Hunter Valley
phone (02) 6579 1193 **fax** (02) 6579 1269 **open** Weekends 10–5 by appointment
winemaker Tamburlaine (Contract) **production** 2000 **est.** 1987
product range ($15–20 CD) Semillon, Unwooded Semillon, Chardonnay, Chardonnay Semillon, Shiraz.
summary John Holdsworth established the Hollyclare Vineyard (now totalling 3 hectares of chardonnay, semillon and shiraz) ten years ago, but the Hollyclare label is a relatively new one on the market. While the wines are made under contract at Tamburlaine, Hollyclare has its own dedicated wine tanks and all of the wines are estate-grown.

holly folly   NR

649 Campersic Road, Baskerville, WA 6056 **region** Swan District
phone (08) 9296 2043 **fax** (08) 9296 2043 **open** By appointment
winemaker Peter Hollingworth **production** 400 **est.** 1995
product range ($7.50–15 ML) Dry White, Verdelho (Barrel Fermented and Barrel Aged), Marsanne, Marsanne Viognier, Méthode Champenoise, Light Red.
summary Peter Hollingworth clearly has a sense of humour and a sense of perspective. He began the establishment of the 11.5 hectares of vineyards (planted to chenin blanc, chardonnay, viognier, marsanne, verdelho, petit verdot, grenache and merlot) in 1995, but it was not until 2000 that the necessary producer's licence was obtained, and in October of that year he embarked upon the limited release of the 400-case production, destined mainly for friends and acquaintances. Most of the grapes are sold to other producers.

holm oak   ★★★★☆

RSD 256, Rowella, West Tamar, Tas 7270 **region** Northern Tasmania
phone (03) 6394 7577 **fax** (03) 6394 7350 **open** 7 days 10–5
winemaker Nick Butler, Julian Alcorso **production** 3000 **est.** 1983
product range ($16–27 R) Riesling, Chardonnay, Reserve Chardonnay, Tyrian Rosé, Pinot Noir, Cabernet Sauvignon.
summary The Butler family produces tremendously rich and strongly flavoured red wines from the vineyard on the banks of the Tamar River, and which takes its name from the grove of oak trees planted around the turn of the century and originally intended for the making of tennis racquets. The white wines, too, led by Riesling, have also impressed over the past few years.

Holm Oak Riesling

ΨΨΨΨ 2001 Light straw-green; a light and bright bouquet with fresh mineral aromas leads into a tight, well-balanced and constructed palate, with good length. **rating: 88**

best drinking 2002–2006 **best vintages** '99, '00 **drink with** Sweet and sour pork • $22

Holm Oak Pinot Noir

▼▼▼▼▽ **2000** Medium red-purple; the intense and complex bouquet has spicy overtones to the fruit; the powerful, intense and grippy palate has enormous impact. Yet another wine from the vintage which pushes the envelope without, however, destroying it. **rating: 92**

best drinking 2003–2009 best vintages '98, '99 drink with Breast of duck • $26

Holm Oak Cabernet Sauvignon

▼▼▼▼▽ **2000** Full red-purple; the aromas range through cassis, mint, earth and oak, leading into a full-bodied palate with dark currant fruit; both the tannins and the oak are already nicely balanced and integrated. **rating: 92**

best drinking 2004–2010 best vintages '00 drink with Sirloin • $27

home hill ★★★★

73 Nairn Street, Ranelagh, Tas 7109 **region** Southern Tasmania
phone (03) 6264 1028 **fax** (03) 6264 1069 **open** 7 days 10–5
winemaker Michael Vishacki, Stefano Lubiana (Contract), Jim Chatto (Contract) **production** 1900 **est.** 1994
product range ($12–30 ML) Chardonnay, Kelly Cuvée, Dry White, Pinot Noir; Kelly's Reserve Chardonnay and Pinot Noir.
summary Terry and Rosemary Bennett planted their first 0.5 hectare of vines in 1994 on gentle slopes in the beautiful Huon Valley. The plantings were quickly extended to 3 hectares, with another hectare planted in 1999. A 70-seat winery restaurant is open for lunch Wednesday to Sunday and dinner on Saturday.

Home Hill Kelly Cuvée

▼▼▼▼ **1999** Light to medium yellow-straw; the bouquet is solid, with distinct bready autolysis aromas, the palate solid, quite full and firm; all in all, at the bigger end of town, and not over-burdened with finesse. **rating: 88**

best drinking 2002–2004 best vintages NA drink with Carpaccio of salmon • $25

Home Hill Pinot Noir

▼▼▼▼▽ **2000** Medium red-purple; a complex bouquet with savoury/briary edges to ripe fruit leads into a very intense and complex palate, with a slightly aggressive finish, but with the near-certainty of coming together exceptionally well with further time in bottle. **rating: 92**

best drinking 2003–2008 best vintages '00 drink with Smoked quail • $25

Kelly's Reserve Pinot Noir

▼▼▼▼▽ **2000** Medium red-purple; very, very ripe fruit moves into anise and other characters seldom encountered in pinot noir; the massively potent palate takes no prisoners, yet manages to avoid outright dry red character. It will be more than interesting to see how the wine develops over a long time in bottle. **rating: 92**

best drinking 2005–2010 best vintages '00 drink with Leave it in the cellar • $30

honeytree estate ★★★★

16 Gillards Road, Pokolbin, NSW 2320 **region** Lower Hunter Valley
phone (02) 4998 7693 **fax** (02) 4998 7693 **open** Wed–Thurs 11–4, Fri–Sun 10–5
winemaker Contract **production** 3600 **est.** 1970
product range ($18–25 CD) Semillon, Shiraz, Cabernet Sauvignon.
summary The Honeytree Estate vineyard was first planted in 1970, and for a period of time wines were produced under the Honeytree Estate label. It then disappeared, but has since been revived. Its 10 hectares of vines are of shiraz, cabernet sauvignon, semillon and a little clairette, known in the Hunter Valley as blanquette, a variety which has been in existence there for well over a century. Jancis Robinson comments that the wine 'tends to be very high in alcohol, a little low in acid and to oxidise dangerously fast', but in a sign of the times, the first Honeytree Clairette sold out so quickly (in 4 weeks) that 2.2 hectares of vineyard has been grafted over to additional clairette. The 2000 vintage wines are particularly good.

Honeytree Estate Semillon

▼▼▼▼ **2000** Light green-yellow; a clean, soft bouquet with a touch of tropical fruit is certainly ripe (12.2° alcohol). The palate is similarly rich and ripe; while it doesn't burn, nor does it have the length and finesse of the slower maturing wines. Thoroughly acceptable in a drink-now alternative mode. **rating: 85**

best drinking 2002–2004 best vintages NA drink with Thai chicken • $18

Honeytree Estate Shiraz
♥♥♥♥♡ **2000** Medium red-purple; harmonious dark berry, plum and spice fruit aromas flow into a supple, rich and smooth palate, with more sweet berry fruit and fine tannins; flavoursome yet elegant. **rating:** 90
best drinking 2004–2014 **best vintages** '00 **drink with** Shepherd's pie • $20

Honeytree Estate Cabernet Sauvignon
♥♥♥♥♡ **2000** Medium to full red-purple; clean, sweet dark berry fruit shows perfect ripeness on the bouquet; layer-upon-layer of dark cassis/blackberry fruit to the palate is in no way over-extracted. Gold medals 2002 Sydney International Wine Competition and Hunter Valley Boutique Wine Show – and deserved them both. **rating:** 93
best drinking 2005–2015 **best vintages** '00 **drink with** Lamb casserole • $25

hope estate ★★★☆
Cobcroft Road, Broke, NSW 2330 **region** Lower Hunter Valley
phone (02) 6579 1161 **fax** (02) 6579 1373 **open** 7 days 10–4
winemaker Josh Steele **production** 30 000 **est.** 1996
product range ($15 CD) Semillon, Verdelho, Chardonnay, Shiraz, Merlot.
summary Pharmacist Michael Hope has come a long way since acquiring his first vineyard in the Hunter Valley in 1994. The Hunter Valley empire now encompasses three substantial vineyards and the former Saxonvale Winery, acquired in 1996, renamed Hope Estate, and refurbished at a cost of over $1 million. That, however, proved to be only the first step, for Hope has acquired most of the assets of the former public-listed Vincorp, including its Donnybrook Vineyard in Western Australia, and a $6 million acquisition of the Virgin Hills brand, its original 14-hectare vineyard, another nearby 32-hectare vineyard at Glenhope, a lease of the historic winery, and the acquisition of all Virgin Hills stocks. In the middle of all this, Hope Estate has managed to produce some excellent wines. Exports to the US, the UK, Japan, Singapore and Hong Kong.

Hope Estate Semillon
♥♥♥♥ **2001** Pale straw-green; the dry herb, mineral and slate aromas have weight; the palate has flavour but lacks sharp focus. 12° alcohol Semillon is often less appealing than the lower alcohol version. **rating:** 85
best drinking 2001–2004 **best vintages** NA **drink with** Balmain bugs • $15

Hope Estate Chardonnay
♥♥♥♥ **2000** Medium yellow-green; strong barrel ferment oak aromas overwhelm the fruit on the bouquet, but the fruit makes a surprising comeback on the palate, which has length and intensity, not to mention considerable complexity. **rating:** 88
best drinking 2001–2003 **best vintages** '99 **drink with** Rich seafood • $15

Hope Estate Merlot
♥♥♥♥ **2000** Medium purple-red; dusty vanilla oak plus ripe berry fruit on the bouquet are followed by sweet blackcurrant/small berry fruit and vanilla oak on the palate. Does not say a great deal about Merlot, but has plenty of flavour. **rating:** 86
best drinking 2002–2006 **best vintages** NA **drink with** Rack of veal • $15

hoppers hill vineyards NR
Googodery Road, Cumnock, NSW 2867 **region** Central Ranges Zone
phone (02) 6367 7270 **open** Weekends 11–5
winemaker Robert Gilmore **production** NFP **est.** 1990
product range ($10–12 CD) Chardonnay, Sauvignon Blanc, Dry White, Cabernet Franc Merlot, Cabernet Sauvignon.
summary The Gilmores planted their vineyard in 1980, using organic growing methods, and using no preservatives or filtration in the winery, which was established in 1990. Not surprisingly, the wines cannot be judged or assessed against normal standards, but may have appeal in a niche market.

horndale NR
Fraser Avenue, Happy Valley, SA 5159 **region** McLaren Vale
phone (08) 8387 0033 **fax** (08) 8387 0033 **open** Mon–Sat 9–6, Sun and public holidays 10–5.30
winemaker Phil Albrecht **production** NFP **est.** 1896

product range ($8.90–17.90 CD) Riesling, Colombard Semillon Chardonnay, Semillon Chardonnay, Chardonnay, Shiraz Cabernet, Cabernet Merlot, Shiraz Grenache, Cabernet Sauvignon Cabernet Franc, Cabernet Sauvignon; a wide range of dessert and fortified wines.

summary Established in 1896, and has remained continuously in production in one way or another since that time, but there have been a number of changes of ownership and direction, and the wines are only available from the cellar door and by mail order. A personal connection is the Horndale Brandy my father used to buy 60 years ago, although it no longer appears on the extensive price list.

horseshoe vineyard NR

Horseshoe Road, Horseshoe Valley via Denman, NSW 2328 **region** Upper Hunter Valley
phone (02) 6547 3528 **open** Weekends 9–5
winemaker John Hordern **production** NFP **est.** 1986
product range ($13–18 CD) Classic Hunter Semillon, Chardonnay Semillon, Chardonnay, Pinot Noir.
summary Fell by the wayside after its wonderful start in 1986, with rich, full-flavoured, barrel-fermented Semillons and Chardonnays. The '87 Semillon was exhibited in the Museum Class at the 1996 Hunter Valley Wine Show and was still drinking beautifully, winning a strong silver medal. These days John Hordern's main occupation seems to be as a highly successful contract winemaker, particularly for Penmara.

houghton ★★★★★

Dale Road, Middle Swan, WA 6056 **region** Swan District
phone (08) 9274 5100 **fax** (08) 9274 5372 **open** 7 days 10–5, except Christmas Day and Good Friday
winemaker Larry Cherubino, Ross Pymment, Simon Osicka **production** 300 000 **est.** 1836
product range ($9.90–93.95 R) Semillon Sauvignon Blanc, Chardonnay Verdelho, White Burgundy, Show Reserve White Burgundy, Chardonnay, Late Picked Verdelho, Shiraz, Reserve Grenache, Cabernet Shiraz Merlot; Crofters Semillon Sauvignon Blanc, Chardonnay, Cabernet Merlot; finally, the super-premium Jack Mann (Cabernet blend).
summary The five-star rating may seem extreme but is very deliberate, in part justified by Houghton White Burgundy, one of Australia's largest-selling white wines – it is almost entirely consumed within days of purchase, but it is superlative with seven or so years bottle age. To borrow a phrase of the late Jack Mann, 'There are no bad wines here.' The Jack Mann red, Houghton Reserve Shiraz, the Margaret River reds and Frankland Riesling are all of the highest quality.

Houghton Frankland River Riesling

▼▼▼▼▼ 2001 Pale straw-green; a spotlessly clean, crisp, direct bouquet leads into a super-refined palate with apple, lime and a wisp of passionfruit; very long carry and finish. **rating:** 94

best drinking 2001–2010 **best vintages** '01 **drink with** Blue-lipped mussels • $21.95

Houghton Crofters Semillon Sauvignon Blanc

▼▼▼▼▽ 2001 Bright green-yellow; quite intense lemony/citrussy fruit and a whiff of oak on the bouquet flow into a lively, fresh palate with lemony acidity. **rating:** 90

best drinking 2001–2003 **best vintages** '96, '01 **drink with** Lemon chicken • $15.50

Houghton White Burgundy

▼▼▼▼ 2001 Fragrant, distinct passionfruit aromas are replicated with the gentle tropical/passionfruit flavours of the finely structured, clean palate. **rating:** 87

best drinking 2001–2007 **best vintages** '83, '87, '89, '91, '93, '95, '99, '00, '01 **drink with** Fish, chicken or veal • $10.50

Houghton Shiraz

▼▼▼▼ 2000 Medium to full red-purple; chocolate liqueur aromas, plus cherry, earth and vanilla on the bouquet are followed by a medium-bodied palate with good length, honest flavour and soft tannins. Particularly good value. **rating:** 86

best drinking 2001–2004 **best vintages** NA **drink with** Meat pie • $11.50

Houghton Frankland Shiraz

▼▼▼▼▼ 1999 Deep red-purple; smooth, deep black cherry fruit with touches of licorice and spice are revealed on the bouquet; the palate has abundant depth and extract, without harshness. Black fruits, spice and a subliminal hint of sweet earth/forest run through the long palate, with oak playing a pure support role.

Two gold medals, including 2001 Royal Sydney Wine Show tell only part of the tale. Starred in the 2002 Divine State of Origin challenge.   **rating:** 94

best drinking 2004–2014 **best vintages** '95, '99 **drink with** Aged beef • $28.99

Houghton Cellar Reserve Grenache
TTTT 1998 Medium to full red-purple; the bouquet and palate offer lots of rich, sweet, dark berry fruit which is, however, dominated by oak and oak tannins. It is just possible the wine could develop into a unique style.   **rating:** 85

best drinking 2003–2010 **best vintages** NA **drink with** Jugged hare • $17.95

Houghton Jack Mann Cabernet Blend
TTTTT 1998 Strong purple-red; fine blackcurrant/cassis fruit with subtle oak on the bouquet is followed by a palate with excellent balance and focus, centred on cassis/blackberry fruit supported by ripe tannins and restrained but positive oak. A wine of the highest quality, although I don't think the label works or does justice to the wine. Multiple trophy winner, including Tucker Seabrook Caon Trophy.   **rating:** 95

best drinking 2003–2023 **best vintages** '94, '95, '96, '98 **drink with** Fillet of lamb • $93.95

Houghton Margaret River Cabernet Sauvignon
TTTTT 1999 A massive dark berry/blackcurrant/chocolate charged bouquet foretells a similarly awesome but luscious palate, with loads of sweet dark berry fruit. Amazingly, the tannins are soft, the oak submerged in the fruit.   **rating:** 95

best drinking 2004–2014 **best vintages** '99 **drink with** Braised ox tail • $27.95

🐌 house of certain views   ★★★★

1238 Milbrodale Road, Broke, NSW 2330 **region** Lower Hunter Valley
phone (02) 6579 1317 **fax** (02) 6579 1317 **open** Not
winemaker Andrew Margan **production** 3000 **est.** 2001
product range ($30–38 R) Coonabarabran Sauvignon Blanc, Orange Shiraz, Mt Kaputar Merlot, Coonabarabran Cabernet Sauvignon.
summary A stand-alone business owned by Andrew and Lisa Margan, with a fascinating portfolio of wines based on exclusive or fairly new wine growing regions on the western side of the Great Dividing Range. The selection of the vineyard sites (via contract growers) involves a careful correlation of latitude, altitude, soil type and variety – the French catch it all in the single word 'terroir'. The initial releases are particularly impressive given the youth of the vines; one can only imagine the venture will go from strength to strength. The packaging of the wines, incidentally, is brilliant.

House of Certain Views Orange Shiraz
TTTT 1999 Vivid red-purple, particularly striking given its age; a youthful, clean and exuberant bouquet of raspberry and blackberry is faithfully repeated on the youthful palate with abundant juicy berry fruit. All in all, well removed from the mainstream.   **rating:** 88

best drinking 2003–2007 **best vintages** NA **drink with** Beef braised in red wine • $38

House of Certain Views Mt Kaputar Merlot
TTTTY 2000 Medium to full red-purple; a rich and ripe bouquet with spicy berry fruit to the fore, a touch of oak following up on the rear, then a particularly complex palate offering an interplay of dark fruits and olive/savoury aspects, all supported by gentle tannins running through to the finish. Trophy winner at the 2001 Boutique Wine Show.   **rating:** 90

best drinking 2003–2008 **best vintages** NA **drink with** Moroccan lamb • $38

House of Certain Views Coonabarabran Cabernet Sauvignon
TTTT 2000 Medium red-purple; a cedary/spicy/savoury bouquet, not the least green, indeed verging on the overripe, is followed by a ripe, almost jammy, palate with a flood of sweet cassis/berry fruit. That fruit has literally eaten the oak, which is not at all prominent.   **rating:** 87

best drinking 2003–2008 **best vintages** NA **drink with** Rare roast beef • $38

howard park (denmark)   ★★★★☆

Scotsdale Road, Denmark, WA 6333 **region** Great Southern
phone (08) 9848 2345 **fax** (08) 9848 2064 **open** 7 days 10–5
winemaker Michael Kerrigan, James Kellie **production** 100 000 **est.** 1986

product range ($17–75 R) Madfish Premium White, Chardonnay, Premium Red and Shiraz provide low-priced volume; limited quantities of Howard Park Riesling, Chardonnay, Botrytis Semillon, Leston Shiraz, Scotsdale Shiraz, Cabernet Sauvignon Merlot, Leston Cabernet Sauvignon, Scotsdale Cabernet Sauvignon.

summary In the wake of its acquisition by the Burch family, the emphasis has switched from the Great Southern; a splendid new winery has been constructed in the Margaret River region (incorporating Feng Shui principles) to complement the (near new) Denmark winery. Howard Park has 230 hectares of estate and selected long-term contract vineyards in all of the best regions for cool-climate fruit production in southern Western Australia. The philosophy is to source fruit from the region best suited to a particular variety, thus flagship Howard Park Cabernet Merlot has Cabernet Sauvignon from Margaret River and Mount Barker with Cabernet Franc from the Frankland River and Merlot from Pemberton. Exports to the US, Canada, New Zealand, the UK, Belgium, Switzerland, Spain, Italy, Indonesia, Malaysia, Singapore, Hong Kong and Japan.

Howard Park Riesling

▼▼▼▼ **2001** Light to medium green-yellow; the moderately intense and clean bouquet has nicely ripened fruit varietal aroma, but the palate has fearsome acidity, in similar vein to the 2000 vintage. It is difficult to imagine that the wine will ever soften or come back into balance. **rating:** 86

best drinking 2005–2010 **best vintages** '91, '93, '94, '95, '96, '97, '98, '99 **drink with** Fresh asparagus, Asian seafood • $24.50

Howard Park Leston Shiraz

▼▼▼▼▽ **2000** Medium red-purple; the bouquet offers a mix of mint, red berry and leaf, attesting to a moderately cool climate; the palate is sweetened up with nice oak, and taken more into the mainstream quality style. **rating:** 91

best drinking 2005–2010 **best vintages** '99, '00 **drink with** Spiced lamb with couscous • $35

howard park (margaret river) ★★★★☆

Miamup Road, Cowaramup, WA 6284 **region** Margaret River
phone (08) 9755 9988 **fax** (08) 9755 9048 **open** 7 days 10–5
winemaker Michael Kerrigan, James Kellie **production** 100 000 **est.** 1986
product range ($18–74 R) Madfish Premium White, Chardonnay, Premium Red and Shiraz provide low-priced volume; limited quantities of Howard Park Riesling, Chardonnay, Botrytis Semillon, Leston Shiraz, Scotsdale Shiraz, Cabernet Sauvignon Merlot, Leston Scotsdale Cabernet Sauvignon.

summary In the wake of its acquisition by the Birch family, the emphasis has switched from the Great Southern; a splendid new winery has been constructed in the Margaret River region (incorporating Feng Shui principles) to complement the (near new) Denmark winery. Howard Park has 230 hectares of estate and selected long-term contract vineyards in all of the best regions for cool climate fruit production in southern Western Australia. The philosophy is to source fruit from the region best suited to a particular variety, thus flagship Howard Park Cabernet Merlot has Cabernet Sauvignon from Margaret River and Mount Barker with Cabernet Franc from the Frankland River and Merlot from Pemberton. Exports to the US, Canada, New Zealand, UK, Belgium, Switzerland,Spain, Italy, Indonesia, Malaysia, Singapore, Hong Kong and Japan.

Howard Park Madfish Premium White

▼▼▼▼▽ **2001** Light green-yellow; a direct, fresh bouquet with a mix of nectarine and citrus fruit aromas leads into a palate with excellent intensity and persistence to the lemony, lingering flavour. Ideal summer white. **rating:** 90

best drinking 2001–2003 **best vintages** '00, '01 **drink with** Chicken • $17.99

Howard Park Scotsdale Shiraz

▼▼▼▼▼ **2000** Medium to full red-purple; a fragrant, almost flowery, bouquet with spicy berry aromas, then an elegant but intense and perfectly poised palate. Here the driver is the red cherry fruit; the tannins are supple, the oak exemplary. **rating:** 96

best drinking 2005–2015 **best vintages** '00 **drink with** Spit-roasted baby lamb • $35

Howard Park Cabernet Sauvignon Merlot

▼▼▼▼▼ **1999** Medium red-purple; fresh, crushed red berry aromas and subtle oak lead into a palate bounding with red fruits and some fine, savoury flavours, supported by convincing oak and tannin inputs. **rating:** 94

best drinking 2004–2014 **best vintages** '86, '88, '89, '90, '92, '93, '94, '96, '98, '99 **drink with** Lamb fillets, mature cheddar • $73.99

howards way vineyard ★★★★

Cobcroft Road, Broke, NSW 2330 **region** Lower Hunter Valley
phone (02) 4998 1336 **fax** (02) 4938 3775 **open** Not
winemaker Andrew Margan (Contract) **production** 3500 **est.** NA
product range ($15–20 ML) Semillon, Pinot Noir, Shiraz.
summary Yet another of the dozens of new vineyards and labels that have appeared in the Hunter Valley in the latter part of the 1990s. Eight hectares of shiraz, 3 hectares of pinot noir and 2 hectares of semillon provide a substantial base, and retail distribution began in 1999.

Howards Way Semillon
▼▼▼▼ 1999 Medium yellow-green; the bouquet is clean, with lemony fruit, the palate having good depth of flavour and balance. Very probably moving into the difficult transition stage between youth and maturity.

rating: 86

best drinking 2003–2007 **best vintages** NA **drink with** Summer salad • NA

Howards Way Shiraz
▼▼▼▼♀ 1999 Bright purple-red; clean dark cherry fruit with a hint of spice on the bouquet is followed by a rich and luscious palate with plenty of flavour and structure, although pushed by oak.   **rating:** 90

best drinking 2004–2009 **best vintages** '99 **drink with** Rich casserole • NA

howarth's pycnantha hill   NR

Benbournie Road, Clare, SA 5453 **region** Clare Valley
phone (08) 8842 2137 **fax** (08) 8842 2137 **open** Not
winemaker Jim Howarth **production** 800 **est.** 1997
product range ($11–15 R) Riesling, Chardonnay, Shiraz, Cabernet Sauvignon.
summary The Howarth family progressively established 2.4 hectares of vineyard from 1987, making its first commercial vintage ten years later, in 1997. *Acacia pycnantha* is the botanic name for the golden wattle which grows wild over the hills of the Howarth farm, and they say it was 'a natural choice to name our vineyards Pycnantha Hill'. I am not too sure that marketing gurus would agree, but there we go.

🐌 howcroft estate   NR

Cnr Buckingham and Scows Roads, Mundulla, SA 5270 **region** Limestone Coast Zone
phone (08) 8753 4000 **fax** (08) 8753 4000 **open** Not
winemaker Peter Hall **production** 220 000 **est.** 1998
product range ($16 R) Shiraz, Petit Verdot, Merlot, Cabernet.
summary The largest producer in the nascent Bordertown region in the Limestone Coast Zone. It draws upon 121 hectares of shiraz, 50 hectares of merlot, 46 hectares of cabernet sauvignon and 18 hectares of petit verdot. All of the wines are very competitively priced, and the major focus is on export markets.

hugh hamilton ★★★

McMurtrie Road, McLaren Vale, SA 5171 **region** McLaren Vale
phone (08) 8323 8689 **fax** (08) 8323 9488 **open** Mon–Fri 10–5, weekends and public holidays 11–5
winemaker Hugh Hamilton **production** 8500 **est.** 1992
product range ($14.50–19.50 R) Chenin Blanc, Unwooded Chardonnay, Shiraz, Merlot, Cabernet Sauvignon, Sparkling Shiraz.
summary Hugh Hamilton is a member of the famous Hamilton winemaking family, there being an intense (and well-known) competitive spirit existing between various members – notably between Richard and Hugh – which can only be good for the consumer.

hugo ★★★★

Elliott Road, McLaren Flat, SA 5171 **region** McLaren Vale
phone (08) 8383 0098 **fax** (08) 8383 0446 **open** Mon–Fri 9.30–5, Sat 12–5, Sun 10.30–5
winemaker John Hugo **production** 10 000 **est.** 1982
product range ($15–38 R) Sauvignon Blanc, Unwooded Chardonnay, Reserve Shiraz, Shiraz, Grenache, Cabernet Sauvignon, Port.
summary A winery which came from relative obscurity to prominence in the late 1980s with some lovely ripe, sweet reds which, while strongly American-oak-influenced, were quite outstanding. Has picked up the pace again after a dull period in the mid-1990s. There are 32 hectares of estate plantings, with part of the grape production sold to others. The wines are exported to the US, Canada, the UK, Germany and Singapore.

Hugo Sauvignon Blanc

♥♥♥♥ **2001** Light green-yellow; a delicate and fresh bouquet with light, aromatic hints of passionfruit and citrus tightens up more on the palate in a minerally mode. Has length and grip, but is not flashy. Well made in a year which dry-roasted the white varieties.   **rating:** 87

best drinking 2002–2003 **best vintages** NA **drink with** King George whiting • $17

Hugo Reserve Shiraz

♥♥♥♥ **2000** Full red-purple; concentrated blackberry/plum/cherry fruit with positive but not overly aggressive oak on the bouquet, then a sweet, ripe plum/blackberry palate with slightly dusty oak. A genuine Reserve, way in front of the varietal release.   **rating:** 89

♥♥♥♥♡ **1998** Dense red-purple; a massive and concentrated bouquet with blackberry/cherry fruit and lots of vanilla from new American oak is followed by similarly awesome, rich and concentrated palate in Henry VIII style, and a mere 14.5° alcohol. Balanced to a degree by tangy acidity.   **rating:** 90

best drinking 2006–2012 **best vintages** '98 **drink with** A haunch of beef • $38

Hugo Cabernet Sauvignon

♥♥♥♥ **2000** Medium red-purple; the bouquet is clean, moderately intense, with fresh red and blackcurrant fruit, and regional dark chocolate adding another layer of flavour on the palate. Fine tannins, neatly judged oak.   **rating:** 87

♥♥♥♥♡ **1999** Medium to full red-purple; fragrant cassis aromas and nicely handled oak flow into a palate with good structure, clear, ripe berry varietal character, and neatly balanced tannins.   **rating:** 93

best drinking 2004–2011 **best vintages** '90, '92, '94, '98, '99, '00 **drink with** Rump steak • $20

hungerford hill   ★★★☆

McDonalds Road, Pokolbin, NSW 2320 **region** Lower Hunter Valley
phone 1300 651 650 **fax** (02) 4998 7682 **open** Mon–Fri 9–4.30, weekends 10–4.30
winemaker Phillip John **production** 30 000 **est.** 1967
product range ($13–23 R) Tumbarumba Chardonnay, Sauvignon Blanc, Pinot Gris and Pinot Noir; Cowra Chardonnay, Cowra Verdelho, Young Chardonnay, Young Semillon, Late Picked Semillon, Late Picked Riesling, Griffith Botrytis Semillon, Cabernet Merlot, Hunter Shiraz, Hilltops Shiraz, Hilltops Cabernet Sauvignon, Adelaide Hills–McLaren Vale Cabernet. Additions following the Cassegrain acquisition will include Hunter Valley Semillon, a Shiraz and Merlot from Orange, plus a Watervale Riesling.
summary Saved from death when Cassegrain acquired the brand and cellar door from Southcorp in February 2002. The product range previously appearing under the Hungerford Hill label will be maintained, and new wines added; all will be made at the Cassegrain winery in the Hastings Valley under the supervision of Phillip John.

🐾 hunting lodge estate   NR

703 Mt Kilcoy Road, Mount Kilcoy, Qld 4515 **region** South Burnett
phone (07) 5498 1243 **fax** (07) 5498 1243 **open** Wed–Sun 10–5
winemaker Brian Wilson **production** 3300 **est.** 1999
product range ($14–25 CD) Mauritius Traminer Riesling, Serengeti Oaked Chardonnay, Kalahari Unoaked Chardonnay, Simpson Red, Zambezi Cabernet Merlot, Cape Cabernet Sauvignon, Hunters Cabernet Sauvignon, Nairobi Tawny Port, Estate Tawny Port.
summary Yet another new player in the rapidly expanding Queensland wine industry, established in 1999 with plantings of 1 hectare each of verdelho, merlot and cabernet sauvignon. However, is offering a range of wines ranging from 1997 to 1999, including 'our famous Nairobi Port'; the names of the table wines all crosslink both to hunting and South Africa whence, one imagines, the owners originated.

huntington estate   ★★★★☆

Cassilis Road, Mudgee, NSW 2850 **region** Mudgee
phone (02) 6373 3825 **fax** (02) 6373 3730 **open** Mon–Fri 9–5, Sat 10–5, Sun 10–3
winemaker Susie Roberts **production** 20 000 **est.** 1969
product range ($8.80–30 ML) Semillon, Semillon Chardonnay, Dry White Semillon Chardonnay, Chardonnay, Rosé Dry, Rosé, Sweet White Blend; red wines are released under bin numbers (FB = full-bodied, MB = medium-bodied) comprising Shiraz, Dry Red Shiraz Cabernet, Cabernet Shiraz Merlot, Cabernet Sauvignon.

summary The remarkable Roberts family members have a passion for wine which is equalled only by their passion for music, with the Huntington Music Festival a major annual event. The red wines of Huntington Estate are outstanding and sell for absurdly low prices. The wines are seldom exported; almost all are sold via the cellar door and the mailing list.

Huntington Estate Semillon

TTTT **2001** Bin W1. Light green-yellow; the bouquet shows distinct varietal herbaceousness, with similar flavours on the palate, balanced by what seems to be a touch of subliminal sweetness.   **rating:** 89

best drinking 2003–2009 **best vintages** NA **drink with** Smoked trout • $12.50

Huntington Estate Shiraz

TTTTY **1999** Bin FB45. Medium red-purple; the bouquet offers an attractive mix of cedary/savoury/spicy notes with fresh fruit; the well-balanced and smooth plum and cherry palate has neatly judged oak. Like so many of the 1999 wines from Huntington, a very good outcome for an indifferent vintage.   **rating:** 90

best drinking 2004–2008 **best vintages** '74, '75, '78, '79, '84, '90, '91, '93, '94, '95, '97 **drink with** Kangaroo fillet • $16.50

Huntington Estate Special Reserve Shiraz

TTTTT **2000** Bin FB12. Medium to full red-purple; the bouquet exudes sweet cherry/berry fruit and quite pronounced vanilla oak, and the palate has rich fruit and depth which sustains the quite obvious oak, tannins and acidity. An outstanding success in a dismal vintage for shiraz.   **rating:** 94

TTTTT **1999** Bin FB33. Dense red-purple; the big, rich, powerfully dense bouquet of prune, plum and oak is mirrored in the rich and concentrated palate, led by chocolate, prune and plum flavours; abundant oak and tannins for the long haul.   **rating:** 94

TTTTT **1999** Bin FB34. Medium to full red-purple; powerful, robust dark berry and plum intermingle with American oak on the bouquet, with more of the same on the full-bodied, rich and complex palate, laden with dark berry and dark chocolate. Like its sister wine, a gold medal winner at the 2001 Mudgee Wine Show.   **rating:** 94

best drinking 2005–2012 **best vintages** '93, '99, '00 **drink with** Venison • $25

Huntington Estate Cabernet Sauvignon

TTTT **1999** Bin FB31. Medium red-purple; a gently complex bouquet ranging through berry, spice, earth, cedar and vanilla provides a replay on the palate, plus fine, ripe tannins and nice oak to finish.   **rating:** 88

best drinking 2004–2009 **best vintages** '74, '79, '81, '84, '89, '90, '94, '95, '97 **drink with** Grilled rump steak • $17.50

Huntington Estate Special Reserve Cabernet Sauvignon

TTTTY **1999** Bin FB35. Medium to full red-purple; fragrant, red berry fruit with touches of leaf, mint and earth, then a palate veering more towards a mix of blackberry and blackcurrant, supported by fine tannins. Medium-bodied more than full-bodied perhaps, but that is of no particular moment.   **rating:** 90

TTTT **1999** Bin FB36. Medium to full red-purple; a savoury, powerful bouquet showing blackberry and a touch of dark chocolate, the palate goes hither and thither, with a slightly sharper profile and finish which belies the bouquet, and yet is perhaps more elegant than the Bin 35, but without its sweet fruit. Should settle down with further time in bottle.   **rating:** 88

best drinking 2004–2014 **best vintages** '99 **drink with** Rib of beef • $30

huntleigh vineyards   ★★★☆

38 Tunnecliffes Lane, Heathcote, Vic 3523 **region** Heathcote
phone (03) 5433 2795 **fax** (03) 5433 2795 **open** 7 days 10–5.30
winemaker Leigh Hunt **production** 500 **est.** 1975
product range ($13–20 CD) Traminer, Shiraz, Cabernet Sauvignon.
summary The wines are all made at the winery by former stockbroker Leigh Hunt from 5 hectares of estate-grown grapes, the last-tasted Cabernet Sauvignon (1998) being of exemplary quality.

hunt's foxhaven estate   NR

Canal Rocks Road, Yallingup, WA 6282 **region** Margaret River
phone (08) 9755 2232 **fax** (08) 9255 2249 **open** Weekends, holidays 11–5 or by appointment
winemaker David Hunt **production** 1000 **est.** 1978

product range ($12–15 CD) Riesling (dry and sweet), Semillon, Canal Rocks White, Yallingup Classic, Noble Riesling, Hunting Pink, Cabernet Sauvignon.
summary Draws upon 4 hectares of vines progressively established, the oldest being 25-year-old riesling. All of the wine is sold through the cellar door and by mail order.

hurley vineyard   NR

101 Balnarring Road, Balnarring, Vic 3926 **region** Mornington Peninsula
phone (03) 9608 8220 **fax** (03) 9608 7293 **open** Not
winemaker Contract **production** NA **est.** 1998
product range Pinot Noir.
summary Hurley Vineyard has been established by Melbourne Queens Counsel Kevin Bell. Four hectares of pinot noir were planted in 1998; no tastings to date.

hutton vale vineyard   NR

'Hutton Vale', Stone Jar Road, Angaston, SA 5353 **region** Eden Valley
phone (08) 8564 8270 **fax** (08) 8564 8385 **open** By appointment
winemaker David Powell, Chris Ringland, Caroline Dunn **production** 500 **est.** 1994
product range ($19–39 ML) Riesling, Shiraz, Grenache Mataro.
summary John Howard Angas (who arrived in South Australia in 1843, aged 19, charged with the responsibility of looking after the affairs of his father, George Fife Angas) named part of the family estate Hutton Vale. It is here that John Angas, John Howard's great-great-grandson, and wife Jan tend a little over 26 hectares of vines and produce (or, at least, Jan does) a range of jams, chutneys and preserves. Almost all of the grapes are sold, a tiny quantity being made by the Who's Who of the Barossa Valley, notably David Powell of Torbreck, Chris Ringland of Rockford and Caroline Dunn of Beringer Blass. Most of the wine is sold by mail order, and what is left is exported. I haven't tasted the wines, but I'm prepared to wager they are of outstanding quality.

ibis wines   ★★★

239 Kearneys Drive, Orange, NSW 2800 **region** Orange
phone (02) 6362 3257 **fax** (02) 6362 5779 **open** Weekends and public holidays 11–5 or by appointment
winemaker Phil Stevenson **production** 1100 **est.** 1988
product range ($12–25 CD) Riesling, Chardonnay, Dry Muscat, Pinot Noir, Kanjara Shiraz, Cabernet Sauvignon, Cabernet Franc; Habitat Sauvignon Blanc, Pagan (Pinot Noir Cabernet blend), Merlot.
summary Ibis Wines is located just north of Orange (near the botanic gardens) on what was once a family orchard. Planting of the vineyard commenced in 1988, and a new winery was completed on the property in 1998. The grapes are sourced from the home vineyards at an altitude of 800 metres, from the Habitat Vineyard at 1100 metres on Mount Canobolas (pinot noir and merlot) and from the Kanjara Vineyard (shiraz). Wine quality has shown steady improvement over the past couple of years.

immerse in the yarra valley   NR

1548 Melba Highway, Yarra Glen, Vic 3775 **region** Yarra Valley
phone (03) 5965 2444 **fax** (03) 5965 2460 **open** Wed–Sun 12–5
winemaker Contract **production** 1000 **est.** 1989
product range Sauvignon Blanc, Chardonnay, Pinot Noir, Shiraz.
summary Steve and Helen Miles have purchased the restaurant, accommodation and function complex previous known as Lovey's. It will feature a cafe/restaurant/cooking school run by Gary Cooper, sustained by an organic market garden. A spa-based health farm has eight rooms, with a full range of services. I have to say that the name chosen both for the facility and for the wines is as far left of centre as it is possible to go. As previously, a substantial portion of the grapes produced are sold to other makers in the Yarra Valley.

inchiquin wines   ★★★☆

PO Box 865, Clare, SA 5453 **region** Clare Valley
phone (08) 8843 4210 **open** Not
winemaker Stephen McInerney **production** 500 **est.** 1998
product range ($13–20 ML) Riesling, Cabernet Shiraz.

summary Stephen McInerney learnt his trade on the winery floor in various parts of the world: his first experience came in 1985 at Jim Barry Wines. He spent a number of years there before moving to Pikes. In the intervening period he worked as a flying winemaker in France, Oregon, Spain and Argentina. He is now assistant winemaker at the large, new Kirribilly Winery in the Clare Valley. He established Inchiquin Wines with his partner Kate Strachan, who has great industry credentials herself, primarily as the viticulturist for Taylor's (previously Southcorp), which has the largest vineyards in the Clare Valley. The wines, incidentally, are made by Stephen McInerney at Pikes.

Inchiquin Shiraz Cabernet

▼▼▼▼ **2000** Strong red-purple; youthful, dark, dense black cherry and blackberry aromas and flavours are a promising start, but the wine does tail off somewhat on the finish. **rating:** 87

best drinking 2003–2007 **best vintages** NA **drink with** Leave it in the cellar • $17

indigo ridge ★★★

Icely Road, Orange, NSW 2800 **region** Orange
phone (02) 6362 1851 **fax** (02) 6362 1851 **open** First weekend of the month 12–5 or by appointment
winemaker Jon Reynolds (Contract) **production** 600 **est.** 1995
product range ($15–27 ML) Sauvignon Blanc, Cabernet Sauvignon, Ophir Gold.
summary Indigo Ridge has 4 hectares each of sauvignon blanc and cabernet sauvignon; production is still very small, and all of the wines are sold through the cellar door and by mail order, with limited on and off-premise distribution in Orange and Sydney.

indijup point NR

Caves Road, Wilyabrup, WA 6280 **region** Margaret River
phone 0408 955 770 **fax** (08) 9386 8352 **open** By appointment
winemaker Belinda Gould, Michael Standish **production** 1000 **est.** 1993
product range ($15–20 ML) Sauvignon Blanc, Semillon Sauvignon Blanc, Shiraz, Cabernets Merlot.
summary The development of the substantial Indijup Point vineyard began in 1993; the plantings now comprise 5 hectares of cabernet sauvignon, 3 hectares each of shiraz and cabernet franc, 2 hectares of merlot and 1 hectare each of sauvignon blanc, pinot noir and semillon. Most of the grapes are sold to other makers, with a small amount reserved for mail order sale and other local distribution. An extensive native garden surrounds the property, which has views to the adjacent Leeuwin Naturaliste National Park.

inglewood vineyards ★★★☆

Yarrawa Road, Denman, NSW 2328 **region** Upper Hunter Valley
phone (02) 6547 2556 **fax** (02) 6547 2546 **open** Not
winemaker Gary Reed (Contract) **production** 25 000 **est.** 1988
product range ($7.50–20 R) Atmosphere Coastal White and Inland Red; Two Rivers Stone's Throw Semillon, Wild Fire Unwooded Chardonnay, Two Rivers Lightning Strike Chardonnay, Hidden Hive Verdelho, Rocky Crossing Cabernet Sauvignon, Back Track Cabernets; Reserve Hunter Semillon, Hunter Chardonnay, Hunter Shiraz and McLaren Vale/Hunter Cabernet Sauvignon; also Tulloch wines.
summary A significant addition to the viticultural scene in the Upper Hunter Valley, with almost 170 hectares of vineyards established, involving a total investment of around $7 million. Part of the fruit is sold to Southcorp under long-term contracts, but part is made under contract for the expanding winemaking and marketing operations of Inglewood. The emphasis is on Chardonnay and Semillon, and the wines have been medal winners in the wine show circuit. In early 2002 Inglewood acquired the Tulloch brand from Southcorp; it has taken the decision to separately market and distribute the Tulloch brand (through Angove's).

Inglewood Vineyards Two Rivers Stone's Throw Semillon

▼▼▼▼ **2001** Light to medium straw-yellow; the bouquet is clean, with quite ripe but nonetheless lemony fruit aromatics; the palate is lemony, crisp and lively. **rating:** 86

best drinking 2002–2006 **best vintages** NA **drink with** Antipasto • $12.50

Tulloch Verdelho

▼▼▼▽ **2001** Medium yellow-green; the bouquet is clean, with gentle fruit salad aromas, and nothing remarkable; the palate presents no surprises; no wood, of course, simply a well-balanced dry table wine with no particular character or individuality. How it won the Schenker Perpetual Trophy for the Best Medium Bodied Dry White Table Wine in the 2001 Sydney International Wine Competition, coupled with the Kemeny perpetual Trophy for Best Value Dry Table Wine in all category divisions, is beyond my comprehension. **rating:** 84

best drinking 2002–2003 **best vintages** NA **drink with** Takeaway • $13.99

Inglewood Two Rivers Lightning Strike Chardonnay

ΤΤΤΤΥ **2000** Light to medium green-yellow; clean, fresh nectarine fruit, the palate fresh, long and lively, again with nectarine fruit to the fore; if there is any oak in the wine, it is certainly not obvious. **rating:** 90

best drinking 2001–2003 **best vintages** '00 **drink with** Grilled calamari • $12.50

inigo wines   NR

Lot 2 New England Highway, Glen Aplin, Qld, 4382 **region** Granite Belt
phone (07) 3397 6425 **fax** (07) 3397 5280 **open** Fri 12-3, weekends 10–5 or by appointment
winemaker Janis Carter **production** 450 **est.** 1996
product range ($16–18 CD) Sauvignon Blanc, Semillon Sauvignon Blanc, Verdelho, Cabernet Shiraz Merlot, Cabernet Merlot.
summary The property and winery operate as a kind of home-stay operation, and anyone staying at the Chateau Bernard and St Ignatius Vineyard Retreat (Inigo's home) can help in the winery.

innisfail vineyards   NR

Cross Street, Batesford, Vic 3221 **region** Geelong
phone (03) 5276 1258 **fax** (03) 5276 1258 **open** By appointment
winemaker Nick Farr **production** 2000 **est.** 1980
product range ($15–25 ML) Riesling, Chardonnay, Pinot Noir, Cabernet Sauvignon Merlot.
summary This 6-hectare vineyard released its first wines in 1988, made in a small but modern winery on site, with a chewy, complex Chardonnay from both 1989 and 1990 attesting to the quality of the vineyard. No tastings for many years, however.

ironbark ridge vineyard   NR

Middle Road Mail Service 825, Purga, Qld 4306 **region** Queensland Coastal
phone (07) 5464 6787 **fax** (07) 5464 6858 **open** By appointment
winemaker Mark Ravenscroft (Contract) **production** 250 **est.** 1984
product range ($15–28 ML) Chardonnay, Reserve Chardonnay, Shiraz, Vintage Port.
summary Ipswich is situated on the coastal side of the Great Dividing Range, and the high summer humidity and rainfall will inevitably provide challenges for viticulture here. On the evidence of the '98 Chardonnay, Ironbark Ridge is capable of producing Chardonnay equal to the best from Queensland.

iron pot bay wines   ★★★★

766 Deviot Road, Deviot, Tas 7275 **region** Northern Tasmania
phone (03) 6394 7320 **fax** (03) 6394 7346 **open** Thurs–Sun 11–5 Sept-May (except Christmas Day and Good Friday), June–Aug by appointment
winemaker Russell Cook **production** 2000 **est.** 1988
product range ($18–25 CD) Traminer, Semillon Sauvignon Blanc, Pinot Grigio, Unwooded Chardonnay, Kyra Sparkling Vintage.
summary Iron Pot Bay is now part of the syndicate which has established Rosevears Estate, with its large, state-of-the-art winery erected on the banks of the Tamar. The vineyard takes its name from a bay on the Tamar River and is strongly maritime-influenced, producing delicate but intensely flavoured unwooded white wines.

ironwood estate   NR

RMB 1288, Porongurup, WA 6234 **region** Great Southern
phone (08) 9853 1126 **fax** (08) 9853 1172 **open** By appointment
winemaker Robert Lee, John Wade (Consultant) **production** 1000 **est.** 1996
product range ($14.50–19.50 CD) Riesling, Chardonnay, Reserve Chardonnay, Late Harest, Rocky Rosé, Shiraz, Merlot, Cabernet Merlot, Cabernet Sauvignon.
summary Ironwood Estate was established in 1996 when the first wines were made from purchased grapes. In the same year chardonnay, shiraz and cabernet sauvignon were planted on a northern slope of the

Porongurup Range. The twin peaks of the Porongurups rise above the vineyard and provide the basis for the label design. The first estate-grown grapes were vinified at the new Porongurup Winery, erected for the 1999 vintage and jointly owned by Jingalla and Chatsfield Wines.

Ironwood Estate Reserve Chardonnay

▼▼▼▽ **2001** Medium straw-yellow; strong, sawdusty/spicy oak dominates the bouquet, although on the palate nectarine fruit makes a partial comeback; there is every chance the balance will improve over the next 12 months or so.　　　　　　　　　　　　　　　　　　　　　　　　　　　**rating:** 83

best drinking 2003–2004 **best vintages** NA **drink with** Chinese prawns • $18.95

irvine　　　★★★★

Roeslers Road, Eden Valley, SA 5235 **region** Eden Valley
phone (08) 8564 1046 **fax** (08) 8564 1314 **open** Not
winemaker James Irvine, Joanne Irvine **production** 7000 **est.** 1980
product range ($15–100 R) Under the cheaper Eden Crest label: Unwooded Chardonnay, Pinot Gris, Merlot, Merlot Cabernet, Zinfandel Merlot, Meslier Brut; under the premium James Irvine label: Pinot Meslier, Merlot Brut and (at the top of the tree) Grand Merlot.
summary Industry veteran Jim Irvine, who has successfully guided the destiny of so many SA wineries, quietly introduced his own label in 1991, although the vineyard from which the wines are sourced was first planted in 1983 and now comprises a patchwork quilt of a little over 12 hectares of vines. The flagship is the rich Grand Merlot. Much of the production is exported to Germany, Switzerland, the US, Japan, Taiwan, New Zealand, Hong Kong and Singapore.

Irvine Eden Crest Pinot Gris

▼▼▼▼ **2001** Pale straw-bronze; the bouquet is typically neutral, faintly oily; the palate is driven by mouthfeel and structure more than the peach skin flavour, with rich, sweet viscosity from the 14° alcohol.　　**rating:** 87

best drinking 2001–2004 **best vintages** NA **drink with** Yakitori chicken • $26

James Irvine Grand Merlot

▼▼▼▼▽ **1998** Medium red, with some purple; the moderately intense and complex bouquet shows the extended barrel maturation yet does not unduly compromise the fruit, which really flowers on the palate. Here, most attractive sweet berry is married with totally integrated and sympathetic oak, helping to provide a mix of savoury and cedary overtones.　　　　　　　　　　　　　　　　　　　**rating:** 90

best drinking 2003–2008 **best vintages** '96, '97, '98 **drink with** Venison • $100

Irvine Eden Crest Merlot Cabernet

▼▼▼▼ **2000** Medium red-purple; the soft bouquet has a mix of leafy, spicy, plum and mulberry aromas; the palate has ripe, slightly jammy plum and mint fruit flavours, tightened up on the finish by good acidity.　　　　　　　　　　　　　　　　　　　　　　　　　　　　　　　**rating:** 89

best drinking 2002–2006 **best vintages** '97 **drink with** Rabbit in herbs and red wine • $28

✿ irymple estate winery　　　NR

2086 Karadoc Avenue, Irymple, Vic 3498 **region** Murray Darling
phone (03) 5024 5759 **fax** (03) 5024 5759 **open** Not
winemaker Contract **production** 1500 **est.** 1999
product range ($5.50 R) Chardonnay, Shiraz.
summary Irymple is a paradox. On the one hand, it is estate-based, with only 2 hectares each of chardonnay and shiraz, and less than 1 hectare of merlot and cabernet sauvignon. On the other hand, the contract-made wines are sold in the old-fashioned way at distinctly old-fashioned prices: in the case of the Chardonnay, either cleanskin at under $5 a bottle; labelled at a little over $5 a bottle; or in a 10-litre cask costing $21.30. The Shiraz is offered only cleanskin or labelled, but at the same price as the Chardonnay. Wine quality is appropriate to the price.

island brook estate　　　NR

Lot 817 Bussell Highway, Metricup, WA 6280 **region** Margaret River
phone (08) 9755 7501 **fax** (08) 9755 7008 **open** 7 days 10–5
winemaker Mark Shepherd **production** NA **est.** 1985
product range Semillon, Chardonnay, Verdelho, Merlot, Cabernet Sauvignon.

summary Linda and Peter Jenkins purchased Island Brook from Ken and Judy Brook in early 2001, and have undertaken major renovations, including extensive vineyard re-trellising, before opening their cellar door in November 2001.

ivanhoe wines   NR

Marrowbone Road, Pokolbin, NSW 2320 **region** Lower Hunter Valley
phone (02) 4998 7325 **fax** (02) 4998 7848 **open** 7 days 10–5
winemaker Stephen Drayton, Tracy Drayton **production** 7000 **est.** 1995
product range ($15–27 CD) Various varietal wines under the Ivanhoe and Stephen Drayton Signature Series, including Semillon, Verdelho, Chardonnay, Late Picked Gewürztraminer, Chambourcin, Shiraz, Cabernet Sauvignon.
summary Stephen Drayton is the son of the late Reg Drayton and, with wife Tracy, is the third branch of the family to be actively involved in winemaking in the Hunter Valley. The property on which the vineyard is situated has been called Ivanhoe for over 140 years, and 25 hectares of 30-year-old vines provide high-quality fruit for the label. The plans are to build a replica of the old homestead (burnt down, along with much of the winery, in the 1968 bushfires) to operate as a sales area.

Ivanhoe Stephen Drayton Shiraz
▼▼▼▼ **2000** Good red-purple; lots of berry and licorice fruit aromas on the bouquet announce an attractive, fruit-driven palate, finishing with relatively soft tannins.   **rating:** 88
best drinking 2003–2008 **best vintages** NA **drink with** Spaghetti bolognese • $18

jackson's hill vineyard   ★★★☆

Mount View Road, Mount View, NSW 2321 **region** Lower Hunter Valley
phone (02) 4990 1273 **fax** (02) 4991 3233 **open** 7 days 10–5
winemaker Mike Winborne **production** 1200 **est.** 1984
product range ($16–24 CD) Semillon, Shiraz, Cabernet Franc, Cabernet Sauvignon.
summary One of the newer arrivals on the spectacularly scenic Mount View Road, making small quantities of estage-grown (3 hectares) wine sold exclusively through the cellar door and specialising in Cabernet Franc. Jackson's Hill also produces marvellous home-made chocolates.

Jackson's Hill Semillon
▼▼▼▼ **2000** Light green-yellow; a powerful, ultra-herbaceous bouquet is reflected in the long, intense palate, with impeccable balance.   **rating:** 87
best drinking 2002–2007 **best vintages** NA **drink with** Sashimi • $16

Jackson's Hill Cabernet Franc
▼▼▼▼ **2000** Light to medium red-purple; the bouquet is quite fragrant, with spice and light red berry aromas, leading logically into a light to medium-bodied palate featuring redcurrant, leaf and mint flavours. **rating:** 85
best drinking 2003–2007 **best vintages** '91, '94, '95 **drink with** Smoked lamb • $22

jadran   NR

445 Reservoir Road, Orange Grove, WA 6109 **region** Perth Hills
phone (08) 9459 1110 **open** Mon–Sat 10–8, Sun 11–5
winemaker Steve Radojkovich **production** NFP **est.** 1967
product range ($6–12 CD) Riesling, Hermitage, generic red and white table wines, Sparkling, Fortifieds.
summary A quite substantial operation which basically services local clientele, occasionally producing wines of quite surprising quality from a variety of fruit sources.

james estate   ★★★★

951 Bylong Valley Way, Baerami via Denman, NSW 2333 **region** Upper Hunter Valley
phone (02) 6547 5168 **fax** (02) 6547 5164 **open** 7 days 10–4.30
winemaker Peter Orr, Matthew Carter **production** 100 000 **est.** 1971
product range ($10–20 R) Semillon, Verdelho Chardonnay, Late Harvest Sylvaner, Grand Cuvée, Shiraz, Merlot, Cabernet Sauvignon; Reserve Chardonnay, Shiraz; Sundara Chardonnay Semillon, Shiraz Cabernet.
summary A substantial viticultural enterprise with 98 hectares of vineyards planted to ten varieties. Since a change of ownership in 1997 there have been many innovations, including the appointment of Peter Orr as winemaker after a winemaking career with McWilliam's Mount Pleasant and thereafter Allandale Wines,

and the complete revamping and repackaging of the wines. In December 2000 the company issued a prospectus, seeking to raise just under $5 million to fund the development of over 80 hectares of new vineyards which will substantially increase winery production. Exports to the US.

James Estate Semillon

ŦŦŦŦ 2000 Light to medium green-straw; the mineral and citrus bouquet is firm and solid, rather than fragrant and floral; the palate has good intensity, weight, length and grip, carrying its 12° alcohol quite well. Two gold medals and a trophy from the 2000 Hunter Valley Boutique Wine Show. **rating: 89**

best drinking 2002–2005 **best vintages** NA **drink with** Grilled calamari salad • $14

James Estate Compass Verdelho

ŦŦŦŦ 2000 Light to medium yellow-green; very ripe, sweet, fruit salad/dried fruits/tropical aromas are reflected in the deep palate and, almost inevitably, in the slightly heavy finish. Nonetheless, a Verdelho with attitude. Trophy for Best Verdelho of Show at the 2001 Perth Royal Wine Show. **rating: 85**

best drinking 2001–2002 **best vintages** NA **drink with** Takeaway • $15

James Estate Shiraz

ŦŦŦŦ 2000 Bright, light to medium red-purple; the bouquet has clean, fresh cherry fruit and French and American oak inputs, followed by a nicely balanced and composed palate showing clear cherry and spice fruit. Good value. **rating: 88**

best drinking 2003–2007 **best vintages** NA **drink with** Pasta • $15

James Estate Reserve Frankland River Shiraz

ŦŦŦŦŸ 2000 Light to medium red-purple; the bouquet is fresh, with some spicy notes and subtle, cedary oak, the palate picking up the pace with intense, spicy redcurrant and cherry fruit, and considerable length and persistence. **rating: 92**

best drinking 2003–2008 **best vintages** NA **drink with** Baked ham • $20

James Estate Cabernet Sauvignon

ŦŦŦŦ 2000 Light to medium red-purple; a fresh, light red berry bouquet, then red berry and mint fruit on the palate, are all presented in a simple mode, the saving grace being gentle but obvious tannins on the finish to provide some structure (though not complexity). **rating: 85**

best drinking 2003–2007 **best vintages** NA **drink with** Pizza • $15

jamiesons run winery ★★★☆

Penola–Naracoorte Road, Coonawarra, SA 5263 **region** Coonawarra
phone (08) 8736 3380 **fax** (08) 8736 3307 **open** Mon–Fri 9–4.30, weekends 10–4
winemaker Andrew Hales **production** NFP **est.** 1955
product range ($13–45 R) Jamiesons Run Chardonnay, McShane's Block Shiraz, Coonawarra Red, Coonawarra Merlot, Coonawarra Reserve, Alexander Block Cabernet. Also made are Mildara Coonawarra Cabernet Sauvignon, Robertson's Well Shiraz and Cabernet Sauvignon, Jimmy Watson Chardonnay and Cabernet Shiraz and Greg Norman Estates Yarra Valley Chardonnay and Limestone Coast Cabernet Merlot.
summary Once the prized possession of a stand-alone Mildara, which spawned a child called Jamiesons Run to fill the need for a cost-effective second label. Now the name Mildara is very nearly part of ancient wine history, and the child has usurped the parent. Worldwide distribution via Beringer Blass.

Jamiesons Run Sauvignon Blanc

ŦŦŦŦ 2001 Light to medium green-yellow; light but clear varietal character in the gooseberry/canned fruit spectrum. The palate is light, fresh and crisp, with acidity and residual sugar poised perfectly for the mass market. **rating: 86**

best drinking 2001–2002 **best vintages** NA **drink with** Seafood • $14.99

Jamiesons Run Chardonnay

ŦŦŦŸ 2001 Light green-yellow; a clean, light, fresh bouquet with smooth, nectarine/melon fruit is followed by a bracingly fresh palate, a little on the tart side. **rating: 84**

best drinking 2001–2002 **best vintages** NA **drink with** Oysters • $14.99

Jamiesons Run Coonawarra Red

TTTT 1999 Medium red-purple; some bottle-developed savoury characters, with hints of leaf and earth, run through the bouquet, but the palate sweetens up somewhat, aided by oak and touches of mint.   **rating:** 85

best drinking 2001–2003 **best vintages** '86, '88, '90, '91, '93, '96, '98 **drink with** Mediterranean, Italian cuisine • $15

Jamiesons Run Reserve Red

TTTT 1999 Medium red-purple; a fragrant bouquet ranging from red berry through to leaf and mint is an uncertain start, but riper flavours come through on the palate, with complex blackberry/blackcurrant fruit, well-handled oak and ripe tannins.   **rating:** 89

best drinking 2004–2009 **best vintages** '95, '96, '98 **drink with** Porterhouse steak • $45

Jimmy Watson Dry Red Cabernet Shiraz

TTTY 1999 Light to medium red, with some purple remaining. The bouquet is light, dusty/earthy, with touches of mint. There is rather more dark berry, chocolate and earth fruit on the palate, showing gentle oak and tannin management.   **rating:** 84

best drinking 2002–2005 **best vintages** NA **drink with** Spaghetti bolognese • $14

Mildara Coonawarra Cabernet Sauvignon

TTTT 1999 Medium red-purple; the moderately intense, clean and quite fragrant bouquet has red and blackberry fruit, the palate following on with bright, fresh red berry and mint flavours (vaguely recalling the famous 1963 Peppermint Pattie) then a brisk finish.   **rating:** 86

best drinking 2003–2008 **best vintages** '63, '86, '88, '90, '91, '98 **drink with** Beef casserole • $20

Robertson's Well Cabernet Sauvignon

TTTT 1999 Medium red-purple; a quite complex bouquet, very different from that of the Mildara Coonawarra Cabernet, with cedar and earth aromas; the solid palate is again more complex, but then unbalanced by the tannins. A blend of the two wines might have been very synergistic.   **rating:** 86

best drinking 2004–2009 **best vintages** NA **drink with** Lamb Provencale • $19

jane brook estate ★★★

229 Toodyay Road, Middle Swan, WA 6056 **region** Swan District
phone (08) 9274 1432 **fax** (08) 9274 1211 **open** Mon–Fri 10–5, weekends and public holidays 12–5
winemaker Julie White, David Atkinson **production** 15 000 **est.** 1972
product range ($17.50–29 CD) Pemberton Swan Valley Sauvignon Blanc, James Vineyard Verdelho, James Vineyard Chardonnay, Atkinson Shiraz, Mountjoy Cabernet Merlot, Elizabeth Jane Mèthode Champenoise.
summary An attractive winery which relies in part on substantial cellar-door trade and in part on varying export markets, with much work having been invested in the Japanese market in recent years. It has established a vineyard in the Margaret River and is also now sourcing fruit from Pemberton, Ferguson Valley and Arthur River. Exports to Japan, Singapore and Malaysia, with a gift service available to the UK.

Jane Brook James Vineyard Verdelho

TTTY 2001 Light green-yellow; the fruit salad and lemon aromas of the bouquet have the faintest touch of reduction; the palate is bright and lively, with crisp, tangy, grassy flavours.   **rating:** 83

best drinking 2002–2003 **best vintages** NA **drink with** Takeaway chicken • $17.50

Jane Brook Estate James Vineyard Chardonnay

TTTT 2000 Medium yellow-green; the clean bouquet shows attractive, ripe nectarine and melon fruit supported by a touch of oak; the neatly structured palate has clean fruit, good acidity and length, once again coupled with well handled oak. Like the Westfield Chardonnay, shows what the Swan Valley can deliver with this variety.   **rating:** 88

best drinking 2002–2005 **best vintages** NA **drink with** Roast pork • $18

Jane Brook Estate Mountjoy Cabernet Merlot

TTTY 2000 Medium red-purple; light, earthy berry and a touch of mint on the bouquet lead into a palate with gently sweet berry fruit, an echo of the earthy character of the bouquet, and soft tannins to close.   **rating:** 83

best drinking 2002–2005 **best vintages** NA **drink with** Wood-fired pizza • $19

jardee NR

Old School House, Jardee, WA 6258 **region** Manjimup
phone (08) 9777 1552 **fax** (08) 9777 1552 **open** Not
winemaker Barrie Smith **production** 510 **est.** 1994
product range ($18–22 R) Chardonnay, Pinot Noir.
summary Jardee is a pioneering mill town. The wines are in fact made in tiny quantities from purchased fruit, the operation being a part-time interest for proprietor Steve Miolin.

jasper hill ★★★★★

Drummonds Lane, Heathcote, Vic 3523 **region** Heathcote
phone (03) 5433 2528 **fax** (03) 5433 3143 **open** By appointment
winemaker Ron Laughton **production** 3000 **est.** 1975
product range ($17–79 R) Georgia's Paddock Riesling, Georgia's Paddock Shiraz, Emily's Paddock Shiraz Cabernet Franc.
summary The red wines of Jasper Hill are highly regarded and much sought after, invariably selling out at the cellar door and through the mailing list within a short time of release. These are wonderful wines in admittedly Leviathan mould, reflecting the very low yields and the care and attention given to them by Ron Laughton. The oak is not overdone, and the fruit flavours show Central Victoria at its best.

Jasper Hill Georgia's Paddock Shiraz

▼▼▼▼▼ **2000** Strong purple-red; youthful, juicy, berry fruit aromas, the oak well-balanced and integrated. As always, the palate is crammed with ripe fruit and a fair dollop of vanilla oak, but has good balance and structure. Seems a little more elegant. **rating:** 94
▼▼▼▼▼ **1999** Dense purple-red; an almost impenetrable array of black fruits dominate the bouquet, with some savoury aspects, and well-balanced and integrated oak. The strong, dense and potent palate has lots of bitter chocolate flavours along with the riper black fruit spectrum of the bouquet; a long, lingering finish has powerful but balanced tannins, and likewise oak. I have beaten the alcohol horse enough to say no more. **rating:** 94
▼▼▼▼▼ **1998** Dense purple-red; a rich, ripe bouquet has a cascade of aromas running through leather, licorice, prune and plum, slightly more savoury, perhaps, than Emily's of the same vintage. The palate is loaded with intensely rich and sweet blackberry, plum, prune and spice flavours; the tannins are balanced, as is the oak, but it is undeniable that you feel the alcohol. **rating:** 94
best drinking 2007–2017 **best vintages** '90, '91, '93, '95, '96, '97, '98, '99, '00 **drink with** Wild duck • $60

Jasper Hill Emily's Paddock Shiraz Cabernet Franc

▼▼▼▼▼ **1999** Dense purple-red; the immensely complex and rich bouquet has a range of spice/heather/herb/plum aromas, with a slightly savoury substrate. The palate has an arpeggio of flavours centred around notes of dark chocolate and prune, but absolutely not limited to those characters. Oak and tannins well managed and well-balanced. **rating:** 94
▼▼▼▼▼ **1998** Dark, deep red-purple; the bouquet has everything: plum, prune, spice, blackberry, licorice and lots of shoe leather aromas (sweet, not sour). The massively flavoured palate has all the flavours imaginable, but with high-toned spiced/brandied prune and plum flavours, mixed with dark chocolate, predominant. **rating:** 94
best drinking 2006–2016 **best vintages** '90, '91, '93, '95, '96, '97, '98, '99 **drink with** Rare eye fillet of beef • $79

jasper valley NR

RMB 880, Croziers Road, Berry, NSW 2535 **region** Shoalhaven
phone (02) 4464 1596 **fax** (02) 4464 1596 **open** 7 days 9.30–5.30
winemaker Contract **production** 1100 **est.** 1976
product range ($4.20–12 CD) White Burgundy, Riesling, Traminer Riesling, Moselle, Summer Red, Cabernet Sauvignon, Port; also non-alcoholic fruit wines.
summary A strongly tourist-oriented winery with most of its wine purchased as cleanskins from other makers. Features around 1 hectare of lawns, barbecue facilities, and sweeping views.

jeanneret wines ★★★★

Jeanneret Road, Sevenhill, SA 5453 **region** Clare Valley
phone (08) 8843 4308 **fax** (08) 8843 4251 **open** Mon–Fri 11–5, weekends and public holidays 10–5
winemaker Ben Jeanneret **production** 4500 **est.** 1992

product range ($15–55 CD) Riesling, Semillon, Chardonnay, Sparkling Grenache, Grenache Shiraz, Shiraz, Denis Reserve Shiraz, Cabernet Sauvignon.

summary Jeanneret's fully self-contained winery has a most attractive outdoor tasting area and equally attractive picnic facilities situated on the edge of a small lake surrounded by bushland. While it did not open the business until October 1994, its first wine was in fact made in 1992 (Shiraz), and it has already established a loyal following. National wholesale distribution; exports to Canada, Malaysia, Switzerland and the UK.

Jeanneret Riesling

TTTT 2001 Light to medium yellow-green; a clean mix of lime and a little mineral on the bouquet leads into a palate with abundant flavour through to the middle, but does hang around slightly on the finish and aftertaste. **rating:** 86

best drinking 2001–2005 **best vintages** NA **drink with** Shellfish • $15

Jeanneret Chardonnay

TTTT 2001 Bright yellow-green; the bouquet is quite complex, with good fruit and oak balance and integration. The palate has an extra degree of complexity, and weight; very well made, and Clare Valley chardonnay simply does not come better than this. Barrel fermentation, lees contact and partial mlf have all played a part. **rating:** 89

best drinking 2002–2005 **best vintages** '01 **drink with** Barossa chicken • $20

Jeanneret Shiraz

TTTTY 2000 Medium to full red-purple; ripe plum, prune and dark chocolate aromas are followed by a ripe, succulent palate with excellent tannin structure and depth. **rating:** 92

best drinking 2004–2011 **best vintages** '00 **drink with** Beef stew with olives • $20

Jeanneret Denis Reserve Shiraz

TTTT 1998 Medium red-purple; the bouquet is clean and firm, with some herbal notes lurking in the background. The palate is very elegant, with raspberry and cherry fruit flavours, light to medium tannins and subtle oak. A wine which shows that old vines do not necessarily produce blockbuster fruit. **rating:** 88

best drinking 2003–2013 **best vintages** NA **drink with** Rack of veal • $55

Jeanneret Grenache Shiraz

TTTT 2000 Medium red-purple; there are leather, spice and black plum fruit on both bouquet and palate; nicely balanced overall, and not too extractive. **rating:** 86

best drinking 2001–2002 **best vintages** NA **drink with** Braised duck • $16

jeir creek ★★★

Gooda Creek Road, Murrumbateman, NSW 2582 **region** Canberra District
phone (02) 6227 5999 **fax** (02) 6227 5900 **open** Fri–Sun, holidays 10–5
winemaker Rob Howell **production** 4500 **est.** 1984
product range ($16–22 CD) Riesling, Sauvignon Blanc, Chardonnay, Botrytis Semillon Sauvignon Blanc, Pinot Noir, Shiraz, Cabernet Merlot.
summary Rob Howell came to part-time winemaking through a love of drinking fine wine, and is intent on improving both the quality and consistency of his wines. Jeir Creek is now a substantial (and still growing) business, with the vineyard plantings increased to 11 hectares by the establishment of more cabernet sauvignon, shiraz and merlot.

jenke vineyards ★★★☆

Barossa Valley Way, Rowland Flat, SA 5352 **region** Barossa Valley
phone (08) 8524 4154 **fax** (08) 8524 5044 **open** 7 days 11–5
winemaker Kym Jenke **production** 9000 **est.** 1989
product range ($13.50–40 CD) Riesling, Semillon, Kalte Ente Sparkling Shiraz, Shiraz, Grenache, Mourvedre, Merlot, Cabernet Franc, Cabernet Sauvignon.
summary The Jenkes have been vignerons in the Barossa since 1854 and have over 45 hectares of vineyards; a small part of the production is now made and marketed through a charming restored stone cottage cellar door. Wholesale distribution in Victoria and NSW; exports to the UK, the US, Switzerland, Belgium, Germany, New Zealand, Singapore and Thailand.

Jenke Kalte Ente Sparkling Shiraz

YYYY 1996 Medium red; berry, earth, spice and vanilla aromas are followed by a complex palate, neither too heavy nor too sweet; spent 4½ years on lees and was liqueured with Jenke 1981 Vintage Port. Well above the average, callow sparkling red. **rating: 87**

best drinking 2002–2003 **best vintages** NA **drink with** Hot hors d'oeuvres • $40

jester hill wines   NR

Mount Stirling Road, Glen Aplin, Qld 4381 **region** Granite Belt
phone (07) 4683 4380 **fax** (02) 6622 3190 **open** Fri–Sun 10–4
winemaker Mark Ravenscroft **production** 850 **est.** 1993
product range ($12–18 ML) Sauvignon Blanc, Chardonnay, Sparkling Shiraz, Shiraz, Cabernet Sauvignon, Fortified Shiraz.
summary A family-run vineyard situated in the pretty valley of Glen Aplin in the Granite Belt. The owners, John and Genevieve Ashwell, aim to concentrate on small quantities of premium-quality wines reflecting the full-bodied style of the region. Believing that good wine is made in the vineyard, John and Genevieve spent the first 7 years establishing healthy, strong vines on well-drained soil.

Jester Hill Shiraz

YYYY 2000 Bright purple-red of medium depth; clean, pleasant red berry and earth varietal aromas with an airbrush of oak lead into a light-bodied palate, with clean, fresh berry fruit. Not complex, but commendable. **rating: 83**

best drinking 2003–2006 **best vintages** NA **drink with** Light red meat dishes • $18

jim barry wines   ★★★★☆

Main North Road, Clare, SA 5453 **region** Clare Valley
phone (08) 8842 2261 **fax** (08) 8842 3752 **open** Mon–Fri 9–5, weekends, holidays 9–4
winemaker Mark Barry **production** 40 000 **est.** 1959
product range ($10–150 ML) Watervale Riesling, Clare Valley Chardonnay, Unwooded Chardonnay, Lavendar Hill, Noble Riesling, McCrae Wood Shiraz, The Armagh (Shiraz), McCrae Wood Cabernet Sauvignon, Clare Valley Cabernet Sauvignon, Cabernet Sauvignon Shiraz, McCrae Wood Cabernet Malbec, Fortifieds.
summary The Armagh and the McCrae Wood range continue to stand out as the very best wines from Jim Barry, exceptionally concentrated and full-flavoured. The remainder are seldom less than adequate, but do vary somewhat from one vintage to the next. Has an exceptional viticultural resource base of 247 hectares of mature Clare Valley vineyards. Exports to the UK, much of Europe, North America, Japan and Southeast Asia.

Jim Barry Watervale Riesling

YYYYY 2001 Bright light green-yellow; the smooth bouquet has sweet lime juice aromas; the palate is fresh, well-balanced with attractive lime and lemon flavours, and has a lingering, almost silky finish. Should develop quickly. **rating: 92**

best drinking 2001–2007 **best vintages** '83, '86, '89, '91, '94, '95, '99, '01 **drink with** Salmon and asparagus terrine • $14.95

Jim Barry McCrae Wood Shiraz

YYYY 1999 Medium red-purple; obvious American oak and the typical vineyard touch of mint on the bouquet are followed by scented, sweet fruit on the entry to the palate, chopped off by a somewhat abrupt finish. **rating: 86**

best drinking 2004–2009 **best vintages** '92, '93, '94, '95, '97, '98 **drink with** Jugged hare • $39.95

Jim Barry The Armagh Shiraz

YYYYY 1999 Deep red-purple; a powerful, complex ripe bouquet offers licorice, prune, plum, sweet cherry and spice, all of which come through on the massively built yet balanced palate. The big end of town, to be sure, but an exceptionally good example. Unanimous gold medal 2001 Clare Valley Regional Wine Show. **rating: 95**

best drinking 2005–2015 **best vintages** '89, '90, '91, '92, '93, '95, '96, '98, '99 **drink with** The richest game dish possible • $150

Jim Barry Cabernet Sauvignon Shiraz

ŸŸŸŸ **2000** Good red-purple; licorice, prune and mint aromas are followed by a ripe, glossy, plummy/minty palate which opens well but tails off slightly on the finish. **rating:** 86

best drinking 2002–2006 **best vintages** '99 **drink with** Irish stew • $14.95

Jim Barry McCrae Wood Cabernet Sauvignon

ŸŸŸŸŸ **1998** Very good red-purple colour; spotlessly clean, powerful cassis/blackcurrant aromas on the bouquet are followed by a rich, chunky and ripe palate, laden with cassis and hints of chocolate. Well-handled oak. Trophy winner (Best Cabernet) at the 2001 Clare Valley Regional Wine Show. **rating:** 95

best drinking 2004–2014 **best vintages** '98 **drink with** Roast kid • $35

jindalee estate ★★★★☆

265 Ballan Road, Moorabool, North Geelong, Vic 3221 **region** Geelong
phone (03) 5276 1280 **fax** (03) 5276 1537 **open** 7 days 10–5
winemaker Scott Ireland **production** 403 000 **est.** 1997
product range ($9.50–19.50 ML) Chardonnay, Shiraz, Merlot, Cabernet Sauvignon; under the Fettlers Rest label are Gewürztraminer, Chardonnay, Pinot Noir, Shiraz, Cabernet Shiraz.
summary Jindalee Wines made its debut with the 1997 vintage. It is part of the Littore Group, which currently has 500 hectares of premium-wine grapes in wine production and under development in the Riverland. Corporate offices are now at the former Idyll Vineyard, acquired by Jindalee in late 1997. Here 13 hectares of estate vineyards are being re-trellised and upgraded, and a premium Jindalee Estate range is now made. The Jindalee Estate Chardonnay can offer spectacular value, as it did in 2001. Retail distribution through Red + White and Options Wines (SA); exports to the UK, the US and Canada.

Fettlers Rest Gewürztraminer

ŸŸŸŸ **2001** Extremely pale colour; quite intense spicy, rose petal varietal aromas preceding a palate with a touch of sweetness, the sweetness coming more on the entry than the finish; well made in typical delicate style, and particularly good value. **rating:** 87

best drinking 2002–2004 **best vintages** NA **drink with** Lightly spiced Asian • $16

Jindalee Estate Chardonnay

ŸŸŸŸ **2001** Light to medium yellow-green; well-balanced stone fruit and slightly smoky oak aromas lead into a light to medium-bodied palate with melon, stone fruit and a hint of oak; excellent mouthfeel and acidity to close. Exceptional sophistication at this price level, and quite unbeatable value. **rating:** 89

best drinking 2002–2003 **best vintages** '01 **drink with** Takeaway chicken • $9.50

Fettlers Rest Pinot Noir

ŸŸŸŸŸ **2000** Medium red-purple; attractive earthy/spicy/savoury/plummy aromas on the bouquet lead into a palate with excellent length and structure; spicy/savoury/foresty notes to the black plum fruit, and good acidity. **rating:** 93

best drinking 2001–2005 **best vintages** '00 **drink with** Roast pigeon • $19.50

Fettlers Rest Shiraz

ŸŸŸŸŸ **2000** Medium to full red-purple; complex dark fruits/plum/savoury fruit aromas and attractive oak lead into a palate with excellent complexity, balance and structure; dark plum fruit is supported by fine tannins and high-quality, integrated oak. Once again, top value. **rating:** 93

best drinking 2004–2010 **best vintages** '99, '00 **drink with** Yearling steak • $19.50

Fettlers Rest Cabernet Shiraz

ŸŸŸŸ **1998** Light to medium red-purple; fresh red berry fruit and subtle oak on the bouquet are repeated on the palate. The flavour is nice enough, but the wine is pretty light on, lacking structure. **rating:** 84

best drinking 2001–2003 **best vintages** NA **drink with** Pasta • $19.50

jindi creek NR

426 Turner Road, Denmark, WA 6333 **region** Great Southern
phone (08) 9848 1113 **fax** (08) 9848 1844 **open** Thurs–Mon 11–4.30 Oct–July
winemaker Brendon Smith **production** 600 **est.** 1996
product range ($15–20 CD) Semillon Sauvignon Blanc, Semillon Wooded Chardonnay, Verdelho Chardonnay, Chardonnay, Pinot Noir, Shiraz, Cabernet Sauvignon.

summary The Ponsfords (Nick, Rosemary and son Andrew) used to run a stock fencing contract business, and Rosemary always had an interest in cooking and hospitality. They decided that moving into winemaking and running a restaurant would be an easier life, and now wryly admit 'how wrong can you be!?' They have planted 5.5 hectares of chardonnay, semillon, sauvignon blanc, pinot noir, merlot and cabernet sauvignon, with a few rows of verdelho and marsanne, but up to this point of time have sold part of the crop to other wineries. They hope that in the future a newly formed co-operative will allow all of the estate production to be vinified, and at that stage may need to look beyond the cellar door and restaurant through which all of the present output is sold.

jingalla ★★★★

RMB 1316, Bolganup Dam Road, Porongurup, WA 6324 **region** Great Southern
phone (08) 9853 1023 **fax** (08) 9853 1023 **open** 7 days 10.30–5
winemaker Robert Lee, John Wade (Consultant) **production** 4000 **est.** 1979
product range ($12–45 CD) Great Southern White and Red, Riesling, Riesling Reserve, Semillon, Verdelho, Late Harvest, Botrytis, Shiraz Reserve, Cabernet Rouge, Cabernet Sauvignon, Tawny Port, Liqueur Muscat.
summary Jingalla is a family-run business, owned and run by Geoff and Nita Clarke and Barry and Shelley Coad, the latter the ever-energetic wine marketer of the business. The 8 hectares of hillside vineyards are low-yielding, with the white wines succeeding best, but it also produces some lovely red wines. A partner in the new Porongurups Winery, which means it no longer has to rely on contract winemaking. National distribution; exports to the UK, Canada and Taiwan.

Jingalla Riesling Reserve
▼▼▼▼▽ **2001** Light green-straw; a crisp and fine, gently fragrant lime blossom bouquet, then a nicely poised wine on the palate, flowing through to the finish. An admirable mix of flavour and delicacy. **rating:** 91

best drinking 2002–2010 **best vintages** '01 **drink with** Crayfish • $16

Jingalla Verdelho
▼▼▼▽ **2000** Light straw-green; the addition of 10 per cent Sauvignon Blanc adds complexity to the bouquet, with primarily tropical fruit aromas, then a sauvignon bite; the light to medium-bodied palate does not have quite as much personality as the bouquet, but is distinctly better than average. **rating:** 84

best drinking 2002–2004 **best vintages** '90, '91, '94, '96 **drink with** Caesar salad • $18

Jingalla Shiraz Reserve
▼▼▼▼ **1999** Medium red-purple; fragrant aromas vaguely reminiscent of the Australian bush and perhaps pine needle, with a more conventional spicy, cedary end. The light to medium-bodied palate has plenty of red fruit flavours in a high-toned frame; full of interest, though unusual. **rating:** 88

best drinking 2003–2009 **best vintages** '94, '98 **drink with** Ox tail • $23

jinglers creek vineyard NR

288 Relbia Road, Relbia, Tas 7258 **region** Northern Tasmania
phone (03) 6344 3966 **fax** (03) 6344 3966 **open** Not
winemaker Graham Wiltshire **production** NA **est.** 1998
product range ($25 R) Pinot Noir.
summary One of the newest arrivals on the Tasmanian scene, with 2 hectares of pinot noir, pinot gris and chardonnay. Winemaking is done by industry veteran Graham Wiltshire, who knows more about growing grapes and making wine in Tasmania than any other active winemaker.

jinks creek winery ★★★★☆

Tonimbuk Road, Tonimbuk, Vic 3815 **region** Gippsland
phone (03) 5629 8502 **fax** (03) 5629 8551 **open** By appointment
winemaker Andrew Clarke **production** 600 **est.** 1981
product range ($17.50–28 CD) Sauvignon Blanc, Pinot Noir, Gippsland Shiraz, Yarra Valley Shiraz.
summary Jinks Creek Winery is situated between Gembrook and Bunyip, bordering the evocatively named Bunyip State Park. While the winery was not built until 1992, planting of the 2.5-hectare vineyard started back in 1981 and all of the wines are estate-grown. The 'sold out' sign goes up each year, small wonder in vintages such as 2000.

Jinks Creek Gippsland Pinot Noir

♥♥♥♥♡ 2000 Good red-purple; an appealing balance of cherry/plum fruit and integrated oak on the bouquet, then a very powerful, ripe palate with an array of berry flavours and even chocolate, reflecting the seven different clones planted; the alcohol (13.8°) kicks slightly on the finish, but there is every prospect the wine will age well.　　　　　**rating:** 90

best drinking 2003–2007 **best vintages** NA **drink with** Braised duck • $22

Jinks Creek Gippsland Shiraz

♥♥♥♥♡ 2000 Deep purple-red; super-ripe blackberry and prune aromas with nice oak lead into a very ripe, multi-faceted array of dark, small berry fruits, and plenty of complex structure.　　　　　**rating:** 92

best drinking 2005–2010 **best vintages** '00 **drink with** Braised oxtail • $20

Jinks Creek Yarra Valley Shiraz

♥♥♥♥♥ 2000 Full red-purple; a clean, rich bouquet with black fruits, plums and chocolate, then a super-powerful, concentrated and rich yet not over-extracted palate, the tannins in particular being quite soft. Outstanding, even by the standards of the vintage.　　　　　**rating:** 94

best drinking 2005–2015 **best vintages** '00 **drink with** Jugged hare • $28

joadja vineyards　　　NR

Joadja Road, Berrima, NSW 2577 **region** South Coast Zone
phone (02) 4878 5236 **fax** (02) 4878 5236 **open** 7 days 10–5
winemaker Kim Moginie **production** 2000 **est.** 1983
product range ($13–21 CD) Classic Dry White, Sauvignon Blanc, Chardonnay, Botrytis Autumn Riesling, Sauternes, Classic Dry Red, Cabernet Malbec, Christopher Tawny Port.
summary The strikingly labelled Joadja Vineyards wines, first made in 1990, are principally drawn from 7 hectares of estate vineyards situated in the cool hills adjacent to Berrima. Both the reds and the whites have a consistent eucalypt/peppermint character which is clearly a product of the climate and (possibly) soil.

john gehrig wines　　　★★☆

Oxley–Milawa Road, Oxley, Vic 3678 **region** King Valley
phone (03) 5727 3395 **fax** (03) 5727 3699 **open** 7 days 9–5
winemaker John Gehrig **production** 5600 **est.** 1976
product range ($9–25 CD) Riesling, Oxley Dry White, Chenin Blanc, Chardonnay, Pinot Victoria, Late Harvest Riesling, Pinot Noir Brut, Oxley Rosé, Pinot Noir, King River Red, Border Blend, Merlot, Cabernet Merlot, Fortifieds.
summary Honest, if seldom exciting, wines; the occasional Chardonnay, Pinot Noir, Merlot and Cabernet Merlot have, however, risen above their station.

jollymont　　　★★★☆

145 Pullens Road, Woodbridge, Tas 7162 **region** Southern Tasmania
phone (03) 6267 4594 **fax** (03) 6267 4594 **open** Not
winemaker Andrew Hood (Contract) **production** 20 **est.** 1990
product range ($20–25 R) Chardonnay, Pinot Noir.
summary However briefly, Jollymont displaced Scarp Valley as the smallest producer in Australia, its 1998 vintage (the first) producing ten cases, the next 20. The vines are not irrigated, nor will they be, and Peter and Heather Kreet do not intend to sell any wine younger than three to 4 years old. Their aim is to produce wines of maximum intensity and complexity.

jollymont Pinot Noir

♥♥♥♥ 2000 Medium red-purple; ripe, juicy cherry and plum fruit aromas are followed by a potent palate, with undeniably ripe fruit balanced by bright acidity; some interpret these characters as porty/stewy, but I don't.　　　　　**rating:** 88

best drinking 2002–2005 **best vintages** NA **drink with** Pasta • NA

jones winery　　　NR

Jones Road, Rutherglen, Vic 3685 **region** Rutherglen
phone (02) 6032 8496 **fax** (02) 6032 8495 **open** Fri–Sun and public holidays 10–5 (closed Christmas Day, Boxing Day, New Year's Day and Good Friday)
winemaker Mandy Jones **production** 600 **est.** 1864

product range ($14–35 CD) Annie's Dry White, Shiraz, LJ Shiraz, Fortified.
summary Late in 1998 the winery was purchased from Les Jones by Leanne Schoen and Mandy and Arthur Jones (nieces and nephew of Les). They are planning to refurbish the winery, and to concentrate on Shiraz and the styles of wine that the winery is known for. All wine is sold through the cellar door.

judds warby range estate ★★★★

Jones Road, Taminick via Glenrowan, Vic 3675 **region** Glenrowan
phone (03) 5765 2314 **open** Wed–Sun 9–5
winemaker Ralph Judd **production** 500 **est.** 1989
product range ($15 CD) Shiraz, Durif.
summary Ralph and Margaret Judd began the development of their vineyard in 1989 as contract growers for Southcorp. They have gradually expanded the plantings to 4 hectares of shiraz and 0.5 hectare of durif; they also have 100 vines each of zinfandel, ruby cabernet, cabernet sauvignon, petit verdot, nebbiolo, tempranillo and sangiovese for evaluation. Up until 1995 all of the grapes were fermented and then sent by tanker to Southcorp, but in 1996 the Judds made their first barrel of wine, and have now moved to opening a small cellar door sales facility. The wines are monumental in flavour and depth, in best Glenrowan tradition, and will richly repay extended cellaring.

Judds Warby Range Estate Shiraz

▼▼▼▼ **2001** Medium to full red-purple; voluminous dark berry, dark chocolate and sweet earth aromas precede a rich, ripe, dark and dense palate, everything traditional Glenrowan Shiraz should be. Obviously enough, still very youthful and, equally obviously, with a long future provided the apparently low levels of SO$_2$ stand up. **rating:** 89

best drinking 2005–2015 **best vintages** NA **drink with** Braised beef with olives • $15

Judds Warby Range Estate Durif

▼▼▼▼▽ **2001** Deep, inky red purple; rich, dense blackberry and chocolate fruit on the bouquet, then tremendous depth to lusciously ripe fruit in the mouth, with chewy tannins and barely perceptible oak. Great flavour, although there is a faint question mark on the sufficiency of the SO$_2$. **rating:** 90

best drinking 2005–2015 **best vintages** NA **drink with** Rare rump • $15

juniper estate ★★★★

Harmans Road South, Cowaramup, WA 6284 **region** Margaret River
phone (08) 9755 9000 **fax** (08) 9755 9100 **open** 7 days 10–5
winemaker Mark Messenger **production** 10 000 **est.** 1998
product range ($13–30 ML) Under the Juniper Crossing label are Semillon Sauvignon Blanc, Chenin Blanc, Chardonnay, Late Harvest Riesling, Shiraz, Cabernet Sauvignon; Juniper Estate Riesling, Semillon, Cabernet Sauvignon; Wright's White Port.
summary This is the reincarnation of Wrights, which was sold by founders Henry and Maureen Wright in 1998. The 10-hectare vineyard has been retrellised, and the last 1.5 hectares of plantable land has seen the key plantings of shiraz and cabernet sauvignon increase a little. A major building programme was completed in February 2000, giving Juniper Estate a new 250-tonne capacity winery, barrel hall and cellar-door facility. The Juniper family is a famous one in the Margaret River region, its strong artistic bent evident in the immaculate packaging and background material. Juniper Crossing wines use a mix of estate-grown and contract-purchased grapes from other Margaret River vineyards. The Juniper Estate releases are made only from the 25-year-old estate plantings. Exports to the UK.

Juniper Estate Riesling

▼▼▼▼ **2001** Pale straw-green; the bouquet is clean, firm and not at all aromatic; restrained mineral and lime flavours have a faintly chalky finish to the palate. Needs time. **rating:** 86

best drinking 2003–2008 **best vintages** NA **drink with** Tuna salad • $13.50

Juniper Estate Semillon

▼▼▼▼▽ **2001** Light green-yellow; the bouquet has a delicate yet complex web of citrus fruit and lightly smoky barrel ferment oak; the palate has excellent balance, retaining grassy varietal character with intensity, complexity and length. Will flourish with age. **rating:** 93

best drinking 2002–2006 **best vintages** '01 **drink with** Marron • $22

Juniper Crossing Chardonnay

ŶŶŶŶ 2000 Light to medium green-yellow; toasty, charry oak and complex, tangy fruit provide a powerful opening, although there is less of that power on the fore palate, before picking up the pace – perhaps a little too much – on the back palate and finish, ending slightly hot from the 14.5° alcohol.   **rating: 86**

best drinking 2002–2004 **best vintages** NA **drink with** Charcoal grilled chicken • $18.50

Juniper Crossing Shiraz

ŶŶŶŶŶ 2000 Bright purple-red; dark cherry fruit has faintly gamey overtones, with a subtle mix of French and American oak on the bouquet. Very ripe black cherry fruit marks the entry to the palate, which then tightens up nicely, with fine tannins on the finish. Quite elegant.   **rating: 90**

best drinking 2004–2009 **best vintages** '00 **drink with** Venison pie • $19

Juniper Estate Cabernet Sauvignon

ŶŶŶŶŶ 1999 Medium to full red-purple; the complex bouquet has abundant blackcurrant/blackberry varietal fruit; the very powerful palate has firm savoury/earthy/blackberry fruit, the tannins are likewise firm but fine, the oak influence throughout being subtle.   **rating: 92**

best drinking 2004–2010 **best vintages** '99 **drink with** Lamb shanks • NA

Juniper Crossing Cabernet Sauvignon

ŶŶŶŶ 2000 Medium purple-red; the bouquet has a mix of dark berry fruit and touches of chocolate and vanilla; the palate has clear-cut cassis berry fruit and fine-grained tannins, but overall is a fraction lean. May well fill out with more time in bottle.   **rating: 88**

best drinking 2004–2009 **best vintages** NA **drink with** Roast beef • $19

jyt wines   NR

De Beyers Road, Pokolbin, NSW 2320 **region** Lower Hunter Valley
phone (02) 4998 7528 **fax** (02) 4998 7370 **open** Thurs–Tues 10–5
winemaker Jay Tulloch, Julie Tulloch **production** 1750 **est.** 1996
product range ($16.50 CD) Semillon, Verdelho, Chardonnay, Pink.
summary When Jay Tulloch left in 1996, it marked the end of a 100-year, multi-generational association with JY Tulloch and Sons (formerly part of the Southcorp wine group). However, it did not mark the end of the Tulloch family's involvement with the wine industry, for he and wife Julie have established a 3-hectare hillside vineyard on the picturesque De Beyers Road which (appropriately) overlooks the old Tulloch winery. Here they have planted 0.6 hectare each of semillon, chardonnay, verdelho, shiraz and sangiovese.

JYT Semillon

ŶŶŶŶ 2001 Light green-yellow; a minerally bouquet with hints of herb and grass is followed by a firm palate, with good length and intensity, and crisp acidity. All the building blocks are there for a wine which will flower with age in bottle.   **rating: 85**

best drinking 2004–2009 **best vintages** NA **drink with** Light seafood dishes • $16.50

kaesler wines   ★★★★☆

Barossa Valley Way, Nuriootpa, SA 5355 **region** Barossa Valley
phone (08) 8562 4488 **fax** (08) 8562 4499 **open** Mon–Sat 10–5, Sunday and public holidays 11.30–4
winemaker Reid Bosward **production** 12 000 **est.** 1990
product range ($7.50–155 CD) Riesling, Home Block Semillon, Old Vine Semillon, Prestige Semillon, Stonehorse Late Harvest, Reid's Rasp, Stonehorse Gilt-Finish, Stonehorse Shiraz, Old Vine Shiraz, Old Bastard Shiraz, Old Vine Grenache, Single Wire Merlot, Cabernet Sauvignon, Tawny Port, Cottage Block Fortified White.
summary Toby and Treena Hueppauff purchased Kaesler Farm, with its 12 hectares of vines (since doubled to over 24 hectares), in 1985, and since 1990 have been producing wine under the Kaesler label. The original vineyard was established by the Kaesler family in 1893, and 1.6 hectares of shiraz continues in production. The winery has an à la carte restaurant offering both indoor and outdoor dining; there is also accommodation.

Kaesler Old Vine Semillon

ŶŶŶŶ 2001 Light to medium yellow-green; clean citrus, grass and herb aromas, then a palate of good depth and flavour tracking the bouquet; has good length, and will become very powerful with some years in bottle. From 40-year-old vines.   **rating: 86**

best drinking 2002–2004 **best vintages** NA **drink with** Baked ham • $19

Kaesler Old Vine Shiraz

TTTTT 1999 Medium to full red-purple; a rich blend of ripe plum and dark berry fruit, supported by gentle oak, on the bouquet leads into a luscious and rich palate, which is not the least jammy. Ripe, sweet tannins and well-handled oak round off a wine which rises well above the reputation of the vintage, and which also seems to have risen well above its previous price. **rating: 94**

best drinking 2004–2014 **best vintages** '98, '99 **drink with** Buffalo steak • $70

Kaesler Stonehorse Shiraz

TTTT 1999 Medium red-purple; a fragrant bouquet with red berry fruit and touches of licorice and spice, then a palate with plenty of weight and substance to the ripe red berry/plum fruit, closing with balanced tannins. **rating: 89**

TTTTY 1998 Medium to full red-purple; ripe cherry, chocolate and vanilla aromas are followed by a long and lively palate with masses of ripe (but not overripe) fruit; good length, and sustained fruit flavour. The oak has certainly left its mark on the wine, if only because of the length of maturation. **rating: 90**

best drinking 2004–2009 **best vintages** '98 **drink with** Beef casserole • $34

Kaesler Old Vine Grenache

TTTT 2000 Medium red-purple; the fresh bouquet shows good varietal character in a ripe, rich, juicy berry style. There is abundant concentration of both fruit and tannins on the palate; this is exactly what old vine Grenache should be like. **rating: 89**

best drinking 2002–2009 **best vintages** '00 **drink with** Game pie • $20

Kaesler Cabernet Sauvignon

TTTT 2000 Medium red-purple; light, fresh red berry/cassis fruit on the bouquet is reflected in the pleasant, elegant light to medium-bodied palate with its red fruit flavours and soft tannins. Not complex, simply enjoyable. **rating: 86**

best drinking 2003–2007 **best vintages** NA **drink with** Grilled lamb chops • $25

kaiser stuhl ★ ★ ☆

Tanunda Road, Nuriootpa, SA 5355 **region** Barossa Valley
phone (08) 8560 9389 **fax** (08) 8568 9489 **open** Mon–Sat 10–5, Sun 11–5
winemaker Nigel Logos **production** 1.3 million **est.** 1931
product range ($4–16 R) Black Forest, generic whites under bin numbers, Claret Bin 33, Bin 44 Riesling, Bin 55 Moselle, Bin 66 Burgundy, Bin 77 Chablis, Sparkling; also extensive cask and flagon range.
summary Part of the Southcorp Wines empire but a shadow of its former self, with its once-famous Green Ribbon Riesling and Red Ribbon Shiraz no more. Essentially provides flagon-quality wines in bottles at competitive prices.

kalari vineyards   NR

120 Carro Park Road, Cowra, NSW 2794 **region** Cowra
phone (02) 6342 1465 **fax** (02) 6342 1465 **open** Fri–Mon 10–4
winemaker Jill Lindsay, Jon Reynolds (Contract) **production** 1200 **est.** 1995
product range ($14–19 ML) Semillon, Verdelho, Chardonnay, Late Picked Verdelho, Shiraz, Fortelho (fortified Verdelho).
summary Kalari Vineyards is yet another of the new brands to appear in the Cowra region. Fifteen and a half hectares of vines have been established, with a Verdelho, Chardonnay and Shiraz being included in the initial release.

🐚 kamberra   NR

Corner Northbourne Avenue and Fleminton Road, Lyneham, ACT 26002 **region** Canberra District
phone (02) 6262 2333 **fax** (02) 6262 2300 **open** 7 days 10–5
winemaker Alex McKay, Ed Carr, Glenn James, Stephen Pannel **production** 50 000 **est.** 2000
product range ($12–30 R) The wines come in two ranges, at the bottom the Meeting Place label of Sauvignon Blanc, Chardonnay, Pinot Noir Chardonnay, Shiraz, Cabernet Sauvignon; the premium range is under the Kamberra label comprising Riesling, Chardonnay, Pinot Noir Chardonnay, Shiraz, Cabernet Sauvignon.

summary Kamberra is part of the BRL Hardy group, established in 2000 with the planting of 40 hectares of vines and a new winery within the ACT, only a few hundred metres away from the showground facilities where the national wine show is held every year. The two 100 per cent estate-grown wines are Riesling and Shiraz, but most of the wines have a Kamberra component.

kangarilla road vineyard & winery ★★★★

Kangarilla Road, McLaren Vale, SA 5171 **region** McLaren Vale
phone (08) 8383 0533 **fax** (08) 8383 0044 **open** Mon–Fri 9–5, weekends 11–5
winemaker Kevin O'Brien **production** 20 000 **est.** 1975
product range ($12–28 CD) Chardonnay, Viognier, Zinfandel, Shiraz, Cabernet Sauvignon, Tawny Port, Vintage Port.
summary Kangarilla Road Vineyard & Winery was formerly known as Stevens Cambrai. Long-time industry identity Kevin O'Brien and wife Helen purchased the property in July 1997, and have now fully established the strikingly labelled Kangarilla Road brand in place of Cambrai. Exports to the US and the UK.

Kangarilla Road Chardonnay

TTTY 2001 Light green-yellow; a light, crisp and citrussy bouquet precisely matches the lively nectarine and citrus-flavoured palate. Thirty per cent of the wine is in fact barrel-fermented, but the oak contribution goes more to texture than to flavour. **rating:** 84

best drinking 2002–2003 **best vintages** NA **drink with** Pasta marinara • $15

Kangarilla Road Shiraz

TTTT 2000 Medium to full red-purple; a powerful bouquet with concentrated blackberry and plum fruit is replicated on the palate; overall has some earthy austerity; subtle oak. **rating:** 87
TTTTY 1999 Medium to full red, the purple starting to diminish; strong, dark cherry/berry fruit has splashes of licorice, earth and spice on the bouquet; the expansive palate has abundant ripe, juicy, berry fruit and soft tannins. Fruit, rather than oak, driven. **rating:** 90

best drinking 2004–2009 **best vintages** '97, '99 **drink with** Barbecued beef • $20

kangaroo island vines ★★★★

c/o 413 Payneham Road, Felixstow, SA 5070 **region** Kangaroo Island
phone (08) 8365 3411 **fax** (08) 8336 2462 **open** Not
winemaker Caj Amadio **production** 600 **est.** 1990
product range ($20–25 ML) Island Sting, Kate's Block Shiraz, Florance Cabernet Merlot, Special Reserve Cabernet Merlot.
summary Kangaroo Island is another venture of Caj and Genny Amadio, with the wines being sold through the Chain of Ponds cellar door. The Amadios have been the focal point of the development of vineyards on Kangaroo Island, producing the wines not only from their own tiny planting of 450 vines on a quarter of an acre, but buying grapes from other vignerons on the island. The tiny quantities of wine so far produced strongly support the notion that Kangaroo Island has an excellent climate for Bordeaux-style reds, particularly the excellent Special Reserve Cabernet Merlot.

Kangaroo Island Vines Kate's Block Shiraz

TTTTY 1999 Medium red-purple; a clean, stylish and complex bouquet with berry, spice, earth and cedar/vanilla oak aromas, flowing into a palate with dark cherry, chocolate and cedar, then fine, ripe tannins, all in a light to medium-bodied mould. Has improved wonderfully over the last 12 months. **rating:** 93

best drinking 2004–2009 **best vintages** '99 **drink with** Bratwurst sausages • $25

Kangaroo Island Vines Florance Cabernet Merlot

TTTT 1999 Medium to full red-purple; the very ripe fruit the wine displayed when young is still there, but has settled down in a cedar, cassis, cigar box mix. The palate, likewise, has good structure and cedary/savoury flavours; the fruit can only be described as quite dry, not withstanding its ripeness, perhaps a legacy of the tannins of youth. Once again, great improvement over the past 12 months. **rating:** 89

best drinking 2004–2009 **best vintages** '97 **drink with** Braised lamb • $25

kangderaar vineyard NR

Wehla–Kingower Road, Rheola, Vic 3517 **region** Bendigo
phone (03) 5438 8292 **fax** (03) 5438 8292 **open** Mon–Sat 9–5, Sun 10–5
winemaker James Nealy **production** 800 **est.** 1980

product range ($10–18 CD) Riesling Traminer, Sauvignon Blanc, Chardonnay, Carmine, Cabernet Merlot, Rheola Gold (White Port), Vintage Port (Touriga).
summary The 4.5-hectare vineyard is situated at Rheola, near the Melville Caves, said to have been the hideout of the bushranger Captain Melville in the 1850s, and surrounded by the Kooyoora State Park. It is owned by James and Christine Nealy.

kanjara   NR

Cargo Road, Orange, NSW 2800 **region** Orange
phone (02) 6365 6148 **fax** (02) 6365 6148 **open** Not
winemaker Jan Carter, Mark Davidson (Contract) **production** 130 **est.** 1994
product range ($14.50–16 ML) Riesling, Chardonnay, Shiraz, Tiffin Cabernet Sauvignon.
summary Since 1994 Kanjara has progressively established 2.5 hectares of riesling, shiraz and cabernet sauvignon. Grapes have been produced on a commercial basis for 4 years, but the first wines (Riesling, Shiraz and Cabernet Sauvignon) were released at the 2001 October Winefest at Orange.

kara kara vineyard   ★★★★

Sunraysia Highway, St Arnaud, Vic 3478 (10 km sth St Arnaud) **region** Pyrenees
phone (03) 5496 3294 **fax** (03) 5496 3294 **open** Mon–Fri 10.30–6, weekends 9–6
winemaker John Ellis, Steve Zsigmond **production** 2500 **est.** 1977
product range ($18–24 CD) Semillon Chardonnay, Sauvignon Blanc, Chardonnay, Shiraz, Shiraz Cabernet, Cabernet Sauvignon.
summary Hungarian-born Steve Zsigmond comes from a long line of vignerons and sees Kara Kara as the eventual retirement occupation for himself and wife Marlene. He is a graduate of the Adelaide University Roseworthy campus wine marketing course, and worked for Yalumba and Negociants as a sales manager in Adelaide and Perth. He looks after sales and marketing from the Melbourne premises of Kara Kara, and the wine is contract-made by John Ellis, with consistent results. Draws upon 9 hectares of estate plantings.

Kara Kara Shiraz

▼▼▼▼▽ **2000** Dense red-purple; powerful, deep, dark berry fruit and subtle oak on the bouquet flow into a powerful but not extractive palate, with layers of dark plum and blackberry fruit; by far the best wine from Kara Kara to date.   **rating:** 91

best drinking 2005–2015 **best vintages** '00 **drink with** Beef casserole • $24

Kara Kara Vineyard Cabernet Sauvignon

▼▼▼▼ **2000** Youthful, bright purple-red; fresh, cassis/blackcurrant fruit on the bouquet is followed by a light to medium-bodied palate, spotlessly clean, and simply needing time for the fresh fruit to marry with the savoury tannins on the finish.   **rating:** 88

best drinking 2005–2010 **best vintages** NA **drink with** T-bone steak • $24

karina vineyard   ★★★★

35 Harrisons Road, Dromana, Vic 3936 **region** Mornington Peninsula
phone (03) 5981 0137 **fax** (03) 5981 0137 **open** Weekends 11–5, 7 days in January
winemaker Gerard Terpstra **production** 2000 **est.** 1984
product range ($12–19 CD) Riesling, Sauvignon Blanc, Chardonnay, Pinot Noir, Cabernet Merlot.
summary A typical Mornington Peninsula vineyard, situated in the Dromana/Red Hill area on rising, north-facing slopes, just 3 kilometres from the shores of Port Phillip Bay, immaculately tended and with picturesque garden surrounds. Fragrant Riesling and cashew-accented Chardonnay are usually its best wines. Exports to Japan.

Karina Riesling

▼▼▼▼▽ **2001** Light green-yellow; fresh, crisp apple and slate aromas lead into a delicate and fine palate with crisp apple and hints of passionfruit and citrus, finishing with good acidity. Altogether elegant.   **rating:** 92
▼▼▼▼ **1999** Medium yellow-green; a complex bouquet with an obvious botrytis influence giving exotic overtones, including a hint of plastic. The distinctly Germanic palate has lime/tropical fruit flavours; overall, coming from left field, but on the other hand, continuing the Karina tradition of producing strongly flavoured Riesling.   **rating:** 88

best drinking 2002–2007 **best vintages** '94, '97, '98, '01 **drink with** Crab, mussels • $15

Karina Sauvignon Blanc

TTTT 2000 Light straw-green; a clean, moderately intense bouquet with a mix of gooseberry and passionfruit is followed by a similarly flavoured palate, bolstered by some residual sugar.   **rating:** 85

best drinking 2001–2003 **best vintages** '98 **drink with** Saffron mussels • $19

Karina Chardonnay

TTTT 2000 Medium yellow-green; a complex, toasty bouquet with spicy barrel-ferment characters dominant, but a palate which is much better balanced, offering citrus/melon fruit, a touch of cashew and controlled oak.   **rating:** 88

best drinking 2002–2003 **best vintages** '91, '92, '94, '96, '97 **drink with** Grilled spatchcock • $19

karl seppelt ★★★☆

Ross Dewells Road, Springton, SA 5235 **region** Eden Valley
phone (08) 8568 2378 **fax** (08) 8568 2799 **open** 7 days 10–5
winemaker Karl Seppelt **production** 5000 **est.** 1981
product range ($16–25 CD) Riesling, Chardonnay, Chardonnay Brut, Brut Sauvage, Sparkling Shiraz, Shiraz, Merlot, Cabernet Sauvignon, Fino Sherry, Vintage Port, Tawny Port, Liqueur Muscat.
summary After experimenting with various label designs and names, Karl Seppelt (former marketing director of Seppelt) has decided to discontinue the brand name Grand Cru (although retaining it as a business name) and to henceforth market the wines from his estate vineyards under his own name. The wines are now made at a small winery constructed on the property. The quality is highly consistent across the range, and the wines are exported to Canada, Germany and Japan.

karrivale ★★★★☆

Woodlands Road, Porongurup, WA 6324 **region** Great Southern
phone (08) 9481 2856 **fax** (08) 9481 2857 **open** Wed–Sun 10–5
winemaker Gavin Berry (Contract) **production** 1170 **est.** 1979
product range ($12–18 CD) Riesling, Chardonnay.
summary A tiny Riesling specialist in the wilds of the Porongurups forced to change its name from Narang because Lindemans felt it could be confused with its (now defunct) Nyrang Shiraz brand; truly a strange world. This beautifully sited vineyard and its long-lived Riesling were acquired by Dr Peter Honey prior to the 2001 vintage.

karriview ★★★★☆

RMB 913 Roberts Road, Denmark, WA 6333 **region** Great Southern
phone (08) 9840 9381 **fax** (08) 9840 9381 **open** Summer school holidays 7 days 11–4, Feb–Dec Fri–Tues 11–4
winemaker Elisabeth Smith **production** 800 **est.** 1986
product range ($26.50–33 R) Chardonnay, Pinot Noir.
summary One and a quarter hectares each of immaculately tended pinot noir and chardonnay on ultra-close spacing produce tiny quantities of two wines of remarkable intensity, quality and style. Available only from the winery, but worth the effort. There is some vintage variation; the winery rating is based upon the successes, not the disappointments. Typically, back vintages are available; with age, the Pinot Noir acquires strong foresty characters which are quite Burgundian.

Karriview Chardonnay

TTTTT 1999 Medium to full yellow-green; as one expects from this vineyard, a powerful and concentrated bouquet driven by melon/citrus fruit, and oak in the background. Rich, mouthfilling fruit floods the mouth, providing a great example of a big style which is essentially fruit-driven, although there is a substrate of oak.   **rating:** 94

best drinking 2001–2004 **best vintages** '90, '92, '93, '95, '98, '99 **drink with** Marron, yabbies • $26.50

katnook estate ★★★★

Riddoch Highway, Coonawarra, SA 5263 **region** Coonawarra
phone (08) 8737 2394 **fax** (08) 8737 2397 **open** Mon–Fri 9–4.30, weekends 10–4.30
winemaker Wayne Stehbens **production** 70 000 **est.** 1979
product range ($19–85 R) Under the premium Katnook label: Riesling, Sauvignon Blanc, Chardonnay, Chardonnay Brut, Shiraz, Merlot, Cabernet Sauvignon, Odyssey (super-premium Cabernet) and Prodigy

(super-premium Shiraz); under the Riddoch label: Semillon, Sauvignon Blanc, Chardonnay, Sparkling Shiraz, Shiraz, Cabernet Shiraz and Cabernet Merlot.

summary Still one of the largest contract grape growers and suppliers in Coonawarra, selling more than half of its grape production to others. The historic stone woolshed in which the second vintage in Coonawarra (1896) was made and which has served Katnook since 1980 is being restored. Together, the 1997 launch of the flagship Odyssey and the 2000 follow-up with Prodigy Shiraz point the way for a higher profile for the winemaking side of the venture. In a surprise (and not widely publicised) move, Freixenet, the Spanish cava producer, has recently acquired 60 per cent of Katnook. Exports to the UK, Europe, Asia and the US.

Katnook Estate Riesling

▼▼▼▼ **2001** Light to medium green-yellow; lime, herb and mineral aromas, with a touch of spice, intermingle, leading into a palate of moderate length, framed in a noticeably dry style throughout. Obvious development potential. **rating:** 87

best drinking 2003–2008 **best vintages** '00 **drink with** Vegetable terrine • $19

Katnook Estate Sauvignon Blanc

▼▼▼▼ **2001** Light green-yellow; the bouquet is predominantly in the grassy/herbal spectrum, with passionfruit also present. The palate, however, is tending a little broad, with a slightly spongy finish. **rating:** 86

best drinking 2001–2002 **best vintages** '84, '86, '90, '92, '94, '95, '96, '98 **drink with** Oysters • $25

Riddoch Chardonnay

▼▼▼▼ **1999** Medium yellow-green; the bouquet is clean, with melon fruit and just a touch of cashew nut; the palate follows down the same track, with the ripe, sweet melon fruit driving the flavour, and just a touch of oak making its present felt on the finish. **rating:** 85

best drinking 2001–2004 **best vintages** NA **drink with** Pasta carbonara • $17

Katnook Estate Shiraz

▼▼▼▼ **1999** Medium red-purple; distinctly savoury/earthy/spicy aromas make the running before the fruit of the bouquet, and the palate moves down much the same track, elegant but savoury; without the core of sweet fruit of the 1998, which is not surprising. **rating:** 88

best drinking 2004–2011 **best vintages** '98 **drink with** Rack of veal • $40

Katnook Estate Prodigy Shiraz

▼▼▼▼ **1998** Medium to full red-purple; potent oak sits on top of the fruit on the bouquet; the texture and structure of the palate are excellent, with sweet tannins, but once again the flavours of the oak swamp those of the fruit. Others, I am sure, will happily accept the amount of oak and rate my judgement as harsh. **rating:** 89

best drinking 2003–2013 **best vintages** '97 **drink with** Wild game • $85

Riddoch Shiraz

▼▼▼▼ **1999** Medium red-purple; the moderately intense bouquet has a range of savoury/spicy aromatics, partly from the fruit and partly from the oak. The palate ranges through cedar, spice, cherry and raspberry, finishing with soft, almost silky, tannins. **rating:** 88

best drinking 2002–2006 **best vintages** NA **drink with** Barbecued steak • $19.95

Katnook Estate Riddoch Cabernet Shiraz

▼▼▼♀ **1999** Medium to full red-purple; there is plenty of ripe black cherry fruit on the bouquet, complexed by a mix of savoury and vanilla notes; these carry through to the palate, where some chocolate also comes into play. The structure and tannins are adequate. Workmanlike. **rating:** 84

best drinking 2002–2006 **best vintages** NA **drink with** Barbecued meat • $19.95

Katnook Estate Odyssey Cabernet Sauvignon

▼▼▼▼▼ **1997** Medium red-purple; lots of dusty/spicy/cedary/vanilla oak sit on top of blackberry fruit on the bouquet; the palate offers a powerful and intense mix of the foregoing, and is well structured; simply oak rather than fruit-driven. **rating:** 94

best drinking 2002–2012 **best vintages** '91, '92, '94, '96, '97 **drink with** Yearling beef • $80

kay bros amery ★★★★

Kay Road, McLaren Vale, SA 5171 **region** McLaren Vale
phone (08) 8323 8211 **fax** (08) 8323 9199 **open** Mon–Fri 9–5, weekends and public holidays 12–5
winemaker Colin Kay **production** 8000 **est.** 1890

product range ($16–39 CD) Late Harvest Sauvignon Blanc, Shiraz, Block 6 Shiraz, Hillside Shiraz, Merlot, Cabernet Sauvignon; Founders Very Old Tawny Solera, Liqueur Muscat.

summary A traditional winery with a rich history and nearly 20 hectares of priceless old vines; while the white wines have been variable, the red wines and fortified wines can be very good. Of particular interest is Block 6 Shiraz, made from 100-year-old vines; both vines and wine are going from strength to strength. Exports to New Zealand, Singapore, the US and Canada.

Kay Bros Amery Shiraz

▼▼▼▼ 1999 Strong red-purple; ripe blackberry, chocolate and a hint of spice on the bouquet lead into a palate with an array of ripe flavours in the same chocolate, plum and blackberry spectrum; excellent tannins and subtle oak. Impressive value.   **rating:** 92

best drinking 2004–2010 **best vintages** '98, '99 **drink with** Prime rib • $22

Kay Bros Amery Hillside Shiraz

▼▼▼▼ 1999 Medium to full red-purple; concentrated prune, dark plum and chocolate aromas foretell a super-concentrated palate redolent with dark chocolate and blackberry; the 15° alcohol is evident, but certainly within bounds for this style.   **rating:** 91

best drinking 2004–2014 **best vintages** '98, '99 **drink with** Braised beef • $30

Kay Bros Amery Cabernet Sauvignon

▼▼▼ 1999 Medium red-purple, holding its hue well; a cedary, earthy, blackberry mix on the bouquet flows through to the opening blackberry and chocolate of the palate before mouth-ripping tannins take over.   **rating:** 84

best drinking 2005–2010 **best vintages** '98 **drink with** Leave it in the cellar • $22

keith tulloch wine   ★★★★★

Lilywood Farm, O'Connors Road, Pokolbin, NSW 2320 **region** Lower Hunter Valley
phone (02) 4990 7867 **fax** (02) 4990 7171 **open** Not
winemaker Keith Tulloch **production** 5500 **est.** 1997
product range ($15–48 R) Under the Keith Tulloch label: Semillon, Chardonnay, Kester Shiraz, Merlot, Forres Blend (Cabernet Sauvignon, Petit Verdot, Merlot); Perdiem label has Verdelho, Chardonnay, Shiraz, Cabernet Sauvignon.

summary Keith Tulloch is, of course, a member of the Tulloch family which has played such a lead role in the Hunter Valley for over a century. Formerly a winemaker at Lindemans and then Rothbury Estate, he is responsible for the production of Evans Family Wines as well as developing his own label since 1997. Currently, moves are underway to centralise all of the winemaking at Hunter Ridge Winery, where he will be permanently based. I cannot remember being more impressed with an initial release of wines than I was with those under the Keith Tulloch label. The only problem is the small scale of their production, like that of Jeffrey Grosset in his early days. There is the same almost obsessive attention to detail, the same almost ascetic intellectual approach, the same refusal to accept anything but the best.

Keith Tulloch Chardonnay

▼▼▼▼▼ 2001 Medium yellow-green; a subtle but complex bouquet, the nectarine fruit framed with a delicate touch of spicy oak; the fine palate, with citrus, melon and nectarine, is intense and long, displaying true elegance.   **rating:** 94

best drinking 2002–2005 **best vintages** '98, '01 **drink with** Blue-eyed cod • $30

Keith Tulloch Kester Shiraz

▼▼▼▼ 2000 Medium to full red-purple; the powerful dark berry fruit of the bouquet has a light savoury/tobacco regional edge; the luscious, ripe palate shows a similar mix of powerful fruit woven through with discrete oak.   **rating:** 91

best drinking 2005–2015 **best vintages** '98, '99, '00 **drink with** Rare fillet of beef • $48

Keith Tulloch Merlot

▼▼▼▼ 2000 Medium red-purple; clean, fresh, bright berry fruit on the bouquet introduces a palate with harmonious texture and flavour, the sole limitations in the wine lying with the choice of region and variety.   **rating:** 88

best drinking 2003–2008 **best vintages** NA **drink with** Rabbit or hare • $27

Keith Tulloch Forres Blend

▼▼▼▼▼ **2000** Dense red-purple; deep, ripe blackberry and blackcurrant fruit on the bouquet flow into a potent, ripe, deep, multi-layered palate, adding a touch of chocolate and finishing with ripe tannins. Cabernet Sauvignon with a dash of Petit Verdot and Merlot. **rating:** 94

best drinking 2005–2015 **best vintages** '00 **drink with** Saddle of lamb • $35

kellermeister ★★★

Barossa Valley Highway, Lyndoch, SA 5351 **region** Barossa Valley
phone (08) 8524 4303 **fax** (08) 8524 4880 **open** 7 days 9–6
winemaker Trevor Jones **production** 8000 **est.** 1970
product range ($8.50–26.50 CD) High Country Riesling, Show Reserve Riesling, Abendlese, Frontignan Spätlese and Auslese, Late Harvest Sylvaner, Cabernet Rosé, Black Sash Shiraz, Cabernet Sauvignon, Cabernet Shiraz, Sparkling and Fortifieds; also the Trevor Jones range (under his own label) of Virgin Chardonnay, Riesling, Cabernet Merlot and Dry Grown Barossa Shiraz.
summary Specialises in older vintage wines made in traditional fashion, an extraordinary array of which are on offer at enticing prices. There is always a range of vintages available; the wines are soft and generous, if very traditional, in style.

Kellermeister Roger's Reserve Semillon

▼▼▼▽ **2001** Light to medium yellow-green; the bouquet is quite powerful, in a herbaceous mould; abundant CO_2 on the palate heightens the acidity, and makes the wine somewhat spiky. However, this is a recipe which will pay off in the long term, when the wine will almost certainly merit significantly higher points. **rating:** 84

best drinking 2004–2011 **best vintages** NA **drink with** Leave it in the cellar • NA

kellybrook ★★★☆

Fulford Road, Wonga Park, Vic 3115 **region** Yarra Valley
phone (03) 9722 1304 **fax** (03) 9722 2092 **open** Tues–Sat 9–6, Sun 11–6, Mon 11–5
winemaker Darren Kelly, Philip Kelly **production** 4000 **est.** 1960
product range ($16–45 CD) Riesling, Gewürztraminer, Chardonnay, Pinot Noir, Shiraz, Cabernet Merlot, Brut Pinot Noir Chardonnay, Champagne Cider, Apple Brandy, Liqueur Muscat, Old Vintage Tawny Port.
summary The 8-hectare vineyard is situated at Wonga Park, the entrance to the principal wine growing areas of the Yarra Valley, and is replete with picnic area and a full-scale restaurant. As well as table wine, a very competent producer of both cider and apple brandy (in Calvados style). Retail distribution through Victoria, NSW and Queensland; exports to the UK.

kelly's creek ★★★★

RSD 226a Lower Whitehills Road, Relbia, Tas 7258 **region** Northern Tasmania
phone (03) 6234 9696 **fax** (03) 6231 6222 **open** Not
winemaker Andrew Hood (Contract) **production** 650 **est.** 1992
product range ($15–17 R) Riesling, Chardonnay, Pinot Noir, Cabernet Sauvignon.
summary Kelly's Creek draws on 1 hectare of riesling and 0.2 hectare each of chardonnay, pinot noir and cabernet sauvignon. Its majority owner is Darryl Johnson, who runs the vineyard, with help from Guy Wagner, who describes himself as 'merely a marketing minion'. Small quantities of Riesling are made for Kelly's Creek; all vintages having had notable success at the Tasmanian Wines Show.

kelman vineyards ★★★☆

Cnr Oakey Creek and Mount View Roads, Pokolbin, NSW 2320 **region** Lower Hunter Valley
phone (02) 4991 5456 **fax** (02) 4991 7555 **open** 7 days 10–5
winemaker Simon Gilbert (Contract) **production** 3000 **est.** 1999
product range ($14.50–20 CD) Orchard Block Semillon, Pond Block Chardonnay, Lakeview Lane Shiraz.
summary The Kelman Vineyards is a California-type development on the outskirts of Cessnock. A 40-hectare property has been subdivided into 80 residential development lots, but with 8 hectares of vines wending between the lots under common ownership. In a sign of the times, part of the chardonnay has already been grafted across to shiraz before coming into full production, and the vineyard has the potential to ultimately produce 8000 cases a year. In the meantime, each owner will receive 12 cases a year of the wines produced by the vineyard, with the balance being available for sale via mail order (phone 02 4991 5456 for details) and through a single Sydney retail outlet. The Chardonnay is a nice, fresh wine, with light melon fruit, free of the dreaded oak chips.

Kelman Estate Orchard Block Semillon

ŦŦŦŦŸ **2001** Very pale straw-green; a bright, fresh and clean bouquet with faint lemony aromas, then a pure, unforced palate with a long finish thanks to excellent acidity. Disciplined winemaking ensures that the wine will develop very well. **rating:** 90

best drinking 2004–2010 **best vintages** '01 **drink with** Marinated scallop sashimi • $18.50

Kelman Vineyards Lakeview Lane Shiraz

ŦŦŦŸ **2000** Light to medium purple-red; earthy cherry aromas on the bouquet are reflected in the relatively simple and direct palate, with its soft, red cherry fruit; it is evident that the American oak was not new, which is appropriate given the relatively light weight of the wine. **rating:** 84

best drinking 2001–2004 **best vintages** NA **drink with** Braised pork neck • $21.50

kenilworth bluff wines NR

Lot 13 Bluff Road, Kenilworth, Qld 4574 **region** Queensland Coastal
phone (07) 5472 3723 **open** Fri–Sun 10–4 and by appointment
winemaker Bruce Humphery-Smith (Contract) **production** NA **est.** 1993
product range ($13–16 CD) Semillon, Chardonnay, Shiraz, Merlot, Cabernet Sauvignon.
summary Brian and Colleen Marsh modestly describe themselves as 'little more than hobbyists at this point in time' but also admit that 'our wines show tremendous promise'. They began planting the vineyards in 1993 in a hidden valley at the foot of Kenilworth Bluff, and now have 4 hectares (shiraz, cabernet sauvignon, merlot, semillon, chardonnay) coming into bearing. Presently the wines are made off-site by Bruce Humphery-Smith, but one day the Marshes hope it will be feasible to establish an on-site winery.

kennedys keilor valley NR

Lot 3 Overnewton Road, Keilor, Vic 3036 **region** Sunbury
phone (03) 9311 6246 **fax** (03) 9331 6246 **open** By appointment
winemaker Peter Dredge **production** 300 **est.** 1994
product range ($16 CD) Chardonnay.
summary A small Chardonnay specialist, producing its only wine from 1.8 hectares of estate vineyards.

kevin sobels wines NR

Cnr Broke and Halls Roads, Pokolbin, NSW 2320 **region** Lower Hunter Valley
phone (02) 4998 7766 **fax** (02) 4998 7475 **open** 7 days (no fixed hours)
winemaker Kevin Sobels **production** 9000 **est.** 1992
product range ($15–25 CD) Gewürztraminer, Semillon, Verdelho, Chardonnay, Sparkling Burgundy, Traminer (Sticky), Rosé, Pinot Noir, Shiraz, Cabernet Shiraz, Oak Aged Port.
summary Veteran winemaker Kevin Sobels has found yet another home, drawing upon 8 hectares of vineyards (originally planted by the Ross Jones family) to produce wines sold almost entirely through the cellar door and by mail order, with limited retail representation. The cellar door offers light meals and picnic and barbecue facilities.

kies family wines NR

Barossa Valley Way, Lyndoch, SA 5381 **region** Barossa Valley
phone (08) 8524 4110 **fax** (08) 8524 4110 **open** 7 days 9.30–4.30
winemaker Jim Irvine **production** 2500 **est.** 1969
product range ($7–18 CD) Riesling, Unwooded Semillon, Wooded Semillon, White Barossa (sweet), Sparkling Heysen Gold, Old Bush Vine Grenache, Boutique Red, Lyndoch Creek Merlot, Klauber Block Shiraz, Dedication Shiraz, Tawny Port, White Muscat.
summary The Kies family has been resident in the Barossa Valley since 1857, with the present generation of winemakers being the fifth, their children the sixth. Until 1969 the family sold almost all the grapes to others, but in that year they launched their own brand, Karrawirra. The co-existence of Killawarra forced a name change in 1983 to Redgum Vineyard, and this business was in turn subsequently sold. Later still, Kies Family Wines opened for business, drawing upon vineyards up to 100 years old which had remained in the family throughout the changes, and offering a wide range of wines through the 1880 vintage cellar door. Exports to the UK, the US, Canada, Malaysia and Singapore.

kilgour estate NR

85 McAdams Lane, Bellarine, Vic 3223 **region** Geelong
phone (03) 5251 2223 **fax** (03) 5251 2223 **open** Wed–Sun 10.30–6, 7 days in Jan
winemaker John Ellis (Consultant) **production** 2000 **est.** 1989
product range Chardonnay, Pinot Noir.
summary Kilgour Estate has 7 hectares of vines, and the wines are contract-made by John Ellis at Hanging Rock. Fruit-driven Pinot Noir and Chardonnay are winery specialties, the Pinot Noir having won at least one gold medal.

kilikanoon ★★★★

Penna Lane, Penwortham, SA 5453 **region** Clare Valley
phone (08) 8843 4377 **fax** (08) 8843 4377 **open** Weekends and public holidays 11–5
winemaker Kevin Mitchell **production** 5000 **est.** 1997
product range ($15–25 CD) Morts Block Riesling, Semillon, Adelaide Hills Sauvignon Blanc, Second Fiddle Grenache Rosé, Prodigal Grenache, Oracle Shiraz, Siblings (Grenache, Shiraz, Cabernet Sauvignon), Cabernet Sauvignon.
summary Kilikanoon has 11 hectares of estate vineyards at Leasingham and Penwortham. Wholesale distribution in SA, Victoria and WA; exports to the US, Canada, the UK, Germany, Switzerland and Hong Kong.

Kilikanoon Morts Block Riesling

▼▼▼▼ **2001** Medium to full yellow-green; a solid bouquet, but a question mark on volatile acidity, which also raises its head on the solid, sweet fruit of the palate, with lime juice and more tropical characters. Polarised opinion at the 2001 Clare Valley Regional Wine Show. **rating:** 88

best drinking 2001–2005 **best vintages** NA **drink with** Sushi • $18

Kilikanoon Second Fiddle Grenache Rosé

▼▼▼▽ **2001** Light red-purple; a clean, fresh and lively bouquet is followed by a palate with enjoyable cherry/raspberry fruit well-balanced by acidity; cleverly named; another string to Grenache's impressive bow. **rating:** 84

best drinking 2002–2003 **best vintages** NA **drink with** Serve chilled with cold meat salad • $17

killawarra ★★★☆

Tanunda Road, Nuriootpa, SA 5355 **region** Barossa Valley
phone (08) 8560 9389 **fax** (08) 8562 1669 **open** See Penfolds
winemaker Steve Goodwin **production** 205 000 **est.** 1975
product range ($9–15 R) Only Sparkling wines: Non Vintage Brut, Vintage Brut, Brut Cremant, Premier Brut and Reserve Brut; also Non Vintage Sparkling Burgundy, Killawarra 'K' series Vintage Pinot Noir Chardonnay and Sparkling Shiraz Cabernet.
summary Purely a Southcorp brand dedicated to sparkling wine, without any particular presence in terms of either vineyards or winery, but increasingly styled in a mode different from the Seaview or Seppelt wines. As one would expect, the wines are competitively priced, and what is more, perform well in national wine shows. Whether it has a future as a brand, I do not know.

Killawarra K Series Vintage Pinot Noir Chardonnay

▼▼▼▼ **1998** Bronze; a big, ripe style with a mix of biscuity and slightly vegetal notes on the bouquet; the palate is powerful, but doesn't flow as easily as the best around its price point. **rating:** 85

best drinking 2001–2002 **best vintages** NA **drink with** Sautéed prawns • $14

killerby ★★★★

Caves Road, Wilyabrup, WA 6280 **region** Margaret River
phone 1800 655 722 **fax** 1800 679 578 **open** Not
winemaker Mark Matthews **production** 15 000 **est.** 1973
product range ($23.20–30 CD) Semillon, Semillon Sauvignon Blanc, Sauvignon Blanc, Chardonnay, Shiraz, Cabernet Sauvignon and budget-priced April Class (Traminer Semillon Chardonnay).
summary Has moved from Geographe to the Margaret River following the acquisition of a long-established vineyard on Caves Road with 23-year-old chardonnay vines. It continues to own its substantial and mature vineyards in Geographe, where the wines are still made. Exports to the US and Denmark.

kimbarra wines ★★★★

422 Barkly Street, Ararat, Vic 3377 **region** Grampians
phone (03) 5352 2238 **fax** (03) 5342 1950 **open** Mon–Fri 9–5
winemaker Peter Leeke **production** 900 **est.** 1990
product range ($10–18 CD) Riesling, Late Picked Riesling, Shiraz, Cabernet Sauvignon.
summary Peter and David Leeke have established 12 hectares of riesling, shiraz and cabernet sauvignon, the three varieties overall which have proved best suited to the Grampians region. The well-made wines deserve a wider audience.

Kimbarra Riesling

♥♥♥♥ **2001** Light green-yellow; clean, crisp apple and mineral aromas lead into an intense and firm palate with the texture and structure built around a mineral core; excellent value. **rating:** 87

best drinking 2003–2008 **best vintages** NA **drink with** Sashimi • $12

Kimbarra Shiraz

♥♥♥♥ **1999** Medium red, the purple starting to fade as the wine develops; a moderately intense bouquet with attractive cedary, spicy aromas, then a similarly textured palate with a range of cedar, spice, vanilla and red berry fruit; distinctly soft tannins maintain the style. **rating:** 88

best drinking 2003–2008 **best vintages** NA **drink with** Lasagne • $18

Kimbarra Cabernet Sauvignon

♥♥♥♥♡ **1999** Medium to full red-purple, holding its hue well; firm blackberry and blackcurrant fruit drives the bouquet and the palate, which has very good texture and mouthfeel, aided by ripe, fine tannins. **rating:** 92

best drinking 2004–2009 **best vintages** '99 **drink with** Rack of lamb • $18

king river estate ★★★

RMB 9300, Wangaratta, Vic 3677 **region** King Valley
phone (03) 5729 3689 **fax** (03) 5729 3688 **open** Weekends or by appointment
winemaker Trevor Knaggs **production** 2500 **est.** 1996
product range ($18–22 CD) Verdelho, Chardonnay, Nancy Shiraz, Merlot, Cabernet Sauvignon.
summary Trevor Knaggs, with the assistance of his father Collin (sic) began the establishment of King River Estate in 1990, making the first wines in 1996. The initial plantings were of 3.3 hectares each of chardonnay and cabernet sauvignon, followed by 8 hectares of merlot and 3 hectares of shiraz. More recent plantings have extended the varietal range with verdelho, viognier, barbera and sangiovese, lifting the total plantings to a substantial 18 hectares. Home-stay accommodation is available in the farm-style guesthouse. Needless to say, bookings are essential.

King River Estate Chardonnay

♥♥♥♡ **2000** Light green-yellow; the moderately intense bouquet has some complexity from a touch of bready/yeasty character which may or may not derive from the wild yeast used to initiate fermentation. The palate goes along the same lines, not having a lot of flavour, but with pleasing balance and texture, the finish likewise. **rating:** 83

♥♥♥♡ **1999** Medium yellow-green; tangy nectarine/citrus fruit on the bouquet leads into a palate with plenty of honest varietal fruit flavour and minimal oak impact. Has developed well, though best drunk soon. **rating:** 84

best drinking 2002–2004 **best vintages** NA **drink with** Coquilles St Jacques • $18

kings creek winery ★★★★☆

237 Myers Road, Bittern, Vic 3918 **region** Mornington Peninsula
phone (03) 5983 2102 **fax** (03) 5983 5153 **open** Weekends 11–5
winemaker Brien Cole **production** 3500 **est.** 1981
product range ($16–30 R) Sauvignon Blanc, Chardonnay, Reserve Chardonnay, Pinot Noir, Reserve Pinot Noir, Shiraz, Cabernet Sauvignon.
summary Kings Creek was originally operated by the Bell, Glover and Perraton families; ownership now rests with Kings Creek Winery Pty Ltd. Planting commenced in 1981, and the vines are now fully mature. Since 1990 the quality of the wines, particularly of the Pinot Noir and Chardonnay, has provided excellent value for money. Limited retail distribution in NSW and Victoria.

Kings Creek Reserve Chardonnay

♥♥♥♥♡ **2000** Light to medium green-yellow; the aromatic but relatively light bouquet has citrussy melon fruit and nicely controlled oak. The elegant and understated palate has good texture, with cashew, melon and citrus. All in all, shows the finesse gained from whole bunch-pressing. **rating:** 90

best drinking 2003–2007 **best vintages** NA **drink with** Steamed fish Chinese-style • $22

Kings Creek Reserve Pinot Noir

♥♥♥♥♥ **2000** Bright purple-red; a complex, fragrant bouquet of dark plum and spice then a palate with excellent fruit-weight and varietal character, showing ripe (but not jammy) plum, fine tannins and subtle spicy oak. **rating:** 95

best drinking 2002–2006 **best vintages** '99, '00 **drink with** Roast pigeon • $30

🦘 kings of kangaroo ground   NR

15 Graham Road, Kangaroo Ground, Vic 3097 **region** Yarra Valley
phone (03) 9712 0666 **fax** (03) 9712 0566 **open** Not
winemaker Ken King, Geoff Anson, Neil Johannesen **production** 700 **est.** 1990
product range ($15–30 ML) Chardonnay, Pinot Noir, Multi-vintage Pinot Noir, Nutfield Shiraz, Nutfield Cabernet.
summary Ken King's involvement in wine began back in 1984 as an amateur member of the Eltham and District Winemakers Guild. Around that time, the Guild was asked to manage a tiny (0.3 of an acre) experimental vineyard planted on the rich volcanic soil of Kangaroo Ground. In 1988 Ken King purchased a little under 3 hectares of similar land, which he describes as 'chocolate cake', and established 1 hectare of chardonnay and 0.6 hectares of pinot noir in 1990. Up until 2000, the grapes were sold to Diamond Valley, but each year King retained sufficient grapes to produce a barrel or two of Pinot Noir per vintage, and to begin experimenting with multi-vintage blends of pinot with up to 5 years of continuous ageing in French barriques. The wines have been well received at amateur wine shows, and King expects to have a cellar door complex by Christmas 2002.

kingsley   ★★★☆

6 Kingsley Court, Portland, Vic 3305 **region** Henty
phone (03) 5523 1864 **fax** (03) 5523 1644 **open** 7 days 1–4
winemaker Contract **production** 1200 **est.** 1983
product range ($12–21 CD) Riesling, Botrytis Riesling, Late Harvest Riesling, Laura Kate Chardonnay, Cabernet Sauvignon.
summary Only a small part of the 10 hectares is made into wine under contract, the remainder being sold as grapes. Older vintages are sometimes available at the cellar door, and tasting is strongly recommended, as there appears to be significant vintage variation. The rating is a compromise between the best of the wines (for which tasting notes appear) and those which have failed to make the grade in bottle.

Kingsley Riesling

♥♥♥♥♡ **2001** Light green-yellow; a powerful mineral/herbal bouquet leads into a palate with lots of presence, offering an intense mix of mineral, herb and lime. **rating:** 91

♥♥♥♥ **2000** Medium to full yellow-green, quite advanced in colour; a tropical bouquet, with undertones of kerosene, and the possibility of botrytis. The palate is utterly different from the 2001: it is soft, and old-style, with traditional kerosene-like flavours. **rating:** 85

best drinking 2003–2007 **best vintages** '01 **drink with** Chargrilled octopus salad • $12

Kingsley Botrytis Riesling

♥♥♥♥♡ **1998** Glowing yellow-green; intense botrytis/cumquat/marmalade aromas lead into a palate which is complex but not overly sweet; good length. **rating:** 90

best drinking 2002–2003 **best vintages** NA **drink with** Fruit flan • $14

kingston estate   ★★★

PO Box 67, Kingston-on-Murray, SA 5331 **region** Riverland
phone (08) 8583 0500 **fax** (08) 8583 0505 **open** By appointment
winemaker Bill Moularadellis, Rod Chapman **production** 100 000 **est.** 1979
product range ($10–33 R) Verdelho, Chardonnay, Semillon Sauvignon Blanc, Shiraz, Cabernet Sauvignon, Merlot; Tessera (Cabernet blend); Sarantos Soft Press Chardonnay and Merlot; Special Releases

of Saprian NV, Durif, Zinfandel and Viognier; Reserve range of Chardonnay, Shiraz, Merlot and Petit Verdot; Ashwood Grove Chardonnay, Shiraz; Chambers Creek Chardonnay, Cabernet Sauvignon.

summary Kingston Estate is a substantial and successful Riverland winery, crushing 10 000 tonnes a year and exporting 80 per cent of its production. It is only in recent years that it has turned its attention to the domestic market, with national distribution. It has also set up long-term purchase contracts with growers in the Clare Valley, Adelaide Hills, Langhorne Creek and Mount Benson, and embarked on a programme of expanding its varietal range, and seems to have seized the opportunity of significantly increasing its prices.

Kingston Estate Ashwood Grove Chardonnay

ΨΨΨΨ 2000 Light to medium yellow-green; well-balanced light fruit and subtle oak are followed by a palate with threshold sweetness, well made at its price.   **rating:** 83

best drinking 2001–2002 **best vintages** NA **drink with** Takeaway • $12

Kingston Estate Ashwood Grove Shiraz

ΨΨΨΨ 2000 Medium to full red-purple; slightly leafy overtones to the fruit on the bouquet is followed by a palate with pleasant cherry fruit, and mercifully restrained oak. Does not have a great deal of structural complexity, but that is hardly to be expected in this price range.   **rating:** 82

best drinking 2001–2002 **best vintages** NA **drink with** Pizza • $12

Kingston Estate Tessera Cabernet Blend

ΨΨΨΨ 1998 Light to medium red-purple; while light, the bouquet is aromatic, with leafy/minty berry fruit, reflected in the lively, juicy, tangy flavours of the palate. While the wine apparently received some new oak maturation, it is the fruit which provides the character and flavour.   **rating:** 84

best drinking 2002–2006 **best vintages** '99 **drink with** Spaghetti Bolognese • $14.95

kingtree wines   NR

Kingtree Road, Wellington Mills via Dardanup, WA 6326 **region** Geographe
phone (08) 9728 3050 **fax** (08) 9728 3113 **open** 7 days 12–5.30
winemaker Contract **production** 1000 **est.** 1991
product range ($16–20 CD) Riesling, Sauvignon Blanc, Gerrasse White, Cabernet Merlot.
summary Kingtree Wines, with 2.5 hectares of estate plantings, is part of the Kingtree Lodge development, a 4 and a half-star luxury retreat in dense Jarrah forest.

kinvarra estate   NR

RMB 5141, New Norfolk, Tas 7140 **region** Southern Tasmania
phone (03) 6286 1333 **fax** (03) 6286 2026 **open** Not
winemaker Andrew Hood **production** 90 **est.** 1990
product range ($13.50–15 ML) Riesling, Pinot Noir.
summary Kinvarra is the part-time occupation of David and Sue Bevan, with their wonderful 1827 homestead depicted on the label. There is only 1 hectare of vines, half riesling and half pinot noir, and most of the crop is sold to Wellington Wines.

kirkham estate   NR

3 Argyle Street, Camden, NSW 2570 **region** South Coast Zone
phone (02) 4655 7722 **fax** (02) 4655 7722 **open** 7 days 11–5
winemaker Stan Aliprandi **production** 3000 **est.** 1993
product range ($6-15.50 CD) Estate range of Traminer Riesling, Semillon, Semillon Chardonnay, Chardonnay, Sparkling Pinot Noir White, Sparkling Pinot Noir Pink, Old Gold Botrytis Semillon, White Lambrusco, Lambrusco, Pinot Noir, Shiraz, Merlot, Cabernet Sauvignon, Port; Camden Vale range of Semillon Chardonnay, Classic Dry White, Classic Dry Red, Cabernet Shiraz.
summary Kirkham Estate is one of six or so wine producers near Camden, a far cry from the 18 producers of the mid-nineteenth century but still indicative of the growth of vineyards and winemakers everywhere. It is the venture of Stan Aliprandi, a former Riverina winemaker with an interesting career going back over 30 years. It draws upon 9 hectares of vineyards, planted to chardonnay, semillon, verdelho, petit verdot, shiraz, merlot, pinot noir and cabernet sauvignon, supplemented, it would seem, by grapes (and wines) purchased elsewhere.

kirwan's bridge wines   NR

Lobb's Lane/Kirwan's Bridge Road, Nagambie, Vic 3608 **region** Goulburn Valley
phone (03) 5794 1777 **fax** (03) 5794 1993 **open** 7 days 10–5
winemaker Anna Hubbard **production** 1500 **est.** 1997
product range ($15–35 ML) Riesling, Marsanne, Shiraz, Merlot.
summary A major development, with over 35 hectares planted, and a major emphasis on the Rhône varietals (7.9 hectares marsanne, 2.7 hectares viognier, with 1.3 hectares of roussanne to be planted 2001; and 11.2 hectares shiraz, 2.7 hectares mourvedre and 2.5 hectares grenache). A side bet on 4.8 hectares cabernet sauvignon, 2.4 hectares merlot and 1.3 hectares riesling rounds off the planting. The cellar door complex includes a restaurant (open for lunch and dinner Thursday to Sunday – dinner bookings essential), conference facility and art gallery.

knappstein lenswood vineyards   ★★★★★

Crofts Road, Lenswood, SA 5240 **region** Adelaide Hills
phone (08) 8389 8111 **fax** (08) 8389 8555 **open** By appointment
winemaker Tim Knappstein **production** 10 000 **est.** 1981
product range ($23–51 R) Semillon, Sauvignon Blanc, Chardonnay, Pinot Noir, The Palatine.
summary Knappstein Lenswood Vineyards is now the sole (and full-time) occupation of Tim and Annie Knappstein, Tim Knappstein having retired from the winery which bears his name in the Clare Valley, and having sold most of the Clare vineyards to Petaluma (along with the wine business). With 25.5 hectares of close-planted, vertically trained vineyards maintained to Knappstein's exacting standards the business will undoubtedly add to the reputation of the Adelaide Hills as an ultra-premium area. Complex Chardonnay, intense Sauvignon Blanc and broodingly powerful yet stylish Pinot Noir are trailblazers. The wines are exported to the UK, the US, Canada, Japan, Belgium, Switzerland, Germany, Japan and Singapore.

Knappstein Lenswood Vineyards Sauvignon Blanc

▼▼▼▼▽ **2001** Light green-straw; there is a slightly reductive edge to the powerful fruit of the bouquet, and good length to the lemony/citrussy palate. Others will be more tolerant of the reductive edge, which many see as part and parcel of varietal character.   **rating:** 90

best drinking 2001–2002 **best vintages** '94, '95, '97, '98, '01 **drink with** Shellfish • $22

Knappstein Lenswood Vineyards Chardonnay

▼▼▼▼▽ **2000** Glowing yellow-green; a complex, powerful bouquet with nectarine, citrus and fig interwoven with oak then an impressively powerful, rich and complex palate, with a V8 engine throbbing away gently on the massive mid-palate.   **rating:** 93

best drinking 2003–2008 **best vintages** '93, '94, '95, '96, '97, '98, '99, '00 **drink with** Terrine of smoked salmon • $31.53

Knappstein Lenswood Vineyards Pinot Noir

▼▼▼▼▼ **2000** Medium to full red-purple; the initially shy bouquet gave spicy, cedary, woodsy, briary aromas, but after being stirred and metaphorically poked, allowed the underlying plummy fruit to come through strongly. The palate needed no such coaxing; it is long, intense, rich and powerful, with a lovely interplay of ripe plum and more foresty characters.   **rating:** 95

best drinking 2003–2008 **best vintages** '91, '93, '94, '95, '96, '97, '98, '99, '00 **drink with** Wild mushroom risotto • $47.20

Knappstein Lenswood Vineyards The Palatine

▼▼▼▼ **1999** Medium red-purple; the bouquet is clean, offering fragrant red and black berry fruit; there is a sweet array of red berry fruit, in a quite different spectrum from the '98; soft, fine tannins and subtle oak round off the finish.   **rating:** 89

best drinking 2004–2009 **best vintages** '97, '98, '99 **drink with** Roast venison • $51.20

knappstein wines   ★★★★☆

2 Pioneer Avenue, Clare, SA 5453 **region** Clare Valley
phone (08) 8842 2600 **fax** (08) 8842 3831 **open** Mon–Fri 9–5, Sat 11–5, Sun and public holidays 11–4
winemaker Andrew Hardy **production** 50 000 **est.** 1976
product range ($17–39 R) Hand Picked Riesling, Dry Style Gewürztraminer, Semillon Sauvignon Blanc, Chardonnay, Shiraz, Chainsaw Shiraz, Enterprise Shiraz, Cabernet Merlot, Enterprise Cabernet Sauvignon.

summary Very much part of the Petaluma empire, with Andrew Hardy now a veteran of the region. The 100 hectares of mature estate vineyards in prime locations supply grapes both for the Knappstein brand and for wider Petaluma use. The current releases are particularly impressive. The wines are exported to the UK and much of Europe and Asia.

Knappstein Hand Picked Riesling

▼▼▼▼ 2001 Light to medium green-yellow; the bouquet is complex, with some spicy characters which seem to be yeast-influenced, and which intensify on the palate, interfering with the varietal fruit flavour. Stelvin-capped. **rating:** 85

best drinking 2003–2007 **best vintages** '77, '78, '79, '80, '83, '86, '90, '93, '94, '96, '97 **drink with** Salads of all kinds • $19.99

Knappstein Semillon Sauvignon Blanc

▼▼▼▼▽ 2001 Bright, light green-yellow; a complex, rich and ripe bouquet with neatly interwoven citrus and oak; then a generously flavoured and mouthfilling palate, fruit-driven by ripe citrus, and a classic dry finish. **rating:** 91

best drinking 2002–2004 **best vintages** '98, '00, '01 **drink with** Rich fish dishes • $18.99

Knappstein Wines Clare Valley Shiraz

▼▼▼▼ 2000 Light to medium purple-red; the moderately intense bouquet has a clean and fresh array of small red fruits, the faintest hint of earth and subtle oak. The palate is still to settle down, the components still to integrate, but this will happen, without question. The generous fruit and tannins are there. **rating:** 89

best drinking 2004–2009 **best vintages** '98 **drink with** Moroccan lamb • $20.99

Knappstein Enterprise Shiraz

▼▼▼▼▽ 1999 Excellent, full red-purple; the bouquet offers concentrated deep plum and black cherry fruit plus a touch of earth; the palate is at once powerful and concentrated, yet classically restrained; skilled use of French oak is complemented by well-balanced tannins. **rating:** 93

best drinking 2004–2014 **best vintages** '94, '96, '97, '98, '99 **drink with** Rich red meat dishes • $38.99

Knappstein Cabernet Merlot

▼▼▼▼▽ 1999 Medium red-purple; clean, fresh red and dark berry aromas and subtle oak lead into a palate with balanced sweet blackberry and raspberry fruit and perfectly balanced tannins. Has excellent mouthfeel and harmony. **rating:** 91

best drinking 2002–2009 **best vintages** '99 **drink with** Roast veal • $21

Knappstein Enterprise Cabernet Sauvignon

▼▼▼▼▽ 1999 Medium to full red-purple; smooth, almost glossy, blackcurrant and blackberry fruit on the bouquet is replicated with the same ripe cassis flavours, then powerful tannins take over; needs a decade. **rating:** 90

best drinking 2004–2014 **best vintages** '96, '98, '99 **drink with** Thick-cut lamb loin chops • $38.99

knight granite hills ★★★★

1481 Burke and Wills Track, Baynton, Kyneton, Vic 3444 **region** Macedon Ranges
phone (03) 5423 7264 **fax** (03) 5423 7288 **open** Mon–Sat 10–6, Sun 12–6
winemaker Llew Knight **production** 7000 **est.** 1970
product range ($13.90–39.30 R) Riesling, Chardonnay, Pinot Noir, Shiraz, Cabernet Sauvignon, Sparkling.
summary Knight Granite Hills was one of the early pacesetters, indeed the first pacesetter, for cool-climate spicy Shiraz and intense Riesling. Revived marketing in a buoyant market and the introduction of the lesser-priced (but short-lived) MICA range have resulted in greater activity; plantings remain the same, at 9 hectares of mature, low-yielding vineyards.

Knight Granite Hills Shiraz

▼▼▼▼▼ 1998 Medium to full red-purple; a clean, ripe, black cherry bouquet is reflected in the ripe black cherry and raspberry flavours of the palate, deliciously complexed by touches of spice and silky tannins; has excellent balance and length, and fully deserves its trophy at the 2001 Macedon Ranges Wine Exhibition. **rating:** 94

best drinking 2003–2008 **best vintages** '81, '82, '88, '91, '92, '95, '98 **drink with** Lasagne • $26.60

Knight Granite Hills Cabernet Sauvignon

♥♥♥♥ 1998 Medium red-purple; the clean bouquet has the fresh fruit character which seems to mark the Knight Granite Hills wines, with red berry and cassis supported by just a touch of oak. The palate reproduces the bouquet, with a lively cool-climate profile; crisp acidity on the finish.   **rating:** 86

best drinking 2004–2010 **best vintages** NA **drink with** Lamb fillet • $22.60

knights eurunderee flats   NR

655 Henry Lawson Drive, Mudgee, NSW 2850 **region** Mudgee
phone (02) 6373 3954 **fax** (02) 6373 3750 **open** Fri–Wed 10–4, Sat 10–5
winemaker Peter Knights **production** 1500 **est.** 1985
product range ($11–19 CD) Riesling, Sauvignon Blanc, Shiraz, Merlin Rouge, Cabernet Sauvignon, Round Table Tawny, Lancelot's Liqueur.
summary Sometimes called Knights Vines, although the wines are marketed under the Eurunderee Flats label. There are 5 hectares of vineyards producing white wines of variable quality, and rather better dry red table wines.

knowland estate   NR

Mount Vincent Road, Running Stream, NSW 2850 **region** Mudgee
phone (02) 6358 8420 **fax** (02) 6358 8423 **open** By appointment
winemaker Peter Knowland **production** 250 **est.** 1990
product range ($12.50–18 CD) Mt Vincent Semillon, Mt Vincent Sauvignon Blanc, Orange Pinot Noir, Mt Vincent Pinot Noir, Wellington Cabernet.
summary The former Mount Vincent Winery, which sells much of its grape production from the 3.5 hectares of vineyards to other makers but which proposes to increase production under its own label.

Mount Vincent Semillon

♥♥♥♡ 2001 Light straw-green; the light bouquet has touches of herb and hay; the light but clean palate is lifted by a touch of sweet fruit on the middle; nicely balanced.   **rating:** 84

best drinking 2003–2008 **best vintages** NA **drink with** Pasta • NA

kominos wines   NR

New England Highway, Severnlea, Qld 4352 **region** Granite Belt
phone (07) 4683 4311 **fax** (07) 4683 4291 **open** 7 days 9–5
winemaker Tony Comino **production** 4000 **est.** 1976
product range ($12–20 CD) Semillon, Sauvignon Blanc, Sauvignon Semillon, Chenin Blanc Semillon Sauvignon Blanc, Chardonnay, Vin Doux, Nouvelle, Shiraz, Shiraz Cabernet, Merlot, Cabernet Franc, Cabernet Sauvignon.
summary Tony Comino is a dedicated viticulturist and winemaker and, together with his father, he has battled hard to prevent ACI obtaining a monopoly on glass production in Australia, foreseeing many of the things which have in fact occurred. However, Kominos keeps a very low profile, selling all of its wine through the cellar door and the mailing list. No recent tastings.

kongwak hills winery   NR

1030 Korumburra–Wonthaggi Road, Kongwak, Vic 3951 **region** Gippsland
phone (03) 5657 3267 **fax** (03) 5657 3267 **open** Weekends and public holidays 10–5
winemaker Peter Kimmer **production** 600 **est.** 1989
product range ($10–25 CD) Riesling, Pinot Noir, Shiraz, Cabernet Malbec.
summary Peter and Jenny Kimmer started the development of their vineyard in 1989 and now have 0.5 hectare each of cabernet sauvignon, shiraz and pinot noir, together with lesser quantities of malbec, merlot and riesling. Most of the wines are sold at the cellar door, with limited distribution in Melbourne through Woods Wines Pty Ltd of Fitzroy.

🐝 kooyong   ★★★★

110 Hunts Road, Tuerong, Vic 3933 **region** Mornington Peninsula
phone (03) 5989 7355 **fax** (03) 5989 7677 **open** Not
winemaker Sandro Mosele **production** 3000 **est.** 1996
product range ($36–41 R) Chardonnay, Pinot Noir.

summary Kooyong, owned by Chris and Gail Aylward, is one of the larger new entrants on the Mornington Peninsula scene, releasing its first wines in June 2001. Thirty-four hectares of vines are in bearing, two-thirds pinot noir, and one-third chardonnay. Winemaker Sandro Mosele is a graduate of Charles Sturt University, having previously gained a science degree. He has worked at Rochford and learnt from Sergio Carlei, of Green Vineyards, and makes the wine at the on-site winery. Production will increase to 10 000 cases from the first vintage (1999) of 1000 cases. The wines are distributed through Negociants Australia, and the quality is impressive.

Kooyong Chardonnay

TTTTY 1999 Light to medium green-yellow; light, smoky/tangy barrel-ferment aromas over citrus-tinged fruit on the bouquet lead into a fresh and lively light to medium-bodied palate with melon and citrus flavours. Has excellent length and balance.   rating: 90

best drinking 2001–2005 best vintages NA drink with White-fleshed fish and beurre blanc • $37

Kooyong Pinot Noir

TTTT 1999 Light to medium red; light, spicy/savoury overtones on the bouquet are within the varietal spectrum; the palate is likewise savoury, spicy and tangy, giving the impression that it should be drunk before the red fruit flavours fade.   rating: 87

best drinking 2001–2003 best vintages NA drink with Smoked quail • $42

koppamurra wines   ★★★☆

Joanna via Naracoorte, SA 5271 region Wrattonbully
phone (08) 8357 9533 fax (08) 8271 0726 open By appointment
winemaker John Greenshields production 3000 est. 1973
product range ($9–25.00 ML) Riesling, Chardonnay, Late Harvest Riesling, Dry Red, Pinot Meunier, Shiraz, Cabernet Merlot, Merlot, Cabernet Sauvignon, Barrel Selection Cabernet Sauvignon, Two Cabernets, McLaren Vale Muscat.
summary Which Hollywood actress was it who said 'I don't care what they say about me, as long as they spell my name right'? This might be the motto for Koppamurra Wines, which became embroiled in a bitter argument over the use of the name Koppamurra for the region in which its vineyards are situated and which, through what seems to be sheer bloody-mindedness by various of the parties involved, is now known as Wrattonbully. The wines have limited retail distribution in the eastern states, and are exported to the US.

Koppamurra Wines Barrel Selection Cabernet Sauvignon

TTTT 2000 Medium red, with just a touch of purple; the berry fruit of the bouquet has gently earthy/savoury overtones supported by a touch of oak; the palate offers much more than the bouquet, with plenty of sweet, luscious cassis and berry fruit offset by touches of olive and herb.   rating: 87

best drinking 2003–2008 best vintages NA drink with Fillet steak • $25

kopparossa estate   ★★★☆

Bells Road, Naracoorte, SA 5271 region Wrattonbully
phone 1800 620 936 fax (08) 8762 0937 open Not
winemaker Gavin Hogg, Mike Press production 5000 est. 1996
product range ($15–25 CD) Coonawarra range of Chardonnay, Shiraz, Cabernet Sauvignon Merlot; Limestone Coast range of Shiraz, Merlot, Cabernet Sauvignon.
summary Industry veteran winemakers Mike Press and Gavin Hogg have formed a partnership to establish an 80-hectare vineyard of cabernet sauvignon (35 hectares), shiraz (21 hectares), merlot (12 hectares) and petit verdot (2 hectares). They have put their money on the proposition that Wrattonbully is a red wine region, but are not averse to taking advantage of the ready supply of locally grown chardonnay. In March 2002 expressions of interest were being sought for the possible purchase of the property.

Kopparossa Estate Coonawarra Shiraz

TTTY 1999 Medium to full red-purple; the bouquet is lively, tangy and spicy, with hints of blossom and brush alongside glints of red berry fruit. The palate is relatively light, but with very savoury/woodsy characters in a pleasant but unusual mode.   rating: 84

best drinking 2002–2006 best vintages NA drink with Slowly braised beef • $20

kraanwood ★★★★☆

8 Woodies Place, Richmond, Tas 7025 **region** Southern Tasmania
phone (03) 6260 2540 **open** Not
winemaker Frank van der Kraan **production** 150 **est.** 1994
product range ($16.20–25 ML) Schönburger, Montage, Unwooded Chardonnay, Pinot Noir.
summary Frank van der Kraan and wife Barbara established their 0.5-hectare vineyard Kraanwood between 1994 and 1995, with approximately equal plantings of pinot noir, chardonnay and cabernet sauvignon. Frank van der Kraan also manages the 1-hectare Pembroke Vineyard, and procures from it small quantities of schönburger, chardonnay, riesling and sauvignon blanc.

Kraanwood Pinot Noir

▼▼▼▼▼ **2000** Medium red-purple; a fragrant, stylish and complex bouquet with sour cherry, plum and spice aromatics is followed by a palate with excellent texture, weight, structure and length. Gold medal 2002 Tasmanian Wines Show. **rating:** 94

best drinking 2002–2007 **best vintages** '00 **drink with** Jugged hare • $25

🐚 kreglinger estate NR

Limestone Coast Road, Mount Benson, SA 5265 **region** Mount Benson
phone (08) 8768 5080 **fax** (08) 8768 5083 **open** Not
winemaker Ralph Fowler **production** 120 000 **est.** 2000
product range Riesling, Sauvignon Blanc, Pinot Gris, Shiraz, Merlot, Cabernet Sauvignon.
summary This is by far the largest and most important development in the Mount Benson region. It is ultimately owned by a privately held Belgian company, G & C Kreglinger, established in 1797. Kreglinger Australia was established in 1893 as an agribusiness export company specialising in sheep skins. In early 2002 Kreglinger Australia acquired Pipers Brook Vineyard; it will maintain the separate brands of each venture. The Mount Benson side commenced in 2000 with the development of a 160-hectare vineyard and 2000-tonne winery, primarily aimed at the export market.

🐚 krinklewood ★★★★

712 Wollombi Road, Broke, NSW 2330 **region** Lower Hunter Valley
phone (02) 9969 1311 **fax** (02) 9968 3435 **open** Saturdays, long weekends and by appointment
winemaker Simon Gilbert, Adrian Lockhart **production** 2000 **est.** 1981
product range ($18–22 ML) Semillon, Verdelho, Chardonnay.
summary Rod and Suzanne Windrim first ventured to the Hunter Valley in 1981, establishing Krinklewood Cottage at Pokolbin and a 1-hectare vineyard. In 1996 they sold that property and moved to the Broke/Fordwich region, where they planted 17.5 hectares; Dr Richard Smart was their viticultural consultant. They struck gold with their first vintage in 2000, the Chardonnay winning a Blue/Gold medal at the 2002 Sydney International Wine Competition, the 2001 Verdelho being similarly rewarded at the same show. Leading restaurant listings of the imaginatively packaged wines have followed, as have favourable reviews in various magazines.

Krinklewood Semillon

▼▼▼▼▽ **2001** Light straw-green; a clean, intense, herb and citrus bouquet is followed by a light to medium-bodied well-balanced palate which has length and flows smoothly, some fruit sweetness offsetting the bone-dry finish. **rating:** 92

▼▼▼▼▽ **2000** Light straw-green; the bouquet is intensely herb and mineral, with some citrus, and is followed by a well-balanced palate, with similar structure and feel to the 2001, perhaps fractionally firmer. **rating:** 91

best drinking 2004–2010 **best vintages** '00, '01 **drink with** Leave it in the cellar • $18

Krinklewood Chardonnay

▼▼▼▼ **2000** Light to medium yellow-green; the bouquet is driven by fresh, lively melon and citrus fruit, as is the long, crisp palate, with subtle French oak adding a degree of complexity, and finishing with excellent acidity. Belies its 13.5° alcohol, and should develop relatively slowly. **rating:** 89

best drinking 2002–2005 **best vintages** NA **drink with** Salmon risotto • $22

kulkunbulla ★★★★

Brokenback Estate, Lot 1 Broke Road, Pokolbin, NSW 2320 **region** Lower Hunter Valley
phone (02) 4998 7140 **fax** (02) 4998 7142 **open** Since July 2002
winemaker Rhys Eather, Gavin Lennard **production** 5000 **est.** 1996

product range ($14–40 ML) Hunter Valley Semillon, Orion's Gate Semillon, The Glandore Semillon, Hunter Valley Chardonnay, Nullarbor Chardonnay, Orion's Gate Chardonnay, The Brokenback Chardonnay, Botrytis Semillon, Shiraz.

summary Kulkunbulla is owned by a relatively small Sydney-based company headed by Gavin Lennard, which has purchased part of the Brokenback Estate in the Hunter Valley formerly owned by Rothbury. For the time being all Kulkunbulla's wines are sold by mail order, though a sophisticated brochure entitled *Vinsight*. Retail distribution in Victoria and Queensland.

Kulkunbulla Hunter Valley Semillon

▼▼▼▼ **2000** Light straw-green; the bouquet is clean, with crisp, mineral notes and a faint whiff of spice; the bone-dry, lemon and mineral-flavoured palate carries its atypically high 12.5° alcohol very well, but is still likely to develop reasonably quickly. **rating:** 88

best drinking 2001–2005 **best vintages** NA **drink with** Seafood salad • $23

Kulkunbulla The Glandore Semillon

▼▼▼▼ **2001** Light to medium yellow-green; the bouquet is surprisingly rich and soft, almost into tropical; the wine is likewise soft and full in the mouth; an ideal Semillon for those who don't want to wait. For the record, hand-picked from three rows of old vines, with only free-run juice used. Eleven degrees alcohol. **rating:** 87

best drinking 2002–2004 **best vintages** '98, '99, '00 **drink with** Balmain bugs • $29.95

Kulkunbulla Hunter Valley Chardonnay

▼▼▼▼▽ **2000** Light green-yellow; a complex bouquet with tangy/smoky overtones to the melon and citrus fruit allied with some cashew is a striking start to the wine; the palate is more delicate than the bouquet, moving through stone fruit and citrus on the fore-palate then cashew and creamy characters on the finish. Impressive. **rating:** 91

best drinking 2001–2004 **best vintages** '98, '00 **drink with** Rich seafood • $29

Kulkunbulla Orion's Gate Chardonnay

▼▼▼▼ **2000** Medium yellow-green; gentle, light melon fruit and a light touch of oak on the bouquet are followed by a light to medium-bodied palate of fair length, with stone fruit and peach flavours augmented by that light touch of oak. **rating:** 85

best drinking 2001–2003 **best vintages** NA **drink with** Sautéed chicken • $19

Kulkunbulla The Brokenback Chardonnay

▼▼▼▽ **2000** Medium yellow-green; the bouquet is complex, with well-balanced and integrated winemaker thumbprints; the palate is rich and full-bodied, with yellow peach and fig fruit supported by well-judged oak. Will never be better than it is right now. **rating:** 92

best drinking 2001–2002 **best vintages** '98, '00 **drink with** Pan-fried chicken • $35

Kulkunbulla Shiraz

▼▼▼▽ **2000** Light to medium red-purple; a clean but surprisingly light bouquet with a regional mix of fruit and leather. The light to medium-bodied palate has fruit and slightly dusty tannins still needing to mesh; pleasant medium-term drinking. **rating:** 83

best drinking 2003–2006 **best vintages** NA **drink with** Porterhouse steak • $29.95

kyeema estate ★★★☆

43 Shumack Street, Weetangera, ACT 2614 **region** Canberra District
phone (02) 6254 7557 (ah) **fax** (02) 6254 7536 **open** Not
winemaker Andrew McEwin **production** 750 **est.** 1986
product range ($22 ML) Chardonnay, Shiraz, Merlot, Cabernet Merlot.

summary Part-time winemaker, part-time wine critic (with *Winewise* magazine) Andrew McEwin produces wines full of flavour and character; every wine released under the Kyeema Estate label has won a show award of some description. Limited retail distribution in Brisbane and exports to California (The Grateful Palate).

laanecoorie NR

4834 Bendigo/Maryborough Road, Betley, Vic 3472 **region** Bendigo
phone (03) 5468 7260 **fax** (03) 5468 7388 **open** Most weekends and by appointment
winemaker John Ellis (Contract) **production** 1500 **est.** 1982

product range ($20 R) A single Bordeaux-blend dry red of Cabernet Franc, Cabernet Sauvignon and Merlot in roughly equal proportions.
summary John McQuilten's 9-hectare vineyard produces grapes of high quality, and competent contract-winemaking by John Ellis at Hanging Rock has done the rest; no recent tastings.

la cantina king valley   NR

Honey's Lane, RMB 9460, King Valley, Vic 3678 **region** King Valley
phone (03) 5729 3615 **fax** (03) 5729 3613 **open** 7 days 10–5
winemaker Gino Corsini **production** 1500 **est.** 1996
product range ($10–14 CD) Riesling, Dry Red, Shiraz, Dolcetto, Cabernet Sauvignon.
summary Gino and Peter Corsini have 22 hectares of riesling, chardonnay, shiraz, merlot and cabernet sauvignon, selling most but making a small amount on site in a winery 'made of Glenrowan granite stone in traditional Tuscan style'. The wines are made without the use of sulphur dioxide; in other words, they are organic.

lake barrington estate   ★★★★

1133–1136 West Kentish Road, West Kentish, Tas 7306 **region** Northern Tasmania
phone (03) 6491 1249 **fax** (03) 6334 2892 **open** Tues–Sun 10–5 (Nov–Apr)
winemaker Steve Lubiana (Sparkling), Andrew Hood (Table), both Contract **production** 600 **est.** 1986
product range ($18–33 CD) Riesling, Chardonnay, Pinot Noir, Alexandra (Sparkling).
summary Lake Barrington Estate is owned by the vivacious and energetic Maree Taylor, and takes its name from the adjacent Lake Barrington, 30 kilometres south of Devonport, on the northern coast of Tasmania. There are picnic facilities at the 3-hectare vineyard, and, needless to say, the scenery is very beautiful.

Lake Barrington Estate Chardonnay

▼▼▼▼▽ **2000** Medium yellow-green; strong barrel-ferment oak characters on the bouquet and palate are major contributors to a complex and powerful wine, but there is sufficient fruit and acidity to carry the oak. A bold style, which won a gold medal at the 2002 Tasmanian Wines Show.   **rating: 92**

best drinking 2002–2005 **best vintages** '98, '00 **drink with** Brains in black butter • $24

lake breeze wines   ★★★★

Step Road, Langhorne Creek, SA 5255 **region** Langhorne Creek
phone (08) 8537 3017 **fax** (08) 8537 3267 **open** 7 days 10–5
winemaker Greg Follett **production** 12 000 **est.** 1987
product range ($11–38 CD) Chardonnay, White Frontignac, Grenache, Cabernet Sauvignon, Bernoota (Cabernet Shiraz), Old Windmill Tawny Port. The premium Winemaker's Selection range was introduced in 1996 with Shiraz and Cabernet Sauvignon.
summary The Folletts have been farmers at Langhorne Creek since 1880, grape growers since the 1930s. Since 1987 a small proportion of their grapes has been made into wine, and a cellar door sales facility was opened in early 1991. The quality of the releases has been exemplary; the red wines are particularly appealing. Retail distribution in Victoria, NSW, Queensland and WA is now augmented by exports to the US, the UK, Switzerland, Denmark and France.

Lake Breeze Bernoota Cabernet Shiraz

▼▼▼▼▽ **2000** Medium red-purple; the complex bouquet has a range of dark, small berries, spice, chocolate and cedar; the palate has considerable depth, structure and power, with fruit, oak and tannins all coalescing.   **rating: 90**

best drinking 2005–2010 **best vintages** '87, '88, '90, '92, '98, '00 **drink with** Braised beef • $21

Lake Breeze Cabernet Sauvignon

▼▼▼▼▽ **2000** Medium to full red-purple; like the Bernoota of the same vintage, a complex bouquet with blackberry, blackcurrant, spice, cedar and licorice; the palate follows through logically with dark fruits held in a solid structure, rounded off by fine, savoury tannins.   **rating: 90**

▼▼▼▼ **1999** Light to medium red-purple; the fresh, moderately intense bouquet is a fraction callow/earthy, while on the palate, youthful red berry and mint fruit flavours are still settling down. It is far from certain that time will sort out the problems, but it is not impossible.   **rating: 85**

best drinking 2005–2010 **best vintages** '87, '88, '90, '95, '96, '98 **drink with** Smoked kangaroo fillet • $24

lake george winery　　NR

Federal Highway, Collector, NSW 2581 **region** Canberra District
phone (02) 4848 0039 **fax** (02) 4848 0039 **open** Not
winemaker Angus Campbell **production** 750 **est.** 1971
product range ($28.50–49.50 R) Chardonnay, Semillon, Sauternes, Pinot Noir, Cabernet Sauvignon, Merlot, Fortifieds.
summary Dr Edgar Riek was an inquisitive, iconoclastic winemaker who was not content with his role as godfather and founder of the Canberra district; he was forever experimenting and innovating. His fortified wines, vintaged in northeastern Victoria but matured at Lake George, were very good. He has sold the winery, but for the time being continues as a consultant. No recent tastings.

lake moodemere vineyard　　NR

McDonalds Road, Rutherglen, Vic 3685 **region** Rutherglen
phone (02) 6032 9449 **fax** (02) 6032 9449 **open** Fri–Mon 10–5
winemaker Michael Chambers **production** 3000 **est.** 1995
product range ($13.50–16 CD) Riesling, Chardonnay, Late Harvest Biancone, Shiraz, Cabernet Sauvignon.
summary Michael, Belinda, Peter and Helen Chambers are all members of the famous Chambers family of Rutherglen. They have 17 hectares of vineyards (tended by Peter), and Lake Moodemere Homestead is in its 14th year as a bed and breakfast facility.

lake's folly　　★★★★★

Broke Road, Pokolbin, NSW 2320 **region** Lower Hunter Valley
phone (02) 4998 7507 **fax** (02) 4998 7322 **open** Mon–Sat 10–4
winemaker Rodney Kempe, Stephen Lake (Consultant) **production** 5000 **est.** 1963
product range ($40 CD) Chardonnay and Cabernets.
summary The first of the weekend wineries to produce wines for commercial sale, and long revered for its Cabernet Sauvignon and thereafter its Chardonnay. Very properly, terroir and climate produce a distinct regional influence and thereby a distinctive wine style. Some find this attractive, others are less tolerant. The winery continues to enjoy an incredibly loyal clientele, with much of each year's wine selling out quickly by mail order. A little of the wine finds its way to the UK. Lake's Folly has been sold, but Stephen Lake continues as a consultant. The winery was purchased by Perth businessman Peter Fogarty. Mr Fogarty's family company has previously established the Millbrook Winery in the Perth Hills, so is no stranger to the joys and agonies of running a small winery.

Lake's Folly Chardonnay
TTTTT 2000 Light to medium yellow-green; a very complex yet subtle bouquet has a seamless stream of melon, fig and cashew; the palate has powerful flavour from ripe melon and fig fruit, a hint of creamy cashew, good oak and a long finish.　　**rating:** 94
best drinking 2003–2008 **best vintages** '81, '82, '83, '84, '86, '89, '92, '96, '97, '99, '00 **drink with** Sweetbreads • $40

Lake's Folly Cabernets
TTTT 2000 Light to medium red-purple; the bouquet is quite earthy and very regional; blackberry and blackcurrant fruit come through with more precision on the palate, but overall the wine is still very earthy. Unless a poor bottle, something of a disappointment from the outstanding 2000 vintage.　　**rating:** 87
best drinking 2005–2010 **best vintages** '69, '75, '81, '87, '89, '91, '97, '98 **drink with** Rabbit, hare • $40

lamont wines　　▲▲▲▲

85 Bisdee Road, Millendon, WA 6056 **region** Swan District
phone (08) 9296 4485 **fax** (08) 9296 1663 **open** Wed–Sun 10–5
winemaker Mark Warren **production** 9000 **est.** 1978
product range ($9–28 CD) Riesling, Barrel Fermented Semillon, Quartet, Chenin Blanc, Verdelho, Barrel Fermented Chardonnay, Mèthode Champenoise, Cabernet Mèthode Champenoise, Sparkling Burgundy, Sweet White, Late Picked, Light Red Cabernet, Shiraz, Cabernet Merlot, Cabernet Sauvignon, Family Reserve; Fortifieds, including Flor Fino, Amontillado and Reserve Sherry (Oloroso style).
summary Corin Lamont is the daughter of the late Jack Mann, and oversees the making of wines in a style which would have pleased her father. Lamont also boasts a superb restaurant run by granddaughter Kate Lamont. with a gallery for the sale and promotion of local arts. The wines are going from strength to strength, utilising both estate-grown and contract-grown (from southern regions) grapes. Exports to the US.

Lamont Barrel Fermented Semillon
▼▼▼▼ 2001 Light green-yellow; the bouquet is fine and intense, with a beautifully balanced and integrated touch of oak. The oak in no way imperils the crisp, lively and long palate, which has an excellent finish and aftertaste. **rating:** 93

best drinking 2001–2008 **best vintages** '00, '01 **drink with** Trout pate • $18

Lamont Chenin Blanc
▼▼▼ 2001 Light green-yellow; the bouquet is light, with distinctly lemony overtones adding to the overall impression of freshness. The palate is firm, with touches of slate and mineral to the lemon/fruit salad flavours, augmented by a touch of CO_2. **rating:** 84

best drinking 2001–2004 **best vintages** NA **drink with** Seafood platter • $15

Lamont Verdelho
▼▼▼▼ 2001 Light green-yellow; the intense bouquet has a lemony lift which adds to its appeal, but the palate is even better, with harmonious lemon fruit-pastille flavours and a clean finish. **rating:** 88

best drinking 2001–2005 **best vintages** NA **drink with** Smoked chicken • $15

Lamont Barrel Fermented Chardonnay
▼▼▼▼ 2000 Medium yellow-green; the bouquet is quite tangy and complex, the oak subtle. The palate has good flow and feel, in a rich, round, regional style. **rating:** 87

best drinking 2001–2004 **best vintages** '97, '99, '00 **drink with** Grilled Swan Valley marron • $20

Lamont Shiraz
▼▼▼▼ 1999 Full red-purple; a powerful and deep bouquet with ripe plum, earth and oak aromas is followed by a big, rich palate which, unfortunately, shows the overenthusiastic use of slightly pencilly/charry oak. **rating:** 85

best drinking 2004–2009 **best vintages** NA **drink with** Beef Bordelaise • $24

Lamont Family Reserve
▼▼▼▼ 1999 Medium purple-red; a high-toned and fragrant bouquet is followed by a palate with considerable length and vibrancy, once again driven by its spicy/berry fruit. **rating:** 92

best drinking 2004–2009 **best vintages** '99 **drink with** Ragout of venison • $28

Lamont Cabernet Merlot
▼▼▼▼ 1999 Medium purple-red, bright and vibrant; the moderately intense bouquet is fine and elegant, driven by its dark berry fruit; savoury, dark berry fruit stands at the core of the well-structured palate, with excellent tannins and controlled oak. **rating:** 89

best drinking 2004–2009 **best vintages** NA **drink with** Chargrilled beef fillet with field mushrooms • $15

langanook wines ★★★
Faraday Road RSD 181, Castlemaine, Vic 3450 **region** Bendigo
phone (03) 5474 8250 **open** Weekends 11–5
winemaker Matt Hunter **production** 750 **est.** 1985
product range ($16.50–31 ML) Chardonnay, Syrah, Cabernet Sauvignon, Reserve Cabernet Sauvignon Blend.
summary The Langanook vineyard was established back in 1985 (the first wines coming much later), at an altitude of 450 metres on the slopes of Mount Alexander.

langbrook estate vineyard NR
65 Summerhill Road, Yarra Junction, Vic 3797 **region** Yarra Valley
phone (03) 5967 1320 **fax** (03) 5967 1182 **open** By appointment
winemaker Martin Williams **production** 360 **est.** 1996
product range ($18 R) Sauvignon Blanc.
summary Langbrook Estate has 9 hectares of pinot noir, 5 hectares of sauvignon blanc, 4 hectares each of chardonnay and merlot and 1 hectare of cabernet sauvignon planted, which will provide the base for a substantial output in future years, although the only wine as yet is Sauvignon Blanc, which in 2001 was made in an ultra-delicate style. A bed and breakfast cottage and studio joins the many wine-linked bed and breakfast operations in the Yarra Valley.

langmeil winery ★★★☆

Cnr Para and Langmeil Roads, Tanunda, SA 5352 **region** Barossa Valley
phone (08) 8563 2595 **fax** (08) 8563 3622 **open** 7 days 11–4.30
winemaker Paul Lindner **production** 15 000 **est.** 1996
product range ($14.50–48 CD) White Frontignac, Semillon, Chardonnay, Bella Rouge Cabernet Sauvignon (Rosé style), Valley Floor Shiraz, The Freedom Shiraz, Three Gardens Shiraz Grenache Mourvèdre, The Fifth Wave Grenache, Cabernet Sauvignon, Ondenc Cuvée, Liqueur Shiraz Tawny, Paradale Tawny.
summary Vines were first planted at Langmeil in the 1840s, and the first winery on the site, known as Paradale Wines, opened in 1932. In 1996 cousins Carl and Richard Lindner, along with brother-in-law Chris Bitter, formed a partnership to acquire and refurbish the winery and its 5-hectare vineyard planted to shiraz, including 2 hectares planted in 1846. This vineyard has now been supplemented by another vineyard acquired in 1998, taking total plantings to 14.5 hectares and including cabernet sauvignon and grenache, moving towards a 4-star rating. Distribution in NSW and Vic; exports to the US, Canada, France, Holland, Malaysia, Taiwan and New Zealand.

Langmeil The Freedom Shiraz

▼▼▼▼ **1999** Full red-purple; intense dark fruit aromas lead into a powerfully flavoured palate which is curiously short on structure, resulting in a slightly hollow mouthfeel. That said, the flavour is good. **rating:** 87

best drinking 2003–2008 **best vintages** '98 **drink with** Smoked Barossa sausage • $48

Langmeil Valley Floor Shiraz

▼▼▼▼▽ **2000** Medium red-purple; a fragrant and expressive bouquet with cherry and plum fruit, then a sweet but not jammy palate that flows well across the tongue. Judicious oak use. Gold medal winner at the 2002 Sydney International Wine Competition. **rating:** 92

best drinking 2004–2009 **best vintages** '00 **drink with** Ravioli • $22.50

Langmeil Three Gardens Shiraz Grenache Mourvèdre

▼▼▼▼ **2000** Light to medium red-purple; the bouquet is relatively light and juicy, with some of the confection and mint characters typical of these varieties grown in the Barossa. The flavours of the palate follow suit, but it does flow, and is well-balanced and quite appealing, with touches of sweet vanilla on the finish. **rating:** 85

best drinking 2002–2003 **best vintages** NA **drink with** Osso buco • $16.50

Langmeil The Fifth Wave Grenache

▼▼▼▼ **1999** Medium red-purple; the ripe, juicy, berry fruit of the bouquet is typical of the variety; the palate has much more structure than is often the case, with darker berry fruit and brisk acidity. **rating:** 86

best drinking 2002–2006 **best vintages** NA **drink with** Coq au vin • $28

lark hill ★★★★★

RMB Bungendore Road, Bungendore, NSW 2621 **region** Canberra District
phone (02) 6238 1393 **fax** (02) 6238 1393 **open** Wed–Mon 10–5
winemaker Dr David Carpenter, Sue Carpenter **production** 4000 **est.** 1978
product range ($14–45 ML) Riesling, Sauvignon Blanc, Chardonnay, Late Harvest (dessert wine), Pinot Noir, Exultation Pinot Noir, Shiraz, Cabernet Merlot, The Canberra Fizz.
summary The Lark Hill vineyard is situated at an altitude of 860 metres, level with the observation deck on Black Mountain Tower, and offers splendid views of the Lake George Escarpment. Right from the outset, the Carpenters have made wines of real quality, style and elegance but have defied all the odds (and conventional thinking) with the quality of their Pinot Noirs, the high quality of the other wines coming as no surprise. Exports to the UK.

Lark Hill Riesling

▼▼▼▼▼ **2001** Light green-yellow; an aromatic, floral though quite delicate bouquet with lime blossom leads into a well-balanced, fruit-forward palate which nonetheless has delicacy and excellent overall structure. **rating:** 94
▼▼▼▼▽ **2000** Light to medium yellow-green; the clean, crisp, lemon and lime bouquet flows through into the palate, which has lovely fruit carry in the same flavour spectrum. **rating:** 93

best drinking 2002–2007 **best vintages** '88, '91, '92, '93, '94, '00, '01 **drink with** Gazpacho • $20

Lark Hill Chardonnay

TTTTY **2000** Light to medium yellow-green; a clean bouquet with a subtle interplay of cashew, melon and oak; a similarly stylish palate, light melon and cashew providing good mouthfeel. **rating:** 93

best drinking 2002–2005 **best vintages** '89, '91, '92, '93, '95, '00 **drink with** Crispy chicken • $26

Lark Hill Pinot Noir

TTTTY **2000** Strong purple-red; the bouquet is clean, with strong plummy fruit but no spicy characters yet emerging. The palate reflects the bouquet, with rich, ripe plummy fruit in a generous, full-bodied mode; good length and acidity, and should develop complexity over the next few years. **rating:** 91

best drinking 2002–2006 **best vintages** '96, '97, '99, '00 **drink with** Venison • $27

Lark Hill Exultation Pinot Noir

TTTTY **2000** Medium red-purple; a highly aromatic bouquet with tobacco, leaf, plum, spice and strawberry all to be found. The palate, while essentially in the savoury/spicy spectrum, offers the same array of exotic flavours, with good texture and feel. **rating:** 92

best drinking 2002–2006 **best vintages** '00 **drink with** Breast of duck • $45

Lark Hill Shiraz

TTTTY **2000** Medium to full purple-red; solid, ripe damson plum and dark berry fruit on the bouquet lead into a well-crafted palate with plum, dark berry and chocolate fruit flavours, finished off with soft, fine tannins and integrated oak. **rating:** 90

TTTT **1999** Medium purple-red; a clean, moderately intense bouquet is driven by its black cherry fruit, as is the light to medium-bodied palate, with a mixture of black cherry and spice. Controlled oak use throughout. **rating:** 88

best drinking 2004–2009 **best vintages** NA **drink with** Fillet of beef • $28

lashmar ★★★

c/o 24 Lindsay Terrace, Belair, SA 5052 **region** Warehouse
phone (08) 8278 3669 **fax** (08) 8278 3998 **open** Not
winemaker Colin Cooter, Contract **production** 500 **est.** 1996
product range ($35 R) Three Valleys Shiraz, Kangaroo Island Cabernet Sauvignon sourced from various regions in South Australia, including Kangaroo Island, McLaren Vale and the Eden and Clare Valleys.
summary Colin and Bronwyn Cooter (who are also part of the Lengs & Cooter business) are the driving force behind Antechamber Bay Wines. The wines are in fact labelled and branded Lashmar; the Kangaroo Island Cabernet Sauvignon comes from vines planted in 1991 on the Lashmar family property, on the extreme eastern end of Kangaroo Island, overlooking Antechamber Bay. The first commercial wines were made in 1999 and released in October 2000. To give the business added volume, a second wine, known as Three Valleys Shiraz, and coming from mainland regions of Eden Valley, Clare Valley and McLaren Vale, is also made. Exports to the US, Canada and Singapore.

latara NR

Cnr McDonalds and Deaseys Roads, Pokolbin, NSW 2320 **region** Lower Hunter Valley
phone (02) 4998 7320 **open** Sat 9–5, Sun 9–4
winemaker Iain Riggs (Contract) **production** 250 **est.** 1979
product range ($9.50–11 CD) Semillon, Cabernet Sauvignon, Shiraz.
summary The bulk of the grapes produced on the 5-hectare Latara vineyard, which was planted in 1979, are sold to Brokenwood. A small quantity is vinified for Latara and sold under its label. As one would expect, the wines are very competently made, and are of show medal standard.

laurel bank ★★★☆

130 Black Snake Lane, Granton, Tas 7030 **region** Southern Tasmania
phone (03) 6263 5977 **fax** (03) 6263 3117 **open** By appointment
winemaker Andrew Hood (Contract) **production** 800 **est.** 1987
product range ($17–23 R) Sauvignon Blanc, Pinot Noir, Cabernet Sauvignon Merlot.
summary Laurel (hence Laurel Bank) and Kerry Carland began planting their 3-hectare vineyard in 1986. They delayed the first release of their wines for some years, and (by virtue of the number of entries they were able to make) won the trophy for Most Successful Exhibitor at the 1995 Royal Hobart Wine Show. Things have settled down since; wine quality is solid and reliable.

Laurel Bank Pinot Noir

▼▼▼▼ **2000** Medium red-purple; while on the lighter side, the bouquet has spicy fragrance and a pleasant touch of oak, the palate continuing in lighter style, but with some sweetness and length. **rating:** 85

best drinking 2002–2005 **best vintages** '94, '95, '97 **drink with** Tasmanian venison • $21

Laurel Bank Cabernet Sauvignon Merlot

▼▼▼▼ **2000** Bright purple-red; the moderately intense bouquet has a range of fragrant berry, leaf and spice aromas, the oak coming up strongly on the palate with a desirable sweetening effect on the fruit. A cleverly made wine. **rating:** 88

best drinking 2004–2009 **best vintages** '98 **drink with** Stuffed shoulder of lamb • $23

lauren brook   ★★★

Eedle Terrace, Bridgetown, WA 6255 **region** Blackwood Valley
phone (08) 9761 2676 **fax** (08) 9761 1879 **open** Fri–Wed 11–4.30
winemaker Stephen Bullied **production** 500 **est.** 1993
product range ($17–23 CD) Chardonnay, Bridgetown Classic, Cabernet Sauvignon.
summary Lauren Brook is established on the banks of the beautiful Blackwood River, and is the only commercial winery in the Bridgetown subregion of Mount Barker. An 80-year-old barn on the property has been renovated to contain a micro-winery and a small gallery. There is 1 hectare of estate chardonnay, supplemented by grapes purchased locally.

lawrence victor estate   NR

Penola Road, Naracoorte, SA 5271 **region** Wrattonbully
phone (08) 8739 7276 **fax** (08) 8739 7344 **open** Not
winemaker Neil Dodderidge (Contract) **production** 1600 **est.** 1994
product range ($18–30 R) Shiraz, Cabernet Sauvignon.
summary Lawrence Victor Estate is part of a large SA company principally engaged in the harvesting and transportation of soft wood plantation logging. The company was established by Lawrence Victor Dohnt in 1932, and the estate has been named in his honour by the third generation of the family. Although only a small part of the group's activities, the plantings (principally contracted to Southcorp) are substantial, with 11 hectares of shiraz and 20 hectares of cabernet sauvignon established between 1994 and 1999. An additional 12 hectares of cabernet sauvignon and 6 hectares of pinot noir were planted in 2000.

lawson's hill   ★★★

Henry Lawson Drive, Eurunderee, Mudgee, NSW 2850 **region** Mudgee
phone (02) 6373 3953 **fax** (02) 6373 3948 **open** Mon, Thurs, Fri, Sat 10–4.30, Sun 10–4
winemaker Various Contract and Jose Grace **production** 3500 **est.** 1985
product range ($11–39 CD) Chardonnay, Verdelho, Sauvignon Blanc, Riesling, Traminer Riesling, Louisa Rosé, Cabernet Merlot, Pinot Noir Gamay, Reserve Dryland Cabernet Sauvignon, Port.
summary Former music director and arranger (for musical acts in Sydney clubs) Jose Grace and wife June run a strongly tourist-oriented operation situated next door to the Henry Lawson Memorial, offering a kaleidoscopic array of wines, produced from 8 hectares of vineyard, and made under contract. The red wines are richly representative of the deeply coloured, flavoursome Mudgee style.

leasingham   ★★★★☆

7 Dominic Street, Clare, SA 5453 **region** Clare Valley
phone (08) 8842 2555 **fax** (08) 8842 3293 **open** Mon–Fri 8.30–5.30, weekends 10–4
winemaker Kerri Thompson **production** 70 000 **est.** 1893
product range ($12.99–45.99 R) Classic Clare Riesling, Shiraz, Sparkling Shiraz and Cabernet Sauvignon at the top end; mid-range Bin 7 Riesling, Bin 37 Chardonnay, Bin 23 Semillon, Bin 56 Cabernet Malbec, Bin 61 Shiraz; low-priced Hutt Creek Riesling, Sauvignon Blanc, Shiraz Cabernet; also Bastion Shiraz Cabernet.
summary Successive big-company ownerships and various peregrinations in labelling and branding have not resulted in any permanent loss of identity or quality. With a core of high-quality, aged vineyards to draw on, Leasingham is in fact going from strength to strength under BRL Hardy's direction. The stentorian red wines take no prisoners, compacting densely rich fruit and layer upon layer of oak into every long-lived bottle, and the Bin 7 Riesling often excels.

Leasingham Bin 7 Riesling

TTTT 2001 Light green-yellow; complex mineral, talc and lime aromas are followed by a firm, minerally palate. Early in its life the CO_2 spritz was intrusive; this apart, the wine is still not up to the brilliant 2000. **rating:** 87

best drinking 2003–2008 **best vintages** '97, '00 **drink with** Vegetable terrine • $14

Leasingham Classic Clare Sparkling Shiraz

TTTTY 1994 Medium red, with a tinge of purple; the base wine appears to have backed away from the heavy oak of prior releases; complex spicy/earthy shiraz on the palate with just a hint of vanilla; the time on lees has worked well. **rating:** 91

best drinking 2002–2007 **best vintages** '94 **drink with** Borscht • $37

Leasingham Trial Bin Botrytis Semillon

TTTTY 1997 Deep gold; cumquat and mandarin aromas on the bouquet are followed by a striking palate, with many layers of flavour, tightened and held together by good acidity. **rating:** 91

best drinking 2001–2004 **best vintages** '97 **drink with** Fruit tart • NA

Leasingham Bin 61 Shiraz

TTTTY 1998 Deep, dark red-purple; a rich and ripe bouquet with plum and blackberry fruit mingles with lots of American oak. A powerful, opulent palate, again with lashings of oak and fruit, cries out for time to soften and build complexity. Two trophies at the 2000 Brisbane Wine Show. **rating:** 90

best drinking 2003–2013 **best vintages** '88, '90, '91, '93, '94, '96, '99 **drink with** Spiced lamb kebabs • $19

leconfield ★★★★

Riddoch Highway, Coonawarra, SA 5263 **region** Coonawarra
phone (08) 8737 2326 **fax** (08) 8737 2285 **open** 7 days 10–5
winemaker Paul Gordon **production** 31 500 **est.** 1974
product range ($17.95–30 CD) Old Vines Riesling, Noble Harvest, Chardonnay, Shiraz, Merlot, Cabernets.
summary A distinguished estate with a proud, even if relatively short, history. Long renowned for its Cabernet Sauvignon, its repertoire has steadily grown, with the emphasis on single varietal wines. The style overall is fruit rather than oak-driven. Exports to Canada, the US, Asia, the UK and Europe.

Leconfield Old Vines Riesling

TTTT 2001 Light straw-green; a clean and flowery bouquet with a mix of herbal/slatey/minerally/blossom aromas; the delicate palate is fresh and flavoursome, and will flower given time. Stelvin-capped. **rating:** 89

best drinking 2004–2010 **best vintages** NA **drink with** Seafood salad • $17.95

Leconfield Chardonnay

TTTT 2000 Light green-yellow; nutty/cashew barrel-ferment/mlf influences on the bouquet come to the fore; the palate has light stone fruit, but lacks intensity, possibly due to the winemaking techniques **rating:** 87

best drinking 2001–2003 **best vintages** '98 **drink with** Chicken pasta • $18.95

Leconfield Shiraz

TTTT 2000 Medium red-purple; a markedly complex bouquet with spice, leaf and lesser touches of mint and game, then a palate with all of the foregoing in a lively fashion, speaking both of the vineyard and the vintage. **rating:** 86

best drinking 2002–2005 **best vintages** '88, '90, '91, '94, '95, '96 **drink with** Beef casserole • $29.95

Leconfield Merlot

TTTT 2000 Light to medium red-purple; multifaceted aromas, with earthy, spicy, cedary and savoury characters on one side, and red berry fruit on the other; the palate picks up that red berry fruit, being sweeter than expected; quite delicate, but fine and long, as befits the variety. **rating:** 89

best drinking 2004–2008 **best vintages** '97, '98, '00 **drink with** Duck casserole • $29.95

Leconfield Cabernets

TTTY 1999 Medium red, already showing some shift away from purple-red; a light spicy/leafy/savoury bouquet is followed by a palate with a similar spectrum of flavours, lacking generosity and weight. **rating:** 83

best drinking 2003–2006 **best vintages** '80, '82, '88, '90, '95 **drink with** Yearling steak, mild cheddar • $30

☙ ledaswan ★★★

179 Memorial Avenue, Baskerville, WA 6065 **region** Swan District
phone (08) 9296 0216 **open** Fri–Tues and public holidays 11–5
winemaker Duncan Harris **production** 250 **est.** 1998
product range ($15–19 CD) Chenin Blanc, Shiraz, Pedro Ximinez.
summary LedaSwan claims to be the smallest winery in the Swan Valley. It uses organically grown grapes, partly coming from its own vineyard, and partly contract-grown; the intention is to move to 100 per cent estate-grown in the future, utilising the 3 hectares of estate vineyards. Duncan Harris Moved from the coast to Baskerville in 1998, and retired from engineering in 2001 to become a full-time vintner, winning several awards. Tours of the underground cellar are offered.

LedaSwan Shiraz

♥♥♥♡ 2000 Light to medium red-purple; a fresh, clean and light bouquet is followed by a light to medium-bodied palate, with cherry fruit outweighed by pervasive tannins; time will help.   **rating:** 83
♥♥♥♡ 1999 Quite strong red-purple; the bouquet has concentrated, earthy, savoury black fruit, the palate correspondingly having ripe jammy berry flavours, but with a curious hole in the mid-palate, something which one more normally associates with Cabernet Sauvignon than Shiraz.   **rating:** 84

best drinking 2003–2007 **best vintages** NA **drink with** Long-braised beef and tomato • $19

leeuwin estate ★★★★★

Stevens Road, Margaret River, WA 6285 **region** Margaret River
phone (08) 9759 0000 **fax** (08) 9759 0001 **open** 7 days 10–4.30
winemaker Bob Cartwright **production** 64 000 **est.** 1974
product range ($19–76 CD) Art Series Riesling, Sauvignon Blanc, Chardonnay, Pinot Noir, Cabernet Sauvignon; Brut; Prelude Vineyards Classic Dry White, Chardonnay, Cabernet Merlot and Siblings Sauvignon Blanc Semillon are lower-priced alternatives.
summary Leeuwin Estate's Chardonnay is, in my opinion, Australia's finest example based on the wines of the last 20 vintages, and it is this wine alone which demands a five-star rating for the winery. The Cabernet Sauvignon can be an excellent wine with great style and character in warmer vintages. Almost inevitably, the other wines in the portfolio are not in the same Olympian class, although the Prelude Chardonnay and Sauvignon Blanc are impressive at their lower price level. Exports to all major markets.

Leeuwin Estate Art Series Riesling

♥♥♥♥ 2001 Light straw-green; the bouquet is not as aromatic as it is in some years, with a restrained mix of herb, mineral and lime, but the well-balanced and fluid palate is beguiling, with a gentle touch of passionfruit.   **rating:** 89

best drinking 2002–2005 **best vintages** '99 **drink with** Margaret River marron • $22

Leeuwin Estate Art Series Sauvignon Blanc

♥♥♥♥ 2001 Very light straw-green; the aromatic bouquet is distinctly herbal/grassy, the brisk and lively palate following suit with lemony grassy flavours. Quite different from the 2000.   **rating:** 88
♥♥♥♥ 2000 Light green-yellow; a crisp and pleasantly lifted bouquet of herb, asparagus and mineral is a promising start, and the palate is crisp and lively, with similar flavours, limited only by slightly congested acidity on the finish.   **rating:** 89

best drinking 2002–2003 **best vintages** '95, '97, '99 **drink with** Asian • $31

Leeuwin Estate Siblings Sauvignon Blanc Semillon

♥♥♥♥ 2001 Pale straw-green; pronounced grassy/herbal aromatics are followed by a lively and crisp palate in precisely the same flavour spectrum.   **rating:** 89

best drinking 2001–2003 **best vintages** '00 **drink with** Vichysoisse • $21

Leeuwin Estate Prelude Vineyards Classic Dry White

♥♥♥♥ 2001 Light green-yellow; the clean, firm and brisk bouquet has a light mix of grass and passionfruit aromas, characters which also define the palate, which finishes with good acidity. Sauvignon Blanc dominates the blend.   **rating:** 85

best drinking 2002–2003 **best vintages** NA **drink with** Scampi • $19

Leeuwin Estate Art Series Chardonnay

TTTTT 1999 Brilliant pale straw-green; a delicate and restrained bouquet is completely at odds with the 14.5° alcohol, as are the youthful, vibrant grapefruit, nectarine and melon fruit of the palate. This could develop into something quite special, even by the standards of Leeuwin. **rating:** 96

best drinking 2004–2014 **best vintages** '80, '81, '82, '83, '85, '87, '89, '90, '92, '94, '95, '96, '97, '98, '99 **drink with** Tempura • $77

Leeuwin Estate Prelude Vineyards Chardonnay

TTTT 2001 Light green-yellow; the fresh bouquet has hints of smoky oak intermingling with the citrus and nectarine fruit, the delicate palate ranging from light grapefruit through to gentle tropical flavours, the oak held well in restraint. **rating:** 87

TTTT 2000 Light green-yellow; a light, fresh bouquet with restrained citrus and stone fruit aromas is followed by a palate which is still fresh, crisp and youthful, and which may build more complexity with time. **rating:** 88

best drinking 2002–2004 **best vintages** '95, '96 **drink with** Sashimi • $30

Leeuwin Estate Pinot Chardonnay Brut

TTTTY 1998 Light straw-green; a crisp and fresh bouquet has citrus, lemon and a subliminal hint of strawberry; the crisp and crunchy palate has offsetting bready/yeasty flavours and a crisp, dry finish. A 60/40 blend of Pinot Noir and Chardonnay from the Great Southern given 22 months on lees. **rating:** 91

best drinking 2002–2003 **best vintages** '98 **drink with** Aperitif • $34

Leeuwin Estate Art Series Pinot Noir

TTTT 2000 Light to medium red-purple; a clean, light bouquet with faintly aromatic/foresty overtones, then a palate with more presence thanks to tangy/foresty varietal character, and fine but persistent tannins. **rating:** 85

best drinking 2002–2006 **best vintages** NA **drink with** Braised quail • $37

Leeuwin Estate Prelude Vineyards Cabernet Merlot

TTTT 1999 Medium red-purple; the elegant bouquet has attractively sweet but fine fruit allied with subtle oak; the palate moves up a notch, with a mix of blackcurrant, a touch of chocolate, and savoury tannins to close. **rating:** 89

best drinking 2004–2009 **best vintages** NA **drink with** Roast kid • $30

lefroy brook   NR

Glauder Road, Pemberton, WA 6260 **region** Pemberton
phone (08) 9386 8385 **open** Not
winemaker Peter Fimmel (Contract) **production** 350 **est.** 1982
product range ($21.95 R) Chardonnay, Pinot Noir.
summary Owned by Perth residents Pat and Barbara Holt, the former a graduate in biochemistry and microbiology working in medical research but with a passion for Burgundy. The 1.5 hectares of vines are now both netted and fenced with steel mesh, producing wines which, on tastings to date, are outside the mainstream.

legana vineyard   NR

24 Vale Street, Prospect Vale, Tas 7250 **region** Northern Tasmania
phone (03) 6344 8030 **fax** (03) 6343 2937 **open** By appointment
winemaker Richard Richardson (Contract) **production** 150 **est.** 1966
product range ($21–22 R) Pinot Noir, Cabernet Sauvignon.
summary The Legana vineyard was the first established in the Tamar Valley, planted in 1966 by Graham Wiltshire, and provided the first Heemskerk wines. In 1983 Heemskerk moved to the Pipers River region, and Steven Hyde (Rotherhythe) leased the Legana vineyard until 1994. In May of that year Kurt and Kaye Beyer acquired the vineyard and began its rehabilitation, with rich dividends now being paid.

leland estate   ★★★☆

PO Lenswood, SA 5240 **region** Adelaide Hills
phone (08) 8389 6928 **open** Not
winemaker Robb Cootes **production** 1200 **est.** 1986
product range ($13.50–18.50 CD) Sauvignon Blanc, Pinot Noir, Adele (Sparkling).

summary Former Yalumba senior winemaker Robb Cootes, with a Master of Science degree, deliberately opted out of mainstream life when he established Leland Estate, living in a split-level, one-roomed house built from timber salvaged from trees killed in the Ash Wednesday bushfires. The Sauvignon Blanc is usually good. Retail distribution in Victoria, NSW and Queensland via Prime Wines; exports to Malaysia, Singapore and Hong Kong.

le 'mins winery   NR

40 Lemins Road, Waurn Ponds, Vic 3216 **region** Geelong
phone (03) 5241 8168 **open** Not
winemaker Steve Jones **production** 150 **est.** 1994
product range ($15 R) Pinot Noir.
summary Steve Jones presides over 0.5 hectare of pinot noir planted in 1998 to the MV6 clone, and 0.25 hectare of the same variety planted 4 years earlier to Burgundy clone 114. The tiny production is made for Le 'Mins at Prince Albert Vineyard, and the wine is basically sold by word of mouth.

lengs & cooter   ★★★☆

24 Lindsay Terrace, Belair, SA 5042 **region** Warehouse
phone (08) 8278 3998 **fax** (08) 8278 3998 **open** Not
winemaker Contract **production** 2750 **est.** 1993
product range ($12–47 ML) Watervale Riesling, Clare Valley Semillon, Clare Valley Old Vines Shiraz, Reserve Shiraz, Victor (Grenache Shiraz), Swinton (Cabernet blend).
summary Carel Lengs and Colin Cooter began making wine as a hobby in the early 1980s. Each had (and has) a full-time occupation outside the wine industry, and it was all strictly for fun. One thing has led to another, and although they still possess neither vineyards nor what might truly be described as a winery, the wines have graduated to big boy status, winning gold medals at national wine shows and receiving critical acclaim from writers across Australia. Exports to the UK, Canada and Singapore.

Lengs & Cooter Watervale Riesling

▼▼▼▼ **2001** Light yellow-green; a clean, though not particularly aromatic bouquet leads into a palate with pleasant fruit, well enough balanced but lacking the thrust of the best wines of the vintage.   **rating:** 86

best drinking 2001–2005 **best vintages** '98 **drink with** Summer salads • $13

Lengs & Cooter Clare Valley Old Vines Shiraz

▼▼▼▼ **2000** Medium to full purple-red; rich black fruits and plum aromas lead into a palate with strong minty overtones to the berry fruit. This is a particular facet of shiraz which some enjoy; others (such as myself) are less enthusiastic.   **rating:** 87

best drinking 2004–2009 **best vintages** '96, '99 **drink with** Rib of beef • $25

lenton brae wines   ★★★★☆

Wilyabrup Valley, Margaret River, WA 6285 **region** Margaret River
phone (08) 9755 6255 **fax** (08) 9755 6268 **open** 7 days 10–6
winemaker Edward Tomlinson **production** 8000 **est.** 1983
product range ($15–30 CD) Semillon Sauvignon Blanc, Sauvignon Blanc, Chardonnay, Late Harvest Semillon, Shiraz (Fergusson Valley), Margaret River (Cabernet Sauvignon), Cabernet Merlot.
summary Former architect, town planner and wine activist Bruce Tomlinson built a strikingly beautiful winery but would not stand for criticism of his wines or politics. Son Edward is more relaxed, and is in fact making wines which require no criticism. Retail distribution through all states, and exports to the UK, Singapore and Canada.

Lenton Brae Semillon Sauvignon Blanc

▼▼▼▼ **2001** Light to medium green-yellow; a light, clean and fresh bouquet runs through into the palate, with intermediate fruit ripeness providing a mix of grassy and gooseberry flavours; good length, though not quite up to the standard of the 2000.   **rating:** 88

best drinking 2001–2003 **best vintages** '94, '95, '00 **drink with** Asian dishes • $18

Lenton Brae Chardonnay

▼▼▼▼▼ **2000** Light to medium yellow-green; the bouquet is subtle, with good integration of figgy fruit and cashew-accented barrel-ferment and malolactic fermentation aromas. The wine flows fluidly across the palate, with melon, nectarine and fig fruit supported by excellent acidity and freshness.   **rating:** 94

best drinking 2001–2005 **best vintages** '97, '99, '00 **drink with** Smoked chicken • $27

Lenton Brae Cabernet Merlot

TTTTY 2000 Medium to full red-purple; a complex mix of ripe and more savoury fruit on the bouquet is followed by a palate full of blackberry and blackcurrant fruit, supported by persistent tannins and subtle oak. Great value at this price. **rating: 91**

best drinking 2003–2008 **best vintages** '00 **drink with** Rack of veal • $19

Lenton Brae Margaret River Cabernet Sauvignon

TTTT 1999 Medium red-purple; cedary/savoury overtones to stylish fruit on the bouquet is a promising start, but the oak sweetening intrudes and spoils the flavour balance on the palate. A pity; less new oak would have made a better wine. **rating: 87**

best drinking 2004–2009 **best vintages** '98 **drink with** Grilled beef • $30

leo buring ★★★★☆

Tanunda Road, Nuriootpa, SA 5355 **region** Barossa Valley
phone (08) 8560 9408 **fax** (08) 8563 2804 **open** Mon–Sat 10–5, Sun 1–5
winemaker Geoff Henriks (former) **production** 25 000 **est.** 1931
product range ($10–35.50 R) A very much simplified range of Clare Valley Riesling, Late Picked Clare Valley Riesling, Clare Valley Chardonnay, Clare Valley Semillon, Clare Valley Shiraz, Clare Valley Shiraz Grenache and Barossa Valley Coonawarra Cabernet Sauvignon, all under the split label introduced in 1996; the Aged Show Releases are now under the Leonay Eden Valley label and Leo Buring Eden Valley Riesling.
summary Earns its high rating by virtue of being Australia's foremost producer of Rieslings over a 30-year period, with a rich legacy left by former winemaker John Vickery. But it also has the disconcerting habit of bobbing up here and there with very good wines made from other varieties, even if not so consistently. It will be interesting to see what the future holds for the wines (other than the Riesling) in the wake of the Southcorp/Rosemount merger.

Leo Buring Leonay Riesling

TTTTT 1998 Great colour is an enticing start; the bouquet has a classic lime and mineral mix. The refreshing, almost light, palate has nigh-on perfect balance in a bone-dry style, then a lingering finish. **rating: 94**

best drinking 2001–2010 **best vintages** '70, '72, '75, '77, '79, '90, '91, '92, '94, '95, '97, '98 **drink with** Baked fish, Chinese style • $35.50

lerida estate NR

The Wineries, Old Federal Highway, Collector, NSW 2581 **region** Canberra District
phone 0419 246 149 **fax** (02) 6295 6676 **open** By appointment
winemaker Angus Campbell **production** 1500 **est.** 1999
product range ($15–22 CD) Sauvignon Blanc, Unoaked Chardonnay, Cabernet Sauvignon.
summary Lerida Estate continues the planting of vineyards along the escarpment sloping down to Lake George. It is immediately to the south of the Lake George vineyard established by Edgar Riek 30 years ago. Inspired by Edgar Riek's success with pinot noir, Lerida founder Jim Lumbers has planted 6 hectares of pinot noir, together with 1 hectare each of chardonnay and merlot, and 0.5 hectare of pinot gris. The only Lake George wine so far released has been an unwooded Chardonnay, the other wines coming from elsewhere. The intention is to ultimately rely entirely on estate-grown grapes for the Lerida label, with a second label (Gryphon) for wines made from purchased grapes. An open-air winery was put in place for the 2000 and 2001 vintages, and a Glen Murcott-designed tasting, barrel and function room is being erected on site.

lethbridge wines ★★★★

74 Burrows Road, Lethbridge, Vic 3222 **region** Geelong
phone (03) 5281 7221 **fax** (03) 5281 7221 **open** Fri–Sun 10.30–5 first and third weekends of each month
winemaker Ray Nadeson, Maree Collis **production** 1500 **est.** 1996
product range ($20–38 CD) Pinot Gris, Pinot Noir, Shiraz, Merlot.
summary Lethbridge has been established by three scientists: Ray Nadeson, Maree Collis and Adrian Thomas. In Ray Nadeson's words 'Our belief is that the best wines express the unique character of special places. With this in mind our philosophy is to practise organic principles in the vineyard complemented by traditional winemaking techniques to allow the unique character of the site to be expressed in our fruit and captured in our wine.' As well as understanding the importance of terroir, the partners have built a unique load-bearing straw-bale winery, designed to recreate the controlled environment of cellars and caves in Europe. Winemaking is no less ecological: hand picking, indigenous yeast fermentations, small open fermenters, pigeage (treading the grapes) and minimal handling of the wine throughout the maturation process are all part and parcel of the Lethbridge approach.

Lethbridge Pinot Gris

▼▼▼▼ 2001 Very pale; gently aromatic apple blossom leads into a delicate but long palate with apple, almond and citrus; a well-made and well-balanced wine, particularly with its acidity.　　**rating: 87**

best drinking 2002–2004　**best vintages** NA　**drink with** Delicate seafood • $19.95

Lethbridge Pinot Noir

▼▼▼▼▽ 2000 Strong red-purple; a clean and sweet bouquet with dark plum, hints of spice and forest, and subtle oak. The plummy fruit comes through on the palate, which has excellent balance and structure, but is still firm and needs a year or two to soften and show its best, which will be very good indeed.　　**rating: 93**

best drinking 2003–2007　**best vintages** '00　**drink with** Duck risotto • $27.95

leura glen estate　　★★★☆

260 Green Gully Road, Glenlyon, Vic 3461　**region** Macedon Ranges
phone (03) 5348 7785　**fax** (03) 5348 4077　**open** Weekends and public holidays 11–5 or by appointment
winemaker Graham Ellender　**production** 1000　**est.** 1996
product range ($16–35 CD) Chardonnay, Estate Chardonnay, Loddon Falls Pinot Noir, Shiraz, Cabernet Franc, Cabernet Sauvignon; also wines under Glenlyon Vintners label.
summary Former senior lecturer in dental science at the University of Melbourne Graham Ellender moved to Daylesford with wife Jenny with the twofold purpose of escaping academia and starting a vineyard and winery. The Ellenders have established 4 hectares of pinot noir, chardonnay, sauvignon blanc and pinot gris, and also shiraz and sauvignon blanc from Cowra, cabernet sauvignon from Harcourt, cabernet franc from Macedon and pinot noir from Narre Warren. These wines are made by Graham Ellender, and are released under the Glenlyon Vintners label; the estate-grown products are released under the Leura Glen Estate label.

Leura Glen Estate Artist Series Chardonnay

▼▼▼▼ 2001 Light straw-green; a fresh and lively bouquet with clean citrus fruit is followed by a palate reflecting the ultra-cool climate; it is flinty and lemony like traditional Chablis, also having some length.
　　rating: 86

best drinking 2002–2004　**best vintages** NA　**drink with** Green-lipped mussels • $25

Leura Glen Estate Loddon Falls Ballarat Chardonnay

▼▼▼▽ 2001 Light to medium yellow-green; the clean bouquet has oak and gentle nectarine, with nectarine also present on the palate; there is also slightly fuzzy vanilla oak, suggesting slightly dubious oak selection.
　　rating: 84

best drinking 2002–2004　**best vintages** NA　**drink with** Chinese dumplings • $18

Leura Glen Estate Loddon Falls Pinot Noir

▼▼▼▼ 2000 Bright purple-red; a smooth, sweet bouquet with a mix of plum and cherry fruit, then a palate with good weight and texture; not particularly intense, but with some foresty complexity to suggest short-term cellaring will be worthwhile. Overall, an impressive debut.　　**rating: 87**

best drinking 2001–2004　**best vintages** NA　**drink with** Braised duck • $35

Leura Glen Estate Loddon Falls Shiraz

▼▼▼▼ 2000 Bright red-purple; opens with generous ripe, dark cherry and plum fruit on the bouquet, a touch of oak adding complexity. There is similarly plenty of flavour on the palate, although a slight touch of CO_2 on the finish is distracting. Should settle down well with time in bottle.　　**rating: 87**

best drinking 2004–2008　best vintages NA　drink with Devilled kidneys • $18

liebich wein　　★★★☆

Steingarten Road, Rowland Flat, SA 5352　**region** Barossa Valley
phone (08) 8524 4543　**fax** (08) 8524 4543　**open** Weekends 11–5, Mon–Fri 11–5, appointments advisable
winemaker Ron Liebich　**production** 1600　**est.** 1992
product range ($9–35 CD) Riesling of the Valleys (a blend of Barossa and Clare Valley Riesling), Unwooded Semillon, Cameo Spätlese, Spätlese Traminer, Fortified Semillon, Leveret Shiraz, The Darkie Shiraz, The Potter's Merlot, The Lofty Cabernet Sauvignon, Tawny Port, Benno Port, Vintage Port, Muscat; bulk port constitutes major sales.

summary Liebich Wein is Barossa Deutsch for 'Love I wine'. The Liebich family have been grape growers and winemakers at Rowland Flat since 1919, with CW 'Darky' Liebich one of the great local characters. His nephew Ron Liebich commenced making wine in 1969, but it was not until 1992 that he and his wife Janet began selling wine under the Liebich Wein label. Exports to the US and Germany.

Liebich Wein Riesling Of The Valleys

TTTY **2001** Light to medium straw-green; a solid, clean bouquet which is not particularly aromatic, matched by a firm palate with predominantly mineral flavours, together with some herbal notes. **rating:** 84

best drinking 2002–2007 **best vintages** NA **drink with** Salmon tartare • $13.50

Liebich Wein The Darkie Shiraz

TTTTY **2000** Medium to full red-purple; the complex and savoury bouquet ranges through chocolate, berry, spice and licorice, moving into a powerful palate which adds black cherry to the range of flavours promised by the bouquet. The particularly good finish is intense, but not tannic. From 30-year-old vines yielding 1 tonne per acre. **rating:** 91

best drinking 2005–2015 **best vintages** '00 **drink with** Chargrilled rump • $35

lilac hill estate ★★★

55 Benara Road, Caversham, WA 6055 **region** Swan District
phone (08) 9378 9945 **fax** (08) 9378 9946 **open** Tues–Sun 10.30–5.00
winemaker Stephen Murfit **production** 6500 **est.** 1998
product range ($12–16 R) Semillon, Chenin Blanc, Verdelho, Chardonnay Verdelho, Chardonnay, Late Picked Frontignan, Zinfandel, Shiraz, Cabernet Merlot, Old Tawny Port.
summary Lilac Hill Estate is part of the renaissance which is sweeping the Swan Valley. Just when it seemed the region would die a lingering death, supported only by Houghton, Sandalford and the remnants of the once Yugoslav-dominated cellar-door trade, wine tourism has changed the entire scene. Thus Lilac Hill Estate, drawing in part on 4 hectares of estate vineyards, has already built a substantial business, relying on cellar-door trade and limited retail distribution in Perth.

Lilac Hill Estate Semillon

TTTY **2000** Full yellow-green, very forward but bright. Both the bouquet and palate show a great deal of vanilla oak. **rating:** 82

best drinking 2001–2002 **best vintages** NA **drink with** KFC • $25

Lilac Hill Estate Verdelho

TTTY **2000** The colour is reasonably developed for a young wine, medium to full yellow-green. The bouquet shows some bottle-developed aromas, but seems to be in transition between the aromaticity of youth and the complexity of age. The palate shows this to be the case, with honeyed overtones to the ripe fruit and good length. **rating:** 84

best drinking 2001–2003 **best vintages** NA **drink with** Crumbed brains • $14

lillydale vineyards ★★★★

45 Davross Court, Seville, Vic 3139 **region** Yarra Valley
phone (03) 5964 2016 **fax** (03) 5964 3009 **open** 7 days 11–5
winemaker Jim Brayne, Max McWilliam **production** NFP **est.** 1975
product range ($14–23 R) Gewürztraminer, Sauvignon Blanc, Chardonnay, Pinot Noir, Cabernet Merlot.
summary Acquired by McWilliam's Wines in 1994; Max McWilliam is in charge of the business. With a number of other major developments, notably Coonawarra and Barwang, on its plate, McWilliam's has adopted a softly, softly approach to Lillydale Vineyards; a winery restaurant opened in February 1997.

Lillydale Sauvignon Blanc

TTTT **2001** Light straw-green; the bouquet is clean, crisp and light, not displaying a lot of fruit character, but there is more on the palate, where crisp grassy lemony flavours run through to a cleansing, brisk finish. **rating:** 87

best drinking 2002–2003 **best vintages** '98, '99 **drink with** Delicate fish dishes • $18

Lillydale Chardonnay

▼▼▼▼▽ 2000 Light to medium green-yellow; a fine, classic, elegant Yarra Valley style with melon and citrus fruit aromas repeated on the palate. Seems to dip slightly on the mid-palate, but then reasserts itself on a long finish with sustained acidity, and an assured cellaring future. Excellent value for money. **rating: 90**

best drinking 2001–2006 **best vintages** '86, '88, '90, '91, '97, '98, '00 **drink with** Avocado • $17.50

Lillydale Vineyards Cabernet Merlot

▼▼▼▼ 2000 Medium to full red-purple; nicely ripened and quite sweet dark berry fruit aromas are reflected in the ripe, blackberry and blackcurrant-flavoured palate, supported by fine, ripe tannins. **rating: 89**

best drinking 2004–2008 **best vintages** '00 **drink with** Young veal • $23

lillypilly estate ★★★☆

Lillypilly Road, Leeton, NSW 2705 **region** Riverina
phone (02) 6953 4069 **fax** (02) 6953 4980 **open** Mon–Sat 10–5.30, Sun by appointment
winemaker Robert Fiumara **production** 8000 **est.** 1982
product range ($11.50–22.50 CD) Semillon, Sauvignon Blanc, Chardonnay, Tramillon® (Traminer Semillon), Spätlese Lexia, Noble Riesling, Noble Muscat of Alexandria, Noble Harvest, Red Velvet® (medium sweet red), Shiraz, Cabernet Sauvignon, Tawny Port, VP (Fortified Shiraz).
summary Apart from occasional Vintage Ports, the best wines by far are the botrytised white wines, with the Noble Muscat of Alexandria unique to the winery; these wines have both style and intensity of flavour and can age well. The Noble Semillon and Noble Traminer add strings to the bow. Exports to the US and Canada.

Lillypilly Estate Tramillon®

▼▼▼▼ 2001 Brilliant green-yellow; intense, spicy gewürztraminer aromas on the bouquet are followed by an equally intense spice and lemon-flavoured palate; substantial residual sugar on the finish is part and parcel of the style, a blend of gewürztraminer and semillon. **rating: 87**

best drinking 2002–2003 **best vintages** NA **drink with** Gently spiced Asian dishes • $11.50

Lillypilly Chardonnay

▼▼▼▼▽ 2000 Medium yellow-green; some nutty/smoky oak inputs on the bouquet add interest to the light citrus and melon fruit of the palate. Pleasant drink-now style. **rating: 84**

best drinking 2002–2003 **best vintages** NA **drink with** White-fleshed fish • $12.50

Lillypilly Estate Noble Muscat of Alexandria

▼▼▼▼▽ 1998 Bright gold; the clean bouquet is surprisingly subdued, lacking the grapey fruit of the variety; on the other hand, the payback comes in the lively peachy/lemony palate, and the slow rate of development, in contrast to the Noble Riesling. **rating: 84**

best drinking 2002–2004 **best vintages** '85, '87, '90, '96 **drink with** Tarte Tatin • $16.50

Lillypilly Estate Noble Riesling

▼▼▼▼ 2001 Very advanced golden colour; a richly complex mandarin and cumquat bouquet translates into an almost raisined palate, counterbalanced by good acidity, which also contributes to the length of the wine. Emphatic drink now. **rating: 85**

best drinking 2002–2003 **best vintages** NA **drink with** Poached peaches • $13.50

Lillypilly Estate Noble Harvest

▼▼▼▼ 1999 Golden orange; an exotic mix of tropical, honey and cumquat aromas, lifted by a degree of volatile acidity, is followed a very intense and rich palate with the sweetness balanced by acidity; high botrytis influence, and a confronting style. **rating: 87**

best drinking 2001–2002 **best vintages** NA **drink with** Rich desserts • $22.50

Lillypilly Estate Cabernet Sauvignon

▼▼▼▼▽ 2000 Medium red-purple; clean, fresh berry aromatics lead into a light to medium-bodied palate, with direct blackberry and low tannins. **rating: 83**

best drinking 2002–2004 **best vintages** NA **drink with** Big Mac • $13.50

Lillypilly Estate VP

▼▼▼▼ 1995 Medium red; the bouquet has some Christmas cake complexity; the palate has powerful, clean spirit in a relatively dry framework, and more of those Christmas cake flavours. **rating: 86**

best drinking 2002–2003 **best vintages** NA **drink with** Cake and coffee • $10

lindemans (coonawarra)   ★★★★☆

Main Penola–Naracoorte Road, Coonawarra, SA 5263 **region** Coonawarra
phone (02) 4998 7684 **fax** (02) 4998 7682 **open** Not
winemaker Greg Clayfield **production** 15 000 **est.** 1908
product range ($10–50 R) Under the new Coonawarra Vineyard label, Riesling, Sauvignon Blanc, Coonawarra Limestone Ridge Shiraz Cabernet; then come the premium red trio of Pyrus (Cabernet blend), Limestone Ridge (Shiraz Cabernet), and St George (Cabernet Sauvignon).
summary Lindemans is clearly the strongest brand other than Penfolds (and perhaps Rosémount) in the Southcorp Group, with some great vineyards and a great history. The Coonawarra vineyards are of ever-increasing significance because of the move towards regional identity in the all-important export markets, which has led to the emergence of a new range of regional/varietal labels. Whether the fullest potential of the vineyards (from a viticultural viewpoint) is being realised is a matter of debate. Worldwide distribution.

lindemans (hunter valley)   NR

McDonalds Road, Pokolbin, NSW 2320 **region** Lower Hunter Valley
phone (02) 4998 7684 **fax** (02) 4998 7682 **open** 7 days 10–5
winemaker Philip Shaw **production** 12 000 **est.** 1843
product range ($8–38 R) Hunter Valley Semillon, Shiraz and Reserve Semillon.
summary One way or another, I have intersected with the Hunter Valley in general and Lindemans in particular for over 45 years. It is now but a shadow of its former self, no longer made in the Lower Hunter, its once mighty Semillon seemingly headed for oblivion.

lindemans (karadoc)   ★★★☆

Edey Road, Karadoc via Mildura, Vic 3496 **region** Murray Darling
phone (03) 5051 3333 **fax** (03) 5051 3390 **open** Wed–Sun 10–4
winemaker Greg Clayfield **production** 8 million **est.** 1974
product range ($7–11 R) Bin 23 Riesling, Bin 65 Chardonnay (one of the biggest-selling Chardonnay brands in the world), Bin 95 Sauvignon Blanc, Bin 99 Pinot Noir, Bin 45 Cabernet Sauvignon, Bin 50 Shiraz, Bin 40 Merlot are the most important in terms of volume; Cawarra range of Colombard Chardonnay, Classic Dry White, Traminer Riesling, Shiraz Cabernet and Merlot; also Nyrang Semillon and Shiraz. Karadoc; also produces the great fortified wines, including the premium Fino, Amontillado and Oloroso Sherries, Old Liqueur Muscat, Tokay, Madeira and fine Tawny Ports.
summary Now the production centre for all of the Lindemans and Leo Buring wines, with the exception of special lines made in the Coonawarra and Hunter wineries. The biggest and most modern single facility in Australia, allowing all-important economies of scale, and the major processing centre for the beverage wine sector (casks, flagons and low-priced bottles) of the Southcorp empire. Its achievement in making several million cases of Bin 65 Chardonnay a year is extraordinary given the quality and consistency of the wines. Worldwide distribution. The Cawarra Cafe is open Monday to Friday 10–2 pm.

Lindemans Bin 95 Sauvignon Blanc

▼▼▼▽ 2001 Light to medium yellow-green; the bouquet is clean, but has relatively subdued fruit varietal character; the palate is lifted by a faint touch of sweetness on the finish, and is well directed at its target market. How it won a silver medal at the Hobart Wine Show is beyond my comprehension.   **rating:** 82

best drinking 2002–2003 **best vintages** NA **drink with** Seafood • $8.50

Lindemans Bin 65 Chardonnay

▼▼▼▽ 2001 Medium yellow-green; there seems to be slightly more obvious oak on the bouquet than in prior vintages, but the palate is well put together, with nectarine and white peach flavours; it is deserving of its two bronze medals.   **rating:** 84

best drinking 2002–2003 **best vintages** NA **drink with** Virtually anything you choose • $10

Lindemans Bin 50 Shiraz

▼▼▼▽ 2001 Light purple-red; light juicy berry aromas lead into a palate with more flavour centred on soft, sweet fruit. Well priced.   **rating:** 82

best drinking 2002–2003 **best vintages** NA **drink with** Pasta with meat sauce • $8.50

lindemans (padthaway) ★★★★

Naracoorte Road, Padthaway, SA 5271 **region** Padthaway
phone (02) 4998 7684 **fax** (02) 4998 7682 **open** Not
winemaker Greg Clayfield **production** 68 000 **est.** 1908
product range ($11–15 R) Lindemans Padthaway Vineyard Sauvignon Blanc, Verdelho, Chardonnay, Pinot Noir, Cabernet Merlot and Botrytis Riesling; also Reserve Chardonnay, Limestone Coast Chardonnay, Limestone Coast Shiraz and Padthaway Merlot.
summary Lindemans Padthaway Chardonnay is one of the best-performing premium Chardonnays on the market in Australia, with an exceptional capacity to age. All of the wines under the Padthaway label offer consistent quality and value for money.

Lindemans Limestone Coast Chardonnay

♥♥♥♥ **2001** Medium yellow-green; the bouquet is of light to medium intensity, with pleasant melon fruit and the barest whiff of oak. The palate is pleasant and well-balanced in a light-bodied, no-frills style.   **rating:** 85

best drinking 2001–2002 **best vintages** NA **drink with** Takeaway • $11

Lindemans Padthaway Reserve Chardonnay

♥♥♥♥ **2001** Light to medium yellow-green; there are obvious barrel-ferment influences on the nectarine and grapefruit aromas of the bouquet, but the oak is less assertive on the palate, where grapefruit and citrus flavours provide a firm but pleasant mouthfeel.   **rating:** 87

best drinking 2002–2004 **best vintages** NA **drink with** Roast chicken • NA

Lindemans Padthaway Shiraz

♥♥♥♥ **1999** Youthful and quite deep red-purple; rich plummy/spicy fruit is accompanied by a hint of vanilla bean oak; the palate shows fully ripe fruit flavours, and here the oak is subservient. Well priced.   **rating:** 86
♥♥♥♥♥ **1998** Medium red-purple; the bouquet has soft, dark plum fruit and gentle oak, the palate pleasant plum and chocolate fruit and soft, ripe tannins. A fruit-driven, attractive early-drinking style.   **rating:** 90

best drinking 2002–2005 **best vintages** NA **drink with** Pizza • $15

Lindemans Padthaway Reserve Shiraz

♥♥♥♥ **1999** Bright purple-red; the moderately intense bouquet features bonded plummy fruit and oak; there is then a mix of plum and earthy flavours on the medium-bodied palate, finishing with fractionally gritty tannins.   **rating:** 86

best drinking 2003–2006 **best vintages** NA **drink with** Scotch fillet • NA

☙ lindrum   NR

c/o Level 29, Chifley Tower, 2 Chifley Square, Sydney, NSW 2000 **region** Warehouse
phone (02) 9375 2185 **fax** (02) 9375 2121 **open** Not
winemaker Michael Potts (Contract) **production** 8200 **est.** 2001
product range ($17–95 ML) Clara Semillon Chardonnay, Frederick III Chardonnay, Walter Shiraz, Horace Cabernet Shiraz.
summary The Lindrum story is a fascinating one; few Australians will not have heard of Walter Lindrum, who reigned as World Professional Billiards and Snooker Champion for over 30 years. What few would know is that his great-grandfather Frederick Wilhelm von Lindrum was a renowned vigneron in Norwood, South Australia, and also became Australia's first professional billiards champion, beating the English champion, John Roberts, in 1869. The wines are made from purchased grapes by contract winemaker Michael Potts at Potts' Bleasdale Winery, with an active website helping the marketing effort, which is otherwise through retail accounts.

lirralirra estate   ★★★

Paynes Road, Lilydale, Vic 3140 **region** Yarra Valley
phone (03) 9735 0224 **fax** (03) 9735 0224 **open** Weekends and holidays 10–6, Jan 7 days
winemaker Alan Smith **production** 300 **est.** 1981
product range ($17–25 CD) Sauvignon Blanc, Semillon Sauvignon Blanc, Pinot Noir, Cabernets.
summary Twenty years ago I wrote that the Yarra Valley was a viticultural Garden of Eden; little did I know. The trials and tribulations of Lirralirra over the past ten years have been awesome, yet Alan Smith retains a sense of proportion and faith in the future. All I can say is he deserves every success that comes his way.

Lirralirra Pinot Noir

TTTT 2000 Light to medium purple-red; clean, light, cherry plum aromas show nicely ripened fruit, but not the density of most of the Yarra Valley Pinots of the vintage. The palate picks up the pace somewhat, with nice plummy fruit, but not a lot of complexity. The 15° alcohol is extraordinary; by rights the wine should have been porty, but it is not. **rating: 86**

best drinking 2002–2004 **best vintages** NA **drink with** Smoked quail • $25

little river wines NR

Cnr West Swan and Forest Roads, Henley Brook, WA 6055 **region** Swan District
phone (08) 9296 4462 **fax** (08) 9296 1022 **open** 7 days 10–5
winemaker Bruno de Tastes **production** 3500 **est.** 1934
product range ($13.50–22.50 CD) Chenin Blanc, Viognier, Chardonnay, Brut de Brut, Vin Doux Late Harvest, Noble Classic, Old Vines Shiraz, Cabernet Sauvignon.
summary Following several quick changes of ownership (and of consultant winemakers), the former Glenalwyn now has as its winemaker the eponymously named Count Bruno de Tastes. I, however, have had no recent tastes.

little's winery ★★★☆

Lot 3 Palmers Lane, Pokolbin, NSW 2320 **region** Lower Hunter Valley
phone (02) 4998 7626 **fax** (02) 4998 7867 **open** 7 days 10–4.30
winemaker Ian Little, Suzanne Little **production** 12 000 **est.** 1984
product range ($16–22 R) Premium Hunter Valley range of Gewürztraminer, Semillon Chardonnay, Shiraz, Cabernet Shiraz Merlot; Reserve range of Semillon, Chardonnay and Shiraz.
summary A successful cellar-door operation with friendly service and friendly wines: aromatic, fresh and sometimes slightly sweet white wines, light, inoffensive red wines in the premium range, and fuller, more structured wines in the Reserve range. Has grown steadily, with 41 hectares of estate vineyards; another 44 hectares of vineyards are leased. The wines are exported to the US, Canada, the UK and Hong Kong.

Little's Reserve Semillon

TTTTY 2000 Pale straw-green; the bouquet is typically light, with mineral/stony and crisp apple aromatics; a particularly fresh and lively palate, with apple and a touch of citrus; finishes with crisp, lingering acidity. **rating: 90**

best drinking 2004–2010 **best vintages** '00 **drink with** Summer salad • $18

Little's Reserve Chardonnay

TTTT 2000 Light to medium yellow-green; melon, fig and smoky cashew of light to medium intensity lead into a smooth, light to medium-bodied palate in a relatively understated mode which augurs well for future bottle development (and higher points). **rating: 86**

best drinking 2003–2007 **best vintages** NA **drink with** Full-flavoured fish • $22

logan wines ★★★☆

Ground Floor, 160 Sailor's Bay Road, Northbridge, NSW 2063 (postal) **region** Orange
phone (02) 9958 6844 **fax** (02) 9958 1258 **open** Not
winemaker Peter Logan **production** 17 000 **est.** 1997
product range ($15–27 R) Sauvignon Blanc, Chardonnay, Reserve Chardonnay, Weemala Chardonnay, Shiraz, Weemala Shiraz, Weemala Merlot, Cabernet Merlot.
summary Logan wines is a family operation, founded by businessman Mal Logan assisted by three of his children: Peter, who just happens to be an oenology graduate from the University of Adelaide, Greg (advertising) and Kylie (office administrator). Retail distribution in all states; exports to the UK, the US, Canada, the Philippines and New Zealand.

Logan Orange Sauvignon Blanc

TTTT 2001 Light green-yellow; a highly spicy, floral bouquet with passionfruit and spice has gewürztraminer overtones; the lively, light to medium-bodied palate has a similar, somewhat odd, blend of flavours. **rating: 87**

best drinking 2002–2003 **best vintages** NA **drink with** Chinese fried dumplings • $18.95

Logan Reserve Orange Chardonnay

▼▼▼▼ 1999 Bright yellow-green; the bouquet is particularly attractive, with excellent fruit and oak balance and integration; similarly, the melon and cashew flavours of the palate are harmonious and balanced.

rating: 88

best drinking 2002–2004 best vintages '98 drink with Pan-fried veal • $23.95

Logan Weemala Hunter Valley Chardonnay

▼▼▼▼ 2000 Bright, light straw-green; a clean, fresh, delicately sweet, nectarine-accented bouquet is followed by a fruit-driven palate with pleasant mouthfeel and flavour. **rating:** 86

best drinking 2002–2003 best vintages NA drink with Chicken kebabs • $14.95

Logan Weemala Merlot

▼▼▼▽ 2000 Light to medium red-purple; the bouquet offers berry fruit with some hints of olive in varietal mode; the palate has quite pleasant, sweetly savoury fruit, finishing with soft, fine tannins. **rating:** 84

best drinking 2002–2004 best vintages NA drink with Roast pheasant • $14.95

london lodge estate   NR

Muswellbrook Road, Gungal, NSW 2333 **region** Upper Hunter Valley
phone (02) 6547 6122 **fax** (02) 6547 6122 **open** 7 days 10–9
winemaker Gary Reed **production** NA **est.** 1988
product range NA
summary The 16-hectare vineyard of Stephen and Joanne Horner is planted to chardonnay, pinot noir, shiraz and cabernet sauvignon, and sold through a cellar door (and restaurant) with a full array of tourist attractions, including arts and crafts.

long gully estate   ★★★★

Long Gully Road, Healesville, Vic 3777 **region** Yarra Valley
phone (03) 9510 5798 **fax** (03) 9510 9859 **open** 7 days 11–5
winemaker Peter Florance, Luke Houlihan **production** 25 000 **est.** 1982
product range ($15–30 CD) Riesling, Victoria Collection Chardonnay, Chardonnay, Sauvignon Blanc, Sauvignon Blanc Semillon, Pinot Noir, Shiraz, Merlot, Irma's Cabernet, Victoria Collection Cabernet Sauvignon; Reserve Ice Riesling, Reserve Merlot.
summary One of the larger (but by no means largest) of the Yarra Valley producers which have successfully established a number of export markets over recent years. Wine quality has risen, doubtless due to a core of mature vineyards; the winery is able to offer a range of wines with 2–3 years bottle age. Recent vineyard extensions underline the commercial success of Long Gully. Exports to the UK, Switzerland and Germany.

Long Gully Sauvignon Blanc

▼▼▼▼ 2000 Bright, light green-yellow; pronounced grassy aromas lead into a light to medium-bodied palate, again with predominantly grassy flavours, which result in a faint bitterness on the finish. **rating:** 86

best drinking 2002–2003 best vintages NA drink with Shellfish • $18

Long Gully Chardonnay

▼▼▼▼ 2000 Medium yellow-green; the clean bouquet offers melon, fig and a touch of cashew, the palate with similar cashew and melon flavours; seems to show a little of the heat of 2000, although only 13°. **rating:** 87

best drinking 2002–2004 best vintages '89, '92, '93, '94 drink with Abalone • $22

Long Gully Estate Shiraz

▼▼▼▽ 1999 Medium to full red-purple; a cedary, spicy, earthy bouquet leads into a palate that is in two parts: initially with slightly stewed plum fruit, then an earthy, savoury finish. **rating:** 84

best drinking 2002–2007 best vintages '97 drink with Civet of venison • $22

Long Gully Estate Reserve Merlot

▼▼▼▼▽ 1999 Medium red, showing some development; the bouquet offers a nice mix of berry, olive, earth and spice; the palate has considerable length, prolonged by lingering, savoury tannins; altogether very interesting. **rating:** 90

best drinking 2002–2008 best vintages '99 drink with Braised veal • $30

Long Gully Estate Irma's Cabernet
▼▼▼▼▽ 1999 Medium to full red-purple; an excellent spice, cedar and blackberry bouquet, then a palate with remarkable depth and sweetness to the round, velvety, blackberry fruit. A triumph for the vintage. **rating:** 93

best drinking 2005–2015 **best vintages** '97, '98, '99 **drink with** Yarra Valley venison • $25

longleat ★★★☆
105 Old Weir Road, Murchison, Vic 3610 **region** Goulburn Valley
phone (03) 5826 2294 **fax** (03) 5826 2510 **open** Weekends and public holidays 10–5
winemaker David Traeger (Contract) **production** 3000 **est.** 1975
product range ($10–28 CD) River's Edge Riesling, Founder's Reserve Semillon, Semillon Sauvignon Blanc, Murchison Mill Shiraz, Old Weir Road Shiraz, Campbell's Bend Cabernet Sauvignon.
summary Longleat has a 7.5-hectare vineyard, largely planted over 25 years ago. This provides the riesling, semillon, shiraz and cabernet, with small amounts of sauvignon blanc bought in. All of the production goes to make the Longleat wines, which are now distributed nationally by Alepat Taylor, and exported to Malaysia and the US.

Longleat River's Edge Riesling
▼▼▼▼ 2000 Light to medium green-yellow; a potent, big and perhaps slightly old-fashioned bouquet, with a touch of kerosene starting to develop, then a palate with lots of grip, all adding up to a food style. **rating:** 85

best drinking 2002–2005 **best vintages** '85, '86, '87, '93, '94, '98 **drink with** Strongly flavoured fish dishes • $15.50

Longleat Semillon Sauvignon Blanc
▼▼▼▽ 2000 Bright, light green-yellow; a fresh, quite firm bouquet with mineral and herb aromas; the palate has crisp, grassy herb flavours, finishing with a flick of mineral.   **rating:** 84

best drinking 2002–2004 **best vintages** NA **drink with** Seafood salad • $15

Longleat Murchison Mill Shiraz
▼▼▼▼ 1999 Medium red-purple; the solid, savoury bouquet is reluctant to release aromas, but there are notes of earth and spice; the fruit comes up well on the palate, with dark berry at its core, surrounded by more savoury characters.   **rating:** 86

best drinking 2004–2009 **best vintages** NA **drink with** Grilled T-bone • $20

Longleat Old Weir Road Shiraz
▼▼▼▼ 1999 Full red-purple, deeper than the Murchison Mill. A solid and deep bouquet with a mix of chocolate, berry, earth and oak flows naturally into the quite powerful palate, with layers of dark berry and plum fruit, controlled tannins, and minimal oak.   **rating:** 89

best drinking 2004–2014 **best vintages** NA **drink with** Venison • $28

Longleat Campbell's Bend Cabernet Sauvignon
▼▼▼▼▽ 1999 Medium to full red-purple; the solid bouquet has savoury/earthy blackberry fruit aromas; the palate has lots of weight and power, the flavours tracking the bouquet; ripe tannins and subtle oak complete the picture for a well-priced wine.   **rating:** 90

best drinking 2004–2009 **best vintages** '82, '84, '86, '91, '98, '99 **drink with** Lamb casserole • $22

🐚 long point vineyard ★★★
6 Cooinda Plance, Lake Cathie, NSW 2445 **region** Hastings River
phone (02) 6585 4598 **fax** (02) 6584 8915 **open** Weekends and public holidays 10–6
winemaker Graeme Davies **production** 500 **est.** 1995
product range ($12–14 ML) Chardonnay, Shiraz, Duet Cabernet Sauvignon Chambourcin. Also ginger beer, mead and orange liqueur.
summary In turning their dream into reality, Graeme (an educational psychologist) and Helen (chartered accountant) Davies took no chances. After becoming interested in wine as consumers through wine appreciation courses the Davies moved from Brisbane so that 36-year-old Graeme could begin his study for a postgraduate diploma in wine from Roseworthy. Late in 1993 they purchased a 5-hectare property near Lake Cathie, progressively establishing 2 hectares of chardonnay, shiraz, chambourcin, cabernet sauvignon and frontignac. As well as having a full-time job at Cassegrain and establishing the vineyard, Graeme Davies self-built the house designed by Helen with a pyramid-shaped roof and an underground cellar. All of the wines are made on-site.

Long Point Vineyard Duet Cabernet Sauvignon Chambourcin

▼▼▼▽ **2001** Medium purple-red; the bouquet has some faintly gamey complexity, presumably deriving from the chambourcin; the palate is fruit-driven, with the cabernet coming more into play via herbaceous notes and slightly pointed acidity on the finish. **rating:** 84

best drinking 2002–2003 **best vintages** NA **drink with** Chump chops • $16

🐌 longview vineyard NR

Pound Road, Macclesfield, SA 5153 **region** Adelaide Hills
phone (08) 8388 9694 **fax** (08) 8388 9693 **open** By appointment
winemaker Shaw & Smith, Kangarilla, d'Arenberg (Contract) **production** 1500 **est.** 1995
product range ($10–19 ML) Iron Knob Riesling, Beau Sea Viognier, Blue Cow Unwooded Chardonnay, Red Bucket Shiraz, Epitome Red, Nebbiolo, Zinfandel, Devil's Elbow Cabernet.
summary In a strange twist of fate, Longview Vineyard came to be through the success of Two Dogs lemon-flavoured alcohol drink created by Duncan MacGillivray, sold in 1995 to the Pernod Ricard Groupe (also the owners of Orlando). Nearly 50 hectares have been planted, with shiraz and cabernet sauvignon accounting for more than half, followed by significant plantings of chardonnay and merlot, with smaller plantings of viognier, semillon, riesling, sauvignon blanc, zinfandel and nebbiolo. The majority of the production is sold to Rosemount, but $1.2 million has been invested in establishing a cellar door and function area, barrel rooms and an overall administration centre for the Group activities. All of the buildings enjoy a spectacular view over the Coorong and Lake Alexandrina.

lost lake vineyard & winery NR

Lot 3 Vasse Highway, Pemberton, WA 6260 **region** Pemberton
phone (08) 9776 1251 **fax** (08) 9776 1919 **open** By appointment
winemaker Contract **production** 3500 **est.** 1990
product range ($16–27 CD) Sauvignon Blanc, Semillon Chardonnay, Chardonnay, Pinot Noir, Shiraz.
summary Previously known as Eastbrook Estate, this vineyard's origins go back to 1990 and to the acquisition of an 80-hectare farming property which was subdivided into three portions: 16 hectares, now known as Picardy, were acquired by Dr Bill Pannell; 18 hectares became the base for Lost Lake; and the remainder was sold. The initial plantings in 1990 were of pinot noir and chardonnay, followed by shiraz, sauvignon blanc, merlot and cabernet sauvignon between 1996 and 1998. Just under 8 hectares are now planted. A jarrah pole and cedar winery with a crush capacity of 300 tonnes was built in 1995, together with a restaurant which seats 150 people; it is open 6 days a week for lunch and for dinner on Friday and Saturday nights. In 1999 the business was acquired by four Perth investors.

lost valley winery ★★★☆

Strath Creek, Vic 3658 **region** Central Victorian High Country
phone (03) 9592 3531 **fax** (03) 9592 6396 **open** Not
winemaker Alex White (Contract) **production** 1200 **est.** 1995
product range ($24–34 R) Verdelho, Shiraz, Merlot, Cortese.
summary Dr Robert Ippaso planted the Lost Valley vineyard at an elevation of 450 metres on the slopes of Mount Tallarook, with 1.5 hectares of shiraz and 0.75 hectare each of merlot and verdelho. The 1.5 hectares of cortese is the only such planting in Australia. It pays homage to Dr Ippaso's birthplace, Savoie, in the Franco-Italian Alps, where cortese flourishes. Exports to the UK.

Lost Valley Cortese

▼▼▼▼ **2001** Light green-yellow; crisp and clean, with a mix of grassy, herbaceous, citrus and apple aromas, akin to Sauvignon Blanc. The palate tracks the bouquet, and has more presence, fruit depth and interest than many of the trendy new varieties; good finish. 3000 bottles produced. **rating:** 87

best drinking 2002–2007 **best vintages** NA **drink with** Light seafood • $30

Lost Valley Winery Shiraz

▼▼▼▼ **2000** Dense red-purple; blackberry, plum and licorice aromas on both the bouquet and palate mark a powerful and concentrated wine with subtle oak, but still impossibly young. When mature, would almost certainly rate significantly higher points. **rating:** 89

best drinking 2005–2015 **best vintages** NA **drink with** Leave it in the cellar • $34

Lost Valley Winery Merlot

▼▼▼♈ **2000** Medium red-purple; the light bouquet has fresh berry fruit and a touch of mint, the palate echoing the bouquet with lively, minty, almost lemony fruit flavours, needing more structure. **rating:** 83

best drinking 2002–2006 **best vintages** NA **drink with** Saltimbocca • $34

louis-laval wines   NR

160 Cobcroft Road, Broke, NSW 2330 **region** Lower Hunter Valley
phone (02) 6579 1105 **fax** (02) 6579 1105 **open** By appointment
winemaker Roy Meyer **production** 600 **est.** 1987
product range ($25 CD) Shiraz, Cabernet Sauvignon.
summary It is ironic that the winery name should have associations with Alfa Laval, the giant Swiss food and wine machinery firm. Roy Meyer runs an organic vineyard (using only sulphur and copper sprays) and is proud of the fact that the winery has no refrigeration and no stainless steel. The wines produced from the 2.5-hectare vineyard are fermented in open barrels or cement tanks, and maturation is handled entirely in oak. At its first entry into the Hunter Valley Small Winemakers Show, the 1998 Cabernet Sauvignon won a silver medal, and the 1998 Shiraz a bronze medal.

lovegrove vineyard and winery   ★★★☆

1420 Heidelberg–Kinglake Road, Cottles Bridge, Vic 3099 **region** Yarra Valley
phone (03) 9718 1569 **fax** (03) 9718 1028 **open** Weekends and public holidays 11–6, Mon–Fri by appointment
winemaker Stephen Bennett **production** 1500 **est.** 1983
product range ($15–32 CD) Sauvignon Blanc, Chardonnay, Quest Chardonnay, Paradis, Petillant Méthode Champenoise, Pinot Noir, Merlot, Cabernet Merlot.
summary Lovegrove is a long-established winery in the Diamond Valley subregion, and while production is limited, it offers the visitor much to enjoy: picturesque gardens overlooking the Kinglake Ranges; antipasto, soup and cheese lunch; barbecue and picnic tables; and live music on the second Sunday of the month. Art exhibitions are also staged, and the winery caters for private functions. The wines are produced from 4 hectares of estate plantings which are now fully mature, and a range of vintages is available.

lowe family wines   ★★★★

Tinga Lane, Mudgee, NSW 2850 **region** Mudgee
phone (02) 6372 0800 **fax** (02) 6372 0811 **open** Fri–Mon 10–5 or by appointment
winemaker David Lowe, Jane Wilson **production** 4000 **est.** 1987
product range ($21–28 ML) Semillon, Chardonnay, Shiraz, Merlot, Orange Red (Cabernet blend), Yacht Club Port; also Peppers Creek wines (Hunter Valley) Rosé, Merlot and Shiraz.
summary Former Rothbury winemaker David Lowe and Jane Wilson make the Lowe Family Wines at two locations, principally at their purpose-built winery at Mudgee, but also with a shop-front in the Hunter Valley via the former Peppers Creek.

Lowe Family Chardonnay

▼▼▼▼♈ **1999** Medium yellow-green; a smooth, subtle yet complex bouquet with cashew, melon and a hint of oak seamlessly woven together. The palate is fresh, offering citrus, melon and cashew; good length and feel. Whole bunch-pressed, wild yeast and barrel-fermented, and a blend of Hunter Valley, Mudgee and Orange grapes.   **rating:** 91

best drinking 2002–2005 **best vintages** '99 **drink with** Balmain bugs • $23

lowe family wines (hunter valley)   ★★★★

Cnr Broke Road/Ekerts Lane, Pokolbin, NSW 2320 **region** Lower Hunter Valley
phone (02) 4998 7121 **fax** (02) 4998 7121 **open** Wed–Mon 10–5
winemaker David Lowe, Jane Wilson **production** 2500 **est.** 1987
product range ($15–25 CD) Semillon, Chardonnay, Shiraz, Merlot, Orange Red (Cabernet blend), Yacht Club Port; also Peppers Creek wines (Hunter Valley) Rosé, Merlot and Shiraz.
summary The former Peppers Creek winery has been acquired by David Lowe and Jane Wilson, and is now the Hunter Valley base for Lowe Family Wines. For the time being the Peppers Creek brand is being maintained.

Lowe Family Hunter Valley Semillon

▼▼▼▼▽ **2001** Light to medium yellow-green; a clean, crisp and correct bouquet with delicate herb and grass aromas, the palate basically replaying the bouquet, but showing some riper notes which add to the appeal and balance. **rating:** 90

best drinking 2004–2010 **best vintages** '01 **drink with** Fried chicken • $21

Lowe Family Hunter Valley Shiraz

▼▼▼▼ **2000** Bright red-purple; a solid, ripe bouquet with black berry and plum over an earth and spice substrate; the palate offers powerful, solid fruit backed by persistent, savoury tannins; needs time. **rating:** 87

best drinking 2005–2012 **best vintages** NA **drink with** Leave it in the cellar • $25

☙ loxley vineyard   NR

362 Pastoria East Road, Pipers Creek near Kyneton, Vic 3444 **region** Macedon Ranges
phone (03) 9616 6598 **fax** (03) 9614 2249 **open** Not
winemaker John Ellis, Llew Knight (Contract) **production** NA **est.** 1999
product range Riesling, Sparkling, Pinot Noir, Merlot.
summary A partnership is developing a vineyard/resort/entertainment complex at Loxley. Seventeen hectares of vineyard have been planted, and contract winemaking arranged through John Ellis and Llew Knight. Wines will be produced under two labels, as part of the crop is being sold to John Ellis of Hanging Rock. The first commercial releases are expected in 2003–4.

☙ lucas estate wines   NR

Donges Road, Severnlea, Qld 4352 **region** Granite Belt
phone (07) 4683 6365 **fax** (07) 4683 6356 **open** 7 days 10–5
winemaker Peter Lucas **production** 250 **est.** 1999
product range ($10–20 ML) Chardonnay, Rosé, Shiraz, Merlot, Oaked Merlot, Cabernet Merlot, Cabernet Shiraz, Cabernet Sauvignon, Muscat, Vintage Port.
summary Peter and Robyn Lucas purchased the property on which their vineyard and winery is now established in 1994 in the wake of Peter's redundancy from his former occupation. Establishing the vineyard has been both slow and difficult, with drought-retarded growth, rabbit and wallaby attacks, and then drought-breaking rain-promoted fungal diseases inside the shields which had been put around the vines to stop rabbit and wallaby attack. Then, as everywhere, there are the birds. However, 2.5 hectares of chardonnay, merlot, shiraz, cabernet sauvignon, verdelho and muscat hamburg have been established, and the first good vintage came in 2000.

lyre bird hill   ★★★

Inverloch Road, Koonwarra, Vic 3954 **region** Gippsland
phone (03) 5664 3204 **fax** (03) 5664 3206 **open** Weekends and public holidays 10–5 or by appointment
winemaker Owen Schmidt **production** 2500 **est.** 1986
product range ($12–35 CD) Riesling, Riesling Cellar Reserve, Traminer, Sauvignon Blanc, Bowers Bouquet (white blend), Chardonnay, Pinot Noir, Pinot Noir Cellar Reserve, Shiraz, Cabernet Sauvignon, Salut! (Cabernet Sauvignon Shiraz Merlot), Rhapsody (Sparkling), Phantasy (Sparkling), Golden Nectar (Dessert).
summary Former Melbourne professionals Owen and Robyn Schmidt make small quantities of estate-grown wine (the vineyard is 2.4 hectares in size), and offers accommodation for three couples (RACV 4-star rating) in their spacious guesthouse and self-contained cottage. Various weather-related viticulture problems have seen the Schmidts supplement their estate-grown intake with grapes from contract growers in Gippsland and the Yarra Valley.

mcalister vineyards   NR

Golden Beach Road, Longford, Vic 3851 **region** Gippsland
phone (03) 5149 7229 **fax** (03) 5149 7229 **open** By appointment
winemaker Peter Edwards **production** 550 **est.** 1975
product range A single wine, The McAlister, a blend of Cabernet Sauvignon, Cabernet Franc and Merlot.
summary The McAlister Vineyards actively shun publicity or exposure which, on the basis of prior tastings, is a pity.

macaw creek wines ★★★★

Macaw Creek Road, Riverton, SA 5412 **region** Mount Lofty Ranges Zone
phone (08) 8847 2237 **fax** (08) 8847 2237 **open** Sun and public holidays 11–4
winemaker Rodney Hooper **production** 1500 **est.** 1992
product range ($13–35 CD) Riesling, Sauvignon Blanc Semillon, Predro Ximinez (sweet white), Yoolang Preservative Free Shiraz, Shiraz, Reserve Shiraz Cabernet, Grenache Shiraz.
summary The property on which Macaw Creek Wines is established has been owned by the Hooper family since the 1805s, but development of the estate vineyards did not begin until 1995; ten hectares have been planted since that time, with a further 20 hectares planted in the winter/spring of 1999. Rodney and Miriam Hooper established the Macaw Creek brand previously (in 1992) with wines made from grapes from other regions, including the Preservative-Free Yoolang Cabernet Shiraz. Rodney Hooper is a highly qualified and skilled winemaker with experience in many parts of Australia and internationally in Germany, France and the US. Exports to the UK, US and Malaysia.

Macaw Creek Riesling

▼▼▼▼♀ **2001** Light green-yellow; a clean bouquet offering lime, apple and herb aromas, then a palate with good intensity, length and weight; a stylish dry Riesling with well above average structure.   **rating:** 92

best drinking 2003–2010 **best vintages** '98, '01 **drink with** Lebanese dips • $14

Macaw Creek Wines Grenache Shiraz

▼▼▼▼ **2001** Bright red-purple; the bouquet is clean, with fresh red and black berry fruit; the palate opens well, but falls away slightly on the finish. That apart, a good example of a light-bodied, early-drinking red.   **rating:** 86

best drinking 2001–2002 **best vintages** NA **drink with** Takeaway • $14

mcgee wines NR

1710 Wattlevale Road, Nagambie, Vic 3608 **region** Goulburn Valley
phone (03) 5794 1530 **fax** (03) 5794 1530 **open** By appointment
winemaker Don Lewis (Contract) **production** 750 **est.** 1995
product range ($15.95 R) Chardonnay, Shiraz, Cabernet Sauvignon.
summary Andrew McGee and partner Kerry Smith (the latter the viticulturist) have established 12 hectares of vines on the banks of the Goulburn River, the majority planted to shiraz, with lesser quantities of grenache, viogner and mourvèdre. Currently, 95 per cent of the production is sold to Mitchelton, where the McGee wines are presently made, but the plan is for the partners to make the wine for themselves in the future, and to increase production. The wines are distributed through Woods Wines, 35 Greeves Street, Fitzroy.

mcguigan wines ★★★★

PO Box 300, Cessnock, NSW 2335 **region** Lower Hunter Valley
phone (02) 4998 7700 **fax** (02) 4998 7401 **open** 7 days 10–5
winemaker Brian McGuigan, Peter Hall, Thomas Jung, Brod Vallance **production** 1.2 million **est.** 1992
product range ($10–49.50 ML) The wines are sold in several price brackets: the Black Label range of Verdelho Chardonnay, Chardonnay, Traminer Riesling, Sparkling Chardonnay, Sparkling Shiraz and Black Label Red; the Bin range of 2000 Shiraz, 3000 Merlot, 4000 Cabernet Sauvignon, 5000 Malbec, 6000 Verdelho, 7000 Chardonnay, 8000 Sauvignon Blanc, 9000 Semillon; Vineyard Selection Gewürztraminer, Late Picked Semillon, Chambourcin and Cabernet Merlot; Shareholder range of Semillon, Lisa (sparkling) and Show Traminer Late Picked; Superior Verdelho and Superior Verdot; finally the Personal Reserve range with Chardonnay, Louis (sparkling), Botrytis Semillon, Shiraz, Cabernet Sauvignon and Port; also Howcroft Estate Shiraz, Cabernet; Genus 4 Old Vine Chardonnay, Shiraz and Cabernet Sauvignon.
summary A publicly listed company which is the ultimate logical expression of Brian McGuigan's marketing drive and vision, on a par with that of Wolf Blass in his heyday. Highly successful in its chosen niche market. Has been particularly active in export markets, notably the US and more recently China. The current range of wines, spanning the 1998–2000 vintages, commands respect.

McGuigan Bin 9000 Semillon

▼▼▼▼♀ **1999** Light to medium yellow-green; the clean bouquet is still fresh, with herb and grass aromatics; the palate provides more of the same, developing slowly but surely; it is still in the primary phase, but has considerable character. A re-release of the wine, which has won multiple wine show awards including a gold medal at the 2001 Canberra National Wine Show.   **rating:** 92

best drinking 2002–2009 **best vintages** '99, '00 **drink with** Balmain bugs • $13.50

McGuigan Bin 8000 Sauvignon Blanc

ŸŸŸŸ **2001** Pale straw-green; a light and fresh bouquet, with touches of passionfruit, is followed by a crisp, minerally palate; not a great deal of fruit focus, but a nice seafood style. **rating: 85**

best drinking 2001–2002 **best vintages** NA **drink with** Trout mousse • $13.50

McGuigan Bin 6000 Verdelho

ŸŸŸŸ **2001** Light to medium yellow-green; while far from complex, has above average fruit aromas; the palate is clean and correct, its gentle fruit salad flavours providing a pretty good example of a variety which finds its true expression as a fortified wine on the island of Madeira, and which arguably has no business making table wine. On the other hand, it is preferable to Chenin Blanc. **rating: 84**

best drinking 2002–2003 **best vintages** NA **drink with** Anything • $15.50

McGuigan Bin 7000 Chardonnay

ŸŸŸŸ **2001** Medium yellow-green; strong, toasty/dusty oak on the bouquet, allied with some melon, then a palate with nectarine and melon fruit which makes a partial comeback from the oak domination of the bouquet, with crisp acid on the finish. The performance of the outstanding 2000 wine suggests it could improve significantly in bottle, although the 2001 vintage (for Chardonnay) was not in the class of the 2000. **rating: 85**

ŸŸŸŸŸ **2000** Medium yellow-green; the bouquet is clean and smooth, with attractive nectarine fruit, smoky barrel-ferment oak, and just a hint of creaminess from the mlf. The palate is very well-balanced, with gentle peach and nectarine flavour, hints of cashew, and subtle oak. An altogether distinguished show career was capped by a trophy at the 2001 National Wine Show in November 2001. **rating: 94**

best drinking 2002–2003 **best vintages** '00 **drink with** Breast of chicken • $13.50

McGuigan Genus 4 Old Vine Chardonnay

ŸŸŸŸ **2001** Medium yellow-green, showing some development, but retaining brightness; the bouquet is complex, with tangy barrel-ferment characters in a quasi-Burgundian style. The palate, too, is in a challenging mode, perhaps reflecting a touch of botrytis, but also suggesting some lateral thinking (and practices) in the winery. Nearly, but not quite, comes off. **rating: 86**

ŸŸŸŸŸ **2000** Medium yellow-green; a complex wine with the type of aromas one expects from wild yeast initiation, the palate with a rarely encountered level of flavour and complexity. Top gold medal 2001 Hunter Valley Wine Show. **rating: 94**

best drinking 2002–2004 **best vintages** NA **drink with** Marinated spatchcock • $22

McGuigan Late Picked Traminer

ŸŸŸŸ **2001** Medium yellow-green; a spicy, tangy bouquet and palate, showing good varietal character throughout, as well as good balance. **rating: 88**

best drinking 2001–2004 **best vintages** NA **drink with** Poached pears • $17

McGuigan Genus 4 Old Vine Shiraz

ŸŸŸŸŸ **2000** Deep, bright purple-red; a distinctly regional bouquet that retains varietal character, and offers a mix of dark plum, sweet earth, leather and licorice. The stylish, medium-bodied palate focusses on plum, cherry and spice fruit, with just the right amount of oak. **rating: 90**

best drinking 2005–2010 **best vintages** '00 **drink with** Jugged hare • $22

Howcroft Estate Shiraz

ŸŸŸŸ **2000** Medium red-purple; a clean, moderately intense bouquet with some red berry fruit and soft earthy/oaky overtones on the bouquet; the palate is pleasant, plain and inoffensive. **rating: 83**

ŸŸŸŸŸ **1999** Medium red, with some purple hues remaining. The bouquet is solid, with a mix of dark berry and dark chocolate fruit supported by vanilla oak. The abundantly flavoured palate has voluminous ripe and sweet cherry and chocolate fruit flavours, with a well-judged touch of oak. **rating: 90**

best drinking 2002–2005 **best vintages** NA **drink with** Braised ox cheek • $18

McGuigan Verdot Superior

ŸŸŸŸ **2000** Strong colour; deep, dark, ripe berry fruit and gentle oak on the bouquet are followed by a lusciously ripe and plummy palate. Little or no varietal character, but no cause for complaint at this price. **rating: 86**

best drinking 2002–2007 **best vintages** NA **drink with** Devilled kidneys • $15

McGuigan Genus 4 Old Vine Cabernet Sauvignon

▼▼▼▼▽ **2000** Full red-purple; powerful blackberry, blackcurrant and briar aromas come through strongly on the textured, rich palate; tasted blind, few if any would pick it as a Hunter Cabernet. Fine tannins complete a most attractive wine. **rating:** 91

best drinking 2005–2015 **best vintages** '00 **drink with** Lamb shoulder with garlic and rosemary • NA

Howcroft Estate Cabernet

▼▼▼▼ **2000** Full red-purple; the bouquet is rich, with firm blackberry/mulberry fruit; the palate follows down precisely the same track in a fruit-forward style; plenty of depth, good tannins and neatly judged oak. **rating:** 87

▼▼▼▼ **1999** Light to medium red-purple; the bouquet offers clean, fresh, red berry fruit, nicely ripe but not heavy. The palate is similarly fresh and elegant, with a light touch of French oak and gentle tannins. **rating:** 87

best drinking 2004–2010 **best vintages** NA **drink with** Rack of veal • $18

mcivor creek NR

Costerfield Road, Heathcote, Vic 3523 **region** Heathcote
phone (03) 5433 3000 **fax** (03) 5433 3456 **open** 7 days 10–5.30
winemaker Peter Turley **production** 5000 **est.** 1973
product range ($12.50–27.50 CD) Chardonnay, Shiraz, Cabernet Shiraz, Fine Old Tawny Port.
summary The beautifully situated McIvor Creek winery is well worth a visit and does offer wines in diverse styles; the red wines are the most regional. Peter Turley has 5 hectares of cabernet sauvignon together with 2.5 hectares of cabernet franc and merlot, and supplements his intake with grapes from other growers. No recent tastings.

mclaren vale iii associates NR

130 Main Road, McLaren Vale, SA 5171 **region** McLaren Vale
phone 1800 501 513 **fax** (08) 8323 7422 **open** Mon–Fri 9–5, tasting by appointment
winemaker Brian Light **production** 12 000 **est.** 1999
product range ($17–27.50 ML) Semillon Sauvignon Blanc, Chenin Blanc, Chardonnay, Sparkling Chardonnay Pinot, The Third Degree, Shiraz, Indent Shiraz, Grenache, Merlot.
summary The three associates in question all have a decade or more of wine industry experience; Mary Greer is managing partner, Reginald Wymond chairing partner, and Christopher Fox partner. The partnership owns 25 hectares of vines spanning two vineyards, one owned by Mary and John Greer, the other by Reg and Sue Wymond. Nineteen of the 25 hectares are planted to mainstream red varieties, with shiraz leading the way. The label was first introduced in 1999, the aim being to produce affordable quality wine. Exports to California.

🐌 mcleish estate ★★★★

Lot 3 De Beyers Road, Pokolbin, NSW 2320 **region** Lower Hunter Valley
phone (02) 4998 7754 **fax** (02) 4998 7754 **open** 7 days 10–5, or by appointment
winemaker Andrew Thomas **production** NA **est.** 1985
product range ($14–30 CD) Semillon, Semillon Chardonnay, Verdelho, Verdelho Chardonnay, Chardonnay, Botrytis Semillon, Shiraz, Cabernet Sauvignon.
summary Bob and Maryanne McLeish commenced the establishment of their vineyard in 1985, and have progressively planted 9 hectares of grapes. They have now moved to opening up their cellar door to the public, having accumulated a number of awards for their wines.

McLeish Estate Semillon

▼▼▼▼▼ **2001** Light to medium green-yellow; the powerful lemony bouquet heralds a powerful, long and intense palate with lemon and herb flavours and excellent balance. Top gold medal in its class 2001 Hunter Valley Wine Show. **rating:** 95

best drinking 2002–2009 **best vintages** '01 **drink with** Tuna sashimi • $30

mcmanus NR

Rogers Road, Yenda, NSW 2681 **region** Riverina
phone (02) 6968 1064 **open** 7 days 9–5
winemaker Dr David McManus **production** 500 **est.** 1972

product range ($4–8 CD) Chardonnay, Chardonnay Semillon, Malbec, Merlot, Shiraz, Pinot Malbec Shiraz; many named after family members.

summary An extremely idiosyncratic winery run by Griffith GP Dr David McManus, his sister and other family members. Natural winemaking methods lead to considerable variation in quality, but the prices are from another era; some of the vintages likewise.

mcpherson wines ★★★

PO Box 529, Artarmon, NSW 1570 (postal) **region** Goulburn Valley
phone (02) 9436 1644 **fax** (02) 9436 3144 **open** Not
winemaker Guido Vazzoler, Andrew Dean, Andrew McPherson **production** 300 000 **est.** 1993
product range ($7.99–16.99 R) Semillon Chardonnay, Chardonnay, Reserve Goulburn Valley Chardonnay, Shiraz, Reserve Goulburn Valley Shiraz, Merlot, Shiraz Cabernet, Cabernet Sauvignon.
summary McPherson Wines is little known in Australia but is, by any standards, a substantial business. Its wines are almost entirely produced for the export market, with Dan Murphy being the sole (and exclusive) retail source in Australia. The wines are made at various locations from contract-grown grapes and represent good value at their price point. For the record, McPherson Wines is a joint venture between Andrew McPherson and Alister Purbrick of Tahbilk. Both have had a lifetime of experience in the industry. Exports to the US, Scandinavia and New Zealand.

McPherson Wines Murray Darling Chardonnay

▼▼▼▽ 2000 Medium yellow-green; the clean bouquet offers pleasant nectarine fruit and minimal oak; the fruit-driven palate is holding very well for its age. The wine represents excellent value. **rating:** 84

best drinking 2002–2003 **best vintages** NA **drink with** Takeaway • $7.99

McPherson Reserve Goulburn Valley Chardonnay

▼▼▼▽ 2000 Light to medium yellow-green; some smoky/charry oak mixes with light fruit on the bouquet; the palate is slightly tighter than the varietal in a firm, crisp understated fashion, making it less immediately user-friendly. **rating:** 84

best drinking 2002–2004 **best vintages** NA **drink with** Grilled spatchcock • $16.99

McPherson Reserve Goulburn Valley Shiraz

▼▼▼▼ 2000 Medium red-purple; the firm bouquet has fairly articulated cherry varietal fruit and a neatly balanced touch of oak. The palate opens with the same fruit flavours; the tannins on the finish are slightly aggressive given the fruit weight, but should settle down with time in bottle. **rating:** 86

best drinking 2003–2007 **best vintages** NA **drink with** Grilled chump chops • $16.99

⊗ macquariedale estate ★★★★

170 Sweetwater Road, Rothbury, NSW 2335 **region** Lower Hunter Valley
phone (02) 6574 7012 **fax** (02) 6574 7013 **open** By appointment
winemaker Ross McDonald **production** 6000 **est.** 1993
product range ($12–23 ML) Old Vine Semillon, Premium Blend Semillon Chardonnay, 4 Winds Chardonnay, Macqblush (Rosé), Thomas Shiraz, Matthew Merlot, Cabernet Sauvignon.
summary Macquariedale is an acorn to oak story, beginning with a small hobby vineyard in Branxton many years ago, and now extending to three vineyards around the Lower Hunter with a total 15 hectares of semillon, chardonnay, shiraz, merlot and cabernet sauvignon. This has led to Ross McDonald and his family leaving a busy Sydney life for that of a full-time grape grower and winemaker. The wines are sold by mailing list, through the Boutique Wine Centre in Pokolbin or via the 30 or so restaurants that list the wines. Those restaurants have included such icons as Banc and Bathers Pavilion. Limited exports to the US via Scott Street Portfolio, San Francisco.

Macquariedale Estate Old Vine Semillon

▼▼▼▼ 2000 Light green-yellow; quite intense lime and mineral aromas lead into a palate with similar ripe lemon/lime flavours and good length and persistence. **rating:** 88

▼▼▼▼ 1999 Medium yellow-green; the bouquet offers a mix of toast, flint and mineral; the palate moves up significantly, with lots of flavour and a slight overall sweetness. **rating:** 87

best drinking 2001–2004 **best vintages** NA **drink with** Cold salmon salad • $15

Macquariedale Estate 4 Winds Chardonnay

▼▼▼▼ **2000** Light to medium yellow-green; the bouquet is tight, quite tangy, the oak subtle; the palate isn't particularly rich, but is well-balanced, and offers some cellaring potential. **rating:** 87

best drinking 2001–2003 **best vintages** NA **drink with** Stir-fried prawns • $15

Macquariedale Estate Matthew Merlot

▼▼▼▼♡ **2000** Medium purple-red; the bouquet offers a mix of spicy oak and sweet berry and plum fruit which move through into the deep fruit and big frame of the palate. If there be a criticism, it is that the wine is slightly short, but that is of minor moment. **rating:** 90

best drinking 2003–2009 **best vintages** NA **drink with** Braised beef • $22.80

mcwilliam's ★★★★☆

Jack McWilliam Road, Hanwood, NSW 2680 **region** Riverina
phone (02) 6963 0001 **fax** (02) 6963 0002 **open** Mon–Sat 9–5
winemaker Jim Brayne, Simon Crook **production** NFP **est.** 1916
product range ($6–40 R) A disciplined and easy-to-follow product range (all varietally identified) commencing with Hillside casks; Inheritance Range; Hanwood; Charles King; JJ McWilliams (first released 1996); Winemaker's Reserve Chardonnay and Cabernet Shiraz; and Regional Collection Limited Release Hunter Valley Chardonnay, Eden Valley Riesling and JJ McWilliam Riverina Botrytis Semillon. Also superb fortified wines, including MCW11 Liqueur Muscat and 10-Year-Old Hanwood Tawny Port and a much larger range of Sherries, which still form an important part of the business.
summary The best wines to emanate from the Hanwood winery are from other regions, notably the Barwang Vineyard at Hilltops in NSW, Coonawarra and Eden Valley; as McWilliam's viticultural resources have expanded, so have they been able to produce regional blends from across southeastern Australia under the Hanwood label; in the last few years, these have been startlingly good. Exports to many countries, the most important being the UK, the US (via major distribution joint ventures with Jim Beam and Gallo respectively), Germany and New Zealand.

McWilliam's Clare Riesling

▼▼▼▼♡ **2001** Light green-yellow; a spotlessly clean, but quite firm, bouquet has a mix of citrus and mineral, the palate having abundant flavour without being too heavy; attractive mouthfeel already; a now or later style. Stelvin-capped. **rating:** 93

best drinking 2002–2010 **best vintages** '01 **drink with** Caesar salad • $18

McWilliam's Hunter Semillon

▼▼▼▼▼ **2001** Light green-yellow; the quite intense bouquet, ranging through citrus, herb and spice, is followed by a crisp, intense and lively palate; excellent balance and length. **rating:** 94

best drinking 2002–2012 **best vintages** '00, '01 **drink with** Blue-eye cod • $18

McWilliam's Margaret River Semillon Sauvignon Blanc

▼▼▼▼ **2001** Light green-yellow; a very light and fresh grassy bouquet with some asparagus aromatics is, as one would expect, repeated on the well-made palate, with its mix of asparagus and gooseberry flavours. **rating:** 87

best drinking 2001–2003 **best vintages** NA **drink with** Asian seafood • $18

McWilliam's Hanwood Chardonnay

▼▼▼▼ **2001** Smooth melon and nectarine fruit coupled with creamy, nutty nuances and a touch of oak, all adding depth and complexity. As ever, exceptional value. **rating:** 88

best drinking 2001–2002 **best vintages** '99, '00, '01 **drink with** Fresh pasta • $11.50

McWilliam's Margaret River Chardonnay

▼▼▼▼♡ **2000** Light to medium yellow-green; light, clean fruit and just a hint of oak on the bouquet are followed by a clean, fresh, light palate; well made but lacking intensity and weight; very probably from young vines. **rating:** 84

best drinking 2001–2004 **best vintages** NA **drink with** Light seafood • $18

McWilliam's Limited Release Botrytis Semillon

▼▼▼▼♡ **1998** Golden bronze; a complex and intense bouquet of mandarin and cumquat is followed by a rich palate with honey, mead, cumquat and mandarin fruit tied together by good acidity. Winner of a trophy and 10 gold medals, mainly at lesser shows. **rating:** 91

best drinking 2002–2003 **best vintages** '98 **drink with** Rich dessert • $20.50

McWilliam's Coonawarra Shiraz

ŸŸŸŸ 1999 Medium red-purple; light, simple, juicy berry fruit aromas are repeated on the light to medium-bodied palate. Part of the new Regional Collection range from McWilliam's, some of which offer excellent value for money. This wine is less convincing. **rating: 84**

best drinking 2001–2003 **best vintages** NA **drink with** Roast veal • $18

McWilliam's Hanwood Shiraz

ŸŸŸŸ 2000 Light to medium red-purple; a light, clean, fresh and simple bouquet leads into a no-frills palate, with fresh cherry fruit and restrained oak. Good value. **rating: 83**

best drinking 2001–2002 **best vintages** NA **drink with** Pizza • $11.50

McWilliam's McLaren Vale Grenache

ŸŸŸŸ 2000 Medium red-purple; fresh, moderately intense, juicy berry varietal aromas lead into a lively, fresh, jammy/berry/spicy palate which, however, is not heavy. The jammy characters are a legitimate part of the grenache varietal make-up. **rating: 87**

best drinking 2001–2003 **best vintages** NA **drink with** Devilled kidneys • $16.95

McWilliam's Coonawarra Cabernet Sauvignon

ŸŸŸŸ 1999 Light to medium red-purple; the clean, moderately intense bouquet has gentle red berry/cassis fruit supported by a touch of oak. The palate has a mix of red berry, savoury and chocolatey flavours, essentially fruit-driven, and finishes with fine tannins. **rating: 87**

best drinking 2003–2007 **best vintages** NA **drink with** Lamb shanks on risotto • $18

McWilliam's Family Reserve Oak Aged Muscat

ŸŸŸŸ NV Red hues are still showing in the colour, indicating a youthful wine; the bouquet has intense, raisiny varietal character, quite remarkable given its Riverland provenance. The palate, likewise, has a heap of raisiny fruit; good for drinking, pouring on ice cream or dousing cakes. Top value. **rating: 85**

best drinking 2002–2003 **best vintages** NA **drink with** Nuts, dried fruits • $13

McWilliam's Amontillado Sherry

ŸŸŸŸŸ NV Golden yellow; a quite complex mix of rancio and flor characters on the bouquet leads into a long and intense palate, neither sweet nor dry, with dry biscuity characters coming on the aftertaste. Great balance is the feature of the wine. **rating: 90**

best drinking 2002–2003 **best vintages** NA **drink with** Winter aperitif • $18

mcwilliam's mount pleasant ★★★★★

Marrowbone Road, Pokolbin, NSW 2320 **region** Lower Hunter Valley
phone (02) 4998 7505 **fax** (02) 4998 7761 **open** 7 days 10–5
winemaker Phillip Ryan, Scott Stephens **production** NFP **est.** 1921
product range ($10–45 R) Much simplified and rationalised over the past year. The base range now comprises Mount Pleasant Elizabeth, Philip Shiraz, Late Harvest Dessert Wine, Semillon Sauvignon Blanc, Verdelho, Chardonnay, Unwooded Chardonnay, Pinot Chardonnay, Sparkling Pinot Noir, Merlot; then individual vineyard wines, Rosehill Shiraz, Old Paddock & Old Hill Shiraz, Lovedale Semillon (previously known as Anne), then Maurice O'Shea Chardonnay, Shiraz; finally, Museum releases of Elizabeth, Lovedale Semillon, Late Harvest Reserve.
summary McWilliam's Elizabeth and the glorious Lovedale Semillon are generally commercially available with many years of bottle age, and are undervalued and underpriced treasures with a consistently superb show record. The three individual vineyard wines, together with the Maurice O'Shea memorial wines, add to the lustre of this proud name. Exports to many countries, the most important being the UK, the US, Germany and New Zealand.

McWilliam's Mount Pleasant Elizabeth

ŸŸŸŸŸ 1998 Bright yellow-green; the herb and grass aromas of youth are already being joined by the first signs of honey and toast, while acidity, emphasised by diminishing spritz, will guarantee the future. **rating: 94**

best drinking 2001–2008 **best vintages** '75, '81, '82, '83, '86, '89, '90, '91, '93, '94, '95, '96, '97, '98 **drink with** Pan-fried veal • $17.50

McWilliam's Mount Pleasant Lovedale Semillon

▼▼▼▼▼ **1997** Brilliant green-yellow; a very complex and powerful bouquet with a touch of French white Bordeaux character; the palate is commensurately intense, powerful and long, finishing with crisp, lemony acidity. A particularly interesting and very good Lovedale. **rating:** 95

▼▼▼▼▼ **1996** Brilliant green-yellow; intense, fragrant lemon/lemon rind/toast aromas are followed by a delicate, daisy-fresh palate, like Brokenwood's ILR with a touch of CO_2 yet to disappear. **rating:** 96

best drinking 2002–2012 **best vintages** '69, '72, '74, '75, '79, '84, '86, '95, '96, '97 **drink with** Fine fish dishes • $41

McWilliam's Mount Pleasant Hunter Valley Chardonnay

▼▼▼▽ **1999** Glowing yellow-green; the moderately intense bouquet has peachy, honeyed fruit but slightly plain oak; the palate unfolds with far richer, peach-driven flavour, balanced by acidity. **rating:** 84

best drinking 2001–2002 **best vintages** '98 **drink with** Chargrilled calamari • $14

McWilliam's Mount Pleasant Maurice O'Shea Chardonnay

▼▼▼▼▽ **1999** Medium to full yellow-green; a complex bouquet with spicy oak woven through ripe, melon fruit is followed by a rich and generous palate; here tropical/melon fruit is supported by touches of vanilla spice from the oak. **rating:** 91

best drinking 2001–2003 **best vintages** '98, '99 **drink with** Roast pork • $33

McWilliam's Mount Pleasant Maurice O'Shea Shiraz

▼▼▼▼▼ **1998** The savoury, complex spice, licorice and earth aromas are reflected in the latent power of the long, lingering, intense palate, with fine tannins running through its length. **rating:** 96

best drinking 2005–2020 **best vintages** '98 **drink with** Ragout of veal • $35

McWilliam's Mount Pleasant OP & OH Shiraz

▼▼▼▼▼ **1998** Full red-purple; a concentrated bouquet with a mix of dark berry, blackberry, plum, spice and earth leads into a wine with masses of flavour reflecting the bouquet; a great example of style and terroir coming from old vines; excellent balance to the finish. **rating:** 94

best drinking 2008 – 2020 **best vintages** '65, '66, '67, '79, '85, '87, '90, '91, '94, '95, '96, '98 **drink with** Roast veal • $37

McWilliam's Mount Pleasant Philip Shiraz

▼▼▼▽ **1997** Light to medium red; a light, earthy, leathery bouquet in traditional style is followed by a medium-bodied palate displaying a mix of earth, leather and spice in an ultra-traditional style. Made and matured to be ready for immediate consumption, but I am not convinced that either McWilliam's or the consumer is necessarily getting the best out of the delayed release. **rating:** 84

best drinking 2001–2002 **best vintages** NA **drink with** Chargrilled fillet • $18

McWilliam's Mount Pleasant Roséhill Shiraz

▼▼▼▼ **1999** Medium red-purple; the moderately intense bouquet shows distinctly earthy/regional fruit characters, as does the palate, which is silky and savoury, and not the least flamboyant. **rating:** 89

best drinking 2004–2014 **best vintages** '59, '65, '66, '67, '75, '95, '96, '99 **drink with** Marinated spatchcock • $29

McWilliam's Mount Pleasant Merlot

▼▼▼▼ **2000** Light to medium red-purple; a quite fragrant bouquet with a mix of berry, olive and spice supported by subtle oak flows into a light to medium-bodied palate, with gently ripe and supple berry fruit; fine-grained tannins run through the finish. Has a freshness which the Philip does not have. **rating:** 87

best drinking 2001–2003 **best vintages** '96 **drink with** Rabbit • $18

madew wines ★★★☆

Westering, Federal Highway, Lake George, NSW 2581 **region** Canberra District
phone (02) 4848 0026 **open** Weekends, public holidays 11–5
winemaker David Madew **production** 2500 **est.** 1984
product range ($13–20 CD) Riesling, Reserve Riesling, Semillon, Chardonnay, Phoenix (Botrytis Chardonnay), Dry Red, Merlot, Cabernets.
summary Madew Wines bowed to the urban pressure of Queanbeyan and purchased the Westering Vineyard from Captain G P Hood some years ago. Plantings there have now increased to 9.5 hectares, with 1 hectare each of shiraz and pinot gris coming into bearing. Madew's restaurant, grapefoodwine, which is open Friday to Saturday for lunch and dinner and Sunday for breakfast and lunch, won the Best Restaurant in a Winery award in 2001, and also hosts monthly music concerts.

Madew Reserve Riesling

▼▼▼▼ **2001** Very developed yellow-straw; unusual, aromatic spicy aromas, then a full-flavoured palate with herb, spice and a touch of sweetness. The palate is fractionally short, possibly linked to the colour problem; nonetheless, has lots of flavour. **rating:** 85

best drinking 2002–2003 **best vintages** NA **drink with** Rich Chinese • $25

Madew Pinot Gris

▼▼▼▽ **2001** A slight bronze caste to the colour is totally acceptable given the variety; obvious barrel-ferment spicy oak produces a complex bouquet; the palate is flavoursome, but much of the flavour derives from the oak. An alternative face for Pinot Gris. **rating:** 84

best drinking 2002–2004 **best vintages** NA **drink with** Chinese prawns • $20

Madew Botrytis Riesling

▼▼▼▼ **1999** Medium yellow-green; the bouquet is quite rich, with a touch of toffee over sweet lime fruit; the palate is of spätlese sweetness, with crisp acidity giving the wine good balance. **rating:** 86

best drinking 2002–2003 **best vintages** NA **drink with** Poached fruit • $20

Madew Shiraz

▼▼▼▽ **2000** Medium red-purple; slightly stewed fruit plum and blackberry aromas are followed by a palate which likewise shows very ripe flavours, a touch of chocolate, and ripe tannins on the finish. **rating:** 84

best drinking 2002–2005 **best vintages** NA **drink with** Braised beef • $25

Madew Merlot

▼▼▼▼ **1999** Medium red-purple; sweet dark berry/blackcurrant fruit on the bouquet is followed by a quite powerful palate, with the varietal fruit coming through with slightly savoury touches, and lingering, fine tannins. Has much better weight than the 2000 vintage. **rating:** 87

best drinking 2003–2007 **best vintages** NA **drink with** Ragout of lamb • $30

maglieri of mclaren vale ★★★★

Douglas Gully Road, McLaren Flat, SA 5171 **region** McLaren Vale
phone (08) 8383 0177 **fax** (08) 8383 0735 **open** Mon–Sat 9–4, Sun 12–4
winemaker Trevor Tucker **production** NFP **est.** 1972
product range ($5.50–47 R) Produces a range of Italian-derived styles for specialty markets within Australia, and is increasingly known for the quality of its varietal table wines, spearheaded by Semillon, Chardonnay, Merlot, Cabernet Sauvignon and Shiraz, the last released in two guises: as a simple varietal, and as the top-end Steve Maglieri. Typically several vintages available at any one time.
summary Was one of the better-kept secrets among the wine cognoscenti, but not among the many customers who drink thousands of cases of white and red Lambrusco every year, an example of niche marketing at its profitable best. It was a formula which proved irresistible to Beringer Blass, which acquired Maglieri in 1999. Its dry red wines are invariably generously proportioned and full of character, the Shiraz particularly so.

Maglieri Shiraz

▼▼▼▼▽ **2000** Medium to full red-purple; the bouquet exudes; dark berry, dark chocolate and some vanilla; the palate is rich, mouthfilling and ripe (14°), the French and American oak well-integrated. Has both varietal and region typicity. **rating:** 90

best drinking 2004–2009 **best vintages** '90, '91, '93, '95, '96, '97, '98, '00 **drink with** Ravioli • $19

Maglieri Steve Maglieri Shiraz

▼▼▼▼ **1999** Full red-purple; a powerful, chocolatey, dark berry bouquet is followed by a palate with pristine regional bitter chocolate flavours running throughout. A prime example of terroir speaking. **rating:** 88

best drinking 2004–2009 **best vintages** '91, '93, '94, '95 **drink with** Bistecca fiorentina • $45

Maglieri Cabernet Sauvignon

▼▼▼▼▽ **1999** Medium to full red-purple; ripe blackberry, plum and prune fruit aromas introduce a fleshy and ripe palate with a near-identical range of flavours supported by a deft touch of vanilla oak. All works very well. **rating:** 90

best drinking 2003–2008 **best vintages** '90, '91, '95, '97, '99 **drink with** Parmesan cheese • $21

main ridge estate ★★★★☆

80 William Road, Red Hill, Vic 3937 **region** Mornington Peninsula
phone (03) 5989 2686 **fax** (03) 5931 0000 **open** Mon–Fri 12–4, weekends 12–5
winemaker Nat White **production** 1200 **est.** 1975
product range ($32–47 CD) Chardonnay, Pinot Noir, Half Acre Pinot Noir.
summary Nat White gives meticulous attention to every aspect of his viticulture and winemaking, doing annual battle with one of the coolest sites on the Peninsula. The same attention to detail extends to the winery and the winemaking. Minuscule production; domestic sales through cellar door and mail order, exports to Singapore.

Main Ridge Chardonnay

TTTTY **2000** Medium yellow-green; the moderately intense bouquet has spotlessly clean fig and melon fruit woven through nutty/creamy oak and malolactic characters. The palate is similarly bright, clean and focussed, offering melon layered with cashew, fig and subtle oak flavours. **rating:** 90

best drinking 2002–2006 **best vintages** '91, '92, '94, '96, '97 '98, '99, '00 **drink with** Sweetbreads • $42

Main Ridge Half Acre Pinot Noir

TTTTY **2000** Medium red-purple; an ultra-complex bouquet with a mix of rich forest, plum, fraise du bois and a touch of smoky oak to the bouquet; the medium-bodied palate is still fairly tight, with some cherry coming through as well as the wild strawberry and plum. **rating:** 90

best drinking 2002–2006 **best vintages** '97, '99, '00 **drink with** Grilled salmon • $47

maiolo wines ★★★

Bussell Highway, Carbunup River, WA 6282 **region** Margaret River
phone (08) 9755 1060 **fax** (08) 9755 1060 **open** 7 days 10–5
winemaker Charles Maiolo **production** 3500 **est.** 1999
product range ($16–26 CD) Semillon Sauvignon Blanc, Chardonnay, Pinot Noir, Shiraz, Cabernet Sauvignon.
summary Charles Maiolo has established a 28-hectare vineyard planted to semillon, sauvignon blanc, chardonnay, pinot noir, shiraz, merlot and cabernet sauvignon. He has a wine science degree from Charles Sturt, and presides over a winery with a capacity of 250 to 300 tonnes. As the vines are still coming into bearing, production will increase from the present level of around 50 tonnes to over 200 tonnes, with the option of selling surplus grapes. The red wines, in particular, show great promise, with Shiraz and Cabernet Sauvignon to the fore. The white wines have a constant thread of reduction and are less appealing. The wines are distributed in WA and NSW.

Maiolo Shiraz

TTTT **2000** Medium red-purple; the moderately intense bouquet is quite complex, with savoury/spicy edges to red berry fruit; the medium-bodied palate shows nice varietal cherry fruit, a touch of spice, and neatly balanced oak and tannins. **rating:** 86

best drinking 2003–2008 **best vintages** NA **drink with** Lamb shanks • $22

Maiolo Cabernet Sauvignon

TTTT **2000** Medium red-purple; a clean bouquet with hints of olive and earth to the black fruits; the palate follows on logically, showing cassis, a touch of mulberry and subtle oak. Just a fraction simple overall. **rating:** 85

best drinking 2003–2008 **best vintages** NA **drink with** White Rocks veal • $26

majella ★★★★☆

Lynn Road, Coonawarra, SA 5263 **region** Coonawarra
phone (08) 8736 3055 **fax** (08) 8736 3057 **open** 7 days 10–4.30
winemaker Bruce Gregory **production** 10 000 **est.** 1969
product range ($16–55 CD) Riesling, Sparkling Shiraz, Shiraz, The Malleea Shiraz Cabernet, Cabernet Sauvignon.
summary Majella is one of the more important contract grape growers in Coonawarra, with 61 hectares of vineyard, principally shiraz and cabernet sauvignon, and with a little riesling and merlot in production and now fully mature. Common gossip has it that part finds its way into the Wynns John Riddoch Cabernet Sauvignon and Michael Shiraz, or their equivalent within the Southcorp Group. Production under the

Majella label is increasing as long-term supply contracts expire. Production under the Majella label has increased substantially over the past few years, rising from 2000 to 10 000 cases, with exports to the UK, the US, Singapore, Malaysia and Hong Kong.

Majella Riesling

TTTT 2001 Light green-yellow; the tight and fresh bouquet is slightly firmer than most Coonawarra Rieslings, with some slate and a hint of spice. The palate is similarly tight, predominantly in the mineral and apple spectrum; not at all heavy, and may well blossom with a few years in bottle.　　　　rating: 84

best drinking 2004–2009 best vintages NA drink with Chinese steamed dumplings • $16

Majella Shiraz

TTTT 1999 Medium red-purple; the clean, fruit-driven, fresh berry bouquet is followed by a lively palate, with a notably intense entry into the mouth, flowing through to the finish on the back of fine tannins and subtle oak.　　　　rating: 91

best drinking 2004–2010 best vintages '97, '98, '99 drink with Lamb chops • $25

Majella The Malleea Shiraz Cabernet

TTTT 1999 Medium to full red-purple; a luscious mix of blackberry, cassis and plum on the bouquet is followed by a palate with slightly more savoury overtones, which is no bad thing. The judicious use of oak and balanced tannins round off a distinguished wine from a vintage which had a difficult act to follow. rating: 93

best drinking 2004–2014 best vintages '96, '97, '98, '99 drink with Marinated beef • $55

Majella Cabernet Sauvignon

TTTT 1999 Medium to full red-purple; savoury, earthy cabernet aromas with touches of spice from the oak are followed by lively, juicy blackcurrant, blackberry and spice flavours; the oak has been well-integrated.

rating: 89

best drinking 2004–2010 best vintages '93, '94, '96, '98 drink with Rack of lamb • $29

malcolm creek vineyard　　★★★☆

Bonython Road, Kersbrook, SA 5231 region Adelaide Hills
phone (08) 8389 3235 fax (08) 8389 3235 open Weekends and public holidays 11–5 or by appointment
winemaker Reg Tolley production 700 est. 1982
product range ($19–22 R) Chardonnay, Cabernet Sauvignon.
summary Malcolm Creek is the retirement venture of Reg Tolley, and keeps a low profile. However, the wines are invariably well made and develop gracefully; they are worth seeking out, and are usually available with some extra bottle age at a very modest price. Exports to the UK.

maleny mountain wines　　NR

269 Landsborough Road, Maleny, Qld 4551 region Queensland Coastal
phone (07) 5429 6300 fax (07) 5429 6331 open 7 days 10–5
winemaker Gerry Pagano production 1280 est. 2000
product range ($16.50–25 CD) Semillon, Semillon Chardonnay, Verdelho, Semillon Botrytis, Nerina Sunrise Chardonnay Merlot, Shiraz, Shiraz Cabernet, Merlot, Cabernet Merlot, Glasshouse Tawny Port.
summary The Pagano family's forebears made wine on the foothills of Mount Etna for many generations, and the family has been involved in the Australian wine industry for over 40 years. But it was not until 11 years ago that father Sebastian and wife Maria Pagano saw the Maleny area with its Glasshouse Mountain and surrounding Blackall Range, reminiscent of a scaled-down Mount Etna. They have now planted 4 hectares of chambourcin on site, and opened a tasting room in the shape of a giant barrel; the chambourcin is yet to come into production, but there is a wide range of wines sourced from elsewhere in Australia. In best Queensland tradition, there are plenty of attractions for tourists, including vineyard tours, light focaccia lunches through Monday to Saturday, and a continental buffet lunch on Sunday.

maling family estate　　★★★☆

Waverley-Honour, Palmers Lane, Pokolbin, NSW 2320 region Lower Hunter Valley
phone (02) 4998 7953 fax (02) 4998 7952 open 7 days 10–5
winemaker Gary Reed (Contract) production 4500 est. 1989
product range ($35–72 CD) Waverley Estate Semillon, Chardonnay, Sparkling, Hermitage, Cabernet Sauvignon.

summary The word 'unique' is in the same category as 'passion': a grossly overused cliche. Nonetheless, unique is the only word to describe the Maling Family Estate operation, which dates back at the very least to 1989 and arguably to 1971, when the core of the existing vineyard was planted. In 1989 Terry Maling and family acquired the vineyard, which has since been increased to 21.5 hectares of shiraz, semillon, chardonnay and cabernet sauvignon. The large house-cum-cellar-door-restaurant-bed-and-breakfast complex has been constructed with materials from damaged heritage buildings from the 1989 Newcastle earthquake. Building materials include huge grey sandstone blocks, some blazed with convict tally markings, the big doors and roof trusses coming from Newcastle bond stores built c1860. 1989 not only marked the Newcastle earthquake, but the first vintage of Maling Estate Wines which, from that year onwards, have been made by Gary Reed. Remarkably, none of the wines was offered for sale until the end of 1999, and since 2000 a range of vintages have been on sale.

malmsbury estate vineyard ★★★

Calder Highway, Malmsbury, Vic 3446 **region** Macedon Ranges
phone 0417 325 773 **fax** (03) 5423 2243 **open** Not
winemaker David Watson (former) **production** 550 **est.** 1989
product range ($15–19 R) Under the Lord Malmsbury label: Chardonnay, Pinot Noir, Classic Red.
summary David Rush and family planted 2 hectares in total of chardonnay, pinot noir, malbec, merlot, cabernet franc, shiraz and cabernet sauvignon in 1989. The vineyard is not irrigated, and the plantings have taken some time to come into commercial bearing, although the first experimental wine was made back in 1993.

Lord Malmsbury Cabernets

▼▼▼▽ **1999** Medium red-purple; the bouquet is sweetened by a touch of oak which is, however, not entirely compatible with the character of the fruit. Thus on the palate pleasant berry fruit is ill at ease with the slightly pencilly character of that oak. **rating: 84**

best drinking 2003–2007 **best vintages** NA **drink with** Lamb cutlets • NA

mandurang valley wines NR

77 Fadersons Lane, Mandurang, Vic 3551 **region** Bendigo
phone (03) 5439 5367 **fax** (03) 5439 3850 **open** Weekends 11–5
winemaker Wes Vine **production** 1200 **est.** 1994
product range ($13–18 CD) Riesling, Pinot Noir, Shiraz, Cabernet Sauvignon.
summary The eponymously named Wes and Pamela Vine have slowly built Mandurang Valley Wines, utilising 2.5 hectares of estate vines and a further 6 hectares of estate-grown grapes. As from Easter 2001 they have been offering cafe lunches to complement the outdoor seating and barbecue facilities already in existence. The wines are chiefly sold at the cellar door and by mailing list, with limited Melbourne distribution through Bacchus Wines, Armadale.

mann NR

105 Memorial Avenue, Baskerville, WA 6056 **region** Swan District
phone (08) 9296 4348 **fax** (08) 9296 4348 **open** Weekends 10–5 and by appointment from 1 Aug until sold out
winemaker Dorham Mann **production** 550 **est.** 1988
product range ($16 CD) Mèthode Champenoise.
summary Industry veteran Dorham Mann has established a one-wine label for what must be Australia's most unusual wine: a dry, only faintly pink, sparkling wine made exclusively from cabernet sauvignon grown on the 2.4-hectare estate surrounding the cellar door. Dorham Mann explains, 'Our family has made and enjoyed the style for more than 30 years, although just in a private capacity until recently.'

mansfield wines ★★★☆

204 Eurunderee Road, Mudgee, NSW 2850 **region** Mudgee
phone (02) 6373 3871 **fax** (02) 6373 3708 **open** Thurs–Mon 10–5, or by appointment
winemaker Bob Heslop **production** 3000 **est.** 1975
product range ($7–20 CD) Sauvignon Blanc, Frontignac, Chardonnay, Spectabilis White (semi-sweet), Sparkling Muscat, Spectabilis Red, Shiraz, Shiraz Cabernet, Touriga, Zinfandel, Cabernet Sauvignon Merlot, and a selection of fortified wines.

summary Mansfield Wines is one of the old-style wineries, offering a mix of varietal and generic table wines at low prices, and an even larger range of miscellaneous fortified wines, not all of which are locally produced. Distribution is through the cellar door and various regional outlets.

Mansfield Wines Frontignac

ŸŸŸŸ **2001** Light yellow-green; the bouquet and palate show the spicy/grapey varietal character of frontignac, but do so in a relatively light mode. **rating:** 82

best drinking 2001–2002 **best vintages** NA **drink with** Asian • $14

Mansfield Wines Cabernet Sauvignon Merlot

ŸŸŸŸŸ **1999** Medium red-purple; a clean bouquet, moderately intense, with a mix of berry and mint; the palate is elegant, with restrained berry and mint flavours, well weighted tannins and subtle oak. **rating:** 91

best drinking 2004–2009 **best vintages** '99 **drink with** Fillet of lamb • $19

Mansfield Wines Vintage Port

ŸŸŸŸ **2001** Light, bright red-purple; fresh cherry fruit and just a touch of spirit on the bouquet are repeated on the palate, producing a thoroughly interesting outcome. Presumably intended as an early-release, early-drinking style. **rating:** 82

best drinking 2002–2003 **best vintages** NA **drink with** Aperitif or soft cheese • $18

mantons creek vineyard NR

Tucks Road, Main Ridge, Vic 3928 **region** Mornington Peninsula
phone (03) 5989 6264 **fax** (03) 5959 6060 **open** 7 days 10–5
winemaker Alex White (Contract) **production** 5000 **est.** 1998
product range ($15–25 CD) Sauvignon Blanc, Muscat, Pinot Gris, Chardonnay, Tempranillo, Pinot Noir.
summary The substantial Mantons Creek Vineyard was established in the early 1990s, with the grapes from the first 5 years' production being sold to other makers. Since that time events have moved quickly: the label was launched in 1998 and a restaurant-cum-tasting room was opened in December 1998, boasting two chefs with impeccable credentials. The 14-hectare vineyard includes 3 hectares of tempranillo, which John Williams says grows well in the cool climate of the Mornington Peninsula, making a very rich style of wine with great flavour. I am yet to taste it.

margan family winegrowers ★★★★

1238 Milbrodale Road, Broke, NSW 2330 **region** Lower Hunter Valley
phone (02) 6579 1317 **fax** (02) 6579 1317 **open** Mon–Fri 9–5
winemaker Andrew Margan **production** 40 000 **est.** 1997
product range ($17–25 R) Semillon, Verdelho, Chardonnay, Botrytis Semillon, Shiraz, Shiraz Saignée, Merlot, Cabernet Sauvignon.
summary Andrew Margan followed in his father's footsteps by entering the wine industry 20 years ago; he has covered a great deal of territory since, working as a flying winemaker in Europe, then for Tyrrell's, first as a winemaker then as marketing manager. His wife Lisa, too, has had many years of experience in restaurants and marketing. They now have 10 hectares of fully yielding vines at their 50-hectare Ceres Hill homestead property at Broke, and lease the nearby Vere Vineyard of 13 hectares. The first stage of a 700-tonne on-site winery was completed in 1998, the first wines having been made elsewhere in 1997. Wine quality (and the packaging) is consistently good. Exports to the UK, the US, Canada and the Netherlands.

Margan Family Semillon

ŸŸŸŸŸ **2001** Light green-yellow; youthful, but already showing quite intense lemony varietal character; the palate likewise is starting to flex its muscles; it is long and multiflavoured, with a faintly grippy finish which may well soften back into the wine with further time. **rating:** 90

best drinking 2002–2007 **best vintages** '99, '00 **drink with** Rich seafood • $17

Margan Family Verdelho

ŸŸŸŸ **2001** Light to medium yellow-green; the moderately intense bouquet is clean, with fruit salad aromas, swelling somewhat on the palate with a range of fruit salad, nectarine and citrus fruit; good balance. **rating:** 86

best drinking 2001–2002 **best vintages** NA **drink with** Asian • $17

Margan Family Chardonnay
YYYY 2001 Medium yellow-green; a very complex bouquet with lots of toasty oak, but also powerful fruit. The palate is abundantly flavoured, with rich, yellow peach fruit flavours and complementary toasty oak. A quick- developing style best enjoyed now. **rating: 88**

best drinking 2001–2002 **best vintages** '98, '01 **drink with** Breast of chicken • $18

Margan Family Botrytis Semillon
YYYYY 2000 Orange-gold; a complex and fragrant bouquet of cumquat and honeycomb is followed by a long, intense and complex palate. Gold medal 2001 Hunter Valley Wine Show. **rating: 93**

best drinking 2001–2004 **best vintages** NA **drink with** Fruit tart • $25

Margan Family Shiraz
YYYY 2000 Medium to full purple-red; strong, dark fruit, with regional earthy overtones is followed by a palate still in its infancy, but well constructed and with good length. A good outcome for a challenging vintage. **rating: 88**

best drinking 2005–2010 **best vintages** '99 **drink with** Braised lamb shanks • $20

Margan Family Shiraz Saignée
YYYY 2001 Vivid red-purple; there is quite powerful fruit on the bouquet offering a mix of berry, earth and spice; the palate is well-balanced, and most definitely not sweet; best served slightly chilled. **rating: 85**

best drinking 2001–2002 **best vintages** NA **drink with** Barbecue • $17

Margan Family Cabernet Sauvignon
YYYY 2000 Dense red-purple; a powerful, herby/earthy aroma with savoury aspects is offset by a touch of vanillin oak. The palate has plenty of blackcurrant/blackberry fruit at its core, surrounded at the moment by tannins and some American oak. Here, too, patience will be rewarded. **rating: 89**

best drinking 2005–2015 **best vintages** '00 **drink with** Braised ox cheek • $20

marienberg ★★★
2 Chalk Hill Road, McLaren Vale, SA 5171 **region** McLaren Vale
phone (08) 8323 9666 **fax** (08) 8323 9600 **open** 7 days 10–5
winemaker Grant Burge (Contract) **production** 30 000 **est.** 1966
product range ($11.95-19.95 R) Cottage Classic range of Riesling, Sauvignon Blanc Semillon, Unwooded Chardonnay, Cabernet Grenache Mourvèdre; Reserve Chardonnay, Shiraz and Cabernet Sauvignon; also Late Picked Frontignac, Nicolle Mèthode Traditionale and Tawny Port.
summary The Marienberg brand was purchased by the Hill International group of companies in late 1991 following the retirement of founder and Australia's first female winemaker, Ursula Pridham. Releases under the new regime have been honest, if unashamedly commercial, wines. The Reserve wines do offer a significant lift in quality above the basic range, reflecting the recent acquisition of the 33-hectare Douglas Gully Vineyard (up to 40 years old) in the foothills of McLaren Vale. The financial problems of Hill International may lead to an ownership change. The wines are exported to the US, Canada, Brazil, the UK, Denmark, Germany, Switzerland, Hong Kong, Indonesia, Fiji, Singapore, Thailand and New Zealand.

Marienberg Reserve Chardonnay
YYYY 1998 Medium to full yellow-green; the bouquet is full, with soft peachy fruit, and somewhat plain. Lots of sweet fruit and oak coalesce on the generously flavoured palate, which, however, lacks piquancy and was probably better 12 months after it was made. **rating: 82**

best drinking 2000–2001 **best vintages** NA **drink with** Calamari • $17.95

Marienberg Reserve Shiraz
YYYY 1999 Medium red-purple; fresh cherry/berry fruit lies at the core of both the bouquet and palate; the latter is nicely balanced, with fine, soft tannins. **rating: 89**

best drinking 2003–2008 **best vintages** NA **drink with** Lamb chops • $19.95

Marienberg Reserve Cabernet Sauvignon
YYYY 1996 Medium red; the soft bouquet has an attractive range of bottle-developed cedary/gently earthy varietal fruit; is the palate similarly soft, with cedary/earthy varietal fruit and gentle tannins. Attractively priced and ready to roll. **rating: 85**

best drinking 2000–2003 **best vintages** '96 **drink with** Rib of beef • $19.95

mariners rest NR

Jamakarri Farm, Roberts Road, Denmark, WA 6333 **region** Great Southern
phone (08) 9840 9324 **fax** (08) 9840 9321 **open** 7 days 11–5
winemaker Brenden Smith **production** 750 **est.** 1996
product range ($15–22.50 R) Chardonnay, Southern White, Autumn Gold, Autumn Red, Southern Red, Pinot Noir, Nelson's Blood (Tawny Port).
summary Mariners Rest is the reincarnation of the now defunct Golden Rise winery. A new 2.5-hectare vineyard was planted in the spring of 1997, and a slightly odd selection of replacement wines is being marketed.

marion's vineyard ★★★☆

Foreshore Drive, Deviot, Tas 7275 **region** Northern Tasmania
phone (03) 6394 7434 **fax** (03) 6394 7434 **open** 7 days 10–5
winemaker Mark Semmens, Marion Semmens **production** 2000 **est.** 1980
product range ($15–30 ML) Chardonnay, Müller Thurgau, Pinot Noir, Cabernet Sauvignon.
summary The irrepressible Mark Semmens and indefatigable wife Marion have one of the most beautifully situated vineyards and wineries in Australia on the banks of the Tamar River. As well as an outdoor restaurant and accommodation, there is a jetty and a stage – indeed, life is a stage for Mark Semmens.

maritime estate ★★★☆

Tucks Road, Red Hill, Vic 3937 **region** Mornington Peninsula
phone (03) 9848 2926 **fax** (03) 9882 8325 **open** Weekends and public holidays 11–5, 7 days Dec 27–Jan 26
winemaker Contract **production** 2000 **est.** 1988
product range ($16–29 CD) Chardonnay DR (unwooded), Chardonnay AR, Pinot Gris LAR, Pinot Noir NR.
summary John and Linda Ruljancich have enjoyed great success since their first vintage in 1994, no doubt due in part to skilled contract-winemaking but also to the situation of their vineyard, which looks across the hills and valleys of the Red Hill subregion.

Maritime Estate Chardonnay AR
▼▼▼▼ 2000 Light to medium yellow-green; quite complex, smoky overtones to the melon, nectarine and citrus fruit of the bouquet are followed by a fresh palate with citrus, nectarine, a touch of cashew, and crunchy/lemony acidity on the finish. **rating:** 85
best drinking 2002–2004 **best vintages** '95 **drink with** Calamari • $26

Maritime Estate Pinot Noir NR
▼▼▼▼▽ 2000 Light to medium red-purple; the bouquet has a fragrant mix of plum, spice and forest aromas; the light to medium-bodied palate has good length and flavour; spicy plum and cherry fruit are followed by a tangy, lively finish. **rating:** 90
best drinking 2002–2005 **best vintages** '00 **drink with** Breast of squab • $28

markwood estate NR

Morris Lane, Markwood, Vic 3678 **region** King Valley
phone (03) 5727 0361 **fax** (03) 5727 0361 **open** 7 days 9–5
winemaker Rick Morris **production** 100 **est.** 1971
product range ($15–30 CD) Rhine Riesling, Cabernet Sauvignon, White Port, Old Tawny Port.
summary A member of the famous Morris family, Rick Morris shuns publicity and relies virtually exclusively on cellar-door sales for what is a small output. Of a range of table and fortified wines tasted several years ago, the Old Tawny Port (a cross between Port and Muscat, showing more of the character of the latter than the former) and a White Port (seemingly made from Muscadelle) were the best.

marribrook ★★★★

Albany Highway, Kendenup, WA 6323 **region** Great Southern
phone (08) 9851 4651 **fax** (08) 9851 4652 **open** Wed–Sun and public holidays 10.30–4.30
winemaker Gavin Berry **production** 2200 **est.** 1990

product range ($14–25 CD) Semillon Sauvignon Blanc, Stirling White (Semillon), Botanica Chardonnay, Reserve Chardonnay, Marsanne, Cabernet Malbec Merlot.

summary The Brooks family purchased the former Marron View 5.6-hectare vineyard from Kim Hart in 1994 and renamed the venture Marribrook Wines. Those wines are now made by Gavin Berry at Plantagenet, having been made at Alkoomi up to 1994. The Brooks have purchased an additional property on the Albany Highway north of Mount Barker and immediately south of Gilbert's Wines. Cellar-door sales have moved to this location, and a dedicated cellar-door sales building encompassing a small restaurant and gallery was completed in 2000, with great views out to the Stirling Range. Retail distribution in WA and Victoria, exports through International Winex Corporation.

Marribrook Semillon Sauvignon Blanc

TTTT 2001 Very pale straw-green; delicate herb, grass and lemon aromas lead into a light but firm palate with similar herb/grass flavours, all in all possessing some relatively austere authority.   **rating:** 85

best drinking 2002–2003 **best vintages** NA **drink with** Shellfish • $15

Marribrook Marsanne

TTTT 2000 Light to medium yellow-green; a pleasant array of dried fruit (apricot, apple, pear) aromas, then a fresh palate which picks up the bouquet, has balanced acidity and is not phenolic. Well made.   **rating:** 86

best drinking 2002–2005 **best vintages** '97 **drink with** Antipasto • $14

Marribrook Marsanne Oaked

TTTT 2000 Light to medium yellow-green; the oak is quite subtle but does slightly mask the delicate fruit; the palate works better, the oak marginally sweetening the finish, or at least appearing so to do. A trading–off: more complexity, less of the delicate varietal fruit.   **rating:** 86

best drinking 2002–2004 **best vintages** NA **drink with** Antipasto • $19

Marribrook Reserve Chardonnay

TTTTY 2000 Light to medium green-yellow; a fine but aromatic bouquet with stone fruit, citrus and underlying barrel ferment characters, then a palate with good length, fruit to the fore, minimal oak and a lingering aftertaste. Gold medal 2001 Adelaide Wine Show.   **rating:** 92

best drinking 2003–2007 **best vintages** '98, '01 **drink with** Slow-cooked Atlantic salmon • $21

Marribrook Cabernet Malbec Merlot

TTTTY 1999 Medium to full red-purple; the complex bouquet has dark berry fruits and evident charry oak; the palate has abundant flavour, good balance between the blackberry fruit and oak, and ripe tannins to close. Gold medal 2001 West Australian Wine Show. A 61/20/18 per cent blend of the three varieties.   **rating:** 90

best drinking 2004–2009 **best vintages** '99 **drink with** Venison • $16

marsh estate   ★★★

Deasey Road, Pokolbin, NSW 2320 **region** Lower Hunter Valley
phone (02) 4998 7587 **fax** (02) 4998 7884 **open** Mon–Fri 10–4.30, weekends 10–5
winemaker Peter Marsh **production** 4000 **est.** 1971
product range ($18–25 CD) Semillon, Private Bin Semillon, Chardonnay (oaked and unoaked), Semillon Sauternes, Shiraz (Private Bin, Vat S and Vat R), Cabernet Sauvignon, Champagne Brut, Andrew IV Vintage Port.
summary Through sheer consistency and unrelenting hard work, the Marsh family (who purchased the former Quentin Estate in 1978) has built up a sufficiently loyal cellar-door and mailing list clientele to allow all of their considerable production to be sold direct. Wine style is always direct, with oak playing a minimal role and prolonged cellaring paying handsome dividends. No recent tastings.

martins hill wines   ★★★☆

Sydney Road, Mudgee, NSW 2850 **region** Mudgee
phone (02) 6373 1248 **fax** (02) 6373 1248 **open** Not
winemaker Pieter Van Gent (Contract) **production** 700 **est.** 1985
product range ($13–16 R) Sauvignon Blanc, Pinot Noir.
summary Janette Kenworthy and Michael Sweeny are committed organic grape growers and are members of the Organic Vignerons Association. It is a tiny operation at the moment, with only 0.5 hectare each of sauvignon blanc and pinot noir in production, but with an additional hectare of cabernet sauvignon to produce its first grapes in the year 2000, and 1.5 hectares of shiraz in 2001. While there is no cellar door (only a mailing list), organic vineyard tours and talks can be arranged by appointment.

marybrook vineyards NR

Vasse–Yallingup Road, Marybrook, WA 6280 **region** Margaret River
phone (08) 9755 1143 **fax** (08) 9755 1112 **open** Fri–Mon 10–5, school holidays 7 days 10–5
winemaker Aub House **production** 2000 **est.** 1986
product range ($11–26.50 CD) Verdelho, Chardonnay, Classic White, Nectosia (sweet), Grenache, Cabernet, Cabernet Franc, Temptation (sweet red), Ruby Jetty Port, Liqueur Muscat.
summary It is easy to confuse Marybrook Vineyards with Marybrook Estate; they are in fact separate operations. Maribrook Vineyards is owned by Aub and Jan House. Eight hectares of vineyards are in production, with back vintages usually available.

🐚 mary byrnes wine NR

Rees Road, Ballandean, Qld 4382 **region** Granite Belt
phone (07) 4684 1111 **fax** (07) 4684 1312 **open** Weekends and public holidays 10–5, or by appointment
winemaker Mary Byrnes **production** 1500 **est.** 1991
product range ($15–20 CD) Rosé, Shiraz, Liqueur Muscat.
summary Mary Byrnes, who has a wine science degree, acquired her property in 1991, subsequently planting 4 hectares of shiraz, and 1 hectare each of marsanne, viognier, roussanne and mourvèdre, topping the planting off with 0.5 hectare of grenache and 0.5 hectare of black hamburg muscat. She has deliberately grown the vines without irrigation, thereby limiting yield and (in her words) ensuring a distinctive regional quality and flavour. The wines are sold via mail order and the cellar door.

massoni wines ★★★★

32 Brasser Avenue, Dromana, Vic 3936 **region** Mornington Peninsula
phone (03) 5981 8008 **fax** (03) 5981 8015 **open** By appointment
winemaker Ian Home, Sam Tyrrell **production** 6000 **est.** 1984
product range ($17–40 R) Chardonnay, Pinot Noir, Lectus Cuvée are the top wines; also Homes Chardonnay, Pinot Noir, Shiraz, Merlot and Cabernet Merlot.
summary The changes have continued to flow after Ian Home (best known as the founder of Yellowglen) acquired the remaining 50 per cent of Massoni from former restaurateur Leon Massoni. There are now two ranges of wines, and (quite sensibly) the Shiraz and Cabernet Merlot releases are in whole or in part sourced from outside the Mornington Peninsula (from Langhorne Creek). The flagships continue to be the Chardonnay, Pinot Noir and Lectus Cuvée. Exports to the US.

Homes Chardonnay
TTTT 2000 Light to medium green-yellow; a clean and crisp bouquet opens with melon and grapefruit, with hints of smoky oak and cashew mlf. The elegant, light to medium-bodied palate is focussed on cool-grown citrussy fruit, with an appropriately subtle touch of oak. **rating:** 88
best drinking 2001–2005 **best vintages** NA **drink with** Stir-fried prawns • $19

Massoni Main Creek Pinot Noir
TTTT 1999 Light to medium red, with just a touch of purple remaining. The clean, gentle bouquet shows clear strawberry/cherry fruit and neatly controlled oak. The palate has a slightly more savoury cast to it, with good balance and length, aided by feathery tannins on the finish. **rating:** 87
best drinking 2001–2004 **best vintages** '91, '92, '93, '94, '96, '97 **drink with** Pot-roasted quail • $40

Homes Pinot Noir
TTTT 2000 Medium red, showing the first signs of development as the purple drops out. The very ripe strawberry and cherry fruit of the bouquet flows through into the palate, where some greener, stemmy characters make their appearance towards the slightly tart finish. If it all comes together, could be quite delicious. **rating:** 87
best drinking 2001–2004 **best vintages** NA **drink with** Smoked duck • $19

matilda's meadow ★★★☆

Eladon Brook Estate, RMB 654 Hamilton Road, Denmark, WA 6333 **region** Great Southern
phone (08) 9848 1951 **fax** (08) 9848 1957 **open** 7 days 10–5
winemaker Brenden Smith **production** 1500 **est.** 1990

product range ($13–25 CD) Semillon Sauvignon Blanc, Unwooded Chardonnay, Late Picked Riesling, Autumn Amethyst (light red), Pinot Noir, Cabernet Sauvignon Shiraz, Cabernet Sauvignon Cabernet Franc, Tawny Port Muscat blend.

summary Former hotelier Don Turnbull and oil-industry executive Pamela Meldrum have quickly established a thriving business at Matilda's Meadow, based on 6 hectares of estate plantings and with a restaurant offering morning and afternoon teas and lunches every day.

Matilda's Meadow Unwooded Chardonnay

▼▼▼▽ **2001** Bright, light green-yellow; varietally correct melon and citrus fruit aromas are followed by a fresh palate, inevitably lacking complexity, but with nice fruit and fair length. **rating:** 84

best drinking 2002–2004 **best vintages** NA **drink with** Tempura • $16

Matilda's Meadow Cabernet Sauvignon Cabernet Franc

▼▼▼▽ **2000** Medium red-purple; the clean bouquet has cedary fragrance; the palate has a mix of berry, mint and chocolate, finishing with fine tannins and the barest suggestion of oak. **rating:** 84

best drinking 2003–2006 **best vintages** '95, '98 **drink with** Beef sirloin • $22.50

Matilda's Meadow Cabernet Sauvignon Shiraz

▼▼▼▼ **2000** Medium red-purple; distinct spice from the shiraz component is offset against the fresh, dark berry cabernet fruit aromas. The palate has good substance, with sweet berry fruit and ripe tannins, the oak merely an observer. **rating:** 88

best drinking 2004–2008 **best vintages** NA **drink with** Devilled kidneys • $22

mawarra NR

69 Short Road, Gisborne, Vic 3437 **region** Macedon Ranges
phone (03) 5428 2228 **fax** (03) 9621 1413 **open** 7 days 10–5
winemaker John Ellis (Contract) **production** 1000 **est.** 1978
product range Semillon, Chardonnay, Pinot Noir.
summary Bob Nixon began the development of Mawarra way back in 1978, planting his dream vineyard row by row, then acre by acre. The early years were difficult, but he persevered, and has now established chardonnay, semillon and pinot noir. A cellar door was always part of the scheme, and he just happens to be married to Barbara Nixon, founder of Victoria Winery Tours – she has been in and out of cellar doors around Australia with greater frequency than any other living person. So it is that the tasting room has 8 foot wide shaded verandahs, plenty of windows and sweeping views of the Chardonnay Bowl and Semillon Flats. Deli-style foods are offered, all pre-packaged, featuring meats, cheese, antipasto and biscuits.

Mawarra Chardonnay Semillon

▼▼▼▼ **1998** Light to medium yellow-green; lemony/herbal/grassy aromas lead into a palate still very crisp and fresh, the flavours following on precisely from the bouquet. **rating:** 85

best drinking 2001–2004 **best vintages** NA **drink with** Vegetable terrine • NA

mawson ridge NR

24–28 Main Road, Hahndorf, SA 5066 **region** Adelaide Hills
phone (08) 8362 7826 **fax** (08) 8362 7588 **open** By appointment
winemaker Nepenthe (contract) **production** 400 **est.** 1998
product range ($18–30 R) Sauvignon Blanc, Chardonnay, Pinot Noir.
summary You might be forgiven for thinking the winery name carries the cool-climate association a little bit too far. In fact, Sir Douglas Mawson, also a conservationist and forester, arrived in the Lenswood region in the early 1930s, harvesting the native stringybarks for hardwood and replanting the cleared land with pine trees. A hut that Mawson built on the property still stands today on Mawson Road, the road which the vineyard fronts. Here Raymond and Madeline Marin have established 3.5 hectares of vines, with contract winemaking by Peter Leske of Nepenthe Vineyards.

🐌 maximilian's vineyard ★★★★

Main Road, Verdun, SA 5245 **region** Adelaide Hills
phone (08) 8388 7777 **fax** (08) 8388 1371 **open** Wed–Sun 10–5
winemaker Contract **production** 1500 **est.** 1994
product range ($19–21 CD) Chardonnay, Cabernet Sauvignon.

summary Maximilian and Louise Hruska opened Maximilian's Restaurant in 1976, accommodated in a homestead built in 1851. Two hectares of chardonnay and 6 hectares of cabernet sauvignon were planted in 1994, and surround the restaurant. The Cabernet Sauvignon is made by Grant Burge, the Chardonnay at Scarpantoni Estate under the direction of the Hruskas' eldest son Paul. Since graduating from Roseworthy, Paul Hruska has completed vintages in Burgundy, Spain, Margaret River and the Clare Valley, and when he finally decides to come home, an on-site winery will be developed.

Maximilian's Vineyard Chardonnay

TTTT 2000 Light to medium yellow-green; the bouquet has obvious charry barrel–ferment oak, but it is not totally over the top; the palate is quite sophisticated, with creamy/nutty characters, and again some charry oak; the underlying intensity of the fruit results in a fairly stylish wine, especially in food context. **rating:** 88

best drinking 2001–2003 **best vintages** NA **drink with** Prawns Florentine • $21.50

maxwell wines ★★★☆

Olivers Road, McLaren Vale, SA 5171 **region** McLaren Vale
phone (08) 8323 8200 **fax** (08) 8323 8900 **open** 7 days 10–5
winemaker Mark Day, Mark Maxwell **production** 10 000 **est.** 1979
product range ($8–28 CD) Under the Maxwell Wines brand, Twenty 20 Semillon, Verdelho, Frontignac Spätlese, Chardonnay, Cabernet Merlot, Reserve Shiraz; Ellen Street Shiraz, 4 Roads Shiraz, Lime Cave Cabernet Sauvignon; and excellent Dry Mead, Honey Mead, Spiced Mead, Liqueur Mead and Old Tawny Port.
summary Maxwell Wines has come a long way since opening for business in 1979 using an amazing array of Heath Robinson equipment in cramped surroundings. A state-of-the-art and infinitely larger winery was built on a new site in time for the 1997 vintage, which was appropriate for a brand which has produced some excellent white and red wines in recent years. Exports to the US, Canada, the UK, Switzerland, Austria, Germany, Belgium, Hong Kong, Singapore, Thailand and New Zealand.

Maxwell Ellen Street Shiraz

TTTT 1999 Medium red-purple; the moderately intense bouquet has simple berry fruit and slightly edgy oak, but the palate comes up with much more sweet fruit, although the oak is still a touch raspy. Should settle down with time. **rating:** 88

best drinking 2004–2009 **best vintages** '82, '88, '91, '92, '94, '98 **drink with** Kangaroo • $24.99

Maxwell 4 Roads Shiraz

TTTT 2000 Medium to full red-purple; a ripe bouquet has a mix of prune, dried fruit and spice aromas; the palate is fleshy and mouthfilling, with more of those prune and chocolate flavours. A very flavoursome early- drinking style. **rating:** 85

best drinking 2001–2003 **best vintages** NA **drink with** Steak and kidney pie • $17.50

Maxwell Lime Cave Cabernet Sauvignon

TTTT 2000 Medium to full red-purple; clean, nicely ripened cassis fruit on the bouquet is followed by a firm palate, with cassis berry flavours but a somewhat angular structure that needs to soften and loosen up. **rating:** 85

best drinking 2004–2009 **best vintages** NA **drink with** Stir-fried beef • $23

m. chapoutier australia ★★★★☆

PO Box 437, Robe, SA 5276 (postal) **region** Mount Benson
phone (08) 8768 5076 **fax** (08) 8768 5073 **open** Not
winemaker Jean Philippe Archambaud **production** 5000 **est.** 1998
product range ($25–28 R) Shiraz, Cabernet Sauvignon.
summary This is one of several winemaking ventures the famous Rhône Valley firm of M. Chapoutier is establishing in Australia. A large vineyard comprising 15 hectares of shiraz, 10 hectares of cabernet sauvignon, 4 hectares each of marsanne and viognier and 2 hectares of sauvignon blanc is in the course of establishment, using biodynamic farming methods. For the time being winemaker Jean Philippe Archambaud makes the wines at nearby Cape Jaffa; exports to Europe, Asia, the US, New Zealand, Kong Kong, Japan, Singapore and Indonesia. Australian distribution through David Ridge Wines and Aria Wine Co.

M. Chapoutier Australia Mount Benson Shiraz

TTTTY **2000** Deep, vibrant purple-red, the signature of this wine; the satin-smooth bouquet is driven by red berry fruit; the palate has abundant, deliciously sweet, dark cherry fruit sustained by very good tannins and oak. Has improved with each succeeding vintage. **rating:** 93

best drinking 2003–2010 **best vintages** '99, '00 **drink with** Osso buco • $24

M. Chapoutier Australia Mount Benson Cabernet Sauvignon

TTTT **2000** Dense red-purple; the bouquet has a strange aroma, ever so faintly fishy, but also earthy. The palate throws off the question marks of the bouquet, with concentrated cassis/blackberry fruit which is almost essency, accompanied by a touch of spice. A difficult wine to give points to – you could add or subtract several points either way. **rating:** 89

best drinking 2004–2010 **best vintages** NA **drink with** Roast lamb • $27

meadowbank estate ★★★★☆

699 Richmond Road, Cambridge, Tas 7170 **region** Southern Tasmania
phone (03) 6248 4484 **fax** (03) 6248 4485 **open** 7 days 10–5
winemaker Andrew Hood (Contract) **production** 6000 **est.** 1974
product range ($22–32 CD) Riesling, Sauvignon Blanc, Unwooded Chardonnay, Grace Elizabeth Chardonnay, Mardi Mèthode Champenoise, Pinot Noir, Henry James Pinot Noir, Cabernet Sauvignon.
summary Now an important part of the Ellis family business on what was once (but is no more) a large grazing property on the banks of the Derwent. Increased plantings are being established under contract to BRL Hardy, and a splendid new winery has been built to handle the increased production, with wine quality consistently excellent. The winery has expansive entertainment and function facilities, capable of handling up to 1000 people, and offers an ongoing arts and music programme throughout the year, plus a large restaurant that is open 7 days.

Meadowbank Sauvignon Blanc

TTTTY **2001** Pale straw-green; a striking and aromatic bouquet of passionfruit and gooseberry leads into a fresh, lively and elegant palate with a mix of passionfruit and a hint of green grass, which in no way detracts. **rating:** 91

best drinking 2001–2003 **best vintages** '01 **drink with** Tuna sashimi • $25

Meadowbank Unwooded Chardonnay

TTTY **2001** Light to medium green-yellow; an elegant and aromatic bouquet with stone fruit and citrus changes little on the palate, providing citrus/melon fruit and a distinctly minerally finish. **rating:** 84

best drinking 2002–2004 **best vintages** NA **drink with** Diced chicken • $24

Meadowbank Grace Elizabeth Chardonnay

TTTT **2001** Very light green-straw; a delicate, restrained bouquet with crisp melon and citrus supported by the faintest backdrop of oak, then a similarly delicate, balanced and restrained palate in slow-developing mode; will offer more in the years ahead. **rating:** 89

TTTTT **2000** Light but bright colour; it has fresh, fine, nectarine/stonefruit aromas, and an elegant palate, modulated and rounded. Fruit-driven, but with real finesse and length. Trophy Best White Wine, 2002 Tasmanian Wines Show. **rating:** 95

best drinking 2004–2009 **best vintages** '93, '95, '97, '00 **drink with** Fresh Tasmanian salmon • $30

Meadowbank Wines Mardi Mèthode Champenoise

TTTT **1999** Light to medium yellow-green; there are faintly hard, minerally aspects to the bouquet, but a very different expression on the palate, with much sweeter fruit and balancing dosage. Strong silver medal 2001 Tasmanian Wines Show. **rating:** 89

best drinking 2002–2003 **best vintages** NA **drink with** Shellfish • $32

Meadowbank Pinot Noir

TTTTY **2001** Excellent purple-red; the bouquet is clean, with plum, dark cherry fruit and subtle oak in a linear style; there is more texture and structure to the plummy palate, with very fine tannins and sure oak handling. **rating:** 90

TTTT **2000** Light to medium red-purple; the moderately intense bouquet is clean and fresh, the fruit coming bursting through on the palate with an array of sweet, ripe plum and red cherry fruit, promising further development and increased complexity with a few years' bottle age. **rating:** 88

best drinking 2003–2007 **best vintages** '98, '00, '01 **drink with** Roast squab • $26

Meadowbank Henry James Pinot Noir
▼▼▼▼▽ **2000** Light to medium red-purple; the stylish bouquet is moderately intense, with savoury/sappy/spicy aromas and hints of the plum which comes through on the medium-weight palate; a savoury/spicy finish. **rating:** 90

best drinking 2002–2005 **best vintages** '94, '98, '99, '00 **drink with** Rabbit casserole • $33

Meadowbank Cabernet Sauvignon
▼▼▼▼▽ **2000** Youthful, medium purple-red; a clean and fresh bouquet with bright red berry fruits, then a similarly focussed palate with fresh, sweet fruit and quite supple, fine tannins. Excellent outcome for the variety in the Tasmanian context. **rating:** 90

best drinking 2004–2010 **best vintages** '99, '00 **drink with** Barbecued steak • $26

meerea park ★★★★
Lot 3 Palmers Lane, Pokolbin, NSW 2320 **region** Lower Hunter Valley
phone (02) 4998 7474 **fax** (02) 4930 7100 **open** At The Boutique Wine Centre, Broke Road, Pokolbin 9–5
winemaker Rhys Eather **production** 10 000 **est.** 1991
product range ($18.50–45 R) Epoch Semillon, Lindsay Hill Viognier, Alexander Munro Chardonnay, The Aunts Shiraz, Alexander Munro Shiraz, Cabernet Merlot.
summary An interesting operation, selling its substantial production primarily through The Boutique Wine Centre, Broke Road, Pokolbin, and by mailing list. All of the wines are produced from grapes purchased from growers, primarily in the Broke/Fordwich region, but also from as far afield as McLaren Vale, the Barossa Valley, Mudgee and Orange. It is the brainchild of Rhys Eather, great-grandson of Alexander Munro, a leading vigneron in the middle of the 19th century, and who makes the wine in Simon Gilbert's contract winery. Retail distribution through the principal states, and the wines are exported to the UK, Switzerland, the US, New Zealand and Asia.

Meerea Park Epoch Semillon
▼▼▼▼ **2001** Light to medium yellow-green; a clean, quite sweet and fragrant bouquet with lemony/citrussy fruit; the tangy palate is lifted by a touch of spritz which also serves to highlight some minerally notes and lengthen the finish. **rating:** 88
▼▼▼▼ **2000** Light to medium green-yellow; the ripe, clean bouquet has pronounced citrus tones; the palate has well above average density of flavour, promising relatively quick development in an alternative but worthwhile style, which can only come from vintages such as 2000. **rating:** 89

best drinking 2002–2005 **best vintages** '00 **drink with** Lemon chicken • $18.50

Meerea Park Alexander Munro Chardonnay
▼▼▼▼ **2000** Light green-yellow; strong, smoky barrel-ferment oak comes through strongly on the bouquet, but fresh melon fruit and a touch of citrus make a strong comeback on the palate, where the oak is less assertive though certainly present. well-balanced acidity. **rating:** 87

best drinking 2002–2004 **best vintages** NA **drink with** Marinated octopus • $25

Meerea Park Alexander Munro Shiraz
▼▼▼▼ **1999** Strong, bright red-purple; a strong and moderately complex bouquet with dark berries in nicely ripened mode. The textured, powerful palate has rich plum fruit, well-integrated oak and sustaining tannins. **rating:** 89

best drinking 2004–2011 **best vintages** '97, '98, '99 **drink with** Braised beef • $45

Meerea Park The Aunts Shiraz
▼▼▼▼ **2000** Bright purple-red; clean, moderately sweet dark berry and plum fruit on the bouquet, with subtle oak, precede a palate which is slightly firmer than the bouquet suggests, although still in the plum spectrum. Needs time for some faint green tinges to be absorbed. **rating:** 86
▼▼▼▼ **1999** Medium red-purple; the moderately intense bouquet has dark, slightly foresty, fruit aromas offset by a touch of vanilla oak. The medium to full-bodied palate is, once again, centred around plum and raspberry fruit; the oak is well-balanced and well-integrated. **rating:** 87

best drinking 2002–2009 **best vintages** NA **drink with** Braised beef • $30

Meerea Park Cabernet Merlot
ŦŦŦŦ **2000** Medium red-purple; clean, firm raspberry and redcurrant fruit carries the bouquet. An interesting wine on the palate, where tannins grip early and then seem to recede, helped in part by some deft oak use. A blend of Langhorne Creek, Hunter Valley and Orange grapes. **rating:** 85

best drinking 2003–2007 **best vintages** NA **drink with** Braised veal • $22

melaleuca grove ★★★★

8 Melaleuca Court, Rowville, Vic 3178 **region** Central Victorian High Country
phone (03) 9752 7928 **fax** (03) 9752 7928 **open** Not
winemaker Jeff Wright **production** 800 **est.** 1999
product range ($16 ML) Chardonnay, Shiraz, Cabernet Sauvignon.
summary Jeff and Anne Wright are both honours graduates in biochemistry who have succumbed to the lure of winemaking after lengthy careers elsewhere. He commenced his winemaking apprenticeship in 1997 at Green Vineyards, backed up by further vintage work in 1999 and 2000 at Bianchet and Yarra Valley Hills, both in the Yarra Valley. At the same time he began the external Bachelor of Applied Science (Wine Science) course at Charles Sturt University, while continuing to work in biochemistry in the public hospital system. In both 1999 and 2000 the Wrights purchased grapes from Thomson's Vineyard at Limestone (near Yea) in the Central Victorian Mountain Country region, releasing their first two wines from the 1999 vintage. They are available through slected Melbourne retailers and restaurants, and by mailing list.

Melaleuca Grove Yea Valley Chardonnay
ŦŦŦŦ **2000** Light to medium yellow-green; the bouquet offers a subtle interplay of oak and malolactic influences; the palate is in similar mode, with sweet melon fruit and nicely controlled inputs, giving a rounded, sophisticated feel. **rating:** 89

best drinking 2002–2004 **best vintages** NA **drink with** Mussel soup • $16

Melaleuca Grove Yea Valley Cabernet Sauvignon
ŦŦŦŦ **2000** Medium purple-red; clean, moderately intense cassis/red berry aromas are followed logically by a palate with nicely ripened cassis fruit, subtle oak and good tannins. **rating:** 87

best drinking 2002–2007 **best vintages** NA **drink with** Barbecued lamb chops • $16

merrebee estate ★★★☆

Lot 3339 St Werburghs Road, Mount Barker, WA 6234 **region** Great Southern
phone (08) 9851 2424 **fax** (08) 9851 2425 **open** By appointment
winemaker Brenden Smith (Contract) **production** 3000 **est.** 1986
product range ($15–23 CD) Riesling, Giles Point Sauvignon Blanc Chardonnay, Chardonnay, Giles Point Unwooded Chardonnay, Mount Barker Chardonnay, Shiraz.
summary Planting of the Merrebee Estate vineyards commenced in 1986; it has now reached a little under 9 hectares. The wines are available from selected retailers in WA and from Rathdowne Cellars, Melbourne, and Ultimo Wine Centre, Sydney; exports to the US, Canada and Sweden.

merricks estate ★★★☆

Thompsons Lane, Merricks, Vic 3916 **region** Mornington Peninsula
phone (03) 5989 8416 **fax** (03) 9606 9090 **open** First weekend of each month, each weekend in Jan and public holiday weekends 12–5
winemaker Paul Evans **production** 2500 **est.** 1977
product range ($28–33 CD) Chardonnay, Pinot Noir, Shiraz, Cabernet Sauvignon.
summary Melbourne solicitor George Kefford, together with wife Jacquie, runs Merricks Estate as a weekend and holiday enterprise, as a relief from professional practice. Right from the outset it has produced distinctive, spicy, cool-climate Shiraz which has accumulated an impressive array of show trophies and gold medals.

merrivale wines ★★★

Olivers Road, McLaren Vale, SA 5171 **region** McLaren Vale
phone (08) 8323 9196 **fax** (08) 8323 9746 **open** 7 days 11–5
winemaker Contract **production** 10 000 **est.** 1971

product range ($10–18 CD) Under the Tapestry label Riesling, Chardonnay, Tapestry Spätlese, Tapestry Shiraz, Tapestry Cabernet Shiraz, Tapestry Cabernet Sauvignon, Muscat of Alexandria, Old Tawny Port, Brian Light Reserve Shiraz.

summary After a relatively brief period of ownership by Brian Light and family, the winery has been acquired by the Gerard family, former owners of Chapel Hill.

merum ★★★★☆

Hillbrook Road, Quinninup, WA 6258 **region** Manjimup

phone (08) 9776 6011 **fax** (08) 9776 6022 **open** By appointment

winemaker Jan Davies **production** 1000 **est.** 1996

product range ($22–28 ML) Semillon, Shiraz.

summary Merum was founded by the late Maria Melsom (formerly winemaker at Driftwood Estate) and Michael Melsom (former vineyard manager for Voyager Estate, both in the Margaret River region). The 6.3 hectares of vineyard (3.3 shiraz, 2 semillon, 1 chardonnay) was planted in 1996, and the first wine made in 1999. The quality of the wines so far released has been truly excellent. The tragic death of Maria Melsom through a car accident in 2001 leaves Michael with a tough job, but he intends to carry on the work. (In the first printing of the 2003 *Wine Companion* I incorrectly wrote that it was Michael who died, and I wish to publicly apologise for the undoubted hurt and embarrassment this error has caused.)

metcalfe valley NR

283 Metcalfe–Malmsbury Road, Metcalfe, Vic 3448 **region** Macedon Ranges

phone NA **open** Not

winemaker John Frederickson **production** 100 **est.** 1994

product range Shiraz.

summary John Frederickson (a social worker in the drug and alcohol area) and wife Marilyn Frederickson (a children's literacy consultant) began the development of their 6-hectare vineyard 7 years ago. It is situated in the far northeast corner of what may become the Macedon Ranges region, hard up against the Heathcote/Bendigo boundaries. Shiraz is typically harvested in the last week of April, underlining the unambiguously cool nature of the region. Most of the production is sold to Virgin Hills, but over the 2000 and 2001 vintages, a tiny amount has been kept back and made into wine by John Frederickson. Refined but spicy and complex, it is worth pursuing.

Metcalfe Valley Shiraz

TTTTY **2000** Medium to full red-purple; cool climate spicy/gamey/savoury/plummy aromas flow through in abundance to the palate, which has soft tannins and subtle oak to support the complexity of the fruit. This is the climate speaking, not brettanomyces, as some might suggest. **rating:** 90

best drinking 2003–2009 **best vintages** '00 **drink with** Game pie • NA

metier wines ★★★★★

Tarraford Vineyard, 440 Healesville Road, Yarra Glen, Vic 3775 **region** Yarra Valley

phone (03) 5962 2461 **fax** (03) 5962 2194 **open** Not

winemaker Martin Williams **production** 1400 **est.** 1995

product range ($29.50–35 R) Viognier, Tarraford Vineyard Chardonnay, Schoolhouse Vineyard Chardonnay, Tarraford Vineyard Pinot Noir.

summary Metier is the French word for craft, trade or profession; the business is that of Yarra Valley-based winemaker Martin Williams MW, who has notched up an array of degrees and winemaking stints in France, California and Australia which are, not to put too fine a word on it, extraordinary. The focus of Metier is to produce individual vineyard wines, initially based on grapes from the Tarraford and Schoolhouse Vineyards, both in the Yarra Valley. The quality of the Viognier, Pinot Noir and Chardonnay is extremely high.

Metier Wines Pinot Noir

TTTTT **1999** Medium red-purple; complex, ripe dark plum and spices on the bouquet play again on the very powerful, very complex palate which, while slightly grippy, is most impressive. Needs time. **rating:** 94

best drinking 2003–2009 **best vintages** '99 **drink with** Roast squab • $35

miceli ★★★★

60 Main Creek Road, Arthurs Seat, Vic 3936 **region** Mornington Peninsula
phone (03) 5989 2755 **fax** (03) 5989 2755 **open** First weekend each month 12–5, public holidays, and also every weekend and by appointment in Jan
winemaker Anthony Miceli **production** 1500 **est.** 1991
product range ($17–25 CD) Iolanda's Pinot Grigio, Unwooded Chardonnay, Olivia's Chardonnay, Lucy's Choice Pinot Noir.
summary This may be a part-time labour of love for general practitioner Dr Anthony Miceli, but this hasn't prevented him taking the whole venture very seriously. He acquired the property in 1989 specifically for the purpose of establishing a vineyard, carrying out the first plantings of 1.8 hectares in November 1991, followed by a further hectare of pinot gris in 1997. Ultimately the vineyard will be increased to 5 hectares, with a projected production of 2500–3000 cases a year. Between 1991 and 1997 Dr Miceli enrolled in and thereafter graduated from the Wine Science course at Charles Sturt University, and thus manages both vineyard and winery. Retail distribution through fine wine outlets and restaurants in Melbourne.

michelini wines ★★★

Great Alpine Road, Myrtleford, Vic 3737 **region** Alpine Valleys
phone (03) 5751 1990 **fax** (03) 5751 1410 **open** 7 days 10–5 (except Christmas Day and New Year's Day)
winemaker Greg O'Keefe (Contract) **production** 3500 **est.** 1982
product range ($13.50–20 CD) Riesling, Unwooded Chardonnay, Chardonnay, Pinot Noir, Marzemino, Shiraz, Merlot, Cabernet Sauvignon, Fragolino.
summary The Michelini family are among the best-known grape growers in the Buckland Valley of northeast Victoria. Having migrated from Italy in 1949, the Michelinis originally grew tobacco, diversifying into vineyards in 1982. A little over 42 hectares of vineyard have been established on terra rossa soil at an altitude of 300 metres, mostly with frontage to the Buckland River. The major part of the production is sold (to Orlando and others), but since 1996 an on-site winery has permitted the Michelinis to vinify part of their production. The winery in fact has capacity to handle 1000 tonnes of fruit, thereby eliminating the problem of moving grapes out of a declared phylloxera area.

Michelini Cabernet Sauvignon

▼▼▼▽ **1999** Medium red, with just a touch of purple. The bouquet has a mix of light raspberry/blackcurrant fruit with more leafy/earthy/cedary overtones. On the palate, pleasant raspberry and red and blackcurrant fruit flavours are supported by gentle tannins and subtle oak. **rating:** 84

best drinking 2003–2007 **best vintages** NA **drink with** Ragout of veal • $18.50

middlebrook NR

RSD 43, Sand Road, McLaren Vale, SA 5171 **region** McLaren Vale
phone (08) 8383 0600 **fax** (08) 8383 0557 **open** Mon–Fri 9–5, weekends 10–5
winemaker Joseph Cogno **production** 12,000 **est.** 1947
product range ($14–20 CD) At the top come Middlebrook Pinot Chardonnay, Unwooded Semillon, Sauvignon Blanc, Chardonnay, Frontignac, Shiraz and Cabernet Sauvignon; then cheaper wines under the Cogno label.
summary After a brief period of ownership by industry veteran Bill Clappis (who renovated and reopened the winery), ownership has now passed to the Cogno Brothers Family, which has been winemaking at Cobbity near Camden, NSW, since 1964. Through Middlebrook, the family has become one of the largest producers of Lambrusco in Australia; it is available Australia-wide through Liquorland stores. Many other wines (18 in all) are produced under the Cogno Brothers label; while the Middlebrook cask hall has been given over to production of the Medlow chocolate range. The top wines are still sold under the Middlebrook label.

middleton estate NR

Flagstaff Hill Road, Middleton, SA 5213 **region** Currency Creek
phone (08) 8555 4136 **fax** (08) 8555 4108 **open** Fri–Sun 11–5
winemaker Nigel Catt **production** 3000 **est.** 1979
product range ($9–16 CD) Riesling, Sauvignon Blanc, Semillon Sauvignon Blanc, Cabernet Hermitage.
summary Nigel Catt has demonstrated his winemaking skills at Andrew Garrett and elsewhere, so wine quality should be good; despite its decade of production, I have never seen or tasted its wines. A winery restaurant helps the business turnover.

milburn park ★★★

Campbell Avenue, Irymple, Vic 3498 **region** Murray Darling
phone (03) 5024 6800 **fax** (03) 5024 6605 **open** Mon–Sat 10–4.30
winemaker Krister Jonsson, Gary Magilton **production** 2 million **est.** 1977
product range ($4–15 R) Top-end wines under the Milburn Park label are Chardonnay, Pinot Noir Chardonnay, Shiraz and Cabernet Sauvignon; then comes the standard Salisbury Estate range of Riesling Dry, Sauvignon Blanc, Chardonnay, Shiraz, Merlot, Grenache, Cabernet Sauvignon, Cabernet Merlot; then there is the Castle Ridge range, consisting of Colombard Chardonnay, Shiraz Malbec Mourvèdre; Acacia Ridge non-vintage generics bring up the rear, with two wines in the Tennyson Vineyard off to one side.
summary Part of a widespread group of companies owned by Cranswick Premium Wines Limited, with a strong export focus.

Salisbury Estate Merlot

▼▼▼▽ 2001 Light to medium red-purple; sweet, juicy berry fruit on the bouquet, then light but very sweet berry fruit on the palate, combined with a touch of oak, all adding up to a cleverly made wine which represents good value. **rating:** 82

best drinking 2002–2003 **best vintages** NA **drink with** Takeaway • $9

mildara (murray darling) ★★★

Wentworth Road, Merbein, Vic 3505 **region** Murray Darling
phone (03) 5021 9332 **fax** (03) 5021 1300 **open** Mon–Fri 9–5, weekends 10–4
winemaker David Tierney **production** NFP **est.** 1888
product range ($10.50–27.50 R) Under the Mildara label are Chardonnay, Shiraz, Coonawarra Cabernet Sauvignon; Half Mile Creek Verdelho, Chardonnay, Shiraz, Cabernet Merlot; Mount Helen Chardonnay, Cabernet Sauvignon Merlot; Church Hill Chardonnay, Cabernet Shiraz; also makes fine Sherries (Chestnut Teal, George and Supreme) and superb Pot Still Brandy.
summary A somewhat antiquated Merbein facility remains the overall group production centre, although all of its premium wines are sourced from and made at Coonawarra.

Mildara Mount Helen Chardonnay

▼▼▼▼ 2000 Medium yellow-green; the moderately intense bouquet is clean and smooth, but somewhat simple; the palate is a replay, with smooth stone fruit flavours in an uncomplicated style. **rating:** 86

best drinking 2001–2002 **best vintages** NA **drink with** Salmon pizza • $21

Mount Helen Cabernet Merlot

▼▼▼▼▽ 1998 Medium to full red-purple; it has attractive, gently cedary/spicy fruit and oak aromas flowing into an elegant, medium-bodied palate with ripe berry/cassis fruit, fine tannins and good length.

rating: 93

best drinking 2003–2008 **best vintages** '98 **drink with** Lamb shoulder • $24

milford vineyard ★★★★

Tasman Highway, Cambridge, Tas 7170 **region** Southern Tasmania
phone (03) 6248 5029 **fax** (03) 6224 2331 **open** Not
winemaker Andrew Hood (Contract) **production** 200 **est.** 1984
product range ($21.75 R) Pinot Noir.
summary Given the tiny production, Milford is understandably not open to the public, the excellent Pinot Noir being quickly sold by word of mouth. The 150-hectare grazing property (the oldest Southdown sheep stud in Australia) has been in Charlie Lewis's family since 1830. Only 15 minutes from Hobart, and with an absolute water frontage to the tidal estuary of the Coal River, it is a striking site. The vineyard is established on a patch of 5-foot-deep sand over a clay base with lots of lime impregnation.

Milford Vineyard Pinot Noir

▼▼▼▼ 2000 Light to medium red-purple; a clean, slightly simple bouquet with cherry fruit, then a pleasant and correct palate with more of the cherry promised by the bouquet, but lacking the intensity of the better wines of the vintage. **rating:** 85

best drinking 2002–2003 **best vintages** '96, '98 **drink with** Ravioli • $22

milimani estate NR

92 The Forest Road, Bungendore, NSW 2621 **region** Canberra District
phone (02) 6238 1421 **fax** (02) 6238 1424 **open** Weekends and public holidays 10–4
winemaker Lark Hill (Contract) **production** 700 **est.** 1989
product range ($12.50–17 CD) Sauvignon Blanc, Chardonnay, Pinot Noir, Cabernet Franc Merlot.
summary The Preston family (Mary, David and Rosemary) have established a 4-hectare vineyard planted to sauvignon blanc, chardonnay, pinot noir, merlot and cabernet franc. Contract winemaking at Lark Hill guarantees the quality of the wine.

millers samphire NR

Cnr Watts Gully and Robertson Roads, Kersbrook, SA 5231 **region** Adelaide Hills
phone (08) 8389 3183 **fax** (08) 8389 3183 **open** 7 days 9–5 by appointment
winemaker Tom Miller **production** 70 **est.** 1982
product range ($9 CD) Riesling.
summary Next after Scarp Valley, one of the smallest wineries in Australia offering wine for sale; pottery also helps. Tom Miller has an interesting and diverse CV, with an early interest in matters alcoholic leading to the premature but happy death of a laboratory rat at Adelaide University and his enforced switch from biochemistry to mechanical engineering. The Riesling is a high-flavoured wine with crushed herb and lime aromas and flavours.

millfield ★★★☆

Lot 341 Mount View Road, Millfield, NSW 2325 **region** Lower Hunter Valley
phone (02) 4998 1571 **fax** (02) 4998 0172 **open** Fri–Sun 10–4
winemaker David Lowe **production** 5000 **est.** 1997
product range ($19.50–23 CD) Semillon, Chardonnay, Shiraz.
summary Situated on the picturesque Mount View Road, Millfield made its market debut in June 2000. The neatly labelled and packaged wines have won gold medals and trophies right from the first vintage in 1998, and praise from winewriters and critics both in Australia and the UK. The wines are sold both through the cellar door and by mailing list, and through a limited number of fine wine retail outlets and top-quality restaurants. Exports to the UK through Corney & Barrow.

Millfield Semillon

▼▼▼▽ **2001** Light to medium green-yellow; the bouquet is quite full and soft, with citrus and a touch of mineral; the palate is light, clean, smooth and well-balanced. **rating:** 84

best drinking 2002–2007 **best vintages** '98, '99 **drink with** Fresh asparagus with hollandaise sauce • $19.50

Millfield Shiraz

▼▼▼▼ **2000** Medium red-purple; plum, mint and cherry aromas are out of the Hunter mainstream, more often encountered in cooler southern regions. On the palate, quite penetrating fruit flavours in a similar taste spectrum underpin the bouquet, with touches of cedar here and there. **rating:** 87

best drinking 2003–2008 **best vintages** NA **drink with** Beef stroganoff • $23

millinup estate ★★★★

RMB 1280 Porongurup Road, Porongurup, WA 6324 **region** Great Southern
phone (08) 9853 1105 **fax** (08) 9853 1105 **open** Weekends 10–5
winemaker Rob Lee (Contract) **production** 200 **est.** 1989
product range ($14–20 CD) Twin Peaks Riesling, Old Cottage Riesling, Cabernet Sauvignon Merlot, Cabernet Sauvignon Cabernet Franc Merlot.
summary The Millinup Estate vineyard was planted in 1978, when it was called Point Creek. Owners Peter and Lesley Thorn purchased it in 1989, renaming it and having the limited production (from 0.5 hectare of riesling, supplemented by purchased red grapes) vinified at Plantagenet.

Millinup Estate Riesling

▼▼▼▼▽ **2000** Light green-yellow; the initially shy, crisp bouquet progressively opens up, initially with gentle, flowery apple aromas and then with some passionfruit to go with the underlying mineral. The palate, too, is very much on the delicate side; it is light, firm and crisp, the fruit intensity fractionally light, but persistent. **rating:** 90

best drinking 2001–2004 **best vintages** '00 **drink with** Trout mousse • $16

minot vineyard   NR

PO Box 683, Margaret River, WA 6285 **region** Margaret River
phone (08) 9757 3579 **fax** (08) 9757 2361 **open** By appointment
winemaker Various Contract **production** 1000 **est.** 1986
product range ($13–20 ML) Semillon Sauvignon Blanc, Cabernet Sauvignon.
summary Minot, which takes its name from a small chateau in the Loire Valley in France, is the husband and wife venture of the Miles family, producing just two wines from the 4.2-hectare plantings of semillon, sauvignon blanc and cabernet sauvignon.

mintaro wines   ★★★☆

Leasingham Road, Mintaro, SA 5415 **region** Clare Valley
phone (08) 8843 9046 **fax** (08) 8843 9050 **open** 7 days 9–5
winemaker Peter Houldsworth **production** 5000 **est.** 1984
product range ($16–24 CD) Riesling, Semillon Chardonnay, Late Picked Riesling, Anastasia's Sparkling Cabernet Shiraz, Shiraz, Reserve Shiraz, Cabernet Sauvignon, Cabernet.
summary Has produced some very good Riesling over the years, developing well in bottle. The red wines are formidable, massive in body and extract, built for the long haul.

miramar   ★★★☆

Henry Lawson Drive, Mudgee, NSW 2850 **region** Mudgee
phone (02) 6373 3874 **fax** (02) 6373 3854 **open** 7 days 9–5
winemaker Ian MacRae **production** 8000 **est.** 1977
product range ($11–35 CD) Riesling, Semillon, Sauvignon Blanc, Chardonnay, Fumé Blanc, Eurunderee Rosé, Shiraz, Cabernet Sauvignon; Doux Blanc (sweet white), Encore and Encore Rouge (Sparkling).
summary Industry veteran Ian MacRae has demonstrated his skill with every type of wine over the decades, ranging from Rosé to Chardonnay to full-bodied reds. All have shone under the Miramar label at one time or another, although the Ides of March are pointing more to the red than the white wines these days. A substantial part of the production from the 33 hectares of estate vineyard is sold to others, the best being retained for Miramar's own use.

miranda wines (barossa)   ★★★★

Barossa Highway, Rowland Flat, SA 5352 **region** Barossa Valley
phone (08) 8524 4537 **fax** (08) 8524 4066 **open** Mon–Fri 10–4.30, weekends 11–4
winemaker Gary Wall, Richard Langford, Mark Murray **production** NFP **est.** 1919
product range ($15–33 R) Premium Late Harvest Riesling; the Grey Series of Riesling, Semillon, Sauvignon Blanc, Chardonnay, Shiraz, Bush Vine Grenache and Cabernet Sauvignon; followed by Show Reserve range of Chardonnay, Old Vine Shiraz and Shiraz Cabernet; The Drainings (Shiraz Cabernet blend).
summary Increasingly absorbed into the Miranda Wine Group since its acquisition, drawing on grapes produced both in the Barossa Valley and throughout other parts of southeast Australia. The accent is on value for money, with consistent show success underlining the quality. Exports to the UK.

Miranda Eden Valley Riesling

▼▼▼▼▽ 2001 Light to medium yellow-green; a firm, very correct bouquet with relatively tight lime and mineral aromas, then a fresh palate with some CO_2 spritz, again quite tight, but with evenly flowing lime juice fruit. Good potential for the medium term; trophy at the 2001 Queensland Wine Show. Well priced.
rating: 91

best drinking 2002–2008 best vintages '01 drink with Salmon roulade $15

Miranda Rovalley Ridge Riesling

▼▼▼▼ 2001 Medium yellow-green; the bouquet is clean and quite rich, with flowery, lime-accented fruit; the palate is soft and flavoursome, tailing off on the finish ever so slightly. An early-developing style.   **rating:** 88
best drinking 2001–2004 best vintages NA drink with Fresh asparagus • $15

Miranda Sparkling Shiraz

▼▼▼▽ 1997 Light to medium red; a light, spicy/berry bouquet with a hint of oak leads into a relatively gentle palate with appealing spicy flavours and soft structure. Not in your face like so many sparkling red wines. A gold medal at the 2001 Cowra Wine Show may have been generous, but you can't complain at the price.   **rating:** 84
best drinking 2002–2003 best vintages NA drink with Hors d'oeuvres • $15

miranda wines (griffith)   ★★★

57 Jondaryan Avenue, Griffith, NSW 2680 **region** Riverina
phone (02) 6960 3000 **fax** (02) 6962 6944 **open** 7 days 9–5
winemaker Gary Wall, Sam F Miranda **production** NFP **est.** 1939
product range ($5–25 R) Top of the range is Show Reserve Chardonnay, Old Vine Shiraz, Shiraz Cabernet; Golden Botrytis; Mirool Creek Dry White, Chardonnay and Cabernet Shiraz; Somerton Riesling Traminer, Semillon Chardonnay, Chardonnay and Shiraz Cabernet; also lower-priced Christy's Land and assorted varietals, generics, sparkling and ports.
summary Miranda Wines continues its aggressive and successful growth strategy, having opened a new winery in the King Valley in 1998 and previously expanded winemaking operations into the Barossa Valley. A veritable cascade of wines now appear under the various brand names, the majority representing good value for money. Exports to Europe, the UK, Canada and the US.

Miranda Somerton Chardonnay

TTTT 2000 Light to medium yellow-green; the clean bouquet has light melon fruit; the palate has good intensity and a degree of sweetness, part from fruit and part from a touch of unfermented sugar. **rating:** 83
best drinking 2001–2002 **best vintages** NA **drink with** KFC • $6.99

Miranda Mirool Creek Reserve Durif

TTTT 2001 Youthful purple-red; the bouquet opens with sweet raspberry fruit, moving more to blackcurrant on the palate, with nicely balanced and handled extract; notwithstanding the variety, an attractive early-consumption style. **rating:** 85
best drinking 2002–2003 **best vintages** NA **drink with** Grilled T-bone • $9.95

miranda wines (king valley)   ★★★

Cnr Snow and Whitfield Roads, Oxley, Vic 3768 **region** King Valley
phone (03) 5727 3399 **fax** (03) 5727 3851 **open** 7 days 10–5
winemaker Luis F Simian (Snr), Luis F Simian, Gary Wall **production** NFP **est.** 1998
product range ($14–20 R) The High Country series of Riesling, Sauvignon Blanc, Chardonnay, Merlot, Shiraz, Cabernet Sauvignon, Dark Horse Cabernet Franc Malbec.
summary Miranda now has three quite separate winemaking entities: the original (and largest) in Griffith; the next in the Barossa Valley; and the most recent in the King Valley. It is at the latter winery that the High Country range is made, using 37 hectares of estate vineyards, supplemented by grapes purchased from elsewhere, including the Kiewa Valley.

Miranda High Country Sauvignon Blanc

TTTT 2000 Light to medium yellow-green; the crisp, light and clean bouquet has grassy/herbal/asparagus aromatics; the palate follows down the same track, being fresh and light, and well-balanced. **rating:** 85
best drinking 2001–2002 **best vintages** NA **drink with** Shellfish • $11.95

Miranda High Country Shiraz

TTTT 1999 Medium red-purple; light, fresh cherry fruit and a flick of oak on the bouquet lead into a light to medium-bodied palate, well crafted in an easy-drinking style, finishing with soft tannins. From the King, Ovens and Kiewa Valleys. **rating:** 84
best drinking 2002–2003 **best vintages** NA **drink with** Grilled meat • $19.95

mistletoe wines   ★★★☆

771 Hermitage Road, Pokolbin, NSW 2320 **region** Lower Hunter Valley
phone (02) 4998 7770 **fax** (02) 4998 7792 **open** 7 days 10–6
winemaker John Cassegrain (Contract) **production** 2500 **est.** 1989
product range ($16–20 CD) Semillon, Silvereye Semillon, Chardonnay, Reserve Chardonnay, The Rosé, Shiraz.
summary Mistletoe Wines, owned by Ken and Gwen Sloan, can trace its history back to 1909, when a substantial vineyard was planted on what was then called Mistletoe Farm. The Mistletoe Farm brand made a brief appearance in the late 1970s but then disappeared; it has now been revived under the Mistletoe Wines label by the Sloans, with contract winemaking providing consistent results. No retail distribution, but worldwide delivery service available ex winery. The art gallery features works by local artists.

Mistletoe Semillon

TTTT 2000 Light straw-green; the clean, quite ripe bouquet has soft, citrus aromas; the palate likewise has plenty of flavour, is well-balanced and has some 'squeaky' mouthfeel. In transition between young and old; well made. **rating: 88**

best drinking 2002–2006 **best vintages** '97 **drink with** Crab, Balmain bugs • $16

Mistletoe The Rosé

TTTP 2001 Light red, with just a tinge of purple; the bouquet is clean though not particularly aromatic; a well- made and balanced wine on the palate, with subliminal sweetness to the berry fruit providing a drop-dead cellar- door style, doubtless helped by avant-garde labelling. For the record, made from 100 per cent Hunter Valley shiraz. Serve slightly chilled. **rating: 83**

best drinking 2002–2003 **best vintages** NA **drink with** Summer cold cuts • $16

Mistletoe Shiraz

TTTT 2000 Bright purple-red, deep but clear; a clean, smooth bouquet with dark plum and blackberry fruit supported by gentle oak. A supple, fruit-driven palate in medium-bodied mode finishes with fine, ripe tannins. Another well-made wine. **rating: 88**

best drinking 2004–2014 **best vintages** NA **drink with** Rare beef • $20

mitchell ★★★★☆

Hughes Park Road, Sevenhill via Clare, SA 5453 **region** Clare Valley
phone (08) 8843 4258 **fax** (08) 8843 4340 **open** 7 days 10–4
winemaker Andrew Mitchell **production** 30 000 **est.** 1975
product range ($17–25 CD) Watervale Riesling, The Growers Semillon, Noble Semillon, Sparkling Peppertree, The Growers Grenache, Peppertree Vineyard Shiraz, Sevenhill Cabernet Sauvignon.
summary For long one of the stalwarts of the Clare Valley, producing long-lived Rieslings and Cabernet Sauvignons in classic regional style but having extended the range with very creditable Semillon and Shiraz. A lovely old stone apple shed provides the cellar door and upper section of the compact winery. Production has increased by 50 per cent over the past few years, and as well as national retail distribution, the wines are exported to the US.

Mitchell Watervale Riesling

TTTTT 2001 Light to medium green-yellow; a firm, crisp, herbal/mineral bouquet, then a powerful and concentrated palate with a lime-juice base, and a long, tight finish. **rating: 94**

best drinking 2004–2011 **best vintages** '78, '84, '90, '92, '93, '94, '95, '00, '01 **drink with** Grilled fish • $19

Mitchell Peppertree Vineyard Shiraz

TTTT 2000 Bright, youthful red-purple; clean berry/cherry fruit with touches of spice, cedar and leaf on the bouquet; tannins run through the palate and into the aftertaste, giving a savoury austerity to the wine. **rating: 87**

best drinking 2004–2009 **best vintages** '84, '86, '87, '94, '95, '96, '99 **drink with** Devilled kidneys • $25

mitchelton ★★★★

Mitchellstown via Nagambie, Vic 3608 **region** Goulburn Valley
phone (03) 5736 2222 **fax** (03) 5736 2266 **open** 7 days 10–5
winemaker Don Lewis, Toby Barlow **production** 200 000 **est.** 1969
product range ($9.95–50 CD) Top-of-the-range is Print Shiraz; then come Chardonnay, Viognier, Shiraz, Airstrip Marsanne Roussanne Viognier, Shiraz, Crescent Shiraz Mourvèdre Grenache, Cabernet Sauvignon, next Blackwood Park Riesling, Blackwood Park Botrytis Riesling; Preece range of Sauvignon Blanc, Chardonnay, Sparkling Chardonnay Pinot Noir, Pinot Noir, Shiraz, Merlot, Cabernet Sauvignon; and finally Thomas Mitchell range of Marsanne, Chardonnay, Shiraz, Cabernet Sauvignon Shiraz.
summary Acquired by Petaluma in 1994, having already put the runs on the board in no uncertain fashion with the gifted winemaker Don Lewis. Boasts an impressive array of wines across a broad spectrum of style and price, but each carefully aimed at a market niche. The wines are exported to Europe, the UK, Asia and the US.

Mitchelton Blackwood Park Riesling

TTTTP 2001 Light to medium yellow-green; clean, moderately aromatic, with lime, apple and some mineral threaded through the aromas; the palate is at once delicate yet quite intense, with a mix of lime and more minerally notes providing good structure. **rating: 91**

best drinking 2001–2005 **best vintages** '85, '90, '91, '92, '94, '95, '96, '98, '99, '00, '01 **drink with** Sashimi • $14.95

Mitchelton Airstrip Marsanne Roussanne Viognier

▼▼▼♀ 2000 Medium yellow-green; the bouquet is quite rich and powerful, with touches of apricot and peach. The entry to the palate is powerful, but the mid-palate and finish don't flow, tailing off somewhat.

rating: 84

best drinking **best vintages** NA **drink with** Rich pasta • $26

Mitchelton Viognier

▼▼▼▼ 2000 Glowing yellow-green; the bouquet is clean, smooth and ripe, with hints of apricot and fruit pastille. The palate is quite chunky, with some dried fruit flavours and a soft finish.

rating: 86

best drinking 2001–2003 **best vintages** NA **drink with** Barbecued pork fillet with honey mustard • $22

Mitchelton Chardonnay

▼▼▼♀ 1999 Medium to full yellow-green, quite advanced. Toasty, ripe, buttery, peachy fruit aromas are almost Hunter Valley-like; the palate has pleasant balance and acidity, but is somewhat nondescript.

rating: 83

best drinking 2001–2003 **best vintages** '81, '85, '90, '91, '92, '97 **drink with** Chicken and creamy pasta • $20

Mitchelton Blackwood Park Botrytis Riesling

▼▼▼▼♀ 2001 Bright green-yellow; fragrant lime marmalade aromatics flow into a nicely balanced palate with lime juice flavours, good varietal character and neatly balanced acidity; not aggressively sweet.

rating: 90

best drinking 2002–2006 **best vintages** '01 **drink with** Scallops in bechamel sauce • $14

Mitchelton Shiraz

▼▼▼▼ 1999 Medium to full red-purple; a moderately intense mix of red berry and more savoury/dusty aromas is followed by a palate with good structure and balance, with flavours of cherry and mulberry; good length, oak integration and tannin balance.

rating: 88

best drinking 2004–2009 **best vintages** NA **drink with** Braised duck • $22

Mitchelton Print Shiraz

▼▼▼▼♀ 1997 Medium red-purple; a clean, smooth, dark cherry/plum bouquet with subtly integrated oak is followed by a well-balanced, dark fruit-accented palate, which has elegance and persistence, and fine tannins.

rating: 92

best drinking 2002–2009 **best vintages** '81, '82, '90, '91, '92, '95, '96 **drink with** Marinated venison • $50

Mitchelton Crescent Shiraz Mourvedre Grenache

▼▼▼▼ 1999 Medium red, with the purples starting to fade. The bouquet is clean, light and spicy, the palate is fresh and lively, with spicy/juicy berry flavours and minimal oak influence, providing a very attractive, early-drinking style.

rating: 89

best drinking 2002–2005 **best vintages** NA **drink with** Barbecued lamb cutlets • $26

Mitchelton Cabernet Sauvignon

▼▼▼♀ 1997 Medium red, starting to move towards brick; a cedary/savoury/earthy bouquet is followed by a palate with blackberry/cassis fruits, complexed by a range of cedary, earthy, herbal, meaty flavours. Somewhere left of centre.

rating: 83

best drinking 2002–2006 **best vintages** '96 **drink with** Lamb casserole • $22

molly morgan vineyard ★★★★

Talga Road, Lovedale, NSW 2321 **region** Lower Hunter Valley
phone (02) 9816 4088 **fax** (02) 9816 2680 **open** By appointment
winemaker Sarah-Kate Wilson (Contract) **production** 4500 **est.** 1963
product range ($18–21 ML) Joe's Block Semillon, Old Vines Semillon, Semillon Sauvignon Blanc, Chardonnay, Shiraz.
summary Molly Morgan has been acquired by Andrew and Hady Simon, who established the Camperdown Cellars Group in 1971, becoming the largest retailer in Australia before moving on to other pursuits, and handing the business over to John Baker, one of Australia's best-known fine wine retailers, who owned or managed Quaffers, Double Bay Cellars, the Newport Bottler and Grape Fellas (Epping) at various times. The property is planted to 5.5 hectares of 25-year-old unirrigated semillon, which goes to make the Old Vines Semillon, 0.8 hectare for Joe's Block Semillon, 2.5 hectares of chardonnay and 1.2 hectares of shiraz. The wines are contract-made (as has always been the case, in fact, but to a high standard). Exports to the US.

Molly Morgan Joe's Block Semillon

TTTTT 2001 Light green-yellow; a firm, crisp bouquet with a mix of mineral and lemon is followed by a lively, crisp and attractive palate, with a mix of lemon, mineral and grass flavours. Has abundant potential.

rating: 90

best drinking 2003–2008 **best vintages** '99, '00, '01 **drink with** Seafood • $19

Molly Morgan Old Vines Semillon

TTTT 2001 Light to medium green-yellow; there is quite intense herbal/mineral fruit on both the bouquet and long palate; a touch of CO_2 while a little disruptive now, will help the wine's longevity.

rating: 86

best drinking 2003–2010 **best vintages** '98, '99, '00 **drink with** Calamari • $19

monahan estate ★★★☆

Lot 1 Wilderness Road, Rothbury, NSW 2320 **region** Lower Hunter Valley
phone (02) 4930 9070 **fax** (02) 4930 7679 **open** Thurs–Sun 10–5
winemaker Monarch Winemaking Services **production** 2000 **est.** 1997
product range ($12–13 CD) Semillon, Old Bridge Semillon, Old Bridge Unwooded Chardonnay.
summary Matthew Monahan acquired his property on Wilderness Road in 1997, establishing 6 hectares of semillon and chardonnay under the guidance of veteran Hunter Valley viticulturist Keith Holder. In 1999 he entered into a partnership with husband and wife team of John and Trish Graham. They now manage the property, which is bordered by Black Creek in the Lovedale district, an area noted for its high-quality semillon. The old bridge adjoining the property is displayed on the wine labels; the wines themselves have been consistent silver and bronze medal winners at the Hunter Valley Wine Show.

Monahan Estate Semillon

TTTTT 2001 Light to medium yellow-green; a spotlessly clean bouquet with mineral, citrus and grass aromas; the palate is lively, quite long and well-balanced. **rating:** 90

best drinking 2002–2008 **best vintages** NA **drink with** Summer salads • $12

Monahan Estate Old Bridge Chardonnay

TTTT 2001 Light to medium yellow-green; the bouquet shows some obvious oak, though not over the top, and allows the citrussy/lemony fruit of the palate to come through quite clearly. An unusual style, possibly picked a little green, and certainly having high acidity. Sensibly priced. **rating:** 83

best drinking 2002–2004 **best vintages** NA **drink with** Tempura fish • $13

monbulk winery ★★☆

Macclesfield Road, Monbulk, Vic 3793 **region** Yarra Valley
phone (03) 9756 6965 **fax** (03) 9756 6965 **open** Weekends and public holidays 12–5 or by appointment
winemaker Paul Jabornik **production** 800 **est.** 1984
product range ($11.90–16.50 CD) Chardonnay, Riesling, Pinot Noir, Shiraz, Cabernet Sauvignon; also fruit wines including Kiwifruit, Strawberry, Blackberry, Raspberry and Plum.
summary Originally concentrated on kiwifruit wines but now extending to table wines; the very cool Monbulk subregion should be capable of producing wines of distinctive style, but the table wines are (unfortunately) not of the same standard as the kiwifruit wines, which are quite delicious.

monichino wines ★★★☆

1820 Berrys Road, Katunga, Vic 3640 **region** Goulburn Valley
phone (03) 5864 6452 **fax** (03) 5864 6538 **open** Mon–Sat 9–5, Sun 10–5
winemaker Carlo Monichino, Terry Monichino **production** 17 000 **est.** 1962
product range ($10–45 CD) Riesling, Semillon Sauvignon Blanc, Sauvignon Blanc, Chardonnay, Botrytis Semillon, Orange Muscat, Golden Lexia, Rosé Petals Spätlese, Shiraz, Merlot, Malbec, Carlo's Pressings, Rosso Dolce, Cabernet Sauvignon, Italian Stubby; various Ports and Fortifieds; bulk sales also available.
summary A winery which has quietly made some clean, fresh wines in which the fruit character is carefully preserved, and has shown a deft touch with its Botrytis Semillon.

Monichino Chardonnay

ŸŸŸŸ 2001 Medium to full green-yellow; smoky oak opens proceedings on the bouquet, with some stone fruit lurking underneath; that stone fruit and a touch of citrus come through strongly on the clean, well-balanced palate. **rating:** 87

best drinking 2002–2003 **best vintages** NA **drink with** Poached chicken • NA

Monichino Botrytis Semillon

ŸŸŸŸŸ 2001 Excellent yellow-green, not too deep; intense and complex botrytis results in a tangy/citrussy bouquet; on the palate, super-intense sweetness is balanced by high acidity. A very good wine which should mature well over the short term. **rating:** 90

best drinking 2002–2005 **best vintages** '01 **drink with** Rich desserts • $15

montagne view estate   NR

555 Hermitage Road, Pokolbin, NSW 2320 **region** Lower Hunter Valley
phone (02) 4998 7822 **fax** (02) 6574 7276 **open** 7 days 10–5
winemaker Greg Silkman (Contract) **production** 500 **est.** 1993
product range ($20–25 CD) Edith Margaret Chardonnay, Vivian Laurie Merlot.
summary The major investment and principal business of Montagne View is the eight-studio/suite guesthouse sitting among the 5 hectares of vines. There is also a high-quality restaurant (Brents) offering the prospect of all-inclusive gourmet weekends for around $550 per couple. The estate wines are sold through the restaurant and the cellar door, with other local wines available in the restaurant.

montalto vineyards   ★★★★☆

33 Shoreham Road, Red Hill South, Vic 3937 **region** Mornington Peninsula
phone (03) 5989 8412 **fax** (03) 5989 8417 **open** 7 days 12–5
winemaker Daniel Green **production** 3000 **est.** 1998
product range ($16.50–28 CD) Riesling, Chardonnay, Pinot Noir; second label Pennon Riesling, Semillon Sauvignon Blanc, Cuvée One, Pinot Meunier Rosé and Pinot Noir.
summary John Mitchell and family established Montalto Vineyards in 1998, although the core of the vineyard goes back to 1986. There are 5 hectares of chardonnay and 4 hectares of pinot noir, with 0.5 hectare each of semillon, riesling and pinot meunier. Intensive vineyard work opens up the canopy, with yields ranging between 1.5 and 2.5 tonnes per acre, and the majority of the fruit hand-harvested. Wines are released under two labels, Montalto and Pennon, the latter effectively a lower-priced, second label. The restaurant, open daily for lunch and on Friday and Saturday evenings, also features guest chefs and cooking classes. A winery to watch.

Montalto Pennon Mornington Peninsula Riesling

ŸŸŸŸ 2001 Pale straw-green; the very light and delicate bouquet has mineral aromas; the fruit is yet to express itself, but sweet apple flavours on entry and the mid-palate are reassuring, as is the well-balanced, dry finish. Guaranteed to grow with age in bottle. **rating:** 89

best drinking 2004–2010 **best vintages** NA **drink with** Shellfish • $16.50

Montalto Pennon Semillon Sauvignon Blanc

ŸŸŸŸ 2001 Light straw-green; distinct grassy/herbaceous aromas drive the bouquet, but the fruit sweetens up remarkably on the palate, with an almost silky texture to the ripe citrus flavours. **rating:** 88

best drinking 2002–2004 **best vintages** NA **drink with** Tempura • $16.50

Montalto Chardonnay

ŸŸŸŸ 2000 Light green-yellow; the bouquet offers citrus and melon, and then some mineral lift; the palate performs similarly, with lively, lemony/citrussy tang and grip, in somewhat unusual style, particularly for the vintage. Whole bunch-pressing and malolactic fermentation are part of the winery thumbprints. **rating:** 87

best drinking 2002–2004 **best vintages** NA **drink with** Flathead fillets • $23.50

Montalto Pennon Pinot Meunier Rosé

ŸŸŸŸ 2001 Light, bright pink; the bouquet is firm, with quite minerally/earthy aromas; the palate is fresh, clean and lively, with strawberry/rose petal flavours. well-balanced. **rating:** 86

best drinking 2002–2003 **best vintages** NA **drink with** Antipasto • $16.50

Montalto Pinot Noir

▼▼▼▼ 2000 Bright red-purple; a ripe and complex bouquet with rich dark plum fruit and spice flows through into full, unctuously ripe plummy fruit on the palate; silky texture and a dash of spice. **rating:** 95

best drinking 2003–2007 **best vintages** '00 **drink with** Breast of squab • $25

Montalto Pennon Pinot Noir

▼▼▼▼▼ 2000 Medium to full red-purple; some foresty edges to the rich, ripe, plummy fruit of the bouquet precede a palate likewise flooded with very ripe plum fruit; good texture and mouthfeel. Another exceptionally good Pinot from a great vintage. **rating:** 94

best drinking 2003–2006 **best vintages** '00 **drink with** Wild mushroom risotto • $18.50

montara ★★★☆

Chalambar Road, Ararat, Vic 3377 **region** Grampians
phone (03) 5352 3868 **fax** (03) 5352 4968 **open** Mon–Sat 10–5, Sun 12–4
winemaker Mike McRae **production** NFP **est.** 1970
product range ($13.50–22 CD) Riesling, Chardonnay, Pinot Noir, Shiraz, Cabernet Sauvignon; 'M' range of Chardonnay, Pinot Noir, Pinot Shiraz.
summary Achieved considerable attention for its Pinot Noirs during the 1980s, but other regions (and other makers) have come along since. It continues to produce wines of distinctive style, and smart new label designs do help. Limited national distribution; exports to the UK, Switzerland, Canada and Hong Kong.

montgomery's hill ★★★☆

Hassell Highway, Upper Kalgan, Albany, WA 6330 **region** Great Southern
phone (08) 9844 3715 **fax** (08) 9844 1104 **open** 7 days 11–5
winemaker Robert Lee (Porongurup Winery), John Wade (Consultant) **production** 2000 **est.** 1996
product range ($15–22.50 R) Sauvignon Blanc, Chardonnay, Unwooded Chardonnay, Cabernet Franc, Cabernets.
summary Montgomery's Hill is situated 16 kilometres northeast of Albany on a north-facing slope on the banks of the Kalgan River. The vineyard is on an area which was previously an apple orchard, and is a diversification for the third generation of the Montgomery family, which owns the property. Chardonnay, cabernet sauvignon and cabernet franc were planted in 1996, followed by sauvignon blanc, shiraz and merlot in 1997. The 1998 wines were contract-made by Brenden Smith at West Cape Howe Wines, but since 1999 Montgomery's Hill has been made at the new Porongurup Winery.

Montgomery's Hill Chardonnay

▼▼▼▼ 2000 Light green-yellow; clean, light, fresh citrus aromas on the bouquet flow into a melon, stone fruit and citrus-flavoured palate. The oak in which the wine was fermented seems to have all but disappeared, but it does have pleasant mouthfeel. **rating:** 86

best drinking 2001–2004 **best vintages** NA **drink with** Stir-fried chicken and cashews • $18.50

Montgomery's Hill Cabernet Franc

▼▼▼▼ 2000 Medium red-purple; slightly dusty oak and red berry fruit on the bouquet give no hint of the palate flavour, which builds, deepens and ripens, with good tannin structure and length. A convincing example of an often disappointing varietal red. **rating:** 87

best drinking 2002–2007 **best vintages** NA **drink with** Wood-fired pizza • $16.50

monument vineyard NR

Cnr Escort Way and Manildra Road, Cudal, NSW 2864 **region** Central Ranges Zone
phone (02) 6364 2294 **fax** (02) 6364 2069 **open** By appointment
winemaker Alison Eisermann **production** 900 **est.** 1998
product range ($12–20 CD) Pinot Noir, Shiraz, Hospital Hill Shiraz, Sangiovese, Cabernet Sauvignon.
summary In the early 1990s five mature-age students at Charles Sturt University, successful in their own professions, decided to form a partnership to develop a vineyard and winery on a scale that they could not afford individually, but could do collectively. After a lengthy search, a large property at Cudal was identified, with ideal terra rossa basalt-derived soil over a limestone base. The property now has 108 hectares under vine, as a result of planting in the spring of 1998 and 1999.

moondah brook ★★★★

c/o Houghton, Dale Road, Middle Swan, WA 6056 **region** Swan District
phone (08) 9274 5372 **fax** (08) 9274 5372 **open** Not
winemaker Larry Cherubino **production** 60 000 **est.** 1968
product range ($10–17 R) Chardonnay, Chenin Blanc, Verdelho, Sauvignon Blanc, Shiraz, Cabernet Sauvignon, Maritime (Sparkling); also occasional Show Reserve releases of Chenin Blanc and Verdelho.
summary Part of the BRL Hardy wine group which has its own special character, as it draws part of its fruit from the large Gingin vineyard, 70 kilometres north of the Swan Valley, and part from the Margaret River and Great Southern. In recent times it has excelled even its own reputation for reliability with some quite lovely wines, in particular honeyed, aged Chenin Blanc and finely structured Cabernet Sauvignon.

Moondah Brook Chenin Blanc

▼▼▼▼ **2001** Light to medium yellow-green; the bouquet is quite complex, strongly hinting that the wine has not simply been stainless steel-fermented and then bottled. Flavoursome fruit salad aromas and flavours are but part of the story, with some textural richness, possibly coming from partial barrel fermentation and/or maturation. Looks as if it could develop into something well above average.   **rating:** 86
▼▼▼▼ **2000** Light to medium green-yellow; the bouquet is quite fragrant with lifted citrus and fruit salad aromatics, but the palate, while clean, is still to build complexity and depth – which it will surely do.   **rating:** 85

best drinking 2002–2007 **best vintages** '80, '87, '89, '91, '93, '94, '97 **drink with** Cold marron salad • $14.99

Moondah Brook Chardonnay

▼▼▼▼ **2001** Light to medium green-yellow; a fruit-driven bouquet offers melon with a light tropical overlay; attractive, flavoursome nectarine and melon fruit on the palate are clean and fresh.   **rating:** 86

best drinking 2001–2003 **best vintages** '95 **drink with** Marron • $11.75

Moondah Brook Shiraz

▼▼▼▼ **2000** Solid dark berry fruit aromas, with hints of earth and vanilla, lead into a full-flavoured, dense but not jammy palate with dark plum, prune and blackberry fruit.   **rating:** 89
▼▼▼▼▽ **1999** Medium to full red-purple; a ripe, dense bouquet laden with black cherry and chocolate fruit flows through seamlessly into a full-flavoured palate where some slightly savoury characters add to the complexity; the tannins are well-balanced, the oak relatively subtle. Great value.   **rating:** 90

best drinking 2003–2008 **best vintages** '99, '00 **drink with** Barbecued T-bone • $14.95

Moondah Brook Cabernet Sauvignon

▼▼▼▼ **2000** Medium to full red-purple; clean, ripe blackberry/blackcurrant fruit on the bouquet is followed by a well-balanced and crafted palate, as smooth as the proverbial baby's bottom. Light to medium-bodied, with the dusting of tannin and oak wholly appropriate for the fruit weight.   **rating:** 87
▼▼▼▼▽ **1999** Medium to full red-purple; powerful blackberry/cassis backed by oak on the bouquet flows through to the robust, rich palate with blackberry fruit, touches of prune and chocolate, lingering tannins and good oak.   **rating:** 90

best drinking 2002–2007 **best vintages** '82, '88, '91, '93, '94, '96, '97, '98, '99 **drink with** Braised lamb with couscous • $18.99

moondarra   NR

Browns Road, Moondarra, Vic 3825 **region** Gippsland
phone (03) 9598 3049 **fax** (03) 9598 3049 **open** Not
winemaker Neil Prentice **production** NA **est.** 1991
product range ($90 R) Samba Side Pinot Noir, Conception Pinot Noir, Holly's Garden Pinot Noir.
summary In 1991 Neil Prentice and family established their Moondarra Vineyard in Gippsland, planted to 11 low-yielding clones of pinot noir. The vines are not irrigated, and vineyard management is predicated on the minimum use of any sprays, with the aim of ultimately moving to Biodynamic/Pagan farming methods. The winemaking techniques are strongly influenced by the practices of controversial Lebanese-born Burgundy consultant Guy Accad, with 10 days' pre-fermentation maceration and whole bunches added prior to fermentation. The wines are distributed in Melbourne and Sydney by Select Vineyards, go to Japan via Vintage Cellars, and to Hong Kong and Belgium. And yes, the $90 a bottle (or $1000 per dozen) is indeed the price.

Moondarra Conception Pinot Noir

ŢŢŢŢŶ 1999 Medium purple-red; the complex bouquet has a range of forest, plum and spice aromas; the palate is complex and powerful, with the savoury/foresty tannins doubtless coming from the whole bunch/stem components in the winemaking. It will be interesting to watch the development of the wine.

rating: 90

best drinking 2001–2006 **best vintages** '99 **drink with** Braised quail • $90

🐂 moonrakers   NR

321 Raymond Road, Gunns Plains, Tas 7315 **region** Northern Tasmania
phone (03) 6429 1186 **open** 7 days 9–5
winemaker Richard Richardson (Contract) **production** 300 **est.** 1997
product range ($15–25 CD) Chardonnay, Pinot Noir.
summary Stephen and Diana Usher came from Wiltshire in England, where a local legend was told of illegal smuggling of kegs of brandy which were thrown into a pond to avoid detection. Later that night, when the coast was clear, the smugglers began the job of raking the kegs out of the pond, only to be surprised by the customs officers. Asked what they were doing, the smugglers replied they were trying to rake the moon reflected in the water. Taking them to be idiot fools from the village, the excise men rode off. The Ushers should have no such problem, having planted only 0.5 a hectare each of chardonnay and pinot noir on a north-facing slope above the picturesque valley of Gunns Plains. The deep loam over limestone soil holds much promise.

moonshine valley winery   NR

374 Mons Road, Forest Glen, Buderim, Qld 4556 **region** Queensland Coastal
phone (07) 5445 1198 **fax** (07) 5445 1799 **open** Mon–Fri 10–4, weekends 10–5
winemaker Tom Weidmann **production** 3000 **est.** 1985
product range ($10–30 CD) A kaleidoscopic array of basically fruit-based wines, including White Moon, Red Moon, Chardonnay, Shiraz, Shiraz Cabernet Merlot. Liqueurs are Limoncello, Almondo, Espresso; Old Buderim Ginger, Strawberry Port, Old Ned (spirit), Porto Rubino, Ruby Moon Port (Shiraz Durif Sangiovese).
summary Frederick Houweling brings a European background to his making of these fruit-based wines. The winery is situated on a large property among natural lakes and forest, and also offers a restaurant, cafeteria, and souvenir shop.

moorebank vineyard   NR

Palmers Lane, Pokolbin, NSW 2320 **region** Lower Hunter Valley
phone (02) 4998 7610 **fax** (02) 4998 7367 **open** Fri–Mon 10–5 or by appointment
winemaker Iain Riggs (Contract) **production** 2000 **est.** 1977
product range ($19.50–24.50 CD) Chardonnay, Summar Semillon, Gewürztraminer, Merlot, now sold in the narrow 500 ml Italian glass bottle known as Bellissima.
summary Ian Burgess and Debra Moore own a mature 5.5-hectare vineyard with a small cellar-door operation offering immaculately packaged wines in avant-garde style. The peachy Chardonnay has been a medal winner at Hunter Valley Wine Shows.

moorilla estate   ★★★★☆

655 Main Road, Berriedale, Tas 7011 **region** Southern Tasmania
phone (03) 6277 9900 **fax** (03) 6249 4093 **open** 7 days 10–5
winemaker Michael Glover **production** 15 000 **est.** 1958
product range ($9–50 ML) Riesling, Gewürztraminer, White Label Chardonnay, Black Label Chardonnay, Botrytis Riesling, Black Label Pinot Noir, White Label Pinot Noir, Cabernet Sauvignon, Millennium Cuvée 2, Vintage Brut; Reserve wines include Pinot Noir, Syrah and Cabernet Sauvignon.
summary Moorilla Estate is an icon in the Tasmanian wine industry and is thriving. Wine quality continues to be unimpeachable, while the opening of the museum in the marvellous Alcorso house designed by Sir Roy Grounds adds even more attraction for visitors to the estate, a mere 15–20 minutes from Hobart. Five-star self-contained chalets are available, with a restaurant open for lunch 7 days a week.

Moorilla Estate Riesling

ŦŦŦŦŸ **2001** Light green-yellow; the bouquet is clean and firm, quite intense, with pure mineral, apple and lime aromas. The palate is well-balanced, with a long carry and good aftertaste. Silver medal 2002 Tasmanian Wines Show. **rating:** 93

best drinking 2002–2007 **best vintages** '81, '82, '90, '91, '93, '94, '95, '97, '98, '99, '01 **drink with** Asparagus • $22.50

Moorilla Estate Brut

ŦŦŦŦŦ **1998** Medium yellow-straw; the complex bouquet has a whiff of aldehyde, almost certainly intentional. The palate is complex, with some real Champagne characters, in a nutty/wet dog spectrum. Trophy winner 2002 Tasmanian Wines Show. **rating:** 94

best drinking 2002–2004 **best vintages** NA **drink with** Rich canapes • $28.50

Moorilla Estate Syrah

ŦŦŦŦŸ **2000** Inky purple; clean, deep, dark berry fruit on the bouquet is followed by an utterly remarkable palate, as rich, dense and concentrated as both the colour and bouquet promise. While it is dense, it is not over-extractive; its only drawback early in its life is a lack of light and shade. **rating:** 92

best drinking 2005–2010 **best vintages** '00 **drink with** Leave it in the cellar • $50

Moorilla Estate Reserve Merlot

ŦŦŦŦ **1999** Medium purple-red; clean, fresh, sweet berry fruit and subtle aroma is followed by a palate with an attractive grainy structure altogether appropriate to the variety, and with (an acceptable) tweak of acidity on the finish. **rating:** 88

best drinking 2003–2007 **best vintages** NA **drink with** Rack of veal • $45

Moorilla Estate Cabernet Sauvignon

ŦŦŦŦŦ **1999** Excellent red-purple; strong and clear; pure cassis/currant fruit and subtle oak drive the clean bouquet; the palate is beautifully balanced and composed, revolving around the flavours promised by the bouquet. A truly lovely wine in the Tasmanian context. **rating:** 94

best drinking 2004–2010 **best vintages** '98, '99 **drink with** Marinated venison • $28.50

moorooduc estate ★★★★★

501 Derril Road, Moorooduc, Vic 3936 **region** Mornington Peninsula
phone (03) 5971 8506 **fax** (03) 5971 8550 **open** Weekends 11–5
winemaker Dr Richard McIntyre **production** 6000 **est.** 1983
product range ($20–46 CD) Sauvignon Blanc Semillon, Johnson Vineyard Pinot Gris, Chardonnay, Wild Yeast Chardonnay, Devil Bend Creek Chardonnay, Pinot Noir, Wild Yeast Pinot Noir, Devil Bend Pinot Noir, Shiraz, Cabernet.
summary Dr Richard McIntyre regularly produces one of the richest and most complex Chardonnays in the region, with grapefruit/peach fruit set against sumptuous spicy oak, and that hallmark soft nutty/creamy/regional texture. As well as retail distribution, the wines are exported through Trembath and Taylor.

Moorooduc Estate Chardonnay

ŦŦŦŦŸ **1999** Medium to full yellow-green; a rich, complex and toasty bouquet, coming in part from bottle development, and in part from ripe fruit. The palate is very attractive and harmonious, offering stone fruits, fig and cashew, plus perfectly balanced oak and acidity. **rating:** 91

best drinking 2002–2005 **best vintages** '88, '90, '91, '92, '93, '94, '95, '97, '98, '99 **drink with** Grilled spatchcock • $30

Moorooduc Estate Wild Yeast Chardonnay

ŦŦŦŦŸ **1999** Medium to full yellow-green; the rich and complex bouquet is very similar to that of the 'standard' Chardonnay; the palate is more complex, but not necessarily more attractive; it is simply different, with more nutty/spicy characters. **rating:** 90

best drinking 2002–2005 **best vintages** '98 **drink with** Grilled spatchcock • $45

Moorooduc Estate Devil Bend Creek Pinot Noir

ŦŦŦŦŸ **2001** Bright, brilliant purple-red, suggesting a relatively low pH. Clean and fresh cherry fruit on the bouquet leads into a palate with high-toned cherry fruit, then a dash of stem and spice on the finish. Compelling as an early-drinking style, but also has some future. **rating:** 92

🍷🍷🍷🍸 **2000** Medium red-purple; a fragrant, fresh, fruit-driven strawberry/cherry bouquet is followed by a palate which builds complexity, as it moves more to plum in flavour; good length and acidity. **rating:** 92

best drinking 2002–2005 **best vintages** '00, '01 **drink with** Pastrami/antipasto • $20

Moorooduc Estate Wild Yeast Pinot Noir

🍷🍷🍷🍷🍷 **2000** Light in colour and body, has tremendous intensity to its fragrant, savoury foresty bouquet and its complex, beguiling and long sappy/savoury foresty palate. **rating:** 95

best drinking 2001–2005 **best vintages** '00 **drink with** Duck salad • $46

Moorooduc Estate Shiraz

🍷🍷🍷🍷 **2000** Medium purple-red; the moderately intense bouquet has red cherry/berry fruit, but no spice; the clean palate has ripish red cherry fruit, but not a great deal of structure or tannin. **rating:** 86

best drinking 2002–2006 **best vintages** NA **drink with** Roast pigeon • $36

morgan simpson ★★★☆

PO Box 39, Kensington Park, SA 5068 (postal) **region** McLaren Vale
phone (08) 8364 3645 **fax** (08) 8364 3645 **open** Not
winemaker Richard Simpson **production** 1200 **est.** 1998
product range ($9.50–15 ML) Chardonnay, Stone Hill Shiraz, Row 42 Cabernet Sauvignon.
summary Morgan Simpson is a joint venture between SA businessman George Morgan and winemaker Richard Simpson, who is a wine science graduate from Charles Sturt University. Their grapes are sourced from the Clos Robert Vineyard (where the wine is made) established by Robert Alan Simpson in 1972. The partners say, 'As we gain knowledge and experience of winemaking we intend to increase both the range and quality of our products. Our current plan is to provided drinkable wines at a reasonable price.' They have succeeded admirably with the small quantities of wine so far released, and intend to limit production to its present level of around 1200 cases per year. The value for money of these wines is second to none.

Morgan Simpson Chardonnay

🍷🍷🍷🍷 **2000** Light straw-green; the moderately intense bouquet has light peach/stone fruit and subtle oak; the unforced palate has attractively rounded and integrated fruit and oak; a bargain at the price. **rating:** 85

best drinking 2002–2003 **best vintages** NA **drink with** Pasta • $9.50

Morgan Simpson Stone Hill Shiraz

🍷🍷🍷🍷 **2000** Medium to full red-purple; black fruits and chocolate aromas plus subtle oak on the bouquet move into a sweet and supple palate with a rich, plummy mid-palate, closing with soft tannins and subtle oak. Another great bargain. **rating:** 89

best drinking 2002–2006 **best vintages** NA **drink with** Italian sausages • $15

Morgan Simpson Row 42 Cabernet Sauvignon

🍷🍷🍷🍷 **2000** Medium red-purple; obvious vanilla oak on the bouquet does not obscure the clean, ripe fruit, and indeed on the palate there is abundant, sweet, jammy, berry fruit and a touch of vanilla. Great value at the price, and I suspect others will in any event give it even higher points. **rating:** 85

best drinking 2002–2005 **best vintages** NA **drink with** Braised ox cheek • $15

morialta vineyard NR

195 Norton Summit Road, Norton Summit, SA 5136 **region** Adelaide Hills
phone (08) 8390 1061 **fax** (08) 8390 1585 **open** By appointment
winemaker Jeffrey Grosset (Contract) **production** 500 **est.** 1989
product range ($15–22 R) Sauvignon Blanc, Unwooded Chardonnay, Chardonnay, Pinot Noir Rosé.
summary Morialta Vineyard was planted in 1989 on a site first planted to vines in the 1860s by John Baker, who named his property Morialta Farm. The Bunya pine depicted on the label is one of the few surviving trees from that era, and indeed one of the few surviving trees of that genus. The 20-hectare property has 11 hectares under vine, planted to chardonnay, pinot noir, cabernet sauvignon, sauvignon blanc, shiraz and merlot. Most of the grapes are sold to Southcorp. Given the age of the vineyard and contract winemaking by Jeffrey Grosset, it is not surprising the wines have done well in the Adelaide Hills Wine Show. They are sold through selected restaurants in Adelaide as well as by mail order.

morningside wines ★★★★

711 Middle Tea Tree Road, Tea Tree, Tas 7017 **region** Southern Tasmania
phone (03) 6268 1748 **fax** (03) 6268 1748 **open** By appointment
winemaker Peter Bosworth **production** 500 **est.** 1980
product range ($17–29 ML) Riesling, Chardonnay, Pinot Noir, Cabernet Sauvignon.
summary The name 'Morningside' was given to the old property on which the vineyard stands because it gets the morning sun first – the property on the other side of the valley was known as 'Eveningside'. Consistent with the observation of the early settlers, the Morningside grapes achieve full maturity with good colour and varietal flavour. Production is as yet tiny but will increase as the 2-hectare vineyard matures. Retail distribution through Sutherland Cellars, Melbourne and the Tasmanian Wine Centre.

Morningside Wines Riesling

▼▼▼▼▼ 2001 Light straw-green; an aromatic and penetrating bouquet with hints of herb and slate is followed by a palate which has the focus, intensity and length missing from many wines of the vintage, although even here there is a faint question on the slightly soft finish. Gold medal at the 2002 Tasmanian Wines Show. **rating:** 94

best drinking 2002–2006 **best vintages** '01 **drink with** Shellfish • $17

Morningside Pinot Noir

▼▼▼▼ 2000 Medium purple-red; a quite complex sappy/briary/woody bouquet is repeated on the palate; yet another facet of the 2000 vintage which particularly appealed to Larry McKenna, the New Zealand judge at the 2002 Tasmanian Wines Show. **rating:** 85

best drinking 2002–2006 **best vintages** '99 **drink with** Roast quail • $29

mornington estate ★★★☆

c/o Dromana Estate, Harrison's Road and Bittern–Dromana Road, Dromana, Vic 3936 **region** Mornington Peninsula
phone (03) 5987 3800 **fax** (03) 5981 0714 **open** At Dromana Estate 7 days 11–4
winemaker Gary Crittenden, Judy Gifford Watson **production** 6000 **est.** 1989
product range ($17–20 CD) Chardonnay, Sauvignon Blanc, Pinot Noir, Shiraz.
summary As with so many Mornington Peninsula vineyards, a high degree of viticultural expertise, care and attention is needed to get to first base. With a little over 20 hectares in production, it is one of the larger vineyards on the Peninsula and is an important part of the publicly-listed Dromana Estate group. Exports to the UK.

Mornington Estate Sauvignon Blanc

▼▼▼▼ 2001 Light straw-green; the bouquet is light and crisp, as is the palate, which has quite attractive lemony flavours, but is not particularly varietal. **rating:** 85

best drinking 2001–2002 **best vintages** NA **drink with** Seafood • $17

Mornington Estate Chardonnay

▼▼▼▼ 2001 Light green-yellow; a light, delicate bouquet with stone fruit and a whisper of French oak; the palate is well-balanced in a light mode, with melon and stone fruit to the fore. **rating:** 85

best drinking 2002–2004 **best vintages** '91, '93, '94 **drink with** Mussels • $20

Mornington Estate Pinot Noir

▼▼▼▼ 2001 Youthful purple-red; fresh, lively cherry and strawberry aromas backed by a hint of charry oak lead into a medium-bodied fresh palate, with direct fruit and good length. **rating:** 89
▼▼▼▼ 2000 Light to medium red-purple; a clean, fresh and light bouquet is rather simple, but does offer clear varietal character, the palate providing more of the same. Will develop a little extra complexity over the short term. **rating:** 86
▼▼▼▽ 1999 Light red; the clean but very light bouquet has faint cherry aromas; the palate has cherry/cherry pip, but not a lot of power or concentration. **rating:** 83

best drinking 2002–2004 **best vintages** '94, '95, '01 **drink with** Cold meat salad • $20

Mornington Estate Shiraz

▼▼▼▼ 2000 Medium red-purple; the bouquet is of light to medium intensity, with a mix of berry, spice and earth, the palate showing classic cool-climate fruit character in a black cherry, spice and licorice spectrum, supported by subtle oak. Excellent value. **rating:** 87

best drinking 2003–2008 **best vintages** NA **drink with** Lamb kebabs • $20

morris ★★★★★

Mia Mia Vineyard, Rutherglen, Vic 3685 **region** Rutherglen
phone (02) 6026 7303 **fax** (02) 6026 7445 **open** Mon–Sat 9–5, Sun 10–5
winemaker David Morris **production** NFP **est.** 1859
product range ($11–46 R) Table wines include Chardonnay, Sparkling Shiraz Durif, Shiraz, Rutherglen Durif, Rutherglen Blue Imperial Cinsaut, Cabernet Sauvignon; then fortified wines, comprising Black Label Liqueur Muscat, Liqueur Muscat, Premium Liqueur Muscat, Liqueur Tokay, Premium Liqueur Tokay, Premium Amontillado, Black Label Tawny Port, Old Tawny Port; tiny quantities of Show Reserve are released from time to time, mainly ex-winery.
summary One of the greatest of the fortified winemakers, some would say the greatest. If you wish to test that view, try the Old Premium Muscat and Old Premium Tokay, which are absolute bargains given their age and quality, and which give rise to the winery rating. The table wines are dependable, the white wines all being made by owner Orlando.

Morris Liqueur Tokay

▼▼▼▼▽ NV Light to medium golden-brown; a fragrant bouquet with fresh tea-leaf varietal aroma. There is masses of flavour on the palate, yet the wine is quite fresh, with archetypal cold tea and butterscotch flavours; the mid-palate sweetness is followed by a cleansing, crisp finish. **rating:** 90

best drinking 2002–2010 **best vintages** NA **drink with** Either aperitif or at the end of the meal • $15.95

Morris Old Premium Liqueur Tokay (500 ml)

▼▼▼▼▼ NV The mahogany colour has an olive rim, a sure sign of age and quality in such wines. The bouquet offers rich, toffee and Christmas cake fruit, but not so much of the cold tea varietal character. A rich and concentrated palate with more of the cake and toffee flavours follows through with good length and acidity. A little more varietal definition would have resulted in even higher points. **rating:** 94

best drinking 2001–2002 **best vintages** NA **drink with** Coffee • $45

Morris Liqueur Muscat

▼▼▼▼▽ NVLight to medium red-brown; clearly articulated, lively, raisiny muscat varietal aromas. In the mouth you can literally taste the grapes, as if you are chewing on an explosively rich raisin; great length, and perfect balance. **rating:** 91

best drinking 2002–2010 **best vintages** NA **drink with** Aperitif or digestif • $15.95

Morris Old Premium Liqueur Muscat

▼▼▼▼▼ NV Medium to full tawny, with a hint of olive on the rim. A rich bouquet with complex caramel, toffee and coffee aromas intermingling with the raisins. The palate shows more of the raisiny varietal fruit, although the complexity of the bouquet does repeat itself. A great example of blending. **rating:** 95

best drinking 2002–2003 **best vintages** NA **drink with** Coffee, petits 4s • $45.95

Morris Old Premium Amontillado Sherry

▼▼▼▼▽ NV Golden brown; a classic nutty bouquet proclaims the age of the blend, but without any sign of staleness. The palate has all the complexity, length and rancio one could wish for, and is gently sweet on the mid-palate, and dry on the finish. The one question is the strong, biscuity aftertaste, a character which makers of this style of wine regard as perfectly acceptable. **rating:** 90

best drinking 2001–2002 **best vintages** NA **drink with** Winter aperitif • $45.95

morrisons riverview estate NR

Lot 2 Merool Lane, Moama, NSW 2731 **region** Perricoota
phone (03) 5480 0126 **fax** (03) 5480 7144 **open** 7 days 10–5
winemaker John Ellis **production** 2500 **est.** 1996
product range ($14–22 CD) Semillon, Sauvignon Blanc, Sauvignon Blanc Semillon, Pink Fronti, Adonis (late harvest Sauvignon Blanc), Shiraz, Cabernet Sauvignon Shiraz, Cabernet Sauvignon, Isaac White Port, Muscat.
summary Alistair and Leslie Morrison purchased this historic piece of land in 1995. Plantings began in 1996 with shiraz and cabernet sauvignon, followed in 1997 by sauvignon blanc and frontignac, and grenache in 1998, totalling 6 hectares. The cellar door opened in spring 2000, serving light lunches, platters, picnic baskets, coffee and gourmet cakes; wines are sold by the glass, bottle or box and tastings are free of charge.

moss brothers ★★★★☆

Caves Road, Wilyabrup, WA 6280 **region** Margaret River
phone (08) 9755 6270 **fax** (08) 9755 6298 **open** 7 days 10–5
winemaker David Moss **production** 14 000 **est.** 1984
product range ($14–37 ML) Semillon, Sauvignon Blanc, Semillon Sauvignon Blanc, Verdelho, Oaked
Chardonnay, Non Wooded Chardonnay, Moses Rock White, Drummond Hill White, NV Pinot Noir,
Shiraz, Cabernet Merlot, Drummond Hill Red, Cellar Door Red, Moses Rock Red (the last two are
unusual blends, Moses Rock including Merlot, Pinot Noir, Grenache and Cabernet Franc).
summary Established by long-term viticulturist Jeff Moss and his family, notably sons Peter and David and
Roseworthy graduate daughter Jane. A 100-tonne rammed-earth winery was constructed in 1992 and
draws upon both estate-grown and purchased grapes. Wine quality has improved dramatically, first the
white wines, and more recently the reds. National wholesale distribution; exports to the UK, Europe, the
US, Malaysia, Philippines, and Singapore.

Moss Brothers Semillon

▼▼▼▼ 2001 Medium yellow-green; an aromatic, sweet citrus and herb bouquet is followed by a full-
flavoured and complex palate ranging through herb and spice, but with a slightly grippy finish. **rating:** 88

best drinking 2003–2007 **best vintages** '98, '99 **drink with** Fried chicken • $17.95

Moss Brothers Shiraz

▼▼▼▼▽ 2000 Medium to full red-purple; the bouquet offers complexity, with dark cherry fruit and
touches of vanilla oak; the palate has good weight and fruit ripeness, and is round and fleshy, but far from
jammy. Both the extract and oak management are good. **rating:** 90

best drinking 2003–2009 **best vintages** '99, '00 **drink with** Game pie • $29.95

Moss Brothers Cabernet Sauvignon Merlot

▼▼▼▼▼ 1999 Medium to full red-purple; the first whiff of the bouquet signals an outstanding wine, with
great balance between the varietal fruit inputs and oak, ranging through cedar, blackberry and
blackcurrant; the richly textured and structured palate lives up the bouquet, with layers of dark berry fruit,
excellent, ripe tannins and good oak. **rating:** 95

best drinking 2003–2008 **best vintages** '98 **drink with** Beef Wellington • $35

moss wood ★★★★★

Metricup Road, Wilyabrup, WA 6280 **region** Margaret River
phone (08) 9755 6266 **fax** (08) 9755 6303 **open** By appointment
winemaker Keith Mugford **production** 6000 **est.** 1969
product range ($25.50–77 R) Semillon, Chardonnay, Lefroy Brook Vineyard Chardonnay, Pinot Noir,
Cabernet Sauvignon, Glenmore Vineyard Cabernet Sauvignon.
summary Widely regarded as one of the best wineries in the region, capable of producing glorious
Semillon (the best outside the Hunter Valley) in both oaked and unoaked forms, unctuous Chardonnay and
elegant, gently herbaceous, superfine Cabernet Sauvignon which lives for many years. Exports to the UK,
the US, Switzerland, Germany, Denmark, Belgium, France, Japan, Hong Kong, Indonesia, Malaysia,
Singapore and New Zealand.

Moss Wood Semillon

▼▼▼▼▽ 2001 Light to medium yellow-green; restrained grass and herb aromas in classic Margaret River
varietal style, then a palate with considerable depth and a bone-dry finish after fruit and alcohol sweetness
(14.5°) on the mid to back palate. **rating:** 90

best drinking 2003–2008 **best vintages** '81, '82, '83, '84, '86, '87, '92, '94, '95, '97, '98, '99 **drink with** Crab,
lobster • $28

Moss Wood Glenmore Vineyard Cabernet Sauvignon

▼▼▼▼▽ 2000 Medium red-purple; the moderately intense bouquet offers a mix of red and blackcurrant
fruit supported by subtle oak; the palate moves along the same road, with gently sweet, attractive
cassis/redcurrant fruit and fine oak. An attractive wine. **rating:** 91

best drinking 2004–2010 **best vintages** '99, '00 **drink with** Roast venison • $35

mountadam ★★★★☆

High Eden Road, High Eden Ridge, SA 5235 **region** Eden Valley
phone (08) 8564 1101 **fax** (08) 8361 3400 **open** 7 days 11–4
winemaker Adam Wynn, Andrew Ewart **production** 45 000 **est.** 1972
product range ($13–52 CD) Under the premium Mountadam label are Riesling, Chardonnay, Pinot Noir Chardonnay, Pinot Noir, The Red (50 per cent Merlot, 50 per cent Cabernet), Merlot, Cabernet Sauvignon; under the David Wynn label are Chardonnay, Shiraz, Patriarch Shiraz; under organically grown Eden Ridge label are Sauvignon Blanc, Cabernet Sauvignon; also Ratafia Chardonnay and Pinot Noir.
summary One of the leading small wineries, founded by David Wynn and run by winemaker son Adam Wynn, initially offering only the Mountadam range at relatively high prices. The subsequent development of the three ranges of wines has been very successful, judged from both a winemaking and a wine-marketing viewpoint. Mountadam has built up an extensive export network over many years, with the US, Canada, Hong Kong, Japan and the UK being the major markets, but extending across the breadth of Europe and most Asian markets. This will doubtless be strengthened following the acquisition of Mountadam by Cape Mentelle in 2000.

Mountadam Eden Valley Riesling

▼▼▼▼▽ **2001** Light green-straw; fresh, spotlessly clean and pure lime, apple and pear aromas are followed by a precise and firm palate; it is quite intense and austere, but has obvious ageing potential.   **rating: 92**
best drinking 2004–2014 **best vintages** '01 **drink with** Caesar salad • $24

Mountadam Pinot Noir

▼▼▼▼ **1999** Medium red-purple; a clean rather than complex bouquet, but with attractive cherry and plum fruit; the palate is a logical follow-on, with primary fruit developing slowly. By far the best Mountadam Pinot Noir to date.   **rating: 89**
best drinking 2002–2007 **best vintages** '99 **drink with** Rabbit pie • $36

mount alexander vineyard ★★☆

Calder Highway, North Harcourt, Vic 3453 **region** Bendigo
phone (03) 5474 2262 **fax** (03) 5474 2553 **open** 7 days 10–5.30
winemaker Keith Walkden **production** 6000 **est.** 1984
product range ($10–14 CD) A wide range of various table wines, sparkling, fortifieds, meads and liqueurs.
summary A substantial operation with large vineyards with 17 hectares planted to all the right varieties. It is several years since I have tasted the wines, but a recent report gives me no reason to suppose they have changed much.

mount anakie wines ★★☆

Staughton Vale Road, Anakie, Vic 3221 **region** Geelong
phone (03) 5284 1452 **fax** (03) 5284 1405 **open** Tues–Sun 11–6
winemaker Otto Zambelli **production** 6000 **est.** 1968
product range ($10–18 R) Biancone, Riesling, Semillon, Chardonnay, Dolcetto, Shiraz, Cabernet Franc, Cabernet Sauvignon.
summary Also known as Zambelli Estate. Once produced some excellent wines (under its various ownerships and winemakers), all distinguished by their depth and intensity of flavour. No recent tastings; prior to that, the wines tasted were but a shadow of their former quality. The level of activity seems relatively low.

mount avoca vineyard ★★★☆

Moates Lane, Avoca, Vic 3467 **region** Pyrenees
phone (03) 5465 3282 **fax** (03) 5465 3544 **open** Mon–Fri 9–5, weekends 10–5
winemaker Matthew Barry **production** 18 000 **est.** 1970
product range ($11–45 R) Sauvignon Blanc, Chardonnay, Rhapsody, Trioss White, Trioss Red, Shiraz, Cabernet; Reserve range of Noble Semillon, Merlot, Shiraz, Cabernet, Cabernet Franc, Arda's Choice (Cabernet Sauvignon Cabernet Franc Merlot), Millennium.
summary A substantial winery which has for long been one of the stalwarts of the Pyrenees region, and is steadily growing, with 23.7 hectares of vineyards. There has been a significant refinement in the style and flavour of the red wines over the past few years. I suspect a lot of worthwhile work has gone into barrel selection and maintenance. Acquired by Barrington Estate in 2002.

Mount Avoca Chardonnay

♥♥♥♥ 2000 Light straw-green; an up-and-down bouquet with citrus, mineral, mlf influences and slightly pencilly oak, then a palate which is initially somewhat mute, but has good balance; the fruit finally comes through on the finish. **rating:** 86

best drinking 2002–2004 **best vintages** NA **drink with** Creamy pasta • $20.70

Mount Avoca Reserve Shiraz

♥♥♥♥♥ 1998 Medium red-purple; the bouquet has a mix of small, red berry, cherry and plum fruit offset by cedar and vanilla aromas; the palate offers plenty of mouthfilling flavour, showing chocolate, vanilla, red berry and soft ripe tannins. **rating:** 90

best drinking 2003–2008 **best vintages** '97, '98 **drink with** Braised ox cheek • $34

mount beckworth ★★★★☆

RMB 915 Learmonth Road, Tourello via Ballarat, Vic 3363 **region** Ballarat
phone (03) 5343 4207 **fax** (03) 5343 4207 **open** Weekends 10–6 and by appointment
winemaker Paul Lesock **production** 1000 **est.** 1984
product range ($15–18 CD) Unwooded Chardonnay, Pinot Noir, Shiraz, Cabernet Merlot.
summary The 4-hectare Mount Beckworth vineyard was planted between 1984 and 1985, but it was not until 1995 that the full range of wines under the Mount Beckworth label appeared. Until that time much of the production was sold to Seppelt Great Western for sparkling wine use. It is owned and managed by Paul Lesock, who studied viticulture at Charles Sturt University, and his wife Jane. The wines reflect the very cool climate (except in years such as 2000). Limited Victorian retail distribution.

Mount Beckworth Pinot Noir

♥♥♥♥♥ 2000 Bright purple-red; fragrant and stylish sappy/foresty aromas over red fruits on the bouquet are followed by a palate with all of the foregoing in an intense Burgundian style; great length, fine tannins and outstanding value. **rating:** 92

best drinking 2002–2005 **best vintages** '96, '98, '00 **drink with** Venison ragout • $18

Mount Beckworth Shiraz

♥♥♥♥♥ 2000 Dense purple-red; a fragrant and complex bouquet with dark plum, licorice and spice is shadowed by the palate, which texturally has some affinities with the Pinot Noir, as it is intense but not tannic. A lovely red wine from an exceptional vintage. **rating:** 94

best drinking 2003–2008 **best vintages** '95, '00 **drink with** Marinated beef • $18

mount broke wines ★★★☆

Adams Peak Road, Broke, NSW 2330 **region** Lower Hunter Valley
phone (02) 6579 1313 **fax** (02) 6579 1313 **open** Weekends and public holidays 9.30–5
winemaker Contract **production** 840 **est.** 1997
product range ($17–24.50 R) River Bank Verdelho, River Bank Shiraz, Black Pine Ridge Merlot, Harrowby Cabernet Merlot.
summary Phil and Jo McNamara began planting their 9.6-hectare vineyard to shiraz, merlot, verdelho, barbera, semillon, chardonnay and cabernet sauvignon in 1997 on the west side of Woollamai Brook. It is early days, but they have already established a wine club and have opened The Cow Cafe, with wine tasting and wine function capacity. The Shiraz has starred since 1999.

Mount Broke River Bank Verdelho

♥♥♥♥ 2001 Medium green-yellow; the clean bouquet has the usual fruit salad fruit, with an added touch of citrus; much the same play occurs on the palate, where the citrus accents give the wine some life and interest. **rating:** 84

best drinking 2002–2003 **best vintages** NA **drink with** Pasta • $17

Mount Broke Wines River Bank Shiraz

♥♥♥♥ 2001 Strong purple-red; rich, concentrated dark berry, licorice and oak aromas flow into a palate as powerful and as ripe as the bouquet suggests, with super-abundant fruit supported by tannins and oak. **rating:** 90

best drinking 2005–2015 **best vintages** '99, '01 **drink with** Barbecued rump • $24.50

🐚 mount cathedral vineyards ★★★☆

125 Knafl Road, Taggerty, Vic 3714 **region** Central Victorian High Country
phone 0409 354 069 **fax** (03) 9354 0994 **open** By appointment
winemaker Oscar Rosa, Nick Arena **production** 500 **est.** 1995
product range ($20–35 ML) Chardonnay, Merlot.
summary The Rosa and Arena families established Mount Cathedral Vineyards 1995, the vines being planted at an elevation of 300 metres on the north face of Mount Cathedral. The first plantings were of 1.2 hectares of merlot and 0.8 hectare of chardonnay, followed by 2.5 hectare of cabernet sauvignon and 0.5 hectare of cabernet franc in 1996. Oscar Rosa, chief winemaker, has completed two TAFE courses in viticulture and winemaking, and is currently in his fifth year of the Bachelor of Wine Science course at Charles Sturt University. He gained practical experience working at Yering Station during 1998 and 1999. The initial releases from 2000 are an impressive start.

Mount Cathedral Vineyards Chardonnay

▼▼▼▽ **2000** Light green-yellow; the bouquet is clean, but the fruit seems to have been suppressed, perhaps by the malolactic fermentation, possibly by bottling shock. The palate is quite crisp, clean and fresh, the sophisticated winemaking once again coming through. I am not convinced the base material had sufficient power to absorb all of the winemaker inputs. **rating:** 84

best drinking 2002–2006 **best vintages** NA **drink with** Deep-fried calamari • $20

Mount Cathedral Vineyards Merlot

▼▼▼▼ **2000** Medium red-purple; strong oak is the first impression on the bouquet, then rich fruit underneath. The palate has plenty of depth, flavour and structure, also showing a varietally correct twist of olive on the finish. **rating:** 87

best drinking 2004–2010 **best vintages** NA **drink with** Lamb Provençale • $35

mount charlie winery ★★★

228 Mount Charlie Road, Riddells Creek, Vic 3431 **region** Macedon Ranges
phone (03) 5428 6946 **fax** (03) 5428 6946 **open** Weekends by appointment
winemaker Trefor Morgan **production** 600 **est.** 1991
product range ($20–22 CD) Sauvignon Blanc, Chardonnay, Red (Shiraz Merlot Cabernet blend).
summary Mount Charlie's wines are sold principally by mail order and through selected restaurants. A futures programme encourages mailing list sales with a discount of over 25 per cent on the ultimate release price. Owner/winemaker Trefor Morgan is perhaps better known as a Professor of Physiology at Melbourne University.

Mount Charlie Chardonnay

▼▼▼▽ **2000** Light to medium yellow-green; a clean, light bouquet has melon and just a touch of cashew; the palate is yet to build complexity or depth. Should do so with a few years in bottle. **rating:** 83

best drinking 2002–2006 **best vintages** NA **drink with** Summer salad • $22

🐚 mount delancey winery NR

60 De Lancey Road, Wandin North, Vic 3139 **region** Yarra Valley
phone (03) 5964 4964 **open** Weekends 10–5.30 or by appointment
winemaker Jordan Metlikovec **production** 200 **est.** 1985
product range ($10–20 CD) Chardonnay, Pinot Noir, Cabernet Sauvignon; also fruit wines.
summary Jordan Metlikovec makes a tiny quantity of wine and fruit wine from a mixed planting of 1 hectare which includes chardonnay, pinot noir and cabernet sauvignon, purchasing approximately 2 tonnes of grapes from other small Yarra Valley vineyards and berry growers.

mount duneed ★★☆

Feehan's Road, Mount Duneed, Vic 3216 **region** Geelong
phone (03) 5264 1281 **fax** (03) 5264 1281 **open** Public holidays and weekends 11–5 or by appointment
winemaker Ken Campbell, John Darling **production** 1000 **est.** 1970
product range ($10–18 CD) Semillon, Sauvignon Blanc, Riesling, Botrytis Semillon, Malbec, Cabernet Malbec, Cabernet Sauvignon.

summary Rather idiosyncratic wines are the order of the day, some of which can develop surprisingly well in bottle; the Botrytis Noble Rot Semillon has, from time to time, been of very high quality. A significant part of the production from the 7.5 hectares of vineyards is sold to others.

mount eliza estate   NR

Cnr Sunnyside Road and Nepean Highway, Mount Eliza, Vic 3930 **region** Mornington Peninsula
phone (03) 9787 0663 **fax** (03) 9781 2106 **open** 7 days 11–5
winemaker Scott Ireland (Contract) **production** 2500 **est.** 1997
product range ($16–35 CD) Riesling, Sauvignon Blanc, Chardonnay, Pinot Noir, Magnus Maximus Pinot Noir, Shiraz.
summary Robert and Jenny Thurley planted the 7.84-hectare vineyard at Mount Eliza Estate in 1997; the varieties are riesling, chardonnay, sauvignon blanc, shiraz, pinot noir and cabernet sauvignon. Son James, presently studying viticulture, has worked at the vineyard since day one under the direction of viticulturist Graeme Harrip, making the business a family affair. The cellar door, which has great views across Port Phillip Bay to the Melbourne city skyline, was opened in November 2000. The contract winemaker is Scott Ireland, of Provenance, who has had many years' experience in making wines from the Port Phillip Zone.

mount eyre vineyard   ★★★☆

1325 Broke Road, Broke, NSW 2330 **region** Lower Hunter Valley
phone 0438 683 973 **fax** (02) 9744 3508 **open** By appointment
winemaker Stephen Hagan (Contract) **production** 9000 **est.** 1996
product range ($14–35 CD) Released under three labels: the Mount Eyre range of Semillon, Semillon Chardonnay, Unwooded Chardonnay; Three Ponds Semillon, Chardonnay, Shiraz; and Neptune (Sparkling Semillon).
summary Dr Aniello Inannuzzi's 24-hectare estate at Broke is planted to semillon, chardonnay, shiraz, cabernet franc and cabernet sauvignon, the wines being contract-made off-site.

Mount Eyre Vineyard Three Ponds Chardonnay
▼▼▼▼ **2000** Light to medium yellow-green; the bouquet offers complexity, with nutty/cashew overtones to light melon fruit. The palate has good texture and structure, a touch of sweetness not detracting, although the oak is slightly persistent.   **rating: 86**

best drinking 2001–2004 **best vintages** NA **drink with** Cheese gnocchi • $20

mountford   ★★★

Bamess Road, West Pemberton, WA 6260 **region** Pemberton
phone (08) 9776 1345 **fax** (08) 9776 1345 **open** 7 days 10–4
winemaker Andrew Mountford, Saxon Mountford **production** 3000 **est.** 1987
product range ($16.50–35 CD) Sauvignon Blanc, Unwooded Chardonnay, Wood Aged Chardonnay, Pinot Noir, Reserve Merlot, Cabernet Merlot.
summary English born and trained Andrew Mountford and wife Sue migrated to Australia in 1983, first endeavouring to set up a winery at Mudgee and thereafter moving to Pemberton with far greater success. Their strikingly packaged wines are produced from 6 hectares of permanently netted, dry-grown vineyards. Exports to the UK.

Mountford Reserve Merlot
▼▼▼▼ **2000** Light to medium red-purple; savoury, earthy, woodsy aromas are a distinctly legitimate manifestation of merlot varietal character; the taut, savoury/spicy/foresty/tangy palate is likewise in varietal mode, and a stylish one at that. Much more concentration than the other Mountford wines.   **rating: 87**

best drinking 2003–2008 **best vintages** NA **drink with** White Rocks veal • $35

mount gisborne wines   NR

83 Waterson Road, Gisborne, Vic 3437 **region** Macedon Ranges
phone (03) 5428 2834 **fax** (03) 5428 2834 **open** By appointment
winemaker Stuart Anderson **production** 1200 **est.** 1986
product range ($25–40 CD) Chardonnay, Pinot Noir, Pinot Noir Limited Release.
summary Mount Gisborne Wines is very much a weekend and holiday occupation for proprietor David Ell, who makes the wines from the 7-hectare vineyard under the watchful and skilled eye of industry veteran Stuart Anderson, now living in semi-retirement high in the Macedon Hills.

mount horrocks ★★★★☆

The Old Railway Station, Curling Street, Auburn, SA 5451 **region** Clare Valley
phone (08) 8849 2243 **fax** (08) 8849 2265 **open** Weekends and public holidays 10–5
winemaker Stephanie Toole **production** 4500 **est.** 1982
product range ($19.50–38 ML) Watervale Riesling, Semillon, Chardonnay, Cordon Cut Riesling, Shiraz, Cabernet Merlot.
summary Mount Horrocks has well and truly established its own identity in recent years, aided by positive marketing and, equally importantly, wine quality which has resulted in both show success and critical acclaim. Exports to the UK, the US, Germany, Switzerland, Holland, Italy, France, New Zealand, Malaysia, Singapore and Japan. Lunches available on weekends.

Mount Horrocks Watervale Riesling

▼▼▼▼♀ 2001 Light green-yellow; the bouquet has an interesting mix of mineral, slate and blossom aromas; the palate is particularly long and quite powerful, with good balance and excellent persistence of flavour.
rating: 92

best drinking 2001–2007 **best vintages** '86, '87, '90, '93, '94, '97, '01 **drink with** Thai or Chinese soup • $25.95

Mount Horrocks Semillon

▼▼▼▼♀ 2000 Light to medium yellow-green; the bouquet is clean, firm and solid, with some mineral undertones, and not particularly aromatic. The palate has been very well constructed, not unlike a cross between traditional Hunter style and that of the Adelaide Hills. Should develop very well; the oak has in no sense been overplayed.
rating: 90

best drinking 2002–2007 **best vintages** '97, '99, '00 **drink with** Pan-fried fish • $25

Mount Horrocks Cordon Cut Riesling

▼▼▼▼♀ 2001 Glowing yellow-green; a rich, honeyed bouquet, with touches of lime, is followed by a rich palate with great length and intensity, the sweetness perfectly balanced by crisp acidity.
rating: 93

best drinking 2001–2004 **best vintages** '00, '01 **drink with** Pavlova • $32

Mount Horrocks Shiraz

▼▼▼▼ 1999 Medium purple-red; there is good balance and integration between the cherry/plum fruit and oak; the palate is still tight and firm, with the acidity showing on the finish; needs time to soften and open up, but is well focussed, and has an assured future.
rating: 89

best drinking 2004–2009 **best vintages** '98 **drink with** Steak and kidney pie • $38

Mount Horrocks Cabernet Merlot

▼▼▼▼♀ 1999 Medium to full red-purple; the bouquet is clean, with sweet red berry and cassis fruit supported by gentle oak, swelling into an attractive palate with more of the cassis/berry fruit flavours, fine tannins, and sure oak handling. The 18th vintage of this wine, which Stephanie O'Toole believes is one of the best so far, a judgement which seems eminently reasonable to me.
rating: 91

best drinking 2004–2009 **best vintages** '99 **drink with** Ragout of veal • $30

mount ida ★★★★

Northern Highway, Heathcote, Vic 3253 **region** Heathcote
phone NA **open** Not
winemaker Matt Steel **production** NFP **est.** 1978
product range ($40 R) Shiraz.
summary Established by the famous artist Leonard French and Dr James Munro but purchased by Tisdall after the 1987 bushfires and thereafter by Beringer Blass when it acquired Tisdall. Up to the time of the fires, wonderfully smooth, rich red wines with almost voluptuous sweet, minty fruit were the hallmark. After a brief period during which the name was used as a simple brand (with various wines released,) has returned to a single estate-grown wine.

Mount Ida Shiraz

▼▼▼▼ 1999 Medium to full red-purple; a wine with lots of activity on both bouquet and palate, opening with licorice and black cherry, before moving through to a slightly extractive finish which needs time to soften and settle down, which it almost certainly will.
rating: 87

best drinking 2004–2009 **best vintages** '98 **drink with** Australian Parmesan • $39.99

mountilford NR

Mount Vincent Road, Ilford, NSW 2850 **region** Mudgee
phone (02) 6358 8544 **fax** (02) 6358 8544 **open** 7 days 10–4
winemaker Don Cumming **production** NFP **est.** 1985
product range ($12–22 CD) Riesling, Highland White, Windamere, Sylvaner, Chardonnay, Pinot Noir, Pinot Shiraz, Cabernet Shiraz, Jubilation Cabernet Shiraz, Sir Alexander Port, Lady Alex.
summary Surprisingly large cellar-door operation which has grown significantly over the past few years. I have not, however, had the opportunity to taste the wines.

mount langi ghiran vineyards ★★★★★

Warrak Road, Buangor, Vic 3375 **region** Grampians
phone (03) 5354 3207 **fax** (03) 5354 3277 **open** Mon–Fri 9–5, weekends 12–5
winemaker Trevor Mast, Andrew McLoughney **production** 45 000 **est.** 1969
product range ($17–55 ML) Riesling, Pinot Gris, Joanna Cabernet Sauvignon; under Langi label Shiraz and Cabernet Merlot; Nut Tree Block Sangiovese, Cliff Edge Shiraz.
summary A maker of outstanding cool-climate peppery Shiraz, crammed with flavour and vinosity, and very good Cabernet Sauvignon. The Shiraz points the way for cool-climate examples of the variety, for weight, texture and fruit richness all accompany the vibrant pepper-spice aroma and flavour. Now partly owned by Trevor Mast, and partly by German wine entrepreneur Riquet Hess; the most tangible sign of the partnership has been the erection of a totally new, state-of-the-art winery, not to mention the expansion of the estate vineyards to over 60 hectares and the establishment of an export network throughout the US, the UK, Asia, Europe, New Zealand and Canada.

Mount Langi Ghiran Pinot Gris

▼▼▼▼ 2001 The faintly pink tinge comes from the colour of the skin of the grape, not from oxidation; light strawberry and spice aromas are followed by quite remarkable peachy/strawberry flavours, somewhat out of left field; the 13.5° alcohol seems to give a slightly hot finish to this curate's egg. **rating:** 87

best drinking 2001–2002 **best vintages** NA **drink with** Antipasto • $22

mount lofty ranges vineyard ★★★★

Harris Road, Lenswood, SA 5240 **region** Adelaide Hills
phone (08) 8389 8339 **fax** (08) 8389 8349 **open** Weekends 11–5
winemaker Nepenthe (Contract) **production** 1200 **est.** 1992
product range ($16–20 CD) Five Vines Riesling, Sauvignon Blanc, Chardonnay, Old Pump Shed Pinot Noir.
summary Mount Lofty Ranges is owned by Alan Herath and Jan Reed, who have been involved from the outset in planting, training and nurturing the 4.5-hectare vineyard. Both have professional careers but are intending to become full-time vignerons in the not too distant future. Skilled winemaking by Peter Leske at Nepenthe has already brought rewards and recognition to the vineyard.

Mount Lofty Five Vines Riesling

▼▼▼▼ 2001 Light straw-green; the clean, firm mineral/slate bouquet is repeated on the firm, minerally palate, with bracing grip on the finish. Definitely needs time, but will repay cellaring. **rating:** 85

best drinking 2004–2009 **best vintages** '99 **drink with** Vegetable terrine • $16

Mount Lofty Sauvignon Blanc

▼▼▼▽ 2001 Water white, with an almost grey tinge; the delicate bouquet has faint whiffs of passionfruit and kiwifruit, characters which lurk in the painfully shy palate. **rating:** 84

best drinking 2002–2004 **best vintages** NA **drink with** Blue swimmer crab • $16

Mount Lofty Chardonnay

▼▼▼▼ 2000 Light to medium yellow-green; a quite complex bouquet with melon, cashew and nutty oak, then a palate led by ripe stone fruit and melon, with notes of cream and nutty oak leading to an appealing overall softness. **rating:** 88

best drinking 2003–2006 **best vintages** NA **drink with** Sweetbreads • $16

Mount Lofty Old Pump Shed Pinot Noir

ŢŢŢŢŸ 2000 Medium red, with some purple remaining; an aromatic, savoury/woodsy bouquet with some spice and lift, then a tangy, savoury, spicy palate, with an almost lemony flavour, finishing with fine tannins and controlled oak. Stylish.   **rating: 91**

best drinking 2002–2005 **best vintages** '98, '00 **drink with** Braised ox cheek • $20

mount macedon   ★ ★ ★ ☆

Bawden Road, Mount Macedon, Vic 3441 **region** Macedon Ranges
phone (03) 5427 2735 **fax** (03) 5427 1071 **open** 7 days 10–5
winemaker Ian Deacon **production** 4500 **est.** 1989
product range ($16–30 CD) Unwooded Chardonnay, Chardonnay, Winemaker's Reserve Chardonnay, Brut, Pinot Noir Saignée Rosé, Pinot Noir, Shiraz, Cabernet Merlot.
summary Don and Pam Ludbey have established a substantial operation at Mount Macedon drawing upon two separate vineyards; Mount Macedon and Hay Hill. In all, they have a little over 11 hectares under vine. Ian Deacon has made wine in the Yarra Valley and surrounding cool regions for many years; his experience shows through in the wines, which, while not particularly rich or full, have a touch of elegance.

Mount Macedon Brut

ŢŢŢŢ NV Light to medium yellow-green; the bouquet has attractive bready/yeasty autolysis characters; the palate opens well with good fruit, but tails off on the finish.   **rating: 86**

best drinking 2001–2003 **best vintages** NA **drink with** Aperitif • $30

mount majura vineyard   ★ ★ ★ ★

RMB 314 Majura Road, Majura, ACT 2609 **region** Canberra District
phone 0403 355 682 **fax** (02) 6262 4288 **open** Not
winemaker Dr Frank van de Loo, (Dr Roger Harris, Consultant) **production** 700 **est.** 1988
product range ($20–25 R) Chardonnay, Pinot Noir, Cabernet Franc Merlot.
summary The first vines were planted in 1988 by Dinny Killen on a site on her family property which had been especially recommended by Dr Edgar Riek; its attractions were red soil of volcanic origin over limestone, the reasonably steep east and northeast slopes providing an element of frost protection. The 1-hectare vineyard was planted to pinot noir, chardonnay and merlot in equal quantities; the pinot noir grapes were sold to Lark Hill and used in their award-winning Pinot Noir, while the chardonnay and merlot were made for Mount Majura by Lark Hill, both wines enjoying show success. The syndicate which purchased the property in 1999 has extended the plantings, and Dr Frank van de Loo makes the wines in leased space at Brindabella Hills, with consultancy advice from Roger Harris.

Mount Majura Chardonnay

ŢŢŢŢ 2000 Light to medium yellow-green; complex barrel fermentation and malolactic fermentation characters provide a mix of nectarine and cashew on the bouquet; the winemaker's thumbprints are also very evident on the figgy/cashew/creamy palate; all in all a sophisticated package.   **rating: 88**

best drinking 2002–2004 **best vintages** NA **drink with** Abalone • $25

Mount Majura Pinot Noir

ŢŢŢŢ 2000 Light to medium red-purple; foresty, savoury, spicy aromas carry through to the entry of the palate before plum and dark fruit flavours take over, finishing with the barest suggestion of vanilla oak.   **rating: 87**

best drinking 2002–2005 **best vintages** NA **drink with** Roast quail • $25

mount mary   ★ ★ ★ ★ ★

Coldstream West Road, Lilydale, Vic 3140 **region** Yarra Valley
phone (03) 9739 1761 **fax** (03) 9739 0137 **open** Not
winemaker Dr John Middleton **production** 3000 **est.** 1971
product range ($32–80 ML) Chardonnay, Triolet (Sauvignon Blanc, Semillon, Muscadelle), Pinot Noir, Cabernets Quintet (Bordeaux-blend).
summary Superbly refined, elegant and intense Cabernets and usually outstanding and long-lived Pinot Noirs fully justify Mount Mary's exalted reputation. The Triolet blend is very good, more recent vintages of Chardonnay likewise. Limited quantities of the wines are sold through the wholesale/retail distribution system in Victoria, NSW, QLD, and SA.

Mount Mary Pinot Noir
▼▼▼▼▼ **1999** Excellent hue: bright, light to medium red-purple. Pure varietal character is evident on the bouquet with fragrant plum and cherry fruit. Stylish palate has the hallmark silky mouthfeel in a light to medium-bodied frame. Very interesting to taste the wine so young (April 2001), as you can see the breed of the wine, and the pure fruit with which it starts. Shows absolutely no sign of any vintage problems. **rating:** 94

best drinking 2003–2009 **best vintages** '79, '85, '86, '89, '91, '99 **drink with** Breast of squab • $80

mount moliagul ★★★☆

Clay Gully Lane, Moliagul, Vic 3472 **region** Bendigo
phone (03) 9809 2113 **open** Mon–Fri 12–5 or by appointment
winemaker Terry Flora **production** 200 **est.** 1991
product range ($16–22 ML) Unwooded Chardonnay, Pinot Noir, Shiraz, Cabernet Sauvignon.
summary Terry and Bozenka Flora began the establishment of their tiny vineyard in 1991, gradually planting 0.5 hectare each of shiraz and cabernet sauvignon, and 0.2 hectare of chardonnay. Terry Flora has completed two winemaking courses, one with Winery Supplies and the other at Dookie College, and has learnt his craft very well. In 1998 and 2000, Mount Moliagul won the trophy for Best Red Wine of Show at the Victorian Wines Show. The cellar door opened in December 2001.

Mount Moliagul Unwooded Chardonnay
▼▼▼▼ **2001** Excellent, glowing green-yellow; the bouquet is slightly subdued, possibly through bottling shock and/or free SO$_2$. The palate is fine, tight and elegant, with light citrus and melon fruit, and is well-balanced. An impressive example of unwooded Chardonnay. **rating:** 86

best drinking 2001–2003 **best vintages** NA **drink with** Warm seafood • $16

Mount Moliagul Shiraz
▼▼▼▼ **2000** Bright, medium red-purple; savoury, spicy fruit and oak intermingle on the bouquet and palate; there are interesting savoury/briary tones to the fruit, but I am not entirely convinced by the choice of oak. **rating:** 85

best drinking 2003–2009 **best vintages** NA **drink with** Designer sausages • $18

Mount Moliagul Cabernet Sauvignon
▼▼▼▼▽ **2000** Excellent, youthful purple-red; clean, ripe cassis/blackcurrant fruit and subtle oak on the bouquet, followed by a substantial palate with abundant berry fruit, tannins and oak. Simply needs time to knit and open up. **rating:** 90

best drinking 2004–2010 **best vintages** '00 **drink with** Beef casserole • $22

mount panorama winery NR

117 Mountain Straight, Mount Panorama, Bathurst, NSW 2795 **region** Southern New South Wales Zone
phone (02) 6331 5368 **fax** (02) 6331 5368 **open** 7 days 10.30–5
winemaker Bill Stuart, Deborah Stuart **production** 600 **est.** 1991
product range ($9–20 CD) Riesling, Unwooded Chardonnay, Chardonnay, Shiraz, Cabernet Sauvignon, Old Sweet Tawny, Honey Wine.
summary For all the obvious reasons, Mount Panorama Winery makes full use of its setting on Mountain Straight after the 'Hell Corner' on the inside of the famous motor racing circuit. Bill and Deborah Stuart are wholly responsible for the production of the wine, from picking and using the hand-operated basket press through to bottling, labelling, etc. They are gradually extending both the size and scope of the cellar-door facilities to take advantage of the tourist opportunities of the site.

mount prior vineyard ★★★☆

Gooramadda Road, Rutherglen, Vic 3685 **region** Rutherglen
phone (02) 6026 5591 **fax** (02) 6026 5590 **open** 7 days 9–5
winemaker James Ashe, Nick Henry **production** 15 000 **est.** 1860
product range ($13–40 CD) Chenin Blanc, Classic Ibis Dry White, Semillon Chardonnay, Chardonnay, Sparkling Shiraz Durif, Brut Cuvée, Late Picked Riesling, Noble Gold, Classic Ibis Dry Red, Shiraz, Durif, Merlot Limited Release, Cabernet Merlot, Port, Muscat, Tokay.
summary A full-scale tourist facility, with yet more in the pipeline. Full accommodation packages at the historic Mount Prior House; a restaurant operating weekends under the direction of Trish Hennessy (for groups of six or more), with 4 consecutive *Age Good Food Guide* awards to its credit; picnic and barbecue

facilities; and a gift shop. The wines are basically sold through the cellar door and by an active mailing list. The already substantial 40 hectares of vineyards were expanded by a further 5 hectares of durif planted in 1998, a mark both of the success of Mount Prior and of the interest in Durif.

Mount Prior Chardonnay

▼▼▼▽ NV 1999 Medium yellow-green; the bouquet has obvious bottle-developed toasty/honeyed aromas, the palate dutifully following with solid, honest bottle-developed flavour in a slightly old-fashioned 'white burgundy' style. **rating:** 84

best drinking 2002–2003 **best vintages** '98 **drink with** Rich chicken or veal • $16

Mount Prior Sparkling Shiraz Durif

▼▼▼▼ NV Dense red-purple; a massive berry and chocolate bouquet is followed by an equally huge chocolate, prune and plum palate, with relatively low gas levels. Totally idiosyncratic, but works well. **rating:** 89

best drinking 2003–2010 **best vintages** NA **drink with** Borscht • $22

Mount Prior Durif

▼▼▼▼ 1999 Dark red-purple; deep plume/prune/licorice/chocolate fruit aromas are very typical of the variety, and the solidly built palate, with a similar array of flavours, does not stray into over-extraction; the tannins are not overblown. **rating:** 86

best drinking 2004–2014 **best vintages** NA **drink with** Richest meat or strongest cheese • $25

Mount Prior Vineyard Director's Selection Muscat (375 ml)

▼▼▼▼ NV Medium to full red; clean spirit, raisin and honey aromas, then a palate with greater density than the price would suggest, showing some older material with the predominantly fresh younger components; excellent value. **rating:** 86

best drinking 2002–2003 **best vintages** NA **drink with** Chocolate • $13

Mount Prior Vineyard Reserve Port Museum Release

▼▼▼▼ NV Medium to full red; Christmas cake, spice and aromas show the obvious wood age of the wine, those characters coming through on the palate but with special emphasis on chocolate, spice and biscuit. **rating:** 88

best drinking 2002–2003 **best vintages** NA **drink with** Rich cakes, nuts • $40

mount tamborine winery   NR

32 Hartley Road, Mount Tamborine, Qld 4272 **region** Queensland Coastal
phone (07) 5545 3981 **fax** (07) 5545 3311 **open** 7 days 10–4
winemaker Stuart Pierce **production** 8000 **est.** 1993
product range ($10–40 ML) Hinterland Selection of Semillon, Classic Dry Red, Sweet Red; Cedar Ridge Selection of Sauvignon Blanc Chardonnay, Unwooded Chardonnay, Oaked Chardonnay, Blanc de Blanc, Black Shiraz, Shiraz Cabernet, Grenache Cabernet Merlot, Cabernet Sauvignon; Tehembrin Reserve Selection of Sparkling Merlot, Imperial Reserve, Merlot; also Daisy Chardonnay, Lily the Pink Rosé, Frontignac (dessert style), Bush Turkey Port, Mountain Muscat.
summary Mount Tamborine Winery draws upon 3 hectares of estate plantings adjacent to the winery, 30 hectares in Stanthorpe, and also purchases wine from the King Valley, Cowra and the Riverland to produce a wide range of wine styles. The Chardonnay and Merlot have both had success in Queensland wine shows and competitions, and the wines are sold locally and exported to Southeast Asia. It is a sister company to Barambah Ridge, both operations being owned by Tambarambah Limited.

Mount Tamborine Tehembrin Merlot

▼▼▼▽ 1999 Light to medium red-purple, the clean bouquet offers some earth/olive/savoury varietal character; the light to medium-bodied palate is sweetened up by American oak. Competently made, but it is hard to take the wine seriously when it is offered in one of those tall, skinny bottles better suited to olive oil. **rating:** 83

best drinking 2002–2005 **best vintages** NA **drink with** Yearling beef • $33

mount trio vineyard   ★★★☆

Cnr Castle Rock and Porongurup Roads, Porongurup WA 6324 **region** Great Southern
phone (08) 9853 1136 **fax** (08) 9853 1120 **open** By appointment
winemaker Gavin Berry **production** 4500 **est.** 1989
product range ($14–18 R) Sauvignon Blanc, Chardonnay, Pinot Noir, Cabernet Merlot.

summary Mount Trio was established by Gavin Berry and Gill Graham shortly after they moved to the Mount Barker district in late 1988. Gavin Berry was assistant winemaker to John Wade, and Gill managed the cellar-door sales. Gavin is now senior winemaker and managing director of Plantagenet, and Gill is the mother of two young children. In the meantime they have slowly built up the Mount Trio business, based in part upon estate plantings of 2 hectares of pinot noir and 0.5 hectare of chardonnay and in part on purchased grapes. An additional 6 hectares was planted in the spring of 1999, and plans are to ultimately increase production to around 5000 cases.

Mount Trio Vineyard Sauvignon Blanc

♥♥♥♡ **2001** Light green-yellow; a crisp, very light bouquet with faint mineral aromas, then a palate where the fruit flavour is not obvious; however, the wine does have considerable length, helped by lemony/minerally acidity. **rating:** 84

best drinking 2002–2003 **best vintages** NA **drink with** Shellfish • $14

Mount Trio Chardonnay

♥♥♥♥ **2000** Medium yellow-green; gentle, but quite complex, citrus fruit aromas and subtle barrel-ferment inputs to the bouquet run through into the palate, with grapefruit, melon and cashew intermingling before brisk acidity on the finish. **rating:** 87

best drinking 2003–2007 **best vintages** '98 **drink with** Tempura • $16

Mount Trio Cabernet Merlot

♥♥♥♡ **1999** Medium red-purple; both the bouquet and palate are at the savoury end of the spectrum, with leafy/cedary aromas and flavours supported by gently cedary oak and fine tannins. Very much in a Bordeaux mould. **rating:** 84

best drinking 2003–2007 **best vintages** NA **drink with** Yearling beef • $18

mount view estate ★★★★☆

Mount View Road, Mount View, NSW 2325 **region** Lower Hunter Valley
phone (02) 4990 3307 **fax** (02) 4991 1289 **open** 7 days 10–5
winemaker Andrew Thomas **production** 3500 **est.** 1971
product range ($10–40 CD) Reserve Semillon, Reserve Verdelho, Chardonnay Semillon, Reserve Chardonnay, Rosé, Pinot Noir, Shiraz, Reserve Shiraz, Merlot, Cabernet Sauvignon, Liqueur Verdelho, Tawny Port.
summary The Tulloch family no longer owns nor has any interest in Mount View Estate following its sudden sale in 2000, but winemaking has passed to the capable hands of former Tyrrell's winemaker Andrew Thomas. The 30-year-old vines are paying big dividends.

Mount View Estate Reserve Semillon

♥♥♥♥♡ **2001** Light to medium yellow-green; the firm bouquet has a predominance of grassy/mineral aromas, and then a hint of lemon; the wine has above average palate weight and feel, with ripe citrus/lemon fruit, and will develop more quickly than many of its 2001 counterparts. Perhaps the 12.1° alcohol has something to do with it. A very useful wine. **rating:** 91

best drinking 2002–2006 **best vintages** '01 **drink with** Balmain bugs • $16

Mount View Estate Reserve Chardonnay

♥♥♥♥♡ **2001** Light straw-green; the clean and fresh bouquet is driven by nectarine and citrus fruit, with minimal oak; an elegant, restrained wine on the palate, with a subtle blend of inputs, and which actually needs some time. Fermented in new and used French oak, and lees-contacted. **rating:** 90

best drinking 2003–2005 **best vintages** NA **drink with** Poached chicken • $14

Mount View Estate Pinot Noir

♥♥♥♥ **2000** Medium to full red-purple; a solid bouquet with some ripe cherry fruit; the powerful palate has some vestiges of varietal character, but is far better assessed as a generic dry red wine than as Pinot Noir. Will become more regional as it ages. **rating:** 87

best drinking 2003–2007 **best vintages** NA **drink with** Kangaroo fillet • $13

Mount View Estate Reserve Shiraz

♥♥♥♥♡ **2000** Medium red-purple; the moderately intense bouquet is spotlessly clean, with dark cherry and plum fruit supported by gentle oak. The medium to full-bodied palate is rich, but has clear varietal expression, the region only (yet) manifesting itself in the slightly earthy tannins. **rating:** 92

best drinking 2005–2012 **best vintages** '97, '00 **drink with** Fillet mignon • $16

Mount View Estate Merlot

ŸŸŸŸ 2000 Medium red-purple; the bouquet is foresty, and fractionally hard, but there is attractive sweet berry fruit on the palate, and the tannins are present but under control.　　　　**rating:** 84

best drinking 2002–2006 **best vintages** NA **drink with** Yearling steak • $40

Mount View Estate Cabernet Sauvignon

ŸŸŸŸ 2000 Medium to full red-purple; the depth and ripeness of the blackcurrant and cassis fruit on the bouquet is surprising, even for 2000; the ripe fruit comes through on the palate with a slightly crushed ant character, steadied by soft, fine and ripe tannins on the finish.　　　　**rating:** 89

best drinking 2006–2011 **best vintages** NA **drink with** Daube of lamb • $18

mountview wines　　　★★★

Mount Stirling Road, Glen Aplin, Qld 4381 **region** Granite Belt
phone (07) 4683 4316 **fax** (07) 4683 4111 **open** Fri–Mon 9.30–4.30, 7 days during school and public holidays
winemaker Phillipa Hambleton **production** 1250 **est.** 1990
product range ($10–18 CD) Chardonnay Semillon Sauvignon Blanc, First Pick (Chardonnay blend), Emu Swamp White, Chardonnay Royal (sparkling), Bianco Bubbles (sparkling), Blanc de Blancs, Sparkling Perry, Short Flat White (dessert), Cerise (light red), Short Flat Red (light red), Shiraz, Merlot, Cabernet Merlot, Shiraz Royal (sparkling).
summary Mountview Wines has changed hands and is now owned by Pauline Stewart. I have no reason to suppose the quality of the Shiraz (in particular) has diminished.

mount vincent mead　　　NR

Common Road, Mudgee, NSW 2850 **region** Mudgee
phone (02) 6372 3184 **fax** (02) 6372 3184 **open** Mon–Sat 10–5, Sun 10–4
winemaker Sue Nevell **production** 2000 **est.** 1972
product range ($12–33 CD) Honey Nectar, Napunya Dry Mead, Napunya Medium Sweet, Stringy Bark Medium Sweet, Napunya Sweet Metheglin, Yellow Box Liqueur Mead and Red Hot Devil (spiced). Each of these is vintage-dated.
summary Now only produces meads, which can be absolutely outstanding, dramatically reflecting the impact of the different plants from which the bees have collected their nectar. Self-contained accommodation is available.

mount william winery　　　★★★

Mount William Road, Tantaraboo, Vic 3764 **region** Macedon Ranges
phone (03) 5429 1595 **fax** (03) 5429 1998 **open** Weekends 11–5
winemaker Murray Cousins, Hanging Rock (Contract) **production** 2500 **est.** 1987
product range ($15–30 CD) Bedbur's Riesling, Stuart's Block Semillon, Chardonnay, Macedon Sparkling Chardonnay, Blanc de Blanc, Louis Clare Sparkling Red, Pinot Noir, Cabernets.
summary Adrienne and Murray Cousins established 7 hectares of vineyards between 1987 and 1999, planted to pinot noir, cabernet franc, merlot, semillon and chardonnay. The wines are made under contract (Hanging Rock) and are sold through a stone tasting room/cellar-door facility which was completed in 1992, and also through a number of fine wine retailers around Melbourne.

mudgee wines　　　NR

Henry Lawson Drive, Mudgee, NSW 2850 **region** Mudgee
phone (02) 6372 2258 **open** Thurs–Mon 10–5, holidays 7 days
winemaker David Conway **production** 600 **est.** 1963
product range ($9–15 CD) Chardonnay, Gewürztraminer, Trebbiano, Riesling, Rosé, Shiraz, Pinot Noir, Cabernet Sauvignon.
summary Following the acquisition of Mudgee Wines by the Conway family, the organic winemaking practices of the former owner, Jennifer Meek, have been discontinued, with conventional viticultural and winemaking practices now adopted.

🐝 mulligan wongara vineyard   NR

603 Grenfell Road, Cowra, NSW 2794 **region** Cowra
phone (02) 6342 9334 **fax** (02) 9810 4697 **open** Not
winemaker David Carpenter, Sue Carpenter, Jon Reynolds (all Contract) **production** 2500 **est.** 1993
product range ($14–20 R) Chardonnay, Unwooded Chardonnay, Shiraz, Cabernet Sauvignon.
summary Andrew and Emma Mulligan began the establishment of their 16-hectare vineyard in 1993. Plantings now comprise chardonnay (8 hectares), shiraz (3.5 hectares), cabernet (3.5 hectares) and sangiovese (1 hectare); a significant proportion of the grapes is sold to others, the wines being made under contract by David and Sue Carpenter at Lark Hill, and by Jon Reynolds at Reynolds. The wines are stocked by Vintage Cellars, and the plans are to open a cellar door sometime in 2002, plus a substantial underground storage area capable of holding up to 10 000 cases.

mulyan   ★★★☆

North Logan Road, Cowra, NSW 2794 **region** Cowra
phone (02) 6342 1289 **fax** (02) 6341 1015 **open** Sat–Mon and public holidays 10–5 or by appointment Mon–Fri
winemaker Simon Gilbert (Contract) **production** 3200 **est.** 1994
product range ($14–18 R) Chardonnay, Bushrangers Bounty Chardonnay, Shiraz, Bushrangers Bounty Shiraz.
summary Mulyan is a 1350-hectare grazing property purchased by the Fagan family in 1886 from Dr William Redfern, a leading 19th century figure in Australian history. The current-generation owners, Peter and Jenni Fagan, began the establishment of 45 hectares of shiraz in 1994, and intend increasing the vineyard area to 100 hectares. Presently there are 28.8 hectares of shiraz and 14.8 hectares of chardonnay, with an experimental plot of sangiovese. The label features a statue of the Roman God Mercury which has stood in the Mulyan homestead garden since being brought back from Italy in 1912 by Peter Fagan's grandmother. The wines have limited Sydney retail distribution and are also available through the Quarry Cellars in Cowra.

Mulyan Bushrangers Bounty Chardonnay

▼▼▼▼ 2000 Bright, light green-yellow; the clean, light bouquet shows melon and a hint of citrus; the palate is very light but well made, clean and fresh, and has nice acidity. Good winemaking; the limitations of the wine lie firstly in the vineyard, and secondly in the unoaked style.   **rating:** 83

best drinking 2002–2003 **best vintages** NA **drink with** Fish and chips • $14

Mulyan Cowra Chardonnay

▼▼▼▼ 2000 Bright, light green-yellow; the clean bouquet offers a subtle blend of fruit and the French oak in which the wine was fermented and matured; the palate is still very fresh, and though light, has complexity in an understated way, here deriving from the partial malolactic fermentation. It is easy to see why the wine has won show medals, albeit no golds.   **rating:** 86

best drinking 2002–2003 **best vintages** NA **drink with** Creamy pasta • $18

munari wines   ★★★★

1129 Northern Highway, Heathcote, Vic 3523 **region** Bendigo
phone (03) 5433 3366 **fax** (03) 5433 3095 **open** 7 days 10–5
winemaker Adrian Munari, Deborah Munari **production** 1500 **est.** 1993
product range ($20–30 CD) Chardonnay, Marsanne, Shiraz, Schoolhouse Red, Cabernet Sauvignon.
summary Adrian and Deborah Munari made a singularly impressive entry into the winemaking scene, with both their initial vintages winning an impressive array of show medals, and have carried on in similar vein since then. With a little under 8 hectares of estate vines, production will be limited, but the wines are well worth seeking out.

Munari Shiraz

▼▼▼▼▼ 2000 Medium to full red-purple; opens with fragrant berry fruit and obvious vanilla oak on the bouquet, then a medium-bodied palate, with the fruit flavours tracking the bouquet, and the oak less evident. Long and with some finesse, carrying its 13.5° alcohol with ease.   **rating:** 90

best drinking 2005–2010 **best vintages** '99, '00 **drink with** Barbecued lamb • $25

Munari Schoolhouse Red

ŸŸŸŸ **2000** Medium red-purple; the bouquet is clean, with quite spicy overtones to the berry fruit and subtle oak; the medium-bodied palate has an array of fresh berry flavours reflecting the blend of shiraz, cabernet sauvignon, merlot and malbec in a 50/20/20/10 ratio. **rating:** 86

best drinking 2002–2005 **best vintages** NA **drink with** Baby rack of lamb • $25

Munari Cabernet Sauvignon

ŸŸŸŸŸ **2000** Medium red-purple; the moderately intense bouquet has clean blackcurrant/cassis fruit; the palate has an attractively sweet mix of blackcurrant and blackberry, neatly supported by good tannins and gentle oak. **rating:** 91

best drinking 2005–2010 **best vintages** NA **drink with** Lamb casserole • $30

mundrakoona estate   NR

Sir Charles Moses Lane, Old Hume Highway, Woodlands via Mittagong, NSW 2575 **region** Southern New South Wales Zone
phone (02) 4872 1311 **fax** (02) 4872 1322 **open** Weekends and public holidays 9–6
winemaker Anton Balog **production** 1800 **est.** 1997
product range ($18–32 CD) Riesling, Sauvignon Blanc, Reserve Chardonnay, Nouveau Rouge, Reserve Cabernet Sauvignon Merlot.
summary During 1998 and 1999 Anton Balog progressively planted 3.2 hectares of pinot noir, sauvignon blanc and tempranillo at an altitude of 680 metres. He is using wild yeast ferments, hand-plunging and other 'natural' winemaking techniques, with the aim of producing Burgundian-style Pinot and Chardonnay and Bordeaux-style Sauvignon Blanc and Cabernet Sauvignon. For the foreseeable future, estate production will be supplemented by grapes grown from local Southern Highlands vineyards.

murdoch hill   NR

Mappinga Road, Woodside, SA 5244 **region** Adelaide Hills
phone (08) 8389 7081 **fax** (08) 8389 7991 **open** By appointment
winemaker Brian Light (Contract) **production** 1500 **est.** 1998
product range ($19.95–24.95 R) Sauvignon Blanc, Cabernet Sauvignon.
summary A little over 21 hectares of vines have been established on the undulating, gum-studded countryside of the Erinka property, owned by the Downer family, 4 kilometres east of Oakbank. In descending order of importance, the varieties established are sauvignon blanc, shiraz, cabernet sauvignon and chardonnay. The wines are distributed by Australian Prestige Wines in Melbourne and Sydney.

murdock   ★★★★☆

Riddoch Highway, Coonawarra, SA 5263 **region** Coonawarra
phone (08) 8737 3700 **fax** (08) 8737 2107 **open** Not
winemaker Peter Bissell (Contract) **production** 1700 **est.** 1998
product range ($42 CD) Cabernet Sauvignon.
summary The Murdock family has established 10.4 hectares of cabernet sauvignon, 2 hectares of shiraz, 1 hectare of merlot, and 0.5 hectare each of chardonnay and riesling, and produces small quantities of an outstanding Cabernet Sauvignon, contract-made by Peter Bissell at Balnaves. The labels, incidentally, are ultra-minimalist; no flood of propaganda here.

Murdock Cabernet Sauvignon

ŸŸŸŸŸ **1999** Full red-purple; a clean, powerful bouquet with classic blackberry/currant/earth Coonawarra cabernet aromas. The palate has ripe, but not jammy fruit, almost velvety; cassis and mulberry flavours dominate, with fine tannins on the finish. Double gold at the 2000 Sydney International Wine Competition, a great achievement for the vintage. **rating:** 94

ŸŸŸŸŸ **1998** Medium to full red-purple; the rich, ripe and dense bouquet has an array of dark berry, blackberry, mulberry and chocolate aromas; the palate is ripe and mouthfilling, with blackcurrant/cassis fruit and well- controlled oak. **rating:** 94

best drinking 2003–2008 **best vintages** '98, '99 **drink with** Aged fillet of beef • $42

murrindindi   ★★★★

Cummins Lane, Murrindindi, Vic 3717 **region** Central Victorian High Country
phone (03) 5797 8217 **fax** (03) 5797 8422 **open** Not

winemaker Alan Cuthbertson **production** 2000 **est.** 1979
product range ($22 R) Chardonnay, Cabernets Merlot.
summary Situated in an unequivocally cool climate, which means that special care has to be taken with the viticulture to produce ripe fruit flavours. In more recent vintages, Murrindindi has succeeded handsomely in so doing. Limited Sydney and Melbourne distribution through Wine Source.

Murrindindi Chardonnay

▼▼▼▼♡ 1999 Medium to full yellow-green; a complex mix of citrus and melon fruit and spicy French oak on the bouquet leads into a palate which is full flavoured, yet balanced and elegant. The citrus and melon fruit provide good mouthfeel, and at only 12.5°, alcohol heat or burn is not in the picture. Has developed significantly over the past 12 months. Very nice wine. **rating:** 92

best drinking 2002–2004 **best vintages** '84, '90, '91, '92, '93, '96, '97, '99 **drink with** Mussels • $24

Murrindindi Cabernets Merlot

▼▼▼▼♡ 1998 Medium red-purple; the bouquet has ripe, earthy, blackberry fruit and gentle oak; the palate offers gentle blackberry and dark chocolate fruit, fine tannins, and excellent balance and structure. A very nice wine in a sophisticated mould. **rating:** 90

best drinking 2003–2008 **best vintages** '92, '93, '98 **drink with** Rib of beef • $24

murrumbateman winery   NR

Barton Highway, Murrumbateman, NSW 2582 **region** Canberra District
phone (02) 6227 5584 **open** Thurs–Mon 10–5
winemaker Duncan Leslie **production** 1500 **est.** 1972
product range ($14–30 CD) Riesling, Sauvignon Blanc, Sally's Sweet White, Rosé, Shiraz, Cabernet Merlot, Mead, Fortifieds and Sparkling.
summary Revived after a change of ownership, the Murrumbateman Winery draws upon 4.5 hectares of vineyards, and also incorporates an à la carte restaurant and function room, together with picnic and barbecue areas.

🌿 naked range wines   ★★★☆

125 Rifle Range Road, Smiths Gully, Vic, 3760 **region** Yarra Valley
phone (03) 9710 1575 **fax** (03) 9710 1655 **open** By appointment
winemaker Robert Dolan, Kate Goodman **production** 1500 **est.** 1996
product range ($16–20 ML) Sauvignon Blanc, Pinot Noir, Cabernet Sauvignon.
summary Mike Jansz began the establishment of the Jansz Estate vineyard in 1996 at Smiths Gully, in the Diamond Valley subregion of the Yarra Valley. He has established 7 hectares of vineyard, one-third planted to sauvignon blanc, a small patch to pinot noir and the remainder to cabernet sauvignon (predominant), merlot and cabernet franc. The wines are made at the Yarra Hill winery by former Yarra Ridge winemaker Rob Dolan, and marketed under the striking Naked Range label, one calculated to give the United States BATF cardiac arrest if ever the wines were to be exported there. In the meantime, distribution is by mail order and direct to restaurants and specialty wine shops from the estate.

Naked Range Sauvignon Blanc

▼▼▼▼ 2001 Light green-yellow; the bouquet is quite powerful, with a mix of grass, herb and asparagus; the same flavours come through on the palate, which, while having a slightly phenolic finish, also has abundant character. **rating:** 86

best drinking 2002–2003 **best vintages** NA **drink with** Shellfish • $16

Naked Range Chardonnay

▼▼▼▼ 2000 Medium yellow-green; nutty oak and malolactic influences dominate the bouquet; some cashew and melon are present on the understated and quite harmonious palate, the only problem being a lack of fruit intensity. **rating:** 86

best drinking 2002–2005 **best vintages** NA **drink with** Seafood pasta • $18

Naked Range Pinot Noir

▼▼▼▼♡ 2001 Quite deep red; a highly fragrant and potent bouquet with a mix of plummy, sappy and spicy aromas is followed by a palate which flows directly on from the bouquet, and makes a major statement. Excellent value. **rating:** 90

best drinking 2002–2006 **best vintages** '01 **drink with** Smoked duck • $20

Naked Range Cabernet Sauvignon

♥♥♥♡ **2000** Bright red-purple of medium depth; the bouquet offers clean, fresh, red berry fruit aromas in a direct, rather than complex, fashion; the palate is fleshed out with a touch of vanilla oak, but again direct, and finishing with a tweak of acidity. **rating:** 84

best drinking 2002–2005 **best vintages** NA **drink with** Spaghetti bolognese • $18

nandroya estate NR

262 Sandfly Road, Margate, Tas 7054 **region** Southern Tasmania
phone (03) 6267 2377 **open** By appointment
winemaker Andrew Hood (Contract) **production** 200 **est.** 1995
product range ($18–25 CD) Sauvignon Blanc, Pinot Noir.
summary John Rees and family have established 0.5 hectare each of sauvignon blanc and pinot noir, the wines being sold through the cellar door and to one or two local restaurants. The Reeses regard it as a holiday and retirement project, and modestly wonder whether they deserve inclusion in this work. They certainly do, for wineries of this size are an indispensable part of the Tasmanian fabric.

narkoojee ★★★★

1110 Francis Road, Glengarry, Vic 3854 **region** Gippsland
phone (03) 5192 4257 **fax** (03) 5192 4257 **open** 9–5 by appointment
winemaker Harry Friend, Axel Friend **production** 1200 **est.** 1981
product range ($14–30 CD) Chardonnay, Trafalgar Chardonnay, The Rosé, The Athelstan Merlot, Cabernets.
summary Narkoojee Vineyard is within easy reach of the old goldmining town of Walhalla, and looks out over the Strzelecki Ranges. The wines are produced from a little over 4 hectares of estate vineyards. Harry Friend was an amateur winemaker of note before turning to commercial winemaking with Narkoojee, his skills showing through with all the wines, none more so than the Chardonnay.

Narkoojee Chardonnay

♥♥♥♥♡ **2000** Medium to full yellow-green; a complex and rich bouquet with excellent fruit and oak balance and integration is followed by a similarly rich and full palate, with ripe fig and peach flavours, and plenty of supporting texture. **rating:** 93

best drinking 2001–2006 **best vintages** '87, '89, '92, '93, '94, '97, '99, '00 **drink with** Salmon pizza • $28

nashdale wines NR

Borenore Lane, Nashdale, NSW 2800 **region** Orange
phone (02) 6365 2463 **fax** (02) 6361 4495 **open** Weekends 2–6
winemaker Mark Davidson (Contract) **production** 1000 **est.** 1990
product range ($10–25 CD) Riesling, Sauvignon Blanc, Chardonnay, Pinot Noir, Cabernet Sauvignon.
summary Orange solicitor Edward Fardell commenced establishing the 10-hectare Nashdale Vineyard in 1990. At an elevation of 1000 metres, it offers panoramic views of Mount Canobolas and the Lidster Valley, with a restaurant-cafe open on weekends.

neagles rock vineyards ★★★★

Lots 1 and 2 Main North Road, Clare, SA 5453 **region** Clare Valley
phone (08) 8843 4020 **fax** (08) 8843 4021 **open** 7 days 10–5
winemaker Neil Pike (Contract), Steve Wiblin **production** 4000 **est.** 1997
product range ($15–25 CD) Riesling, Semillon, Chardonnay, Pinot Noir, Sparkling, Sweet Dorothy Botrytis Riesling, Shiraz, Grenache, Cabernet Sauvignon, Richard Lincoln Liqueur Tawny Port.
summary Owner-partners Jane Willson and Steve Wiblin have taken the plunge in a major way, simultaneously raising a young family, and resuscitating two old vineyards, and – for good measure – stripping a dilapidated house to the barest of bones and turning it into a first-rate, airy restaurant-cum-cellar door (which I wholeheartedly recommend). They bring 35 years of industry experience to Neagles Rock. Jane Willson held a senior marketing position with Southcorp before heading up Negociants Australia's Sales and Marketing team in a 15-year career which brought her unqualified respect. Steve Wiblin's 20-year career spanned Guinness to Grange, public companies to small ones, marketing to finance. Exports to the US and Belgium.

Neagles Rock Shiraz

▼▼▼▼ **2000** Medium red-purple; the soft plum and cherry fruit, allied with some vanilla oak, of the bouquet flows through into a medium-bodied palate with a soft profile and gentle fruit; all in all, very different from the '99 wine. **rating:** 86

best drinking 2004–2008 **best vintages** NA **drink with** Patience • $22.50

Neagles Rock Grenache

▼▼▼▼ **2001** Appealing, bright colour; plum, cherry and spice aromas intensify on the light to medium-bodied palate. Well above average early-drinking style. **rating:** 87

best drinking 2001–2002 **best vintages** NA **drink with** Takeaway • $17.50

Neagles Rock Cabernet Sauvignon

▼▼▼▼ **2000** Medium purple-red; the moderately intense bouquet is spotlessly clean, foreshadowing the pleasing redcurrant fruit on the supple and sweet palate, which finishes with soft tannins. **rating:** 89

best drinking 2003–2009 **best vintages** NA **drink with** Lamb shanks • $22.50

needham estate wines NR

Ingoldby Road, McLaren Flat, SA 5171 **region** McLaren Vale
phone (08) 8383 0301 **fax** (08) 8383 0301 **open** Not
winemaker Contract **production** 2800 **est.** 1997
product range ($17–25 R) Albertus Shiraz, White House Shiraz.
summary Clive Needham has two vineyards; the first, of 4 hectares, is newly planted and will come into full production in 2001. The second has less than 0.5 hectare of 100-year-old shiraz vines, which go to produce the White House Shiraz, with an annual production of only 120 cases.

neighbours vineyards NR

75 Fullarton Road, Kent Town, SA 5067 (postal) **region** McLaren Vale
phone (08) 8331 8656 **fax** (08) 8331 8443 **open** Not
winemaker Chester Osborn **production** 500 **est.** 1995
product range ($26 ML) Shiraz.
summary Esteemed (and dare I say now senior) journalist Bob Mayne planted 1.6 hectares of Shiraz in McLaren Vale in 1995, without any clear objective in mind, and certainly not venturing into winemaking. However, one thing leads to another, and in 1998 he formed Neighbours Vineyards Pty Ltd, its 14 shareholders all being McLaren Vale grape growers. By 2001 their combined production had risen to 120 tonnes, with more to come in the future. 1998 was the first small production, 1999 the second vintage.

Neighbours Vineyards Shiraz

▼▼▼▽ **1999** Medium red-purple; the moderately intense bouquet has red berry fruit with slightly gamey overtones, no doubt a function of the vintage. The palate, likewise, has pleasant red berry fruit, but slightly gamey characters also make their presence felt. **rating:** 84

best drinking 2002–2006 **best vintages** NA **drink with** Veal shanks • $26

nepenthe vineyards ★★★★☆

Vickers Road, Lenswood, SA 5240 **region** Adelaide Hills
phone (08) 8431 7588 **fax** (08) 8431 7688 **open** By appointment
winemaker Peter Leske **production** 40 000 **est.** 1994
product range ($18–50 R) Riesling, Semillon, Sauvignon Blanc, Unwooded Chardonnay, Chardonnay, Pinot Gris, Pinot Noir, Zinfandel, The Rogue, The Fugue (Cabernet Merlot).
summary The Tweddell family has established a little over 60 hectares of close-planted vineyards at Lenswood since 1994, with an exotic array of varieties reflected in the wines. In late 1996 it obtained the second licence to build a winery in the Adelaide Hills, Petaluma being the only other successful applicant, back in 1978. A 500-tonne winery has been constructed, with Peter Leske in charge of winemaking. Nepenthe has quickly established itself as one of the most exciting new wineries in Australia. Distribution through most states, and exports to the UK, the US, Switzerland, Belgium, Italy, Austria, Japan and Hong Kong.

Nepenthe Vineyards Adelaide Hills Riesling

TTTTT 2001 Light green-yellow; the crisp, clean bouquet has mineral, herb and faintly spicy aromas; the palate is remarkably intense and focussed, fresh as a daisy, with bright, lingering acidity and a guaranteed future. Stelvin finished. **rating: 94**

best drinking 2003–2010 **best vintages** '98, '99, '00, '01 **drink with** Sashimi • $19

Nepenthe Vineyards Semillon

TTTT 2000 Light to medium green-yellow; a clean, gently lemony bouquet with a near-subliminal touch of oak is followed by a powerful and intense palate, the high alcohol (13.5°) making its presence felt on the aftertaste, but not before. **rating: 88**

best drinking 2001–2004 **best vintages** '97 **drink with** Sautéed veal • $22

Nepenthe Vineyards Sauvignon Blanc

TTTT 2001 Very light green-yellow; a pungent bouquet with passionfruit, gooseberry and a touch of matchstick is followed by a crisp palate, with lighter fruit flavours than the bouquet promises, but also escaping from the touch of reduction of the bouquet, and further redeemed by length. A good outcome for an unfriendly vintage. **rating: 86**

best drinking 2001–2002 **best vintages** NA **drink with** Poached scallops in white sauce • $19

Nepenthe Vineyards Chardonnay

TTTTT 2000 Medium to full yellow-green; strong barrel-ferment/malolactic-ferment influences provide a complex, nutty/toasty bouquet. The long and lingering palate has excellent acidity to balance the flavours promised by the bouquet, and which duly present themselves. **rating: 94**

best drinking 2001–2005 **best vintages** '99, '00 **drink with** Chinese steamed fish • $25

Nepenthe Vineyards Pinot Noir

TTTTT 2000 Medium red-purple; plum and mint aromas combine with a touch of savoury/spicy oak on the bouquet; the complex palate has a mix of plum, cherry, mint and more savoury/foresty characters; excellent length and persistence. **rating: 94**

best drinking 2002–2007 **best vintages** '99, '00 **drink with** Confit of duck • $29

Nepenthe The Rogue

TTTT 2000 Medium to full red-purple; there are hard to place, slightly dusty overtones, possibly from the oak, but possibly from the fruit, a blend of merlot and cabernet sauvignon. Bright raspberry/blackberry fruit greets the entry to the palate, but the wine then tails off on the back palate and finish. **rating: 85**

best drinking 2003–2007 **best vintages** NA **drink with** Braised beef • $18

Nepenthe Vineyards The Fugue Cabernet Merlot

TTTT 1999 Medium to full red-purple; blackberry and chocolate fruit swirl through cedar and vanilla oak inputs on the bouquet. The palate has lively fruit, with slightly grippy acidity, and needs time to settle down. **rating: 88**

best drinking 2004–2009 **best vintages** '98 **drink with** Kangaroo fillet • $30

newstead winery NR

Tivey Street, Newstead, Vic 3462 **region** Bendigo
phone (03) 5476 2733 **fax** (03) 5476 2536 **open** Weekends and public holidays 10–5
winemaker Ron Snep, Cliff Stubbs **production** 1500 **est.** 1994
product range ($15–16 CD) Welshman's Reef Semillon, Barrel Fermented Semillon, Unwooded Chardonnay, Cabernet Sauvignon; Burnt Acre Riesling, Shiraz.
summary Newstead Winery is established in the old Newstead Butter Factory, drawing upon two distinct vineyards at Welshman's Reef (near Maldon) and Burnt Acre Vineyard at Marong, west of Bendigo. Vineyard designations are used for each of the wines.

next generation wines NR

Gomersal Road, Lyndoch, SA 5351 **region** Barossa Valley
phone (08) 8524 0444 **fax** (08) 8524 0400 **open** By appointment
winemaker Natasha Mooney **production** 50 000 **est.** 2001
product range Fox Gordon Premium range of Barossa Valley Shiraz, Barossa Valley Cabernet Merlot; NXG VinFive range of Semillon Chardonnay, Chardonnay, Shiraz, Shiraz Cabernet, Cabernet Merlot,

Cabernet Sauvignon; Flinders Reach range of Chardonnay, Shiraz, Shiraz Cabernet, Cabernet Sauvignon; and Stockmans Post range, with Australian Dry White, Australian Dry Red.

summary The venture is the brainchild of wine industry professionals Sam Atkins and David Cumming, with many years experience between them working for some of Australia's largest companies. The appointment of Natasha Mooney, previously chief winemaker at Barossa Valley Estate, adds significantly to the venture. As at the end of 2001, all of the NXG wines had been exported to the United Kingdom under the Phoenix brand. There they sell for less than ten pounds. However, domestic sales are planned to commence sometime prior to the end of 2002.

nicholson river ★★★★☆

Liddells Road, Nicholson, Vic 3882 **region** Gippsland
phone (03) 5156 8241 **fax** (03) 5156 8433 **open** 7 days 10–4 for sales, tastings by appointment
winemaker Ken Eckersley **production** 2500 **est.** 1978
product range ($15–45 CD) Semillon Sauvignon Blanc, Chardonnay, Gippsland Chardonnay, Botrytis Semillon, Cuvée (Pinot Noir Chardonnay), Sparkling Pinot Noir, Pinot Noir, Gippsland Pinot Noir, The Nicholson (Pinot Noir Merlot); second label Montview Chardonnay, Pinot Noir and Cabernet Merlot.
summary The fierce commitment to quality in the face of the temperamental Gippsland climate and the frustratingly small production has been handsomely repaid by some stupendous Chardonnays, mostly sold through the cellar door; a little is exported to the UK, Thailand and the US. Ken Eckersley does not refer to his Chardonnays as white wines but as gold wines, and lists them accordingly in his newsletter.

Nicholson River Chardonnay
▼▼▼▼▽ **2000** Medium to full yellow-green, bright and – by the standards of Nicholson River – quite restrained. The complex, rich bouquet exudes ripe chardonnay and toasty/buttery notes; the equally complex palate is rich and ripe, soft and full on the mid-palate, but shortens slightly on the finish.   **rating:** 90
best drinking 2002–2006 **best vintages** '86, '87, '92, '94, '97, '00 **drink with** Pheasant with truffles • $45

Nicholson River The Nicholson Pinot Noir Merlot
▼▼▼▼▽ **1999** Medium red-purple, the hue still bright; the bouquet offers clean, lifted, spicy/cherry/plum aromas with a nicely controlled touch of oak. The lively, savoury palate has cherry with a touch of lemon; a perverse blend of Pinot Noir and Merlot which works surprisingly well. Spends 18 months in oak. **rating:** 93
best drinking 2002–2006 **best vintages** '99 **drink with** Smoked quail • $37

Nicholson River Pinot Noir
▼▼▼▼▽ **1999** Medium red-purple, fractionally more advanced than The Nicholson. An array of briary/foresty/spicy aromas dance alongside dark berry/plum/cherry on the bouquet. Comes through strongly on the palate, with considerable length and presence, in a slightly riper (and fractionally less stylish) mode than The Nicholson.   **rating:** 91
best drinking 2003–2008 **best vintages** '99 **drink with** Game • $35

Nicholson River Montview Pinot Noir
▼▼▼▼ **1999** Medium red-purple; gently savoury/foresty/earthy tones mix with black cherry on the bouquet; the palate has savoury/foresty varietal character in abundance, although finishing with slightly grippy tannins. Made from contract-grown Gippsland fruit.   **rating:** 87
best drinking 2002–2006 **best vintages** NA **drink with** Duck risotto • $22

nightingale wines ★★★★

1239 Milbrodale Road, Broke, NSW 2330 **region** Lower Hunter Valley
phone (02) 6579 1499 **fax** (02) 6579 1477 **open** Wed–Sun 10–4
winemaker Andrew Margan (Contract) **production** 2400 **est.** 1997
product range ($17–19 CD) Semillon, Verdelho, Unwooded Chardonnay, Chardonnay, Sparkling, Botrytis Semillon, Shiraz, Merlot, Cabernet Sauvignon, Port.
summary Paul and Gail Nightingale have wasted no time since establishing their business in 1997. They have planted 3 hectares each of verdelho and merlot, 2 hectares of shiraz, 1.5 hectares each of chardonnay and cabernet sauvignon and 1 hectare of chambourcin. The wines are contract made by Andrew Margan, and are sold only through the cellar door, an actively promoted wine club, and to selected local restaurants.

Nightingale Merlot

♥♥♥♥♡ **2000** Medium purple-red; youthful, rich fruit on the bouquet leads into a luscious palate with redcurrant, raspberry and chocolate fruit, girdled by soft tannins. Topped its class at the 2001 Hunter Valley Wine Show, with a strong silver medal. **rating:** 90

best drinking 2002–2007 **best vintages** '00 **drink with** Braised ox tail • $19

ninth island ★★★★

Baxter's Road, Pipers River, Tas 7252 **region** Northern Tasmania
phone (03) 6382 7122 **fax** (03) 6382 7231 **open** Not
winemaker Andrew Pirie **production** 14 000 **est.** 1999
product range ($18.14–24 R) Riesling, Chardonnay, Sauvignon Blanc, Straits Dry White, Botrytis Riesling, Pinot Noir, Cuvée Tasmania, Tamar Cabernets.
summary This is the former Rochecombe Vineyard, the Rochecombe brand having been discontinued. There is a sharing of vineyards and of winery facilities within the Pipers Brook Group; the Ninth Island Wines, however, have their own identity.

Ninth Island Riesling

♥♥♥♥ **2001** Light green-yellow; the bouquet shows ripe fruit with tropical overtones, suggestive of some botrytis. The palate follows down a similar track; fractionally oily, and again showing some signs of botrytis or similar inputs. **rating:** 85

best drinking 2002–2004 **best vintages** NA **drink with** Trout mousse • $21.95

Ninth Island Brut

♥♥♥♥♡ **NV** Medium yellow-green; the bouquet is clean, with quite ripe citrus and melon aromas; the thoroughly pleasing palate has excellent balance and length in an easy-drinking style. Some clever winemaking at work here. **rating:** 92

best drinking 2002–2004 **best vintages** NA **drink with** Shellfish • $21.95

Ninth Island Botrytis Riesling

♥♥♥♥♡ **2000** Glowing green-yellow; intense botrytis lime juice aromas, plus a little cumquat, lead into a luscious palate with lime, pineapple and cumquat flavours. A little more acidity might have produced the perfect wine. **rating:** 92

best drinking 2001–2005 **best vintages** '00 **drink with** Fruit tart • $19.95

Ninth Island Pinot Noir

♥♥♥♥ **2001** Very good, deep colour for Pinot Noir; lots of ripe plummy fruit in a direct mode, then a touch of spice on the bouquet; the palate, likewise, has above average depth, and Ninth Island must have threaded the needle vintage-wise. The mouthfeel is still on the firm side, and a year or so in bottle will improve the wine out of sight. **rating:** 89

best drinking 2002–2005 **best vintages** '00, '01 **drink with** Osso buco • $23.65

noon winery ★★★★

Rifle Range Road, McLaren Vale, SA 5171 **region** McLaren Vale
phone (08) 8323 8290 **fax** (08) 8323 8290 **open** Weekends 10–5 from November (while stock is available)
winemaker Drew Noon **production** 2000 **est.** 1976
product range ($15–20 CD) One Night (Rosé), Solaire Reserve Grenache, Eclipse (Grenache Shiraz), Reserve Shiraz, Reserve Cabernet Sauvignon, Vintage Port.
summary Drew Noon has returned to McLaren Vale having spent many years as a consultant oenologist and viticulturist in Victoria, thereafter as winemaker at Cassegrain, and purchased Noon's from his parents (though father David still keeps an eye on things). Some spectacular and unusual wines have followed, such as the 17.9° alcohol Solaire Grenache, styled like an Italian Amarone. Low prices mean each year's release sells out in 4 to 5 weeks. In 1998 Drew Noon gained the coveted Master of Wine (MW) award. Exports to the UK, the US, Canada, Germany, Switzerland, Belgium and New Zealand.

no regrets vineyard ★★★★★

40 Dillons Hill Road, Glaziers Bay, Tas 7109 **region** Southern Tasmania
phone (03) 6295 1509 **fax** (03) 6295 1509 **open** By appointment, also at Salamanca Market, Hobart most Saturdays

winemaker Andrew Hood (Contract), Eric Phillips **production** NA **est.** 2000
product range ($12–40 CD) Riesling, Gewürztraminer, Triple S (Sylvaner Semillon Sauvignon Blanc), Sylvaner, Chardonnay, Miss Otis (Sparkling), Pinot Noir.
summary Having sold Elsewhere Vineyard, Eric and Jette Phillips have turned around and planted another vineyard almost next door, called No Regrets. This is their 'retirement' vineyard, because they will be producing only 1 wine from the one hectare of pinot noir newly planted. The first vintage came in 2002; in the meantime they were selling residual stock from their days at Elsewhere Vineyard. The last wines from the old venture were the 2000 Riesling and the superb 2000 Pinot Noir. The wines are also available most Saturdays at Hobart's Salamanca Market.

No Regrets Riesling
▼▼▼▼ **2000** Light to medium yellow-green; the bouquet is quite rich, with some sinewy herb aromas threaded through the dominant lime. The palate is powerful but generous, with rich, mouthfilling lime-accented fruit in typical vintage style. **rating:** 92
best drinking 2001–2006 **best vintages** '00 **drink with** Sashimi • $18

No Regrets Miss Otis Sparkling
▼▼▼▼ **1998** Light straw-green; a clean and quite complex bouquet with hints of hay and cashew, suggesting malolactic influences. The mouth-caressing palate is round, almost velvety, particularly rare for a Tasmanian sparkling wine, yet not the least bit sweet. **rating:** 93
best drinking 2002–2004 **best vintages** '98 **drink with** Rich canapes • $20

No Regrets Pinot Noir
▼▼▼▼▼ **2000** Medium red, with the purple just starting to diminish; a fragrant and stylish bouquet has a mix of savoury, leafy and spicy aromas underpinned by sweet damson plum and strawberry fruit. The palate really takes off, with masses of character and style, yet retaining elegance, the whole anchored around the mix of ripe (but not overripe) spicy/plummy fruit. Multiple trophy winner, including Best Wine of Show at the 2002 Tasmanian Wines Show. **rating:** 96
best drinking 2002–2007 **best vintages** '00 **drink with** Rare roast squab • $40

nuggetty vineyard ★★★☆
280 Maldon–Shelbourne Road, Nuggetty, Vic 3463 **region** Bendigo
phone (03) 5475 1347 **fax** (03) 5475 1647 **open** Weekends and public holidays 10–4 or by appointment
winemaker Greg Dedman, Jackie Dedman **production** 1000 **est.** 1993
product range ($15–25 CD) Semillon, Shiraz.
summary The family-owned vineyard was established in 1994 by Greg and Jackie Dedman. Greg (a Charles Sturt University graduate) is also chief winemaker at Charles Sturt University and the winemaking degree at Blue Pyrenees Estate, while Jackie (having spent 18 months at Bowen Estate in 1997–98) has simultaneously undertaken the wine marketing degree at Charles Sturt University and the winemaking degree at the University of Adelaide. They share the vineyard and winery tasks, which include 6 hectares of estate plantings (semillon, shiraz and cabernet sauvignon). Mailing list and cellar door sales are available while stocks last.

Nuggetty Vineyard Barrel-Fermented Semillon
▼▼▼▼ **2000** Light to medium yellow-green; the bouquet is quite complex, the barrel-ferment inputs obvious but not excessive; the varietal character of the semillon comes through strongly on the palate, which has good length. An impressive wine, and a bargain at the price. **rating:** 89
best drinking 2002–2005 **best vintages** NA **drink with** Avocado • $15

Nuggetty Vineyard Shiraz
▼▼▼▼ **2000** Deep, dense red-purple; the solid bouquet ranges through earthy, plummy and berry aromas, supported by subtle oak. The palate is powerful, but distinctly under-worked and jagged. **rating:** 82
best drinking 2004–2008 **best vintages** NA **drink with** Steak and kidney pie • $25

🦘 nursery ridge estate ★★★
Calder Highway, Red Cliffs, Vic 3496 **region** Murray Darling
phone (03) 5024 3311 **fax** (03) 5024 3311 **open** By appointment
winemaker Donna Stephens **production** 1100 **est.** 1999
product range ($14–16 R) Sparkling Shiraz, Cassia Street Shiraz, Shiraz Cabernet, Petit Verdot, Cottrell's Hill Cabernet Sauvignon, Parb's Cabernet Sauvignon.

summary The estate takes its name from the fact that it is situated on the site of the original vine nursery at Red Cliffs. It is a family-owned and operated affair, with shiraz, cabernet sauvignon, chardonnay and petit verdot in production, and viognier planted in 2001. A cellar door and new winery site on the Calder Highway, Red Cliffs, opened prior to the end of 2001. The well-priced wines are usually well made, with greater richness and depth of fruit flavour than most other wines from the region, although I didn't know what to make of the incredibly dense and powerful 2001 Petit Verdot. Production is planned to rise from the 60 tonnes in 2002 to a total of 250 tonnes.

Nursery Ridge Estate Cassia Street Shiraz

TTTY 1999 Medium red-purple; soft, savoury/oaky aromas do have some sweetness in the background, and the palate continues to develop the richness, with a touch of chocolate, and more weight than expected. **rating:** 84

best drinking 2002–2005 **best vintages** NA **drink with** Rare roast beef • $16

Nursery Ridge Estate Parb's Cabernet Sauvignon

TTTT 2000 Bright red-purple; the bouquet is moderately intense, with ripe, slightly savoury varietal character, the oak balanced. The palate has remarkable richness and sweetness through to the mid-palate, softening slightly thereafter, but with good oak handling and soft tannins. **rating:** 86

best drinking 2003–2008 **best vintages** NA **drink with** Barbecued T-bone • $15

oakover estate ★★★☆

14 Yukich Close, Middle Swan, WA 6056 **region** Swan District
phone (08) 9274 0777 **fax** (08) 9274 0788 **open** 7 days 11–5
winemaker Julie White (Contract) **production** 3500 **est.** 1990
product range ($16.50–22.50 CD) Verdelho, Chenin Blanc, S.V. Classic (Chardonnay Chenin Blanc), Chardonnay, Shiraz, Cabernet Sauvignon.
summary Owned by the Yukich family, part of the long-established Dalmatian Coast/Croatian cultural group in the Swan Valley, with its roots going back to the early 1900s. However, Oakover Estate is very much part of the new wave in the Swan Valley, with a very large vineyard holding of 64 hectares, planted predominantly to chardonnay, shiraz, chenin blanc and verdelho. Part of the production is sold to others; the talented Julie White is contract winemaker for the 3500 cases or so sold through the cellar door and the large, new cafe/restaurant and function centre in the heart of the vineyard.

Oakover Estate Chenin Blanc

TTTT 1998 Medium to full yellow-green; a rich and complex bouquet with honeyed fruit salad aromas are followed by a rich, supple and mouthfilling palate with masses of flavour. **rating:** 89

best drinking 2001–2004 **best vintages** '98 **drink with** Creamy seafood pasta • $16.50

Oakover Estate Verdelho

TTTT 2001 Light green-yellow; a fresh and crisp bouquet has some gooseberry/citrus overtones not unlike Sauvignon Blanc; the distinctly fruity and moderately long palate is freshened by CO_2 which will disappear as the wine matures. **rating:** 86

best drinking 2001–2005 **best vintages** NA **drink with** Prosciutto and melon • $16.50

oakridge estate ★★★☆

864 Maroondah Highway, Coldstream, Vic 3770 **region** Yarra Valley
phone (03) 9739 1920 **fax** (03) 9739 1923 **open** 7 days 10–5
winemaker Steve Warne **production** NFP **est.** 1982
product range ($16.50–29.75 R) Sauvignon Blanc, Chardonnay, Pinot Noir, Double Fermented Pinot Noir, Shiraz, Merlot, Cabernet Merlot, Cabernet Sauvignon; Reserve Chardonnay, Merlot and Cabernet Sauvignon.
summary The 1997 capital raising by Oakridge Vineyards Limited led to the opening of a new winery in 1998 on a prominent Maroondah Highway site. In 2001 the then struggling company was acquired by Evans & Tate.

Oakridge Estate Sauvignon Blanc

TTTT 2001 Light green-yellow; the bouquet offers a mix of light gooseberry and tropical edges; the palate has light varietal character, flowing well and providing good mouthfeel. **rating:** 86

best drinking 2001–2002 **best vintages** NA **drink with** Yarra Valley yabbies • $16.50

Oakridge Estate Yarra Valley Shiraz

▼▼▼▼ 2000 Medium red-purple; the bouquet is somewhat closed, but the oak is evident, coming through strongly on the palate along with red and black cherry fruit. Needs patience. **rating:** 85

best drinking 2004–2009 **best vintages** '98 **drink with** Lamb stew • $29.75

Oakridge Estate Yarra Valley Merlot

▼▼▼▼▽ 2000 Medium red-purple; a rich, complex berry and olive bouquet, ripe but not heavy, leads into a well-handled palate, showing good varietal character, good oak handling and fine tannins. **rating:** 91

best drinking 2004–2009 **best vintages** '98, '00 **drink with** Roast veal • $29.75

Oakridge Estate Cabernet Sauvignon

▼▼▼▼ 2000 Medium red-purple; a mix of savoury, earthy and fractionally gamey canopy-derived aromas is followed logically enough on the palate, with a somewhat soft and slightly short finish. **rating:** 85

best drinking 2003–2008 **best vintages** NA **drink with** Pizza • $29.75

oakvale ★★★★

Broke Road, Pokolbin, NSW 2320 **region** Lower Hunter Valley
phone (02) 4998 7520 **fax** (02) 4998 7077 **open** 7 days 9–6
winemaker Cameron Webster **production** 20 000 **est.** 1893
product range ($17–30 CD) Gold Rock range of Semillon Chardonnay, Verdelho, French Oak Chardonnay, Shiraz; Reserve range of Elliott's Well Semillon, Peach Tree Chardonnay, Peppercorn Shiraz
summary All of the literature and promotional material emphasises the fact that Oakvale has been family-owned since 1893. What it does not mention is that three quite unrelated families have been the owners: first, and for much of the time, the Elliott family; then former Sydney solicitor Barry Shields; and, since 1999, Richard and Mary Owens, who also own the separately-run Milbrovale winery at Broke. Be that as it may, the original slab hut homestead of the Elliott family which is now a museum, and the atmospheric Oakvale winery, are in the 'must visit' category. The winery complex offers a delicatessen, coffee shop, a book shop and has picnic and playground facilities. Live entertainment each weekend between 11 am and 3 pm. Exports to the UK and the US.

Oakvale Elliott's Well Semillon

▼▼▼▼▽ 1998 Medium green-yellow; the smooth bouquet is developing well, having reached the citrus and honey stage, the toast still to come. The palate provides more of the same, still with years in front of it, but all the right things are happening. **rating:** 90

best drinking 2002–2008 **best vintages** NA **drink with** Salmon risotto • $24.99

Oakvale Gold Rock Verdelho

▼▼▼▽ 2001 Light to medium yellow-green; clean, soft fruit salad aromas so typical of the variety lead into a nicely made light to medium-bodied palate, with gentle fruit salad. A blue gold medal at the 2001 Sydney International Wine Competition, presumably on the principle of the dog preaching. **rating:** 84

best drinking 2002–2003 **best vintages** NA **drink with** Takeaway • $17

Oakvale Peach Tree Chardonnay

▼▼▼▼ 2000 Surprisingly light straw-green; a very youthful, light and undeveloped bouquet, then a similarly light palate, with gently sweet nectarine fruit and good acidity. Not the style one expects from the Hunter; developing slowly and may end up as something special. **rating:** 85

best drinking 2002–2005 **best vintages** NA **drink with** Pan-fried veal • $29.99

Oakvale Gold Rock Shiraz

▼▼▼▼ 2000 Bright red-purple, with a fresher hue than the Peppercorn Shiraz. The moderately intense, clean and smooth bouquet has gentle black cherry and subtle oak, the palate likewise showing a mix of black and red cherry fruit, finishing with soft, fine tannins. **rating:** 86

best drinking 2002–2004 **best vintages** NA **drink with** Mixed grill • $17

Oakvale Peppercorn Shiraz

▼▼▼▼▽ 2000 Medium red-purple; solid dark berry/cherry fruit on the bouquet is followed by a richly concentrated and textured palate with a mix of black cherry and blackberry; good oak and sustained tannins. **rating:** 90

best drinking 2005–2015 **best vintages** '00 **drink with** Teppanyaki beef • $29.99

old caves   NR

New England Highway, Stanthorpe, Qld 4380 **region** Granite Belt
phone (07) 4681 1494 **fax** (07) 4681 2722 **open** Mon–Sat 9–5, Sun 10–5
winemaker David Zanatta **production** 2200 **est.** 1980
product range ($7.50–13.50 CD) Chardonnay, Classic Dry White, Light Red, Shiraz, Cabernet Sauvignon and a range of generic wines in both bottle and flagon, including fortifieds.
summary Has a strictly local, relatively uncritical and evidently loyal clientele.

old kent river   ★★★★

Turpin Road, Rocky Gully, WA 6397 **region** Great Southern
phone (08) 9855 1589 **fax** (08) 9855 1660 **open** At South Coast Highway, Kent River Wed–Sun 9–5 (extended hours during tourist season)
winemaker Alkoomi (Contract), Michael Staniford **production** 2500 **est.** 1985
product range ($17–50 CD) Sauvignon Blanc, Chardonnay, Pinot Noir, Reserve Pinot Noir, Shiraz, Diamontina (Sparkling).
summary Mark and Debbie Noack have done it tough all of their relatively young lives but have earned respect from their neighbours and from the other producers to whom they sell more than half the production from the 16.5-hectare vineyard established on their sheep property. 'Grapes,' they used to say, 'saved us from bankruptcy.' Exports to Canada, the UK, the Netherlands and Hong Kong.

Old Kent River Sauvignon Blanc

▼▼▼▼ 2001 Light green-yellow; quite intense grassy/gooseberry fruit aromas are followed by a palate with good flavour, length and balance, and providing yet more of the grass and gooseberry of the bouquet.

rating: 89

best drinking 2002–2003 **best vintages** NA **drink with** Chinese dumplings • $17

Old Kent River Reserve Pinot Noir

▼▼▼▼ 2000 Deep purple-red, still holding bright, primary hue; a savoury, spicy bouquet with dark berry fruits lurks underneath. A very powerful wine in the mouth, tightly knitted, and must be given time. I suspect the wine has high acidity and low pH, which lead to a certain hardness. Only 200 cases made.   **rating:** 89

best drinking 2004–2009 **best vintages** NA **drink with** Game • $50

old loddon wines   NR

5 Serpentine Road, Bridgewater, Vic 3516 **region** Bendigo
phone (03) 5437 3197 **fax** (03) 5437 3201 **open** Weekends 10–5, Mon–Fri by appointment
winemaker Russell Burdett **production** 5000 **est.** 1995
product range ($12–15 CD) Merlot Shiraz, Merlot Cabernet Franc, Cabernet Franc, Cabernet Sauvignon.
summary Russell and Jill Burdett began planting 3 hectares of cabernet franc, merlot, cabernet sauvignon and shiraz in 1987 on the banks of the Loddon River at Bridgewater. Until 1995 all of the grapes were sold to other makers (including Passing Clouds), but in that year the Burdetts began to vinify part of the production, and have steadily increased their own wine production since that time, with the assistance of their daughters Brooke and Lisa. All of the wine is sold through the cellar door and by mailing list.

old station vineyard   ★★★☆

St Vincent Street, Watervale, SA 5452 **region** Clare Valley
phone 0414 441 925 **fax** (02) 9144 1925 **open** Not
winemaker David O'Leary, Nick Walker **production** 2000 **est.** 1926
product range ($12–20 ML) Watervale Riesling, Watervale Free Run Rosé, Grenache Shiraz, Shiraz.
summary When Bill and Noel Ireland decided to retire from the Sydney retail scene in 1996 to go all the way up (or down) the production stream to become grape growers and winemakers, they did not muck around. In 1995 they had purchased a 6-hectare, 70-year-old vineyard at Watervale and formed a significantly larger joint venture in the Margaret River region, which has given birth to Flinders Bay wines. In their first year of shows the Old Station Vineyard wines won two gold, three silver and eight bronze medals, a reflection of the strength of old vines and the skills of contract winemaking at Quelltaler. I just wonder what Bill Ireland feels now about retailers who slash and burn the theoretical retail price of his wines.

Old Station Vineyard Grenache Shiraz

TTTY 2000 Medium red-purple; a highly aromatic bouquet is reflected in the juicy/berry/minty palate. Strongly expressive of Grenache. **rating: 84**

best drinking 2001–2002 **best vintages** '98, '99 **drink with** Game casserole • $15

old stornoway vineyard   NR

370 Relbia Road, Relbia, Tas 7258 **region** Northern Tasmania
phone (03) 6343 4742 **fax** (03) 6343 4743 **open** 7 days 10–5
winemaker Julian Alcorso (Contract) **production** 2750 **est.** 1998
product range ($17–18 CD) Sauvignon Blanc, Unwooded Chardonnay, Chardonnay, Pinot Noir.
summary Old Stornoway Vineyard is headed for big things, having planted 10.6 hectares of vines in 1998 and 49.4 hectares in 1999. Pinot noir (33 ha), chardonnay (12 ha), pinot meunier (6.5 ha), riesling (3.5 ha), pinot gris (3.4 ha) and traminer (0.6 ha) will come into full bearing within a few years; the recently completed cellar-door facilities include a cafe/restaurant.

o'leary walker wines   ★★★★☆

Main Road, Leasingham, SA 5452 (PO Box 49, Watervale, SA 5452) **region** Clare Valley
phone (08) 8333 3309 **fax** (08) 8333 0072 **open** Not
winemaker David O'Leary, Nick Walker **production** 8000 **est.** 2001
product range ($18.50–21 R) Watervale Riesling, Watervale Semillon, Adelaide Hills Sauvignon Blanc, Adelaide Hills Chardonnay, Clare Valley Cabernet Merlot.
summary David O'Leary and Nick Walker have more than 30 years' combined experience as winemakers working for some of the biggest Australian wine groups. They have taken the plunge and backed themselves to establish their own winery and brand. Their main vineyard is at Watervale in the Clare Valley, with over 36 hectares of riesling, shiraz, cabernet sauvignon, merlot and semillon. In the Adelaide Hills they have established 14 hectares of chardonnay, cabernet sauvignon, pinot noir, shiraz, sauvignon blanc and merlot. Winemaking skills are not in doubt, nor is the quality of the vineyards, and the wine prices are highly competitive.

O'Leary Walker Watervale Riesling

TTTTT 2001 Light green-yellow; the spotlessly correct and crisp bouquet with apple and citrus aromas lays the foundation for a long, lingering and intense palate with a faint touch of CO_2 which will stand the wine in good stead in the years ahead. The finish is nigh on perfect, notwithstanding that touch of spritz. **rating: 94**

best drinking 2002–2010 **best vintages** '01 **drink with** Fresh asparagus • $18.50

O'Leary Walker Watervale Semillon

TTTT 2001 Medium to full yellow-green; the bouquet is solid, clean, and not particularly aromatic; the palate is excellently balanced in a big-framed style. Lemon/lemon tart flavours will progressively develop over the short to medium term. **rating: 89**

best drinking 2002–2005 **best vintages** NA **drink with** Creamy pasta • $18.50

O'Leary Walker Adelaide Hills Sauvignon Blanc

TTTTY 2001 Light green-yellow; the strongly varietal bouquet has a mix of passionfruit, gooseberry and a hint of compost; a lively and intense palate with lemony flavours joining those of the bouquet; the long finish with minerally acidity; not only suited to, but positively demands, food. **rating: 90**

best drinking 2002–2004 **best vintages** '01 **drink with** Thai prawns • $19.50

O'Leary Walker Adelaide Hills Chardonnay

TTTT 2001 Light green-yellow; delicate aromas of citrus, nectarine and melon, and even more subtle oak, are reflected on the palate, which lacks fruit depth, but has length, and may surprise with a few years in bottle. **rating: 85**

best drinking 2002–2005 **best vintages** NA **drink with** Blue swimmer crab • $20.50

O'Leary Walker Clare Valley Cabernet Merlot

TTTT 2000 Medium purple-red; clean, fresh, clear red berry/raspberry/cassis fruit aromatics are followed by a similarly attractive clean and fresh palate which is as yet a little disjointed, but which will undoubtedly come together with time in bottle. The oak has been cleverly handled, adding complexity without threatening the integrity of the fruit. **rating: 88**

best drinking 2003–2008 **best vintages** NA **drink with** Rack of veal • $19.50

olive farm ★★★

77 Great Eastern Highway, South Guildford, WA 6055 **region** Swan District
phone (08) 9277 2989 **fax** (08) 9277 6828 **open** Wed–Sun 10–5.30 Cellar Sales, 11.30–2.30 Cafe
winemaker Ian Yurisich **production** 3500 **est.** 1829
product range ($11.50–35 CD) Traminer, Sauvignon Blanc Semillon, Chenin Blanc, Classic White, Verdelho, Unwooded Chardonnay, Chardonnay, Sauterne Style, Pinot Noir, Shiraz, Merlot, Cabernet Shiraz Merlot, Cabernet Sauvignon, Fortifieds, Sparkling.
summary The oldest winery in Australia in use today, and arguably the least communicative. The ultra-low profile in no way inhibits flourishing cellar-door sales. The wines come from 14 hectares of estate plantings of 11 different varieties.

Olive Farm Chenin Blanc

ΨΨΨΨ **2000** Light green-yellow; a clean, rich, tropical fruit salad bouquet is followed by a palate with abundant and rich flavour, bolstered further by a flick of sweetness. An excellent example of unwooded, early-drinking Chenin Blanc. **rating:** 85

best drinking 2001–2004 **best vintages** NA **drink with** Trout mousse • $14.50

Olive Farm Shiraz

ΨΨΨΨ **1999** Medium red-purple; a ripe bouquet with dark berry, prune and molasses aromas is followed by a palate with abundant sweet fruit, but not a lot of structural complexity. **rating:** 83

best drinking 2002–2005 **best vintages** NA **drink with** Meat-based pasta • $15.50

Olive Farm Merlot

ΨΨΨΨ **2000** Medium red, with some purple tints remaining; the bouquet shows surprising varietal character, with a mix of savoury and dark berry aromatics. The palate is very ripe and sweet, far from classical, but has appeal nonetheless. **rating:** 85

best drinking 2002–2007 **best vintages** NA **drink with** Chargrilled beef fillet • $15.50

oliverhill NR

Seaview Road, McLaren Vale, SA 5171 **region** McLaren Vale
phone (08) 8323 8922 **open** 7 days 10–5
winemaker Stuart Miller **production** 1300 **est.** 1973
product range ($5–11 CD) Great Outdoors White and Red, Chardonnay, Shiraz Cabernet, Port, Muscat.
summary Oliverhill has changed hands but otherwise continues an operation aimed almost entirely at the local tourist trade.

olivers taranga vineyards ★★★★

Olivers Road, McLaren Vale, SA 5171 **region** McLaren Vale
phone (08) 8323 8498 **fax** (08) 8323 7498 **open** Not
winemaker Corinna Rayment, Mike Farmilo **production** 1500 **est.** 1839
product range ($16.50 R) Shiraz, HJ Reserve Shiraz.
summary 1839 was the year in which William and Elizabeth Oliver arrived from Scotland to settle at McLaren Vale. Six generations later, members of the family are still living on the Whitehill and Taranga farms, 2 kilometres north of McLaren Vale. The Taranga property has 10 varieties planted on 62 hectares; historically, grapes from the property have been sold to up to five different wineries, but since 1994 some of the old vine shiraz has been made under the Oliver's Taranga label. From the 2000 vintage, the wine has been made by Mike Farmilo at Boar's Rock together with Corinna Rayment (the Oliver family's first winemaker and sixth generation family member). Exports to Belgium, Canada, Singapore, Germany, New Zealand, Switzerland, Thailand and the US.

Olivers Taranga Vineyards Shiraz

ΨΨΨΨΨ **1999** Medium red-purple; a complex bouquet with scented sweet leather, earth and ripe, concentrated berry fruit. The palate is a replay, with lots of satisfaction in a traditional American oaked style, the fruit well and truly supporting the oak. Excellent value. **rating:** 90

best drinking 2004–2011 **best vintages** '99 **drink with** Rare roast beef • $16.50

olssens of watervale ★★★☆

Government Road, Watervale, SA 5452 **region** Clare Valley
phone (08) 8843 0065 **fax** (08) 8843 0065 **open** Fri–Mon and public holidays 11–5 or by appointment

winemaker Contract **production** 1000 **est.** 1994
product range ($13–20 CD) Riesling, Semillon, Botrytised Riesling, Cabernet Sauvignon Cabernet Franc Merlot.
summary Kevin and Helen Olssen first visited the Clare Valley in December 1986. Within 2 weeks they and their family decided to sell their Adelaide home and purchased a property in a small, isolated valley 3 kilometres north of the township of Watervale. Between 1987 and 1993 production from the 5-hectare vineyard was sold to other makers, but in 1993 the decision was taken to produce wine under the Olssen label.

Olssens of Watervale Cabernet Sauvignon Cabernet Franc Merlot

YYYY 1999 Medium red, with some of the purple starting to fade; a quite complex array of savoury aromas come through on the palate, with an added touch of spice; nicely structured and balanced.   **rating:** 86

best drinking 2003–2007 **best vintages** NA **drink with** Rack of lamb with fresh rosemary • $20

orani vineyard   NR

Arthur Highway, Sorrel, Tas 7172 **region** Southern Tasmania
phone (03) 6225 0330 **fax** (03) 6225 0330 **open** Weekends and public holidays 9.30–6.30
winemaker Various Contract **production** NA **est.** 1986
product range ($15.60–18.35 R) Riesling, Chardonnay, Pinot Noir.
summary The first commercial release from Orani was of a 1992 Pinot Noir, with Chardonnay and Riesling following in the years thereafter. Since that time Orani has continued to do well with its Pinot Noirs, including a ripe, plummy, highly flavoured wine from the 1999 vintage. Owned by Tony and Angela McDermott, the latter the President of the Royal Hobart Wine Show.

orlando   ★★★★☆

Jacob's Creek Visitor Centre, Barossa Valley Way, Rowland Flat, SA 5352 **region** Barossa Valley
phone (08) 8521 3000 **fax** (08) 8521 3003 **open** 7 days 10–5
winemaker Philip Laffer, Bernard Hicken, Sam Kurtz **production** NFP **est.** 1847
product range ($8–60 R) The table wines are sold in 4 ranges: first the national and international best-selling Jacob's Creek Semillon Sauvignon Blanc, Semillon Chardonnay, Chardonnay, Riesling, Shiraz Cabernet and Grenache Shiraz and special Limited Releases; then the Gramp's range of Chardonnay, Botrytis Semillon, Grenache and Cabernet Merlot; next the Saint range – St Helga Eden Valley Riesling, St Hilary Padthaway Chardonnay, St Hugo Coonawarra Cabernet Sauvignon; finally the premium range of Steingarten Riesling, Jacaranda Ridge Cabernet Sauvignon and Lawson's Padthaway Shiraz; sparkling wines are under the Trilogy and Carrington labels.
summary Jacob's Creek is one of the largest-selling brands in the world and is almost exclusively responsible for driving the fortunes of this Pernod Ricard-owned company. A colossus in the export game, chiefly to the UK and Europe, but also to the US and Asia. In the latter part of the 1990s (and into 2000) wine quality across the full spectrum from Jacob's Creek upwards has been exemplary.

Orlando Jacob's Creek Riesling

YYYY 2001 Almost water-white in colour; a spotlessly clean, pure, crisp minerally bouquet is followed by a neatly proportioned palate with good length. excellent value, though (at least at this juncture) not in the class of the 2000 vintage.   **rating:** 86

best drinking 2001–2005 **best vintages** '00 **drink with** Salads, seafood • $8

Orlando Jacob's Creek Reserve Riesling

YYYYY 2001 Bright, light green-yellow; the fresh, bright, citrus, apple and herb leads into a tight palate, with excellent structure through a mix of citrus and mineral flavours; long, well-balanced finish.**rating:** 91

best drinking 2001–2006 **best vintages** '01 **drink with** Avocado salad • $15

Orlando Jacob's Creek Semillon Chardonnay

YYYY 2001 Light green-yellow; a crisp, light lemony/minerally bouquet is followed by a palate with pleasant citrussy flavours, good mouthfeel and balance. More like a Semillon Sauvignon Blanc blend, but nonetheless won silver medals at Hobart and Perth wine shows in 2001.   **rating:** 84

best drinking 2002–2003 **best vintages** NA **drink with** Seafood takeaway • $8

Orlando Jacob's Creek Chardonnay

ΨΨΨΨ 2001 Light green-yellow, the clean bouquet features subtle oak on more than adequate fruit, repeated in the mouth with plenty of sweet melon/stone fruit flavour and a nicely judged flick of oak.　**rating: 87**

best drinking 2001–2002 **best vintages** '00, '01 **drink with** Whatever takes your fancy • $8

Orlando Jacob's Creek Reserve Chardonnay

ΨΨΨΨ 2000 Light to medium green-yellow; clean melon fruit and a well-judged touch of oak on the bouquet are followed by a neatly balanced and weighted palate, offering fresh melon and stone fruit flavours, closing with crisp acidity.　**rating: 88**

best drinking 2001–2003 **best vintages** NA **drink with** Sautéed prawns • $14.95

Orlando St Hilary Padthaway Chardonnay

ΨΨΨΨΨ 2000 Light to medium green-yellow; a fragrant bouquet, with regional grapefruit aromas and restrained barrel-ferment treatment leads into a light to medium-bodied palate, with fresh fruit and a touch of cashew. Needed a touch more bite for top points.　**rating: 90**

best drinking 2001–2003 **best vintages** '96, '00 **drink with** Veal • $18

Orlando Gramp's Botrytis Semillon

ΨΨΨΨΨ 1999 Medium yellow-green; an intense and complex bouquet with botrytis-derived cumquat and mandarin aromas, characters which replay on the long palate; not over-oaked; drink immediately.**rating: 90**

best drinking 2002–2003 **best vintages** '97, '99 **drink with** Baked apple • $16

Orlando Jacob's Creek Reserve Shiraz

ΨΨΨΨ 1999 Good colour and a bouquet flooded with ripe, dark plum and prune leads logically into a palate with luscious ripe fruit offset by appropriately persistent tannins and subtle oak.　**rating: 89**

best drinking 2003–2008 **best vintages** '98, '99 **drink with** Rare roast beef • $15

Orlando Lawson's Padthaway Shiraz

ΨΨΨΨΨ 1996 Medium red-purple; the powerful bouquet is loaded with American oak, as is the palate. On the other side of the ledger come lashings of fruit; altogether, a big, big style.　**rating: 92**

best drinking 2006–2016 **best vintages** '88, '90, '91, '93, '94, '95, '96 **drink with** Beef stroganoff • $60

Orlando Trilogy

ΨΨΨΨ 1999 Medium red-purple; the bouquet is clean and smooth, with well-integrated fruit and oak, and a faintly savoury background. There are some nice black fruit flavours on the palate, but (not surprisingly) the wine falls well short of the utterly exceptional 1998 vintage.　**rating: 85**

best drinking 2002–2006 **best vintages** '98 **drink with** Roast shoulder of lamb • $13

Orlando Gramp's Cabernet Merlot

ΨΨΨΨ 1999 Medium to full red-purple; ripe, smooth, blackcurrant/berry/raspberry fruit on the bouquet comes through on a palate with lots of texture and structure. The tannins are a fraction abrasive, and one wonders whether they will soften or not. Good value, though, continuing the tradition for this wine.

rating: 87

best drinking 2004–2009 **best vintages** '98 **drink with** Butterfly leg of lamb • $16

Orlando Jacaranda Ridge Cabernet Sauvignon

ΨΨΨΨΨ 1997 Medium red-purple; a fragrant bouquet of cedar, spice and berry; ripe berry/chocolate/mocha flavours lead the way on the palate, finishing with moderately persistent tannins; controlled oak.　**rating: 92**

best drinking 2004–2009 **best vintages** '86, '88, '90, '94, '96, '97 **drink with** Grilled beef • $55

Orlando Jacob's Creek Reserve Cabernet Sauvignon

ΨΨΨΨ 1999 Medium red-purple; the bouquet is smooth, with ripe berry fruit and well-integrated oak. A powerful wine, unexpectedly dominated by tannins; needs to improve and probably will, but not to the level of the '98.　**rating: 85**

best drinking 2004–2009 **best vintages** '98 **drink with** Braised oxtail • $15

Orlando St Hugo Cabernet Sauvignon

ΨΨΨΨΨ 1999 Medium red-purple; the elegant bouquet has good fruit ripeness, which flows through into the mid-palate of the wine. The oak has been well handled, the wine finishing with pleasantly dry, savoury tannins. An excellent follow up to the outstanding '98 vintage.　**rating: 93**

best drinking 2004–2009 **best vintages** '86, '88, '90, '91, '92, '94, '96, '98, '99 **drink with** Rack of lamb • $32

osborns ★★★★

166 Foxeys Road, Merricks North, Vic 3926 **region** Mornington Peninsula
phone (03) 5989 7417 **fax** (03) 5989 7510 **open** First weekend of each month, holiday weekends and by appointment
winemaker Richard McIntyre (Consultant) **production** 1500 **est.** 1988
product range ($21.50–25 CD) Chardonnay, Pinot Noir, Cabernet Merlot, 'Sticky' (Botrytis Semillon Chardonnay).
summary Frank and Pamela Osborn are now Mornington Peninsula veterans, having purchased the vineyard land in Ellerina Road in 1988 and (with help from son Guy) planted the vineyard over the following 4 years. The first release of wines in 1997 offered six vintages each of Chardonnay and Pinot Noir and five vintages of Cabernet Sauvignon, quite a debut. Part of the production from the 5.5 hectares of vineyards is sold to others, but increasing amounts are made and marketed under the Osborns label.

Osborns Chardonnay

▼▼▼▼ **2000** Medium yellow-green; nectarine and cashew aromas are mixed with subtle, slightly smoky, oak on the bouquet, moving to peach on the palate, which is once again backed by quality French oak. **rating:** 88
▼▼▼▼▽ **1999** Medium yellow-green; from start to finish, the wine counterpoises perfectly balanced and integrated oak with cashew, fig and melon aromas and flavours, smooth and supple on the palate. **rating:** 93

best drinking 2002–2005 **best vintages** '97, '98, '99 **drink with** Sautéed scallops • $21.50

Osborns Pinot Noir

▼▼▼▼▽ **2000** Bright red-purple; the bouquet has penetrating, plummy varietal character with sappy/savoury/lemony adjuncts; there is good depth and length to the flavour on the palate, rippling through plum, spice and a touch of forest, then a fractionally firm finish. **rating:** 91

best drinking 2002–2006 **best vintages** '97, '00 **drink with** Grilled quail • $25

Osborns Cabernet Merlot

▼▼▼▼ **1998** Light to medium red-purple; a savoury/briary/woodsy bouquet is followed by a palate with more fruit intensity and length than the bouquet suggests, and while still in a savoury mode, with plenty of merlot varietal character. **rating:** 86

best drinking 2001–2005 **best vintages** NA **drink with** Slow-braised beef • $23

o'shea & murphy rosebery hill vineyard ★★★★

Rosebery Hill, Pastoria Road, Pipers Creek, Vic 3444 **region** Macedon Ranges
phone (03) 5423 5253 **fax** (03) 5424 5253 **open** By appointment
winemaker Barry Murphy, John O'Shea **production** 1250 **est.** 1984
product range ($22 R) Cabernet Sauvignon Cabernet Franc Merlot.
summary Planting of the 8-hectare vineyard began in 1984 on a north-facing slope of red basalt soil which runs between the 600 and 875 metre elevation line; it is believed that the hill was the site of a volcanic eruption seven million years ago. The vines were established without the aid of irrigation (and remain unirrigated), and produced the first small crop in 1990. No grapes were produced between 1993 and 1995 owing to mildew: Murphy and O'Shea say, 'We tried to produce fruit with no sprays at all, and learned the hard way.' Part of the current production is made for the O'Shea & Murphy Rosebery Hill label, and part is sold to others, all of whom attest to the quality of the fruit.

O'Shea & Murphy Rosebery Hill Vineyard Cabernet Sauvignon Cabernet Franc Merlot

▼▼▼▼▽ **1998** Amazing youthful colour and hue; a clean, fresh bouquet is followed by a relatively light-bodied palate with gently sweet berry fruit and minimal tannins. Has some Chinon characters. **rating:** 93

best drinking 2002–2005 **best vintages** NA **drink with** Antipasto • $20

oyster cove vineyard NR

134 Manuka Road, Oyster Cove, Tas 7054 **region** Southern Tasmania
phone (03) 6267 4512 **fax** (03) 6267 4635 **open** By appointment
winemaker Andrew Hood **production** 100 **est.** 1994
product range ($15–20 CD) Chardonnay, Pinot Noir.

summary The striking label of Oyster Cove, with a yacht reflected in mirror-calm water, is wholly appropriate, for Jean and Rod Ledingham have been quietly growing tiny quantities of grapes from the 1 hectare of chardonnay and pinot noir since 1994.

padthaway estate ★★★★

Riddoch Highway, Padthaway, SA 5271 **region** Padthaway
phone (08) 8734 3148 **fax** (08) 8734 3188 **open** 7 days 10–4
winemaker Nigel Catt, Ulrich Grey-Smith **production** 6000 **est.** 1980
product range ($14.95–22 R) Eliza Pinot Chardonnay Cuvée, Eliza Pinot Noir Brut, Eliza Sparkling Burgundy, Eliza Chardonnay (wooded and unwooded); Chardonnay, Unwooded Chardonnay, St Elgin Merlot, Cabernet Sauvignon.
summary For many years, until the opening of Stonehaven, the only functioning winery in Padthaway, set in the superb grounds of the Estate in a large and gracious old stone woolshed; the homestead is in the Relais et Chateaux mould, offering luxurious accommodation and fine food. Sparkling wines are the specialty of the Estate. Padthaway Estate also acts as a tasting centre for other Padthaway-region wines. National retail distribution; exports to the UK.

Padthaway Estate Chardonnay

TTTTY **2000** Medium yellow-green; the bouquet is complex, with smoky/tangy aromas reflecting the interplay of terroir with chardonnay. The light to medium-bodied palate is lively and fresh, with tangy citrus and stone fruit flavours to the fore. Clever winemaking has got the oak/fruit balance spot on. **rating:** 90

best drinking 2001–2004 **best vintages** '00 **drink with** Robe crayfish • $18.95

Padthaway Estate St Elgin Merlot

TTTTY **2000** Medium red-purple; fragrant, savoury/cedary edges to bright red fruit aromas, then a palate with excellent mouthfeel, fine and supple, plus fresh berry fruit and well-handled oak. Great value. **rating:** 91

best drinking 2003–2009 **best vintages** '00 **drink with** Braised beef • $19

Padthaway Estate Cabernet Sauvignon

TTTT **2000** Medium red-purple; the moderately intense bouquet has red berry/cassis fruit with touches of earth and leaf; the light to medium-bodied palate has similar well-balanced flavours, supported by quite ripe tannins. **rating:** 85

best drinking 2005–2010 **best vintages** NA **drink with** Beef roulade • $18.95

palandri wines ★★★☆

Bussell Highway, Cowaramup, WA 6284 **region** Margaret River
phone (08) 9755 5711 **fax** (08) 9755 5722 **open** Mon–Fri 10–5, weekends and public holidays 9–5
winemaker Tony Carapetis, Sarah Siddons **production** 240 000 **est.** 2000
product range ($15–25 R) Under the lower-priced Aurora label are Semillon Sauvignon Blanc, Semillon Chardonnay, Chardonnay, Shiraz, Merlot, Cabernet Shiraz; the flagship Palandri range consists of Riesling, Semillon, Sauvignon Blanc, Chardonnay, Shiraz, Cabernet Merlot, Cabernet Sauvignon.
summary A state-of-the-art winery, completed just prior to the 2000 vintage, has a capacity of 2500 tonnes. The vineyards which are scheduled to supply Palandri Wines with 50 per cent of its intake are situated in the Frankland River subregion of the Great Southern. 150 hectares of vines were planted at Frankland River in September 1999; the major varieties are shiraz, merlot, cabernet sauvignon, riesling, chardonnay and sauvignon blanc. A further 60 hectares were planted in early September 2000, making this the largest single vineyard developed in WA. A second block has been purchased south of the Frankland River vineyard, and a further 140 hectares are being developed there. It has also acquired Rosabrook Estate, but had placed it back on the market within a year. Palandri is a business driven by sales and marketing to a degree not hitherto seen in Australia.

Palandri Sauvignon Blanc

TTTY **2001** Light green-yellow; the moderately intense bouquet has straightforward gooseberry fruit; the palate continues the theme with a mix of gooseberry and more tropical flavours, held back by a slightly fuzzy finish. **rating:** 83
TTTT **2000** Light green-yellow; the crisp, fresh, moderately intense bouquet has direct fruit; the palate follows suit with good varietal fruit and fair length. **rating:** 87

best drinking 2002–2003 **best vintages** NA **drink with** Shellfish • $20

Palandri Chardonnay

▼▼▼▼ 2000 Light green-yellow; light, clean melon and citrus fruit with minimal oak influence on the bouquet is mirrored on the light, fresh palate, again with subtle oak.   **rating:** 85

best drinking 2001–2002 **best vintages** NA **drink with** Pan-fried fish • $22

Palandri Cabernet Merlot

▼▼▼▼ 2000 Medium red-purple; a clean, fresh bouquet with red berry, raspberry and redcurrant fruit aromas is followed by a light to medium-bodied palate, with similar fruit flavours to those of the bouquet, finishing with gentle tannins.   **rating:** 86

best drinking 2002–2006 **best vintages** NA **drink with** Lamb shanks • $25

Palandri Aurora Cabernet Shiraz

▼▼▼▼ 2000 Medium red-purple; the moderately intense bouquet has slightly lifted, fresh berry aromatics; the medium-bodied, straightforward palate has sweet, ripe raspberry fruit and soft tannins.   **rating:** 85

best drinking 2002–2005 **best vintages** NA **drink with** Lamb cutlets • $15

palmara   ★★★☆

1314 Richmond Road, Richmond, Tas 7025 **region** Southern Tasmania
phone (03) 6260 2462 **fax** (03) 6260 2462 **open** Sept–May 7 days 12–6
winemaker Allan Bird **production** 300 **est.** 1985
product range ($15.50–32.50 CD) Montage, Chardonnay, Exotica (Siegerrebe), Pinot Noir, Cabernet Sauvignon.
summary Allan Bird makes the Palmara wines in tiny quantities. (The vineyard is slightly less than 1 hectare in total.) The Pinot Noir has performed well since 1990. The Exotica Siegerrebe blend is unchallenged as Australia's most exotic and unusual wine, with pungent jujube/lanolin aromas and flavours.

palmer wines   ★★★★

Caves Road, Wilyabrup, WA 6280 **region** Margaret River
phone (08) 9756 7388 **fax** (08) 9756 7399 **open** 7 days 10–5
winemaker Bernard Abbott, Cathy Oates (Contract) **production** 5000 **est.** 1977
product range ($16–45 R) Sauvignon Blanc, Semillon Sauvignon Blanc, Chardonnay, Shiraz, Merlot, Shiraz Cabernet, Cabernet Sauvignon.
summary Stephen and Helen Palmer planted their first hectare of vines way back in 1977, but a series of events (including a cyclone and grasshopper plagues) caused them to lose interest and instead turn to thoroughbred horses. But with encouragement from Dr Michael Peterkin of Pierro, and after a gap of almost ten years, they again turned to viticulture and now have 15 hectares planted to the classic varieties. A new cellar door/art gallery/cafe complex opened in April 2002, with accommodation units to follow in late 2002, along with full resort facilities.

Palmer Sauvignon Blanc

▼▼▼▼ 2001 Light green-yellow; the delicate bouquet is clean, but the varietal aromas are suppressed; the palate makes a partial comeback, with grass and a touch of passionfruit providing pleasant mouthfeel.   **rating:** 85

best drinking 2002–2003 **best vintages** NA **drink with** Scampi • $16

Palmer Shiraz

▼▼▼▼ 2000 Medium red-purple; attractive blackberry/plum fruit and vanilla oak, then a medium-bodied palate with plum, chocolate and, once again, a touch of vanilla; quite elegant, and quite different from the '99 vintage.   **rating:** 88

best drinking 2004–2009 **best vintages** '99 **drink with** Marinated beef • $36

pankhurst   ★★★☆

Old Woodgrove, Woodgrove Road, Hall, NSW 2618 **region** Canberra District
phone (02) 6230 2592 **fax** (02) 6230 2592 **open** Weekends, public holidays and by appointment
winemaker Dr David Carpenter, Sue Carpenter (Contract) **production** 4000 **est.** 1986
product range ($15–25 CD) Sauvignon Blanc Semillon, Chardonnay, Pinot Noir, Cabernet Sauvignon.
summary Agricultural scientist and consultant Allan Pankhurst and wife Christine (with a degree in pharmaceutical science) have established a 5.7-hectare split canopy vineyard. Tastings of the first wines

produced showed considerable promise. In recent years Pankhurst has shared success with Lark Hill in the production of surprisingly good Pinot Noir – surprising given the climatic limitations. Says Christine Pankhurst, 'it is the result of good viticulture here and great winemaking at Lark Hill', and she may well be right.

Pankhurst Sauvignon Blanc Semillon

TTTT 2001 Light straw-green; the crisp, clean bouquet has a range of mineral, herbaceous and grassy aromas; the same somewhat reserved fruit characters come through on the nicely balanced palate, finishing with good acidity. Well made.   **rating:** 87

best drinking 2002–2003 **best vintages** NA **drink with** Light seafood • $15

Pankhurst Cabernet Merlot

TTTT 2000 Medium to full red-purple; typical blackberry and blackcurrant fruit aromas are followed by a quite substantial and concentrated palate with austere tannins and oak in the background. A blend of 84 per cent Cabernet Sauvignon and 16 per cent Merlot.   **rating:** 87

best drinking 2005–2010 **best vintages** NA **drink with** Leg of lamb • $18

panorama   ★★★★☆

RSD 297 Lower Wattle Grove, Cradoc, Tas 7109 **region** Southern Tasmania
phone (03) 6266 3409 **fax** (03) 6266 3482 **open** Wed-Mon 10–5
winemaker Michael Vishacki **production** 2250 **est.** 1974
product range ($10–35 CD) Sauvignon Blanc, Chardonnay, Reserve Chardonnay, Pinot Noir, Cabernet Sauvignon.
summary Michael and Sharon Vishacki purchased Panorama from Steve Ferencz 3 years ago, and have since spent considerable sums in building a brand new winery and an attractive cellar-door sales outlet, and in trebling the vineyard size.

Panorama Reserve Chardonnay

TTTT 2000 Pale straw-green; the bouquet has light melon and stone fruit, a touch of oak, a hint of malolactic character, but is not particularly intense. A fine, elegant palate in typical Tasmanian style, with fairly brisk acidity.   **rating:** 85

best drinking 2001–2005 **best vintages** NA **drink with** Shellfish • $35

Panorama Pinot Noir

TTTTT 2000 Medium to full red-purple; the rich and dense bouquet offers ripe, dark plum and a nice touch of oak; the mouthfilling, rich and soft palate has a touch of bitter chocolate, and avoids any jammy flavours. Gold medal at the 2002 Tasmanian Wines Show.   **rating:** 94

best drinking 2002–2007 **best vintages** '90, '91, '92, '93, '98 **drink with** Duck casserole • $35

panton hill winery   NR

145 Manuka Road, Panton Hill, Vic 3759 **region** Yarra Valley
phone (03) 9719 7342 **fax** (03) 9719 7362 **open** Weekends 11–5
winemaker Dr Teunis AP Kwak **production** 750 **est.** 1988
product range ($18–28 CD) Chardonnay, Sparkling Cabernet Franc, Pinot Noir, Cabernet Franc, Cabernet Sauvignon Merlot Franc.
summary Melbourne academic Dr Teunis Kwak has a 4.5 hectare fully mature vineyard, part planted in 1976, the remainder in 1988. Part of the production is sold to others, part retained for the Panton Hill label. The vineyard is a picturesque one, established on a fairly steep hillside, and there is a large stone hall available for functions.

paracombe wines   ★★★★

Main Road, Paracombe, SA 5132 **region** Adelaide Hills
phone (08) 8380 5058 **fax** (08) 8380 5488 **open** Not
winemaker Paul Drogemuller **production** 3000 **est.** 1983
product range ($20–26 R) Sauvignon Blanc, Chardonnay, Pinot Chardonnay Mèthode Champenoise, Sparkling Shiraz, Shiraz, Somerville Shiraz Limited Release, Cabernet Franc, Cabernet Sauvignon.

summary The Drogemuller family have established 12 hectares of vineyards at Paracombe, reviving a famous name in SA wine history. The wines are stylish and consistent, and are sold by mail order and through retailers in SA. Exports to the US, Malaysia, Sweden and the UK.

Paracombe Sauvignon Blanc

▼▼▼▼♀ 2001 Pale straw-green; a typically clean and fresh bouquet with some mineral alongside apple and gooseberry aromas; the intense, firm palate has pronounced mineral flavours and the considerable length usually evident in this particular wine.   **rating:** 91

best drinking 2002–2003 **best vintages** '95, '96, '97, '01 **drink with** Trout mousse • $20

Paracombe Chardonnay

▼▼▼▼ 2000 Light to medium yellow-green; barrel fermentation in French oak and malolactic fermentation invests the bouquet with a mix of citrus, cashew and well-integrated oak; the palate is complex yet elegant, with all of the components coming together well.   **rating:** 89

best drinking 2002–2004 **best vintages** NA **drink with** Seafood risotto • $24

Paracombe Shiraz

▼▼▼▼ 1999 Medium purple-red; the bouquet is quite aromatic, featuring ripe, almost stewed, plum with touches of mint; notwithstanding its 14.5° alcohol, the palate is more restrained, with plum, mint and some minerally grip on the finish.   **rating:** 86

best drinking 2004–2009 **best vintages** '98 **drink with** Moroccan lamb • $26

Paracombe Cabernet Franc

▼▼▼▼ 2000 Light to medium red-purple; the blackcurrant, mulberry and spice aromas of the bouquet are sweeter and riper than usual; the palate likewise has surprising sweetness and concentration, adding bitter chocolate, vanilla and cedar rather than the more usual olive and earth flavours. Needs time.   **rating:** 88

best drinking 2004–2009 **best vintages** NA **drink with** Pastrami • $26

paradise enough   ★★★☆

Stewarts Road, Kongwak, Vic 3951 **region** Gippsland
phone (03) 5657 4241 **fax** (03) 5657 4229 **open** Sun, public holidays 12–5
winemaker John Bell, Sue Armstrong **production** 600 **est.** 1987
product range ($13–25 CD) Chardonnay, Reserve Chardonnay, Pinot Noir, Cabernet Merlot, Pinot Chardonnay.
summary Phillip Jones of Bass Phillip persuaded John Bell and Sue Armstrong to establish their small vineyard on a substantial dairy and beef cattle property.

paringa estate   ★★★★★

44 Paringa Road, Red Hill South, Vic 3937 **region** Mornington Peninsula
phone (03) 5989 2669 **fax** (03) 5931 0135 **open** 7 days 11–5
winemaker Lindsay McCall **production** 6500 **est** 1985
product range ($15–52.50 CD) Peninsula range of Chardonnay, Pinot Noir, Shiraz; Estate range of White Pinot, Pinot Gris, Chardonnay, Pinot Noir, Shiraz; Sparkling Shiraz, Cabernet Sauvignon.
summary No longer a rising star but a star shining more brightly than any other in the Mornington Peninsula firmament. As recent vintages have emphasised, the Mornington Peninsula region is sensitive to growing season conditions, with problems in 1995 and 1996, but having a succession of warm, dry vintages until 2002. Paringa shines most brightly in the warmer years. The restaurant is open seven days 10–3.

Paringa Estate Pinot Gris

▼▼▼▼ 2001 Full-on straw-pink; the light mix of apple, pear and strawberry aromas is followed by a powerful palate, with good feel and balance, neither hot nor phenolic.   **rating:** 88

best drinking 2002–2005 **best vintages** NA **drink with** Smoked salmon • $20

Paringa Estate Chardonnay

▼▼▼▼♀ 2000 Medium yellow-green; concentrated melon, fig and nectarine fruit reflect the barrel fermentation in French oak and 20 per cent malolactic fermentation; there is a replay on the palate, with melon and stone fruit with flecks of cashew, finishing with bright, lemony acidity.   **rating:** 92

best drinking 2002–2005 **best vintages** '91, '92, '93, '94, '96, '97, '00 **drink with** Pan-fried veal with abalone mushrooms • $15

Paringa Estate Pinot Noir

❔❔❔❔ **2000** Medium purple-red; a rich, complex, high-toned plum and spice bouquet leads into a powerfully framed palate, crawling with character and with ripe plummy fruit running right through to the emphatic finish. **rating: 95**

best drinking 2002–2007 **best vintages** '88, '90, '91, '92, '93, '95, '97, '99, '00 **drink with** Braised duck and wild mushrooms • $52.50

Paringa Estate Shiraz

❔❔❔❔❔ **2000** Medium to full purple-red; a concentrated and powerful dark cherry bouquet is followed by an equally powerful palate with masses of black cherry fruit, the tannins ripe but soft; less spice than usual, but highly rated by other critics. **rating: 92**

best drinking 2003–2010 **best vintages** '91, '92, '93, '94, '97, '00 **drink with** Stir-fried beef • $42.50

parker coonawarra estate ★★★★★

Riddoch Highway, Coonawarra, SA 5263 **region** Coonawarra
phone (08) 8737 3525 **fax** (08) 8737 3527 **open** 7 days 10–4
winemaker Chris Cameron **production** 5000 **est.** 1985
product range ($30–79 R) Terra Rossa Merlot, Terra Rossa First Growth, Terra Rossa Cabernet Sauvignon.
summary Parker Coonawarra Estate is now a 50/50 joint venture between founder John Parker and family and James Fairfax. It is by this mechanism that Pepper Tree in the Hunter Valley (controlled by James Fairfax) has its Coonawarra stake. It has also led to the highly regarded wines being made by Pepper Tree winemaker Chris Cameron, albeit using the Balnaves winery in Coonawarra to do so. Exports to the UK, Switzerland, Germany, Japan, Taiwan, Hong Kong, Singapore, Malaysia and Indonesia.

Parker Coonawarra Estate Terra Rossa First Growth

❔❔❔❔❔ **1999** Dark, dense red; the bouquet exudes ripe blackberry and chocolate aromas, with no green characters whatsoever. The palate is similarly dense and ripe (not jammy), with the flavours promised by the bouquet; fine tannins and good oak handling round off a classy wine. **rating: 93**

best drinking 2004–2014 **best vintages** '91, '96, '98, '99 **drink with** Prime rib of beef • $79

Parker Coonawarra Estate Terra Rossa Cabernet Sauvignon

❔❔❔❔❔ **1999** As dark and dense as its sister wine from 1999 (Terra Rossa First Growth); powerful blackberry and blackcurrant fruit with savoury aspects on the bouquet lead into a well-balanced and constructed palate, with luscious blackberry fruit supported by clever oak and tannin management. **rating: 94**

best drinking 2004–2014 **best vintages** '99 **drink with** Beef in black bean sauce • $36

park wines NR

RMB 6291, Sanatorium Road, Allan's Flat, Yackandandah, Vic 3691 **region** Alpine Valleys
phone (02) 6027 1564 **fax** (02) 6027 1561 **open** Weekends and public holidays 10–5
winemaker Rod Park, Julia Park **production** NA **est.** 1995
product range ($16–17 CD) Chardonnay, Cabernet Sauvignon.
summary Rod and Julia Park have a 6-hectare vineyard of riesling, chardonnay, merlot, cabernet franc and cabernet sauvignon, set in the beautiful hill country of the Ovens Valley. Part of the vineyard is still coming into bearing, and the business is still in its infancy.

passing clouds ★★★★

RMB 440 Kurting Road, Kingower, Vic 3517 **region** Bendigo
phone (03) 5438 8257 **fax** (03) 5438 8246 **open** Weekends 12–5, Mon–Fri by appointment
winemaker Graeme Leith **production** 4000 **est.** 1974
product range ($17–30 CD) Red wine specialist; principal wines include Pinot Noir, Shiraz, Grenache, Merlot, Graeme's Blend (Shiraz Cabernet), Angel Blend (Cabernet), Cabernet Shiraz, Cabernet Sauvignon; Chardonnay and Sauvignon Blanc from the Goulburn Valley.
summary Graeme Leith is one of the great personalities of the industry, with a superb sense of humour, and he makes lovely regional reds with cassis, berry and mint fruit. His smiling, bearded face adorned the front cover of many of the Victorian Tourist Bureau's excellent tourist publications for several years. Exports to the US.

Passing Clouds Graeme's Blend Shiraz Cabernet

YYYY 2000 Full red-purple; a dense and rich bouquet with a range of savoury/earthy/dark berry fruit, then a palate with ripe plum and prune fruit; lacks a little continuity as yet, but will come together in bottle. **rating:** 88

best drinking 2005–2010 **best vintages** '81, '82, '86, '90, '91, '92, '94, '97, '98 **drink with** Yearling steak or veal • $25

Passing Clouds Angel Blend

YYYYY 2000 Medium to full red-purple; cassis/blackberry with a nice hint of cedar, and little or none of the mint which can sometimes dominate. The palate has dark savoury fruit, a touch of chocolate, fine tannins and cedary oak. Quality wine. **rating:** 90

best drinking 2005–2010 **best vintages** '90, '91, '92, '94, '96, '97, '00 **drink with** Wild duck • $30

paternoster   NR

17 Paternoster Road, Emerald, Vic 3782 **region** Yarra Valley
phone (03) 5968 3197 **fax** (03) 5968 3197 **open** Weekends 11–6
winemaker Philip Hession **production** 700 **est.** 1985
product range ($15–120 CD) Lily, Chardonnay, Jack of Hearts Chardonnay, Rosemary, Pinot Noir, Pinot Noir Reserve, Jack of Hearts Pinot Noir, Queen Jane Pinot Noir, Jack of Hearts Shiraz, Cabernets, Jack of Hearts Cabernets, Tawny Port.
summary The densely planted, non-irrigated vines (at a density of 5000 vines to the hectare) cascade down a steep hillside at Emerald in one of the coolest parts of the Yarra Valley. Pinot Noir is the specialty of the winery, which produces intensely flavoured wines with a strong eucalypt mint overlay reminiscent of the wines of Delatite. No recent tastings; there also seems to be some dispute as to whether or not Paternoster falls within the Yarra Valley.

patrick creek vineyard   NR

Springfield Park, North Down, Tas 7307 **region** Northern Tasmania
phone (03) 6424 6979 **fax** (03) 6424 6380 **open** By appointment
winemaker Andrew Hood (Contract) **production** 350 **est.** 1990
product range ($15 CD) Semillon, Chardonnay, Classic Dry White, Pinot Noir.
summary Patrick Creek Vineyard came into being in 1990, when Pat and Kay Walker established high-density plantings of chardonnay, pinot noir, semillon and sauvignon blanc in a 1-hectare vineyard.

patritti wines   ★★☆

13–23 Clacton Road, Dover Gardens, SA 5048 **region** Adelaide Zone
phone (08) 8296 8261 **fax** (08) 8296 5088 **open** Mon–Sat 9–6
winemaker G Patritti, J Patritti **production** 100 000 **est.** 1926
product range ($3–9 CD) A kaleidoscopic array of table, sparkling, fortified and flavoured wines (and spirits) offered in bottle and flagon. The table wines are sold under the Blewitt Springs Estate, Patritti and Billabong Wines brands.
summary A traditional, family-owned business offering wines at modest prices, but with impressive vineyard holdings of 10 hectares of shiraz in Blewitt Springs and 6 hectares of grenache at Aldinga North.

pattersons   ★★★★

St Werburghs Road, Mount Barker, WA 6234 **region** Great Southern
phone (08) 9851 2063 **fax** (08) 9851 2063 **open** Sat–Wed 10–5 or by appointment
winemaker Plantagenet (Contract) **production** 2000 **est.** 1982
product range ($15–29 CD) Chardonnay, Unwooded Chardonnay, Pattersons Curse Chardonnay, Sparkling Shiraz, Pinot Noir, Shiraz, Pattersons Curse Shiraz.
summary Schoolteachers Sue and Arthur Patterson have grown chardonnay, shiraz and pinot noir and grazed cattle as a weekend relaxation for a decade. The cellar door is in a recently completed and very beautiful rammed-earth house, and a number of vintages are on sale at any one time. Good Chardonnay and Shiraz have been complemented by the occasional spectacular Pinot Noir. Retail distribution in NSW, WA and Victoria.

Pattersons Shiraz

TTTT 1997 A quite fragrant bouquet with a typical estate array of savoury/earthy/spicy aromas leads into a light to medium-bodied palate with pleasantly sweet fruit surrounded by the aromas of the bouquet.

rating: 89

best drinking 2000 – 2005 **best vintages** '90, '93, '94, '96, '97 **drink with** Duck casserole • $25

paul conti wines ★★★★

529 Wanneroo Road, Woodvale, WA 6026 **region** Greater Perth Zone
phone (08) 9409 9160 **fax** (08) 9309 1634 **open** Mon–Sat 9.30–5.30, Sun by appointment
winemaker Paul Conti, Jason Conti **production** 7000 **est.** 1948
product range ($14–26 CD) The Tuarts Chenin Blanc, The Tuarts Unwooded Chardonnay, The Tuarts Chardonnay, Nero Sparkling Shiraz, Late Harvest Muscat Fronti, Medici Ridge Pinot Noir, Old Vine Grenache Shiraz, Medici Ridge Shiraz, Mariginiup Shiraz, The Tuarts Cabernet Sauvignon, White Port, Reserve Port, Reserve Muscat.
summary Third-generation winemaker Jason Conti has now assumed day-to-day control of winemaking, although father Paul (who succeeded his father in 1968) remains interested and involved in the business. Over the years Paul Conti challenged and redefined industry perceptions and standards; the challenge for Jason Conti (which he shows every sign of meeting) will be to achieve the same degree of success in a relentlessly and increasingly competitive market environment. Exports to the UK, Denmark, Singapore, Malaysia and Japan.

Paul Conti Wines The Tuarts Chenin Blanc

TTTY 2001 Light green-yellow; the bouquet is aromatic, with ripe peach/tropical aromas, with an exotic overtone vaguely reminiscent of durian. The same exotic mix of tropical fruits, including guava and durian, comes through on the palate, which has good length and acidity.

rating: 84

best drinking 2001–2004 **best vintages** NA **drink with** Antipasto • $14.90

Paul Conti The Tuarts Chardonnay

TTTTY 2001 Light to medium yellow-green; the bouquet has melon, nectarine and citrus fruit accompanied by a light touch of oak; the elegant, finely balanced, delicate but long palate provides a replay of the flavours of the bouquet, once again with well-integrated oak.

rating: 90

best drinking 2002–2005 **best vintages** '01 **drink with** Calamari • $19.99

Paul Conti Wines Medici Ridge Pinot Noir

TTTY 2000 Light red; the bouquet is quite spicy/brambly; the palate is light and lacks concentration, but does have varietal character in a cherry/spicy/brambly mode.

rating: 83

best drinking 2001–2003 **best vintages** '99 **drink with** Coq au vin • $19.99

Paul Conti Wines Mariginiup Shiraz

TTTTY 1999 Deep red-purple; the complex bouquet has an abundance of dark berry/mulberry fruits supported by subtle oak; the palate ripples with rich, dark berry/savoury/dark chocolate flavours. Good tannin and extract management round off a classy wine.

rating: 91

best drinking 2004–2009 **best vintages** '98, '99 **drink with** Grilled steak • $26

Paul Conti Wines Medici Ridge Shiraz

TTTT 1999 Youthful, medium to full red-purple; clean black cherry fruit, a hint of spice and a whiff of oak introduce an elegant, nicely weighted and balanced palate, with background hints of spice and game.

rating: 89

best drinking 2003–2008 **best vintages** NA **drink with** Braised quail • $19.99

Paul Conti The Tuarts Cabernet Sauvignon

TTTT 2000 Medium red-purple; light, spicy, savoury, cedary aromas join gentle redcurrant fruit on the palate, which finishes with fine tannins and hints of cedar and vanilla.

rating: 85

best drinking 2003–2008 **best vintages** NA **drink with** Osso buco • $19.99

paulett ★★★☆

Polish Hill Road, Polish Hill River, SA 5453 **region** Clare Valley
phone (08) 8843 4328 **fax** (08) 8843 4202 **open** 7 days 10–5
winemaker Neil Paulett **production** 12 500 **est.** 1983

product range ($15–42 CD) Riesling, Polish Hill River Riesling, Sauvignon Blanc, Unwooded Chardonnay, Late Harvest Riesling, Clare Blue Sparkling Shiraz, Shiraz, Andreas Shiraz, Cabernet Merlot.

summary The completion of the winery and cellar-door sales facility in 1992 marked the end of a development project which began back in 1982, when Neil and Alison Paulett purchased a 47-hectare property with a small patch of old vines (now extended to 14.4. hectares) and a house in a grove of trees (which were almost immediately burnt by the 1983 bushfires). The beautifully situated winery is one of the features of the scenic Polish Hill River region, as are its Riesling and its Cabernet Merlot. Exports to the UK, the US, Germany and New Zealand.

Paulett Polish Hill River Riesling

▼▼▼▽ **2001** Light green-yellow; the bouquet is clean, but very shy, the varietal fruit aromatics still locked up; the same is largely true of the palate, which has good balance and structure, but which is going through the sulks, from which it will emerge in a few years' time; the future is underwritten by the Stelvin cap. **rating: 84**

best drinking 2003–2008 **best vintages** '84, '90, '92, '93, '95, '96, '98, '00 **drink with** Quiche Lorraine • $18

paul osicka ★★★★

Majors Creek Vineyard at Graytown, Vic 3608 **region** Heathcote
phone (03) 5794 9235 **fax** (03) 5794 9288 **open** Mon–Sat 10–5, Sun 12–5
winemaker Paul Osicka **production** NFP **est.** 1955
product range ($14–25 CD) Chardonnay, Riesling, Cabernet Sauvignon, Shiraz.
summary A low-profile producer but reliable, particularly when it comes to its smooth but rich Shiraz. The wines are distributed in Melbourne and Sydney by Australian Prestige Wines, with exports to the UK, Hong Kong and Japan.

Paul Osicka Heathcote Shiraz

▼▼▼▼▽ **2000** Excellent, bright purple-red; smooth dark cherry fruit and touches of plum and spice on the bouquet; the palate is more refined and savoury than the bouquet suggests, with barely perceptible oak.
rating: 91

▼▼▼▼▽ **1999** Medium red-purple; there is abundant fruit on the clean bouquet, with ripe, dark berry and raspberry aromas. The same lively, sweet berry fruit comes through strongly on the medium-bodied palate, with supple tannins and the gentlest hint of oak all contributing to the structure of the wine. **rating: 91**

best drinking 2005–2011 **best vintages** '96, '99, '00 **drink with** Kangaroo fillet • $22

paxton wines ★★★★

Sand Road, McLaren Vale, SA 5171 **region** McLaren Vale
phone (08) 8323 8645 **fax** (08) 8323 8903 **open** Not
winemaker Contract **production** 600 **est.** 1997
product range ($35 ML) Shiraz.
summary David Paxton is one of Australia's best-known viticulturists and consultants. He founded Paxton Vineyards in McLaren Vale with his family in 1979, and has since been involved in various capacities in the establishment and management of vineyards in the Adelaide Hills, Coonawarra, The Clare Valley, The Yarra Valley, Margaret River and Great Southern regions. The family vineyards in McLaren Vale remain the centre of attention, and are still contract-growers for others. However, as a means of promoting the quality of the grapes produced by the vineyards, Paxton Wines has ventured into small-scale winemaking (via contract) with an initial release of Shiraz. There are plans to increase the range in the future, but the volume of production of each wine will remain small. Exports to the US.

Paxton McLaren Vale Shiraz

▼▼▼▼▽ **1999** Strong, deep, bright red-purple; the fruit aromas are primarily in the plum/berry spectrum, with just a touch of mint; the rich berry and dark chocolate flavours of the bouquet are powerful, but not over-extracted or over-oaked. Fine tannins round off an impressive wine. **rating: 90**

best drinking 2004–2010 **best vintages** '98, '99 **drink with** Roast lamb • $35

peacock hill vineyard NR

Cnr Branxton Road and Palmers Lane, Pokolbin, NSW 2320 **region** Lower Hunter Valley
phone (02) 4998 7661 **fax** (02) 4998 7661 **open** Thurs-Mon, public and school holidays 10–5, or by appointment
winemaker Bill Sneddon, Steve Langham **production** 1800 **est.** 1969

product range ($15–28 CD) Absent Friends Unoaked Chardonnay, Reserve Chardonnay, Untamed Chardonnay, Top Block Chardonnay, Jaan Shiraz, Cabernet Sauvignon Shiraz, Faith Cabernet Sauvignon.

summary The Peacock Hill Vineyard was first planted in 1969 as part of the Rothbury Estate, originally being owned by a separate syndicate but then moving under the direct control and ownership of Rothbury. After several further changes of ownership as Rothbury sold many of its vineyards, George Tsiros and Silvi Laumets acquired the 8-hectare property in October 1995. Since that time they have rejuvenated the vineyard and built a small but attractive accommodation lodge for two people, and have a tennis court and petanque rink for their exclusive enjoyment. Over the years, Peacock Hill has been a consistent medal winner in local wine shows.

pearson vineyards   NR

Main North Road, Penwortham, SA 5453 **region** Clare Valley
phone (08) 8843 4234 **fax** (08) 8843 4141 **open** Mon–Fri 11–5, weekends 10–5
winemaker Jim Pearson **production** 800 **est.** 1993
product range ($13–18 CD) Riesling, Late Harvest Riesling, Cabernet Franc, Cabernet Sauvignon.
summary Jim Pearson makes the Pearson Vineyard wines at Mintaro Cellars. The 1.5-hectare estate vineyards surround the beautiful little stone house which acts as a cellar door and which appears on the cover of my book, *The Wines, The History, The Vignerons of the Clare Valley.*

peel estate   ★★★★

Fletcher Road, Baldivis, WA 6171 **region** Peel
phone (08) 9524 1221 **fax** (08) 9524 1625 **open** 7 days 10–5
winemaker Will Nairn **production** 8000 **est.** 1974
product range ($14–55 R) Chardonnay, Chenin Blanc, Wood Matured Chenin Blanc, Verdelho, Pichet Premium White, Pichet Premium Red, Shiraz, Zinfandel, Cabernet Sauvignon, Baroque Shiraz Cremant, Vintage Port.
summary The winery rating is given for its Shiraz, a wine of considerable finesse and with a remarkably consistent track record. Every year Will Nairn holds a Great Shiraz Tasting for 6-year-old Australian Shirazs, and pits Peel Estate (in a blind tasting attended by 60 or so people) against Australia's best. It is never disgraced. The white wines are workmanlike, the wood-matured Chenin Blanc another winery specialty, although not achieving the excellence of the Shiraz. At five years of age it will typically show well, with black cherry and chocolate flavours, a strong dash of American oak, and surprising youth. There is limited retail distribution, and exports to the UK, Malaysia and Hong Kong.

Peel Estate Wood Matured Chenin Blanc

▼▼▼▼ **1999** Medium to full yellow-straw; the bouquet is solid, the oak integrated but dominant. The palate is rich, soft and opulent, in an ultimate food style, with oak and alcohol (14.5°) providing a blast of flavour. Long a specialty of the winery. **rating:** 85

best drinking 2002–2004 **best vintages** NA **drink with** Stuffed roast spatchcock • $22

Peel Estate Verdelho

▼▼▼▼ **2001** Light but bright yellow-green; the bouquet is moderately rich, with some tropical fruit salad aromas; the palate is rich and ripe, again with tropical fruit salad; mouthfilling, and carries its 14° alcohol well. **rating:** 85

best drinking 2002–2005 **best vintages** NA **drink with** Pan-fried veal • $17

Peel Estate Chardonnay

▼▼▼▼ **1999** Medium yellow-green; the bouquet has some complexity, with attractive lees-contact aromas. The palate, likewise, has good mouthfeel and length, with ripe peach and nectarine fruit; gentle oak. **rating:** 86

best drinking 2002–2004 **best vintages** '98 **drink with** Smoked chicken • $22

Peel Estate Shiraz

▼▼▼▼▽ **1998** Medium purple-red; a spotlessly clean bouquet features dark cherry fruit with touches of spice and vanilla; the powerful palate retains finesse, with silky, dark cherry fruit, fine tannins and length. **rating:** 93

best drinking 2002–2008 **best vintages** '93, '94, '96, '98 **drink with** Leg of lamb • $39

Peel Estate Pichet Premium Red

♥♥♥♥ **2000** Medium red-purple; the bouquet has quite attractive fruit, with the barest hint of shaded character. The palate provides quite a surprise, with ripe, sweet berry fruit and good mouthfeel. A blend of Cabernet Franc and Merlot. **rating:** 85

best drinking 2002–2003 **best vintages** NA **drink with** Pizza • $16

Peel Estate Cabernet Sauvignon

♥♥♥♥♀ **1999** Medium red-purple; some slightly smoky/savoury overtones to the underlying blackcurrant fruit. The palate has good structure, mouthfeel and balance; dark fruits, a hint of earth, and fine, ripe tannins round off a good wine. **rating:** 90

best drinking 2003–2008 **best vintages** '97 **drink with** Herbed rack of lamb • $31.50

peerick vineyard ★★★☆

Wild Dog Track, Moonambel, Vic 3478 **region** Pyrenees
phone (03) 9817 1611 **fax** (03) 9817 1611 **open** Weekends 11–4
winemaker Contract **production** 1300 **est.** 1990
product range ($12.75–25 CD) Sauvignon Blanc, Viognier, Shiraz, Cabernet Sauvignon.
summary Peerick is the venture of Chris Jessup and his wife Meryl. They have mildly trimmed their Joseph's coat vineyard by increasing the plantings to 5.95 hectares and eliminating the malbec and semillon, but still manage to grow cabernet sauvignon, shiraz, cabernet franc, merlot, sauvignon blanc and viognier.

Peerick Vineyard Viognier

♥♥♥♀ **2001** Light to medium yellow-green; the complex bouquet mixes touches of oak spice with faintly peachy fruit; the palate is weighty, with that typical viognier feel, and the heat on the finish comes from the 14.5° alcohol. One hundred per cent barrel fermentation in new French oak, and partial malolactic fermentation, add to the total impact, but tend to obscure varietal flavour. **rating:** 84

best drinking 2002–2004 **best vintages** NA **drink with** Roast turkey • $25

Peerick Vineyard Shiraz

♥♥♥♥ **1999** Medium red-purple; a complex mix of ripe dark berry, plum and licorice aromas move through into the palate, there joined by a touch of chocolate; good extract and oak handling throughout. **rating:** 88

best drinking 2004–2009 **best vintages** NA **drink with** Braised venison • $25

☙ pegeric vineyard NR

640 Trentham Tylden Road, Tylden, Vic 3444 **region** Macedon Ranges
phone (03) 9354 4961 **fax** (03) 9354 4961 **open** Not
winemaker Llew Knight, Ian Guntar, Chris Cormack **production** 100 **est.** 1991
product range ($65 ML) Pinot Noir.
summary Owner and viticulturist Chris Cormack accumulated an oenological degree and experience in every facet of the wine industry here and overseas before beginning the establishment of the close-planted, non-irrigated, low yielding Pegeric Vineyard at an altitude of 640 metres on red volcanic basalt soil. None of the wines has so far been released; the first vintage to be offered will be the 1998. As a separate exercise, Chris Cormack has also made several vintages of a cross-regional blend of Cabernet Shiraz named Tumbetin.

pembroke NR

Richmond Road, Cambridge, Tas 7170 **region** Southern Tasmania
phone (03) 6248 5139 **fax** (03) 6234 5481 **open** By appointment
winemaker Andrew Hood (Contract) **production** 500 **est.** 1980
product range ($22.50 ML) Pinot Noir.
summary The 1-hectare Pembroke vineyard was established in 1980 by the McKay and Hawker families, and is still owned by them. It is predominantly planted to pinot noir, with tiny quantities of chardonnay, riesling and sauvignon blanc.

Pembroke Pinot Noir

♥♥♥♀ **2000** Light to medium red-purple; light, leafy, minty overtones to spicy, savoury underbrush aromas and flavours result in an interesting wine which in more normal vintages might gain significantly higher points. **rating:** 84

best drinking 2002–2004 **best vintages** '98 **drink with** Quail risotto • $22.50

🐦 penbro vineyard   NR

Cnr Melba Highway and Murrindindi Road, Glenburn, Vic 3717 **region** Central Victorian High Country
phone (03) 9817 2158 **fax** (03) 9817 7015 **open** Not
winemaker Martin Williams (Contract) **production** 3000 **est.** 1997
product range Chardonnay, Unwooded Chardonnay, Pinot Noir, Shiraz, Merlot, Cabernet Sauvignon.
summary Since 1997 Penbro has established 40 hectares of chardonnay, pinot noir, merlot, cabernet
sauvignon and shiraz. The Unwooded Chardonnay from both 2000 and 2001 won medals at the Victorian
Wine Show in the year of making. The first wines were released in March 2002.

pendarves estate   ★★★☆

110 Old North Road, Belford, NSW 2335 **region** Lower Hunter Valley
phone (02) 6574 7222 **fax** (02) 9970 6152 **open** Weekends 11–5, Mon–Fri by appointment
winemaker Greg Silkman (Contract) **production** 11 000 **est.** 1986
product range ($18–25 CD) An unusual portfolio of Semillon, Sauvignon Blanc, Verdelho, Unoaked
Chardonnay, Chardonnay, Pinot Noir, Chambourcin, Shiraz, Merlot Malbec Cabernet.
summary The perpetual-motion general practitioner and founder of the Australian Medical Friends of
Wine, Dr Philip Norrie, is a born communicator and marketer as well as a wine historian of note. He also
happens to be a passionate advocate of the virtues of Verdelho, inspired in part by the high regard held for
that variety by vignerons around the turn of the century. His ambassadorship for the cause of wine and
health in both Australia and overseas has led to the development of a joint venture for the production and
export distribution of a large- volume brand called 'The Wine Doctor', and to the establishment of export
markets in Singapore, the UK, Germany, China and Malyasia (as well as national distribution).

penfolds   ★★★★★

Tanunda Road, Nuriootpa, SA 5355 **region** Barossa Valley
phone (08) 8568 9290 **fax** (08) 8568 9493 **open** Mon–Fri 10–5, weekends and public holidays 11–5
winemaker John Duval **production** 1.4 million **est.** 1844
product range ($9–300 R) Kalimna Bin 28 Shiraz, 128 Coonawarra Shiraz, 389 Cabernet Shiraz, 407
Cabernet Sauvignon, 707 Cabernet Sauvignon and Special Show Bin reds. Brands include Minchinbury
Sparkling; Rawson's Retreat Chardonnay, Semillon Chardonnay and Cabernet Shiraz; Penfolds The Valleys
Chardonnay, Old Vine Barossa Valley Semillon and Old Vine Barossa Valley Shiraz Grenache Mourvèdre;
Koonunga Hill Shiraz Cabernet, Semillon Sauvignon Blanc, Chardonnay, and Cabernet Merlot; Magill
Estate; Clare Estate Chardonnay; Clare Valley Reserve Aged Riesling, Eden Valley Riesling, Adelaide Hills
Chardonnay, Adelaide Hills Semillon, Barossa Valley Semillon Chardonnay, RWT Barossa Valley Shiraz,
Trial Bins Semillon; St Henri Cabernet Shiraz; Yattarna Chardonnay, Grange. Also various export-only
labels. Finally, Grandfather Port and Great Grandfather Port.
summary Senior among the numerous wine companies or stand-alone brands in Southcorp Wines and
undoubtedly one of the top wine companies in the world in terms of quality, product range and exports.
The consistency of the quality of the red wines and their value for money is recognised worldwide. Headed
by the development of the ultra-premium Yattarna Chardonnay, Penfolds has also steadily raised the quality
of its white wines. Following the acquisition of Rosemount Estate by Southcorp in 2001, there has been
even greater focus on the three leading brands of Penfolds, Lindemans and Rosemount, with the sale of
some lesser brands and the deletion of others.

Penfolds Clare Valley Reserve Aged Riesling
♥♥♥♥ 1997 Glowing yellow-green; a very toasty bouquet with some bottle-developed kerosene aromas is
followed by a palate with much more lime fruit than the bouquet suggests, although the toasty characters
are still there. **rating: 89**
best drinking 2001–2004 **best vintages** NA **drink with** Smoked fish • $25

Penfolds Eden Valley Reserve Riesling
♥♥♥♥♡ 2001 Light to medium green-yellow; a powerful bouquet with solid, ripe lime aromas; the palate
is more reserved, with quite tight lime and apple flavours; all waiting to happen. **rating: 90**
best drinking 2004–2009 **best vintages** '99, '01 **drink with** Mussells in white wine • $25

Penfolds Adelaide Hills Semillon

ⵊⵊⵊⵊⵊ **2000** Light green-yellow; a smooth and complex bouquet with excellent balance and integration of lemony fruit and oak; the palate is smooth, clean and well balanced, with medium weight and a long finish. **rating:** 93

best drinking 2002–2007 **best vintages** '00 **drink with** Prawn risotto • $28

Penfolds Yattarna Chardonnay

ⵊⵊⵊⵊⵊ **1998** Light green-yellow; the bouquet is extremely fine and tight, with ever so subtle oak. The palate is exceptionally delicate yet intense, with nettle and citrus flavours running through to an extremely long finish. This wine will surely live for upwards of 20 years. **rating:** 94

best drinking 2003–2018 **best vintages** '95, '96, '97 **drink with** Rack of veal • $100

Penfolds Bin 128 Coonawarra Shiraz

ⵊⵊⵊⵊⵊ **1999** Medium red-purple; smooth plum fruit with a hint of mulberry and soft oak leads into a well-balanced palate, with skilled oak handling, soft, ripe tannins and gentle plummy fruit. **rating:** 90

best drinking 2003–2009 **best vintages** '63, '66, '80, '86, '89, '90, '91, '93, '94, '96, '98 **drink with** Veal; mild cheddar • $23

Penfolds Kalimna Bin 28 Shiraz

ⵊⵊⵊⵊⵊ **1999** Medium red-purple; well-balanced and integrated fruit and oak, in typical Penfolds style, mark the bouquet; the palate has good weight and structure, with ripe plum and dark berry fruit; overall, soft and approachable. **rating:** 91

best drinking 2002–2009 **best vintages** '64, '66, '71, '80, '81, '83, '86, '90, '91, '94, '95, '96, '98, '99 **drink with** Lamb or beef casserole • $23

Penfolds RWT Shiraz

ⵊⵊⵊⵊⵊ **1998** Medium to full red-purple; the powerful, rich and complex bouquet offers ripe fruit and lots of oak. The deep, strongly structured palate has the abundant fruit the bouquet promised, but the overall impact of the oak and tannin extract needs time to settle down. **rating:** 90

best drinking 2005–2013 **best vintages** '97 **drink with** Roast veal • $110

Penfolds Old Vine Barossa Valley Bin 138 Shiraz Mourvèdre Grenache

ⵊⵊⵊⵊ **1999** Medium red-purple; some spicy/juicy aromas flow into a palate which opens with ripe, juicy fruit, but has a somewhat rough finish. **rating:** 85

best drinking 2003–2007 **best vintages** '98 **drink with** Rich stews • $23

Penfolds Koonunga Hill Shiraz Cabernet

ⵊⵊⵊⵊ **2000** Medium red-purple, the bouquet has smooth, sweet, dark berry fruit and subtle oak; the palate has good structure, richness and weight, thanks to dark berry and chocolate flavours and balanced tannins. **rating:** 89

best drinking 2002–2007 **best vintages** '82, '87, '90, '91, '92, '94, '96, '98, '00 **drink with** All red meat, cheese • $15

Penfolds Koonunga Hill Cabernet Merlot

ⵊⵊⵊⵊ **2001** Medium to full red-purple; solid, dark fruit aromas and the barest touch of oak on the bouquet are followed by a berry/plum palate with good length and structure; not sweet, and works well. A further brand extension for the Koonunga Hill range. **rating:** 86

best drinking 2003–2007 **best vintages** NA **drink with** Braised lamb • $15

Penfolds Bin 389 Cabernet Shiraz

ⵊⵊⵊⵊ **1999** Medium red-purple; the bouquet is, by the standards of the brand, somewhat light and plain, with slightly dusty oak. A pleasant, medium-bodied and well-balanced wine in the mouth, finishing with surprisingly soft tannins. This may turn out to be a harsh description and rating. **rating:** 86

best drinking 2004–2009 **best vintages** '66, '70, '71, '86, '90, '93, '94, '96, '98 **drink with** Double lamb loin chops • $38

Penfolds Rawson's Retreat Cabernet Shiraz

ⵊⵊⵊⵊ **2000** Light to medium red, with some purple hints; the bouquet has quite ripe, dark fruit; the palate has more structure and texture than expected, thanks to the dark berry fruit and balanced tannins. Good value. **rating:** 85

best drinking 2001–2003 **best vintages** NA **drink with** Pizza • $12

Penfolds Bin 407 Cabernet Sauvignon

▼▼▼▼▽ **1999** Medium red-purple; the bouquet offers sweet cassis berry fruit and subtle oak flowing on well into the attractive, sweet, redcurrant-flavoured palate. Soft tannins and gentle oak add to the appeal; significantly better than the 1999 Bin 389. **rating:** 90

best drinking 2004–2009 **best vintages** '90, '91, '92, '93, '94, '96, '98 **drink with** Venison, kangaroo fillet • $28

Penfolds Bin 707 Cabernet Sauvignon

▼▼▼▼▼ **1999** Medium to full red-purple; ripe blackberry/earthy varietal character on the bouquet, then a palate with great depth and power, supported by controlled, savoury tannins and lingering blackberry fruit. The oak handling throughout cannot be faulted. **rating:** 94

best drinking 2005–2015 **best vintages** '66, '80, '84, '86, '88, '90, '92, '93, '94, '96, '97, '99 **drink with** Rare scotch fillet • NA

penley estate ★★★★☆

McLeans Road, Coonawarra, SA 5263 **region** Coonawarra
phone (08) 8736 3211 **fax** (08) 8736 3124 **open** 7 days, 10–4
winemaker Kym Tolley **production** 20 000 **est.** 1988
product range ($18–65 R) Chardonnay, Hyland Shiraz, Ausvetia Shiraz, Shiraz Cabernet Sauvignon, Merlot, Merlot, Reserve Cabernet Sauvignon, Phoenix Cabernet Sauvignon, Traditional Method Pinot Noir Chardonnay.
summary Owner winemaker Kym Tolley describes himself as a fifth-generation winemaker, the family tree involving both the Penfolds and the Tolleys. He worked for 17 years in the industry before establishing Penley Estate and has made every post a winner since, producing a succession of rich, complex, full-bodied red wines and stylish Chardonnays. Now ranks as one of the best wineries in Coonawarra, drawing upon 91 precious hectares of estate plantings. Exports to the UK, Switzerland, Austria, Luxembourg, California, Canada, Malaysia, Singapore and Hong Kong.

🐾 penmara NR

Bridge Street, Muswellbrook, NSW 2333 **region** Upper Hunter Valley
phone (02) 9362 5157 **fax** (02) 9362 5157 **open** Not
winemaker John Horden **production** 30 000 **est.** 2000
product range The wines are made in three levels: at the bottom is the Five Families range; next in the ladder is the Reserve range; and finally comes the Individual Vineyard range, made only in exceptional vintages. The varieties offered including Semillon, Verdelho, Shiraz, Merlot, Cabernet Sauvignon.
summary Penmara was formed with the banner '5 Vineyards: 1 Vision'. In fact a sixth vineyard has already joined the group, the vineyards pooling most of their grapes, with a central processing facility, and marketing focussed exclusively on exports. The members are Lilyvale Vineyards, in the Northern Slopes region near Tenterfield; Tangaratta Vineyards at Tamworth; Birnam Wood, Rothbury Ridge and Martindale Vineyards in the Hunter Valley; and Highland Heritage at Orange. In all, these vineyards give Penmara access to 128 hectares of shiraz, chardonnay, cabernet sauvignon, semillon, verdelho and merlot. Exports to the US, Canada, Singapore and Japan.

🐾 penna lane wines ★★★☆

Lot 51 Penna Lane, Penwortham via Clare, SA 5453 **region** Clare Valley
phone (08) 8843 4364 **fax** (08) 8843 4349 **open** Thurs–Sun and public holidays 11–5 or by appointment
winemaker Contract **production** 1800 **est.** 1998
product range ($15–20 CD) Riesling, Semillon, Shiraz, Cabernet Sauvignon.
summary Ray and Lynette Klavin, then living and working near Waikerie in the Riverland, purchased their 14-hectare property in the Skilly Hills in 1993. It was covered with rubbish, Salvation Jane, a derelict dairy and a tumbledown piggery, and every weekend they travelled from Waikerie to clean up the property, initially living in a tent and thereafter moving into the dairy, which had more recently been used as a shearing shed. Planting began in 1996, and in 1997 the family moved to the region, Lynette to take up a teaching position and Ray to work at Knappstein Wines. Ray had enrolled at Roseworthy in 1991, and met Stephen Stafford-Brookes, another mature-age student. Both graduated from Roseworthy in 1993, having already formed a winemaking joint venture for Penna Lane. Picnic and barbecue facilities are available at the cellar door, and light lunches are served. Exports to the US.

Penna Lane Riesling

▼▼▼▼ **2001** Light to medium green-yellow; a solid bouquet, but not a lot of character showing early in its life; the palate has more character and flavour, with attractive, squeaky mouthfeel. Stelvin closure. **rating:** 86

best drinking 2002–2007 **best vintages** NA **drink with** Fresh asparagus • $16

Penna Lane Semillon

▼▼▼▼ **2001** Light to medium yellow-green; the clean and ripe bouquet offers citrus, and even a touch of melon, with the barest touch of smoky oak lurking in the background. The palate has a similar elegant and subtle approach, reflecting the partial barrel fermentation and 4 months on lees in 2-year-old French barriques. **rating:** 87

best drinking 2002–2005 **best vintages** NA **drink with** Calamari • $16

Penna Lane Shiraz

▼▼▼▽ **2000** Medium red-purple; the bouquet is clean and fresh, with dark berry fruit aromas; the palate is rather less appealing: it is slightly minty, and with a relatively simple structure. **rating:** 84

best drinking 2002–2005 **best vintages** NA **drink with** Yearling beef • $20

Penna Lane Cabernet Sauvignon

▼▼▼▼ **2000** Red-purple; a clean bouquet, with sweet redcurrant fruit, is followed by ripe berry and chocolate fruit on the palate, which has some depth, and finishes with soft tannins. **rating:** 88

best drinking 2003–2008 **best vintages** NA **drink with** Steak and kidney pie • $20

penny's hill ★★★☆

Main Road, McLaren Vale, SA 5171 **region** McLaren Vale
phone (08) 8362 1077 **fax** (08) 8362 2766 **open** 7 days 10–5, except Christmas Day and Good Friday
winemaker Ben Riggs (Contract) **production** 6500 **est.** 1988
product range ($14–37.50 ML) Goss Corner Semillon, Chardonnay, Nobilis Botrytis Semillon, Shiraz, Grenache, Specialized Shiraz Cabernet Merlot, Fine Old Tawny, Fortified Shiraz.
summary Penny's Hill is owned by Adelaide advertising agency businessman Tony Parkinson and his wife Susie. The Penny's Hill vineyard is 43.5 hectares and, unusually for McLaren Vale, is close-planted with a thin vertical trellis/thin vertical canopy, the work of consultant viticulturist David Paxton. The innovative red dot packaging was the inspiration of Tony Parkinson, recalling the red dot 'sold' sign on pictures in an art gallery and now giving rise to the Red Dot Art Galley opening at Penny's Hill. Exports to the UK and the US.

Penny's Hill Goss Corner Semillon

▼▼▼▼ **2000** Medium yellow-green, somewhat developed; firm herb/grass aromas are at odds with the colour and the palate, which is slightly soft and diffuse in terms of structure, although the herb/grass flavours of the bouquet do come through to provide positive varietal character. **rating:** 85

best drinking 2002–2004 **best vintages** NA **drink with** Rich fish dishes • $14

Penny's Hill Chardonnay

▼▼▼▽ **2000** Medium to full yellow green; ripe yellow peach and smoky oak aromas are quite complex; a similarly rich, soft and ripe palate has lots of flavour, but a somewhat congested finish. **rating:** 84

best drinking 2002–2003 **best vintages** NA **drink with** Smoked chicken • $18

Penny's Hill Nobilis Botrytis Semillon

▼▼▼▼ **1999** Medium to full yellow-green; tropical fruit and peach aromas seem to speak of late harvest as much as botrytis; the same slightly simple fruit characters come through on the palate, but good acidity contributes to a fine, cleansing finish. **rating:** 85

best drinking 2002–2003 **best vintages** NA **drink with** Rich ice cream • $22

Penny's Hill Shiraz

▼▼▼▼ **1999** Medium red-purple; savoury, earthy, chocolatey, berry aromas are also reflected in the smooth, medium-bodied palate with its supple blend of berry/plum/chocolate/vanilla, plus good tannin and oak management. **rating:** 87

best drinking 2003–2009 **best vintages** '97, '98 **drink with** Roast ox kidney • $25

Penny's Hill Grenache

▼▼▼▼ **2000** Medium red-purple; a strong and fragrant bouquet with clear-cut jammy grenache varietal character is mirrored on the medium-bodied palate; definitely a wine for grenache devotees. **rating:** 85

best drinking 2002–2005 **best vintages** NA **drink with** Game • $20

Penny's Hill Vintage Fortified Shiraz

ŸŸŸŸ 1998 Dense, youthful purple-red; the bouquet has firm, dark berry fruit with neutral spirit; the powerful, pleasingly dry-style palate needs 10 years, but could be a real surprise.   **rating:** 87

best drinking 2008–2015 **best vintages** NA **drink with** Blue cheese; nuts • $25

pennyweight winery ★★★☆

Pennyweight Lane, Beechworth, Vic 3747 **region** Beechworth
phone (03) 5728 1747 **fax** (03) 5728 1704 **open** 7 days 10–5
winemaker Stephen Newton Morris **production** 1000 **est.** 1982
product range ($15–28 CD) The table wines include Beechworth Riesling, Semillon Sauvignon Blanc, Gamay (light red), Pinot Noir, Shiraz; also important is the range of Oloroso, Fino and Amontillado Sherries and a range of Ports – Old Tawny, Ruby, Gold and Muscat.
summary Pennyweight was established by Stephen Morris, great-grandson of G F Morris, founder of Morris Wines. The 3 hectares of vines are not irrigated and are organically grown. The business is run by Stephen, together with his wife Elizabeth and their three sons; Elizabeth Morris says, 'It's a perfect world', suggesting that Pennyweight is more than happy with its lot in life.

Pennyweight Beechworth Pinot Noir

ŸŸŸŸ 2000 Medium to full red; a solid, foresty, briary bouquet with rich plum at its core, then a ripe, solid palate with rich plum fruit in an ultra-generous style. Still retains varietal character, although it teeters on the brink of dry red, and is stylistically not dissimilar to some of the ripe-year Giacondas.   **rating:** 87

best drinking 2002–2006 **best vintages** NA **drink with** Game • $25

penwortham wines NR

Government Road, Penwortham, SA 5453 **region** Clare Valley
phone (08) 8843 4345 **open** Sat 10–5, Sun, holidays 10–4
winemaker Richard Hughes **production** 1000 **est.** 1985
product range ($13–16 CD) Riesling, Cabernet Sauvignon, Shiraz.
summary Richard Hughes has progressively established 12 hectares of riesling, semillon, verdelho, shiraz and cabernet sauvignon, selling most of the grapes and making restricted quantities of wine from the remainder.

🦘 peos estate NR

Graphite Road, Manjimup, WA 6258 **region** Manjimup
phone (08) 9772 1378 **fax** (08) 9772 1372 **open** 7 days 10–4
winemaker Bernard Abbott (Contract) **production** 1200 **est.** 1996
product range ($15–30 CD) Unwooded Chardonnay, 4 Aces Shiraz, Cabernet Sauvignon.
summary The Peos family has farmed the West Manjimup district for 50 years, the third generation of four brothers commencing the development of a substantial vineyard in 1996. In all, there is a little over 33 hectares of vines, with shiraz (10 hectares), merlot (7 hectares), chardonnay (6.5 hectares), cabernet sauvignon (4 hectares) and pinot noir, sauvignon blanc and verdelho (2 hectares each). Part of the production is sold, and part is made by Bernard Abbott.

pepper tree wines ★★★☆

Halls Road, Pokolbin, NSW 2320 **region** Lower Hunter Valley
phone (02) 4998 7539 **fax** (02) 4998 7746 **open** Mon–Fri 9–5, weekends 9.30–5
winemaker Chris Cameron **production** 43 200 **est.** 1993
product range ($12–60 CD) Lake Chardonnay, PT Shiraz Merlot, Mulberry Row (Grenache Shiraz Cabernet); Reserve range of Clare Semillon, Sauvignon Blanc, Verdelho Semillon, Chardonnay, Merlot, Cabernet Franc, Cabernet Sauvignon.
summary The Pepper Tree winery is situated in the complex which also contains The Convent guesthouse and Roberts Restaurant. The company which now owns Pepper Tree made a decisive move in 1996, formalising the acquisition of a major interest in the Parker (Coonawarra) Estate vineyards, having previously purchased some of the fruit from those vineyards. Pepper Tree has made a determined, and quite successful, effort to establish its reputation as one of Australia's leading producers of Merlot. It also has an amazing array of Reserve wines. The new Audrey Wilkinson winery is in the same ownership. Exports to the US, the UK, Denmark, Switzerland, New Zeland, Singapore, Indonesia, Malaysia, China and Japan.

Pepper Tree Reserve Sauvignon Blanc

ŦŦŦŦ 2001 Light green-yellow; ultra-light aromas of passionfruit lead into a palate which is quite intense, yet hard to define or describe, other than that it is largely acid-driven. No regional claim or acknowledgement is made anywhere on the bottle. **rating: 85**

best drinking 2002–2004 best vintages NA drink with Seafood • $20

Pepper Tree Reserve Verdelho Semillon

ŦŦŦŦ 2001 Light green-yellow; a clean, light, fresh citrus-tinged bouquet; the palate is lively and crisp, showing more affinity with Semillon than Verdelho, notwithstanding the fact that Verdelho must be the dominant component. A Reserve blend of this nature is a breathtaking oxymoron. **rating: 85**

best drinking 2002–2003 best vintages NA drink with Takeaway • $20

Pepper Tree McLaren Vale Merlot

ŦŦŦŦ 1999 Medium red-purple; some fragrance and spice, with good varietal character on the bouquet is repeated on the palate, where there are gently savoury/olive edges to fine red fruit. Ironically, not given the Reserve benediction. **rating: 88**

best drinking 2004–2009 best vintages NA drink with Braised veal • $27

Pepper Tree Reserve Coonawarra Cabernet Sauvignon

ŦŦŦŦŸ 1999 Medium red-purple; the bouquet is clean, still to develop aromatics, but with abundant blackcurrant/blackberry/redcurrant fruit. The firm, clean, medium-bodied palate is beautifully focussed on cabernet varietal fruit, the oak playing a pure support role. Not in the class of the Olympian '98, but a very good wine, and clearly the flagship of the Pepper Tree range. **rating: 90**

best drinking 2004–2008 best vintages '98, '99 drink with Fillet steak • $60

perrini estate ★★★

Bower Road, Meadows, SA 5201 **region** Adelaide Hills
phone (08) 8388 3210 **fax** (08) 8388 3210 **open** Wed–Sun and public holidays 10–5
winemaker Antonio Perrini **production** 3500 **est.** 1997
product range ($13–21.50 CD) Semillon Sauvignon Blanc, Unwooded Chardonnay, Shiraz, Merlot, Cabernet Sauvignon, Tony's Blend, Tawny Port.
summary Perrini Estate is very much a family affair; Tony and Connie Perrini had spent their working life in the retail food business, and Tony purchased the land in 1988 as a hobby farm and retirement home (or so Tony told Connie). In 1990 Tony planted his first few grapevines, began to read everything he could about making wine, and thereafter obtained vintage experience at a local winery. Next came highly successful entries into amateur winemaker competitions, and that was that. Together the family established the 6 hectares of vineyard and built the winery and cellar door, culminating in the first commercial releases of the 1997 vintage, and steadily increasing production thereafter. Exports to Singapore.

pertaringa ★★★★

Cnr Hunt and Rifle Range Roads, McLaren Vale, SA 5171 **region** McLaren Vale
phone (08) 8323 8125 **fax** (08) 8323 7766 **open** Mon–Fri 10–5, weekends and public holidays 11–5
winemaker Geoff Hardy, Ben Riggs **production** 6000 **est.** 1980
product range ($14–28 R) Barrel Fermented Semillon, Sauvignon Blanc, Shiraz, Cabernet Sauvignon, Liqueur Frontignac; Grandis Red (Merlot blend), Grandis White (Semillon).
summary The Pertaringa wines are made from part of the grapes grown by leading viticulturists Geoff Hardy and Ian Leask. The Pertaringa vineyard of 31 hectares was acquired in 1980 and rejuvenated; establishment of the ultra-cool Kuitpo vineyard in the Adelaide Hills began in 1987; it now supplies leading makers such as Southcorp and Petaluma. Retail distribution through SA, NSW, Vic and Qld; exports to the UK, the US, Canada, Denmark, Germany, Hong Kong, Japan and New Zealand.

Pertaringa Shiraz

ŦŦŦŦŸ 2000 Medium red-purple; the moderately intense bouquet has dark berry fruit, with hints of raspberry and vanilla; the palate offers dark berry, touches of bitter chocolate, fine tannins and subtle vanilla oak. **rating: 90**

best drinking 2005–2010 best vintages '97, '98, '99, '00 drink with Beef casserole • $28

peschar's ★★★☆

179 Wambo Road, Bulga, NSW 2330 **region** Lower Hunter Valley
phone (02) 4927 1588 **fax** (02) 4927 1589 **open** Not
winemaker Tyrrell's (Contract) **production** 8000 **est.** 1995
product range ($14–18.50 ML) Chardonnay, Shiraz, Cabernet Merlot.
summary In 1995 John and Mary Peschar purchased the historic Meerea Park property, which had been in the ownership of the Eather family; the name continues to be used by the Eathers for a quite separate winemaking operation. The property acquired by the Peschars is situated at the foot of the Wollemi National Park, which rises steeply behind the vineyard, the latter being planted on sandy alluvial soils. There are 16 hectares of chardonnay, the wine being contract-made by Tyrrell's. While the focus is on Chardonnay, the Peschars have sourced 6 hectares of vines in the Limestone Coast Zone of SA for the production of Shiraz and Cabernet Merlot.

petaluma ★★★★★

Spring Gully Road, Piccadilly, SA 5151 **region** Adelaide Hills
phone (08) 8339 4122 **fax** (08) 8339 5253 **open** At Bridgewater Mill
winemaker Brian Croser **production** 30 000 **est.** 1976
product range ($19–90 R) Riesling, Chardonnay, Coonawarra (Cabernet Blend), Croser (Sparkling); Second label Sharefarmers White and Red. Bridgewater Mill is another label – see separate entry.
summary The Petaluma empire comprises Knappstein Wines, Mitchelton, Stonier and Smithbrook. In late 2001 the Petaluma group was acquired by New Zealand brewer Lion Nathan; they left Brian Croser as (non-executive) Chairman. Croser has never compromised his fierce commitment to quality, and doubtless never will. The Riesling is almost monotonously good; the Chardonnay is the big mover, going from strength to strength; the Merlot is another marvellously succulent wine to buy without hesitation. Exports to the UK and the US.

Petaluma Riesling

TTTTT 2001 Brian Croser has written of the climatic trials of the 2001 vintage in the Clare Valley, and rightly pointed to the unexpectedly excellent outcome. This is truly delicious, with fresh, crisp passionfruit and apple blossom aromas; the wine literally dances on the tongue with all the flavours promised by the bouquet.   **rating:** 95

best drinking 2002–2011 **best vintages** '80, '85, '86, '88, '90, '92, '93, '94, '95, '97, '98, '99, '00, '01 **drink with** Blue swimmer crab • $21

Petaluma Viognier

TTTTT 2001 Light to medium yellow-green; a fragrant bouquet with ripe apple/apple cake fruit and spice is followed by a powerful palate, increasing its impact on the finish, and braced by good acidity. **rating:** 92

best drinking 2001–2005 **best vintages** '99, '01 **drink with** Stuffed pig's trotter • $30

Petaluma Chardonnay

TTTTT 1999 Medium yellow-green; a complex array of melon, fig and cashew aromas with the oak barely noticeable is followed by a typically elegant and subtle palate, at once complex yet understated; its best years are in front of it.   **rating:** 92

best drinking 2002–2007 **best vintages** '87, '90, '91, '92, '95, '96, '99 **drink with** Slow-roasted Tasmanian salmon • $38

Petaluma Croser LD

TTTTT 1992 Light to medium green-yellow; gently toasty/bready notes to the fine citrus/melon fruit on the bouquet foreshadow a palate which is still remarkably elegant, fine and long, has fully lived up to its early rating, the extra years on yeast lees in no way diminishing the finesse or the fruit. Disgorged October 2001.   **rating:** 94

best drinking 2002–2003 **best vintages** NA **drink with** Aperitif, seafood • $45

Petaluma Shiraz

TTTTT 1999 Medium red-purple; fragrant, red cherry fruit with a substrate of spice on the bouquet, then a powerfully structured and layered palate, with abundant dark cherry fruit plus splashes of spice and oak.

rating: 95

best drinking 2003–2010 **best vintages** '99 **drink with** Lamb casserole • $43

Petaluma Coonawarra

🍷🍷🍷🍷🍷 1999 Medium to full red-purple; even by the standards of Petaluma, a particularly complex bouquet of blackberry and plum fruit with outstanding oak balance and integration. The palate is very concentrated, with quite surprising tannins enfolding the core of sweet fruit; demands patience. **rating:** 93

best drinking 2004–2019 **best vintages** '79, '86, '88, '90, '91, '92, '95, '97, '98, '99 **drink with** Saddle of lamb • $58

peter lehmann   ★★★★

Para Road, Tanunda, SA 5352 **region** Barossa Valley
phone (08) 8563 2500 **fax** (08) 8563 3402 **open** Mon–Fri 9.30–5, weekends and public holidays 10.30–4.30
winemaker Peter Lehmann, Andrew Wigan, Peter Scholz, Leonie Lange, Ian Hongell
production 200 000 **est.** 1979
product range ($11–65 CD) Barossa/Eden Valley Riesling, Blue Eden Riesling, Barossa Semillon, Chenin Blanc, Semillon Chardonnay, Chardonnay, Clancy's Classic Dry White, Late Harvest Frontignac, Noble Semillon, Pinot Noir Cuvée, Grenache, Merlot, Seven Surveys Dry Red, Barossa Shiraz, Cabernet Sauvignon, Clancy's Red, Bin AD 2015 Vintage Port, Old Tawny, Liqueur Muscat. Premium wines are Reserve Riesling, Reserve Chardonnay, Mentor, Stonewell Shiraz, Eight Songs Shiraz, Black Queen Sparkling Shiraz.
summary Public listing on the stock exchange has not altered the essential nature of the company, which is resolutely and single-mindedly focussed on Peter Lehmann's beloved Barossa Valley. Some of the top-of-the-range wines are seriously good, and the base range is highly rated by the *Wine Spectator* and the International Wine and Spirit Competition. Exports to the UK through its own subsidiary; also to New Zealand, Europe, Asia, the South Pacific and the US.

Peter Lehmann Riesling

🍷🍷🍷🍷 2001 Light to medium green-yellow; the bouquet is quite firm, with a mix of herbal and riper fruit aromas; the solidly built palate offers cheerful early drinking. **rating:** 84

best drinking 2001–2002 **best vintages** '00 **drink with** Dim sims • $11.95

Peter Lehmann Blue Eden Riesling

🍷🍷🍷🍷 2001 Light green-yellow; the fine lime/citrus bouquet is absolutely typical of the best Eden Valley wines; the palate is fresh and lively, with more of those lime/citrus flavours, but at this juncture the CO_2 spritz is distracting. Together with the Stelvin closure, the CO_2 will guarantee a long life; if given 4–5 years in bottle, it would receive much higher points. **rating:** 88

best drinking 2005–2015 **best vintages** NA **drink with** Sashimi • $20

Peter Lehmann The Barossa Semillon

🍷🍷🍷🍷 2001 Light but intense green-yellow; a moderately intense, fresh, unforced bouquet with citrus and lemon varietal character; the wine flows evenly across the palate, with plenty of flavour, length and balance. For all that, to be drunk sooner rather than later. **rating:** 88

best drinking 2001–2002 **best vintages** NA **drink with** Seafood • $11.95

Peter Lehmann Chardonnay

🍷🍷🍷🍷 2001 Medium yellow-green; the light bouquet offers modest melon fruit, the palate showing a faint touch of oak, but not a lot of varietal flavour. One the other hand, it does have good length, is not forced, and will look better with another 12 months under its belt. **rating:** 83

🍷🍷🍷🍷 2000 Medium green-yellow, bright and promising; the attractive, fruit-driven bouquet and palate offer melon and nectarine varietal fruit; a light to medium-bodied wine with no frills or pretensions. **rating:** 86

best drinking 2003–2004 **best vintages** NA **drink with** Pasta • $15

Peter Lehmann Cabernet Sauvignon

🍷🍷🍷🍷 2000 Medium red-purple; the bouquet shows fairly obvious dusty/chippy oak, but on the palate black and redcurrant fruit make their presence felt; still fractionally hard in the mouth. **rating:** 84

best drinking 2003–2007 **best vintages** NA **drink with** Steak and kidney pie • $22

peterson champagne house   NR

Cnr Broke and Branxton Roads, Pokolbin, NSW 2320 **region** Lower Hunter Valley
phone (02) 4998 7881 **fax** (02) 4998 7882 **open** 7 days 9–5
winemaker Gary Reed **production** 10 000 **est.** 1994

product range ($14–28 CD) Sparkling whites include First Creek, Sparkling Ambrosia, Chardonnay Pinot Noir, Semillon Pinot, Chardonnay Blanc de Blanc Millennium, Pinot Noir Chardonnay Meunier; sparkling reds, Sparkling Shiraz, Sparkling Chambourcin, Rouge Ambrosia and Sparkling Merlot; also table wine Chardonnay and Pinot Noir.

summary Prominently and provocatively situated on the corner of Broke and Branxton Roads as one enters the main vineyard and winery district in the Lower Hunter Valley. It is an extension of the Peterson family empire and, no doubt, very deliberately aimed at the tourist. While the dreaded word 'Champagne' has been retained in the business name, the wine labels now simply say Peterson House, which is a big step in the right direction. Almost all of the wine is sold through the cellar door and the wine club mailing list.

petersons ★★★★

Mount View Road, Mount View, NSW 2325 **region** Lower Hunter Valley
phone (02) 4990 1704 **fax** (02) 4991 1344 **open** Mon–Sat 9–5, Sun 10–5
winemaker Colin Peterson, Gary Reed **production** 15 000 **est.** 1971
product range ($19–48 CD) Semillon, Shirley Semillon, Verdelho, Viognier, Vintage Chardonnay, Cuvée Chardonnay, Samantha Sparkling, Botrytis Semillon, Rosé, Shiraz, Back Block Shiraz, Ian's Selection Shiraz, Cabernet Sauvignon, Back Block Cabernet Sauvignon, Muscat, Vintage Port.
summary Has a distinctly lower profile these days; no doubt the booming Hunter Valley wine tourism industry soaks up much of the wine at the cellar door. The trophy won at the 2001 Hunter Valley Wine Show joins countless others on the Petersons shelves.

Petersons Back Block Shiraz

▼▼▼▼▼ **2000** Dense purple-red; deep and powerful black cherry fruit (and oak) on the bouquet lead into a very powerful but complex and well-balanced palate offering black cherry, blackberry and chocolate fruit supported by excellent tannins and oak. Trophy winner 2001 Hunter Valley Wine Show. **rating: 95**

best drinking 2004–2014 **best vintages** '93, '00 **drink with** Angus beef • $43

pewsey vale ★★★★☆

PO Box 10, Angaston, SA 5353 **region** Eden Valley
phone (08) 8561 3200 **fax** (08) 8561 3393 **open** At Yalumba
winemaker Louisa Rosé **production** 25 000 **est.** 1961
product range ($15–25 R) Riesling, The Contour Riesling, Cabernet Sauvignon.
summary Pewsey Vale was a famous vineyard established in 1847 by Joseph Gilbert, and it was appropriate that when S Smith & Son (Yalumba) began the renaissance of the high Adelaide Hills plantings in 1961, they should do so by purchasing Pewsey Vale and establishing 59 hectares of riesling and cabernet sauvignon. After a dip in form, Pewsey Vale has empahtically bounced back to its very best. Exports to all major markets.

Pewsey Vale Riesling

▼▼▼▼▽ **2001** Medium yellow-green; a clean bouquet with herb, lemon, lime and a hint of spice is followed by a lively, fresh and intense palate with lime-juicy fruit and slight touch of CO_2. **rating: 91**

best drinking 2001–2006 **best vintages** '69, '99, '00, '01 **drink with** Vegetable terrine • $14.95

Pewsey Vale The Contour Riesling

▼▼▼▼▼ **1997** Excellent green-yellow; a complex, powerful bouquet with a mix of lime and toast is followed by a palate with buckets of flavour, and with that delicious lime and toast mix. A wine from the museum reserve which shows, if proof be needed, that of course wines finished with a Stelvin cap develop in bottle. **rating: 94**

best drinking 2001–2007 **best vintages** '95, '97 **drink with** Pan-fried flathead • $24.95

pteitter ★★★

Distillery Road, Wahgunyah, Vic 3687 **region** Rutherglen
phone (02) 6033 2805 **fax** (02) 6033 3158 **open** Mon–Sat 9–5, Sun 11–4
winemaker Christopher Pfeiffer **production** 27 500 **est.** 1984
product range ($11.50–46.50 R) Under the Pfeiffer label Riesling, Chardonnay Semillon, Chardonnay, Frontignac, Auslese Tokay, Ensemble (light Rosé-style), Gamay, Pinot Noir, Shiraz, Merlot, Cabernet Sauvignon, Christopher's Vintage Port, Old Distillery Tawny, Old Distillery Classic Tokay, Old Distillery Classic Muscat, Old Distillery Liqueur Gold (all cellar door only); Vintage Reserve range of Chardonnay, Sparkling Brut, Sparkling Pinot Noir, The Piper; also the Carlyle range of Riesling, Chardonnay, Marsanne, Late Harvest Riesling, Shiraz, Cabernet Sauvignon and Classic Rutherglen Muscat, sold through retail and export.

summary Ex-Lindeman fortified winemaker Chris Pfeiffer occupies one of the historic wineries (built 1880) which abound in northeast Victoria and which is worth a visit on this score alone. The fortified wines are good, and the table wines have improved considerably over recent vintages, drawing upon 32 hectares of estate plantings. The winery offers barbecue facilities, a children's playground, gourmet picnic hampers, and dinners (by arrangement). Exports to the UK, Canada, Singapore and Taiwan (under the Carlyle label).

Pfeiffer Gamay

▼▼▼▽ **2000** Bright purple-red; the bouquet is firm, clean and bright; the palate has attractive soft, sweet raspberry fruit, very much true to type for this Beaujolais variety. **rating:** 84

best drinking 2001–2002 **best vintages** NA **drink with** Warm duck salad • $15.50

pfitzner ★★★★

6B, 39–45 Jeffcott Street, North Adelaide, SA 5006 (postal) **region** Adelaide Hills
phone (08) 8267 5404 **fax** (08) 8267 5404 **open** Not
winemaker Petaluma (Contract) **production** 1500 **est.** 1996
product range ($16.50–19.95 R) Sauvignon Blanc, Chardonnay, Pinot Noir, Merlot.
summary The subtitle to the Pfitzner name is Eric's Vineyard. The late Eric Pfitzner purchased and aggregated a number of small, subdivided farmlets to protect the beauty of the Piccadilly Valley from ugly rural development. His three sons inherited the vision, with a little under 6 hectares of vineyard planted principally to chardonnay and pinot noir, plus small amounts of sauvignon blanc and merlot. Half the total property has been planted, the remainder preserving the natural eucalypt forest. The wines are made by Brian Croser at Petaluma, and roughly half the production is sold in the UK. The remainder is sold through retail outlets in Adelaide, Sydney, Melbourne and Perth.

Pfitzner Eric's Vineyard Sauvignon Blanc

▼▼▼▼ **2000** Medium yellow-green; a powerful bouquet with gooseberry and asparagus aromas, the palate lighter and crisper than the bouquet suggests; nonetheless, very flavoursome and not phenolic. **rating:** 88

best drinking 2002–2003 **best vintages** NA **drink with** Shellfish • $16.50

Pfitzner Eric's Vineyard Chardonnay

▼▼▼▼▽ **1999** Medium yellow-green; the clean bouquet offers neatly balanced melon fruit and subtle, spicy French oak; a complete wine, with a fine array of cashew, melon, fig and faintly creamy flavours. **rating:** 92

best drinking 2002–2005 **best vintages** '98, '99 **drink with** Terrine of scallops • $19.95

Pfitzner Eric's Vineyard Pinot Noir

▼▼▼▽ **1999** Light to medium red-purple; the bouquet is clean and fresh, but subdued; a savoury palate with a slightly dry finish, although the tannins are not aggressive. **rating:** 84

best drinking 2002–2004 **best vintages** NA **drink with** Smoked quail • $19.95

phaedrus estate ★★★☆

220 Mornington–Tyabb Road, Moorooduc, Vic 3933 **region** Mornington Peninsula
phone (03) 5978 8134 **fax** (03) 5978 8134 **open** Weekends and public holidays 11–5
winemaker Ewan Campbell, Maitena Zantvoort **production** 600 **est.** 1997
product range ($14–18 R) Semillon Sauvignon Blanc, Chardonnay, Pinot Noir, Shiraz.
summary Ewan Campbell and Maitena Zantvoort established Phaedrus Estate in 1997. At that time both had already had winemaking experience with large wine companies, and were at the point of finishing their wine science degrees at Adelaide University. They decided they wished to (in their words) 'produce ultra-premium wine with distinctive and unique varietal flavours, which offer serious (and lighthearted) wine drinkers an alternative to mainstream commercial styles'. Campbell and Zantvoort believe that quality wines are made in a process involving both art and science, and I don't have any argument with that.

Phaedrus Estate Chardonnay

▼▼▼▼ **2000** Light to medium green-yellow; subtle melon and cashew aromas are very typical of the Mornington Peninsula, and accurately predict the palate. The texture is complex and well-balanced, but the varietal fruit flavour slightly diminished. **rating:** 85

best drinking 2001–2004 **best vintages** NA **drink with** Fish cakes • $16

Phaedrus Estate Pinot Noir

▼▼▼▼ **2000** Medium to full red-purple; abundant dark plum/spice/berry on the bouquet are followed by a powerful palate with plum together with hints of nutmeg and anise, giving the wine real presence. **rating:** 87

best drinking 2001–2005 **best vintages** NA **drink with** Smoked quail • $18

phillip island vineyard ★★★★☆

Berrys Beach Road, Phillip Island, Vic **region** Gippsland
phone (03) 5956 8465 **fax** (03) 5956 8465 **open** 7 days 11–7 (Nov–March) 11–5 (April–Oct)
winemaker David Lance, James Lance **production** 3500 **est.** 1993
product range ($17–42.50 CD) Sea Spray (Sparkling), Sauvignon Blanc, Cape Woolamai (Semillon Sauvignon Blanc), Summerland (Chardonnay), Newhaven (Riesling Traminer), Botrytis Chardonnay, Pinot Noir, The Nobbies (Pinot Noir), Merlot, Berry's Beach (Cabernet Sauvignon), Western Port, Pyramid Rock.
summary 1997 marked the first harvest from the 2.5 hectares of the Phillip Island vineyard, which is totally enclosed in the permanent silon net which acts as both a windbreak and protection against birds. The quality of the wines across the board make it clear; this is definitely not a tourist-trap cellar door; it is a serious producer of quality wine. In early 2002 it was offered for sale to allow the founding Lance family to concentrate all their efforts on Diamond Valley. Exports to Southeast Asia.

Phillip Island Sauvignon Blanc

▼▼▼▼▽ **2001** Light green-yellow; a fresh, delicate, flowery passionfruit-driven bouquet shows excellent varietal character, as does the palate. Here grassy pea pod and passionfruit flavours provide a neat interplay in a wine with above average intensity and length. **rating:** 91

best drinking 2001–2002 **best vintages** '97, '99, '00, '01 **drink with** Fresh crab • $30

Phillip Island Vineyard Chardonnay

▼▼▼▼▽ **2000** Light to medium green-yellow; a complex, tangy bouquet with a mix of melon and citrus fruit is followed by a typically stylish and elegant palate, with good intensity and balance; the oak plays a pure support role. **rating:** 90

best drinking 2001–2005 **best vintages** '98, '00 **drink with** Sautéed prawns • $27

Phillip Island Vineyard Pinot Noir

▼▼▼▼▽ **2000** Excellent purple-red; spice, plum and black cherry fruit aromas in an overall sweet spectrum on the bouquet move into a wine with concentration of plummy fruit on the entry and mid-palate, tailing off every so slightly on the finish. **rating:** 93

best drinking 2002–2006 **best vintages** NA **drink with** Smoked quail • $42.50

Phillip Island Vineyard The Nobbies Pinot Noir

▼▼▼▼▽ **2000** Light to medium red-purple; spicy/foresty/savoury aromas are reflected on the palate, which has length and intensity in a savoury mode, with some wood strawberries peeping through. **rating:** 91

best drinking 2001–2004 **best vintages** '96, '98, '00 **drink with** Smoked quail • $27.50

Phillip Island Vineyard Merlot

▼▼▼▼ **2000** Medium purple-red; the bouquet is fresh, with a mix of spicy notes and sweet blackberry fruit; the palate offers a slight mix of sweet and sour fruit, accentuated perhaps by the initial sweetness, which is followed by a slightly lean finish. **rating:** 87

best drinking 2003–2007 **best vintages** '98 **drink with** Roast veal • $37.50

piano gully ★★★★

Piano Gully Road, Manjimup, WA 6258 **region** Manjimup
phone (08) 9772 3140 **fax** (08) 9316 0336 **open** By appointment
winemaker Michael Staniford (Contract) **production** 6000 **est.** 1987
product range ($15–25 R) Chardonnay Sauvignon Blanc, Chardonnay, Pemberton Red, Pinot Noir, Cabernet Sauvignon Shiraz, Cabernet Sauvignon.
summary The 4 hectare vineyard was established in 1987 on rich karri loam, 10 kilometres south of Manjimup, with the first wine made from the 1991 vintage. A change of ownership and winemaker has seen a dramatic lift in wine quality. For the record, the name of the road (and hence the winery) commemorates the shipping of a piano from England by one of the first settlers in the region. The horse and cart carrying the piano on the last leg of the long journey were within sight of their destination when the piano fell from the cart and was destroyed.

Piano Gully Chardonnay

▼▼▼▼▽ **2000** Light to medium yellow-green; the bouquet is quite complex, with a seamless mix of fruit, oak and creamy malolactic characters, all well-balanced. The palate has good intensity and length, showing citrus/grapefruit flavours supported by crisp acidity and subtle oak. **rating:** 91

best drinking 2002–2005 **best vintages** '99, '00 **drink with** Marron • $25

Piano Gully Pinot Noir

▼▼▼▼ 2000 Light red; an almost ethereal bouquet with overtones of crushed lemon leaves is an altogether unconventional opening to a wine which has more fruit and length on the palate, albeit in a distinctly savoury, tangy style. Unconventionally appealing. **rating: 85**

best drinking 2001–2002 **best vintages** NA **drink with** Quail salad • $25

Piano Gully Pemberton Red

▼▼▼▼ 2000 Light, bright red-purple; light, fresh, juicy/spicy/berry aromas are followed by a supple, smooth, light-bodied palate that works really well. **rating: 89**

best drinking 2001–2002 **best vintages** NA **drink with** Terrine, antipasto • $18

Piano Gully Cabernet Sauvignon Shiraz

▼▼▼▽ 1999 Medium red-purple; dusty oak (probably American) intrudes on the bouquet, and while there is fresh fruit on the medium-bodied palate, the oak does not flatter the wine; light tannins to close. **rating: 84**

best drinking 2002–2006 **best vintages** NA **drink with** Lamb tagine • $20

pibbin   NR

Greenhill Road, Balhannah, SA 5242 **region** Adelaide Hills
phone (08) 8388 4794 **fax** (08) 8398 0015 **open** Weekends 11–5.30
winemaker Roger Salkeld **production** 1500 **est.** 1991
product range ($15–22 CD) Pinot Noir, Rosé Pinot Noir, White Pinot, Sparkling Pinot.
summary The 7-hectare Pibbin vineyard, near Verdun, is managed on organic principles; owners Roger and Lindy Salkeld explain that the name 'Pibbin' is a corruption of a negro-spiritual word for Heaven, adding that while the wines may not have achieved that lofty status yet, the vineyard has. Pibbin has made a name for itself for producing massive, dense Pinot Noir in a style radically different from that of the rest of the Adelaide Hills.

picardy   ★★★★

Cnr Vasse Highway and Eastbrook Road, Pemberton, WA 6260 **region** Pemberton
phone (08) 9776 0036 **fax** (08) 9776 0245 **open** By appointment
winemaker Bill Pannell, Dan Pannell **production** 5000 **est.** 1993
product range ($35.95 CD) Chardonnay, Pinot Noir, Shiraz, Cabernet Merlot.
summary Picardy is owned by Dr Bill Pannell and his wife Sandra, who were the founders of Moss Wood winery in the Margaret River region (in 1969). Picardy reflects Bill Pannell's view that the Pemberton area will prove to be one of the best regions in Australia for Pinot Noir and Chardonnay, but it is perhaps significant that the wines to be released include a Shiraz, and a Bordeaux-blend of 50 per cent Merlot, 25 per cent Cabernet Franc and 25 per cent Cabernet Sauvignon. Time will tell whether Pemberton has more Burgundy, Rhône or Bordeaux in its veins. It has lost no time in setting up national distribution, and exports to the UK, the US, Japan, Singapore, Malaysia, Indonesia and Hong Kong.

Picardy Pinot Noir

▼▼▼▽ 2000 Light purple-red; the bouquet has bright cherry/cherry blossom aromas and a substrate of charry oak which in no way prepares you for the strong, charry oak which dominates the palate. There really isn't enough fruit density to sustain the oak. **rating: 84**

best drinking 2002–2003 **best vintages** NA **drink with** Braised pheasant • $35.95

Picardy Shiraz

▼▼▼▼▼ 2000 Vivid purple-red; a rich, deep and complex bouquet with black fruits and spice; the palate provides more of the same dark fruits, supported by fine, savoury tannins which run through the length of the palate; good oak handling. **rating: 94**

best drinking 2004–2010 **best vintages** '97, '00 **drink with** Moroccan lamb • $35.95

picarus   NR

Winetrust Estate, Caves Road, Naracoorte, SA 5271 **region** Limestone Coast Zone
phone (02) 9816 4088 **fax** (02) 9816 2680 **open** Not
winemaker John Baruzzi **production** 5000 **est.** 1998
product range ($25–80 R) Limestone Coast Chardonnay, Limestone Coast Shiraz, Reserve A Padthaway Shiraz, Limestone Coast Cabernet Sauvignon, Reserve 1 Coonawarra Cabernet Sauvignon.

summary Picarus is a partnership between Hunter winemaker John Baruzzi and long-term marketer Mark Arnold. They have established 12 hectares of vineyards (4 hectares each of chardonnay, shiraz and cabernet sauvignon) in the Limestone Coast region and supplement the production from these vineyards with contract-grown grapes in Coonawarra and Padthaway. The wines are distributed nationally through the National Liquor Company in Sydney and Melbourne. Marketing and brand management is provided by WineTrust Estate, which brings together Picarus, Aruna and Ocean Grove.

piccadilly fields   NR

185 Piccadilly Road, Piccadilly, SA 5151 **region** Adelaide Hills
phone (08) 8370 8800 **fax** (08) 8232 5395 **open** Not
winemaker Sam Virgara **production** 3000 **est.** 1989
product range ($17.95 ML) Chardonnay, Merlot Cabernet Franc Cabernet Sauvignon.
summary Piccadilly Fields draws upon a very substantial vineyard, with much of the production being sold to Petaluma. The plantings include 10 hectares of pinot meunier, 8 hectares of pinot noir, 5 hectares each of chardonnay, merlot and sauvignon blanc, 2 hectares of cabernet franc and 1 hectare of cabernet sauvignon.

pierro   ★★★★☆

Caves Road, Wilyabrup via Cowaramup, WA 6284 **region** Margaret River
phone (08) 9755 6220 **fax** (08) 9755 6308 **open** 7 days 10–5
winemaker Dr Michael Peterkin **production** 7500 **est.** 1979
product range ($24.90–49.50 R) Chardonnay, Semillon Sauvignon Blanc LTC, Pinot Noir, Cabernets, Cabernet Merlot.
summary Dr Michael Peterkin is another of the legion of Margaret River medical practitioners who, for good measure, married into the Cullen family. Pierro is renowned for its stylish white wines, which often exhibit tremendous complexity. The Chardonnay can be monumental in its weight and complexity. The wines are exported to the UK, the US, Japan and Indonesia.

Pierro Semillon Sauvignon Blanc LTC

ΥΥΥΥΥ 2001 An outstanding success this vintage, the clean and concentrated bouquet of lemon/citrus and gooseberry flowing into a harmonious palate, with oak an impeccably behaved observer.   **rating:** 94

best drinking 2001–2005 **best vintages** '87, '89, '90, '94, '95, '97, '01 **drink with** Turkey breast • $22.30

Pierro Chardonnay

ΥΥΥΥΥ 2000 Light to medium yellow-green; suave and subtle citrus and melon fruit, with hints of spicy oak on the bouquet, is followed by a palate much more in the Pierro style: ultra-powerful, full-frontal, the finish marked by a twist of alcohol.   **rating:** 91

best drinking 2001–2004 **best vintages** '86, '87, '89, '90, '92, '94, '95, '96, '00 **drink with** Seafood pasta • $35

piesse brook   ★★★

226 Aldersyde Road, Bickley, WA 6076 **region** Perth Hills
phone (08) 9293 3309 **fax** (08) 9293 3309 **open** Sat 1–5, Sun, public holidays 10–5 and by appointment
winemaker Di Bray, Ray Boyanich, Michael Davies (Consultant) **production** 1200 **est.** 1974
product range ($10–22.50 CD) Chardonnay, Shiraz, Brian Murphy Reserve Shiraz, Merlot, Cabernet Sauvignon, Cabernet Merlot, Cabernet Shiraz, Cabernova (early-drinking style).
summary Surprisingly good red wines made in tiny quantities, and which have received consistent accolades over the years. The first Chardonnay was made in 1993; a trophy-winning Shiraz was produced in 1995. Now has 4 hectares of chardonnay, shiraz, merlot and cabernet sauvignon under vine.

Piesse Brook Brian Murphy Reserve Shiraz

ΥΥΥΥ 1998 Medium red, quite developed for its age. The bouquet is clean, predominantly savoury, but with some sweet berry notes; the solid, savoury palate is a replay of the bouquet, with a flicker of sweetness on the mid-palate before quite persistent tannins come on the finish.   **rating:** 85

best drinking 2003–2008 **best vintages** NA **drink with** Rib of beef • $22.50

Piesse Brook Cabernet Merlot

ΥΥΥΥ 1998 Medium red; the aromas of the bouquet are in the savoury/cedary/spicy end of the spectrum, but are not green, and flow through directly into the light to medium-bodied palate with additional hints of bitter chocolate. Attractive, gently ripe tannins run through to the finish.   **rating:** 85

best drinking 2002–2007 **best vintages** NA **drink with** Ragout of veal • NA

pieter van gent ★★★☆

Black Springs Road, Mudgee, NSW 2850 **region** Mudgee
phone (02) 6373 3807 **fax** (02) 6373 3910 **open** Mon–Sat 9–5, Sun 11–4
winemaker Pieter van Gent, Philip van Gent **production** 15 000 **est.** 1978
product range ($11.50–24 CD) The dry wines are Verdelho, Chardonnay, Müller Thurgau, Shiraz, Shiraz Cabernet and Cabernet Sauvignon; the Flower of Florence, Angelic White and Sundance Soft Red all have varying degrees of sweetness; fortified wines are the specialty, including Pipeclay Port, Mudgee White Port, Cornelius Port, Mudgee Oloroso, Mistella, Pipeclay Vermouth.
summary Many years ago Pieter van Gent worked for Lindemans, before joining Craigmoor then moving to his own winery in 1979. Here, he and his family have forged a strong following, notably for their fortified wines.

Pieter van Gent Chardonnay

▼▼▼▼♈ **2000** Light to medium yellow-green; the bouquet offers fragrant, aromatic stone fruit; the palate has excellent length and drive, and like the bouquet relies entirely on its fruit. **rating:** 90
best drinking 2002–2005 **best vintages** '99, '00 **drink with** Carpaccio of salmon • $17.50

Pieter van Gent Matador Shiraz

▼▼▼♈ **2000** Medium red-purple; the bouquet is clean, with a degree of vanilla oak which does not overwhelm the light cherry/berry fruit; the same restrained hand is evident on the palate, which, while not deep or powerful, is well-balanced. **rating:** 84
best drinking 2003–2006 **best vintages** NA **drink with** Spaghetti bolognese • $16.50

piggs peake NR

697 Hermitage Road, Pokolbin, NSW 2320 **region** Lower Hunter Valley
phone (02) 6574 7000 **fax** (02) 6574 7070 **open** Mon–Sat 10–4, Sun 10–3
winemaker Steve Dodd, Lesley Minter **production** 5000 **est.** 1998
product range ($14–20 CD) Pokolbin Semillon, Lovedale Semillon, Pokolbin Verdelho, Rylstone Chardonnay, Lovedale Premium Chardonnay, Mudgee Botrytis Semillon, Hunter Valley Shiraz, Hunter Valley Merlot, Mudgee Tempranillo Cabernet.
summary The derivation of the name remains a mystery to me, and if it is a local landmark, I have not heard of it. Certain it is that it is one of the newest wineries to be constructed in the Hunter Valley, sourcing most of its grapes from other growers to complement the hectare of estate plantings.

pikes ★★★☆

Polish Hill River Road, Sevenhill, SA 5453 **region** Clare Valley
phone (08) 8843 4370 **fax** (08) 8843 4353 **open** 7 days 10–4
winemaker Neil Pike, John Trotter **production** 35 000 **est.** 1984
product range ($15–22 R) Riesling, Reserve Riesling, Sauvignon Blanc, Sauvignon Blanc Semillon, Chardonnay, Shiraz, Shiraz Grenache Mourvèdre, Cabernet Sauvignon.
summary Owned by the Pike brothers, one of whom (Andrew) was for many years the senior viticulturist with Southcorp; the other (Neil) is a former winemaker at Mitchell. Pikes now has its own winery, with Neil Pike presiding. Generously constructed and flavoured wines are the order of the day. The wines are exported to the UK, the US, Canada, Japan, Switzerland, Germany, New Zealand, Malaysia, Singapore and Belgium.

Pikes Riesling

▼▼▼♈ **2001** Light green-yellow; a crisp, clean and relatively light bouquet with fresh minerally notes is followed by a palate which repeats the bouquet, but lacks concentration. **rating:** 83
best drinking 2001–2004 **best vintages** '86, '90, '92, '93, '95, '97, '00 **drink with** Lightly spiced chicken salad • $18.99

pinelli NR

30 Bennett Street, Caversham, WA 6055 **region** Swan District
phone (08) 9279 6818 **fax** (08) 9377 4259 **open** 7 days 10–6
winemaker Robert Pinelli **production** 7000 **est.** 1979

product range ($5–16 CD) Limited table wine range centred on Chenin Blanc, Chardonnay, Shiraz and Cabernet Sauvignon, and an extensive range of fortified wines, including Cabernet-based Vintage Port. The wines have won a number of medals at the Perth Show in recent years.

summary Dominic Pinelli and son Robert – the latter a Roseworthy Agricultural College graduate – sell 75 per cent of their production in flagons but are seeking to place more emphasis on bottled-wine sales in the wake of recent show successes with Chenin Blanc.

pipers brook vineyard ★★★★★

1216 Pipers Brook Road, Pipers Brook, Tas 7254 **region** Northern Tasmania
phone (03) 6382 7527 **fax** (03) 6382 7226 **open** 7 days 10–5
winemaker Andrew Pirie **production** 60 000 **est.** 1974
product range ($22.95–70 R) A three-tier range. The basic Estate varietals of Riesling, Gewürztraminer, Sauvignon Blanc, Pinot Gris, Chardonnay and Pinot Noir; next Reserve Chardonnay and Pinot Noir; then Single Site Riesling, Chardonnay and Pinot Noir.
summary The Pipers Brook Tasmanian empire has over 220 hectares of vineyard supporting the Pipers Brook and Ninth Island labels (see separate entry for Ninth Island), with the major focus, of course, being on Pipers Brook. As ever, fastidious viticulture and winemaking, immaculate packaging and enterprising marketing constitute a potent and effective blend. Piper Brook operates three cellar-door outlets: one at headquarters, one at Strathlyn (phone 03 6330 2388), the third at Ninth Island. The wines are exported to the UK, the US, Japan, Canada and Singapore, and are distributed throughout Australia by S Smith & Son. In 2001 it became yet another company to fall prey to a takeover, in this instance by Belgian-owned sheepskin business Kreglinger, which has also established a large winery and vineyard at Mount Benson in SA.

Pipers Brook Vineyard Estate Riesling

▼▼▼▼▽ **2001** Light to medium green-yellow; a fragrant yet delicate, Germanic-lime bouquet merges into a pure, clean and crisp palate which builds intensity progressively towards the finish.   **rating:** 93

best drinking 2003–2010 **best vintages** '82, '91, '92, '93, '94, '98, '99, '00 **drink with** Pan-fried scallops • $23.60

Pipers Brook Vineyard Estate Gewürztraminer

▼▼▼▼▽ **2001** So pale it is almost colourless; a fragrant and flowery bouquet of spice and rose petal aromas, delicate but pure, are followed by a very delicate palate, which doesn't quite deliver on the promise of the bouquet, but is nonetheless of high quality.   **rating:** 90

best drinking 2002–2005 **best vintages** '99, '00, '01 **drink with** Duck liver pâté • $27.80

Pipers Brook Vineyard Estate Chardonnay

▼▼▼▼▼ **2000** Medium green-yellow; the clean and elegant bouquet has citrus and nectarine fruit, with subtle oak influences throughout. The palate is rounded but fresh, and still tight; some malolactic cashew comes on the finish, adding to the texture and flavour.   **rating:** 94

best drinking 2001–2007 **best vintages** '82, '88, '91, '92, '93, '94, '97, '98, '99, '00 **drink with** Tasmanian lobster • $34.65

Pipers Brook Vineyard Reserve Chardonnay

▼▼▼▼▼ **1999** Light to medium yellow-green; a clean, quite brisk bouquet with citrus, herb and melon aromas leads into a complex palate, with a nice touch of spicy oak adding to the appeal of the fruit; very good balance and length; immaculate winemaking.   **rating:** 95

best drinking 2001–2005 **best vintages** '98, '99 **drink with** Salmon with sorrel cream sauce • $45.65

Pipers Brook The Summit Chardonnay

▼▼▼▼▽ **1999** Light to medium yellow-green; the bouquet has some slightly herbal overtones – typical of very cool-grown chardonnay – to the citrus and melon fruit, nuances of almond/cashew, and balanced and integrated oak. The palate is very subtle and sophisticated, again with those nutty cashew characters, and brisk acidity. A slight reservation is that I might have expected a touch more fruit.   **rating:** 90

best drinking 2004–2014 **best vintages** '97, '98 **drink with** Grilled Tasmanian lobster • $66.50

Pipers Brook Cuvée Clarke

▼▼▼▼▼ **2000** Glowing green-yellow; a complex and intensely fragrant bouquet offers apricot, honey, pineapple and lime, which flow through to the lime and honey bouquet. The wine has exceptional balance and intensity, with a long, lingering finish, the acid perfect. (A late-harvest, fully botrytised wine rarely made.)   **rating:** 95

best drinking 2001–2007 **best vintages** NA **drink with** Citrus crème brûlée • $33.95

Pipers Brook Pirie Cuvée

▼▼▼▼▼ 1997 Light to medium yellow-green; a restrained, elegant, yet complex bouquet with biscuity aromas is followed by a similarly restrained, super-elegant palate, marked by great length and typical Tasmanian acidity. **rating:** 94

best drinking 2002–2007 **best vintages** '95, '96, '97 **drink with** Tasmanian oysters • $55

Pipers Brook Vineyard Estate Pinot Noir

▼▼▼▼▽ 2000 Youthful, light to medium purple-red; tangy, minty/leafy overtones to strawberry fruit on the bouquet are followed by a delicate, fresh and lively palate with cherry/strawberry fruit; early-maturing style. **rating:** 90

best drinking 2001–2004 **best vintages** '99, '00 **drink with** Chinese roast duck • $34.65

Pipers Brook Vineyard Reserve Pinot Noir

▼▼▼▼▽ 1999 Medium red-purple; savoury/foresty/stemmy/tobacco aromas repeat on the long and savoury palate, with fine tannins and faintly citrussy acidity. **rating:** 92

best drinking 2002–2007 **best vintages** '99 **drink with** Barbecued boned quail • $45.65

Pipers Brook Vineyard The Blackwood Pinot Noir

▼▼▼▼▼ 1999 Medium to full red-purple; lovely spicy, sweet plum fruit with neatly balanced oak comes through faithfully on the palate, which exudes ripe but not jammy pinot fruit. It comes as no surprise to find the alcohol is 14.4 per cent, but the wine does carry that alcohol with ease. **rating:** 94

best drinking 2002–2007 **best vintages** '99 **drink with** Barbecued boned quail and blackcurrant jus • $66.50

Pipers Brook Vineyard The Lyre Pinot Noir

▼▼▼▼▼ 1999 Strongly coloured; the powerful, complex spicy/tangy/savoury bouquet is less opulently sweet than The Blackwood, but has a remarkably intense, complex and structured palate, finishing with fine, lingering tannins. **rating:** 96

best drinking 2002–2012 **best vintages** '99 **drink with** Coq au vin • $69.20

piromit wines NR

113 Hanwood Avenue, Hanwood, NSW 2680 **region** Riverina
phone (02) 6963 0200 **fax** (02) 6963 0277 **open** Mon–Fri 9–5
winemaker Dom Piromalli, Pat Mittiga **production** 60 000 **est.** 1998
product range ($8–17 CD) Semillon, Old Briggie Semillon Chardonnay, Colombard Chardonnay, Chardonnay, Botrytis Semillon, Shiraz, Old Briggie Shiraz Cabernet, Cabernet Merlot, Cabernet Sauvignon.
summary I simply cannot resist quoting directly from the background information kindly supplied to me. 'Piromit Wines is a relatively new boutique winery situated in Hanwood, New South Wales. The winery complex, which crushed 1000 tonnes this season (2000), was built for the 1999 vintage on a 14-acre site which was until recently used as a drive-in. Previous to this, wines were made on our 100-acre vineyard. The winery site is being developed into an innovative tourist attraction complete with an Italian restaurant and landscaped formal gardens.' It is safe to say that this extends the concept of a boutique winery into new territory, but then it is a big country. It is a family business run by Pat Mittiga, Dom Piromalli and Paul Hudson.

pirramimma ★★★★

Johnston Road, McLaren Vale, SA 5171 **region** McLaren Vale
phone (08) 8323 8205 **fax** (08) 8323 9224 **open** Mon–Fri 9–5, Sat 11–5, Sun, public holidays 11.30–4
winemaker Geoff Johnston **production** 30 000 **est.** 1892
product range ($10–26 R) Stocks Hill Semillon Chardonnay, Adelaide Hills Semillon, McLaren Vale Semillon, Stocks Hill Semillon Chardonnay, Hillsview Chardonnay, Stocks Hill Shiraz, Petit Verdot, Hillsview Cabernet Merlot, Cabernet Sauvignon, Ports.
summary An operation with large vineyard holdings of very high quality and a winery which devotes much of its considerable capacity to contract-processing fruit for others. In terms of the brand, has been a consistent under-performer during the 1990s. The marketing of the brand does scant justice to the very considerable resources available to it, notably its gold medal Petit Verdot and fine, elegant Chardonnay. Exports to the UK, New Zealand, Germany, Switzerland and the US.

Pirramimma Reserve Petit Verdot

▼▼▼▼▼ **1999** Excellent, bright, deep purple red; the bouquet is powerful, with dark chocolate, blackberry and some spice. The palate has excellent red and black berry fruit flavours, with a touch of chocolate so typical of McLaren Vale, finishing with fine, lingering tannins, and easily carrying its alcohol of 14°. **rating:** 94

best drinking 2004–2009 **best vintages** '95, '99 **drink with** Grilled lamb chops • $26

pizzini ★★★

King Valley Road, Wangaratta, Vic 3768 **region** King Valley
phone (03) 5729 8278 **fax** (03) 5729 8495 **open** 7 days 12–5
winemaker Alfred Pizzini, Joel Pizzini, Mark Walpole **production** 8000 **est.** 1980
product range ($12–40 CD) Riesling, Sauvignon Blanc, Alfred Pizzini Chardonnay, Sangiovese, Nebbiolo, Alfred Pizzini Shiraz Cabernet, Cabernet, Shiraz.
summary Fred and Katrina Pizzini have been grape growers in the King Valley for over 20 years, with 66 hectares of vineyard. Grape growing (rather than winemaking) still continues to be the major focus of activity, but their move into winemaking has been particularly successful, and I can personally vouch for their Italian cooking skills. It is not surprising, then, that their wines should span both Italian and traditional varieties.

plantagenet ★★★★

Albany Highway, Mount Barker, WA 6324 **region** Great Southern
phone (08) 9851 2150 **fax** (08) 9851 1839 **open** Mon–Fri 9–5, weekends 10–4
winemaker Gavin Berry **production** 55 000 **est.** 1974
product range ($16.50–38 CD) Riesling, Omrah Sauvignon Blanc, Omrah Chardonnay (unoaked), Mount Barker Chardonnay, Fronti, Fine White, Fine Red, Pinot Noir, Shiraz, Henry II, Cabernet Sauvignon, Mount Barker Brut; Breakaway Fine White and Fine Red.
summary The senior winery in the Mount Barker region, and making superb wines across the full spectrum of variety and style – highly aromatic Riesling, tangy citrus-tinged Chardonnay, glorious Rhône-style Shiraz and ultra-stylish Cabernet Sauvignon. Exports to the US, the UK, Germany, Austria, Singapore, Japan, Switzerland and Hong Kong.

Plantagenet Mount Barker Chardonnay

▼▼▼▼ **2000** Light to medium green-yellow; the fresh bouquet has an appealing mix of tangy fruit and barrel-ferment oak influences; the tangy grapefruit flavours drive the crisp, long palate, which is still developing complexity. **rating:** 87

best drinking 2002–2006 **best vintages** '81, '83, '86, '92, '94, '95 **drink with** Breast of chicken • $23

Plantagenet Mount Barker Pinot Noir

▼▼▼▼ **2000** Light red, with the colour already starting to change; a light, dusty, savoury bouquet is followed by a palate showing the best varietal character since the '94 vintage, with savoury, mint overtones. **rating:** 87

best drinking 2001–2004 **best vintages** '94 **drink with** Chargrilled salmon • $25

Plantagenet Mount Barker Shiraz

▼▼▼▼▼ **1999** Medium red-purple; a moderately intense and quite fragrant bouquet has a mix of spicy, earthy, juicy, berry fruit; the palate has excellent texture and structure, with red berry fruit, spice, fine tannins and subtle oak. The only caveat is that it may develop relatively quickly. **rating:** 94

best drinking 2003–2009 **best vintages** '82, '83, '85, '88, '89, '90, '91, '93, '94, '96, '98, '99 **drink with** Hare, squab • $38

Plantagenet Omrah Shiraz

▼▼▼▼ **2000** Medium to full red-purple; the bouquet opens with clean, ripe and sweet fruit woven through vanilla oak; the fleshy palate has similarly sweet and ripe fruit, with attractive tannins in support. **rating:** 88

best drinking 2002–2006 **best vintages** '99 **drink with** Lamb shashlik • $19.50

Plantagenet Omrah Cabernet Merlot

▼▼▼▼▽ **2000** Light to medium red; the light, savoury/earthy bouquet is followed by a tangy, leafy, savoury palate which is almost lemony. A skewed wine which some will actually enjoy. **rating:** 84

best drinking 2003–2006 **best vintages** '99 **drink with** Fish with red wine sauce • $17.50

platt's   NR

Mudgee Road, Gulgong, NSW 2852 **region** Mudgee
phone (02) 6374 1700 **fax** (02) 6372 1055 **open** 7 days 9–5
winemaker Barry Platt **production** 4000 **est.** 1983
product range ($9–12 CD) Chardonnay, Semillon, Gewürztraminer, Cabernet Sauvignon.
summary No recent tastings; problems with oak handling marked the last wines, tasted some years ago.

plunkett   ★★★☆

Lambing Gully Road, Avenel, Vic 3664 **region** Central Victorian High Country
phone (03) 5796 2150 **fax** (03) 5796 2147 **open** 7 days 11–5
winemaker Sam Plunkett **production** 10 000 **est.** 1980
product range ($15–35 CD) The top-of-the-range wines are released under the Strathbogie Ranges label, with Riesling, Chardonnay, Reserve Shiraz, Merlot, Cabernet Merlot, Sparkling Chardonnay Pinot; standard wines under the Blackwood Ridge brand are Gewürztraminer, Semillon, Sauvignon Blanc Semillon, Unwooded Chardonnay, Botrytis Gewürztraminer, Pinot Noir, Shiraz.
summary The Plunkett family first planted grapes way back in 1968, establishing 7.5 hectares with 25 experimental varieties. Commercial plantings commenced in 1980, with 100 hectares now under vine, and more coming. While holding a vigneron's licence since 1985, the Plunketts did not commence serious marketing of the wines until 1992, and have now settled down into producing an array of wines which are pleasant and well-priced. Wholesale distribution to all states; exports to Malaysia, Canada and Hong Kong.

Plunkett Strathbogie Ranges Riesling

▼▼▼▼ **2001** Light green-yellow; a firm, minerally and slightly muted bouquet does have hints of passionfruit poking through; residual sugar is overplayed on the palate, but will greatly appeal to those who taste it at the cellar door.   **rating:** 85

best drinking 2001–2005 **best vintages** NA **drink with** Prosciutto and melon • $16

Plunkett Strathbogie Ranges Reserve Shiraz

▼▼▼▼ **1999** Medium to full red-purple; there is a complex array of aromas on the bouquet, moving through spice, berry, mint and leaf, the palate following on with lively, spicy/savoury highlights to the core of sweet berry fruit. Fine tannins and well-integrated oak complete the picture.   **rating:** 89

best drinking 2004–2009 **best vintages** '98, '99 **drink with** Rich Lebanese dishes • $35

Plunkett Strathbogie Ranges Merlot

▼▼▼▽ **1999** Signs of premature colour change, but it is doubtful whether the pH is, as the winery background information suggests, 6.5. The aromatic bouquet has a range of spicy/leafy/minty fruit magnified on the highly flavoured palate. A wine right on the edge in every respect.   **rating:** 84

best drinking 2002–2006 **best vintages** NA **drink with** Smoked lamb • $18

poet's corner wines   ★★★★☆

Craigmoor Road, Mudgee, NSW 2850 **region** Mudgee
phone (02) 6372 2208 **fax** (02) 6372 4464 **open** Mon–Fri 10–4.30, weekends and public holidays 10–4
winemaker James Manners **production** NFP **est.** 1858
product range ($10–22 R) Semillon Sauvignon Blanc Chardonnay, Unwooded Chardonnay, Shiraz Cabernet Sauvignon Cabernet Franc; PC range of Chardonnay, Merlot, Pinot Chardonnay; Henry Lawson range of Semillon, Chardonnay, Shiraz, Cabernet Sauvignon; also home to the Craigmoor and Montrose labels.
summary Poet's Corner is located in one of the oldest wineries in Australia to remain in more or less continuous production: Craigmoor (as it was previously known) was built by Adam Roth in 1858/1860; his grandson Jack Roth ran the winery until the early 1960s. It is the public face for Poet's Corner, Montrose and Craigmoor wines, all of which are made at the more modern Montrose winery (which is not open to the public).

Henry Lawson Semillon

▼▼▼▼▽ **1999** Excellent light green-yellow; the bouquet has a powerful and complex mix of mineral, slate and herb, the palate following down the same flavour track.   **rating:** 93

best drinking 2004–2010 **best vintages** '00 **drink with** Tempura • $15.95

Poet's Corner Semillon Sauvignon Blanc Chardonnay

♥♥♥♥ 2001 Light green-yellow; delicate passionfruit and citrus aromas flow into a crisp, clean and lively palate, finishing with lemony acidity. Unwooded. **rating: 85**

best drinking 2002–2003 best vintages NA drink with Seafood • $10

Poet's Corner PC Chardonnay

♥♥♥♥♡ 1999 Medium to full green-yellow; a complex, rich bouquet with obvious barrel-ferment and bottle maturation characters surrounding the ripe peach fruit; a luscious, soft palate with exceedingly smooth fruit still holding its position. Trophy 2000 Royal Melbourne Wine Show, top gold 2000 Royal Sydney Wine Show.. **rating: 90**

best drinking 2002–2003 best vintages NA drink with Pan-fried chicken • $12

Montrose Black Shiraz

♥♥♥♥♥ 1999 Intense, deep purple-red; rich, dark fruits in a berry/cherry spectrum have a subtle oak backdrop on the bouquet; the palate is concentrated and rich, with berry/cherry fruit counterbalanced by gentle savoury tannins and a touch of oak on the finish. Two gold medals, including 2000 Mudgee Wine Show. **rating: 94**

♥♥♥♥♡ 1998 Medium to full red, with some purple hues remaining; a complex and rich bouquet starting to show some bottle development to the black cherry, plum and chocolate fruit. Rich chocolatey/berry fruit on the palate is ever so slightly compromised by fractionally furry tannins, but it is highly probable that further bottle age will smooth these over. **rating: 92**

♥♥♥♥♥ 1997 Medium red-purple; a touch of Rhône Valley licorice adds to the appeal of both the bouquet and the palate; attractive fruit flavours run through a beautifully structured and complex palate, with outstanding mouthfeel. Gold medal and trophy winner Mudgee Wines Show 2000. **rating: 95**

best drinking 2004–2009 best vintages '97, '98 drink with Beef with olives and red wine • $19

Montrose Barbera

♥♥♥♥ 1999 Medium red-purple; significantly less ripe than the '97, with slightly earthy/leafy edges to the aroma; the palate offers a clean mix of earth, leaf, blackberry and fine tannins. **rating: 85**

best drinking 2003–2008 best vintages NA drink with Bistecca fiorentina • $22

Poet's Corner PC Merlot

♥♥♥♥ 2000 Light to medium purple-red; light, fresh red berry with some savoury notes; the medium-bodied palate has quite good structure, texture and length, although the oak flavour is not convincing. **rating: 85**

best drinking 2003–2007 best vintages NA drink with Veal chop • $12

pokolbin estate   ★★☆

McDonalds Road, Pokolbin, NSW 2320 **region** Lower Hunter Valley
phone (02) 4998 7524 **fax** (02) 4998 7765 **open** 7 days 10–6
winemaker Contract **production** 2500 **est.** 1980
product range ($15–40 CD) Riesling, Semillon, Chardonnay, Show Reserve Chardonnay, Late Picked Riesling, Dessert Verdelho, Shiraz; Port.
summary An unusual outlet, offering own-label wines made under contract by Trevor Drayton, together with other Hunter Valley wines; also cheap varietal 'cleanskins'. Wine quality under the Pokolbin Estate label has been very modest, although the 1997 Hunter Riesling (perversely, true Riesling, not Semillon) won a silver medal and was the top-pointed wine in its class at the 1997 Hunter Valley Wine Show. No recent news.

ﾑ pontville station   ★★★★

948 Midland Highway, Pontville, Tas 7030 **region** Southern Tasmania
phone (03) 6268 1635 **open** Not
winemaker Peter Rundle **production** 90 **est.** 1990
product range ($17–25 ML) Dessert Riesling, Pinot Noir.
summary Peter and Jane Rundle have a tiny vineyard of 0.5 hectare, mainly planted to pinot noir. Because the vineyard has been established in a frost-prone site, they have from time to time purchased small quantities of grapes from other growers, but in February 2002 they were able to make the first commercial vineyard release, hot on the heels of winning a silver medal with each wine at the 2002 Tasmanian Wines Show: the Pinot Noir in one of the strongest Pinot classes ever seen in Australia, and the Dessert Riesling coming second in its class.

Pontville Station Dessert Riesling

ᵀᵀᵀᵀ **2001** Light green-yellow; attractive lime aromas lead into a lime sherbet/fizz-flavoured palate; good acidity, balance and length.   **rating:** 89

best drinking 2002–2005 **best vintages** NA **drink with** Fruit flan • $17

Pontville Station Pinot Noir

ᵀᵀᵀᵀᵀ **2000** Medium red-purple; a silky smooth bouquet with rich plum and black cherry fruit is echoed on the rich palate, with voluminous fruit running through to fine tannins on the finish. **rating:** 91

best drinking 2002–2007 **best vintages** '00 **drink with** Braised quail • $25

poole's rock ★★★★

'Glen Elgin', De Beyers Road, Pokolbin, NSW 2320 **region** Lower Hunter Valley
phone (02) 9667 1622 **fax** (02) 9667 1442 **open** As from 30 June 2003
winemaker Patrick Auld **production** 60 000 **est.** 1988
product range ($25.95 R) Chardonnay.
summary Sydney merchant banker David Clarke has had a long involvement with the wine industry. The 18-hectare Poole's Rock vineyard, planted purely to chardonnay, is his personal venture, the resource initially bolstered by the acquisition of the larger, adjoining Simon Whitlam Vineyard. However, the purchase of the 74-hectare Glen Elgin Estate, upon which the 2500-tone former Tulloch winery is situated, takes Poole's Rock (and its associated brand, Cockfighter's Ghost) into another dimension. The sale terms provide that Poole's Rock will not have access to the winery until the 2003 vintage, nor the cellar door until 30 June 2003. The wine has retail distribution throughout Australia and is exported to the UK, the US, Canada, New Zealand and Asia.

Poole's Rock Chardonnay

ᵀᵀᵀᵀᵀ **1999** Glowing yellow-green; a complex bouquet with obvious charry barrel-ferment inputs giving a distinctly nutty cast to the tangy fruit; a flavoursome but not heavy palate, basically driven by tangy fruit and sustained by good acidity, notwithstanding all that barrel work in the background.   **rating:** 90

best drinking 2002–2003 **best vintages** '92, '93, '95, '98, '99 **drink with** Creamy pasta • $25.95

pooley wines ★★★★

Cooinda Vale Vineyard, Barton Vale Road, Campania, Tas 7026 **region** Southern Tasmania
phone (03) 6224 3591 **fax** (03) 6224 3591 **open** Wed–Sun 10–5
winemaker Mat Pooley, Andrew Hood (Contract) **production** 1000 **est.** 1985
product range ($15–24 CD) Cooinda Vale Riesling, Coal River Riesling, Coal River Chardonnay, Nellie's Nest Pinot Noir, Cooinda Vale Pinot Noir; Reserve Range of Cooinda Vale Riesling, Cooinda Vale Pinot Noir.
summary Three generations of the Pooley family have been involved in the development of the Cooinda Vale Estate; it was indeed under the Cooinda Vale label that the winery was previously known. After a tentative start on a small scale, plantings have now reached 8 hectares on a property which covers both sides of the Coal River in a region which is substantially warmer and drier than most people realise. The wines have limited retail distribution in Victoria (Southern Fine Wines) and of course in Tasmania.

Pooley Wines Coal River Chardonnay

ᵀᵀᵀᵀᵀ **2000** Medium green-yellow, bright and clear; the bouquet exhibits very good fruit and oak balance and integration, just as it did 12 months ago, but it is the palate which has filled out and gained length, without losing the harmony and elegance it had as a young wine.   **rating:** 91

best drinking 2002–2005 **best vintages** '00 **drink with** Breast of chicken • $22

Pooley Wines Cooinda Vale Pinot Noir

ᵀᵀᵀᵀ **2000** Bright red-purple; the bouquet offers a complex mix of savoury/briary aromas on the one side, and plummy/black cherry on the other. It is the savoury aspects which come through most strongly on the relatively dry but well-balanced palate. Definitely at the austere end of the spectrum from the 2000 vintage.   **rating:** 88

best drinking 2002–2005 **best vintages** NA **drink with** Smoked quail • NA

poplar bend NR

RMB 8655 Main Creek Road, Main Ridge, Vic 3928 **region** Mornington Peninsula
phone (03) 5989 6046 **fax** (03) 5989 6460 **open** Weekends and public holidays 10–5 and by appointment
winemaker David Briggs **production** 350 **est.** 1988

product range ($16–28 ML) Pineau Chloe, Cabernet Chloe, Sparkling Chloe, Pinot Noir, Cellar Reserve Pinot Noir, Cabernet Shiraz.

summary Poplar Bend was the child of Melbourne journalist, author and raconteur Keith Dunstan and wife, Marie, who moved into full-scale retirement in 1997, selling Poplar Bend to David Briggs. The changes are few; the label still depicts Chloe in all her glory, which could be calculated to send the worthy inhabitants of the Bureau of Alcohol, Tobacco and Firearms (of the US) into a state of cataleptic shock.

port phillip estate ★★★★☆

261 Red Hill Road, Red Hill, Vic 3937 **region** Mornington Peninsula
phone (03) 5989 2708 **fax** (03) 5989 3017 **open** Weekends and public holidays 11–5
winemaker Lindsay McCall (Contract) **production** 4000 **est.** 1987
product range ($20–35 R) Sauvignon Blanc, Chardonnay, Pinot Noir, Reserve Pinot Noir, Reserve Shiraz, Shiraz.
summary Established by leading Melbourne QC Jeffrey Sher, who, after some prevarication, sold the estate to Giorgio and Dianne Gjergja in February 2000. The Gjergjas are rightly more than content with the quality and style of the wines; the main changes are enhanced cellar door facilities and redesigned labels.

Port Phillip Estate Sauvignon Blanc
▼▼▼▼ 2000 Medium yellow-green; opulent, decadent, tropical fruit aromas are followed by a rich, opulent palate, which, almost inevitably, has a slightly thick finish. **rating: 86**
best drinking 2002–2003 **best vintages** NA **drink with** Shellfish • $20

Port Phillip Estate Pinot Noir Reserve
▼▼▼▼▼ 2000 Bright, strong red-purple; a fragrant, ultra-ripe black cherry, blood plum and spice bouquet is repeated on the intense, multi-layered palate; excellent acidity adds to the length of a striking wine. **rating: 94**
best drinking 2002–2006 **best vintages** '97, '98, '99, '00 **drink with** Duck • $35

Port Phillip Estate Reserve Shiraz
▼▼▼▼▼ 2000 Medium red-purple; complex, very spicy multi-aromatics, then spice, black fruits, bitter chocolate and licorice feature on the palate, which has great texture and soft, fluffy tannins. **rating: 94**
best drinking 2005–2012 **best vintages** '97, '00 **drink with** Braised oxtail • $35

portree ★★★☆

72 Powells Track via Mount William Road, Lancefield, Vic 3455 **region** Macedon Ranges
phone (03) 5429 1422 **fax** (03) 5429 2205 **open** Weekends and public holidays 11–5
winemaker Ken Murchison **production** 800 **est.** 1983
product range ($15–35 CD) Chardonnay, Greenstone Chardonnay (unoaked), Macedon (Blanc de Blanc), Pinot Noir, Damask (Cabernet Franc Rosé), Quarry Red (Cabernet Franc Merlot).
summary Owner Ken Murchison selected his 4-hectare Macedon vineyard after studying viticulture at Charles Sturt University and being strongly influenced by Dr Andrew Pirie's doctoral thesis. All of the wines show distinct cool-climate characteristics, the Quarry Red having clear similarities to the wines of Chinon in the Loire Valley. However, it is Chardonnay that Portree has done best with; it is its principal wine (in terms of volume). As from the 1998 vintage, the wines have been made at an on-site winery.

port stephens wines NR

69 Nelson Bay Road, Bobs Farm, NSW 2316 **region** Northern Rivers Zone
phone (02) 4982 6411 **fax** (02) 4982 6766 **open** 7 days 10–5
winemaker Contract **production** 3500 **est.** 1984
product range ($10–21.50 CD) Chardonnay, Tri-Blend, Tomaree White, Late Harvest, Golden Sands, Shiraz, Cabernet Merlot, Cabernet Sauvignon, Sparkling and Fortifieds.
summary Planting of the quite substantial Port Stephens Wines vineyard began in 1984, and there are now 4 hectares of vines in production. The wines are made under contract by John Baruzzi at Wilderness Estate in the Hunter Valley, but are sold through an attractive, dedicated cellar-door sales outlet on-site.

pothana ★★★★☆

Carramar, Belford, NSW 2335 **region** Lower Hunter Valley
phone (02) 6574 7164 **fax** (02) 6574 7209 **open** By appointment
winemaker David Hook **production** 5000 **est.** 1984

product range ($14–30 R) Pothana Semillon, Chardonnay, Shiraz; also The Gorge range of Semillon, Semillon Sauvignon Blanc, Verdelho, Unwooded Chardonnay, Chardonnay, Pinot Noir, Shiraz. All are estate-grown; the Pothana range is produced in tiny quantities (250 cases) and then only in the best vintages.
summary David Hook has over 20 years' experience – as a winemaker for Tyrrell's and Lake's Folly, also doing the full flying winemaker bit, with jobs in Bordeaux, the Rhône Valley, Spain, the US and Georgia. He and his family began the establishment of the vineyard (in 1984) and the winery (in 1990). The wines are available by mailing list, but have distribution by Grapelink in NSW and Vic, and Prime Wines in Qld and Tas.

Pothana Belford Semillon

ŸŸŸŸ **2001** Very light straw-green; a clean, vibrant and crisp bouquet with lemon and grass aromas is followed by a palate with classic young semillon fruit flavour and vibrant, lemony acidity. **rating: 94**
ŸŸŸŸŸ **2000** Light straw-green; the bouquet is starting to develop some depth, with lemon and lanolin aromas; the palate, while delicate, has a touch of fruit sweetness on the mid-palate and overall is a total contrast in style to the 2001, partly due to the much higher alcohol (12.5°) and the warmer growing conditions for the 2000. **rating: 94**
best drinking 2006–2011 **best vintages** '00, '01 **drink with** Green salad • $22

Pothana Belford Chardonnay

ŸŸŸŸŸ **2001** Medium yellow-green; moderately intense, smooth white peach aromas mingle with well-balanced and integrated oak on the bouquet; the palate is well constructed and balanced, with attractive creamy nuances and, once again, subtle oak. **rating: 90**
ŸŸŸŸŸ **2000** Excellent bright, light yellow-green; an understated bouquet, fresh and clean, with nectarine fruit, is followed by a delicate, well-balanced palate showing sophisticated winemaking, and developing slowly; firmer than the 2001, and with a longer life in front of it. **rating: 90**
best drinking 2002–2005 **best vintages** '00, '01 **drink with** Fresh yabbies • $30

The Gorge Chardonnay

ŸŸŸŸŸ **2001** Light to medium yellow-green; fresh citrus and nectarine fruit aromas are repeated on the fresh, fruit-driven palate; pleasant unoaked style. **rating: 84**
best drinking 2002–2003 **best vintages** NA **drink with** Salmon pizza • $14

Pothana Shiraz

ŸŸŸŸŸ **2000** Medium to full red-purple; clean, smooth dark cherry and plum fruit intermingle with touches of regional earth on the bouquet; the rounded, rich and ripe – but not jammy – palate has the tannins to sustain the wine for the long term. **rating: 93**
ŸŸŸŸŸ **1999** Medium red-purple; a complex bouquet with savoury regional overtones coming through the mix of berry, earth, spice and leather is followed by a similarly complex and savoury palate, clearly reflecting the terroir, and in quite different style from the 2000. **rating: 90**
best drinking 2005–2015 **best vintages** '99, '00 **drink with** Braised oxtail • $30

The Gorge Shiraz

ŸŸŸŸ **2000** Medium to full red-purple; very ripe, prune and plum fruit aromas suggest some shrivel or raisining of the grapes; the fruit driven palate has masses of rich, plummy flavour; very good value. **rating: 88**
best drinking 2005–2010 **best vintages** NA **drink with** Rack of lamb • $16

potters clay vineyards ★★★

Main Road, Willunga, SA 5172 **region** McLaren Vale
phone (08) 8556 2799 **fax** (08) 8556 2922 **open** Not
winemaker John Bruschi **production** 900 **est.** 1994
product range ($15.90–16.90 R) Chardonnay, Shiraz, Merlot Cabernet Franc.
summary John and Donna Bruschi are second generation grapegrowers who assumed full ownership of the 16-hectare Potters Clay Vineyard in 1994 with the aim of establishing their own winery and label. In 1999 construction of stage one of a two-stage boutique winery was completed. Stage one is a winery production facility, stage two (at some future date) is to be a cellar door, restaurant and garden/picnic area. At least this is in the correct order; all too often it is the cellar door and restaurant which come first. The clever packaging and high-quality promotional literature should do much to enhance sales.

powercourt vineyard NR

2 McEwans Road, Legana, Tas 7277 **region** Northern Tasmania
phone (03) 6330 1225 **fax** (03) 6330 2161 **open** By appointment

winemaker Ralph Power **production** 1000 **est.** 1972
product range ($18 CD) Pinot Noir, Cabernet Pinot, Cabernet Sauvignon.
summary A long-established but ultra-low profile winery with a mostly local clientele, plus retail distribution in Canberra.

preston peak ★★★

31 Preston Peak Lane, Toowoomba, Qld 4352 **region** Granite Belt
phone (07) 4630 9499 **fax** (07) 4630 9499 **open** Wed–Fri 11–3, weekends 10–5
winemaker Philippa Hambleton, Rod MacPherson **production** 5500 **est.** 1994
product range ($11–28 CD) Code Flag White, Reserve Chardonnay, Leaf Series Chardonnay, Code Flag Red, Wild Flower White, Wild Flower Red, Venus, Leaf Series Shiraz, Cabernet Merlot, Cabernets, sparkling and fortified.
summary The ambitious growth plans of dentist owners Ashley Smith and Kym Thumpkin have seemingly slowed to a more realistic level; winemaking continues at Wyberba, with the proposed winery at Toowoomba on hold, but cellar door sales take place there.

Preston Peak Reserve Shiraz

▼▼▼▽ **1999** Light to medium red-purple; a clean, fresh bouquet with light red cherry fruit is followed by a fresh, clean, direct and simple palate.   **rating: 83**

best drinking 2001–2004 **best vintages** NA **drink with** Spaghetti bolognese • $28

Preston Peak Leaf Series Cabernet Merlot

▼▼▼▽ **2000** Light to medium red-purple; the clean, light bouquet offers fresh berry fruit which is also present on the early palate, although the finish is rather fuzzy and blurred.   **rating: 82**

best drinking 2001–2004 **best vintages** NA **drink with** Pasta • $19

primo estate ★★★★★

Old Port Wakefield Road, Virginia, SA 5120 **region** Adelaide Plains
phone (08) 8380 9442 **fax** (08) 8380 9696 **open** June–Aug Mon–Sat 10–4, Sep–May Mon–Fri 10–4
winemaker Joseph Grilli **production** 20 000 **est.** 1979
product range ($13–55 R) La Biondina Colombard, Joseph La Magia Botrytis Riesling, Il Briccone Shiraz Sangiovese, Joseph Moda Amarone Cabernet Merlot, Joseph The Fronti, Joseph Sparkling Red.
summary Roseworthy dux Joe Grilli has risen way above the constraints of the hot Adelaide Plains to produce an innovative and always excellent range of wines. The biennial release of the Joseph Sparkling Red (in its tall Italian glass bottle) is eagerly awaited, the wine immediately selling out. Also unusual and highly regarded are the vintage-dated extra virgin olive oils. However, the core lies with the zingy, fresh Colombard, the velvet-smooth Adelaide Shiraz and the distinguished, complex Joseph Cabernet Merlot. National distribution through Negociants; exports to the UK, Asia, Europe and Japan.

Primo Estate La Biondina Colombard

▼▼▼▼▽ **2001** Excellent green-yellow; the fresh, lively and tangy bouquet with its citrus/mineral mix reminiscent of Sauvignon Blanc, is followed by an abundantly flavoured but fresh palate with a twist of spritz.

rating: 92

best drinking 2001–2002 **best vintages** '99, '00, '01 **drink with** Shellfish • $14.50

Primo Estate Joseph Sparkling Red

▼▼▼▼▽ **NV** Medium red-purple; the complex mix of berry, sweet earth and touches of leather and spice on the bouquet is followed by a similarly complex palate with berry fruit to the fore, then hints of spice and chocolate, and a nice, dry finish. Has the texture, balance and appeal which so many sparkling red wines utterly fail to produce.   **rating: 92**

best drinking 2002–2010 **best vintages** NA **drink with** Borscht • $55

Primo Estate Il Briccone Shiraz Sangiovese

▼▼▼▼▽ **2000** Medium purple-red; the fragrant cherry/cherry pip bouquet is bright and fresh; the palate follows on logically, with an attractive, early drinking mix of savoury and fresh cherry fruit.   **rating: 90**

best drinking 2001–2003 **best vintages** '00 **drink with** Bruschetta • $20

Primo Estate Joseph Moda Amarone Cabernet Merlot

TTTTY **1999** Medium red, starting to show some development. The bouquet is complex, with ripe plum and blackberry, supported by touches of prune, spice and cedar. Then follows noticeably ripe fruit on the mid-palate in a plummy/pruney spectrum, with savoury tannins providing balance to the finish. **rating:** 90

best drinking 2003–2009 **best vintages** '81, '84, '86, '90, '91, '93, '94, '95, '96, '97, '98 **drink with** Bistecca Fiorentina • $45

prince albert ★★★★☆

100 Lemins Road, Waurn Ponds, Vic 3216 **region** Geelong
phone (03) 5241 8091 **fax** (03) 5241 8091 **open** By appointment
winemaker Bruce Hyett **production** 500 **est.** 1975
product range ($29 ML) Pinot Noir.
summary Australia's true Pinot Noir specialist (it has only ever made the one wine), which also made much of the early running with the variety: the wines always show good varietal character and have rebounded after a dull patch in the second half of the 1980s. In 1998 the vineyard and winery were certified organic by OVAA Inc. Apart from the mailing list, the wine is sold through fine wine retailers in Sydney and Melbourne, with a little finding its way to the UK.

provenance wines ★★★☆

PO Box 74, Bannockburn, Vic 3331 **region** Geelong
phone (03) 5281 7477 **fax** (03) 5281 7377 **open** Not
winemaker Scott Ireland **production** 1200 **est.** 1995
product range ($22–27 R) Pinot Gris, Chardonnay, Pinot Noir, Merlot, Shiraz.
summary Provenance is the reborn Melbourne Wine Company, with Scott Ireland its principal and sole winemaker. All of the wine is sourced from the Geelong region, and is competently made as one would expect from such an experienced winemaker. Scott Ireland also contract-makes for others.

Provenance Pinot Gris

TTTT **2000** Bronze pink; rose petal, peach skin and apple aromas are followed by a palate with power and grip if not a little grippy. All in all, certainly not short on authority or interest. **rating:** 87

best drinking 2001–2004 **best vintages** NA **drink with** Seafood risotto • $23

providence vineyards ★★★★★

236 Lalla Road, Lalla, Tas 7267 **region** Northern Tasmania
phone (03) 6395 1290 **fax** (03) 6395 1290 **open** 7 days 10–5
winemaker Andrew Hood (Contract) **production** 600 **est.** 1956
product range ($17–35 CD) Riesling, Semillon, Botrytis Semillon, Chardonnay, Pinot Noir; in exceptional years may be released under the Miguet label.
summary Providence incorporates the pioneer vineyard of Frenchman Jean Miguet, now owned by the Bryce family, which purchased it in 1980. The original 1.3-hectare vineyard has been expanded to a little over 3 hectares, as well as grafting over unsuitable grenache and cabernet (left from the original plantings) to chardonnay and pinot noir and semillon. Miguet in fact called the vineyard 'La Provence', reminding him of the part of France whence he came, but after 40 years the French authorities forced a name change to Providence.

Providence Botrytis Semillon

TTTT **2001** Medium yellow-green; an unusually complex bouquet, with a mix of strong, spicy oak and lanolin overlying the fruit. The palate is less complex, but is intensely sweet, and also quite oaky. **rating:** 87

best drinking 2002–2005 **best vintages** NA **drink with** Rich tart • $21.50

Providence Miguet Reserve Pinot Noir

TTTTT **2000** Medium red-purple; the smooth bouquet has perfectly ripened plum fruit at its heart, with a touch of spice around the perimeter; the palate is in typical Miguet Reserve style, with plum and spice flavours, perfectly ripened fruit and fine tannins contributing to the silky texture. Perhaps not quite up to the 1999 vintage, but a great wine nonetheless. Gold medal at the 2002 Tasmanian Wines Show. **rating:** 95

TTTTT **1999** Medium red-purple; the bouquet is both complex and potent, with spice, licorice and a hint of game; the palate is at once very complex yet elegant, the complexity coming from the plum, spice and ripe fruit flavours, the elegance from the silky texture and fine tannin finish. **rating:** 97

best drinking 2002–2007 **best vintages** '99, '00 **drink with** Breast of duck • $34

punters corner ★★★★☆

Cnr Riddoch Highway and Racecourse Road, Coonawarra, SA 5263 **region** Coonawarra
phone (08) 8737 2007 **fax** (08) 8737 3138 **open** 7 days 10–5
winemaker Peter Bissell (Contract) **production** 10 000 **est.** 1988
product range ($12–60 CD) Riesling, Chardonnay, Shiraz, Spartacus Reserve Shiraz, Cabernet Merlot,
Cabernet Sauvignon, Cabernet.
summary The quaintly named Punters Corner started life in 1975 as James Haselgrove, but in 1992 was
acquired by a group of investors who quite evidently had few delusions about the uncertainties of
viticulture and winemaking, even in a district as distinguished as Coonawarra. The arrival of Peter Bissell as
winemaker at Balnaves paid immediate (and continuing) dividends. Sophisticated packaging and label design
add to the appeal of the wines. National retail distribution; exports to the US, Canada, Malaysia, Singapore,
Japan, New Zealand, Belgium, Switzerland, Italy and Holland.

Punters Corner Chardonnay

TTTT 2000 Light to medium yellow-green; a clean, smooth bouquet with nectarine interwoven with
subtle vanilla oak is followed by a lively, fresh, nectarine-accented palate, finishing with good acidity and a
background hint of vanilla. **rating:** 88

best drinking 2001–2004 **best vintages** NA **drink with** Creamed scallops • $20

Punters Corner Shiraz

TTTTY 2000 Full red-purple; has dark berry fruit and touches of earth and chocolate on both the bouquet
and palate, the latter having good texture and weight. Impressive for an intermediate vintage. **rating:** 91

best drinking 2005–2010 **best vintages** '97, '00 **drink with** Game pie • $29

Punters Corner Spartacus Reserve Shiraz

TTTTT 2000 Full red-purple; the bouquet has more concentrated fruit than the varietal, but with a similar
set of aromas. Delicious dark cherry and plum fruit are the core of a fruit-dominant palate, complemented
by subtle oak and fine tannins. **rating:** 95

TTTTT 1999 Dense red-purple; the bouquet is crammed with rich and ripe blackberry, chocolate and
vanilla aromatics; the palate is mouthfilling, but shows exemplary handling of the total extract. Dark berry
fruits and harmonious oak feature in an unusually supple wine. **rating:** 95

best drinking 2005–2015 **best vintages** '98, '99, '00 **drink with** Aged Warrnambool T-bone • $60

Punters Corner Cabernet Sauvignon

TTTTY 2000 Dense red-purple; in the mainstream of the Punters Corner style, with ripe blackcurrant,
cassis and mulberry fruit on the bouquet, and similar dense flavours plus a touch of dark chocolate on the
palate; again consistently with the style, oak is present but plays a secondary role. **rating:** 91

TTTTY 1999 Medium to full red-purple; ripe, cassis/blackberry fruit aromas are neatly set against gently
spicy oak on the bouquet. The palate offers sweet, ripe yet savoury blackcurrant fruit; the structure, length
and tannin management are exemplary. **rating:** 93

best drinking 2005–2012 **best vintages** '98, '99, '00 **drink with** Yearling beef • $30

Punters Corner Cabernet

TTTTY 2000 Medium to full red-purple; ripe, sweet blackberry and cassis fruit on the bouquet are
followed by a sweet, ripe and supple palate with a mix of cassis and blackberry fruit, then fine tannins to
close. **rating:** 90

TTTT 1999 Medium red-purple; the overall cast of the aromas of the bouquet is distinctly sweet, with a
mix of cassis, berry and even licorice; the palate follows through with savoury/spicy red and blackberry
fruit, supported by fine, silky tannins on the finish. **rating:** 89

best drinking 2005 2011 best vintages '00 drink with Spiced rack of lamb • $25

🐀 pyrenees ridge vineyard ★★★★

Lot 6 Caralulup Road, Bung Bong via Avoca, Vic 3467 **region** Pyrenees
phone (03) 5465 3710 **fax** (03) 5465 3320 **open** By appointment
winemaker Graeme Jukes **production** 500 **est.** 1998
product range ($28 R) Shiraz, Cabernet Shiraz, Cabernet Sauvignon.
summary Notwithstanding the quite extensive winemaking experience (and formal training) of Graeme
Jukes, this is small-scale winemaking in the raw, an estate-based version of the French garagiste winemaking
approach. Together with wife Sally-Ann, Graeme Jukes has planted 1.5 hectares of cabernet sauvignon and

0.5 hectare of shiraz, with a further hectare of shiraz to be planted in 2002; the cabernet intake is supplemented by purchases from other growers in the region. Australian Prestige Wines distributes limited quantities of the wine in Melbourne, with a tiny percentage going overseas; the rest is sold by mail order, but a cellar door is to be opened before the end of 2002.

Pyrenees Ridge Vineyard Cabernet Shiraz

ꔛꔛꔛꔛ **2000** Dense red-purple; powerful blackberry and plum fruit plus plenty of oak on the bouquet are followed by a dense, concentrated, chewy palate which demands 5 years' (minimum) cellaring, but which will amply repay patience. **rating: 89**

best drinking 2005–2015 **best vintages** NA **drink with** Marinated venison • $28

queen adelaide ★★☆

Sturt Highway, Waikerie, SA 5330 **region** Barossa Valley
phone (08) 8541 2588 **fax** (08) 8541 3877 **open** Not
winemaker Peter Gajewski, Sue Franke **production** 800 000 **est.** 1858
product range ($6–7 R) Rhine Riesling, Chenin Blanc, Semillon Chardonnay, Chardonnay, Spätlese Lexia, Sauvignon Blanc, Regency Red, Shiraz, Grenache Pinot Noir, Cabernet Sauvignon.
summary The famous brand established by Woodley Wines and some years ago subsumed into the Seppelt and now Southcorp Group. It is a pure brand, without any particular home either in terms of winemaking or fruit sources, but is hugely successful; Queen Adelaide Chardonnay is and has for some time been the largest-selling bottled white wine in Australia. The move away from agglomerate to synthetic corks should end the glue-taint problems of prior years.

Queen Adelaide Pinot Noir

ꔛꔛꔛꔛ **2001** Medium red-purple; the bouquet is clean, with light red fruit aromas; the palate has attractive fruit and some tannins. There is no varietal character, but at this price it probably barely matters. **rating: 82**

best drinking 2001–2002 **best vintages** NA **drink with** Summer lunches • $7

raleigh winery NR

Queen Street, Raleigh, NSW 2454 **region** Northern Rivers Zone
phone (02) 6655 4388 **fax** (02) 6655 4265 **open** 7 days 10–5
winemaker Lavinia Dingle **production** 1000 **est.** 1982
product range ($13–25 CD) Semillon Chardonnay, Traminer Riesling, Rouge (Rosé), Late Harvest, Shiraz Cabernet Merlot, Port.
summary Raleigh Winery lays claim to being Australia's most easterly vineyard. The vineyard was initiated in 1982 and was purchased by Lavinia and Neil Dingle in 1989, with the wine produced in part from 1 hectare of vines planted to no less than 6 varieties. The wines have won bronze medals at the Griffith Wine Show.

ralph fowler wines NR

Limestone Coast Road, Mount Benson, SA 5265 **region** Mount Benson
phone (08) 8365 6968 **fax** (08) 8365 2516 **open** Mon–Fri 9–5
winemaker Ralph Fowler **production** 6500 **est.** 1999
product range ($18–38 R) Limestone Coast Sauvignon Blanc, Limestone Coast Shiraz, Limestone Coast Cabernet Sauvignon.
summary Established in February 1999 by the Fowler family, headed by well-known winemaker Ralph Fowler, with wife Deborah and children Sarah (currently studying Wine Science) and James. All are involved in the 40-hectare vineyard property at Mount Benson. Ralph Fowler began his winemaking career at Tyrrell's, moving to the position of chief winemaker before moving to Hungerford Hill, and then the Hamilton/Leconfield group. He thus brings great experience to the venture. Interestingly, he has planted two varieties to provide the flagship wines: shiraz and viognier.

ramsay's vin rosé ★★★

30 St Helier Road, The Gurdies, Vic 3984 **region** Gippsland
phone (03) 5997 6531 **fax** (03) 5997 6158 **open** Wed–Mon 12–5
winemaker Dianne Ramsay, Roger Cutler **production** 220 **est.** 1995
product range ($8–18 CD) Riesling, Satin Rosé (dry), Satin Rosé (sweet), Cabernet Sauvignon.

summary The slightly curious name (which looks decidedly strange in conjunction with Riesling and Cabernet Sauvignon) stems from the original intention of Alan and Dianne Ramsay to grow roses on a commercial scale on their property. Frank Cutler, at Western Port Winery, persuaded them to plant wine grapes instead, establishing the first 2 hectares of vines in 1995. They opened their micro winery in 1999, and now also have 4 two-bedroom self-contained units set around their 800-bush rose garden. The pinot noir and chardonnay are sold to Diamond Valley, so for the time being the range of wines released is limited to Riesling, a Cabernet Franc–based Rosé and Cabernet Sauvignon, with a Merlot maturing in barrel. Ultimately, the Ramsays hope to use all of the estate grapes for their wines.

ravenswood lane ★★★★☆

Ravenswood Lane, Hahndorf, SA 5245 **region** Adelaide Hills
phone (08) 8388 1250 **fax** (08) 8388 7233 **open** Not
winemaker Robert Mann, Stephen Pannell (Red), Glenn James (White) at Hardys **production** 12 800 **est.** 1993
product range ($18–49 R) The Gathering Sauvignon Blanc, Beginning Chardonnay, Reunion Shiraz; Starvedog Lane Sauvignon Blanc, Chardonnay, Sparkling, Shiraz, Cabernet Sauvignon, Sparkling.
summary With their sales and marketing background, John and Helen Edwards opted for a major lifestyle change when they began the establishment of the first of the present 28.1 hectares of vineyards in 1993. Initially, part of the production was sold to BRL Hardy, but now some of the wine is made for release under the Ravenswood Lane label. A joint venture with BRL Hardy is Starvedog Lane, producing wines from a patchwork of vineyards throughout the Adelaide Hills. Exports to the UK and Singapore.

Starvedog Lane Sauvignon Blanc

TTTTY 2001 Light green-straw; the moderately intense bouquet has a range of ripe gooseberry and rather more tropical aromas; the palate has good length and intensity, with attractive lemony fruit and that squeaky acidity which comes as you move the wine around your mouth. **rating: 93**
best drinking 2001–2003 **best vintages** '01 **drink with** Marinated fish • $19

Ravenswood Lane The Gathering Sauvignon Blanc

TTTY 2001 Medium yellow-green; the bouquet is clean, moderately intense, but not showing a great deal of varietal character. The palate provides more of the same, with fair length and balance; appears to be a victim of the vintage. **rating: 84**
best drinking 2001–2002 **best vintages** '99, '00 **drink with** Coquilles St Jacque • $25

Starvedog Lane Chardonnay Pinot Noir Pinot Meunier

TTTT 1998 Pale straw-green; the bouquet is fine and well balanced, with a touch of tangy complexity. The palate is driven by fresh fruit and lively acidity; it is very direct, and needs a few more winemaking thumbprints for top points. **rating: 88**
best drinking 2001–2002 **best vintages** NA **drink with** Aperitif • $27

Starvedog Lane Shiraz

TTTTY 1999 Medium red-purple; a fruit-driven, moderately intense, fresh red berry bouquet is followed by a palate with more substance, thanks in part to some clever use of oak. **rating: 92**
best drinking 2003–2008 **best vintages** '97, '98, '99 **drink with** Turkish lamb pizza • $27

ray-monde NR

250 Dalrymple Road, Sunbury, Vic 3429 **region** Sunbury
phone (03) 5428 2657 **fax** (03) 5428 3390 **open** Sundays or by appointment
winemaker John Lakey **production** 700 **est.** 1900
product range ($25–27 CD) Pinot Noir.
summary The Lakey family has established 5 hectares of pinot noir on their 230-hectare grazing property at an altitude of 400 metres. Initially the grapes were sold to Domaine Chandon, but in 1994 son John Lakey (who had gained experience at Tarrawarra, Rochford, Virgin Hills and Coonawarra, plus a vintage in Burgundy) commenced making the wine – and very competently.

reads NR

Evans Lane, Oxley, Vic 3678 **region** King Valley
phone (03) 5727 3386 **fax** (03) 5727 3559 **open** Mon–Sat 9–5, Sun 10–6
winemaker Kenneth Read **production** 1900 **est.** 1972

product range ($7.50–13 CD) Riesling, Chardonnay, Sauvignon Blanc, Crouchen, Cabernet Shiraz, Cabernet Sauvignon, Port.

summary Limited tastings have not impressed, but there may be a jewel lurking somewhere, such as the medal-winning though long-gone 1990 Sauvignon Blanc. No tastings for some time.

redbank winery ★★★★

Sunraysia Highway, Redbank, Vic 3467 **region** Pyrenees
phone (03) 5467 7255 **fax** (03) 5467 7248 **open** Mon–Sat 9–5, Sun 10–5
winemaker Neill Robb **production** 58 000 **est.** 1973
product range ($12–50 R) The range centres on a series of evocatively named red wines, with Sally's Paddock the flagship; then Rising Chardonnay, Sunday Morning Pinot Gris, Frenchman's Pinot Noir, Fighting Flat Shiraz and Percydale Cabernet Merlot. Long Paddock Shiraz Cabernet, Long Paddock Chardonnay and Emily Pinot Chardonnay Brut Cuvée are cheaper, larger-volume second labels.
summary Neill Robb makes very concentrated wines, full of character; the levels of volatile acidity can sometimes be intrusive but are probably of more concern to technical tasters than to the general public. Sally's Paddock is the star, a single vineyard block with an esoteric mix of cabernet, shiraz and malbec which over the years has produced many great wines.

red clay estate ★★★☆

269 Henry Lawson Drive, Mudgee, NSW 2850 **region** Mudgee
phone (02) 6372 4569 **fax** (02) 6372 4596 **open** Jan–Sept 7 days 10–5, Oct–Dec Mon–Fri 10–5 or by appointment
winemaker Ken Heslop **production** NA **est.** 1997
product range Cabernet Shiraz Merlot.
summary Ken Heslop and Annette Bailey are among the recent arrivals in Mudgee, with a 2.5-hectare vineyard planted to a diverse range of varieties. The wines are exclusively sold through the cellar door and by mail order.

Red Clay Estate Cabernet Merlot

▼▼▼▼ 2000 Medium to full red-purple; a big, powerful wine with plenty of red and black berry fruit supported by very evident vanilla oak. **rating:** 87

best drinking 2004–2010 **best vintages** NA **drink with** Smoked lamb • $20

red edge ★★★★★

Golden Gully Road, Heathcote, Vic 3523 **region** Bendigo
phone (03) 9337 5695 **fax** (03) 9337 7550 **open** By appointment
winemaker Peter Dredge, Judy Dredge **production** 500 **est.** 1971
product range ($29–40 R) Shiraz, Cabernet Sauvignon.
summary Red Edge is a new name on the scene, but the vineyard dates back to 1971, at the renaissance of the Victorian wine industry. In the early 1980s it produced the wonderful wines of Flynn & Williams; it has now been rehabilitated by Peter and Judy Dredge, and produced two quite lovely wines in their inaugural 1997 vintage. For the time being, at least, Peter Dredge continues to keep body and soul together by making the wines at Wildwood and at Witchmount Estate, Rockbank. Trying to eke a living out of 500 cases of what in these days are moderately priced wines is simply not possible.

Red Edge Shiraz

▼▼▼▼▼ 2000 Impenetrable stygian purple-red; staining the glass as you swirl the wine. Luscious, almost essency, plum and blackberry fruit exude from the bouquet, foretelling a quite massive wine on the palate, as concentrated and as powerful as they come, with drying, spicy tannins on the finish. The wine is neither fined nor filtered, and notwithstanding the fact that Robert Parker must surely give the wine 100 points, it might have benefited from one or the other. As it is, leave it undisturbed for not less than 10 years and then kill an ox. **rating:** 94

best drinking 2010–2020 **best vintages** '97, '98, '99, '00 **drink with** Leave it in the cellar • $40

Red Edge Cabernet Sauvignon

▼▼▼▼ 2000 Deep, dark purple-red; dark blackberry/blackcurrant fruit on the bouquet has eaten up the oak, but on the palate the tannins really take over, eating up the fruit. Certainly give it 10 years if you decide to buy it, but I have reservations about the tannins ever softening before the fruit fades. **rating:** 89

best drinking 2010–2025 **best vintages** '97, '98, '99 **drink with** Leave it in the cellar • $37

redgate ★★★★

Boodjidup Road, Margaret River, WA 6285 **region** Margaret River
phone (08) 9757 6488 **fax** (08) 9757 6308 **open** 7 days 10–5
winemaker Andrew Forsell **production** 14 000 **est.** 1977
product range ($14–32.50 CD) Sauvignon Blanc Reserve, Chardonnay, OFS Semillon, Chenin, Late
Harvest Riesling, Pinot Noir, Cabernet Franc, Cabernet Merlot, Cabernet Sauvignon, White Port.
summary Twenty hectares of vineyard provide the base for a substantial winery, which probably has a lower
profile than it deserves. The wines do have limited distribution in the eastern states, and export markets in
Singapore, Hong Kong, Canada, Japan, Denmark, Switzerland and the UK have been established.

Redgate Sauvignon Blanc Reserve

♥♥♥♥♡ **2000** Light green-yellow; a complex mix of gooseberry-accented fruit and spicy nutmeg oak on
the bouquet is repeated on the palate; the clever use of oak doesn't swamped the fruit, and the wine has a
lively, fresh, dry finish. **rating:** 91

best drinking 2001–2003 **best vintages** '99, '00 **drink with** Creamy seafood pasta • $17

Redgate Cabernet Merlot

♥♥♥♥ **1999** Medium red-purple; the tangy, spicy bouquet shows a strong Merlot influence; the palate has
a range of essentially spicy and savoury characters, sweetened up by a gentle hint of vanilla oak. **rating:** 85

best drinking 2003–2007 **best vintages** NA **drink with** Marinated venison • $26

red hill estate ★★★★

53 Redhill–Shoreham Road, Red Hill South, Vic 3937 **region** Mornington Peninsula
phone (03) 5989 2838 **fax** (03) 5989 2855 **open** 7 days 11–5
winemaker Michael Kyberd **production** 20 000 **est.** 1989
product range ($15–36 CD) Particular emphasis on Méthode Champenoise, but also producing
Unoaked Chardonnay, Chardonnay, Riesling, Sauvignon Blanc, Hill Block Pinot (Rosé), Pinot Noir and
Cabernet Sauvignon; also Muscat (from Rutherglen material) available cellar-door only.
summary Sir Peter Derham and family completed the construction of an on-site winery in time for the
1993 vintage, ending a period in which the wines were made at various wineries under contract
arrangements. The 10-hectare vineyard is one of the larger plantings on the Mornington Peninsula, and the
tasting room and restaurant have a superb view across the vineyard to Westernport Bay and Phillip Island.
Production continues to surge, and the winery goes from strength to strength.

Red Hill Estate Chardonnay

♥♥♥♥♡ **2000** Light to medium green-yellow; tangy, citrussy stone fruit aromas are supported by subtle oak
and malolactic influences on the bouquet. The palate is fresh, clean and crisp, with very similar citrus and
stone fruit flavours; good length and acidity. **rating:** 92

best drinking 2001–2005 **best vintages** '98, '00 **drink with** Seafood • $20

Red Hill Estate Blanc de Blanc

♥♥♥♥ **1998** Medium yellow-green; the intense, fruit-driven bouquet exudes melon and citrus; the palate is
bright, with extra length and focus, and just a hint of creamy/nutty complexity, presumably from yeast
autolysis rather than malolactic fermentation which, so far as I know, is not part of this style. **rating:** 89

best drinking 2002–2003 **best vintages** NA **drink with** Aperitif • $26

Red Hill Estate Pinot Noir

♥♥♥♥ **2000** Medium red-purple; the moderately intense bouquet offers a mix of red fruit and forest
aromas; the palate is fresh and still quite firm; cherry/strawberry fruit has a particularly lively finish and
aftertaste. The wine is still to build its latent complexity. **rating:** 87

best drinking 2002–2006 **best vintages** '99 **drink with** Tea-smoked duck • $20

Red Hill Estate Shiraz

♥♥♥♥ **2000** Medium to full red-purple; the very ripe bouquet is a reflection of the warm vintage, with dark
cherry/berry fruit and no spice obvious. The rich, ripe palate opens with plummy fruit, then a touch of
spice, rounded off with soft, ripe tannins. The 14° alcohol reflects the unusually warm vintage. **rating:** 88

best drinking 2003–2008 **best vintages** NA **drink with** Game pie • $25

red rock winery   NR

Red Rock Reserve Road, Alvie, Vic 3249 **region** Geelong
phone (03) 5234 8382 **open** Wed–Sun 10–5
winemaker Rohan Little **production** 5000 **est.** 1981
product range ($15–25 R) Semillon Sauvignon, Chardonnay, Pinot Noir, Shiraz, also MC (Méthode Champenoise).
summary The former Barongvale Estate, with 8 hectares of sauvignon blanc, semillon, pinot noir, and shiraz; a part-time occupation for Rohan Little, with wines sold under both the Red Rock and Otway Vineyards labels. The winery cafe opened in early 2002.

redman   ★★★★

Riddoch Highway, Coonawarra, SA 5253 **region** Coonawarra
phone (08) 8736 3331 **fax** (08) 8736 3013 **open** Mon–Fri 9–5, weekends 10–4
winemaker Bruce Redman, Malcolm Redman **production** 18 000 **est.** 1966
product range ($13–25.95 R) Shiraz, Cabernet Sauvignon Merlot, Cabernet Sauvignon.
summary After a prolonged period of mediocrity, the Redman wines are showing sporadic signs of improvement, partly through the introduction of modest amounts of new oak, even if principally American. It would be nice to say the wines now reflect the full potential of the vineyard, but there is still some way to go.

reedy creek vineyard   NR

Reedy Creek via Tenterfield, NSW 2372 **region** Northern Slopes Zone
phone (02) 6737 5221 **fax** (02) 6737 5200 **open** 7 days 9–5
winemaker Contract **production** 2800 **est.** 1971
product range ($13–17 CD) Bianco Alpino, Chardonnay, Unwooded Chardonnay, Rosso Alpino, Shiraz Mourvèdre, Old Vine Shiraz, Merlot, Durif, Liqueur Muscat, Red Deer Port.
summary Like so many Italian settlers in the Australian countryside, the De Stefani family has been growing grapes and making wine for its own consumption for over 30 years at its Reedy Creek property near Tenterfield, in the far north of NSW. What is more, like their compatriots in the King Valley, the family's principal activity until 1993 was growing tobacco; the continued rationalisation of the tobacco industry prompted the De Stefanis to turn a hobby into a commercial exercise. The vineyard has now been expanded to 6.1 hectares, and the first commercial vintage of Shiraz was made in 1995, with Chardonnay following in 1998. The wines are sold through the cellar door, from the maturation cellar which was opened in 1997.

rees miller estate   ★★★☆

5355 Goulburn Highway, Yea, Vic 3717 **region** Central Victorian High Country
phone (03) 5797 2101 **fax** (03) 5797 3276 **open** Weekends and public holidays 10–5
winemaker David Miller **production** 1000 **est.** 1996
product range ($22–40 CD) Meadows Hill Chardonnay, Pinot Noir, Manytrees Shiraz Viognier, Eildon Shiraz.
summary Partners Sylke Rees and David Miller purchased the 64-hectare property in 1998, with 1 hectare of pinot noir (planted in 1996). They have since extended the plantings with another block of pinot noir, 3 hectares of cabernet sauvignon, 1 hectare each of merlot and shiraz, and 0.5 hectare of cabernet franc, all of which came into production in 2002. The property was originally used for grazing; the sheep on the property are now Wiltshire Horn and Dorper, which shed their own wool. This has enabled the partners to convert the shearing shed into a cellar and cellar door, building a small adjacent winery. Sylke Rees has completed a Diploma of Viticulture and manages the vineyard, and both of them have completed short courses in winemaking, which is under David Miller's control. The cellar door opened in August 2001.

Rees Miller Estate Meadows Hill Chardonnay

♥♥♥♡ **2000** Bright, light to medium green-yellow; some smoky barrel-ferment characters join with citrus fruit on the bouquet, then melon and citrus plus barrel-ferment on the palate; the wine softens/cloys slightly on the finish.   **rating: 84**
best drinking 2001–2003 **best vintages** NA **drink with** Chinese-style prawns • $25

Rees Miller Estate Eildon Shiraz

♥♥♥♥ **2000** Appealing purple-red; the bouquet is clean, with a direct thrust of plum, mint and cherry supported by nicely weighted oak. Ripe plum and raspberry flavours are supported by soft tannins which run through from the mid-palate onwards, the oak handling once again being spot on.   **rating: 89**
best drinking 2001–2010 **best vintages** NA **drink with** Braised ox tail • $22

Rees Miller Estate Manytrees Shiraz Viognier

TTTTY 2000 Medium to full red-purple; smooth, clean dark berry, plum and spice fruit are perfectly balanced and integrated with vanilla oak on the bouquet. The palate is luscious, but not jammy, with interesting cool- climate flavours underwritten by complex, fine tannins. **rating:** 90

best drinking 2003–2010 **best vintages** NA **drink with** Braised duck • $40

reg drayton wines ★★★☆

Cnr Pokolbin Mountain and McDonalds Roads, Pokolbin, NSW 2320 **region** Lower Hunter Valley
phone (02) 4998 7523 **fax** (02) 4998 7523 **open** 7 days 10–5
winemaker James Estate (Contract) **production** 4000 **est.** 1989
product range ($17–28 CD) Lambkin Semillon, Lambkin Verdelho, Pokolbin Hills Chardonnay, Pokolbin Hills Chardonnay Semillon, Pamela Robyn Sparkling Chardonnay, Three Sons Shiraz, Pokolbin Hills Shiraz, Pokolbin Hills Cabernet Shiraz, Port.
summary Reg and Pam Drayton were among the victims of the Seaview/Lord Howe Island air crash in October 1984, having established Reg Drayton Wines after selling their interest in the long-established Drayton Family Winery. Their daughter Robyn (a fifth-generation Drayton and billed as the Hunter's first female vigneron) and husband Craig continue the business, which draws chiefly upon the Pokolbin Hills Estate but also takes fruit from the historic Lambkin Estate vineyard. The wines are made for them at James Estate.

reilly's wines ★★★☆

Cnr Hill and Burra Streets, Mintaro, SA 5415 **region** Clare Valley
phone (08) 8843 9013 **fax** (08) 8843 9013 **open** 7 days 10–5
winemaker Justin Ardill **production** 5000 **est.** 1994
product range ($12–40 CD) Watervale Riesling, Semillon, St Clare Semillon, Chardonnay, Sparkling Grenache, Late Picked Riesling, Old Bushvine Grenache, Block 1919 Grenache Shiraz, Clare Valley Shiraz, Dry Land Shiraz, Cabernet Sauvignon, Port.
summary Justin and Julie Ardill are relative newcomers in the Clare Valley, with only half a dozen or so vintages under their belt. An unusual sideline of Reilly's Cottage is the production of an Extra Virgin Olive Oil; unusual in that it is made from wild olives found in the Mintaro district of the Clare Valley. Exports to the US, Ireland, Malaysia and Singapore.

Reilly's Shiraz

TTTT 1998 Medium red; there is a mix of minty/berry/savoury aromas, starting to show some bottle development. The palate has a mix of soft leather and earth notes together with black cherry fruit, which has seemingly swallowed up most of the American oak. **rating:** 85

best drinking 2001–2006 **best vintages** NA **drink with** Spaghetti bolognese • $25

Reilly's Dry Land Shiraz

TTTTY 1999 Good red-purple; a very powerful, earthy bouquet, bordering on astringency, is followed by a full-on palate, crammed with chocolate, blackberry and tannins. Could develop into something special in the long term. **rating:** 90

best drinking 2005–2015 **best vintages** NA **drink with** Leave it in the cellar • NA

Reilly's Dry Land Cabernet Sauvignon

TTTT 1999 Medium red-purple; the earthy/savoury/oaky aromas of the bouquet come through on the palate, which has fair length and depth, but is by no means luscious. **rating:** 85

best drinking 2003–2007 best vintages NA drink with Pastrami • NA

☜ reschke wines ★★★★☆

'Rocky Castle', Rocky Castle Road, Coonawarra, SA 5263 **region** Coonawarra
phone (08) 8363 3343 **fax** (08) 8363 9949 **open** Not
winemaker Martin Williams MW (Contract) **production** 1500 **est.** 1998
product range ($100 ML) Empyrean Cabernet Sauvignon.
summary It's not often that the first release from a new winery is priced at $100 per bottle, but that is precisely what Reschke Wines has achieved. The family has been a landholder in the Coonawarra region for almost 100 years, with a large landholding which is partly terra rossa, part woodland. Fifteen and a half hectares of merlot, 105 hectares of cabernet sauvignon, 0.5 hectare of cabernet franc and 2.5 hectares of

shiraz are in production, with a further 26 hectares planted prior to the end of 2001, mostly to shiraz, and with a little petit verdot. The first release of 1998 Empyrean Cabernet Sauvignon, immaculately packaged, was an exceptionally good wine; the 1999 was a partial return to earth.

Reschke Empyrean Cabernet Sauvignon

TTTT 1999 Medium to full red-purple; a complex, quite aromatic bouquet with smooth berry fruit, cedar and vanilla oak, then a light to medium-bodied palate, with flavours in the berry/mint/leaf spectrum; pleasant mouthfeel and good length. To put it mildly, fully priced. **rating:** 87

TTTTY 1998 Dense purple-red; ultra-ripe, yet not jammy, cassis/blackberry fruit on the bouquet repeats on the ultra-rich mix of blackberry, blackcurrant, chocolate and cedar on the palate; lingering tannins, and a pronounced alcohol nip on the finish. There is doubtless a lot of new oak in the wine, but the fruit has utterly soaked up that oak. **rating:** 93

best drinking 2003–2008 **best vintages** '98 **drink with** Spit-roasted haunch of beef • $100

reynell ★★★★

Reynell Road, Reynella, SA 5161 **region** McLaren Vale
phone (08) 8392 2222 **fax** (08) 8392 2202 **open** 7 days 10–4, except public holidays
winemaker Stephen Pannell **production** NFP **est.** 1838
product range ($40.99 R) Basket Pressed Shiraz, Basket Pressed Merlot, Basket Pressed Cabernet Sauvignon.
summary Reynell is the name under which all wines from the historic Reynella winery (once called Chateau Reynella) are released. What is more, the range of wines was compressed and taken into the super-premium category with the introduction of the Basket Pressed range in 1997.

Reynell Basket Pressed Shiraz

TTTT 1999 Medium to full purple-red; clean dark berry and plum fruit aromas flow through from the bouquet into the palate, the latter ever so slightly marred by slightly green tannins. Nonetheless, a more than useful wine. **rating:** 88

best drinking 2004–2009 **best vintages** '94, '95, '96 **drink with** Barbecued rump steak • $40.99

reynolds ★★★★

'Quondong', Cargo Road, Cudal, NSW 2864 **region** Orange
phone (02) 6364 2330 **fax** (02) 6364 2388 **open** Not
winemaker Jon Reynolds, Nic Millichip, Tony Cosgriff **production** 50 000 **est.** 1989
product range ($15–28.99 CD) Wines from Orange are Sauvignon Blanc, Chardonnay, Merlot, Cabernet Sauvignon and the Portrait series of Moon Shadow Chardonnay, Marble Man Merlot and The Jezebel Cabernet Sauvignon; Handpicked Orange Sauvignon Blanc Semillon and Handpicked Cabernet Merlot.
summary In 2000 the Reynolds brand was acquired by Cabonne Limited. Later that year Cabonne Limited, which joined the stock markets in 1999, announced a global alliance with Trinchero's Family Estates of the US, best known as the owner of America's biggest brand, Sutter Home. Cabonne is the ninth-largest vineyard operator in Australia, with 900 hectares of vineyards at Molong, near Orange. Its 20 000-tonne winery should place it among the top 20 companies in Australia (by volume) in 2002. As a result, volumes will be lifted to 100 000 cases in the first year of the US distribution, with a target of 380 000 cases per annum within five years. Exports to the UK will be even greater, with sales projected to reach 480 000 cases over the same period. The Reynolds Yarraman label is being phased out in consequence.

Reynolds Handpicked Sauvignon Blanc Semillon

TTTT 2001 Light green-yellow; the bouquet is clean, with somewhat anonymous fruit varietal character, but the wine moves up a notch on the palate, with ripe citrus and grass flavours, plenty of depth, and a harmonious finish. **rating:** 88

best drinking 2001–2002 **best vintages** NA **drink with** Chinese dumplings • $15

Reynolds Moon Shadow Chardonnay

TTTTT 1999 Medium yellow-green; a stylish and aromatic bouquet with stone fruit dominant, and hints of barrel-ferment in the background. The palate is immaculately structured and balanced, in an elegant and unforced style, with a seamless marriage of stone fruit, cashew and oak. **rating:** 94

best drinking 2001–2004 **best vintages** '99 **drink with** Chinese-style steamed fish • $24.99

Reynolds Marble Man Merlot

▼▼▼▼ 1999 Medium red-purple; gentle mulberry and spice aromas have slight gamey overtones; the palate has a mix of leaf, berry and more savoury flavours. The structure of the wine is wholly appropriate to Merlot, with fine tannins, and the French oak not overplayed. **rating:** 88

best drinking 2002–2007 **best vintages** NA **drink with** Roast veal • $28.99

Reynolds The Jezebel Cabernet Sauvignon

▼▼▼▽ 1999 Medium to full red-purple; lifted blackberry/cedary/savoury aromas lead into a palate with fairly pointed acidity, which makes the wine user-unfriendly at this point of time. **rating:** 84

best drinking 2004–2009 **best vintages** NA **drink with** Devilled kidneys • $28.99

🍇 ribarits estate wines   NR

Sturt Highway, Trentham Cliffs, NSW 2738 **region** Murray Darling
phone 0409 330 997 **fax** (03) 5024 0332 **open** Not
winemaker Contract **production** 4000 **est.** 1998
product range ($6.25–6.75 ML) Chardonnay, Shiraz, Merlot, Cabernet Sauvignon.
summary Adrian Ribarits has developed over 82 hectares of chardonnay, merlot, shiraz and cabernet sauvignon, primarily as a contract grapegrower for Simeon Wines. A small part of the grape production is vinified for Ribarits Estate and sold by mail order at yesterday's prices.

ribbon vale estate   ★★★☆

Lot 5 Caves Road, Wilyabrup via Cowaramup, WA 6284 **region** Margaret River
phone (08) 9755 6272 **fax** (08) 9755 6337 **open** 7 days 10–4
winemaker Keith Mugford **production** 5000 **est.** 1977
product range ($17.50–23 CD) Semillon Sauvignon Blanc, Merlot, Cabernet Sauvignon Merlot Cabernet Franc.
summary Acquired by Moss Wood in 2001. While the separate identity of Ribbon Vale is being maintained, a 5-year programme has been initiated to redefine the vineyard and wine style with the same quality criteria as Moss Wood itself. In the meantime, the product range has been shortened to three wines.

Ribbon Vale Estate Semillon Sauvignon Blanc

▼▼▼▼ 2001 Light to medium yellow-green; the moderately intense bouquet offers asparagus, lemon and mineral, with a hint of the reductive character which is often part and parcel of this style, followed by a lively, lemony palate still, however, showing the ghost of the reduced characters of the bouquet. **rating:** 85

best drinking 2001–2003 **best vintages** NA **drink with** Asparagus terrine • $19

richfield vineyard   NR

Bruxner Highway, Tenterfield, NSW 2372 **region** Northern Slopes Zone
phone (02) 6737 5888 **fax** (02) 6737 5898 **open** Not
winemaker John Cassegrain **production** NA **est.** 1997
product range Chardonnay, Shiraz, Merlot, Cabernet Sauvignon, with the first releases still in the pipeline.
summary Richfield is owned by Corporation Franco Asiatique, headquartered in Singapore. Bernard Forey is the majority shareholder of the company, and now lives in Brisbane. Denis Parsons, of Bald Mountain Vineyards, is a director and shareholder of the company, and is in charge of management of its operations, as it is only 20 minutes' drive south of Bald Mountain. It is located in a picturesque section of Tenterfield Creek, just to the west of the town of Tenterfield. A substantial vineyard has been established, comprising shiraz (11.1 ha), cabernet sauvignon (4.3 ha), merlot (3.7 ha), ruby cabernet (3.1 ha), semillon (2.9 ha), chardonnay (2.0 ha) and verdelho (1.3 ha). The first vintage was made in 2000, and it is expected that the bulk of Richfield's sales will come from the export markets of Southeast Asia.

richmond grove   ★★★★

Para Road, Tanunda, SA 5352 **region** Barossa Valley
phone (08) 8563 7300 **fax** (08) 8563 2804 **open** Mon–Fri 10–5, weekends and public holidays 10.30–4.30
winemaker John Vickery **production** NFP **est.** 1977
product range ($12–18 R) Watervale Riesling, Barossa Riesling, Hunter Valley Semillon, Marlborough Sauvignon Blanc, Verdelho, McLaren Vale Chardonnay, French Cask Chardonnay, Chardonnay Pinot, Barossa Shiraz, Coonawarra Shiraz, Cabernet Merlot, Coonawarra Cabernet Sauvignon.

summary Richmond Grove now has two homes, including this one in the Barossa Valley where John Vickery presides. It is owned by Orlando Wyndham and draws its grapes from diverse sources. The Richmond Grove Barossa Valley and Watervale Rieslings made by John Vickery represent excellent value for money (for Riesling) year in, year out. If these were the only wines produced by Richmond Grove, it would have five-star rating. Exports to the UK.

Richmond Grove French Cask Chardonnay

▼▼▼▼ **2001** Light to medium green-yellow; the bouquet is clean, light, and tending neutral, with just a faint hint of oak. The light to medium-bodied palate, however, is particularly well put together, with seductive melon and nectarine fruit running through a wine of good length. Two trophies at the Queensland Wine Show and various other medals and awards attest to the excellent value the wine offers.   **rating:** 87

best drinking 2001–2002 **best vintages** '01 **drink with** Pan-fried veal • $12

Richmond Grove McLaren Vale Chardonnay

▼▼▼▽ **2000** Light to medium yellow-green; the moderately intense bouquet has a mix of melon and citrus fruit married with subtle oak. The palate is pleasant, clean and unforced, but is not particularly intense. Given the Rolls Royce treatment in the winery, one can only assume a reasonably high crop level.   **rating:** 83

best drinking 2001–2003 **best vintages** NA **drink with** Fish and chips • $15

Richmond Grove Barossa Shiraz

▼▼▼▼ **1999** Strong red-purple, holding its hue well; high-toned berry fruit and subtle oak on the bouquet are followed by a palate with powerful fruit, still in its primary phase, and with some spicy characters adding interest. Good value.   **rating:** 87

best drinking 2003–2009 **best vintages** '98 **drink with** Marinated game • $18

Richmond Grove Coonawarra Shiraz

▼▼▼▼▽ **1999** Medium red-purple, like the Barossa wine of the same vintage, holding its hue well. The moderately intense, clean bouquet has fresh berry fruit; the palate is likewise firm and relatively unevolved, but well balanced. Consistent silver medal winner.   **rating:** 90

best drinking 2003–2008 **best vintages** NA **drink with** Braised beef • $18

richmond park vineyard   ★★★★

Logie Road, Richmond, Tas 7025 **region** Southern Tasmania
phone (03) 6265 2949 **fax** (03) 6265 3166 **open** Not
winemaker Andrew Hood (Contract) **production** 600 **est.** 1989
product range ($9–20ML) Chardonnay, Pinot Noir.
summary A small vineyard owned by Tony Park, which gives the clue to the clever name.

Richmond Park Pinot Noir

▼▼▼▼▽ **2000** Bright purple-red; the fresh, tangy bouquet ranges through sour cherry, plum, mint and spice; the elegant and perfectly balanced palate has good length.   **rating:** 92

best drinking 2002–2007 **best vintages** '00 **drink with** Roast duck • $20

⬥ ridgeback wines   ★★★★

New Chum Gully Estate, Howards Road, Panton Hill, Vic 3759 **region** Yarra Valley
phone (03) 9719 7687 **fax** (03) 9719 7667 **open** By appointment
winemaker Martin Williams, Dan Crane **production** 1000 **est.** 2000
product range ($23–29 ML) Chardonnay, Pinot Noir, Merlot, Cabernet Sauvignon.
summary Ron and Lynne Collings purchased their Panton Hill property in March 1990, clearing the land and making it ready for the first vine planting in 1992. Now there are a little over 4 hectares on the hillside slopes beneath their house, and Ron has completed the degree in wine growing at Charles Sturt University, winning the Dean's Award for Academic Excellence. Most of the grapes were sold to Coldstream Hills, but Ron Collings made small batches of wine himself each year, which ultimately led to the decision to establish the Ridgeback label, with contract winemaking, although Collings is never far from the scene at vintage. The name, incidentally, is intended to reflect in part the rolling hillside of Panton Hill, and to salute the Collings' Rhodesian Ridgeback dog.

Ridgeback Chardonnay

ŸŸŸŸ 2000 Light to medium yellow-green; the fresh bouquet has fig, melon and cashew; the palate has good structure, balance and mouthfeel, the flavours tracking the aromas of the bouquet; skilled use of oak throughout.   **rating:** 91

best drinking 2002–2004 **best vintages** '00 **drink with** Crumbed brains • $23

Ridgeback Pinot Noir

ŸŸŸŸ 2000 Deep red-purple; a complex array of savoury, spicy, black plum aromas feed into a palate with abundant flavour; foresty/plummy fruit is followed by tannins which are slightly over the top. May settle down with time in bottle.   **rating:** 89

best drinking 2003–2007 **best vintages** NA **drink with** Braised duck • $25

Ridgeback Merlot

ŸŸŸŸ 2000 Light to medium red-purple; the relatively light bouquet has a mix of leaf, mint and berry aromas which stream through into the palate, which has some red fruit, and correct tannin structure.   **rating:** 84

best drinking 2003–2006 **best vintages** NA **drink with** Braised veal • $29

Ridgeback Cabernet Sauvignon

ŸŸŸŸ 2000 Medium red-purple; the moderately intense bouquet has blackberry/blackcurrant tinged with touches of varietal earth; the same fruit flavours come through on the palate, which gains structure through slightly savoury tannins; good length.   **rating:** 87

best drinking 2004–2009 **best vintages** NA **drink with** Roast kid • $25

rimfire vineyards ★★★

Bismarck Street, MacLagan, Qld 4352 **region** Queensland Zone
phone (07) 4692 1129 **fax** (07) 4692 1260 **open** 7 days 10–5
winemaker Tony Connellan **production** 6000 **est.** 1991
product range ($10–16 CD) Verdelho, Chardonnay, Marsanne Chardonnay, Pioneer White, Country Rosé, Ruby Cabernet, Shiraz; Fortifieds.
summary The Connellan family (parents Margaret and Tony and children Michelle, Peter and Louise) began planting the 12-hectare, 14-variety Rimfire Vineyards in 1991 as a means of diversification of their very large (1500-hectare) cattle stud in the foothills of the Bunya Mountains, 45 minutes' drive northeast of Toowoomba. Increasingly producing a kaleidoscopic array of all manner of wines, the majority without any regional claim of origin. The Black Bull Cafe is open daily 10–5, with a blackboard menu and wine by the glass. Annual Jazz on the Lawn concert each spring.

rivendell ★★★

Lot 328 Wildwood Road, Yallingup, WA 6282 **region** Margaret River
phone (08) 9755 2235 **fax** (08) 9755 2295 **open** 7 days 10–5
winemaker Mike Davies, Jan Davies (Contract) **production** 2750 **est.** 1987
product range ($12.50–14.50 CD) Semillon Sauvignon Blanc, Honeysuckle Late Harvest Semillon, Verdelho, Shiraz Cabernet.
summary With 13.5 hectares of vineyards coming into bearing, production for Rivendell will increase significantly over the coming years. The cellar-door sales facility is in a garden setting, complete with restaurant. An unusual sideline is the sale of 50 types of preserves, jams and chutneys. No recent tastings.

riverbank estate NR

126 Hamersley Road, Caversham, WA 6055 **region** Swan District
phone (08) 9377 1805 **fax** (08) 9377 2168 **open** Weekends and public holidays 10–5
winemaker Robert James Bond **production** 3500 **est.** 1993
product range ($12–16 CD) Semillon, Verdelho, Chenin, Chardonnay, Classic Sweet White, Pinot Noir, Grenache Shiraz, Shiraz, Cabernet, Fortified Muscat, Fortified Shiraz.
summary Robert Bond, a graduate of Charles Sturt University and a Swan Valley viticulturist for 20 years, established RiverBank Estate in 1993. He draws upon 11 hectares of estate plantings and, in his words, 'The wines are unashamedly full-bodied, produced from ripe grapes in what is recognised as a hot grape growing region.' Wines extending back over every vintage back to 1994 were available at the cellar door in August 2001.

riverina estate ★★★☆

700 Kidman Way, Griffith, NSW 2680 **region** Riverina
phone (02) 6962 4122 **fax** (02) 6962 4628 **open** 7 days 9–5.30
winemaker Sam Trimboli **production** 3 million **est.** 1969
product range ($4–28 CD) An extensive range of varietal wines with Warburn Estate Semillon, Verdelho, Chardonnay, Shiraz, Durif, Merlot, Cabernet Merlot; Ridgewood Estate Chardonnay, Grenache Mataro; Ballingal Estate Traminer, Semillon, Semillon of the Riverina, Semillon Chardonnay, Sauvignon Blanc, Marsanne, Chardonnay, Shiraz, Merlot, Barbera, Cabernet Sauvignon; 1164 Semillon, Shiraz; Nonno Guiseppi Semillon Verdelho, Cabernet Durif Merlot; Three Corners and Lizard Ridge ranges with Semillon Sauvignon Blanc, Semillon Chardonnay, Chardonnay, Shiraz, Shiraz Cabernet, Merlot; Bushmans Gully Bin 157 Crisp Dry White, Bin 158 Soft Dry Red, Semillon Chardonnay, Shiraz Cabernet; Montello Classic Dry White, Botrytis Semillon, Botrytis Sauvignon Blanc. There is also a range of sparkling wines and fortifieds in both bottle and cask.
summary One of the large producers of the region, drawing upon 1100 hectares of estate plantings. While much of the wine is sold in bulk to other producers, selected parcels of the best of the grapes are made into table wines, with quite spectacular success. At the 1997 National Wine Show, Riverina Wines won an astonishing six gold medals, topping no less than 4 classes. That success has, it seems, given rise to the introduction of the Show Reserve wines, and while the 1997 success has not been equalled since, the top wines continue to impress. Exports to the UK and Canada.

Riverina Estate 1164 Shiraz

TTTT **1998** Strong, bright colour; spicy cherry fruit and oak on the bouquet are followed by a full-bodied palate, with layers of fruit, and slightly drying tannins on the finish. An impressive effort. **rating:** 88

best drinking 2003–2007 **best vintages** NA **drink with** Grilled T-bone • $27.95

riversands vineyards NR

Whytes Road, St George, Qld 4487 **region** Queensland Zone
phone (07) 4625 3643 **fax** (07) 4625 5043 **open** Mon–Sat 8–6, Sun 9–4
winemaker Ballandean Estate (Contract) **production** 3500 **est.** 1990
product range ($11–20 CD) Sauvignon Blanc Semillon, Explorers Chardonnay, Major Mitchell White, Three Rivers Red, Dr Seidel's Soft Red, Ellen Meacle Merlot, Golden Liqueur Muscat, Gaolhouse Port.
summary Riversands is situated on the banks of the Balonne River near St George, in the southwest corner of Queensland. It is a mixed wine grape and table grape business, acquired by present owners Alison and David Blacket in 1996. The wines are very competently made under contract at Ballandean Estate and have already accumulated a number of silver and bronze medals. The Chardonnay is particularly meritorious.

roberts estate wines ★★☆

Game Street, Merbein, Vic 3505 **region** Murray Darling
phone (03) 5024 2944 **fax** (03) 5024 2877 **open** Not
winemaker Ian McElhinney **production** 80 000 **est.** 1998
product range ($8–10 R) Chardonnay, Merlot, Shiraz, Cabernet Sauvignon; under the Denbeigh label Chardonnay, Semillon Chardonnay, Colombard Chardonnay, Shiraz, Cabernet Sauvignon, Shiraz Cabernet.
summary A very large winery acting as a processing point for grapes grown up and down the Murray River. Over 10 000 tonnes are crushed each vintage; much of the wine is sold in bulk to others, but some is exported under the Denbeigh and Kombacy labels.

robinsons family vineyards ★★★

Curtin Road, Ballandean, Qld 4382 **region** Granite Belt
phone (07) 4684 1216 **fax** (07) 4684 1216 **open** 7 days 9–5
winemaker Craig Robinson **production** 3000 **est.** 1969
product range ($14–20 CD) Sauvignon Blanc Semillon, Chardonnay, Unwooded Chardonnay, Lyra Dry White, Traminer, Late Harvest Traminer, Shiraz, Shiraz Cabernet, Cabernet Sauvignon, Sparkling.
summary One of the pioneers of the Granite Belt. The conjunction of a picture of a hibiscus and 'cool climate' in prominent typeface on the labels is a strange one, but then that has always been the nature of Robinsons Family Vineyards. The red wines can be very good, particularly when not overly extracted and tannic.

robinvale ★★★

Sea Lake Road, Robinvale, Vic 3549 **region** Murray Darling
phone (03) 5026 3955 **fax** (03) 5026 1123 **open** Mon–Fri 9–6, Sun 1–6
winemaker Bill Caracatsanoudis **production** 15 000 **est.** 1976
product range ($8.50–20 CD) A unique offering of white, red and fortified wines, the majority estate-grown under the internationally recognised Bio-Dynamic Demeter Grade A requirements, the highest level. In addition, a number are Kosher wines, and all are certified free of any genetically modified organisms.
summary Robinvale was one of the first Australian wineries to be fully accredited with the Biodynamic Agricultural Association of Australia. Most, but not all, of the wines are produced from organically grown grapes, with certain of the wines made preservative-free. Production has increased dramatically, no doubt reflecting the interest in organic and biodynamic viticulture and winemaking. Exports to the UK and Japan.

🐚 roche wines NR

Broke Wines, Pokolbin, NSW 2320 **region** Lower Hunter Valley
phone (02) 4998 7600 **fax** (02) 4998 7706 **open** 7 days 10–5
winemaker Jim Chatto, Greg Silkman (Contract) **production** 8500 **est.** 1999
product range ($20–35 ML) Tallawanta range of Unwooded Chardonnay, Semillon, Shiraz.
summary Roche Wines, with its production of 8500 cases from 7 hectares each of semillon and shiraz and 5 hectares of chardonnay, is but the tip of the iceberg of the massive investment made by Bill Roche in the Pokolbin subregion. He has transformed the old Hungerford Hill development on the corner of Broke and McDonalds Roads, and built a luxurious resort hotel with extensive gardens and an Irish pub on the old Tallawanta Vineyard, as well as resuscitating the vines on Tallawanta. The wines are all sold on-site through the various outlets in the overall development.

Roche Wines Tallawanta Semillon

▼▼▼▼ **2001** Medium straw-yellow; both the bouquet and palate have above average weight and depth to the lemony/grassy fruit; should develop well over the medium term. **rating:** 85

best drinking 2002–2006 **best vintages** NA **drink with** Sauteed prawns • $24

rochford ★★★★☆

Romsey Park, Rochford, Vic 3442 **region** Macedon Ranges
phone (03) 5429 1428 **fax** (03) 5429 2356 **open** 7 days 10–4
winemaker David Creed **production** 6000 **est.** 1983
product range ($13–35 R) Riesling, Chardonnay, Macedon Blanc de Blanc, Pinot Noir, Cabernet Sauvignon; Romsey Park label includes Riesling, Pinot Grigio, Chardonnay, Pinot Noir, Merlot, Cabernet Sauvignon.
summary Since acquiring Rochford in early 1998, Helmut Konecsny and Yvonne Lodoco-Konecsny have made a substantial investment in the estate vineyards, but have been more than content to leave the style unchanged, with David Creed continuing as winemaker. The emphasis is on Chardonnay and Pinot Noir, and as the new plantings come into bearing, so will production increase. Following the acquisition of Eyton-on-Yarra in late 2001, winemaking will move to that site still under the direction of David Creed.

Rochford Pinot Gris

▼▼▼▼ **2001** Pale partridge eye; has an aromatic, apple blossom bouquet, and a well-balanced palate with crisp apple and crunchy pear flavours, with a twist of alcohol on the finish. **rating:** 86

best drinking 2001–2002 **best vintages** NA **drink with** Seafood risotto • $22

Rochford Chardonnay

▼▼▼▼ **2000** Light to medium yellow-green; mineral, cashew and melon aromas are followed by a typically delicate but well-balanced palate with a nice mix of fruit and mlf-induced cashew. **rating:** 88

best drinking 2003–2008 **best vintages** '99 **drink with** Fresh abalone • $25

Rochford Pinot Noir

▼▼▼▼▼ **2000** Medium red-purple; a clean bouquet with most attractive plummy/cherry fruit is complexed by a neat touch of toasty oak. The palate is smooth, with perfectly ripened fruit, and the silky texture and length of top-class Pinot Noir. A multiple trophy winner, first at the 2001 Royal Melbourne Wine Show (Best Pinot Noir of Show) and then at the 2001 Macedon Ranges Wine Exhibition for Best Wine of Show. **rating:** 94

best drinking 2002–2007 **best vintages** '91, '92, '93, '95, '96, '98, '99, '00 **drink with** Jugged hare • $35

Rochford Cabernet Merlot

TTTTT **1998** Medium red-purple; quite complex black and red fruit aromas foretell a palate with good richness and weight centred on ripe red berry fruit, finishing with subtle oak. **rating:** 90

best drinking 2003–2008 **best vintages** NA **drink with** Yearling beef • $25

rockfield estate vineyard NR

Rosa Glen Road, Margaret River, WA 6285 **region** Margaret River
phone (08) 9757 5092 **fax** (08) 9757 5092 **open** 7 days 10–5
winemaker Mike Lemmes **production** 2000 **est.** 1997
product range ($16–18 CD) Semillon, Semillon Sauvignon Blanc, Autumn Harvest Semillon, Rosa (Rosé), Cabernet Shiraz, Reserve Cabernet.
summary Rockfield Estate Vineyard is very much a family affair. Dr Andrew Gaman wears the hats of chief executive officer, assistant winemaker and co-marketing manager; wife Anne Gaman is a director; Alex Gaman and Nick McPherson are viticulturists, Andrew Gaman Jr is also an assistant winemaker and Anna Walter (née Gaman) helps Dr Andrew Gaman with the marketing. The Chapman Brook meanders through the property, the vines running from its banks up to the wooded slopes above the valley floor, and the winery offers light refreshments and food from the cafe throughout the day.

rockford ★★★★☆

Krondorf Road, Tanunda, SA 5352 **region** Barossa Valley
phone (08) 8563 2720 **fax** (08) 8563 3787 **open** Mon–Sat 11–5
winemaker Robert O'Callaghan, Chris Ringland **production** 19 000 **est.** 1984
product range ($10.50–45 CD) Eden Valley Riesling, Local Growers Semillon, Alicante Bouchet, White Frontignac, Basket Press Shiraz, Sparkling Black Shiraz, Dry Country Grenache, Cabernet Sauvignon, Tawny Port.
summary The wines are sold through Adelaide retailers only (and the cellar door) and are unknown to most eastern Australian wine drinkers, which is a great pity, because these are some of the most individual, spectacularly flavoured wines made in the Barossa today, with an emphasis on old, low-yielding dry-land vineyards. This SA slur on the palates of Vic and NSW is exacerbated by the fact that the wines are exported to Switzerland, the UK and New Zealand; it all goes to show that we need proper authority to protect our living treasures.

Rockford Black Shiraz

TTTTT NV Dark red, but with some brick hues evident. There is an attractive mix of spice and earth aromas on the bouquet, but the palate is something else, with that fine, faintly spicy, faintly earthy taste of mature Shiraz of the old Great Western style. It is neither heavy nor sweet, and has tremendous balance and length. **rating:** 94

best drinking 2002–2003 **best vintages** NA **drink with** Needs no accompaniment • NA

roehr NR

Roehr Road, Ebenezer near Nuriootpa, SA 5355 **region** Barossa Valley
phone (08) 8565 6242 **fax** (08) 8565 6242 **open** Not
winemaker Contract **production** 300 **est.** 1995
product range Elmor's Ebenezer Old Vine Shiraz.
summary Karl Wilhelm Roehr arrived in Australia in 1841, and was among the earliest settlers at Ebenezer in the northern end of the Barossa Valley. His great-great-grandson, Elmor Roehr, is the custodian of 20 hectares of shiraz, grenache, mataro and chardonnay on a vineyard passed down through the generations. In 1995 he decided to venture into winemaking, and produced a Shiraz from 80-year-old vines which typically crop at less than 1.5 tonnes to the acre. It is sold exclusively in Germany and the US.

romavilla NR

Northern Road, Roma, Qld 4455 **region** Queensland Zone
phone (07) 4622 1822 **fax** (07) 4622 1822 **open** Mon–Fri 8–5, Sat 9–12, 2–4
winemaker David Wall, Richard Wall **production** 2500 **est.** 1863
product range ($12–40 CD) An extensive range of varietal and generic table wines, including Rhine Riesling, Crouchen, Chenin Blanc, Reserve Chenin Blanc, Viognier, Reserve Chardonnay, Rosé, Maranoa Shiraz, Cellarman's Shiraz and fortified wine styles, including Madeira and Tawny Port, are on sale at the winery; the Very Old Tawny Port is made from a blend of material ranging in age from 10–25 years.

summary An amazing historic relic, seemingly untouched since its 19th-century heyday, producing conventional table wines but still providing some extraordinary fortifieds, including a truly stylish Madeira made from riesling and syrian (the latter variety originating in Persia). David Wall has now been joined by son Richard in the business, which will hopefully ensure continuity for this important part of Australian wine history.

rosabrook estate ★★★★☆

Rosa Brook Road, Margaret River, WA 6285 **region** Margaret River
phone (08) 9757 2286 **fax** (08) 9757 3634 **open** 7 days 10–4
winemaker Simon Keall **production** 4000 **est.** 1980
product range ($15–22 CD) Semillon Sauvignon Blanc, Chardonnay, Autumn Harvest Riesling, Botrytis Riesling, Shiraz, Cabernet Merlot.
summary The 14-hectare Rosabrook Estate vineyards have been established progressively since 1980, with seven varieties planted. The cellar-door facility is housed in what was Margaret River's first commercial abattoir, built in the early 1930s; a new winery was constructed in 1993. It has been acquired by the rapidly expanding Palandri Wines, which should find the quality of the Rosabrook wines very useful.

ⓦ rosebrook estate NR

1090 Maitlandvale Road, Rosebrook, NSW 2320 **region** Lower Hunter Valley
phone (02) 4930 1114 **fax** (02) 4930 1690 **open** By appointment
winemaker Graeme Levick **production** 1200 **est.** 2000
product range ($15 CD) Verdelho, Chardonnay, Shiraz, Muscat.
summary Graeme and Tania Levick run Rosebrook Estate and Hunter River Retreat as parallel operations. These include self-contained cottages, horse-riding, tennis, canoeing, swimming, bushwalking, fishing, riverside picnic area, recreation room and minibus for winery tours and transport to functions or events in the area. Somewhere in the middle of all of this they have established 2.5 hectares each of chardonnay and verdelho, purchasing shiraz and muscat to complete the product range.

rosemount estate (hunter valley) ★★★★

Rosemount Road, Denman, NSW 2328 **region** Upper Hunter Valley
phone (02) 6549 6400 **fax** (02) 6549 6499 **open** 7 days 10–4
winemaker Philip Shaw **production** Over 2 million **est.** 1969
product range ($8.99–55.99 R) A very large range of wines which in almost all instances are varietally identified, sometimes with the conjunction of vineyards at the top end of the range, and which in the case of the lower-priced volume varietals increasingly come from all parts of southeast Australia. Names and label designs change regularly, but the emphasis remains on the classic varietals. Roxburgh Chardonnay is the white flag-bearer; Mountain Blue Shiraz Cabernet is the real leader. Chardonnay, Shiraz and Cabernet Sauvignon under the standard labels consistently excellent at the price. In 1997 a Yarra Valley Chardonnay was added to the regional range, which also encompasses Coonawarra, Orange and Mudgee (Hill of Gold).
summary Rosemount Estate has achieved a miraculous balancing act over the past years maintaining – indeed improving – wine quality while presiding over an ever-expanding empire and dramatically increasing production. The wines are consistently of excellent value; all have real character and individuality; not a few are startlingly good. The outcome was the merger with Southcorp in March 2001; while in financial terms Southcorp was the acquirer, most of the key management positions within the merged group are held by Rosemount executives. Exports to the UK and the US.

Rosemount Estate Diamond Label Riesling

♥♥♥♥ **2001** Light to medium yellow-green; a quite classic bouquet opens with slate/mineral then provides some citrus blossom; the palate loosens up and spreads out somewhat on the finish, but, all in all, something of a surprise packet. **rating:** 88

best drinking 2001–2003 **best vintages** NA **drink with** Takeaway seafood • $15

Rosemount Estate Diamond Label Sauvignon Blanc

♥♥♥♥ **2001** Light green-yellow; crisp grass, apple and gooseberry aromas are followed by a fresh and lively palate, with some grassy notes offset by a touch of residual sweetness. **rating:** 85

best drinking 2001–2002 **best vintages** NA **drink with** Steamed fish • $15

Rosemount Estate Diamond Label Semillon Chardonnay

TTTY 2001 Light to medium yellow-green; has some quite lively and tangy aromatics; the light to medium-bodied palate is clean and pleasant; no frills, but no nonsense either. **rating: 84**

best drinking 2001–2002 **best vintages** NA **drink with** Takeaway • $11

Hill of Gold Mudgee Chardonnay

TTTY 2000 Light to medium yellow-green; the bouquet has attractive, smoky barrel-ferment notes providing a touch of smoky/char over the melon fruit. However, the palate doesn't deliver on the promise of the bouquet, for the fruit is simply not there. **rating: 84**

best drinking 2001–2003 **best vintages** NA **drink with** Pasta • $20

Rosemount Estate Rose Label Orange Vineyard Chardonnay

TTTTY 2000 Light to medium yellow-green; clean stone fruit/melon with the barest twist of oak on the bouquet precedes a palate with very good mouthfeel and balance; it is long, and driven by its pure, fine fruit. **rating: 93**

best drinking 2001–2005 **best vintages** '92, '95, '96, '97, '99, '00 **drink with** Oyster soup • $22

Rosemount Estate Show Reserve Chardonnay

TTTT 2000 Light to medium green-yellow; the bouquet is light and clean, tending neutral, the light to medium-bodied palate unforced, fresh and lively. It is highly likely that the wine will transform itself over the next 12 months. **rating: 87**

best drinking 2002–2005 **best vintages** '97, '99 **drink with** Pan-fried veal • $25

Rosemount Estate Yarra Valley Chardonnay

TTTT 2000 Medium yellow-green; the bouquet initially offers light melon fruit and barely perceptible oak, but the aromatics build as the wine sits in the glass. While light and elegant, the palate has soaked up the oak to a surprising degree. Has time in front of it. **rating: 88**

best drinking 2001–2004 **best vintages** NA **drink with** Pasta • $16

Rosemount Estate Kirri Billi Vintage Brut

TTTT 1998 Strong straw-pink; a highly aromatic and fruity bouquet is followed by a surprisingly fresh and direct palate, lacking the textural complexity one might expect from prolonged lees contact. **rating: 86**

best drinking 2001–2002 **best vintages** NA **drink with** Aperitif • $23

Rosemount Estate Pinot Noir

TTTY 2000 Medium to full red-purple; the bouquet offers plenty of fruit but not much varietal character; the palate is a replay, with sweet fruit, nice balance and flavour; a light to medium-bodied dry red. **rating: 84**

best drinking 2001–2003 **best vintages** NA **drink with** Duck • $15

Rosemount Estate Diamond Label Shiraz

TTTT 2000 Medium red-purple; the moderately intense bouquet does offer some complexity, via savoury edges to the berry fruit. Similarly, clever winemaking has delivered both flavour and structure complexity, with dark berry flavours, a touch of chocolate, and soft but perceptible tannins. **rating: 87**

best drinking 2002–2006 **best vintages** '88, '90, '91, '92, '94, '96, '98, '99, '00 **drink with** Lamb shanks • $16

Rosemount Estate Hill of Gold Mudgee Shiraz

TTTTY 1999 Medium to full red-purple; clean, smooth black fruit aromas, quite ripe, and positive oak lead into a palate with attractively sweet and smooth red and black fruit flavours; soft tannins. Trophy at Cowra and double gold at the 2001 Sydney International Wine Competition. **rating: 91**

best drinking 2002–2010 **best vintages** '98, '99 **drink with** Braised ox cheek • $19

Rosemount Estate Rose Label Orange Vineyard Shiraz

TTTT 1999 Medium red, with the purple starting to diminish; the bouquet is light, with some cherry fruit, but lacks focus; the palate has more substance, thanks in part to some clever use of oak. **rating: 85**

best drinking 2002–2007 **best vintages** '97 **drink with** Moroccan lamb • $31

Rosemount Estate Diamond Label Shiraz Cabernet

TTTY 2001 Medium purple-red; there is a curious dusty nutmeg scent together with the fresh fruit of the bouquet; the palate likewise offers very fresh fruit, but has a distinct residual sugar sweetness to the finish which will appeal to some, not others. **rating: 83**

best drinking 2001–2002 **best vintages** '96, '98, '99 **drink with** Lasagne • $10

Rosemount Estate Mountain Blue Shiraz Cabernet

ᵀᵀᵀᵀᵧ 1999 Medium to full red-purple; a clean, solid bouquet with nicely ripened cassis/berry fruit and well-balanced oak; the palate has abundant fresh, lively fruit which drives the wine, rather than oak or tannin; good length, and a gold medal winner, 2000 Mudgee Wine Show. A success in a difficult vintage. **rating: 91**

best drinking 2004–2009 **best vintages** '95, '96, '97, '98, '99 **drink with** Barbecued beef • $45

Rosemount Estate Diamond Label Merlot

ᵀᵀᵀᵀ 2000 Medium red-purple; a clean, straightforward bouquet is followed by a light to medium-bodied palate, with pleasing texture and structure; the only shortcoming is a lack of clear varietal character to the fruit. **rating: 85**

best drinking 2001–2003 **best vintages** NA **drink with** Veal • $15

Rosemount Estate Rose Label Orange Vineyard Merlot

ᵀᵀᵀᵀ 1998 Medium red-purple; oak unduly dominates the bouquet, but on the palate quite powerful sweet fruit joins the fray, together with oak and an acid tweak on the finish. Plenty of all-up flavour. **rating: 87**

best drinking 2003–2007 **best vintages** NA **drink with** Ragout of lamb • $31

Rosemount Estate Diamond Label Cabernet Sauvignon

ᵀᵀᵀᵀ 2000 Medium red-purple; the moderately intense bouquet has dark blackcurrant and cassis varietal fruit supported by subtle oak. The palate offers plenty of extract and fruit, significantly the best of the Diamond Label range from 2000, largely free of the sweetness so evident in others. **rating: 86**

best drinking 2002–2005 **best vintages** '86, '88, '90, '92, '93, '94, '96 **drink with** Rare sirloin steak • $15

Rosemount Estate Hill of Gold Mudgee Cabernet Sauvignon

ᵀᵀᵀᵀᵧ 1999 Medium red-purple; the clean, moderately intense bouquet has a mix of red and blackcurrant fruit with a varietal earthy substrate; the nicely balanced and constructed palate has a mix of red berry and mint flavours with fine, emery paper tannins. **rating: 90**

best drinking 2003–2009 **best vintages** '98 **drink with** Roast lamb • $20

Rosemount Estate Rose Label Orange Vineyard Cabernet Sauvignon

ᵀᵀᵀᵀ 1998 Medium red-purple; the moderately intense bouquet has a mix of cedary/spicy/slightly savoury/dark berry fruit aromas, building presence on the palate, with plenty of quite sweet dark berry fruit and surprisingly pronounced tannins on the finish. Will amply repay cellaring. **rating: 89**

best drinking 2003–2013 **best vintages** '96, '97 **drink with** Roast lamb shoulder • $22

rosemount estate (mclaren vale)   ★★★★★

Ingoldby Road, McLaren Vale, SA 5171 **region** McLaren Vale
phone (08) 8383 0001 **fax** (08) 8383 0456 **open** Mon–Fri 10–4.30, weekends and public holidays 11–4.30
winemaker Charles Whish **production** 1 million **est.** 1888
product range ($20–69.99 CD) Ryecroft Unwooded Chardonnay, Balmoral Syrah, Show Reserve Shiraz, GSM (Grenache Shiraz Mourvèdre blend), Traditional (Cabernet blend); Ryecroft Flame Tree White, Cabernet Shiraz.
summary The specialist red wine arm of Rosemount Estate, responsible for its prestigious Balmoral Syrah, Show Reserve Shiraz and GSM, as well as most of the other McLaren Vale-based Rosemount brands.

Ryecroft Flame Tree White

ᵀᵀᵀᵧ 2001 Light green-yellow; the bouquet is clean and fresh with tropical passionfruit aromas; the palate has pleasant fruit, nicely balanced; rises well above its price station, and great value. **rating: 84**

best drinking 2001–2002 **best vintages** NA **drink with** Takeaway • $8

Ryecroft Reserve Chardonnay

ᵀᵀᵀᵀ 2000 Medium yellow-green; a complex bouquet, very smoky and very tangy, takes the wine to the limits; similar smoky/tangy flavours on the palate are in stark contrast to the Hunter Valley Show Reserve Chardonnay of Rosemount. Rolls Royce winemaking treatment for a wine retailing for less than $20. **rating: 87**

best drinking 2001–2004 **best vintages** NA **drink with** King George whiting • $19

Rosemount Estate Show Reserve Shiraz

▼▼▼▼▼ 1999 Medium to full red-purple; a skilfully crafted wine, with smooth, ripe, dark cherry and plum fruit on the bouquet, joined by a touch of mint on the palate. An elegant style, and not overwhelmed by oak. I accorded it significantly higher points than my fellow judges at the 2001 Great Australian Shiraz Challenge. **rating: 94**

▼▼▼▼▼ 1998 Medium red-purple; as one would expect from such an outstanding vintage, a rich and ripe bouquet with a mix of black cherry and blackberry fruit. The palate provides no surprises, with abundant ripe (but not jammy) red fruits supported by well-balanced tannins and vanilla oak which does not go over the top. Presented itself very well at the 2001 Great Australian Shiraz Challenge, scoring gold medal points on my scoresheet in both the first and second round of judging. **rating: 94**

best drinking 2004–2009 best vintages '90, '91, '93, '94, '95, '98, '99 drink with Braised ox cheek • $30

Rosemount Estate Balmoral Syrah

▼▼▼▼▼ 1999 Strong red-purple; an aromatic, high-toned cherry fruit and vanilla oak bouquet; the palate is intense, but not overly extracted, with layers of black cherry fruit, tannins, oak and alcohol all in balance. An outstanding success for the vintage. **rating: 94**

best drinking 2004–2014 best vintages '86, '87, '88, '89, '91, '93, '95, '96, '97, '98, '99 drink with Chargrilled rump • $64

Rosemount Estate GSM

▼▼▼▼▽ 1999 Medium red-purple; the bouquet has an array of berry, game, spice, mint, licorice and oak; the big chewy palate is complex and rich, with distinct gamey varietal character playing its part. **rating: 91**

best drinking 2004–2009 best vintages '94, '95, '96, '99 drink with Beef with olives • $27

Rosemount Estate Traditional Cabernet Blend

▼▼▼▼▽ 1999 Medium red-purple; the bouquet offers a mix of savoury/earthy/spicy overtones to ripe berry fruit; the palate swells with masses of quite striking sweet, dark berry fruit flavour; the tannins are ripe and soft, the oak subservient. **rating: 91**

best drinking 2004–2009 best vintages '91, '94, '95, '96, '97, '98, '99 drink with Chargrilled beef • $22

Rosemount Estate Coonawarra Show Reserve Cabernet Sauvignon

▼▼▼▼▽ 1999 Medium red-purple; rich, dark fruit aromas are joined by touches of leather and cedar on the bouquet; the palate has abundant flavour, some slightly sharp/angular characters needing to settle down with bottle age. **rating: 90**

▼▼▼▼▽ 1998 Medium red-purple; the moderately intense bouquet has smooth red berry/cassis/mulberry fruit plus gentle oak; the medium-bodied palate is nicely balanced and composed, with cassis/currant fruit supported by soft tannins and gentle oak. **rating: 92**

best drinking 2004–2009 best vintages '98 drink with Steak with mushrooms • $25.90

🐦 rosenvale wines NR

Lot 385 Railway Terrace, Nuriootpa, SA 5355 **region** Barossa Valley
phone 0407 390 788 **fax** (08) 8565 7206 **open** By appointment
winemaker James Rosenzweig, John Zilm **production** 1000 **est.** 2000
product range ($8–29.80 ML) Semillon, Chardonnay, Barrel Fermented Chardonnay, Shiraz.
summary The Rosenzweig family has 80 hectares of vineyards, some old and some new, planted to chardonnay, semillon, pinot noir, grenache, shiraz and cabernet sauvignon. Most of the grapes have been sold, from the inaugural 1999 vintage released in 2000. The white wines are cheap, but far from convincing; the shiraz, by contrast, is excellent.

Rosenvale Shiraz

▼▼▼▼ 1999 Dense red-purple; the rich and deep bouquet has a mix of black cherry and dark chocolate aromas which come through even more strongly (if it were possible) on the palate, with its luscious, sweet black fruits and controlled oak. **rating: 89**

best drinking 2004–2014 best vintages '99 drink with Rich game • $29.80

rosevears estate ★★★★

1a Waldhorn Drive, Rosevears, Tas 7277 **region** Northern Tasmania
phone (03) 6330 1800 **fax** (03) 6330 1810 **open** 7 days 10–4
winemaker James Chatto (Consultant) **production** 10 000 **est.** 1999

product range ($18–35 CD) Riesling, Sauvignon Blanc, Unwooded Chardonnay, Rosé, Pinot Noir, Notley Gorge Cabernet Sauvignon.

summary The multi-million dollar Rosevears Estate winery and restaurant complex was opened by the Tasmanian premier in November 1999. Built on a steep hillside overlooking the Tamar River, it is certain to make a lasting and important contribution to the Tasmanian wine industry. It is owned by a syndicate of investors headed by Dr Mike Beamish, and incorporates both Notley Gorge and Ironpot Bay. The inaugural winemaker was the youthful Jim Chatto (now a consultant), who brought with him large winery experience gained in the Hunter Valley and an extremely acute palate.

Rosevears Estate Riesling

▼▼▼▼ **2000** Pale straw-green; a light, crisp bouquet with a mix of herb and mineral aromas is logically followed by a fresh, crisp and neatly balanced palate. Developing slowly, and it will be interesting to see whether the apparent lack of fruit depth fills out with time in bottle. **rating:** 89

best drinking 2002–2007 **best vintages** NA **drink with** Seafood salad • $20

Rosevears Estate Pinot Noir

▼▼▼▼ **2000** Medium purple-red; the clean and smooth bouquet has ripe plum and black cherry fruit; the palate opens with plenty of substance and richness, but finishes with slightly tough tannins. Time will be on its side. **rating:** 88

best drinking 2003–2008 **best vintages** NA **drink with** Braised venison • $35

Rosevears Estate Cabernet Sauvignon

▼▼▼▼ **2000** Medium to full red-purple; very strong charry oak dominates the bouquet, but not the complex, youthful palate; the wine does dip in the middle, and is quite tannic on the finish; it needs time to resolve itself. May well improve dramatically with that time. **rating:** 86

best drinking 2005–2010 **best vintages** NA **drink with** Rump steak • $22

Notley Gorge Cabernet Sauvignon

▼▼▼▼ **2000** Medium red-purple; a clean bouquet with a mix of earth and berry typical of the variety, then a nicely weighted palate with tannins which are slightly grippy, but will soften and come into balance. **rating:** 87

best drinking 2004–2009 **best vintages** NA **drink with** Rare eye fillet • $30

rosewhite vineyards   NR

Happy Valley Road, Rosewhite via Myrtleford, Vic 3737 **region** Alpine Valleys
phone (03) 5752 1077 **open** Weekends and public holidays 10–5, 7 days January
winemaker Joan Mullett **production** 700 **est.** 1983
product range ($10 CD) Traminer, Chardonnay, Pinot Noir, Shiraz, Cabernet Sauvignon, Tawny Port.
summary After careers with the Victorian Department of Agriculture, agricultural scientists Ron and Joan Mullett began the establishment of Rosewhite in 1983. They have since established a little over 2 hectares of vineyards at an altitude of 300 metres.

rosily vineyard   ★★★★

Yelveton Road, Wilyabrup, WA 6284 **region** Margaret River
phone (08) 9755 6336 **fax** (08) 9485 0772 **open** By appointment
winemaker Mike Lemmes, Dan Pannell (Consultant) **production** 7000 **est.** 1994
product range ($11.50–22 ML) Semillon, Semillon Sauvignon Blanc, Sauvignon Blanc, Chardonnay, Shiraz, Cabernet Merlot, Cabernet Sauvignon.
summary The partnership of Mike and Barb Scott and Ken and Dot Allan acquired the Rosily Vineyard site in 1994. Under the direction of consultant Dan Pannell (of the Pannell family), 12 hectares of vineyard were planted over the next 3 years: first up sauvignon blanc, semillon, chardonnay and cabernet sauvignon, and thereafter merlot, shiraz and a little grenache and cabernet franc. The first crops were sold to other makers in the region, but in 1999 Rosily built a winery with 120-tonne capacity, and is now moving to fully utilise that capacity.

Rosily Vineyard Shiraz

▼▼▼▼ **2000** Vivid red-purple; the clean and aromatic bouquet offers sweet cherry, a hint of spice and subtle oak; the medium-bodied palate has good mouthfeel, soft and quite silky, with a positive contribution from well-handled oak. The first vintage; also contains a touch of grenache. **rating:** 89

best drinking 2004–2009 **best vintages** NA **drink with** Coq au vin • $22

Rosily Vineyard Cabernet Merlot

♥♥♥♥♡ 2000 Medium red-purple; a complex bouquet with blackberry, cassis, spice and earth aromas, with a similar array of flavours on a long palate with a lingering, savoury finish. Spent 19 months in new French oak, yet is in no way over-oaked. A fifty/fifty blend; 325 cases made. **rating: 90**

best drinking 2004–2009 **best vintages** '00 **drink with** Marinated beef • $22

Rosily Vineyard Cabernet Sauvignon

♥♥♥♥ 2000 Youthful red-purple; a clean, fresh cassis and blackcurrant bouquet with a nice touch of oak is followed by a palate with quite potent fruit in a light to medium-bodied mould. It has a real edge of the earthy austerity of classic cool-grown cabernet. Like the Cabernet Merlot, 19 months in new oak; 375 cases made. **rating: 89**

best drinking 2004–2010 **best vintages** NA **drink with** Shoulder of lamb • $22

ross estate wines ★★★☆

Barossa Valley Way, Lyndoch, SA 5351 **region** Barossa Valley
phone (08) 8524 4033 **fax** (08) 8524 4533 **open** Tue–Sat 10–5, Sun 1–5
winemaker Rod Chapman **production** 10 000 **est.** 1999
product range ($13–26 CD) Riesling, Semillon, Semillon Sauvignon Blanc, Sauvignon Blanc Semillon, Chardonnay, Beekeeper's Blend (Late Harvest), Shiraz, Tempranillo Graciano, Old Vine Grenache, Merlot, Cabernet Sauvignon Cabernet Franc Merlot, Cabernet Sauvignon.
summary Darius and Pauline Ross laid the foundation for Ross Estate Wines when they purchased 43 hectares of vines which included blocks of 75 and 90-year-old grenache. Also included were blocks of 30-year-old riesling and semillon, and 13-year-old merlot. The remaining vines were removed and planted with chardonnay, sauvignon blanc, cabernet sauvignon, cabernet franc and shiraz, which are now 7 years old. A winery was built in time for the 1998 vintage, and a tasting room was opened in 1999. The immensely experienced Rod Chapman, with 38 vintages under his belt, including 18 years as red winemaker with Southcorp/Penfolds, is in charge of winemaking. Production is rising rapidly, with over 30 000 cases by 2002, as other family vineyards come in to full production. Exports to the US.

rossetto ★★★

Farm 576 Rossetto Road, Beelbangera, NSW 2686 **region** Riverina
phone (02) 6966 0200 **fax** (02) 6966 0298 **open** Mon–Sat 8.30–5.30
winemaker Belinda Morandin **production** 400 000 **est.** 1930
product range ($5.75–20.85 R) Several ranges, the commercial Wattle Glen series ($5.75), the Mirror Lake range ($8.30), the Silky Oak range ($8.35-$9.90), the Promenade Range of Semillon, Semillon Riverina, Chardonnay, Botrytis Semillon, Shiraz, Cabernet Merlot ($13–$20.85) and Mitchell Brooke Limited Release Shiraz (McLaren Vale); also fortifieds and sparkling.
summary Another family-owned and run Riverina winery endeavouring to lift the profile of its wines, although not having the same spectacular success as Riverina Wines. Rossetto does have distributors in each state and exports to New Zealand, Asia and Europe, but much of the total production is sold in bulk to other makers.

Rossetto Promenade Semillon

♥♥♥♥ 2001 Light to medium yellow-green; faintly toasty aromas, together with some mineral, lead into a wine with excellent mouthfeel and attractive fruit, almost Riesling-like in character. Will probably develop more quickly than one might expect from its present structure. **rating: 86**

best drinking 2002–2005 **best vintages** NA **drink with** Summer salad • $15.95

ross hill vineyard NR

62 Griffin Road via Ammerdown, Orange, NSW 2800 **region** Orange
phone (02) 6360 0175 **fax** (02) 6360 0175 **open** By appointment
winemaker David Lowe, Stephen Doyle (Contract) **production** 1500 **est.** 1994
product range ($15–22 CD) Sauvignon Blanc, Chardonnay, Rosé, Shiraz, Merlot, Cabernet Franc, Cabernet Sauvignon.
summary Peter and Terri Robson began planting 12 hectares of vines in 1994. Chardonnay, sauvignon blanc, merlot, cabernet sauvignon, shiraz and cabernet franc have been established on gentle north-facing slopes at an elevation of 800 metres. No insecticides are used in the vineyard, the grapes are hand-picked and the vines hand-pruned. Ross Hill also has an olive grove with Italian oil varieties, and the Spanish variety, manzanilla, which is also a popular table olive.

rothbury estate ★★★★☆

Broke Road, Pokolbin, NSW 2320 **region** Lower Hunter Valley
phone (02) 4998 7363 **fax** (02) 4993 3559 **open** 7 days 9.30–4.30
winemaker Neil McGuigan **production** NFP **est.** 1968
product range ($8.90–35 R) At the top comes the Individual Vineyard range of Hunter Valley Semillon, Chardonnay and Shiraz; next the Hunter Valley range of varietals; and finally varietals from Mudgee and Cowra.
summary Rothbury celebrated its 30th birthday in 1998, albeit not quite in the fashion that founder and previous chief executive Len Evans would have wished. After a protracted and at times bitter takeover battle, it became part of the Beringer Blass empire. Quality has bounced back dramatically since the advent of Neil McGuigan as winemaker.

Rothbury Estate Brokenback Semillon
ΨΨΨΨΨ 2000 The very pure bouquet has an array of grass, herb and citrus aromas, matched by the clarity of the palate, with its excellent mouthfeel, balance and length. **rating:** 95
best drinking 2001–2010 **best vintages** '97, '98, '00 **drink with** Grilled flathead • $20

Rothbury Estate Hunter Valley Semillon
ΨΨΨΨΨ 2001 Light green-yellow; the powerful bouquet has floral lemon and herb aromatics; the excellent palate has crisp lime and lemon flavours running through to a long finish. Gold medal 2001 Hunter Valley Wine Show. **rating:** 94
best drinking 2003–2010 **best vintages** '72, '73, '74, '76, '79, '94, '97, '98, '00, '01 **drink with** Smoked eel • $20

Rothbury Estate Neil McGuigan Series Semillon
ΨΨΨΨΨ 2001 Light to medium yellow-green; unusually complex and ripe fruit aromas, even verging into the tropical, are an altogether different take on the normal Hunter 2001 Semillons. The palate has plenty of flavour, is more lemony than the bouquet and hence more conventional, but is still ripe; will develop moderately quickly. Surprising, given it is only 10.7° alcohol. **rating:** 90
best drinking 2002–2007 **best vintages** NA **drink with** Green-lipped mussels • $18

Rothbury Estate Wine Society Black Label Semillon
ΨΨΨΨ 2001 Light to medium green-yellow; pungent herb/herbaceous aromas are striking, as is the intense, powerfully structured and long palate, sustained by high acidity. Outstanding potential. **rating:** 89
best drinking 2004–2011 **best vintages** NA **drink with** Blue swimmer crab • $20

Rothbury Wine Society Gerry Sissingh Collection Semillon
ΨΨΨΨΨ 2001 Light straw-green; a classically clean, pure and correct aroma of herb, lemon and slate is followed by a beautifully balanced and tightly focussed wine, with tingling but not abrasive acidity; a classic cellaring prospect. **rating:** 93
best drinking 2006–2016 **best vintages** '01 **drink with** Leave it in the cellar • $26

Rothbury Estate Verdelho
ΨΨΨΨ 2001 Light green-yellow; a crisp mix of mineral and lemon on the bouquet, then fresh and clean citrus-tinged fruit salad on the palate. Did not come up with a trophy at the Perth Show (like the 2000), but did receive a silver medal at the 2001 Hunter Valley Wine Show. One way or another, I must be missing something. **rating:** 85
best drinking 2002–2003 **best vintages** NA **drink with** Pasta • $13

Rothbury Estate Brokenback Chardonnay
ΨΨΨΨΨ 2000 Light to medium green-yellow; the clean, gentle, melon fruit on the bouquet has background hints of spice and fig; the fresh, elegant and attractive palate has stone fruit and citrus, as well as echoes of the bouquet, with good balance and length. Comes together exceptionally well. **rating:** 91
best drinking 2001–2002 **best vintages** NA **drink with** Chicken ravioli • $23

Rothbury Estate Neil McGuigan Series Mudgee Chardonnay
ΨΨΨΨ 2001 Light to medium yellow-green; the bouquet is clean but is tending neutral, with ultra-subtle fruit and oak; the palate, likewise, is lively and fresh, but not particularly varietal. **rating:** 85
best drinking 2002–2003 **best vintages** NA **drink with** Pasta • $18

Rothbury Estate Brokenback Shiraz

▼▼▼▼▽ **2000** Light to medium purple-red; a light and vibrant bouquet with distinct spicy characters, wrongly suggesting that this wine might have come from a cool climate. The palate is spotlessly clean, with good fruit and oak balance and integration. **rating:** 90

best drinking 2005–2010 **best vintages** '00 **drink with** Shepherd's pie • $35

Rothbury Estate Old Liqueur Aleatico

▼▼▼▼ **NV** Medium red-purple; a strongly raisined bouquet, intense and different from the northeast Victorian fortifieds. The palate is similarly raisiny, with high acidity to provide balance. Striking wine produced from an old aleatico vineyard in Mudgee, a variety introduced by Dr Thomas Fiaschi in the 19th century. Available at the cellar door only; strongly recommended for wine students. **rating:** 89

best drinking 2002–2003 **best vintages** NA **drink with** Biscuits, cakes, nuts • $16

rothbury ridge   NR

Talga Road, Rothbury, NSW 2320 **region** Lower Hunter Valley
phone (02) 4930 7122 **fax** (02) 4930 7198 **open** Mon–Sat 9–5, Sun 10–5
winemaker Peter Jorgensen **production** 10 000 **est.** 1988
product range ($15–28 ML) Stanleigh Park Reserve Semillon, Mary FDW Chablis Style, Anne Chardonnay Semillon, Steven FBW Chardonnay, Mount Royal Reserve Durif, Early Release Chambourcin, Edgar Chambourcin, James Shiraz Chambourcin, Mount Royal Reserve Chambourcin, Joye Cabernet Sauvignon, Mount Royal Mèthode Champenoise.
summary Rothbury Ridge has an extraordinarily eclectic choice of varieties planted, with between 1.2 hectares and 2.4 hectares each of chardonnay, semillon, verdelho, chambourcin, durif, shiraz and cabernet sauvignon.

rotherhythe   ★★★★

Hendersons Lane, Gravelly Beach, Exeter, Tas 7251 **region** Northern Tasmania
phone (03) 6394 4869 **open** By appointment
winemaker Steven Hyde **production** 1600 **est.** 1976
product range ($16–26.95 CD) Chardonnay, Pinot Noir, Cabernet Sauvignon, Pinot Chardonnay.
summary At the 1996 Tasmanian Wines Show Rotherhythe swept all before it, winning trophies galore. Ironically, two days later Dr Steven Hyde sold the vineyard, although he has retained all of the existing wine stocks and will remain involved in the winemaking for some time to come. In both 1997 and again in 1998 Rotherhythe was awarded the trophy for Most Successful Exhibitor at the Tasmanian Wines Show. Since then the pace has slowed.

rothvale vineyard   ★★★★

Deasy's Road, Pokolbin, NSW 2320 **region** Lower Hunter Valley
phone (02) 4998 7290 **fax** (02) 4998 7290 **open** 7 days 10–5
winemaker Max Patton, Luke Patton **production** 5000 **est.** 1978
product range ($18–35 CD) Vat 8 Semillon, Barrel Fermented Semillon, Angus's Semillon Chardonnay, Unwooded Chardonnay, Lightly Oaked Chardonnay, Reserve Chardonnay A (American Oak), Reserve Chardonnay F (French Oak), Annie's Dry Red, Tilda's Shiraz, Luke's Shiraz, Cabernet Sauvignon.
summary Owned and operated by the Patton family, headed by Max Patton, who has the fascinating academic qualifications of BV Sc, M Sc London, BA Hons Canterbury, the scientific part of which has no doubt come in useful for his winemaking. The wines are sold only through the cellar door and direct to an imposing list of restaurants in the Hunter Valley and Sydney. Rothvale also has 4 vineyard cottages available for bed and breakfast accommodation. The wines have already accumulated an impressive array of medals.

Rothvale Vineyard Barrel Fermented Semillon

▼▼▼▼ **2000** Medium yellow-green; the complex oak on the bouquet is very evident but quite well-integrated, announcing a palate which is a rich, juicy style, utterly atypical for the Hunter Valley. 13.6° alcohol takes it into a different league and into an emphatic drink-now style. **rating:** 85

best drinking 2001–2002 **best vintages** NA **drink with** Roast chicken • $28

Rothvale Vineyard Vat 8 Semillon

▼▼▼▽ **2000** Medium yellow-green; the big, powerful, slightly broad bouquet is much more akin to a Barossa Valley Semillon than the Hunter Valley. Solid grass and citrus flavours hang around the mouth on the finish; unquestionably, best with food. A pretty cheeky price. **rating:** 84

best drinking 2001–2002 **best vintages** NA **drink with** KFC • $25

Rothvale Unwooded Chardonnay

▼▼▼▼ **2001** Medium to full yellow-green; the bouquet has some suggestions of complexity, possibly deriving from lees contact; pleasant nectarine and white peach fruit on the palate and a crisp finish make for a good early-drinking style. **rating:** 86

▼▼▼▼ **2000** Glowing yellow-green; masses of rich, ripe yellow peach and tropical fruit on the bouquet lead into an incredibly rich, rollicking food style, very much the product of the hot, dry vintage. Drink immediately. **rating:** 86

best drinking 2001–2002 **best vintages** '99, '01 **drink with** Trout mousse • $18

Rothvale Vineyard Reserve Chardonnay F

▼▼▼▼ **2000** Medium yellow-green; the bouquet solid peachy fruit, the oak handling infinitely better than that of the sister wine, Reserve Chardonnay A. A massively viscous wine in the mouth, which goes close to carrying the alcohol, and certainly demands full-flavoured food. **rating:** 85

best drinking 2001–2002 **best vintages** '99 **drink with** Pasta carbonara • $28

Rothvale Vineyard Tilda's Shiraz

▼▼▼▼▽ **2000** Medium to full red-purple; the complex bouquet ranges through spicy black cherry and mulberry fruit, together with vanilla notes from the oak. The palate is a replay, with a complex chord of spice, vanilla, blackberry and mulberry. **rating:** 90

best drinking 2005–2015 **best vintages** '99, '00 **drink with** Leave it in the cellar • $28

Rothvale Vineyard Annie's Dry Red

▼▼▼▼ **2000** Dense red-purple; the full and sweet bouquet has blackberry, plum, mulberry and vanilla aromas; the dense and concentrated palate has an abundance of sweet fruit on the mid-palate and ample tannins and oak. Toughens up slightly on the finish. **rating:** 88

best drinking 2005–2012 **best vintages** '99 **drink with** High-flavoured red meat dishes • NA

Rothvale Vineyard Cabernet Sauvignon

▼▼▼▼▽ **2000** Inky, dense red-purple; the bouquet is flooded with ripe cassis/blackcurrant fruit; the full-bodied palate is likewise crammed with fruit, bitter chocolate and extract. Essentially well-balanced despite its size, and despite tannins on the finish which are slightly drying, and need to soften with bottle age. **rating:** 91

best drinking 2005–2015 **best vintages** '98, '00 **drink with** Roast kid • $30

rouge homme ★★★☆

Riddoch Highway, Coonawarra, SA 5263 **region** Coonawarra
phone (08) 8736 3205 **fax** (08) 8736 3250 **open** Not
winemaker Paul Gordon, Brett Sharpe **production** 64 000 **est.** 1954
product range ($11–18 R) Semillon, Chardonnay, Unoaked Chardonnay, Pinot Noir, Reserve Pinot Noir, Shiraz Cabernet, Cabernet Merlot, Cabernet Sauvignon.
summary From time to time I have described Rouge Homme as the warrior brand of the Lindeman Group Coonawarra operations. In recent times it has proved a formidable warrior, particularly with its Cabernet and Cabernet blend wines, which benefited from the 1996 and 1998 vintages. The winery was sold in March 2002 but the brand and stock retained, its future direction and positioning not entirely clear.

Rouge Homme Shiraz Cabernet

▼▼▼▽ **1999** Medium to full red-purple; there is well-balanced and integrated fruit and oak to the bouquet, then abundant flavour on the palate, chained by slightly sticky, oppressive oak. **rating:** 84

best drinking 2003–2008 **best vintages** '88, '90, '91, '92, '94, '98 **drink with** King Island cheddar • $14.65

Rouge Homme Cabernet Sauvignon

▼▼▼▼▽ **1999** Flooded with ripe blackcurrant/berry fruit aromas which flow through to the palate. Rich fruit, sweet oak nuances and ripe tannins all add to the appeal. **rating:** 92

best drinking 2002–2010 **best vintages** '88, '90, '91, '94, '96, '98, '99 **drink with** Steak and kidney pie • $18

roundstone winery & vineyard ★★★☆

54 Willow Bend Drive, Yarra Glen, Vic 3775 **region** Yarra Valley
phone (03) 9730 1181 **fax** (03) 9730 1151 **open** Thurs–Sun and public holidays 10–5 or by appointment
winemaker John Derwin, Rob Dolan **production** 1400 **est.** 1998
product range ($15–35 CD) Charmed Chardonnay, Rosé, Pinot Noir, Rubies Pinot Noir, Shiraz Cabernet.
summary John and Lynne Derwin have moved quickly since establishing Roundstone, planting 7.5 hectares of vineyard (half to pinot noir with a mix of the best clones), building a small winery, and opening a cellar door and restaurant situated on the side of a dam. The Derwins prune the vineyard and enlist the aid of friends to pick the grapes; John makes the wine, with advice from Rob Dolan and Guy Lamothe, and Lynne is the chef and sommelier. Her pride and joy is a shearers' stove which was used at the Yarra Glen Grand Hotel for 100 years before being abandoned, and which is now at the centre of the kitchen. The restaurant opened in December 2001, and I haven't yet had the opportunity of tasting the food, but if it is as good as the wine, custom will be brisk.

Roundstone Charmed Chardonnay

▼▼▼▼ **2000** Light green-yellow; the bouquet is fresh and crisp, with tangy citrus and grapefruit aromas coming through clearly on the light-bodied palate which, while lacking complexity, has fair length. **rating: 85**

best drinking 2002–2004 **best vintages** NA **drink with** Sushi • $18

Roundstone Rosé

▼▼▼▼ **2001** Very light red; a fragrant bouquet of cherry blossom and lime, then a clean, well-balanced palate; all in all, an impressive rosé style, well made. **rating: 86**

best drinking 2002–2003 **best vintages** NA **drink with** Summer salad • $15

Roundstone Pinot Noir

▼▼▼▽ **2000** Light to medium red-purple; there are soft foresty overtones to the bouquet, but the firmly textured palate still has a fractionally hard profile. Needs time to soften in bottle, but there isn't a great deal of fruit to lengthen the window of best-drinking opportunity. **rating: 84**

best drinking 2002–2004 **best vintages** NA **drink with** Cold cuts • $22

Roundstone Rubies Pinot Noir

▼▼▼▼ **2000** Bright, medium red-purple; the bouquet, while only moderately intense, has attractive plum fruit, a hint of forest, and subtle oak. There is good depth to the plummy fruit on the palate, which finishes with fine tannins and neatly handled oak. A superior wine. **rating: 89**

best drinking 2002–2005 **best vintages** NA **drink with** Breast of duck • $35

rumbalara ★★☆

Fletcher Road, Fletcher, Qld 4381 **region** Granite Belt
phone (07) 4684 1206 **fax** (07) 4684 1299 **open** 7 days 9–5
winemaker Bob Gray **production** 1500 **est.** 1974
product range ($11.50–19.50 CD) Barrel Fermented Semillon, Granitegolde, Light Shiraz, Cabernet Sauvignon, Pinot Noir, Cabernet Shiraz and a range of Fortified wines, Cider and Vermouth.
summary Has produced some of the Granite Belt's finest honeyed Semillon and silky, red berry Cabernet Sauvignon, but quality does vary. The winery incorporates a spacious restaurant, and there are also barbecue and picnic facilities. No recent tastings.

rumball sparkling wines NR

55 Charles Street, Norwood, SA 5067 **region** Other Wineries of SA
phone (08) 8332 2761 **fax** (08) 8364 0188 **open** Mon–Fri 9–5
winemaker Peter Rumball **production** 8000 **est.** 1988
product range ($20 R) Sparkling Shiraz (also available in half bottles, magnums and jeroboams).
summary Peter Rumball has been making and selling sparkling wine for as long as I can remember, but has led a somewhat peripatetic life, starting in the Clare Valley but now operating one of the 12 Mèthode Champenoise lines in Australia, situated in the Adelaide suburb of Norwood. The grapes are purchased and the wines made under the supervision of Peter Rumball. His particular specialty has always been Sparkling Shiraz, long before it became 'flavour of the month'. National retail distribution through Tucker Seabrook, and exports to Japan and the US.

🐦 russet ridge ★★★★

Cnr Caves Road and Riddoch Highway, Naracoorte, SA 5271 **region** Wrattonbully
phone (08) 8762 0114 **fax** (08) 8762 0341 **open** Thurs–Mon 11–4.30
winemaker Philip Laffer, Sam Kurtz **production** NFP **est.** 2000
product range ($16 R) Coonawarra Chardonnay, Coonawarra Cabernet Shiraz Merlot.
summary This is the former Heathfield Ridge winery, built in 1998 as a contract crush and winemaking facility for multiple clients, but purchased by Orlando in 2000. It is the only winery in the large Wrattonbully region, and also receives Orlando's Coonawarra and Padthaway grapes, and other Limestone Coast fruit.

🐦 rutherglen estates ★★★

Cnr Great Northern Road and Murray Valley Highway, Rutherglen, Vic 3685 **region** Rutherglen
phone (02) 6032 8516 **fax** (02) 6032 8517 **open** Not
winemaker Nick Butler, David Valentine **production** 25 000 **est.** 2000
product range ($12–16 R) Chardonnay Marsanne, Shiraz, Shiraz Mourvèdre, Durif, Sangiovese.
summary The Rutherglen Estates brand is an offshoot of a far larger contract crush and make business, with a winery capacity of 4000 tonnes (roughly equivalent to 280 000 cases). Rutherglen is in a declared phylloxera region, which means all of the grapes grown within that region have to be vinified within it, itself a guarantee of business for ventures such as Rutherglen Estates. It also means that some of the best available material can be allocated for the brand, with an interesting mix of varieties.

Rutherglen Estates Sangiovese

▼▼▼▽ **2001** Light to medium red-purple; the bouquet has some fragrance, with light earthy berry aromas; the palate has a touch of maraschino cherry, vanilla oak, and soft, fine tannins. As with all the first vintage of Rutherglen Estates wines, not a lot of concentration, but what is there is appealing. **rating:** 83

best drinking 2002–2004 **best vintages** NA **drink with** Lasagne • NA

ryland river NR

RMB 8945, Main Creek Road, Main Ridge, Vic 3928 **region** Mornington Peninsula
phone (03) 5989 6098 **fax** (03) 9899 0184 **open** Weekends and public holidays 10–5 or by appointment
winemaker John W Bray **production** 2000 **est.** 1986
product range ($15–30 CD) Semillon Sauvignon Blanc, Chardonnay, Cabernet Sauvignon, Jack's Delight Tawny Port and Muscat.
summary John Bray has been operating Ryland River at Main Ridge on the Mornington Peninsula for a number of years, but not without a degree of controversy over the distinction between Ryland River wines produced from Mornington Peninsula grapes and those produced from grapes purchased from other regions. A large lake with catch-your-own trout and a cheese house are general tourist attractions.

rymill ★★★★

The Riddoch Run Vineyards, Riddoch Highway, Coonawarra, SA 5263 **region** Coonawarra
phone (08) 8736 5001 **fax** (08) 8736 5040 **open** 7 days 10–5
winemaker John Innes **production** 50 000 **est.** 1970
product range ($12–28.50 CD) March Traminer, Sauvignon Blanc, Chardonnay, Pinot Noir Chardonnay, The Bees Knees Sparkling Red, June Traminer Late Harvest, Shiraz, MC2 (Merlot Cabernet Sauvignon Cabernet Franc), Cabernet Sauvignon.
summary The Rymills are descendants of John Riddoch and have long owned some of the finest Coonawarra soil, upon which they have grown grapes since 1970, with present plantings of 165 hectares. Peter Rymill made a small amount of Cabernet Sauvignon in 1987 but has since plunged headlong into commercial production, with winemaker John Innes presiding over the striking winery portrayed on the label. Australian distribution is through Negociants Australia; exports go to all of the major markets in Europe and Asia.

Rymill Sauvignon Blanc

▼▼▼▼ **2001** Light green-yellow; pleasant gooseberry-accented aromatics are clearly varietal; the palate is somewhat lighter than the bouquet suggests, and rather less focussed, but does have pleasant, soft flavour.
rating: 86

best drinking 2001–2002 **best vintages** NA **drink with** Yabbies • $15

Rymill Shiraz

TTTT **1999** Medium to full red-purple; a smooth, moderately intense bouquet with plummy/spicy fruit and delicate cedary oak, then a fresh, light to medium-bodied and well-balanced palate with plum and dark cherry fruit supported by perfectly judged oak.   **rating:** 89

best drinking 2004–2009 **best vintages** '90, '91, '92, '95, '97, '98, '99 **drink with** Stuffed eggplant • $23

Rymill MC2

TTTTY **2000** Medium to full red-purple; clean, fragrant, blackberry/blackcurrant/cassis aromas, then attractive, ripe cassis fruit; fine, ripe tannins and subtle oak. Continues the success story for this label in a fairly ordinary vintage.   **rating:** 90

best drinking 2004–2009 **best vintages** '99, '00 **drink with** Marinated beef • $19

Rymill Cabernet Sauvignon

TTTT **1999** Medium red-purple; a cedary, savoury, earthy bouquet, then a powerful palate with cedary/savoury edges to the blackberry fruit; austere, but has length and character.   **rating:** 88

best drinking 2004–2010 **best vintages** '90, '93, '98 **drink with** Mushroom risotto • $28.50

saddlers creek ★★★★

Marrowbone Road, Pokolbin, NSW 2320 **region** Lower Hunter Valley
phone (02) 4991 1770 **fax** (02) 4991 2482 **open** 7 days 9–5
winemaker John Johnstone **production** 15 000 **est.** 1989
product range ($18–50 CD) Marrowbone Chardonnay, Pinot Noir, Bluegrass Cabernet Sauvignon; Equus Shiraz; Verdelho, Classic Hunter Semillon, Reserve Selection Sauvignon Blanc, Botrytis Semillon, Classical Gas (Mèthode Champenoise), Single Vineyard Hunter Shiraz, Reserve Selection Merlot, Langhorne Reserve Cabernet; Liqueur Muscat.
summary Made an impressive entrance to the district with consistently full-flavoured and rich wines, and has continued on in much the same vein, with good wines across the spectrum. Limited retail distribution in NSW, Qld and Vic.

Saddlers Creek Classic Hunter Semillon

TTTTY **2001** Pale straw; the bouquet is relatively subdued, the wine coming alive on the long and intense palate, with a near-subliminal hint of sweetness. Gold medal winner 2001 Liquorland National Wine Show.   **rating:** 92

best drinking 2002–2006 **best vintages** '01 **drink with** Shellfish • $17.50

Saddlers Creek Marrowbone Chardonnay

TTTT **2000** Light to medium yellow-green; both the bouquet and palate show citrussy fruit, the palate, in particular, having finesse and length. Developing nicely, and slightly atypical for the 2000 vintage from the Hunter Valley.   **rating:** 85

best drinking 2001–2004 **best vintages** '95, '97 **drink with** Bone marrow in brioche • $25

Saddlers Creek Equus Shiraz

TTTT **1999** Medium red, with a touch of purple; abundant earthy/oaky/savoury aromas move into the medium-bodied palate where chocolate and berry join the fray; good tannin management, likewise oak.
rating: 86

TTTT **1998** Deeply coloured; from the big end of town, with a deep and powerful bouquet and palate, all in all needing a gentler touch – or much patience.   **rating:** 88

best drinking 2004–2009 **best vintages** NA **drink with** Braised oxtail • $50

Saddlers Creek Bluegrass Cabernet Sauvignon

TTTTY **1996** Medium red, showing the expected development. The bouquet is slightly weedy, but the palate another thing again, with sweet berry fruit and fine tannins combining in stylish fashion. **rating:** 91

best drinking 2001–2005 **best vintages** '96 **drink with** Yearling steak • $26

🐢 st anne's vineyards ★★★

Corner of Perricoota Road and 24 Lane, Moama, NSW 2731 **region** Perricoota
phone (03) 5480 0099 **fax** (03) 5480 0077 **open** 7 days 9–5, except Christmas Day, Good Friday and Anzac Day
winemaker Richard McLean **production** 20 000 **est.** 1972

product range ($14–25 CD) Pericoota Semillon, Chardonnay, Grenache Shiraz Mourvèdre, Shiraz, Cabernet Franc, Cabernet, Dulcet I (late harvest Riesling), Dulcett II (dessert style Semillon), Tawny Port, Belle Tawny, Liqueur Tawny.

summary St Anne's is by far the most active member of the newly registered (under the Geographic Indications Legislation) region in southern NSW. Richard McLean has established 80 hectares of estate vineyards, with another 120 hectares of grower vineyards to draw upon. Shiraz, cabernet sauvignon, grenache and mourvèdre account for over 75 per cent of the plantings, but there is a spread of the usual white wines and few red exotics. The wines are all competently made.

St Anne's Chardonnay

▼▼▼▽ 2000 Medium yellow-green; the bouquet has neatly balanced stone fruit and oak aromas leading into a clean palate which has good flavour until the very finish, when oak-derived phenolics take over. **rating:** 83

best drinking 2001–2002 **best vintages** NA **drink with** Pasta carbonara • $16

St Anne's Shiraz

▼▼▼▽ 2000 Medium red-purple; the bouquet has masses of ripe, almost essency fruit in a high-toned register; on the palate, obvious oak inputs provide the framework and a fair bit of the flavour. **rating:** 83

best drinking 2002–2005 **best vintages** NA **drink with** Beef casserole • $19.50

st gregory's   NR

Bringalbert South Road, Bringalbert South via Apsley, Vic 3319 **region** Henty
phone (03) 5586 5225 **open** By appointment
winemaker Gregory Flynn **production** NFP **est.** 1983
product range ($14 ML) Port.
summary Unique Port-only operation selling its limited production direct to enthusiasts (by mailing list).

st hallett   ★★★★

St Hallett's Road, Tanunda, SA 5352 **region** Barossa Valley
phone (08) 8563 7000 **fax** (08) 8563 7001 **open** Mon-Sat 9–5, Sun and public holidays 10–5
winemaker Stuart Blackwell, Di Ferguson **production** 65 000 **est.** 1944
product range ($11–55 CD) Poacher's Blend (White), Eden Valley Riesling, Semillon Sauvignon Blanc, Semillon Select, Sweet Meredith, The Garden Chardonnay, The Black Barossa Sparkling Shiraz, Gamekeeper's Reserve (Red), Faith Shiraz, Blackwell Shiraz, Old Block Shiraz, Cabernet Shiraz, Cabernet Sauvignon, The Reward Cabernet, Fortifieds.
summary Nothing succeeds like success. St Hallett merged with Tatachilla to form Banksia Wines, which was then acquired by New Zealand's thirsty Lion Nathan. St Hallett understandably continues to ride the Shiraz fashion wave, but all its wines are honest and well-priced. It has established its own distribution network in the UK, and actively exports to Europe, North America and Asia.

St Hallett Eden Valley Riesling

▼▼▼▼▽ 2001 Light green-yellow; the solid bouquet has hints of spice over lime and apple fruit, the palate offering plenty of sweet lime fruit, particularly on the back palate, before tightening up with a pleasantly firm finish. Drink now style, but a good one. **rating:** 90

best drinking 2001–2004 **best vintages** '97, '01 **drink with** Crab • $15.95

St Hallett Barossa Sauvignon Blanc Semillon

▼▼▼▼ 2001 Semillon Sauvignon Blanc. Medium yellow-green; a solid, quite ripe bouquet with citrus running into tropical fruit, then a similarly honest, medium-bodied but full-flavoured palate making for easy drinking. **rating:** 85

best drinking 2002–2003 **best vintages** NA **drink with** Fish and chips • $14.50

St Hallett Blackwell Shiraz

▼▼▼▼ 1998 Strong red-purple; a complex array of dark fruits, licorice and vanilla on the bouquet is followed by a high-flavoured palate, showing plenty of dark fruit, and ever-so-slightly pencilly/dusty oak on the finish. **rating:** 87

best drinking 2003–2008 **best vintages** '96 **drink with** Lamb shanks • $26.80

St Hallett Faith Shiraz

TTTT 2000 Bright red-purple; clean, direct and ripe black cherry fruit with slightly spicy/savoury overtones, then a light to medium-bodied palate with cherry and mint fruit, and crisp acidity. Just there; not a particularly easy vintage. **rating: 85**

best drinking 2004–2008 **best vintages** NA **drink with** Italian • $19.30

St Hallett Old Block Shiraz

TTTTT 1998 Medium red-purple; excellent dark cherry fruit is seamlessly woven through gently sweet oak on the bouquet; the palate has exemplary depth and structure thanks to bountiful soft tannins and positive though not aggressive oak. Up to its very best form, and has developed beautifully over the past 12 months. **rating: 95**

best drinking 2003–2013 **best vintages** '80, '84, '87, '88, '90, '91, '93, '94, '96, '97, '98 **drink with** Kangaroo, game • $55

St Hallett Cabernet Sauvignon

TTTT 1999 Medium red-purple; the light bouquet has clean, fresh cassis/berry fruit, building on the juicy/berry palate which has rather more length and weight than the bouquet suggests; the oak input is minimal throughout. **rating: 87**

best drinking 2002–2007 **best vintages** NA **drink with** Parmesan cheese • $21.50

st huberts ★★★☆

Maroondah Highway, Coldstream, Vic 3770 **region** Yarra Valley
phone (03) 9739 1118 **fax** (03) 9739 1096 **open** Mon–Fri 9–5, weekends 10.30–5.30
winemaker Matt Steel **production** NFP **est.** 1966
product range ($19.50–43 R) Sauvignon Blanc, Roussane, Chardonnay, Pinot Chardonnay, Pinot Noir, Cabernet Merlot, Cabernet Sauvignon, Reserve Cabernet Sauvignon.
summary The changes have come thick and fast at St Huberts, which is now part of the Beringer Blass group. It has produced some quite lovely wines, notably Chardonnay and Cabernet Sauvignon, but the brand is slowly but surely losing its direction and meaning.

St Huberts Sauvignon Blanc

TTTT 2001 Light green-yellow; the bouquet is clean and fresh, the varietal character lacking intensity, perhaps, but present nonetheless. The palate has a mix of crisp peapod, asparagus and a faint tropical underlay, finishing dry. **rating: 84**

best drinking 2002–2003 **best vintages** NA **drink with** Summer salads • $20

St Huberts Chardonnay

TTTT 2001 Medium yellow-green; smooth, gently ripe melon and subtle oak are a promising opening, but the fresh palate lacks concentration. **rating: 84**

best drinking 2001–2003 **best vintages** '88, '90, '91, '92, '93, '94, '95, '97 **drink with** Yabbies • $20

St Huberts Pinot Noir Chardonnay

TTTT 1998 Very pale straw-green; the lemony/leafy/citrussy bouquet is followed by a palate with good mouthfeel, with touches of melon and strawberry and faint nuances of cream. The label very precisely describes the varietal mix of 57 per cent Pinot Noir and 43 per cent Chardonnay, but does not disclose whether or not this is a Yarra Valley sparkling. **rating: 87**

best drinking 2002–2004 **best vintages** NA **drink with** Aperitif • $31

St Huberts Pinot Noir

TTTTT 2000 Striking medium to full red-purple; the bouquet has concentrated, ripe blood plum fruit, the palate in powerful, full-on style; masses of extract, and will have particular appeal to those who enjoy full-bodied Pinots. **rating: 91**

best drinking 2003–2008 **best vintages** '00 **drink with** Strong red meat dishes • $22

st ignatius vineyard ★★★

Sunraysia Highway, Avoca, Vic 3467 **region** Pyrenees
phone (03) 5465 3542 **fax** (03) 5465 3542 **open** 7 days 10–5
winemaker Enrique Diaz **production** 700 **est.** 1992
product range ($18–22 CD) Released under their own labels are Graveyard Hill Chardonnay, Djarmbee Shiraz and Hangmans Gully Cabernet Sauvignon.

summary Silvia and husband Enrique Diaz began the establishment of their vineyard, winery and restaurant complex in 1992. They have established shiraz (the major planting at 3.2 hectares), chardonnay (1.6 hectares), cabernet sauvignon (1 hectare) and sauvignon blanc (0.4 hectares) in bearing, with merlot (1.6 hectares) and sangiovese (0.2 hectares) planted but not yet in production. The vineyard has already received three primary production awards, and all of the wine is made on-site by Enrique Diaz.

st leonards   ★★★

Wahgunyah, Vic 3687 **region** Rutherglen
phone (02) 6033 1004 **fax** (02) 6033 3636 **open** 7 days 11–5
winemaker Peter Brown **production** NFP **est.** 1860
product range ($13.50–45 CD) Muscadello, Semillon, Chenin Blanc, Sauvignon Blanc, Chardonnay, Orange Muscat, Pinot Noir, Shiraz, Classic Rutherglen Muscat.
summary An old favourite, relaunched in late 1997 with a range of three premium wines cleverly marketed through a singularly attractive cellar door and bistro at the historic winery on the banks of the Murray. All Saints and St Leonards are now wholly owned by Peter Brown; the vast majority of the wines are sold through cellar door and by mailing list.

St Leonards Orange Muscat

♈♈♈♈ **2001** Light yellow-green; a gently fruity bouquet with tropical fruit salad characters is effectively repeated on the palate, which finishes dry and is nicely balanced; all in all, possessing some individuality.

rating: 84

best drinking 2002–2003 **best vintages** NA **drink with** Pancakes • $13.90

St Leonards Pinot Noir

♈♈♈♈ **2000** Light to medium red-purple; a spicy, savoury bouquet with a hint of cherry is followed by a palate which is a major surprise, showing evidence of efforts in the winery to focus on style, and investing the wine with some tangy/savoury fruit.   **rating:** 83

best drinking 2002–2003 **best vintages** NA **drink with** Smoked quail • $18.60

St Leonards Wahgunyah Shiraz

♈♈♈♈ **1997** Medium red-purple, holding its hue well. The bouquet is powerful, showing ripe fruit and vanilla oak, a big, somewhat old fashioned, jammy, oaky red wine style. A re-release, and fully priced.   **rating:** 85

best drinking 2002–2007 **best vintages** NA **drink with** Braised beef • $45

st mary's   NR

V & A Lane, via Coonawarra, SA 5277 **region** Limestone Coast Zone
phone (08) 8736 6070 **fax** (08) 8736 6045 **open** 7 days 10–4
winemaker Barry Mulligan **production** 4000 **est.** 1986
product range ($12–22 CD) Shiraz, Merlot, Cabernet Sauvignon.
summary The Mulligan family has lived in the Penola/Coonawarra region since 1909. In 1937 a 250-hectare property 15 kms to the west of Penola, including an 80-hectare ridge of terra rossa over limestone, was purchased for grazing. The ridge was cleared; the remainder of the property was untouched and is now a private wildlife sanctuary. In 1986 Barry and Glenys Mulligan planted shiraz and cabernet sauvignon on the ridge, followed by merlot in the early 1990s. The first wines were made in 1990, and national distribution began in 1992, followed by exports in 1996. It remains a wholly estate-based operation.

st matthias   ★★★★☆

113 Rosevears Drive, Rosevears, Tas 7277 **region** Northern Tasmania
phone (03) 6330 1700 **fax** (03) 6330 1975 **open** 7 days 10–5
winemaker Michael Glover **production** 4000 **est.** 1983
product range ($9.35–24 CD) Riesling, Chardonnay, Pinot Noir, St Matthias (Cabernet blend).
summary After an uncomfortable period in the wilderness following the sale of the vineyard to Moorilla Estate, and the disposal of the wine made by the previous owners under the St Matthias label, Moorilla has re-introduced the label, and markets a full range of competitively priced wines which are in fact made at Moorilla Estate.

St Matthias Riesling

ŦŦŦŦ♈ **2001** Light green-yellow; lifted passionfruit and apple blossom aromatics introduce a palate with most attractive flavours tracking those of the bouquet, a veritable cornucopia of fruits, too much so for some palates (but not mine). **rating: 93**

best drinking 2002–2005 **best vintages** '97, '99, '01 **drink with** Salmon mousse • $18

St Matthias Cabernet Blend

ŦŦŦŦ♈ **1999** Medium red-purple; a fragrant bouquet, with sweet red berry aromas and just a touch of olive/green leaf. The palate is driven by a mix of sweet, fragrant berry fruit and neatly handled oak, finishing with fine tannins. Gold medal Tasmanian Wines Show 2002. **rating: 93**

best drinking 2004–2010 **best vintages** '99 **drink with** Lamb shanks • $24

st peters edenhope wines   NR

Whitton Stock Route, Yenda, NSW 2681 **region** Riverina
phone (02) 4285 3180 **fax** (02) 4285 3180 **open** Mon–Fri 9–5
winemaker Contract **production** 4000 **est.** 1977
product range ($8–20 CD) A wide variety of wines under the St Peters, Edenhope, Yenda Vineyards and Wilton Estate labels.
summary Draws grapes and wine from various parts of southern Australia and NSW for its dry table wines, most of which are sold overseas through Australian Prestige Wines.

salem bridge wines   ★★★☆

Salem Bridge Road, Lower Hermitage, SA 5131 **region** Adelaide Hills
phone (08) 8380 5240 **fax** (08) 8380 5240 **open** Not
winemaker Barry Miller **production** 300 **est.** 1989
product range ($19 R) Cabernet Franc.
summary Barry Miller acquired the 45-hectare Salem Bridge property in the Adelaide Hills of South Australia in 1988. A little under two hectares of cabernet franc were planted in 1989, and cabernet franc has been the only commercial release prior to 1999. However, a further 14 hectares have been planted to cabernet sauvignon, shiraz and merlot, with a Shiraz and Cabernet Sauvignon release in the pipeline. The wine is made off site by contract-winemaking, with input from Barry Miller.

🐚 salena estate   ★★★

Bookpurnong Road, Loxton, SA 5343 **region** Riverland
phone (08) 8584 1333 **fax** (08) 8584 1388 **open** Mon–Fri 8.30–5
winemaker Grant Semmens **production** 130 000 **est.** 1998
product range ($13–32 CD) At the bottom is the Salena Estate range of Chardonnay, Shiraz, Merlot, Cabernet Sauvignon; next is Ellen Landing Shiraz, Petit Verdot, Cabernet Sauvignon; at the top is the Bookpurnong Hill range of Shiraz, Block 267 (blend of Cabernet Sauvignon, Petit Verdot, Merlot, Shiraz), Cabernet Sauvignon; Amore Fortified Chardonnay.
summary This business, established in 1998, encapsulates the hectic rate of growth across the entire Australian wine industry. Its 1998 crush was 300 tonnes, and by 2001 it was processing 7000 tonnes. This was in part produced from over 200 hectares of estate vineyards, supplemented by grapes purchased from other growers. It is the venture of Bob and Sylvia Franchitto, the estate being named after their daughter Salena. Export distribution to the US, UK, Sweden, Malaysia, Hong Kong and Singapore has already been established to supplement local distribution; it is the export market which will take the lion's share.

Salena Estate Chardonnay

ŦŦŦŦ **2001** Medium yellow-green, quite advanced; the bouquet shows ripe melon fruit, with some oak said to be French; the palate has plenty of peachy fruit weight, linked with a hint of spicy oak. Drink soonest if not yesterday, but very good value, and with a number of show medals to its credit. **rating: 85**

best drinking 2002–2003 **best vintages** NA **drink with** Deep-fried chicken • $13

Salena Estate Ellen Landing Shiraz

ŦŦŦ♈ **2000** Light to medium red-purple; the bouquet has some savoury complexity and a touch of oak, the palate with more concentration than the varietal (and cheaper) version, but still with a hint of sweet and sour characters. **rating: 84**

best drinking 2002–2005 **best vintages** NA **drink with** Barbecue • $18

Salena Estate Bookpurnong Hill Cabernet Sauvignon

▼▼▼▽ **1998** Light to medium red-purple; pleasant, sweet cassis/berry aromas and a dusting of vanilla oak on the bouquet are followed by a mix of sweet berry fruit and vanilla oak on the palate, with some tannins; not particularly concentrated, but well enough balanced. **rating:** 84

best drinking 2002–2004 **best vintages** NA **drink with** Pasta • $32

Salena Estate Ellen Landing Cabernet Sauvignon

▼▼▼▼ **2000** Medium red-purple; ripe, slightly jammy confection aspects to the cassis fruit of the bouquet, but has character; the palate, similarly, has substance and some structure, with ripe tannins and a hint of cedar on the finish. **rating:** 85

best drinking 2002–2005 **best vintages** NA **drink with** Lamb casserole • $18

salitage ★★★★

Vasse Highway, Pemberton, WA 6260 **region** Pemberton
phone (08) 9776 1771 **fax** (08) 9776 1772 **open** 7 days 10–4
winemaker Patrick Coutts **production** 20 000 **est.** 1989
product range ($16–35 R) Chardonnay, Unwooded Chardonnay, Pinot Noir, Pemberton (Cabernet blend); Treehouse range Chardonnay Verdelho, Pinot Noir, Shiraz and Cabernets.
summary Salitage is the showpiece of Pemberton. If it had failed to live up to expectations, it is a fair bet the same fate would have befallen the whole of the Pemberton region. The quality and style of Salitage did vary substantially, presumably in response to vintage conditions and yields, but since 1999 seems to have found its way, with a succession of attractive wines. Key retail distribution in all states, and exports to New Zealand, Taiwan, Singapore, Japan, Hong Kong, Philippines, Malaysia, Germany, Switzerland, Canada, Denmark, Korea and Netherlands.

Salitage Treehouse Chardonnay Verdelho

▼▼▼▼ **2000** Medium yellow-green; the bouquet is soft, but quite fruity, with peachy/tropical fruit. There is more of the same on the palate, with plenty of easy-drinking flavour. **rating:** 85

best drinking 2001–2002 **best vintages** NA **drink with** Pasta marinara • $16

Salitage Chardonnay

▼▼▼▼ **2000** Medium yellow-green; the bouquet offers an exotic mix of spicy nutmeg oak and tangy grapefruit, the palate equally high flavoured, but with a slight confection overhang. **rating:** 89

best drinking 2001–2004 **best vintages** '98 **drink with** Turkey breast • $30

Salitage Pinot Noir

▼▼▼▼▽ **2000** Light to medium red-purple; a quite fragrant bouquet in the savoury/spicy end of the spectrum is followed by a palate with convincing flavour and structure in a lighter-bodied mode; strawberry and cherry flavours, and subtle oak. Another success for Salitage. **rating:** 92

best drinking 2002–2005 **best vintages** '93, '94, '99, '00 **drink with** Barbecued quail • $34

Salitage Pemberton Cabernet Blend

▼▼▼▼ **1999** Medium red-purple; the bouquet is relatively light, with slightly simple but clean, fresh berry fruit. A user-friendly style palate, with sweet berry fruit, sweet oak, and soft, ripe tannins. **rating:** 88

best drinking 2003–2008 **best vintages** '96 **drink with** Rolled shoulder of lamb • $32

saltram ★★★★☆

Salters Gully, Nuriootpa, SA 5355 **region** Barossa Valley
phone (08) 8564 3355 **fax** (08) 8564 2209 **open** 7 days 10–3
winemaker Nigel Dolan **production** NFP **est.** 1859
product range ($10–49.95 R) At the top is No. 1 Shiraz; then Mamre Brook, now 100 per cent Barossa and comprising Chardonnay, Shiraz and Cabernet Sauvignon; Metala Black Label and White Label; and the Saltram Classic range sourced from southeast Australia; also Pepperjack range with Shiraz and Cabernet Sauvignon.
summary There is no doubt that Saltram has taken giant strides towards regaining the reputation it held 30 or so years ago. Under Nigel Dolan's stewardship, grape sourcing has come back to the Barossa Valley for the flagship wines, a fact of which he is rightly proud. The red wines, in particular, have enjoyed great show success over the past few years, with No. 1 Shiraz, Mamre Brook and Metala leading the charge.

Saltram Pepperjack Grenache Rosé

▼▼▼▼ **2001** Light to medium purple-red; a fresh, clean bouquet with sweet small berry aromas, the palate with clearly articulated juicy/jammy, gently sweet fruit. There never has been any question about the suitability of grenache for this style of wine. **rating:** 86

best drinking 2002–2003 **best vintages** NA **drink with** Mediterranean food • $10

Saltram Mamre Brook Shiraz

▼▼▼▼▽ **1999** Medium red-purple; quite ripe, dark berry fruit aromas, with chocolate nuances flow into a palate with luscious, but not jammy, fruit, subtle oak and soft tannins. A major success for the vintage. **rating:** 92

best drinking 2004–2009 **best vintages** '98, '99 **drink with** Grilled calf's liver • $19

Saltram No. 1 Reserve Shiraz

▼▼▼▼▼ **1998** Excellent red-purple colour; a clean, rich, round and full bouquet is followed by a luscious and rich palate, full of black cherry and chocolate fruit, oak and tannins. At the big end of town, and will richly repay extended cellaring. Trophy winner 2001 Barossa Wine Show and gold medal 2001 Great Australian Shiraz Challenge. **rating:** 95

best drinking 2005–2018 **best vintages** '96, '97, '98 **drink with** Richly sauced casserole • $39.99

Pepperjack Barossa Shiraz

▼▼▼▼ **1999** Medium red-purple; the moderately intense, clean bouquet seems to open up and grow in fragrance as the wine airs; the palate has good substance with honest fruit, oak and tannins. **rating:** 87

▼▼▼▼ **1998** Medium red-purple; a moderately intense, clean bouquet, then a soft palate with ripe, savoury/chocolatey fruit, finishing with soft tannins. Minimal oak influence throughout. **rating:** 87

best drinking 2003–2008 **best vintages** '96 **drink with** Pepper steak • $20

Mamre Brook Cabernet Sauvignon

▼▼▼▼▽ **2000** Medium red-purple; an attractive, moderately intense bouquet with sweet cassis fruit and gentle oak, leading into a palate with good texture and luscious cassis fruit in the middle, finishing with fine tannins and neatly judged oak. **rating:** 90

▼▼▼▼ **1999** Medium red-purple; earthy/blackberry varietal fruit on the bouquet is followed by a smooth, sweet, juicy red berry palate with some tannins to lose; the oak input is controlled throughout. **rating:** 87

best drinking 2004–2011 **best vintages** '96, '98, '00 **drink with** Roast kid • $19.50

sandalford ★★★★

West Swan Road, Caversham, WA 6055 **region** Swan District
phone (08) 9374 9374 **fax** (08) 9274 2154 **open** 7 days 10–5
winemaker Paul Boulden **production** 80 000 **est.** 1840
product range ($12.95–35 R) At the bottom end under the Caversham label Chenin Verdelho, Late Harvest Cabernet Shiraz; then the 1840 Collection of Semillon Sauvignon Blanc, Chardonnay and Cabernet Merlot; under the premium range Margaret River Mount Barker Riesling, Margaret River Verdelho, Mount Barker Margaret River Chardonnay, Mount Barker Margaret River Shiraz, Mount Barker Margaret River Cabernet Sauvignon; also excellent fortifieds, notably Sandalera; also the new Element brand including Chenin Verdelho, Chardonnay and Cabernet Shiraz.
summary The installation of a new winemaking team headed by the energetic Paul Boulden, and continuing winery upgrading has meant that wine quality has continued to improve year by year, with good wines across the whole portfolio. The quality of the labelling and packaging has also taken a giant leap forwards. Exports to the UK, Switzerland, US, Japan, Singapore and Hong Kong.

Sandalford Margaret River Mount Barker Riesling

▼▼▼▼▽ **2001** Light green-yellow; the bouquet has a highly aromatic mix of herb, lime, blossom and mineral, moving more towards toast and mineral on the palate, which has bracing acidity. Should flower with time. **rating:** 91

best drinking 2003–2008 **best vintages** '92, '96, '01 **drink with** Chinese prawns • $22

Sandalford Semillon Sauvignon Blanc

▼▼▼▼ **2001** Light green-yellow; once again, the bouquet has a mix of blossom, passionfruit, lemon and grass, the palate well-balanced, fresh, clean and lively; gently sweet fruit runs through the mid-palate. **rating:** 89

best drinking 2001–2002 **best vintages** NA **drink with** Crab souffle • $18

Sandalford Classic Dry White

♈♈♈♈ **2001** Light to medium green-yellow; clean and fresh, with some light, ripe gooseberry aromas along with a touch of passionfruit; the palate has good length and, in particular, aftertaste. **rating:** 86

best drinking 2002–2003 **best vintages** NA **drink with** Trout mousse • $18.50

Sandalford Element Chardonnay

♈♈♈♈ **2000** Light to medium green-yellow; the bouquet is clean, not particularly complex, but the oak is neatly balanced with the fruit. The wine comes into its own on the palate, with good mid-palate flavour to the peach and nectarine fruit; likewise, good balance and length. **rating:** 87

best drinking 2001–2002 **best vintages** NA **drink with** Slow-roasted salmon • $13

Sandalford Margaret River Chardonnay

♈♈♈♈♈ **2001** Medium yellow-green; a complex bouquet with smoky barrel-ferment oak surrounding melon fruit; then a palate with good length and good acidity, with citrus/melon/stone fruit flavours to the fore, and oak less immediately obvious. **rating:** 92

best drinking 2002–2005 **best vintages** '01 **drink with** Chicken salad • $29.50

Sandalford Mount Barker Margaret River Shiraz

♈♈♈♈ **1999** Light to medium red-purple; a scented and fragrant bouquet with small, red berry fruits and some spice is followed by a mix of red berry, mint, spice and leaf on the palate, then sweet vanilla oak and soft tannins to conclude. Seems slightly unfocussed. **rating:** 87

best drinking 2003–2008 **best vintages** '94, '95, '97 **drink with** Lamb chops • $24.50

Sandalford Element Shiraz Cabernet

♈♈♈♈ **2001** Light to medium red-purple; light, juicy berry fruit on the bouquet is a simple enough start, but there is slightly more weight and push on the palate, which, while not complex, shows clever winemaking; good value. **rating:** 85

best drinking 2002–2003 **best vintages** NA **drink with** Steak and kidney pie • $12.50

Sandalford Cabernet Sauvignon

♈♈♈♈ **1999** Medium purple-red; smooth, redcurrant/blackberry fruit aromas flow into a gentle, red berry palate with quite savoury tannins, subtle oak and good acidity. **rating:** 88

best drinking 2003–2009 **best vintages** NA **drink with** Roast leg of lamb • $25

sandalyn wilderness estate   NR

Wilderness Road, Rothbury, NSW 2321 **region** Lower Hunter Valley
phone (02) 4930 7611 **fax** (02) 4930 7611 **open** 7 days 10–5
winemaker Adrian Sheridan (Contract) **production** 4000 **est.** 1988
product range ($16–22 CD) Semillon, Verdelho, Semillon Verdelho, Chardonnay, Semillon Late Harvest, Pinot Noir, Conservatory Shiraz, Sparkling.
summary Sandra and Lindsay Whaling preside over the picturesque cellar-door building of Sandalyn on the evocatively named Wilderness Road, where you will find a one-hole golf range and views to the Wattagan, Brokenback and Molly Morgan ranges. The estate has 8.85 hectares of vineyards.

sand hills vineyard   ★★☆

Sandhills Road, Forbes, NSW 2871 **region** Lachlan Valley
phone (02) 6852 1437 **fax** (02) 6852 4401 **open** Mon–Sat 9–5, Sun 12–5
winemaker Jill Lindsay **production** 1000 **est.** 1920
product range ($9–16 CD) Classic Dry White, Chardonnay, Colombard Semillon, Banderra The White, Vat 1 Dry Red, Dry Red, Pinot Noir, Shiraz Cabernet, Cabernet Shiraz, Banderra The Red, Oloroso Cream Sherry, Lucien Tawny Port.
summary Having purchased Sand Hills from long-term owner Jacques Genet, the Saleh family has replanted the vineyard to appropriate varieties, with over six hectares of premium varieties having been established. Winemaking is carried out by Jill Lindsay of Woodonga Hill.

sandhurst ridge   ★★★

156 Forest Drive, Marong, Vic 3515 **region** Bendigo
phone (03) 5435 2534 **fax** (03) 5435 2548 **open** Weekends 1–5 and by appointment
winemaker Paul Greblo, George Greblo **production** 2000 **est.** 1990

product range ($17–28 CD) Sauvignon Blanc, Chardonnay, Shiraz, Reserve Shiraz, Merlot, Cabernet Sauvignon.

summary The four Greblo brothers, with combined experience in business, agriculture, science and construction and development began the establishment of Sandhurst Ridge in 1990 with the planting of the first 2 hectares of shiraz and cabernet sauvignon. Those plantings have now been increased to over 6 hectares, principally cabernet and shiraz, but with small amounts of merlot, sauvignon blanc and chardonnay. The fully equipped winery was completed in 1996 with a cellar capacity of 400 barriques. The white wines are not up to standard, but there is no problem with the reds, which, on their own, would give the winery a significantly higher rating.

Sandhurst Ridge Reserve Shiraz

▼▼▼▼▽ **2000** Dense red-purple; dark berry and plum fruit teams with well-integrated oak on the bouquet. The palate provides more of the same, with rich, sweet, but not jammy dark plum fruit, ripe tannins and an appropriate jab of American oak in which the wine spent 12 months. **rating:** 90

best drinking 2005–2015 **best vintages** '00 **drink with** Aged venison • $28

Sandhurst Ridge Merlot

▼▼▼▽ **2000** Medium red-purple; the moderately intense bouquet has some savoury/leafy edges to the fruit, characters which come through in the minty/leafy aspects of the berry fruit. Partially varietal, no doubt, and the wine should have been ripe at 13.2°. **rating:** 83

best drinking 2003–2007 **best vintages** NA **drink with** Lamb shanks • $26

Sandhurst Ridge Cabernet Sauvignon

▼▼▼▼ **2000** Medium red-purple; clean and quite fragrant dark berry/currant fruit is echoed on the palate, which has a fragrant mix of spice, chocolate, berry and fine tannins; restrained oak handling adds to the elegance. **rating:** 87

best drinking 2004–2009 **best vintages** NA **drink with** Parmesan or aged cheddar • $26

sandstone ★★★

PO Box 558, Busselton, WA 6280 **region** Margaret River
phone (08) 9755 6271 **fax** (08) 9755 6292 **open** By appointment
winemaker Mike Davies, Jan Davies **production** 2000 **est.** 1988
product range ($22–27.50 ML) Semillon, Cabernet Sauvignon.
summary The family operation of consultant-winemakers Mike and Jan Davies, who also operate very successful mobile bottling plants. It will eventually be estate-based following the planting of 6 hectares of semillon and 2 hectares of cabernet sauvignon in 2002.

Sandstone Semillon

▼▼▼▽ **1999** Medium to full yellow-green; a solid, tangy bouquet with some old oak influence is followed by a solid, 4-square palate which, if nothing else, will age slowly. **rating:** 84

best drinking 2002–2005 **best vintages** '92, '93 **drink with** Avocado with seafood • $22

sandy farm vineyard NR

RMB 3734 Sandy Farm Road, Denver via Daylesford, Vic 3641 **region** Macedon Ranges
phone (03) 5348 7610 **open** Weekends 10–5 or by appointment
winemaker Peter Comisel **production** 800 **est.** 1988
product range ($15–20 CD) Pinot Noir, Merlot, Cabernet Sauvignon.
summary Peter Covell has a small, basic winery in which he makes preservative-free Cabernet Sauvignon, Merlot and Pinot Noir, attracting a loyal local following.

saracen estates ★★★☆

Bussell Highway/Gale Road, Metricup, WA 6280 **region** Margaret River
phone (08) 9321 2167 **fax** (08) 9321 2224 **open** By appointment
winemaker Dorham Mann **production** 12 000 **est.** 1998
product range ($15–25 R) Sauvignon Blanc, Classic Dry White, Chardonnay, Classic Dry Red, Cabernet Sauvignon.
summary The Cazzolli and Saraceni families have established 40 hectares of vines on their 80-hectare property at Metricup, with a restaurant and cellar door scheduled to be opened by the end of 2002. The

name not only echoes one of the founding families, but also pays tribute to the Saracens, one of the most advanced races in cultural and social terms at the time of the Crusades. The business has lost no time in securing eastern states distribution, with exports to the UK, Singapore and Malaysia.

Saracen Estates Sauvignon Blanc

▼▼▼▼ 2000 Light straw-green; a brisk, minerally bouquet with hints of herb leads into a crisp, direct palate which does not have a lot of fruit intensity per se. It is highly probable there is an element of young vine influence here. **rating: 85**

best drinking 2001–2002 **best vintages** NA **drink with** Marinated scallops • $20

Saracen Estates Classic Dry White

▼▼▼▽ 2000 Light straw-green; a grassy, lemony bouquet with flecks of mineral and herb is followed by a wine with a pleasant mid-palate, albeit fairly light-bodied, trailing off towards the finish. **rating: 84**

best drinking 2001–2002 **best vintages** NA **drink with** Cold seafood • $16

Saracen Estates Chardonnay

▼▼▼▼ 2000 Light to medium yellow-green; the aromatic bouquet offers melon, stone fruit and a light touch of French oak; the light to medium-bodied palate is clean, fresh and well-balanced, with the flavours replicating the bouquet. **rating: 86**

best drinking 2002–2006 **best vintages** NA **drink with** Green-lipped mussels • $20

Saracen Estates Classic Dry Red

▼▼▼▽ 1999 Medium red-purple; sweet berry and plum drive the moderately intense bouquet, with a flick of oak in the background. The firm and youthful palate has dark berry fruit on the mid-palate, the finish lacking the structure and density one obtains from mature vines. **rating: 84**

best drinking 2001–2004 **best vintages** NA **drink with** Spicy hamburger • $17

Saracen Estates Cabernet Sauvignon

▼▼▼▼▽ 1999 Bright red-purple; the bouquet is clean, bright and fresh with red and blackberry fruits, the palate well composed, with gently ripe cassis berry fruit, fine tannins and neatly balanced and integrated oak. **rating: 90**

best drinking 2003–2009 **best vintages** '99 **drink with** White Rocks veal • $23

sarsfield estate ★★★☆

345 Duncan Road, Sarsfield, Vic 3875 **region** Gippsland
phone (03) 5156 8962 **fax** (03) 5156 8970 **open** By appointment
winemaker Dr Suzanne Rutschmann **production** 1000 **est.** 1995
product range ($17.50–20 CD) Pinot Noir, Cabernets Shiraz Merlot.
summary The property is owned by Suzanne Rutschmann, who has a PhD in Chemistry, a Diploma in Horticulture and a BSc (Wine Science) from Charles Sturt University, and by Swiss-born Peter Albrecht, a civil and structural engineer who has also undertaken various courses in agriculture and viticulture. For a part-time occupation, these are exceptionally impressive credentials. Their 2-hectare vineyard was planted between 1991 and 1998; the first vintage made at the winery was 1998, the grapes being sold to others in previous years. High quality packaging a plus.

Sarsfield Estate Pinot Noir

▼▼▼▼▽ 2000 Good red-purple; the bouquet is not particularly aromatic, but does have some foresty/savoury elements; elegant, plummy varietal fruit comes through strongly on the palate, which has good length and balance, the oak being held nicely in restraint. Very impressive. **rating: 92**

best drinking 2002–2005 **best vintages** '00 **drink with** Braised duck • $20

Sarsfield Estate Cabernets Shiraz Merlot

▼▼▼▽ 2000 Light to medium red-purple; the light, earthy/leafy/spicy bouquet leads into a palate with a similar flavour spectrum; well made, but lacks flesh/ripeness. Very similar to the 1999 vintage, but a little more going for it. **rating: 84**

best drinking 2004–2008 **best vintages** NA **drink with** Shoulder of lamb • $17.50

scarborough ★★★★

Gillards Road, Pokolbin, NSW 2321 **region** Lower Hunter Valley
phone (02) 4998 7563 **fax** (02) 4998 7786 **open** 7 days 9–5
winemaker Ian Scarborough **production** 12 000 **est.** 1985

product range ($19–23 CD) Semillon, Blue Silver Label Chardonnay, Gold Label Chardonnay, Pinot Noir.
summary Ian Scarborough put his white winemaking skills beyond doubt during his years as a consultant, and has brought all of those skills to his own label. He makes two radically different styles of Chardonnay, the Blue Silver Label in a light, elegant, Chablis style for the export market and a much richer, strongly barrel-fermented wine (with a mustard/gold label) for the Australian market. However, the real excitement lies with the future and the portion of the old Lindemans Sunshine Vineyard which he has purchased (after it lay fallow for 30 years) and planted with semillon and (quixotically) pinot noir. If history is any guide, the semillon coming from this vineyard should be wonderful.

Scarborough Blue Silver Label Chardonnay

TTTT **2000** Light to medium yellow-green; a fragrant, clean nectarine fruit-driven bouquet, then a similarly bright and fresh palate with crisp acidity and little or no evidence of oak.   **rating:** 87

best drinking 2002–2003 **best vintages** NA **drink with** Grilled flathead • $19

Scarborough Gold Label Chardonnay

TTTTY **1999** Medium to full yellow-green; a complex, potent rich wine with sweet French barrel-ferment oak coming through strongly on the bouquet. Very well made, with lots of flavour and character on the palate; good balance between the ripe nectarine peach fruit and oak. The two Chardonnays are indeed two style opposites.   **rating:** 93

best drinking 2002–2003 **best vintages** '87, '89, '91, '94, '96, '98 **drink with** Rich white meat dishes • $23

scarpantoni estate   ★★★☆

Scarpantoni Drive, McLaren Flat, SA 5171 **region** McLaren Vale
phone (08) 8383 0186 **fax** (08) 8383 0490 **open** Mon–Fri 10–5, weekends 11–5
winemaker Michael Scarpantoni, Filippo Scarpantoni **production** 25 000 **est.** 1979
product range ($6-36 CD) Block 1 Riesling, Sauvignon Blanc, Unwooded Chardonnay, Chardonnay, Fleurieu Brut, Black Tempest (sparkling), Botrytis Riesling, Fiori, Gamay, School Block (Shiraz Cabernet Merlot), Block 3 Shiraz, Showcroft (Shiraz Grenache Gamay), Cabernet Sauvignon, Estate Reserve, Tawny Port, Vintage Port, V.P. Shiraz.
summary While an erratic producer at times, and not helped by the earlier use of agglomerate corks, has made some excellent wines in recent years which – if repeated – would earn the winery an even higher rating.

scarp valley vineyard   ★★★★

8 Robertson Road, Gooseberry Hill, WA 6076 **region** Perth Hills
phone (08) 9454 5748 **open** By appointment
winemaker Contract **production** 25 **est.** 1978
product range ($20 ML) Darling Range Hermitage.
summary Owner Robert Duncan presides over what has to be one of the smallest producers in Australia, with one-quarter acre of shiraz and 30 cabernet sauvignon vines producing a single cask of wine each year if the birds do not get the grapes first. The property, which has views all the way to the city of Perth, and cannot be built out, was being offered for sale in March 2002.

Scarp Valley Darling Range Hermitage

TTTTY **2001** Dense, inky purple-red; powerful dark berry fruit on the bouquet leads into a lush and equally powerful palate, with some tannin grip on the finish, and well handled oak throughout. The best yet from Scarp Valley, and demands patience.   **rating:** 90

best drinking 2006–2016 **best vintages** '01 **drink with** Fillet steak • $20

schild estate wines   ★★★☆

Cnr Barossa Valley Way and Lyndoch Valley Road, Lyndoch, SA 5351 **region** Barossa Valley
phone (08) 8524 5560 **fax** (08) 8524 4333 **open** 7 days 11–5
winemaker Rod Chapman (Contract) **production** 5500 **est.** 1998
product range ($13–23 ML) Barossa Valley Riesling, Eden Valley Riesling, Semillon, Chardonnay, Shiraz, Cabernet Sauvignon.
summary Ed Schild has been a Barossa Valley grape grower who first planted a small vineyard at Rowland Flat in 1952, steadily increasing his vineyard holdings over the past 40 years to their present level of 125 hectares. Currently only ten per cent of the production from these vineyards are used to produce Schild Estate Wines, but the plans are to steadily increase this percentage. The flagship wine will be made from

150-year-old shiraz vines on the Moorooroo Block, due for release late 2002. The cellar door sales is situated in what was the old ANZ Bank at Lyndoch, and provides the sort of ambience which can only be found in the Barossa Valley. Exports to Malaysia and the US.

Schild Estate Barossa Valley Riesling

▼▼▼▽ **2001** Light to medium yellow-green; the bouquet offers a mix of ripe, tropical fruit aromas on the one hand, and lime on the other. The palate picks up on those aromas, but is broad, soft and slightly short. A difficult vintage, to be sure. **rating:** 84

best drinking 2002–2003 **best vintages** NA **drink with** Stuffed eggplant • $15

Schild Estate Semillon

▼▼▼▼▽ **2000** Light to medium yellow-green; a complex bouquet, with some slightly reductive and/or solids fermentation aromas which, strangely enough, add to the appeal, rather than detract. The palate reinforces the impression of the bouquet, with length and intensity. **rating:** 90

best drinking 2002–2006 **best vintages** '00 **drink with** Smoked eel • $15

Schild Estate Shiraz

▼▼▼▽ **2000** Bright colour; the bouquet has a mix of ribena and chocolate, the solid palate providing more of the same in a slightly extractive mould. There is no question 2000 produced some unusual flavours in Barossa Shiraz. **rating:** 84

best drinking 2003–2007 **best vintages** NA **drink with** Barossa sausage • $23

Schild Estate Cabernet Sauvignon

▼▼▼▼ **2000** Medium red-purple; the bouquet has a mix of dark berry fruits and touches of forest and earth; the pleasantly soft palate has sweet berry fruit and vanilla oak, finishing with soft tannins. Not in the class of the excellent '99 vintage. **rating:** 86

best drinking 2004–2010 **best vintages** '99 **drink with** Roast lamb • $23

❧ schindler northway downs ★★★★

437 Stumpy Gully Road, Balnarring, Vic 3926 **region** Mornington Peninsula
phone (03) 5983 1945 **fax** (03) 9580 4262 **open** First weekend each month
winemaker Tammy Schindler-Hands **production** 450 **est.** 1996
product range ($18–22 ML) Schindler Chardonnay, Pinot Noir.
summary Establishment of the vineyard by the Schindler family began in 1996 with the planting of the first 2 hectares of pinot noir and chardonnay. A further 4 hectares of pinot noir were planted on an ideal north-facing slope in 1999, and the first vintage followed in 2000. The cellar door was subsequently established, and opens on the first weekend of each month, offering Austrian food and live Austrian music on the Sunday.

Schindler Northway Downs Chardonnay

▼▼▼▼ **2001** Light straw-green; a highly aromatic bouquet offering citrus, nectarine and even passionfruit, the oak barely evident, leads into a high-flavoured palate, all in all suggesting the impact of botrytis. **rating:** 89
▼▼▼▼▽ **2000** Light to medium green-yellow; some bottle development starting to appear on the bouquet, plus gentle malolactic fermentation/new oak adding spice to the nectarine fruit. The wine has excellent mouthfeel, with creamy/cashew malolactic characters, then nectarine fruit running through a long finish. **rating:** 93

best drinking 2002–2004 **best vintages** '00 **drink with** Marinated calamari • $18

Schindler Northway Downs Pinot Noir

▼▼▼▼▽ **2000** Excellent purple-red; rich, ripe spicy plum fruit aromas and a touch of oak lead into a palate with excellent depth and structure, featuring dark plum and soft, spicy tannins throughout; good length. **rating:** 93

best drinking 2002–2005 **best vintages** '00 **drink with** Wild mushroom risotto • $22

schmidts tarchalice ★★★

Research Road, Vine Vale via Tanunda, SA 5352 **region** Barossa Valley
phone (08) 8563 3005 **fax** (08) 8563 0667 **open** Mon–Sat 10–5, Sun 12–5
winemaker Christopher Schmidt **production** 1500 **est.** 1984
product range ($8.50–19.75 CD) Barossa Riesling, Eden Valley Riesling, Barossa Chardonnay, Barossa Semillon, Auslese Riesling, Shiraz Cabernet/Cabernet Franc, 4 different Ports and Old Liqueur Frontignac; Magna Carta Shiraz, Carta's Choice Shiraz Cabernet.
summary Typically has a range of fully mature wines at low prices available at cellar door.

scotchmans hill ★★★★

190 Scotchmans Road, Drysdale, Vic 3222 **region** Geelong
phone (03) 5251 3176 **fax** (03) 5253 1743 **open** 7 days 10.30–5.30
winemaker Robin Brockett **production** 65 000 **est.** 1982
product range ($16.50–29.50 CD) Sauvignon Blanc, Chardonnay, Pinot Noir, Cabernet Sauvignon
Merlot; Swan Bay range of Sauvignon Blanc Semillon, Chardonnay, Pinot Noir, Shiraz.
summary Situated on the Bellarine Peninsula, southeast of Geelong, with a well-equipped winery and
first class vineyards. It is a consistent performer with its Pinot Noir and has a strong following in both
Melbourne and Sydney for its astutely priced, competently made wines. A doubling in production has seen
the establishment of export markets to the UK and The Netherlands. The second label of Spray Farm takes
its name from a National Trust property with panoramic views of Port Phillip Bay and Melbourne, which
has also been planted to vines by the Brown family and is run as a distinct vineyard and brand operation.
The same 4 varieties are produced but at a lower price-point across the range.

Scotchmans Hill Pinot Noir

▼▼▼▼♀ **2000** Medium red-purple; spicy/savoury overtones to nicely ripened plummy fruit on the bouquet
is followed by a similar mix of savoury/foresty and riper plummy fruit flavours on the palate; gentle oak.

rating: 93

best drinking 2001–2004 **best vintages** '91, '92, '94, '97, '98, '00 **drink with** Squab • $29.50

scotts brook NR

Scotts Brook Road, Boyup Brook, WA 6244 **region** Blackwood Valley
phone (08) 9765 3014 **fax** (08) 9765 3015 **open** Weekends, school holidays 10–5 or by appointment
winemaker Aquila Estate (Contract) **production** 2000 **est.** 1987
product range ($11–19 CD) Riesling, Autumn Harvest White, Chardonnay, Cabernet Sauvignon.
summary The Scotts Brook winery at Boyup Brook (equidistant between the Margaret River and Great
Southern regions) has been developed by local schoolteachers Brian Walker and wife Kerry – hence the
opening hours during school holidays. There are 17.5 hectares of vineyards, but the majority of the
production is sold to other winemakers, with limited quantities being made by contract.

seldom seen vineyard ★★★☆

Cnr Gulgong and Hill End Roads, Mudgee, NSW 2850 **region** Mudgee
phone (02) 6372 0839 **fax** (02) 6372 1055 **open** 7 days 9.30–5
winemaker Barry Platt, Marcus Platt **production** 3000 **est.** 1987
product range ($10–19 CD) Unwooded Semillon, Semillon, Chardonnay Semillon, Unwooded
Chardonnay, Chardonnay, Autumn Harvest (dessert), Cabernet Sauvignon Shiraz, Liqueur Muscat.
summary A substantial grape grower (with 18 hectares of vineyards) which reserves a proportion of its
crop for making and release under its own label.

seppelt ★★★★★

RSD Seppeltsfield via Nuriootpa, SA 5355 **region** Barossa Valley
phone (08) 8568 6217 **fax** (08) 8562 8333 **open** 7 days 11–5
winemaker James Godfrey **production** NFP **est.** 1851
product range ($8–500 R) The great wines of Seppeltsfield are first and foremost Para Liqueur Port
(bottling 119), Para Liqueur 21 Year Old, Vintage Tawny, Show Tawny Port DP90, Rutherglen Show Muscat,
Rutherglen Show Tokay, Mount Rufus Finest Tawny Port DP4, Trafford DP30, Seppeltsfield Fino Sherry,
Show Amontillado DP116, Show Fino DP117, Show Oloroso DP38, Seppelt Show Vintage Shiraz, Dorrien
Cabernet Sauvignon. The other wines in the Seppelt portfolio are handled at Great Western. The 100 Year
Old Para Liqueur Port is the $500 a bottle (375 ml) jewel in the crown, the current vintage being the 1901.
summary A multi-million-dollar expansion and renovation programme has seen the historic Seppeltsfield
winery become the production centre for the Seppelt wines, adding another dimension to what was already
the most historic and beautiful major winery in Australia. It is now home to some of the world's unique
fortified wines, nurtured and protected by the passionate James Godfrey. Worldwide distribution.

Seppelt Rutherglen Show Tokay DP57

▼▼▼▼▼ NV Mahogany gold; complex, sweet and rich tea-leaf, raisin and plum pudding aromas are followed
by an equally complex, multiflavoured palate which leaves the mouth fresh, thanks to its perfect balance.

rating: 94

best drinking 2002–2019 **best vintages** NA **drink with** Fine, dark chocolate • NA

Seppelt Show Reserve Muscat

❦❦❦❦❦ NV Deep mahogany brown, with a mix of gold and green on the rim. Rich, raisined, spicy plum pudding aromas are lifted by perfectly balanced and integrated spirit. The powerful, complex and rich palate – plum pudding and Christmas cake – has a very long, lingering finish. **rating:** 96

best drinking 2002–2002 **best vintages** NA **drink with** Dried fruits • NA

Seppelt Amontillado Sherry DP116

❦❦❦❦❦ NV Bright mid-gold; the bouquet has a lovely touch of honey over the bite of the rancio; the very elegant, very fresh palate finishes distinctly dry after the mellowness of the bouquet and mid-palate. This is as it should be. **rating:** 94

best drinking 2002–2003 **best vintages** NA **drink with** A great winter aperitif • NA

Seppelt Show Fino Sherry DP117

❦❦❦❦❦ NV Brilliant green-yellow; the bouquet is strong and stylish, with that faintly nutty, faintly tangy cut which is the hallmark of Fino Sherry. The palate is intense and racy, the flavour lingering in the mouth long after the wine is swallowed, but not so long to stop you taking the next mouthful. **rating:** 96

best drinking 2002–2003 **best vintages** NA **drink with** Olives, tapas • NA

Seppelt Show Oloroso Sherry DP38

❦❦❦❦❦ NV Golden brown; nutty rancio complexity, with just a hint of sweetness, introduce a finely balanced palate with a constant interplay between nutty, honeyed sweetness and drier, rancio characters. **rating:** 95

best drinking 2002–2003 **best vintages** NA **drink with** Sweet biscuits • NA

Seppelt Show Tawny Port DP90

❦❦❦❦❦ NV The tawny hues are rimmed with olive-green, immediately proclaiming the age of the wine. The bouquet is fine, fragrant and penetrating, much closer to the Tawny Ports of Portugal than most Australian wines. The palate offers flavours of spice, butterscotch and more nutty characters, but it is the length of flavour and finish which is absolutely remarkable. Given its age, arguably the most undervalued wine on the Australian market today. **rating:** 97

best drinking 2002–2003 **best vintages** NA **drink with** Dried fruits and nuts • NA

Seppelt 100 Year Old Para Liqueur Port

❦❦❦❦❦ 1897 Dark olive-brown, tinged with green, and pours like viscous oil; the bouquet leaps out of the glass, with cascades of aroma; plum pudding, toffee and the works lifted by the touch of volatility one always encounters. The tiniest sip is overwhelming, drawing saliva from every corner of the mouth; incredibly concentrated and essency. **rating:** 94

best drinking 2002–2017 **best vintages** 1886, 1887, 1890, 1892, 1894, 1897 **drink with** The finest quality double expresso coffee • NA

Seppelt Para Liqueur Port

❦❦❦❦❦ NV Dark mahogany tinged with green; the bouquet is complex, and both richer and sweeter than DP90 with malt, butterscotch and strong rancio characters. The palate has complex structure and great power, yet paradoxically has an almost dry finish, and no biscuity aftertaste. **rating:** 94

best drinking 2002–2003 **best vintages** NA **drink with** Coffee, chocolate • NA

seppelt great western ★★★★★

Moyston Road, Great Western via Ararat, Vic 3377 **region** Grampians
phone (03) 5361 2222 **fax** (03) 5361 2200 **open** 7 days 10–5
winemaker Paul Lapsley **production** 2 million **est.** 1865
product range ($8–61 R) Mèthode Champenoise comprising (from the bottom up) Brut Reserve, Imperial Reserve, Rosé Reserve, Grande Reserve, Fleur de Lys, Original Sparkling Shiraz, Show Sparkling Shiraz Great Western Vineyard, Show Sparkling Reserve Drumborg Blanc de Blancs and Salinger; table wines include Sheeoak Spring Riesling, Drumborg Riesling, Partalunga Sauvignon Blanc, Drumborg Sauvignon Blanc, Mornington Peninsula Pinot Gris, Drumborg Pinot Grigio, Eden Valley Botrytis Gewürztraminer, Sunday Creek Pinot Noir, Drumborg Pinot Noir, Chalambar Shiraz, Great Western Shiraz, Harpers Range Cabernet Sauvignon, Drumborg Cabernet Sauvignon, Dorrien Cabernet Sauvignon.
summary Australia's best-known producer of sparkling wine, always immaculate in its given price range but also producing excellent Great Western-sourced table wines, especially long-lived Shiraz and Australia's best Sparkling Shirazs. The somewhat cluttered product range and ever-changing labels are likely to be significantly pruned and stabilised under the new Rosemount regime.

Seppelt Drumborg Riesling

TTTTY **2000** Light straw-green; a crisp bouquet with freshly cut green apple and floral notes is followed by a palate with pronounced apple and underlying citrus, with a vaguely musky overtone. An unusual wine for the vineyard, but certainly has character, the finish dry. **rating:** 90

TTTTT **1999** Light green-yellow; a classic and intense mix of lime, passionfruit, mineral and toast on the bouquet is followed by a tight, beautifully modulated palate with exceptional length. Has been a prolific trophy winner already; perhaps closing down as it enters the transition phase, and all it needs is time in bottle. **rating:** 94

best drinking 2004–2010 **best vintages** '98 **drink with** Chinese prawns with cashews • $25

Seppelt Drumborg Chardonnay

TTTTT **2000** Light to medium yellow-green; a complex yet elegant bouquet, with excellent fruit intensity and balance, offering melon, fig and a hint of butterscotch. The palate, likewise, has good balance and length, showing no sign of excess alcohol or heat, and beautifully balanced fruit and oak. (Not yet released.) **rating:** 95

best drinking 2003–2008 **best vintages** '00 **drink with** Pan-fried veal • $25

Seppelt Salinger Mèthode Champenoise

TTTTY **1995** Bright yellow-green, the fresh lemony/citrussy bouquet is complexed by delicate bready/creamy/yeasty autolysis characters, the palate with Salinger's hallmark harmony and finesse. **rating:** 93

best drinking 2001–2002 **best vintages** '88, '89, '90, '91, '93, '94, '95 **drink with** Aperitif, oysters, shellfish • $26.50

Seppelt Fleur de Lys Pinot Noir Chardonnay

TTTT **1995** Medium to full yellow-green; the bouquet is solid, with some bready aromas, the palate with fair flavour and length, though perhaps less powerful than one might expect from a wine of this age. **rating:** 86

best drinking 2001–2002 **best vintages** '93, '94 **drink with** Oysters or shellfish • $17

Seppelt Fleur de Lys Chardonnay Pinot

TTTT **NV** Light to medium yellow-green; the bouquet is quite complex, with rich toasty/bready aromas, the well-balanced palate more delicate than the bouquet suggests it will be, but by no means to its disadvantage. **rating:** 88

best drinking 2001–2002 **best vintages** NA **drink with** Hors d'oeuvres • $12

Seppelt Drumborg Pinot Noir

TTTTY **1999** Medium red-purple; a stylish, tangy/savoury bouquet is followed by a long, medium–bodied palate, predominantly savoury but with some wood strawberry flavours; fine tannin extract and good acidity. One of the few very good Pinot Noirs from the 1999 vintage. **rating:** 93

best drinking 2001–2005 **best vintages** '99 **drink with** Rare duck breast • $42.70

Seppelt Great Western Shiraz

TTTTT **1997** Old vines and 18 months in new French oak produce a wondrously complex array of dark berry, plum, leather, licorice and chocolate aromas and flavours, the concentration of the fruit offset by savoury tannins. **rating:** 96

best drinking 2004–2017 **best vintages** '54, '56, '60, '63, '71, '84, '85, '86, '91, '93, '95, '96, '97 **drink with** Braised ox cheek • $37.30

Seppelt Chalambar Shiraz

TTTTY **1999** Medium red-purple; fresh red and black berry fruit with some spicy aromas are followed by a well-balanced palate with ripe cherry, plum and prune fruit; soft tannins, and more accessible than previous vintages. **rating:** 91

best drinking 2003–2013 **best vintages** '53–63, '91, '93, '94, '95, '96, '97, '98, '99 **drink with** Braised game dishes • $23

⚘ serafino wines ★★★☆

McLarens on the Lake, Kangarilla Road, McLaren Vale, SA 5171 **region** McLaren Vale
phone (08) 8323 0157 **fax** (08) 8323 9010 **open** Mon–Fri 10–5, weekends and public holidays 10–4.30
winemaker Scott Rawlinson **production** 17 000 **est.** 2000
product range ($12–21 ML) Serafino range of Semillon, Chardonnay, Shiraz, Merlot, Cabernet Sauvignon; McLarens on the Lake range of Chardonnay, Chardonnay Pinot NV Brut, Reserve Chardonnay Pinot, Cabernet Shiraz Merlot, Old Tawny Port.

summary In the wake of the sale of Maglieri Wines to Beringer Blass in 1998, Maglieri founder Steve Maglieri acquired the McLarens on the Lake complex which had originally been established by Andrew Garrett. The accommodation has been upgraded and a larger winery was commissioned prior to the 2002 vintage. The operation draws upon 40 hectares each of shiraz and cabernet sauvignon, 7 hectares of chardonnay, 2 hectares each of merlot, semillon, barbera, nebbiolo and sangiovese, and 1 hectare of grenache. Part of the grape production will be sold to others, the remainder to produce wines under the Serafino and McLarens on the Lake labels. Exports to the UK, US, Asia, Italy and New Zealand.

Serafino Shiraz

TTTT▽ **1999** Medium red; the bouquet has lifted vanillin aromatics; the palate, while similarly oaky, has very attractive red cherry and plum fruit, finishing with soft tannins. A trophy and gold medal McLaren Vale Wine Show 2001. **rating:** 90

TTTT 1998 Full red-purple; strong, slightly pencilly American oak on both bouquet and palate needs to integrate with the abundant and lush sweet cherry/berry fruit which is as yet enveloped by that oak.
rating: 87

best drinking 2002–2007 **best vintages** NA **drink with** Steak and kidney pie • $21

serventy ★ ★ ☆

Valley Home Vineyard, Rocky Road, Forest Grove, WA 6286 **region** Margaret River
phone (08) 9757 7534 **fax** (08) 9757 7534 **open** Fri–Sun, holidays 10–4
winemaker Peter Serventy **production** 1500 **est.** 1984
product range ($15 CD) Chardonnay, Pinot Noir, Shiraz.
summary Peter Serventy is nephew of the famous naturalist Vincent Serventy and son of ornithologist Dominic Serventy. It is hardly surprising, then, that Serventy should practise strict organic viticulture, using neither herbicides nor pesticides. The wines, too, are made with a minimum of sulphur dioxide, added late in the piece and never exceeding 30 parts per million.

settlers ridge NR

54b Bussell Highway, Cowaramup, WA 6284 **region** Margaret River
phone (08) 9755 5883 **fax** (08) 9755 5883 **open** 7 days 10–5
winemaker Wayne Nobbs **production** 3200 **est.** 1994
product range ($15–27 CD) Chenin Blanc, Sauvignon Blanc, Shiraz, Merlot, Sangiovese Novello, Cabernet Sauvignon.
summary Wayne and Kaye Nobbs have established what they say is the only winery in WA with organic certification and the only winery in Australia with dual classification from NASAA (National Association for Sustainable Agriculture Australia) and OVAA (Organic Vignerons Association of Australia Inc.). They have seven hectares of vineyard, including shiraz, cabernet sauvignon, merlot, sangiovese, malbec, chenin blanc and sauvignon blanc. Exports to Germany.

settlers rise montville ★ ★ ★

249 Western Avenue, Montville, Qld 4560 **region** Queensland Coastal
phone (07) 5478 5558 **fax** (07) 5478 5655 **open** 7 days 10–5
winemaker Peter Scudamore-Smith (Contract) **production** 3000 **est.** 1998
product range ($11.50–26.50 CD) Queensland Classic White, Blackall Range White, Sauvignon Blanc, Semillon Chardonnay, Verdelho, Chardonnay, Reserve Shiraz, Shiraz Cabernet, Lake Baroon Cabernet Merlot, Tawny Port.
summary Settlers Rise is located in the beautiful highlands of the Blackall Range, 75 minutes drive north of Brisbane and 20 minutes from the Sunshine Coast. A little over a hectare of chardonnay, verdelho, shiraz and cabernet sauvignon have been planted at an elevation of 450 metres on the deep basalt soils of the property. First settled in 1887, Montville has gradually become a tourist destination, with a substantial local arts and crafts industry and a flourishing bed and breakfast and lodge accommodation infrastructure.

Settlers Rise Montville Chardonnay

TTT▽ **2000** Medium yellow-green; the light bouquet gains some complexity from the subtle touch of barrel ferment oak; the palate has pleasant balance and texture; there is not a lot of fruit, but the wine is well made. Partially barrel-fermented, and seven months on lees in French oak. **rating:** 84

best drinking 2002–2003 **best vintages** NA **drink with** Mud crab • $18.50

Settlers Rise Montville Reserve Shiraz

TTTT 2000 Medium red-purple; the bouquet has an array of savoury, cedary, spicy, earthy, vanillin aromas which also come through strongly on the palate, where there is some red berry fruit lurking. Overall, the wine is oak-pushed, but cleverly done. A blend of Burnett, Inglewood and Montville fruit which spent 17 months in a mix of new French and American oak. **rating: 85**

best drinking 2002–2007 **best vintages** NA **drink with** Smoked lamb • $26.50

Settlers Rise Montville Lake Baroon Cabernet Merlot

TTTT 2000 Medium red-purple; a clean bouquet, with nicely balanced dark berry fruit and oak; attractive fruit comes through initially on the palate, with oak and oak tannins coming through strongly on the finish, but well within bounds. The best of a neat range of wines; a 50/50 blend sourced from North Burnett and the Granite Belt, which spends 10 months in new French and American oak. **rating: 87**

best drinking 2004–2009 **best vintages** NA **drink with** Boned leg of lamb • $18.50

sevenhill cellars ★★★★

College Road, Sevenhill, SA 5453 **region** Clare Valley
phone (08) 8843 4222 **fax** (08) 8843 4382 **open** Mon–Fri 9–4.30, Saturday and public holidays 10–4
winemaker Brother John May, John Monten **production** 20 000 **est.** 1851
product range ($8–20 CD) Riesling, Gewürztraminer, Semillon, St Aloysius (Chenin Blanc, Chardonnay, Verdelho blend), College White, Verdelho, Botrytis Semillon, Shiraz, Shiraz Touriga Malbec, Merlot, Cabernet Sauvignon, St Ignatius (Cabernet Sauvignon Malbec Cabernet Franc Merlot blend), Fortifieds, Sacramental Wine.
summary One of the historical treasures of Australia; the oft-photographed stone wine cellars are the oldest in the Clare Valley, and winemaking is still carried out under the direction of the Jesuitical Manresa Society and in particular Brother John May. Quality is very good, particularly that of the powerful Shiraz, all the wines reflecting the estate-grown grapes from old vines. Extensive retail distribution throughout all states; exports to New Zealand, Switzerland, Germany and Ireland.

Sevenhill Cellars Riesling

TTTTT 2001 Light green-yellow, it has a classic mix of lime, mineral, toast and spice, the fruit flavours exploding on the palate, giving the wine great length and balance. **rating: 95**

best drinking 2001–2010 **best vintages** '87, '89, '91, '92, '94, '97, '01 **drink with** Sashimi • $19.95

Sevenhill Cellars Botrytis Semillon

TTTT 2001 Medium yellow-green; the bouquet shows complexity, undoubtedly triggered by botrytis. The palate is profoundly sweet, but really needs more acidity to provide balance. **rating: 84**

best drinking 2001–2004 **best vintages** NA **drink with** Crème brûlée • NA

Sevenhill Cellars Cabernet Shiraz

TTTT 1999 Medium red-purple; the bouquet is quite scented, with an array of complex earthy/savoury aromas. The same characters come through on the savoury/briary/brambly palate, which finishes with soft, ripe tannins. **rating: 85**

best drinking 2003–2007 **best vintages** NA **drink with** Designer sausages • NA

sevenoaks wines NR

304 Doyles Creek Road, Jerrys Plains, NSW 2330 **region** Lower Hunter Valley
phone (02) 9579 5325 **open** By appointment, phone (02) 6576 4285
winemaker John Hordern (Contract) **production** 1300 **est.** 1997
product range ($15–24 CD) Vino Estivo Sangiovese, Rows 1 to 26 Shiraz.
summary Robert and Deborah Sharp established Sevenoaks Wines in 1997 with the original intention of selling the grapes to other winemakers. With only 1.85 hectares of shiraz, 1.45 hectares of sangiovese and 0.25 hectares of petit verdot, it was inevitable the wine from their grapes would be blended with many others, so in 2000 the Sharps changed course, retaining John Hordern as contract winemaker. The vineyard is part of a 68-hectare property which abuts the Wollemi National Park at the bottom of the slopes that rise to be Mount Woodlands.

Sevenoaks Rows 1 to 26 Shiraz

❦❦❦❦ 2000 Medium red-purple; the bouquet is fragrant, but is showing a lot of oak, apparently American. The palate has interesting texture and structure, possessing finesse as well as lots of fruit and soft oak flavour. **rating:** 86

best drinking 2003–2008 **best vintages** NA **drink with** Beef bourgignon • $24

severn brae estate   NR

Lot 2 Back Creek Road (Mount Tully Road), Severnlea, Qld 4352 **region** Granite Belt
phone (07) 4683 5292 **fax** (07) 3391 3821 **open** Mon–Fri 12–3, weekends 10–5, or by appointment
winemaker Bruce Humphery-Smith **production** 1400 **est.** 1987
product range ($14–16 ML) Murray Grey White, Unwooded Chardonnay, Estate Chardonnay, Light Fruity Red, Merlot Sangiovese, Reserve Shiraz; Liqueur Muscat and Chardonnay.
summary Patrick and Bruce Humphery-Smith have established 5.5 hectares of chardonnay with relatively close spacing and trained on a high two-tier trellis. Winery and cellar-door facilities were completed in time for the 1995 vintage.

seville estate   ★★★★★

Linwood Road, Seville, Vic 3139 **region** Yarra Valley
phone (03) 5964 2622 **fax** (03) 5964 2633 **open** Weekends and public holidays 10–5
winemaker Iain Riggs **production** 5000 **est.** 1970
product range ($12–35 ML) Chardonnay Sauvignon Blanc, Chardonnay, Pinot Noir, Shiraz, Cabernet Sauvignon; new GP label of Chardonnay Semillon and Cabernet Sauvignon in honour of winery founder Dr Peter McMahon.
summary In February 1997 a controlling interest in Seville Estate was acquired by Brokenwood (of the Hunter Valley) and interests associated with Brokenwood. I was one of the founding partners of Brokenwood, and the acquisition meant that the wheel had turned full circle. This apart, Seville Estate has added significantly to the top-end of the Brokenwood portfolio, without in any way competing with the existing styles. Hit a purple patch with its 2000 vintage wines.

Seville Estate Chardonnay

❦❦❦❦❦ 2000 Medium yellow-green; ripe stone fruit and melon aromas lead into a palate with that tactile/squeaky mouthfeel; good length, building progressively after a quiet start; impeccable oak handling throughout. **rating:** 92

best drinking 2002–2006 **best vintages** '99, '00 **drink with** Yabbies or marron • $23.50

Seville Estate Pinot Noir

❦❦❦❦❦ 2000 Good colour, clean cherry and plum fruit, and sympathetic oak handling lead into a palate with harmonious mouthfeel and balance, sustained by sweet plum and spice fruit. Oozes development potential. **rating:** 94

best drinking 2003–2009 **best vintages** '00 **drink with** Rare breast of squab • $23.50

Seville Estate Shiraz

❦❦❦❦❦ 2000 Medium to full purple-red; spotlessly clean, rich and sweet black cherry/raspberry fruit is followed by a palate with excellent weight and balance, again with sweet, black cherry/raspberry/plum fruit and vanilla oak, but no spice. 14° alcohol may tell that tale. Has elegance, despite the alcohol. **rating:** 94

best drinking 2003–2010 **best vintages** '88, '90, '91, '92, '93, '94, '97, '00 **drink with** Pot-au-feu • $23.50

Seville Estate Reserve Cabernet Sauvignon

❦❦❦❦ 1999 Medium red-purple; the bouquet offers a mix of cedary/toasty/spicy oak plus sweet cassis berry fruit; the light to medium-bodied palate is clean, with pleasantly sweet berry fruit, and low tannins. Carries its remarkable 14° alcohol with ease. **rating:** 89

best drinking 2004–2009 **best vintages** NA **drink with** Spring lamb • $35

shadowfax vineyard and winery   ★★★★☆

K Road, Werribee, Vic 3030 **region** Geelong
phone (03) 9731 4420 **fax** (03) 9731 4421 **open** 7 days 11–5
winemaker Matt Harrop **production** 15 000 **est.** 2000
product range ($18–58 CD) Riesling, Sauvignon Blanc, Sauvignon Blanc Semillon, Pinot Gris, Chardonnay, Pinot Noir, Geelong Pinot Noir, McLaren Vale Shiraz, Yarra Valley Cabernet Sauvignon.

summary Shadowfax is part of an awesome development at Werribee Park, a mere 20 minutes from Melbourne towards Geelong. The truly striking winery, designed by Wood Marsh architects, was erected in time for the 2000 vintage crush, adjacent to the extraordinary 60-room private home built in the 1880s by the Chirnside family and known as The Mansion. It was then the centrepiece of a 40 000-hectare pastoral empire, and the appropriately magnificent gardens were part of the reason why the property was acquired by Parks Victoria in the early 1970s. The Mansion is now The Mansion Hotel, with 92 rooms and suites, with the emphasis on conference bookings during the week, and general tourism on the weekend. The striking packaging of the wines, and the quality of the first releases, all underline the thoroughly serious nature of this quite amazing venture. Exports to the UK.

Shadowfax Geelong Pinot Gris

ᵀᵀᵀᵀ 2001 Light straw-green; a range of dried fruit, spices, peach skin and berry aromatics lead into a palate with abundant character and weight, but is not particularly focussed. One cannot help but wonder whether a slightly less exuberant fermentation would have helped on this score. **rating:** 86

best drinking 2001–2002 **best vintages** NA **drink with** Mediterranean food • $24

Shadowfax Chardonnay

ᵀᵀᵀᵀ 2000 Light to medium yellow-green; complex barrel-ferment influences come through on intense melon and cashew fruit on the bouquet. The palate is more fruit-driven than the bouquet, and has a particularly attractive mid-palate and finish. A truly stylish wine. **rating:** 93

best drinking 2001–2005 **best vintages** '00 **drink with** Rock lobster • $28.50

Shadowfax Vineyard and Winery Pinot Noir

ᵀᵀᵀᵀ 2000 Medium red-purple; plum and vanilla oak intermingle on the bouquet, leading into a palate with generous, sweet cherry/plum fruit and a well-structured, long finish. **rating:** 90

best drinking 2001–2005 **best vintages** '00 **drink with** Braised duck Chinese-style • $30

Shadowfax Geelong Pinot Noir

ᵀᵀᵀᵀᵀ 2000 Medium red, with a touch of purple remaining; a fragrant, warm and spicy bouquet shows the excellent use of French oak; the palate is in similar mode, with lovely warmth to the plum and spice fruit cradled in a silky texture. **rating:** 94

best drinking 2002–2005 **best vintages** '00 **drink with** Duck confit • $55

Shadowfax McLaren Vale Shiraz

ᵀᵀᵀᵀ 2000 Medium to full red-purple; quite ripe and luscious raspberry, plum and spice aromas lead into a rounded, light to medium-bodied palate, which has a curiously light entry to the mouth, picking up thereafter, finishing with subtle oak and soft tannins. **rating:** 87

best drinking 2003–2007 **best vintages** NA **drink with** Venison • $33

Shadowfax Yarra Valley Cabernet Sauvignon

ᵀᵀᵀᵀᵀ 2000 Medium to full red-purple; a complex blend of blackcurrant fruit and spicy, slightly charry, oak on the bouquet leads into a palate with great depth to the layered blackberry and blackcurrant fruit; long and flavoursome, with well controlled extract. A top result from a top vintage. **rating:** 94

best drinking 2005–2015 **best vintages** '00 **drink with** Barbecued butterfly leg of lamb • $30

shantell ★★★★☆

1974 Melba Highway, Dixons Creek, Vic 3775 **region** Yarra Valley
phone (03) 5965 2264 **fax** (03) 5965 2331 **open** 7 days 10.30–5
winemaker Shan Shanmugam, Turid Shanmugam **production** 2500 **est.** 1980
product range ($15–32 CD) Semillon, Chardonnay, Glenlea Chardonnay, Pinot Noir, Shiraz, Cabernet Sauvignon, Sparkling.
summary The substantial and now fully mature Shantell vineyards provide the winery with a high-quality fruit source; part is sold to other Yarra Valley makers, the remainder vinified at Shantell. In January 1998 Shantell opened a new cellar door situated at 1974 Melba Highway, 50 metres along a service road from the highway proper. Chardonnay, Semillon and Cabernet Sauvignon are its benchmark wines, sturdily reliable, sometimes outstanding (witness the 1997 and 2000 Chardonnay). An on-site cafe provides light lunches. Domestic and international distribution through Australian Prestige Wines.

Shantell Semillon

TTTTY **2000** Glowing yellow-green; complex, powerful tangy fruit on the bouquet is followed by a remarkably powerful and intense palate, with a mix of citrus and mineral. **rating:** 93

best drinking 2002–2006 **best vintages** '88, '90, '91, '92, '93, '97, '00 **drink with** Abalone • $15

Shantell Chardonnay

TTTTT **2000** Light to medium green-yellow; the spotlessly clean, fruit-driven bouquet ranges through nectarine, melon and citrus, the same intense varietal fruit driving the long and perfectly balanced palate; the oak is there for reasons of texture and structure as much as flavour. Super wine. **rating:** 94

best drinking 2002–2007 **best vintages** '90, '92, '94, '97, '98, '99, '00 **drink with** Yarra Valley smoked trout • $24

sharmans ★★★★

Glenbothy, 175 Glenwood Road, Relbia, Tas 7258 **region** Northern Tasmania
phone (03) 6343 0773 **fax** (03) 6343 0773 **open** Weekends by appointment
winemaker James Chatto, Rosevears Estate (Contract) **production** 700 **est.** 1987
product range ($15–25 ML) Riesling, Sauvignon Blanc, Chardonnay, Noble Late Harvest, Pinot Noir, Cabernet Sauvignon, Shaman.
summary Mike Sharman has very probably pioneered one of the more interesting wine regions of Tasmania, not far south of Launceston but with a distinctly warmer climate than (say) Pipers Brook. Ideal north-facing slopes are home to a vineyard now approaching 3 hectares, most still to come into bearing. The few wines produced in sufficient quantity to be sold promise much for the future.

Sharmans Riesling

TTTTY **2000** Light green-yellow; an intense bouquet in classic mould has contrasting highlights of lime and kerosene, the abundantly flavoured palate replicating the bouquet. Very strong silver medal Tasmanian Wines Show 2002. **rating:** 93

best drinking 2002–2005 **best vintages** '00 **drink with** Sashimi • $16

Sharmans Chardonnay

TTTY **2000** Light green-yellow; both the bouquet and palate are crisp and citrussy, the oak subtle, and overall still to show much development. May well surprise with another two years or so in bottle. **rating:** 84

best drinking 2002–2005 **best vintages** NA **drink with** Angel hair pasta • $18

shaw & smith ★★★★★

Lot 4 Jones Road, Balhannah, SA 5242 **region** Adelaide Hills
phone (08) 8398 0500 **fax** (08) 8398 0600 **open** Weekends 10–4
winemaker Martin Shaw, Willy Lunn **production** 30 000 **est.** 1989
product range ($17–32 ML) Sauvignon Blanc, Unoaked Chardonnay, Reserve Chardonnay, M3 Vineyard Chardonnay, Merlot; also Incognito range of Riesling, Chardonnay, Merlot.
summary Has progressively moved from a contract grape-grown base to estate production. First came the development of a 40-hectare vineyard at Balhannah in the Adelaide Hills, followed by the erection prior to the 2000 vintage of a state-of-the-art, beautifully designed and executed winery at Balhannah, ending the long period of tenancy at Petaluma. While wine quality has been exemplary, the perfectionism of Martin Shaw will now receive full play. The wines have wide international distribution including the UK, Japan, US, Canada, Hong Kong, Japan and Singpaore.

Incognito Riesling

TTTT **2001** Light straw-green; a clean, lively, fine lime and apple bouquet, then a delicate, fine and crisp palate, finishing with minerally acidity, has all that is needed to age with grace. **rating:** 89

best drinking 2002–2010 **best vintages** NA **drink with** Blue swimmer crab • $17

Shaw & Smith Sauvignon Blanc

TTTTT **2001** Pale straw-green; an intensely fragrant bouquet offers a mix of passionfruit, kiwifruit and gooseberry, followed by a crisp and lively palate with good length and acidity. Must be one of the best, if not the best, Sauvignon Blancs from the 2001 vintage. **rating:** 94

best drinking 2001–2002 **best vintages** '92, '93, '95, '97, '99, '00, '01 **drink with** Poached mussels • $22

Shaw & Smith Unoaked Chardonnay

▼▼▼▼ **2001** Light green-yellow; a faintly smoky/tangy edge to the citrus fruit of the bouquet adds interest; citrus/nectarine/apple flavours make for a palate with good length and balanced acidity.　　**rating:** 88

best drinking 2001–2004 **best vintages** '00 **drink with** Pan-fried scallops • $18

Incognito Chardonnay

▼▼▼▼ **2001** Light to medium yellow-green; stylish and restrained use of French oak and barrel-fermentation set the scene for a finely chiselled, crisp, nectarine-flavoured palate, with the same oak inputs as are evident on the bouquet.　　**rating:** 89

best drinking 2001–2004 **best vintages** '00 **drink with** Fresh mussels • $20

Shaw & Smith M3 Vineyard Chardonnay

▼▼▼▼▼ **2000** A fine, fresh and restrained bouquet with delicately aromatic melon and nectarine is logically followed by an elegant, long and restrained palate, with the barrel and malolactic inputs present but subjugated to the fruit.　　**rating:** 94

best drinking 2003–2008 **best vintages** '00 **drink with** Lobster salad • $35

Shaw & Smith Merlot

▼▼▼▼▼ **2000** Medium red-purple; a fine, spotlessly clean bouquet with ripe dark berry fruit and a delicate filigree of spice and oak, then a palate with excellent small red fruit flavours, perfect oak balance and integration, fine tannins, and a long, silky finish. Brave winemaking (one month on skins post fermentation) has given rise to a near-freakish outcome for an indifferent vintage.　　**rating:** 94

best drinking 2005–2010 **best vintages** '00 **drink with** Veal saltimbocca • $32

Incognito Merlot

▼▼▼▼ **2000** Bright red-purple; fresh, lively berry fruit, yet not callow. The palate has fresh, lively, juicy berry fruit with soft tannins and little or no oak evident. A brasserie bull's eye.　　**rating:** 88

best drinking 2002–2003 **best vintages** '98, '99 **drink with** All things Italian • $19

shottesbrooke　　★ ★ ★ ☆

Bagshaws Road, McLaren Flat, SA 5171 **region** McLaren Vale
phone (08) 8383 0002 **fax** (08) 8383 0222 **open** Mon–Fri 10–4.30, weekends and public holidays 11–5
winemaker Nick Holmes **production** 10 000 **est.** 1984
product range ($15–35 CD) Fleurieu Sauvignon Blanc, Chardonnay, Shiraz, Eliza Reserve Shiraz, Merlot, Cabernet Merlot Malbec, Bernesh Bray Liqueur Tawny.
summary Now the full-time business of former Ryecroft winemaker Nick Holmes; the grapes grown on his vineyard at Myoponga, at their best, show clear berry fruit, subtle oak and a touch of elegance. A compact, handsome new winery was erected prior to the 1997 vintage. Exports to the UK, US and Canada supplement distribution through all Australian states.

Shottesbrooke Chardonnay

▼▼▼▼ **2001** Light straw-green; a very light bouquet with citrus and herb aromas, and a typically fresh, elegant and lively palate, right in the Shottesbrooke style.　　**rating:** 85

best drinking 2002–2004 **best vintages** NA **drink with** King George whiting • $15.50

Shottesbrooke Shiraz

▼▼▼▼ **2000** Medium red-purple; notwithstanding the 14.5° alcohol, the bouquet is light, with aromas of spice and leaf; dark cherry, spice and earth flavours come through on the palate, which utterly belies its alcohol, and is in the mainstream Shottesbrooke style.　　**rating:** 85

best drinking 2003–2006 **best vintages** NA **drink with** Osso buco • $18

Shottesbrooke Cabernet Sauvignon Merlot Malbec

▼▼▼▽ **1998** Medium red-purple; an archetypal Australian version of the classic Bordeaux blend, with a mix of leaf, herb and some red berry fruit to the bouquet. The palate comes as a surprise, with grippy tannins throwing it out of balance at the present time. There are some red fruit flavours in the core, and the tannins will partially, at least, resolve with time.　　**rating:** 83

best drinking 2003–2008 **best vintages** '97 **drink with** Yearling steak • $18.50

silk hill   NR

324 Motor Road, Deviot, Tas 7275 (postal) **region** Northern Tasmania
phone (03) 6394 7385 **fax** (03) 6326 2350 **open** Thurs–Sun 9–5
winemaker Gavin Scott **production** 200 **est.** 1990
product range Pinot Noir.
summary Pharmacist Gavin Scott has been a weekend and holiday viticulturist for many years, having established the Glengarry Vineyard, which he sold, and then establishing the one-hectare Silk Hill (formerly Silkwood Vineyard) in 1989, planted exclusively to pinot noir. Growing and making Pinot Noir and fishing will keep him occupied when he sells his pharmacy business.

silvan winery   NR

Lilydale–Silvan Road, Silvan, Vic 3795 **region** Yarra Valley
phone (03) 9737 9392 **open** Weekends, public holidays 11–6
winemaker John Vigliaroni **production** 500 **est.** 1993
product range ($8 CD) Chardonnay, Pinot Noir, Cabernet, Cabernet Shiraz Merlot, Merlot.
summary One of the newer and smaller of the Yarra Valley wineries; tastings are held in the Vigliaronis' spacious Italian villa, being offered for sale by Auction in March 2001.

simon gilbert wines   ★★★☆

1220 Sydney Road, Mudgee, NSW 2850 **region** Mudgee
phone (02) 9958 1322 **fax** (02) 8920 1333 **open** Not
winemaker Simon Gilbert **production** 50 000 **est.** 1993
product range ($14–50 R) Card Series Semillon Sauvignon Blanc, Chardonnay, Shiraz, Cabernet Merlot; Family Selection Orange Pinot Noir, Wongalere McLaren Vale Shiraz, Mudgee Shiraz, McLaren Vale Grenache Shiraz Mourvèdre, Central Ranges Cabernet Merlot, Abbaston Cabernet Sauvignon.
summary The transition from a converted butter factory at Muswellbrook to a spectacularly sited, state-of-the-art $10 million winery at Mudgee represents the culmination of a family winemaking history dating back to 1847, when forbear Captain Joseph Gilbert commenced the establishment of a splendid vineyard and winery at Pewsey Vale, in the East Barossa Ranges. Simon Gilbert Wines is now a significant public company listed on the Stock Exchange with a primary base of large scale contract winemaking for others, but with plans to rapidly develop a three-tiered range of proprietary wines sourced from grapes grown in premium regions around south east Australia and from the 40 hectares of hillside vineyards surrounding the winery. A spacious cellar door and restaurant overlooking the micro valley in which the winery is situated will open when turning lanes from the highway are completed. Exports to the UK, US, Canada, Singapore and Finland.

Simon Gilbert Hunter Chardonnay

♥♥♥♥ **1999** Light to medium yellow-green; the bouquet has distinctly tangy/citrussy overtones to the fruit, supported by subliminal French oak; the light to medium-bodied palate likewise has fresh citrus and nectarine flavours to the fore, providing pleasing mouthfeel. The oak is barely perceptible. The slow rate of development is impressive.   **rating:** 88

best drinking 2002–2005 **best vintages** NA **drink with** Grilled fish • $15

simon hackett   ★★★☆

Budgens Road, McLaren Vale, SA 5171 **region** McLaren Vale
phone (08) 8323 7712 **fax** (08) 8323 7713 **open** Wed–Sun 11–5
winemaker Simon Hackett **production** 20 000 **est.** 1981
product range ($12–35 R) Barossa Valley Semillon, Barossa Valley Chardonnay, McLaren Vale Shiraz, McLaren Vale Anthony's Reserve Shiraz, McLaren Vale Old Vine Grenache, McLaren Vale Foggo Road Cabernet Sauvignon.
summary In 1998 Simon Hackett acquired the former Taranga winery in McLaren Vale, which has made his winemaking life a great deal easier. He also has eight hectares of estate vines and has contract growers in McLaren Vale, the Adelaide Hills and the Barossa Valley, with another 32 hectares of vines.

Simon Hackett Bright View Barossa Valley Semillon

♥♥♥♥ **2001** Glowing medium to full yellow-green, distinctly advanced; the solid bouquet has some citrus, and also explains the colour, which has come through skin contact prior to pressing and fermentation. The palate provides rich, mouthfilling flavour in an early-drinking style. If cellared, the phenolics will catch up with it.   **rating:** 86

best drinking 2002–2003 **best vintages** NA **drink with** KFC • $12

Simon Hackett Bright View Barossa Valley Chardonnay

TTTT 2001 Medium to full yellow-green; a solid, not particularly aromatic bouquet does show good fruit and oak integration. The palate hangs together well, with subdued melon and nectarine fruit, plus gentle French and American oak inputs. A surprise packet, but still for early drinking. **rating: 88**

best drinking 2002–2003 **best vintages** NA **drink with** Braised veal • $12

Simon Hackett McLaren Vale Shiraz

TTTT 2001 Medium to full red-purple; ripe, dark berry fruit and just a hint of oak; there is mouthfilling fruit on entry, rapidly followed by powerful tannins suggesting the wine be left strictly alone for at least five years. **rating: 86**

best drinking 2006–2011 **best vintages** NA **drink with** Lamb cutlets • $15

Simon Hackett McLaren Vale Anthony's Reserve Shiraz

TTTT 1999 Medium red-purple; a moderately intense bouquet with savoury, earthy overtones and a hint of chocolate leads into a medium to full-bodied palate, starting with savoury/chocolatey flavours, then with strong, grippy tannins. Approach with caution. **rating: 85**

best drinking 2005–2010 **best vintages** '98 **drink with** Kangaroo fillet • $25

Simon Hackett Foggo Road Cabernet Sauvignon

TTTT 1999 Medium red; a solid bouquet with blackberry and earth aromas offset by vanilla oak is followed by a palate with a range of cedary, spicy, chocolate, vanilla and blackberry flavours. **rating: 86**

best drinking 2005–2010 **best vintages** NA **drink with** Roast lamb • $35

sinclair wines   NR

Graphite Road, Glenoran, WA 6258 **region** Manjimup
phone (08) 9421 1399 **fax** (08) 9421 1191 **open** By appointment
winemaker Brenden Smith (Contract) **production** 2500 **est.** 1994
product range ($15–22 CD) Sauvignon Blanc, Semillon Sauvignon, Chardonnay, Rosé of Glenoran, Cabernet Sauvignon.
summary Sinclair Wines is the child of Darelle Sinclair, a science teacher, wine educator and graduate viticulturist from Charles Sturt University, and John Healy, a lawyer, traditional jazz musician and graduand wine marketing student of Adelaide University, Roseworthy Campus. Five hectares of estate plantings are in production.

Sinclair Chardonnay

TTTY 1999 Medium to full yellow-green; toasty barrel ferment aromas mingle with ripe, white peach fruit, the palate providing a similar mix of peach and toasty oak, with a fractionally hollow mid-palate. **rating: 84**

best drinking 2001–2003 **best vintages** NA **drink with** • NA

sirromet wines   ★★★☆

850–938 Mount Cotton Road, Mount Cotton, Qld 4165 **region** Queensland Coastal
phone (07) 3206 2999 **fax** (07) 3206 0900 **open** 7 days 10–5
winemaker Adam Chapman, Alain Rousseau, Craig Stevenson **production** 80 000 **est.** 1998
product range ($12–30 CD) Perfect Day range of Semillon Verdelho Chardonnay, Harvest White, Chardonnay, Harvest Red, Shiraz Cabernet Merlot; Vineyard Selection range of Sauvignon Blanc Semillon, Chardonnay, Pinot Chardonnay Sparkling, Teewah, Chambourcin, Cabernet Sauvignon, Seven Scenes range of Chardonnay, Pinot Chardonnay Sparkling, Shiraz, Finito Muscat; and Private Bin TM at the top.
summary This is an unambiguously ambitious venture, with the professed aim of creating Queensland's premier winery. The Morris family, founders of Sirromet Wines, which owns Mount Cotton Estate, retained a leading architect to design the striking state-of-the-art winery with a 80 000-case production capacity; the state's foremost viticultural consultant to plant the three major vineyards which total 100 hectares, and the most skilled winemaker practising in Qld, Adam Chapman, to make the wine. It has a 200-seat restaurant; a wine club offering all sorts of benefits to its members; and is firmly aimed at the domestic and international tourist market, taking advantage of its situation half way between Brisbane and the Gold Coast. The intention is to move to a predominantly estate-based operation as quickly as the vineyards (planted to 14 varieties) come into production. Both the consistency and quality of the wines release so far and their modest pricing bodes well for the future.

Sirromet Queensland Semillon

ΨΨΨΨ 2001 Light to medium yellow-green; a firm, clean, crisp and correct bouquet leads into a palate with quite intense grassy varietal fruit and good acidity; a serious, well made wine in every way. **rating:** 89

best drinking 2002–2006 **best vintages** NA **drink with** Shellfish • $16

Sirromet Sauvignon Blanc Semillon

ΨΨΨΨ 2001 Light green-yellow; crisp, fine fruit on the bouquet, then a well made and balanced palate, with hints of tropical fruit coming through, and a clean, focussed finish. A blend of sauvignon blanc from Orange and semillon from the Granite Belt. **rating:** 86

best drinking 2002–2004 **best vintages** NA **drink with** Barramundi • $16

Sirromet Seven Scenes Shiraz

ΨΨΨΨ 2000 Medium red-purple; the moderately intense and savoury bouquet has reasonable complexity, and some attractive cedary notes from the oak. The palate veers towards primary fruit, with a mix of cherry, mint and leaf, then a brisk finish. One hundred per cent Granite Belt. **rating:** 86

best drinking 2002–2005 **best vintages** NA **drink with** Barbecued rib of beef • $25

Sirromet Queensland Cabernet Merlot

ΨΨΨΨ 2000 Medium red-purple; red berry fruit mingles with more cedary, savoury, spicy aromas before flowing into a well-balanced, light to medium-bodied palate, offering redcurrant fruit, soft tannins and a clever touch of oak. **rating:** 87

best drinking 2003–2007 **best vintages** NA **drink with** Lamb shanks in red wine sauce • $16

sittella wines   NR

100 Barrett Road, Herne Hill, WA 6056 **region** Swan District
phone (08) 9296 2600 **fax** (08) 9473 0774 **open** Wed–Sun and most public holidays 11–5
winemaker Julie White **production** 3500 **est.** 1998
product range ($13.50–18 CD) Chenin Blanc, Verdelho, Unwooded Chardonnay, Chardonnay, Silk, Shiraz, Cabernet Sauvignon.
summary Perth couple Simon and Maaike Berns acquired a 7-hectare block (with 2 hectares of vines) at Herne Hill, making the first wine in February 1998 and opening the most attractive cellar-door facility later in the year. They also own the 5-hectare Wildberry Springs Estate vineyard in the Margaret River region, which commenced to provide grapes from the 1999 vintage.

Sittella Silk

ΨΨΨΨ 2001 Pale green-yellow; a fragrant, highly protected, tangy bouquet with passionfruit overtones is followed by a palate with all of the flavours promised by the bouquet, and above-average length. **rating:** 87

best drinking 2001–2003 **best vintages** NA **drink with** Tuna sashimi • $13.50

Sittella Verdelho

ΨΨΨΨ 2000 Light to medium green-yellow; the bouquet has tangy citrussy/lemony aromas moving on to a wine with an extra degree of mid-palate texture and flavour, and a moderately firm finish. **rating:** 85

best drinking 2001–2004 **best vintages** NA **drink with** Veal parmigiana • $14

Sittella Chardonnay

ΨΨΨΨ 2000 Medium yellow-green; the fruit is slightly suppressed, although the toasty oak is by no means overplayed. A big, full-frontal style on the palate, with a slightly fat finish suggesting that some skin contact may also have been used. **rating:** 84

best drinking 2001–2002 **best vintages** NA **drink with** Smoked salmon and cucumber salad • $15.75

s kidman wines   NR

Riddoch Highway, Coonawarra, SA 5263 **region** Coonawarra
phone (08) 8736 5071 **fax** (08) 8736 5070 **open** 7 days 9–5
winemaker John Innes (Contract) **production** 8000 **est.** 1984
product range ($13–19 CD) Riesling, Sauvignon Blanc, Shiraz, Cabernet Sauvignon.
summary One of the district pioneers, with a 16-hectare estate vineyard which is now fully mature. No recent tastings; limited retail distribution in Melbourne and Adelaide.

skillogalee ★★★★☆

Off Hughes Park Road, Sevenhill via Clare, SA 5453 **region** Clare Valley
phone (08) 8843 4311 **fax** (08) 8843 4343 **open** 7 days 10–5
winemaker Dave Palmer **production** 7000 **est.** 1970
product range ($13.50–24.50 CD) Riesling, Late Picked Riesling, Gewürztraminer, Chardonnay, Sparkling Riesling, Shiraz, The Cabernets, Fortifieds.
summary David and Diana Palmer purchased the small hillside stone winery from the George family at the end of the 1980s and have capitalised to the full on the exceptional fruit quality of the Skillogalee vineyards. The winery also has a well-patronised lunchtime restaurant. All of the wines are generous and full-flavoured, particularly the reds.

Skillogalee Riesling

TTTTY 2001 Light green-yellow; the firm bouquet has mainstream Clare Valley mineral, herb and toast aromatics, the palate opening up somewhat with lime and a touch of apple; overall, quite generous, with good flow and mouthfeel. **rating:** 92
best drinking 2003–2008 **best vintages** '80, '84, '87, '90, '92, '97, '99, '01 **drink with** Quiche Lorraine • $17

Skillogalee The Cabernets

TTTT 1999 Medium to full red; solid blackberry fruit on the bouquet is followed by a rich, ripe and complex palate, with good structure and tannin management. Built to last, but well-balanced. **rating:** 89
best drinking 2004–2009 **best vintages** '84, '87, '90, '93, '96, '97, '98 **drink with** Yearling steak • $24.50

smithbrook ★★★★

Smith Brook Road, Middlesex via Manjimup, WA 6258 **region** Manjimup
phone (08) 9772 3557 **fax** (08) 9772 3579 **open** By appointment
winemaker Michael Symons **production** 10 000 **est.** 1988
product range ($16.50–24.50 R) Sauvignon Blanc, Chardonnay, Merlot, Cabernet Merlot, Cabernet Sauvignon.
summary Smithbrook is a major player in the Manjimup region, with 60 hectares of vines in production. A majority interest was acquired by Petaluma in 1997 but will continue its role as a contract grower for other companies, as well as supplying Petaluma's needs and making relatively small amounts of wine under its own label. Perhaps the most significant change has been the removal of Pinot Noir from the current range of products, and the introduction of Merlot. National distribution through Negociants; exports to UK and Japan.

Smithbrook Cabernet Sauvignon

TTTT 1999 Strong red-purple; gentle cassis and berry aromas, sweet but not jammy, supported by a touch of oak, lead into a palate with abundant cassis, blackcurrant and blackberry fruit, which dips slightly on the mid to back palate, and is then picked up by fine tannins and oak on the finish. **rating:** 88
best drinking 2003–2008 **best vintages** NA **drink with** Beef in red wine sauce • $24.50

smithleigh vineyard NR

53 Osborne Road, Lane Cove, NSW 2066 (postal) **region** Lower Hunter Valley
phone 0418 484 565 **fax** (02) 9420 2014 **open** Not
winemaker Andrew Margan (Contract) **production** 3000 **est.** 1997
product range ($14–16 CD) Old Vine Hunter Semillon, Verdelho, Chardonnay, Shiraz.
summary As the name suggests, a partnership between Rod and Ivija Smith and John and Jan Leigh, which purchased the long-established vineyard from Southcorp in 1996. A lot of work in the vineyard, and skilled contract winemaking by Andrew Margan has produced the right outcomes.

SmithLeigh Semillon

TTTT 2001 Bright, light green-yellow; an aromatic lemony/lime bouquet is followed by a quite full, almost luscious palate, with lots of depth. One wonders whether there is some botrytis assistance. **rating:** 88
TTTT 1999 Medium to full yellow-green; gentle toasty aromas are starting to develop on the clean bouquet, the palate is gentle, light to medium-bodied mode, smooth and lemony. **rating:** 87
best drinking 2002–2006 **best vintages** NA **drink with** Smoked fish • $14

SmithLeigh Shiraz

TTTT 1999 Medium red-purple; the bouquet has regional aromas of sweet leather, spice and earth, the palate following on in soft, pleasant, savoury regional style. Well made, not forced to be something it isn't. **rating:** 85
best drinking 2003–2007 **best vintages** NA **drink with** Smoked beef • $16

snowy river winery   NR

Rockwell Road, Berridale, NSW 2628 **region** Southern New South Wales Zone
phone (02) 6456 5041 **fax** (02) 6456 5005 **open** Wed–Sun, 7 days during school holidays
winemaker Manfred Plumecke **production** 2500 **est.** 1984
product range ($10–20 CD) Snowy White, Alpine Dry White, Sauvignon Blanc Chardonnay, Sylvaner
Muller Thurgau, Sieger Rebe [sic], Rhine Riesling Auslese, Noble Riesling, Snow Bruska, Snowy Port,
Tawny Port.
summary An operation which relies entirely on the substantial tourist trade passing through or near
Berridale on the way to the Snowy Mountains. The product range is, to put it mildly, eclectic; all the wines
are said to be made on site, and the grapes for all of the white varietals are estate-grown.

somerset hill wines   ★★★

891 McLeod Road, Denmark, WA 6333 **region** Great Southern
phone (08) 9840 9388 **fax** (08) 9840 9394 **open** 7 days 11–5
winemaker Brenden Smith (Contract) **production** 3600 **est.** 1995
product range ($18–35 CD) Semillon, Sauvignon Blanc, Harmony (Semillon Sauvignon Blanc),
Chardonnay (Unwooded), Constellation (Sparkling), Pinot Noir.
summary Graham Upson commenced planting 11 hectares of pinot noir, chardonnay, semillon, merlot
and sauvignon blanc in 1995, and Somerset Hill Wines duly opened its limestone cellar-door sales area with
sweeping views out over the ocean. Limited retail distribution in Melbourne and Sydney, and is also
exported to the UK.

Somerset Hill Unwooded Chardonnay

▼▼▼▽ **2001** Light to medium yellow-green; the bouquet is quite complex and rich, but with faintly
funky/leesy overtones, unusual for unwooded Chardonnay. The palate is similarly well endowed, but again
slightly rustic. Not dissimilar to the preceding vintage.   **rating:** 83

best drinking 2002–2003 **best vintages** NA **drink with** Vegetable terrine • $19.50

sorrenberg   NR

Alma Road, Beechworth, Vic 3747 **region** Beechworth
phone (03) 5728 2278 **fax** (03) 5728 2278 **open** Mon–Fri by appointment, most weekends 1–5
(phone first)
winemaker Barry Morey **production** 1500 **est.** 1986
product range ($20–32 CD) Sauvignon Blanc Semillon, Chardonnay, Gamay, Cabernet Sauvignon,
Havelock Hills Shiraz, Cabernet Merlot Franc.
summary Barry and Jan Morey made their first wines in 1989 from the 2.5-hectare vineyard situated on
the outskirts of Beechworth. No recent tastings, but the wines have a good reputation and loyal clientele.

spring vale vineyards   ★★★★☆

130 Spring Vale Road, Cranbrook, Tas 7190 **region** Southern Tasmania
phone (03) 6257 8208 **fax** (03) 6257 8598 **open** Weekends, holidays 10–5 by appointment
winemaker Kristen Lyne **production** 3000 **est.** 1986
product range ($13.50–35 CD) Gewürztraminer, Chardonnay, Pinot Gris, Pinot Noir, Baudin
Chardonnay and Pinot Noir.
summary Rodney Lyne has progressively established 1.5 hectares each of pinot noir and chardonnay and
then added half a hectare each of gewürztraminer and pinot gris; the latter produced a first crop in 1998.
After frost problems, Spring Vale was enjoying the fruits of excellent vintages from 1997 to 2000 before
frost returned to devastate 2001. Exports to the UK.

Spring Vale Chardonnay

▼▼▼▼▽ **2000** Light to medium yellow-green; toasty oak and subdued fruit on the bouquet move up a gear on
the palate, with nectarine, peach and a hint of vanilla. Another attractive wine from this vineyard.   **rating:** 90

best drinking 2002–2005 **best vintages** '97, '99, '00 **drink with** Veal or pork • $25

Spring Vale Pinot Noir

▼▼▼▼▽ **2000** Medium red-purple; the bouquet is clean, but by the standards of the vintage, quite light, with
some leafy nuances. The palate is much more compelling, with lots of character, style and length.   **rating:** 90

best drinking 2002–2006 **best vintages** '00 **drink with** Smoked quail • $35

springviews wine ★★★★

Woodlands Road, Porongurup, WA 6324 **region** Great Southern
phone (08) 9853 2088 **fax** (08) 9853 2098 **open** 7 days 10–5
winemaker Howard Park (Contract) **production** 420 **est.** 1994
product range ($16–20 CD) Riesling, Chardonnay, Cabernet Sauvignon.
summary Andy and Alice Colquhoun planted their 5-hectare vineyard (2 hectares each of chardonnay and cabernet sauvignon and 1 hectare of riesling) in 1994. The wine is contract made and is sold through the cellar door and mailing list.

stanley brothers ★★★

Barossa Valley Way, Tanunda, SA 5352 **region** Barossa Valley
phone (08) 8563 3375 **fax** (08) 8563 3758 **open** 7 days 9–5
winemaker Lindsay Stanley **production** 10 000 **est.** 1994
product range ($11–25 CD) Sylvaner, Full Sister Semillon, Chardonnay Pristine, John Hancock Shiraz, Thoroughbred Cabernet Sauvignon, Cabernet Shiraz, Late Harvest Sylvaner, NV Black Sheep, Sparkling, Fortifieds.
summary Former Anglesey winemaker and industry veteran Lindsay Stanley established his own business in the Barossa Valley when he purchased (and renamed) the former Kroemer Estate in late 1994. As one would expect, the wines are competently made. Twenty one hectares of estate plantings have provided virtually all of the grapes for the business. Exports to Canada, France, Hong Kong, Singapore and the US.

stanthorpe wine co NR

Granite Belt Drive, Thulimbah, Qld 4377 **region** Granite Belt
phone (07) 4683 2011 **fax** (07) 4683 2600 **open** 7 days 9–5
winemaker Contract **production** 2000 **est.** 1997
product range ($12–45 CD) Semillon, Semillon Chardonnay, Sauvignon Blanc, Chardonnay, Sweet White, Sweet Red, Shiraz Pinot Noir (sparkling), Emily Rosé, Shiraz, Reserve Shiraz, Shiraz Cabernet Sauvignon, Reserve Merlot, Cabernets Merlot, Liqueur Muscat, Tawny Port.
summary The Stanthorpe Wine Centre does a bit of everything. Its ten partners are mainly professional people who work in Brisbane, but who share a love of wine. They decided to establish a business which would offer wine education, sell other wines of the region, and have wines contract-made for the Centre's own label. The partners have also established a vineyard with 3 hectares of shiraz, 2 hectares each of cabernet sauvignon and merlot, and 1 hectare each of petit verdot, tempranillo and verdelho, and plan to set up a small, specialised winemaking facility to make the wine from this vineyard under the Summit Estate label.

stanton & killeen wines ★★★★★

Jacks Road, Murray Valley Highway, Rutherglen, Vic 3685 **region** Rutherglen
phone (02) 6032 9457 **fax** (02) 6032 8018 **open** Mon–Sat 9–5, Sun 10–5
winemaker Chris Killeen **production** 13 000 **est.** 1875
product range ($10.50–75 CD) A red wine and fortified wine specialist, though offering Chardonnay, Riesling, White Frontignac, Auslese Tokay and Parkview Dry White as well as Parkview Dry Red, Moodemere Shiraz, Cabernet Franc Merlot, Cabernet Shiraz, Shiraz, Durif; fortifieds include Rutherglen White Port, Rutherglen Ruby Port, Rutherglen Muscat; Classic Rutherglen Tawny, Tokay and Muscat, Grand Rutherglen Muscat, Rare Rutherglen Muscat.
summary Chris Killeen has skilfully expanded the portfolio of Stanton & Killeen but without in any way compromising its reputation as a traditional maker of smooth, rich reds, some of Australia's best Vintage Ports, and attractive, fruity Muscats and Tokays. All in all, deserves far greater recognition. Exports to the UK and US.

Stanton & Killeen Moodemere Shiraz

▼▼▼▼▽ 2000 Medium to full red-purple; ripe, deep plum and prune fruit and subliminal oak on the bouquet leads into a massive palate, rich and plummy, with lingering fine tannins and subtle oak. **rating:** 90
best drinking 2005–2015 **best vintages** '00 **drink with** Rump steak • $17.50

Stanton & Killeen Shiraz Durif

▼▼▼▼▽ 2000 Dense red-purple; there is a mix of deep, dark chocolate, blackberry and prune on the bouquet; the palate is densely packed with flavour, yet not extractive, the tannins soft and ripe, the oak where it should be. **rating:** 91
best drinking 2005–2015 **best vintages** '00 **drink with** Whole roasted ox kidney • $17.50

Stanton & Killeen Tawny Port

ＹＹＹＹＹ NV Medium red-tawny; the bouquet is clean with nice butterscotch overtones and, like the palate, shows positive but not aggressive rancio. **rating:** 93

best drinking 2002–2003 **best vintages** NA **drink with** Aperitif or coffee • NA

staughton vale vineyard NR

20 Staughton Vale Road, Anakie, Vic 3221 **region** Geelong
phone (03) 5284 1477 **fax** (03) 5284 1229 **open** Fri–Mon and public holidays 10–5 or by appointment
winemaker Paul Chambers **production** 2000 **est.** 1986
product range ($14–20 ML) Riesling, Pinot Noir, Staughton (Merlot blend), Tawny Port, Liqueur Shiraz.
summary Paul Chambers has 6 hectares of grapes, with the accent on the classic Bordeaux mix of cabernet sauvignon, merlot, cabernet franc and petit verdot, although chardonnay and pinot noir are also planted. Weekend lunches available at the Staughton Cottage Restaurant.

steels creek estate NR

1 Sewell Road, Steels Creek, Vic 3775 **region** Yarra Valley
phone (03) 5965 2448 **fax** (03) 5965 2448 **open** Weekends and public holidays 10–6 or by appointment
winemaker Simon Peirce **production** 400 **est.** 1981
product range ($16–25 CD) Colombard, YV Chardonnay, Shiraz, Cabernet Sauvignon.
summary Established by brother and sister team Simon and Kerri Peirce. While only a tiny operation, with 1.7 hectares of vineyard planted at various times between 1981 and 1994, Steels Creek Estate has an on-site winery where the wines are made with assistance from consultants, but increasingly by Simon Peirce, who has completed his associate diploma in Applied Science (Wine-growing) at Charles Sturt University.

stefano lubiana ★★★★

60 Rowbottoms Road, Granton, Tas 7030 **region** Southern Tasmania
phone (03) 6263 7457 **fax** (03) 6263 7430 **open** 7 days 10–5 (closed public holidays)
winemaker Steve Lubiana **production** 8000 **est.** 1990
product range ($24–49 R) Riesling, Sauvignon Blanc, Pinot Grigio, Sur Lie Chardonnay, Chardonnay, Vintage Brut, NV Brut, Pinot Noir, Primavera Pinot Noir.
summary Steve Lubiana has moved from one extreme to the other, having run Lubiana Wines at Moorook in the SA Riverland for many years before moving to Granton to set up a substantial winery. The estate-produced Stefano Lubiano wines come from ten hectares of beautifully located vineyards sloping down to the Derwent River. All the Lubiana wines are immaculately crafted. Exports to the UK and the US.

Stefano Lubiana Riesling

ＹＹＹＹ 2001 Light green-yellow; the bouquet has mineral, apple, pear and herb, flavours which come through on the delicate but long palate. The temptation to bulk up the palate with residual sugar has been resisted, the only question mark being a whisper of reduction. **rating:** 87

best drinking 2003–2010 **best vintages** '00, '01 **drink with** Tempura • $26

Stefano Lubiana Sauvignon Blanc

ＹＹＹＹ 2001 Light green-yellow; a light, crisp, minerally bouquet does not have over-much varietal character or fruit, nor does the palate add a great deal to the equation. On the other hand, the wine has been immaculately handled in the winery and the lack of varietal sauvignon punch is commonplace in Tas. **rating:** 85

best drinking 2002–2005 **best vintages** NA **drink with** Shellfish • $26

Stefano Lubiana Pinot Grigio

ＹＹＹＹ 2001 Light green-yellow; light, crisp, apple and mineral aromas are followed by an austere palate with some weight and grip, but little distinctive fruit. Grigio indeed. **rating:** 85

best drinking 2002–2003 **best vintages** NA **drink with** Antipasto • $27

Stefano Lubiana Chardonnay

ＹＹＹＹ 2000 Light to medium yellow-green; a light, sophisticated bouquet with fig and creamy characters, with obvious but well handled barrel-ferment flavours coming through on the palate. The only drawback is the slightly hot finish from the towering 14.5° alcohol. **rating:** 89

best drinking 2002–2004 **best vintages** NA **drink with** Chinese prawns • $42

Stefano Lubiana Sur Lie Chardonnay

TTTT 2000 Light straw-yellow; the bouquet has a mix of crisp apple, pear and stone fruit, with just a dusting of oak. The elegant palate has a similar fruit register; a nicely balanced, elegant, cool-grown style. **rating:** 89

best drinking 2002–2006 **best vintages** NA **drink with** Steamed mussels • $24

Stefano Lubiana NV Brut

TTTT NV Light to medium yellow-green; clean and crisp citrus and stone fruit aromas lead into a crisp, elegant and direct palate, not particularly complex, but with appealing, bright flavour. **rating:** 87

best drinking 2002–2004 **best vintages** NA **drink with** Aperitif • $33

Stefano Lubiana Pinot Noir

TTTT 2000 Medium red-purple; the smooth, clean bouquet does not seem to have the impact of many of the wines of the vintage, but bounces back strongly on the powerful, fleshy palate with excellent definition and varietal flavour. **rating:** 89

best drinking 2002–2007 **best vintages** '98, '99 **drink with** Jugged hare • $44

Stefano Lubiana Primavera Pinot Noir

TTTTY 2000 Startlingly deep purple-red; a concentrated bouquet of ripe black cherry fruit with briary overtones is followed by a palate in similar massive mode. The wine obviously needs time, but where precisely it will head I simply don't know. The rating is nothing but a compromise for a quite unique wine. **rating:** 90

best drinking 2004–2010 **best vintages** '99, '00 **drink with** Leave it in the cellar • $25

steins ★★★★

Pipeclay Lane, Mudgee, NSW 2850 **region** Mudgee
phone (02) 6373 3991 **fax** (02) 6373 3709 **open** 7 days 10–4.30
winemaker Robert Stein, Michael Slater **production** 5000 **est.** 1976
product range ($10–25 CD) Semillon, Semillon Riesling, Semillon Chardonnay, Chardonnay, Late Harvest Gewürztraminer, Rosé, Mt Buckaroo Dry Red, Shiraz, Reserve Shiraz, Cabernet Sauvignon and a range of Muscats and Ports.
summary The sweeping panorama from the winery is its own reward for cellar-door visitors. Right from the outset Steins has been a substantial operation but has managed to sell the greater part of its production direct from the winery by mail order and cellar door, with limited retail distribution in Sydney, Vic and SA. Wine quality has been very good from time to time, with the Shiraz and Chardonnay variously coming out on top.

Robert Stein Chardonnay

TTTT 2000 Light green-yellow; the light, clean bouquet offers melon and a gentle touch of oak; the palate is well-balanced in a slightly austere fruit mode, perhaps reflecting the difficult vintage Mudgee encountered. **rating:** 85

best drinking 2002–2004 **best vintages** '95 **drink with** Creamy pasta • $14

Robert Stein Shiraz

TTTTY 2000 Light to medium red-purple; a light array of leafy/minty/earthy/berry aromas are reflected in the palate, which lacks fruit concentration and full ripeness, but has been well handled in the winery. The difficult vintage evident once again. **rating:** 84

best drinking 2002–2005 **best vintages** '91 **drink with** Lamb • $16

Steins Cabernet Sauvignon

TTTTY 1999 Medium to full red-purple; solid blackberry and blackcurrant fruit aromas on the bouquet flow through to into a similarly flavoured palate with a touch of chocolate and good tannin and oak management into the bargain. An elegant style which needs more than a casual sip to reveal its true quality. **rating:** 93

best drinking 2004–2014 **best vintages** '99 **drink with** Rack of lamb • $16

stellar ridge estate ★★★

Clews Road, Cowaramup, WA 6284 **region** Margaret River
phone (08) 9755 5635 **fax** (08) 9755 5636 **open** 7 days 10–5
winemaker Bernie Abbott **production** 1500 **est.** 1994

product range ($14–25 CD) Sauvignon Blanc, Verdelho, Unwooded Chardonnay, Late Harvest Sauvignon Blanc, Shiraz, Cabernet Sauvignon; also estate-grown varietally identified olive oil (Pendolino, Leccino, Frantolo, WA Mission).

summary Colin and Helene Hellier acquired a 49-hectare grazing property at Cowaramup in 1993 which included 2.5 hectares of chardonnay and sauvignon blanc planted in 1987. A large dam was constructed in 1994, and the following year 11 hectares of new vineyards and 4 hectares of olive trees were planted; 1.6 hectares of zinfandel followed in 1996, bringing total plantings to 15.1 hectares. The majority of the 100 tonne grape production is sold to other local wineries, with 14 to 15 tonnes being retained for the Stellar Ridge label. The wines are sold exclusively through cellar door and mailing list.

Stellar Ridge Estate Sauvignon Blanc

TTTT 2001 Extremely pale colour; the light bouquet has a mix of grassy and more tropical fruit aromas, the palate with a similar mix in a soft but not flabby frame. Scores for delicacy rather than intensity or power. **rating:** 85

best drinking 2002–2003 **best vintages** NA **drink with** Light seafood • $16

Stellar Ridge Estate Shiraz

TTTY 2000 Light to medium red-purple; the bouquet is of light to moderate intensity, displaying berry, leaf and a touch of mint. There is slightly more fruit weight on the palate than the bouquet suggests, once again in a berry/mint/leaf/earthy spectrum suggesting less than perfect ripeness. **rating:** 83

best drinking 2003–2007 **best vintages** NA **drink with** Lamb shanks • $25

stephen john wines ★★★★

Government Road, Watervale, SA 5452 **region** Clare Valley
phone (08) 8843 0105 **fax** (08) 8843 0105 **open** 7 days 11–5
winemaker Stephen John **production** 7500 **est.** 1994
product range ($13–40 CD) Watervale Riesling, Semillon Sauvignon Blanc, Blanc de Blanc, Traugott Cuvée Sparkling Burgundy, Clare Valley Shiraz, Estate Reserve Shiraz, Merlot, Clare Valley Cabernet Sauvignon, Estate Reserve Cabernet Sauvignon.

summary The John family is one of the best-known names in the Barossa Valley, with branches running Australia's best cooperage (AP John & Sons) and providing the chief winemaker of Lindemans (Philip John) and the former chief winemaker of Quelltaler (Stephen John). Stephen and Rita John have now formed their own family business in the Clare Valley, based on a 6-hectare vineyard overlooking the town of Watervale and supplemented by modest intake from a few local growers. The cellar-door sales area is housed in an 80-year-old stable which has been renovated and is full of rustic charm. The significantly increased production and good quality of the current releases has led to the appointment of distributors in each of the eastern states, and exports to the US, Malaysia and Singapore.

Stephen John Watervale Riesling

TTTTY 2001 Light to medium green-yellow; clean, crisp lime and mineral bouquet aromas are followed by a palate with plenty of flavour and focus, with attractively ripe fruit running through to a long finish. **rating:** 90

best drinking 2002–2007 **best vintages** '01 **drink with** Steamed asparagus • $15

Stephen John Semillon Sauvignon Blanc

TTTT 2001 Light green-yellow; the clean bouquet has attractive aromatic gooseberry fruit, the fresh, well-balanced palate in a fruit-forward style. This is by far the best white wine (other than Riesling) so far from Stephen John. A blend of 80 per cent Clare Valley semillon and 20 per cent Adelaide Hills sauvignon blanc, the latter contributing significantly. **rating:** 88

best drinking 2002–2004 **best vintages** NA **drink with** Terrine of asparagus and eggplant • $15

Stephen John Clare Valley Shiraz

TTTT 1999 Medium red-purple; the moderately intense bouquet has earthy/berry fruit, the medium-bodied palate presently in straightforward regional style, but with potential to build complexity with time in bottle. **rating:** 85

best drinking 2004–2009 **best vintages** NA **drink with** Moussaka • $20

Stephen John Merlot

TTTT 2001 Deep, youthful purple-red; a mix of rich, clean dark berry and dark chocolate aromas lead into a luscious palate with red and dark berry fruit, finishing with slightly dusty tannins. Once again, there is far more fruit character here than in many of the prior releases. **rating:** 87

best drinking 2005–2010 **best vintages** NA **drink with** Braised beef • $15

🐝 step road winery ★★★☆

Davidson Road, Langhorne Creek, SA 5255 **region** Langhorne Creek
phone (08) 8537 3342 **fax** (08) 8537 3357 **open** 7 days 9–4.30
winemaker Rob Dundon **production** 55 000 **est.** 1998
product range ($12–19.50 CD) The economy second label is Red Wing, with Chardonnay and Cabernet Sauvignon; under the Step Road Label Sauvignon Blanc (Adelaide Hills), Shiraz (McLaren Vale), Sangiovese (Langhorne Creek) and Cabernet Sauvignon (McLaren Vale).
summary Step Road has 30 hectares of vineyard in Langhorne Creek, and 40 hectares in the Adelaide Hills, supplementing the production from those vineyards with cabernet sauvignon and shiraz purchased from McLaren Vale. It is an autonomous business, but operationally part of the Beresford Wines group. The wines are distributed nationally by Red + White.

Step Road Adelaide Hills Sauvignon Blanc

▼▼▼▼ **2001** Light straw-green; a firm, minerally bouquet, almost earthy, but the fresh, delicate palate frees up somewhat, finishing with lingering acidity. **rating:** 88

best drinking 2002–2003 **best vintages** NA **drink with** King George whiting • $17.50

Step Road McLaren Vale Shiraz

▼▼▼▼ **2000** Medium red-purple; the balance of fruit and oak on the bouquet is good, as is the integration of oak. Ripe plummy/spicy fruit and fine tannins contribute to the good texture of a well made wine. **rating:** 87

best drinking 2004–2009 **best vintages** NA **drink with** Braised beef • $19.50

Step Road Langhorne Creek Sangiovese

▼▼▼▽ **2000** Medium red-purple; some savoury/leafy/earthy/tobacco varietal character on the bouquet comes through in a savoury, tangy palate with fine tannins; lacks depth, but has length. **rating:** 84

best drinking 2001–2005 **best vintages** NA **drink with** Vitella tonnato • $17.50

Step Road McLaren Vale Cabernet Sauvignon

▼▼▼▼ **2000** Bright red-purple; fresh, direct, clean cassis berry aromas, supported by gentle oak, lead through into a smooth and supple palate with ripe cabernet fruit flavours; good structure and length. **rating:** 88

best drinking 2004–2009 **best vintages** NA **drink with** Shoulder of lamb • $19.50

sterling heights NR

Faulkners Road, Winkleigh, Tas 7275 **region** Northern Tasmania
phone (03) 6396 3214 **fax** (03) 6396 3214 **open** By appointment
winemaker Moorilla Estate (Contract) **production** 400 **est.** 1988
product range ($14–16 CD) Riesling, Chardonnay, Breton Rosé, Pinot Noir.
summary With 2 hectares of vines, Sterling Heights will always be a small fish in a small pond. However, the early releases had considerable success in wine shows, and the quality was all one could expect. The wines are also available through Hartzview Wine Centre. No recent tastings.

🐝 sticks ★★★☆

The YarraHill, 10 St Huberts Road, Coldstream, Vic 3770 **region** Yarra Valley
phone (03) 9739 0666 **fax** (03) 9739 0633 **open** Not
winemaker Rob Dolan **production** 10 000 **est.** 2001
product range ($16–19 R) Sauvignon Blanc Semillon, Chardonnay, Pinot Noir, Merlot, Cabernet Sauvignon.
summary Rob Dolan, the affable, towering (former) long-serving winemaker at Yarra Ridge, has always had the nickname Sticks, doubtless recognising his long legs. Since leaving Yarra Ridge several years ago, he has made wine first at Dominion and now at The YarraHill. But he has also decided to produce his own range of wines, which he makes at The YarraHill, the grapes being chosen from 100 hectares spread across three Yarra Valley vineyards. The wines are keenly priced, the packaging excellent, and national distribution through Red+White should all contribute to rapid growth for the brand.

Sticks Sauvignon Blanc Semillon

▼▼▼▼ **2001** Light green-yellow; the relatively complex bouquet has plenty of weight, suggestive of a small percentage of barrel ferment. The palate, likewise, is high-flavoured, with ripe apple and gooseberry flavours, together with a hint of sweetness cleverly aimed at the cellar door. **rating:** 85

best drinking 2001–2002 **best vintages** NA **drink with** Pasta marinara • $15

Sticks Chardonnay

ŢŢŢŢ 2000 Light green-yellow; a fresh, crisp, light melon bouquet and minimal oak is reflected in the palate, braced by a touch of lemony acidity on the finish.　　　　**rating:** 85

best drinking 2001–2003　**best vintages** NA　**drink with** Weiner schnitzel • $15

Sticks Pinot Noir

ŢŢŢŢ 2000 Light to medium red-purple; the bouquet is somewhat closed with plummy fruit and a hint of spice, aromas reflected in the plummy/spicy palate which is, however, quite firm, and needs time to evolve.　**rating:** 86

best drinking 2002–2005　**best vintages** NA　**drink with** Braised quail • $18

Sticks Cabernet Sauvignon

ŢŢŢŢ 2000 Medium red-purple; the bouquet is light, with slightly herbaceous/minty aspects repeated on the palate, with some pleasant, sweet berry fruit. Lacks depth.　　　**rating:** 83

best drinking 2002–2004　**best vintages** NA　**drink with** Yearling steak • $18

stone bridge estate　　　NR

RMB 189 Holleys Road, Manjimup, WA 6258 **region** Manjimup
phone (08) 9773 1371 **fax** (08) 9773 1309 **open** By appointment
winemaker Syd Hooker, Kate Hooker **production** 3000 **est.** 1991
product range ($20–30 R) Sauvignon Blanc Semillon, Mèthode Champenoise, Shiraz, Cabernet Merlot Malbec.
summary Syd and Sue Hooker purchased the property on which Stone Bridge Estate is established in 1990, and planted the first vines that year. A subsequent planting in 1996 has increased the vineyard size to 8 hectares, with shiraz (2 hectares) a total of 1.7 hectares of pinot noir and chardonnay, 1.6 hectares of the four Bordeaux varieties, 1 hectare each of semillon, sauvignon blanc and sangiovese. The pinot noir and chardonnay go to provide the Mèthode Champenoise, made (on site, like all the other wines) by daughter Kate, a graduate winemaker and viticulturist from the Lycée Viticole d'Avize in Champagne.

stonehaven　　　★★★★

Riddoch Highway, Padthaway, SA 5271 **region** Padthaway
phone (08) 8765 6140 **fax** (08) 8765 6137 **open** 7 days 10–4
winemaker Tom Newton, Susanne Bell, Adrienne Cross **production** NFP **est.** 1998
product range ($15–35 R) Padthaway Unwooded Chardonnay, Cabernet Merlot, Chardonnay, Limestone Coast Chardonnay, Limestone Coast Vigonier, Shiraz, Limestone Coast Shiraz, Padthaway Cabernet Sauvignon, Limited Release Chardonnay.
summary It is, to say the least, strange that it should have taken 30 years for a substantial winery to be built at Padthaway. However, when BRL Hardy took the decision, it was no half measure: $20 million has been invested in what is the largest greenfields winery built in Australia for more than 20 years. Exports to the US, Canada and UK.

Stonehaven Limestone Coast Viognier

ŢŢŢŢ 2001 Light to medium yellow-green; quite intense, sweet multi-aromatics to the bouquet feed into a palate with abundant apricot, peach and fruit pastille flavours. One of the best examples of Viognier, and not oak-pushed. Gold medals in Perth and Canberra 2001.　　　**rating:** 89

best drinking 2002–2004　**best vintages** NA　**drink with** Rich seafood • $17.99

Stonehaven Limestone Coast Chardonnay

ŢŢŢŢ 2000 Medium yellow-green; melon and nectarine fruit has a slightly charry/smoky/burnt match background, the palate crisp and intense, driven by its nectarine and citrus fruit, and largely devoid of the reduction apparent on the bouquet.　　　**rating:** 85

best drinking 2001–2003　**best vintages** NA　**drink with** Fresh crab cakes • $16.95

Stonehaven Limestone Coast Shiraz

ŢŢŢŢ 1999 Medium purple-red; a complex, ripe and rich bouquet with slightly gamey overtones to the dark berry fruit is followed by a massive wine on the palate quite extractive and tannic, and requiring both faith and patience.　　　**rating:** 84

best drinking 2004–2009　**best vintages** '98　**drink with** Traditional Aussie meat pie • $17.99

stonemont ★★★

421 Rochford Road, Rochford, Vic 3442 **region** Macedon Ranges
phone (03) 5429 1540 **fax** (03) 5429 1878 **open** By appointment
winemaker Contract **production** 500 **est.** 1997
product range ($18–25 R) Chardonnay, Sparkling Macedon, Pinot Noir.
summary Ray and Gail Hicks began the establishment of their vineyard in 1993, extending plantings to a total of 1.5 hectares each of chardonnay and pinot noir in 1996. The tiny production of Chardonnay, Pinot Noir and Sparkling Macedon is contract-made by various Macedon Ranges winemakers, and the wines are sold by mail order and (by appointment) through the cellar door, which is situated in a heritage stone barn on the vineyard site.

Stonemont Chardonnay

▼▼▼▽ **2000** Medium to full yellow-green; the bouquet has a slightly austere, herbaceous edge, yet is quite complex. The melon and cashew flavours of the palate have unusual length, suggesting a clever balance between a touch of sugar and the typically high acidity of the region. **rating:** 84

best drinking 2001–2005 **best vintages** NA **drink with** Fish terrine • $18

Stonemont Sparkling Macedon

▼▼▼▽ **1998** Pale straw-green; a clean, fragrant, citrus-driven bouquet leads into a strongly lemony/citrussy palate, with fair balance and length. **rating:** 83

best drinking 2001–2004 **best vintages** NA **drink with** Aperitif • $25

stone ridge ★★★☆

35 Limberlost Road, Glen Aplin, Qld 4381 **region** Granite Belt
phone (07) 4683 4211 **fax** (07) 4683 4211 **open** 7 days 10–5
winemaker Jim Lawrie, Anne Kennedy **production** 2100 **est.** 1981
product range ($10–60 CD) Semillon, Marsanne, Viognier, Chardonnay, Pinot Noir, Shiraz, Cabernet Malbec, Cabernet Sauvignon, Mount Sterling Dry Red Shiraz.
summary Spicy Shiraz is the specialty of the doll's-house-sized winery, but the portfolio has progressively expanded over recent years to include two whites and the only Stanthorpe region Cabernet Malbec (and occasionally a straight varietal Malbec).

Stone Ridge Marsanne

▼▼▼▼▽ **2000** Glowing yellow-green; the aromas show attractive bottle-developed characters, with a mix of citrus blossom and apple. Citrus and apple come through on the palate, which has excellent mouthfeel, and is well made. There is just a slightly concern that the SO_2 may be on the low side. **rating:** 90

best drinking 2002–2003 **best vintages** NA **drink with** Queensland mud crab • $25

Stone Ridge Pinot Noir

▼▼▼▼ **2000** Medium red; some tea leaf and forest edges to the ripe plum of the bouquet work well; the palate is ripe, with some vestiges of varietal character, and is well enough balanced. I suppose the price is a case of the dog preaching. **rating:** 85

best drinking 2002–2003 **best vintages** NA **drink with** Braised duck • $60

stoney rise ★★★☆

PO Box 442, Robe, SA 5276 **region** Mount Benson
phone (08) 8768 6106 **fax** (08) 8768 6106 **open** By appointment
winemaker Matt Lowe **production** 1000 **est.** 2000
product range ($15–20 ML) Sauvignon Blanc, Cotes du Robe Shiraz.
summary Matt Lowe and Joe Holyman met as 14-year-old school boys in Tasmania before they headed off in different directions, Joe Holyman to establish a record of the most number of catches by a wicket keeper on debut in first-class cricket, Matt Lowe to see the world. They came together once again at Roseworthy undertaking the marketing degree, leading to positions as sales representatives. Matt then trained to be a chef, while Joe set off for a series of vintages in Burgundy, Provence and the Douro Valley. Their paths crossed again when they both began working at Cape Jaffa Wines at Robe on the Limestone Coast, and to the establishment of their own brand as a side interest.

Stoney Rise Sauvignon Blanc

TTTY 2001 Light to medium green-yellow; the bouquet is quite full, with a mix of ripe gooseberry and grass aromas, rather than tropical. The palate is soft, ripe, slightly broad and sweet; gives the impression earlier picking would have benefitted the wine. **rating: 84**

best drinking 2001–2002 **best vintages** NA **drink with** Seafood • $17

Stoney Rise Cotes du Robe Shiraz

TTTT 2000 Vivid, youthful purple-red; fresh, spicy, savoury aromas on the bouquet lead through to a rich, full and deep berry (plum and blackberry) fruit on the palate, with good acidity and length. A most interesting, youthful wine. **rating: 89**

best drinking 2003–2008 **best vintages** NA **drink with** Game pie • $20

stonier wines ★★★★☆

362 Frankston–Flinders Road, Merricks, Vic 3916 **region** Mornington Peninsula
phone (03) 5989 8300 **fax** (03) 5989 8709 **open** 7 days 12–5 (summer 11–5) (except Christmas Day)
winemaker Tod Dexter, Geraldine McFaul **production** 25 000 **est.** 1978
product range ($19–45 CD) Chardonnay, Reserve Chardonnay, Pinot Noir, Reserve Pinot Noir.
summary Looked at across the range, Stonier and Paringa Estate are now the pre-eminent wineries in the Mornington Peninsula; Stoniers' standing is in turn based more or less equally on its Chardonnay and Pinot Noir under the Reserve label. The acquisition of a 70 per cent interest by Petaluma in 1998 has given both Stonier (and the Mornington Peninsula as a whole) even greater credibility than hitherto. Exports to the UK, Canada, Belgium, Germany, Italy, Netherlands, New Zealand, Malaysia, Hong Kong, Singapore and Japan.

Stonier Chardonnay

TTTTY 2000 Light to medium yellow-green; tangy citrus/grapefruit/nectarine fruit and barely perceptible oak on the bouquet. An attractive, fresh fruit-driven palate precisely tracking the bouquet results in a thoroughly nice wine. **rating: 90**

best drinking 2001–2004 **best vintages** '91, '93, '94, '97, '98, '00 **drink with** Pasta, rich seafood • $19

Stonier Reserve Chardonnay

TTTTY 2000 Light green-yellow; smoky barrel-ferment aromas surround the citrus and nectarine fruit of the bouquet, then a fine, long, intense, fruit-driven palate still needing to soften and open up a little. **rating: 93**

best drinking 2002–2006 **best vintages** '86, '88, '91, '93, '94, '95, '96, '97, '98, '99, '00 **drink with** Milk-fed veal • $36

Stonier Pinot Noir

TTTTY 2000 Excellent purple-red; the bouquet is tangy, with lifted aromatics, the palate intense, tight and with excellent length. The plummy fruit is still bound up, and the wine will transform itself over the next 12–18 months in bottle. **rating: 93**

best drinking 2001–2005 **best vintages** '92, '94, '95, '97, '00 **drink with** Game of any kind • $23

Stonier Reserve Pinot Noir

TTTTY 2000 Light to medium red-purple; a clean, bright and fragrant bouquet with strawberry, plum, leaf and mint is followed by a lively, fresh, juicy/berry/minty fruit-flavoured palate which does, however, lighten off slightly on the finish. **rating: 91**

best drinking 2001–2005 **best vintages** '90, '91, '92, '94, '95, '97, '99, '00 **drink with** Coq au vin • $45

stratherne vale estate NR

Campbell Street, Caballing, WA 6312 **region** Central Western Australia Zone
phone (08) 9881 2140 **fax** (08) 9881 3122 **open** Not
winemaker James Pennington (Contract) **production** 600 **est.** 1980
product range A single red wine made from a blend of Cabernet Sauvignon, Zinfandel, Merlot and Shiraz.
summary Stratherne Vale Estate stretches the viticultural map of Australia yet further. It is situated near Narrogin, which is north of the Great Southern region and south of the most generous extension of the Darling Ranges. The closest viticultural region of note is at Wandering, to the northeast.

☙ strathewen hills ★★★★

1090 Strathewen Road, Strathewen, Vic 3099 **region** Yarra Valley
phone (03) 9714 8464 **fax** (03) 9714 8464 **open** By appointment
winemaker William Christophersen **production** NA **est.** 1991

product range ($45–75 R) Chardonnay, Tribal Elder Shiraz, Merlot Cabernets.

summary Joan and William (who I have always called Bill) Christophersen began the slow process of establishing Strathewen Hills in 1991. The vineyard was established with ultra-close spacing, with 3 hectares planted predominantly to pinot noir, chardonnay, shiraz, merlot and small amounts of cabernet sauvignon, cabernet franc and a few bits and pieces, but frost caused persistent losses until protective sprinklers were installed. The first two commercial releases from the 2000 vintage are excellent wines, bearing testimony both to Bill Christophersen's undoubted skills as a winemaker, and the ideal vintage. They also operate Sugar Loaf Cottage, a two-bedroom, self-contained bed and breakfast.

Strathewen Hills Chardonnay

TTTT 2001 Medium to full yellow-green; stone fruit, melon and a hint of fig on the bouquet also come through on the palate, which is not particularly intense, but well made. The oak influence throughout is minimal, adding textural rather than flavour complexity. **rating:** 85

best drinking 2003–2006 **best vintages** NA **drink with** Smoked trout • NA

Strathewen Hills Tribal Elder Shiraz

TTTTY 2000 Medium to full purple-red; the bouquet is clean, with ripe, small black fruit aromas, a hint of fruit spice, and subtle oak. The fully ripe, strong black cherry fruit on the palate is supported by ample tannins and just a hint of oak; very impressive. **rating:** 90

best drinking 2003–2008 **best vintages** '00 **drink with** Smoked lamb • $70

Strathewen Hills Merlot Cabernet

TTTTY 2000 Medium to full red-purple; the ripe, cassis, blackberry fruit with slightly savoury/spicy overtones leads into a well-constructed and balanced medium-bodied palate, with good length and integration of oak and tannins. **rating:** 90

best drinking 2003–2008 **best vintages** '00 **drink with** Rack of lamb • $45

strathkellar   NR

Murray Valley Highway, Cobram, Vic 3644 **region** Goulburn Valley
phone (03) 5873 5274 **fax** (03) 5873 5270 **open** 7 days 10–5
winemaker Tahbilk (Contract) **production** 2000 **est.** 1990
product range ($10–18 CD) Chenin Blanc, Chardonnay, Sparkling Brut Reserve, Sparkling Shiraz, Late Picked Chenin Blanc, Sweet Muscatel, Shiraz, Grenache Shiraz Mataro, Muscat, Tokay, Putters Port, Old Putters Port.

summary Dick Parkes planted his 6-hectare vineyard to chardonnay, shiraz and chenin blanc in 1990, and has the wine contract-made at Tahbilk by Alister Purbrick. The fact that the wines are made at Tahbilk is a sure guarantee of quality, and the prices are modest.

straws lane   ★★★

1282 Mount Macedon Road, Hesket, Vic 3442 **region** Macedon Ranges
phone (03) 9654 9380 **fax** (03) 9663 6300 **open** Weekends and public holidays 10–4, or by appointment
winemaker Stuart Anderson, John Ellis **production** 1000 **est.** 1987
product range ($24–40 R) Gewürztraminer, Macedon Blanc de Noirs, Pinot Noir.

summary The Straws Lane vineyard was planted 12 years ago, but the Straws Lane label is a relatively new arrival on the scene; after a highly successful 1995 vintage, adverse weather in 1996 and 1997 meant that little or no wine was made in those years, but the pace picked up again with subsequent vintages. Stuart Anderson guides the making of the Pinot Noir, Hanging Rock Winery handles the Gewürztraminer and the sparkling wine base, and Cope-Williams looks after the tiraging and maturation of the sparkling wine. It's good to have co-operative neighbours.

Straws Lane Blanc de Noirs RD

TTTT 1996 Excellent mousse and pale straw-gold colour. The bouquet opens with strong bready autolysis, then hints of strawberry reflecting the pinot noir base; good style. The palate in this recently disgorged version has penetrating acidity, with what seems to be a much lower dosage than that given to the wine first disgorged and released over a year ago. A compromise between the two versions might have given the very best result, but this is a good wine. **rating:** 87

best drinking 2002–2006 **best vintages** NA **drink with** Shellfish, oysters • $40

Straws Lane Gewürztraminer

ŦŦŦŦ **2001** Exceedingly pale straw-green; a fresh flinty/minerally/spicy bouquet is followed by a palate with some length and grip, although the latent fruit is still to develop full varietal character. Was the public choice at the 2001 Macedon Ranges Wine Exhibition dinner. **rating: 85**

best drinking 2001–2006 **best vintages** NA **drink with** Chinese prawns • $24

Straws Lane Pinot Noir

ŦŦŦŶ **2000** Medium red-purple; the bouquet is complex, with the slightly green stalky/foresty characters which seem to be the mark of the estate. The palate has lots of grip and length, and will always walk on the green side, but never be short of character. **rating: 84**

ŦŦŦŦ **1999** Medium red, with just a touch of purple; the palate is soft, plummy, with slightly savoury aspects. Some minty notes on the palate strongly suggest the grapes were not 100 per cent ripe. **rating: 83**

best drinking 2002–2007 **best vintages** '98 **drink with** Ragout of veal • $31

stringy brae ★★★★

Sawmill Road, Sevenhill, SA 5453 **region** Clare Valley
phone (08) 8843 4313 **fax** (08) 8843 4319 **open** Weekends and public holidays 10–5, Mon–Fri refer to road sign
winemaker Contract (Mitchell) **production** 1500 **est.** 1991
product range ($15–48 CD) Riesling, Sparkling Riesling, Shiraz, Black Knight Shiraz, Mote Hill, Cabernet Sauvignon.
summary Donald and Sally Willson have established over 9 hectares of vineyards that since the 1996 vintage have produced all the grapes for their wines. (Previously grapes from Langhorne Creek were used.) The Australian domestic market is serviced direct by mail order, but the wines are exported to the UK, New Zealand and the US.

Stringy Brae Riesling

ŦŦŦŦŦ **2001** Light green-yellow; a spotlessly clean, bright and fresh bouquet offers lemon, spice and slate aromas, then the palate is classic Clare Valley style, tight, long and bone dry, with great structure and length. Unusually for the Clare Valley, picked at only 10.5° baume, and also dressed in a smart new package. **rating: 94**

best drinking 2001–2006 **best vintages** '01 **drink with** Asparagus • $16

stuart range estates ★★★

67 William Street, Kingaroy, Qld 4610 **region** South Burnett
phone (07) 4162 3711 **fax** (07) 4162 4811 **open** 7 days 9–5
winemaker Charles Pregenzer **production** 5000 **est.** 1997
product range ($9–18 CD) Semillon, Verdelho, Chardonnay, Goodger Chardonnay, Range White and Range Red (both semi-sweet), Shiraz, Goodger Shiraz, Cabernet Merlot, Cabernet Sauvignon, Blue Moon Liqueur, Explorer Tawny Port.
summary Stuart Range Estates is a prime example of the extent and pace of change in the Qld wine industry, coming from nowhere in 1997 to crushing just under 120 tonnes of grapes in its inaugural vintage in 1998. The grapes are supplied by up to seven growers in the South Burnett Valley with 52 hectares planted by 1996. A state-of-the-art winery has been established within an old butter factory building. The barrel-fermented Chardonnay won the trophy for the Best Qld White Wine in the annual Courier-Mail Top 100 Wine Competition some years ago.

Stuart Range Estates Semillon

ŦŦŦŦ **2001** Pale to the point of water white; the bouquet is clean, with light mineral aromas, the palate similarly crisp, clean, but with little fruit push. To be honest, the points are given for what it may become rather than what it is today. **rating: 84**

best drinking 2004–2009 **best vintages** NA **drink with** Blue swimmer crab • $12

Stuart Range Estates Verdelho

ŦŦŦŶ **2001** Light to medium green-yellow; the bouquet is clean and fresh, but with no particular distinction; the palate is likewise fresh, well made and clean, the lack of fruit ripeness perversely making the wine a natural seafood match. **rating: 83**

best drinking 2002–2003 **best vintages** NA **drink with** Seafood salad • $15

Stuart Range Estates Goodger Chardonnay

TTTT 2001 Light to medium yellow-green; the moderately intense but quite complex bouquet shows delicate barrel ferment characters; the palate is fresh and lively, with balanced and integrated fruit and spicy oak, finishing with brisk acidity. **rating:** 85

best drinking 2002–2003 **best vintages** NA **drink with** Chargrilled salmon • $16

Stuart Range Estates South Burnett Cabernet Sauvignon

TTTY 2000 Light to medium red-purple; the bouquet is clean, with rather simple red berry fruit; the palate, likewise, has some varietal character but is structurally simple; neither the palate or bouquet reflect the maturation in French and American oak. **rating:** 83

best drinking 2003–2006 **best vintages** NA **drink with** Roast lamb • $18

stumpy gully ★★★

1247 Stumpy Gully Road, Moorooduc, Vic 3933 **region** Mornington Peninsula
phone (03) 5978 8429 **fax** (03) 5978 8419 **open** Weekends 11–5
winemaker Wendy Zantvoort, Maitena Zantvoort, Ewan Campbell **production** 500 **est.** 1988
product range ($15–30 CD) Riesling, Sauvignon Blanc, Marsanne, Chardonnay, Encore Chardonnay, Pinot Grigio, Pinot Noir Chardonnay, Botrytis Riesling, Pinot Noir, Sangiovese, Shiraz, Merlot, Merlot Cabernet, Cabernet Sauvignon; also Peninsula Panorama Chardonnay and Pinot Noir.
summary When Frank and Wendy Zantvoort began planting their first vineyard in 1989 there were no winemakers in the family; now there are three, plus two viticulturists. Mother Wendy was first to obtain her degree from Charles Sturt University, followed by daughter Maitena, who then married Ewan Campbell, another winemaker. Father Frank and son Michael look after the vineyards. The original vineyard has 9 hectares of vines, but in establishing the new 20-hectare Moorooduc vineyard (first harvest 2001) the Zantvoorts have deliberately gone against prevailing thinking, planting it solely to red varieties, predominately cabernet sauvignon, merlot and shiraz. They believe they have one of the warmest sites on the Peninsula, and that ripening will in fact present no problems. In all they now have ten varieties planted, producing a dozen different wines.

suckfizzle augusta ★★★★☆

Lot 14 Kalkarrie Drive, Augusta, WA 6290 (PO Box 403, Nedlands, WA 6909) **region** Margaret River
phone (08) 9389 6778 **fax** (08) 9389 6728 **open** Not
winemaker Janice McDonald **production** 4000 **est.** 1997
product range ($14.50–41 R) Sauvignon Blanc Semillon, Cabernet Sauvignon; Stella Bella range of Sauvignon Blanc, Chardonnay, Pink Muscat, Cabernet Merlot.
summary First things first. The back label explains: 'the name Suckfizzle has been snaffled from the 14th century monk and medico turned writer Rabelais and his infamous character the great Lord Suckfizzle'. Suckfizzle is the joint venture of two well-known Margaret River winemakers who, in deference to their employers, do not identify themselves on any of the background material or the striking front and back labels of the wines.

Suckfizzle Augusta Stella Bella Sauvignon Blanc

TTTTY 2001 Light green-yellow; the ripe gooseberry fruit has some attractive flowery characters on the bouquet; the light to medium-bodied palate with pleasantly ripe gooseberry fruit, and a clean finish. **rating:** 90

best drinking 2001–2002 **best vintages** NA **drink with** Margaret River abalone • $22

Suckfizzle Augusta Sauvignon Blanc Semillon

TTTT 2001 Light green-yellow; the bouquet is complex, with obvious barrel-ferment oak influences, the palate with nicely ripened fruit still in the shade of the oak. Very much in the Suckfizzle style, tending baroque, and with great character. **rating:** 88

best drinking 2001–2004 **best vintages** '97, '98 **drink with** Marron • $41

summerfield ★★★★☆

Main Road, Moonambel, Vic 3478 **region** Pyrenees
phone (03) 5467 2264 **fax** (03) 5467 2380 **open** 7 days 9–5.30
winemaker Ian Summerfield, Mark Summerfield **production** 3500 **est.** 1979

product range ($10–35 CD) Sauvignon Blanc, Trebbiano, Shiraz, Reserve Shiraz, Cabernet Merlot, Cabernet Sauvignon, Reserve Cabernet.

summary A specialist red wine producer, the particular forte of which is Shiraz. The wines since 1988 have been consistently excellent, luscious and full-bodied and fruit-driven, but with a slice of vanillin oak to top them off. Exports to the US and UK.

Summerfield Shiraz

▼▼▼▼ **2000** Dense, inky colour; then a highly scented bouquet with concentrated fruit and slightly raw American oak. The palate is tremendously concentrated and rich, yet the tannins are soft; higher quality oak would have produced a wine worthy of many years in the cellar. **rating: 89**

best drinking 2004–2010 **best vintages** '79, '83, '88, '91, '92, '93, '94, '96, '97, '99 '00 **drink with** Beef stew • $23

Summerfield Reserve Shiraz

▼▼▼▼▽ **2000** Medium to full red-purple; rich, concentrated, plush dark cherry fruit on the bouquet is followed by a palate crammed with luscious, ripe black cherry fruit offset by powerful tannins. Oak is somewhere there, as is 15° alcohol. A very good example of the big end of town. **rating: 93**

best drinking 2005–2015 **best vintages** '98, '99, '00 **drink with** Venison pie • $35

Summerfield Cabernet Merlot   *150 RRLS*

▼▼▼▼ **2000** Youthful purple-red; a fragrant and intense bouquet, typical of the winery, has masses of juicy berry fruit flowing through into the juicy blackcurrant/cassis/mint-flavoured palate. Just a trifle overwhelming, but will doubtless settle down with age. **rating: 89**

best drinking 2004–2010 **best vintages** NA **drink with** Venison with blackcurrant jus • $23 *26.36*

Summerfield Reserve Cabernet

▼▼▼▼▽ **2000** Dense, impenetrable purple; as the colour suggests, the bouquet is equally dense and powerful, anchored on blackberry fruit. Improbably, the palate moves up another gear, with massively powerful berry/blackberry/mint fruit, although the tannins are surprisingly soft, the oak bringing up the rear. **rating: 93**

best drinking 2010–2020 **best vintages** '00 **drink with** Osso buco • $35

surveyor's hill winery   NR

215 Brooklands Road, Wallaroo, NSW 2618 **region** Canberra District
phone (02) 6230 2046 **fax** (02) 6230 2048 **open** Weekends and public holidays or by appointment
winemaker Dr Roger Harris **production** 1000 **est.** 1986
product range ($10–22 R) Riesling, Sauvignon Blanc, Pinot Noir, Rosado Touriga, Shiraz, Cabernet Merlot.
summary Surveyor's Hill has 10 hectares of vineyard, but most of the grapes are sold to BRL Hardy, which vinifies the remainder for Surveyor's Hill – which should guarantee the quality of the wines sold. Also offers bed and breakfast accommodation.

sutherland smith wines   NR

Cnr Falkners Road and Murray Valley Highway, Rutherglen, Vic 3685 **region** Rutherglen
phone (03) 6032 8177 **fax** (03) 6032 8177 **open** Weekends, public and Victorian school holidays 10–5, other Fridays 11–5
winemaker George Sutherland-Smith **production** 1000 **est.** 1993
product range ($10.90–16.50 CD) Riesling, Josephine (Riesling Traminer), Chardonnay, Merlot, Cabernet Shiraz, Port.
summary George Sutherland-Smith, for decades managing director and winemaker at All Saints, has opened up his own small business at Rutherglen, making wine in the refurbished Emu Plains winery, originally constructed in the 1850s. He draws upon fruit grown in a leased vineyard at Glenrowan and also from grapes grown in the King Valley.

swanbrook estate wines   ★★★☆

38 Swan Street, Henley Brook, WA 6055 **region** Swan District
phone (08) 9296 3100 **fax** (08) 9296 3099 **open** 7 days 10–5
winemaker Rob Marshall **production** 10 000 **est.** 1998

product range ($12–40 CD) Semillon, Classic Dry White, Chenin (wood aged), Verdelho, Chardonnay, Classic Shiraz, Estate Shiraz, Cabernet Merlot.

summary This is the reincarnation of Evans & Tate's Gnangara Winery. It secures most of its grapes from contract growers in the Perth Hills and Swan Valley, but also has the 60-year-old block of shiraz around the winery. A little under 40 per cent of the annual crush is for the Swanbrook label, the remainder being contract winemaking for others. Owner John Andreou (a Perth restaurateur) has invested $2 million in upgrading and expanding the facilities, and former Evans & Tate winemaker Rob Marshall has continued at Swanbrook, providing valuable continuity.

🦢 swan valley wines ★★★

261 Haddrill Road, Baskerville, WA 6065 **region** Swan District
phone (08) 9296 1501 **fax** (08) 9296 1733 **open** Fri–Sun and public holidays 10–5
winemaker Julie White (Contract) **production** 2000 **est.** 1999
product range ($13.50–16.50 CD) Semillon, Chenin Blanc, Shiraz, Grenache, White Port, Tawny Port.
summary Peter and Paula Hoffman, together with sons Paul and Thomas, acquired their 6-hectare property in 1989. It had a long history of grape growing, and the prior owner had registered the name Swan Valley Wines back in 1983. In 1999 the family built a new winery to handle the grapes from 2.3 hectares of chenin blanc, 1.4 hectares of grenache, a little over 0.5 hectares each of semillon, malbec and cabernet sauvignon and a smaller amount of shiraz. South African-trained Julie White is contract winemaker. Exports to Japan.

Swan Valley Wines Semillon

TTTY 2001 Light green-yellow; the bouquet is clean and fresh, moderately intense, with authentic varietal lemon and grass aromas. The palate opens in similar vein, but does, however, thicken on the finish, perhaps reflecting a touch of residual sugar. **rating: 84**

best drinking 2001–2004 **best vintages** NA **drink with** Weiner schnitzel • $15

Swan Valley Wines Chenin Blanc

TTTY 2001 Light green-yellow; the bouquet is tangy/lemony, almost gritty in its intensity; the powerful palate follows suit with a slightly grippy finish notwithstanding the touch of residual sugar. By no means short on flavour. **rating: 81**

best drinking 2001–2003 **best vintages** NA **drink with** Summer salad • $13.50

Swan Valley Wines Shiraz

TTTY 2000 Light to medium red-purple; the bouquet has light cherry, leaf and spice aromas, the light to medium-bodied palate similarly offering light cherry fruit with slightly earthy nuances, but not a great deal of structure. **rating: 83**

best drinking 2002–2005 **best vintages** NA **drink with** Lasagne • $16.50

sylvan springs estates ★★★☆

RSD 405 Blythmans Road, McLaren Flat, SA 5171 **region** McLaren Vale
phone (08) 8383 0500 **fax** (08) 8383 0499 **open** Not
winemaker Brian Light (Consultant) **production** 1000 **est.** 1974
product range ($19.50 R) Shiraz, Cabernet Sauvignon.
summary The Pridmore family has been involved in grape growing and winemaking in McLaren Vale for 4 generations spanning over 100 years. The pioneer was Cyril Pridmore who established The Wattles Winery in 1896, purchasing Sylvan Park, one of the original homesteads in the area, in 1901. The original family land in the township of McLaren Vale was sold in 1978, but not before third generation Digby Pridmore had established new vineyards (in 1974) near Blewitt Springs. When he retired in 1990, his son David purchased the 45-hectare vineyard (planted to 11 different varieties) and, with sister Sally, ventured into winemaking in 1996, with Brian Light as consultant winemaker.

Sylvan Springs Estates Shiraz

TTTT 2000 Medium red-purple; a clean, moderately intense bouquet with a mix of ripe berry, chocolate, spice and vanilla oak, then ripe, fresh plummy/berry fruit, a twitch of regional chocolate, finishing with fine tannins. Spends 18 months in American and a little French oak, and has finesse. **rating: 88**

best drinking 2004–2009 **best vintages** NA **drink with** Steak and kidney pie • $19.50

symphonia wines ★★★★

Boggy Creek Road, Myrrhee, Vic 3732 **region** King Valley
phone (03) 5729 7579 **fax** (03) 5729 7519 **open** By appointment
winemaker Peter Read **production** 750 **est.** 1998
product range ($15–30 CD) Chardonnay Plus, Viognier Petit Manseng, Pinot Grigio, Pinot Chardonnay, Blanc de Blanc, Quintus, Merlot, Merlot Plus, Saperavi, Las Triadas.
summary Peter Read and his family are veterans of the King Valley, commencing the development of their vineyard in 1981 to supply Brown Brothers. As a result of extensive trips to both Western and Eastern Europe, Peter Read embarked on an ambitious project to trial a series of grape varieties little known in this country. The process of evaluation and experimentation continues, but since Symphonia released the first small quantities of wines in mid-1998 and it has built on that start. A number of the wines have great interest and no less merit.

Symphonia Blanc de Blanc

♥♥♥♥ 1998 Light green-yellow, with quite good mousse; clean lemon/citrus aromas, then a quite delicate, crisp and relatively dry palate, with nicely balanced lemony/citrussy fruit. **rating:** 86

best drinking 2002–2003 **best vintages** NA **drink with** Aperitif • $20

Symphonia Pinot Chardonnay

♥♥♥♥ 1997 Light green-yellow, good mousse. A complex and stylish bouquet with some distinctly bready autolysis characters, then a relatively austere palate with slight green tinges, but impressive. **rating:** 87

best drinking 2002–2003 **best vintages** NA **drink with** Oysters • $20

Symphonia Quintus

♥♥♥♥ 2000 Strong red-purple; a complex array of dark berry fruits in a blackberry, plum and prune spectrum mark the bouquet. The same flavours come through on the palate, which has considerable depth, overall more savoury than fruity/jammy, and providing plenty to play with. A blend of merlot, cabernet sauvignon, saperavi, tannat and tempranillo, unique to Symphonia. **rating:** 89

best drinking 2004–2010 **best vintages** '99, '00 **drink with** Pasta with meat sauce • $22

Symphonia Las Triadas

♥♥♥♡ 2000 Medium red-purple; the moderately intense bouquet has some earthy/spicy notes, the medium-bodied palate with hints of licorice, earth and blackberry, finishing with persistent tannins and more than a touch of American oak. A blend of tempranillo, cabernet sauvignon and merlot devised at the Evena Research Station at Navarra in northern Spain. **rating:** 84

best drinking 2003–2007 **best vintages** NA **drink with** Bratwurst • $20

Symphonia Saperavi

♥♥♥♥ 2000 Potent, deep and bright red-purple, living up to the reputation of the variety. The bouquet has an array of dark fruits, blackberry, bramble and spice, the powerful palate with blackberry, plum and impressive tannins. The most widely planted red grape in Russia, the word meaning 'dyer' in Russian. **rating:** 87

best drinking 2004–2010 **best vintages** NA **drink with** Braised ox cheek • $30

Symphonia King Valley Merlot

♥♥♥♥ 2000 Bright red-purple; fresh, red berry fruits plus hints of spice and leaf are an encouraging opening, but the dusty tannins which run through the palate take away from the elegance and varietal character, even if they do add to the total flavours. Subtle oak. **rating:** 85

best drinking 2002–2005 **best vintages** '99 **drink with** Light Italian • $17

tahbilk ★★★★☆

Goulburn Valley Highway, Tabilk, Vic 3608 **region** Goulburn Valley
phone (03) 5794 2555 **fax** (03) 5794 2360 **open** Mon–Sat 9–5, Sun 11–5
winemaker Alister Purbrick, Neil Larson, Alan George **production** 126 000 **est.** 1860
product range ($7.95–99.95 R) Riesling, Marsanne, Roussanne, Viognier, Sauvignon Blanc, Semillon, Verdelho, Chardonnay, Lexia (sweet white), Dulcet (sweet white), Brut Cuvée, Sparkling Lexia, Grenache, Cabernet Franc, Malbec, Merlot, Cabernet Merlot, Shiraz, 1933 Vines Reserve Shiraz, Cabernet Sauvignon; 1860 Vines Shiraz is rare flagship, with a Reserve red released from each vintage; Fortifieds.
summary A winery steeped in tradition (with high National Trust classification), which should be visited at least once by every wine-conscious Australian, and which makes wines – particularly red wines – utterly

in keeping with that tradition. The essence of that heritage comes in the form of the tiny quantities of Shiraz made entirely from vines planted in 1860. Its releases on the market in 2001 and 2002 were all excellent, as if to commemorate the dropping of Chateau from the winery name. As well as Australian national distribution through Tucker Seabrook, Tahbilk has agents in every principal wine market, including the UK, Europe, Asia and North America.

Tahbilk Riesling

 TTTTT 2001 Light to medium yellow-green; the clean, smooth and ripe bouquet has citrus and pineapple aromas, the palate flowing well, with similar ripe fruit then a touch of minerally acidity on the finish. A big, generous wine, continuing the recent run of success for Tahbilk with this variety. **rating: 90**

best drinking 2001–2005 best vintages '86, '90, '92, '94, '99, '00, '01 drink with Seafood salad • $14.95

Tahbilk Semillon

TTTTT 2001 Light to medium green-yellow; a clean, firm bouquet with aromas of lemon and herb leads into a palate with good flavour, depth and length, with richer than average fruit. **rating: 90**

best drinking 2001–2005 best vintages NA drink with Chicken fricassee • $11.95

Tahbilk Marsanne

TTTT 2000 Medium yellow-green; the bouquet is clean, but rather closed, seemingly in transition late in 2001. The palate, however, is quite distinctive in its flavour and structure, offering a mix of honeysuckle and dried flower flavours, then a crisp, bone-dry finish. **rating: 88**

best drinking 2002–2008 best vintages '53, '74, '79, '81, '84, '85, '87, '88, '91, '92, '93, '95, '96, '98, '99 drink with Lighter Italian or Asian dishes • $11.95

Tahbilk Shiraz

TTTTT 1999 Medium red-purple; clean, ripe dark berry/plum fruit with the typical subtle oak of Tahbilk on the bouquet foreshadows a particularly nice wine, centred on plum and chocolate fruit, finishing with fine, earthy tannins and soft oak. Yes, a touch old-fashioned, but a good'un. **rating: 90**

best drinking 2003–2009 best vintages '61, '62, '65, '68, '71, '74, '76, '78, '81, '84, '85, '86, '91, '98, '99 drink with Barbecued T-bone steak • $19.95

Tahbilk 1933 Vines Reserve Shiraz

TTTTT 1996 Medium red; the bouquet is starting to evolve, with clean, scented fruit and hints of sweet leather. An interesting palate with savoury, sweet leather and briar flavours around the core of cherry fruit; has a particularly good finish, and is absolutely the best of the old vine wines to be so far released by Tahbilk. **rating: 94**

best drinking 2002–2016 best vintages '96 drink with Braised ox tail • $53

Tahbilk Cabernet Sauvignon

TTTT 1999 Medium red, with some purple hues remaining; the moderately intense bouquet has a range of savoury/earthy/secondary aromas; there is good depth to the fruit on the palate in a black/dark berry spectrum plus a distinct touch of chocolate. Good tannin balance. **rating: 89**

best drinking 2003–2013 best vintages '65, '71, '72, '75, '76, '78, '79, '86, '90, '92, '97, '98, '99 drink with Strong mature cheddar, stilton • $19.95

tait wines   NR

Yaldara Drive, Lyndoch, SA 5351 **region** Barossa Valley
phone (08) 8524 5000 **fax** (08) 8524 5220 **open** Weekends 11–4 or by appointment
winemaker Bruno Tait **production** 1000 **est.** 1994
product range ($12–27 CD) Chardonnay, Basket Press Shiraz, Basket Press Cabernet Sauvignon.
summary The Tait family has been involved in the wine industry in the Barossa for over 100 years, making not wine but barrels. Their recent venture into winemaking was immediately successful; retail distribution through single outlets in Melbourne, Adelaide and Sydney; exports to the US and Singapore.

Tait Basket Press Shiraz

TTTT 2000 Medium to full red-purple; unusual prune and date aromas and flavours, together with a touch of hay and straw on the palate all attest to very ripe, if not over-ripe grapes, in turn reflected by the alcohol of just under 15°. **rating: 83**

best drinking 2002–2006 best vintages NA drink with Rich game • $25

☙ talga ★★★★

Milbrodale Road, Broke, Hunter Valley, NSW 2330 **region** Canberra District
phone (02) 6579 1111 **fax** (02) 6579 1440 **open** Not
winemaker Suzanne Little **production** 2000 **est.** 1998
product range ($26 ML) Talagandra Chardonnay, Shiraz.
summary Talga is a partnership between two viticulturists – Anne and Anthony Richard – and their daughter and son-in-law, Suzanne and Ian Little, both winemakers at Little's Hunter Valley winery. The vineyard was planted between 1980 and 1996 at an altitude of nearly 700 metres on the slopes of the Gundaroo Valley near Canberra. There is 2.1 hectares of shiraz and 0.9 hectares of chardonnay. The first commercial crop in 1998 was sent to Little's, originally with the intention of using it as part of a blend of other non-Hunter material. However, the quality was such that the parcels were kept separate and the partnership formed. Exports to the US.

Talagandra Chardonnay

▼▼▼▼▽ **2000** Light to medium yellow-green; the bouquet is quite aromatic and intense, with a mix of stone fruit and citrus, precisely replicated in the flavours of the palate. The influence of oak is subtle, and the fruit-driven palate has good length. **rating: 90**

best drinking 2002–2007 **best vintages** '00 **drink with** Carpaccio of salmon • $26

talijancich NR

26 Hyem Road, Herne Hill, WA 6056 **region** Swan District
phone (08) 9296 4289 **fax** (08) 9296 1762 **open** Sun–Fri 11–5
winemaker James Talijancich **production** 10 000 **est.** 1932
product range ($17–135 CD) Verdelho, Voices Dry White, Grenache, Shiraz, Julian James White Liqueur, Julian James Red Liqueur, Liqueur Tokay 375 ml.
summary A former fortified wine specialist (with old Liqueur Tokay) now making a select range of table wines, with particular emphasis on Verdelho – on the third Saturday of August each year there is a tasting of fine three-year-old Verdelho table wines from both Australia and overseas. Also runs an active wine club and exports to China, Japan and Hong Kong.

taliondal NR

240 Old North Road, Rothbury, NSW 2320 **region** Lower Hunter Valley
phone (02) 9427 6812 **fax** (02) 9427 6812 **open** By appointment
winemaker Frank Brady **production** 200 **est.** 1974
product range ($8–15 ML) Traminer, Cab Fizz, Cabernet Sauvignon.
summary The Brady Bunch, headed by Frank Brady, acquired Taliondal in 1974 as a family hideaway. Says Frank Brady, 'When in the Hunter do as the Hunter does', so one hectare of cabernet sauvignon was planted in 1974, and 1.5 hectares of traminer the following year. For many years the family was content to sell the grapes to local vignerons, but now take a small portion of the production and make wine on the property. The Cabernet Sauvignon has been a consistent medal-winner at Hunter shows, the 1998 winning the trophy for Open Vintage Reds at the 1999 Boutique Winemakers Show. This has led to a decision to concentrate on red wine making, and while some Traminer remains for sale, future production will be of the Cabernet Sauvignon only.

tallarook ★★★★

Ennis Road, Tallarook, Vic 3659 **region** Central Victorian High Country
phone (03) 9818 3455 **fax** (03) 9818 3646 **open** Not
winemaker Martin Williams, Daniel Crane **production** 2750 **est.** 1987
product range ($25–27.50 ML) Chardonnay, Marsanne, Pinot Noir, Shiraz, with Viognier and Rousanne on the way.
summary Tallarook has been established on a property between Broadford and Seymour at an elevation of 200-300 metres. 4teen hectares of vines have been planted since 1987, the three principal varieties being chardonnay, shiraz and pinot noir. The retainer of Martin Williams as winemaker in the 1998 vintage brought a substantial change in emphasis, and the subsequent release of an impressive Chardonnay. The wines are mainly sold by mail order; also retail distribution in Melbourne and exports to the UK.

taltarni ★★★★

Taltarni Road, Moonambel, Vic 3478 **region** Pyrenees
phone (03) 5467 2218 **fax** (03) 5467 2306 **open** 7 days 10–5
winemaker Shane Clohesy, Peter Steer, Loic Le Calvez **production** 80 000 **est.** 1972
product range ($10–28 CD) Sauvignon Blanc, Viognier, Late Harvest Riesling, Rosé, Shiraz, Merlot
Cabernet, Merlot, Cabernet Sauvignon; Fiddleback red and white; Brut, Brut Tache; Lalla Gully
Sauvignon Blanc, Chardonnay.
summary In the shadow of the departure of long-serving winemaker and chief executive Dominique
Portet, Taltarni seems to have backed off the high levels of tannin and extract evident in the older vintage
wines, which, after a brief period of uncertainty, seems to be paying off. The addition of the Lalla Gully
vineyard (like Clover Hill, also Tasmanian) has extended the production range. Exports to all the major
markets, including the UK, US, Canada, Japan, Hong Kong, Switzerland, Sweden and extensively
throughout Southeast Asia and Western Europe.

Taltarni Sauvignon Blanc

▼▼▼▼ 2001 Light green-yellow; the bouquet is clean, crisp and minerally, although the fruit is somewhat
repressed. The palate has considerable length, building intensity but then finishing with a hot finish,
reflecting its 14° alcohol. **rating:** 85

best drinking 2001–2002 **best vintages** '96, '97, '98 **drink with** Calamari • $19.50

Lalla Gully Sauvignon Blanc

▼▼▼▼ 2001 Light green-yellow; clean, crisp and fresh range from light citrus through to
gooseberry/tropical, characters sustained through to the crisp, flavoursome mid-palate, although the finish
of the wine is not so clear-cut. **rating:** 86

best drinking 2002–2003 **best vintages** NA **drink with** Deep sea crab • $16

Lalla Gully Chardonnay

▼▼▼▼▽ 1999 Light to medium yellow-green; gentle citrus and melon is neatly married with subtle oak on
the bouquet. The promised elegance comes through on the neatly balanced palate with hints of cashew and
spice, smooth fruit, and good length. **rating:** 90

best drinking 2002–2004 **best vintages** '99 **drink with** Tasmanian lobster • $26.50

Taltarni Brut

▼▼▼▼ 1999 Light straw-green; a bright, fresh, lemony herbaceous bouquet, then a bright, elegant and
lively palate; Chardonnay, Pinot Noir and Pinot Meunier from both Taltarni and Clover Hill vineyards.
Virtually identical to the Brut Tache of the same vintage. **rating:** 87

▼▼▼▼ 1998 Light straw-green; the bouquet is quite complex, with bready notes and touches of citrus. The
palate is lively and crisp with a hint of strawberry, but predominantly citrus-tinged flavours. Fresh and lively.
rating: 87

best drinking 2002–2003 **best vintages** NA **drink with** Oysters, shellfish • $18

Taltarni Brut Tache

▼▼▼▼ 1998 Pale rosé; a quite aromatic bouquet with a mix of strawberry and mineral is followed by a fresh,
strawberry-accented palate with lively, tingling acidity. A new benchmark for Taltarni sparkling. **rating:** 89

best drinking 2001–2002 **best vintages** NA **drink with** Shellfish • $19.50

Taltarni Shiraz

▼▼▼▼ 1999 Medium red-purple; the moderately intense bouquet is clean, but somewhat closed and not
showing much varietal character. The palate has a pleasant mix of red berry fruit, a hint of chocolate, and
far softer tannins and extract than the Taltarni wines of bygone years, and all the better for that. **rating:** 85

best drinking 2004–2009 **best vintages** '84, '88, '90, '91, '92, '96, '98 **drink with** Gippsland blue cheese • $28

Taltarni Merlot

▼▼▼▽ 1998 Light to medium red-purple; a clean, light leafy berry bouquet, then a pleasantly soft palate
ranging through savoury, leafy, berry flavours subtly sweetened by oak, and finishing with soft tannins.
rating: 84

best drinking 2003–2008 **best vintages** NA **drink with** Veal saltimbocca • $28

talunga   NR

Adelaide to Mannum Road (PO Box 134), Gumeracha, SA 5233 **region** Adelaide Hills
phone (08) 8389 1222 **fax** (08) 8389 1233 **open** Wed–Sun and public holidays 10.30–5
winemaker Vince Scaffidi **production** 7000 **est.** 1994
product range ($11.50–29.50 CD) Chardonnay, Yearling Blend, Pinot Noir, Shiraz, Sangiovese Merlot, Cabernet Sauvignon.
summary Talunga owners Vince and Tina Scaffidi have a one-third share of the 62-hectare Gumeracha Vineyards, and it is from these vineyards that the Talunga wines are sourced.

tamar ridge   ★★★★★

Auburn Road, Kayena, Tas 7270 **region** Northern Tasmania
phone (03) 6394 7000 **fax** (03) 6334 6050 **open** 7 days 10–5
winemaker Michael Fogarty **production** 30 000 **est.** 1994
product range ($15–24 CD) Riesling, Sauvignon Blanc, Unwooded Chardonnay, Chardonnay, Pinot Noir, Cabernet Sauvignon, RV (Sparkling); second label Devil's Corner Riesling, Pinot Noir.
summary Tamar Ridge is the most recent venture into wine production of grass-fed-beef magnate Joe Chromy. When he sold Heemskerk and Rochecombe to Pipers Brook in 1998, he retained a substantial vineyard in the Tamar Valley which presently has over 50 hectares in bearing and which is to be increased to 70 hectares over the next two to three years. The new winery, situated on the edge of a large dam (or lake, for that is what it looks like) is a striking piece of architecture, and a large restaurant is planned for the future. The quality of the early releases is impressive; led by consistently superb Rieslings. Exports to Canada, Japan and Singapore.

Tamar Ridge Riesling

TTTTT 2001 Pale green-yellow, the crisp, clean mineral/herb/apple bouquet is followed by a palate with the Tamar Ridge hallmark intensity of lime and apple flavour. Faultless balance and structure.   **rating:** 95

best drinking 2001–2010 **best vintages** '98, '99, '00, '01 **drink with** Blue fin tuna • $19.95

Tamar Ridge Pinot Noir

TTTTT 2000 Medium to full red-purple; seductive, spiced plum aromas and the clever use of oak highlight the bouquet; the palate has abundant flavour, yet also has elegance, length and balance. Gold medal Tasmanian Wines Show 2002.   **rating:** 94

best drinking 2002–2007 **best vintages** '00 **drink with** Venison pie • $22

tamburlaine   ★★★☆

McDonalds Road, Pokolbin, NSW 2320 **region** Lower Hunter Valley
phone (02) 4998 7570 **fax** (02) 4998 7763 **open** 7 days 9.30–5
winemaker Mark Davidson, Michael McManus **production** 60 000 **est.** 1966
product range ($11-24 ML) Quaffing Blue range of: Surprise Semillon, Sweetheart (Verdelho), Chardonnay, Blush (Rosé style), Scarlet (Shiraz), Velvet Cabernet Shiraz; Three Parishes Verdelho; Reserve range of Riesling, Semillon, Sauvignon Blanc, Verdelho, Chardonnay, Shiraz, Syrah, Merlot, Chambourcin, Cabernets, Cabernet Sauvignon.
summary A thriving business which, notwithstanding the fact that it has doubled its already substantial production in recent years, sells over 90 per cent of its wine through cellar door and by mailing list (with an active tasting club members' cellar programme offering wines which are held and matured at Tamburlaine). Unashamedly and deliberately focused on the tourist trade (and, of course, its wine club members).

tanglewood downs   NR

Bulldog Creek Road, Merricks North, Vic 3926 **region** Mornington Peninsula
phone (03) 5974 3325 **fax** (03) 5974 4170 **open** Sun–Mon 12–5
winemaker Ken Bilham, Wendy Bilham **production** 1200 **est.** 1984
product range ($25 CD) Riesling, Gewürztraminer, Chardonnay, Pinot Noir, Cabernet Sauvignon, Cabernet Franc Merlot.
summary One of the smaller and lower-profile wineries on the Mornington Peninsula, with Ken Bilham quietly doing his own thing on 2.5 hectares of estate plantings. Winery lunches and dinners are available by arrangement.

tannery lane vineyard NR
174 Tannery Lane, Mandurang, Vic 3551 **region** Bendigo
phone (03) 5439 3227 **open** By appointment
winemaker Lindsay Ross (Contract) **production** 300 **est.** 1990
product range ($15–23 CD) Sangiovese, Shiraz, Merlot, Cabernet Merlot.
summary In 1990 planting began of the present total of 2 hectares of shiraz, cabernet sauvignon, cabernet franc, sangiovese, merlot and nebbiolo. Their Sangiovese is the only such wine coming from the Bendigo region at the present time. The micro-production is sold through cellar door only and then only while stocks last, which typically is not for very long.

tantemaggie NR
Kemp Road, Pemberton, WA 6260 **region** Pemberton
phone (08) 9776 1164 **fax** (08) 9776 1810 **open** By appointment
winemaker Contract **production** 600 **est.** 1987
product range ($20–25 CD) Verdelho, Cabernet Sauvignon.
summary Tantemaggie was established by the Pottinger family with the help of a bequest from a deceased aunt named Maggie. It is part of a mixed farming operation, and by far the greatest part of the 20 hectares is under long-term contract to Houghton. The bulk of the plantings are cabernet sauvignon and verdelho, the former producing the light-bodied style favoured by the Pottingers.

tarrawarra estate ★★★★☆
Healesville Road, Yarra Glen, Vic 3775 **region** Yarra Valley
phone (03) 5962 3311 **fax** (03) 5962 3887 **open** 7 days 10.30–4.30
winemaker Clare Halloran, Damian North **production** 25 000 **est.** 1983
product range ($23–48 R) Chardonnay and Pinot Noir; also Kidron Chardonnay and Shiraz (kosher).
summary Slowly developing Chardonnay of great structure and complexity is the winery specialty; robust Pinot Noir also needs time and evolves impressively if given it. National retail distribution; exports to the UK, Switzerland, Belgium, Singapore, Hong Kong and the US.

Tarrawarra Estate Kidron Chardonnay
▼▼▼▽ **1999** Light green-yellow; the bouquet offers light fruit with pronounced spicy oak, and the palate is rather light in fruit terms, with peaky acidity. **rating:** 81
best drinking 2000–2003 **best vintages** NA **drink with** Kosher food • NA

tarrington vineyards ★★★★☆
Hamilton Highway, Tarrington, Vic 3301 **region** Henty
phone (03) 5572 4509 **fax** (03) 5572 4509 **open** Weekends and public holidays 11–5, appointments preferred
winemaker Tamara Irish **production** 300 **est.** 1993
product range ($25–35 CD) Chardonnay, Pinot Noir, Cuvée Emilie Pinot Noir.
summary The grape growing and winemaking practices of Burgundy permeate every aspect of Tarrington Vineyards. While its establishment began in 1993, there has been no hurry to bring the vineyard into production. Two varieties only have been planted: pinot noir and chardonnay, with a planting density varying between 3333 and 8170 vines per hectare. There are no less than nine clones in the 2 hectares of pinot noir, and 4 clones in the 1 hectare of chardonnay. The approach to making the Pinot Noir is common in Burgundy, while the unoaked Chardonnay is kept in tank on fine lees for nine months, the traditional method of making Chablis. Everything about the operation speaks of a labour of love, with a high standard of packaging and presentation of all background material. The exemplary wines are to be found on a thoroughly impressive collection of Victoria's top restaurant wine lists.

Tarrington Vineyards Pinot Noir
▼▼▼▼▼ **2000** Medium to full red-purple; complex, spicy/foresty carbonic maceration aromas on the bouquet are the fore-runners of a very powerful palate, with concentrated plummy fruit, long and intense. **rating:** 94
best drinking 2001–2006 **best vintages** '00 **drink with** Braised duck • $24.75

Tarrington Vineyards Cuvée Emilie Pinot Noir

▼▼▼▼▽ **1999** Medium red-purple; the bouquet is complex, with spicy/stalky/plummy aromas, but is less rich than the 2000. The palate, however, has pronounced varietal character in good style, with that hallmark length of top flight Pinot Noir. **rating:** 92

best drinking 2001–2004 **best vintages** '99 **drink with** • NA

tarwin ridge NR

Wintles Road, Leongatha South, Vic 3953 **region** Gippsland
phone (03) 5664 3211 **fax** (03) 5664 3211 **open** Weekends and holidays 10–5
winemaker Brian Anstee **production** 700 **est.** 1983
product range ($16–27 CD) Sauvignon Blanc, White Merlot, Pinot Noir, Pinot Noir Premium, Cabernet Merlot.
summary For the time being Brian Anstee is making his wines at Nicholson River under the gaze of fellow social worker Ken Eckersley; the wines come from two hectares of estate pinot and half a hectare each of cabernet and sauvignon blanc.

tatachilla ★★★★☆

151 Main Road, McLaren Vale, SA 5171 **region** McLaren Vale
phone (08) 8323 8656 **fax** (08) 8323 9096 **open** Mon–Sat 10–5, Sun and public holidays 11–5
winemaker Michael Fragos, Justin McNamee **production** 270 000 **est.** 1901
product range ($14.50–46 R) Adelaide Hills Sauvignon Blanc, Growers (Chenin Blanc Semillon Sauvignon Blanc), Adelaide Hills Chardonnay, McLaren Vale Chardonnay, Padthaway Chardonnay, Pinot Noir NV, Sparkling Malbec, Foundation Shiraz, McLaren Vale Shiraz, Adelaide Hills Merlot, McLaren Vale Merlot, Clarendon Merlot, Keystone (Grenache Shiraz), Partners (Cabernet Sauvignon Shiraz), McLaren Vale Cabernet Sauvignon, Padthaway Cabernet Sauvignon, Tawny Port.
summary Tatachilla was reborn in 1995 but has an at-times tumultuous history going back to 1901. For most of the time between 1901 and 1961 the winery was owned by Penfolds but was closed in that year before being reopened in 1965 as the Southern Vales Co-operative. In the late 1980s it was purchased and renamed The Vales but did not flourish, and in 1993 it was purchased by local grower Vic Zerella and former Kaiser Stuhl chief executive Keith Smith. After extensive renovations, the winery was officially reopened in 1995 and won a number of tourist awards and accolades. Became part of Banksia Wines in 2001, in turn acquired by Lion Nathan in 2002.

Tatachilla Adelaide Hills Sauvignon Blanc

▼▼▼▼ **2001** Light green-yellow; a clean and fresh bouquet with a mix of grass, herb and mineral is basically repeated on the direct and fresh palate. **rating:** 87

best drinking 2001–2002 **best vintages** '99 **drink with** Calamari • $18.95

Tatachilla McLaren Vale Chardonnay

▼▼▼▼ **2001** Medium yellow-green; tangy citrus and melon fruit plus a whisk of oak on the bouquet leads into a tangy, citrussy palate, with complex winemaking techniques peeping through. Subtle oak. **rating:** 86

best drinking 2002–2003 **best vintages** NA **drink with** Pasta • $16.50

Tatachilla Padthaway Chardonnay

▼▼▼▼ **2001** Light to medium yellow-green; a fragrant bouquet with melon and grapefruit aromas to the fore, a subliminal touch of oak coming from the small percentage barrel-fermented in new French oak. The palate is lively but light, with stone fruit/grapefruit flavours, finishing with balanced acidity. **rating:** 86

best drinking 2002–2003 **best vintages** NA **drink with** Richer fish dishes • $15.95

Tatachilla Sparkling Pinot Noir

▼▼▼▼ **NV** Full-on salmon-pink; unmistakable strawberry varietal character on the bouquet fades away somewhat on the delicate palate which lacks intensity and length, although the overall impact is pleasant enough. **rating:** 85

best drinking 2001–2002 **best vintages** NA **drink with** Aperitif • $19.50

Tatachilla Foundation Shiraz

▼▼▼▼▽ **1999** Full red-purple; rich, dark berry fruit with a touch of licorice on the bouquet follows through to the powerful, long and complex palate. The only question comes with the slightly assertive oak on the finish. **rating:** 90

best drinking 2004–2014 **best vintages** '95, '97, '98, '99 **drink with** Kangaroo fillet • $44

Tatachilla Adelaide Hills Merlot

▼▼▼▼▼ 1999 Medium red-purple; a complex bouquet with a mix of savoury berry and sweet spice aromatics, the palate nicely structured and composed, opening soft and gently sweet, then finishing with good tannin structure. Very unlucky to miss the Top 100 2001. **rating: 94**

best drinking 2003–2009 **best vintages** '99 **drink with** Osso buco • $24.50

Tatachilla McLaren Vale Merlot

▼▼▼▼ 2000 Medium red-purple; ripe, dusty fruit aromas and regional chocolate on the bouquet, then a palate with chocolate and plum fruit all add up to a thoroughly enjoyable red wine, but not a great deal of varietal character. **rating: 87**

best drinking 2004–2009 **best vintages** '96, '97, '98, '99 **drink with** Rare rump steak • $22.95

Tatachilla McLaren Vale Padthaway Cabernet Sauvignon

▼▼▼▼ 1999 Medium red-purple; both the bouquet and palate show perfectly ripened cabernet fruit in a distinctly elegant mould. The palate is not at all lush, but the oak handling is good, as is the tannins structure and balance. **rating: 87**

best drinking 2003–2009 **best vintages** NA **drink with** Roast veal • NA

Tatachilla Padthaway Cabernet Sauvignon

▼▼▼▼▽ 2000 Medium to full red-purple; pleasing dark berry/cassis/mulberry aromas and subtle oak lead into a palate that more than lives up to the bouquet, with masses of rich blackberry/cassis/mulberry fruit. Clever winemaking; good value. **rating: 92**

best drinking 2003–2008 **best vintages** '00 **drink with** Beef pie • $21.50

tatehams wines ★★★☆

Main North Road, Auburn, SA 5451 **region** Clare Valley
phone (08) 8849 2030 **fax** (08) 8849 2260 **open** Wed–Sun 10–5
winemaker Mike Jeandupeux **production** 500 **est.** 1998
product range ($11.50–17 CD) Riesling, Shiraz.
summary Mike and Isabel Jeandupeux left the French-speaking part of Switzerland in September 1997 to begin a new life in Australia. They now operate a restaurant and guest house at Auburn, in the southern end of the Clare Valley. The 1863 stone building, which originally operated as a general store and stables, has been completely refurbished, with several buildings offering a variety of upscale accommodation. The winemaking side of the business is effectively an add-on, with most of the wine sold through the restaurant and cellar door, but with a mailing list and limited distribution in Adelaide. The Riesling is particularly attractive.

Tatehams Riesling

▼▼▼▼ 2001 Light green-yellow; a fresh, bright, crisp mineral and apple skin bouquet leads into a classically pure and focussed palate; quite austere, but has length and will develop. **rating: 88**

best drinking 2004–2010 **best vintages** NA **drink with** Vegetable terrine • $15

tawonga vineyard NR

2 Drummond Street, Tawonga, Vic 3697 **region** Alpine Valleys
phone (03) 5754 4945 **open** By appointment
winemaker John Adams **production** 300 **est.** 1994
product range ($12.50–13.75 CD) Verdelho, Shiraz, Merlot.
summary Diz and John Adams made their first wine in 1995, but it was not until 1998 that they finally received their producer's license entitling them to sell the wine they had made. With a planned maximum production of less than 1000 cases, Tawonga has been able to take advantage of the small business tax exemption. In the meantime their handcrafted wines (virtually all of which have won show medals) remain at magically low prices.

taylors ★★★★☆

Taylors Road, Auburn, SA 5451 **region** Clare Valley
phone (08) 8849 2008 **fax** (08) 8849 2240 **open** Mon–Fri 9–5, Sat and public holidays 10–5, Sun 10–4
winemaker Adam Eggins, Craig Grafton **production** 250 000 **est.** 1972
product range ($8.50–50 R) At the top comes the super-premium St Andrews releases of Riesling, Chardonnay, Shiraz and Cabernet Sauvignon, then the premium range consists of Clare Valley Riesling,

Gewürztraminer, Semillon, White Burgundy, Promised Land Unwooded Chardonnay, Chardonnay, Pinot Noir, Shiraz, Promised Land Shiraz Cabernet, Merlot and Cabernet Sauvignon; the lower-priced Clare Valley range consists of Dry White, Sweet White and Classic Dry Red; Wakefield Tawny Port.

summary Taylors continues to flourish and expand, with yet further extensions to its vineyards, now totalling over 500 hectares, by far the largest holding in Clare Valley. There have also been substantial changes on the winemaking front, both in terms of the winemaking team and in terms of the wine style and quality, particularly through the outstanding St Andrews range. Widespread national distribution, with exports to the UK, Ireland, New Zealand and Malaysia.

Taylors Clare Riesling

▼▼▼▼▼ **2001** Excellent green-yellow; clean lime blossom and apple aromas are followed by a lively, fresh lime juicy palate with very good acidity. Subliminal spritz and SO$_2$ will simply serve to sustain the wine over a long period of development. Gold medal 2001 Clare Valley Regional Wine Show. **rating:** 94

best drinking 2001–2010 **best vintages** '82, '87, '92, '93, '94, '96, '99, '01 **drink with** Avocado • $16

Taylors St Andrews Riesling

▼▼▼▼▼ **1996** Brilliant, glowing light to medium green-yellow; the bouquet is still very youthful, with no toast nor kerosene characters developing, still predominantly lime, pear and apple. A classic, long, powerful and focussed palate leaves no doubt the wine is just entering the plateau of maturity. **rating:** 95

best drinking 2002–2011 **best vintages** '96 **drink with** Asparagus risotto • $30

Taylors Gewürztraminer

▼▼▼▼ **2001** Medium yellow-green; overall shows surprisingly clear varietal character, with a spicy lychee bouquet joined by some lime flavours on the palate; good length and acidity. **rating:** 87

best drinking 2001–2003 **best vintages** NA **drink with** Chinese • $14

Taylors Semillon

▼▼▼▼ **2000** Good green-yellow colour; both the bouquet and palate have abundant sweet, citrus-tinged aroma and flavour, and the oak is subtle throughout. **rating:** 89

best drinking 2001–2005 **best vintages** NA **drink with** Rich fish dishes • $15

Taylors Shiraz

▼▼▼▼▽ **2001** Vivid purple-red; the bouquet is flooded with clean, fresh blackberry and raspberry fruit with oak somewhere in the background. The palate has plenty of depth, texture and weight, with delicious raspberry and plum fruit flavours; oak barrel-matured; exceptional value. **rating:** 90

▼▼▼▼ **2000** Youthful purple-red; the bouquet is a touch hard and oaky, but the palate redeems the wine, with plenty of dark cherry/plum fruit and good tannins. **rating:** 87

best drinking 2003–2010 **best vintages** '86, '89, '90, '92, '95, '01 **drink with** Carpaccio of beef • $15

Taylors St Andrews Shiraz

▼▼▼▼▽ **1999** Medium red-purple; dark berry, spice and sweet oak aromas lead into a palate with excellent richness and concentration, basically at the savoury end of the spectrum. I am far from convinced that this represents the same value as the varietal Shiraz, but there is no denying it is a good wine. **rating:** 91

▼▼▼▼▼ **1998** Deep red-purple; an outstanding wine with an abundance of rich, ripe, dark cherry and plum fruit, with great depth and structure to an outstanding palate. Certainly, oak plays a role, but it is both balanced and integrated. Placed first in the 2001 Great Australian Shiraz Challenge. **rating:** 96

best drinking 2004–2011 **best vintages** '98, '99 **drink with** Rump steak • $50

Taylors Merlot

▼▼▼▽ **2001** Medium red-purple; there is plenty of red fruit, but no obvious varietal character to the bouquet; the palate has good texture and weight, but once again is varietally anonymous, and doesn't have the great texture the 1999 vintage had. **rating:** 84

▼▼▼▼ **2000** Deeply coloured; the bouquet is as powerful and strong as the colour suggests, with no obvious varietal character. The palate follows down the same track, with impressive depth and power, thus almost inevitably lacking the finesse which should be part and parcel of Merlot. **rating:** 87

best drinking 2003–2008 **best vintages** '99 **drink with** Veal saltimbocca • $16

Taylors Cabernet Sauvignon

▼▼▼▼▽ **2000** Medium purple-red; fresh, redcurrant fruit with a touch of earth on the bouquet is followed by an unexpectedly ripe berry and chocolate-flavoured palate with fine, soft tannins; sexy stuff, and good value. **rating:** 91

best drinking 2003–2008 **best vintages** '86, '89, '90, '92, '94, '99, '00 **drink with** Mixed grill • $16

Taylors St Andrews Cabernet Sauvignon

TTTTY **1999** Medium red-purple; the bouquet has well-balanced savoury berry fruit and oak, the medium to full-bodied palate showing savoury edges to blackcurrant fruit, and tannins which run through the length without dominating that fruit. Yet another good wine. **rating:** 90

TTTTY **1997** Medium red, showing obvious bottle development. The bouquet has savoury yet gently sweet fruit, with good oak balance and integration; the fine, supple palate offers nicely ripened berry and chocolate fruit, gentle oak and fine tannins. **rating:** 90

best drinking 2004–2009 **best vintages** '97, '99 **drink with** Porterhouse steak and mushrooms • $50

temple bruer ★★★☆

Milang Road, Strathalbyn, SA 5255 **region** Langhorne Creek
phone (08) 8537 0203 **fax** (08) 8537 0131 **open** Mon–Fri 9.30–4.30
winemaker Nick Bruer **production** 14 000 **est.** 1980
product range ($12.80–23.70 R) Riesling, Verdelho, Viognier, Chenin Blanc, Botrytis Riesling, Cornucopia Grenache, Cabernet Merlot, Reserve Merlot, Shiraz Malbec, Sparkling Cabernet Merlot.
summary Always known for its eclectic range of wines, Temple Bruer (which also carries on a substantial business as a vine propagation nursery) has seen a sharp lift in wine quality. Clean, modern redesigned labels add to the appeal of a stimulatingly different range of red wines. Part of the production from the 24 hectares of estate vineyards is sold to others, the remainder being made under the Temple Bruer label. The vineyard is now certified organic.

templer's mill ★★★☆

The University of Sydney, Leeds Parade, Orange, NSW 2800 **region** Orange
phone (02) 6360 5509 **fax** (02) 6360 5698 **open** Mon–Fri 9–4.30 or by appointment
winemaker Jon Reynolds **production** 1500 **est.** 1997
product range ($12.50–16 CD) Sauvignon Blanc, Chardonnay, Shiraz, Cabernet Sauvignon.
summary Templer's Mill is the outcome of a joint venture between winemaker Jon Reynolds, entrepreneur-cum-vigneron Gary Blom (of Barrington Estate in the Upper Hunter Valley) and the Orange campus of the University of Sydney. There were plans to erect a substantial winery, but these have now been abandoned for a number of reasons. For the time being, at least, the label continues, utilising just under 20 hectares of vines grown on the University's property.

Templer's Mill Sauvignon Blanc

TTTT **2000** Light to medium yellow-green; aromatic ripe fruits with apple and passionfruit aromas, then similarly ripe flavours on the mid-palate, lightening off slightly on the clean, crisp finish. **rating:** 87

best drinking 2002–2003 **best vintages** NA **drink with** Sushi • $12.50

tempus two wines ★★★☆

Broke Road, Pokolbin, NSW 2331 **region** Lower Hunter Valley
phone (02) 9818 7222 **fax** (02) 9818 7333 **open** 7 days 9–5
winemaker Peter Hall **production** 36 000 **est.** 1997
product range ($14–28 CD) Varietal range of Eden Valley Riesling, Semillon Sauvignon Blanc, Verdelho, Cowra Chardonnay, Hunter Shiraz, Merlot, Cabernet Shiraz, Cabernet Merlot; Pewter range of Broke Chardonnay, Sparkling Chardonnay, Botrytis Semillon, Vine Vale Shiraz, Hunter Merlot, Hollydene Cabernet Sauvignon, Reserve Hollydene Cabernet Sauvignon.
summary Tempus Two is the new name for Hermitage Road Wines, a piece of doggerel akin to that of Rouge Homme, except that it is not Franglais, but a mix of Latin (Tempus means time) and English. I should not be too critical, however; the change was forced on the winery by the EU Wine Agreement and the prohibition of the use of the word 'hermitage' on Australian wine labels. Nor should the fracas over the labels disguise the fact that some very attractive wines have appeared so far, and will do so in the future, no doubt. Exports to New Zealand and the Philippines.

Tempus Two Somerset Vineyard Verdelho

TTTT **2001** Light to medium green-yellow; the bouquet has the same hints of citrus and spice evident in prior vintages, coupled with a touch of lanolin. The palate, likewise, has some citrus and spice flavours running through to the nicely tuned finish. **rating:** 85

best drinking 2002–2003 **best vintages** NA **drink with** Takeaway • $14

Tempus Two Botrytis Semillon 375 ml

▼▼▼▼ 1999 Glowing yellow-green; the complexity of the fruit on the bouquet shows obvious botrytis; the palate is rather less complex, with peachy fruit, a hint of brandy snap and a soft, easy going finish. **rating:** 85

best drinking 2002–2003 **best vintages** NA **drink with** Home-made ice-cream • $18

Tempus Two Vine Vale Shiraz

▼▼▼▽ 1999 Medium red-purple; the clean bouquet is of light to medium intensity, with slightly simple fruit, but the wine picks up the pace somewhat on the palate with quite ripe, lush fruit in an early drinking style. **rating:** 84

best drinking 2002–2003 **best vintages** NA **drink with** Pizza • $28

Tempus Two Pewter Hunter Merlot

▼▼▼▽ 2000 Medium red-purple; a light, fresh and quite fragrant leafy/berry bouquet, then a palate with similar flavours, but slightly angular and unformed. Short term cellaring should see the wine settle down if one can resist hurling the bowling bottle-shape bottle down the nearest alley. **rating:** 84

best drinking 2002–2005 **best vintages** NA **drink with** Soft cheese • $28

Tempus Two Reserve Hollydene Cabernet Sauvignon

▼▼▼▼▼ 1998 Good colour; a lifted, aromatic bouquet is fruit-driven, as is the palate, with blackberry/blackcurrant/chocolate flavours then savoury tannins on the finish. Unanimous gold medal 2001 Hunter Valley Wine Show. **rating:** 94

best drinking 2003–2008 **best vintages** '98 **drink with** Braised beef in olives • $28

🌿 ten minutes by tractor wine co ★★★★☆

111 Roberts Road, Main Ridge, Vic 3928 **region** Mornington Peninsula
phone (03) 5989 6084 **fax** (03) 5989 6599 **open** Weekends 11–5 Nov-Easter, first weekend of month or by appointment
winemaker Richard McIntyre (Pinot Noir, Chardonnay, Pinot Gris), Alex White (Sauvignon Blanc)
production 2500 **est.** 1999
product range ($18.50–35 CD) Sauvignon Blanc, Pinot Gris, Chardonnay, Botrytised Sauvignon Blanc, Pinot Noir Chardonnay, Pinot Noir; Judd Vineyard Chardonnay, Sauvignon Blanc, Pinot Noir; McCutcheon Vineyard Chardonnay, Pinot Noir; Wallis Vineyard Pinot Gris, Chardonnay, Pinot Noir.
summary This has to be one of the cleverest pieces of marketing I have ever come across, the unforgettable name reinforced by superb graphics. But it also has a particularly clever business plan, and some excellent wines to support the business. The company belongs to the Judd, McCutcheon and Wallis families, each of which established a 6-hectare vineyard a decade ago, but decided to merge the operations in 1999, realising that each of the three properties are only ten minutes by tractor distant from each other. While most of the grapes were and are sold to other winemakers, in 2000 they began making limited quantities of wines under the 10X label (drawing on all three properties) and individual vineyard selection wines from each of the three properties. A number of Melbourne restaurants list the wines, and exports to Hong Kong, San Francisco, New York and London are being developed.

Ten Minutes by Tractor Sauvignon Blanc

▼▼▼▼ 2001 Light straw-green; a spotlessly clean, crisp bouquet falls predominantly in the grass/herb/mineral spectrum, but does have some riper nuances; the palate is correspondingly clean, firm and bright, lemony acidity providing an attractive spine. Made by Alex White. **rating:** 89

best drinking 2002–2003 **best vintages** NA **drink with** Fresh seafood • $18.50

Ten Minutes by Tractor Chardonnay

▼▼▼▼▽ 2000 Medium to full yellow-green, quite developed; complex fig, cashew and ripe peach aromas are followed by a full-bodied palate, again with fig, white peach and melon fruit; good balance and length. Made by Richard McIntyre. **rating:** 92

best drinking 2002–2004 **best vintages** NA **drink with** Lambs brains in black butter • $28

Ten Minutes by Tractor Judd Vineyard Chardonnay

▼▼▼▼▽ 2000 Medium to full yellow; the bouquet has a mix of cashew, yellow peach, fig and subtle oak, the palate the best balanced of the three individual wines, with sweet peachy fruit, good acidity and good length. **rating:** 91

best drinking 2002–2005 **best vintages** '00 **drink with** Calamari • $26

Ten Minutes by Tractor McCutcheon Vineyard Chardonnay

▼▼▼▼ 2000 Fractionally deeper colour, headed more to yellow-straw; a quite powerful bouquet with a mix of nutty fig and more minerally aromas, then a palate which belies the colour, as it has less full-frontal fruit development, yet retains fruit sweetness. **rating:** 88

best drinking 2002–2004 **best vintages** NA **drink with** Crumbed brains • $26

Ten Minutes by Tractor Wallis Vineyard Chardonnay

▼▼▼▼ 2000 Medium to full yellow; the bouquet is rich and smooth, with hints of nut, smoke and fig; a big, solidly ripe palate with nutty melon flavours tightened up by acidity on the finish. **rating:** 88

best drinking 2002–2004 **best vintages** NA **drink with** Creamy pasta • $26

Ten Minutes by Tractor Pinot Noir

▼▼▼▼▼ 2000 Light red-purple; light, spicy/sappy/plummy aromas became increasingly fragrant and complex as the wine sat in the glass; the palate, while light bodied, has great texture and length, with a mix of sappy/savoury characters alongside strawberry, cherry and plum. Fully deserved its gold medal at the 2001 Victorian Wines Show; also demonstrates the danger of judging a Pinot Noir by its colour. **rating:** 94

best drinking 2002–2006 **best vintages** NA **drink with** Grilled Atlantic salmon • $32.50

Ten Minutes by Tractor Judd Vineyard Pinot Noir

▼▼▼▼▼ 2000 Medium red-purple; sweet, complex strawberry and spice aromas lead into a stylish, light to medium-bodied palate, with surprising intensity and length, a touch of dark cherry adding to the complexity of the fruit flavours. **rating:** 94

best drinking 2002–2005 **best vintages** '00 **drink with** Wild mushroom risotto • $29

Ten Minutes by Tractor McCutcheon Vineyard Pinot Noir

▼▼▼▼▽ 2000 Light to medium red-purple; the bouquet has plum, cherry and some savoury notes, the palate with clearly expressed plum and cherry fruit; less complex than the Judd Vineyard but with good structure. Subtle oak. **rating:** 92

best drinking 2002–2005 **best vintages** '00 **drink with** Breast of duck • $29

Ten Minutes by Tractor Wallis Vineyard Pinot Noir

▼▼▼▼▽ 2000 Light to medium purple-red, bright and clear; the bouquet is clean, the most concentrated of the three individual vineyard pinot noirs, not particularly aromatic. The palate is firm and long, sustained by good tannins; the least immediately attractive of the three wines, but may well develop better than the others. Gold medal Concours du Vin Victoria 2000. **rating:** 91

best drinking 2003–2007 **best vintages** '00 **drink with** Braised pigeon • $35

terrace vale ★★★★

Deasey's Lane, Pokolbin, NSW 2321 **region** Lower Hunter Valley
phone (02) 4998 7517 **fax** (02) 4998 7814 **open** 7 days 10–4
winemaker Alain Leprince **production** 8000 **est.** 1971
product range ($14.50–27.50 CD) Gewürztraminer, Semillon, Chardonnay, Unwooded Chardonnay, Fine Hunter White, Shiraz, Pinot Shiraz, Fine Hunter Red, Cabernet Merlot, Chardonnay Pinot Noir Brut, Elizabeth Sauvignon Blanc (dessert), Vintage Port; Family Reserve wines include Campbell's Orchard Semillon, Lachlan's Block Chardonnay and Alexanders Old Vine Shiraz.
summary In April 2001, the Batchelor family acquired Terrace Vale, but little else has changed. Alain Leprince remains as winemaker, and the wines still come from the 30-year-old estate plantings.

Terrace Vale Semillon

▼▼▼▼ 2001 Medium to full yellow-green; a quite full and complex bouquet is matched by a generously flavoured palate, with an extra degree of complexity. **rating:** 85

best drinking 2002–2007 **best vintages** '98 **drink with** Shellfish • $17.50

Terrace Vale Campbell's Orchard Semillon

▼▼▼▼ 1999 Medium yellow-green; an elegant and aromatic wine, with fresh lime, lemon and mineral aromas and flavours, developing nicely. **rating:** 88

best drinking 2002–2008 **best vintages** NA **drink with** Seafood salad • $25

Terrace Vale Lachlans Chardonnay

ΤΤΤΤ 2000 Light to medium green-yellow; an elegant and well-balanced wine with melon and cashew fruit supported by just the right amount of oak. Some sweetness, but not to the point of distraction. Unanimous silver medal 2001 Hunter Valley Wine Show. **rating:** 89

best drinking 2001–2004 **best vintages** NA **drink with** Veal goulash • $27.50

Terrace Vale Alexanders Old Vine Shiraz

ΤΤΤΤΥ 2000 Medium to full red-purple; clean, cherry and plum fruit on the bouquet leads into a harmonious and quite soft palate, with abundant fruit, pleasing oak and gentle tannins. **rating:** 91

best drinking 2004–2010 **best vintages** '00 **drink with** Eye fillet • $27.50

🍇 terra nova estate ★★★☆

60 Banna Avenue, Griffith, NSW 2680 **region** Riverina
phone (02) 6962 1822 **fax** (02) 6962 6392 **open** Mon–Fri 9–5
winemaker John Quarisa, Darren Owers **production** 100 000 **est.** 1999
product range ($14.95–29.95 R) Cookoothama range of Semillon Chardonnay, Chardonnay, Botrytis Semillon, Shiraz, Pigeage Merlot, Cabernet Merlot; Saviours Rock Cabernet Sauvignon.
summary Terra Nova has arrived on the scene like a whirlwind. It is an off-shoot of the Nugan group, a family company established over 60 years ago in Griffith as a broad-based agricultural business. It is headed by Michelle Nugan, inter alia the recipient of an Export Hero Award 2000. Eight years ago the company began developing vineyards, and is now a veritable giant, with 310 hectares at Darlington Point, 52 hectares at Hanwood and 120 hectares at Hillston (all in NSW), 100 hectares in the King Valley, Vic, and 10 hectares in McLaren Vale. In addition, it has contracts in place to buy 1000 tonnes of grapes per year from Coonawarra. It sells part of the production as grapes, part as bulk wine and part under the Cookoothama label (Saviours Rock being the Coonawarra/Limestone Coast label). Ex McWilliam's winemaker John Quarisa is in charge of winemaking and the first wines from the estate have received both show success and highly favourable ratings in wine magazines. Exports to New Zealand.

Terra Nova Estate Cookoothama Semillon Chardonnay

ΤΤΤΥ 2000 Light to medium yellow-green; a light and crisp bouquet with touches of herb and citrus is repeated on the palate, which also has a touch of spice, though no oak is apparent. Thickens slightly on the finish. **rating:** 84

best drinking 2001–2002 **best vintages** NA **drink with** Takeaway • $16.95

Terra Nova Estate Cookoothama Botrytis Semillon

ΤΤΤΤ 1999 Deep gold; powerful, dried mandarin peel and spice come through on the complex bouquet; rich honey, mandarin and spiced peel flavours on the palate are balanced by good acidity on the finish. **rating:** 87

best drinking 2001–2004 **best vintages** NA **drink with** Rich desserts • $22.95

Terra Nova Estate Saviour's Rock Cabernet Sauvignon

ΤΤΤΤ 1999 Medium red-purple; a mix of savoury/earthy/leafy aromas also provide the opening stanza for the palate, joined by some sweet berry fruit, appropriate tannins, and a touch of cedary oak. **rating:** 85

best drinking 2002–2007 **best vintages** NA **drink with** Lamb shashlik • $20.95

t'gallant ★★★★

1385 Mornington–Flinders Road, Main Ridge, Vic 3928 **region** Mornington Peninsula
phone (03) 5989 6565 **fax** (03) 5989 6577 **open** 7 days 10–5
winemaker Kathleen Quealy, Kevin McCarthy **production** 14 000 **est.** 1990
product range ($15–49 R) An ever changing list of names (and avant-garde label designs) but with Unwooded Chardonnay and Pinot Gris at the centre. Labels include McCabe Viognier, The T'Gallant Chardonnay, Pinot Grigio, Tribute Pinot Gris, Imogen Pinot Gris, Celia's White Pinot, Cape Schanck Pinot Grigio Chardonnay, Io Botrytis Pinot Gris, Triumph Late Harvest Pinot Gris, Holystone, Our Romeo, Pinot Noir Cape Schanck Pinot Noir and a range of wines under the Lyncroft label.
summary Husband and wife consultant-winemakers Kathleen Quealy and Kevin McCarthy are starting to carve out an important niche market for the T'Gallant label, noted for its innovative label designs and names. The acquisition of a 15-hectare property, and the planting of 10 hectares of pinot gris gives the business a firm geographic base, as well as providing increased resources for its signature wine. The yearly parade of new (usually beautiful and striking, it is true) labels designed by Ken Cato do not make my life at all easy. No sooner is the database built up than it is discarded for next year's rash of labels. La Baracca Trattoria is open seven days for lunch and for specially booked evening events. Exports to the UK and US.

T'Gallant Cape Schanck Pinot Grigio Chardonnay

▼▼▼▽ **2001** Medium straw colour; some spice on the bouquet is followed by a palate with a mix of chalky grigio feel and flavour, and sweeter melon from the chardonnay; designed by a committee. **rating:** 84

best drinking 2001–2002 **best vintages** '98 **drink with** Virtually anything • $15

T'Gallant Imogen Pinot Gris

▼▼▼▼ **2001** Light to medium green-yellow; a crisp bouquet with spice and apple aromas comes through with similar characters on the palate, which has fair flavour and length, although the finish is not entirely convincing. **rating:** 86

best drinking 2001–2002 **best vintages** NA **drink with** Gravlax • $19.80

T'Gallant Tribute Pinot Gris

▼▼▼▼▽ **2001** Light to medium yellow-green; a powerful and complex wine on both bouquet and palate, reflecting its 14.3° alcohol; demands rich food, with its mix of creamy and unctuous flavour and texture. A tribute to Jean Meyer of Josmeyer, which Kathleen Quealy thinks is the best Tribute to date. **rating:** 90

best drinking 2002–2007 **best vintages** '94, '95, '97 **drink with** Gravlax • $35

T'Gallant Pinot Noir

▼▼▼▼ **2001** Bright, light to medium purple-red. The bouquet offers clean, fresh cherry/cherry pip fruit, the palate following down the same flavour track, though quite firm, and needing time to soften, open up and fully express itself. **rating:** 87

best drinking 2003–2006 **best vintages** '00 **drink with** Breast of duck • $29

T'Gallant Cape Schanck Pinot Noir

▼▼▼▽ **2001** Light to medium red-purple, rose-plus, as it were; strawberry and cherry aromatics lead into a crisp, fruit-driven palate which has quite certainly seen no oak. **rating:** 84

best drinking 2001–2002 **best vintages** NA **drink with** Japanese • $17.80

thalgara estate NR

De Beyers Road, Pokolbin, NSW 2321 **region** Lower Hunter Valley
phone (02) 4998 7717 **fax** (02) 4998 7774 **open** 7 days 10–5
winemaker Steve Lamb **production** 3000 **est.** 1985
product range ($15–30 CD) Chardonnay, Show Reserve Chardonnay, Semillon Chardonnay, Shiraz, Show Reserve Shiraz, Shiraz Cabernet.
summary A low-profile winery which had its moment of glory at the 1997 Hunter Valley Wine Show when it won the Doug Seabrook Memorial Trophy for Best Dry Red of Show with its 1995 Show Reserve Shiraz.

the blok estate NR

Riddoch Highway, Coonawarra, SA 5263 **region** Coonawarra
phone (08) 8737 2734 **fax** (08) 8737 2994 **open** 7 days 10–4
winemaker Contract **production** 1200 **est.** 1999
product range ($16–28 CD) Riesling, Chardonnay, Pinot Chardonnay, Shiraz, Cabernet Sauvignon.
summary Di and John Blok have owned a tiny vineyard planted to cabernet sauvignon for the past five years. They have now decided to take the production from this and from contract-grown grapes elsewhere in Coonawarra for release under their own label. The cellar door is situated in an old stone home which has recently been renovated and surrounded by newly landscaped gardens.

the falls vineyard NR

Longwood-Gobur Road, Longwood East, Vic 3665 **region** Central Victorian High Country
phone (03) 5798 5291 **fax** (03) 5798 5437 **open** 9–5 (phone beforehand)
winemaker Andrew Cameron **production** 1000 **est.** 1969
product range ($10–16 CD) Longwood Shiraz, The Falls Shiraz, Longwood Reserve Shiraz.
summary The Falls Vineyard was planted by Andrew and Elly Cameron way back in 1969, as a minor diversification for their pastoral company. Two hectares of shiraz, originally established on a wide T-trellis, but now converted to vertical spur positioning, provides both the Longwood Shiraz and the Longwood Reserve Shiraz. The wines (showing pronounced cool climate characteristics) are made on-site, but are bottled at Mitchelton. With only 1000 cases per year, the wines are basically sold by word of mouth, and the cellar door is open only if you phone beforehand or take advantage of the bed and breakfast accommodation offered by the Camerons.

the fleurieu ★★★★

Main Road, McLaren Vale, SA 5171 **region** McLaren Vale
phone (08) 8323 8999 **fax** (08) 8323 9332 **open** 7 days 9–5
winemaker Mike Farmilo **production** 3500 **est.** 1994
product range ($18–35 R) Shiraz, released under the Fleurieu and Stump Hill labels.
summary A specialist Shiraz producer, with 6.5 hectares of estate vineyards and contract winemaking by the former long-serving Seaview/Edwards & Chaffey winemaker Mike Farmilo. Exports to the UK, US, Singapore, Hong Kong, Japan, Philippines and Canada.

the gap ★★★

Pomonal Road, Halls Gap, Vic 3381 **region** Grampians
phone (03) 5356 4252 **fax** (03) 5356 4645 **open** Wed–Sun 10–5, 7 days during school and public holidays, closed Christmas Day and Good Friday
winemaker Trevor Mast, Andrew McLoughney **production** 1500 **est.** 1969
product range ($12–26 CD) Chardonnay, Reserve Chardonnay, Late Harvest Riesling, Rosé, Shiraz, Shiraz Grenache, Shiraz Cabernet Sauvignon, Cabernet Sauvignon, Cassel Port; Four Sisters Sauvignon Blanc Semillon and Shiraz; Billi Billi Creek Shiraz Cabernet and Shiraz Grenache Cabernet.
summary The Gap is the reincarnation of Boroka, a spectacularly situated vineyard 5 kilometres east of Halls Gap, with the slopes of the Mount William Range forming a backdrop. The vineyard was planted in 1969 but following its acquisition by Mount Langi Ghiran has been rehabilitated (including transplanted riesling vines), and extensive renovations have been made to the cellar-door sales area which offers estate-grown The Gap wines and a selection of Mount Langi Ghiran and Four Sisters wines.

The Gap Shiraz
TTTY 1999 Slightly dull red-purple; the highly fragrant, spicy and somewhat jammy bouquet is followed by a light-bodied palate with flavours (which reflect the bouquet) in a somewhat unconventional style. **rating:** 83
best drinking 2002–2005 **best vintages** NA **drink with** Designer sausages • $26

The Gap Billi Billi Creek Shiraz Grenache Cabernet
TTTY 1999 Light to medium red-purple; dusty oak and suffuse fruit on the bouquet take a little more direction on the palate with some sweeter fruit notes. Pleasant commercial red which is, however, fully priced. **rating:** 83
best drinking 2001–2002 **best vintages** NA **drink with** Bistro food • $18

The Gap Shiraz Cabernet
TTTY 2000 Medium purple-red; a very youthful, fresh but slightly unformed bouquet with red berry fruit is followed by a light to medium-bodied palate, with simple red berry fruit flavours for every day quaffing. **rating:** 83
best drinking 2002–2003 **best vintages** NA **drink with** Mixed grill • $26

The Gap Cabernet Sauvignon
TTTY 1999 Medium to full red-purple; the berry fruit of the bouquet has minty, spicy, leafy aromas, the palate with more structure, and taking the flavour more to red berry. **rating:** 84
best drinking 2003–2007 **best vintages** NA **drink with** Veal chop • $26

🐚 the garden vineyard NR

174 Graydens Road, Moorooduc, Vic 3933 **region** Mornington Peninsula
phone (03) 5970 0006 **fax** (03) 5978 0049 **open** First weekend of the month 11–5, or by appointment
winemaker Rick McIntyre (Contract) **production** 800 **est.** 1995
product range ($20–30 CD) Pinot Gris, Pinot Noir.
summary This captures the delights of the Mornington Peninsula in so many ways. As the name suggests, it is as much a garden as it is a vineyard; Di and Doug Johnson began the establishment of a walled garden seven years ago, at much the same time as they decided to increase the existing half a hectare of pinot noir (planted in 1989) with an additional hectare of pinot noir and half a hectare of pinot gris. The entrance fee to the garden is $8, but there is no charge for wine tasting. Most visitors end up enjoying both.

the green vineyards and carlei estate ★★★★

1 Albert Road, Upper Beaconsfield, Vic 3808 **region** Yarra Valley
phone (03) 5944 4599 **fax** (03) 5944 4599 **open** Weekends by appointment
winemaker Sergio Carlei **production** 2000 **est.** 1994
product range ($12–25 CD) Yarra Valley Riesling, Mornington Sauvignon Blanc, Yarra Valley Chardonnay, Sunbury Pinot Noir, Heathcote Shiraz, Yarra Valley Cabernets.
summary The Green Vineyards and Carlei Estate has come a long way in a little time, with Sergio Carlei graduating from home winemaking in a suburban garage to his own (real) winery in Upper Beaconsfield, which happens to fall just within the boundaries of the Yarra Valley. As the product range attests, many of the wines come from grapes grown by others, but Carlei does have 2.25 hectares of pinot noir and his preferred source is the Yarra Valley. He has already produced a number of remarkably stylish wines, with more in the pipeline.

the gurdies NR

St Helier Road, The Gurdies, Vic 3984 **region** Gippsland
phone (03) 5997 6208 **fax** (03) 5997 6511 **open** 7 days 10–5 or by appointment
winemaker Peter Kozik **production** 1500 **est.** 1991
product range ($18–25 CD) Riesling, Gurdies Hill White (Chardonnay), Pinot Noir, Reserve Pinot Noir, Shiraz, Merlot, Cabernet Merlot, Gurdies Hill Red (Cabernet Sauvignon Shiraz), Cabernet Sauvignon.
summary The only winery in the southwest Gippsland region, established on the slopes of The Gurdies hills overlooking Westernport Bay and French Island. Plantings of the 3.5-hectare vineyard commenced in 1981, but no fruit was harvested until 1991 owing to bird attack. A winery has been partially completed, and it is intended to increase the vineyards to 25 hectares and ultimately build a restaurant on site.

the mews NR

84 Gibson Street, Kings Meadows, Tas 7249 **region** Northern Tasmania
phone (03) 6344 2780 **fax** (03) 6343 2076 **open** Not
winemaker Graham Wiltshire **production** 300 **est.** 1984
product range Chardonnay.
summary Robin and Anne Holyman have established 0.4 hectares of pinot noir and 9.2 hectares of chardonnay at Kings Meadows, only 4 kilometres from the centre of Launceston. Industry veteran Graham Wiltshire acts as winemaker, and the wines are sold by direct contact with the Holymans.

the minya winery NR

Minya Lane, Connewarre, Vic 3227 **region** Geelong
phone (03) 5264 1397 **fax** (03) 5264 1097 **open** Public holidays or by appointment
winemaker Susan Dans **production** 330 **est.** 1974
product range ($15.50–18 CD) Gewürztraminer, Chardonnay, Shiraz, Grenache, Cabernet Sauvignon Merlot.
summary Geoff Dans first planted vines in 1974 on his family's dairy farm, followed by further plantings in 1982 and 1988. I have not tasted any of the wines, but the concerts staged in summer sound appealing.

the natural wine company ★★★

217 Copley Road, Upper Swan, WA 6069 **region** Swan District
phone (08) 9296 1436 **fax** (08) 9296 1436 **open** Wed–Sun and public holidays 10–5
winemaker Colin Evans **production** 1500 **est.** 1998
product range ($15 CD) Semillon, Chenin Semillon, Chenin Blanc, Verdelho, Unwooded Chardonnay, Chardonnay, Pinot Noir, Shiraz, Cabernet Sauvignon.
summary Owners Colin and Sandra Evans say the name of the business is intended to emphasise that no herbicides or systemic pesticides are used in the vineyard, which is situated on the western slopes of the Darling Range. Weed control is achieved through mulching, and Sandra does the vineyard work and helps with the night shift during vintage. She was also responsible for the koala emerging from the barrel on the unusual label. The vineyard is within a short walk of Bells Rapids and close to the Walunga National Park.

The Natural Wine Company Chenin Blanc

▼▼▼▼ 2001 Light green-yellow; a fresh, tangy bouquet offers a mix of fruit salad and citrus; there is considerable richness and palate-weight to follow. **rating:** 85

best drinking 2001–2004 **best vintages** NA **drink with** Cold meat salad • $15

The Natural Wine Company Verdelho

▼▼▼▽ **2001** Light green-yellow; the bouquet is firm, closed and not particularly aromatic, although touches of mineral and citrus come peeping through. The palate is far more expressive, with distinctive fruit salad and honeysuckle flavours, with the near certainty that the honeyed characters will build with age.   **rating: 84**

best drinking 2001–2004 **best vintages** NA **drink with** Chinese honey prawns • $15

The Natural Wine Company Unwooded Chardonnay

▼▼▼▽ **2001** Light green-yellow; the bouquet is light, fresh and crisp, quite zesty but showing a somewhat unusual face of Chardonnay. The palate has plenty of more conventional flavour in a citrus and melon spectrum, tripping over itself slightly on the faintly sweet/thick finish.   **rating: 83**

best drinking 2001–2002 **best vintages** NA **drink with** Tempura prawns • $15

The Natural Wine Company Chardonnay

▼▼▼▼ **2001** Light straw-green; a clean bouquet with light melon fruit and minimal oak, then a light-bodied palate which surprises as it builds with melon, a hint of cashew, and good balance and length, all providing pleasing mouthfeel.   **rating: 85**

best drinking 2002–2003 **best vintages** NA **drink with** Pasta • $15

The Natural Wine Company Shiraz

▼▼▼▼ **2001** Bright, strong purple-red; a clean and youthful bouquet with quite intense dark plum/berry fruit leads logically into a palate with a powerful expression of the same flavours and balanced extract, but certainly needing time in bottle. Excellent value.   **rating: 88**

best drinking 2004–2009 **best vintages** NA **drink with** Grilled sirloin • $15

the oaks vineyard and winery   ★★★☆

31 Melba Highway, Yering, Vic 3770 **region** Yarra Valley
phone (03) 9739 0070 **fax** (03) 9739 0070 **open** Weekends 10.30–5, or by appointment
winemaker Karen Coulston (Contract) **production** 400 **est.** 2000
product range ($13.50–22.50 ML) Deschamps (Sauvignon Blanc Chardonnay Riesling), Chardonnay, Pinot Noir, Cabernet Sauvignon Merlot.
summary The Oaks has been established in what was originally a Presbyterian Manse, the change in use coming after a long period of neglect, and thus not incurring the wrath of the previous occupants. Owner Pauline Charlton spent 12 months restoring the Victorian homestead to its former glory prior to the opening. An on-site gallery features photographs by Pauline Charlton's daughter, Mackenzie, and fellow students of the Photography Studies College. The vineyard is close-planted, and the wine competently made by contract maker Karen Coulston.

The Oaks Pinot Noir

▼▼▼▼ **2000** Medium red-purple; the moderately intense bouquet has fair varietal character in a gentle plummy mode; the palate starts quietly enough with sweet plummy fruit and a touch of spice, but finishes strongly with good length and aftertaste, always the mark of quality Pinot.   **rating: 87**

best drinking 2002–2005 **best vintages** NA **drink with** Roast quail • $18.50

the silos estate   NR

Princes Highway, Jaspers Brush, NSW 2535 **region** Shoalhaven
phone (02) 4448 6082 **fax** (02) 4448 6246 **open** Wed–Sun 10–5
winemaker Gaynor Sims, Kate Khoury **production** 1000 **est.** 1985
product range ($13–18 CD) Traminer Riesling, Semillon, Chardonnay, Sauvignon Blanc, Wileys Creek Brut, Mostly Malbec, Softly Shiraz, Tawny Port, Liqueur Muscat.
summary Since 1995, Gaynor Sims and Kate Khoury, together with viticulturist Jovica Zecevic, have worked hard to improve the quality of the wine, starting with the 5 hectares of estate vineyards but also in the winery. The winery continues to rely on the tourist trade, however, and the wines do not appear in normal retail channels.

the warren vineyard   NR

Conte Road, Pemberton, WA 6260 **region** Pemberton
phone (08) 9776 1115 **fax** (08) 9776 1115 **open** 7 days 11–5
winemaker Bernard Abbott **production** 400 **est.** 1985
product range ($15–30 CD) Riesling, Cabernet Merlot, Cabernet Blanc.

summary The 1.5-hectare vineyard was established in 1985 and is one of the smallest in the Pemberton region, coming to public notice when its 1991 Cabernet Sauvignon won the award for the Best Red Table Wine from the Pemberton Region at the 1992 SGIO WA Winemakers Exhibition. Bottle-aged Riesling has also had notable success, the 1994 winning the trophy for Best Aged White at the 1998 Qantas Wine Show of WA.

the willows vineyard ★★★★

Light Pass Road, Light Pass, Barossa Valley, SA 5355 **region** Barossa Valley
phone (08) 8562 1080 **fax** (08) 8562 3447 **open** 7 days 10.30–4.30
winemaker Peter Scholz, Michael Scholz **production** 6000 **est.** 1989
product range ($12–28 ML) Riesling, Semillon, The Doctor Sparkling Red, Shiraz, Cabernet Sauvignon.
summary The Scholz family have been grape growers for generations and have almost 40 hectares of vineyards, selling part and retaining part of the crop. Current generation winemakers Peter and Michael Scholz could not resist the temptation to make smooth, well-balanced and flavoursome wines under their own label. These are all marketed with some years bottle age. Exports to the UK, the US and New Zealand.

The Willows Vineyard Semillon

▼▼▼▼▽ 2000 Light to medium yellow-green; the bouquet offers classic mineral and herb aromas which flow through onto the palate, which has good length and style. Was my second highest pointed wine (out of 32) at the 2001 Barossa Wine Show. **rating:** 92

best drinking 2002–2005 best vintages '00 drink with Deep-fried calamari • $13

The Willows Vineyard Shiraz

▼▼▼▽ 1999 Medium red-purple; the aromatic oak on the bouquet is matched by berry fruit; a big, rich and ripe palate finishes with slightly hot alcohol. **rating:** 84
▼▼▼▼ 1998 Medium red-purple; a full-bodied wine, with rich, ripe and luscious fruit is highlighted both on the bouquet and palate with some spicy notes. **rating:** 89

best drinking 2004–2009 best vintages NA drink with Rich Italian dishes • $23

the yarrahill/punt road ★★★★

10 St Huberts Road, Coldstream, Vic 3770 **region** Yarra Valley
phone (03) 9739 0666 **fax** (03) 9739 0633 **open** 7 days 10–5.30
winemaker Rob Dolan, Kate Goodman **production** 6000 **est.** 1999
product range ($18–23 R) Semillon, Sauvignon Blanc, Pinot Gris, Chardonnay, Shiraz, Merlot, Punt Road Cabernet Sauvignon.
summary The YarraHill brings together a syndicate headed by Rob Dolan (as winemaker) and Malcolm Fell (as viticulturist). The venture has been in the pipeline for several years, the wines having been made (under contract) at Yarra Ridge, where Rob Dolan was chief winemaker for a decade. The venture controls three vineyards, the home vineyard of The Yarra Hill (45 hectares), Napoleone (39 hectares) and Briarty Hill (15 hectares). A new winery has been established on St Huberts Road, which processed the 2001 vintage; the cellar door is part of the same complex. As from 2002, the wines will be marketed under the Punt Road brand name; it was felt there were too many producers incorporating the word 'Yarra' in their name.

Punt Road Pinot Gris

▼▼▼▼ 2001 Very light straw-green; a strongly spicy and perfumed bouquet leads into an intense yet delicate palate, which doesn't cloy, and which has nice feel and balance backing up the distinctive bouquet. **rating:** 88

best drinking 2002–2004 best vintages NA drink with Antipasto • $18

Punt Road Shiraz

▼▼▼▼ 2000 Medium purple-red; spicy earthy cherry fruit on the bouquet is mirrored on the palate which has length and a firm finish; subtle use of oak throughout. **rating:** 87

best drinking 2004–2009 best vintages NA drink with Scotch fillet • $23

Punt Road Merlot

▼▼▼▼ 2000 Medium red-purple; there are slightly earthy edges to the small berry fruit of the moderately intense bouquet; the palate opens up more, with lively, sweet raspberry fruit; attractively focussed; light but sufficient tannins. **rating:** 88

best drinking 2003–2007 best vintages NA drink with Beef Provencale • $23

thistle hill ★★★☆

McDonalds Road, Mudgee, NSW 2850 **region** Mudgee
phone (02) 6373 3546 **fax** (02) 6373 3540 **open** 7 days 9–5
winemaker David Robertson **production** 4000 **est.** 1976
product range ($15–23 CD) Riesling, Semillon, Special Reserve Semillon, Chardonnay, Pinot Noir, Cabernet Sauvignon, Dave's Cabernet Sauvignon, Liqueur Muscat.
summary The sudden death of Dave Robertson in September 2001 robbed Mudgee of one of its great characters and wife Lesley and daughters Lucy and Sally of a much-loved husband and father. They have vowed to continue Thistle Hill, selling the back vintages made by Dave until approximately 2004, when wines contract made by Ian McRae (Miramar) from Thistle Hill grapes will come on-stream. With typical Aussie humour, they say they will not rename the property Feminist Hill.

Thistle Hill Semillon

▼▼▼▼ **2001** Medium yellow-green; the bouquet is complex, suggesting a touch of barrel ferment, but without obvious oak aroma. The palate carries on in much the same mode, complex both in terms of taste and structure. **rating:** 88

best drinking 2002–2007 **best vintages** NA **drink with** Vegetable terrine • $15

Thistle Hill Chardonnay

▼▼▼▼ **2000** Medium yellow-green; a solid bouquet, with well-balanced and integrated oak and fruit doesn't quite deliver the intensity expected on the palate, but there is sufficient peach and melon fruit to provide a pleasantly soft mouthfeel. **rating:** 86

best drinking 2002–2004 **best vintages** '84, '86, '88, '92 **drink with** Creamy pasta • $17

Thistle Hill Cabernet Sauvignon

▼▼▼▽ **1999** Light to medium red-purple; light, earthy berry aromas are followed by a palate with more substance, in a restrained varietal savoury/earthy spectrum. Not the easiest of vintages. **rating:** 84

best drinking 2003–2007 **best vintages** '85, '86, '88, '89, '90, '97 **drink with** Barbecued meat • $20

✿ thomas wines ★★★★

C/- The Small Winemakers Centre, McDonalds Road, Pokolbin, NSW 2321 **region** Lower Hunter Valley
phone (02) 4991 6801 **fax** (02) 4991 6801 **open** 7 days 10–5
winemaker Andrew Thomas **production** 1500 **est.** 1997
product range ($20–32 R) Semillon, Shiraz.
summary Andrew Thomas came to the Hunter Valley from McLaren Vale, to join the winemaking team at Tyrrell's. After 13 years with Tyrrell's, he left to undertake contract work and to continue the development of his own winery label, a family affair run by himself and his wife Jo. The Semillon is sourced from a single vineyard owned by local grower Ken Bray, renowned for its quality, while the Shiraz is a blend of 60 per cent Hunter Valley shiraz and 40 per cent McLaren Vale shiraz. The wines are virtually exclusively available at the Small Winemakers Centre, although they can be found on restaurant lists throughout the Hunter Valley.

Thomas Semillon

▼▼▼▼ **2001** Medium green-yellow; after the reductive characters disappear, the quality of the wine shines through, with good depth and concentration in a moderately ripe and quite concentrated palate. **rating:** 87

best drinking 2003–2008 **best vintages** NA **drink with** Sashimi • NA

Thomas Shiraz

▼▼▼▼▼ **2000** Medium to full red-purple; the bouquet is full and rich, with excellent fruit/oak balance and integration, the palate mouthfilling, rich and supple, again exhibiting good oak handling. Good now, but will be even better when it loses its puppy fat. **rating:** 90

best drinking 2004–2009 **best vintages** '00 **drink with** Rump steak • NA

✿ thorn-clarke wines NR

Milton Park, Gawler Park Road, Angaston, SA 5353 **region** Barossa Valley
phone (08) 8564 3373 **fax** (08) 8564 3255 **open** Not
winemaker Jim Irvine (Consultant) **production** NA **est.** 1997
product range Shiraz.

summary To say this is a substantial new venture is to put it mildly. Two hundred and sixty-4 hectares of vineyard has been established, with shiraz (136 hectares), cabernet sauvignon (59 hectares) and merlot (28 hectares) being the principal plantings, supported by lesser amounts of petit verdot, cabernet franc, chardonnay, riesling and pinot gris. The first wines were due to be released in the Australian domestic market in August 2002, and one imagines that exports will also be the focus of attention, particularly given the role of Jim Irvine as consultant winemaker.

Thorn-Clarke Barossa Shiraz

TTTT **1998** Medium red-purple; savoury/cedary aromas are followed by a palate with nice extract and balance, all in all showing elegance even if it is a little on the oaky side.   **rating:** 88

best drinking 2003–2008 **best vintages** NA **drink with** Pastrami • $44.95

thornhill/the berry farm   NR

Bessel Road, Rosa Glen, WA 6285 **region** Margaret River
phone (08) 9757 5054 **fax** (08) 9757 5116 **open** 7 days 10–4.30
winemaker Eion Lindsay **production** NFP **est.** 1990
product range ($11.50–25 CD) Under the Thornhill label Classic Dry Semillon, Sauvignon Blanc, Cabernet Sauvignon, Tickled Pink (Sparkling Cabernet Sauvignon), Still Tickled Pink (Light Cabernet Sauvignon). Under The Berry Farm label a range of fruit-based wines, including Sparkling Strawberry and Plum Port.
summary Although I have not enjoyed the Thornhill table wines, the fruit wines under The Berry Farm label are extraordinarily good. The sparkling strawberry wine has intense strawberry flavour; the plum port likewise, carrying its 16° alcohol with remarkable ease.

three moon creek   NR

Waratah Vineyard, Mungungo, via Monto, Qld 4630 **region** South Burnett
phone (07) 4166 5100 **fax** (07) 4166 5200 **open** Tues–Sun and public holidays 10–5
winemaker Peter Scudamore-Smith (Contract) **production** 500 **est.** 1998
product range ($14–20 CD) Queensland White Blend, Chardonnay, Waratah Estate Verdelho, Gentle Annie, Rosé, Shiraz, Merlot, The Gorge Port.
summary David Bray is one of the doyens of wine journalism in Brisbane, and, indeed, Australia. After decades of writing about wine he and wife Pamela have joined Max Lindsay (Pamela's brother) and partner Lynne Tucker in establishing the Waratah Vineyard and Winery joint venture at Mungungo, near Monto, at the top of the Burnett Valley. The wines are principally sourced from the 4 hectare Waratah Vineyard with 3.2 hectares of vineyard planted to chardonnay, verdelho, semillon, marsanne, viognier, shiraz, merlot and petit verdot, an exotic mix if ever there was one, supplemented by grapes grown at Inglewood and Murgon. The wines are made by the energetic Peter Scudamore-Smith MW.

☙ thumm estate wines   NR

87 Kriedeman Road, Upper Coomera, Qld 4209 **region** Queensland Coastal
phone (07) 5573 6990 **fax** (07) 5573 4099 **open** 7 days 9–5, 9–6 in summer
winemaker Robert Thumm **production** 1000 **est.** 2000
product range ($14–22.50 CD) Riesling, Semillon, Sauvignon Blanc, Unwooded Chardonnay, Chardonnay, Shiraz, Cabernet Sauvignon.
summary Robert Thumm, born in 1950, is the eldest son of Hermann Thumm, founder of Chateau Yaldara in the Barossa Valley, gaining his degree in oenology from the University of Geisenheim, Germany. In 1999, when the family business was sold, he and wife Janet decided to move to Qld, establishing the new winery in a valley below the Tambourine Mountain Tourist Centre. Here they have planted cabernet sauvignon and petit verdot, but also have 1.5 hectares of riesling and 1.2 hectares of sauvignon blanc in production in the Adelaide Hills. The venture, and its associated wine club, is firmly aimed at the general tourist market, Thumm Estate being yet another such venture in this part of Australia which relies so heavily on tourism, and which offers so much to tourists.

tilba valley   NR

Glen Eden Vineyard, 947 Old Highway, Corunna Lake, NSW 2546 **region** South Coast Zone
phone (02) 4473 7308 **fax** (02) 4476 1693 **open** Mon–Sat 10–5, Sun 11–5
winemaker Barry Field **production** 12 000 **est.** 1978

product range ($15–16.50 CD) Traminer Riesling, Semillon, Semillon Chardonnay, Cabernet Shiraz, Tawny Port.

summary A strongly tourist-oriented operation, serving a ploughman's lunch daily from noon to 2 pm. Has 8 hectares of estate vineyards; no recent tastings.

tim adams ★★★★

Warenda Road, Clare, SA 5453 **region** Clare Valley
phone (08) 8842 2429 **fax** (08) 8842 3550 **open** Mon–Fri 10.30–5, weekends 11–5
winemaker Tim Adams **production** 20 000 **est.** 1986
product range ($19–35 R) Riesling, Semillon, The Fergus (Grenache), Shiraz, Aberfeldy Shiraz, Cabernet.
summary Tim and Pam Adams have built a first class business since Tim Adams left his position as winemaker at Leasingham in 1985. Eleven hectares of estate vineyards increasingly provide the wine for the business, supplemented by grapes from local growers. Tim Adams has consistently produced wines of exceptional depth of flavour and he also makes significant quantities of wine under contract for others in the district. Extensive distribution through all Australian states; exports to the UK, US, Netherlands and Sweden.

Tim Adams Riesling

▼▼▼▼ **2001** Light straw-green; the bouquet has a range of mineral and herb aromas intermingling with green lime juice characters; it is the latter which come through on the penetrating palate, with its green lime flavours and good length.   **rating:** 89

best drinking 2006–2010 **best vintages** NA **drink with** Seafood salad • $20

Tim Adams Shiraz

▼▼▼▼ **2000** Medium to full red-purple; the dark, blackberry, plum, spice and vanilla aromas of the bouquet are followed by a powerful palate with blackberry and toasty vanilla oak complemented by soft tannins. **rating:** 88

best drinking 2005–2010 **best vintages** '86, '88, '90, '92, '93, '96 **drink with** Spit-roasted lamb • $26

Tim Adams Aberfeldy Shiraz

▼▼▼▼▽ **1999** Dense, inky red-purple; rich, ripe, powerful plum, blackberry and prune fruit is coupled with masses of American oak on the bouquet. The palate is no less rich and concentrated, with plum and blackberry fruit, and again, lots of American oak. Quite similar to the Leasingham Bin 61, and similarly needs time, and, some would argue, less oak.   **rating:** 90

best drinking 2004–2014 **best vintages** '97, '98, '99 **drink with** Chargrilled rump • $35

Tim Adams The Fergus Grenache

▼▼▼▼ **2000** Medium red-purple; the bouquet has a good depth of ripe and not too jammy fruit, the palate following suit with abundant, complex flavour mouthfilling and soft. The small amounts of Cabernet Sauvignon, Cabernet Franc and Shiraz have done the trick.   **rating:** 87

best drinking 2002–2005 **best vintages** NA **drink with** Game • $23

Tim Adams Cabernet

▼▼▼▼ **2000** Medium to full red-purple; a ripe bouquet with complex blackberry and cassis aromas together with a hint of chocolate, and less assertive oak than is usual. The palate has plenty of berry/cassis fruit on entry, then firm/earthy tannins on the finish to provide structure.   **rating:** 88

best drinking 2005–2010 **best vintages** '86, '88, '90, '92, '94, '98 **drink with** Chargrilled rump steak • $22.95

tim gramp ★★★☆

Mintaro Road, Watervale, SA 5452 **region** Clare Valley
phone (08) 8431 3338 **fax** (08) 0101 0009 **open** Weekends and holidays 10.30–4.30
winemaker Tim Gramp **production** 5000 **est.** 1990
product range ($20–30 R) Watervale Riesling, McLaren Vale Shiraz, Watervale Cabernet Sauvignon, Watervale Pedro Ximinez.
summary Tim Gramp has quietly built up a very successful business with a limited product range, and – by keeping overheads to a minimum – provides good wines at modest prices. The operation is supported by 2 hectares of cabernet sauvignon around the cellar door. Exports to the UK, the US and New Zealand.

Tim Gramp Watervale Riesling

▼▼▼▼ **2001** Medium yellow-green, surprisingly deep; the Stelvin closure guarantees it was this colour when it went to bottle. The full bouquet has lime and tropical aromas, the solid palate big on flavour, less so on finesse. For all that, a legitimate alternative style for early drinking.   **rating:** 86

best drinking 2002–2004 **best vintages** '97, '98 **drink with** Bouillabaisse • $19.80

Tim Gramp Watervale Pedro Ximinez

▼▼▼▼ **2001** Light straw; the bouquet has an unusual array of mead and beeswax aromas, the powerful palate equally unusual, but providing a wine with considerable character as opposed to the normally bland (other than for Sherry) flavour. **rating:** 85

best drinking 2001–2004 **best vintages** NA **drink with** Orange cake • $16

Tim Gramp McLaren Vale Shiraz

▼▼▼▼ **2000** Medium to full red-purple; ripe, savoury/herb/dark chocolate/earth/plum aromas all intermingle on the bouquet. The medium-bodied palate is well-balanced and quite finely structured, particularly by normal McLaren Vale standards. Nice wine. **rating:** 87

best drinking 2003–2009 **best vintages** '91, '92, '94, '96, '97, '98 **drink with** Barbecued, marinated steak • $29.80

Tim Gramp Watervale Cabernet Sauvignon

▼▼▼▼ **2000** Medium red-purple; the clean but somewhat light bouquet has savoury/leafy notes to the fore, replaced by redcurrant/red berry fruit on entry to the mouth, before finishing a little sharpish. **rating:** 85

best drinking 2003–2007 **best vintages** NA **drink with** Barbecued beef • $19.80

tin cows NR

Tarrawarra Estate, Healesville Road, Yarra Glen, Vic 3775 **region** Yarra Valley
phone (03) 5962 3311 **fax** (03) 5962 3887 **open** 7 days 10.30–4.30
winemaker Clare Halloran, Damian North **production** 18 000 **est.** 1983
product range ($23–25 CD) Chardonnay, Pinot Noir, Shiraz, Merlot.
summary Tin Cows (formerly Tunnel Hill) is regarded by Tarrawarra as a separate business, drawing most of its grapes from the 21-hectare Tin Cows Vineyard adjacent to the Maroondah Highway. The wines are intended to be more accessible when young, and are significantly cheaper than the Tarrawarra wines.

tinderbox vineyard ★★★★

Tinderbox, Tas 7054 **region** Southern Tasmania
phone (03) 6229 2994 **fax** (03) 6229 2994 **open** By appointment
winemaker Andrew Hood (Contract) **production** 175 **est.** 1994
product range ($25 CD) Pinot Noir.
summary Liz McGown is a Hobart nurse who has established her 1-hectare vineyard on the slope beneath her house, overlooking the entrance to the Derwent River and the D'Entrecasteaux Channel. The attractive label was designed by Barry Tucker, who was so charmed by Liz McGown's request that he waived his usual (substantial) fee.

Tinderbox Vineyard Pinot Noir

▼▼▼▼ **2000** Medium to full red-purple; powerful, smooth plummy aromas lead into a very ripe and big palate, which is stacked with character and flavour, but is slightly over the top early in its life. Has development potential. **rating:** 88

best drinking 2003–2007 **best vintages** '99 **drink with** Duck casserole • NA

tingle-wood ★★★★☆

Glenrowan Road, Denmark, WA 6333 **region** Great Southern
phone (08) 9840 9218 **fax** (08) 9840 9218 **open** 7 days 9–5
winemaker Brenden Smith (Contract) **production** 1000 **est.** 1976
product range ($15–18 CD) Yellow Tingle Riesling, Tree Top Walk (late harvest), Red Tingle Cabernet Sauvignon Shiraz.
summary An intermittent producer of Riesling of extraordinary quality, although birds and other disasters do intervene and prevent production in some years. The rating is given for the Riesling, which remains a sentimental favourite of mine.

Tingle-Wood Yellow Tingle Riesling

▼▼▼▼▽ **2001** Pale straw-green; voluminous passionfruit, lime blossom and apple aromas on both bouquet and palate start proceedings, the palate sustained by excellent lemony/minerally acidity. **rating:** 91

best drinking 2003–2010 **best vintages** '90, '91, '00, '01 **drink with** Sashimi, fuller-flavoured fish • $17

tinklers vineyard ★★★☆

Pokolbin Mountains Road, Pokolbin, NSW 2330 **region** Lower Hunter Valley
phone (02) 4998 7435 **fax** (02) 4998 7529 **open** 7 days 10–4
winemaker Ian Tinkler **production** 750 **est.** 1997
product range ($11–25 CD) School Block Semillon, Flemings Semillon, Pokolbin Mountains Semillon Verdelho, Lucerne Paddock Verdelho, Mt Bright Chardonnay, Eruptions Sparkling Shiraz, Volcanic Ash (sweet white), Cote D'or Shiraz, Mt Bright Shiraz, U&I Shiraz, Mt Bright Merlot, Pokolbin Mountains Cabernet Merlot, Pokolbin Mountains Cabernet Sauvignon, Usher Gordon Muscat.
summary Brothers Ian and Usher Tinkler own a large (41.5-hectare) vineyard on the slopes of the Pokolbin Mountain Road; most of the production is sold, a small amount being contract-made for cellar door sales.

Tinklers Vineyard U&I Shiraz

♥♥♥♥ **2000** Medium red-purple; the clean bouquet with suave cherry fruit and gently spicy overtones leads into an elegant, fine-boned palate, the fruit complemented by subtle oak and fine tannins. From the 1969 plantings. **rating:** 89

best drinking 2004–2010 **best vintages** '00 **drink with** Lamb Provencale • $20

tinlins NR

Kangarilla Road, McLaren Flat, SA 5171 **region** McLaren Vale
phone (08) 8323 8649 **fax** (08) 8323 9747 **open** 7 days 9–5
winemaker Warren Randall **production** 30 000 **est.** 1977
product range ($1.50–3.40 CD) Generic table, fortified and flavoured wines priced from $3.70 for table wines and $4.50 for fortified wines.
summary A very interesting operation run by former Seppelt sparkling winemaker Warren Randall, drawing upon 100 hectares of estate vineyards, which specialises in bulk-wine sales to the major Australian wine companies. A small proportion of the production is sold direct through the cellar door at mouthwateringly low prices to customers who provide their own containers and purchase by the litre. McLaren Vale's only bulk-wine specialist.

tinonee vineyard NR

Milbrodale Road, Broke, NSW 2330 **region** Lower Hunter Valley
phone (02) 6579 1308 **fax** (02) 6579 1146 **open** Weekends and public holidays 11–4
winemaker Andrew Margan, Ray Merger (Contract) **production** 1000 **est.** 1997
product range ($15–18 CD) Chardonnay, Chardonnay Semillon, Verdelho, Merlot, Shiraz.
summary Ian Craig has established 14 hectares of vineyards on a mix of red volcanic and river flat soils at Broke. Part are in production, with the remainder coming into bearing, ultimately capable of producing 5000 cases of wine per year.

tintilla wines ★★★☆

725 Hermitage Road, Pokolbin, NSW 2320 **region** Lower Hunter Valley
phone 0411 214 478 **fax** (02) 9767 6894 **open** Weekends 10.30–6, by appointment Mon–Fri afternoons
winemaker Greg Silkman, Monarch (Contract) **production** 4200 **est.** 1993
product range ($16–35 CD) Semillon, Rosato di Jupiter, Saphira Sangiovese, Catherine de'M Sangiovese Merlot, Shiraz, Justine Merlot, Reserve Shiraz, Merlot, Eduardo Fortified Semillon, Vintage White Port.
summary The Lusby family has established a 7.5-hectare vineyard (including 1 hectare of sangiovese) on their northeast-facing vineyard, with its red clay and limestone soil. The Shiraz (both varietal and Reserve) is especially commendable. They have also planted an olive grove producing 4 different types of olives, which are cured and sold on the estate.

Tintilla Hunter Semillon

♥♥♥♥ **2001** Light green-yellow; classic lemon, flint and mineral aromas are followed by an intense, long and lingering palate, as yet showing some SO_2, but with outstanding potential. **rating:** 88

best drinking 2004–2010 **best vintages** NA **drink with** Leave it in the cellar • $16.50

Tintilla Rosato di Jupiter

TTTT 2001 Light red; light, crisp cherry pip aromas precede a fresh, clean, cherry-accented palate, with a well-balanced, dry finish. This is the 20 per cent juice run-off of the Saphira Sangiovese, and won a somewhat surprising gold medal at the 2002 Sydney International Wine Competition. **rating: 85**

best drinking 2002–2003 **best vintages** NA **drink with** Antipasto • $16

Tintilla Shiraz

TTTT 2000 Dense red-purple; licorice and dark fruit aromas foreshadow an absolutely massive and very extractive wine on the palate, which needs years to soften, but should do so, simply because of the strength of the fruit. **rating: 87**

best drinking 2005–2015 **best vintages** '98 **drink with** Leave it in the cellar • $25

Tintilla Reserve Shiraz

TTTTY 2000 Medium to full red-purple; a complex array of rich chocolate, earth, blackberry, vanilla and licorice aromas on the bouquet are matched by the abundant flavour and complexity of the palate, which is still a baby; all the components are there to justify long term cellaring. Sophisticated winemaking, with ten per cent carbonic maceration and a mix of new French and American oak. **rating: 91**

best drinking 2005–2015 **best vintages** '00 **drink with** Leave it in the cellar • $25.60

Tintilla Saphira Sangiovese

TTTT 2000 Light to medium red-purple; the light bouquet has earthy, spicy overtones, more regional than varietal; the palate, likewise, offers an interesting spicy/savoury/cherry mix; very fine, soft ripe tannins run through the palate and help the structure. **rating: 85**

best drinking 2003–2007 **best vintages** NA **drink with** Lasagne • $25.60

Tintilla Justine Merlot

TTTY 2000 Some development showing in the colour, the bouquet earthy and regional. The palate is powerful, overly extractive and tannic for a Merlot, but rather better as a durable red wine. **rating: 83**

best drinking 2003–2008 **best vintages** NA **drink with** Leave it in the cellar • $25.60

tipperary hill estate   NR

Alma–Bowendale Road, Alma via Maryborough, Vic 3465 **region** Bendigo
phone (03) 5461 3312 **fax** (03) 5461 3312 **open** Weekends 10–5, or by appointment
winemaker Paul Flowers **production** 300 **est.** 1986
product range ($16–24 CD) Shiraz, Pinot Noir, Cabernets.
summary All of the wine is sold through the cellar door and on-site restaurant, open on Sundays. Says Paul Flowers, production depends 'on the frost, wind and birds', which perhaps explains why this is very much a part-time venture. Situated 7 kilometres west of the city of Maryborough, Tipperary Hill Estate is the only winery operating in the Central Goldfields Shire. Winemaker Paul Flowers built the rough-cut pine winery and the bluestone residential cottage next door with the help of friends. Together with wife Margaret he also operates a restaurant.

tizzana winery   NR

518 Tizzana Road, Ebenezer, NSW 2756 **region** South Coast Zone
phone (02) 4579 1150 **fax** (02) 4579 1216 **open** Weekends, holidays 12–6, or by appointment
winemaker Peter Auld **production** 300 **est.** 1887
product range ($11.50–17 CD) From Tizzana vineyards Rosso di Tizzana (a light, dry Cabernet Sauvignon), Waterloo Shiraz, Sackville Tawny, Vintage Port, Old Liqueur Sweet White and Mrs Fiaschi's Old Sweet Red; the Tizzana Selection from other regions of Traminer Riesling, White Port, Sherry (the latter two from Stanton & Killeen) and then two wines from South Australia under the Hawkesbury History Heritage 2001 Committee (a strange combination), including Federation Semillon Chardonnay and Federation Tawny Port.
summary Tizzana has been a weekend and holiday occupation for Peter Auld for many years now, operating in one of the great historic wineries built (in 1887) by Australia's true renaissance man, Dr Thomas Fiaschi. The wines may not be great, but the ambience is.

tokar estate   NR

6 Maddens Lane, Coldstream, Vic 3770 **region** Yarra Valley
phone (03) 5964 9585 **fax** (03) 9706 4033 **open** Fri–Sun and long weekends 10–5
winemaker Paul Evans **production** 1500 **est.** 1996

product range ($19.50–25 CD) Pinot Noir, Shiraz, Tempranillo, Cabernet Sauvignon.

summary Leon Tokar is one of the number of new arrivals on Maddens Lane, having established over 5 hectares of pinot noir, 2.5 hectares of shiraz, and 2 hectares each of cabernet sauvignon and – interestingly – tempranillo. Part of the grape production is sold to Southcorp, the remainder contract-made. By the end of 2002, if all goes according to plan, a new cellar door, barrel room and restaurant will have opened.

Tokar Estate Pinot Noir

▼▼▼▽ **2000** Medium red with a touch of purple; the ripe bouquet has an exotic array of hay, straw, forest, seaweed and spice; the ripe fruit flavours of the palate are in similar style, suggesting some shrivelled berries; dry tannins to finish.   **rating:** 84

best drinking 2002–2004 **best vintages** NA **drink with** Braised duck • $23.50

Tokar Estate Cabernet Sauvignon

▼▼▼▼ **2000** Medium red-purple; the moderately intense bouquet ranges through savoury, earth, vanilla and dark berry aromas. The palate has a mix of sweet berry and dark chocolate fruit, a dusting of vanilla, and finishing with soft tannins.   **rating:** 86

best drinking 2003–2008 **best vintages** NA **drink with** Lamb shanks • $24

tollana   ★★★★

Tanunda Road, Nuriootpa, SA 5355 **region** Barossa Valley
phone (08) 8560 9408 **fax** (08) 8562 2494 **open** By appointment
winemaker Oliver Crawford **production** 30 000 **est.** 1888
product range ($13–22 R) Eden Valley Riesling, Adelaide Hills Sauvignon Blanc, Eden Valley Adelaide Hills Chardonnay, Botrytis Riesling, Shiraz Bin TR16, Cabernet Sauvignon Bin TR222.
summary As the Southcorp wine group moves to establish regional identity for its wines, Tollana is emphasising its Eden Valley base. Seemingly as a by-product of Penfolds development of Yattarna and related wines, the Tollana Chardonnay style has become more elegant, now standing comfortably alongside the flavoursome Riesling and Shiraz.

Tollana Eden Valley Riesling

▼▼▼▽ **2001** Light to medium green-yellow; the herbaceous/grassy bouquet appears to have some yeast influence; there is fair fruit on the mid-palate, but a slightly grippy finish then ensues. Disappointing.

rating: 84

best drinking 2001–2003 **best vintages** '86, '87, '90, '92, '93, '97 **drink with** Seafood salad • $14

Tollana Eden Valley Adelaide Hills Chardonnay

▼▼▼▼ **2000** Light green-yellow; fine melon, citrus and nectarine fruit on the bouquet is replicated on the palate, which has above average concentration and length. Subtle oak handling throughout; very good value.   **rating:** 88

▼▼▼▼ **1999** Medium yellow-green; clean, largely fruit-driven aromas, then a wine which is still fresh in the mouth, with rounded melon fruit, balanced acidity and gentle oak.   **rating:** 87

best drinking 2002–2005 **best vintages** NA **drink with** Salmon risotto • $14

Tollana Botrytis Riesling (375 ml)

▼▼▼▼▽ **1999** Deep gold; very complex, rich mandarin, cumquat and toffee aromas come through on both bouquet and palate. Very much in the traditional style of this wine, which seems to always have an extra degree of weight and concentration over others in its class.   **rating:** 90

best drinking 2002–2003 **best vintages** '97 **drink with** Poached pears and ice cream • $14

Tollana Cabernet Sauvignon Bin TR222

▼▼▼▼▼ **1999** Strong red-purple, the sweet, dark berry cabernet varietal character of the bouquet continues to run through the medium-bodied palate with a skein of sweet fruit wound through fine tannins and nice oak.   **rating:** 93

best drinking 2002–2007 **best vintages** '86, '88, '90, '91, '92, '93, '95, '96, '98, '99 **drink with** Roast veal • $20

tom's waterhole wines   NR

Felton, Longs Corner Road, Canowindra, NSW 2804 **region** Cowra
phone (02) 6344 1819 **fax** (02) 6344 2172 **open** Weekends 10–5
winemaker Graham Kerr **production** 700 **est.** 1997
product range ($8.50–14 ML) Semillon, Chardonnay, Humpers Dry Red, Shiraz, Humpers Port.

summary Graham Timms and Graham Kerr started the development of Tom's Waterhole Wines in 1997, progressively establishing 3 hectares of shiraz and 2 hectares each of cabernet sauvignon and semillon and 1 hectare of merlot. The planting programme completed in 2001. A decision has been taken to bypass the use of irrigation, and the yields will be low, with an expectation that the small on-site winery will crush around 20 tonnes per year.

toorak estate   NR

Toorak Road, Leeton, NSW 2705 **region** Riverina
phone (02) 6953 2333 **fax** (02) 6953 4454 **open** Mon–Sat 9–5
winemaker Robert Bruno **production** 30 000 **est.** 1965
product range ($4–32 CD) Willandra Leeton Selection range of Traminer Riesling, Semillon Chardonnay, Shiraz, Soft Shiraz, Cabernet Shiraz, Cabernet Merlot; Willandra Estate range of Semillon, Chardonnay, Botrytis Semillon, Shiraz, Cabernet Sauvignon, Muscat of Alexandria; Toorak Varietal range of Traminer Riesling, Semillon Chardonnay; Amesbury Estate range of Classic Dry White, Semillon Sauvignon Blanc, Classic Dry Red, Grenache Shiraz; Frank Bruno Red Lambrusco; Sparkling; Fortifieds.
summary A traditional, long-established Riverina producer with a strong Italian-based clientele around Australia. Production has been increasing significantly, utilising 80 hectares of estate plantings and grapes purchased from other growers.

torbreck vintners   ★★★★★

Roennfeldt Road, Marananga, SA 5352 **region** Barossa Valley
phone (08) 8562 4155 **fax** (08) 8562 4195 **open** By appointment
winemaker David Powell, Dan Standish **production** 8600 **est.** 1994
product range ($27.50–187.50 ML) Marsanne Viognier Rousanne, The Steading (Grenache Shiraz), RunRig (Shiraz Viognier), Juveniles (Grenache, Mataro, Shiraz), Descendant (Shiraz Viognier), The Factor (Shiraz).
summary Torbreck has made a major impact since its first releases in 1997 of a 1995 RunRig and 1996 The Steading. David Powell's family has assembled small patches of old vine shiraz, grenache and mourvedre in the Barossa Valley which they are share-farming, complementing a small vineyard of their own. Each succeeding vintage has added to an extraordinary cult following for the wines, the flames fanned by fulsome praise from Robert Parker and bottles sold at auction in New York for $US1000 each. Powell, however, is keeping a level head, knowing this fever will abate sooner or later. The wines are also exported to Germany, Switzerland, New Zealand and Singapore.

Torbreck Vintners Marsanne Viognier Roussanne

▼▼▼▼ 2001 Light to medium yellow-green; the complex, tangy bouquet gives the impression of subliminal oak, which may or may not be there. The palate scores for the depth and weight of its mouthfeel more than simply the slightly tangy/herbal fruit. Very much in the Torbreck mould. Dave Powell says in the back label 'Since we've had success with a few of the red Rhône varieties, we would thought we would give some of the whites a try'. **rating:** 87

best drinking 2002–2005 **best vintages** NA **drink with** Bouillabaisse • $32.50

Torbreck The Factor Shiraz

▼▼▼▼▼ 1999 Full red-purple; a powerful, dense bouquet with ripe plum to the fore, then gentle spice and positive oak. The smooth palate has plush, ripe, dark berry and plum fruit, fine tannins, and excellent oak integration. **rating:** 95

best drinking 2006–2016 **best vintages** '98, '99 **drink with** Braised ox cheek • $125

Torbreck The RunRig Shiraz Viognier

▼▼▼▼▼ 1999 Full red-purple; a fruit-driven bouquet with a complex array of rich dark berry, plum and spice aromas, then a super-saturated and concentrated palate exuding fruit, spice and soft tannins. One can only imagine that part of the concentration derives from juice run-off. **rating:** 94

best drinking 2005–2020 **best vintages** '96, '97, '98, '99 **drink with** Game • $187.50

Torbreck The Descendant Shiraz Viognier

▼▼▼▼▼ 2000 Dense but bright purple-red; intense damson plum and berry fruit aromas foreshadow an opulently rich but well-structured palate, the oak subservient to the fruit, and finishing with lingering, soft tannins. Slightly lighter in style than the Runrig, but still a massive wine. **rating:** 94

best drinking 2005–2015 **best vintages** '00 **drink with** Leave it in the cellar • $125

Torbreck The Juveniles Grenache Blend

♥♥♥♥ **2001** Light to medium red-purple; a fragrant and clean bouquet with some herb and mint aspects is followed by a palate in which juicy, jammy grenache varietal flavour dominates the wine; zero tannins, the overall effect equivalent to a high octane Rosé, best served slightly chilled. **rating: 85**

best drinking 2002–2003 **best vintages** NA **drink with** Rich pasta • $27.50

Torbreck The Steading Granache Shiraz

♥♥♥♥♀ **2000** Medium red-purple; the fragrant bouquet has juicy/jammy berry fruit supported by subtle oak, the palate with sweet, quite luscious fruit providing good flow and mouthfeel. Carries its 14° alcohol well.

rating: 90

best drinking 2004–2010 **best vintages** '97, '98, '99 **drink with** Lamb Provencale • $32.50

tower estate ★★★★★

Cnr Broke and Hall Roads, Pokolbin, NSW 2320 **region** Lower Hunter Valley
phone (02) 4998 7989 **fax** (02) 4998 7919 **open** 7 days 10–5
winemaker Dan Dineen **production** 10 000 **est.** 1999
product range ($19–35 CD) Clare Valley Riesling, Hunter Valley Semillon, Adelaide Hills Sauvignon Blanc, Hunter Valley Verdelho, Hunter Valley Chardonnay, Yarra Valley Pinot Noir, Hunter Valley Shiraz, Barossa Valley Shiraz, Coonawarra Cabernet Sauvignon, Muscat.
summary Tower Estate is a joint venture headed by Len Evans, featuring a luxury conference centre and accommodation. It draws upon varieties and regions which have a particular synergy, coupled with the enormous knowledge of Len Evans and the winemaking skills of Dan Dineen.

Tower Estate Clare Riesling

♥♥♥♥♀ **2001** Light green-yellow; fragrant lime, passionfruit and apple blossom aromas are followed by a palate with excellent flavour, length and grip. Another surprise packet from the Clare Valley, suggesting that, against all the odds, this was a very good riesling vintage. **rating: 93**

best drinking 2001–2010 **best vintages** '99, '01 **drink with** Antipasto • $24

Tower Estate Hunter Valley Semillon

♥♥♥♥♥ **2001** Light straw-green; the spotlessly clean bouquet with a crisp mix of herb, lemon and mineral then an intense herb and spice palate; excellent acidity runs through a long finish. **rating: 94**

best drinking 2006–2016 **best vintages** '99, '00, '01 **drink with** Fine seafood • $19

Tower Estate Adelaide Hills Sauvignon Blanc

♥♥♥♥♀ **2001** Light green-yellow; a classic gooseberry, asparagus and herb mix on the bouquet; then a palate with plenty of weight and presence thanks to gently sweet fruit and a balanced finish. **rating: 90**

best drinking 2002–2003 **best vintages** '99, '00, '01 **drink with** Pan-fried calamari • $26

Tower Estate Hunter Valley Chardonnay

♥♥♥♥♀ **2000** Medium yellow-green; rich, peach and nectarine fruit given complexity by subtly nutty barrel ferment aromas on the bouquet. Nutty cashew and nectarine flavours provide the wine with good length and weight. Sourced from the Maxwell's Maluna vineyard. **rating: 91**

best drinking 2001–2004 **best vintages** '00 **drink with** Sauteed veal • $26

Tower Estate Barossa Shiraz

♥♥♥♥♀ **2000** Medium to full red-purple; attractive touches of spice and cedar illuminate the bouquet; a cleverly built and constructed palate with dark cherry/berry fruit and silky tannins, the oak held in restraint. **rating: 92**

best drinking 2004–2014 **best vintages** '99, '00 **drink with** Barbecued rump steak • $35

Tower Estate Hunter Valley Shiraz

♥♥♥♥♥ **2000** Excellent purple-red; opulent black cherry and plum fruit on the bouquet is matched with positive but high quality oak. The palate is deceptively smooth and polished for such a young wine, which finishes with fine tannins and just a gentle touch of oak. Deceptive, because it is so easy to drink now you might wrongly imagine it does not have a long future. It does. **rating: 94**

best drinking 2002–2012 **best vintages** '99, '00 **drink with** Rare roast beef • $30

🐦 towerhill estate   NR

Albany Highway, Mount Barker, WA 6324 **region** Great Southern
phone (08) 9851 1488 **fax** (08) 9851 2982 **open** By appointment
winemaker Brenden Smith (Contract) **production** 600 **est.** 1993
product range ($13–20 CD) Riesling, Unwooded Chardonnay, Merlot.
summary The Williams family, headed by Alan and Diane began the establishment of Towerhill Estate in 1993, planting chardonnay (2.5 hectares), cabernet sauvignon (2 hectares), riesling (1 hectare) and merlot (1 hectare). Commencing in 1996, the grapes were sold to other producers, but since 1999 limited quantities have been made under contract by Brenden Smith at West Cape Howe Wines. These wines have had consistent show success at the Qantas Wine Show of WA and sell out quickly through cellar door and local outlets.

trafford hill vineyard   NR

Lot 1 Bower Road, Normanville, SA 5204 **region** Southern Fleurieu
phone (08) 8558 3595 **open** Thurs–Mon and holidays 10.30–5
winemaker John Sanderson **production** 500 **est.** 1996
product range ($6.50–19 ML) Riesling, Sparkling Shiraz, Family Reserve Red, Sam-Jack Tawny Port, Parsons Ghost Liqueur Tawny Port.
summary Irene and John Sanderson have established 2 hectares of vineyard at Normanville, on the coast of the Fleurieu Peninsula near to its southern extremity. Irene carries out all the viticulture, and John Sanderson makes the wine with help from district veteran Allan Dyson. Distribution is through local restaurants, the remainder through mail order and cellar door.

tranquil vale   ★★★☆

325 Pywells Road, Luskintyre, NSW 2321 **region** Lower Hunter Valley
phone (02) 4930 6100 **fax** (02) 4930 6105 **open** Fri–Mon 10–4, or by appointment
winemaker Andrew Margan, David Hook **production** 2000 **est.** 1996
product range ($16–20 ML) Semillon, Chardonnay, Shiraz, Cabernet Shiraz.
summary Phil and Lucy Griffiths purchased the property site-unseen from a description in an old copy of the *Australian Weekend* found in the High Commission Office in London. The vineyard they established is situated on the banks of the Hunter River, opposite Wyndham Estate, on relatively fertile, sandy, clay loam. Irrigation has been installed, and what is known as VSP trellising. Within the blink of an eye, they have become experts, and find themselves 'in the amusing position that people ask us our opinion!' The three luxury, self-contained cottages on site offer the extras of a swimming pool, tennis court, gymnasium, etc and sleep a family or two couples each. Finally, competent contract-winemaking has resulted in the production of good wines, some of which have already had show success.

Tranquil Vale Chardonnay
▼▼▼▼ 2001 Light to medium yellow-green; fresh, clean nectarine and melon fruit on the bouquet is supported by an airbrush of oak. The smooth, gently rounded palate, with melon/nectarine fruit and a similarly subtle oak infusion flows well across the palate   **rating: 88**
best drinking 2002–2003 **best vintages** NA **drink with** Roasted tomato and basil soup • $18

Tranquil Vale Cabernet Shiraz
▼▼▼▼ 2001 Medium red-purple; the bouquet has a mix of savoury red berry fruit and more regional, earthy aromas; the palate moves into a distinctly sweeter red berry fruit spectrum, supported by soft vanilla oak.   **rating: 85**
best drinking 2004–2009 **best vintages** NA **drink with** Roast beef • $16

treen ridge estate   NR

Packer Road, Pemberton, WA 6260 **region** Pemberton
phone (08) 9776 1131 **fax** (08) 9776 0442 **open** Wed–Fri 11–5, weekends 10–5
winemaker Andrew Mountford (Contract) **production** 600 **est.** 1992
product range ($15–25 CD) Riesling, Sauvignon Blanc, Springfield Shiraz, Reserve Vintage Shiraz, Sparkling Shiraz.
summary The Treen Ridge vineyard and three-room accommodation is set between the Treen Brook state forest and The Warren National Park and is operated by Mollie and Barry Scotman.

treeton estate ★★★

North Treeton Road, Cowaramup, WA 6284 **region** Margaret River
phone (08) 9755 5481 **fax** (08) 9755 5051 **open** 7 days 10–6
winemaker David McGowan **production** 3000 **est.** 1984
product range ($15–17 R) Chardonnay, Riesling, Estate White, Petit Rouge, Shiraz, Liqueur Muscat.
summary In 1982 David McGowan and wife Corinne purchased the 30-hectare property upon which Treeton Estate is established, beginning to plant the vines two years later. David has done just about everything in his life, and in the early years was working in Perth, which led to various setbacks for the vineyard. The wines are light and fresh, sometimes rather too much so.

trentham estate ★★★☆

Sturt Highway, Trentham Cliffs, NSW 2738 **region** Murray Darling
phone (03) 5024 8888 **fax** (03) 5024 8800 **open** Mon–Fri 9–5, weekends 9.30–5
winemaker Anthony Murphy, Shane Kerr **production** 50 000 **est.** 1988
product range ($9–19 ML) Riesling, Murphy's Lore Semillon Chardonnay, Sauvignon Blanc, Viognier, Chardonnay, Noble Taminga, Sparkling Ruby, Pinot Noir, Shiraz, Cellar Reserve Shiraz, Murphy's Lore Shiraz Cabernet, Nebbiolo, Merlot, Ruby Cabernet, Cabernet Sauvignon Merlot, Vintage Port, Burke & Wills Tawny Port.
summary Remarkably consistent tasting notes across all wine styles from all vintages since 1989 attest to the expertise of ex-Mildara winemaker Tony Murphy, now making the Trentham wines from his family vineyards. All of the wines, whether at the bottom or top end of the price range, offer great value for money. The winery restaurant is also recommended. National retail distribution; exports to Europe.

Trentham Estate Viognier

▼▼▼▽ 2001 Medium yellow-green; a clean, soft bouquet with hints of fruit pastille in true varietal mode, then a modest entry onto the palate, picking up and finishing well. I'm not too sure that the extra dollars for the V-word are justified, but then that is true of almost all Australian Viogniers made to date. **rating:** 84

best drinking 2002–2003 **best vintages** NA **drink with** Creamy pasta • $17

Trentham Estate Chardonnay

▼▼▼▼ 2001 Medium yellow-green; the bouquet opens quietly, with nice fruit and oak balance, but not a lot happening. The wine moves up a gear on the palate, with lively, tangy, citrussy fruit providing attractive, slightly squeaky, mouthfeel. As ever, good value. **rating:** 86

best drinking 2002–2003 **best vintages** '89, '90, '92, '95, '98, '99, '01 **drink with** Stir-fried abalone • $14

Trentham Estate Noble Taminga (375 ml)

▼▼▼▽ 2000 Bright yellow-green; a clean bouquet with tropical fruit, then a peach and spice-accented palate with moderate sweetness and balanced acidity. Good value. **rating:** 83

best drinking 2002–2003 **best vintages** NA **drink with** Fruit flan • $9

Trentham Estate Cellar Reserve Shiraz

▼▼▼▼ 1998 Medium red-purple; the bouquet has a neat mix of red berry/dark cherry and more savoury notes; the palate initially traps you with its vanilla smoothie flavours and feel, but after a second taste the inherent complexity of the wine asserts itself, as do the ripe tannins on the close. Made from 50-year-old vines; good value. **rating:** 89

best drinking 2002–2007 **best vintages** NA **drink with** Barbecued beef • $19

Trentham Estate Nebbiolo

▼▼▼▽ 2000 Light to medium red-purple, slightly jammy/cooked overtones to spicy, almost lemony aromas underneath. A touch of oak and slightly jammy fruit on the palate provide sweetening; nebbiolo texture is there, though not so much the flavour. **rating:** 84

best drinking 2002–2004 **best vintages** NA **drink with** Porcini risotto • $14.50

trevelen farm ★★★☆

Weir Road, Cranbrook, WA 6321 **region** Great Southern
phone (08) 9826 1052 **fax** (08) 9826 1209 **open** Thu–Mon 10–4.30 or by appointment
winemaker Michael Staniford (Contract) **production** 4000 **est.** 1993
product range ($16–18 R) Riesling, Sauvignon Blanc Semillon, Chardonnay, Cabernet Sauvignon Merlot.

summary John and Katie Sprigg, together with their family, operate a 1300-hectare wool, meat and grain-producing farm, run on environmental principles with sustainable agriculture at its heart. As a minor, but highly successful, diversification they established 5 hectares of sauvignon blanc, riesling, chardonnay, cabernet sauvignon and merlot in 1993, adding 1.5 hectares of shiraz in 2000. Vines, it seems, are in the genes, for John Sprigg's great- great-grandparents established 20 hectares of vines at Happy Valley, SA, in the 1870s. The quality of the wines is as consistent as the prices are modest, and visitors to the cellar door have the added attraction of both garden and forest walks, the latter among 130 hectares of remnant bush which harbours many different orchids which flower from May to December.

Trevelen Farm Riesling
▼▼▼▼ 2001 Light straw-green; the clean, light bouquet has a mix of apple blossom and delicate lime, the fine, delicate, quite intense palate with tingling acidity on the finish. **rating: 88**

best drinking 2002–2007 best vintages '00 drink with Fresh asparagus • $16

Trevelen Farm Sauvignon Blanc Semillon
▼▼▼▼ 2001 Light green-yellow; a clean, crisp bouquet has relatively little fruit aromatics, but the wine opens up on the palate with sweet citrus and a touch of passionfruit providing pleasant mouthfeel through to the finish. **rating: 86**

best drinking 2002–2003 best vintages NA drink with Sauteed scallops • $16

Trevelen Farm Chardonnay
▼▼▼▽ 2001 Light green-yellow; the tangy bouquet has nectarine and citrus, some barrel-ferment inputs, and then a slightly vegetal cast. The palate is tight, citrussy, proclaiming its cool climate, before finishing with pungent acidity. Not really ripe, and it is probable the acidity will well outlive the fruit. **rating: 84**

best drinking 2002–2004 best vintages NA drink with Sweetbreads • $17

Trevelen Farm Cabernet Merlot
▼▼▼▼ 2000 Medium red-purple; red berry fruit with a touch of vanilla on the bouquet leads into an attractively ripe palate with an array of redcurrant, mulberry and blackcurrant fruit, complemented by soft tannins and oak, with a quite sweet finish (fruit, not residual sugar). **rating: 87**

best drinking 2003–2008 best vintages NA drink with Leg of lamb • $18

trevor jones ★★★☆
Barossa Valley Highway, Lyndoch, SA 5351 **region** Barossa Valley
phone (08) 8524 4303 **fax** (08) 8524 4880 **open** 7 days 9–6
winemaker Trevor Jones **production** 2000 **est.** 1996
product range ($15–39 CD) Riesling, Virgin Chardonnay, Dry Grown Shiraz, Cabernet Merlot.
summary Trevor Jones is an industry veteran, with vast experience in handling fruit from the Barossa Valley, Eden Valley and Adelaide Hills. He has finally taken the step of introducing his own strikingly designed label, using grapes purchased from various contract growers, with the first wines going on sale in 1996. Exports to the US (very successful) and Japan.

Trevor Jones Dry Grown Barossa Shiraz
▼▼▼▽ 1998 Full red-purple; a massive wine, with huge extract of leather and prune aromas and flavours. Very much in the Battlestar Galactica style favoured by Robert Parker et al. **rating: 83**

best drinking 2008–2018 best vintages '95, '96 drink with Beef Wellington • $39

tuck's ridge ★★★★
37 Shoreham Road, Red Hill South, Vic 3937 **region** Mornington Peninsula
phone (03) 5989 8660 **fax** (03) 5989 8579 **open** 7 days 12–5
winemaker Phillip Kittle **production** 12 000 **est.** 1988
product range ($14–45 CD) Riesling, Chardonnay, Pinot Noir, Altera Pinot Noir,Callanans Road Pinot Noir, A Trial Selection Pinot Noir, Reserve Pinot Noir, Merlot; under the Prentice brand Victoria Chardonnay, Whitfield Pinot Gris, Pinot Noir, Nebbiolo.
summary After an initial burst of frenetic activity following its launch in July 1993, Tuck's Ridge has slowed down a little. Nonetheless, plantings have been increased to a little over 25 hectares, making it one of the largest vineyards in production on the Mornington Peninsula, with wine quality to match. Rumours of a sale in early 2002 turned out to be entirely wrong. Tuck's Ridge has sold its Red Hill vineyard for $2.4 million, and used the proceeds to retire debt and acquire the Prentice wine brand, which will henceforth be available both at retail and through the Tuck's Ridge cellar door.

Tuck's Ridge Riesling

▼▼▼▼ **2001** Light straw-green; the bouquet is clean, with some flinty mineral aromas, but neutral fruit. The firm palate is predominantly flinty/minerally, again lacking fruit flavour, though well enough made. Could develop more with time in bottle. **rating:** 85

▼▼▼▼▽ **2000** Very pale straw-green; exceptionally youthful, fresh and crisp, with some apple aromas; the delicate and fresh palate has a mix of sweet apple and passionfruit flavours; all in all, has affinities with the Coonawarra style of Riesling. **rating:** 91

best drinking 2002–2005 **best vintages** '00 **drink with** Fresh asparagus • $19

Tuck's Ridge Chardonnay

▼▼▼▼ **2000** Light green-yellow; a clean, crisp bouquet which is not especially fruity, although nectarine and melon are certainly there; the palate is pleasant, but lacks intensity; on the other hand, the oak handling is good. **rating:** 85

best drinking 2002–2004 **best vintages** '99 **drink with** Thai cuisine • NA

Prentice Whitlands Pinot Noir

▼▼▼▼ **1999** Medium red-purple; the moderately intense bouquet has some plummy/savoury varietal character, the palate nicely focussed and correct, yet seems to have lost the edge of fruit complexity which it probably once had. That said, the best by far from the King Valley/Whitlands region so far. **rating:** 87

best drinking 2001–2004 **best vintages** NA **drink with** Smoked chicken • $25

Tuck's Ridge Merlot

▼▼▼▼ **2000** Medium red, starting to lose its purple hues; a savoury/leafy/olivaceous/earthy bouquet which is strongly varietal and attractive is somewhat let down by the palate, where the green notes tend towards sharpness. **rating:** 85

best drinking 2002–2005 **best vintages** NA **drink with** Braised veal • NA

tumbarumba wine cellars   NR

Sunnyside, Albury Close, Tumbarumba, NSW 2653 **region** Tumbarumba
phone (02) 6948 3055 **fax** (02) 6948 3055 **open** Weekends and public holidays, or by appointment
winemaker Charles Sturt University (Contract) **production** 600 **est.** 1990
product range ($15–25) Chardonnay, Pinot Noir and Pinot Chardonnay sparkling wines under the Black Range label, with further individual labels likely for the future.
summary Tumbarumba Cellars has taken over the former George Martins Winery (itself established in 1990) to provide an outlet for wines made from Tumbarumba region grapes. It is essentially a co-operative venture, involving local growers and businessmen, and with modest aspirations to growth.

tumbarumba wine estates   NR

Maragle Valley via Tumbarumba, NSW 2653 **region** Tumbarumba
phone (02) 6948 4457 **fax** (02) 6948 4457 **open** Not
winemaker Charles Sturt University (Contract) **production** NA **est.** 1995
product range Chardonnay, Pinot Chardonnay Sparkling.
summary Having established his vineyards progressively since 1982, Frank Minutello decided to seek to add value (and interest) to the enterprise by having a small proportion of his production vinified at Charles Sturt University, commencing with the 1995 vintage. The wines are sold by mail order and from The Elms Restaurant in Tumbarumba.

turkey flat   ★★★★☆

Bethany Road, Tanunda, SA 5352 **region** Barossa Valley
phone (08) 8563 2851 **fax** (08) 8563 3610 **open** 7 days 11–5
winemaker Peter Schell **production** 12 000 **est.** 1990
product range ($12–32 R) Semillon, Rosé, Grenache Noir, Butchers Block (Mataro Shiraz Grenache blend), Shiraz, Cabernet Sauvignon.
summary The establishment date of Turkey Flat is given as 1990 but it might equally well have been 1870 (or thereabouts), when the Schulz family purchased the Turkey Flat vineyard, or 1847, when the vineyard was first planted to the very shiraz which still grows today. In addition there are 8 hectares of very old grenache and 8 hectares of much younger semillon and cabernet sauvignon, together with a total of 7.3 hectares of mourvèdre, dolcetto and (a recent arrival) marsanne. An on-site winery completed just prior to the 2001 vintage will give Turkey Flat even greater control over its wine production. Retail distribution in Adelaide, Melbourne and Sydney; exports to the US, the UK and Belgium.

Turkey Flat Semillon Marsanne

TTTT 2001 Medium yellow-green; a complex bouquet with ripe citrus/citrus rind and a background wash of oak from partial barrel fermentation in French oak. A solid wine in the mouth, with good texture and structure; particularly good value.   **rating:** 86

best drinking 2002–2003 **best vintages** NA **drink with** Roast turkey breast • $12

Turkey Flat Rosé

TTTTY 2001 Vivid, light purple-red; the bouquet offers an exotic mix of crushed rose petals and citrus, merging into a mix of cherries, spices and leaves on the vibrant palate.   **rating:** 90

best drinking 2001–2002 **best vintages** '99, '00 **drink with** Nothing or anything • $14

Turkey Flat Shiraz

TTTTT 2000 Medium to full red-purple; an ultra-smooth bouquet with rich, dark plum fruit, then a perfectly assembled palate with a core of dark, satiny fruit, sweet but in no way jammy. Oak travels in the back of the plane.   **rating:** 94

TTTTT 1999 The spotlessly clean, scented bouquet offers an array of cherry, spice, earth and vanilla; the particularly harmonious balance and extract of the palate is constructed around the red berry fruit at its core, amplified by spice, chocolate and soft tannins. A bargain in these days of stratospheric prices for 100-year-old vine Shiraz.   **rating:** 94

best drinking 2005–2015 **best vintages** '90, '92, '93, '94, '98, '99, '00 **drink with** Braised beef • $32

Turkey Flat Butchers Block (Matro, Shiraz, Grenache Blend)

TTTT 2000 Bright, light to medium red-purple; a spotlessly clean and fragrant bouquet with ripe berry and spice, then a palate with attractive fruit flavours; as ever structurally slightly weak, for reasons I do not know.   **rating:** 87

TTTT 1999 Medium red-purple; clean, juicy berry and plum fruit aromas lead into a soft, round, juicy palate, with touches of mint and very fine tannins. Oak makes a minimal impact.   **rating:** 87

best drinking 2002–2007 **best vintages** NA **drink with** Mushroom risotto • $25

Turkey Flat Cabernet Sauvignon

TTTT 2000 Medium red-purple, with some development evident. Savoury/earthy/cedary notes over a core of varietal fruit on the bouquet, then a nicely framed, savoury palate with a mix of berry, earth and bitter chocolate.   **rating:** 88

TTTT 1999 Medium red, with the purple starting to shift; spicy/leafy/earthy aromas of light to moderate intensity are repeated on the palate which, like the bouquet, is of light to medium body. There are some blackberry and chocolate flavours in the background, but in this vintage doesn't sing.   **rating:** 86

best drinking 2005–2010 **best vintages** '97 **drink with** Roast leg of lamb • $27

turramurra estate   ★★★☆

RMB 4327 Wallaces Road, Dromana, Vic 3926 **region** Mornington Peninsula
phone (03) 5987 1146 **fax** (03) 5987 1286 **open** 12–5 first weekend of the month or by appointment
winemaker David Leslie **production** 6000 **est.** 1989
product range ($26–40 CD) Sauvignon Blanc, Chardonnay, Pinot Noir, Shiraz, Cabernet Sauvignon.
summary Dr David Leslie gave up his job as a medical practitioner after completing the Bachelor of Applied Science (Wine Science) at Charles Sturt University to concentrate on developing the family's 10-hectare estate at Dromana. Wife Paula is the viticulturist. Limited retail distribution in Melbourne and Sydney; exports to the UK.

Turramurra Estate Sauvignon Blanc

TTTT 1999 Light yellow-green; light mineral and herb fruit aromatics, together with oak spices lead into a palate which is intriguingly subdued and quite minerally, and not at all threatened by the oak. The suspicion has to be that the wine is going through transition, or, at the very least, may have had more to say 12 months ago.   **rating:** 85

best drinking 2001–2002 **best vintages** NA **drink with** Creamy seafood pasta • $28

Turramurra Estate Pinot Noir

TTTT 1999 Light to medium red-purple; an undeniably complex bouquet with dusty, savoury, foresty aromatics is followed by a palate with a core of plummy fruit with the aromas of the bouquet surrounding that core. A powerful statement of style, which won a gold medal at the Royal Adelaide Wine Show in 2000.   **rating:** 88

best drinking 2001–2003 **best vintages** '97, '98 **drink with** Double-cooked veal shank • $40

12 acres ★★★

Nagambie–Rushworth Road, Bailieston, Vic 3608 **region** Goulburn Valley
phone (03) 5794 2020 **fax** (03) 5794 2020 **open** Thurs–Mon 10–6, July weekends only
winemaker Peter Prygodicz, Jana Prygodicz **production** 700 **est.** 1994
product range ($9–16 CD) Shiraz, Merlot, Grenache, Bailieston Red, Cabernet Franc, Cabernet Sauvignon.
summary The charmingly named 12 Acres is a red wine specialist, with Peter and Jana Prygodicz making the wines on site in a tiny winery. The wines could benefit from renewal of the oak in which they are matured; the underlying fruit is good.

☙ twelve staves wine company ★★★☆

Kangarilla Road, McLaren Vale, SA 5171 **region** McLaren Vale
phone (08) 8270 4387 **fax** (08) 8270 4387 **open** Not
winemaker Peter Dennis, Brian Light (Consultant) **production** 1500 **est.** 1997
product range ($17 R) Grenache.
summary Twelve Staves has a single vineyard block of a little under 5 hectares of 70-year-old, bush-pruned grenache vines. The highly experienced team of Peter Dennis and Brian Light (in a consulting role) produce an appealing wine in a lighter mode which has an eclectic range of retail outlets on the east coast, and limited exports.

Twelve Staves Grenache

▼▼▼▼ **2000** Light to medium red-purple; the bouquet opens with juicy berry aromas, then shows a touch of dusty vanilla oak; a lively, juicy cherry/berry-flavoured palate without excessive tannin extract or oak provides an admirable, relatively light-bodied luncheon/cafe style. **rating:** 85

best drinking 2001–2004 **best vintages** NA **drink with** Light red meat dishes • $17

twin bays NR

Lot 1 Martin Road, Yankalilla, SA 5203 **region** Southern Fleurieu
phone (08) 8267 2844 **fax** (08) 8239 0877 **open** Weekends and holidays
winemaker Bruno Giorgio, Alan Dyson **production** 1000 **est.** 1989
product range ($11–23 CD) Riesling, Liqueur Riesling, Shiraz, Wild Grenache, Cabernet Shiraz, Cabernet Sauvignon, Fortifieds.
summary Adelaide doctor and specialist Bruno Giorgio, together with wife Ginny, began the establishment of their vineyard back in 1989, but have opted to keep it small (and beautiful). The principal plantings are of cabernet sauvignon, with lesser amounts of shiraz and riesling, taking the total plantings to 2 hectares. It was the first vineyard to be established in the Yankalilla district of the Fleurieu Peninsula, and has spectacular views from the vineyard sited on the slopes above Normanville, taking in hills, valleys, the coastal plains, and the rugged Rapid Bay and more tranquil Lady Bay as the prime focus. The cellar door features the ocean views, the wines on sale being complemented by red and white wine vinegar, Fleurieu olive oil and other local souvenirs.

twin valley estate NR

Hoffnungsthal Road, Lyndoch, SA 5351 **region** Barossa Valley
phone (08) 8524 4584 **fax** (08) 8524 4978 **open** Weekends 10–5
winemaker Fernando Martin, Kay Martin **production** 3500 **est.** 1990
product range ($9–18 CD) Traminer, Frontignac Spätlese, Eden Valley Riesling, Semillon Chardonnay, Cabernet Sauvignon Franc, Classic Burgundy, Pinot Cabernet, White Port, Martin's Mead.
summary While Fernando Martin has always had his sights set firmly on the tourist trade, the Twin Valley Estate wines are more than acceptable, the spicy, limey Frontignac Spätlese being a particularly good example of its kind.

2 bud spur ★★★★★

Unit 2, 8 Binney Court, Sandy Bay, Tas 7005 (postal) **region** Southern Tasmania
phone (03) 6225 0711 **fax** (03) 6233 3477 **open** Not
winemaker Michael Vishacki **production** 300 **est.** 1996
product range ($20 ML) Sauvignon Blanc, Chardonnay, Pinot Noir.

summary Phil Barker and Anne Lasala commenced establishing 2.2 hectares of vineyard in 1996. Phil Barker has the most extraordinary qualifications, having worked as a chef for over ten years after acquiring a PhD in botany, and is now a botanist with the Tasmanian Parks and Wildlife Department. There was some agonising about the name; originally named Latitude, it has now become 2 Bud Spur, a term viticulturists are very familiar with, but which will intrigue the average wine drinker. The rating, incidentally, is given for its Pinot Noir.

2 Bud Spur Pinot Noir

▼▼▼▼▼ **2000** Medium to full red-purple; a very ripe and dense bouquet exudes plum and blackberry; the palate has rich, complex and powerful as the bouquet promises, with mouthfilling dark fruits and soft tannins. Chairman's Trophy at Tasmanian Wines Show 2002. **rating:** 95

best drinking 2002–2008 **best vintages** '00 **drink with** Venison • NA

tyrrell's ★★★★★

Broke Road, Pokolbin, NSW 2321 **region** Lower Hunter Valley
phone (02) 4993 7000 **fax** (02) 4998 7723 **open** Mon–Sat 8–5
winemaker Andrew Spinaze, Mark Richardson **production** 800 000 **est.** 1858
product range ($7–50 R) At the bottom end the large-volume Long Flat White, Chardonnay and Red; next in price is Traditional Range of Traminer Riesling, Twin Wells Chardonnay, Twin Wells Shiraz Cabernet; then Old Winery Semillon, Semillon Sauvignon Blanc, Chardonnay Semillon, Verdelho, Chardonnay, Pinot Noir, Shiraz, Cabernet Merlot; Rufus Stone Heathcote Shiraz, Rufus Stone McLaren Shiraz, Rufus Stone McLaren Vale Merlot; next the Individual Vineyard range of wines including Lost Block Semillon, Shee-Oak Chardonnay, Moon Mountain Chardonnay, Eclipse Pinot Noir, Brokenback Shiraz; then Reserve Stevens range of Semillon, Shiraz; at the very top Vat 1 Semillon, Vat 47 Chardonnay, Vat 6 Pinot Noir, Vat 8 Shiraz Cabernet, Vat 9 Shiraz. Also Sparkling, Fortifieds.
summary An extraordinary family winery which has grown up from an insignificant base in 1960 to become one of the most influential mid-sized companies. Its wines range from cheap, volume-driven Long Flat White up to the super-premium Vat 47 Chardonnay and Vat 1 Semillon, a promiscuous gatherer of trophies and gold medals as it ages. There is a similar range of price and style with the red wines, and in recent years Tyrrell's has simply never faltered within the parameters of price and style. Exports to all of the major markets throughout North America, Europe and Southeast Asia.

Tyrrell's Lost Block Semillon

▼▼▼▼▼ **2001** Light to medium yellow-green; for such a young wine, a complex and quite rich mix of herb and lightly browned toast. Long, intense lemon and herb flavours have subliminal fruit sweetness on the palate, but a bone dry finish. **rating:** 94

best drinking 2003–2011 **best vintages** '93, '94, '96, '97, '99, '00, '01 **drink with** Calamari • $20

Tyrrell's Old Winery Semillon

▼▼▼▼ **2001** Light green-yellow; a clean, fresh bouquet offers pure varietal character with its mix of lemon and herb; the palate is very lively, the spritz-tingle not overplayed. **rating:** 87

best drinking 2001–2003 **best vintages** '99 **drink with** Cold seafood • $14

Tyrrell's Stevens Reserve Semillon

▼▼▼▼▽ **1998** Light to medium green-yellow; the bouquet is clean and firm, still quite youthful; no toast yet, nor even honey. The palate is likewise still developing, but has impeccable balance with soft citrus fruit on the mid-palate braced with fresh, crisp acidity on the finish. Right in the Stevens style slot. **rating:** 93

best drinking 2003–2013 **best vintages** '96, '97, '98 **drink with** Balmain bugs • $25

Tyrrell's Vat 1 Semillon

▼▼▼▼▼ **1997** Light to medium yellow-green; has come through its transition phase and out of its shell to a remarkable degree over the past 12 months. A particularly complex bouquet with toasty/smoky characters, then a palate which opens with a similar range of flavours before tightening up and focussing with minerally notes and a long, piercing finish. **rating:** 94

▼▼▼▼▼ **1996** Glowing yellow-green, the still-tight bouquet has abundant ripe, tangy, citrus and honey aromas, the outstanding palate long and concentrated, citrussy, and sustained by minerally acidity on the finish. **rating:** 96

best drinking 2003–2013 **best vintages** '75, '76, '77, '86, '87, '89, '90, '91, '92, '93, '94, '95, '96, '97 **drink with** Calamari • $48

Tyrrell's Old Winery Chardonnay

ᵀᵀᵀᵀ 2001 Light to medium yellow-green; a smooth, clean bouquet with some interesting herbal hints; the palate is lively, fresh and tangy, with good length and mouthfeel.   **rating:** 86

best drinking 2001–2003 **best vintages** '97 **drink with** Turkey breast • $14

Tyrrell's Shee-Oak Chardonnay

ᵀᵀᵀᵀᵧ 2001 Medium yellow-green; scented, spicy/oily aromatics are an uncertain opening, but the palate is tangy, high flavoured, with intense fruit and length; an unwooded Chardonnay on steroids.   **rating:** 90

best drinking 2001–2002 **best vintages** '97, '01 **drink with** Steamed fish • $20

Tyrrell's Vat 47 Chardonnay

ᵀᵀᵀᵀᵀ 2000 Medium yellow-green; a fine, elegant, silky smooth bouquet offers melon, stone fruit and positive but integrated oak. The palate has great balance, but also intensity and life; nectarine, stone fruit, a touch of cream and good acidity to close.   **rating:** 95

best drinking 2002–2004 **best vintages** '73, '79, '84, '90, '92, '95, '97, '99, '00 **drink with** Fresh, slow-cooked salmon • $48

Tyrrell's Rufus Stone Heathcote Shiraz

ᵀᵀᵀᵀ 1999 Medium to full red-purple; clean, ripe red berry and plum fruit with a mix of spice and vanilla oak on the bouquet flows into a ripe, luscious, but medium-bodied palate with good balance and structure.   **rating:** 89

best drinking 2004–2011 **best vintages** '97, '98, '99 **drink with** Pot-roasted quail • $23

Tyrrell's Rufus Stone McLaren Vale Shiraz

ᵀᵀᵀᵀ 2000 Moderately intense but bright purple-red; the bouquet is quite fragrant, showing damson plum and minimal oak, the medium-bodied palate offering clean, fresh fruit, subtle oak and soft tannins. Like the Heathcote Shiraz, far, far lighter than prior vintages, and far from typical of McLaren Vale. Presumably the vintage at work.   **rating:** 86

best drinking 2002–2006 **best vintages** NA **drink with** Beef Bordelaise • $23

Tyrrell's Stevens Shiraz

ᵀᵀᵀᵀ 1998 Medium purple-red; clean, fresh berry fruit with some plum and subtle oak on the bouquet, then a palate with more power thanks to another layer of fruit and some of the earthy, regional Hunter grip.   **rating:** 88

best drinking 2003–2013 **best vintages** '94, '95 **drink with** Moroccan lamb • $30

Tyrrell's Vat 9 Shiraz

ᵀᵀᵀᵀᵧ 1997 Medium red-purple; the bouquet is distinctly riper than the 1996, with strong, plummy fruit, and even a touch of prune. Spice, plum and prune fruit on the palate is complemented by an attractive touch of sweet oak and ripe tannins. An excellent outcome for a less than perfect vintage.   **rating:** 91

ᵀᵀᵀᵀᵧ 1996 Medium red, with just a touch of purple; the bouquet has typically restrained earthy Hunter Valley varietal character, the palate picking up a gear, with fresh cherry fruit and savoury spices, finishing with quite bright acidity and subtle oak. A wine which encourages the second glass, with the length of the palate becoming ever more apparent.   **rating:** 92

best drinking 2002–2007 **best vintages** '81, '83, '85, '87, '89, '90, '91, '92 **drink with** Venison • $48

Tyrrell's Vat 8 Shiraz Cabernet

ᵀᵀᵀᵀᵧ 1998 Medium to full red-purple; the bouquet is smooth, with sweet red berry fruit and quite pronounced cedary oak. The palate has plenty of depth and richness, with cassis, spice and savoury characters, rounded off with more cedary oak.   **rating:** 93

best drinking 2003–2013 **best vintages** '97, '98 **drink with** Yearling steak • $50

Tyrrell's Rufus Stone McLaren Vale Merlot

ᵀᵀᵀᵀ 2000 Medium red-purple; the clean, moderately intense bouquet has a range of leafy/earthy aromas within the expected varietal spectrum; the palate has much sweeter fruit than the bouquet suggests, gliding across the tongue. Makes the Rufus Stone Shiraz of the same vintage even more anomalous.   **rating:** 89

best drinking 2004–2008 **best vintages** '99 **drink with** Rack of veal • $25

uleybury wines ★★★☆

Uley Road, Uleybury, SA 5114 **region** Mount Lofty Ranges Zone
phone (08) 8280 7335 **fax** (08) 8280 7925 **open** Since June 2002
winemaker Tony Pipicella **production** 5000 **est.** 1995
product range ($16.50–19.50 R) Semillon, Uley Chapel Shiraz, Grenache, Grenache Shiraz, Cabernet Sauvignon.
summary The Pipicella family – headed by Italian-born Tony – has established nearly 45 hectares of vineyard near the township of One Tree Hill in the Mt Lofty Ranges. Ten varieties have been planted, with more planned. Daughter Natalie Pipicella, who has completed the wine marketing course at the University of South Australia, was responsible for overseeing the design of labels, the promotion and advertising, and the creation of the website. The wines are currently being made off-site under the direction of Tony Pipicella. A cellar door opened in June 2002; an on-site winery will follow.

Uleybury Semillon

▼▼▼▼ 2001 Light to medium yellow-green; despite being made in an unoaked style, both the bouquet and palate have a layered and textured richness and complexity akin to that of white Bordeaux. Herb and citrus aromas, and a long palate, have garnered gold and silver medals early in the life of the wine. **rating:** 89

best drinking 2002–2006 **best vintages** NA **drink with** Antipasto • $19.50

Uleybury Grenache

▼▼▼▽ 2000 Light to medium red-purple; the fragrant bouquet has unmistakable jammy/raspberry varietal fruit, the palate in the same spectrum, offering sweet berry tinged with spice. Well priced for casual drinking. **rating:** 83

best drinking 2002–2003 **best vintages** NA **drink with** Takeaway • $11.90

undercliff NR

Yango Creek Road, Wollombi, NSW 2325 **region** Lower Hunter Valley
phone (02) 4998 3322 **fax** (02) 4998 3322 **open** Weekends 10–4 or by appointment
winemaker David Carrick **production** 1400 **est.** 1990
product range ($15–20 CD) Semillon, Shiraz, Sparkling Shiraz.
summary Peter and Lesley Chase now own Undercliff, but it continues to function as both winery cellar door and art gallery. The wines, produced from 2.5 hectares of estate vineyards, have won a number of awards in recent years at the Hunter Valley Wine Show and the Hunter Valley Small Winemakers Show. All of the wine is sold through cellar door.

upper reach vineyard ★★★★

77 Memorial Avenue, Baskerville, WA 6056 **region** Swan District
phone (08) 9296 0078 **fax** (08) 9296 0278 **open** Thu-Sun and public holidays 11–5
winemaker Derek Pearse, John Grifiths **production** 2000 **est.** 1996
product range ($13–18 CD) Verdelho, Chenin Blanc, Unwooded Chardonnay, Reserve Chardonnay, Shiraz, Cabernet Sauvignon.
summary The 10-hectare property, situated on the banks of the upper reaches of the Swan River, was purchased by Laura Rowe and Derek Pearse in 1996. 4 hectares of 12-year-old chardonnay made up the original vineyard, being expanded with 1.5 hectares of shiraz and 1 hectare of cabernet sauvignon, with plans for trials of merlot, zinfandel and barbera in the pipeline. The partners also own 4 hectares of vineyard in the Margaret River region planted to shiraz, cabernet sauvignon, merlot and semillon, but the releases so far have been drawn from the Swan Valley vineyards. The fish on the label, incidentally, is black bream, which can be found in the pools of the Swan River during the summer months.

Upper Reach Vineyard Verdelho

▼▼▼▼▽ 2000 Light to medium green-yellow; a clean, attractive bouquet with a mix of citrus, fruit salad and honeysuckle aromas is followed by a palate with excellent balance, length and mouthfeel, wending its way smoothly through fruit salad flavours. **rating:** 90

best drinking 2001–2005 **best vintages** '00 **drink with** Avocado terrine • $12

Upper Reach Vineyard Unwooded Chardonnay

▼▼▼▼ 2001 Light green-yellow; a clean and fragrant bouquet with a mix of nectarine and citrus flows through to an elegant, fresh unforced example of unwooded Chardonnay which succeeds admirably. **rating:** 86

best drinking 2001–2003 **best vintages** NA **drink with** Summer salad • $13

Upper Reach Vineyard Reserve Chardonnay

♥♥♥♥ 2000 Light to medium green-yellow; the bouquet is clean, with harmonious and subtle oak inputs. Nectarine and citrus fruit on the palate has good length before an ever-so-faintly grippy finish. **rating:** 88

best drinking 2001–2003 **best vintages** NA **drink with** White rocks veal • $16

Upper Reach Vineyard Shiraz

♥♥♥♥ 2000 Bright and clear purple-red. A fresh and clean bouquet with attractive red cherry/berry is followed by a well-modulated and balanced palate, offering savoury touches to the cherry fruit, complemented by fine tannins on the finish. **rating:** 87

♥♥♥♥ 1999 Medium red-purple; complex leathery/savoury/earthy aromas are developing as the wine starts to age in bottle; the palate has plenty of depth, power and extract, with spicy/earthy overtones to its red and black cherry fruit. **rating:** 88

best drinking 2003–2007 **best vintages** NA **drink with** Yearling beef • $17

Upper Reach Vineyard Cabernet Sauvignon

♥♥♥♥ 2000 Light to medium red-purple; light berry aromatics, together with touches of earth and cedar, on the bouquet are reflected in the palate, which has good structure and fine tannins. Yet another appealing wine from Upper Reach. **rating:** 86

♥♥♥♥ 1999 Medium red-purple; a gentle mix of blackberry, cedar, earth and vanilla is followed by a palate which mirrors the bouquet, with excellent oak balance and integration, and above average length. **rating:** 88

best drinking 2003–2008 **best vintages** NA **drink with** Rack of lamb • $15

vale view wines   NR

5 Berrys Road, Vale View, Qld 4352 **region** Queensland Zone
phone (07) 4696 2282 **fax** (07) 4696 2039 **open** Weekends and public holidays 10–5, 7 days during school holidays, or by appointment
winemaker Giovanni Chersini, Hazel Chersini **production** 600 **est.** 1999
product range ($9–17 CD) Semillon, Chardonnay, Wooded Chardonnay, Shiraz, Cabernet Sauvignon, Dolce Rosso, Muscat, fruit wines.
summary Giovanni (John) Chersini was born in Valle d'Isria (then in Italy but now part of Croatia) in a wine-growing region. Visits by John, wife Hazel and son Matthew to John's birthplace inspired the planting of a few experimental vines in 1991, and to the subsequent expansion of the vineyard to its present 2.4 hectares of cabernet sauvignon, shiraz, chardonnay, semillon and frontignac. A family affair it may be, but it is also a multicultural one in the fullest sense of the word: both Hazel and Matthew are nearing completion of the external course in wine science at Charles Sturt University, while John prefers to adhere to the philosophies and practices inherited from his forebears.

van de scheur   NR

O'Connors Lane, Pokolbin, NSW 2321 **region** Lower Hunter Valley
phone (02) 4998 7789 **fax** (02) 4998 7789 **open** Weekends 10–5
winemaker Kees Van De Scheur **production** 2000 **est.** 1995
product range ($16.50 CD) Semillon, Chardonnay, Shiraz.
summary Kees Van De Scheur is a Hunter Valley veteran, having spent the last 25 years in the Hunter Valley, first with the Robson Vineyard and then Briar Ridge, before leaving in November 1993 to establish his own winery and label. He has purchased part of the historic Ingleside property established by vigneron Frederick Ingle in 1872. After a hiatus of 60 years, vines have returned, with an initial planting of a little over 1 hectare (semillon, chardonnay and shiraz) since increased to 4 hectares.

varrenti wines   NR

Glenheather, Blackwood Road, Dunkeld, Vic 3294 **region** Grampians
phone (03) 5577 2368 **fax** (03) 5577 2367 **open** 7 days 12–3
winemaker Ettore Varrenti **production** NA **est.** 1999
product range ($12–14.99 R) Grenache, Grenache Shiraz, Cabernet Shiraz.
summary Ettore Varrenti has established 4 hectares of pinot noir, malbec, shiraz and cabernet sauvignon at the extreme southern end of the Grampians National Park. It is remote from any other winery, and appears to be on the edge of the Grampians region.

vasse felix ★★★★

Cnr Caves Road and Harmans Road South, Wilyabrup, WA 6284 **region** Margaret River
phone (08) 9756 5000 **fax** (08) 9755 5425 **open** 7 days 10–5
winemaker Clive Otto, Will Shields, David Dowden **production** 125 000 **est.** 1967
product range ($19–65 R) Classic Dry White, Semillon, Chardonnay, Heytesbury Chardonnay, NV Extra Brut, Noble Riesling, Classic Dry Red, Shiraz, Cabernet Merlot, Cabernet Sauvignon, Heytesbury (Cabernet blend).
summary In 1999 the production of Vasse Felix wines moved to a new 2000-tonne winery; the old winery is dedicated entirely to the restaurant and tasting rooms. A relatively new 140-hectare vineyard at Jindong in the north of the Margaret River supplies a large part of the increased fruit intake. National Australian distribution; exports to the US, UK, Europe and Asia.

Vasse Felix Semillon
▼▼▼▼ **2001** Light to medium yellow-green; strong, spicy barrel-ferment oak dominates the bouquet; fruit makes a partial comeback on the palate, but overall, the semillon merely seems to be a vehicle for the expansive (and expensive) use of oak. **rating:** 85
best drinking 2002–2005 **best vintages** '92, '93, '95, '96, '99 **drink with** Coquilles St Jacques • $22.50

Vasse Felix Chardonnay
▼▼▼▼ **2000** Medium yellow-green; a solid bouquet with ripe peach, fig and cashew fruit is followed by a similarly bold, ripe palate, with fair length. **rating:** 89
best drinking 2001–2003 **best vintages** '99 **drink with** Pork chops • $22.50

Vasse Felix Heytesbury Chardonnay
▼▼▼▼ **2000** Light to medium yellow-green; a sophisticated and complex bouquet with a range of spicy/nutmeg barrel ferment inputs on the melon and cashew base. The palate wanders away, with ripe, slightly alcoholic fruit and intrusive oak. A pity after the promising start. **rating:** 88
best drinking 2001–2003 **best vintages** '97, '98, '99 **drink with** Rich seafood • $35

Vasse Felix Noble Riesling 375 ml
▼▼▼▼ **2000** Very advanced golden hue; intense botrytis leads to a high-toned bouquet right on the razor's edge; the palate is powerful, rich and intense, but one wonders whether some of rot was less than noble. **rating:** 89
best drinking 2002–2004 **best vintages** '98 **drink with** Fresh fruit • $19

Vasse Felix Shiraz
▼▼▼▽ **2000** Medium red-purple; there is plenty of dusty/vanilla oak on the bouquet and palate, so much so that the earthy/oaky characters unduly dominate the wine. **rating:** 84
best drinking 2003–2007 **best vintages** '83, '85, '88, '90, '91, '92, '94, '96, '99 **drink with** Rich casseroles • $38

Vasse Felix Heytesbury
▼▼▼▼▼ **1999** Medium to full red-purple; the intense bouquet is driven primarily by blackberry and blackcurrant fruit, the oak present but well controlled; the medium to full-bodied palate has abundant, sweet (not jammy) berry fruit, the oak again in balance, the tannins particularly so. Seductively rich; most unlucky to miss out on the 2001 Top 100. **rating:** 95
best drinking 2004–2014 **best vintages** '95, '96, '97, '98, '99 **drink with** Beef Bordelaise • $35

Vasse Felix Cabernet Sauvignon
▼▼▼▼ **2000** Medium red-purple; the moderately intense bouquet has a mix of blackberry fruit and more savoury characters, the palate picking up those savoury notes with slightly spicy/leafy notes; not as ripe or charming as the '99 wine. **rating:** 85
best drinking 2005–2009 **best vintages** '85, '88, '90, '91, '94, '95, '96, '99 **drink with** Lamb cutlets • $30

vasse river wines NR

Bussell Highway, Carbunup, WA 6280 **region** Margaret River
phone (08) 9755 1111 **fax** (08) 9755 1111 **open** 7 days 10–5
winemaker Robert Credaro, Bernie Stanlake **production** 3500 **est.** 1993
product range ($14–20 CD) Semillon Sauvignon Blanc, Verdelho, Chardonnay, Shiraz, Ruby Red, Cabernet Merlot.

summary This is a major and rapidly growing business owned by the Credaro Family. Forty-five hectares of chardonnay, semillon, verdelho, sauvignon blanc, cabernet sauvignon, merlot and shiraz have been established on the typical gravelly red loam soils of the region. These plantings will be in full production by 2005, and it is intended to build a new winery and cellar door sales area prior to that time.

veritas ★★★★

94 Langmeil Road, Tanunda, SA 5352 **region** Barossa Valley
phone (08) 8562 3300 **fax** (08) 8562 1177 **open** Mon–Fri 9–5, weekends 11–5
winemaker Rolf Binder, Christa Deans **production** 14 000 **est.** 1955
product range ($10–30 CD) Riesling, Semillon, JJ Hahn Semillon, Chardonnay, Cabernet Shiraz, Cabernet Merlot, Binder's Bull's Blood, Shiraz Mourvèdre Pressings, Fortifieds.
summary The Hungarian influence is obvious in the naming of some of the wines, but Australian technology is paramount in shaping the generally very good quality. Veritas has 28 hectares of estate vineyards to draw on. A near-doubling of production has coincided with the establishment of export markets to the UK, Germany, Switzerland, Belgium, The Netherlands and the US.

Veritas Semillon

▼▼▼▼ **2001** Medium to full yellow-green; the powerful, herbaceous bouquet is followed by a full-bodied palate which has attractive freshness and length. The wine has a great deal of character already, and is one of those Semillons which is best drunk young. **rating:** 89

best drinking 2001–2003 **best vintages** NA **drink with** Smoked salmon pizza • $15

Veritas JJ Hahn Semillon

▼▼▼▼ **2001** Light yellow-green; both the bouquet and palate offer very pleasant, drink now characters, the palate with both flavour and length. **rating:** 85

best drinking 2001–2004 **best vintages** NA **drink with** Antipasto • $20

verona vineyard NR

Small Winemakers Centre, McDonalds Road, Pokolbin, NSW 2321 **region** Lower Hunter Valley
phone (02) 4998 7668 **fax** (02) 4998 7430 **open** 7 days 10–5
winemaker Greg Silkman, Gary Reed (Contract) **production** NA **est.** 1972
product range ($15–18.50 CD) Produces two ranges: under the Verona label are Verdelho, Semillon and Shiraz; also Tallamurra Verdelho, Chardonnay and Shiraz.
summary Verona has had a chequered history, and is still a significant business acting, as it does, as a sales point for a number of other Hunter Valley winemakers from its premises in McDonalds Road, directly opposite Brokenwood. The Verona wines come from 22 hectares at Muswellbrook, and 5 hectares surrounding the winery.

vicarys NR

Northern Road, Luddenham, NSW 2745 **region** South Coast Zone
phone (02) 4773 4161 **fax** (02) 4773 4411 **open** Mon–Fri 9–5, weekends 10–5
winemaker Chris Niccol **production** 1700 **est.** 1923
product range ($12–36 CD) Chardonnay, Semillon, Riesling, Gewürztraminer, Fume Blanc, Cabernet Sauvignon, Shiraz Cabernet Merlot, Sparkling, Fortifieds.
summary Vicarys justifiably claims to be the Sydney region's oldest continuously operating winery, having been established in a very attractive, large, stone shearing shed built about 1890. Most of the wines come from other parts of Australia, but the winery does draw upon 1 hectare of estate traminer and 3 hectares of chardonnay for those wines, and has produced some good wines of all styles over the years.

vico NR

Farm 1687 Beelbangera Road, Griffith, NSW 2680 **region** Riverina
phone (02) 6962 2849 **open** Mon–Fri 9–5
winemaker Ray Vico **production** 1200 **est.** 1973
product range ($5–15 CD) Semillon, Late Harvest Semillon, Barbera, Cabernet Sauvignon, Liqueur Muscat.
summary Ray Vico has been growing grapes for many years with 9 hectares of vines, more recently deciding to bottle and sell part of the production under the Vico label. From $60 to $70 a dozen for the table wines and $15 per bottle for the 1984 Liqueur Muscat, the prices are positively mouthwatering.

🦎 viking wines NR

RSD 108 Seppeltsfield Road, Marananga, SA 5355 **region** Barossa Valley
phone (08) 8562 3842 **fax** (08) 8562 4266 **open** Not
winemaker Rolf Binder (Contract) **production** 1000 **est.** 1995
product range ($12–50 ML) Dry White, Skumpa Sparkling Chardonnay, Late Harvest Frontignac, Grand Shiraz, Cabernet Sauvignon, Viking Gold White Port.
summary Based upon 40-year-old, dry-grown and near-organic vineyards with a yield of only 1-1.5 tonnes per acre, Viking Wines has been 'discovered' by Robert Parker with inevitable consequences for the price of its top Shiraz. There are in fact 6 hectares of shiraz and 2 of cabernet sauvignon; quaffing white wines are made from purchased grapes. The immensely experienced Rolf Binder is contract winemaker for this operation which sells its wine through the Ultimo Wine Centre in Sydney, by telephone/mail order and of course to the ever-thirsty United States market.

villa primavera NR

Mornington–Flinders Road, Red Hill, Vic 3937 **region** Mornington Peninsula
phone (03) 5989 2129 **fax** (03) 5931 0045 **open** Weekends, public holidays 10–5 and 7 days from Dec 26 to end January
winemaker Gennaro Mazzella **production** 300 **est.** 1984
product range ($18–30 CD) Chardonnay, Pinot Noir, Limoncello, Mèthode Champenoise.
summary A most unusual operation, which is in reality a family Italian-style restaurant at which the wine is principally sold and served, and which offers something totally different on the Mornington Peninsula. A consistent winner of tourism and food awards, it is praised by all who go there, particularly for the concerts staged throughout January each year.

vinden estate ★★★☆

17 Gillards Road, Pokolbin, NSW 2320 **region** Lower Hunter Valley
phone (02) 4998 7410 **fax** (02) 4998 7421 **open** 7 days 10–5
winemaker Guy Vinden, John Baruzzi (Consultant) **production** 1750 **est.** 1998
product range ($19–23 CD) Semillon, Chardonnay, Shiraz.
summary Sandra and Guy Vinden have bought their dream home with landscaped gardens in the foreground and 9 hectares of vineyard with the Brokenback mountain range in the distance. Much of the winemaking is now done on site, and increasingly drawn from the estate vineyards. The wines are available through the cellar door and also via a wine club which offers buying advantages to members. The restaurant, Thai on Gillards Road, is open weekends and public holidays from 10.30 am to 4 pm.

Vinden Estate Semillon
🍷🍷🍷🍷♀ **2001** Very light straw-green; the bouquet is clean, crisp and quite intense, with citrus notes; the palate is more delicate, with mineral and citrus flavours, running through to a long, bone-dry finish. In different style to the 2000.　　　　　**rating:** 92

best drinking 2003–2010 **best vintages** '01 **drink with** Rich fish dishes • $19

Vinden Estate Shiraz
🍷🍷🍷♀ **2000** Light to medium red-purple; the clean, moderately intense bouquet has red berry fruit and light oak, a mix of French and American. The light to medium-bodied palate has cherry and plum fruit on the mid-palate, followed by slightly hard tannins. A pleasant wine, but below expectations for the vintage.　　　　**rating:** 84

best drinking 2004–2008 **best vintages** NA **drink with** Yearling beef • $23

vinifera wines NR

194 Henry Lawson Drive, Mudgee, NSW 2850 **region** Mudgee
phone (02) 6372 2461 **fax** (02) 6372 6731 **open** 7 days 10–5.30
winemaker Steve Dodd, Tony MKendry, Phillip van Gent **production** 2500 **est.** 1997
product range ($14–19 CD) Riesling, Semillon, Chardonnay, Easter (dessert Semillon), Tempranillo, Tempranillo Cabernet Sauvignon Shiraz.
summary Tony and Debbie McKendry have much in common with Dave and Leslie Robertson of Thistle Hill, the latter another Mudgee winery. Dave Robertson lost a leg in a motorcycle accident, and used the compensation proceeds to establish Thistle Hill, turning adversity into good fortune. The McKendry's tell a

similar tale. Having lived in Mudgee for 15 years, Tony McKendry (a regional medical superintendent) and Debbie succumbed to the lure, and planted and tended their small (1.5-hectare) vineyard in 1995. In Debbie's words, 'Tony, in his spare two minutes per day, also decided to start Wine Science at Charles Sturt University in 1992'. She continues, 'His trying to live 27 hours per day (plus our 4 kids!) fell to pieces when he was involved in a severe car smash in 1997. Two months in hospital stopped full-time medical work, and the winery dreams became inevitable.' Here, too, financial compensation finally came through and the small winery was built.

vintina estate   NR

1282 Nepean Highway, Mount Eliza, Vic 3930 **region** Mornington Peninsula
phone (03) 9787 8166 **fax** (03) 9775 2035 **open** 7 days 9–5
winemaker Jim Filippone, Kevin McCarthy (Consultant) **production** 400 **est.** 1985
product range ($12–14 CD) Chardonnay, Semillon, Pinot Gris, Pinot Noir, Cabernet Sauvignon.
summary The initial releases of Vintina (the only wines tasted to date) were mediocre. With competent contract-winemaking, improvement might have been expected. However, no recent tastings.

virage   ★★★

13B Georgette Road, Gracetown, WA 6284 **region** Margaret River
phone (08) 9755 5318 **fax** (08) 9755 5318 **open** Not
winemaker Bernard Abbott **production** 1000 **est.** 1990
product range ($13–20 R) Sauvignon Blanc, Semillon Chardonnay, Traminer Riesling, Cabernet Shiraz Zinfandel, Cabernet Merlot.
summary Former Vasse Felix winemaker Bernard Abbott, together with wife Pascale, acquired (under long-term lease) the former government research station vineyard at Bramley Estate in 1990. Bernard Abbott makes the wines at a local Margaret River winery and sells them by mailing list and direct to retailer and restaurants in Perth, Melbourne and Sydney.

virgin hills   ★★★★★

Salisbury Road, Lauriston West via Kyneton, Vic 3444 **region** Macedon Ranges
phone (03) 5422 7444 **fax** (03) 5422 7400 **open** By appointment
winemaker Josh Steele, Chris Smales **production** 2500 **est.** 1968
product range ($55 R) A single Cabernet Sauvignon Shiraz Merlot Blend called Virgin Hills; occasional limited Reserve release.
summary Virgin Hills has passed through several ownership changes in a short period of time. It is now owned by Michael Hope, who presides over the fast-growing Hope Estate in the Hunter Valley. While there have been one or two raised eyebrows at some of the events in the Hunter Valley several years ago, the quality of the wines currently being made at Hope Estate cannot be questioned, any more than the quality of the 1998 Virgin Hills. So, after some prevarication, the five-star rating remains in place. Exports to the UK and the US.

Virgin Hills Cabernet Sauvignon Shiraz Merlot Blend

▼▼▼▼▽ **1999** Light to medium red-purple; the light but clean bouquet ranges through spice, leaf and cedar; the light to medium-bodied palate has spicy, fine small berry fruit, and very fine tannins. There is no suggestion the wine has been souped up in any way in a rather difficult vintage, and the mouthfeel is particularly pleasing. **rating:** 90
best drinking 2004–2009 **best vintages** '74, '75, '76, '80, '82, '85, '88, '90, '91, '92, '95, '98 **drink with** Duck • NA

voyager estate   ★★★★★

Lot 1 Stevens Road, Margaret River, WA 6285 **region** Margaret River
phone (08) 9757 6354 **fax** (08) 9757 6494 **open** 7 days 10–5
winemaker Cliff Royle **production** 30 000 **est.** 1978
product range ($18.50–80 R) Chenin Blanc, Semillon, Sauvignon Blanc Semillon, Tom Price Sauvignon Blanc Semillon, Tom Price Semillon Sauvignon Blanc, Marsanne, Chardonnay, Shiraz, Cabernet Sauvignon Merlot, Tom Price Cabernet Merlot.
summary Voyager Estate has come a long way since it was acquired by Michael Wright (of the mining family) in May 1991. It now has an important, high quality 63.5-hectare vineyard which puts Voyager Estate in the position of being able to select only the best parcels of fruit for its own label, and to supply

surplus (but high quality) wine to others. The Cape Dutch-style tasting room and vast rose garden are a major tourist attraction, although the winery itself remains in strictly utilitarian form. Exports to the UK, Holland, Switzerland, Singapore, Japan, New Zealand, Canada and the US.

Voyager Estate Sauvignon Blanc Semillon

▼▼▼▼▽ **2001** Light green-yellow; a pronounced herbal edge gives lift to the bouquet, while on the nicely balanced palate lemony/minerally acidity gives length. **rating:** 90

best drinking 2001–2003 **best vintages** '95, '97, '01 **drink with** Marinated octopus • $20

Voyager Estate Tom Price Semillon Sauvignon Blanc

▼▼▼▼▽ **1999** Light straw-green; very complex, spicy barrel-ferment oak and powerful, tangy fruit coalesce on the bouquet; the palate is extremely powerful, long and rich, with some alcohol-derived sweetness. A particularly successful vintage for the wine. **rating:** 93

best drinking 2002–2007 **best vintages** '96, '99 **drink with** Rich seafood • $45

Voyager Estate Chardonnay

▼▼▼▼▼ **2000** Medium green-yellow; the bouquet is complex, with rich barrel ferment characters coupled with intense citrus/nectarine fruit. The long and powerful palate tracks the bouquet, with excellent oak handling not detracting from the quality of the fruit. **rating:** 94

best drinking 2002–2007 **best vintages** '92, '93, '95, '96, '97, '98, '99, '00 **drink with** Braised pork neck • $33

Voyager Estate Shiraz

▼▼▼▼▽ **2000** Medium to full red-purple; ripe, black cherry fruit and sweet oak on the bouquet flow into a palate with dense, dark plum and black cherry fruit then forceful tannins. Needs time, but will repay patience. **rating:** 90

best drinking 2005–2012 **best vintages** '99, '00 **drink with** Barbecued leg of lamb • $28

Voyager Estate Cabernet Sauvignon Merlot

▼▼▼▼▼ **1999** Dense red-purple; the bouquet is packed with dense, ripe blackberry, blackcurrant and chocolate aromas; the powerful palate follows suit precisely, packed with fruit and tannins through a long finish. Needs ten years, and deserves 20. **rating:** 94

best drinking 2009–2019 **best vintages** '91, '93, '97, '98, '99 **drink with** Beef in red wine sauce • $40

Voyager Estate Tom Price Cabernet Sauvignon

▼▼▼▼▽ **1995** Medium red-purple, holding hue well; dark berry fruit is still the driving force on the bouquet, the oak subtle. The palate delivers all the expected power, with dark berry fruit and earthy/savoury/cedary undertones; persistent tannins still need another five years. **rating:** 93

best drinking 2006–2016 **best vintages** '92, '95 **drink with** Grain-fed beef • $80

wa-de-lock ★★★

76 Tyers Street, Stratford, Vic 3862 **region** Gippsland
phone (03) 5145 7050 **fax** (03) 5145 7030 **open** 7 days 10–6, summer weekends 10–8
winemaker Graeme Little **production** 2000 **est.** 1987
product range ($10–28.50 R) Chardonnay, Reserve Chardonnay, Sauvignon Blanc, Pinot Noir, EGL Cabernet Sauvignon, Avon Valley Tawny Port, Noble Sauvignon Blanc.
summary The initial plantings of pinot noir, cabernet sauvignon and sauvignon blanc in 1987 have been progressively expanded by increases in those varieties and the addition of chardonnay, nebbiolo, shiraz, merlot and durif, with 12 hectares under vine, some of it still coming into production. The quality of the wines has improved steadily as Graeme Little's handling of oak has become more assured, and the range of wines has increased. The wines have distributors in Melbourne, Tasmania and Queensland.

wadjekanup river estate NR

Flatrocks Road, Broomehill, WA 6318 **region** Great Southern
phone (08) 9825 3080 **fax** (08) 9825 3007 **open** By appointment
winemaker Michael Staniford (Alkoomi Contract) **production** 400 **est.** 1995
product range ($16–18 CD) Sauvignon Blanc, Shiraz.
summary The Witham family (Scott and Sue, Jim and Ann) began the development of Wadjekanup River Estate in 1995 as a minor diversification for a 3000-hectare wool, prime lamb, beef and cereal cropping enterprise worked by the family. They began with 1.2 hectares of shiraz and sauvignon blanc, since

extended to 8 hectares including a 1-hectare block of merlot with its first production in 2001. The aims for the future include a purpose-built cellar for storage and sales, with a possibility of farm-stay accommodation also being considered. The present wine range of Sauvignon Blanc and Shiraz will be extended with a varietal Merlot, and the possibility of a Semillon or other white somewhere down the track.

wallington wines   NR

Nyrang Creek Vineyard, Canowindra, NSW 2904 **region** Cowra
phone (02) 6344 7153 **fax** (02) 6344 7105 **open** By appointment
winemaker Blair Duncan, Murray Smith (Contract) **production** 1500 **est.** 1992
product range ($12–20 CD) Chardonnay, Shiraz, Cabernet Sauvignon.
summary Anthony and Margaret Wallington commenced the development of their Nyrang Creek Vineyard with 2 hectares of cabernet sauvignon in 1992, followed by 7 hectares of chardonnay in 1994, then shiraz (2 ha) and semillon (0.75 ha) in 1995, 0.75 ha each of cabernet franc and pinot noir in 1998, thereafter adding a mix of grenache, mourvèdre, tempranillo and viognier. Most of the production is sold, but Blair Duncan at Arrowfield makes the Wallington Chardonnay and Murray Smith of Canobolas-Smith Wines at Orange makes the Cabernet Sauvignon and Shiraz. The quality of the wines is such that exports to the US have already commenced.

walsh family winery   NR

90 Walnut Road, Bickley, WA 6076 **region** Perth Hills
phone (08) 9291 7341 **fax** (08) 9291 7341 **open** Weekends 10–5
winemaker Rob Marshall (Contract) **production** 250 **est.** 1995
product range ($15–17 CD) Shiraz.
summary Walsh Family Winery is aptly named: it is a partnership of the Walshes and their eight children. One of those children has established 4.2 hectares of vines near Bridgetown in the Great Southern, the grapes from which form part of the Walsh Family winery intake.

wandering brook estate   NR

PO Box 32, Wandering, WA 6308 **region** Peel
phone (08) 9884 1064 **fax** (08) 9884 1064 **open** Weekends 9.30–6
winemaker Steve Radikovich **production** 2000 **est.** 1989
product range ($10–14.95 CD) Verdelho, Chardonnay, Unwooded Chardonnay, Soft Red and White, Cabernet Sauvignon, Sparkling Verdelho, Port.
summary Laurie and Margaret White have planted 10 hectares of vines on their 130-year-old family property in a move to diversify. Up to 1994 the wines were made at Goundrey, currently at Jadran. Renamed Wandering Brook Estate late in 1994; up till then known as Red Hill Estate.

wandin valley estate   ★★★★

Wilderness Road, Lovedale, NSW 2320 **region** Lower Hunter Valley
phone (02) 4930 7317 **fax** (02) 4930 7814 **open** 7 days 10–5
winemaker Sarah-Kate Wilson, Karl Stockhausen (Consultant) **production** 10 000 **est.** 1973
product range ($13.50–28 CD) Estate Range of Semillon, Verdelho, Chardonnay, Cabernet Malbec Shiraz, Cabernet Merlot, Cabernet Sauvignon and Muscat; top of the range Sparkling Semillon, Reserve Semillon, Reserve Chardonnay, Bridie's Shiraz and Reserve Cabernet Sauvignon.
summary The former Millstone vineyard, now owned by the producer of Australian television's classic 'A Country Practice'. Rapidly developing Chardonnays have been the focal point of Wandin Valley's considerable show success. The estate also boasts a Cope-Williams-type village cricket oval and extensive cottage accommodation. Exports to Malaysia, Canada, Denmark and the UK. The Café Crocodile is open Wednesday-Sunday for lunch, and dinner Friday and Saturday.

Wandin Valley Estate Reserve Semillon

▼▼▼▼ 2001 Light green-straw; a fresh, lively and zesty bouquet with lemon rind and mineral aromatics is followed by a palate with the lemony fruit slightly sweeter than the bouquet, and having good length. Well priced.   **rating:** 89

best drinking 2002–2007 **best vintages** '01 **drink with** Grilled white-fleshed fish and lemon • $25

Wandin Valley WVE Reserve Chardonnay

TTTT 2000 Medium to full yellow-green; the complex bouquet shows strong barrel-ferment inputs onto ripe, peachy fruit; the full-bodied palate, again with ripe, peach and nectarine fruit, finishes with slightly twitchy acidity which suggests the acid may have been corrected late in the piece. Nonetheless, a good wine.

rating: 88

best drinking 2001–2003 **best vintages** '94, '97, '00 **drink with** Barbecued spatchcock • $20

Wandin Valley Estate Bridie's Shiraz

TTTTY 2000 Medium red-purple; ripe dark plum/dried prune aromas with attractive oak and undertones of sweet leather on the bouquet are followed by rich, ripe dark berry fruits on the fore-palate, then gently savoury tannins to close. Good structure.

rating: 90

best drinking 2003–2013 **best vintages** '00 **drink with** Moroccan lamb • $28

waninga ★★★★

Hughes Park Road, Sevenhill via Clare, SA 5453 **region** Clare Valley
phone (08) 8843 4395 **fax** (08) 8843 4395 **open** 7 days 10–5
winemaker Tim Adams, Jeffrey Grosset (Contract) **production** 1500 **est.** 1989
product range ($13–42 CD) Skilly Hills Riesling, Chenin Blanc, Ninnes, Shiraz, Reserve Shiraz, Cabernet Sauvignon, Hilary Port.
summary The large (36.3 hectares) vineyards owned by Waninga were established in 1974, but it was not until 1989 that a portion of the grapes was withheld from sale and vinified for the owners. Since that time, Waninga has produced some quite lovely wines, having wisely opted for very competent contract-winemaking. Exports to the US.

wansbrough wines NR

Richards Road, Ferguson, WA 6236 **region** Geographe
phone (08) 9728 3091 **fax** (08) 9728 3091 **open** Weekends 10–5
winemaker Willespie Wines (Contract) **production** 250 **est.** 1986
product range ($12–18 CD) Riesling, Semillon, Sauvignon Blanc, Constantia (late-picked Semillon), Shiraz Cabernet, Port.
summary Situated east of Dardanup in the picturesque Ferguson Valley, Wansbrough enjoys views of the distant Geographe Bay and the nearer State forest with the Bibblemun Track running along its northern and eastern borders. To taste the wine you need either to order by mail or visit the Wansbrough restaurant on weekends.

wantirna estate NR

Bushy Park Lane, Wantirna South, Vic 3152 **region** Yarra Valley
phone (03) 9801 2367 **fax** (03) 9887 0225 **open** Not
winemaker Reg Egan, Maryann Egan **production** 800 **est.** 1963
product range ($37–105 CD) Isabella Chardonnay, Lily Pinot Noir, Hannah Cabernet Franc Merlot, Amelia Cabernet Sauvignon Merlot.
summary Situated well within the boundaries of the Melbourne metropolitan area, Wantirna Estate is an outpost of the Yarra Valley, and one of the first established in the rebirth of the Valley. In deference to Reg Egan's very firmly held views on the subject, neither the winery nor the wines are rated.

Wantirna Estate Isabella Chardonnay

2000 Light to medium green-yellow; the bouquet offers a complex, subtle mix of melon, fig, cashew and gently smoky oak; the tight, well made palate has good length and acidity.

rating: 0

best drinking 2003–2007 **best vintages** NA **drink with** Pan-fried trout in black butter • $37

Wantirna Estate Lily Pinot Noir

2000 Light to medium red-purple; a complex mix of sappy/foresty/stemmy aromas on the bouquet; the palate opening with red fruits, but the foresty/cigar box characters tend to be the driving force. Belies its 13.6° alcohol.

rating: 0

best drinking 2003–2006 **best vintages** NA **drink with** Peking duck • $45

wards gateway ★★☆

Barossa Valley Highway, Lyndoch, SA 5351 **region** Barossa Valley
phone (08) 8524 4138 **open** 7 days 9–5.30
winemaker Ray Ward (plus Contract) **production** 800 **est.** 1979
product range ($7.50–17 CD) Riesling, Frontignac, Chardonnay, Frontignac Spätlese, Barossa Shiraz, Cabernet Sauvignon, Port.
summary The very old vines surrounding the winery produce the best wines, which are made without frills or new oak and sold without ostentation.

warrabilla ★★★★☆

Murray Valley Highway, Rutherglen, Vic 3685 **region** Rutherglen
phone (02) 6035 7242 **fax** (02) 6035 7298 **open** 7 days 10–5
winemaker Andrew Sutherland Smith **production** 6000 **est.** 1986
product range ($15–24 CD) Chardonnay, KV Brut Rosé, Brimin Shiraz, Reserve Shiraz, Merlot, Reserve Merlot, Reserve Durif, Reserve Cabernet, Vintage Port, Liqueur Muscat.
summary Former All Saints winemaker Andrew Sutherland Smith has leased a small winery at Corowa to make the Warrabilla wines from a 4-hectare vineyard developed by himself and Carol Smith in the Indigo Valley. The red wines are made in open fermenters, hand-plunged and basket-pressed, then matured in quality oak, mainly French. The quality of the Reserve wines is uniformly high, and it is a pleasure to have been able to taste them after many years.

Warrabilla Brimin Shiraz

▼▼▼▽ 2001 Medium purple-red; the light, clean bouquet has plum fruit, which picks up the pace on the ripe palate, with plum jam flavours and minimal tannins. **rating:** 83

best drinking 2002–2005 **best vintages** NA **drink with** Pizza • $15

Warrabilla Reserve Durif

▼▼▼▼▽ 2001 Dense, opaque red-purple; an opulent, deep, dark berry and bitter chocolate bouquet is followed by a tremendously concentrated and chewy, yet not tannic, palate. Here blackberry, chocolate, licorice and subtle French oak all coalesce. For those expecting to live forever, also available in magnum. **rating:** 91

best drinking 2005–2020 **best vintages** '01 **drink with** Rich game dishes • $19

Warrabilla Reserve Merlot

▼▼▼▼ 2001 Medium red-purple; the bouquet is quite savoury, as befits the variety, with a mix of olive, earth, chocolate and red berry aromas. The palate follows down much the same flavour track, with nice weight and extract; well handled oak. **rating:** 88

best drinking 2004–2009 **best vintages** NA **drink with** Ragout of lamb • $19

Warrabilla Reserve Cabernet

▼▼▼▼ 2001 Medium red-purple; a complex array of savoury, cassis, blackberry aromas on the bouquet are followed by a palate with intense flavour, not jammy, but does show the 14.5° alcohol. Once again, good handling of French oak, likewise tannin management. **rating:** 88

best drinking 2005–2011 **best vintages** NA **drink with** Rack of lamb • $19

Warrabilla Liqueur Muscat

▼▼▼▼▽ NV Olive-brown colour attesting to some age. The rich raisin and plum pudding bouquet shows exemplary varietal character, and the palate does not disappoint; rich raisin, toffee and plum pudding flavours providing excellent value. **rating:** 90

best drinking 2002–2003 **best vintages** NA **drink with** Nuts, dried fruits, biscuits • $15

warramate ★★★☆

27 Maddens Lane, Gruyere, Vic 3770 **region** Yarra Valley
phone (03) 5964 9219 **fax** (03) 5964 9219 **open** 7 days 10–6
winemaker David Church **production** 900 **est.** 1970
product range ($20–35 CD) Riesling, Shiraz, Cabernet Sauvignon.
summary Wine quality has been variable in recent years; it would seem that the oak in some of the older barrels is questionable. At their best, the wines reflect the distinguished site on which the vineyard sits. The 2000/2001 extension of the 30-year-old vineyard will lead to greater production in the years ahead.

warraroong estate ★★★★

Wilderness Road, Lovedale, NSW 2321 **region** Lower Hunter Valley
phone (02) 4930 7594 **fax** (02) 4930 7199 **open** Weekends 10–5
winemaker Andrew Thomas **production** 2000 **est.** 1988
product range ($15–40 CD) Semillon, Sauvignon Blanc, Chenin Blanc, Chardonnay, Semillon Mèthode
Champenoise, Ruby Cabernet Mèthode Champenoise, Shiraz, Malbec.
summary Warraroong Estate was formerly Fraser Vineyard and adopted its new name after it changed
hands in 1997. The name 'Warraroong' is an Aboriginal word for hillside, reflecting the southwesterly aspect
of the property looking back towards the Brokenback Range and Watagan Mountains. The label design is
from a painting by local Aboriginal artist Kia Kiro who, while coming from the NT, is living and working
in the Hunter Valley.

Warraroong Estate Shiraz

▼▼▼▼▼ 1998 Medium red-purple; an elegant and stylish wine with a particularly appealing amalgam of
spice, earth, berry and oak on both bouquet and the medium-bodied palate. Trophy winner 2001 Hunter
Valley Wine Show. **rating:** 94

best drinking 2002–2007 **best vintages** '98 **drink with** Roast beef • $40

warrego wines ★★★

Seminary Road, Marburg, Qld 4306 **region** Queensland Coastal
phone (07) 5464 4400 **fax** (07) 5464 4800 **open** 7 days 10–4
winemaker Kevin Watson **production** 2000 **est.** 2000
product range ($13–24 CD) Cane Cutter's Riesling, Sawmill Sauvignon Blanc, Sugar Mill Chardonnay,
Cane Cutter's Cuvée, Cane Cutter's Pinot Noir, Pinot Noir, Seminary Shiraz.
summary Cathy and Kevin Watson have established their small winery in temporary accommodation at
Marburg, which is halfway between Toowoomba and Brisbane, attracted – like so many others – by the
lifestyle opportunities and the tourism potential of southern Qld. Kevin Watson has completed his wine
science degree at Charles Sturt University, and the primary purpose of his business is custom winemaking
for the many small growers in the region. In the meantime, Warrego Wines is sourcing grapes from places as
far away as the Tamar Valley in Tas, shiraz from the Mornington Peninsula and riesling from the Strathbogie
Ranges. Alongside these are wines from locally grown grapes, and the intention is to ultimately become
almost totally reliant on Qld grapes.

Warrego Cane Cutter's Riesling

▼▼▼▽ 2000 Pale straw-green; the bouquet is minerally, with touches of talc, and not a lot of obvious fruit.
The palate is minerally and bone-dry, in an austere style, but nonetheless infinitely preferable to the
alternative of a dose of residual sugar. **rating:** 83

best drinking 2001–2003 **best vintages** NA **drink with** Cold seafood platter • $15.95

Warrego Sawmill Sauvignon Blanc

▼▼▼▽ 2001 Very pale straw-green; the light and grassy bouquet has hints of gooseberry and passionfruit,
with fractionally reduced characters coming through to slightly interrupt the palate flow. **rating:** 83

best drinking 2002–2003 **best vintages** NA **drink with** Green-lipped mussels • $14.95

Warrego Cane Cutter's Pinot Noir

▼▼▼▽ 1999 Light to medium red; a dusty/leafy/woody bouquet is followed by a palate with clear varietal
character in a stemmy/savoury mode. To be drunk sooner rather than later. **rating:** 83

best drinking 2001–2002 **best vintages** NA **drink with** Chinese-style deep-fried quail • $18.95

Warrego Shiraz

▼▼▼▼ 2000 Medium red-purple; the moderately intense bouquet is clean, with cherry-accented fruit and
not particularly spicy. The palate has remarkably sweet cherry fruit balanced by fresh acidity; very much the
product of an ideal year for the later-ripening varieties on the Mornington Peninsula. **rating:** 86

best drinking 2003–2008 **best vintages** NA **drink with** Lasagne • $18.95

warrenmang vineyard resort ★★★★

Mountain Creek Road, Moonambel, Vic 3478 **region** Pyrenees
phone (03) 5467 2233 **fax** (03) 5467 2309 **open** 7 days 10–5
winemaker Luigi Bazzani, Simon Clayfield **production** 12 000 **est.** 1974

product range ($11–55 CD) The wines are released in two ranges: the lower-priced Bazzani white and red blends, Salute Mèthode Champenoise and Vintage Port; then a subtly differing range of wines under the Warrenmang label, predominantly estate-grown and including Sauvignon Blanc, Chardonnay, Late Harvest Traminer, Grand Pyrenees, Shiraz, Cabernet Sauvignon; and, at the top, a flagship wine which varies from time to time.

summary Warrenmang is now the focus of a superb accommodation and restaurant complex created by former restaurateur Luigi Bazzani and wife Athalie, which is in much demand as a conference centre as well as for weekend tourism. The striking black Bazzani label is partly responsible for the growth in the volume of production. However, the real quality comes from the estate-grown wines. Exports to Asia, Europe and the US.

Warrenmang Black Puma Shiraz

TTTT **2000** Medium red-purple; a complex bouquet with spice and black fruits together with slightly tangy overtones, probably deriving from the French oak in which the wine spent 18 months. The palate has good structure, with fine tannins running through its length, giving savoury/briary touches to a wine designed from the ground up to go with food. **rating:** 89

best drinking 2004–2014 **best vintages** '98 **drink with** Venison • $55

Warrenmang Estate Shiraz

TTTT **2000** Medium to full red-purple; clean, dark berry/black cherry fruit with touches of spice on the bouquet; a solidly built and structured palate with ripe tannins running throughout its length, and sweetening from the vanilla oak. The 14.5° alcohol doesn't threaten or unbalance the wine. **rating:** 88

best drinking 2004–2014 **best vintages** '82, '85, '92, '94, '97, '98, '00 **drink with** Kangaroo fillet • $35

Warrenmang Grand Pyrenees

TTTT **1999** Full red-purple; the clean, firm bouquet has dark berry fruits at its core, with hints of herb, spice and cedar; powerful blackberry and blackcurrant fruit arrive on the early and mid-palate, then all-encompassing tannins take over. In radically different style to the '97, demands respect for 20 years. **rating:** 87

best drinking 2015–2025 **best vintages** '97 **drink with** Aged rump • $35

Warrenmang Cabernet Sauvignon

TTTTY **1999** Medium to full red-purple; fully ripe sweet blackberry and chocolate fruit is augmented by gentle oak on the bouquet, followed by similarly attractive sweet blackberry, cassis and chocolate on a long and smooth palate, finishing with nice tannins. **rating:** 93

best drinking 2003–2013 **best vintages** '99 **drink with** Braised beef • $35

warrina wines NR

Back Road, Kootingal, NSW 2352 **region** Northern Slopes Zone
phone (02) 6760 3985 **fax** (02) 6765 5746 **open** Not
winemaker David Nicholls **production** 100 **est.** 1989
product range ($5–12 ML) Sauvignon Blanc, Semillon, Chardonnay, Shiraz, Cabernet Sauvignon.
summary David Nicholls has progressively established a total of 2 hectares of sauvignon blanc, semillon, chardonnay, shiraz and cabernet sauvignon at his vineyard 15 kilometres northeast of Tamworth. Wine prices are low, but the production has seesawed wildly over the years.

waterton estate ★★★★☆

Rowella, Tas 7270 **region** Northern Tasmania
phone (03) 6327 4170 **fax** (03) 6331 9982 **open** Not
winemaker Julian Alcorso, Nick Butler **production** 400 **est.** 1995
product range ($11 ML) Riesling, Chardonnay, Cabernet Sauvignon.
summary The near-invisible Waterton Estate is owned by a seven-member syndicate who doubtless consume much of the annual production themselves, selling the remainder by word of mouth to friends and acquaintances. Contract winemaking by Julian Alcorso and Nick Butler does the rest.

Waterton Estate Riesling

TTTTY **2001** Light green-yellow; a light but appealing mix of passionfruit, apple and citrus on the bouquet is followed by a palate with rather more intensity, life and sharp focus that many wines of the vintage. Not a heavyweight, but well defined. Silver medal 2002 Tasmanian Wines Show. **rating:** 91

best drinking 2002–2006 **best vintages** '01 **drink with** Carpaccio of salmon • NA

Waterton Estate Chardonnay

TTTTY **2000** Medium yellow-green; complex barrel-ferment aromas do not subdue the fruit on the bouquet, the nectarine fruit of the palate likewise with length and touches of sweet nutty/cashew characters to add further interest. Thoroughly nice wine. **rating:** 92

best drinking 2002–2006 **best vintages** '00 **drink with** Smoked trout • NA

water wheel ★★★☆

Bridgewater-on-Loddon, Bridgewater, Vic 3516 **region** Bendigo
phone (03) 5437 3060 **fax** (03) 5437 3082 **open** Oct–Apr 7 days 11–5, May–Sept Mon–Fri 11–5, weekends and public holidays 1-4
winemaker Peter Cumming, Bill Trevaskis **production** 30 000 **est.** 1972
product range ($12–18 R) Bendigo Sauvignon Blanc, Bendigo Chardonnay, Bendigo Shiraz, Bendigo Cabernet Sauvignon.
summary Peter Cumming gained great respect as a winemaker during his 4-year stint with Hickinbotham Winemakers, and his 1989 purchase of Water Wheel was greeted with enthusiasm by followers of his work. The wines are of remarkably consistent quality and modest price, being distributed throughout Australia and with export markets in New Zealand, Asia, UK, Switzerland, Belgium, Austria, US and Canada.

Water Wheel Bendigo Sauvignon Blanc

TTTY **2001** Light green-yellow; a clean, crisp but shy bouquet is followed by a light, crisp palate, with some length, but not a great deal of varietal character. **rating:** 84

best drinking 2001–2002 **best vintages** '00 **drink with** Asian seafood • $12

Water Wheel Chardonnay

TTTT **2001** Light to medium yellow-green; typical Water Wheel style, clean, with light melon fruit and minimal oak, the palate a replay in a straightforward, unpretentious, unforced mode. **rating:** 85

best drinking 2002–2004 **best vintages** NA **drink with** Roast pork • $14

Water Wheel Bendigo Shiraz

TTTY **2000** Medium purple-red; the dark, quite ripe, small berry fruit aromas of the bouquet give no hint of the tannins which come through from the mid-palate on, and which need to soften. **rating:** 84

best drinking 2004–2009 **best vintages** '94, '96, '97, '98, '99 **drink with** Rich meat dishes • $17

Water Wheel Bendigo Cabernet Sauvignon

TTTT **2000** Medium red-purple; a clean, fruit-driven bouquet with red and blackcurrant fruit, that fruit faithfully repeated on the palate, with some tannins to close. As honest and as good value as ever. **rating:** 88
TTTY **1999** Bright purple-red; an earthy/savoury bouquet, with minimal oak, moves through into a savoury/earthy/berry-flavoured palate, the finish rather severe. **rating:** 84

best drinking 2004–2009 **best vintages** '90, '91, '92, '97 **drink with** Yearling steak • $17

waybourne NR

60 Lemins Road, Waurn Ponds, Vic 3221 **region** Geelong
phone (03) 5241 8477 **fax** (03) 5241 8477 **open** By appointment
winemaker David Cowburn (Contract) **production** 730 **est.** 1980
product range ($12–16 ML) Riesling, Trebbiano, Pinot Gris, Cabernet Sauvignon.
summary Owned by Tony and Kay Volpato, who have relied upon external consultants to assist with the winemaking. No recent tastings.

wayne thomas wines ★★★★

26 Kangarilla Road, McLaren Vale, SA 5171 **region** McLaren Vale
phone (08) 8323 9737 **fax** (08) 8323 9737 **open** 7 days 12–5
winemaker Wayne Thomas **production** 5000 **est.** 1994
product range ($14–25 ML) Dry Riesling, Unwooded Chardonnay, Patricia Mèthode Champenoise, Shiraz, Cabernet Sauvignon.
summary Wayne Thomas is a McLaren Vale veteran, having commenced his winemaking career in 1961, working for Stonyfell, Ryecroft and Saltram before establishing Fern Hill with his late wife Pat in 1975. When they sold Fern Hill in April 1994 they started again, launching the Wayne Thomas Wines label, using grapes sourced from ten growers throughout McLaren Vale. The wines are exported to the US, as well as enjoying limited retail distribution through all Australian states except WA.

Wayne Thomas McLaren Vale Shiraz

▼▼▼▼ 2000 Medium purple-red; bright and clear; rich, dark berry fruits are matched with well-integrated and balanced American oak on the bouquet, that oak carrying through to the palate, giving the wine a traditional Australian character. Solid dark plum fruit, with hints of fruit spice, and soft, fine tannins complete the picture.   **rating:** 89

best drinking 2003–2010 **best vintages** '99 **drink with** Wafu beef • $25

wedgetail estate   ★★★★☆

40 Hildebrand Road, Cottles Bridge, Vic 3099 **region** Yarra Valley
phone (03) 9714 8661 **fax** (03) 9714 8676 **open** Weekends and public holidays 11–6, or by appointment, closed 25 Dec–24 Jan
winemaker Guy Lamothe **production** 1500 **est.** 1994
product range ($28–58 R) Old Barrique Chardonnay, Pinot Noir, Reserve Pinot Noir, Cabernet.
summary Canadian-born photographer Guy Lamothe and partner Dena Ashbolt started making wine in the basement of their Carlton home in the 1980s. Insidiously, the idea of their own vineyard started to take hold, and the search for a property began. Then, in their words 'one Sunday, when we were "just out for a drive", we drove past our current home. The slopes are amazing, true goat terrain, and it is on these steep slopes that in 1994 we planted our first block of pinot noir.' While the vines were growing – they now have 5.5 hectares in total – Lamothe enrolled in the winegrowing course at Charles Sturt University, having already gained practical experience working at Tarrawarra in the Yarra Valley, Mornington Peninsula and Meursault. The net result is truly excellent wine. Distributed in NSW and the ACT by The Fine Wine Specalist; exports to Belgium.

Wedgetail Estate Chardonnay

▼▼▼▼ 2000 Medium to full yellow-green; a rich, ripe buttery/figgy/cashew/toasty bouquet leads into a full-bodied palate in rich, ripe style.   **rating:** 89

best drinking 2001–2004 **best vintages** NA **drink with** Sweetbreads • $26

Wedgetail Estate Pinot Noir

▼▼▼▼▼ 2000 A fragrant/savoury/sappy lift to the core of sweet plum on the bouquet and palate is the key to a wine with delicious freshness, fragrance, length and persistence. Drink while the 2000 Reserve (95 points, $55) matures.   **rating:** 94

best drinking 2001–2004 **best vintages** '98, '99, '00 **drink with** Roast quail • $28

Wedgetail Estate Reserve Pinot Noir

▼▼▼▼▼ 2000 Medium red-purple; concentrated, ripe and lusciously sweet plum fruit on the bouquet is precisely matched by the palate, with all of the concentration and richness of the bouquet, adding some savoury characters to the dark plum fruit.   **rating:** 95

best drinking 2004–2010 **best vintages** '99, '00 **drink with** Squab • $55

Wedgetail Estate Cabernet

▼▼▼▼ 2000 Medium purple-red; the bouquet offers a fresh mix of berry, earth and spice, but is not particularly complex. There is a little more weight and depth to the palate, but still a fraction simple, and not in the class of the Pinot Noirs of 2000. For the record, a blend of 85 per cent Cabernet Sauvignon and 15 per cent Shiraz.   **rating:** 85

▼▼▼▼▽ 1999 Medium red-purple; clean, fresh, gently ripe red berry fruit aromas herald an attractive, ripe cassis/berry-accented palate, smooth and supple, with a neatly judged touch of oak tannin.   **rating:** 91

best drinking 2003–2007 **best vintages** '99 **drink with** Kangaroo fillet • $28

wellington   ★★★★☆

Cnr Richmond and Denholms Roads, Cambridge, Tas 7170 **region** Southern Tasmania
phone (03) 6248 5844 **fax** (03) 6248 5855 **open** By appointment
winemaker Andrew Hood **production** 3000 **est.** 1990
product range ($20–25 CD) Riesling, Iced Riesling 375 ml, Chardonnay, Pinot Noir, Ruby Port.
summary Consultant-winemaker Andrew Hood (ex-Charles Sturt University) and wife Jenny have constructed a state-of-the-art winery on land leased from the University of Tasmania. The 3000-case production of Wellington is dwarfed by the 4500 cases contract-made for others, but all the wines are flawlessly crafted.

Wellington Riesling

▼▼▼▼ **2001** Light to medium green-yellow; a firm, correct and tight bouquet with a range of lime and mineral aromas is followed by a surprisingly soft, albeit flavoursome, palate which needs more focus. Part of a very consistent pattern. **rating:** 87

best drinking 2002–2004 **best vintages** '96, '97, '98, '99 **drink with** Sauteed prawns • $20

Wellington Chardonnay

▼▼▼▼▽ **2000** The fragrant stonefruit and citrus aromas, and the barest touch of oak, are followed by a supremely elegant palate, with typical Tasmanian acidity leaving the mouth fresh. **rating:** 93

best drinking 2001–2010 **best vintages** '92, '95, '96, '97, '98, '99, '01 **drink with** Salmon gravlax • $20

Wellington Iced Riesling 375 ml

▼▼▼▼▽ **2001** Light green-yellow; intense lime juice aromas, spotlessly clean, and with hints of spice; then a lingering, intense, finely balanced and harmonious palate with lime juice, a hint of sweetness and acidity woven together. **rating:** 92

best drinking 2002–2005 **best vintages** '97, '98, '99, '01 **drink with** Sorbet • $22

Wellington Pinot Noir

▼▼▼▼▽ **2000** Medium red-purple; the gently sweet and ripe bouquet has a mix of spice, strawberry and cherry, aromas which are the drivers of the seductively sweet cherry and spice palate; good texture, lovely wine in a free-flowing style. **rating:** 91

best drinking 2002–2005 **best vintages** '94, '98, '99, '00 **drink with** Venison fillet • $24

wells parish wines NR

Benerin Estate, Sydney Road, Kandos, NSW 2848 **region** Mudgee
phone (02) 6379 4168 **fax** (02) 6379 4996 **open** By appointment
winemaker Pieter Van Gent **production** 500 **est.** 1995
product range ($17–18 CD) Chardonnay, Cabernet Sauvignon, Strayleaves Vintage Port.
summary Richard and Rachel Trounson, with help from father Barry Trounson, have established 16 hectares of vineyards at Benerin Estate since 1995. Most of the grapes are sold to Southcorp, but small quantities of wine are made for sale under the Wells Parish label. The vineyards are situated at the eastern extremity of the Mudgee region, near Rylstone, and both the soils and climate are distinctly different to those of the traditional Mudgee area.

wendouree ★★★★★

Wendouree Road, Clare, SA 5453 **region** Clare Valley
phone (08) 8842 2896 **open** By appointment
winemaker Tony Brady **production** 2000 **est.** 1895
product range ($15–36 ML) Shiraz, Shiraz Malbec, Shiraz Mataro, Cabernet Malbec, Cabernet Sauvignon, Muscat of Alexandria.
summary The iron fist in a velvet glove best describes these extraordinary wines. They are fashioned with passion and yet precision from the very old vineyard with its unique terroir by Tony and Lita Brady, who rightly see themselves as custodians of a priceless treasure. The 100-year-old stone winery is virtually unchanged from the day it was built; this is in every sense a treasure beyond price. For two reasons, neither Tony Brady nor I see any point in providing tasting notes for the most recently released vintage. Firstly, the wines will have sold out, and moreover, there is no room for newcomers on the mailing list for the next release. Second, all I will ever be able to say is wait for 20 years before drinking the wine.

west cape howe wines ★★★★

PO Box 548, Denmark, WA 6333 **region** Great Southern
phone (08) 9848 2959 **fax** (08) 9848 2903 **open** 7 days 10–5
winemaker Brenden Smith, Dave Cleary **production** 7000 **est.** 1997
product range ($11.75–22 CD) Semillon Sauvignon Blanc, Unwooded Chardonnay, Chardonnay, Late Picked Riesling, Shiraz, Cabernet Merlot, Muscat.
summary Brenden Smith was senior winemaker at Goundrey Wines for many years and has branched into business on his own with a contract-winemaking facility for growers throughout the Great Southern region. West Cape Howe wines are exported to the UK.

West Cape Howe Riesling

▼▼▼▼ 2001 Light to medium green-yellow; the bouquet is clean, firm and crisp, with the fruit aromas presently locked away. The palate, likewise, is fruit-closed, but minerally acidity provides some character and length. **rating: 87**

best drinking 2004–2009 **best vintages** NA **drink with** Shellfish • $15

West Cape Howe Semillon Sauvignon Blanc

▼▼▼▼▽ 2001 Light to medium green-yellow; a crisp and quite aromatic bouquet with a mix of herbaceous, gooseberry and citrus aromas leads into a palate with good mouthfeel, balance and length. Pure fruit flavours run through to a lingering finish. **rating: 90**

best drinking 2002–2003 **best vintages** '01 **drink with** Seafood risotto • $14

West Cape Howe Unwooded Chardonnay

▼▼▼▼ 2001 Light to medium green-yellow; the clean and fresh bouquet offers melon and grapefruit/citrus, the palate with good fruit and mouthfeel, the flavours tracking those of the bouquet. Above average for this style. **rating: 86**

best drinking 2003–2004 **best vintages** NA **drink with** Pan-fried flathead fillets • $14

West Cape Howe Shiraz

▼▼▼▼ 2000 Bright red-purple of medium depth; the bouquet offers a mix of cherry, plum and raspberry fruit and minimal oak; the elegant, medium-bodied palate has pure fruit flavours tracking the bouquet; still quite firm, finishing with fine tannins and crisp acidity. **rating: 87**

best drinking 2003–2008 **best vintages** NA **drink with** Lamb fillets • $15

West Cape Howe Cabernet Merlot

▼▼▼▼ 2001 Bright but deep red-purple; a fragrant, lifted bouquet with cassis and spice is replicated on the palate, which has abundant fruit but is inevitably still very youthful. The points may prove parsimonious. **rating: 86**

best drinking 2005–2010 **best vintages** NA **drink with** Venison with blackcurrant jus • $15

West Cape Howe Cabernet Sauvignon

▼▼▼▼▽ 2000 Medium red-purple; moderately intense, clean, red berry fruit and cedary/pencilly oak in the background of the bouquet leads into a palate with attractive cassis, blackcurrant and dark chocolate fruit, with the oak better integrated and balanced. **rating: 90**

best drinking 2005–2010 **best vintages** '00 **drink with** Game pie • $21

westend estate wines ★★★☆

1283 Brayne Road, Griffith, NSW 2680 **region** Riverina
phone (02) 6964 1506 **fax** (02) 6962 1673 **open** Mon–Fri 8.30–5, Sat 9.30–4
winemaker William Calabria, Bryan Currie **production** 85 000 **est.** 1945
product range ($3.60–20 CD) Outback Traminer Riesling, Semillon Sauvignon Blanc, Shiraz; Richland Chardonnay, Sauvignon Blanc, Shiraz, Merlot, Cabernet Merlot, Cabernet Sauvignon; Port and Liqueur Muscat; are followed by 3 Bridges range of Chardonnay, Shiraz, Durif, Cabernet Sauvignon and Golden Mist Botrytis Semillon.
summary Along with a number of Riverina producers, West End is making a concerted move to lift both the quality and the packaging of its wines, spearheaded by the 3 Bridges range, which has an impressive array of gold medals to its credit since being first released in April 1997. It has also ventured into the export market, with distribution in the UK, the US, Canada, New Zealand, Hong Kong and Switzerland.

Westend 3 Bridges Shiraz

▼▼▼▼ 1999 Medium red-purple; the bouquet and palate have pleasant red fruit characters; while slightly raspy oak distracts, there is above average flavour. **rating: 86**

best drinking 2001–2005 **best vintages** '98 **drink with** Pasta with meat sauce • $20

Westend Estate 3 Bridges Durif

▼▼▼▼ 2000 Medium red-purple; aromatic plum, prune and mint fruit on the bouquet is followed by a flavoursome palate with good structure and a slightly pointed finish. The 3 Bridges label is only given to Westend wines which have won a gold medal, and this wine won its gold at the Royal Adelaide Wine Show in 2001. **rating: 88**

best drinking 2003–2007 **best vintages** NA **drink with** Shepherd's pie • $18.95

☙ western range wines NR

Lot 88 Chittering Road, Lower Chittering, WA 6084 **region** Perth Hills
phone (08) 9571 8800 **fax** (08) 9571 8844 **open** Weekends 11.30–4.30
winemaker Mark Nairn **production** 30 000 **est.** 2001
product range ($13–19 CD) Chardonnay Viognier, Viognier, Verdelho, Shiraz, Carnelian Shiraz, Shiraz Viognier; 8 Vineyard White (Chardonnay Verdelho Chenin Blanc), 8 Vineyard Red (Shiraz Grenache), Grenache.
summary Between the mid-1990s and 2001 several prominent Western Australians, including Marilyn Corderory, Malcolm McCusker, Terry and Kevin Prindiville and Tony Rechner have established approximately 110 hectares of vines (under separate ownerships) in the Perth Hills, with a kaleidoscopic range of varietals. The next step was to join forces to build a substantial winery which is a separate venture to the growers individual vineyards, but which takes the grapes and then markets the wine under the Western Range brand. Winemaker Mark Nairn (son of Will Nairn of Peel Estate) is a Roseworthy graduate who has worked extensively as a flying winemaker throughout the world. All in all, an impressive combination. Distribution through all mainland states, primarily by Australian Liquor Merchants.

westfield ★ ★ ★ ☆

Cnr Memorial Ave and Great Northern Highway, Baskerville, WA 6056 **region** Swan District
phone (08) 9296 4356 **fax** (08) 9296 4356 **open** 7 days 10–5.30
winemaker John Kosovich **production** 11 000 **est.** 1922
product range ($14–48 CD) Chenin Blanc, Verdelho, Unwooded Chardonnay, Chardonnay, Bronze Wing Chardonnay, Late Pick Verdelho, Autumn Harvest, Shiraz, Merlot, Cabernet Sauvignon, Liqueur Muscat.
summary Consistent producer of a surprisingly elegant and complex Chardonnay; the other wines are more variable, but from time to time has made attractive Verdelho and excellent Cabernet Sauvignon. 1998 saw the first release of wines partly or wholly coming from the family's new planting at Pemberton, those being Swan/Pemberton blends released under the Bronze Wing label. Limited retail distribution in Perth, Melbourne and Brisbane.

Westfield Unwooded Chardonnay

▼▼▼▽ **2000** Light straw-green; the bouquet is of light to medium intensity, clean, and with a touch of melon, the palate similarly clean, light and, at the end of the day, somewhat anonymous. **rating:** 82

best drinking 2001–2003 **best vintages** NA **drink with** Light seafood • $16

Westfield Chardonnay

▼▼▼▼ **1998** Medium to full yellow-green; a markedly complex, tangy bouquet strongly suggests barrel ferment of only partially clarified juice at near-ambient temperatures. A striking and powerful palate displays more of the same, all in a Burgundian mould. **rating:** 87

best drinking 2001–2006 **best vintages** Virtually all **drink with** Marron or crayfish • $21.50

Westfield Bronze Wing Shiraz

▼▼▼▼ **1999** Light to medium red-purple; the moderately intense bouquet has some fruit complexity and just a hint of canopy-derived gaminess. The palate is lively and spicy, again showing some tangy/savoury/green edges. **rating:** 85

best drinking 2001–2004 **best vintages** NA **drink with** Prosciutto • $24.50

Westfield Cabernet Sauvignon

▼▼▼▽ **1999** Medium red-purple; earthy varietal fruit on the bouquet is in a slightly surprisingly light mould, the palate likewise with savoury/leafy characters which are not so often encountered in the Swan Valley. **rating:** 83

best drinking 2002–2006 **best vintages** NA **drink with** Marinated beef • $21.50

Westfield Liqueur Muscat

▼▼▼▼▼ **NV** Dark tawny-brown; an intense raisiny bouquet with pronounced rancio is followed by an unctuously rich and sweet raisins-in-brandy palate, quite remarkable for its depth and intensity, and which in no way cloys. **rating:** 95

best drinking 2002–2003 **best vintages** NA **drink with** Coffee and walnuts • $48

🐌 westgate vineyard   NR

'Westgate', RMB 1124, Ararat, Vic 3377 **region** Grampians
phone (03) 5356 2394 **fax** (03) 5356 2594 **open** By appointment
winemaker Bruce Dalkin **production** 200 **est.** 1999
product range ($17–19 CD) Riesling, Cabernet Shiraz.
summary Westgate has been in the Dalkin family ownership since the 1860s, the present owners Bruce and Robyn Dalkin being the sixth generation owners of the property, which today focuses on grape production, a small winery, 4 and a half star accommodation, and wool production. Over 12 hectares of vineyards have been progressively established since 1969, including a key holding of 10 hectares of shiraz. Most of the grapes are sold to Mount Langi Ghiran and Seppelt Great Western, but a vigneron's licence was obtained in 1999 and a small amount of wine is made under the Westgate Vineyard label.

wetherall   ★★★★

Naracoorte Road, Coonawarra, SA 5263 **region** Coonawarra
phone (08) 8737 2104 **fax** (08) 8737 2105 **open** 7 days 10–4
winemaker Michael Wetherall **production** 1500 **est.** 1991
product range ($20–22 CD) Shiraz, Cabernet Sauvignon.
summary The Wetherall family has been growing grapes in Coonawarra for more than 30 years with 115 hectares of mature vines, and Michael Wetherall (a Roseworthy graduate) has been responsible for overseeing wine production since Wetherall extended its operations into winemaking (in a small way) in 1991. Exports to Canada.

Wetherall Shiraz

▼▼▼▼ **2000** Youthful red-purple; the fresh, direct bouquet has red berry/cherry fruit, the oak held in far more restraint than previous vintages. The palate offers a pleasing mix of berry and more savoury flavours, dipping slightly on the mid-palate, but nonetheless well-balanced.   **rating:** 87

best drinking 2004–2010 **best vintages** NA **drink with** Smoked meat • $20

Wetherall Cabernet Sauvignon

▼▼▼▼▽ **2000** Bright, full red-purple; sweet blackberry, blackcurrant and mulberry fruit on the bouquet, then a medium-bodied palate with flavours tracking those of the bouquet. Good tannin and oak management.   **rating:** 90

best drinking 2005–2012 **best vintages** '00 **drink with** Roast beef • $22

wharncliffe   NR

Summerleas Road, Kingston, Tas 7050 **region** Southern Tasmania
phone (03) 6229 7147 **fax** (03) 6229 2298 **open** Not
winemaker Andrew Hood (Contract) **production** 115 **est.** 1990
product range ($20 ML) Chardonnay.
summary With total plantings of 0.75 hectare, Wharncliffe could not exist without the type of contract-winemaking service offered by Andrew Hood, which would be a pity, because the vineyard is beautifully situated on the doorstep of Mount Wellington, the Huon Valley and the Channel regions of southern Tas.

whiskey gully wines   NR

Beverley Road, Severnlea, Qld 4352 **region** Granite Belt
phone (07) 4683 5100 **fax** (07) 4683 5155 **open** 7 days 8.30–5
winemaker Philippa Hambleton, Rod MacPherson **production** 500 **est.** 1997
product range ($12–30 CD) Beverley Chardonnay, Republic Red, Shiraz, Cabernet Sauvignon.
summary Close inspection of the winery letterhead discloses that The Media Mill Pty Ltd trades as Whiskey Gully Wines. It is no surprise, then, to find proprietor John Arlidge saying 'Wine and politics are a heady mix; I have already registered the 2000 Republic Red as a voter in 26 marginal electorates and we are considering nominating it for Liberal Party pre-selection in Bennelong'. Wit to one side, John Arlidge has big plans for Whiskey Gully Wines, with long-range plans to establish 40 hectares of vineyards, extending the varietal range with petit verdot, malbec, merlot, semillon and sauvignon blanc. At present the wines are made off-site, but as production increases (to over 1600 cases within 4 years) on-site winemaking will be progressively introduced.

whispering hills   NR

PO Box 15, Yarra Junction, Vic 3797 **region** Yarra Valley
phone (03) 5964 6070 **fax** (03) 5964 6231 **open** Not
winemaker Murray Lyons, Ron Snep **production** 500 **est.** 1994
product range ($21–24 ML) Chardonnay, Cabernet Sauvignon.
summary The minuscule production of Whispering Hills from its 3.5-hectare vineyard is limited to two wines which are sold by mail order and word of mouth.

whisson lake   NR

PO Box 91, Uraidla, SA 5142 **region** Adelaide Hills
phone (08) 8390 1303 **fax** (08) 8390 3822 **open** By appointment
winemaker Roman Bratasiuk (Contract) **production** 300 **est.** 1985
product range ($27.50–31.50 CD) Pinot Noir.
summary Mark Whisson is primarily a grape grower, with 4.5 hectares of close-planted, steep-sloped north-facing vineyard. A small quantity of the production is made for the Whisson Lake label by Roman Bratasiuk, best known as the owner/winemaker of Clarendon Hills. Tiny quantities are exported to the US and UK.

whistler wines   ★★★☆

Seppeltsfield Road, Marananga, SA 5355 **region** Barossa Valley
phone (08) 8562 4942 **fax** (08) 8562 4943 **open** Weekends and public holidays 10.30–5 or by appointment
winemaker Rolf Binder, Christa Deans (Contract) **production** 950 **est.** 1999
product range ($18–25 CD) Semillon, Sparkling Shiraz, Sparkling Merlot, Shiraz, Merlot, Cabernet Sauvignon.
summary Whistler Wines had a dream start to its life at the 2000 Barossa Valley Wine Show when its 2000 Semillon won trophies for the Best Dry White Semillon and for the Most Outstanding Barossa White Table Wine. Add to that the distinguished US importer Weygandt-Metzler, plus exports to Singapore, and it is no surprise to find the sold out sign going up on the extremely attractive (modern) galvanised iron cellar door building. The operation is presently based on 5 hectares of shiraz and 2 hectares each of semillon, merlot and 1 hectare of cabernet sauvignon, with an additional 4 hectares of grenache, mourvedre and riesling planted in 2001. The hope is to have a restaurant on site by 2004, and to gradually increase production to match already existing market demands.

Whistler Unwooded Semillon
TTTT 2001 One of the features of the wine is its amazing green colour, particularly given its youth. Both the bouquet and palate have abundant flavour, with a slightly grippy finish. One suspects perhaps enzymes and skin contact have been used to bolster the flavour.   **rating:** 86

best drinking 2001–2004 **best vintages** NA **drink with** Stir-fried abalone • $18

Whistler Shiraz
TTTT 1999 Medium to full red; the earth, berry and vanilla aromas of the bouquet are starting to mature, but the palate is much sweeter and riper, with abundant chocolate, ripe berry and flesh coming from the 14.5° alcohol.   **rating:** 88

best drinking 2003–2009 **best vintages** NA **drink with** Steak and kidney pie • $25

Whistler Merlot
TTTT 2000 Medium red-purple; the bouquet is aromatic and tangy, but dominated by the 20 months the wine spent in small oak. The palate is crammed with flavour, showing some positive varietal character, but again buttoned up in an oak overcoat.   **rating:** 87

best drinking 2004–2009 **best vintages** NA **drink with** Roast goose • $22

Whistler Cabernet Sauvignon
TTTY 2000 Medium red-purple; the bouquet has a soft, sweet mix of leather, earth, blackberry and vanilla; the palate is dominated by American oak, the sweet fruit having insufficient power to carry that oak.   **rating:** 84

best drinking 2004–2009 **best vintages** NA **drink with** Smoked lamb • $20

whitehorse wines   NR

4 Reid Park Road, Mount Clear, Vic 3350 **region** Ballarat
phone (03) 5330 1719 **fax** (03) 5330 1288 **open** Weekends 11–5
winemaker Noel Myers **production** 900 **est.** 1981
product range ($10–18 CD) Riesling, Riesling Muller Thurgau, Chardonnay, Pinot Noir, Cabernet Shiraz.
summary The Myers family has moved from grape growing to winemaking, utilising the attractive site on its sloping hillside south of Ballarat. 4 hectares of vines are in production, with pinot noir and chardonnay the principal varieties.

wignalls wines   ★★★★

Chester Pass Road (Highway 1), Albany, WA 6330 **region** Great Southern
phone (08) 9841 2848 **fax** (08) 9842 9003 **open** 7 days 12–4
winemaker Bill Wignall **production** 5000 **est.** 1982
product range ($13.80–25 CD) Albany Dew, Sauvignon Blanc, Low Oaked Chardonnay, Late Harvest Frontignac, Pinot Noir, Reserve Pinot Noir, Shiraz, Cabernet Sauvignon, Tawny Port, White Port.
summary A noted producer of Pinot Noir which has extended the map for the variety in Australia. The Pinots have shown style and flair, but do age fairly quickly. The white wines are elegant, and show the cool climate to good advantage. A new winery was constructed and opened for the 1998 vintage, utilising the production from the 16 hectares of estate plantings. Exports to Japan, Singapore and the UK.

Wignalls Sauvignon Blanc

TTTY **2001** Light green-yellow; the crisp, grassy herbaceous bouquet has more weight on the palate than the bouquet would suggest, even though the flavours are similar.   **rating:** 84

best drinking 2002–2003 **best vintages** NA **drink with** Shellfish • $14.80

Wignalls Pinot Noir

TTTTY **2000** Bright and clear purple-red; fragrant strawberry and cherry fruit on the bouquet, plus a hint of oak, is a gentle start, but the palate builds significantly, with both length and character coming through touches of spice and forest. The best for some time from this once leading producer.   **rating:** 90

best drinking 2002–2005 **best vintages** '85, '86, '88, '91, '93, '95, '97, '00 **drink with** Seared Tasmanian salmon • $21.80

Wignalls Shiraz

TTTT **2000** Medium red-purple; light, clear cherry and spice aromas on the bouquet are matched by the attractive mix of savoury, spicy cherry fruit on the medium-bodied palate; fine tannins and gentle oak round off a nice wine.   **rating:** 87

TTTT **1999** Bright red-purple; the quite fragrant bouquet has attractive sweet cherry fruit; the black cherry, spice and faintly savoury tannins have good mouthfeel; very similar to the 2000, but with that extra touch of intensity.   **rating:** 88

best drinking 2004–2009 **best vintages** NA **drink with** Chicken liver ravioli • $20

🐂 wild broke wines   NR

Milbrodale Road, Broke, NSW 2330 **region** Lower Hunter Valley
phone (02) 6579 1065 **open** Not
winemaker Monarch Winemaking Services **production** 400 **est.** 1999
product range ($40 R) Idlewild Wild Yeast Chardonnay, Late Picked Semillon, Idlewild Cabernet Shiraz.
summary Wild Broke Wines is a spin-off from Ryan Family Wines; it is a partnership between Matthew Ryan (who continues as viticulturist for Ryan Family Wines on Broke Estate and Minimbah Vineyards) and wife Tina Ryan who continues to run Wild Rhino PR Marketing and Events in Sydney. At the present time it draws on 2 hectares of shiraz and cabernet sauvignon, and 1 hectare each of merlot, barbera, chardonnay and tempranillo. The partnership is in the fortunate position of being able to pick and choose the quantity of wine made to reflect vintage conditions.

wild dog   ★★★☆

South Road, Warragul, Vic 3820 **region** Gippsland
phone (03) 5623 1117 **fax** (03) 5623 6402 **open** 7 days 10–5
winemaker John Farrington **production** 3000 **est.** 1982

product range ($12–22 CD) Riesling, Unwooded Chardonnay, Chardonnay, Wild Dog Sparkling, Rosé, Pinot Noir, Shiraz, Cabernet Sauvignon.

summary An aptly named winery which produces somewhat rustic wines from the 12 hectares of estate vineyards; even the Farringtons say that the Shiraz comes 'with a bite', also pointing out that there is minimal handling, fining and filtration.

Wild Dog Shiraz

TTTT 2000 Medium red-purple; aromatic cherry, cherry pip fruit and subtle oak is followed by a fresh and exuberant palate which, although not bottled until October 2001, seemed to need more handling and training, but will likely become more domesticated with time in bottle.   **rating:** 87

best drinking 2004–2009 **best vintages** NA **drink with** Braised beef in red wine • $18

wild duck creek estate   NR

Spring Flat Road, Heathcote, Vic 3523 **region** Heathcote
phone (03) 5433 3133 **fax** (03) 5433 3133 **open** By appointment
winemaker David Anderson **production** 4000 **est.** 1980
product range ($25–75 CD) Springflat Shiraz, Alan's Cabernets, Alan's Cabernets Pressings, The Blend, Duck Muck, Cabernet Sauvignon Reserve, Sparkling Duck 2.
summary The first release of Wild Duck Creek Estate from the 1991 vintage marked the end of 12 years of effort by David and Diana Anderson. They commenced planting the 4.5-hectare vineyard in 1980, made their first tiny quantities of wine in 1986, the first commercial quantities of wine in 1991, and built their winery and cellar-door facility in 1993. Exports to the US (where Duck Muck has become a cult wine), the UK, Belgium, Germany and Singapore.

wilderness estate   NR

Branxton Road, Pokolbin, NSW 2321 **region** Lower Hunter Valley
phone (02) 4998 7755 **fax** (02) 4998 7750 **open** 7 days 9–5
winemaker Josef Lesnik **production** 31 000 **est.** 1986
product range ($11.50–18.50 R) The premium varietal range of Unwooded Semillon, Individual Block Semillon, Unwooded Chardonnay, Reserve Chardonnay, Shiraz, Cabernet Merlot and Merlot is under the Wilderness Estate label; the second Black Creek label encompasses a range of lower-priced varietals with Traminer Riesling, Semillon, Verdelho, Chardonnay, Sparkling Brut, Pinot Noir and Shiraz.
summary Long-term Wyndham Estate winemaker John Baruzzi has formed a 50-50 joint venture with Joe Lesnik, resulting in the former Lesnik Family Winery now renamed Wilderness Estate. The Lesnik label will be phased out, with all wines from the '95 vintage being released either under the Wilderness Estate label or under the Black Creek label. National distribution is supplemented by exports to the US, Canada and the UK. At the time of going to press Wilderness Estate was in the course of being purchased by De Bortoli, and major changes will doubtless follow in due course.

wild soul   NR

Horans Gorge Road, Glen Aplin, Qld 4381 **region** Granite Belt
phone (07) 4683 4201 **fax** (07) 4683 4201 **open** Weekends and public holidays 10–4
winemaker Andy Boullier **production** 400 **est.** 1995
product range ($14–16 CD) Shiraz, Cabernet Sauvignon.
summary Andy and Beth Boullier have been on the land throughout their life, working in various capacities, before buying their small property at Glen Aplin. They have established a little over 1 hectare of vines, more or less equally split between cabernet sauvignon and shiraz, with a little merlot. They use organic principles in growing the fruit which provide challenges to themselves, challenges compounded by birds, drought and kangaroos. A small winery enables Andy Boullier to make the wine on-site; the Shiraz the better of the two wines.

wildwood   ★★★★

St John's Lane, Wildwood, Bulla, Vic 3428 **region** Sunbury
phone (03) 9307 1118 **fax** (03) 9331 1590 **open** 7 days 10–6
winemaker Dr Wayne Stott, Nicholas Blampied-Lane **production** 2000 **est.** 1983
product range ($20–32 CD) Chardonnay, Pinot Noir, Shiraz, Cabernet Franc, Cabernets, Dunalister (a Cabernet Franc with small amounts of Merlot and Malbec).

summary Wildwood is situated just 4 kilometres past Melbourne airport, at an altitude of 130 metres in the Oaklands Valley, which provides unexpected views back to Port Phillip Bay and the Melbourne skyline. Plastic surgeon Wayne Stott has taken what is very much a part-time activity rather more seriously than most by undertaking (and completing) the Wine Science degree at Charles Sturt University. His assistant Nicholas Blampied-Lane is a Flying Winemaker who began his flight at the opposite end to most, gaining his oenology degree at Toulouse before working in Burgundy, California and France. 4 years of drought has cut production and forced the early release of the red wines.

Wildwood Pinot Noir

▼▼▼▽ **2000** Light to medium red-purple; while the bouquet is light and savoury, with not much fruit concentration or varietal character, the palate picks up the pace marginally, with light cherry, plum and mint fruit. The 2000 vintage should have produced a much better result. **rating:** 84

best drinking 2002–2003 **best vintages** '98 **drink with** Duck breast • $30

Wildwood Cabernets

▼▼▼▼▽ **2001** Dense, youthful red-purple; deep, ripe blackberry and cassis fruit on the bouquet is followed by an unusually powerful and concentrated palate reflecting the very low yield; still new-born and not easy to accurately assess. **rating:** 90

▼▼▼▼ **2000** Quite developed colour given its youth; the spicy blackberry fruit of the bouquet shows nicely ripened fruit together with a touch of cedar. Similar cassis, red and blackcurrant fruit flavours come through on the palate, finishing with soft, ripe tannins. **rating:** 89

best drinking 2005–2010 **best vintages** '93, '97, '98, '00, '01 **drink with** Oxtail • $30

wildwood of yallingup NR

Caves Road, Yallingup, WA 6282 **region** Margaret River
phone (08) 9755 2544 **fax** (08) 9755 2644 **open** 7 days 10–4
winemaker NA **production** 5000 **est.** 1984
product range ($14.50–30 CD) Chardonnay, Semillon, Sauvignon Blanc, Chenin Blanc, Shiraz, Cabernet Merlot.
summary Wildwood Winery was part of the Hotham Valley Estate empire, which, like Icarus, flew too close to the sun. This led to the sale of Wildwood as a separate entity; details of the purchaser not being available at the time of going to print.

willespie ★★★★

Harmans Mill Road, Wilyabrup via Cowaramup, WA 6284 **region** Margaret River
phone (08) 9755 6248 **fax** (08) 9755 6210 **open** 7 days 10.30–5
winemaker Kevin Squance **production** 11 000 **est.** 1976
product range ($12.50–50 ML) Riesling, Sauvignon Blanc, Semillon Sauvignon Blanc, Verdelho, Chardonnay, Autumn Whim, Late Harvest Riesling, Shiraz, Merlot, Cabernet Sauvignon, Cabernet Sauvignon Reserve; Harmans Mill White and Harmans Mill Red are cheaper second-label wines; Verdelho White Port, Vintage Port.
summary Willespie has produced many attractive white wines over the years, typically in brisk, herbaceous Margaret River style. All are fruit- rather than oak-driven; the newer Merlot also shows promise. The wines have had such success that the Squance family (which founded and owns Willespie) has substantially increased winery capacity, drawing upon an additional 25 hectares of estate vineyards now in bearing. Exports to Europe, US, Singapore and Hong Kong.

Willespie Sauvignon Blanc

▼▼▼▼ **2001** Light straw-green, a light, crisp and minerally bouquet with subdued fruit is followed by a palate which, likewise, is not highly flavoured, but is well constructed and balanced. **rating:** 85

best drinking 2002–2003 **best vintages** '87, '90, '91, '93, '95, '98 **drink with** Margaret River seafood • $18.50

Willespie Verdelho

▼▼▼▽ **1998** Light to medium green-yellow; the moderately intense bouquet is clean, with that indeterminate fruit salad character of the variety. The palate is pleasant, lengthened and lifted by crisp acidity on the finish. **rating:** 84

best drinking 2001–2003 **best vintages** NA **drink with** Vegetable terrine • $19.50

Willespie Chardonnay

ΨΨΨΨ **1998** Medium yellow-green; the bouquet offers toasty/nutty barrel ferment/bottle development/malolactic influences over the quite rich melon fruit. The palate, likewise, has melon and stone fruit with toasty overtones and a firm finish. **rating:** 86

best drinking 2001–2004 **best vintages** NA **drink with** Slow-roasted salmon • $22.50

Willespie Shiraz

ΨΨΨΨΨ **1999** Deep, youthful red-purple; clean, smooth black cherry and some damson plum aromas flow into a palate of excellent depth to layers of luscious, but not jammy, fruit. Sweet, ripe tannins round off a top-class wine. **rating:** 94

ΨΨΨΨ **1998** Medium to full red-purple; clean raspberry and cherry fruit aromas are supported by subtle oak on the bouquet; the fruit swells dramatically on the palate, almost into Cabernet-like cassis characters which are entirely seductive. The tannins are super-fine, the oak subtle. **rating:** 92

best drinking 2004–2014 **best vintages** '98, '99 **drink with** Beef in red wine sauce • $35

Willespie Cabernets

ΨΨΨΨ **1998** Medium red, with some purple remaining; aromas of spice, earth, dark berry and cedar on the bouquet are followed by a palate with nice sweetness and richness, part fruit and part oak; neatly balanced. **rating:** 87

best drinking 2002–2007 **best vintages** NA **drink with** Marinated lamb • $21

Willespie Cabernet Sauvignon

ΨΨΨΨ **1997** Medium red; a clean bouquet with cedar, leaf, tobacco and earth aromas is followed by a quite intense palate with leafy/cedary/briary overtones to the dark berry fruit, and a slightly piquant finish. **rating:** 88

best drinking 2002–2007 **best vintages** NA **drink with** Butterfly leg of lamb • $32

Willespie Reserve Cabernet Sauvignon

ΨΨΨΨ **1996** Medium red-purple; the clean, firm bouquet has developed some savoury/earthy cabernet aromas; the palate offers fine, gently sweet berry fruit, fine tannins contributing to the long, supple mouthfeel and finish. **rating:** 90

best drinking 2002–2009 **best vintages** '96 **drink with** Braised beef • $50

willow bridge estate ★★★★☆

Gardin Court Drive, Dardanup, WA 6236 **region** Geographe
phone (08) 9728 0055 **fax** (08) 9728 0066 **open** 7 days 10.30–4.30, closed Christmas Day, Boxing Day and Good Friday
winemaker Rob Bowen, David Crawford **production** 25 000 **est.** 1997
product range ($13.50–28 CD) Sauvignon Blanc Semillon, Chenin Blanc, Chardonnay, Shiraz, Merlot, Cabernet Sauvignon; Winemaker's Reserve range of Sauvignon Blanc, Semillon Sauvignon Blanc, Chardonnay, Shiraz, Cabernet Sauvignon Merlot.
summary The Dewar family has followed a fast track in developing Willow Bridge Estate since acquiring their spectacular 180-hectare hillside property in the Ferguson Valley in 1996. Sixty hectares of chardonnay, semillon, sauvignon blanc, shiraz and cabernet sauvignon have already been planted, with tempranillo added in the spring of 2000, and another 10 hectares due to be planted over the next year or two. A state-of-the-art winery has been constructed which will be capable of handling the 1200 to 1500 tonnes expected from the estate plantings by 2004. Winemaker Rob Bowen has had a long and distinguished career, first as winemaker at Plantagenet and thereafter at Capel Vale. Exports to the UK, Germany, Denmark, Singapore, Indonesia and Hong Kong.

Willow Bridge Estate Winemaker's Reserve Sauvignon Blanc

ΨΨΨΨ **2001** Light green-yellow; a complex, rich, ripe gooseberry-accented bouquet, with a hint of smoke, then a flavoursome, fleshy style texturally moving towards Chardonnay, perhaps reflecting its high alcohol of 13.5°. One might be forgiven for thinking a little oak was used, but there is in fact none. **rating:** 88

best drinking 2002–2003 **best vintages** NA **drink with** Rich seafood • $18

Willow Bridge Estate Sauvignon Blanc Semillon

ΨΨΨΨ **2001** Light green-yellow; a clean, fresh, ripe mix of herb, grass and gooseberry leads into a palate with abundant mouthfeel and weight, the alcohol adding a touch of sweetness; overall, quite supple. **rating:** 87

best drinking 2002–2004 **best vintages** '00 **drink with** Fresh abalone • $14.50

Willow Bridge Estate Winemaker's Reserve Semillon Sauvignon Blanc

TTTTY 2001 Light green-yellow; an intense and complex marriage of herbaceous fruit and spicy oak on the bouquet, then a similarly powerful and complex palate, with the fruit intensity easily carrying the oak through to a long and sustained finish. Sixty six per cent barrel-fermented, 33 per cent tank-fermented.   **rating: 93**

best drinking 2002–2005 **best vintages** '01 **drink with** Sugar-cured tuna • $18

Willow Bridge Estate Shiraz

TTTT 2000 Medium red-purple; the cedary/leafy/savoury bouquet has some spicy overtones, the palate moving more to black cherry/raspberry than the bouquet would suggest.   **rating: 86**

best drinking 2003–2007 **best vintages** NA **drink with** Shepherd's pie • $17

Willow Bridge Estate Winemaker's Reserve Shiraz

TTTTT 2000 Medium to full red-purple; smooth, nicely ripened black cherry/raspberry, together with spice and licorice aromas lead into a palate of another depth and dimension, with ripe, plush, plummy fruit and well-handled oak.   **rating: 94**

best drinking 2004–2014 **best vintages** '00 **drink with** Braised oxtail • $28

Willow Bridge Estate Winemaker's Reserve Cabernet Sauvignon Merlot

TTTT 2000 Medium red-purple; the bouquet is quite complex, with an array of briary/savoury/berry aromas to the fore, then a touch of cedar and cigar box. The palate is similar, but all in all is a little tart on both the mid-palate and finish.   **rating: 85**

best drinking 2003–2007 **best vintages** NA **drink with** Cassoulet • $28

willow creek   ★ ★ ★ ☆

166 Balnarring Road, Merricks North, Vic 3926 **region** Mornington Peninsula
phone (03) 5989 7448 **fax** (03) 5989 7584 **open** 7 days 10–5
winemaker Phil Kerney **production** 8000 **est.** 1989
product range ($15–25 ML) Sauvignon Blanc, Unoaked Chardonnay, Tulum Chardonnay, Tulum Brut Sparkling, Rosé, Pinot Noir, Shiraz, Cabernet Sauvignon.
summary Yet another significant player in the Mornington Peninsula area, with 9 hectares of vines planted to cabernet sauvignon, chardonnay and pinot noir. Expansion of the cellar door was completed by January 1998, with a winery constructed for the 1998 vintage. The restaurant is open for lunch seven days and Friday and Saturday nights for dinner. The wines are exported to the US and UK.

Willow Creek Rosé

TTTT 2000 Very pale salmon; a mix of strawberry and more smoky aromas lead into a palate with good acidity and length; lively and fresh, and an appealing summer drink.   **rating: 85**

best drinking 2000–2001 **best vintages** '00 **drink with** Antipasto • $15

willowvale wines   NR

Black Swamp Road, Tenterfield, NSW 2372 **region** Northern Slopes Zone
phone (02) 6736 3589 **fax** (02) 6736 3753 **open** 7 days 9–5
winemaker John Morley **production** 1200 **est.** 1994
product range ($14–25 CD) Federation Classic White, Ambrosia, London Bridge Chardonnay, Late Harvest Riesling, London Bridge Shiraz, London Bridge Dry Red, London Bridge Soft Red, Bushranger Musket, Centenary of Federation Port.
summary John Morley commenced establishing 1.8 hectares of vineyard of equal portions of chardonnay, merlot and cabernet sauvignon in 1994, with further planting in 1999 and 2000. The vineyard is at an altitude of 940 metres and was the first in the growing Tenterfield region. Advanced vineyard climatic monitoring systems have been installed, and a new winery building was constructed and equipped in time for the 2000 vintage.

will taylor wines   ★ ★ ★ ★

1B Victoria Avenue, Unley Park, SA 5061 **region** Warehouse
phone (08) 8271 6122 **fax** (08) 8271 6122 **open** By appointment
winemaker Various contract **production** 1270 **est.** 1997

product range ($20–40 R) Clare Valley Riesling, Hunter Valley Semillon, Adelaide Hills Sauvignon Blanc, Yarra Valley/Geelong Pinot Noir.

summary Will Taylor is a partner in the leading Adelaide law firm Finlaysons and specialises in wine law. Together with Suzanne Taylor, he has established a classic negociant wine business, having wines contract-made to his specification. Moreover, he chooses what he considers to be the best regions for each variety and added a Geelong/Yarra Valley Pinot Noir in 2000. Most of the wine is sold to restaurants, with small volumes sold to a select group of fine wine stores and mail order. Exports to the US.

Will Taylor Clare Valley Riesling

TTTT 2001 Light green-yellow; an aromatic bouquet with ripe apple and citrus aromas is followed by a palate in which the Granny Smith apple flavours are quite pronounced against soft acidity on the finish. Slightly left field. **rating:** 86

best drinking 2003–2007 **best vintages** '00 **drink with** Chargrilled octopus salad • $20.45

Will Taylor Hunter Valley Semillon

TTTTY 2001 Light green-yellow; a delicate but firm bouquet with a mix of lemon and mineral aromas, then a firm, crisp and grassy palate, with lingering acidity and totally appropriate alcohol of 10.6°. Certain to develop; right in the slot of the Hunter style. **rating:** 90

best drinking 2004–2011 **best vintages** '01 **drink with** Light pasta • $20.45

Will Taylor Adelaide Hills Sauvignon Blanc

TTTT 2001 Light to medium green-straw; the bouquet is quite solid but not particularly aromatic, showing some grass/herbaceous characters. The firm, grassy/minerally palate has no tropical fruit characters; a genuine food style. **rating:** 86

best drinking 2002–2004 **best vintages** '00 **drink with** Oysters • $20.45

Will Taylor Yarra Valley/Geelong Pinot Noir

TTTTY 2000 Medium red-purple; an expressive bouquet with spicy/charry oak leads into a complex, savoury and oaky fore palate, supported by lingering plummy/foresty fruit underneath. An undeniably good wine, but less oak might have made it better still. **rating:** 91

best drinking 2002–2006 **best vintages** '00 **drink with** Jugged hare • $39.85

wilmot hills vineyard   NR

407 Back Road, Wilmot, Tas 7310 **region** Northern Tasmania
phone (03) 6492 1193 **fax** (03) 6492 1193 **open** 7 days 9–7
winemaker John Cole, Ruth Cole **production** NA **est.** 1991
product range ($15–18 CD) Muller Thurgau, Pinot Noir, El Nino Pinot Noir, fruit wines and ciders.
summary The beautiful Wilmot Hills Vineyard is situated on the western side of Lake Barrington, not far from the Cradle Mountain road, with marvellous views to Mount Roland and the adjacent peaks. It is very much a family affair, established by John and Ruth Cole, and produces both wine and cider. John Cole spent 18 years in Melbourne participating in engineering design and some graphic art, Ruth working in the hospitality industry for ten years and making fruit wines for 20 years. The neat on-site winery was both designed and built by the Coles, as was much of the wine and cider-making equipment.

wilson vineyard   ★★★★

Polish Hill River, Sevenhill via Clare, SA 5453 **region** Clare Valley
phone (08) 8843 4310 **open** Weekends 10–4 March–November
winemaker John Wilson **production** 4000 **est.** 1974
product range ($14–24.50 CD) Gallery Series Riesling, Daniel Wilson Riesling, Chardonnay, Leucothea (sweet), Shiraz, Hippocrene Sparkling Burgundy.
summary Dr John Wilson is a tireless ambassador for the Clare Valley and for wine (and its beneficial effect on health) in general. His wines were made using techniques and philosophies garnered early in his wine career and can occasionally be idiosyncratic but in recent years have been most impressive. The wines are sold through cellar door and retail in Sydney, Melbourne, Brisbane and Adelaide; no mailing list.

Wilson Vineyard Daniel Wilson Riesling

TTTT 2001 Light to medium green-yellow; a classic, tight herb and mineral bouquet, with plenty of depth to the flavour; an early edge of roughness should settle down with time in bottle. **rating:** 88

best drinking 2003–2010 **best vintages** NA **drink with** Fresh asparagus • $18

Wilson Gallery Series Riesling

TTTT 2001 Light to medium yellow-green; the softly toasty bouquet has lime and tropical fruit, the palate more delicate, with good length and intensity. **rating:** 88

best drinking 2001–2003 **best vintages** '85, '90, '91, '92, '94, '96, '97, '99 **drink with** Japanese cuisine • $19.50

wimbaliri wines ★★★☆

Barton Highway, Murrumbateman, NSW 2582 **region** Canberra District
phone (02) 6227 5921 **fax** (02) 6227 5921 **open** Weekends 11–5 or by appointment
winemaker John Andersen **production** 600 **est.** 1988
product range ($18–21 CD) Chardonnay, Pinot Noir, Merlot, Cabernet Merlot.
summary John and Margaret Andersen moved to the Canberra district in 1987 and commenced the establishment of their vineyard at Murrumbateman in 1988; the property borders two highly regarded Canberra producers, Doonkuna and Clonakilla. The vineyard is close-planted with a vertical trellis system, with a total of 2.2. hectares planted to chardonnay, pinot noir, shiraz, cabernet sauvignon and merlot (plus a few vines of cabernet franc).

Wimbaliri Chardonnay

TTTY 2000 Straw colour; the bouquet is not aromatic, simply showing some bottle development, the basically soft palate with some peachy fruit, but it is hard to see the expected influence of 12 months maturation in new French oak. **rating:** 83

best drinking 2002–2004 **best vintages** NA **drink with** Smoked trout • $18

Wimbaliri Pinot Noir

TTTT 2000 Medium red-purple; the clean, moderately intense bouquet offers a nice mix of plum and a touch of charry oak; the wine comes through quite powerfully on the mid-palate with more plummy fruit, but falls away somewhat on the finish/aftertaste. **rating:** 85

best drinking 2002–2004 **best vintages** NA **drink with** Wild mushroom risotto • $20

Wimbaliri Cabernet Merlot

TTTT 2000 Medium red-purple; clean, gently ripe blackcurrant fruit is accompanied by some earthy notes on the bouquet; there are attractively spicy/cedary edges to the blackcurrant fruit of the palate; good balance and mouthfeel. Consistently the best of the Wimbaliri range, and a blend of 86 per cent Cabernet, 14 per cent Merlot. **rating:** 89

best drinking 2003–2008 **best vintages** NA **drink with** Grilled steak • $21

🐂 winbirra vineyard ★★★☆

173 Point Leo Road, Red Hill South, Vic 3937 (PO Box 130, Red Hill South, Vic 3937)
region Mornington Peninsula
phone (03) 5989 2109 **fax** (03) 5989 2109 **open** By appointment
winemaker Kevin McCarthy (Contract) **production** 450 **est.** 1990
product range ($30 ML) Pinot Noir Pinot Meunier.
summary Winbirra is a small, family-owned and run vineyard which has been producing grapes since 1990, between then and 1997 selling the grapes to local winemakers. Since 1997 the wine has been contract-made by Kevin McCarthy at T'Gallant and sold under the Winbirra label. There is 1.5 hectares of pinot noir (with three clones) and a half a hectare of pinot meunier sourced from Best's vineyard at Great Western. In 1998 the wines were made at separate varietals, but in 1999 and 2000 a single wine composed of 70 per cent pinot noir and 30 per cent pinot meunier was made, both vintages producing wine of convincing quality.

Winbirra Vineyard Pinot Noir Pinot Meunier

TTTT 2000 The slightly dull colour turns out to be a false warning; the tangy/foresty/earthy/spicy aromas of the bouquet are followed by a palate with a substantial volume of earthy/plummy fruit on the mid-palate, suggestive of some whole bunch or whole berry component, and the slightly stalky/foresty undertone which quite possibly comes from the pinot meunier if not from whole berries. **rating:** 88

best drinking 2001–2004 **best vintages** '00 **drink with** Tea-smoked duck • $30

windarra   NR

De Beyers Road, Pokolbin, NSW 2321 **region** Lower Hunter Valley
phone (02) 4998 7648 **fax** (02) 4998 7648 **open** Tues–Sun 10–5
winemaker Tom Andresen-Jung **production** 1650 **est.** 1985
product range ($8–32 CD) Semillon, Semillon Chardonnay, Chardonnay, Reserve Blue Bottle Chardonnay, Rosé, Shiraz, White Liqueur Port, Old Tawny Port, Fair Dinkum Herbal Port, Mead, Gold Wine (Mead, with 22-carat gold flakes).
summary The Andresen family has 6 hectares of semillon, chardonnay and shiraz; the wines are contract made.

windermere wines   ★★★

Lot 3, Watters Road, Ballandean, Qld 4382 **region** Granite Belt
phone (07) 4684 1353 **fax** (07) 4684 1353 **open** 7 days 9.30–5
winemaker Wayne Beecham, Kate Beecham **production** 500 **est.** 1995
product range ($11–17 CD) Chardonnay, Lilybrook DW Chardonnay Semillon, Sangiovese Merlot Cabernet, Millroad DR Cabernet Merlot, Shiraz, Liqueur Muscat; a selection of liqueurs and fruit wines.
summary After spending three years travelling in Europe between 1983 and 1986, Wayne Beecham returned to Australia to take up a position with what was then Thomas Hardy Wines, and specifically to establish the RhineCastle wine distribution in Queensland. During the next seven and a half years he studied wine marketing at Roseworthy while working for Hardys, but in 1993 he, wife Julie and daughter Kate decided to move to the Granite Belt to establish Windermere Wines from the ground up. His long service with Hardys stood him in good stead, landing him a cellar position at Hardys Tintara in the 1994 vintage, working with winemaker David O'Leary. In typical Australian fashion, Wayne Beecham says they decided on the Granite Belt because 'if we were to succeed, we might as well do it in the toughest new region in the industry'.

windowrie estate   NR

Windowrie, Canowindra, NSW 2804 **region** Cowra
phone (02) 6344 3234 **fax** (02) 6344 3227 **open** 7 days 10–6 at the Mill, Vaux Street, Cowra
winemaker Rodney Hooper **production** 35 000 **est.** 1988
product range ($12–21 ML) Chardonnay, Botrytis Sauvignon Blanc, Shiraz; The Mill range of Traminer Riesling, Sauvignon Blanc, Chardonnay, Shiraz and Cabernet Sauvignon Merlot Cabernet Franc.
summary Windowrie Estate was established in 1988 on a substantial grazing property at Canowindra, 30 kilometres north of Cowra and in the same viticultural region. Most of the grapes from the 230-hectare vineyard are sold to other makers, with increasing quantities being made for the Windowrie Estate and The Mill labels, the Chardonnays enjoying show success. The cellar door is situated in a flour mill built in 1861 from local granite. It ceased operations in 1905 and lay unoccupied for 91 years until restored by the O'Dea family.

🐌 windsors edge   ★★★☆

McDonalds Road, Pokolbin, NSW 2320 **region** Lower Hunter Valley
phone (02) 4998 7737 **fax** (02) 4998 7737 **open** Fri–Mon 10–5, or by appointment
winemaker Monarch Wines (Contract), Tim Windsor, Jessie Windsor **production** 3500 **est.** 1996
product range ($14–18 ML) Semillon, Chardonnay, Rosé, Shiraz, Sparkling Shiraz, Coonawarra Cabernet Sauvignon.
summary In 1995 Tim Windsor (a Charles Sturt graduate in winemaking) and wife Jessie (an industrial chemist) purchased the old Black Creek picnic racetrack at the northern end of McDonalds Road in Pokolbin. The first vines were planted in 1996, and to date 17 hectares of shiraz, semillon, chardonnay, tempranillo, tinta cao and touriga are in the ground. Three luxury cottages have been built, followed by a restaurant and cellar door, with a small winery beneath, and the range extended to include a Coonawarra Cabernet Sauvignon, a Chambourcin, and a Tasmanian Pinot. The winemaking, too, has been parceled out: the larger quantities are made by Monarch Wines; the smaller volumes of grapes sourced outside the Hunter are made by Tim and Jessie in the small winery below the restaurant; while the Tinta Cao and Touriga have been sent to the Peter Van Gent Winery in Mudgee to be fortified.

Windsors Edge Semillon

YYYY 2000 Medium to full yellow-green; a developed bouquet with some quasi-Riesling kerosene-type aromas; the palate is powerful, again showing some characters more akin to Riesling, though also offering herb and grass. **rating: 87**

best drinking 2002–2005 **best vintages** NA **drink with** Deep-fried calamari • $15

Windsors Edge Chardonnay

YYYY 2000 Medium yellow-green; the clean, moderately intense bouquet offers nectarine and subtle French oak, that nectarine fruit coming through on the spotlessly clean palate; good balance and mouthfeel. **rating: 88**

best drinking 2002–2004 **best vintages** NA **drink with** Chinese prawns • $16.50

Windsors Edge Coonawarra Cabernet Sauvignon

YYYY 2000 Medium red-purple; quite fine berry fruit is supported by balanced oak on the bouquet; the palate has both depth and length, with fresh cassis fruit flavours and fine tannins. **rating: 87**

best drinking 2004–2009 **best vintages** NA **drink with** Leg of lamb • $18

windy ridge vineyard ★★★

Foster–Fish Creek Road, Foster, Vic 3960 **region** Gippsland
phone (03) 5682 2035 **open** Holiday weekends 10–5
winemaker Graeme Wilson **production** 300 **est.** 1978
product range ($15–35 CD) Traminer, Pinot Noir, Cabernet Sauvignon Malbec, Malbec Cabernet Sauvignon, Vintage Port, Georgia's Liqueur Pinot Noir, Graeme's Late Bottled Vintage Port.
summary The 2.8-hectare Windy Ridge Vineyard was planted between 1978 and 1986, with the first vintage not taking place until 1988. Winemaker Graeme Wilson favours prolonged maturation, part in stainless steel and part in oak, before bottling his wines, typically giving the Pinot Noir three years and the Cabernet two years before bottling.

Windy Ridge Pinot Noir

YYYY 1998 Medium red-purple; an earthy/briary/savoury bouquet is precisely reflected by the palate, strongly savoury, with some style though diminished sweet fruit flavours. Tasted from a 375 ml bottle; 750 ml bottles might well show more fruit. **rating: 86**

best drinking 2002–2003 **best vintages** NA **drink with** Pastrami salad • $30

winewood NR

Sundown Road, Ballandean, Qld 4382 **region** Granite Belt
phone (07) 4684 1187 **fax** (07) 4684 1187 **open** Weekends and public holidays 9–5
winemaker Ian Davis **production** 1000 **est.** 1984
product range ($15–20 CD) Chardonnay, Chardonnay Marsanne, Shiraz Marsanne, MacKenzies Run (Cabernet blend), Muscat.
summary A weekend and holiday activity for schoolteacher Ian Davis and town-planner wife Jeanette; the tiny winery is a model of neatness and precision planning. There is a little over 3 hectares of estate plantings. The use of marsanne with chardonnay and semillon shows an interesting change in direction. All wine sold through cellar door.

winstead ★★★★☆

75 Winstead Road, Bagdad, Tas 7030 **region** Southern Tasmania
phone (03) 6268 6417 **fax** (03) 6268 6417 **open** By appointment
winemaker Andrew Hood (Contract), Neil Snare **production** 730 **est.** 1989
product range ($17–32 CD) Riesling, Ensnared Riesling (Dessert style), Pinot Noir.
summary The good news about Winstead is the outstanding quality of its extremely generous and rich Pinot Noirs, rivalling those of Freycinet for the abundance of their fruit flavour without any sacrifice of varietal character. The bad news is that production is so limited, with only 0.8 hectares of pinot noir and 0.4 ha riesling being tended by fly-fishing devotee Neil Snare and wife Julieanne. Retail distribution in Melbourne.

Winstead Riesling

YYYY 2001 Light green-yellow; the bouquet is clean, with quite positive lime/citrus fruit and a more minerally underlay; the palate, however, veers off in a different direction, with ripe, even cooked, apple flavours. Could quite possibly have been an aberrational bottle. **rating: 85**

best drinking 2002–2005 **best vintages** '98, '99 **drink with** Pan-fried trout • $18

Winstead Pinot Noir

ΨΨΨΨΨ 2000 Medium red-purple; an exceedingly complex bouquet, with a mix of spice, forest and plum aromas bracketed by subtle oak. The palate shows perfectly ripened plummy varietal fruit, woven through with fine tannins. Gold medal Tasmanian Wines Show 2002. **rating:** 94

best drinking 2002–2007 **best vintages** '96, '97, '98, '99, '00 **drink with** Saddle of hare • $32

wirilda creek ★★★

RSD 91, McMurtrie Road, McLaren Vale, SA 5171 **region** McLaren Vale
phone (08) 8323 9688 **fax** (08) 8323 9260 **open** 7 days 10–5
winemaker Kerry Flanagan **production** 1500 **est.** 1993
product range ($13–25 CD) Grape Pickers (Riesling Chardonnay Semillon), Sauvignon Blanc, Verdelho, Shiraz, Shiraz Rare, Cabernet Merlot, Vine Pruners Cabernet Blend, Cabernet Sauvignon Rare, Evening Shadow (Sparkling Shiraz), Fortifieds.
summary Wirilda Creek may be one of the newer arrivals in McLaren Vale but it offers the lot: wine, lunch every day (Pickers Platters reflecting local produce) and accommodation (4 rooms opening onto a private garden courtyard). Co-owner Kerry Flanagan (with partner Karen Shertock) has had great experience in the wine and hospitality industries: a Roseworthy graduate (1980) he has inter alia worked at Penfolds, Coriole and Wirra Wirra and also owned the famous Old Salopian Inn for a period of time. A little under 4 hectares of McLaren Vale estate vineyards have now been joined with a little over 3 hectares of vineyards planted at Antechamber Bay, Kangaroo Island. Limited retail distribution in New South Wales and South Australia; exports to the US.

wirra wirra ★★★★☆

McMurtie Road, McLaren Vale, SA 5171 **region** McLaren Vale
phone (08) 8323 8414 **fax** (08) 8323 8596 **open** Mon–Sat 10–5, Sun 11–5
winemaker Samantha Connew **production** 70 000 **est.** 1969
product range ($14.50–75 R) Hand Picked Riesling, Sauvignon Blanc, Scrubby Rise (Semillon Sauvignon Blanc Chardonnay), Chardonnay, Sexton's Acre Unwooded Chardonnay, The Cousins (Sparkling Pinot Noir Chardonnay), The Anthem (Sparkling Shiraz), Late Picked Riesling, McLaren Vale Shiraz, Chook Block Shiraz, RSW Shiraz, Merlot, Scrubby Rise (Shiraz Cabernet Petit Verdot), Church Block (Cabernet Shiraz Merlot), Penley Coonawarra Cabernet Sauvignon, The Angelus Cabernet Sauvignon, Fortifieds.
summary Long-respected for the consistency of its white wines, Wirra Wirra has now established an equally formidable reputation for its reds. Right across the board, the wines are of exemplary character, quality and style, The Angelus Cabernet Sauvignon and RSW Shiraz battling with each other for supremacy. Long may the battle continue under the direction of the highly respected Tim James, lured from his senior position at BRL Hardy late in 2000. The wines are exported to the US, UK, Switzerland, France, Germany, Netherlands, New Zealand, Hong Kong, Singapore and Malaysia.

Wirra Wirra Hand Picked Riesling

ΨΨΨΨ 2001 Light green-yellow; not particularly aromatic, but clean, and with some ripe citrus aromas; the palate is soft and ripe, with citrus/tropical fruit in a drink-now style. Stelvin-capped. **rating:** 85

best drinking 2001–2003 **best vintages** '82, '89, '91, '92, '94, '96, '97 **drink with** South Australian whiting • $16.99

Wirra Wirra Scrubby Rise

ΨΨΨΨ 2001 Light green-yellow; the bouquet is clean, crisp and neutral, picking up pace on the lively and long palate with nice grassy/lemony notes, sustained by good acidity. **rating:** 85

best drinking 2001–2002 **best vintages** NA **drink with** Shellfish • $15

Wirra Wirra Chook Block Shiraz

ΨΨΨΨΨ 1998 Medium to full red; sweet, dark berry fruit and some chocolate on the bouquet leads into rich, ripe dark berry fruit on the palate with vanilla and abundant, soft tannins. One of the special series wines made by Wirra Wirra, typically in lots of 250 cases or less. **rating:** 95

best drinking 2003–2013 **best vintages** '98 **drink with** Braised lamb shanks • $75

Wirra Wirra McLaren Vale Shiraz

ŸŸŸŸ♡ **1999** Medium red, the purple diminishing. Slightly dusty overtones to the moderately intense fruit on the bouquet blew off after some time in the glass, the palate coming up with sweet black cherry, plum and prune fruit, carrying its typical 14.5° alcohol.   **rating:** 91

best drinking 2004–2009 **best vintages** '99 **drink with** Lamb shanks • $28.50

Wirra Wirra RSW Shiraz

ŸŸŸŸŸ **1999** Medium red-purple; sweet, but not jammy, dark berry/cherry/chocolate fruit to the bouquet, followed by a concentrated but balanced, rich and stylish palate repeating the flavours promised by the bouquet, the oak and tannins well controlled.   **rating:** 94

best drinking 2004–2014 **best vintages** '94, '95, '97, '98, '99 **drink with** Smoked beef • $41.50

Wirra Wirra Church Block Cabernet Shiraz Merlot

ŸŸŸŸ **2000** Medium red-purple; the bouquet has some fragrance and lift, the berry fruit accompanied by earthy, spicy, leafy notes. There is a similar mix on the palate, with redcurrant and black cherry fruit supported by fine tannins.   **rating:** 86

best drinking 2003–2007 **best vintages** '90, '91, '94, '98 **drink with** Pasta bolognese • $19

Wirra Wirra The Angelus Cabernet Sauvignon

ŸŸŸŸ♡ **1999** Medium red-purple; some spicy/cedary overtones to gentle, dark berry fruit on the bouquet, then a mix of sweet spice, chocolate and cedar on the palate, with ripe tannins; against the run of play, almost too sweet.   **rating:** 92

best drinking 2004–2010 **best vintages** '86, '90, '91, '92, '95, '96, '97, '98 **drink with** Spring lamb • $41.50

Wirra Wirra Vineyard Series Penley Cabernet Sauvignon

ŸŸŸŸŸ **1998** Full red-purple, concentrated and dense cassis blackcurrant fruit on the bouquet leads into a luscious, long, smooth, red and blackcurrant palate which has soaked up the new French oak; fine tannins.   **rating:** 97

best drinking 2003–2013 **best vintages** '98 **drink with** Roast rosemary-studded leg of lamb • $67

wise vineyards ★★★

Lot 4 Eagle Bay Road, Dunsborough, WA 6281 **region** Margaret River
phone (08) 9756 8627 **fax** (08) 9756 8770 **open** 7 days 10–5
winemaker Bruce Dukes (Consultant), Andy Coppard, Amanda Kramer **production** 35 000 **est.** 1986
product range ($15–35 CD) Eagle Bay Semillon Sauvignon Blanc, Verdlho, Classic White, Unwooded Chardonnay, Pinot Noir, Classic Red, Eagle Bay Shiraz, Shiraz Cabernet Merlot, Cabernet Sauvignon.
summary Wise Vineyards, headed by Perth entrepreneur Ron Wise, brings together the 20.5-hectare Eagle Bay Vineyard at Meelup, the 10.3-hectare Donnybrook Valley Vineyard at Donnybrook, and the 8-hectare Bramley Estate Vineyard at Margaret River. The on-site restaurant is open daily for lunch, Friday and Saturday for dinner, and Saturday and Sunday for breakfast, and there are five chalets, variously sleeping 2-10 people all within ten minutes walk from the restaurant.

Wise Geographe Verdelho

ŸŸŸŸ **2001** Light green-yellow; some floral/honeysuckle aromas enliven the bouquet, moving on to tropical/pineapple flavours on the fresh palate. Well-balanced, and a nice wine in its class.   **rating:** 85

best drinking 2002–2003 **best vintages** NA **drink with** Chicken yakitori • $18

Wise Pemberton Unwooded Chardonnay

ŸŸŸŸ **2001** Light green-yellow; gentle melon and nectarine fruit on the bouquet comes through in the generously endowed palate; a well above average example of the style.   **rating:** 86

best drinking 2002–2004 **best vintages** NA **drink with** Smoked salmon • $18

witchmount estate ★★★★

557 Leakes Road, Rockbank, Vic 3335 **region** Sunbury
phone (03) 9747 1188 **open** Wed–Sun
winemaker Peter Dredge **production** 2000 **est.** 1991
product range ($25–27 CD) Semillon, Sauvignon Blanc, Chardonnay, Nebbiolo, Shiraz, Cabernet Sauvignon.

summary Gaye and Matt Ramunno operate Witchmount Estate in conjunction with its on-site Italian restaurant and function rooms, which are open from Wednesday to Sunday inclusive for lunch and dinner. Twelve hectares of vines have been established since 1991, with a further 9 hectares currently being planted. Varieties include nebbiolo and the rare northern Italian white grape picolit. Another variety new to the region will be tempranillo.

Witchmount Estate Cabernet Sauvignon

▼▼▼▼▽ **2000** Medium to full red-purple; the bouquet has solid blackberry, blackcurrant and chocolate aromas, the palate flooded with ripe cassis/blackcurrant fruit, rounded off with soft tannins and nicely handled oak. **rating:** 91

best drinking 2004–2010 **best vintages** '00 **drink with** Bistecca fiorentina • NA

wolf blass ★★★★☆

Bilyara Vineyards, Sturt Highway, Nuriootpa, SA 5355 **region** Barossa Valley
phone (08) 8562 1955 **fax** (08) 8562 2156 **open** Mon–Fri 9.15–4.30, weekends 10–4.30
winemaker John Glaetzer (Chief), Wendy Stuckey (White), Caroline Dunn (Red) **production** NFP
est. 1966
product range ($9.95–100 R) White wines under White, Yellow, Green and Gold labels, with emphasis on Riesling and blended Classic Dry White, Gold Label Riesling ; red wines under Red, Yellow, Brown, Grey, Black and Platinum labels with emphasis on Cabernet Sauvignon, Shiraz and blends of these. Also sparkling and fortified wines. The Eaglehawk now roosts here, too, Eaglehawk Chardonnay, Eaglehawk Riesling, Eaglehawk Sauvignon Blanc, Eaglehawk Semillon Sauvignon Blanc, Traminer Riesling, Grenache Shiraz. The Blass range, with its red, minimalist labels in stark contrast to the usual baroque designs so loved by Wolf, is a more recent addition, Vintage Brut, Pinot Chardonnay Brut, Clare Valley Red Label Riesling, Semillon Sauvignon Blanc, Chardonnay,
summary Although merged with Mildara and now under the giant umbrella of Beringer Blass, the brands (as expected) have been left largely intact. The white wines (made by Wendy Stuckey) are particularly impressive, none more so than the Gold Label Riesling. After a short pause, the red wines have improved out of all recognition thanks to the sure touch (and top palate) of Caroline Dunn. Worldwide distribution.

Blass Clare Valley Riesling

▼▼▼▼▽ **2001** Light green-yellow; the spotlessly clean and highly aromatic bouquet offers a mix of lime and lime blossom, the palate lively and fresh, with more lime blossom flavours, though not quite as intense as the bouquet suggests. May well build with time in bottle. Stelvin finished. **rating:** 90

best drinking 2003–2010 **best vintages** '01 **drink with** Crab mornay • $18

Eaglehawk Riesling

▼▼▼▼▽ **2001** The aromatic bouquet ranges through spice, mineral, talc, lime and passionfruit; the fresh, clean and lively palate literally dances on the tongue, but avoids excessive CO_2 spritz. Already a gold medal winner. **rating:** 92

best drinking 2001–2006 **best vintages** '90, '92, '93, '96, '01 **drink with** Asparagus • $9.95

Wolf Blass Gold Label Riesling

▼▼▼▼▼ **2001** Light to medium green-yellow; the bouquet is spicy, with rich lime-accented fruit together with some more minerally characters. The palate is tight and crisp, with excellent acidity surrounding apple and lime fruit, giving that squeaky mouthfeel which is so attractive. **rating:** 94

best drinking 2002–2007 **best vintages** '90, '92, '95, '96, '97, '98, '00, '01 **drink with** Salad Nicoise • $16

Wolf Blass South Australia Riesling

▼▼▼▼▽ **2001** Light green-yellow; the bouquet is classic, with a quite firm minerally frame, the palate opening with abundant lime fruit, then good length and grip to close. **rating:** 91

best drinking 2001–2006 **best vintages** NA **drink with** Fresh asparagus • $12

Blass Eden Valley Gewürztraminer

▼▼▼▼▽ **2001** Light green-yellow; has outstanding varietal character on the highly fragrant bouquet with its mix of spice, lychee and rose petal; the palate does not disappoint, strongly varietal and in no way propped up by residual sugar. Great with any Asian cuisine. **rating:** 91

best drinking 2002–2005 **best vintages** NA **drink with** Chinese • $18

Blass Adelaide Hills Sauvignon Blanc

ŸŸŸŸ **2001** Light green-yellow; quite pronounced gooseberry/passionfruit aromas have a faintly sweaty background, the palate crisp, firm and abundantly flavoured, but unable to completely throw off the touch of sweatiness.   **rating:** 87

best drinking 2002–2003 **best vintages** NA **drink with** Seafood pasta • $18.95

Wolf Blass Frontignac Traminer

ŸŸŸŸ **2001** Light green-yellow; the bouquet is gently spicy with attractive limey fruit, the palate a mix of lime, spice and residual sugar. A particularly good example of its style.   **rating:** 84

best drinking 2001–2002 **best vintages** NA **drink with** Chinese • $12

Blass Adelaide Hills Chardonnay

ŸŸŸŸ **2000** Light to medium green-yellow; the bouquet is utterly dominated by masses of barrel ferment/new oak characters; a complex wine in all respects, with figgy/toasty/cashew flavours but too much oak and winemaker inputs.   **rating:** 86

best drinking 2002–2003 **best vintages** NA **drink with** Rich chicken dishes • $18

Eaglehawk Chardonnay

ŸŸŸŸ **2001** Light to medium yellow-green; pleasant nectarine and melon fruit, with the barest hint of oak, then a lively, juicy, tangy fruit-driven palate all add up to excellent value.   **rating:** 85

best drinking 2001–2002 **best vintages** NA **drink with** KFC • $9.99

Wolf Blass Reserve Eden Valley Chardonnay

ŸŸŸŸ **2001** Light to medium green-yellow; a fresh, quite light bouquet with subtle oak logically feeds into a palate with tight citrus and nectarine fruit; the wine has not been forced by winemaking tricks, but there is not too much there.   **rating:** 85

best drinking 2002–2005 **best vintages** NA **drink with** Gravlax • $17.50

Wolf Blass Vintage Pinot Chardonnay

ŸŸŸŸ **1999** Light green-yellow; the pleasingly complex and intense minerally/citrussy bouquet promises a little more than the palate in fact delivers, but it does have good balance and length in a nice dry style.   **rating:** 87

best drinking 2002–2003 **best vintages** '94 **drink with** Shellfish • $17

Wolf Blass Noble Gold Clare Valley Riesling

ŸŸŸŸ **2001** Light green-yellow; clean albeit light citrus, lemon and honey aromas, then a pleasant entry to the mouth with matching flavours; shortens slightly on the finish.   **rating:** 87

best drinking 2002–2004 **best vintages** NA **drink with** Poached stone fruit • $13.50

Blass Barossa Shiraz

ŸŸŸŸ **1999** Medium red-purple; clean, fresh red berry fruit plus light vanilla oak on the bouquet picks up the pace on the palate, with more richness and concentration to the sweet, black cherry fruit, the oak under control.   **rating:** 89

best drinking 2003–2008 **best vintages** NA **drink with** Yearling beef • $17

Wolf Blass Brown Label Classic Shiraz

ŸŸŸŸŸ **2000** Medium to full purple-red; the moderately intense bouquet has fresh red and dark berry fruit foremost; rich, ripe dark berry fruit allied with a touch of chocolate follow on the palate; the good structure is as much driven by tannins as oak.   **rating:** 91

ŸŸŸŸŸ **1999** Medium to full red-purple; rich cherry and licorice and chocolate fruit aromas lead the bouquet, with similar flavours to be found on the palate. Oak is there in the background, but this is essentially a lovely fruit-drive, elegant wine, reflecting the ongoing changes in winemaking philosophy at Wolf Blass.   **rating:** 92

best drinking 2005–2010 **best vintages** '87, '88, '90, '91, '93, '96, '97, '98, '99, '00 **drink with** Spaghetti bolognese • $32.50

Wolf Blass Green Label Shiraz

ŸŸŸŸ **2000** Medium red-purple; clean, fresh berry fruit and subtle oak on the bouquet is followed by a palate with rather more presence thanks to quite pronounced juicy berry fruit. However, both the bouquet and structure are slightly simple.   **rating:** 86

best drinking 2001–2004 **best vintages** NA **drink with** Takeaway • $15

Wolf Blass Platinum Label Shiraz

ŸŸŸŸŸ 1998 Full purple-red; complex, rich black cherry fruit with hints of licorice and spicy oak on the bouquet foretell a palate with great depth, length, structure and balance. From a single 50-year-old Eden Valley vineyard; spent 18 months in French oak, and won the 2000 Great Australian Shiraz Challenge.   rating: 95

best drinking 2003–2013 best vintages '98 drink with Game pie • $95

Wolf Blass Red Label Shiraz Cabernet

ŸŸŸŸ 2000 Medium to full red-purple; the bouquet has scented, aromatic, slightly chippy/dusty oak, the palate with plenty of raspberry and mint fruit, but thins off on the finish, and the oak is not fully integrated.   rating: 83

best drinking 2002–2004 best vintages NA drink with Takeaway • $12

Wolf Blass Eaglehawk Cabernet Sauvignon

ŸŸŸŸ 2001 Vivid red-purple; juicy berry/rhubarb cabernet fruit aromas are followed by a fresh, young early drinking style with minimal tannin extract. Very good value.   rating: 83

best drinking 2001–2002 best vintages NA drink with Anything • $9.99

Wolf Blass Grey Label Cabernet Sauvignon

ŸŸŸŸŸ 1999 Youthful red-purple, very impressive; ripe cassis/blackcurrant fruit is woven through subtly integrated and balanced oak on the bouquet. A powerful wine on the palate, with lots of dark berry fruit, but also tannins and (of course) oak, the latter derived from the completion of fermentation in a mix of French and American barrels, and 28 months maturation thereafter in those barrels. A long way from the original Wolf Blass style, for the wine still demands time, having developed very well over the past year.   rating: 92

best drinking 2004–2014 best vintages '97, '99 drink with Mixed grill • $37.50

Wolf Blass Platinum Label Cabernet Sauvignon

ŸŸŸŸŸ 1998 Medium to full red-purple; a scented, almost flowery bouquet with a complex array of sweet berry fruit and oak; floods the mouth with rich flavour, some savoury tannins neatly offsetting the fruit sweetness. Once again, sure handling of oak (18 months in new French). From a single 30-year-old vineyard in the Light Pass.   rating: 94

best drinking 2003–2013 best vintages '98 drink with Spit-roasted leg of lamb • $95

Wolf Blass Yellow Label Cabernet Sauvignon

ŸŸŸŸ 2000 Medium red, with just a touch of purple remaining. The distinctly simple bouquet does have pleasantly clean red fruit, and the palate picks up pace with clever winemaking producing some texture. The old warhorse fights on.   rating: 84

best drinking 2002–2004 best vintages '98 drink with Steak and kidney pie • $14

woodend winery   NR

82 Mahoneys Road, Woodend, Vic 3442 region Macedon Ranges
phone (03) 5427 2183 fax (03) 5427 4007 open Not
winemaker Howard Bradfield production 400 est. 1983
product range ($15–30 ML) Unwooded Chardonnay, Pinot Noir, Cabernet Franc.
summary Woodend Winery (for a while known as Bluestone Bridge, a name which had to be relinquished due to trademark problems) draws upon 2.5 hectares of vineyard established way back in 1983, although the winemaking is of much more recent origin. The wines are distributed through wholesaler Australian Prestige Wines.

woodlands   ★★★☆

Cnr Caves and Metricup Roads, Wilyabrup via Cowaramup, WA 6284 region Margaret River
phone (08) 9755 6226 fax (08) 9481 1700 open Weekends by appointment
winemaker David Watson, Mark Lane, Dorham Mann (Consultant) production 3000 est. 1973
product range ($20–45 R) Unwooded Chardonnay, Reserve Chloe Chardonnay, Cabernet Merlot, Margaret Cabernet Merlot, Reserve St Peter Cabernet Merlot,
summary The production (and visibility) of Woodlands have varied over the years, the core of the business lying with 6.8 hectares of cabernet sauvignon, more recently joined by merlot (1.2 ha), malbec (0.8 ha), cabernet franc (0.2 ha), pinot noir (0.2 ha) and chardonnay (0.8 ha), all now in bearing. Exports to the US.

Woodlands Reserve Chloe Chardonnay

▼▼▼▽ 2001 Medium yellow-green; smoky oak and light nectarine fruit merge on the bouquet; the light to medium-bodied palate is nicely balanced and is certainly well made, although it is surprising there is not more fruit concentration. **rating:** 84

best drinking 2002–2005 **best vintages** NA **drink with** Margaret River abalone • $45

Woodlands Cabernet Sauvignon Merlot

▼▼▼▼ 2001 Youthful purple-red; clean, fresh raspberry and redcurrant fruit aromas with barely perceptible oak on the bouquet, then a palate with good mouthfeel for such a young wine, offering the same fresh red berry fruits and soft tannins. **rating:** 85

best drinking 2003–2007 **best vintages** NA **drink with** Lamb shashlick • $20

Woodlands Margaret Cabernet Merlot

▼▼▼▼ 2000 Medium purple-red; as with all the wines, the bouquet is clean, with appealing cassis/raspberry fruit. The palate is still firm and needing time to soften, the firmness being a whole-of-palate character, and not just tannins on the finish. Subtle oak handling throughout. **rating:** 86

best drinking 2004–2011 **best vintages** NA **drink with** Leave it in the cellar • $30

Woodlands Reserve St Peter Cabernet Merlot Malbec

▼▼▼▼ 2001 Medium purple-red; the bouquet has clean, sweet red/blackcurrant/cassis fruit and well-integrated oak; the palate is quite firm and still angular, but has good weight and depth; sure to improve with time in bottle. **rating:** 88

best drinking 2005–2010 **best vintages** NA **drink with** Shoulder of lamb • NA

woodonga hill   NR

Cowra Road, Young, NSW 2594 **region** Hilltops
phone (02) 6382 2972 **fax** (02) 6382 2972 **open** 7 days 9–5
winemaker Jill Lindsay **production** 4000 **est.** 1986
product range ($12.50–21 CD) Dry Rhine Riesling, Sauvignon, Chardonnay, Botrytis Semillon, Auslese Gewürztraminer, Meunier, Shiraz, Vintage Port, Cherry Liqueur Port.
summary Early problems with white wine quality appear to have been surmounted. The wines have won bronze or silver medals at regional wine shows in NSW and Canberra, and Jill Lindsay is also a successful contract-winemaker for other small producers.

wood park   ★★★☆

RMB 1139 Bobinawarrah–Whorouly Road, Milawa, Vic 3678 **region** King Valley
phone (03) 5727 3367 **fax** (03) 5727 3682 **open** At Milawa Cheese Factory
winemaker John Stokes **production** 3500 **est.** 1989
product range ($15–33 CD) Meadow Creek Chardonnay, Pinot Gris, Pinot Noir, Shiraz, Cabernet Shiraz.
summary The first vines were planted at Wood Park in 1989 by John Stokes as part of a diversification programme for his property at Bobinawarrah in the hills of the Lower King Valley to the east of Milawa. The bulk of the 8-hectare production is sold to Brown Brothers, with a further 8 hectares of vineyard being established for Southcorp. In an unusual twist, Stokes acquires his chardonnay from cousin John Leviny, one of the King Valley pioneers, who has his vineyard at Meadow Creek. To complicate matters further, all four vintages of Chardonnay ('95 to '98) were made by Rick Kinzbrunner. Exports to the US and Europe.

Wood Park Meadow Creek Chardonnay

▼▼▼▼ 2000 Medium to full yellow-green; the bouquet has solid stone fruit and light oak, the oak seemingly previously used; the palate is well-balanced with soft cashew, melon and fig, and, once again, a subtle oak infusion. **rating:** 85

best drinking 2002–2004 **best vintages** NA **drink with** Pasta marinara • NA

Wood Park Cabernet Shiraz

▼▼▼▼ 2000 Medium purple-red; here, too, the bouquet is solid, with blackberry fruit and gentle oak; the medium to full-bodied palate opens up with a rich mix of blackberry, and lesser quantities of plum and chocolate; nicely ripened, finishing with good tannins. **rating:** 87

best drinking 2004–2010 **best vintages** NA **drink with** Beef in red wine sauce • NA

woodsmoke estate   NR

Lot 2 Kemp Road, Pemberton, WA 6260 **region** Pemberton
phone (08) 9776 0225 **fax** (08) 9776 0225 **open** By appointment
winemaker Julie White **production** 1500 **est.** 1992
product range ($18–25 CD) Sauvignon Blanc, Semillon, Cabernet blend.
summary The former Jimlee Estate was acquired by the Liebeck family in July 1998 and renamed to WoodSmoke Estate. The current plantings of a little over 2 hectares of semillon, sauvignon blanc, cabernet franc and cabernet sauvignon were expanded with a further 6 acres of cabernet franc and merlot planted in 2000.

woodstock   ★★★☆

Douglas Gully Road, McLaren Flat, SA 5171 **region** McLaren Vale
phone (08) 8383 0156 **fax** (08) 8383 0437 **open** Mon–Fri 9–5, weekends, holidays 12–5
winemaker Scott Collett **production** 30 000 **est.** 1974
product range ($9.95–35 CD) Riesling, Semillon, Douglas Gully Semillon Sauvignon Blanc, Verdelho, Chardonnay, Botrytis Sweet White, Five Feet (Dry Red), Shiraz, Grenache, Douglas Gully Malbec Cabernet Sauvignon Petit Verdot, Cabernet Sauvignon, Vintage Port, Very Old Tawny Port and Muscat. The Stocks Shiraz is a recently introduced flagship.
summary One of the stalwarts of McLaren Vale, producing archetypal, invariably reliable full-bodied red wines and showing versatility with spectacular botrytis sweet whites and high-quality (14-year-old) Tawny Port. Also offers a totally charming reception-cum-restaurant, which understandably does a roaring trade with wedding receptions. Has supplemented its 22 hectares of McLaren Vale vineyards with 10 hectares at its Wirrega Vineyard near Bordertown in the Limestone Coast Zone. The wines are exported to the UK, Switzerland, the US, Canada, New Zealand, Philippines, Malaysia and Singapore.

Woodstock Semillon

♥♥♥♥ **2001** Light green-yellow; the bouquet is light and fresh, with a whiff of gooseberry from the sauvignon blanc; the fresh palate with its gentle fruit again shows the impact of the sauvignon blanc.   **rating:** 85

best drinking 2001–2002 **best vintages** NA **drink with** Shellfish • $14

Woodstock Limestone Coast Verdelho

♥♥♥♡ **2001** Light green-yellow; a quite fragrant bouquet with some grassy/lemony overtones, with similar flavours replaying on the crisp palate, which is almost into sauvignon blanc territory.   **rating:** 84

best drinking 2002–2003 **best vintages** NA **drink with** Seafood • $14

Woodstock Chardonnay

♥♥♥♥ **2000** Bright, light to medium yellow-green; the bouquet offers a subtle combination of fruit and oak, with some nutty/cashew aromas from the barrel and malolactic fermentation. There is an interesting palate, complex, but with the fruit somewhat suppressed by the malolactic fermentation. Packaged in an expensive imported bottle with a Stelvin cap. Will undoubtedly mature at a leisurely pace.   **rating:** 86

best drinking 2002–2008 **best vintages** NA **drink with** Crumbed lambs brains • $16

Woodstock Botrytis

♥♥♥♥ **1999** Golden yellow; complex, ripe tropical/fruit salad aromas suggest a high level of sweetness, but the palate is much lighter than the bouquet suggests, with a nice crisp finish. Provides a good halfway house between dry and fully sweet. A long-established proprietary blend of chenin blanc, riesling and frontignac.   **rating:** 85

best drinking 2002–2003 **best vintages** '90, '91, '92, '93, '95 **drink with** Fruit tart • $13

Woodstock Shiraz

♥♥♥♡ **1999** Medium red-purple; distinctive gamey/earthy overtones to a palate with herb, mint and chocolate flavours all suggest two very different components went into the blend.   **rating:** 84

best drinking 2002–2006 **best vintages** '82, '84, '91, '92, '93, '94 **drink with** Steak in black bean sauce • $20

Woodstock The Stocks Shiraz

♥♥♥♥ **1998** As was the case with the '97 vintage, I find the American oak outweighs the fruit on both bouquet and palate. The other judges at the 2001 Great Australian Shiraz Challenge were far more tolerant of the oak, and it may be my judgement is harsh.   **rating:** 87

best drinking 2003–2008 **best vintages** '91, '94, '95, '96 **drink with** Barbecued steak • $35

Woodstock McLaren Vale Grenache

▼▼▼▼ **1999** Medium red-purple; the sweet, juicy/jammy berry fruit of the bouquet is strongly varietal, the soft, light juicy berry palate occupying a tannin-free zone. Good summer drinking. **rating:** 85

best drinking 2001–2002 **best vintages** NA **drink with** Kangaroo fillet • $15

Woodstock Five Feet

▼▼▼▼ **1999** Medium red-purple; a fragrant, tangy, spicy, savoury bouquet leads into a palate with considerable weight and concentration to the fruit, although the tannin structure is a little deficient. Excellent value in a drink now style. **rating:** 88

best drinking 2001–2004 **best vintages** NA **drink with** Grilled calf's liver • $16

woody nook ★★★★

Metricup Road, Busselton, WA 6280 **region** Margaret River
phone (08) 9755 7547 **fax** (08) 9755 7007 **open** 7 days 10–4.30
winemaker Neil Gallagher **production** 5000 **est.** 1982
product range ($16–28 R) Sauvignon Blanc, Kelly's Farewell (Sauvignon Blanc), Classique (Semillon Sauvignon Blanc Chardonnay), Chenin Blanc, Late Harvest, Shiraz, Merlot, Cabernet Merlot, Cabernet Sauvignon, Nooky Delight; Gallagher's Choice Cabernet Sauvignon is top of the range.
summary This improbably named and not terribly fashionable winery has produced some truly excellent wines over the years, featuring in such diverse competitions as Winewise, the Sheraton Wine Awards and the Qantas West Australian Wines Show. Cabernet Sauvignon has always been its strong point, but it has the habit of bobbing up with excellent white wines in various guises. Since 2000 owned by Peter and Jane Baily, but Neil Gallagher continues as viticulturist, winemaker and minority shareholder. Exports to the US, UK and Hong Kong.

Woody Nook Sauvignon Blanc

▼▼▼▼▽ **2001** Light to medium yellow-green; an aromatic bouquet with passionfruit and slightly smoky/armpit aspects is followed by a quite intense palate, which builds flavour through the mid-palate to the finish. Gold medal 2001 Sheraton Wine Awards. **rating:** 90

best drinking 2002–2003 **best vintages** '95, '01 **drink with** Rich seafood • $21

Woody Nook Shiraz

▼▼▼▼ **2000** Medium to full red-purple; clean, dark cherry, spice and earth aromas flow through into the palate, but the texture doesn't really deliver on the promise of the flavour. **rating:** 85

best drinking 2004–2008 **best vintages** NA **drink with** Steak and kidney pie • $27

Woody Nook Cabernet Merlot

▼▼▼▼ **2000** Medium red-purple; gently ripe blackcurrant, with touches of earth and mint on the bouquet; the palate has similar flavours, with persistent, rubbery-textured tannins. **rating:** 86

best drinking 2004–2009 **best vintages** NA **drink with** Osso buco • $24

Woody Nook Cabernet Sauvignon

▼▼▼▼▽ **2000** Medium red-purple; the bouquet has cassis, dark chocolate and earth supported by neatly handled oak; the powerful and voluminous mix of cassis and dark chocolate fruit on the palate is rounded off by fine, savoury tannins. Woody Nook near its best. **rating:** 92

best drinking 2005–2012 **best vintages** '00 **drink with** Lamb Provencale • $28

wordsworth wines NR

Cnr South Western Highway and Thompson Road, Harvey, WA 6220 **region** Geographe
phone (08) 9773 4576 **fax** (08) 9733 4269 **open** 7 days 10–5
winemaker Tim Mortimer **production** 4000 **est.** 1997
product range ($14.50–25 CD) Chenin Verdelho, Chenin Verdelho Late Harvest, Shiraz, Cabernet Merlot.
summary David Wordsworth has established a substantial business in a relatively short space of time. Twenty three hectares of vines have been planted, with cabernet sauvignon (10 hectares) and shiraz (5 hectares) predominant, and lesser amounts of merlot, zinfandel, petit verdot, chardonnay, chenin blanc and verdelho. The tasting room is built to size, with seating for 40 people, and the wines have had show success in the limited period of time the winery has been operating.

wyanga park   NR

Baades Road, Lakes Entrance, Vic 3909 **region** Gippsland
phone (03) 5155 1508 **fax** (03) 5155 1443 **open** 7 days 9–5
winemaker Graeme Little **production** 5000 **est.** 1970
product range ($8–20 CD) Riesling Traminer, Estate Grown Sauvignon Blanc, Colombard, Estate
Grown Chardonnay, Miriam's Fancy Chardonnay, Rosé, Boobialla (medium-sweet white), Shiraz, Shiraz
Cabernet Sauvignon, Fortifieds.
summary Offers a broad range of wines of diverse provenance directed at the tourist trade; one of the
Chardonnays and the Cabernet Sauvignon are estate-grown. Winery cruises up the north arm of the
Gippsland Lake to Wyanga Park are scheduled 4 days a week throughout the entire year.

wyldcroft estates   NR

98 Stanleys Road, Red Hill South, Vic 3937 **region** Mornington Peninsula
phone (03) 5989 2646 **fax** (03) 5989 2646 **open** Weekends and public holidays 10–5
winemaker Philip Jones (Contract) **production** 700 **est.** 1987
product range ($18–21 CD) Chardonnay, Unwooded Chardonnay, Pinot Noir, Cabernet Sauvignon.
summary Richard Condon and Sharon Stone commenced planting Wyldcroft Estates in 1987, extending
the plantings in 1993 and 1996 to the present total of just over 3 hectares, constructing a mudbrick winery
and cellar door in 1995.

wyndham estate   ★★★★

Dalwood Road, Dalwood, NSW 2335 **region** Lower Hunter Valley
phone (02) 4938 3444 **fax** (02) 4938 3422 **open** Mon–Fri 9.30–5, weekends 10–4
winemaker Brett McKinnon **production** NFP **est.** 1828
product range ($6.95–25 R) In ascending order: Bin TR2 Select White and Select Red; 1828 range of
Semillon Sauvignon Blanc, Semillon Chardonnay, Unwooded Chardonnay, Vintage Brut, Cabernet
Sauvignon Shiraz Ruby Cabernet; Bin 777 Semillon, Bin 111 Verdelho, Bin 222 Chardonnay, Bin 333
Pinot Noir, Bin 555 Shiraz, Bin 999 Merlot, Bin 888 Cabernet Merlot, Bin 444 Cabernet Sauvignon;
Show Reserve range of Semillon, Chardonnay, Shiraz, Cabernet Merlot; Vintage Chardonnay Brut Cuvée.
summary Has risen to the challenge in recent years, its varietal wines smoothly dependable, the Show
Reserves usually justifying their name (and price).

Wyndham Estate Show Reserve Semillon
TTTTY 1997 Bright, light straw-green, exceptional given the age of the wine. A fresh, lively, crisp and delicate
bouquet is amazingly youthful; the palate continues on in the same vein, with light and lively grassy/minerally
flavours. It is not at all clear that it will ever change much, but I'm not sure that matters.   **rating:** 90
best drinking 2002–2007 **best vintages** '97 **drink with** Roast chicken • $22

Wyndham Estate Bin 333 Pinot Noir
TTTY 2001 Light to medium red-purple; the fragrant bouquet has touches of strawberry and cherry, plus
a whiff of savoury earth. The earthy characters tend to take over the palate, which does not have overmuch
structure. Not quite as good as the 2000 vintage, but nonetheless good value at the price.   **rating:** 83
best drinking 2002–2003 **best vintages** NA **drink with** Light meat dishes • $13.99

Wyndham Estate Bin 555 Shiraz
TTTY 2000 Light to medium red-purple; a range of leaf, berry and earth aromas on the bouquet, then
sweet, dark berry fruit coming through as the dominant flavour on the light to medium-bodied palate.
                                                                                                 rating: 84
TTTY 1999 Medium red-purple; a moderately intense bouquet has a mix of cherry, game and spice, much
the same flavours coming through on the soft and easy palate, engineered for early drinking.   **rating:** 83
best drinking 2002–2004 **best vintages** NA **drink with** Barbecued sausages • $13.99

Wyndham Estate Show Reserve Shiraz
TTTT 1997 Medium red-purple; an interesting array of savoury, spicy, gamey, leathery dark fruit aromas
on the bouquet are replayed on the palate; the oak is well-integrated and balanced. Another convincing
Show Reserve wine.   **rating:** 88
best drinking 2003–2008 **best vintages** NA **drink with** Game pie • $25

Wyndham Estate Bin 444 Cabernet Sauvignon

▼▼▼▽ 2000 Medium red-purple; the moderately intense bouquet has earth, blackberry and blackcurrant aromas, the light to medium-bodied palate veering distinctly towards the savoury/earthy end of the spectrum.

rating: 84

best drinking 2003–2007 **best vintages** NA **drink with** Braised beef • $13.99

Wyndham Estate Show Reserve Mudgee Cabernet Sauvignon

▼▼▼▼▽ 1999 Medium to full red, with some purple tints remaining. The bouquet has solid, dark fruit aromas married with touches of savoury oak, the palate nicely weighted and balanced with sweet berry fruit and soft, gently chewy tannins. **rating:** 93

▼▼▼▼▼ 1996 Medium to full red-purple; rich, ripe and generous cassis and chocolate fruit is joined by positive charry oak on the bouquet; plenty happens on the palate, with lots of sweet berry fruit, and that charry oak poking its nose through. Three trophies and ten gold medals is an impressive track record.

rating: 94

best drinking 2009 – **best vintages** '94, '99 **drink with** Game • NA

wynns coonawarra estate ★★★★☆

Memorial Drive, Coonawarra, SA 5263 **region** Coonawarra
phone (08) 8736 3266 **fax** (08) 8736 3202 **open** 7 days 10–5
winemaker Sue Hodder, Sarah Pidgeon **production** 250 000 **est.** 1891
product range ($15.50–89 R) Wynns Coonawarra Estate Riesling, Chardonnay, Shiraz, Cabernet Shiraz Merlot, Cabernet Sauvignon and Black Label Cabernet Sauvignon; Michael Shiraz, John Riddoch Cabernet Sauvignon; also Ovens Valley Shiraz (not sourced from Coonawarra, exclusive to Cellar Door).
summary The large-scale production has in no way prevented Wynns from producing excellent wines covering the full price spectrum from the bargain basement Riesling and Shiraz through to the deluxe John Riddoch Cabernet Sauvignon and Michael Shiraz. Even with steady price increases, Wynns offers extraordinary value for money.

Wynns Coonawarra Estate Riesling

▼▼▼▼▼ 2001 Light straw-green; a crisp, light flowery bouquet with notes of herb and lime, then a palate which moves more into the tropical end of the spectrum, opening up on the well-balanced back palate and finish. Has that extra degree of flowery delicacy particular to Coonawarra. Gold medal and trophy 2001 Limestone Coast Wine Show. **rating:** 94

best drinking 2001–2007 **best vintages** '90, '91, '93, '95, '96, '98, '99, '01 **drink with** King George whiting • $14.50

Wynns Coonawarra Estate Chardonnay

▼▼▼▼▽ 2001 There is abundant rich stonefruit and melon varietal aroma and flavour, yet a restrained complexity, particularly with the nutty/creamy barrel ferment nuances to the palate. **rating:** 92

best drinking 2001–2003 **best vintages** '92, '93, '94, '96, '97, '98, '99, '01 **drink with** Robe lobster • $16

Wynns Coonawarra Estate Shiraz

▼▼▼▼ 2000 Medium to full red-purple; a clean, smooth gently ripe bouquet with black cherry fruit merging with supple, smooth, well-integrated oak, then a firm, fresh, youthful palate needing more time in bottle. The earlier release date has not been without pain. **rating:** 88

best drinking 2003–2010 **best vintages** '54, '55, '62, '65, '70, '85, '86, '89, '90, '91, '93, '94, '96, '98 **drink with** Spiced lamb • $18

Wynns Coonawarra Estate Cabernet Shiraz Merlot

▼▼▼▼ 1999 Medium red-purple; the moderately intense bouquet is firm and clean, with direct red berry fruit, the palate equally firm, with lively red berry fruit and good length. Not particularly complex, however.

rating: 87

best drinking 2004–2009 **best vintages** '86, '88, '90, '91, '92, '96 **drink with** Yearling beef • $19

Wynns Coonawarra Estate Black Label Cabernet Sauvignon

▼▼▼▼▽ 1999 Medium red-purple; the clean, moderately intense bouquet offers a mix of red and blackcurrant and blackberry fruit; a very substantial palate with lots of flavour, extract and tannins promises a long life. Gold medal winner Limestone Coast Wine Show 2001. **rating:** 92

best drinking 2004–2014 **best vintages** '53, '57, '58, '62, '82, '86, '88, '90, '91, '94, '95, '96, '97, '98, '99 **drink with** Roast beef • $32

xanadu wines ★★★★☆

Boodjidup Road, Margaret River, WA 6285 **region** Margaret River
phone (08) 9757 2581 **fax** (08) 9757 3389 **open** 7 days 10–5
winemaker Jurg Muggli, Glenn Goodall **production** 100 000 **est.** 1977
product range ($14–60 R) Semillon, Semillon Sauvignon Blanc, Secession White, Chardonnay, Noble Semillon, Secession Red, Shiraz, Merlot, Secession Merlot, Cabernet Sauvignon, Lagan Estate Cabernet Reserve.
summary Xanadu, once a somewhat quirky, small family winery has reinvented itself with the arrival of substantial outside investment capital and the acquisition of the key brands of Normans Wines of SA. One hundred and thirty hectares of vineyard estate and much expanded winemaking facilities have been complemented by a large, open courtyard, a bar area, new cellar door and a cafe-style restaurant. Wine quality, led by outstanding Merlot, has also risen. Exports to the US, Canada, UK, Holland, Switzerland, Philippines, Malaysia, Hong Kong and Japan.

Xanadu Frankland River Riesling

TTTT 2001 Light green-yellow; clean, fresh herb, citrus and mineral aromas, then a surprisingly full and generous palate, with an Achilles Heel in a slightly phenolic finish making it a drink-now proposition.
rating: 86

best drinking 2002–2003 **best vintages** NA **drink with** Caesar salad • $17

Xanadu Semillon

TTTTT 2000 Medium yellow-green; a particularly complex bouquet with tangy oak certainly evident but which works well is followed by a voluptuously fleshy palate with abundant flavour and totally seductive mouthfeel. An outstanding example of the baroque end of the Semillon spectrum.
rating: 91

best drinking 2001–2004 **best vintages** '96, '97, '98, '99, '00 **drink with** Richer fish dishes • $20

Xanadu Secession

TTTT 2001 Light green-yellow; fragrant lemon blossom and grass aromas are followed by a palate with more verve and length than these licorice allsorts blends normally produce, with a crisp, clean finish. The blend is of Semillon, Sauvignon Blanc, Chenin Blanc and Chardonnay, often called 'classic dry white' in Western Australia. The ridiculous gold stickers on this and other current Xanadu wines are at best tawdry and annoying.
rating: 88

best drinking 2002–2004 **best vintages** '85, '87, '90, '92, '93, '01 **drink with** Crab • $14

Xanadu Chardonnay

TTTTT 2000 Pale but bright green-yellow; a light but complex bouquet with an array of nutty/cashew malolactic influences on fig and melon fruit. A stylish and elegant palate in light to medium-bodied mode, very well made, and with persuasive length.
rating: 94

best drinking 2001–2006 **best vintages** '99, '00 **drink with** White-fleshed fish • $23

Xanadu Shiraz

TTTT 2000 Medium to full red-purple; there are some curious, aromatic herb and spice aromas, plus charry oak, over fresh fruit on the bouquet; a fresh, youthful and lively palate is still all arms and legs, needing time.
rating: 88

best drinking 2003–2008 **best vintages** '99 **drink with** Beef casserole • $23

Xanadu Merlot

TTTTT 2000 Medium red-purple; a moderately intense and quite stylish bouquet has a complex mix of berry and more savoury notes, the same mix of sweet berry, olive and cedar coming through on the palate, finishing with fine, filigreed tannins.
rating: 90

TTTT 1999 Medium red, with the purple starting to subside; an aromatic bouquet with a mix of briary, spicy, tangy, olive-accented fruit leads into a powerful and intense palate in a distinctly savoury mode. A striking wine; Xanadu gets it right when it says 'this is not a Merlot for the faint hearted'.
rating: 88

best drinking 2004–2009 **best vintages** '98, '99, '00 **drink with** Smoked beef • $39.50

yaldara wines ★★★★

Gomersal Road, Lyndoch, SA 5351 **region** Barossa Valley
phone (08) 8524 4200 **fax** (08) 8524 4678 **open** 7 days 9–5
winemaker Matt Tydeman **production** 500 000 **est.** 1947

product range ($10–45 R) A full range of wines under (in ascending order) the Lakewood, Earth's Portrait, Julians, and the super-premium The Farms label.

summary At the very end of 1999 Yaldara became part of the publicly listed Simeon Wines, the intention being that it (Yaldara) should become the quality flagship of the group. Despite much expenditure and the short-lived stay of at least one well known winemaker, the plan failed to deliver the expected benefits. In February 2002 McGuigan Wines made a reverse takeover for Simeon, and the various McGuigan brands will (presumably) fill the role intended for Yaldara.

Yaldara The Farms Barossa Valley Shiraz

▼▼▼▼▽ **1999** Medium to full red-purple; plum, prune, chocolate and licorice fruit aromas flow through on to the powerful, rich fruit-driven palate. Slightly sharp acidity on the finish disrupts the flow, but should settle down with time.   **rating:** 90

best drinking 2004–2009 **best vintages** '97, '98 **drink with** Venison • $35

yalumba   ★★★★☆

Eden Valley Road, Angaston, SA 5353 **region** Barossa Valley
phone (08) 8561 3200 **fax** (08) 8561 3393 **open** Mon–Fri 8.30–5, Sat 10–5, Sun 12–5
winemaker Brian Walsh, Alan Hoey, Louisa Rosé, Hugh Reimers, Kevin Glastonbury, Natalie Fryar
production 900 000 **est.** 1849
product range ($8–90 R) A clearly-structured portfolio arranged by price point, commencing at the bottom with Oxford Landing, then Christobel's, Unwooded Chardonnay and Galway Vintage Shiraz; next varietal wines under the Yalumba Barossa umbrella; then Eden Valley and The Virgilius Viognier; Clare Valley Shiraz and Cabernet Sauvignon; then at the top of the dry table wines, Mawsons Coonawarra Cabernet Shiraz Merlot, The Menzies Coonawarra Cabernet Sauvignon, The Signature Barossa Shiraz and The Octavius Old Vine Barossa Shiraz; a newly added trio of Noble Pick sweet wines and Adelaide Hills Chardonnay and Pinot Noir have joined the roster, and more recently still the Vinnovation series, rounded off with the Yalumba D sparkling wines and fortifieds.

summary Family-owned and run by Robert Hill-Smith; much of its prosperity in the late 1980s and early 1990s turned on the great success of Angas Brut in export markets, but the company has always had a commitment to quality and shown great vision in its selection of vineyard sites, new varieties and brands. In particular, it has always been a serious player at the top end of full-bodied (and full-blooded) Australian reds. Exports to all major markets.

Yalumba Barossa Riesling

▼▼▼▼ **2000** Light green-yellow; the bouquet is clean, with a gentle touch of citrus, the ultra-smooth palate offering citrus, apple and passionfruit flavours in an overall soft, easy style which does no require cellaring.   **rating:** 88

best drinking 2001–2004 **best vintages** NA **drink with** Antipasto • $12

Yalumba Hand Picked Eden Valley Riesling

▼▼▼▼▽ **2000** Light green-straw; a highly aromatic bouquet, predominantly lime, but with touches of spice, leads into a long, bright and crisp palate with apple, citrus and mineral flavours.   **rating:** 92

best drinking 2003–2009 **best vintages** '00 **drink with** Stuffed capsicum • $25

Yalumba Viognier

▼▼▼▼ **2000** Medium yellow-green; the bouquet is quite rich and solid, but not lifted or aromatic. Similarly, there is plenty of presence on the mid-palate with solid fruit, but which thickens somewhat on the finish. Let no one think viognier is an easy grape to handle anywhere in the world.   **rating:** 86

best drinking 2001–2003 **best vintages** NA **drink with** Creamy pasta • $24.95

Yalumba The Virgilius

▼▼▼▼▼ **2000** Medium yellow-green; the bouquet is smooth, quite intense, with a mix of sweet apricot, apple and honey aromas. The palate is powerful, rounded and fleshy, with very good balance in the context of its uncompromising style, and has a long carry and finish. Australian Viognier at its best.   **rating:** 94

best drinking 2001–2005 **best vintages** '99, '00 **drink with** Pork neck • $49.95

Yalumba Adelaide Hills Chardonnay

▼▼▼▼▽ **2000** Light to medium yellow-green; a sophisticated bouquet with subtle mix of barrel ferment and (possibly) malolactic fermentation produces fig, melon and cashew aromas. The palate is similarly fine, with understated fruit yet tremendous complexity.   **rating:** 92

best drinking 2001–2005 **best vintages** '00 **drink with** Crumbed brains • $22.95

Yalumba Barossa Chardonnay

▼▼▼▼ 2001 Medium yellow-green; nectarine and citrus are the drivers on the moderately intense, smooth bouquet, crisping up somewhat on the fresh palate, but otherwise repeating the bouquet; subliminal oak.

rating: 85

best drinking 2001–2002 best vintages NA drink with Creamy pasta • $14.95

Yalumba Oxford Landing Chardonnay

▼▼▼▼ 2001 Bright, light to medium green-yellow; pleasant nectarine/citrus fruit drives the bouquet, the palate with some real texture and structure, adding soft, nutty/figgy characters to the nectarine/citrus fruit of the bouquet. Great value.

rating: 87

best drinking 2002–2004 best vintages NA drink with Everyday food • $7.95

Yalumba D

▼▼▼▼▽ 1998 Light straw-green; while fragrant, fresh and crisp, there are countervailing malolactic edges together with a hint of aldehydes. The palate is very long, crisp and intense with lingering lemony/minerally flavours in a well-balanced framework.

rating: 92

best drinking 2002–2005 best vintages '90, '91, '93, '95, '96, '97, '98 drink with Richer seafood dishes • $19.95

Jansz

▼▼▼▼▼ 1997 Light straw-green; a fragrant array of bready/creamy/citrussy aromas introduce a lively, fresh, super-elegant lemony/citrussy palate with a fine lingering finish.

rating: 95

best drinking 2001–2002 best vintages '96, '97 drink with Shellfish • $32.95

Yalumba D Black

▼▼▼▼ 1998 Medium to full red; the complex array of earthy/stalky/spicy aromas are followed by a palate with abundant licorice, spice and black fruit flavours; a challenging style, which could be something quite special if it spent five or so years on yeast lees.

rating: 89

best drinking 2002–2007 best vintages NA drink with Liver pate • $29.95

Yalumba Adelaide Hills Pinot Noir

▼▼▼▼▽ 2000 Light red; light plummy/savoury/earthy fruit with a hint of mint is followed by a stylish, light to medium-bodied palate with plenty of flavour in that context, with touches of forest, violets and lemon zest. The only question is over the full phenological ripeness of the grapes.

rating: 90

best drinking 2001–2004 best vintages NA drink with Smoked duck breast • $22.95

Yalumba Barossa Valley Shiraz + Viognier

▼▼▼▼▼ 1998 Bright red-purple; the distinctly aromatic, cherry-accented bouquet is almost flowery, the oak perfectly integrated. The palate has excellent richness and a sweet middle of bright, small, red fruits moving through to a fine tannin finish.

rating: 94

best drinking 2002–2010 best vintages '98 drink with Milk-fed lamb • $29

Yalumba Vinnovation Collection Cienna

▼▼▼▼ 2000 Bright purple-red; clean, fresh blackcurrant and earth aromas, followed by an interesting mix of sweet blackcurrant and moderately high acidity on the palate. Moderate tannins help provide balance. Cienna is an Australian-bred cross.

rating: 86

best drinking 2003–2007 best vintages NA drink with Game • $24.95

Yalumba Vinnovation Collection Dolcetto

▼▼▼▼ 2000 Youthful red-purple, moderately deep; a highly expressive bouquet with sweet, juicy berry and mint aromas then a palate which has soft, almost velvety, sweet fruit (not residual sugar), low tannins and subtle oak. A truly amiable wine.

rating: 87

best drinking 2002–2005 best vintages NA drink with Spaghetti bolognese • $24.80

Yalumba Vinnovation Collection Nebbiolo

▼▼▼▼ 2000 Typically light red-purple; the bouquet is less expressive and open than the Dolcetto (not surprising) with a cedary, spicy, savoury aroma spectrum. The palate faithfully follows the bouquet, and has good length and balance.

rating: 87

best drinking 2002–2005 best vintages NA drink with Veal saltimbocca • $24.95

Yalumba Vinnovation Collection Petit Verdot

** TTTT 1999** Strong, bright red-purple; the rich blackberry fruit of the bouquet is at once sweet and ripe, the palate similarly amply endowed with fully ripe, but not jammy, fruit. The acidity for which the variety is known comes through to tidy up the finish. **rating: 88**

best drinking 2004–2009 **best vintages** NA **drink with** Baby lamb • $24.95

Yalumba Growers Bush Vine Grenache

TTTT 2000 Medium red-purple; the bouquet is consistent with prior releases, with a quite complex jammy/spicy/earthy spectrum of aromas. The palate has lots of sweet, slightly jammy, berry fruit yet almost no tannins. A lunch red with high-flavoured dishes. **rating: 86**

best drinking 2001–2003 **best vintages** '97 **drink with** Mildly spiced Indian curry • $16.95

Yalumba Mawsons Cabernet Blend

TTTT 1999 Medium red-purple; slightly dusty/baggy oak does not entirely disguise the ripe cabernet fruit underneath. On the medium to full-bodied palate there is no doubt, the ripe blackberry/blackcurrant fruit taking charge. **rating: 87**

best drinking 2004–2009 **best vintages** '98 **drink with** Barbecued steak • $22.95

yandoit hill vineyard ★★★

Nevens Road, Yandoit Creek, Vic 3461 **region** Bendigo
phone (03) 9379 1763 **fax** (03) 9379 1763 **open** By appointment (special open days for mail list customers)
winemaker Colin Mitchell **production** 300 **est.** 1988
product range ($19–25 CD) Arneis, Merlot, Cabernets, Nebbiolo Cabernet Sauvignon.
summary Colin and Rosa Mitchell commenced the development of Yandoit Hill with the first plantings in 1988 with merlot, and a little under a hectare each of cabernet franc and cabernet sauvignon followed by half a hectare each of arneis (the first planting in Australia), and nebbiolo in 1995. The vineyard is situated 20 kilometres north of Daylesford, roughly halfway from Ballarat to Bendigo and, although situated on the north-facing slope of Yandoit Hill, is in an uncompromisingly cool climate. Colin Mitchell has already discovered that nebbiolo won't ripen to his satisfaction in most years but in vintages like 1988 makes a successful wine.

Yandoit Hill Arneis

TTTY 2001 Light to medium yellow-green; the bouquet is clean, but as with the 2000, not particularly distinctive, showing just a touch of apple blossom. The palate follows suit, crisp and refreshing, with faint touches of apple. **rating: 83**

best drinking 2002–2004 **best vintages** NA **drink with** Shellfish • $25

Yandoit Hill Merlot

TTTY 2000 A similar bright, light to medium red-purple to that displayed by the Nebbiolo Cabernet. The fresh and youthful palate has a mix of berry and leafy aromatics and flavour; well made, but suggesting less than perfect fruit ripeness. **rating: 84**

best drinking 2002–2005 **best vintages** NA **drink with** Baby veal • $25

Yandoit Hill Nebbiolo Cabernet Sauvignon

TTTT 2000 Bright, light to medium red-purple; a lively mix of juicy berry and more earthy notes on the bouquet, then fresh berry fruit with a twist of almost lemony acidity on the finish presumably coming from the nebbiolo, which constitutes 70 per cent of the blend. **rating: 86**

best drinking 2003–2007 **best vintages** NA **drink with** Ravioli • $25

☎ yangarra park ★★★☆

Kangarilla Road, McLaren Vale, SA 5171 **region** McLaren Vale
phone (08) 8383 7459 **fax** (08) 8383 7518 **open** By appointment
winemaker Peter Fraser **production** 220 000 **est.** 2000
product range ($16–25 R) By far the largest part of production is the so-called first tier varietal wines from all over southeastern Australia, comprising Chardonnay, Shiraz, Merlot and Cabernet Sauvignon. There will be a small amount of second tier Reserve wines, likely to account for less than 10 per cent of the total production.
summary This is the Australian operation of Kendall Jackson, one of the leading premium wine producers in California. In December 2000 Kendall-Jackson acquired the 172-hectare Eringa Park vineyard from Normans Wines, 97 hectares are under vine, the oldest dating back to 1923. The name change to Yangarra

Park provides the key estate base for the operation, but it intends to also buy grapes from all of the premium wine-growing regions in southeast Australia with the philosophy that regional blending can enhance both complexity and quality. It's early days yet; some better wines are in the pipeline.

Yangarra Park Chardonnay

▼▼▼▼ **2001** Medium yellow-green; the moderately intense bouquet has well-integrated and balanced nectarine fruit and oak; the same play occurs on the pleasant, neatly balanced palate. Easy drinking style for immediate consumption. **rating:** 85

best drinking 2002–2003 **best vintages** NA **drink with** Grilled chicken • $15.99

Yangarra Park Shiraz

▼▼▼▽ **2001** Medium purple-red; the bouquet is largely driven by the soft plum and berry fruit, although here and on the palate a touch of oak is evident. A round, soft, user-friendly wine. **rating:** 84

▼▼▼▼ **2000** Medium red-purple; the moderately intense bouquet has good cherry varietal character supported by subtle oak; the palate expresses the same fruit characters, but has good depth and texture, the tannins in particular pleasing. **rating:** 87

best drinking 2002–2005 **best vintages** NA **drink with** Tagliatelle • $15.99

Yangarra Park Merlot

▼▼▼▽ **2001** Light to medium red-purple; the fresh, small berry aromas of the bouquet are on the light side, but the palate has more flavour than the bouquet suggests with soft, gently sweet fruit. In the pattern of all of these wines, the oak influence is minimal, the tannins almost but not quite invisible. **rating:** 84

best drinking 2002–2004 **best vintages** NA **drink with** Braised veal • $15.99

Yangarra Park Cabernet Sauvignon

▼▼▼▼ **2001** Light to medium red-purple; a light mix of red berry and more savoury/earthy/leathery aromas lead into a pleasant, soft palate with sweet cassis/blackcurrant fruit, a waft of oak and ultra-light tannins. **rating:** 85

best drinking 2002–2005 **best vintages** NA **drink with** Rack of lamb • $15.99

yarrabank ★★★★☆

38 Melba Highway, Yarra Glen, Vic 3775 **region** Yarra Valley
phone (03) 9730 1107 **fax** (03) 9739 0135 **open** 7 days 10–5
winemaker Claude Thibaut, Tom Carson, Darren Rathbone **production** 2000 **est.** 1993
product range ($30–35 ML) Cuvée, Crème de Cuvée, Brut Cuvée.
summary The 1997 vintage saw the opening of the majestic new winery established as part of a joint venture between the French Champagne house Devaux and Yering Station, and which adds another major dimension to the Yarra Valley. Until 1997 the Yarrabank Cuvée Brut was made under Claude Thibaut's direction at Domaine Chandon, but henceforth the entire operation will be conducted at Yarrabank. four hectares of dedicated 'estate' vineyards have been established at Yering Station; the balance of the intake comes from other growers in the Yarra Valley and southern Vic. Wine quality has been quite outstanding, the wines having a delicacy unmatched by any other Australian sparkling wines.

Yarrabank Brut Cuvée

▼▼▼▼▽ **1998** Light straw-green; a spotlessly clean, fine and restrained bouquet, then a fine, tingling, fresh lemony/citrussy palate, seemingly a little less complex than some of the prior releases, but on the other hand had not had the benefit of cork age when tasted immediately after release. **rating:** 91

best drinking 2002–2004 **best vintages** '93, '94, '95, '97, '98 **drink with** Aperitif, shellfish • $35

yarra burn ★★★★☆

Settlement Road, Yarra Junction, Vic 3797 **region** Yarra Valley
phone (03) 5967 1428 **fax** (03) 5967 1146 **open** 7 days 10–5
winemaker Glenn James, Ed Carr, Stephen Pannell **production** 4500 **est.** 1975
product range ($18–46 R) Sauvignon Blanc Semillon, Chardonnay, Pinot Noir, Chardonnay Pinot Noir, Shiraz, Cabernet Sauvignon, Sparkling Pinot, Chardonnay Pinot; Bastard Hill Chardonnay, Bastard Hill Pinot Noir.
summary Acquired by BRL Hardy in 1995 and, for the time being, the headquarters of Hardys' very substantial Yarra Valley operations, the latter centring on the large production from its Hoddles Creek vineyards. The new brand direction is slowly taking shape; the Bastard Hill Reserve wines are among the significant signs of change. Care needs to be taken in reading the back labels of the red wines other than Pinot Noir. Exports to the UK and US.

Yarra Burn Chardonnay

▼▼▼▽ 2000 Light to medium yellow-green; complex barrel ferment characters introduce the wine which retains elegance and varietal fruit flavour and intensity on both bouquet and palate. Gold medal 2001 Liquorland National Wine Show. **rating:** 92

best drinking 2001–2005 **best vintages** '97, '98, '00 **drink with** Grilled scampi • $18.99

Yarra Burn Bastard Hill Chardonnay

▼▼▼▼▽ 1997 Medium to full yellow-green; a complex, concentrated, fruit-driven bouquet of grapefruit and melon, is followed by an exceptionally rich, complex and concentrated palate with pronounced Burgundian characters. **rating:** 93

best drinking 2002–2004 **best vintages** '95, '97 **drink with** Richly sauced fish • $46

Yarra Burn Pinot Chardonnay Pinot Meunier

▼▼▼▼ 1999 Light straw-green; a fresh, crisp bouquet showing a definite cool-grown backdrop, with some hints of green; a light, fresh bouquet with lemony fruit and acidity is a logical follow-on from the bouquet. **rating:** 88

best drinking 2001–2002 **best vintages** NA **drink with** Aperitif • $24

Yarra Burn Pinot Noir

▼▼▼▼▽ 2000 Medium red-purple; slightly dusty, spicy oak is the first impression, the bouquet thereafter building savoury/tangy/cherry complexity. The medium-bodied palate has good length, and fully reflects the considerable complexity of the bouquet. **rating:** 93

best drinking 2002–2007 **best vintages** '97, '00 **drink with** Ragout of venison • $24

Yarra Burn Shiraz

▼▼▼▼▽ 1999 Medium to full red-purple; complex, ripe licorice and black cherry aromas lead into a palate with an excellent fruit core surrounded by the typically confident oak handling of the BRL Hardy team. **rating:** 93

best drinking 2004–2014 **best vintages** '99 **drink with** Braised beef • $24

yarra edge ★★★☆

PO Box 390, Yarra Glen, Vic 3775 **region** Yarra Valley
phone (03) 9730 1107 **fax** (03) 9739 0135 **open** At Yering Station, 7 days 10–5
winemaker Tom Carson, Darren Rathbone **production** 2000 **est.** 1984
product range ($33 CD) Chardonnay, Pinot Noir, Single Vineyard (Bordeaux blend).
summary Now leased to Yering Station, which makes the wines but continues to use the Yarra Edge brand for grapes from this estate. Tom Carson, Yering Station winemaker, was briefly winemaker/manager at Yarra Edge and knows the property intimately, so the rich style can be expected to continue.

Yarra Edge Single Vineyard

▼▼▼▼ 1997 Distinct colour shift and lightening foreshadows an elegant wine with a mix of savoury/minty/leafy/earthy overtones to the red fruit, all of which is more advanced than one might expect from the '97 vintage. **rating:** 85

best drinking 2001–2004 **best vintages** NA **drink with** Diced lamb • $33

yarraman road estate ★★★☆

Yarraman Road, Wybong, NSW 2333 **region** Upper Hunter Valley
phone (02) 6547 8118 **fax** (02) 6547 8039 **open** 7 days 10–5
winemaker Stephen Hagan **production** 75 000 **est.** 1967
product range ($10.99–24 R) Yarraman Road is the top label with Black Clay Chardonnay and Sandy Slopes Cabernet Shiraz; Barrington Estate is cheaper label; also Narrambla Verdelho and Chardonnay, and The Banjo Shiraz.
summary Yarraman Road/Barrington Estate is the reincarnation of Penfolds Wybong Estate, into which Penfolds poured millions of dollars between 1960 and 1978, then selling the winery and surrounding vineyards to Rosemount Estate. Rosemount removed most of the unproductive vineyards and used the winery for red wine production until 1992, then converting it to pure storage area. In 1994 Gary and Karen Blom purchased the property from Rosemount after they returned from the US, where Australian-born entrepreneur Gary Blom had a highly successful career; their main investment is the IMAX Theatre in Darling Harbour, but they intend to spend $3-4 million in redeveloping Barrington Estate. One physical sign was the purchase of Hay Shed Hill in November 2000. Exports to the UK and Europe.

yarra ridge ★★★★

Glenview Road, Yarra Glen, Vic 3755 **region** Yarra Valley
phone (03) 9730 1022 **fax** (03) 9730 1131 **open** 7 days 10–5
winemaker Matt Steel **production** 40 000 **est.** 1983
product range ($16–42 R) Sauvignon Blanc, Chardonnay, Pinot Noir, Reserve Pinot Noir, Achilles Heel Pinot Noir, Shiraz, Reserve Shiraz, Merlot, Cabernet Sauvignon, Reserve Cabernet Sauvignon; Mount Tanglefoot has been introduced as a second range expressly made from grapes grown in regions other than the Yarra Valley.
summary Under the sole ownership and control of Beringer Blass, with a winery which is strained to its limits. Recent vineyard plantings in the Yarra Valley, and continued purchasing of Yarra Valley grapes, mean that the majority of the wines will continue to be Yarra Valley-sourced.

Yarra Ridge Sauvignon Blanc

▼▼▼▼ **2001** Light green-yellow; a clean, quite ripe bouquet, but with diminished varietal character is followed by a pleasant, easy, soft palate with touches of gooseberry; not concentrated, but balanced. **rating:** 86

best drinking 2001–2002 **best vintages** NA **drink with** Fish and chips • $18

Yarra Ridge Mount Tanglefoot Semillon Sauvignon Blanc

▼▼▼▼ **2001** Light green-yellow; the bouquet is quite fragrant and moderately intense, with grassy/herbal aromas; the palate is well put together, but doesn't quite deliver on the promise of the bouquet, lacking mid-palate fruit and weight. Nonetheless, a thoroughly pleasant wine. **rating:** 87

best drinking 2001–2002 **best vintages** NA **drink with** Seafood risotto • $16

Yarra Ridge Pinot Noir

▼▼▼▼▽ **2000** Medium red-purple; a smooth, ripe bouquet with abundant plummy fruit and subtle oak flows through to a rich, ripe, full-blooded palate with strongly accented varietal fruit and similarly subtle oak. Good development potential. **rating:** 93

best drinking 2002–2007 **best vintages** '91, '92, '93, '96, '00 **drink with** Poultry • $20

Yarra Ridge Mount Tanglefoot Pinot Noir

▼▼▼▼▽ **2000** The bouquet has remarkable varietal character and richness, the palate with its texture, structure and length. Spice, black plums and a hint of tobacco all add to the appeal and to the varietal character. **rating:** 91

best drinking 2002–2006 **best vintages** '00 **drink with** Braised rabbit • $16

Yarra Ridge Reserve Pinot Noir

▼▼▼▼ **2000** Medium to full red; a big, powerful, dark plum/berry fruit bouquet leads into a chunky, powerful palate with lots of ripe, dark fruit; varietal character somewhat blurred. **rating:** 89

best drinking 2002–2007 **best vintages** '94, '96, '97 **drink with** Game, jugged hare • $40

Yarra Ridge Shiraz

▼▼▼▽ **1999** Medium red-purple; the light to moderate aromas offer a mix of berry, together with some leaf and mint; those leafy/minty characters also come through on the palate, which lacks richness, not altogether surprising given the trying vintage. **rating:** 83

best drinking 2002–2006 **best vintages** NA **drink with** Takeaway • $20.95

Yarra Ridge Merlot

▼▼▼▽ **1999** Light to medium red-purple; a fresh, light bouquet with slightly tangy/juicy aspects, the palate tangy and lively, but rather acidic and lean. **rating:** 84

best drinking 2001–2006 **best vintages** '95, '97 **drink with** Rack of veal • $20

yarra track wines ★★★☆

518 Old Healesville Road, Yarra Glen, Vic 3775 **region** Yarra Valley
phone (03) 9730 1349 **fax** (03) 9730 1910 **open** Weekends and public holidays 10–5.30
winemaker Martin Williams MW (Contract) **production** 800 **est.** 1989
product range ($23–25 CD) Chardonnay, Pinot Noir.
summary Jim and Diana Viggers began the establishment of their vineyard back in 1989; it now has 3.1 hectares of chardonnay and 3.4 hectares of pinot noir. The Viggers have chosen a very competent winemaker (Martin Williams from 1999) and intend to increase wine production progressively while selling part of the grape production in the meantime. The wine is sold only through cellar door and through local restaurants.

Yarra Track Chardonnay

TTTT 2001 Light to medium yellow-green; there is a subtle interplay of fruit, mineral, cashew and oak aromas on the bouquet, the palate with elegant melon fruit and a hint of fig. Subtle oak. Carries its 13.8° alcohol well. **rating: 88**

best drinking 2002–2005 **best vintages** NA **drink with** Pan-fried veal • $23

๛ yarra vale   NR

Paynes Road, Seville, Vic 3139 **region** Yarra Valley
phone (03) 9735 1819 **fax** (03) 9737 6565 **open** Not
winemaker Domenic Bucci **production** 1500 **est.** 1982
product range ($13–26 R) Chardonnay, Rosé, Cabernet Sauvignon.
summary This is the second time around for Domenic Bucci, who built the first stage of what is now Eyton-on-Yarra before being compelled to sell the business in the hard times of the early 1990s. He has established 2 hectares of cabernet sauvignon and half a hectare of merlot, supplemented by chardonnay which is supplied in return for his winemaking services to the grower. The wines have retail distribution in Melbourne through Sullivan Wine Agencies and exports via Rubins Productions.

Yarra Vale Chardonnay

TTTT 1999 Light to medium yellow-green; the slightly suppressed fruit has some herbal/green/lemony aspects, but opens up on the palate with classic melon flavours, and just a dusting of oak to add interest. A pleasant wine. **rating: 84**

best drinking 2001–2004 **best vintages** NA **drink with** Deep-fried calamari • $21

Yarra Vale Cabernet Sauvignon

TTTT 1997 Medium red, with just a few purple tones remaining. Subdued blackberry fruit and minimal oak on the bouquet is followed by a palate starting to develop secondary, earthy blackberry fruit flavours plus a touch of dusty oak; a slightly sharp edge on the finish detracts somewhat. **rating: 83**

best drinking 2002–2006 **best vintages** NA **drink with** Roast beef • $26

yarra valley hills   NR

c/o Dromana Estate, Harrison's Road and Bittern–Dromana Road, Dromana, Vic 3936 **region** Yarra Valley
phone (03) 5987 3177 **fax** (03) 5987 3977 **open** Not
winemaker Garry Crittenden, Judy Gifford Watson **production** 6 000 **est.** 1989
product range ($17–21 CD) Sauvignon Blanc, Chardonnay, Pinot Noir, Cabernet Sauvignon.
summary The business of Yarra Valley Hills was acquired by Dromana Estate in 2000. Dromana has kept the Yarra Valley Hills brand, but sold the winery to a syndicate headed by Martin Williams, who will use it to both provide custom crush and make facilities for other Yarra Valley wineries, and (in the case of Martin Williams) to make his own Metier brand.

Yarra Valley Hills Cabernet Sauvignon

TTTT 2000 Medium to full red-purple; the bouquet offers a spectrum of hay, red berry, chocolate and light, spicy oak aromas. Pleasant red berry/cassis fruit on the palate is not particularly concentrated, and comes as a slight let down given the vintage. **rating: 85**

best drinking 2003–2007 **best vintages** NA **drink with** Lamb chops • $21

yarra yarra   ★★★★★

239 Hunts Lane, Steels Creek, Vic 3775 **region** Yarra Valley
phone (03) 5965 2389 **fax** (03) 5965 2006 **open** By appointment
winemaker Ian Maclean **production** NFP **est.** 1979
product range ($30–60 CD) Semillon Sauvignon Blanc, Merlot, Cabernets, Reserve Cabernet Merlot.
summary Notwithstanding its tiny production, the wines of Yarra Yarra have found their way onto a veritable who's who listing of Melbourne's best restaurants. This has encouraged Ian Maclean to increase the estate plantings from 2 hectares to over 7 hectares during the 1996 and 1997 seasons. The demand for the wines continues to exceed supply. Exports to the UK and Singapore.

Yarra Yarra Semillon Sauvignon Blanc

TTTTT 1999 Light green-yellow; an intensely fragrant bouquet with aromas of cut flowers, herbs and lanolin leads into a highly-structured, crisp and lively palate with those distinctive characters of the bouquet repeated, and a mix of spicy and more lemony oak. **rating: 92**

best drinking 2002–2006 **best vintages** '97, '99 **drink with** Wiener schnitzel • $35

Yarra Yarra Cabernets

TTTT 1999 Medium red-purple; a complex bouquet with earth, cedary, blackberry aromas is followed by a balanced palate showing red and black fruits, subtle oak, fine tannins and some acidity on the finish.

rating: 89

TTTTY 1998 Medium purple-red; the immediate impression of the bouquet is strongly reminiscent of Bordeaux, with savoury, dark berry/blackcurrant fruit and subtle oak. The palate is finely structured and styled, neither over, nor under-ripe, and slightly leaner and more racy than so many Australian Cabernets. Sweet French oak on the finish is an excellent counter-poise.

rating: 93

best drinking 2004–2009 **best vintages** '84, '86, '89, '90, '92, '95, '97 **drink with** Osso buco • $45

Yarra Yarra Reserve Cabernet Sauvignon

TTTTY 1999 Medium to full red-purple; dark, sweet blackcurrant, blackberry and cedar aromas on the bouquet, are followed by an aristocratic palate, very long and tightly constructed around a core of blackberry/blackcurrant fruit, finishing with fine tannins. An ideal outcome from a not-so-ideal vintage.

rating: 92

best drinking 2004–2014 **best vintages** '97, '99 **drink with** Braised beef • $60

yarra yering ★★★★★

Briarty Road, Coldstream, Vic 3770 **region** Yarra Valley
phone (03) 5964 9267 **fax** (03) 5964 9239 **open** Not open in 2002, usually first Saturday in May
winemaker Bailey Carrodus **production** NA **est.** 1969
product range Dry White No 1 (Sauvignon Blanc Semillon), Chardonnay, Pinot Noir, Dry Red No 1 (Bordeaux-blend), Dry Red No 2 (Rhône-blend), Merlot (tiny quantities at $100 a bottle), Underhill Shiraz, Underhill 3 Year Cask Shiraz, Portsorts. The portfolio continues to expand, with Dry Red No. 3, Sangiovese and Viognier all making an appearance from the 1998 and/or '99 vintages.
summary Dr Bailey Carrodus makes extremely powerful, occasionally idiosyncratic wines from his 30-year-old, low-yielding unirrigated vineyards. Both red and white wines have an exceptional depth of flavour and richness, although my preference for what I believe to be his great red wines is well known. As he has expanded the size of his vineyards, so has the range of wines become ever more eclectic, none more so than the only Vintage Port being produced in the Yarra Valley. The wines are exported to the UK, US, Switzerland, Germany, Hong Kong, Japan, Malaysia and Singapore.

yass valley wines NR

9 Crisps Lane, Murrumbateman, NSW 2582 **region** Canberra District
phone (02) 6227 5592 **fax** (02) 6227 5592 **open** Wed–Sun and public holidays 11–5 or by appointment
winemaker Michael Withers **production** 670 **est.** 1979
product range ($15–33 CD) Riesling, Semillon, Allegro (white blend), Chardonnay, Barbera, Merlot, Cabernet Sauvignon.
summary Michael Withers and Anne Hillier purchased Yass Valley in January 1991 and have subsequently rehabilitated the existing run-down vineyards and extended the plantings. Mick Withers is a chemist by profession and has completed a Wine Science degree at Charles Sturt University; Anne is a registered psychologist and has completed a Viticulture diploma at Charles Sturt. Crisps Lane Cafe is open weekends and public holidays from 11 am to 5 pm, with an emphasis on local produce. No recent tastings.

yaxley estate ★★★★

31 Dransfield Road, Copping, Tas 7174 **region** Southern Tasmania
phone (03) 6253 5222 **fax** (03) 6253 5222 **open** 7 days 10–6.30
winemaker Andrew Hood (Contract) **production** 333 **est.** 1991
product range ($19.80–25 CD) Pinot Gris, Sauvignon Blanc, Chardonnay, Pinot Noir.
summary While Yaxley Estate was established back in 1991, it was not until 1998 that it offered each of the 4 wines from its vineyard plantings, which total just under 2 hectares. Once again, the small batch handling skills (and patience) of contract-winemaker Andrew Hood have made the venture possible.

Yaxley Estate Pinot Noir

TTTTY 2000 Medium to full red-purple; a very ripe, fruit-driven bouquet offers plum and touches of prune; the palate rich, and full-on with deep, ripe plum fruit, unequivocally at the big end of town, yet it all hangs together.

rating: 92

best drinking 2002–2007 **best vintages** '00 **drink with** Rare roast squab • $25

yellowglen ★★★☆

Whites Road, Smythesdale, Vic 3351 **region** Ballarat
phone (03) 5342 8617 **fax** (03) 5333 7102 **open** Mon–Fri 10–5, weekends 11–5
winemaker Charles Hargraves **production** NFP **est.** 1975
product range ($11–37 R) Grand Cuvée range of Pinot Noir Chardonnay, Brut Cremant, Brut Rosé, Pinot Noir; Premium range of Vintage Brut, Y Premium, Y Sparkling Burgundy, Cuvée Victoria; also Yellow and Red.
summary Just as the overall quality of Australian sparkling wine has improved out of all recognition over the past 15 years, so has that of Yellowglen. Initially the quality lift was apparent at the top end of the range but now extends right to the non-vintage commercial releases.

Yellowglen Hargrave

▼▼▼▼ **1997** Light straw-green; the bouquet is tight, but complex, with a particular spicy edge to the fruit; the palate is elegant, fresh, fine and long, but not quite as complex as the bouquet and three years on yeast lees leads on to expect. Only 400 dozen made, coming exclusively from 2 hectares of close-planted pinot noir and chardonnay planted by Charles (Chilla) Hargrave in 1987.　　**rating: 88**

best drinking 2002–2005 best vintages NA drink with Shellfish • $37

Yellowglen Vintage Cuvée Victoria

▼▼▼▼ **1997** Light to medium green-straw; a crisp, elegant dry bouquet, then a fresh, crisp minerally palate with elegant secondary flavours, yet ending up needing more depth.　　**rating: 89**

best drinking 2001–2002 best vintages '90, '91, '92, '95, '96 drink with Aperitif • $30

Yellowglen Y

▼▼▼▼ **NV** Light green-yellow; a clean bouquet with citrus and a touch of melon, but little or no evidence of autolysis. The palate is clean, delicate and fresh, a little on the simple side, but certainly reflecting its Chardonnay/Pinot Noir base, and easy to drink.　　**rating: 86**

best drinking 2002–2003 best vintages NA drink with Aperitif • $20

Yellowglen Yellow

▼▼▼▽ **NV** Light green-yellow; a quite fragrant, tangy, citrussy/lemony bouquet and a lively, fresh palate with similar flavours, possibly suggesting some riesling. Not particularly 'fizzy', thus in the classic slam-it-down-fast Solo mode. Uncomplicated and quite good value.　　**rating: 82**

best drinking 2002–2003 best vintages NA drink with Summer • $11

Yellowglen Vintage Brut

▼▼▼▼ **1998** Very pale straw-green; a fresh, crisp, restrained minerally bouquet leads directly into a fresh, crisp and extremely delicate palate. Aperitif style.　　**rating: 87**

best drinking 2001–2002 best vintages '88, '90, '92, '94 drink with Aperitif or oysters • $20

yeringberg ★★★★★

Maroondah Highway, Coldstream, Vic 3770 **region** Yarra Valley
phone (03) 9739 1453 **fax** (03) 9739 0048 **open** By appointment
winemaker Guill de Pury **production** 1100 **est.** 1863
product range ($30–45 CD) Chardonnay, Marsanne/Roussanne, Pinot Noir, Yeringberg (Cabernet blend).
summary Makes wines for the new millennium from the low-yielding vines re-established on the heart of what was one of the most famous (and infinitely larger) vineyards of the 19th century. In the riper years, the red wines have a velvety generosity of flavour which is rarely encountered, yet never lose varietal character, while the Yeringberg White takes students of history back to Yeringberg's fame in the 19th century. The wines are exported to the UK, the US, Switzerland, Malaysia, Hong Kong and Singapore.

Yeringberg Marsanne Roussanne

▼▼▼▼ **2001** Light straw-green; aromas of apple, spice and a hint of honeysuckle are followed by a palate which delivers most through its texture and structure rather than its flavour, but will develop over many years.　　**rating: 87**

▼▼▼▽ **2000** Light to medium yellow-green; a scented, floral, lemon blossom bouquet is followed by a palate with excellent mouthfeel, found and quite lush, but not phenolic. A twist of lemony acidity on the finish adds to the appeal of a quite delicious wine, promising much for the future.　　**rating: 93**

best drinking 2005–2015 best vintages '94, '97, '98, '00 drink with Snowy Mountains trout • $30

Yeringberg Chardonnay

YYYYY 2001 Light green-yellow; the bouquet has a mix of melon and citrus, touches of cashew and tinges of oak, the palate the epitome of elegance, lively and fresh. **rating:** 91

YYYYY 2000 Light to medium straw-yellow; in typically understated style, with barrel ferment, malolactic ferment, nutty, cashew and melon aromas interwoven on the bouquet; the palate is rich, with stone fruit and melon supported by excellent oak balance and integration. **rating:** 92

best drinking 2002–2007 **best vintages** '88, '90, '91, '92, '93, '94, '97, '98, '00, '01 **drink with** Sweetbreads • $30

Yeringberg Pinot Noir

YYYY 2000 Medium red-purple; the bouquet is surprisingly closed, although it does have a nice touch of cedar and forest; the medium-bodied palate has pleasant plum and spice flavours running through to its moderately long finish. Nice wine; however, doesn't entirely live up to the vintage. **rating:** 88

YYYY 1999 The hue is quite good, although relatively light; a slightly closed, shy bouquet with cherry and spice leads into a clean palate, with more red cherry fruit, ultra-fine tannins and good length. A good outcome for the vintage. **rating:** 89

best drinking 2003–2006 **best vintages** '97 **drink with** Squab • $45

Yeringberg Dry Red

YYYYY 2000 Light to medium red-purple, lighter than expected; the clean, fresh bouquet is moderately intense, with redcurrant, cassis and blackberry aromas; the palate scores for its elegance, balance and marriage of fruit flavours, tannins and oak, but is not as concentrated as the very best wines of the vintage. **rating:** 92

YYYYY 1999 Deep, dark red-purple; rich, blackberry, blackcurrant and mulberry fruit on the bouquet is followed by a soft, rich and full palate, with hints of plum and chocolate joining the blackberry/blackcurrant of the bouquet. The tannins are soft, the oak balanced; a particularly good outcome. **rating:** 93

best drinking 2005–2010 **best vintages** '85, '86, '88, '90, '91, '93, '94, '97, '98, '99, '00 **drink with** Yarra Valley venison • $45

yering farm   NR

St Huberts Road, Yering, Vic 3770 **region** Yarra Valley
phone (03) 9739 0461 **fax** (03) 9739 0467 **open** 7 days 10–5
winemaker Alan Johns **production** 5000 **est.** 1989
product range ($18–25 ML) Chardonnay, Pinot Noir, Merlot, Cabernet Sauvignon.
summary Alan and Louise Johns established their 12-hectare vineyard in 1989 on the site of the original Yeringa winery built by the Deschamps family in the last century. Between 1992 and 1998 the wines were made by Alan Johns, and since then at Yarra Ridge, which purchases much of the production from the vineyard.

yering range vineyard   NR

14 McIntyre Lane, Coldstream, Vic 3770 **region** Yarra Valley
phone (03) 9739 1172 **fax** (03) 9739 1172 **open** By appointment
winemaker Kevin Ryan, Margaret Ryan **production** 300 **est.** 1989
product range ($18 CD) Cabernet Sauvignon.
summary Yering Range has 2 hectares of cabernet sauvignon under vine, part being sold and part made under the Yering Range label by John Ellis at Hanging Rock. The tiny production is sold through a mailing list.

yering station   ★★★★☆

38 Melba Highway, Yarra Glen, Vic 3775 **region** Yarra Valley
phone (03) 9730 1107 **fax** (03) 9739 0135 **open** 7 days 10–5
winemaker Tom Carson, Dan Buckle, Darren Rathbone **production** 45 000 **est.** 1988
product range ($12.50–55 CD) Baraks Bridge Semillon Sauvignon Blanc, Chardonnay, Botrytis Semillon, Pinot Noir, Shiraz, Cabernet Blend; Yering Station Sauvignon Blanc, Marsanne, Chardonnay, Reserve Chardonnay, Pinot Gris Late Harvest, Pinot Gris Botrytis, Pinot Noir Rosé ED, Pinot Noir, Shiras, Merlot, Cabernet Sauvignon; also Verjuice in 375 ml bottles.
summary The historic Yering Station (or at least the portion of the property on which the cellar-door sales and vineyard are established) was purchased by the Rathbone family in January 1996 and is now the site of a joint venture with the French Champagne house Devaux. A spectacular and very large winery has been erected which handles the Yarrabank sparkling wines and the Yering Station and Yarra Edge table

wines. Has immediately become one of the focal points of the Yarra Valley, particularly with the historic Chateau Yering next door, where luxury accommodation and fine dining is available. Yering Station's own restaurant is open every day for lunch, providing the best cuisine in the Valley. Exports to the US, Canada, the UK, Denmark, Sweden, Malaysia, Singapore, Hong Kong and Japan.

Yering Station Viognier

YYYY **2000** Light green-yellow; the bouquet does have some special fruit aromatics, faintly flowery, and just a hint of barrel-ferment spice; the palate looses some of the focus of the bouquet, but is pleasant enough, again showing some barrel-ferment inputs. **rating:** 85

best drinking 2001–2002 **best vintages** NA **drink with** Yarra Valley salmon • $20

Yering Station Marsanne

YYYY **2000** Light to medium green-yellow; a clean and crisp bouquet with a range of mineral and wild herb aromas leads into a palate which is reasonably neutral in terms of flavour, but has good mouthfeel and balance, offering the prospect of development in bottle. **rating:** 86

best drinking 2002–2007 **best vintages** NA **drink with** Shellfish • $19.50

Yering Station Chardonnay

YYYY **2000** Light to medium yellow-green; very strong, charry barrel-ferment oak dominates the ripe fruit on the bouquet; that fruit comes back on the palate, but still leaves the oak dominant. **rating:** 86

best drinking 2001–2004 **best vintages** '97, '98 **drink with** Poached Tasmanian salmon • $20.50

Yering Station Barak's Bridge Chardonnay

YYYY **2000** Light yellow-green; the bouquet is light, clean and fresh, with archetypal Yarra melon fruit, with a replay of all of this on the fresh, albeit slightly simple, palate. **rating:** 86

best drinking 2001–2003 **best vintages** NA **drink with** Salmon salad • $15.50

Yering Station Reserve Chardonnay

YYYYY **1999** Light to medium yellow-green; a subtle but complex web of barrel ferment, lees and fruit aromas lead into an elegant, gently complex and long palate with cashew, melon and citrus flavours, smoky overtones adding yet further interest. Trophy for Best Yarra Valley Chardonnay at the Southern Victorian Wines Show 2000 and three other gold medals. **rating:** 94

best drinking 2001–2006 **best vintages** '97, '99 **drink with** Pan-fried veal • $50

Yering Station Pinot Gris Botrytis (375 ml)

YYYY **2001** Pale straw-gold; fragrant peach blossom aromas lead into a wine with excellent balance, again with a touch of peach from the botrytis; spätlese sweetness is offset by crisp but not aggressive acidity. **rating:** 88

best drinking 2002–2004 **best vintages** NA **drink with** Fresh fruit • $17.50

Yering Station Pinot Noir ED Rosé

YYYY **2001** Light red, already showing some development; a gentle strawberry and savoury mix on the bouquet leads into a tangy and quite complex palate; surprisingly, there are some light tannins to add structure and interest to a wine of some merit. **rating:** 89

best drinking 2001–2001 **best vintages** NA **drink with** Seafood, Singapore noodles – you name it • $17.50

Yering Station Pinot Noir

YYYY **2000** Light to medium red-purple; spicy oak and light strawberry fruit on the bouquet are followed by a light, spicy, savoury palate which lacks the expected richness of fruit from this vintage. **rating:** 85

best drinking 2001–2003 **best vintages** '91, '94, '96, '97 **drink with** Smoked quail • $23

Yering Station Reserve Pinot Noir

YYYYY **2000** Bright red-purple; aromatic smoky/charry oak and some whole bunch/stalk aromas foreshadow an intense, complex, foresty, tangy palate in Burgundian mould, and representing a very definite statement by the winemaker Tom Carson. The only residual doubt is over the level of oak, which pushes the envelope. **rating:** 94

best drinking 2002–2007 **best vintages** '97, '00 **drink with** Jugged hare • $55

Yering Station Shiraz

YYYY **1999** Medium red-purple; the bouquet ranges through cedar, spice, berry and leaf, with faintly gamey notes in the background. The light to medium-bodied palate reflects the very difficult vintage, lacking sweetness/richness in the mid-palate. **rating:** 84

best drinking 2002–2006 **best vintages** NA **drink with** Grilled calf's liver • $22

Yering Station Barak's Bridge Shiraz

♥♥♥♥ 2000 Medium red-purple; light, cherry fruit with faintly dusty/charry oak in the background leads into a palate with some length, and sweet, albeit relatively light, cherry fruit. Better value than the Yering Station Shiraz of the same vintage. **rating:** 85

best drinking 2001–2003 **best vintages** NA **drink with** Yakitori chicken • $15.50

Yering Station Merlot

♥♥♥♥♀ 2000 Medium red-purple; cedary/spicy oak aromas open the bouquet, with earthy, berry varietal fruit coming in thereafter. The palate has good intensity and length, with savoury overtones to nicely focussed fruit, again showing positive varietal character. **rating:** 91

best drinking 2003–2010 **best vintages** '00 **drink with** White Rocks veal • $23

Yering Station Barak's Bridge Cabernets

♥♥♥♥ 2000 Medium red-purple; the bouquet has a very curious talcum powder scent, the palate much more reassuring than the bouquet, with quite sweet, small red berry fruit and soft tannins. **rating:** 86

best drinking 2001–2003 **best vintages** NA **drink with** Pizza • $15.50

Yering Station Reserve Cabernet Sauvignon

♥♥♥♥ 1999 Medium red-purple; a lifted, leafy/earthy bouquet does not seem at peace with itself, however the palate is better, with fine cassis/blackcurrant fruit, fine tannins and controlled oak. A very good outcome for a troublesome vintage. **rating:** 89

best drinking 2004–2009 **best vintages** NA **drink with** Daube of lamb • $55

yunbar estate ★★★☆

PO Box 64, Port Noarlunga, Sa 5167 **region** Barossa Valley
phone (08) 8327 3987 **fax** (08) 8327 4087 **open** By appointment
winemaker The Bartiers **production** 1000 **est.** 1998
product range ($14–22 CD) Eden Riesling, Bushvines Semillon, Chaste Chardonnay, Sinners Shiraz, Miracle Merlot, Craig's Cabernet.
summary The intruigingly named Sinners Shiraz, the Merlot, Semillon, Riesling and Chardonnay are produced from a total of 8 hectares of contract-grown grapes, the Eden Riesling is made from contract-grown grapes. Sales via the website: www.yunbar.com.

zappacosta estate wines NR

301 Kidman Way, Hanwood, NSW 2680 **region** Riverina
phone (02) 6963 0278 **fax** (02) 6963 0278 **open** 7 days 10–5
winemaker Dino Zappacosta **production** 50 000 **est.** 1956
product range ($12 CD) Riesling, Semillon, Dry White, Shiraz.
summary Zappacosta Estate, briefly known as Hanwood Village Wines, is a relatively new business, with the first release from the 1996 vintage, although the vineyard dates back to 1956.

zarephath wines ★★★☆

Moorialup Road, East Porongurup, WA 6324 **region** Great Southern
phone (08) 9853 1152 **fax** (08) 9841 8124 **open** Wed–Sun 10–4
winemaker Brenden Smith **production** 2000 **est.** 1994
product range ($16.50–24 CD) Riesling, Chardonnay, Unwooded Chardonnay, Pinot Noir, Shiraz, Cabernet Sauvignon.
summary The 9-hectare Zarephath vineyard is owned and operated by Brothers and Sisters of The Christ Circle, a Benedictine community. They say the most outstanding feature of the location is the feeling of peace and tranquility which permeates the site, something I can well believe on the basis of numerous visits to the Porongurups.

Zarephath Riesling

♥♥♥♥ 2001 Light straw-green; tropical lime juice aromas flow through strongly into the mid-palate; a long and intense wine, with mineral coming through on the aftertaste. **rating:** 89

best drinking 2002–2006 **best vintages** '00 **drink with** Chinese prawns • $17

Zarephath Chardonnay

▼▼▼▼ 2001 Light to medium yellow-green; complex smoky/toasty barrel-ferment aromas on the bouquet are also reflected on the palate, where light melon fruit provides the core. Skilfully oak-driven, and does not show its 14° alcohol.   **rating:** 88

best drinking 2002–2004 **best vintages** NA **drink with** Tea-smoked chicken • $21

Zarephath Pinot Noir

▼▼▼▼ 2001 Light red-purple; light strawberry/cherry aromas lead into a palate which, despite 13.9° alcohol, is actually quite delicate. Has reasonable length, but does not sing like the best Pinots.   **rating:** 86

best drinking 2002–2004 **best vintages** NA **drink with** Roast duck • $20

Zarephath Shiraz

▼▼▼▼ 2000 Medium red-purple; the bouquet has a mix of berry, spice and leaf, supported by subtle oak; the palate is only of light to medium body, but is quite firm thanks to savoury tannins. Needs time but will never be fleshy or sweet.   **rating:** 87

best drinking 2004–2008 **best vintages** NA **drink with** Braised veal • $22

Zarephath Cabernet Sauvignon

▼▼▼▼ 2000 Medium to full red-purple; a fragrant bouquet with cedary/savoury aromas is mirrored on the palate, with a mix of woodsy/briary/savoury flavours, all in secondary mode, and consistent with the modest (12.6°) alcohol. Finishes with fine tannins.   **rating:** 86

best drinking 2003–2007 **best vintages** NA **drink with** Rack of lamb • $22

zema estate   ★★★★☆

Riddoch Highway, Coonawarra, SA 5263 **region** Coonawarra
phone (08) 8736 3219 **fax** (08) 8736 3280 **open** 7 days 9–5
winemaker Tom Simons **production** 12 000 **est.** 1982
product range ($20–40 CD) Shiraz, Cabernet Sauvignon, Family Selection Cabernet Sauvignon, Cluny (Cabernet-blend).
summary Zema is one of the last outposts of hand-pruning in Coonawarra, the various members of the Zema family tending a 60-hectare vineyard progressively planted since 1982 in the heart of Coonawarra's terra rossa soil. Winemaking practices are straightforward; if ever there was an example of great wines being made in the vineyard, this is it. Exports to the UK, France, Malaysia, Thailand, Hong Kong and New Zealand.

Zema Estate Shiraz

▼▼▼▼ 2000 Medium red-purple, with a faint touch of gas in the glass; a moderately intense bouquet ranges through plum, spice, cedar and a touch of earth; the smooth medium-bodied palate has plum and mint fruit, generally showing the vintage.   **rating:** 86

▼▼▼▼ 1999 Medium red-purple, not particularly dense. The clean, moderately intense bouquet ranges through blackberry, chocolate and vanilla aromas, the palate adding hints of spice and cigar box to the mix, finishing with fine tannins. A nice wine, but lacks the intensely sweet fruit of the '98 vintage.   **rating:** 88

best drinking 2003–2008 **best vintages** '84, '86, '88, '92, '94, '96, '97, '98 **drink with** Bistecca Fiorentina • $20

Zema Estate Cluny

▼▼▼▼ 2000 Very good red-purple; the bouquet is quite aromatic with red berry, spice and a touch of mint, however the palate has slightly herbal notes, and pronounced acidity on the finish. An up and down wine from an up and down vintage.   **rating:** 87

▼▼▼▼▽ 1999 Medium red-purple; the bouquet is fragrant and lively, with a mix of red fruits, spice and lemon leaf. The palate does not disappoint, with an attractive mix of blackberry and oak; good tannin management and subtle oak play a support role to the very attractive fruit.   **rating:** 90

best drinking 2003–2007 **best vintages** '98, '99 **drink with** Braised lamb • $20

Zema Estate Cabernet Sauvignon

▼▼▼▼ 1999 Medium to full red-purple; strong, blackberry/earthy/savoury fruit aromas are a crystal clear example of the variety. There is abundant blackberry fruit, with touches of bitter chocolate and earth, on the palate which once again shows well managed tannins and oak. Overall, just a little austere, but should open up with time in bottle.   **rating:** 89

best drinking 2004–2009 **best vintages** '84, '86, '88, '92, '93, '96, '97, '98 **drink with** Barbecued leg of lamb • $25.95

Zema Estate Family Selection Cabernet Sauvignon

ŶŶŶŶŶ 1999 Medium to full red-purple; sweet dark berry/blackberry fruit plus a hint of varietal earth on the bouquet leads into a powerful, fairly austere Cabernet Sauvignon with that savoury/earthy edge typical of Coonawarra, particularly as the wine starts to develop in bottle.   **rating: 91**

best drinking 2004–2014 **best vintages** '97, '98 **drink with** Game • $40

ziebarth wines   NR

Foleys Road, Goodger, Qld 4610 **region** South Burnett
phone (07) 4162 3089 **fax** (07) 4162 3084 **open** 7 days 10–5
winemaker John Crane (Contract) **production** 420 **est.** 1998
product range ($13.50–14.50 CD) Semillon, Fairview White, Rosé, Shiraz Cabernet Franc.
summary The 4-hectare vineyard (with 1 hectare each of semillon, cabernet sauvignon, merlot and chardonnay, together with 0.25 hectares of chambourcin) is a minor diversification on a beef cattle property set on the edge of the Stuart Range, and which enjoys superb views. It is a small family operation with the aim of providing a wine experience for visitors, the wines being made for Ziebarth by John Crane at Crane Winery.

🐦 zig zag road   NR

201 Zig Zag Road, Drummond, Vic 3461 **region** Macedon Ranges
phone (03) 5423 9390 **fax** (03) 5423 9390 **open** Weekends and public holidays
winemaker Alan Stevens, Deb Orton **production** 350 **est.** 1972
product range ($20–22 CD) Cabernet Sauvignon.
summary Alan Stevens and Deb Orton purchased the vineyard in 1988; it was then 16 years old, having been established way back in 1972 by Roger Aldridge. The dry-grown vines produce relatively low yields, and until 1996 the grapes were sold to Hanging Rock Winery. In 1996 the decision was taken to manage the property on a full-time basis, and to make the wine on-site, utilising 1 hectare each of shiraz and cabernet sauvignon, 0.5 hectare of pinot noir and 0.25 hectare of merlot.

Zig Zag Road Cabernet Sauvignon

ŶŶŶŶ 1999 Good colour; cassis/berry fruit on the bouquet is followed up by a mix of blackcurrant, earth and a touch of earth on the palate, the tannins fractionally green. For all that, a good outcome for the late ripening cabernet sauvignon in a year such as this.   **rating: 85**

best drinking 2002–2007 **best vintages** NA **drink with** Beef stew • $22

🐦 zilzie wines   ★★★

Lot 66 Kulkyne Way, Karadoc via Red Cliffs, Vic 3496 **region** Murray Darling
phone (03) 5025 8100 **fax** (03) 5025 8116 **open** Not
winemaker Bob Shields, Leigh Sparrow **production** 25 000 **est.** 1999
product range ($10–14 R) The wines are offered under three labels; the export-oriented Forbes Family range of Chardonnay, Shiraz, Merlot, Cabernet Sauvignon; in the middle come the Buloke Reserve Wines, with Sauvignon Blanc, Chardonnay, Shiraz, Petit Verdot, Sangiovese, Merlot, Cabernet Merlot; Zilzie is the top of the range, with Chardonnay, Shiraz, Merlot, Cabernet Sauvignon.
summary The Forbes family has been farming Zilzie Estate since 1911; it is currently run by Ian and Ros Forbes, together with their sons Steven and Andrew. A diverse range of farming activities now include grape growing with 250 hectares of vineyards. Having established a position of a dominant supplier of grapes to Southcorp, Zilzie took the next step of forming a wine company in 1999 and built a winery in 2000 with a present capacity of 16 000 tonnes, but so designed that modules can be added to take it ultimately to 50 000 tonnes. The winery business includes contract storage, contract processing, contract winemaking, bulk wine production and bottled and branded wines. The wines are distributed nationally through Rutherglen Wine and Spirit Company Limited; exports to the UK.

Zilzie Chardonnay

ŶŶŶŶŶ 2001 Medium yellow-green; ripe peach fruit with a touch of vanilla oak drives both the bouquet and palate; the oak does introduce a phenolic background, but there is plenty of flavour. A blend of 87 per cent Chardonnay and 13 per cent other white varieties.   **rating: 83**

best drinking 2002–2003 **best vintages** NA **drink with** KFC • $14

Zilzie Buloke Reserve Petit Verdot

YYYY 2001 Deep, dense purple-red; dark berry/blackberry fruit on the bouquet leads into a palate which is dense and flavourful, though not having much light and shade contrast; soft tannins. A top barbecue red, with excellent value and interest coming through the blend of 91 per cent Petit Verdot, seven per cent Shiraz and two per cent Ruby Cabernet. **rating:** 85

best drinking 2002–2003 **best vintages** NA **drink with** Barbecue • $10

Zilzie Buloke Reserve Sangiovese

YYYY 2001 Medium red-purple; a light bouquet with some cedar and spice aromas, then a light to medium-bodied palate with a gentle mix of sweet berry fruit and spice, the sweetness lingering on the finish. Good value. A blend of 95 per cent Sangiovese and five per cent Petit Verdot. **rating:** 82

best drinking 2002–2003 **best vintages** NA **drink with** Spaghetti bolognese • $10

appendix

grape variety plantings

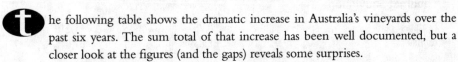he following table shows the dramatic increase in Australia's vineyards over the past six years. The sum total of that increase has been well documented, but a closer look at the figures (and the gaps) reveals some surprises.

Firstly, there is no mention of riesling, simply because there has been no significant net increase in the hectares planted, and production has actually declined markedly since 1996. Precisely the same holds true of grenache, and there has only been a small increase for mourvedre.

Those are the gaps, or, if you wish, the trees. The forest is the relative increase of white and red varieties. (Incidentally, the total white and total red hectares cannot be arrived at by simply adding the varieties shown; you have to include the innumerable varieties not shown.) White grape plantings and tonnage have increased by approximately 20 per cent, red grape plantings and hectares by 300 per cent. Moreover, the variety to show the largest percentage increase is neither shiraz nor cabernet sauvignon, but merlot. That said, it has come from a low base, but now constitutes the third most widely planted variety.

Finally, and to the relief of many in the industry, the rate of increase in plantings finally seems to be slowing down.

wine	1996	1997
Chardonnay		
hectares	11,721	13,713
tonnes	92,258	119,678
Sauvignon Blanc		
hectares	1,538	1,725
tonnes	15,009	13,328
Semillon		
hectares	4,079	4,803
tonnes	45,062	52,829
Total White		
hectares	47,122	50,711
tonnes	516,358	484,030
Cabernet Sauvignon		
hectares	8,752	11,219
tonnes	68,839	67,015
Merlot		
hectares	1,246	2,461
tonnes	9,227	10,331
Pinot Noir		
hectares	1,748	1,896
tonnes	14,801	13,924
Shiraz		
hectares	10,389	13,410
tonnes	81,674	94,848
Total Red		
hectares	30,560	37,763
tonnes	246,043	252,448
Total Grapes		
hectares	77,682	88,474
tonnes	762,401	736,478

1998	1999	2000	2001
14,662	16,855	18,526	18,434
148,515	210,770	201,248	245,199
1,904	2,413	2,706	2,766
18,405	22,834	21,487	25,326
5,287	6,044	6,832	6,803
57,112	80,191	77,506	88,427
50,764	54,990	59,595	57,342
529,463	626,398	592,237	618,266
14,695	21,169	26,674	28,609
91,876	127,494	159,358	249,288
3,802	6,387	8,575	9,330
13,881	31,801	51,269	80,142
2,192	2,996	3,756	4,142
19,123	19,668	19,578	29,514
17,930	25,596	32,327	33,676
131,427	192,330	224,394	311,045
47,675	67,925	86,582	90,933
326,611	449,809	546,348	772,816
98,439	122,915	146,177	148,275
856,074	1,076,207	1,138,585	1,391,082

index

Wine Atlas of Australia and New Zealand

New revised edition

this new edition offers all the detail and research of the previous edition, and more. Including maps of Australia's new wine regions, profiles on Australia and New Zealand's top winemakers and wineries and stunning photographs, the *Wine Atlas of Australia and New Zealand* is an indispensable reference tool.

ISBN: 0 7322 6448 0

Collecting Wine:
You and Your Cellar

a necessity for every wine enthusiast, this book contains valuable information on how to start and maintain a cellar, how to choose white and red wines for cellaring, the most efficient cellar racking systems and the problems a bottle may encounter during its life. It also provides Australian and imported wine vintage charts and recommends wine merchants, auction houses, societies and literature.

ISBN: 0 7322 6528 2